ART & TODAY

ART & TODAY

BY ELEANOR HEARTNEY

Phaidon Press Limited
Regent's Wharf
All Saints Street
London N1 9PA

Phaidon Press Inc.
180 Varick Street
New York, NY 10014

www.phaidon.com

First published 2008

ISBN 978 0 7148 4514 2

A CIP catalogue record for this book is available from the British Library.

Designed by Base
Printed in China

ACKNOWLEDGEMENTS

Art & Today covers the exciting and tumultuous period during which I have been writing about art. It represents an effort to make sense of a massive and ever expanding art world that refuses to stay within any kinds of boundaries. As a result, it is one of those ambitious and possibly foolhardy enterprises whose scope becomes apparent only after one has plunged headlong into it. This has been a long and intense project. The volume you hold in your hands would not have been possible without the immensely detailed efforts of Project Editor Holly LaDue and the perceptive and insightful editing of Jennifer Liese. I would also like to thank those colleagues and friends whose encouragement and moral support helped me through some of the most difficult phases of this project. They include Bruce Altshuler, Debra Balken, Ronald DeFeo, and Michael Rush. And no words of appreciation would be enough to describe the support provided by my ever tolerant partner, Larry Litt.

INTRODUCTION

Until quite recently the history of modern art has been conceived and presented as a chronological progression of art movements. The narrative of modern art as a sequence of stylistic innovations, enshrined in both art history textbooks and museums' permanent collection displays, is commonly known. Any student of art can tick off the highlights: Impressionism, Post-Impressionism, Cubism, Surrealism, Abstract Expressionism, and so on. Further, most understand each of these movements as a daring overthrow of preceding assumptions by a group of like-minded artists whose efforts yielded a coherent tale of artistic experimentation and evolution.

Alfred H. Barr, Jr., first director of the Museum of Modern Art in New York, rendered an early formulation of this conventional wisdom. In 1936 he published a diagram that charted the development of modern art, using arrows and sweeping lines to convey the genealogy of new movements.[1] Barr proposed the narrative of modern art as both exhaustive and generative—before it expired, a prevailing style would beget not just one, but various other styles. For example, Barr drew two lines from Neo-Impressionism, which, in his view, gave birth to both Cubism and Futurism. Cubism, in turn, spawned Dada and Surrealism, while Futurism gave way to Constructivism, the Bauhaus, and Geometric Abstraction.

Barr's notion of art history as a succession of movements implied the inevitability of change, but did not suggest a guiding principle for modern art's evolution. It would take another prominent figure to formulate that principle—the art critic Clement Greenberg, who in 1939 and 1940 published a pair of essays establishing a theory of artistic progress that would prove enormously influential for decades to come.[2] Broadly known as formalism, Greenberg's doctrine was so decisive it holds enormous sway even today. Greenberg argued that modern art represented a decisive break from the Renaissance fixation on illusionism and was moving toward an ideal of "purity," in which painting and sculpture would be pure expressions of their own intrinsic qualities. In practice this meant that they were to be stripped of all associations with other, non-visual arts, such as poetry and music, and all external, representational references, yielding paintings that existed simply as flat, completely self-contained surfaces and sculptures that were solely masses in space. In this scheme, abstraction emerged as modern art's highest achievement and the expression of pure opticality as its rarefied mission.

Greenberg adamantly enforced these criteria and actively promoted artists, such as Jackson Pollock, whose work conveyed them. In other words, he not only identified an ostensibly intrinsic guiding principle, but did his best to make it come true. In Greenberg's wake, movements that did not fit into the purity narrative tended to be dismissed as obscure tributaries leading away from the mainstream development of modern art. Dada, for instance, with its anarchic spirit, sharp political content, and playful appropriation of mass-culture symbols, was often treated in art history texts and permanent collection installations as a dead end or a curious rupture brought on by the extreme socio-political and psychological conditions between the two World Wars. American Regionalism fared even worse, becoming a nonentity despite the fact that one of its masters, Thomas Hart Benton, taught Pollock, the great hero of the standard account of postwar art history.

Despite the appearance of art historical continuity and critical consensus, dissent was brewing. During the 1960s Greenberg's formalism fell largely out of favor, as new developments roundly refuted the principle of purity. Pop art and Minimalism, which appeared at roughly the same time, both attacked, from very different directions, the formalist critical apparatus that had served to explain the evolutionary emergence of Abstract Expressionism. Pop contested the formalist valorization of abstraction by foregrounding the subject—and not just any subject, but the most common products of consumer culture. Minimalism, for its part, reintroduced what second-wave formalist critic Michael Fried condemned as "theatricality," rejecting pure opticality by courting the viewer's physical engagement with the work.[3]

While Pop and Minimalist artists were undoing the master narrative of progress toward ultimate purity, the notion persisted that movements formed as groups of artists with common aims, genealogies, and styles collectively embraced and then rejected approaches to art. By the 1970s, however, even this ordering principle began to unravel. As the art world embraced a series of wildly diverse tendencies, the word "movement" no longer seemed to express the fluidity of the situation. Post-Minimalism, Conceptualism, land art, body art, performance art, "bad painting": if anything united all these efforts, it was an attitude of rebellion not against previous art movements, but against the categorical authority of art history. Artists demanded freedom of expression, and they found radical ways to test the limits of all definitions of art. They rejected the notion of art as an object, rebelled against its status as a marketable commodity, and undermined all existing criteria for judging an artwork's quality. Dismissing hallowed art historical standards of form and content, they engaged in experiments that asked how far you can go and still be making art. By the early 1970s, all of the following were fair game: Dennis Oppenheim presented an artwork that featured a surburn on his chest. Michael Heizer dug a giant hole in the ground. Richard Serra splashed molten lead on walls, while Lawrence Weiner used them as backdrops for lines of text. Vito Acconci followed people in the street.

Despite these efforts to detach everything considered "art-like" from art, the dream of order lingered on through the 1980s. The emergence of Neo-Expressionism, Neo-Geo, and Simulationism seemed to hark back to the coherent movements of old. Julian Schnabel created heroic, paint-slathered canvases that recalled the monumental ambitions of the Abstract Expressionists. Anselm Kiefer placed himself in the bloodline of German Romanticism with canvases clotted with straw, lead, clay, and sand that made reference to German history and mythology. Art again seemed monumental, innovative, and important. But, as art critic Arthur Danto has suggested, there was something oddly artificial about these developments. He describes them as part of an institutional push to "get history back on track" after a period of apparent aimlessness in which the art market all but died. Works by artists such as Schnabel and David Salle were less responses to the evolutionary flow of art history, Danto argued, than to the demands of art collectors and dealers.[4] Still, for a last, brief moment, there was again at least the appearance of consensus in the art world. The artworks and art writing of the time were rife with denunciations of consumer society's commodification of art. Equally pervasive were rejections of the illusion of originality or authenticity that had fueled earlier art movements. These positions were supported by reference to a dense body of post-structural theory that challenged artists and writers to "deconstruct" the hidden meanings of mass media and high culture in order to reveal their complicity in coercive power structures.

Then, sometime in the early 1990s, this sense of unification suddenly collapsed, leaving us in what some commentators call a state of pluralism and others a reign of chaos. This era of profusion, which persists to this day, is characterized by a welter of critical theories accumulated over several decades—post-structural theory, feminism, Marxism, psychoanalysis, formalism, multiculturalism, and analytic philosophy among them—that compete and often conflict. Critics describe artworks, variously and even simultaneously, as reflections of the artist's psycho-social state, as symptoms of ethnocentric patriarchy, as evidence of the disconnect between signifier and sign, or as relatively old-fashioned distillations of the material's inner logic. This theoretical abundance is matched or even superseded by a rampant proliferation of models and media in contemporary art. For example: Damien Hirst's dead cow, bisected and preserved in formaldehyde; Orlan's surgical operations, designed to give her the features of Western art's great beauties; Maurizio Cattelan's sculpture of the Pope knocked down by a meteorite; Rirkrit Tiravanija's communal meals, Nancy Burson's computer-generated glimpses into the viewer's future appearance, Krzysztof Wodiczko's shopping cart outfitted as sleeping quarters for the homeless; and Eduardo Kac's bio-engineered luminescent rabbit.

This inventory raises several questions: How can all of these examples be said to belong to the same discipline? What does it tell us about art today if it can encompass such diversity? Would it be possible to create a contemporary genealogical diagram like Barr's, one that would account for each of these examples as works of art? Such questions are particularly pressing for critics, who in recent years have been beset by a so-called crisis in criticism as the evident loss of consensus about the direction, materials, audience, and purpose of art leaves their statements about value, quality, or meaning on shaky ground indeed. For artists, the amorphous state of contemporary art makes it difficult to know how to proceed, while curators and other art professionals struggle to distinguish art that is meaningful from art that is not. And audiences are often left in a state of complete confusion, without any way to connect the eclectic art of today with the art of the past.

To address such questions, we might ask, How did we get here? In retrospect, we can trace a number of tendencies that came together to undermine and ultimately overthrow the modernist faith in the orderly progression of art. One in particular is the feminist art movement, which emerged in the 1970s and challenged long-sacred notions about the universality of taste, quality, and aesthetic standards. Feminist critics pointed out that the so-called canon—that authoritative catalogue of historic masterpieces and masters (the very words reeked of prejudice)—was far from neutral, and in fact expressed a specific (Eurocentric, male) bias. One seminal essay, written by art historian Linda Nochlin in 1971, asked, with knowing irony, "Why are there no great women artists?"[5] She answered the question by analyzing the institutional barriers that had historically prevented women artists from achieving parity with men. Committed to correcting that situation, feminists demanded not only a wholesale rewriting of art history that acknowledged the existence of forgotten female artists, but also the removal of the structural and psychological barriers that had prevented women from entering the art world in the first place.

Feminism's challenge to received truths coincided with and in part fueled the emergence of another broad phenomenon, postmodernism. As a successor to modernism, postmodernism draws heavily on the characteristics of its namesake—objectivity, unity, rationality—if only to overthrow them. Existing by definition as a set of negations, it is often difficult to say what postmodernism is, and its many potential definitions often surround it in confusion. Regardless, postmodernism, which is largely considered to stem from the globalized, mediated reality of our late-capitalist age, permeates the culture at large. It can be glimpsed in the embrace of representations of reality over the real thing—for instance, in the popularity of planned communities based on nostalgia for a small town utopia that never actually existed, or in the taste for Hollywood-movie versions of history. It is the force that explains the attraction of "reality TV" and the emergence of virtual communities linked only by the Internet. It is the nebulous medium for our increasingly secondhand relationship to society, memory, and each other.

Within the art world, postmodernism is generally identified with a rejection of all things Greenbergian. Thus even as the quintessential modernist ideas have become widely discredited, Greenberg remains the foil against which later developments are described and discussed. As a rejection of Greenbergian formalism, postmodernism takes issue with the modernist principles of purity, authentic experience, and historical progress. These are replaced by the belief that all experience is in some way mediated, that the natural order of things always capitulates to some kind of controlling ideology, and that our sense of self is constructed from the blandishments of mass media and advertising. One of postmodernism's primary targets is the very notion so central to the history of modern art: the master narrative. This term, formulated by French literary theorist Jean-François Lyotard in his 1979 treatise *The Postmodern Condition*, argues that in the postmodern era, comprehensive theories of history, social systems, or science are no longer tenable. Hence, Lyotard asserted, we must abandon universal principles in favor of micro-narratives.[6]

By the 1980s, feminist analysis of modernism's patriarchal biases was adopted by other excluded groups, who also recognized the relativity of the accepted history of art and culture. The focus of traditional art history on white male artists had relegated not only women but also artists of other races and ethnicities to the margins. Multiculturalism challenged this automatic devaluation of the "other," again raising the specter of a mainstream art world riddled with definitions of "quality" that were biased and exclusionary. A high (or low) point in the discussion came when the Museum of Modern Art in New York mounted the ambitious but controversial "'Primitivism' in 20th-Century Art: Affinity of the Tribal and the Modern" in 1984. Designed to trace the impact of African tribal art on such seminal figures as Pablo Picasso and Joan Miró, the exhibition was widely seen to present European artists as singular geniuses and the African artists who preceded them as nameless, existing in some indeterminate past, and acting merely as reflections of a larger cultural zeitgeist.

By the late '80s, with the abrupt end of the cold war, a new condition of the postmodern emerged—globalism. Spurred by the opening of national boundaries, the search for new markets and new sources of cheap labor, and the revolution in electronic communication, globalism has remade the contemporary world. In social terms, its effects have been mixed, and its beneficiaries select. In the art world, globalism has had a singularly productive role in sealing the demise of the Eurocentric narrative of modernism. An expansion of international biennials in places as far flung as São Paulo and Gwangju (and including Manifesta, which itself travels from city to city), the emergence of internationally recognized artists from every corner of the globe, and the increasing mobility of artists, curators, critics, and audiences has forced us to recognize the validity of other narratives, other definitions of art, and other goals, values, and principles.

Which leads to the dilemma posed by this book: How is it possible to write a survey of contemporary art in an era of apparently anarchic pluralism? Clearly, conventional organizational principles no longer apply. Without a master narrative, it no longer makes sense to present contemporary art as a series of movements. The notion of style has been an anachronism for decades. Given the mobility of artists and the global reach of art today, geographical organization doesn't seem viable. And as artists create art using everything from chewing gum to pixels, as they work in various disciplines simultaneously and address issues ranging from cloning to shopping, grouping art by material, genre, or subject all seem equally unsatisfying.

The real issue is that art can no longer be understood as an isolated phenomenon, pursuing its own imperatives without reference to the outside world. Nor can it be seen as a set of developments all arising from a common point. Rather, critics and art historians must now acknowledge that art is as likely to develop as a response to outside forces—changes in technology or geographical vistas, for instance, or the ever-increasing influence of popular culture—as to the dictates of art history or its unraveling. As Lyotard suggested, the master narrative has been replaced by a multiplicity of narratives—ones that may overlap but not necessarily coincide. To reflect the diverse and unruly interactions between art and the world, this book has thus been organized around a set of sixteen themes, each with its own chapter. By no means definitive, each theme is nonetheless prevalent in contemporary art and suggests the way art responds to larger questions that permeate contemporary life.

The book opens with a pair of chapters that considers the continuing sway of two of contemporary art's most influential forebears. Chapter 1, **ART & POPULAR CULTURE**, looks at the legacy of Andy Warhol, which persists in art that speaks to everything from celebrity culture and the pervasive power of the mass media to the destruction of distinctions between high and low culture. Chapter 2, **ART & THE QUOTIDIAN OBJECT**, examines the revolutionary impact of Marcel Duchamp, whose readymades challenged the definition of art as a species of object distinct from everyday life, and whose influence extends to contemporary artists' use of found and industrial objects and their interest in how context determines meaning.

Chapters 3 and 4 address modernism's archetypal polarities: abstraction and representation. **ART & ABSTRACTION** suggests that the once-privileged status of abstraction has long since melted away under the postmodern onslaught. For today's artists, it is simply one in a whole arsenal of potential approaches. Meanwhile, representation, which once promised to represent the visible world, is proposed in **ART & REPRESENTATION** to be as disconnected from "observable reality" as abstraction itself. In the postmodern era, the exposure and dismantling of the conventions of representation have proved to be one of art's most pervasive subjects.

Having established a groundwork in more familiar art historical terms, the book turns to some of the ways in which contemporary art has challenged its own apparent limits, further undermining formalist dictates of purity. Chapter 5, **ART & NARRATIVE**, shows how artists have adopted strategies from cinema, fiction, and theater to tell stories that unfold in time. Chapter 6, **ART & TIME**, takes this notion even further, suggesting how art today draws on the changes to our physiological and psychological perception of time created by advances in science and technology. Virtual reality, instant replay, slow and fast motion, and the Internet are a few of the elements in artworks that mirror this shifting temporal relationship to the world.

Chapter 7, **ART & NATURE AND TECHNOLOGY**, explores the ways in which artists illuminate contemporary anxieties around technology and science, as they advance both for good and ill and threaten two of our most important anchors to reality, nature and the body. Chapter 8, **ART & DEFORMATION**, features art that imagines the outcome of such threats, revealing a fascination with abjection, hybridity, and mutation. These states are not always as gruesome as they might sound; rather, they provide routes to escape the rigidity of reason and logic by putting us back in touch with our animal natures and the inevitable cycles of creation and destruction.

In Chapter 9, **ART & THE BODY**, the human body becomes both art's subject and, in the case of performance art, its medium. Because the body is subject to the strictures of law, politics, and religion, it serves as a vehicle to express contemporary conflicts over social mores, gender definitions, and expressions of sexuality. Chapter 10, **ART & IDENTITY**, further considers contemporary art's complicated interactions with the social and political world, tracing the uneasy evolution from art that celebrates specific identities and asserts the multicultural triumph over modernist universalism to art that expresses postmodern skepticism toward selfhood and posits a more fluid definition of identity.

The next two chapters consider one of the oldest and one of the newest influences in art. Chapter 11, **ART & SPIRITUALITY**, suggests that despite formalism's repudiation of art's spiritual content, deep religious and spiritual beliefs continue to inform the work of contemporary artists. Chapter 12, **ART & GLOBALISM**, presents art that considers the mixed effects of globalism's sudden erasure of national boundaries and the tensions it creates between emerging sets of winners and losers.

Chapter 13, **ART & ARCHITECTURE**, and Chapter 14, **ART & ITS INSTITUTIONS**, reveal contemporary art in a self-reflective mode. The former examines the legacy of modernist architecture's utopian aspirations, and shows how artists find in its failed agendas a potent language for dealing with the complexities of existence. The latter includes artists considering their own role in the art system—how supposedly external factors like art patronage, modes of display, and critical theories play an integral role in shaping contemporary art.

The last two chapters examine the strategies by which artists seek to have an impact on the larger world. Chapter 15, **ART & POLITICS**, looks at the wide variety of approaches artists take as agents of social change. Chapter 16, **ART & AUDIENCE**, describes artists' growing interest in the notion of the artwork as a set of social relationships. It explores a greatly expanded definition of art in which the idea of the art object is all but abandoned; works may involve developing temporary communities, organizing communal activities such as meals, marches, or house-building, or creating conditions for social interaction among strangers.

Beginning with historically rooted themes and arcing toward the more speculative or outward-reaching creations of our time, *Art & Today* explores many of art's most salient issues and articulates the key ways in which artists are re-envisioning art history. The book's time frame is roughly the 1980s to the present, and the focus is primarily on artists who have emerged during that period, though artists of earlier decades are also included when they help elucidate individual themes. Each chapter begins with a sketch of the historical or theoretical context in which its particular theme emerged, followed by a discussion of particular artists who embody and extend the theme.

Though its thematic and geographic reach is wide, *Art & Today* does not claim to be an exhaustive account of the full range of contemporary art and artists. To the contrary, such an attempt would be fruitless in the wake of the demise of the master narrative, when the possibilities for art (not to mention the number of working artists) are ever-expanding. Rather, this book offers a series of mini-narratives that brings together groups of contemporary artists in light of their relationship to some larger concept. The narratives themselves are meant to be suggestive rather than exclusive, and the categorization is porous—on occasion an artist appears in more than one narrative, and in fact many other artists could have inhabited these same stories. Further, other stories could have been included, for instance art and music, or art and language. By necessity, this selective organizational principle means that some noteworthy contemporary artists are not included in these pages because they didn't fit these particular narratives.

As we move further into the twenty-first century, there appears to be more art than ever, from more places than ever, and with a larger audience than ever. Art today is more diverse and contradictory than at any other time in its history. Established genres, mediums, and styles no longer carry deterministic weight among artists. Art transcends old-fashioned limits of time and space, appearing on the Internet, in the landscape, in the sky, and in your head. Art may last for a fraction of a second or it may be designed to outlast human civilization. Art today exists in a state of constant change. Having broken free from one encompassing ideology, it seems unlikely to adopt another. Instead it reaches outward to embrace the larger social, political, economic, and philosophical realities of the world. As *Art & Today* attempts to demonstrate, art is not a single story, it is a tapestry of stories, some of which are interwoven while others develop in relative isolation. Art today is anything but simple. But we can hardly expect simplicity from art when there is nothing simple about the world from which it springs.

ART & POPULAR CULTURE
THE WARHOL EFFECT

In his 1939 manifesto "Avant-garde and Kitsch," critic Clement Greenberg argued fervently and famously that serious critics and artists must strive at all costs to uphold the barrier between high and low culture. Adopting the German term for tasteless and gaudy decoration, he lashed out at "kitsch"—the debasement of low culture represented by "popular, commercial art and literature with their chromeotypes, magazine covers, illustrations, ads, slick and pulp fiction, comics, Tin Pan Alley music, tap dancing, Hollywood movies, etc. etc." The problem with such exemplars of popular taste, according to Greenberg, was their lack of authenticity. "Kitsch," he famously maintained, "is mechanical and operates by formulas. Kitsch is vicarious experience and faked sensations. Kitsch changes according to style but remains always the same. Kitsch is the epitome of all that is spurious in the life of our times. Kitsch pretends to demand nothing of its customers except their money —not even their time."[1]

Kitsch was the weapon of the barbaric hordes eager to breach the ramparts of the avant-garde, and Greenberg would not relent: throughout the 1940s and '50s, he continued to publish essays condemning the sullying influence of mass taste. People listened, especially when the critique of kitsch was linked to cold war assumptions about America's superiority over the tyranny of popular taste in the Soviet Union. But Greenberg's battle against mass taste was successful only to a point: even his favored Abstract Expressionists were not immune to the lure of popular culture. The paintings in Willem de Kooning's famous "Women" series were in part inspired by images of actress Marilyn Monroe. And Jackson Pollock posed for an article in *Life* magazine headlined "Jackson Pollock—Is He the Greatest Living Painter in the United States?" and allowed his paintings to appear in backdrops for fashion shoots.

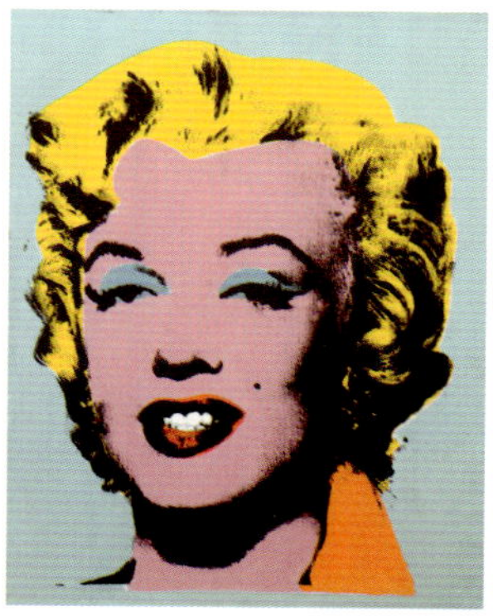

ANDY WARHOL
MINT MARILYN (TURQUOISE MARILYN)
1962
ACRYLIC AND SILKSCREEN INK ON LINEN
20 X 16 IN (50.8 X 40.6 CM)

Nonetheless, it wasn't until the emergence of Andy Warhol in the 1960s that Greenberg's notions of high culture met their ultimate test. Warhol, arguably the most important artist of the latter twentieth century, rode a sea change in the art world and its relationship to contemporary culture as he transformed celebrities and products into icons of Pop art. While by no means the only artist of this time to dismantle the boundary between high and low art, he remains the most protean and inventive in his attack on any notions of purity and elite culture. For defenders of the old faith Greenberg represented, Warhol personified the dreadful decline of art from the exalted heights of Pollock and Mark Rothko to the cesspool of mass taste, commercial co-option, and celebrity worship. But for advocates of the new, emerging art, he was the first artist to clearly understand, harness, and reflect the forces shaping postwar American society.

Today there can be no question about who won the contest between avant-garde and kitsch. When he died in 1987, the shy, standoffish Warhol, who started his career making whimsical drawings of shoes for fashion ads, was as close as any artist could be to a household name. And time has not diminished his fame or influence. His silk-screened paintings of Campbell's soup cans and movie stars, his stiff blond wig, his entourage of divas, drag queens, and hangers-on, and his famously deadpan pronouncements about his life and work remain the stuff of legend both in and outside the art world.

Warhol's continued influence is everywhere, from the 2006 holiday windows at Barneys department store in New York celebrating the "Warhol-idays," to a new line of Levi's jeans decorated with Warhol's images. His themes are the themes of contemporary life. His work and example expose the mechanisms by which collective desires are generated, the way in which our aspirations and self-images are homogenized to better serve the market, and the peculiar deformations of consciousness brought about by life in the "information age." He raises questions about the meanings of freedom, individualism, and equality in a society in which decisions seem shaped by forces beyond our control. He makes us ask whether our materialistic lives render us victims of capitalism or, rather, demonstrate our liberation from want. His obsession with materialism, narcissism, and consumption is shared by us all. In the art world, Warhol's legacy is equally complex and multifaceted. Among the various strains of consciousness that contemporary heirs to the so-called Warhol Effect express in both their work and their identities are the rise of the cult of celebrity, the perception-transforming power of mass media, the leveling of hierarchies, and the merging of art and business. This chapter presents examples of each in turn.

Warhol's most prescient and famous statement was his prediction that "in the future everyone will be famous for 15 minutes."[2] Among the signs that he was on to something: the emergence of "reality TV," which makes stars of ordinary people with no particular fame credentials other than a willingness to expose their most personal activities and desires to the camera; the broadcast of high-profile trials as low comedy, with defendants and witnesses transformed into dubious celebrities; and the intermingling of politics and entertainment as candidates address the electorate on comedy channels and late-night talk shows. An early student of the mechanisms of celebrity, Warhol made it his persistent subject in paintings of Marilyn, Jackie, Liz, and others in the pantheon of one-name stars. One of a series of Marilyn "flavors," *Mint Marilyn (Turquoise Marilyn)*, 1962, reveals how a realistic image is transformed into an iconic one. Based on a publicity still, Warhol cropped the photograph at the base of her neck and applied different flat and exaggerated colors to different parts of her face and background. In this instance, the background is a minty green, her eyes and eyelids bright blue, her hair golden yellow, and the triangle of her collar orange. These colors varied from picture to picture. But celebrity was more than a subject for his work, it was also an elemental aspect of his identity. Despite appearances of nonchalance, Warhol's persona was carefully crafted to suit the media cravings of his day. He presented himself as a kind of court jester to high society, a slave of Hollywood, and the calm center of a whirlpool of decadence. His career, it is now clear, was a series of provocations in the service of publicity. It is no coincidence that when an artist today is accused of peddling in the currency of fame, he or she is likely to be compared to Andy Warhol.

An exceptional reflection of the spirit of Warhol as media-savvy provocateur can be found in the work of artists Gilbert & George. The duo introduced their enduring personae, a pair of "living sculptures," in the late 1960s, when they were still students in art school. This is when they first performed their well-known *Singing*

Sculpture, 1970, in which, with skin painted bronze and outfitted with dapper suits and canes, they danced and sang to the English music hall standard "Underneath the Arches." Their mock bourgeois duds and dandified manner could not have been further from the era's reigning image of the avant-garde artist as an unkempt, macho individualist, and while their work has shifted from performance to images over the years, their selves have remained central to their art. Gilbert & George are best known today for photograph-based "paintings" in which they stand, in suits or in the buff, before montages of images of body fluids, ecclesiastical architecture, "rough trade" (England's young working class boys and men), and the graffitied walls and alleys of the grittier reaches of East London, where the duo continues to live and work. Overlaid with black grids that set off the backgrounds' bright colors, these pieces suggest distinctly unholy stained-glass windows. The title of the 2004 series "Perversive Pictures" underlines the deliberately controversial nature of this newer work's associations. *Clean Me*, 2004, for example, depicts the artists with rolls of toilet paper, against the background of an illuminated halo.

Like Warhol, Gilbert & George are themselves their own best work of art. The same might be said of Julian Schnabel, who burst onto the American art scene in the late 1970s as part of an international revival of expressionist painting. The media portrayed Schnabel as an ultra-macho, swashbuckling painter, a worthy successor to the legendary Pollock. Schnabel created paintings that attested to an outsized ambition and, many noted, displayed an equally outsized ego. He came to fame for his plate paintings, in which he splashed figurative images over wooden armatures covered with broken plates. The effect was powerful, resembling at once rough mosaics, street graffiti, and primitive cave paintings. In time, Schnabel moved on to a variety of other techniques—he drew and wrote over Japanese screens, created word paintings on battered tarpaulin, used fur and velvet as backdrops, made three-dimensional paintings similar to Robert Rauschenberg's "Combines," created huge copies of truly bad thrift-store paintings, and ventured into sculpture with monumental bronze vessels that towered over the heads of viewers like totems.

The boisterous Schnabel is the antithesis of the fey, laconic, anti-expressive Warhol, and therefore a far more likely master of the mechanisms of publicity. Indeed, he has made no bones about courting the limelight. At the height of his fame in the 1980s, Schnabel became the darling of the art press, photographed at home and in the studio with muscles rippling beneath a white T-shirt. Like Warhol, though, Schnabel seemed to present a deliberately empty center, in which irony and self-aggrandizement were mixed in equal measure. His painting, *St. Sebastian—Born in 1951*, 1979, appeared to conflate St. Sebastian, who died for his faith under a rain of arrows, with the artist himself, who was born in 1951. This representation of a scored and fragmented torso thus suggested a coy equation of Schnabel's often hostile reception from critics and the sufferings of the Christian martyrs. Schnabel went even further in his 1981 painting *Portrait of God*, featuring a splash of blue paint on a weathered tarp, which seemed to suggest that the artist maintained a private line to the Almighty. Meanwhile, in his 1987 plate painting *Self-Portrait in Andy's Shadow*, he seemed to acknowledge Warhol as the real patron saint behind his work.

By the mid-'80s, another artist emerged to cement the spirit of the celebrity cult. Jeff Koons, a former Wall Street commodities broker, realized early on that his most marketable commodity was himself. His initial work, created in the context of Simulationism, involved the recontextualization of objects from contemporary life (see chapter 2). However, he quickly perceived the power of the Warholian persona, and began to turn himself into the subject of his art. In 1988, he devised a series of ads that ran in *Flash Art*, *Artforum*, and other art magazines, in which the airbrushed artist appeared with a pair of buxom models and as a teacher in front of a blackboard on which lessons like "Banality as Savior" and "Exploit the Masses" were written. Between 1989 and 1991 Koons created a series of photographs called "Made in Heaven," in which he portrayed himself and the Italian porn star/politician Cicciolina engaged in various sex acts. While some are seriously hardcore, with close-ups of oral sex and penetration, many are curiously sweet. Cicciolina wears a crown of flowers and white silk stockings as she and her partner roll around in an absurdly bucolic garden scene that mixes perversity with Disney-like Edenic innocence. Not surprisingly, critical condemnation of this work produced record crowds and lines around the block at exhibits. In 1991 the pair married, only to be divorced a year later. In 1992 Koons reinscribed the theme of exaggerated innocence onto *Puppy*, a forty-three-foot-high dog shaped topiary covered in seventy thousand seasonal flowers. Originally created for a temporary exhibition in the German city of Bad Arolsen, *Puppy* has subsequently been recreated at venues around the world; its outsized scale, unembarrassed embrace of kitsch, and widespread appeal to treacly tastes have reinforced Koons's reputation as a master publicist and earned him persistent comparisons with Warhol.

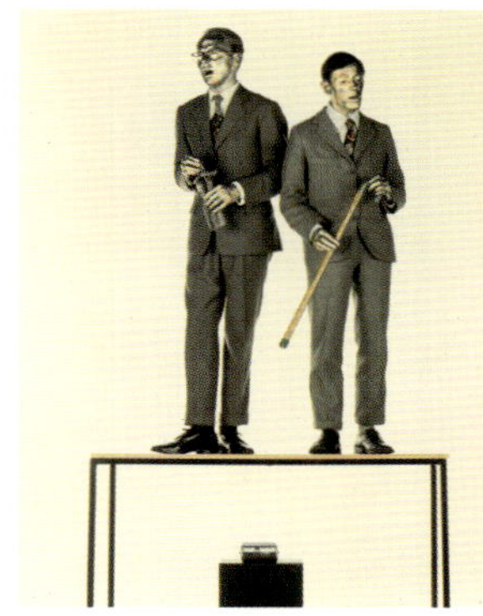

GILBERT & GEORGE
THE SINGING SCULPTURE
1970
LIVE INSTALLATION
LIFE SIZE

A group of artists with a Koonsian grasp of the aesthetics of provocation emerged in the late 1980s in London. Known collectively as the Young British Artists (or more often the YBAs), they took on nearly every taboo—mocking religion, sexual mores, family values, pedophilia, and death. The generally acknowledged leader of the group was Damien Hirst, who in 1988, while still in art school, curated "Freeze," a group exhibition installed in a vacated Port of London building. The show put the YBAs on the map and was regarded as a harbinger of a new generational energy; critics called the YBAs the voice of youth, describing their anarchic, anti-establishment ethos as a reaction by a group of mostly working-class artists to the diminishing sense of opportunity that marked Britain's Thatcher era.

Hirst's own works combine pseudo-philosophic titles with objects designed to stir outrage, disgust, and a heightened awareness of mortality. *A Thousand Years*, 1990, consists of a large vitrine containing a rotting cow's head, flies, maggots, sugar water, and a bug-zapper—a living portrait of a repellent cycle of life. *The Physical Impossibility of Death in the Mind of Someone Living*, 1991, is the name given to a sixteen-foot tiger shark suspended in a vast tank of greenish formaldehyde. *Home Sweet Home*, 1996, is a giant ashtray filled with cigarette butts—a work whose apparent nihilism earned it the cover of critic Donald Kuspit's elegiac tome *The End of Art*. In a related series, Hirst produces abstract paintings of colorful dots that are named after various pharmaceuticals and controlled substances.

JULIAN SCHNABEL

GILBERT & GEORGE

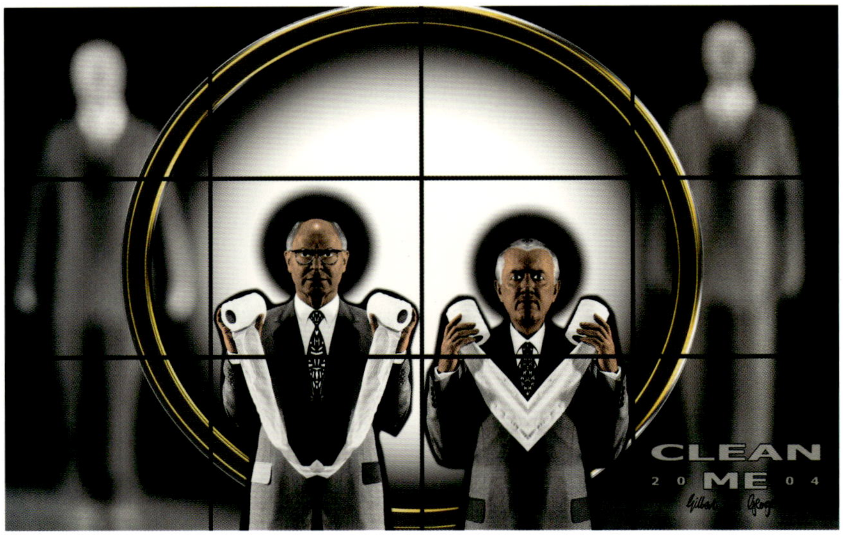

Clean Me, 2004
Mixed media, 74 3/8 x 118 1/8 in (189 x 300 cm)

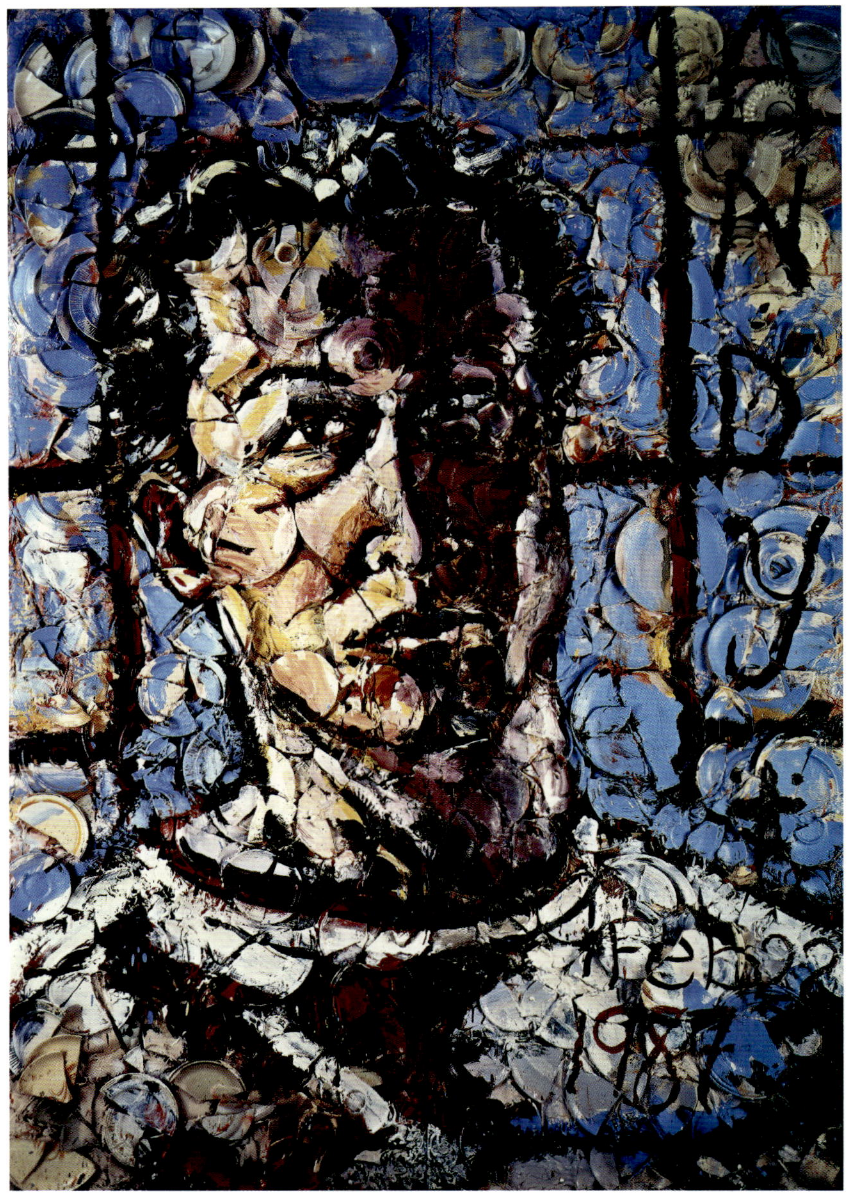

Self-Portrait in Andy's Shadow, 1987
Oil, plates, and Bondo on two wood panels, 103 x 72 x 10 in (261.6 x 182.9 x 25.4 cm)

JEFF KOONS

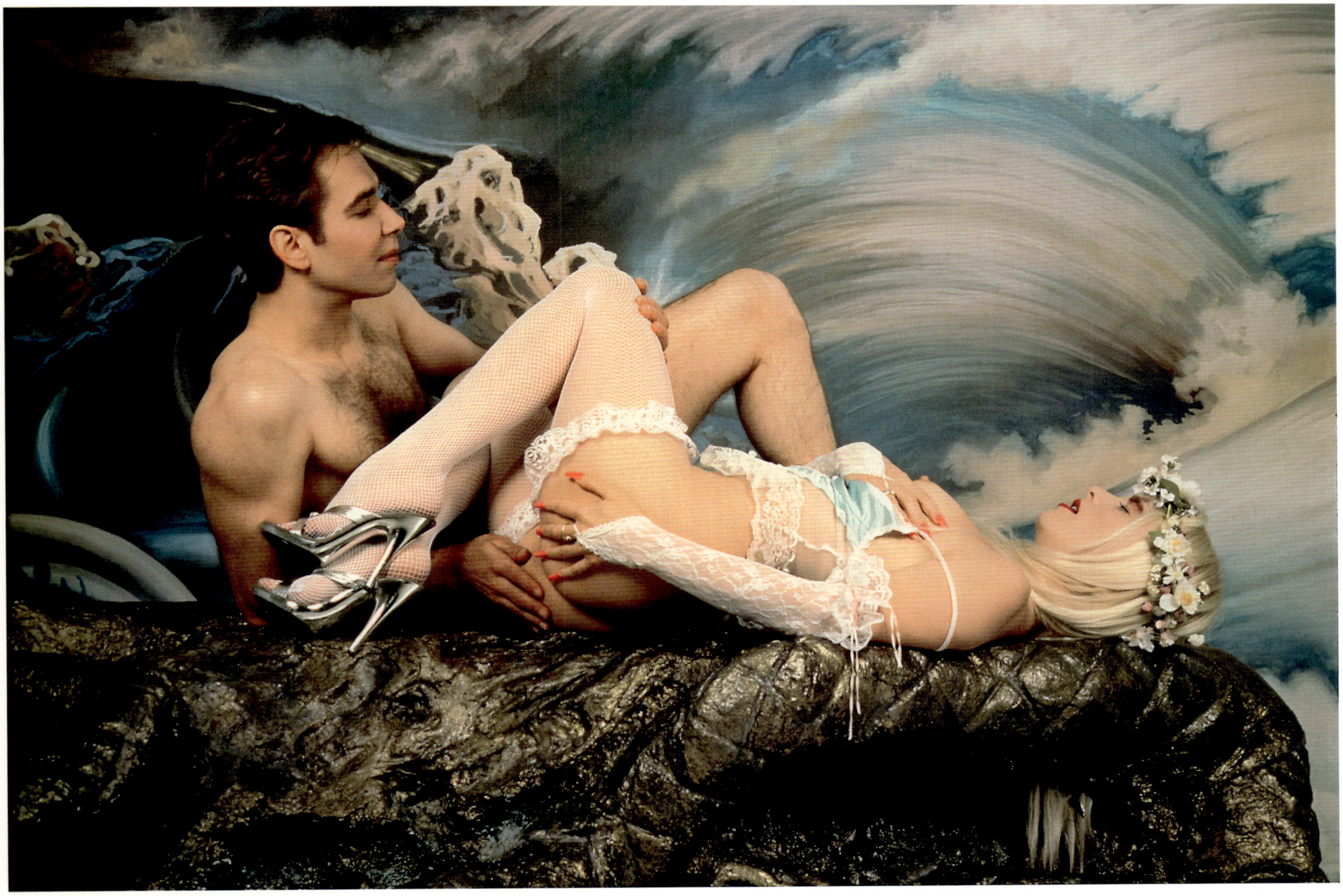

Jeff in the Position of Adam, 1990
Oil on canvas, 96 x 144 in (240 x 370 cm)

JEFF KOONS

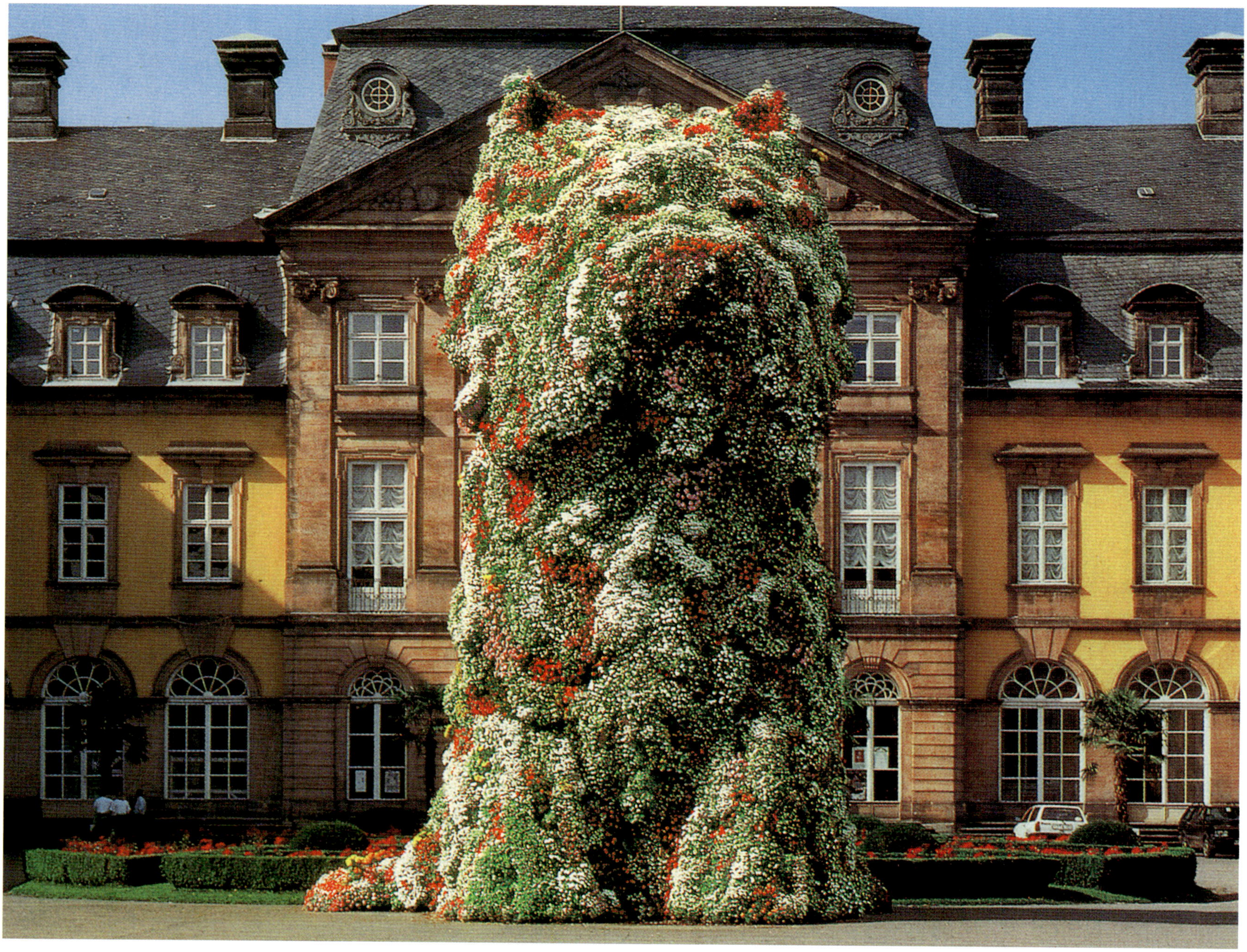

Puppy, 1992
Flowering plants, steel, wood, and soil, 38 ft (11.5 m) high
As installed at Schloss Arolsen, Germany, 1992

After Hirst, the YBA who has most successfully generated a high profile is Tracey Emin. In a move reminiscent of Koons's commodification of his relationship with Cicciolina, Emin has skillfully exploited her personal history and love life. "My Major Retrospective," her first solo exhibition in 1993, was composed of diaries, letters, and other personal mementoes that provided an unflinching confessional on the sexual trauma she suffered as a young girl growing up in Margate, England. Emin's *Everyone I Have Ever Slept With 1963–1995*, 1995, consists of a small tent appliquéd with all of the names in question. With this gesture, Emin turns the tables on male sexual braggadocio, putting her own sexuality on the table to upset the gender power balance. Not surprisingly, her no-holds-barred self-exposure has made Emin a media celebrity known far beyond the confines of the art world.

On the continent, another Warhol heir appeared, Maurizio Cattelan, the artist critic Calvin Tomkins has described as "our reigning artist-provocateur."[3] Cattelan is less interested in pursuing a consistent and recognizable signature style than in providing a kind of signature shock—one that draws intense notice. His sculptures draw on figures and images from the public subconscious, reimagining them in unexpected and disturbing, even blasphemous, forms. One of his best-known works is *La Nona Ora* (The Ninth Hour), 1999, a sculpture depicting Pope John Paul II felled by a meteorite. Other well-known sculptural pieces include *Him*, 2001, in which a suited wax figure of Hitler kneels in prayer, and *Now*, 2004, in which a waxen replica of John F. Kennedy lies in a coffin. Even more provocative are his more theatrical gestures. For the 1993 Venice Biennale, Cattelan rented his allotted exhibition space to a perfume company and pocketed the cash. For the 2004 Whitney Biennial, he allegedly buried a sculpture under the gallery floor, where it purportedly remains to this day. In 1999 he and German curator Jens Hoffmann staged a faux biennial in the Caribbean that was in fact nothing more than an opportunity for invited artists to spend a week in the sun.

Cattelan has also infiltrated many branches of the art world. He co-founded the annual magazine *Charley*, which presents hundreds of emerging and established artists per issue, and *Permanent Food*, described as a "magazine about magazines," both reminiscent of Warhol's *Interview*. He also served as co-curator of the 2006 Berlin Biennial and established a miniuscule but much noticed Chelsea gallery cheekily called The Wrong Gallery. Such tactics have propelled Cattelan to the center of today's celebrity-conscious art world.

Of course, Warhol's legacy goes far beyond his mastery of celebrity. Of equal importance was his understanding of the ways in which television, cinema, and advertising have transformed our consciousness. He once announced in his typically deadpan manner that "people sometimes say the way things happen in movies is unreal, but actually it's the way things happen to you in life that's unreal."[4] This idea finds full expression in the postmodern notion that mass media has trained us to consider second-hand spectacle more real than our own experiences. An early proponent of this view was the Canadian theorist Marshall McLuhan, who achieved a kind of guru status in the 1960s, famously observing that "the medium is the message."[5] McLuhan's general point was that the way in which we get information is more important than its actual content. More specifically, he believed that Gutenberg's fifteenth-century invention of moveable type ushered in an era of private understanding and alienation from society, while, by contrast, the electronic revolution, which brought television to the masses, heralded the onset of a new, connected consciousness, uniting us all (for better and for worse) in what he dubbed "the global village."

By the 1980s Jean Baudrillard eclipsed McLuhan as media guru. The French theorist was equally determinate but far more pessimistic, maintaining that in our post-industrial society reality had been replaced by signs and images that only appear to connect to concrete power relations or even to cause and effect. Politics thus becomes nothing more than a play of symbols, and advertising involves the marketing not of actual products, but of the lifestyle they supposedly will provide. He named such a state "hyper-reality," a realm dominated not by real things and actions, but by mere "simulations" of them.[6] "I never read. I just look at pictures," Warhol said some twenty years before, and it was his genius not only to predict this new state of affairs, but to show us through his works what it meant.[7] His silk-screened portraits, for example, came from newspapers, fanzines, publicity, and advertising photos—but he transformed them. He obscured details, swathing the images in flat colors and repeating them in grids that affirmed the mechanical nature of their reproduction as each successive image became slightly more illegible and indistinct. What was left was less an approximation of the living, breathing original than a trace suited to endless multiplication.

These lessons in the effects of media imagery inspired a host of subsequent artists, foremost among them John Baldessari, who since the 1960s has been exploring the manipulation of consciousness through media. Both through his own innovative work, and as a teacher at the California Institute of the Arts, Baldessari has shaped the thinking of generations of younger artists. Baldessari's "paintings" are composed of juxtaposed, found photographic images, often lifted from obscure Hollywood films, and arranged thematically in such a way that the viewer is compelled to make connections between them. For example, *Heel*, 1986, explores the various meanings of heel—the back of the foot, the command to a dog, a name for a cad—through a series of found images. His canvases, in which things are joined by the most fleeting connections—a similar gesture, a visual pun, an eye-catching background detail—suggest the quick-cut editing popularized by MTV. To look at one of Baldessari's works is to relearn how to read in a nonverbal, nonlinear way.

In a 1990 interview, Baldessari traced his approach to a common contemporary experience: "It's like when I am in an airplane cabin and overhear two conversations: one says something and another one says something else. I could not have thought up those phrases on my own, and I respond to it by connecting one to the other, taking both out of their own context and by making them a part of my imagination."[8]

Baldessari's contemporary, Ed Ruscha, mines a similarly associative vein, and like Baldessari, he has had a crucial influence on younger media-oriented artists. Another longtime California resident, Ruscha is often associated with that state's open space, car culture, and romanticized Hollywood worldview. He is best known for large-scale canvases in which a single word or phrase is superimposed on a glowing field of color. Like Baldessari, Ruscha short-circuits the normal process of reading—words and phrases are no longer transparent vehicles for conjuring up an image or idea but are rather things in themselves. Trompe l'oeil text, painted in liquid spills, as drops of water, or rays of light, synchronizes form to content.

Like Baldessari, Ruscha is indebted to cinema, though in a different way. The vast spaces that his words inhabit bear an unmistakable resemblance to Technicolor movie screens; the words floating on them read like credits, as in *The End*, from 1931.

TRACEY EMIN

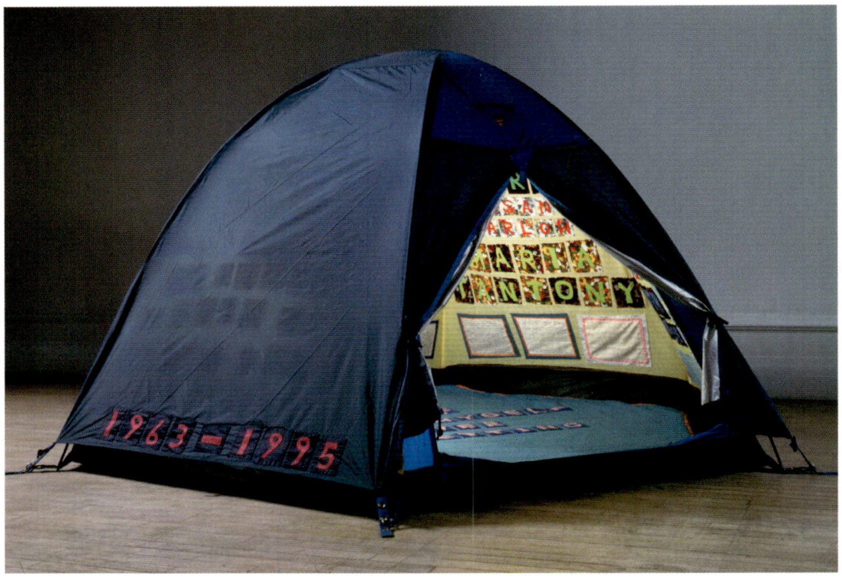

Everyone I Have Ever Slept With 1963–1995, 1995
Appliqued tent, mattress, and light, 48 x 96 1/2 x 84 1/2 in (122 x 245 x 215 cm)
The Saatchi Collection, London, destroyed by fire 2004

DAMIEN HIRST

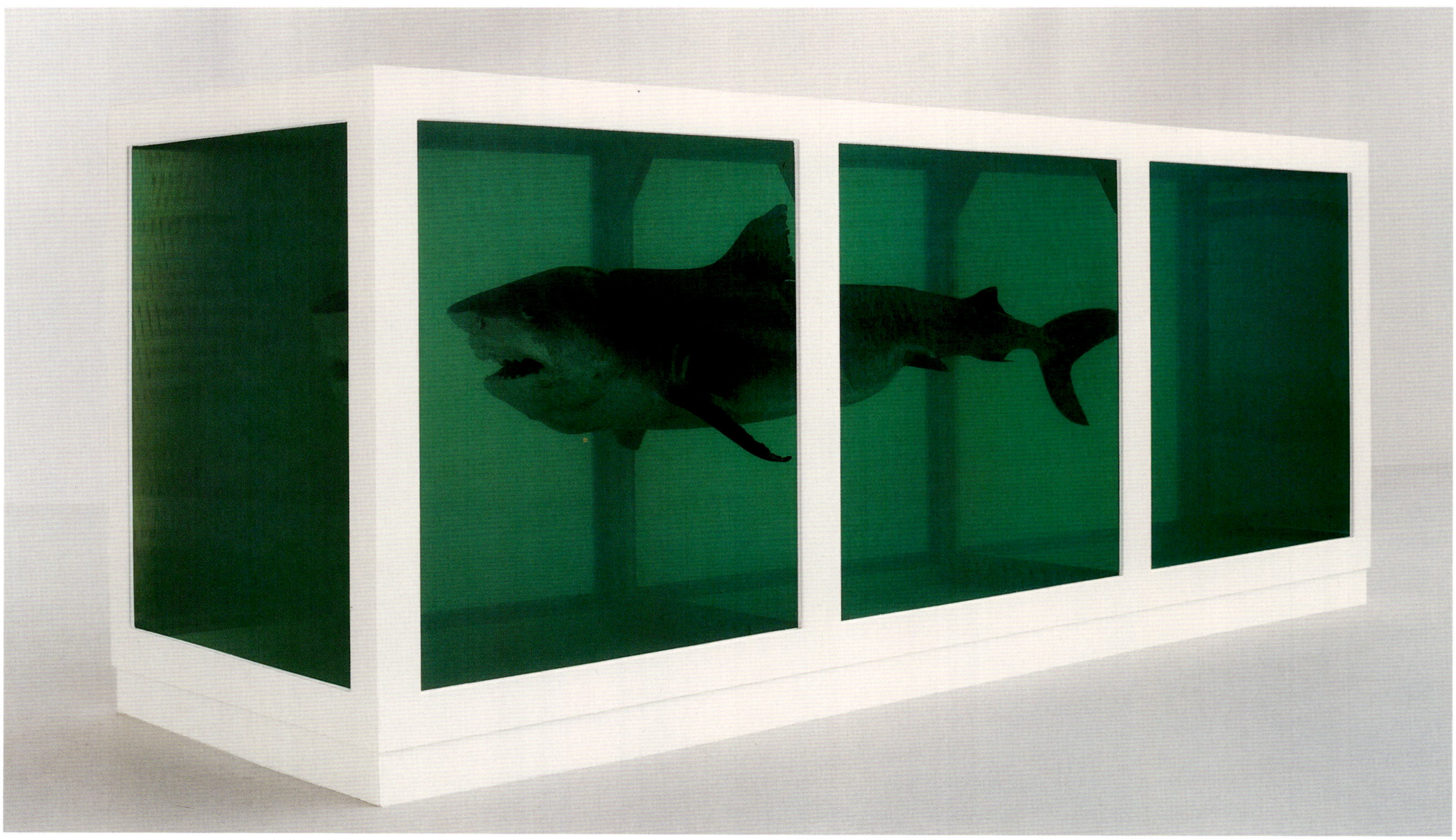

The Physical Impossibility of Death in the Mind of Someone Living, 1991
7 ft x 17 ft x 15 ft 4 in (2.1 x 5.2 x 2.1 m)

MAURIZIO CATTELAN

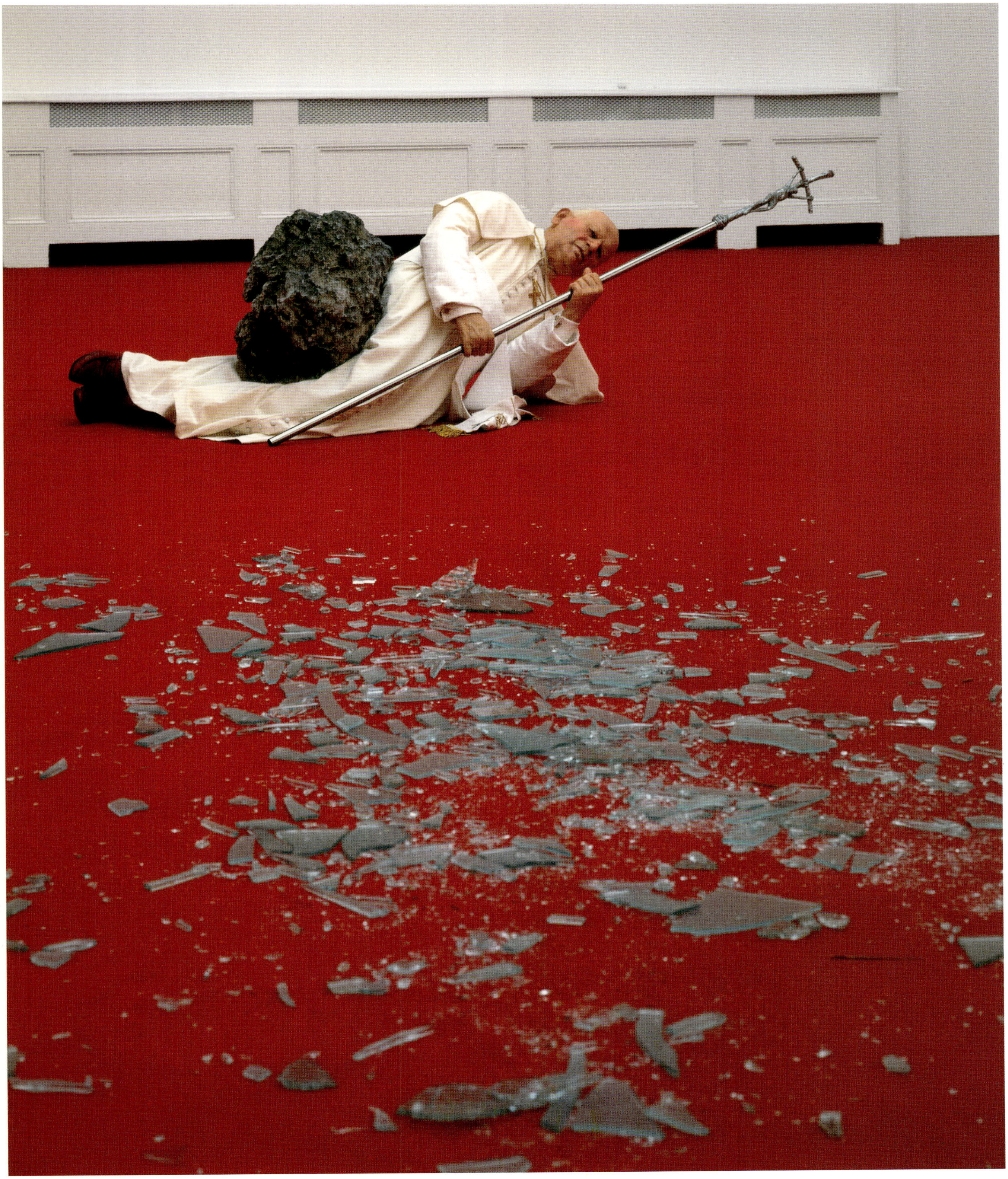

La Nona Ora (The Ninth Hour), 1992
Wax, clothing, polyester resin with metallic powder, volcanic rock, carpet, and glass, life-size

Ruscha also includes certain generic images in his work, most famously in a 1963 series of photographs of twenty-six gasoline stations. But again, as the banality of the subject suggests, these images are to be regarded as abstract symbols rather than things in themselves. As the artist puts it, when he paints a mountain, he is really painting "the idea of the idea of the idea of the mountain."[9] In essence, Ruscha's works suggest nothing more than empty screens on which to project our imaginations, just like the ever-pervasive movies themselves.

The idea that our sense of reality is mediated and even created by language, television, movies, and mass media had a decisive influence on the generation of artists that came of age in the 1980s. Among the more emblematic among them is Richard Prince, who re-photographed and blew up magazine ads that were carefully chosen to highlight the reinvention of American reality through myth. Most famously, he re-photographed the rugged Marlboro Man galloping across the Western landscape or pausing majestically on his horse. As many critics noted, in appropriating the faux cowboy, Prince isolated the perfect metaphor for the mythology of self-sufficiency and individual freedom that informed the Reagan era. Prince's subsequent series have touched on other symbols of American machismo and lowbrow culture. He cannibalized motorcycle magazines for photographs of biker girls straddling motorcycles in overtly sexual poses. He appropriated lurid pulp-fiction covers of voluptuous, sexually voracious nurses. He created huge painterly renderings of sexist Borscht Belt jokes and *Playboy* cartoons. He has also moved to sculpture, celebrating America's car culture with strangely abstract replicas of classic Thunderbird hoods dripping with gestural, expressionistic paint. In each case, his works seem to drain all of the emotional heat from symbols and images normally associated with seduction and desire. By homing in on the tawdry underbelly of popular culture and reflecting it with clinical detachment, Prince makes us consider culture in a different light. We become aware of the way images drawn from advertising, porn, and cartoons meld to create a kind of collective subconscious that shapes the way we think and act.

JOHN BALDESSARI

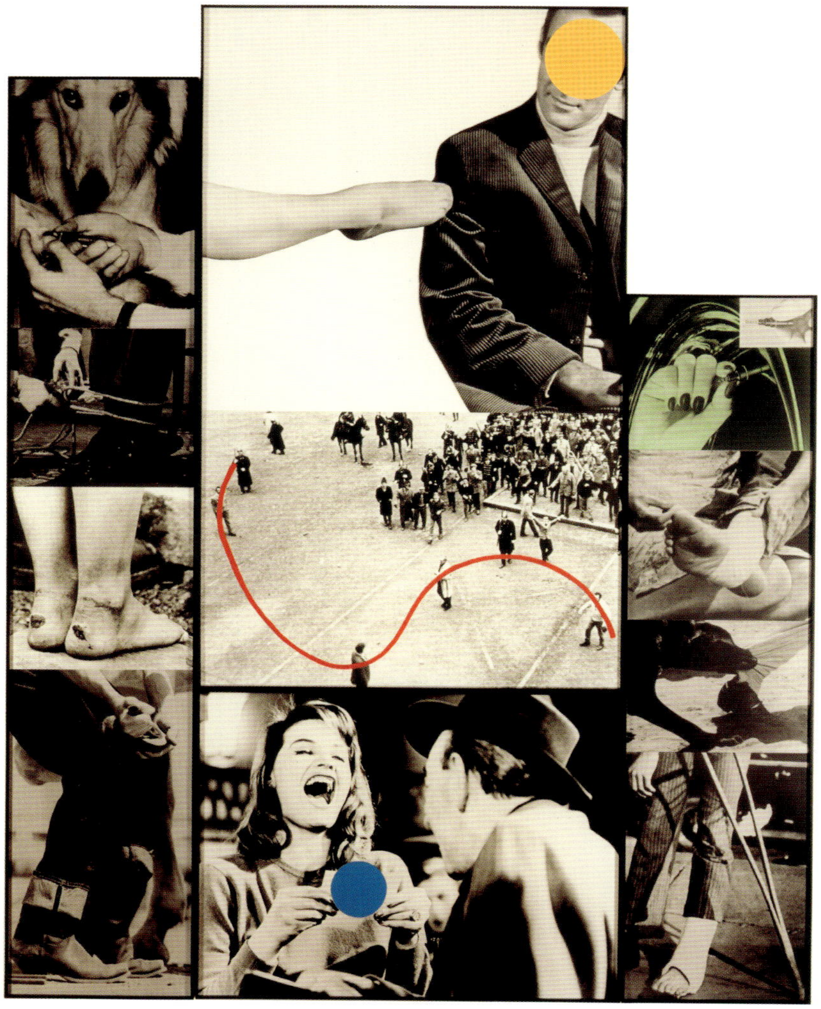

Heel, 1986
Black and white photographs, oil tint, vinyl paint
106 1/2 x 87 in (270.5 x 221 cm)

Robert Longo, an artist of the same milieu as Prince, also responds to media images, mimicking those expressing power and authority from Hollywood, advertising, and other cultural sources. His early-1980s "Men in the City" series consists of life-size charcoal drawings of men and women dressed in elegant corporate attire who writhe in poses that suggest they have just been shot, as in the 1981 work *Untitled*. These arresting high-contrast images approximate the seedy polish of film noir while conveying the precarious nature of the life of the modern corporate warrior.

In 1995 Longo directed a movie that seemed to encapsulate his fascination with Hollywood genre films and second-hand experience. *Johnny Mnemonic* features Keanu Reeves as a high-tech data courier who hires his memory out to the highest corporate bidder. Based on a story by cyberpunk author William Gibson, the film is a pastiche of Hollywood action film conventions, but Longo deliberately alters the pacing in order to undermine the audience's expectation of a thrill every ten minutes. Though he intended the film as a critique of Hollywood's manipulation of viewers' emotions, it was so similar to its pop-culture models that critics failed to detect any difference and generally panned it.

Younger artists who address the reinscription of vision and consciousness draw on new models that go beyond cinema and advertising. Inka Essenhigh, for instance, addresses the swirl of visual influences that come at us through vehicles like comics, the Internet, and video games. Her works are a deliberate mix of high and

ED RUSCHA

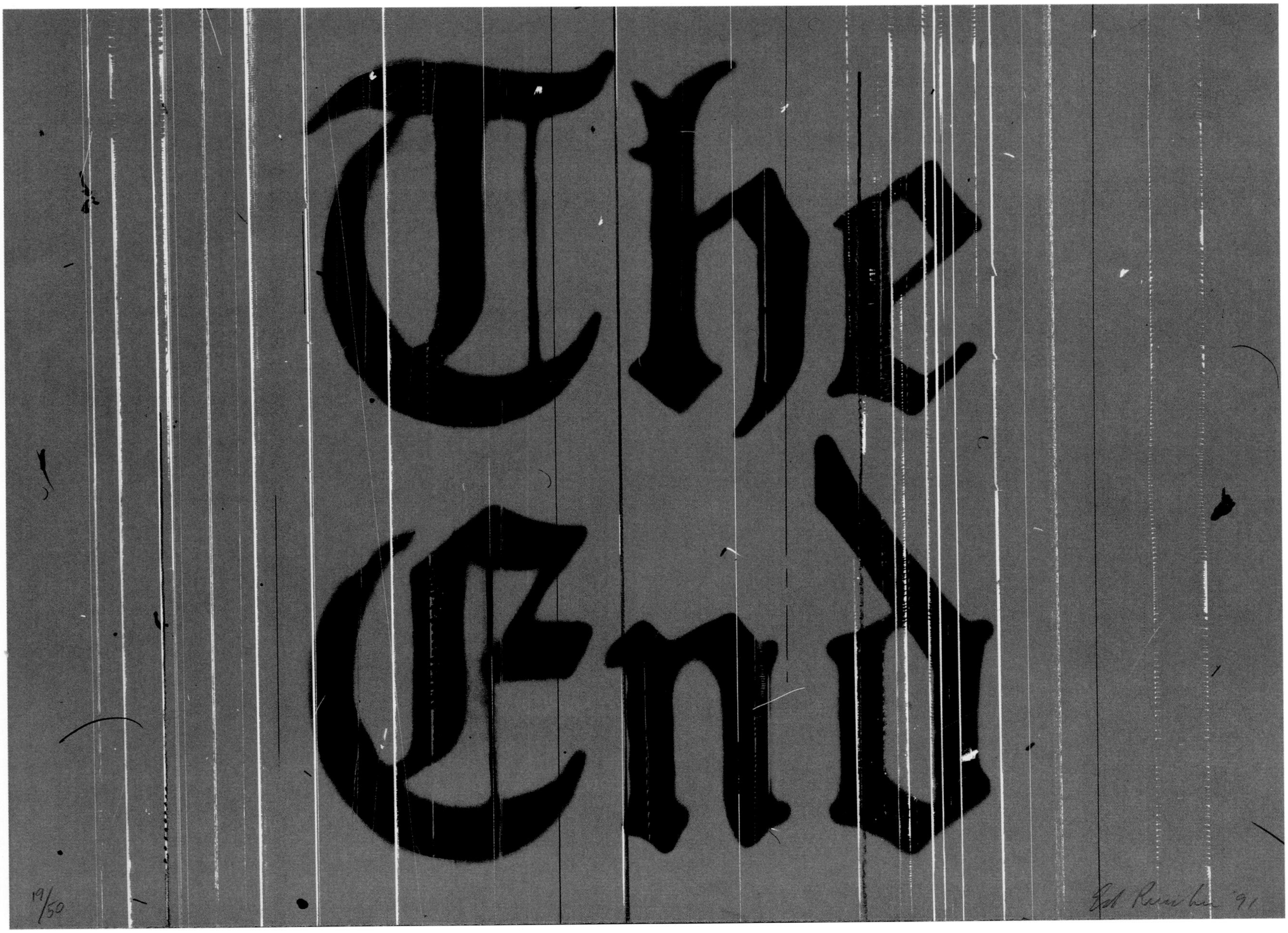

The End, 1991
Acrylic on paper, 26 3/16 x 36 5/8 in (65.5 x 93 cm)

RICHARD PRINCE

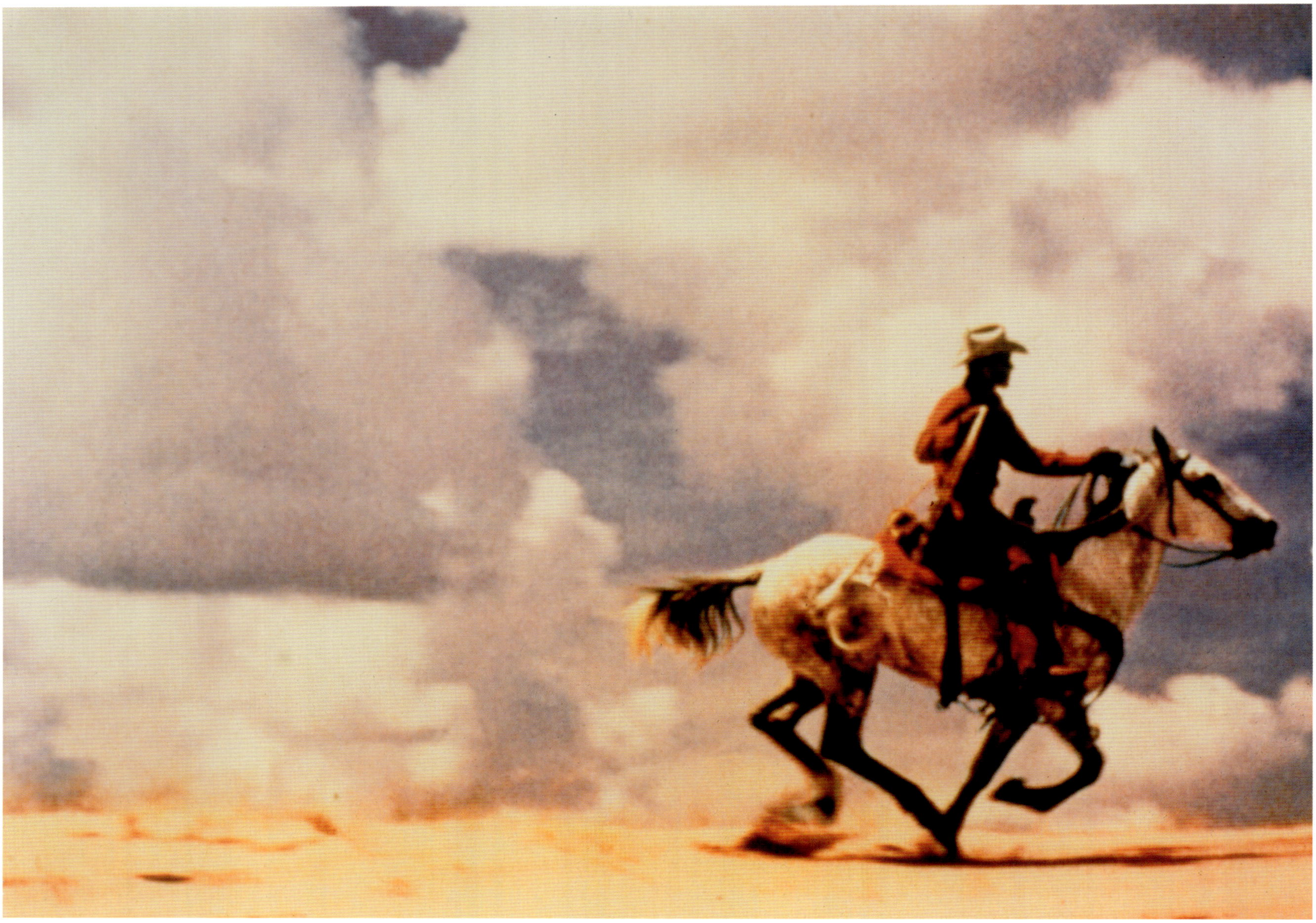

Untitled (Cowboy), 1989
Ektacolor photograph, 50 x 70 in (127 x 177.8 cm)

ROBERT LONGO

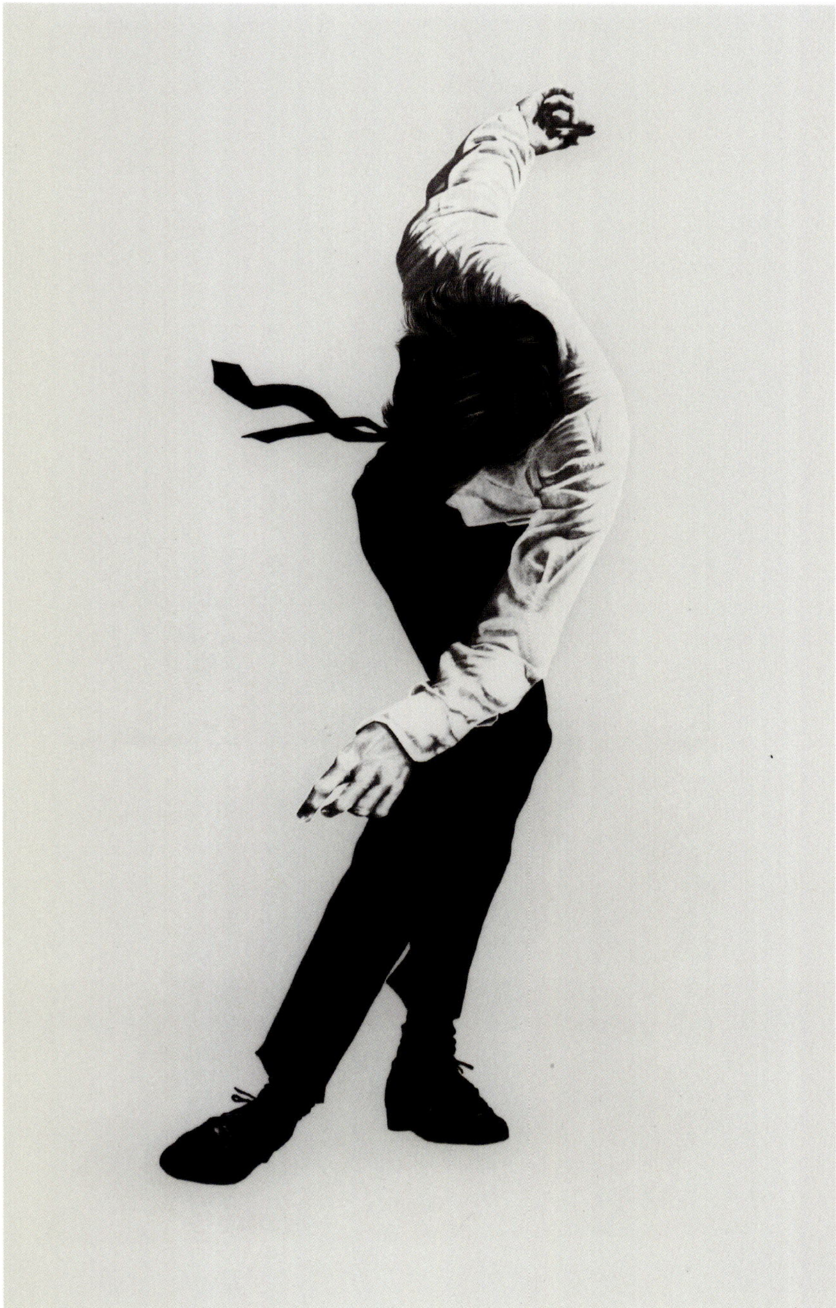

Untitled, 1981
Charcoal and graphite on paper, 96 x 60 in (243.8 x 152.4 cm)

RACHEL HARRISON

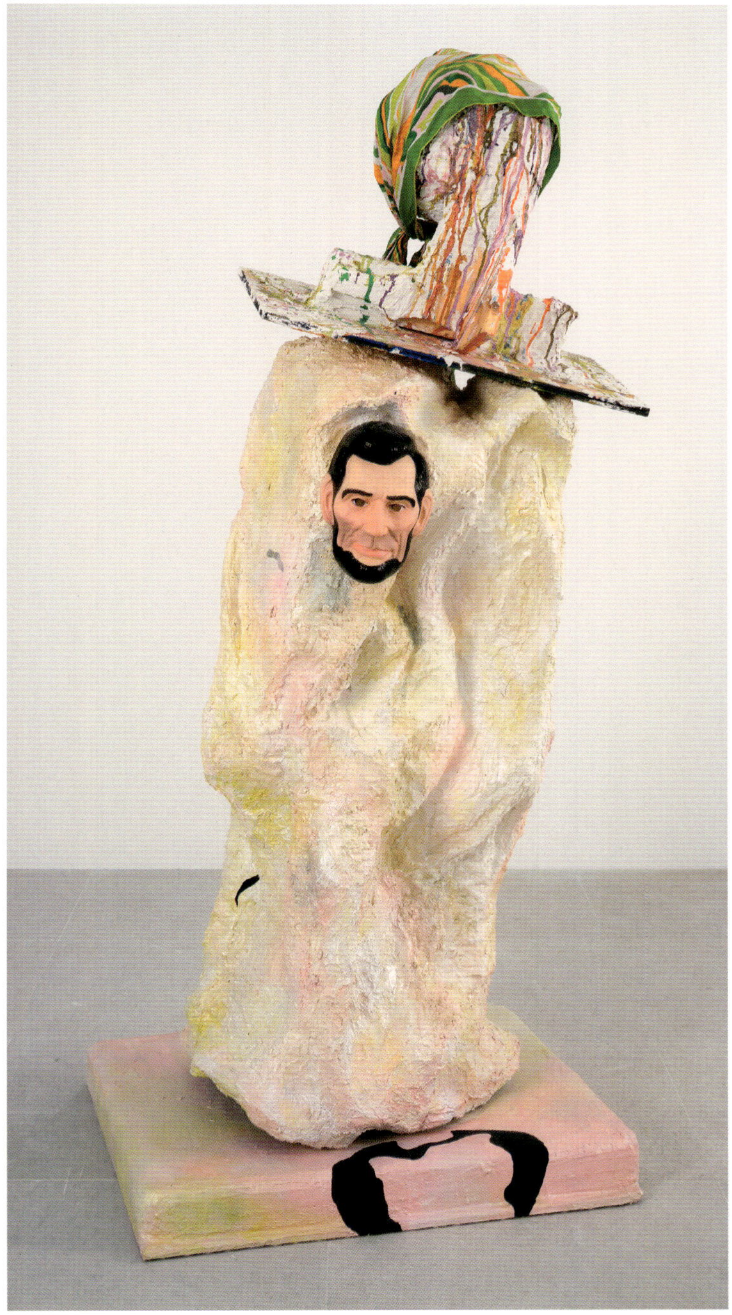

Schmatte with President, 2006
Wood, styrofoam, cement, acrylic, scarf, Lincoln mask
71 x 21 x 27 in (180.3 x 53.3 x 68.8 cm)

low references, absorbing and reworking such diverse sources as Italian Renaissance paintings, Art Nouveau decoration, Japanese Ukiyo-e prints, Persian miniatures, digital animation, and the Surrealism of Salvador Dalí. These multiple sources are assimilated into slick, exotic-looking, highly stylized tableaux of distorted creatures. Like Warhol, Essenhigh elevates the seemingly banal aspects of everyday existence in paintings like *In Bed*, 2005, in which nightmares become palpable presences, enveloping a sleeping woman who seems to have become one with her billowing sheets.

Rachel Harrison is a sculptor who takes Essenhigh's recombinatory images into three dimensions. A self-proclaimed admirer of Baldessari, she mingles blob-like abstract forms with photographs and objects drawn from all reaches of popular culture in a way that makes familiar icons strange and nearly illegible. Among her image bank are gender-specific toys such as Becky, Barbie's wheelchair-bound friend, photos of pop icons such as Michael Jackson, the rock band KISS, Elizabeth Taylor, and Johnny Carson, kitsch statuettes of personages such as the Buddha, and dull consumer products such as canned peas or salsa. These signifiers are embedded in sculptures that make subtle and not always particularly complimentary references to art history—wooden crates that mime Minimalist boxes, for instance, or ungainly Styrofoam and papier-mâché forms in gaudy colors that make a mockery of expressionist sculpture. *Schmatte with President,* 2006, embeds a mask of Abraham Lincoln in an amorphous structure swathed with a rag, undermining his heroic status. Harrison's promiscuous combinations of material, form, and allusion suggest a state of media oversaturation in which icons of past and present commingle in ways that defy logic and memory.

If Warhol introduced a new way of looking at the world, he did it with references to a world that was completely familiar. As he remarked, "The Pop artists did images that anybody walking down Broadway could recognize in a split second—comics, picnic tables, men's trousers, celebrities, shower curtains, refrigerators, Coke bottles—all the great modern things that the Abstract Expressionists tried so hard not to notice at all."[10] The leveling of hierarchies, the celebration of things his predecessors considered outside the parameters of aesthetic appreciation, and the transformation of the street itself into art are among Warhol's important legacies to contemporary art. As he himself suggested, his was a radically egalitarian vision. Drawn from the tabloid newspaper, the supermarket, and the Saturday morning cartoons, his images required no esoteric knowledge or special training.

The legacy of this radical egalitarianism is evident in many strains of contemporary art that incorporate pop culture, but it is especially pronounced in the graffiti art movement of the 1980s, in which inner-city graffiti artists in New York and a few other American cities took an activity considered anti-social or even criminal and turned it into a hot property among the most high-toned art collectors. Young graffitists with names like Lady Pink and Crash took their spray-painted "tags" and images from subway cars, billboards, and buildings straight to canvas and showed their work in blue chip galleries and museums. For a few years critics admired and collectors vied for the works' raw authenticity. By the early 1990s, after the fashion had passed, reporters checking in on the young stars of the movement found that many had slipped back into jobs as bike messengers and delivery boys.

However, in the hands of a few artists—Keith Haring and Jean-Michel Basquiat foremost among them—graffiti art assumed a longer life. Haring, like Basquiat, was not an authentic child of the streets. Born in rural Pennsylvania, he studied commercial art in Pittsburgh, and was among the first art school-trained artists to grasp graffiti's potential as a means of reaching a vast public. Moving to New York in 1978, he studied at the School of Visual Arts, and soon began using the blank, black-papered advertising boards scattered throughout the subway system as "canvases," drawing on them with white chalk, as in *Untitled*, 1984. Response to his outlined, cartoonish drawings of people, dogs, and other creatures was instant, widespread, and positive. Haring cited among his inspirations the sunny characters of Walt Disney, and his subway graffiti had a similar sense of ingratiating good cheer. But there was a darker edge in some works, particularly those created on canvas for more limited, less public consumption. These paintings combined images of mushroom clouds, copulating couples, skeletons, and crucifixes with his signature crawling babies, barking dogs, and running figures. Such works took on big social issues—AIDS, homophobia, drugs, and the threat of nuclear holocaust. But even in these more serious pieces, Haring, who died in 1990 of AIDS-related complications, retained the accessible sense of childlike freedom that was the hallmark of his work.

While Basquiat, like Haring, was considered a "street artist," and was later mythologized as the unschooled wild child of the gritty East Village, he was born in Brooklyn, to a middle-class Haitian father and a Puerto Rican mother. Again like Haring, Basquiat launched his career on the graffiti model. In the late 1970s, he and a friend plastered the tag "SAMO" (his adapted acronym for "Same Old," as in "same ol' shit") over city walls, inscribing them with rebellious pronouncements like "Samo © as an alternative to joe normal and the bourgeoisie fantasy." By 1981, Basquiat had shifted to paintings, but his canvases, like *Untitled*, 1981, retained a loose, raw graffiti feel. Filled with scrawled texts, scratches, and cartoon-like drawings, they combined complex layering with spontaneity. The references were remarkably diverse, ranging from jazz (from heroes such as Miles Davis and Charlie Parker to the very idea of improvisation) to African-American history to cartoon characters, including Porky Pig, Batman, and Dick Tracy, to the American deification of the black athlete to symbols of money and commerce, and even to junk food. Critics discussed the "neo-primitive" nature of his works, constructing a lineage that stretched back to Art Brut and forward to hip hop.

Inside and outside the art world, Basquiat became famous for epitomizing the drug-fueled, unfettered hedonism of the 1980s. In 1985 he was pictured on the cover of the *New York Times Magazine* in his studio, after a night of clubbing, brandishing a brush and costumed in a paint-splattered designer suit. As his fame grew, he was befriended by older successful artists. Warhol in particular acknowledged Basquiat both as heir and competitor by engaging him in a collaborative painting project in which each painted images or texts in their distinctive styles. The poster for the show of these works styled the two as boxers poised for a match. Later, after Basquiat's death in 1988 at age twenty-seven from a heroin overdose, Julian Schnabel directed *Basquiat*, a feature film starring Jeffrey Wright in the lead role. The film also contained a thinly veiled representation of Schnabel himself, played by Gary Oldman, as Basquiat's kindly mentor. David Bowie played Warhol, the father of this holy trinity of celebrity.

While graffiti art was initially identified with New York City, it also found a solid home in San Francisco, where Barry McGee and the late Margaret Kilgallen

INKA ESSENHIGH

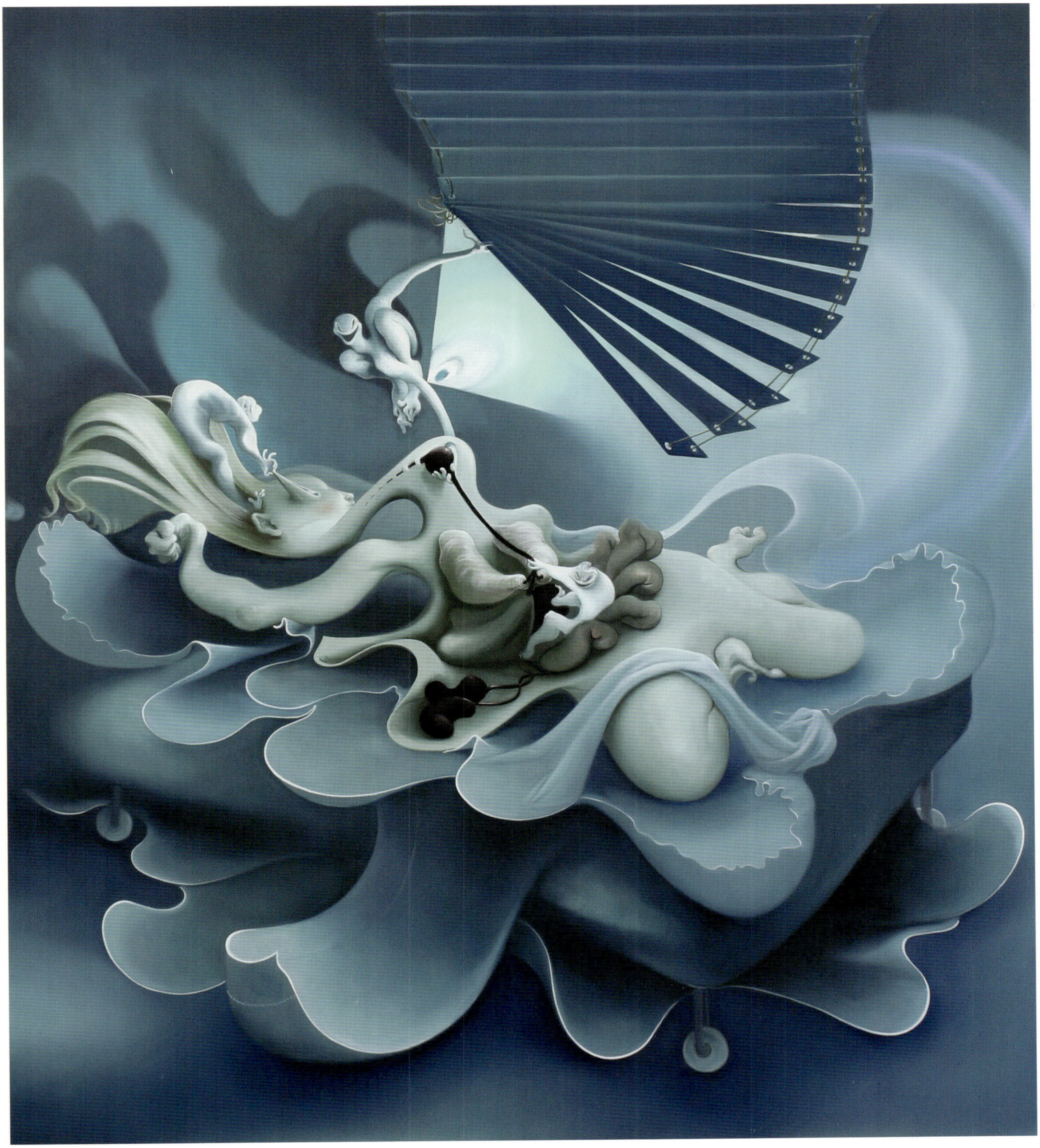

In Bed, 2005
Oil on canvas, 68 x 62 in (172.7 x 157.5 cm)

KEITH HARING

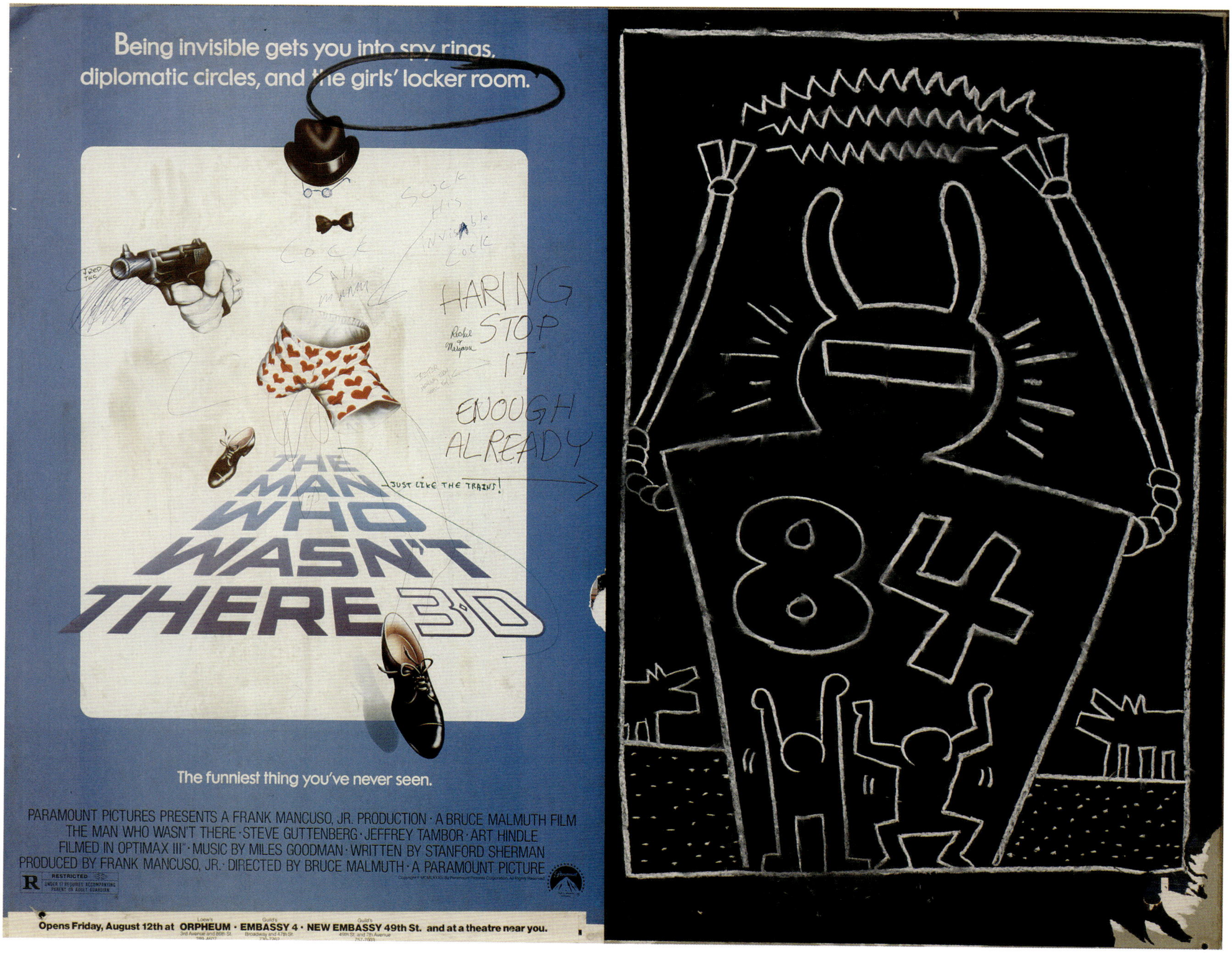

Untitled, 1984
Subway poster, chalk on paper with fiberglass frame, 49 x 68 in (124.4 x 172.7 cm)

JEAN-MICHEL BASQUIAT

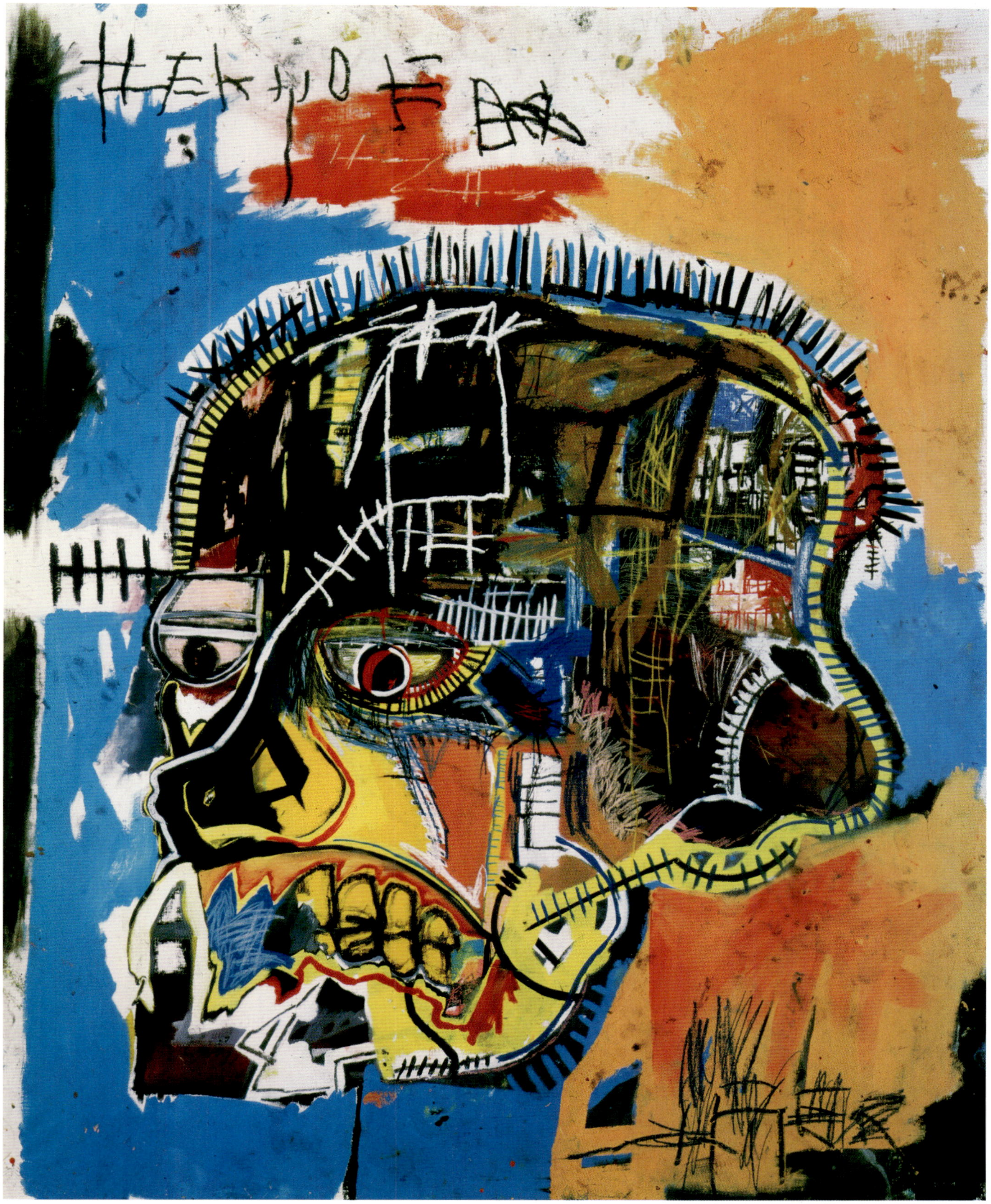

Untitled, 1981
Acrylic and oilstick on canvas, 81 1/2 x 69 1/4 in (207 x 175.8 cm)

RAYMOND PETTIBON

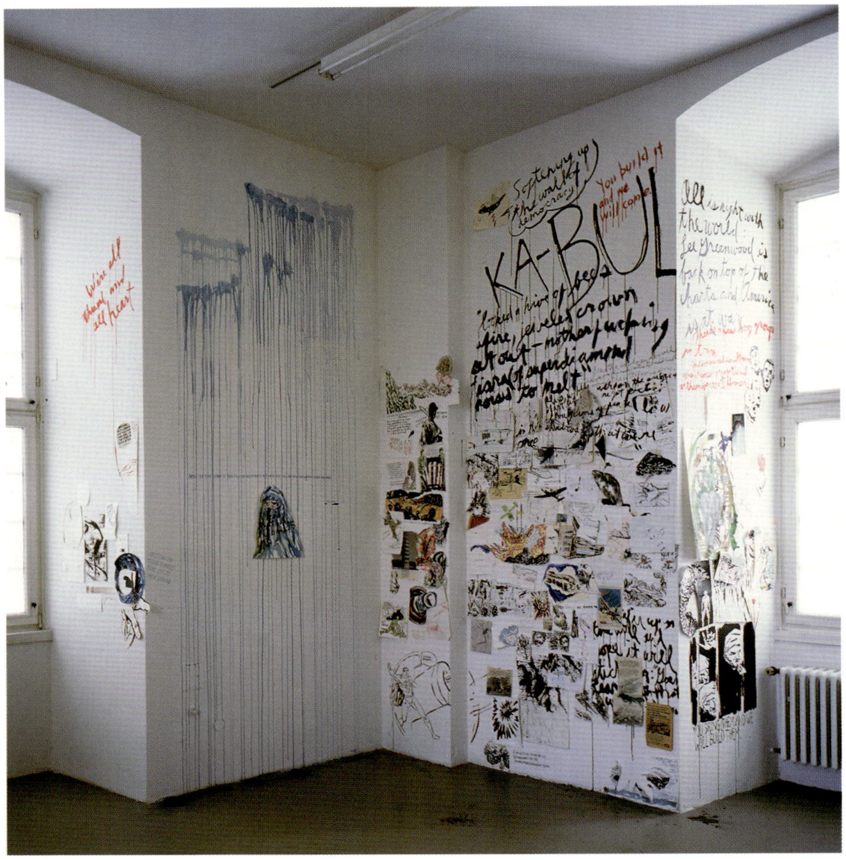

Untitled, 2002
As installed at Documenta 11, Kassel, Germany, 2002

BARRY MCGEE (A.K.A. TWIST)

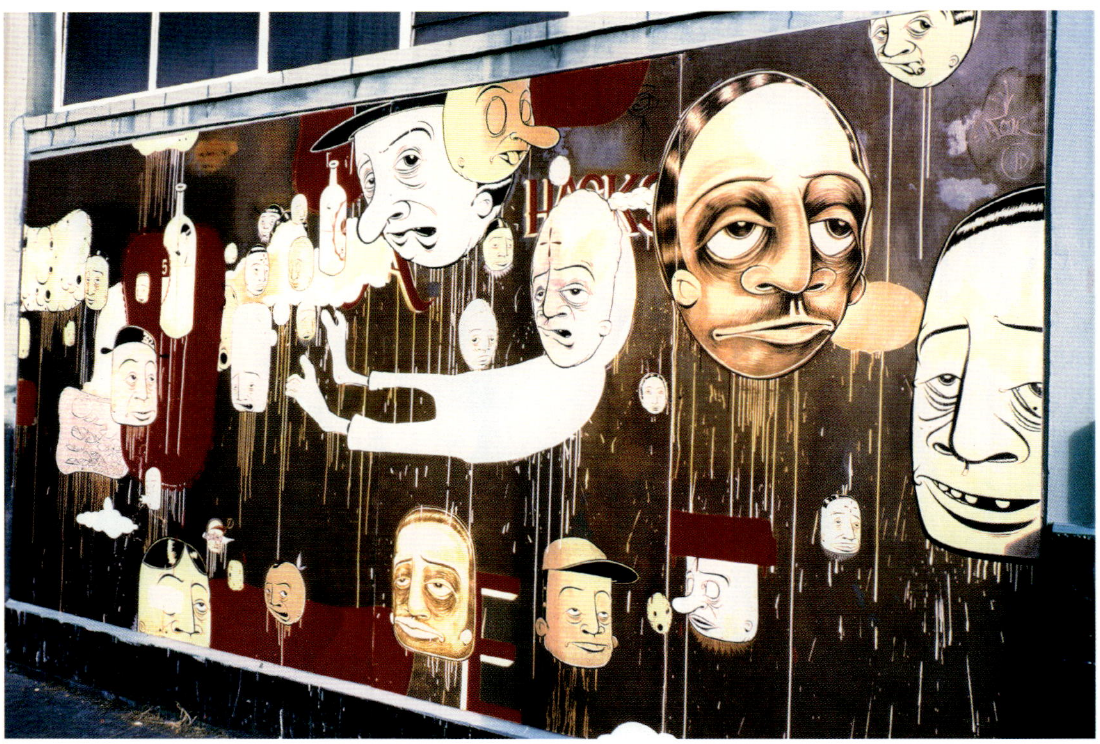

Untitled, 1998
Mural at 1035 Howard Street, San Francisco, stolen August 1999

MARGARET KILGALLEN

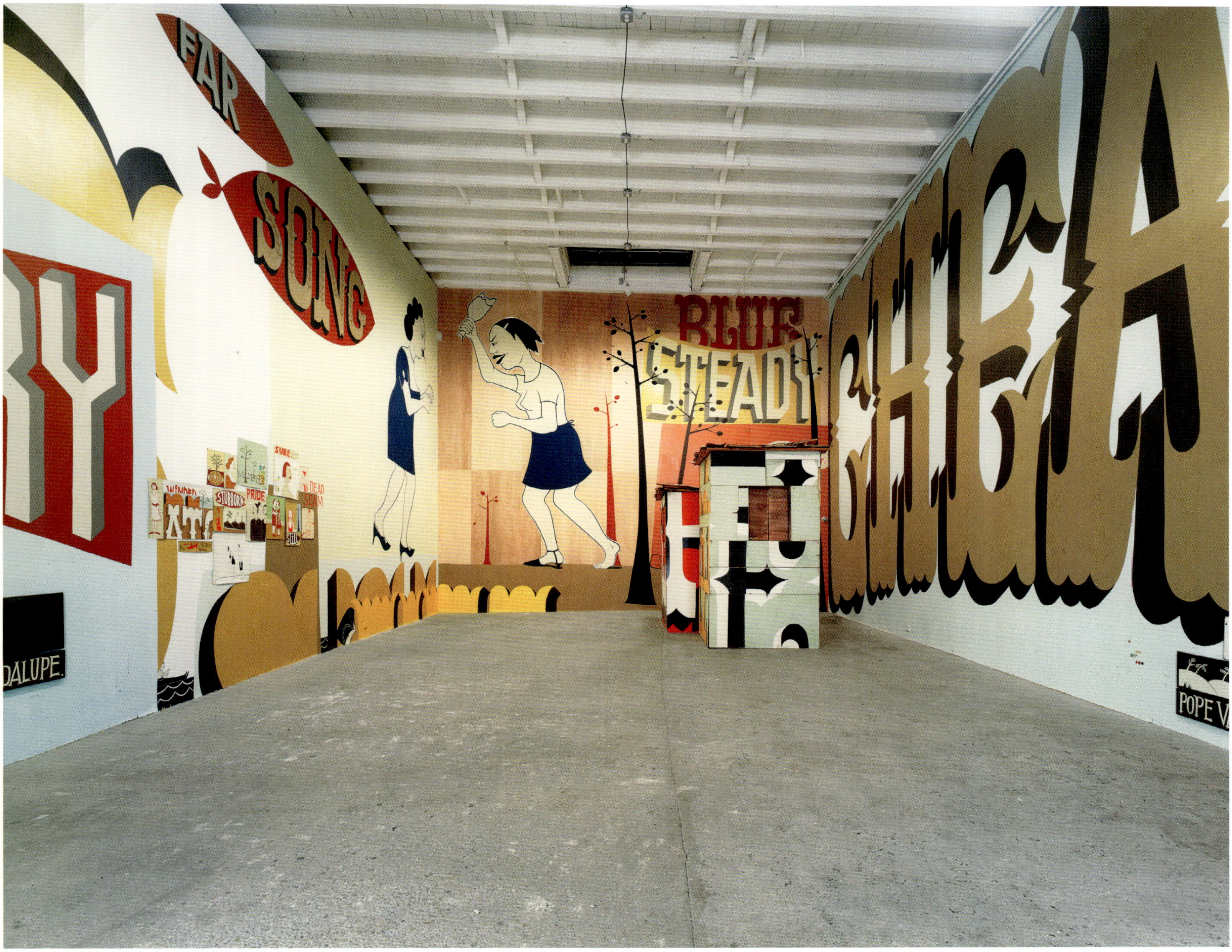

"To Friend and Foe," 1999
As installed at Deitch Projects, New York, September–October 1999

TAKASHI MURAKAMI

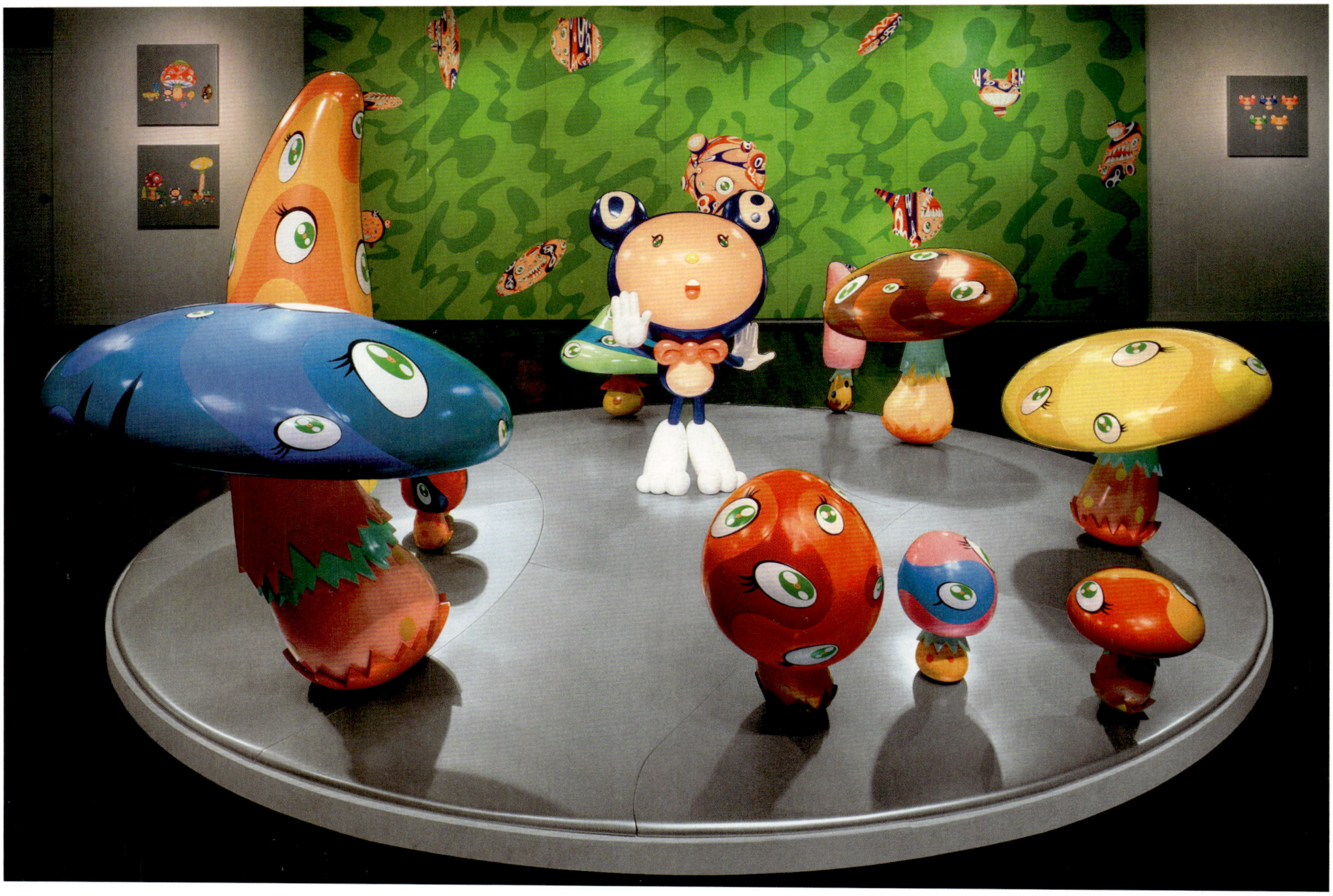

DOB in the Strange Forest, 1999
FRP Resin, fiberglass, and acrylic, 60 x 120 x 120 in (152 x 304 x 304 cm)

stood out among a younger generation of graffiti artists in the 1990s. The couple (who were married, but worked largely independently) came out of the underground music and skateboarding scene to develop a West Coast version of graffiti art. Under the tag name Twist, McGee presented cartoonish old men whose world-weary slumps recalled the sorry characters of cartoonist R. Crumb and painter Philip Guston, as in his 1998 mural *Untitled*, on Howard Street in San Francisco. He also constructs gallery installations that combine painted images with real objects—paint cans, discarded liquor bottles—that capture the same frenetic energy as his outdoor guerrilla works. Kilgallen, who died of cancer in 2001, developed motifs that critics compared to those of Depression-era America: shacks, hobos, signage, and topography that recall small-town, down-and-out America. She combined these with iconic images of powerful but downtrodden women in sweeping murals and gallery installations, such as "To Friend and Foe," her 1999 installation at Deitch Projects in New York. Her works evoked the carnival posters, folk art, and prewar cartoons of supposedly simpler times.

Energetic efforts by city officials to clean up subways and walls, along with inevitable changes in fashion, have dispersed the graffiti energy. But something of that omnivorous, anarchic, populist spirit seems to have mutated into the work of Raymond Pettibon, whose collage-like drawings and wall works recall the tapestry of sketches, scrawls, and fanzine pages that might be tacked willy-nilly on a teenage boy's bedroom wall. Pettibon's work references high and low culture, creating a leveling process by which Gumby meets Socrates, and Saturday morning cartoons mingle with quotations from Proust, Blake, Beckett, and the Bible. One recurring figure is Vavoom, a minor character from *Felix the Cat*. Characters as diverse as Superman, Ronald Reagan, Charles Manson, Jesus Christ, and Elvis Presley also appear. At first glance, Pettibon's whole enterprise seems deliberately adolescent, but in fact the artist is grappling with profound issues. A work created for the 2002 Documenta 11 exhibition in Kassel, Germany, covered a gallery with cartoonish images and phrases drawn directly on the wall. It was populated by superheroes, war scenes, bombs, Arabs, and a drawing of Osama bin Laden before a Nazi flag, and read like a meditation on the new world order following the attacks of September 11.

Finally, rounding out Warhol the celebrity cultist, Warhol the media manipulator, and Warhol the populist, there is Warhol the marketing genius. Warhol once declared: "Business art is the step that comes after Art. I started as a commercial artist, and I want to finish as a business artist.... Being good in business is the most fascinating kind of art."[11] Indeed, Warhol understood the powerful business sense of making a seductive product and of course of mass production: his studio wasn't called the Factory for nothing. Among his most attentive students in this respect is Takashi Murakami, a purveyor of the Japanese fondness for all things cute who draws on the marketable spirit of Hello Kitty, beckoning cat figurines, and the wide-eyed, super-endowed, but childlike superheroes that populate manga cartoons. Murakami's slick graphic paintings and sculpture are filled with images of adorable pandas, mushrooms, flowers, and Japanese-style Mickey Mouses. Murakami has in fact copyrighted this last, customized character, calling him DOB. In *DOB in the Strange Forest*, 1999, the creature is presented in sculptural form, surrounded by a field of giant mushrooms with multiple eyes.

Murakami captures a sense of the voluntary infantilism at the heart of much Japanese pop and consumer culture, but this is not to say he subscribes to it.

SYLVIE FLEURY

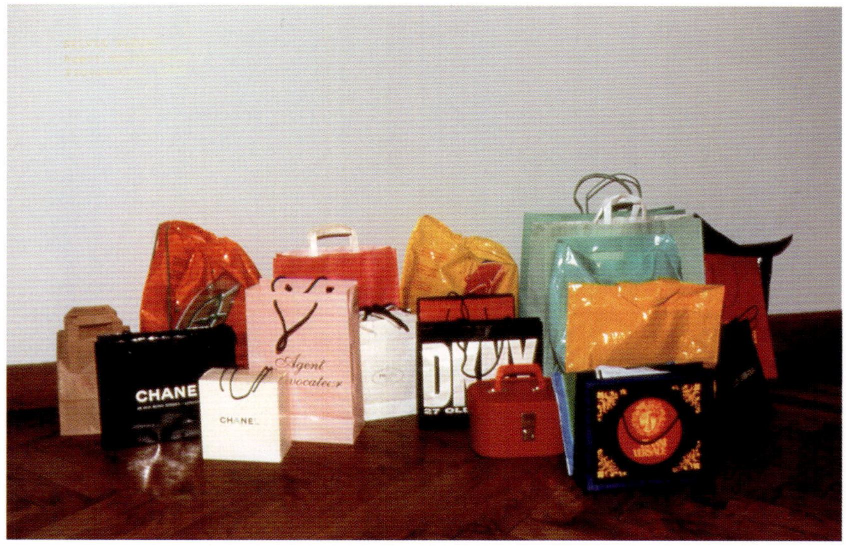

Agent Provocateur, 1995
118 1/8 x 118 1/8 in (300 x 300 cm)

Some critics detect serious social commentary in his works, which exaggerate the extreme materialism of Japanese society. Further, created in the context of a deeply homogenous culture, his imagery purposely confuses gender, racial, and species distinctions. Murakami's Warholian business tendencies come to the fore in his working methods. He maintains an army of assistants and refers to his enterprise, like Warhol did, as a "factory." He also produces a line of factory-fabricated toys, T-shirts, watches, and action figures. And again like Warhol, who began his career as a fashion illustrator, Murakami has hired himself out to the fashion industry, producing designer handbags and accessories for Louis Vuitton that bear a Murakami version of the company's famous LV logo.

The somewhat unsettling synergy between art and commerce is also at the core of the work of Sylvie Fleury, who deliberately confuses the two. For instance, she has linked the signature styles of modernist abstractionists with fashion emblems (Lucio Fontana's slashes become ripped jeans, Piet Mondrian's rigid geometry is softened by fake fur). One installation, *Agent Provocateur*, 1995, consisted simply of shopping bags full of a day's purchases of designer clothing and cosmetics. (Collectors were required to buy the bags without any knowledge of their contents, which sometimes had a higher value than the artwork's purchase price.) Fleury has recreated department-store dressing rooms in art spaces, and has painted classic American cars with nail polish colors and exhibited them in art galleries. In 1999 she presented a series of "Soft Rockets," sculptures accompanied by soundtracks on which slogans from cosmetic and perfume ads are recited. Such works suggest the close link between how art and luxury goods—be they clothing, cars, cosmetics, or shoes—are marketed. Signature styles equal fashion branding. Designer shops and art galleries both cultivate an aura of exclusivity and taste. Luxury cars and blue chip art are equally prestigious collector's items. As with Warhol and Murakami, it is never exactly clear whether Fleury is satirizing or celebrating this tangled state of affairs.

Shopping bags also appear in the work of Brazilian artist Jac Leirner, who strings or sews them together into wall hangings and modular sculpture. She also creates minimalist art out of other objects of consumption. *Lung*, 1987, for example, is an accumulation of three years' worth of cigarette packets, crushed and hung on a string. Leirner has made art out of Brazilian currency rendered useless by devaluation, punching holes in bills and stringing them together into serpentine floor pieces. Other works from the mid-'90s presented arrangements of items acquired on airplanes—slippers, headphones, and disposable razors, for instance—that would be thrown out after one use and thus suggest a culture of excess and waste. (This work brings to mind Warhol's "Time Capsules," cardboard storage boxes containing and preserving forever the otherwise expendable detritus of his studio.)

Where most contemporary artists pursuing a Warholian fascination with commerce have been playful instigators within the art world, Tom Sachs has stirred up much wider and more serious controversy. In 1994 the artist was commissioned to create a holiday window display for Barneys in New York. *Hello Kitty Nativity*—a nativity scene taking place in a McDonald's stable and made entirely of duct tape featuring a haloed Hello Kitty as Baby Jesus, Bart Simpson in triplicate as the Wise Men, and the pop singer Madonna as the Madonna (outfitted in Chanel, Air Jordans, and a headset)—created a furor. Sachs argued that it was intended as a criticism of the commercialization of Christmas, but the conservative Catholic League denounced the display as anti-Christian, and it was quickly dismantled. Sachs is also notorious for the 1999 arrest of his dealer Mary Boone, who was jailed overnight following the opening of his gallery show, which included a collection of live bullets set out in a bowl for visitors to take home in a Hermès knockoff shopping bag. Sachs's provocative works make us uncomfortable—are we being welcomed into an exclusive club or satirized for our desire to belong?

While they are obvious heirs to Warhol, artists such as Fleury, Leirner, and Sachs focus their business and branding concerns not on the middle-class and middle-brow references of Campbell's soup and Brillo pads but on high-end labels such as Hermès, Prada, and Louis Vuitton. In other words, contemporary artists seem less interested in Warholian issues around mass marketing and more obsessed with rarefied status symbols. This shift underlines Warhol's mixed legacy. On one hand, he was the great popularizer, but on the other, he built a career on reinforcing the prestige of our cultural aristocracy, be they Hollywood celebrities, art stars, or supermodels. Artists today are adept at operating between both worlds, mingling high and low, shifting effortlessly from graffiti and B movies to haute couture and art films. But in the end, their impulses seem less democratic than they might at first appear. While Warhol challenged high art by infusing it with the pathos, tacky allure, and shallow sentimentality of mass culture, artists today are frequently drawn to unadulterated expressions of luxury. They traffic in the kind of material Greenberg derided as "high kitsch," performing a sleight of hand, transforming dross into gold with the application of a marketable signature. Greenberg feared that kitsch would overwhelm high art, but even he never foresaw how indistinguishable the two could become.

JAC LEIRNER

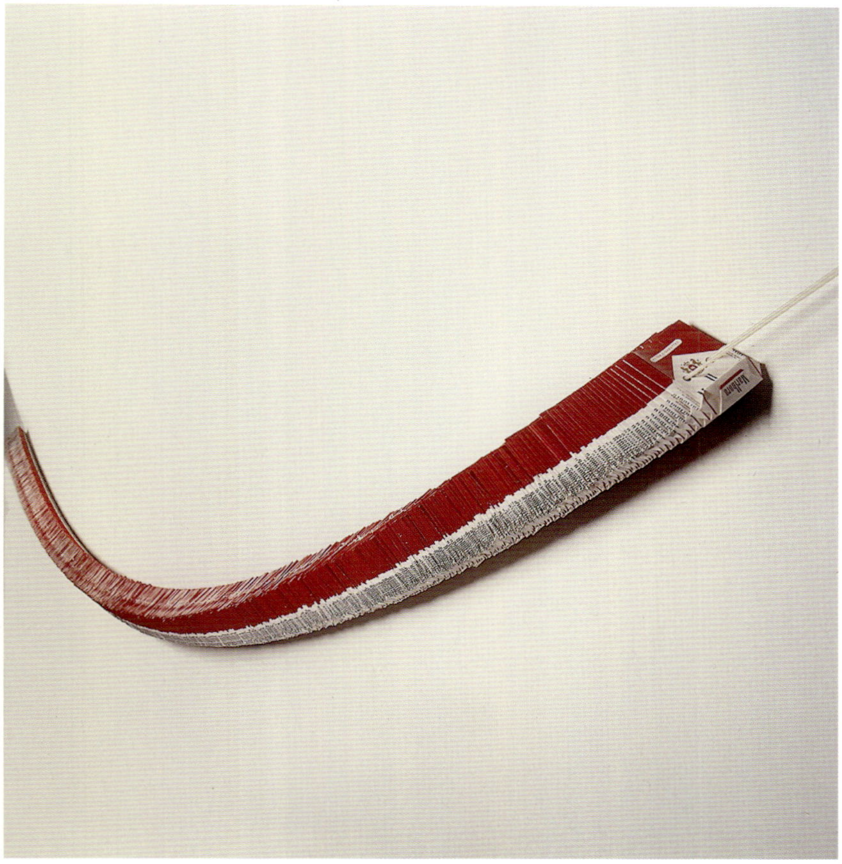

Lung, 1987
Twelve hundred Marlboro cigarette packs strung on a polyurethane cord
Dimensions variable, 14 ft 5 1/4 in (4.4 m) to 15 ft 9 in (4.8 m) wide
The Museum of Modern Art, New York

TOM SACHS

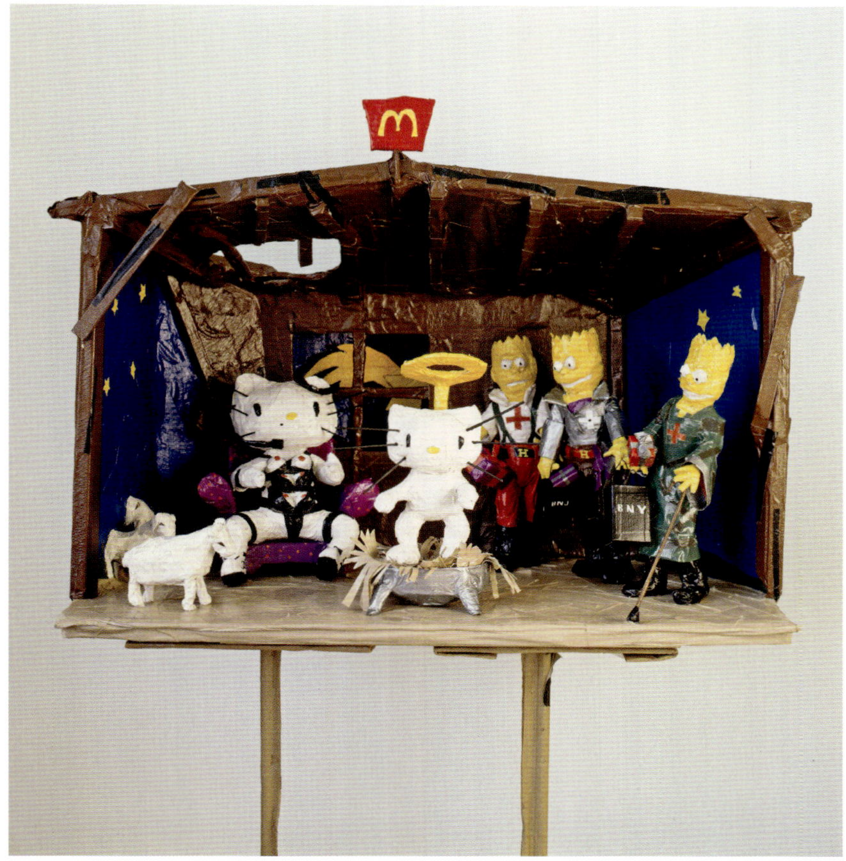

Hello Kitty Nativity, 1994
Duct tape, 48 x 30 x 30 in (121.9 x 76.2 x 76.2 cm)

ART & THE QUOTIDIAN OBJECT

THE TRANSFORMATION OF THE READYMADE

But is it art? The question has resonated ever since Marcel Duchamp famously took a urinal and presented it just as he would any painting or sculpture. For those devoted to the idea of art as a realm apart, where our mundane concerns are burned away in the incandescent heat of pure beauty or transcendent emotion, Duchamp's action is the original sin of modernism. For other observers of contemporary art, however, the idea that a urinal, a soup can, or a Harley Davidson motorcycle might be set alongside the *Mona Lisa* and the Elgin marbles in the pantheon of masterpieces is something to celebrate. Case in point: in 1998 New York's Solomon R. Guggenheim Museum mounted "The Art of the Motorcycle," an exhibition in which fifty state-of-the-art machines were displayed along Frank Lloyd Wright's circular ramp like the gleaming offerings of a dream showroom. In a similar spirit, museums display teapots by Michael Graves (and sell them in museum shops). Of course there's a difference between a sculpture, no matter how utilitarian its source, and a teapot or a motorcycle, and this aestheticization of design objects would appear to be quite contrary to Duchamp's original intentions. As he noted enigmatically in 1961, "The choice of these 'readymades' [Duchamp's word for found-object sculpture] was never esthetic delectation. This choice was based on a reaction of visual indifference with at the same time a total absence of good or bad taste. In fact a complete anesthesia."[1] Clearly, his was a conceptual, not an aesthetic gesture.

The infamous urinal first entered the history of art in 1917, when, under the title *Fountain*, Duchamp submitted it to the first exhibition of the Society of Independent Artists in New York. Signed "R. Mutt" and installed in a rotated position to underscore its distance from the functional object it resembled in every other way, *Fountain* was promptly rejected from the show (whereupon Duchamp resigned from the Society). As might be expected, the rejection ensured more visibility than had the work been accepted, and it gained legendary status in the art world through reproductions in the avant-garde journals of the time. While the original has disappeared, replicas of *Fountain* abound and are in many museum collections. In 1964 Duchamp authorized the production of a set of replicas of all of his original readymades, which include a snow shovel (poetically titled *In Advance of a Broken Arm*), a bottle rack, and a bicycle wheel.

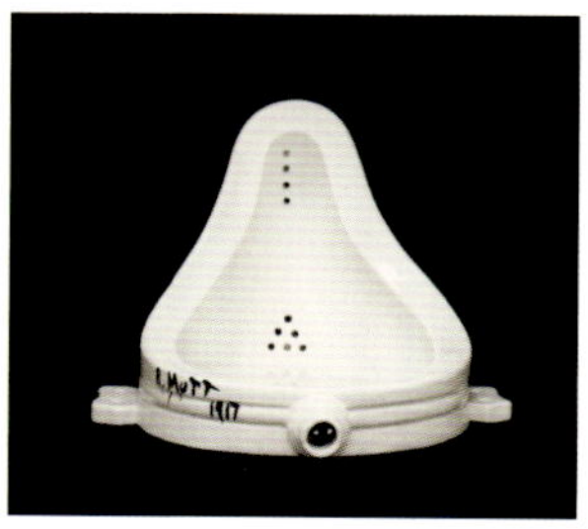

MARCEL DUCHAMP
FOUNTAIN
1917/64
PORCELAIN
HEIGHT 14 IN (33.5 CM)
INDIANA UNIVERSITY ART MUSEUM, BLOOMINGTON

The legacy of Duchamp's readymades is a complex one. On one hand, Duchamp's gesture can be read to mean that anything is art—even, in the right circumstances, the humblest manufactured object. This reading has inspired any number of artists who have unabashedly employed found objects in the creation of high art. But, as the quote above suggests, Duchamp himself preferred to see his readymades as proof that art is in fact no different from anything else in the world. Instead of elevating the commonplace, this interpretation casts art off its pedestal and into everyday life. This attitude had much in common with the anarchic approach of the contemporaneous, European-based Dada movement, whose practitioners (for example Hannah Höch, Raoul Hausmann, Max Ernst, and George Grosz) shared Duchamp's disdain for aesthetics and established institutions. Like Duchamp, the Dadists desired to destroy conventional notions of art, but unlike Duchamp, they tended toward a more overtly political view, relating the high culture they abhorred to the horrors of World War I and its aftermath. More recently, Duchamp's anti-art approach has been reborn in versions of postmodernism devoted to demonstrations of the death of art. The readymade's influence can also be discerned in the formulations of Conceptual artists, who, like Duchamp, reject the "retinal" approach to art in favor of one centered in the mind. According to this view, art is essentially a mental exercise. We turn the urinal or the snow shovel into art simply by regarding it as art.

This last interpretation points to the most radical consequence of the readymade, namely the idea that art resides not in the object itself, but in the meanings we embed in it. Philosopher and art critic Arthur Danto is one of the most articulate and early proponents of this line of thinking. Since the early 1980s, Danto has written frequently about the epiphany he experienced when he first encountered Andy Warhol's 1964 watershed sculpture, *Brillo Box*. That work, a wooden box painted to create a convincing facsimile of just what its title describes, compelled Danto to ask, "Why is this art and not simply a Brillo box?" His answer was that an artwork is an object that physically embodies some superimposed meaning. In other words, Warhol's *Brillo Box* is art and the commercial Brillo box is not because their creators (and their viewers) had completely different intentions.[2]

Some artists and theorists have focused on the political implications of Duchamp's act, envisioning *Fountain* and its fellow readymades as critiques of the system of mass production that was taking hold at the beginning of the twentieth century. In 1936 German critic Walter Benjamin hailed the democratizing effect of these new modes of mass reproduction, photography and film in particular. In his seminal essay of that year, "The Work of Art in the Age of Mechanical Reproduction," he argued that new technology would strip the art object of its precious "aura" of uniqueness and return it to the masses.[3] Benjamin, a Marxist, saw this as a happy development, but many subsequent critics have been less sanguine. In their view, Duchamp's urinal is a symbol of the demise of craft, originality, and personal connection to the fruits of our labor, thus heralding the demise of "authentic" art and the emergence of a dehumanizing cult of pseudo art. Conservative critic Hilton Kramer speaks to this view when he maintains that the problem of Duchamp's followers "was indeed paradoxical: how to honor and participate in the spirit of the master's negation of art while continuing with the creation of art. The solution, of course, was the sham compromise that goes by the name of 'anti-art,' which may best be defined as a species of art that claims, if only provisionally, to be something other than what it is—namely, art—in order to be judged by criteria other than those currently in effect or, better still, not to be judged at all but simply embraced as a form of expression more imperative than mere 'art.'"[4]

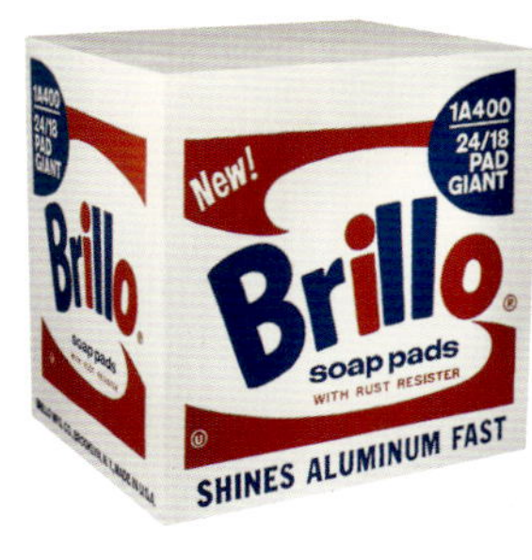

ANDY WARHOL
BRILLO SOAP PADS BOX (STOCKHOLM TYPE)
1964/68
SOAP BOX
12 X 12 X 6 IN
(30 X 30 X 18 CM)

While Duchamp's legacy is complicated and even contradictory, there is no question that the history of modernism and the evolution of art today are unimaginable without him. By blurring the boundary between art and life, Duchamp set the stage for much of what was to come, including Warhol's erasure of distinctions between high and low art, the rise of Conceptual art, and the infusion of materials and forms that were previously foreign to art. Central to this legacy is the acceptance of commonplace manufactured objects into the pantheon of art. (Think of Dan Flavin's sculptures made of standard fluorescent bulbs.) Another offshoot of this strain of Duchampianism is the massing of found objects toward poetic ends, as in the assemblages of French artist Arman, who presented accumulations of corkscrews or packages of aspirin gathered into Plexiglas boxes and sculptures made from dissembled cars, violins, and even whole suites of furniture. However, if Duchamp's influence extends to the widespread use of readymade objects and industrial materials in art, it also can be seen in the contrary impulse to create objects that look like readymades, but are, in a strange convolution of Benjamin's aura, actually handcrafted and unique. Here Duchamp's legacy includes not only Warhol's *Brillo Box*, but iconic works such as Jasper Johns's *Painted Bronze*, 1960, a bronze replica of two ordinary Ballantine Ale beer cans, and Claes Oldenburg's monumental pencils, clothespins, umbrellas, and baseball bats. It also can be seen in Richard Artschwager's faux furniture sculptures—minimalist forms made to resemble chairs, tables, and framed pictures through the artful use of woodgrain–patterned Formica veneer. In short, Duchamp's legacy reaches into many corners of the contemporary art world—extending from the demolition of commonplace assumptions about art's uniqueness to the poetic transformation of humble objects into things of wonder to the revelation of art's commodity status.

Among the most prominent purveyors of the anti-art strain of contemporary art so reviled by Kramer is a small group of conceptually inclined artists who emerged in the 1980s and took the aestheticization of ordinary objects to an absurdist extreme. These artists extended Duchamp's attack on the preciousness of art by exposing the market mechanisms that transform an ordinary object into a work of art. But they also subverted his desire to create a state of complete artistic indifference by endowing the manufactured readymade with the seductive charms reserved for high art. Dubbed "appropriationists," "simulationists," and "commodity critics" by the art media, they contested what they saw as the concocted authenticity of artists like Julian Schnabel. In contrast to the rhetorical and visual heat generated by such contemporaries, they cultivated a cool, cerebral irony, creating works that questioned whether anything could be original. Armed with theoretical arguments culled from Marxist and post-structural theory, they suggested that in a consumer society, we have lost all sense of the distinction between individual and manufactured expressions. The human condition they described was best summed up by a phrase artist Barbara Kruger coined and inscribed on designer shopping bags: "I Shop, Therefore I Am." From this perspective, creativity is indistinguishable not only from production but from consumption, as the act of shopping becomes the postmodern version of democratic choice. In such a climate, our insatiable desire for manufactured products such as running shoes or table lamps becomes a debased substitute for genuine self-expression.

Underscoring this depressing worldview, artists such as Jeff Koons, Haim Steinbach, Ashley Bickerton, and Allan McCollum created works designed to suggest that art was simply one more item in a galaxy of luxury consumer goods. Some appropriated objects and incorporated them as they were, while others replicated them to greater or lesser degrees of faithfulness. Koons did both. In his 1980s "New Hoover" series, for example, he glamorized home appliances, placing brand-new vacuum cleaners in minimalist Plexiglas boxes. In *Three Ball 50/50 Tank*, 1985, he floated basketballs inflated with water and mercury in aquariums full of distilled water and salt so they appeared to be unnaturally suspended. Koons's point seemed to be that the unscathed perfection of the vacuum cleaners and the equilibrium achieved by the basketballs represent exalted states that humans can never hope to achieve, thus demonstrating the superiority of inanimate objects over the mere mortals who own them. Next, Koons moved from real to recreated readymades, recasting a variety of drinking paraphernalia, from plastic buckets to Baccarat crystal decanters, in stainless steel. He hired master ceramicists from Italy to recreate large, exquisitely crafted versions of small ceramic dollar-store tchotchkes, the sort that his well-heeled collectors would abhor in their original forms. With such works he suggested that the real difference between the working and middle classes who buy mass-produced kitsch and the wealthy art world cognoscenti is not taste, but the amount of money they are prepared to spend to outfit and decorate their homes.

Haim Steinbach, who was a decade or so older than the other "commodity critics," emerged in the '80s, and remained committed to the "real" readymade. He first came to art world attention in 1979 with an installation titled "Display #7" that included a wall covered with strips of wallpaper and found objects precisely arranged on shelving. From here, he moved on to his signature works: in *Pink Accent^2*, 1987, latex masks, trash cans, and tea kettles are arranged on top of a minimalist wood shelf. Arrangements of such fetishistic consumer products as lava lamps, digital clocks, running shoes, and rubber Halloween masks placed on streamlined, custom-built shelves incongruously alluded to the minimalist sculptures of Donald Judd. In interviews at the time, he maintained that for him the key issue in art-making was not making, but choice—what and how many objects to buy, where to place one in relationship to another, how many of each object to use in a single piece. Like Koons, Steinbach was particularly attracted to objects with high kitsch content, and he was happy to destabilize distinctions between the art gallery and the department store. In fact, the distinction between his art objects and consumer products was evident only in their pricing. Steinbach's pricing scheme, which he recalled in a 2003 interview, made this crystal and comically clear: "When my work began to be successful, each piece—the shelves with objects—was priced the way you price a work of art: Here's a work of art, and this is what the price is. Of course, that becomes a problem, because if my work is going for $12,000, what happens when you have a group of objects worth $30,000? Do you still sell it at the value of the art? I devised a formula by which there would be a price for the work—plus the price of the objects. Let's say a shelf has three cornflakes boxes and six ceramic ghosts on it. If the ceramic ghosts are $10 apiece, that's $60; the boxes, at $2 each, would make $6, bringing the total of the objects to $66. So if the price of a given work is $12,000, that's $12,066."[5]

Other Simulationist artists chose to tackle the commodification of art by creating the most generic readymades imaginable. In the late 1970s Allan McCollum burst on the scene with sets of "Surrogate Paintings," such as *Collection of Ten Plastic Surrogates*, 1982/91, intentionally fake-looking, small acrylic paintings on wood with monochromatic frames and mats, and either black or colored centers where one would generally expect to find an image. Aside from the absence of any "painting" in the center, these works had all the essential elements of a certified artwork: they were framed, dated, numbered, and signed by the artist, and they were ar-

BARBARA KRUGER

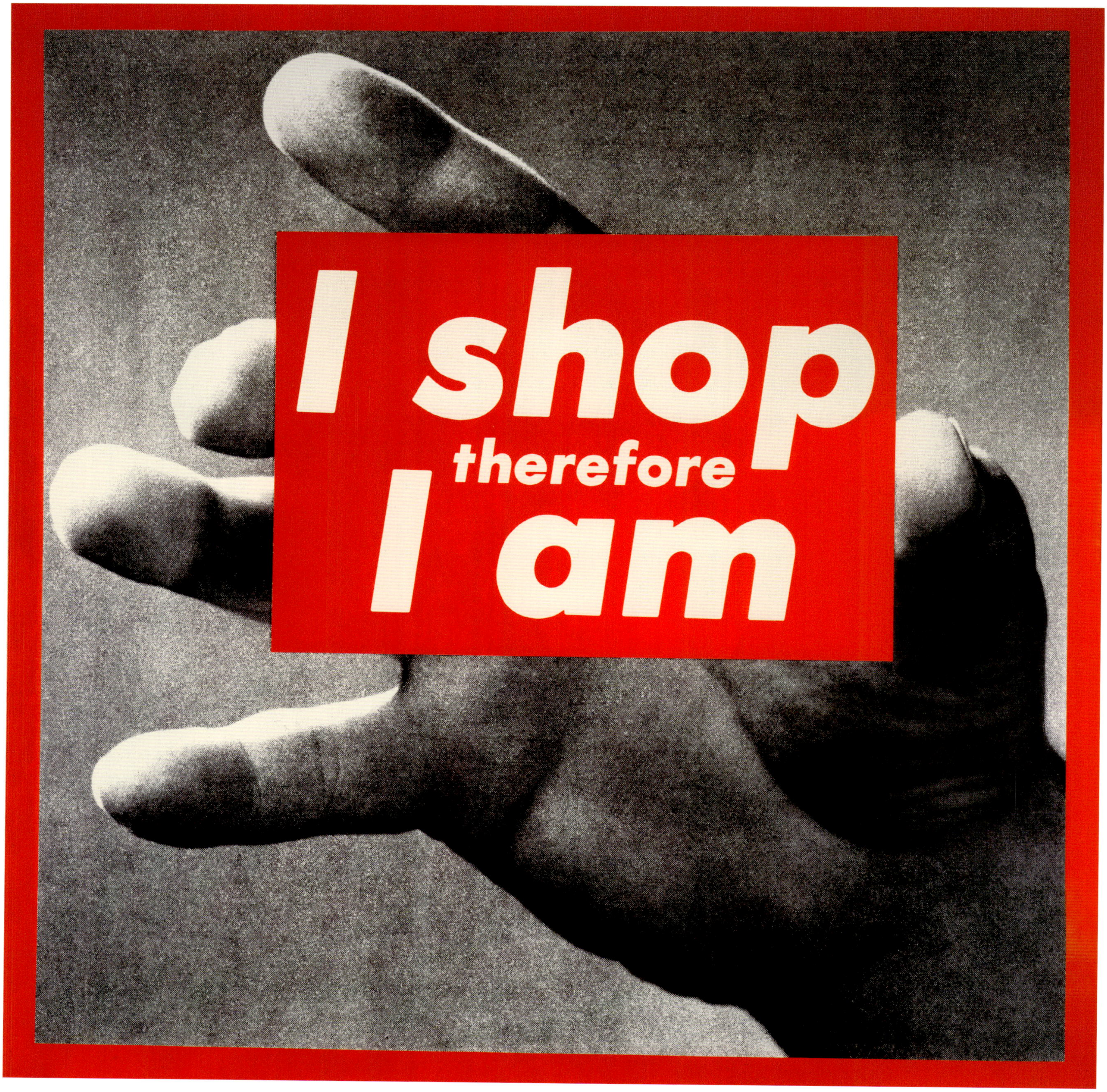

Untitled (I shop therefore I am), 1987
Photographic silkscreen on vinyl, 120 x 120 in (304.8 x 304.8 cm)

JEFF KOONS

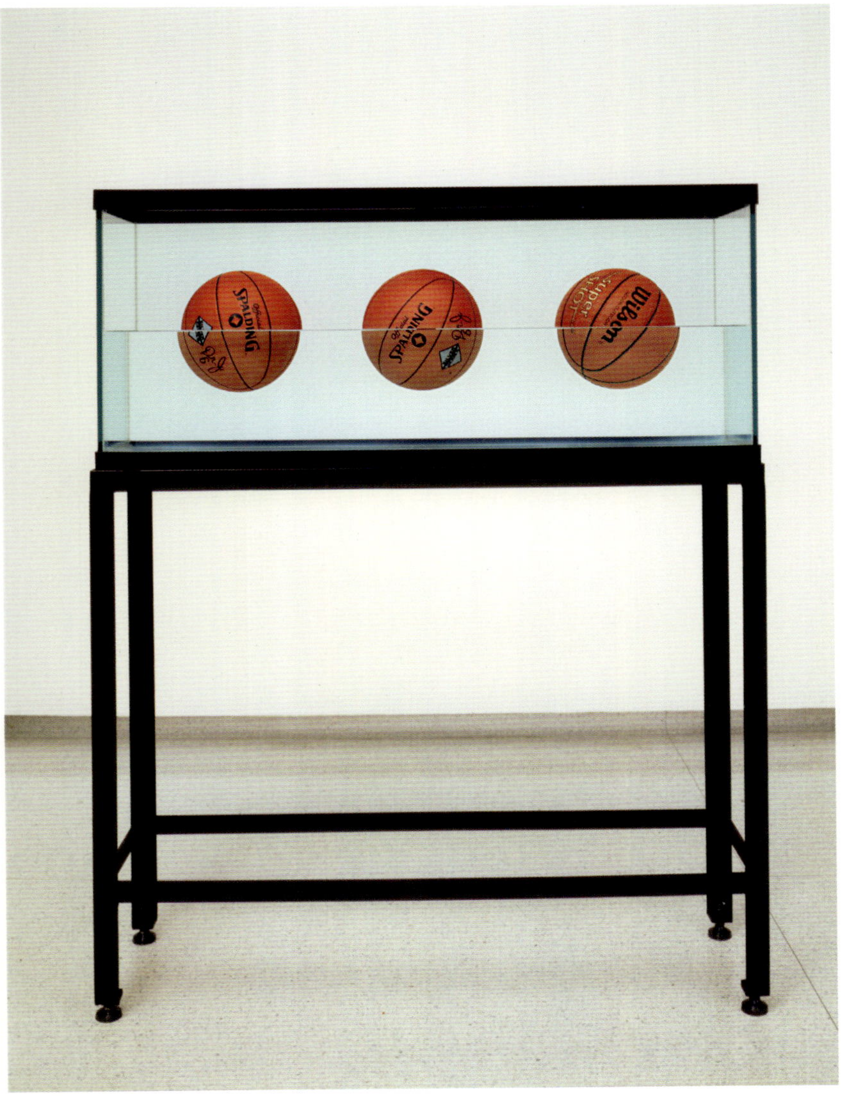

Three Ball 50/50 Tank, 1985
Glass, steel, distilled water, and 3 basketballs
60 1/2 x 48 3/4 x 13 1/4 in (153.7 x 123.8 x 33.7 cm)

ranged on the wall in salon-style groupings. They sold like certified artworks as well, demonstrating that trappings alone are all that matter in creating a marketable work of art.

This lesson also informed the work of Ashley Bickerton, whose painting-sculpture hybrids focused on aspects of the artwork—including installation hardware, materials, and marketing strategies—usually considered extrinsic to its aesthetic meaning. His works resembled footlockers or pinball machines attached to the wall, with large brackets for hanging neatly stored packing materials, oversize handles, digital counters for recording the work's minute-by-minute price increases, and lists of the materials that went into each work and their toxic effects. Their slick surfaces were covered with real and invented corporate logos and painted images that suggested unidentifiable machine parts, and affixed with brightly painted plaster rocks. *Le Art (Composition with Logos #2)*, 1987, for example, is a box attached to the wall with brackets whose front is covered the logos of the companies that manufacture the materials out of which the work was made, including 3M, Winsor and Newton, Liquitex, and the Sturdy Bolt and Nut Company, along with a warning to keep hands off the surface at all times. Contrary to Duchamp works like these demonstrated that erasing the boundary between art and manufactured goods does nothing to decrease its value; instead it remains just as collectible and sought after as ever.

Taking these replicating instincts one step further, Sherrie Levine turned artworks themselves into readymades in what was perceived in the 1980s as an attack on conventional faith in individuality, artistic genius, and originality. Levine rose to fame in the late 1970s with a series of photographs that were simply re-photographs of works by various illustrious art photographers that looked identical to the original. Levine carefully included the name of the original photographer in the title of each work, as in *After Walker Evans*, 1981, or *After Edward Weston*, 1980, which acknowledged their original authorship while claiming them as her own. Rejecting the notion that her images constituted plagiarism, Levine insisted the originals had become new works through her act of re-photographing them. In subsequent works she took on other figures from the modernist canon—repainting works by Malevich, Egon Schiele, and Willem de Kooning, and fabricating forms depicted in Duchamp's *The Large Glass*. As Duchamp himself was the great twentieth-century debunker of artistic originality, this last work placed her in an artistic lineage that rejected the normal claims of lineage. Such pieces assert that the originality that modernism celebrates is merely a myth, and that no artist can avoid borrowing the ideas of others.

Less polemical followers of Duchamp have pursued another aspect of his legacy by celebrating, rather than critiquing, the aestheticization of ordinary objects. Their work explores a "junk aesthetic" in assemblages and installations made exclusively or partly of humble found objects whose original functions are transcended or short-circuited. Thus they recall (though with decidedly different intentions) *Fountain* and the idea that art gains its meaning from the context in which it appears. This direction became widespread in the 1950s and '60s, spawning a diverse set of international movements. In France, the Nouveaux Réalistes, among them Arman, Daniel Spoerri, and Niki de Saint Phalle, made art out of food, trash, and broken machines. Their work was designed to deteriorate, decay, or—in the case of the junk assemblages of Jean Tinguely—literally self-destruct. In Italy, Arte Povera artists such as

HAIM STEINBACH

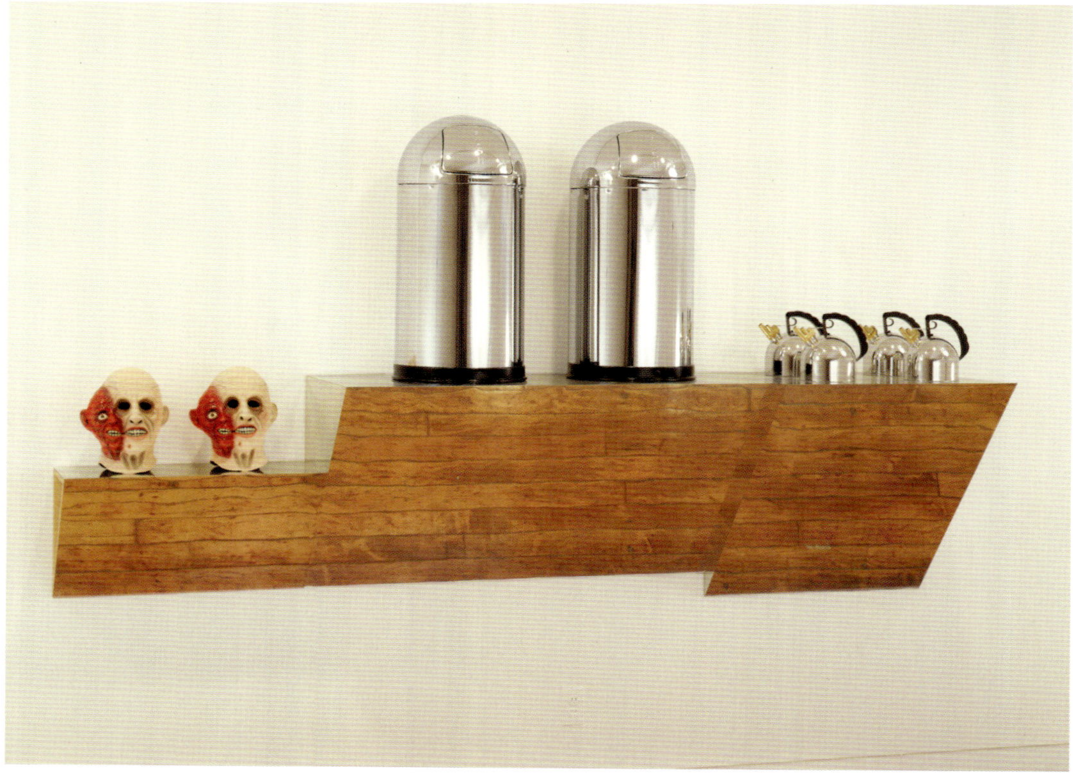

Pink Accent^2, 1987
Chrome laminated wood shelf, latex masks on styrofoam mounts, chrome trash cans, chrome tea kettles, 55 x 110 x 24 in (140 x 280 x 60 cm)

ASHLEY BICKERTON

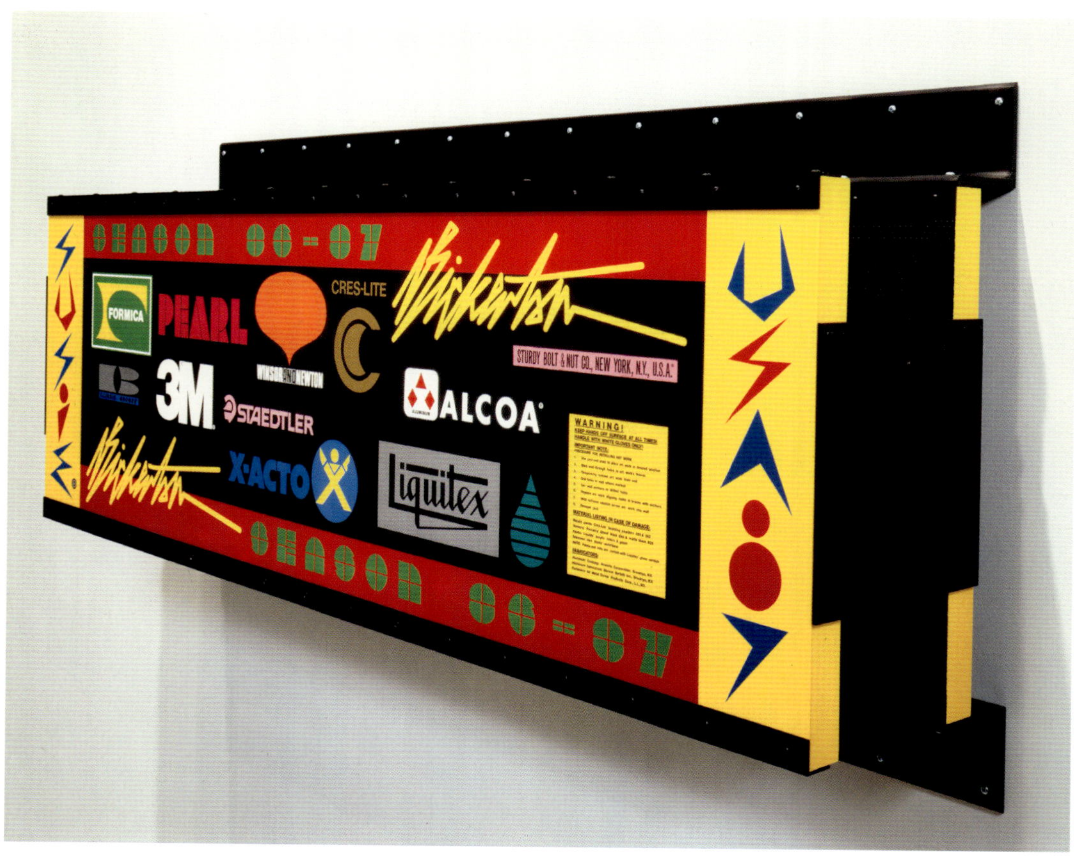

Le Art (Composition With Logos #2), 1987
Silkscreen, acrylic, and bronze powder with lacquer on plywood with anodized aluminum
34 1/2 x 72 x 15 in (88 x 183 x 38 cm)

SHERRIE LEVINE

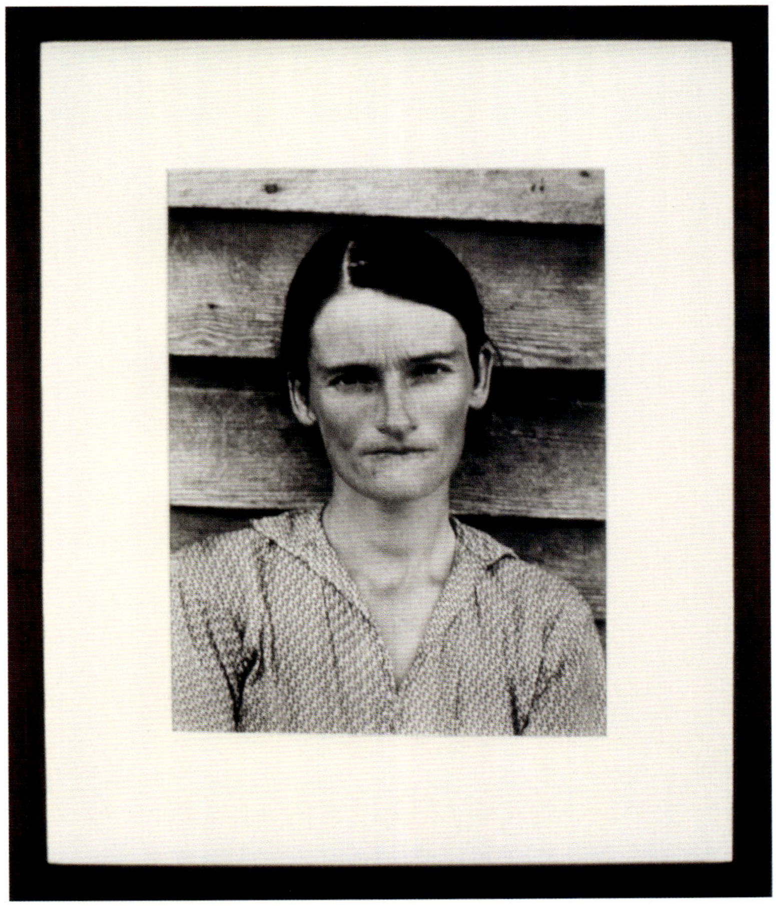

After Walker Evans, 1981
Gelatin silver print, 14 7/8 x 11 5/8 in (37.5 x 29.5 cm)

ALLAN McCOLLUM

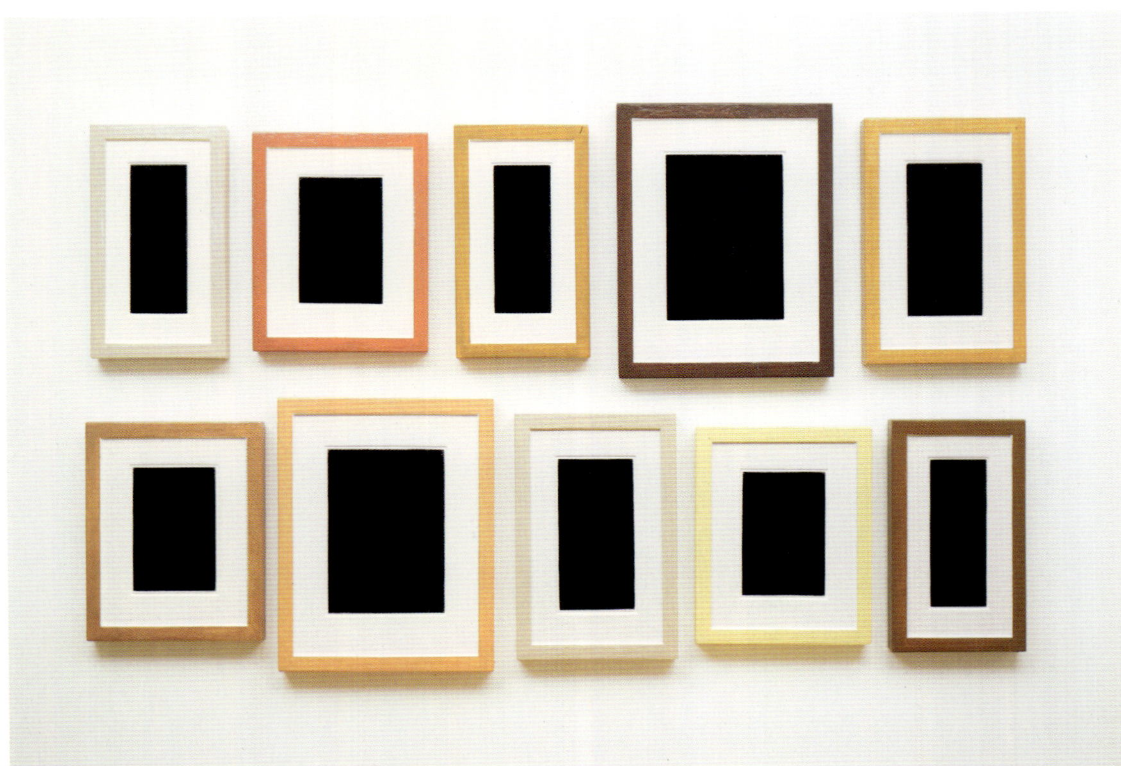

Collection of Ten Plastic Surrogates, 1982/91
Enamel on solid cast hydrostone, 41 3/4 x 71 in (106 x 180.3 cm)

Mario Merz, Jannis Kounellis, and Gilberto Zorio created art out of sheets of glass, umbrellas, bottles, coal, wood, silk, live animals, and plants, and drew on elemental forces—electricity, condensation, evaporation, and fire—to effect changes in their sculpture. In the United States, this approach never took on movement status, though artists such as Jasper Johns and Robert Rauschenberg used everyday objects as both subjects and materials for art, as did Richard Tuttle, who, since the 1960s, has created sculptures and wall drawings made of otherwise inconsequential and often ephemeral materials such as scraps of paper, rope, string, bubble wrap, nails, cardboard, wire, and twigs.

In the 1970s, a similar junk aesthetic appeared in the work of Tony Cragg, who became known for creating silhouette images of human figures, flags, and art icons "drawn" directly on walls or floors with pieces of colorful plastic detritus scavenged from dumpsters and beaches. While they coalesced into single images, these shards retained hints of their former lives as detergent bottles, plastic buckets, sieves, doll legs, and cigarette lighters. In some works Cragg arranged his bits of flotsam and jetsam in all the same color, while in others he presented a rainbow-like progression of hues. In a similar spirit, Cragg created "stacks" of building materials such as broken bricks, cardboard, and rubble, shaping them into minimalist cubes. The works' interest lay in the dissonance between the formal purity of the arrangements and the fact that they were made from garbage. In recent years Cragg has turned from appropriating scavenged objects to making sculptures that resemble them out of traditional art materials such as plaster, clay, iron, bronze, plywood, rubber, granite, marble, and scrap metal. These works bring to mind scientific instruments, machines, simple-celled organisms, or DNA strands. Mixing associations, he shows how functional objects might have erotic undertones, while industrial forms could appear to resemble male and female bodies and masses of manmade materials might assume the outlines of landscape. Thus he suggests that the organic and the manufactured are somehow interchangeable. In the 1997 sculpture *Spyrogyra*, for instance, a winding metal tube is adorned with a radiating spiral of blown-glass bottles in delicate shades of green and white that mimic the colors of the a genus of freshwater green algae referred to in the title. The work refers, of course, to Duchamp's bottle rack, though it has apparently transmuted back to some sort of pre-industrial organic state.

Among a younger generation of artists who use found objects in their work, Jessica Stockholder stands out for her formal rather than associative approach to those objects. Her materials, which are arranged to bring out relationships between color and form, include everything from chairs and tables, curtains and lamps to appliances, electric fans, plastic buckets, and old radios. Her freestanding works have been described as paintings made out of objects, and indeed rather than existing in the round, they often have a definite front and back (though sometimes the back is more interesting than the front). In these works and in her site-specific installations, which might take over an entire room, Stockholder plays with the idea of the stage set, where the "front" brings to mind the careful arrangements of the traditional still life while the "back" recalls the chaotic backstage of a theater, where all the tricks and illusions happen. In *Sam Ran Over Sand or Sand Ran Over Sam*, 2004, for instance, theater lights, electrical cords, furniture, and lamps are arranged against what appears to be the back of a freestanding plywood wall, which unlike the apparent front, is not covered in sheetrock. The sheetrocked side faces a more decorous arrangement including three white Styrofoam obelisks and six orange coolers. Other works hint at cozy domestic interiors that have been invaded by discordant objects and explosions of color. In Stockholder's work the connotations and function of the objects with which she "paints" her sculptures are almost irrelevant. One critic has gone so far as to suggest that she practices a form of visual aphasia (an echo of Duchamp's anesthesia?) in which individual elements are like words severed from their meanings, "so that sense and nonsense bump up against one another, become almost interchangeable."[6]

Sarah Sze practices a similar sort of non-signifying art-making, though her installations are highly animated. She mixes familiar domestic items such as Q-tips, medicine vials, garden hoses, electric fans, and wooden chairs with industrial materials such as bits of hardware, tubing, and aluminum strips and pipes. The works often seem to be bursting out of the wall or floor, like mutant creatures escaping from their cages. Or her materials seem to race through the room, colonizing the ceiling with whirring parts or fluttering bits of paper and cloth. In *Still Life with Flowers*, 1999, the title hardly does justice to the sense of movement conveyed by the elements. Tiny ladders swirl through space, entangling themselves with wooden foldout rulers, plastic leaves, snapshots, and a hanging blue light bulb. Her works are at once miniaturist—full of tiny details such as landscapes created from chewing gum wrappers and candy dots—and monumental in scale, as they overwhelm a room. They always suggest some hidden energy, a mad-scientist quality. Sze has described her aesthetic aspirations as wanting to make works that "look like something someone would create if they were locked for a long time alone in a bathroom."[7]

An equally anarchic spirit animates the work of the duo Peter Fischli and David Weiss. Collaborators since 1979, the artists began by experimenting with the force of gravity in the spirit of children attempting to press natural law to its limits. They piled found tables, chairs, or tires in precarious arrangements, then photographed them just before they collapsed. These experiments lead to their now classic video *Der Lauf der Dinge* (The Way Things Go), 1987, in which the camera dispassionately follows the chain reaction set off by a series of events activated around perilously balanced objects arranged in a large warehouse. The action begins with the descent of a garbage bag suspended by a rope that slowly untwists, lowering the bag until it touches a tire poised at the top of an inclined plank of wood. The tire rolls, and so on, as action unfolds seemingly without any human intervention. One thing literally leads to another: bottles are toppled, balloons inflate and deflate, wire spools unroll, and flammable liquids ignite—as energy is passed from one set-up to the next. In fact, the artists manually pushed things along on occasion, though this is well disguised with deft cuts that give the impression of an unbroken thirty-minute take. *The Way Things Go* suggests a world in which manufactured objects have a life of their own, where humanity, not to mention God, plays only a minor role in "the way things go" in a machine-like universe.

Jason Rhoades, who died in 2006 at the age of forty-one, also brought a childlike energy to his machine-like universes—installations often incorporating toys or made of toy building supplies such as Legos. Described by one critic as "perhaps the most American of contemporary American artists,"[8] Rhoades recreated archetypal American spaces out of scavenged, bought, and manufactured objects, or exotic environs out of archetypally American materials. "Meccatuna," 2003, was a sprawling installation that included cast camel toe bones, dozens of empty tuna cans, hun-

TONY CRAGG

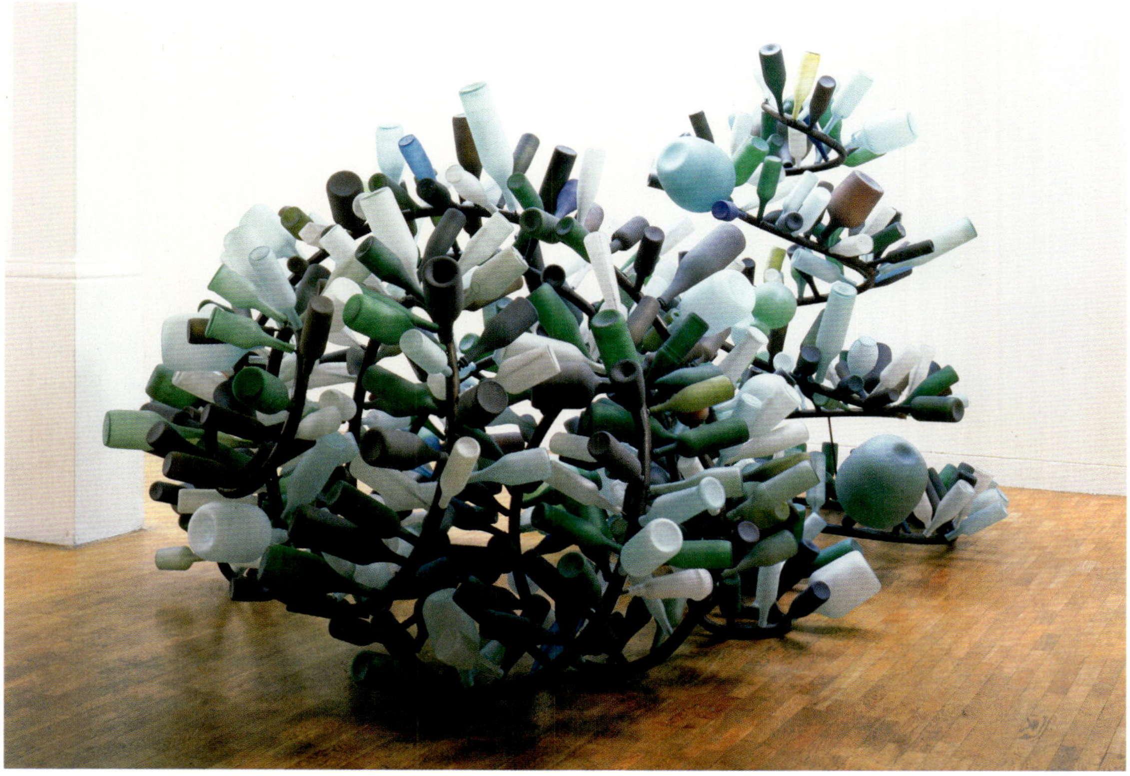

Spyrogyra, 1997
Sandblasted glass, steel, 7 ft 6 in x 18 ft (2.3 x 5.5 m)

JESSICA STOCKHOLDER

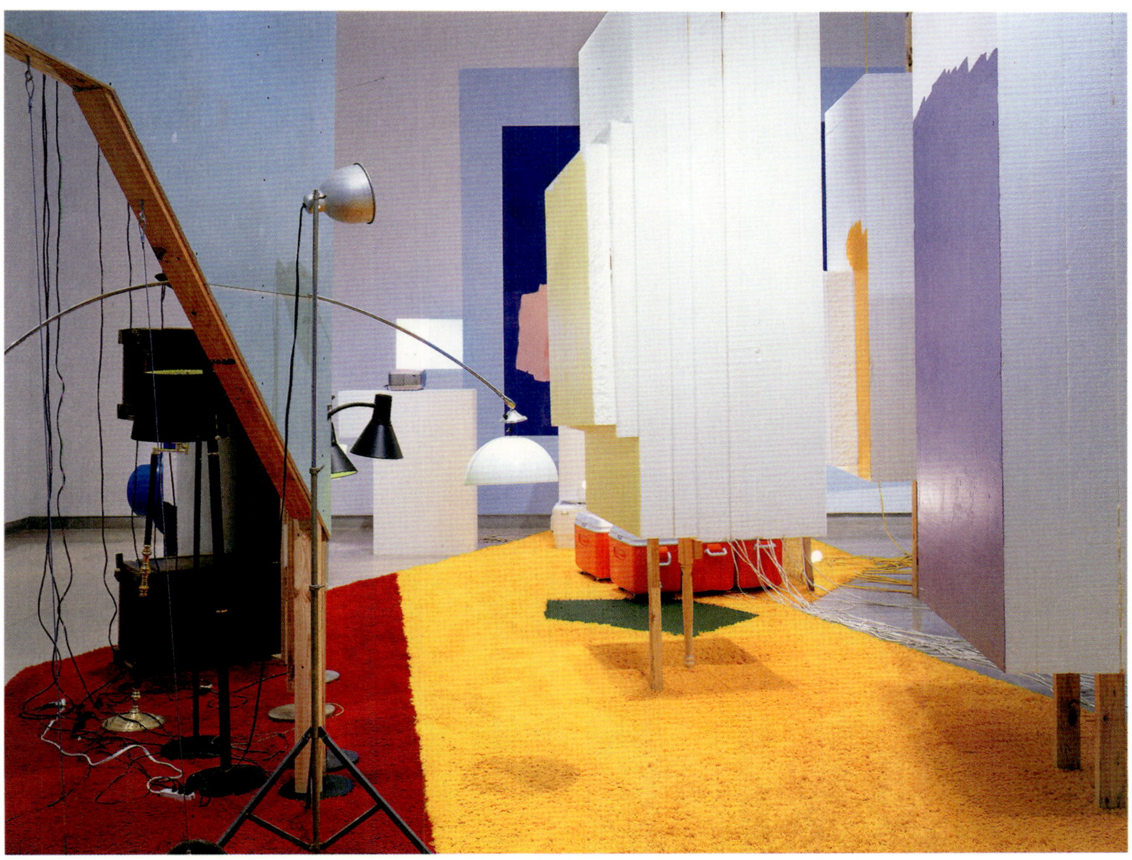

Sam Ran Over Sand or Sand Ran Over Sam, 2004
Carpet, green waterproof sheetrock, theater lights, yellow and white electrical cords, furniture, lamps, Styrofoam, lumber, freezer, digital projector, acrylic paint, coolers, and chicken wire
As installed at Rice University Art Gallery, Houston, Tex., September–October 2004

SARAH SZE

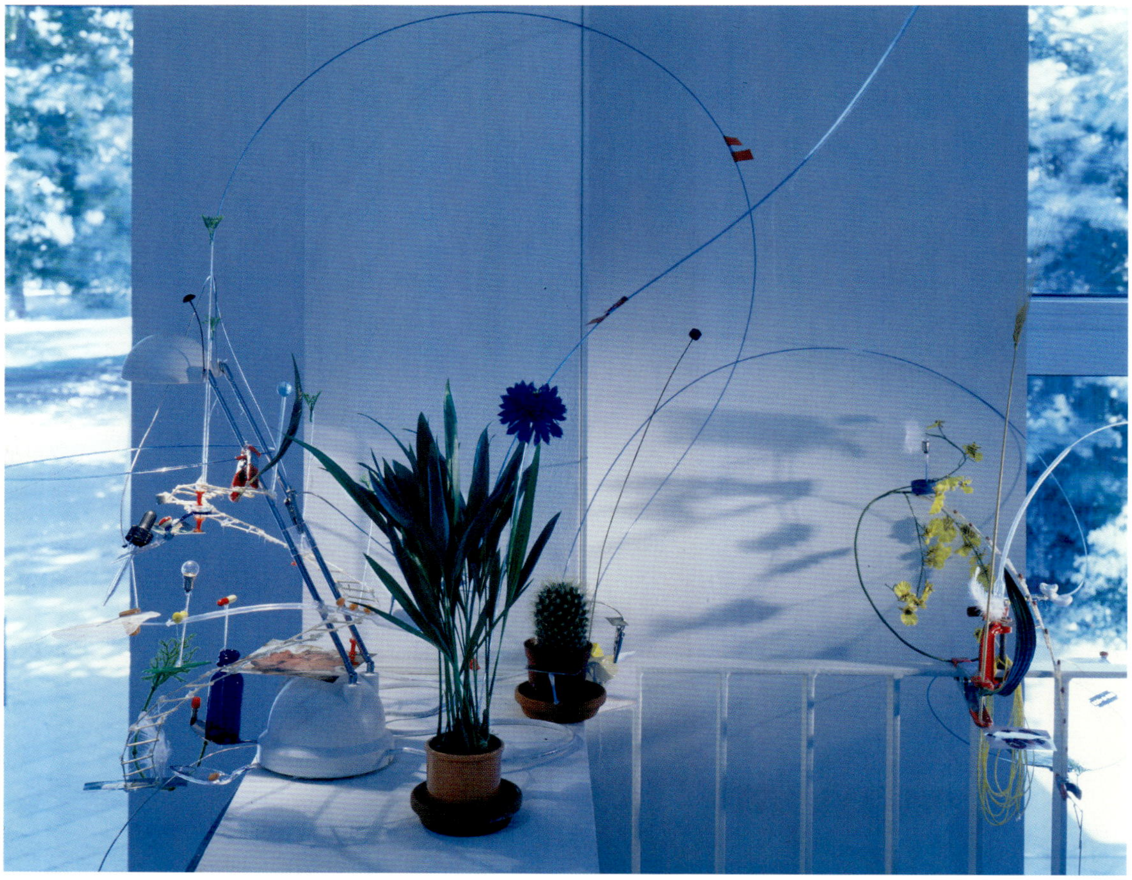

Still Life with Flowers, 1999
Mixed media, dimensions variable

PETER FISCHLI & DAVID WEISS

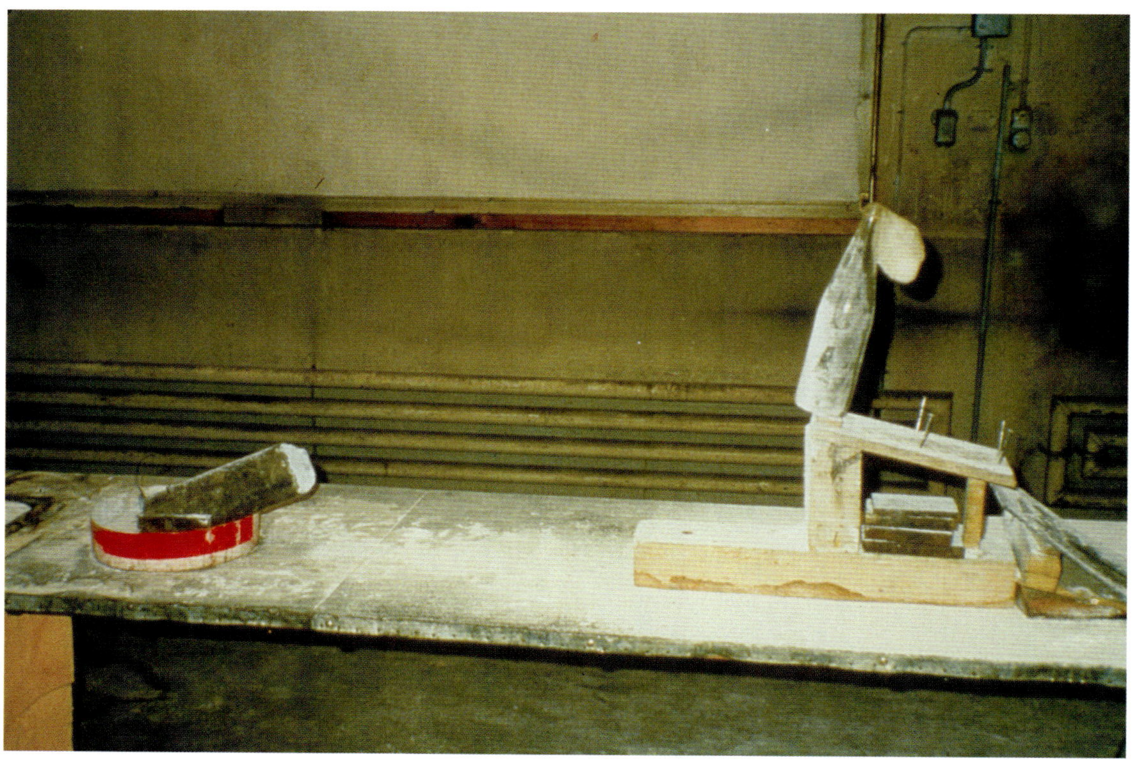

Der Lauf der Dinge (The Way Things Go), 1987
16 mm film, 30 minutes

JASON RHOADES

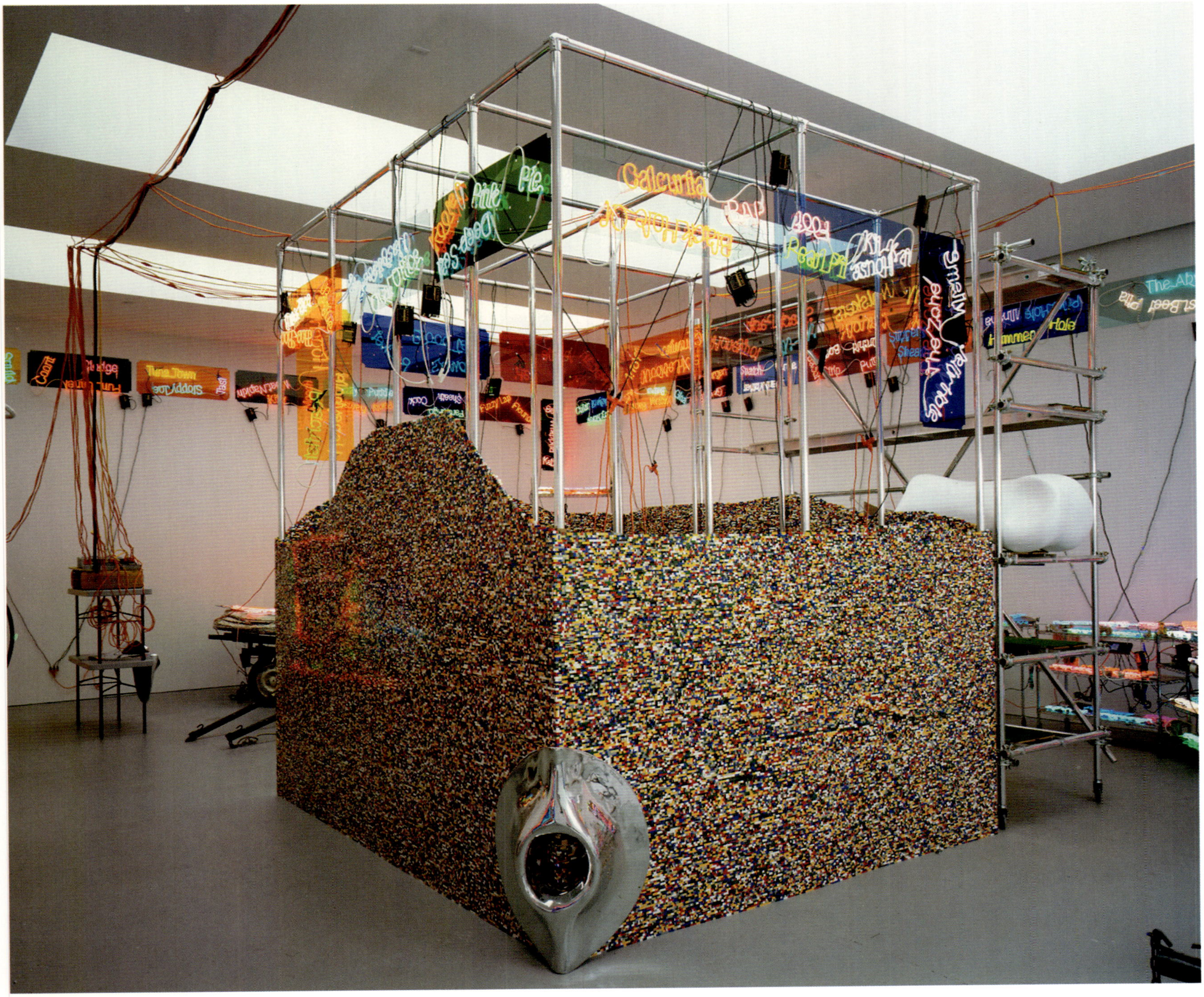

LEGO® Mecca Ka'ba (1/3 scale), 2003
LEGO® pieces, LEGO® Creator plastic tubs, polished aluminum pipes, clamps, 12 neon signs (glass, Plexiglass, wire, transformers, electrical cables), cardboard, Meccavulva (cast polished aluminum), Perfect World Scaffold (polished aluminum pipes, wood, felt, plastic tuna), PeaRoeFoam (dried peas, styrofoam beads, salmon roe, glue), cast fiberglass camel toe
13 ft 6 in x 13 ft 6 in x 11 ft 6 in (4.1 x 4.1 x 3.5 m)
As installed at David Zwirner, New York, September 2003

RONALD JONES

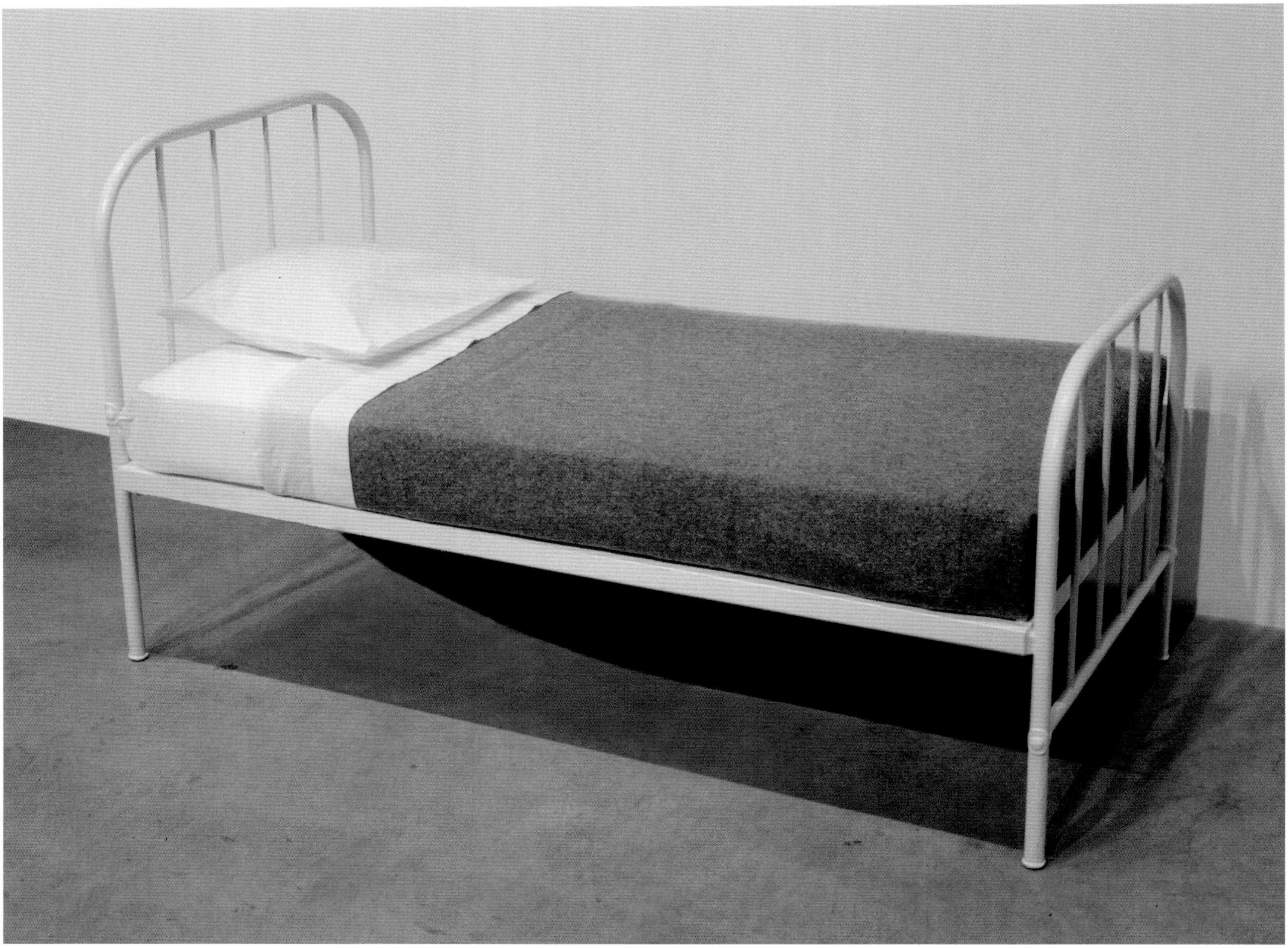

The bed Ethel Rosenberg slept in the night before her execution, 1953–1998, 1998
Painted steel bed frame, mattress, pillow, pillowcase, blanket, sheets
30 1/2 x 27 x 54 1/2 in (77.5 x 68.6 x 138.4 cm)

dreds of ceramic donkeys, neon signs spelling out obscure synonyms for vagina, and in the center of the room, *LEGO® Mecca Ka'ba (1/3 scale),* 2003, a one-third scale replica of the Kaaba, a shrine that is the holiest place in Mecca (here built of a million Legos).The inspiration for the piece was Rhoades's discovery on the Internet that "meccatuna" is a euphemism for vagina, hence his is an absurdist installation that touches on Islam, sex, and consumption.

Sarah Lucas makes equally provocative installations, also choosing readymade elements that are deeply loaded both politically and sexually. Lucas has incorporated materials from food to cigarettes to women's tights into her formally diverse work, using visual puns to suggest the ways in which gender and sexuality pervade contemporary life. For example, she has created the descriptively titled *Beer Can Penis*, 1999, out of two mangled beer cans situated just so. In other works Lucas suggests female forms with stretched-out nylon stockings. These pieces tweak conventional society's discomfort with sexual content, discovering gender in the most ordinary objects.

Moving ever further from Duchampian disinterest and impersonality are artists who treat everyday objects as magnets for memories and associations. In their work objects operate as words do, generating multiple and even contradictory meanings, depending on their contexts. A number of contemporary artists have seized on this resonant aspect of objects to address social and political realities that might otherwise be difficult to express. The most literal proponent of this approach is Ronald Jones, who places apparently ordinary objects together in assemblages that only reveal their meaning when specific historical information—usually tragic or threatening—is provided. In 1998, for instance, he presented scaled-down versions of three beds that wall labels identified as the bed Neil Armstrong slept in his first night back from the moon in 1969, the bed Jack Ruby slept in the night before he shot Lee Harvey Oswald in 1963, and the bed Ethel Rosenberg slept in the night before her execution in 1953. Together the beds evoke turning points in American history, though without the wall texts, they might be regarded as a display of contemporary furniture design.

Dario Robleto deals with political concerns through the poetry of objects as well. In his work, amalgamations of found and altered objects infused with powerful associations are remade into intriguing and beautifully crafted sculptures. For example, a small work with the elaborate title *At War with the Entropy of Nature/ Ghosts Don't Always Want to Come Back*, 2002, looks like a mangled tape cassette. Its wall label notes that it is created from bits of every bone in the human body mixed with trinitite, glass produced from sand that was fused together in the blast for an early atomic bomb test. The non-functional tape is said to contain sounds from various actual battles; it is a compact and elegiac anti-war statement. Robleto compares his process to that of "sampling" in music, and in fact he often uses vinyl records as his raw material.

Cornelia Parker's objects also have significant past lives. In some cases, she displays objects whose ordinary appearance belies a provocative or devastating history. Often placed in museum-style display cases, they resemble archeological artifacts, and again the viewer relies on wall labels to discover the secrets of their previous existence. For instance, Parker has exhibited a glass slide containing a spider that died in Mark Twain's house and a photogram of a feather that escaped from Freud's pillow. In other pieces, she takes familiar objects and subjects them to

SARAH LUCAS

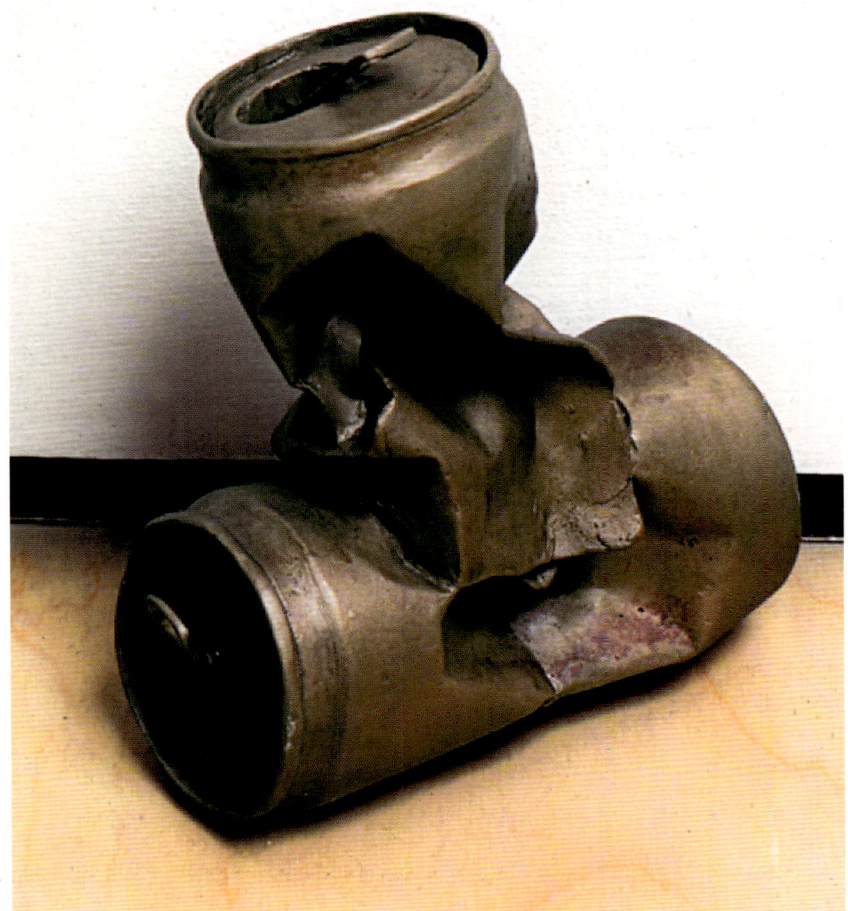

Beer Can Penis, 1999
Bronze, 6 x 5 x 2 3/4 in (15 x 13 x 2.8 cm)

CORNELIA PARKER

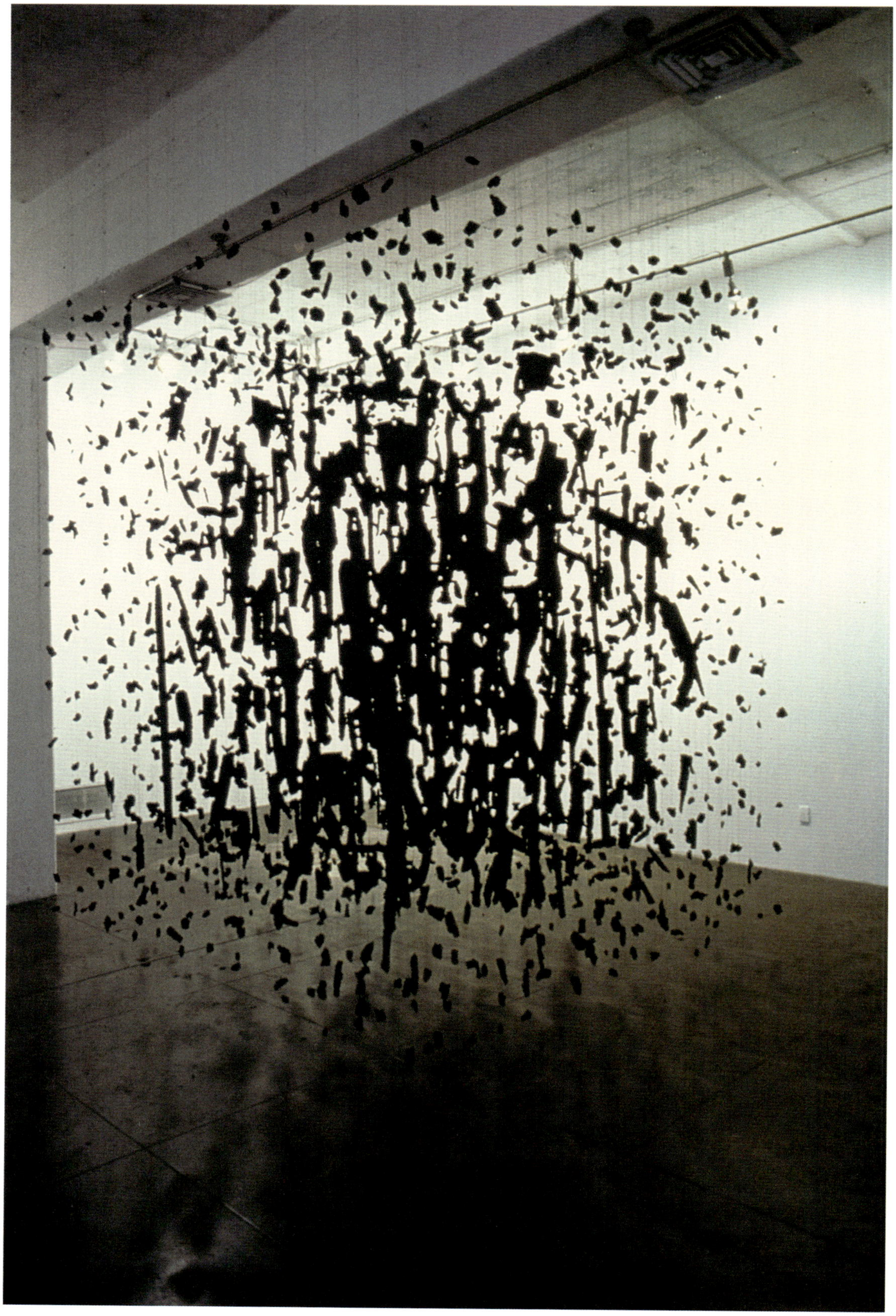

Mass (Colder Darker Matter), 1997
Charcoal retreived from a church struck by lightning, with thanks to the Baptist Church of Lytle, Texas, dimensions variable

DARIO ROBLETO

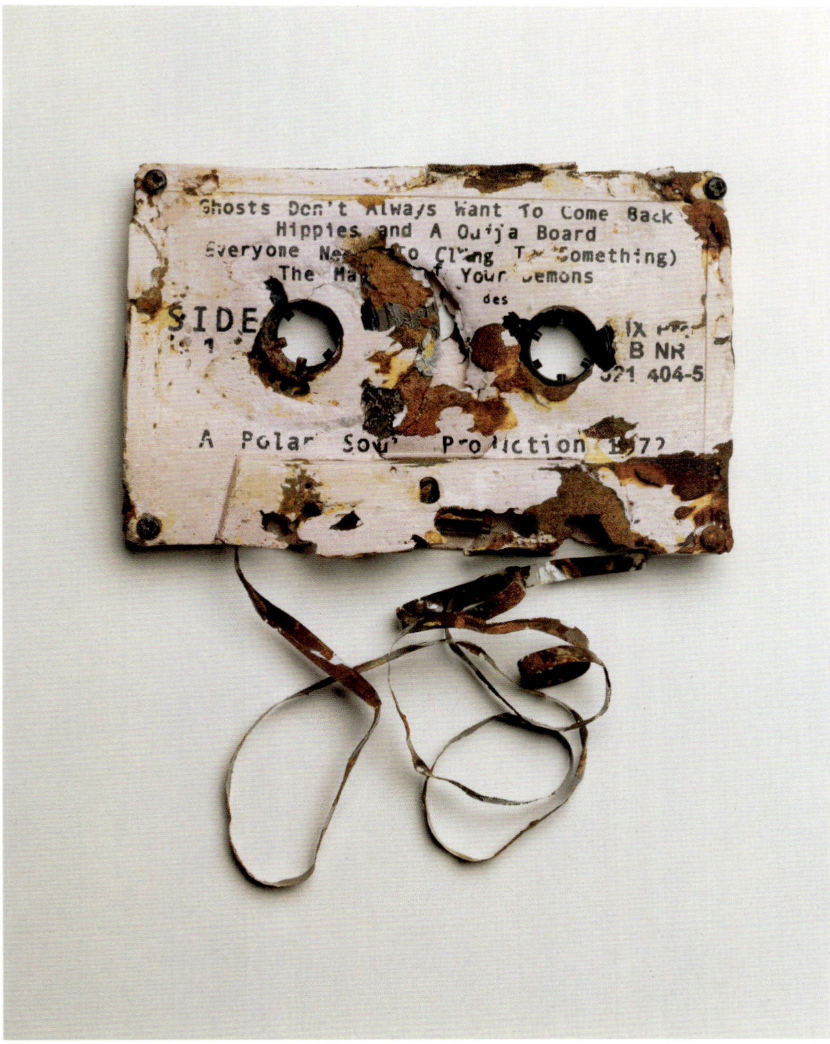

At War With The Entropy Of Nature / Ghosts Don't Always Want To Come Back, 2002
Cassette tape made from carved bone and bone dust from every bone in the body, trinitite, melted and dissoved audio tape of an original composition of military drum marches and soldiers' voices from battlefields of various wars made from E.V.P. recordings (Electronic Voice Phenomena: voices and sounds of the dead or past, detected through magnetic audiotape), metal, screws, rust, letraset, 3 3/4 x 5/8 x 2 1/2 in (9.5 x 1.6 x 6.4 cm)

extreme and even violent transformations. She has spun out the gold in a wedding ring into a single thread that measures the circumference of a living room. She has crushed silver flatware, metal coins, or musical instruments under a steamroller and suspended the distorted remains from the ceiling like a filigree forest of falling leaves. She also exploits the devastations worked by natural forces. *Mass (Colder Darker Matter)*, 1997, consists of the charred remains of a church struck by lightning that hang in mid-air in an approximate replication of the form of the building they once were.

Employing ordinary materials such as bubble gum, toothpaste, pubic hair, soap, aspirin, and masking tape, Tom Friedman makes more subtle transformations to his found objects. At first glance his sculptures appear to be as ordinary as his materials, but a second glance reveals the discrepancy between material and form. For example, a five-inch pink ball stuck in a corner turns out to be made of hundreds of pieces of well-chewed chewing gum, while a minimalist monochrome painting has been "painted" with gel toothpaste. A tiny portrait of the artist is carved from an aspirin tablet. In *Untitled*, 1992, a long, corkscrew-like spiral hanging on the wall is the remains of an entire pencil shaved by a pencil sharpener. Friedman's sculptures share the sense of wonder that one experiences in viewing works by medieval and Renaissance craftsmen who, for example, carved an entire nativity scene in a walnut or the Lord's Prayer on a grain of rice. The difference is that Friedman's works are completely secular—if they produce a sense of awe, it is one completely rooted in the everyday objects of our consumer society.

Tara Donovan creates similarly miraculous transformations in large-scale installations that each rely on a huge accumulation of one extremely ordinary artifact. Among her creations are *Toothpicks*, 2001, a nearly three-foot-square cube of densely packed toothpicks; *Haze*, 2003, a wall encrusted in clear plastic drinking straws; and *Untitled (Plastic Cups)*, 2006, an enormous field of plastic cups that forms a kind of lunar landscape spread across the gallery floor. For this latter work, Donovan arranged the cups in stacks of various heights, creating an undulating mountainous terrain in which the cups closest to the lights suspended from the gallery ceiling seemed to glow, while lower stacks suggest shadowy valleys. The individual cups retained their familiar shape, and hence began to operate a bit like pixels—tiny points that together created the topography of the space. Such works are at once inviting and inaccessible, conveying a sense of fragility and poetry quite at odds with the banality of the material out of which they are created.

Doris Salcedo also uses ordinary objects, but their effect is far from the buoyancy found in the works of Friedman or Donovan. An artist whose sculptures and installations return again and again to the tragic violence that permeates her homeland of Colombia, Salcedo depends on universal understandings of her objects' symbolism to infuse her art with meaning. Worn shoes, doors, tables, chairs, and pressed shirts evoke domesticity, but our comfortable familiarity with such objects is undermined by jarring details. Stacks of freshly pressed shirts pierced with a lance in an untitled work from 1990 commemorate the experience of women who witnessed their husbands being killed on their own doorsteps. Chairs appear in various works. For the 2003 Istanbul Biennial, the artist filled the space between two buildings with a dense pile of 1,550 chairs, which became at once prisons and imprisoned, their chaotic jumbling a metaphor for the helpless entanglement of war.

TOM FRIEDMAN

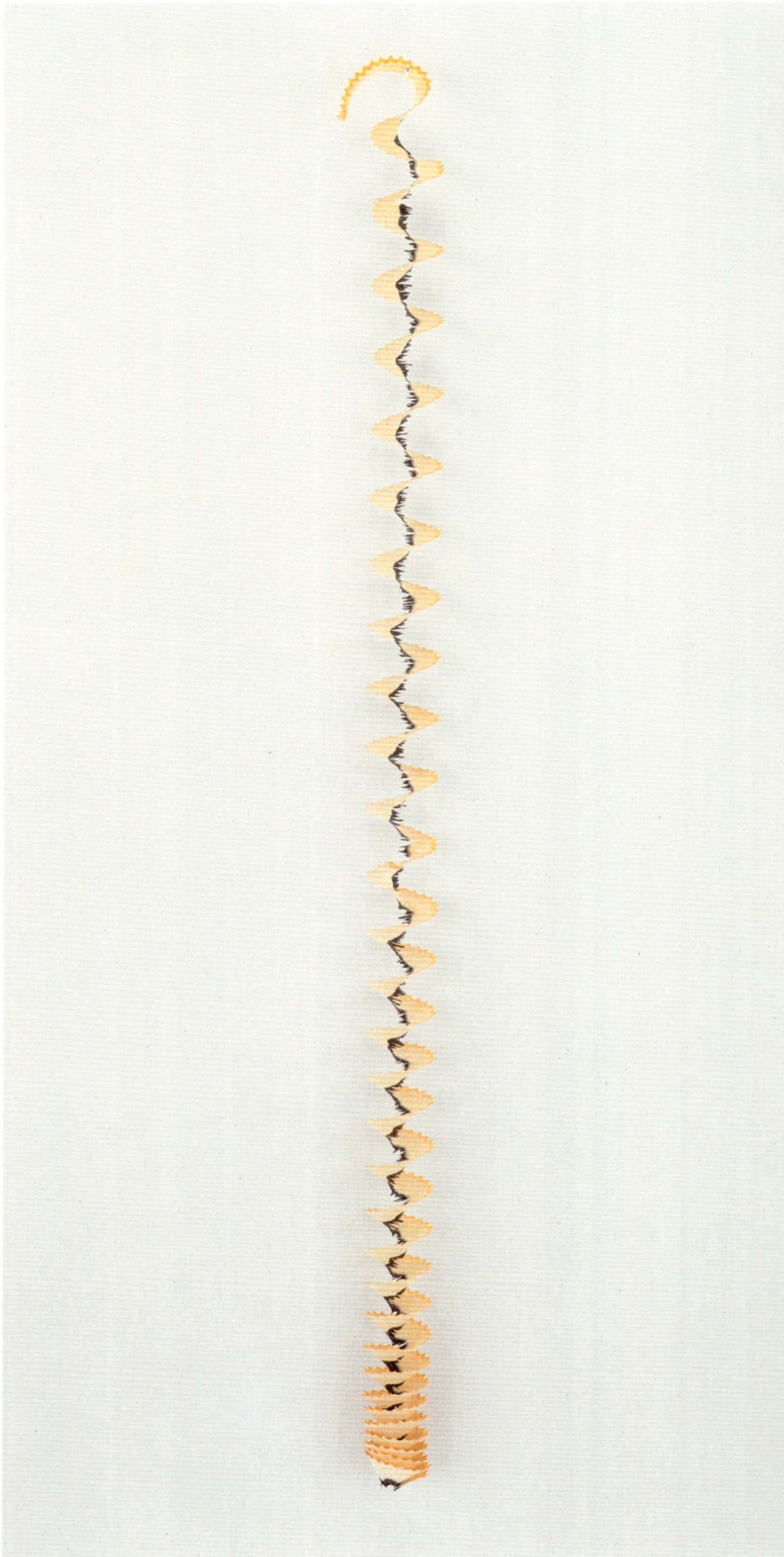

Untitled, 1992
Pencil shaving, 22 x 1 1/2 in (55.9 x 3.8 x 3.8 cm)

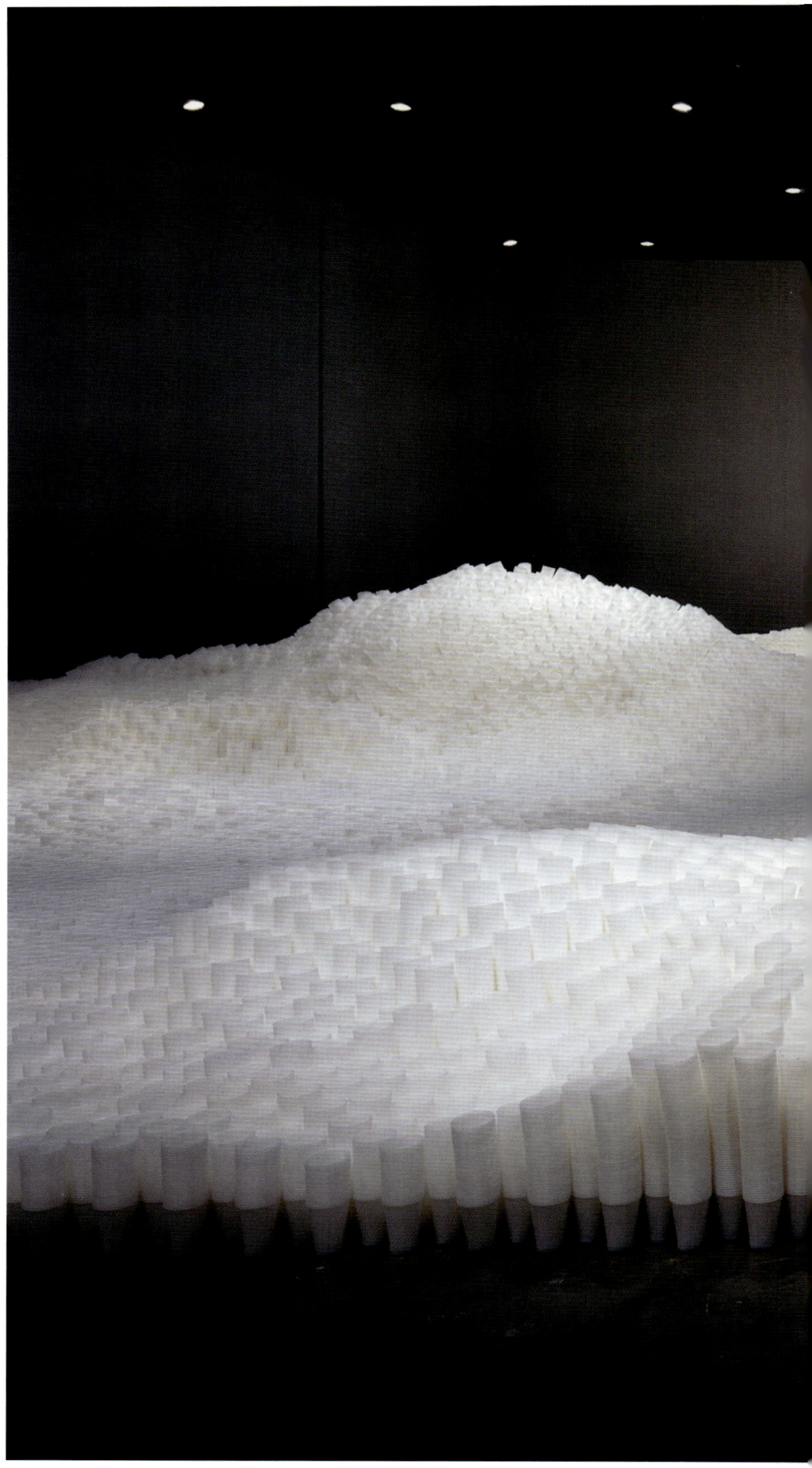

TARA DONOVAN

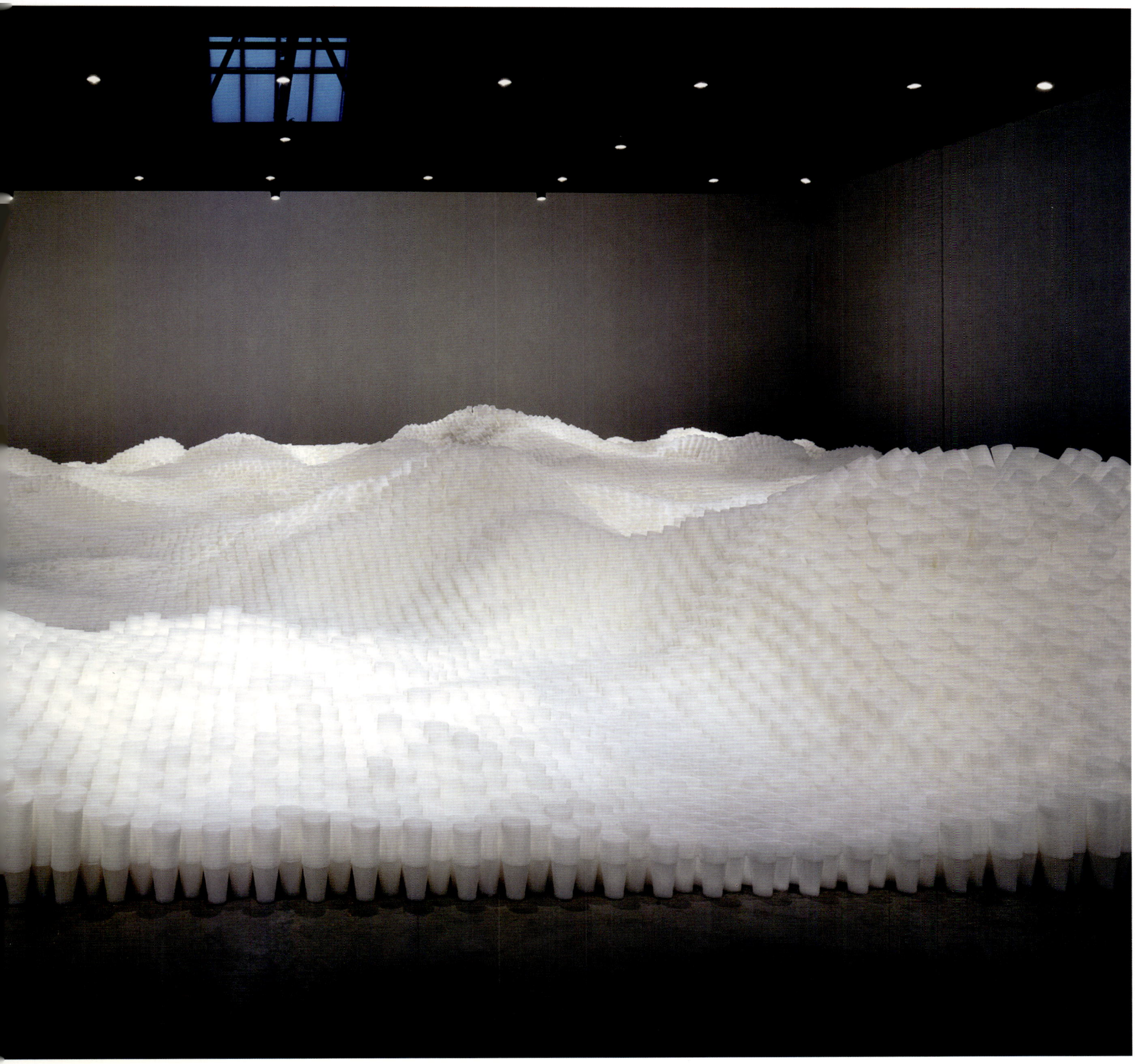

Untitled (Plastic Cups), 2006
Plastic cups, approx. 4 ft x 54 ft 5 in x 49 ft 8 in (1.2 x 16.6 x 15.1 m)
As installed at PaceWildenstein, New York, March–April 2006

DORIS SALCEDO

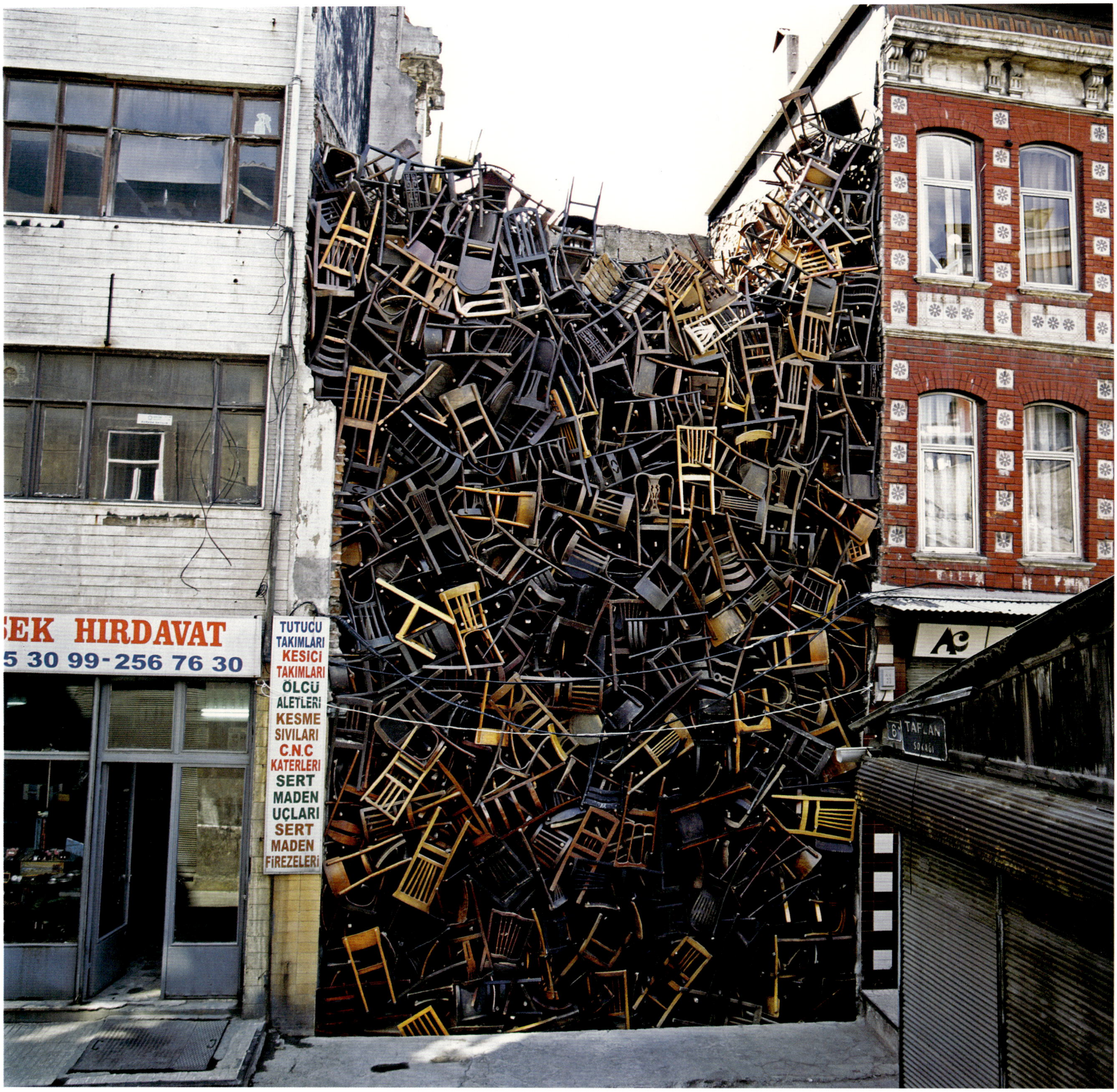

Untitled, 2003
1,550 chairs
As installed at Yemeniciler Caddesi No. 66, Istanbul, for the 8th International Istanbul Biennial, September–November 2003

MONA HATOUM

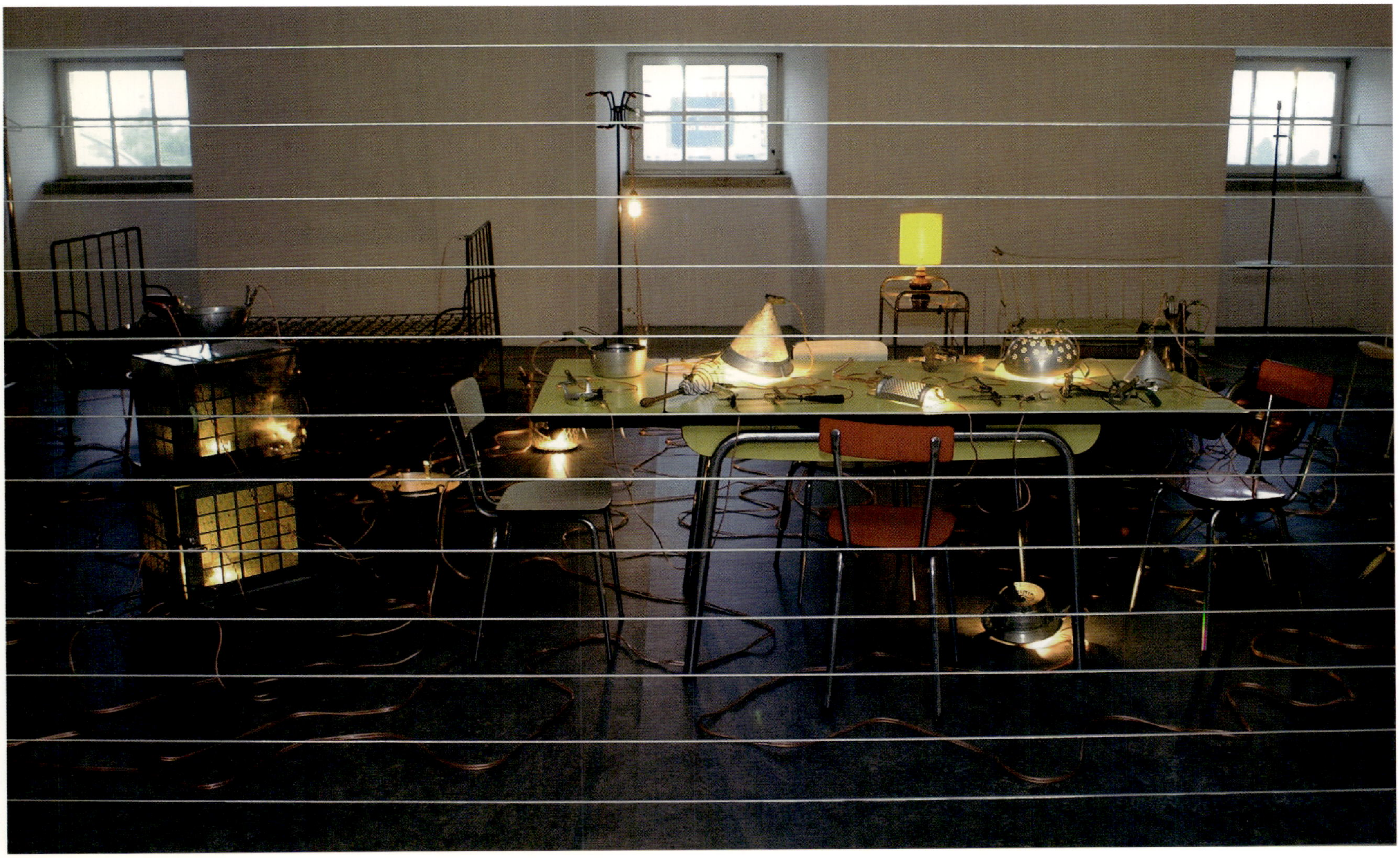

Homebound, 2000
Kitchen utensils, furniture, electric wire, light bulbs, computerized dimmer switch, amplifier, and speakers, dimensions variable
As installed at Documenta 11, Kassel, Germany, 2002

GABRIEL OROZCO

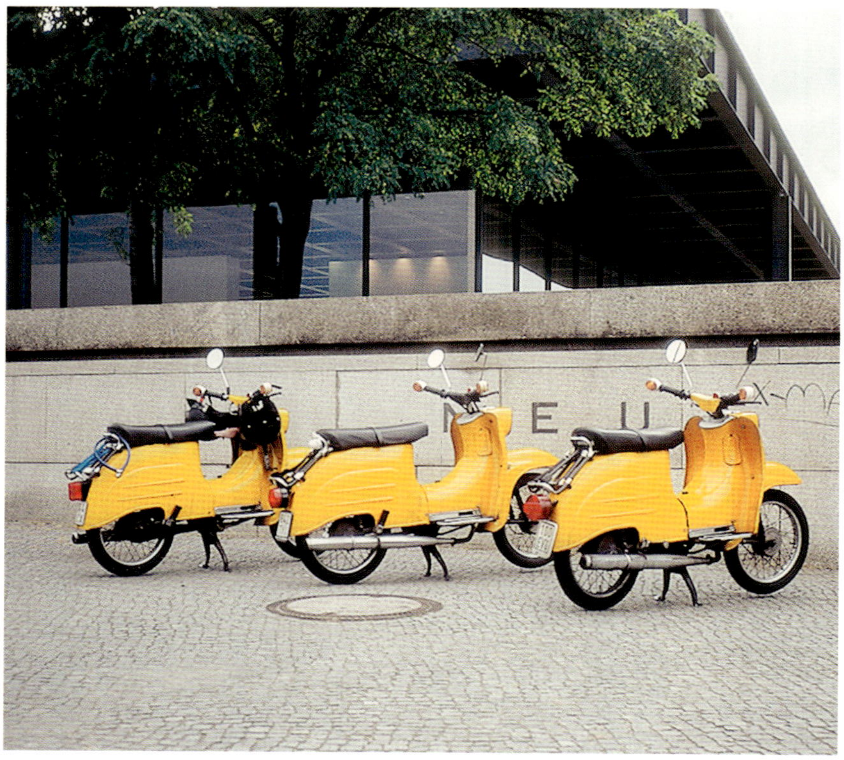

Until You Find Another Yellow Schwalbe, 1995
Set of 40 C-prints, 12 7/16 x 18 5/8 in (31.5 x 47.3 cm)

Domestic objects also become metaphors for dark realities in the work of Mona Hatoum, whose works deal obliquely with the horrors of exile and displacement. In sculptures and installations, Hatoum recycles, recreates, and manipulates objects to conjure up confinement, surveillance, and loss of individual autonomy. In the 2000 installation *Homebound*, Hatoum recreated a domestic interior with furniture, lamps, and other items from the 1950s, the era of her childhood. She made ordinary colanders, meat grinders, and sewing machines appear sinister, cordoning them off with thick cable suggestive of security wire. Set on an unexceptional kitchen table, they were outfitted with electrical cords and wires rigged to make the objects gyrate, emit noises, and light up. By taking objects normally associated with domestic comfort and endowing them with an air of menace, Hatoum invests the supposed serenity of home with anxiety and unrest.

In a related but less apocalyptic way, Gabriel Orozco endows objects with personal and social meanings that express his own sense of displacement in a nomadic art world. In some of his works, he appears to view the world itself as a readymade, for instance in photographs highlighting strange juxtapositions found by chance in the environment, such as an arrangement of twigs on a sidewalk or a bicycle resting on a fallen tree in the desert. For the work, *Until You Find Another Yellow Schwalbe*, 1995, he drove around Rome on a yellow motor scooter and snapped a photograph of every other yellow scooter he saw, as if to establish his own place in this foreign land. In other works, Orozco manipulates or recreates manufactured objects to point to the absurdity of modern life. He has created an oval, pocketless billiard table that defies all the ordinary rules of the game, for instance, and turned yogurt cup lids into minimalist art by installing them on a wall of an otherwise empty gallery. With such works, Orozco violates the rules of functionality to throw light on timeless philosophical and physical questions about humanity.

Diverging from artists who use readymade objects as metaphor are those concerned with craftsmanship in an age of assembly-line manufacturing. These artists extend the critique of mass production broached at the dawn of the industrial age by critics and reformers like William Morris and John Ruskin, Victorian visionaries who sought to recreate a version of the medieval workshop, an alternative to the deadening, homogenizing effects of factory production. Only then could they revive workers' traditional (and idealized) joy in their work. In recent years, a number of artists have echoed this notion. They restore the personalized, psychological dimensions of art-making by meticulously hand-crafting objects that are more commonly produced by machine. Again, this is a reversal of Duchamp's intention. Instead of lowering art to the status of factory goods, contemporary artists who painstakingly recreate mass-market objects elevate articles lifted from everyday life into the aesthetic realm, turning them into precious objects.

A particularly remarkable demonstration of this idea appears in the installations of Liza Lou. Lou creates life-size replicas of whole rooms and environments made entirely of colorful, glittery beads. Her suburban *Kitchen*, 1995, is complete with a beaded refrigerator tacked with beaded notes, a beaded oven whose rack is open to reveal a beaded pie, and even a beaded sink full of dirty beaded dishes and running beaded water flowing from the beaded faucet. Her *Backyard*, 1999, is equally detailed, containing bead-covered patio furniture, a Weber grill with glowing coals, a picnic dinner with sandwiches, corn on the cob, cans of beer, and even thousands of bead-covered blades of grass. Moving from the "female" realm of suburban domes-

LIZA LOU

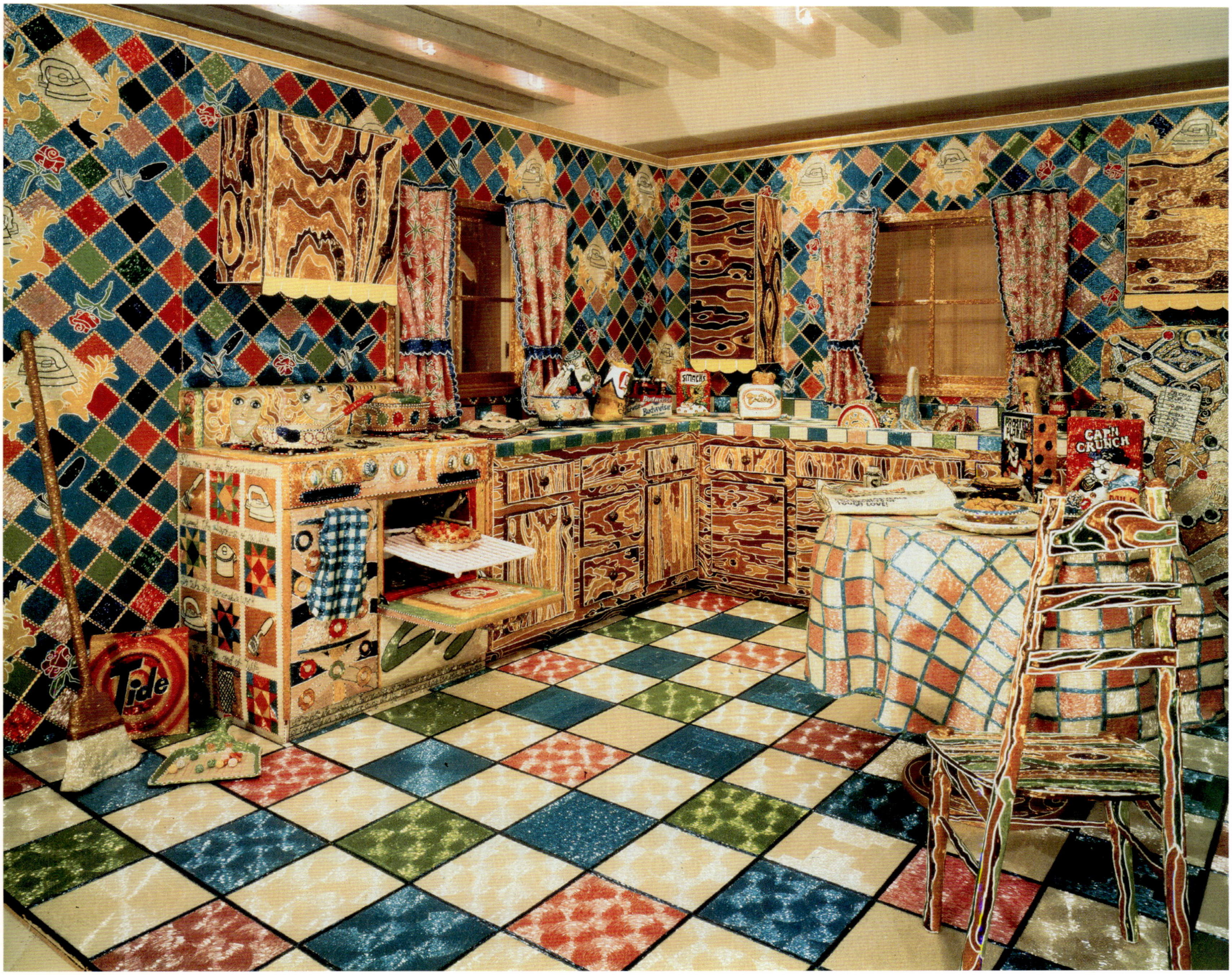

Kitchen, 1991–95
Mixed media and beads, 168 square ft (51.2 square m)

JOSIAH MCELHENY

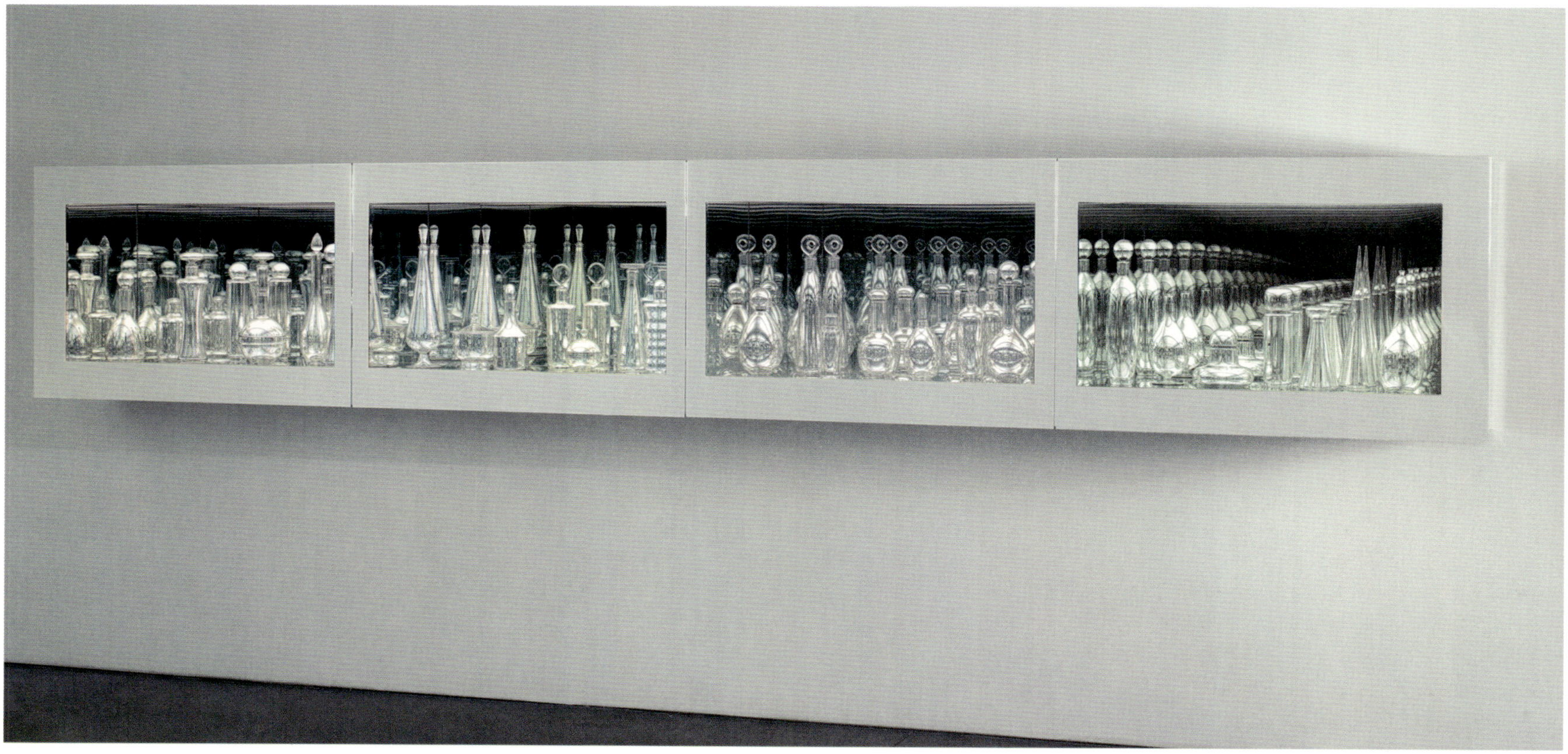

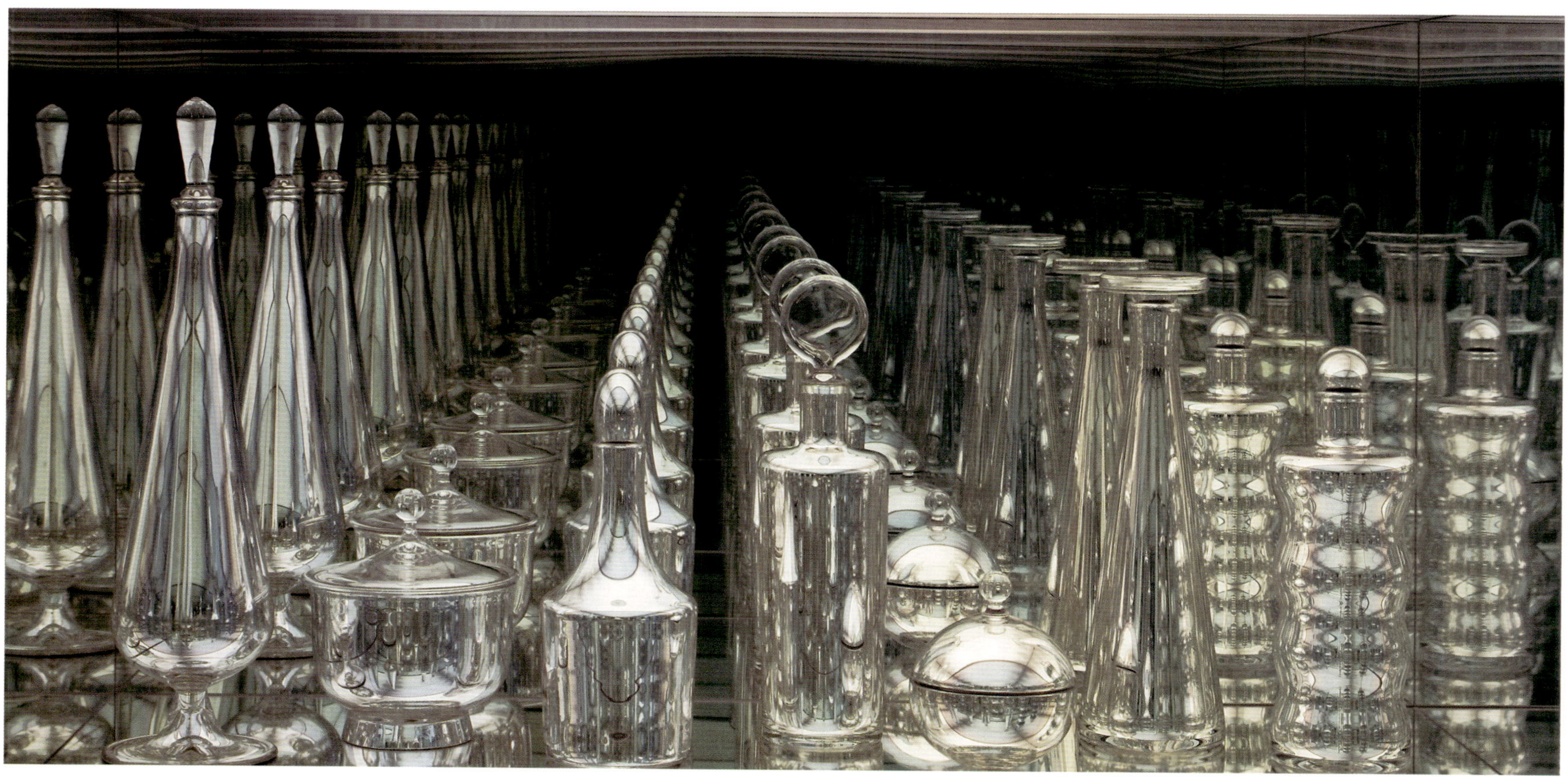

Twentieth Century Modernism, Mirrored and Reflected Infinitely, and detail, 2006
Hand blown mirrored glass, display structure, transparent mirror, and electric lighting
31 1/4 x 188 x 18 3/4 in (79.4 x 477.5 x 47.6 cm)

ticity to a more stereotypically "masculine" realm of the hunting shack, Lou has also beaded the interior of an aluminum Airstream trailer, littering it with beaded girlie magazines, hunting knives, bottles of Jack Daniels, and fishing boots and guns.

The magical quality of Lou's transformations is present too in Josiah McElheny's hand-blown glass sculptures, exquisitely crafted vessels that suggest how objects embody history, memory, and fantasy. Some are based on historical artifacts—recreations of goblets pictured in Renaissance paintings, for instance—or replicate examples of modernist design. Often they convey what the artist calls "historical fictions," intricate stories the artist constructs around the objects, carefully cultivating an air of authenticity supported by seemingly genuine documentation. Whether based on fact or fiction, each of his works is designed to tell a story. He has recreated a "miraculous cup" from a sixteenth-century fresco that supposedly was so strong that when it fell from a tower, it broke the pavement instead of shattering itself. He has devised a chandelier-like sculpture that doubles as a model for the Big Bang, a reimagining of a similarly conceived ceiling fixture designed for New York's Metropolitan Opera House in the mid-1960s. Although he also works with transparent and opaque glass, McElheny is particularly interested in reflective effects. In *Twentieth Century Modernism, Mirrored and Reflected Infinitely*, 2006, he placed twenty-eight mirrored vessels based on various modernist designs in a mirrored case. They reflect each other while also reflecting off of the mirrored case, appearing to multiply into endless rows stretching back into infinity. The work speaks to the transformation of product design wrought by mass production and offers a little essay on the self-reflective nature of modernism.

Objects also stand in for absent bodies in the work of Charles LeDray. Unlike Lou, whose recreations are the same size as the originals they mimic, LeDray frequently miniaturizes familiar objects, for example his doll-size suits of clothing that hang from miniature hangers. Miniaturization makes us look more closely at these garments, which suggest the personality and social status of the person to whom they might belong. LeDray has also created a miniature galaxy of hats and tiny versions of the books, magazines, radios and discarded clothing that one might find spread out on a street vendor's blanket on a city sidewalk. He has carved a tiny tellurian (an apparatus for demonstrating the earth's movement) out of human bone and created an elaborate assemblage out of refashioned velvet-covered ring and bracelet stands found in jewelry store displays. One of his most ambitious works, *Oasis*, 2002, is composed of a glass case with six shelves supporting two thousand tiny hand-thrown ceramic pots whose forms, each different, represent the vast range of historic and geographic varieties of vessels. As with Lou's kitchen and backyard, much of the appeal of this work lies in its sheer obsessiveness and in LeDray's willingness to return to a handmade mode of manufacture to create objects that today are more likely to be mass-produced. His carefully crafted replicas have a strangely melancholy quality—as if they were relics of a lost civilization closely resembling our own.

Changes of scale not only encourage closer viewing, but give new life to replicas of everyday objects. Andreas Slominski remakes mouse, rat, and bird traps into the stuff of nightmare by monumentalizing them. The effects vary from the deeply threatening to the deceptively friendly. Slominski's *Vogelfangstation* (Bird Trapping Station), 1998–99, includes a catching hut for the trap-setter and a series of baited traps, ready to be sprung in the event that a bird wanders into the museum and

CHARLES LEDRAY

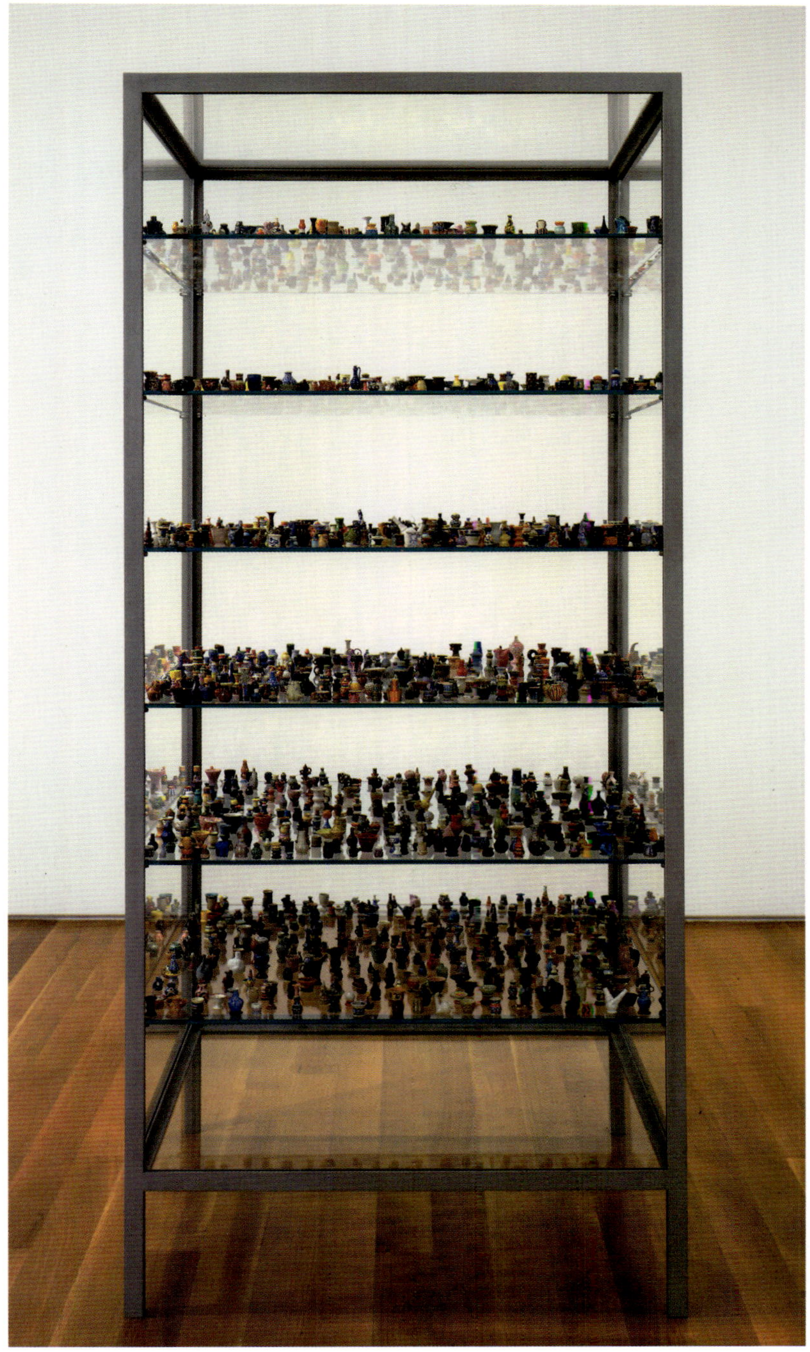

Oasis, 1996–2003
2000 glazed ceramic pots, glass, and steel
96 x 36 x 36 in (243.8 x 91.4 x 91.4 cm)
The Museum of Modern Art, New York

ANDREAS SLOMINSKI

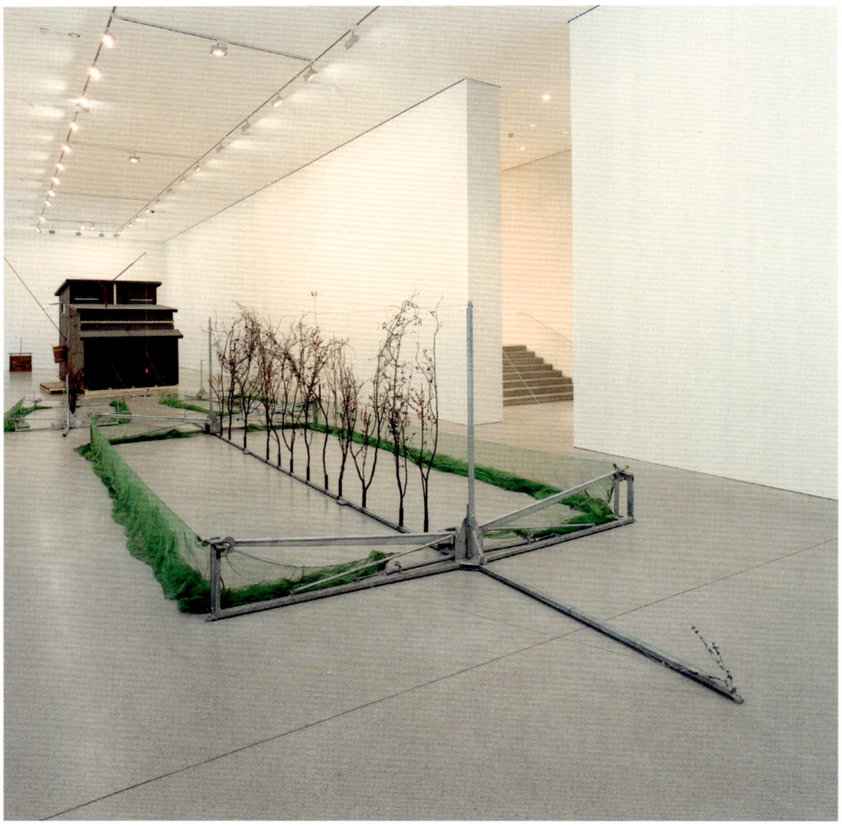

Vogelfangstation (Bird Trapping Station), 1998–99
Metal, wood, and nets (21 parts), dimensions variable
Solomon R. Guggenheim Museum, New York

lands on one of them. The absurdity of the situation is patent, but so is the sense that these things might possibly work were they placed in the wild. All of the traps have a psychological dimension, suggesting that they may at any moment turn on the maker, transforming the hunter into the hunted, just as the mass-produced objects of our desire can entrap us in a constant quest for fulfillment through consumption.

With a similar eye on the effects of altered scale and excess, Katharina Fritsch creates enlarged versions of people, creatures, or religious icons. She adds to their strangeness by multiplying them and giving them the generalized look of statuettes mass-produced from molds. Her sculpture *Rattenkönig* (Rat-King), 1993, composed of a circle of nine-foot-tall black rats facing outward, dwarfs the viewer while evoking the evil kingdom of a fairy tale. A series of oversize Madonnas, modeled after the cheap figurines available at religious shops and shrines and cast in bright-yellow polyester resin, cease to be emblems of worship and become monsters instead. This soulless manufactured quality carries through even in unique sculptures, for example in a six-foot-three black-resin statue of a monk or a red-resin sculpture of an art dealer, who stands as stiff and expressionless as an oversize dollar store tchotchke.

Which brings us back to Duchamp and his cheeky equation of art and the products of mass production, the distinction between which was once utterly sacrosanct. Thanks to Duchamp, today we effortlessly accept arrangements of furniture, plumbing supplies, toothpaste, and food as art. At the same time, we see nothing strange about artists painstakingly recreating objects of manufacture by hand. There is no question that Duchamp forever altered the Western world's vision of art. Yet there is a paradox that supersedes even Duchamp's highly calculated sense of irony. For far from ending art as we know it, Duchamp and his readymades gave it new and highly flexible directions. Both because of and despite Duchamp, the marriage of art and the quotidian object has fed contemporary art's most enduring strategies.

KATHARINA FRITSCH

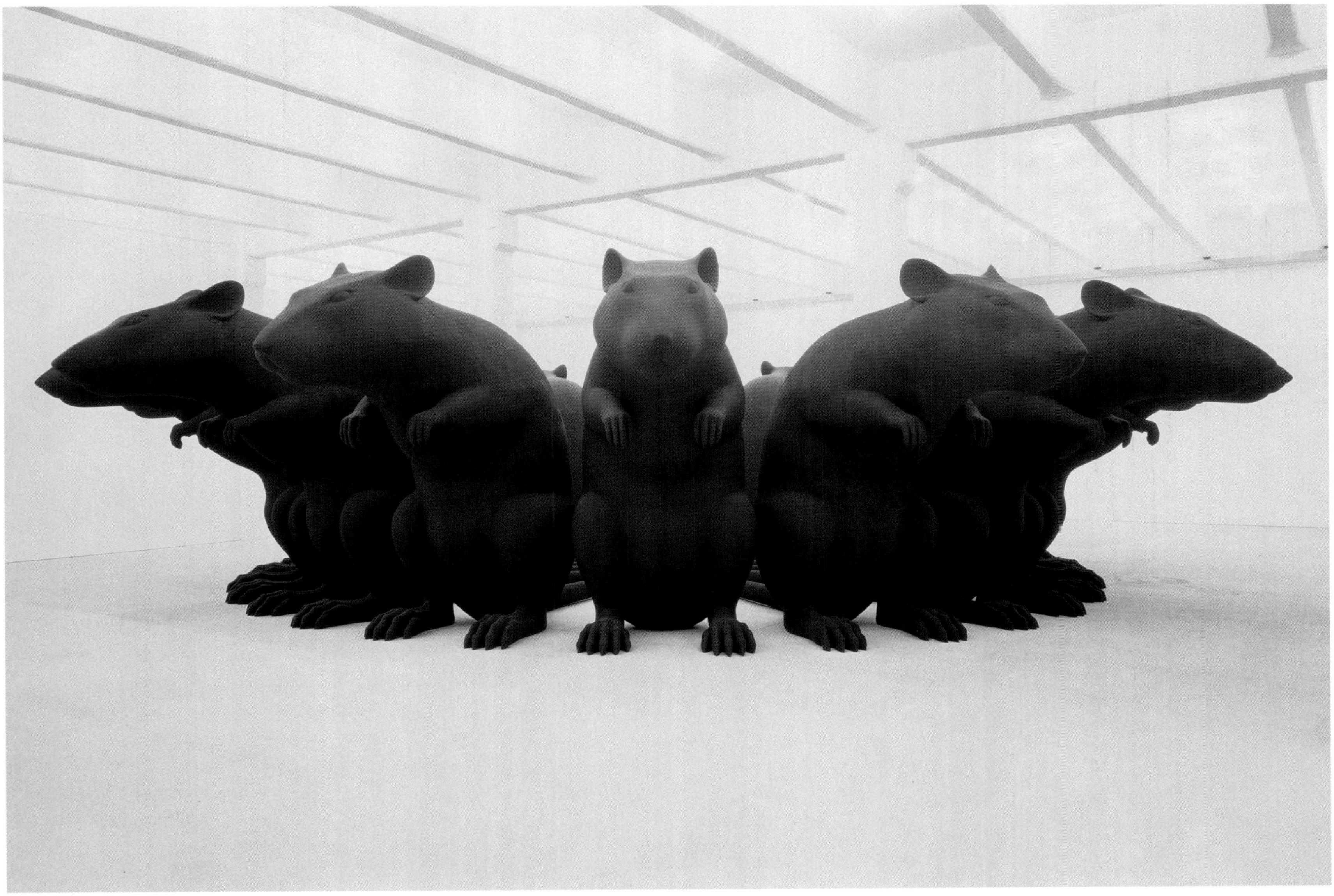

Rattenkönig (Rat-King), 1993
Polyester resin, height 9 ft 2 in (2.8 m) diameter 42 ft 8 in (13 m)
As installed at Dia Center for the Arts, New York, April 1993–June 1994

ART & ABSTRACTION
RETREAT FROM PURITY

Art historians generally agree that the first *truly* abstract works in Western art were created by Wassily Kandinsky in 1911. The Russian painter's abstractions—vibrant, lyrical, and revolutionary—were followed in very short order by equally abstract works by Kazimir Malevich and Piet Mondrian. Why at the beginning of the twentieth century did artists suddenly feel compelled to cast off all vestiges of representation, rejecting a basic principle that had guided Western art for over twenty-five hundred years? This is a question that bewildered art audiences at the time, and it still perplexes visitors to museums today. Theorists on this radical break tend to fall into two camps. On one side are those who align abstraction with a celebration of the new sense of reality that accompanied revolutions in science and technology. In this view, abstraction is a positive response to relativity and atomic theory, which revealed the existence of factors beyond human senses, or reflects artists' embrace of the machine aesthetic of new industries. On the other side are those who see abstraction as a reaction against such new developments. From this perspective, the emergence of "non-objective" art (as it was called before the term "abstraction" came into play) is a search for the unchanging and eternal forms underlying both nature and human consciousness, a rejection of the materialist philosophies introduced by industrialization, and a counterbalancing expression of universal harmonies.

The contradictions that attended the birth of abstraction continue into the present. Abstraction today seems to have as many justifications as it has practitioners. It is regarded alternately as an expression of the individual psyche and a set of conventions that mock true individuality. Some critics argue that abstraction probes the essence of nature, others that it reflects the artifice of the urban world, yet others that it explores a secret world of private feeling. For some it is a harbinger of spiritual truth, for others it offers a celebration of obdurate matter. The forms abstraction takes today are also myriad, drawing on movements as diverse as Constructivism, Abstract Expressionism, Minimalism, color-field painting, Post Minimalism, conceptual abstraction and Simulationism. Perhaps more than any other style in art today, contemporary abstraction can only be understood with reference to its own history.

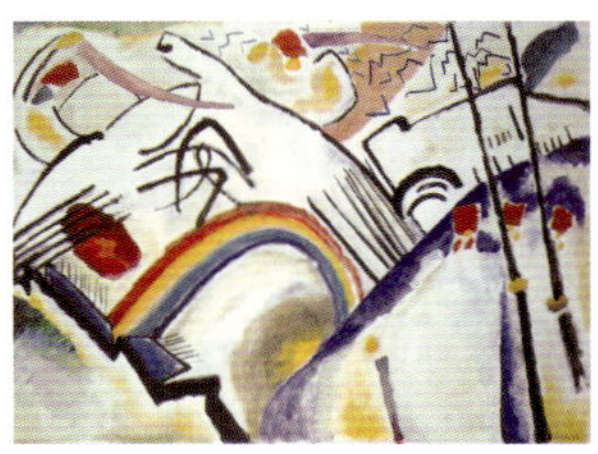

WASSILY KANDINSKY
COSSACKS
1910–11
OIL ON CANVAS
37 1/4 X 51 1/4 IN
(94.6 X 130.2 CM)
TATE, LONDON

The formal roots of contemporary abstraction can be found in its early split onto two different paths, one based on geometric forms and the other on organic ones. In their initial articulations, these approaches pointed to two very different visions of the nature of ultimate realities, though such sharp distinctions began to blur in the hands of subsequent practitioners. Geometric abstraction, which is characterized by clearly defined, angular shapes, was influenced by Plato's argument that the visible world offers only a pale imitation of a set of underlying, universal "forms." Further, at the beginning of the twentieth century, the Russian Theosophist Madame Blavatsky and her associates, who were enormously influential to avant-garde artists of the time, expounded on the mystical nature of color and geometry, investing them with precise metaphysical meaning. In response, artists reduced art to basic colors and forms. Malevich, for instance, referred to the square as "the face of the new art" and the basic component of "world building."[1] He embraced a vision of art that he dubbed Suprematism, which expressed his hope that art would lead people from the materialistic embrace of acquisition and accumulation to a dematerialized realm of pure feeling. To attain this, he created paintings in which pure geometric forms would, in his words, "destroy the antiquated movement of thought according to the laws of causality, the toothless, common sense, the 'symmetrical logic.'"[2] In his *Suprematist Composition* (c.1920–22), for instance, he sets the black square—his emblem of the world of feeling—into a dynamic relationship with other elemental forms. Floating them against a white field, he aims to represent the interplay of between the realm of nonobjective feeling and the void that surrounds it. Mondrian employed geometry to related ends. His compositions of horizontal and vertical lines forming rectangles and squares filled with the primary colors, red, yellow, and blue, were meant to create a state of equilibrium in harmony with the rhythm of the universe. *Composition* (1929) reveals all the elements of his approach, revealing how the radical reduction of colors and shapes can still yield a dynamic structure. He was a leader of the Dutch art movement De Stijl, whose proponents included architects and furniture designers as well as painters, all devoted to the creation of a new utopian society through the introduction of a new order based on simple geometric forms.

Kandinsky was also fascinated with the mystical power of geometry, asserting that the triangle was the sign of the ever-shifting "life of the spirit."[3] He nonetheless espoused a very different approach to abstraction, pointing the way to the emergence of organic abstraction, in which soft-edged, rounded, "natural" forms prevail. Taking music as his model, Kandinsky created paintings full of free-floating lines and patches of vibrant color. For him, the essential nature of the universe was expressed by a state of constant flux. His 1912 essay "Concerning the Spiritual in Art" advised painters to follow their "inner need" and to reject concrete forms in favor of an artistic language of abstract rhythms and harmony.[4] For Kandinsky, abstraction revealed a hidden reality rooted in movement and change rather than in the stable forms of geometry. *Cossacks*, which was painted in the transitional period of 1910-11, combines vestigial figurative elements in the cossacks' lances seen in the right-hand corner, with gestural lines and colors that create an impression of a world in flux. In his preoccupation with movement he was joined by Arthur Dove, who is generally credited with being the first American abstractionist. Dove took his inspiration from the unseen energies of life and growth found in the natural world. Beginning from landscape, he evolved a style in which objects melted away, leaving him, as he noted, with the subjective recollection of "certain sensations [remembered] purely through their form and color."[5]

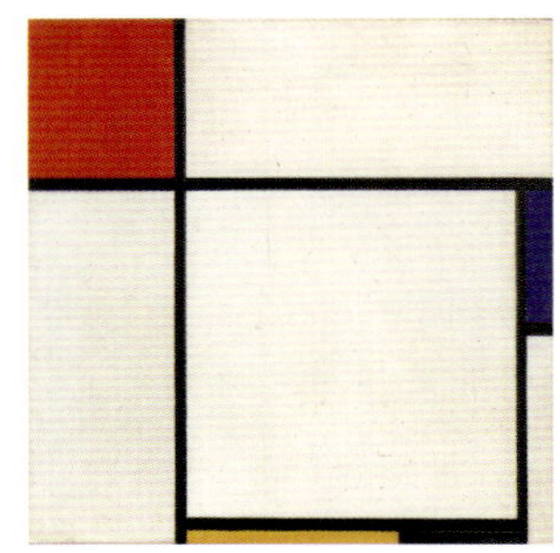

PIET MONDRIAN
COMPOSITION
1929
OIL ON CANVAS
17 3/4 X 17 3/4 IN
(45 X 45 CM)
SOLOMON R. GUGGENHEIM
MUSEUM, NEW YORK

While these two approaches resulted in very distinct looking art, they were united in the belief that abstraction was a manifestation of hidden truths. Practitioners of both the geometric and organic modes believed that they had liberated pure form from extraneous (representational) content so that essential (spiritual) realities could now be directly apprehended. Both groups shared a language of absolutes, the belief that feelings and ideas existed independently of the visible world, and the desire to wrest consciousness free of everyday experience. Under the banner of movements such as Russian Constructivism, the German Bauhaus, Dutch De Stijl and Italian Futurism, various forms of abstraction acted in the service of diverse utopian social programs. The ultimate failure of such social experiments led, however, to a general retreat from utopian thinking by the end of World War II, thus opening the door for the formalist "art for art's sake" that critic Clement Greenberg espoused. Like the early abstractionists, formalist critics advocated the reduction of art to its "essence," but they valorized not truth or spirit but "purity"—the removal from art of narrative, representation, subject, psychology, and spirituality. This purist orientation led to an obsession with opticality, a belief that painting's only relevant concern was the abstract disposition of line, color, shape, and space on a flat canvas.

Greenberg applied his formalism to both organic and geometric styles and supported both the dynamic gestural paintings of Willem de Kooning and Jackson Pollock and the more static geometric works of Barnett Newman and Mark Rothko. Still, regardless of the critic's dictates, the Abstract Expressionists refused to abandon extra-formal concerns. Their own writings about their works expressed a desire to connect with some essential spirituality, primitive myth, or mystical ideal of radical freedom. Subjectivity, explorations of the dream world and the subconscious (a remnant of Surrealism) and private systems of notation and meaning remained. Nonetheless, an offshoot of Abstract Expressionism, known variously as post-painterly abstraction and color-field painting—in which artists soaked pigment into the canvas so that there was no distinction between paint and ground (and therefore none between surface and object)—was seemingly made to order for Greenbergian formalism. (In fact in some ways it was, as Greenberg was notorious for advising artists of this generation to paint their paintings as he saw fit.)

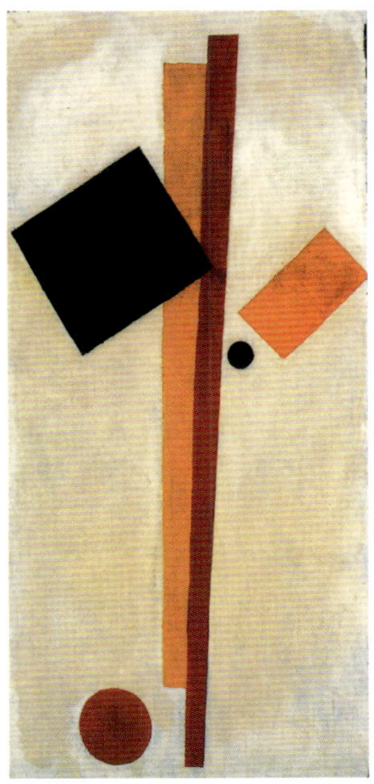

KAZIMIR MALEVICH
SUPREMATIST COMPOSITION
C. 1920–22
OIL ON PANEL
24 3/8 X 11 7/8 IN
(62 X 30 CM)

It is at this point, in the 1960s, that the history of abstraction takes an interesting turn. Always considered radical, revolutionary, and avant-garde, formalist abstraction began to be perceived by younger artists as a conventional, conservative approach to art. Among the most lasting manifestations of this backlash were Pop art, which brought back representational imagery with a vengeance, and Minimalism, whose practitioners perceived the impurity of so-called pure art and took the reductive impulse of formalism to its most extreme logical consequences. Despite the fact that Minimalism is a highly contested entity (very few of the artists associated with the term accept the label), it remains enormously influential. Generally, Minimalism describes work that places real materials in real space, often configuring identical interchangeable parts with machine-like consistency. One of the foremost Minimalists was Carl Andre, who laid modular squares of prefabricated materials—including bricks and tiles of aluminum, zinc, copper, lead, and iron—in continuous grids on the floor. The movement is associated with a resolute rejection of individual subjectivity, the spiritual dimensions of art, and the romantic ethos that characterized the preceding generations of abstractionists. As Frank Stella is often said to have observed of his flat geometric paintings: "What you see is what you see." The experience of this matter-of-factness was not necessarily as neutral as it sounds. An early commentator on the movement, critic Barbara Rose, noted that in the face of Minimalism's "blank, neutral, mechanical impersonality . . . spectators are chilled by its apparent lack of feeling or content."[6]

This effect is evident in the work of two of the most prominent artists associated with Minimalism, Donald Judd and Ellsworth Kelly. Judd, who was both a leading practitioner and a spokesperson for the new approach whose criticism was published in art magazines of the time, rejected the term "Minimalism" and described his sculptures as "specific objects." This term was meant to underscore the literalness of his intentions. Judd worked in three dimensions because he believed that painting would always retain a semblance of illusion, and only objects could be nothing more than what they were. His sculptures are based on the module of the box. Whether made of plywood, aluminum, galvanized steel, or Plexiglas, they embody an ideal of visual and physical clarity. Some sit on the floor, while others—*Untitled*, 1990, for instance—are cantilevered from the wall. Their surfaces vary: some are lacquered like auto bodies, while others are unfinished wood or polished metal. Whatever their material and finish, they retain an industrial quality, eschewing all sense of subjectivity, handcraftsmanship, or conventional aesthetics. In painting, this radically reductive impulse is well represented by Kelly's work. In the early 1960s, Kelly moved from painting flat, hard-edged monochromatic shapes on conventionally shaped canvases to building unusually shaped canvases, which he painted in flat, monochromatic, industrially mixed colors. *Diagonal with Curve III*, 1978, is one example. While they hang on the wall like conventional paintings, his works have nothing to do with conventional illusionism. Instead they participate in the specific objecthood that Judd championed.

Over the years, Minimalism has met challenges on many fronts. As noted in this book's introduction, formalist critic Michael Fried condemned its "theatricality."[7] Feminist critics have taken issue with its supposed neutrality, seeing it instead as an expression of brute force and unencumbered masculinity. A sneaking sense of metaphor has revealed itself as well, sometimes from surprising sources. Kelly has admitted that the eccentric shapes of his monochromatic canvases derive from real world experiences—from the shadow of a barn door, for instance, or the space between two buildings. And even Judd's work, so austere, is praised today for its beauty, a quality Judd would have shunned as emotive. Post-Minimalism undermined its predecessor, bearing associations ranging from Eva Hesse's infusions of bodily references to spilled or otherwise formless shapes by such artists as Richard Serra and Alan Saret, who freed industrial materials from geometry. Then along came postmodernism to further undermine any remaining belief in purity or in abstract art's special relationship to spirituality or universal being. The recent literature on

DONALD JUDD

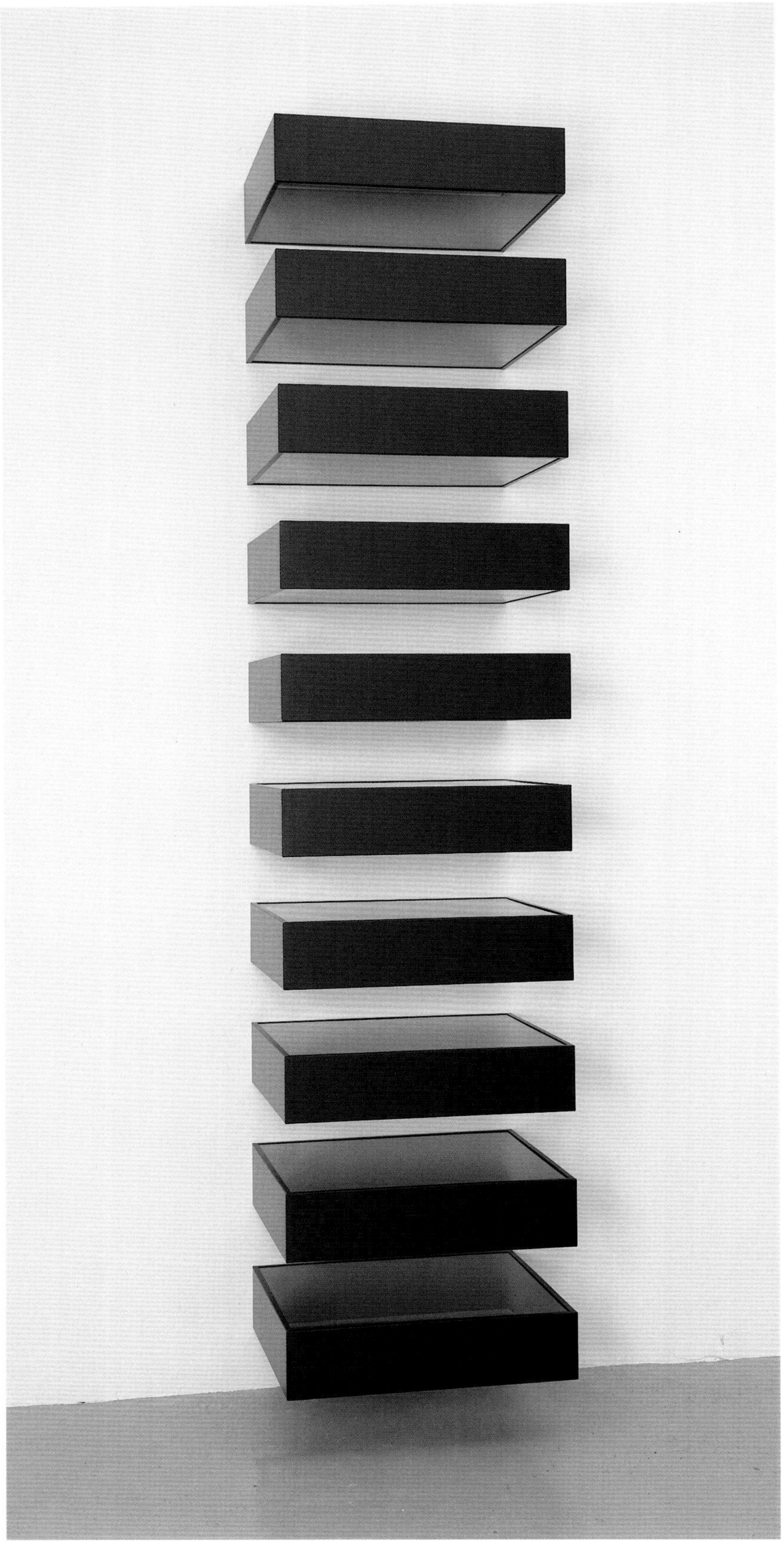

Untitled, 1990
Black anodized aluminum and bronze plexiglas, 10 units, 6 x 27 x 24 in (15 x 68.5 x 61 cm) each

abstraction is full of equivocations, references to "endgame" strategies, and pessimistic discussions about the death of modernism. It would be hard to find an artist today who shares the early modernist belief that abstraction describes the invisible structure of the cosmos. It would be equally difficult to find an art critic or art historian who still sees abstraction as the inevitable outcome of the modernist revolution.

Yet abstract art flourishes. Despite their demotion to the status of simply two more styles among many, both the geometric and the organic traditions, as well as any number of hybrids of the two, are alive and well. Having largely abandoned the metaphysical premises that surrounded abstraction's birth, artists today view the innovations of modernist abstraction as tools to be used for myriad purposes. Both organic and geometric abstraction become starting points for explorations that run far afield of the intentions of their pioneering practitioners. Indeed, for some artists the collapse of the belief systems that sustained modernist abstraction even becomes a part of the painting's content. Others personalize the motifs of organic or geometric abstraction, using them to make private statements that have no claim to sublimity or absolute truth. Yet others combine the organic with the geometric or even abstraction with representation. This latter impulse signals contemporary artists' unwillingness to abandon the visible, contingent world and their recognition that such a departure was always a romantic fantasy. There are even those who apply principles derived from abstraction like seriality and geometric reduction to works that are otherwise quite representational.

Thus, one of the most striking characteristics of abstraction today is its impurity. Manifestos have given way to a situation in which supposedly antithetical impulses can coexist in the same artist or artwork. In sculpture, this is apparent in the work of Richard Deacon and Martin Puryear. Deacon mingles organic form and references to the human body with industrial modes of fabrication. The narrow strips of bent wood in his 1993 sculpture *What Could Make Me Feel This Way 'A,'* seem pure and organic, but closer examination reveals both the screws holding them together and the holes where screws were removed. Martin Puryear's minimal forms are infused with traditional woodworking techniques and African-inspired crafts. In *Untitled*, 1997, a globe of wire mesh covered with tar is, like Deacon's, a combination of industrial materials and organic form. It bears a kinship to modernist abstraction but also has some of the raw power of a tribal artifact.

Among painters, such hybridity is a particular hallmark of the work of Brice Marden, whose canvases encapsulate the historical sweep of modernist abstraction. Marden has moved from making monochromatic paintings in the 1960s to his current preoccupation with looping, organic abstractions inspired in part by Chinese calligraphy. Yet while he has explored both gestural and geometric approaches to abstraction, his underlying motivations bear little relationship to those of the early modernists. Marden's monochromes have thick, waxy surfaces and their colors are always a response to a particular place or a personal memory. He avoids primary colors and instead uses soft shades of gray, green, or tan that reflect nature, evoking evening mist, early spring grass, or the light of Greece, where he has spent summers since the 1970s. In his gestural work, Marden rejects the slashing, swashbuckling strokes of a de Kooning or a Pollock. Instead he suggests the disciplined, rhythmic marks of Asian calligraphy and the restrained and evocative poetry of the eighth-century Chinese poet Han Shan, whose writings have directly influenced Marden's work. Such restraint is evident in

ELLSWORTH KELLY

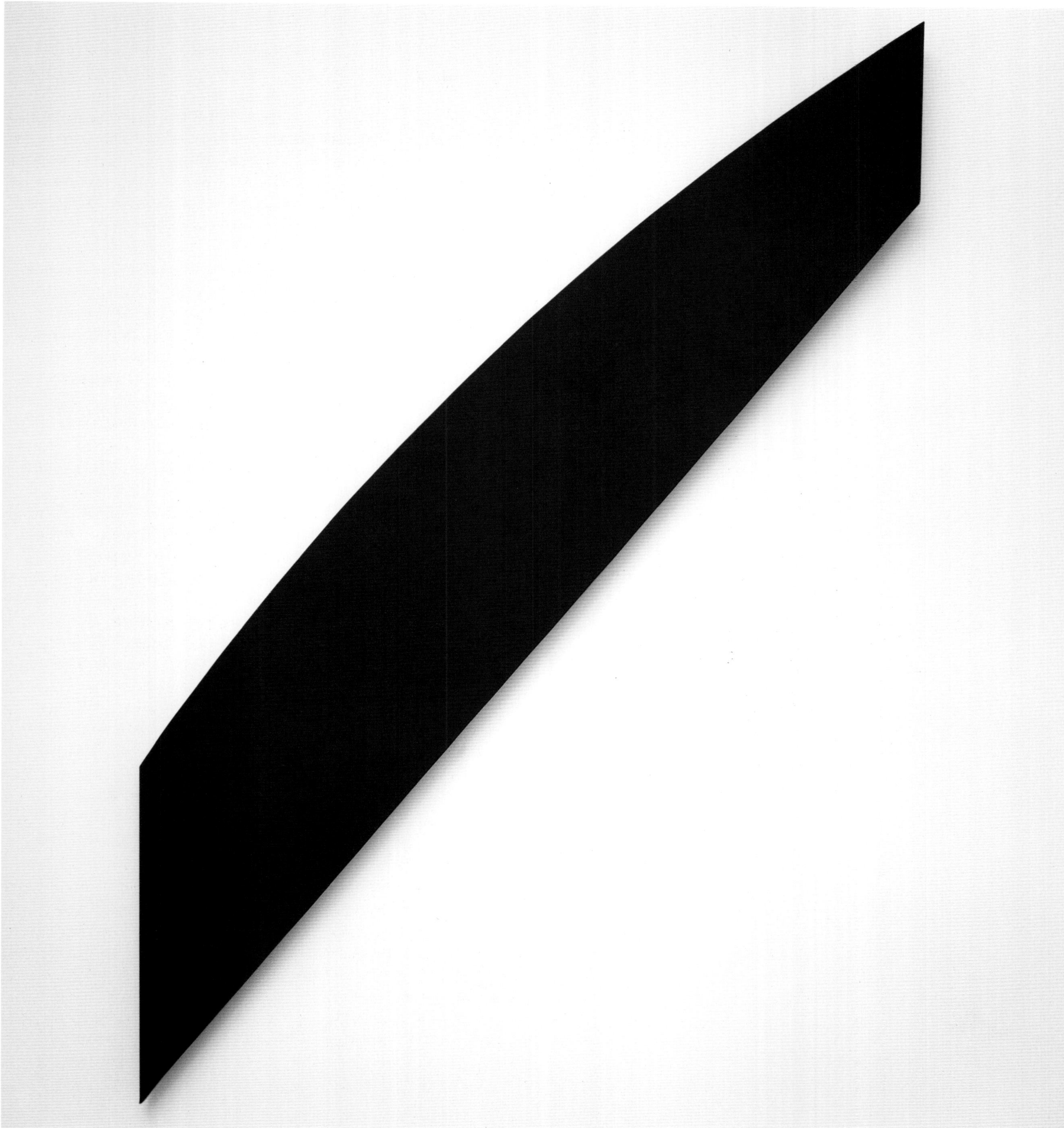

Diagonal with Curve III, 1978
Oil on canvas, 135 in x 99 in (342.9 x 251.5 cm)
Philadelphia Museum of Art, Pa.

MARTIN PURYEAR

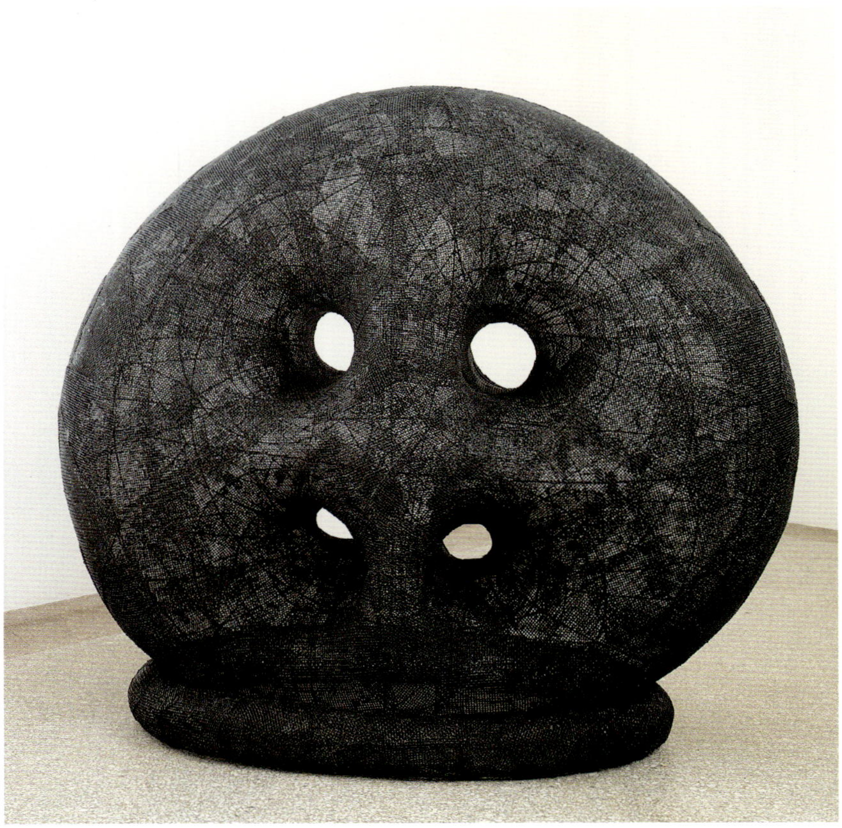

Untitled, 1997
Wire mesh and tar, 66 x 76 1/2 x 37 1/4 in (167.7 x 194.4 x 94.7 cm)

paintings like *Vine*, 1991–93, in which dancing loops of black and blue play over a delicate rose-colored backdrop, seeming at times on the verge of dissolution, looking like traces or ghosts.

Robert Mangold's paintings are also hybrids combining gesture and geometry. The artist began his career making hard-edged abstract paintings in the popular mode of the early 1960s. Eventually these evolved into shaped canvases with monochromatic grounds inscribed with linear geometric shapes. Sometimes these lines play off the hidden supports of the underlying canvas frame. In other paintings they suggest windows or a witty interplay between drawn geometry and the edges of the canvas. Critics interpreted the tilted ovals that appeared frequently on his monochromatic grounds as figural elements. These were followed by long-stemmed spirals that unfurled across multiple panels and elegant curlicues confined to narrow vertical canvases. *Curved Plane/Figure IV (Double Panel)*, 1995, for instance, presents a beautifully modulated set of curls that sweeps over a grey-blue ground. From one perspective, Mangold's work comes out of formalist concerns with line, color, flatness, and measure. But despite the apparent abstraction of his paintings, Mangold, like Marden, bases them on observation and memory. The quiet earth tones relate to nature, while the recent spirals allude to wave patterns, Greek vases, and musical notation.

Another reconciliation practiced by contemporary painters is between the supposedly antithetical approaches of abstraction and representation. As a young student in the 1960s, Thomas Nozkowski studied with various second-generation Abstract Expressionists, but he quickly rejected the attitude of grandiosity that tended to accompany their work. His paintings are easel-size and often painted on canvas board, a material associated with hobbyists and Sunday painters. For Nozkowski, modesty has a political implication, pointing to his resistance to the institutionalization of art. While often set on modulated monochrome grounds, Nozkowski's paintings are full of forms abstracted from the visible world. Some present fragments of latticework, arabesques, and decorative architectural details. Others contain cartoonish curves, marble patterns, and in *Untitled (8-27)*, 2002, shattered shards that recall flagstone walkways. His handling of paint is equally non-formulaic—he makes reference to Abstract Expressionist drips, mingles hard lines with gestural brushstrokes, and preserves the ghostly remnants of earlier states of composition. His paintings are a synthesis of supposed opposites—abstraction and representation, geometry and gesture, the personal and the universal.

Mary Heilmann is of roughly the same generation as Nozkowski, and they share many painterly concerns. In Heilmann's case, though, references to observable reality have feminist overtones. Her brightly colored abstract canvases are full of polka dots, checkerboard patterns, and horizontal bands that echo the designs on Mexican blankets. In the wake of the feminist movement of the 1970s, such references became shorthand for a decorative, female sensibility. These elements are realized with quickly painted, slapped-on brushstrokes that give her canvases a bracing spontaneity. Even when appropriating grids or geometric patterns associated with Minimalism's austerity, Heilmann transforms them into playful reminders of the everyday world. *Green Spiral*, 1988, combines circularity with the minimalist grid, creating a rectilinear spiral which brings to mind a maze or labyrinth.

Another artist of this generation who focuses on mutating patterns is Terry Winters, who has moved in the course of his career from abstracted images inspired

BRICE MARDEN

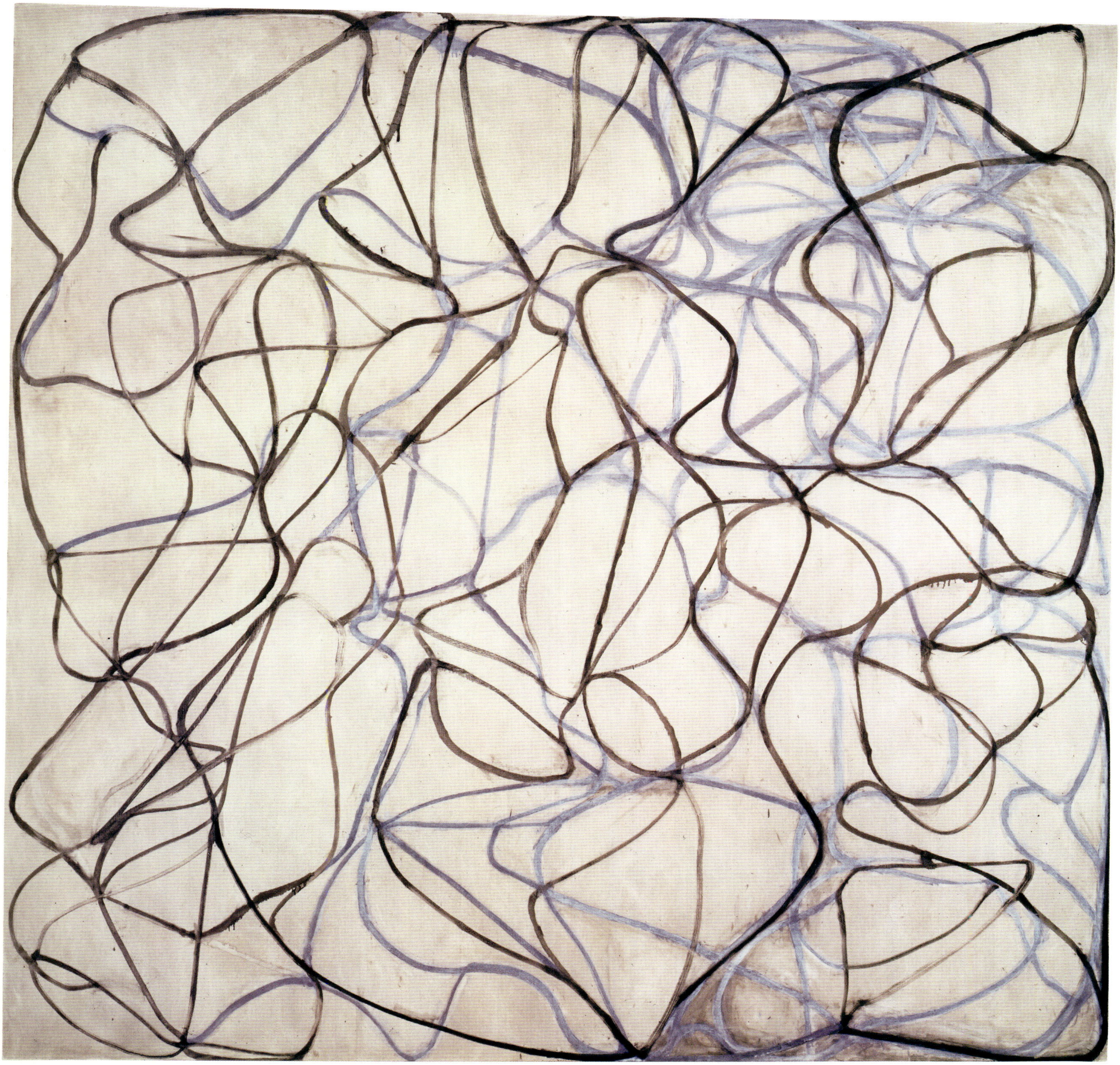

Vine, 1991–93
Oil on linen, 96 x 101 in (243.8 x 256.5 cm)
The Museum of Modern Art, New York

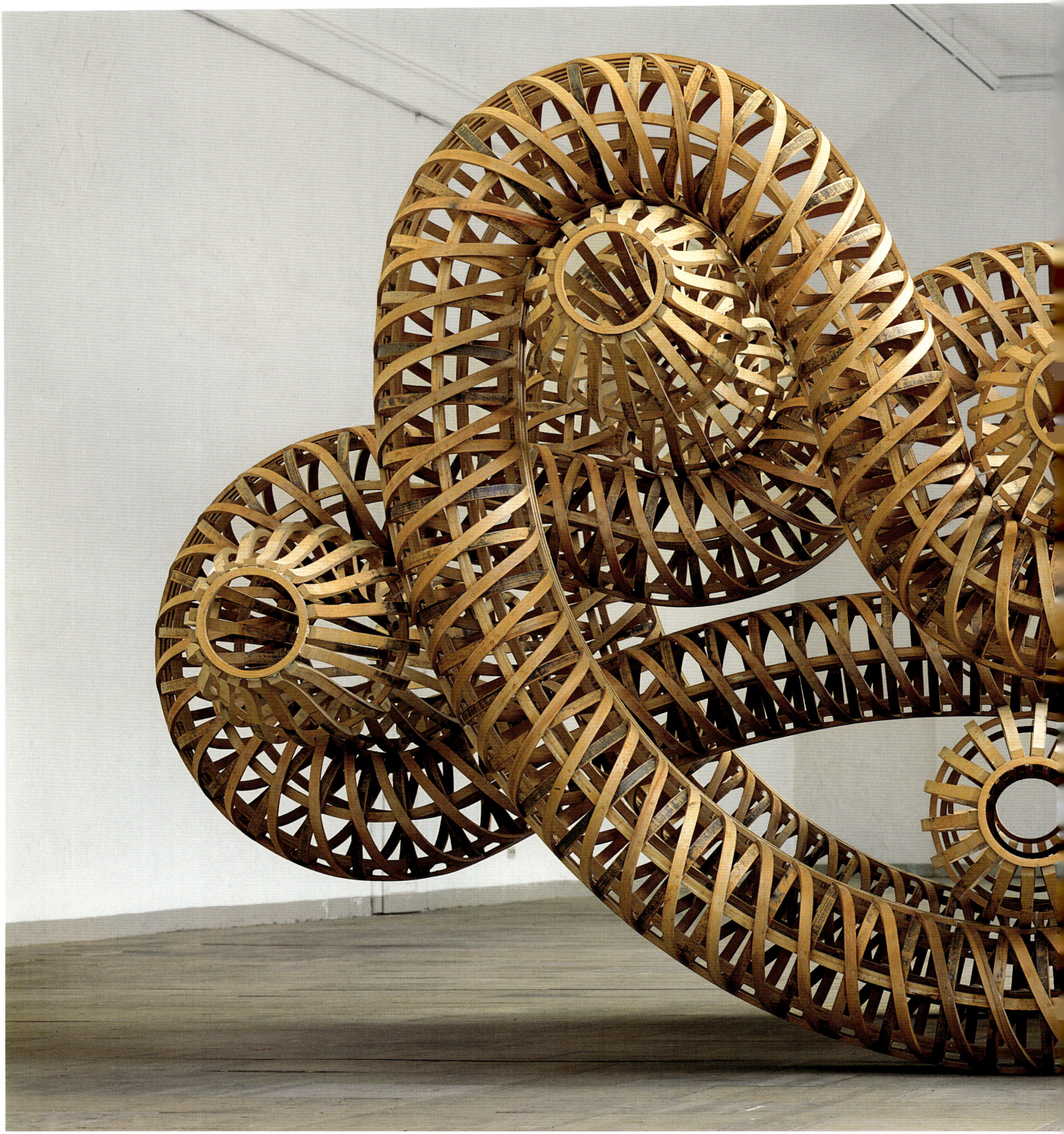

RICHARD DEACON

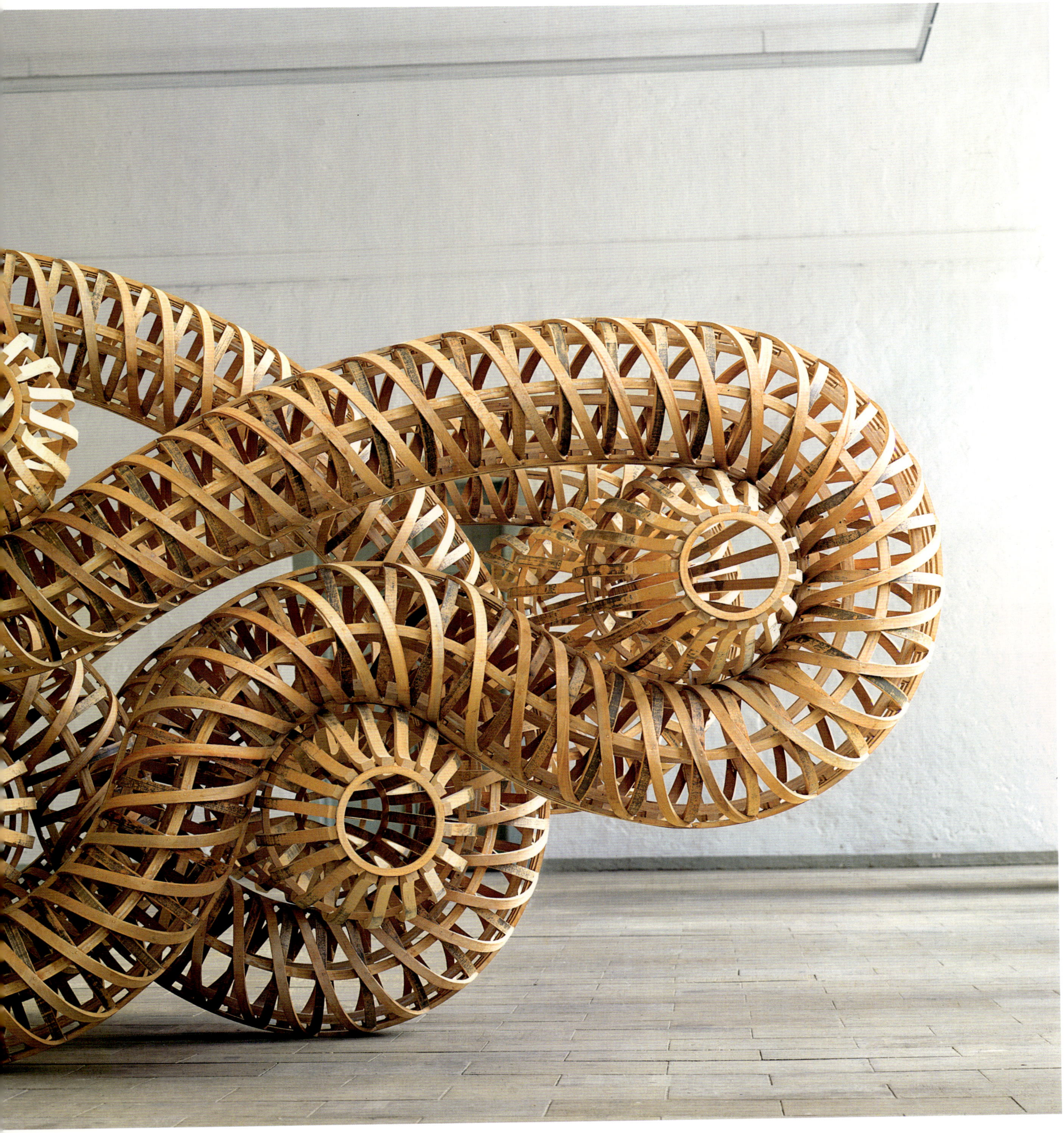

What Could Make Me Feel This Way 'A', 1993
Bentwood, cable ties, screws, 93 ft 10 in x 183 ft 9 in x 158 ft 5 in (28.6 x 56 x 48.3 m)
Sprengel Museum, Hannover, Germany

ROBERT MANGOLD

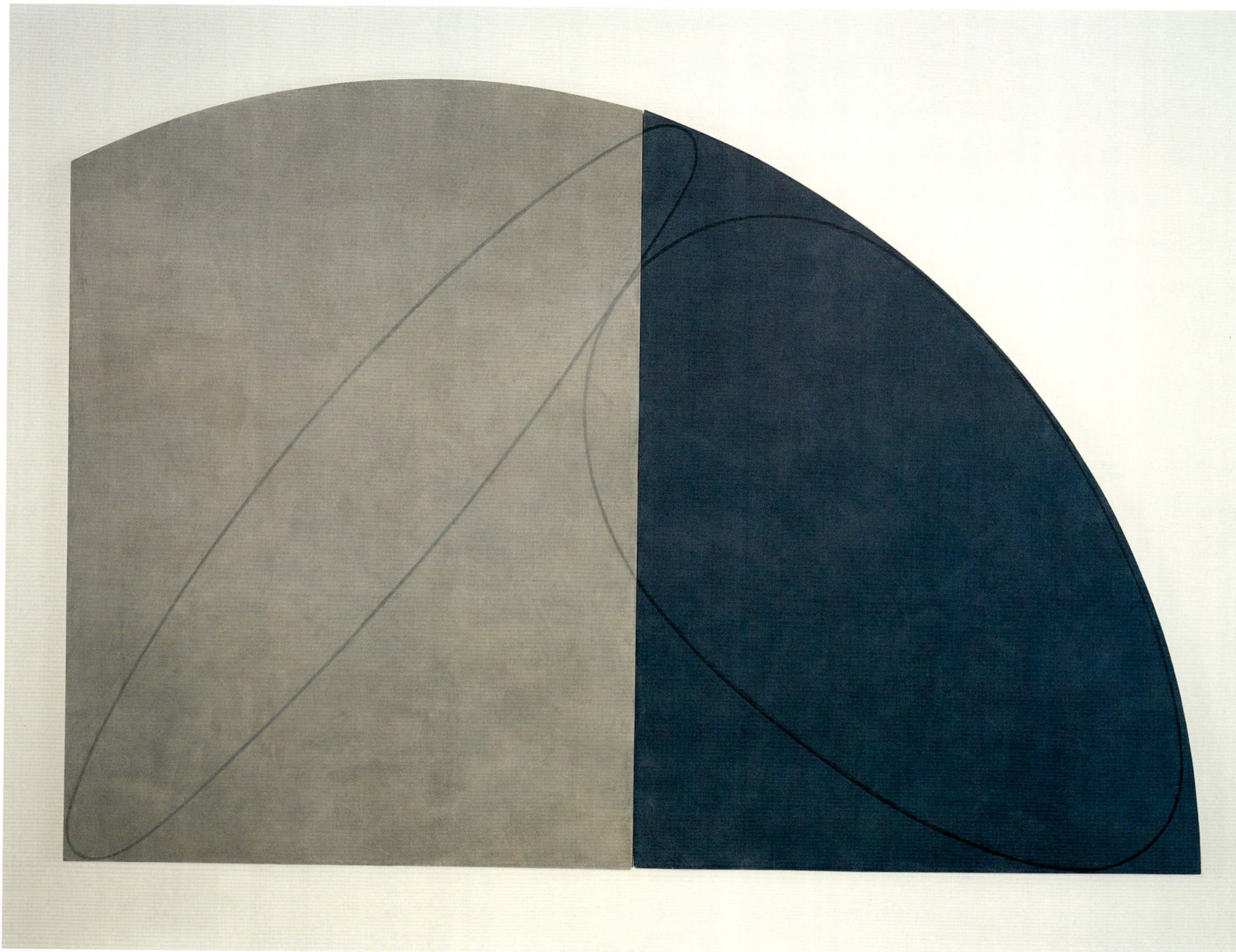

Curved Plane/Figure IV (Double Panel), 1995
Acrylic and pencil on canvas, 98 in x 143 in (248.9 x 363.2 cm)

MARY HEILMANN

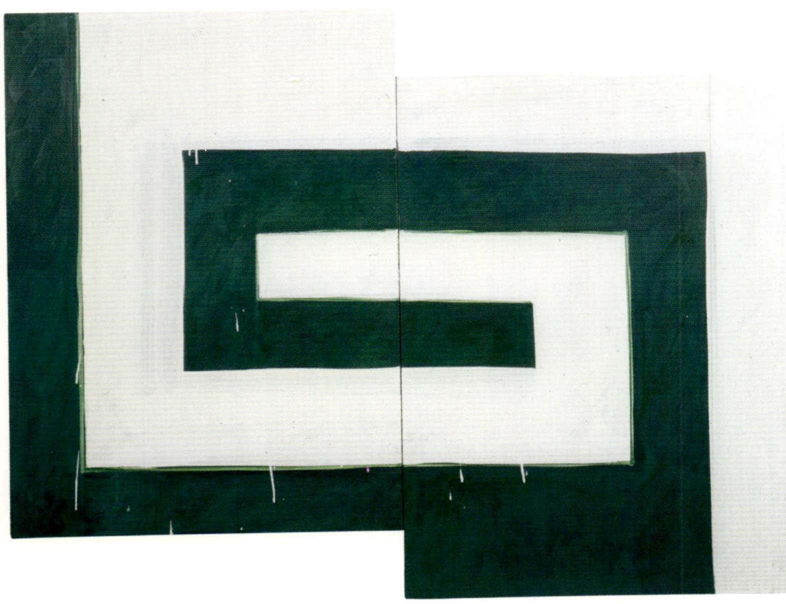

Green Spiral, 1988
Oil on canvas, 45 1/2 x 60 in (115.6 x 152.4 cm)

ROBERT RYMAN

Untitled, 1965
Enamel on stretched raw linen canvas, 10 x 10 in (25.4 x 25.4 cm)

TERRY WINTERS

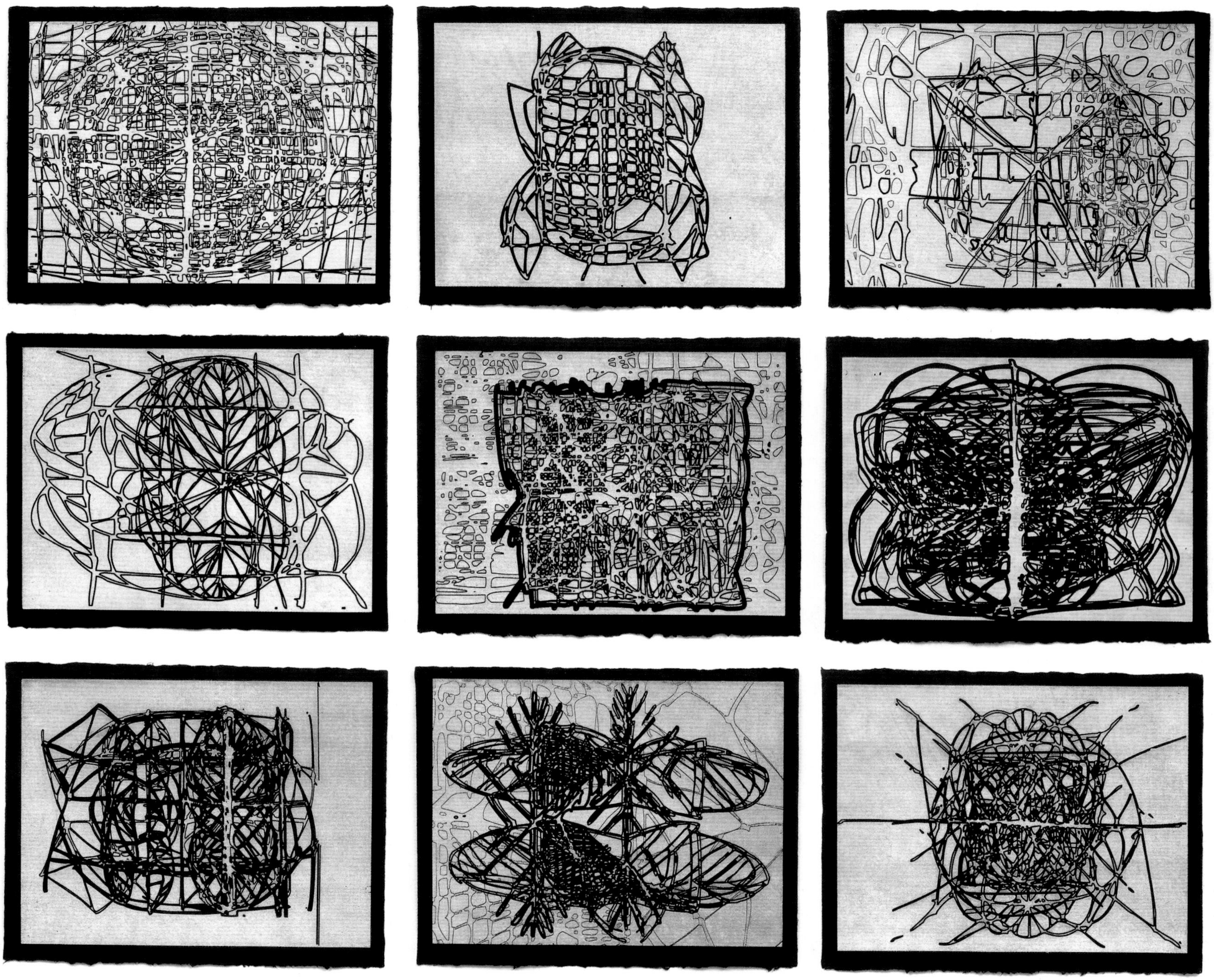

Graphic Primitives, 1998
Portfolio of nine woodcuts on Japanese Kochi paper, each sheet 20 x 26 in (50.8 x 66 cm)

by nature to others based on technology. His early paintings of the 1980s feature schematic, graffiti-like images of pods, seeds, leaves, husks, and shells, suggesting nature's fecundity and its inevitable process of decay. Eventually these abstracted images morphed into densely layered grids, webs, crosshatchings, and spirals that recall diagrams more than allusions to the natural world. They bring to mind any number of manmade or scientific systems—suggesting at times X-rays, blueprints, magnified crystals, or even just a tangle of fishing nets. Drawing on sources as diverse as architectural drawing, medical photography, models of molecular structure, and direct observation, these works suggest that human-generated patterns and systems, no less than natural ones, are subject to processes of decay and regeneration. This is particularly evident in *Graphic Primitives*, 1998, a series of large woodcut prints covered with loosely painted webs, spirals, and cell-like structures that suggest the existence of energy fields extending out beyond the canvas.

For some artists, abstraction can't exist today without acknowledging its failure to apprehend some deeper reality. Robert Ryman, for instance, undermines abstraction's aspiration to transcendence by literally taking a painting apart and showing how it is constructed as an object. Limiting himself almost exclusively to permutations on the theme of the white painting, he clears away the distraction of color to dissect subtle shades of white, varieties of brushstroke, textures, and relationships to the support. Loose white daubs are set on planes of flat linen. Glossy and matte surfaces are juxtaposed. Fasteners and fittings are exposed. *Untitled*, from 1965, presents layers of white stripes, while others are fields of white stipples. Others, painted on sheets of metal, present smooth, machine-like surfaces. Aside from white, there is little continuity from one Ryman painting to another. Some are small, some are large, and some, with their complicated framing devices, teeter on the verge of becoming sculpture. In limiting himself to a white palette, Ryman deliberately invokes the history of monochromatic painting, which is frequently associated with the notion of the absolute, the void, or existential emptiness. Of course the color white itself has poetic associations—with light, purity, and space. Ryman invites these associations only to dismiss them. He rejects all metaphor, insisting that he is a realist. "With realism there is no picture," he notes. "There is no story. And there is no myth. And there is no illusion, above all. So lines are real, and the space is real, the surface is real and there is an interaction between the painting and the wall plane, unlike with abstraction and representation."[8]

A similar disavowal of modernist ideals underlies the work of Günther Förg. There is an arbitrary quality to the stripes and rectangles that are swathed almost lackadaisically across the surfaces of his paintings, and the colors—dirty shades of red, blue, black, and green—are peculiarly inexpressive. Moreover, as his series of small panels advance monotonously across the wall with a sense of military precision in the twenty-two small, lead-sheathed paintings of *Untitled*, 1990, the viewer's attention is deflected away from the individual painting to the architectural space they occupy. To understand what Förg is up to with his paintings, it is important to know that he works in a variety of other modes as well. He creates room-size installations, large wall reliefs of poured lead, and floor-to-ceiling architectural photographs. These latter pieces picture public buildings—notably in Italy and Germany—that date from the 1920s and '30s. Förg focuses on architectural details that emphasize the ordered, often oppressive geometry of these structures. Thus he reminds us that the high ideals of modernism, with its rhetoric of purity, harmony, and unity, turned

THOMAS NOZKOWSKI

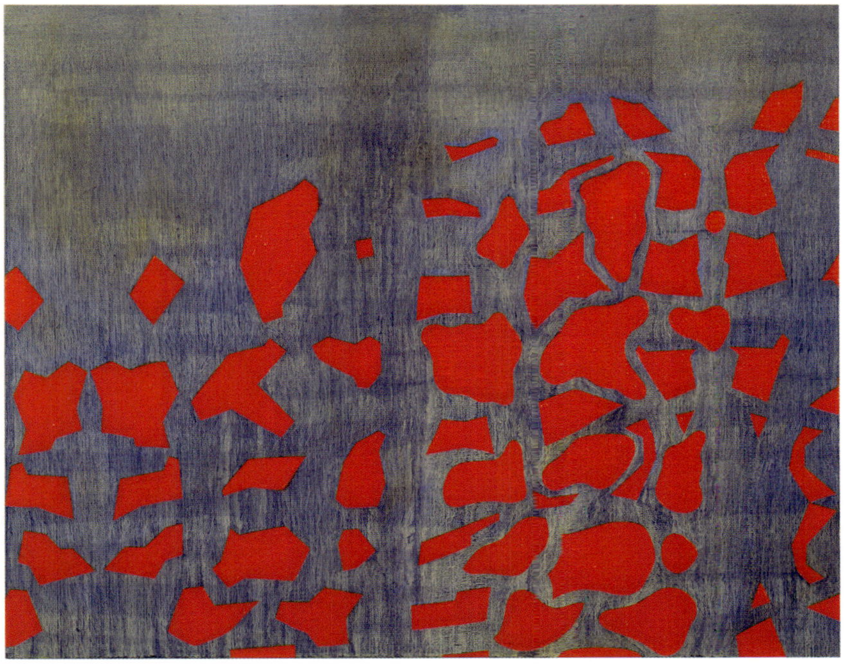

Untitled (8-27), 2002
Oil on linen on panel, 22 x 28 in (55.9 x 71.1 cm)

GÜNTHER FÖRG

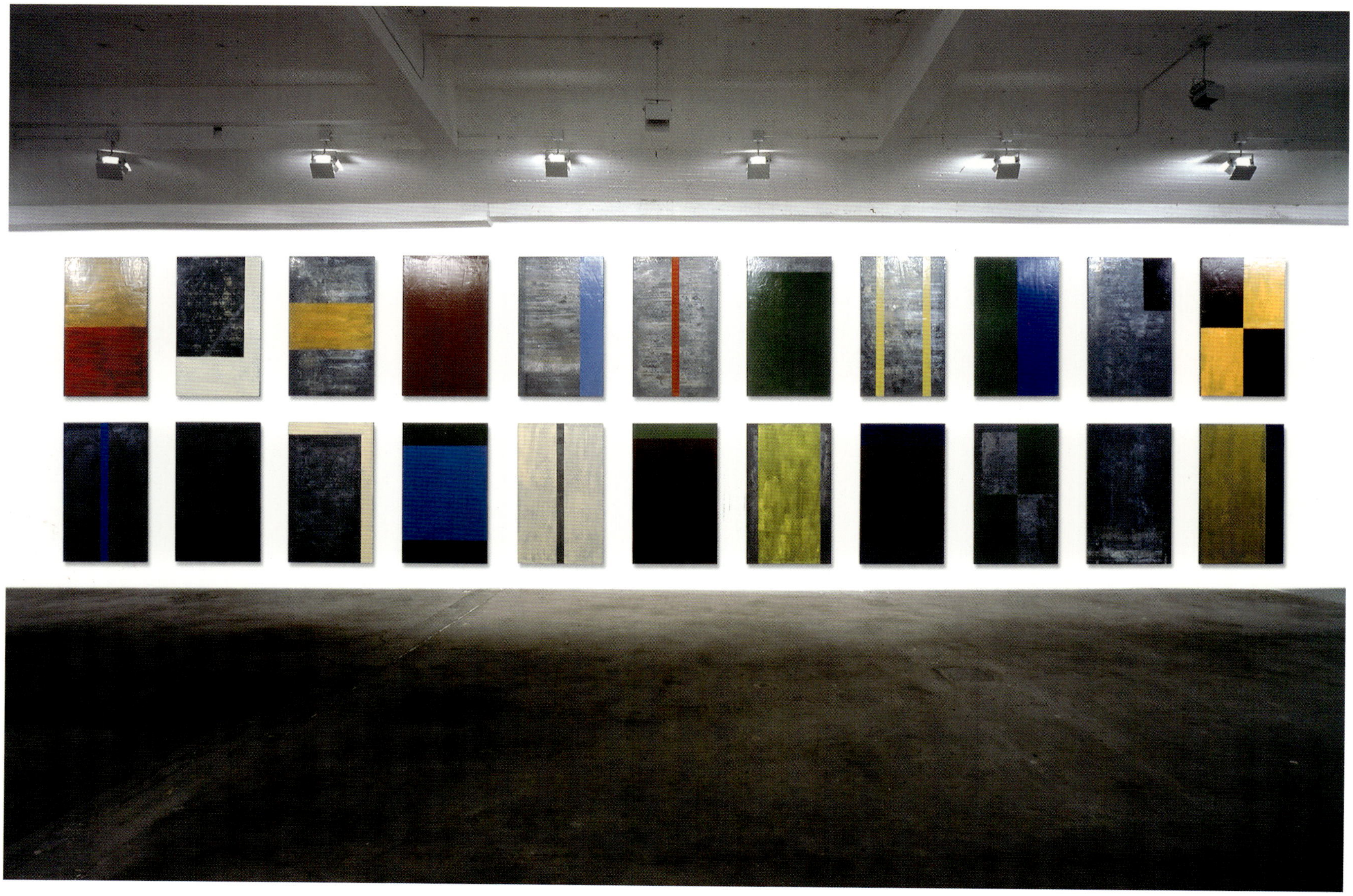

Untitled, 1990
Acrylic and lead mounted on 22 wood panels, 70 3/4 x 43 1/4 in (179.7 x 109.9 cm) each

DAVID REED

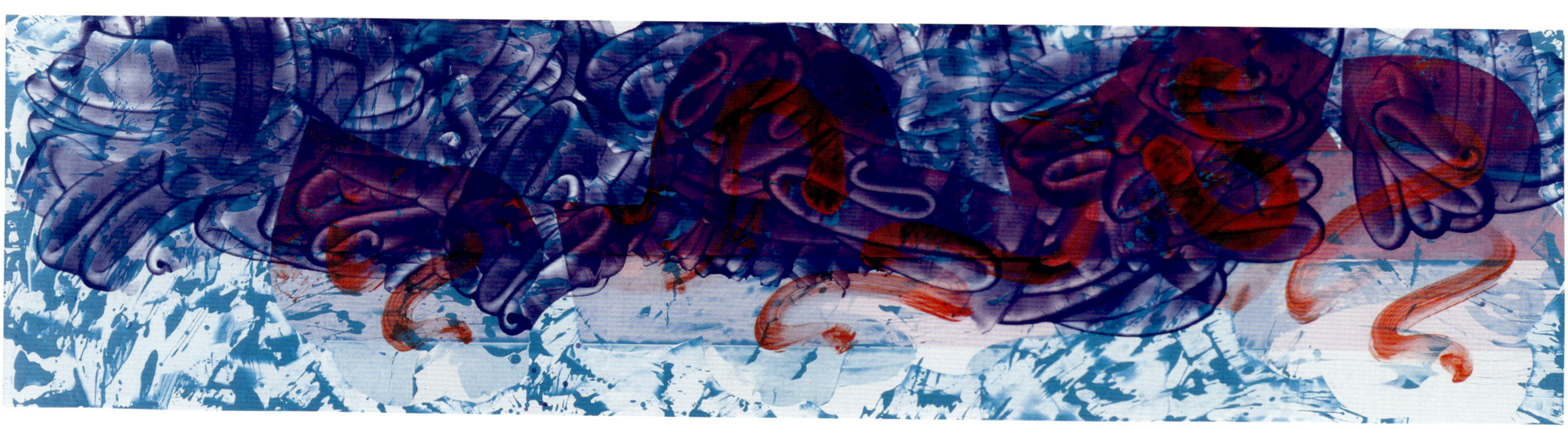

#520, 2004
Oil and alkyd on linen, 3 ft 8 in x 14 ft x 8 in (1.1 x 4.5 m)

BERNARD FRIZE

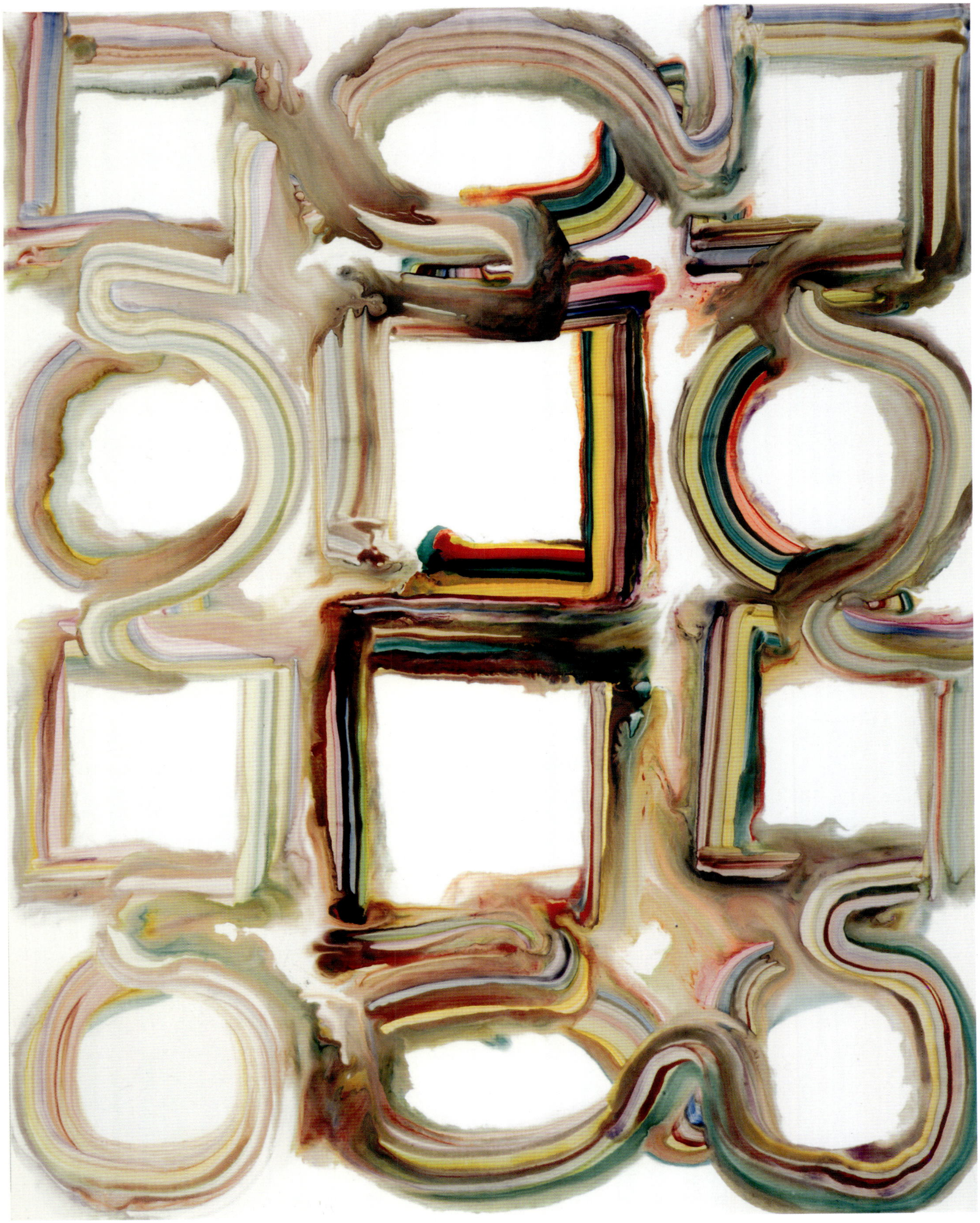

Réciproque, 2000
Acrylic and resin on canvas, 102 x 83 in (259 x 210.8 cm)

out to be disturbingly compatible with Fascism. As a German artist, he is particularly sensitive to the potential ramifications of utopian programs. Directing our attention outward, beyond the picture frame, he reminds us that architecture can bear witness to the most dangerous ambitions.

Förg's opacity and Ryman's physical dissection of painting would seem to place them in the camp of those, like the Minimalist and the Conceptual artists, who reject beauty and personal expression as an artistic goal. (This, despite the fact that many viewers find their work extremely individualistic and beautiful.) The intentional depersonalization of paint is also practiced by David Reed and Bernard Frize. Reed takes the gestural brushstroke, which in the mythology of modernist abstraction is a mark of authentic feeling and subconscious truth, and makes it patently artificial. His paintings, including *#520*, 2004, often feature a slithering ribbon of paint that is laid on with a palette knife rather than a brush. Both the ribbon, which resembles a large brushstroke, and the ground upon which it rests are realized in lurid electric colors. The paint, a mixture of oil and alkyd (a synthetic resin), makes for an unnatural surface resembling slick plastic. Sometimes the slightly raised edges of the brushstroke are enhanced by highlights applied with a spray gun, producing a three-dimensional aura of artifice. Frize moves even further from the old-fashioned fetishization of the artist's physical touch, manipulating paint using a variety of processes of chance. He may create a composition of brightly colored circles by placing "skins" of paint, formed on the surface of open paint cans, directly onto the canvas. Or he may suspend a drying canvas parallel to the floor, with its painted surface facing downward so that gravity pulls at the wet paint, creating a dimpled surface. He also uses a specially designed set of brushes of varying sizes that are each dipped in a different paint color and tied together—as in *Réciproque*, 2000—again distancing painterly work from the painter's hand.

This rhetoric of austerity and depersonalization does not sit well with certain abstract artists who reject end games and anti-aestheticism as limiting and puritanical. For these artists, the tropes of organic abstraction offer a way to revive what they feel is a lost emphasis on visual pleasure. Frequently this desire takes them back to art history for models. One movement younger artists have recently rediscovered after it had been relegated to the periphery of art history is Op Art. During its heyday in the 1960s, Op Art was associated with design more than fine art. Its eye-popping compositions seemed to make the surface of the painting vibrate—a mere novelty to some. But Op Art has an impressive historical pedigree, drawing on De Stijl, Constructivism, and the Bauhaus, and is related, at least in its European versions, to developments in the science of perception. In its purest state, as practiced by such artists as Victor Vasarely, Richard Anuskiewicz, and Michael Kidner, Op Art features pulsing moiré effects, color contrasts adjusted to create afterimages and distortions of perspective, and other forms of optical illusion. Though much of this work is painting, there were also Op Art sculptors, such as Jesús Rafael Soto, a Venezuelan artist who arranged nylon thread, metal rods, and steel and aluminum pieces, which moved or which viewers could move through, affecting perspectival shifts. The most influential Op artist is likely Bridget Riley. Her paintings of mathematically constructed patterns, like *High Sky 2*, 1992, are designed to force the eye to continually adjust its focus. Riley has said that she wants to create a space in which "the mind's eye, or rather, the eye's mind" could move about.[9]

BRIDGET RILEY

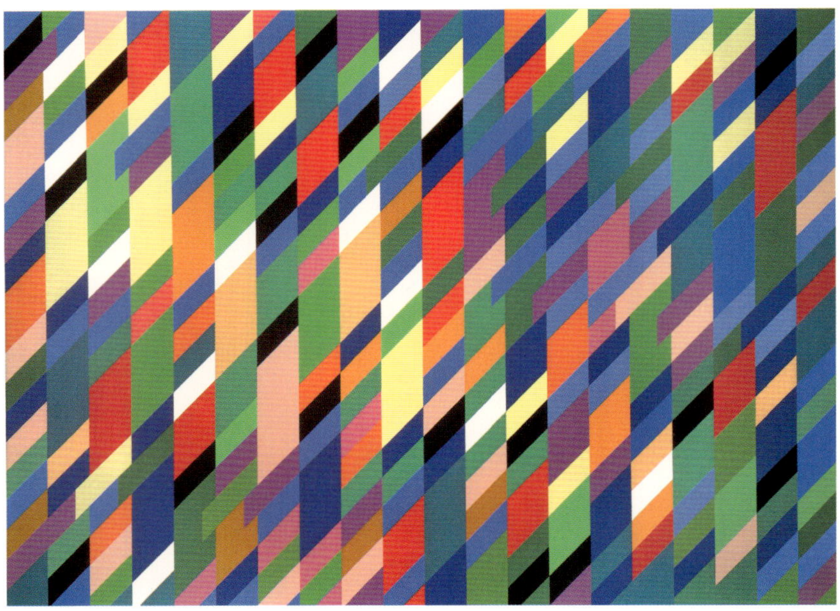

High Sky 2, 1992
Oil on linen, 65 x 89 3/4 in (165 x 228 cm)

PHILIP TAAFFE

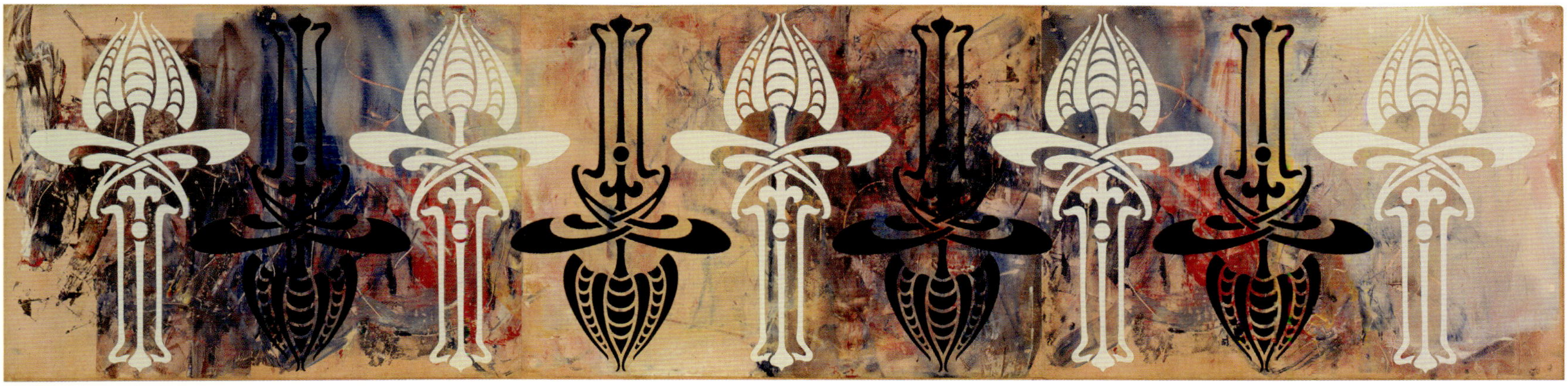

Frieze, 1991–2001
Mixed media on canvas, 28 1/8 x 118 in (71.4 x 299.7 cm)

ROSS BLECKNER

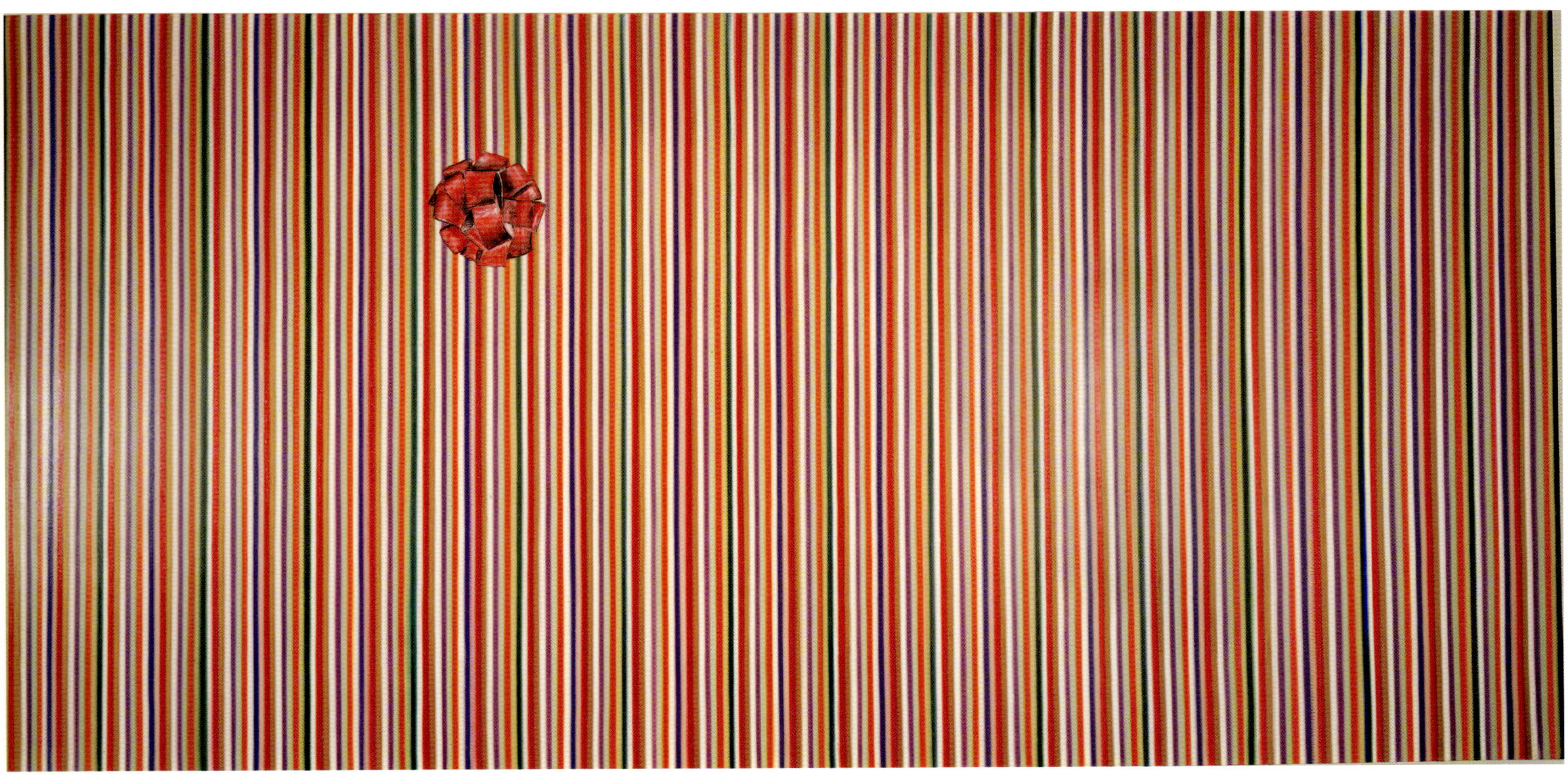

Infatuation, 1986–87
Oil on canvas, 8 ft x 16 ft 8 in (2.4 x 5.1 m)

RICHMOND BURTON

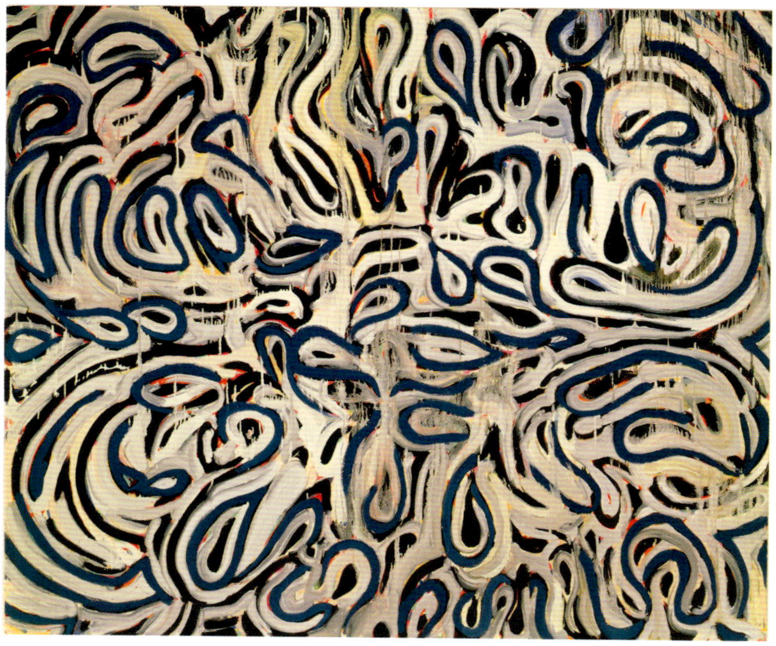

Shivaesque, 1996
Oil on linen, 64 x 78 in (162.6 x 198.1 cm)

TOMMA ABTS

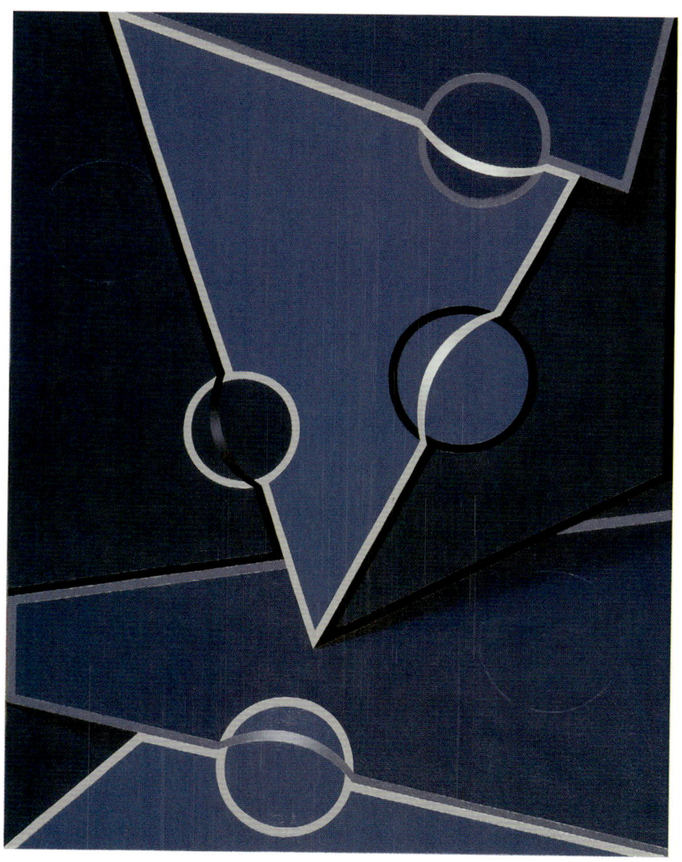

Ebe, 2005
Acrylic and oil on canvas, 18 7/8 x 15 in (48 x 38 cm)

In the popular mind of its time, Op Art was associated with the altered states of consciousness induced by 1960s drug culture. By the 1970s this association with psychedelia became a liability as artists turned to more cerebral, Conceptual approaches to art. But in the 1980s it was exactly Op Art's air of disrepute that attracted younger artists, such as Philip Taaffe and Ross Bleckner, who sought a revival of pleasure in painting. For both of these artists, Op Art is a starting point for paintings that incorporate many other meanings beyond the pure opticality that motivated the progenitors of the style. Taaffe has combined an early interest in Op Art with reworkings of various fields of abstract ornament, among them Islamic architecture, Art Nouveau, and botanical photography. Hints of ferns, serpents, roosters, wrought-iron balustrades, lace collars, and braided ropes are woven together into dazzling, overall-patterned compositions created by a painstaking process of layering, hand-printing, collage, and over-painting, as in *Frieze*, 1991–2001. As with vintage Op Art, his paintings often seem to vibrate, but they diverge by referencing nature and culture. Bleckner combines the jittery stripes of Op Art with repeated images of ribbons, urns, birds, chandeliers, and flowers. In his hands, Op's playfulness offsets meditations on death in the era of AIDS. Appearing in the early 1980s, Bleckner's works were originally taken as ironic dismissals or parodies of the Op Art sensibility, but he clearly has a more loving relationship with his sources. Even when he "ties" a field of Op Art stripes into a red bow in *Infatuation*, 1986–87, the painting's shimmering luminosity removes it from the realm of irony and situates it instead in the realm of spirituality, opticality, and beauty. With these expressive works, Taaffe and Bleckner reinvigorate the notion that art should aspire to beauty, an idea that at times seems to have become almost as disreputable as Op Art itself.

Beauty and sensuousness are also at the heart of Richmond Burton's paintings, in which an almost imperceptible grid at times underlies masses of small, vivid daubs. Circular, triangular, and kidney-shaped swabs of paint in rich colors, occasionally accented with gold, copper, or silver paint, permeate surfaces resembling fields of petals or swirling peacock-feather patterns. These patterns are laid out over the canvas in a semi-regular fashion, allowing geometry and gesture to fight it out or find an uneasy synthesis of order and spontaneity. *Shivaesque*, 1996, for instance, is a field of curvilinear shapes, each with a dark teardrop at the core, which seem to be swirling about in several different directions at once, creating a sense of ripples caught in an eddy. Though Burton doesn't publicly acknowledge a debt to Op Art, as Taaffe and Bleckner do, it is clear that his vibrating surfaces also derive from a desire to cultivate "the eye's mind."

A similar melding of geometry and organic form toward pleasurable effect appears in the paintings of Tomma Abts, whose small, meticulously crafted paintings hover somewhere between these two poles. Abts paints circles, triangles, dynamic rhomboids, and compound, curvilinear forms in muted colors and adjusts them to the shape of the canvas. The hard-edged forms that fill her canvases have a geometrical clarity, but the compositions seem to set them in motion, as planes shear off one another, sliding away or tilting over and under one another. Meanwhile, despite the flatness of the planes themselves, they are arranged in ways that suggest depth, illusion, and even dimensional shadows. *Ebe*, 2005, presents a set of flat triangular planes in shades of blue-gray whose outlines are interrupted by small circles. Despite its flat graphic quality, this work also offers the possibility of a dimensional read, as

FRANK STELLA

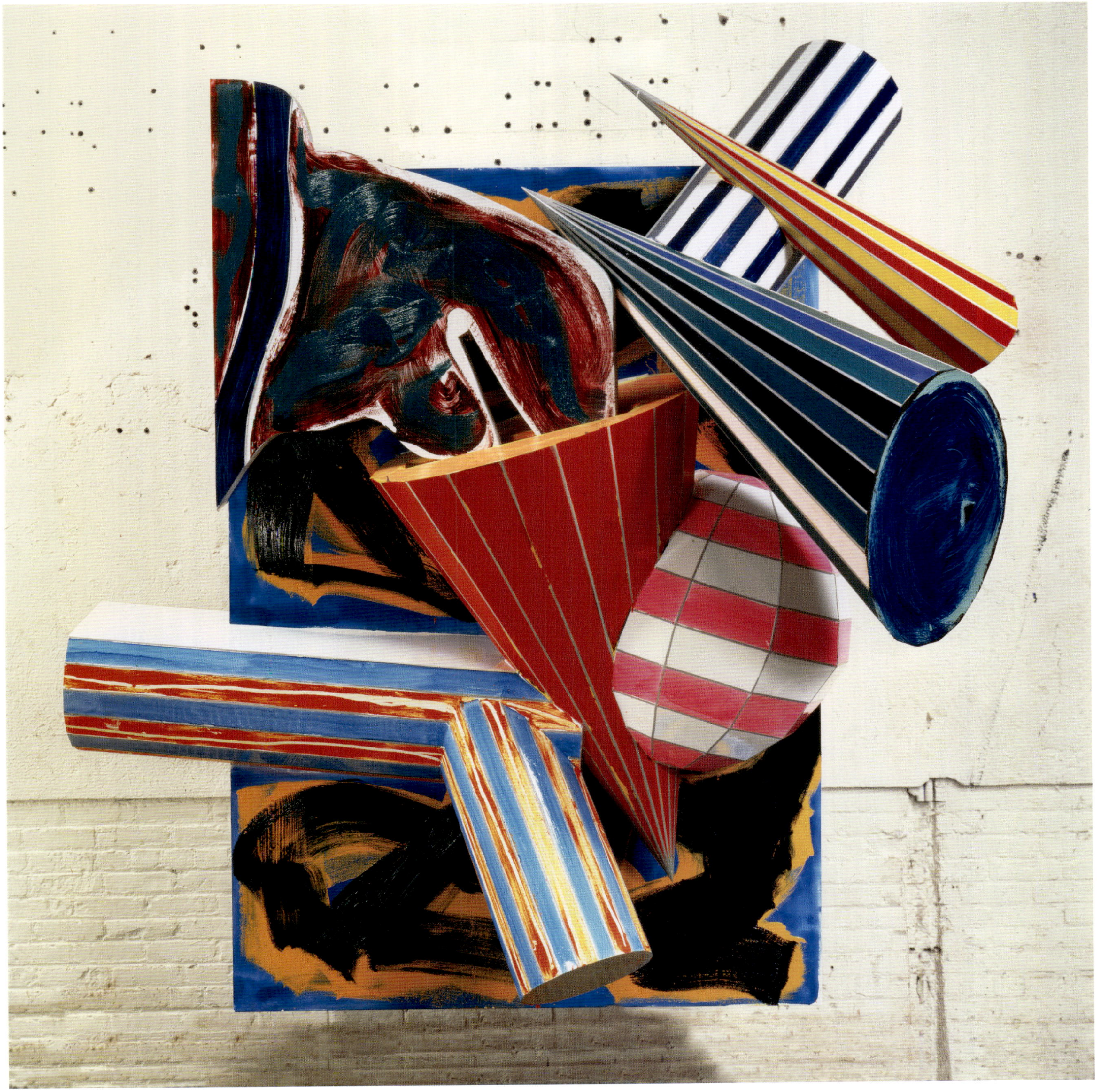

La colomba ladra (#11, 3D-3X), 1987
Paint on aluminum, 97 1/2 x 90 x 63 1/2 in (247.7 x 228.6 x 161.3 cm)

the circles can be seen as spheres and the triangles as pyramidal forms pressing down against the plane beneath it. Abts's paintings seem to pay homage to a variety of early modernist approaches, including Cubism, Futurism, and Constructivism, with a nod as well to the decorative patterned abstraction of the 1970s.

Artists have celebrated opticality in abstraction not only in two but three dimensions as well. One of the most surprising advocates of this approach is Frank Stella, who was initially a devotee of formalist flatness. His early works of the late 1950s were standard squares and rectangles in monochrome black and colors, painted with thin lines that responded to the shape of the canvas. Later these lines evolved into bands of color that articulated increasingly complex canvas shapes. Critics saw such works as resolutely unsymbolic, overlaid with lines that merely served to confirm the canvas's status as object. When Stella burst forth in the '80s with gaudy sculptural paintings like *La colomba ladra (#11, 3D-3X)*, 1987, with its brightly-painted three-dimensional metal reliefs in the forms of columns, waves, and cones, it seemed that he had completely repudiated the formalist faith of his youth. And indeed he had. In a series of lectures at Harvard University, Stella articulated a new philosophy based on the illusionistic space of Baroque painting.[10] He felt that for abstraction to match the impact of the great art of the past, it had to return to such concepts as volume, interior space, and caricature (by which he apparently meant old-fashioned representation), that had been lost in the austerity of formalism. But while returning to deep space and recognizable referents, Stella retained enough of the formalist faith to insist that this "working space" must be real. Hence his works have become ever more sculptural, full of curling metal sheets and lattices of poured lead that swirl out into space with brash abandon.

The notion of "working space" also applies to the exuberant installations of Judy Pfaff and Polly Apfelbaum. Taking over gallery spaces from floor to ceiling and wall to wall, Pfaff creates works that function much like three-dimensional paintings, making lines out of materials such as metal tubing, wood, steel, aluminum, string, and tree branches, and patches of color out of glass globes, puddles of latex, and formed plaster. The installations bring to mind details of Victorian architecture, sea creatures, Tibetan stupas, and Persian patterning. One of Pfaff's most dramatic works commands 700,000 square feet of space in a former railroad terminal in Philadelphia. *Cirque, CIRQUE*, 1995, a permanent installation that is said to include the largest suspended sculpture on earth, is a fantastical concoction of metal coils, arabesques, and serpentine lines that whip through the upper part of a cavernous room. Without a stroke of paint, Pfaff sugests the dance of eye and body associated with Pollock and de Kooning. Apfelbaum's sculptural installations also evoke the image of a painting bursting out into space. In her work, paint is replaced by felt, crepe paper, pom-poms, and fabric cut into shapes such as ovals, floral dingbats, or shamrocks. In *Big Bubbles*, 2000, oblong crosses of synethic velvet, placed in radiating clusters on the floor, produce an eye-popping cracked carpet. Sometimes the colors in these works gradually shift in hue as they travel across the floor. At other times they create a field of stripes. And at still others, the colors spread out to form mandala-like patterns, or mime the garish gaiety of floral wallpaper. Given their placement on the floor, one might trace these works' lineage back to Carl Andre's modular tiles, but the eccentric textures and rich colors—some inherent in the materials and others the product of rich stains and dyes—and energetic scattering bring them closer, again, to the work of the Abstract Expressionists.

Artists like Stella, Pfaff, and Apfelbaum suggest how far organic abstraction has drifted from the philosophy of early modernism. Hidden harmonies of the cosmos or the underlying rhythms of nature are no longer at issue, as artists today tend to regard their organic forms as surface decorations or contingent details borrowed from nature, historical ornament, or the everyday world. Geometric abstraction, especially under the influence of Minimalism, has also undergone radical changes in the hands of contemporary artists. Take, for instance, the grid, one of Minimalism's most venerable tropes, and one of its most aloof, as critic and historian Rosalind Krauss described in 1978: "The grid announces, among other things, modern art's will to silence, its hostility to literature, to narrative, to discourse." She further elaborated that the grid reveals "what art looks like when it turns its back on nature."[11] And yet, like Kandinsky's sweeping arabesques, taken up by contemporary artists in a way that denies his belief in their transcendent spirituality, the grid has been adopted by artists today who deliberately subvert its "hostility."

A startling transformation in the work of Sol LeWitt, one of the progenitors of Minimalism, illustrates the shift. LeWitt, who established his early career with cubes whose white lattice structure formed a three-dimensional grid, set rules and strictly followed them, creating sculptures that presented every possible variation of the cube with one or more of its edges removed. He elaborated on this systemic process by creating wall drawings that were nothing more than a set of instructions about the placement of lines in relationship to each other. In keeping with Minimalism's rejection of gestural "authenticity," he specified that these works were to be executed by a small army of assistants. Over the years LeWitt has persisted with this "hands-off" mode of creation, but the compositions that he directs have changed drastically. Instead of cool, neutral grids of fine lines, his wall drawings now consist of bands of glowing color arranged to suggest stars, arcs, swirls, pinwheels, and various architectural details, as in *Wall Drawing #1118 Whirls*, 2004. Other works, in complete contradiction to Minimalism's rejection of illusionism, suggest three-dimensional pyramids, cubes, or blocks, harking back to the mystical geometry of the early modernists as well as to ancient forms such as the Aztec pyramids. Critics have linked the change in LeWitt's work to his move to Italy, where he has absorbed the rich earth tones of the early Renaissance painters and of the landscape that inspired them. LeWitt himself always acknowledged his embrace of the irrational, the spiritual, and the mystical—the sorts of states, in other words, that Minimalism was designed to overthrow. Already in his 1966 manifesto "Sentences on Conceptual Art," he maintained: "Conceptual artists are mystics rather than rationalists. They leap to conclusions that logic cannot reach."[12]

Agnes Martin is an equally influential grid-maker, who, like LeWitt, has imbued this seemingly impenetrable form with poetry. Again like LeWitt, Martin took the luminous quality of the landscape as inspiration. Her delicately tinted paintings in pale rose, green, and blue are associated with New Mexico, where she lived for decades until her death in 2004 at the age of ninety-two. The underlying structure of all of Martin's paintings is the grid, drawn onto the canvas in pencil lines so fine that they are sometimes almost imperceptible. Martin uses other marks as well, among them parallel lines, dots, and dashes, all of which become the substructure for thinly washed bands of pale color. Her titles, *The Sea*, 2003, *The Harvest*, 1965,

JUDY PFAFF

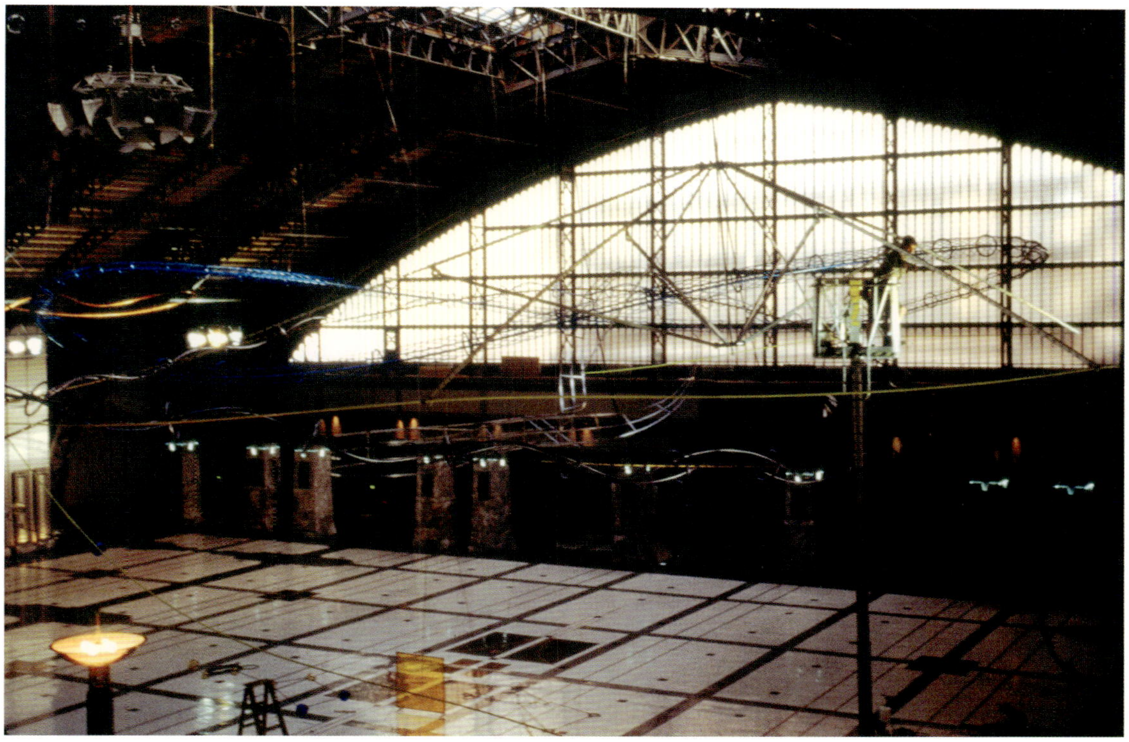

cirque, CIRQUE, 1995
Steel, aluminum, stainless steel cable, urethane glass and lacquer paints
250 x 210 x 40 ft (7.6 x 6.4 x 12.2 m)
Installation at the Pennsylvania Convention Center, Philadelphia

POLLY APFELBAUM

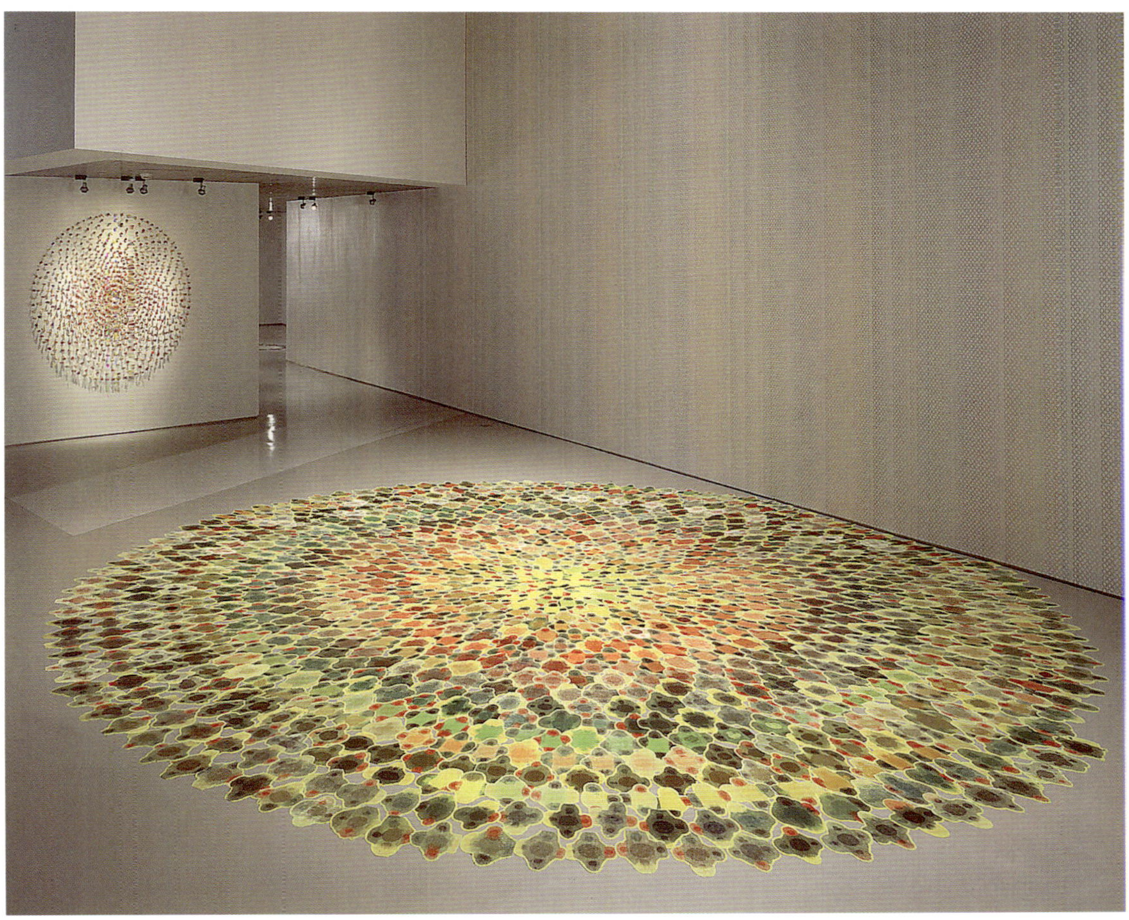

Big Bubbles, 2000
Synthetic velvet and dye, diameter 18 ft (5.5 m)

SOL LEWITT

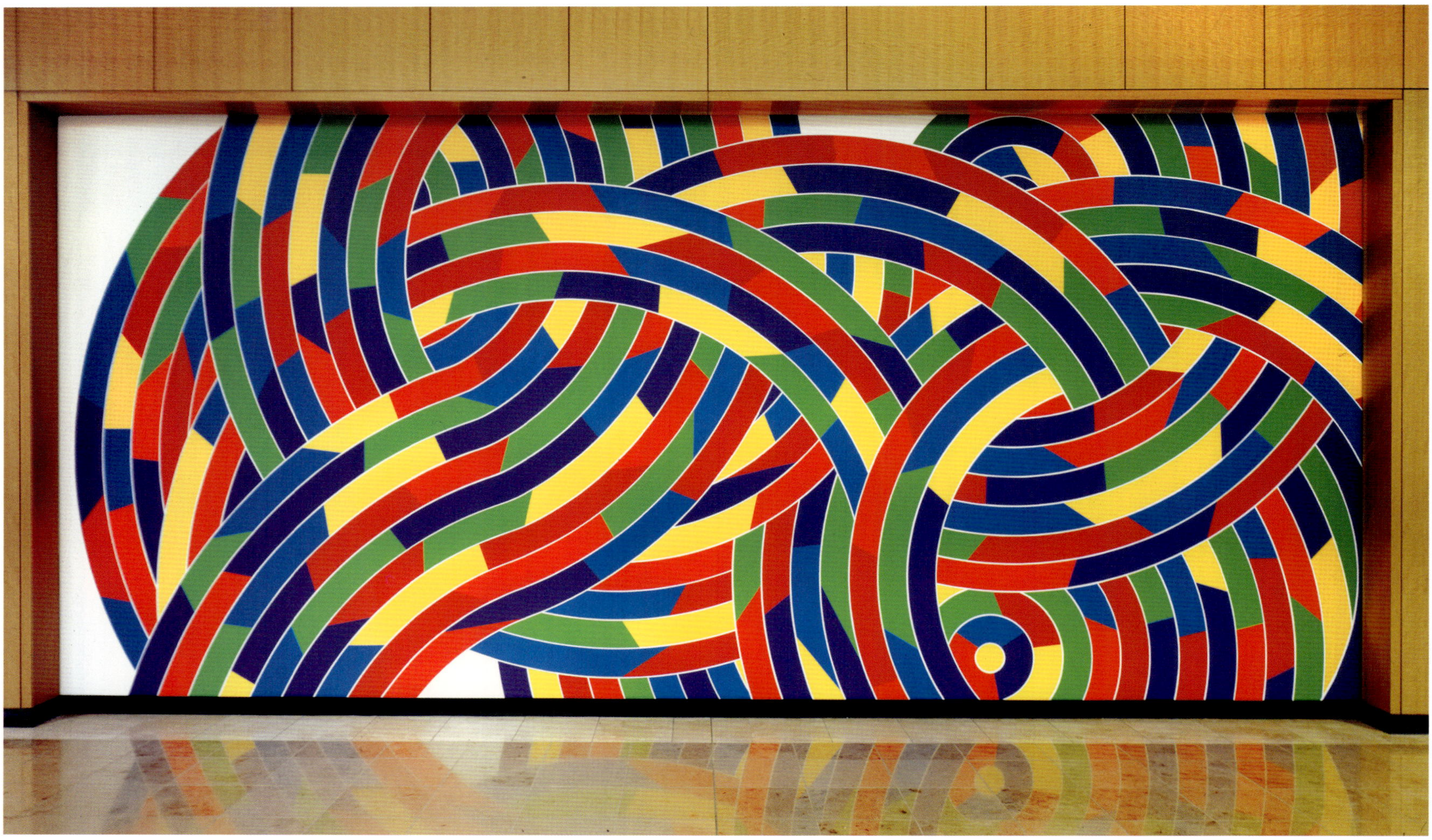

Wall Drawing #1118 Whirls, 2004
Acrylic paint on wall, 10 ft 5 in x 23 ft 4 in (3.2 x 7.1 m)
As installed at Hallmark Fine Arts Collection, Kansas City, Mo., March 2004

AGNES MARTIN

Untitled No. 4, 1984
Acrylic, gesso, and graphite on canvas, 72 x 72 in (183 x 183 cm)

SARAH MORRIS

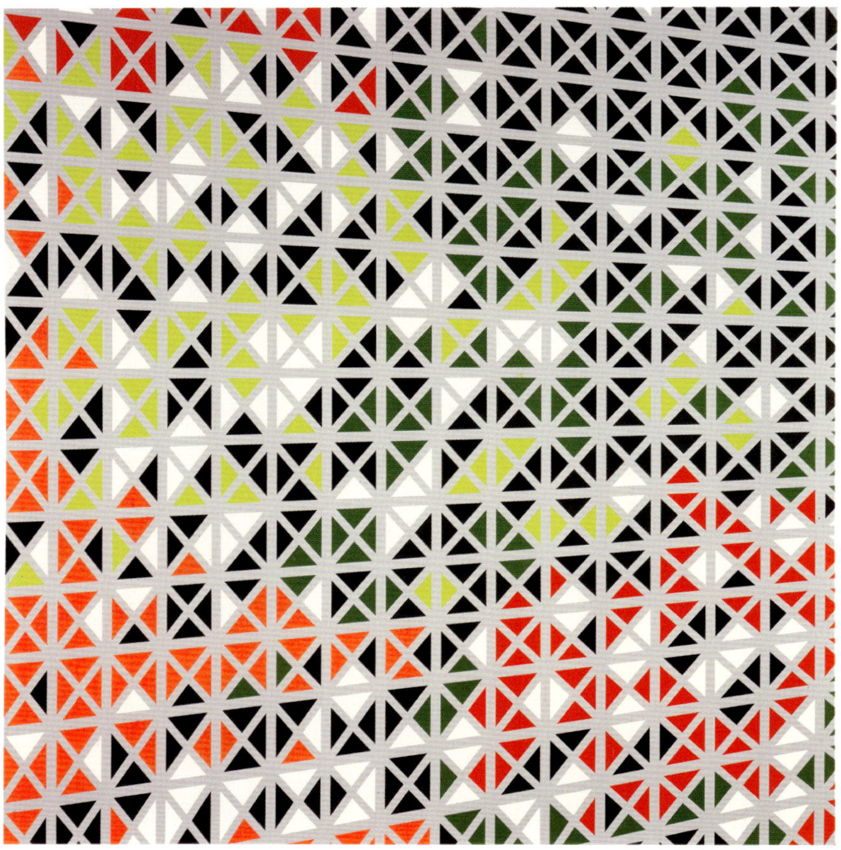

Midtown-Mountain Dew, 1999
Gloss household paint on canvas, 84 x 84 in (213.4 x 213.4 cm)

The Spring, 1959, and *This Rain*, 1960, for instance, suggest the works' roots in the natural world. In another departure from Minimalism, Martin's paintings are profoundly "retinal." For instance, in *Untitled No. 4*, 1984, ninety faintly drawn, evenly spread graphite lines become, from a distance, a subtly uneven field of gray. In many ways, Martin's ambitions recall the transcendental concerns of both the Abstract Expressionists and the early modernists. The artist cited Taoism, Buddhism, and the writings of visionary mystic St. Teresa of Avila as inspirations, and her radiant paintings bear witness to these interests.

LeWitt and Martin softened the grid. Today, one must look to younger artists for the hard-edged, anti-nature grid Krauss described. Sarah Morris, for example, takes as her point of departure the ubiquitous grid of the many-windowed urban building, linking it, as Krauss did, with experiences of modernity. Some works refer to specific New York skyscrapers or the gaudy layers of billboards in Times Square, such as *Midtown-Mountain Dew*, 1999, in which the giant Mountain Dew logo in Times Square is abstracted into an angled grid of gray, black, and bottle green. Others are inspired by Las Vegas casinos and Florida swimming pools. Morris places her brightly colored grids in illusionistic space, pulling the viewer deep into rigidly structured rectilinear spaces that could not be more removed from the natural world. These works are painted in clashing hues of household gloss paint, further distancing them from nature. In their jazzy motion and sharp edges, they feel like heirs to Mondrian's New York-inspired paintings, notably *Broadway Boogie Woogie*, 1942–43. Like Mondrian, Morris translates the energy of the city into paintings that capture the distinctive rhythms of urban life.

Mondrian also haunts the work of Peter Halley, whose garishly colored geometric paintings are clearly "made in New York," and engage the social, political, and philosophical ideals behind modernist abstraction, though without embracing mystical aspirations. Introducing an element of kitsch into the once exalted sphere of geometric abstraction, Halley uses Day-Glo paint and textured, stucco-like surfaces that have more to do with jarring urban facades than transcendence. He further undermines his predecessors' utopian ideals with a set of repeated forms and compositions that suggest what he calls cells, conduits, and circuits. Such references to modern technology put us in mind of our own immersion and dependence on systems of electronic communication, the inhumane logic of the microchip, and the imprisoning grid of the industrial office tower. With titles such as *Optimizer*, 1998, Halley emphasizes how the same motifs that modernists used to evoke the liberating potential of technology are equally useful in suggesting its dark underside.

The grid is a more benign motif in the work of James Siena. In an echo of LeWitt's methodology, he begins each work by formulating a set of structuring devices that set out which forms and shapes he will use as well as which colors and types of lines. Unlike LeWitt, Siena then executes these instructions himself, in small, colorful drawings and paintings that combine the serendipity of hand work with the regular patterning of a mechanical process. For *Untitled Yellow Black*, 1991, the instructions, which are listed on the label that accompanies the work, read: "Endless line containing black. Line made up of acute angles. No lines may cross each other." These dry guidelines yield a surprisingly dynamic painting of a black crystalline form invading a yellow ground. The range of compositions produced by this self-instructional method seems to span the whole history of abstraction. Siena's works include swirling Op Art-like tangles of lines, severe rectilinear compositions that recall

PETER HALLEY

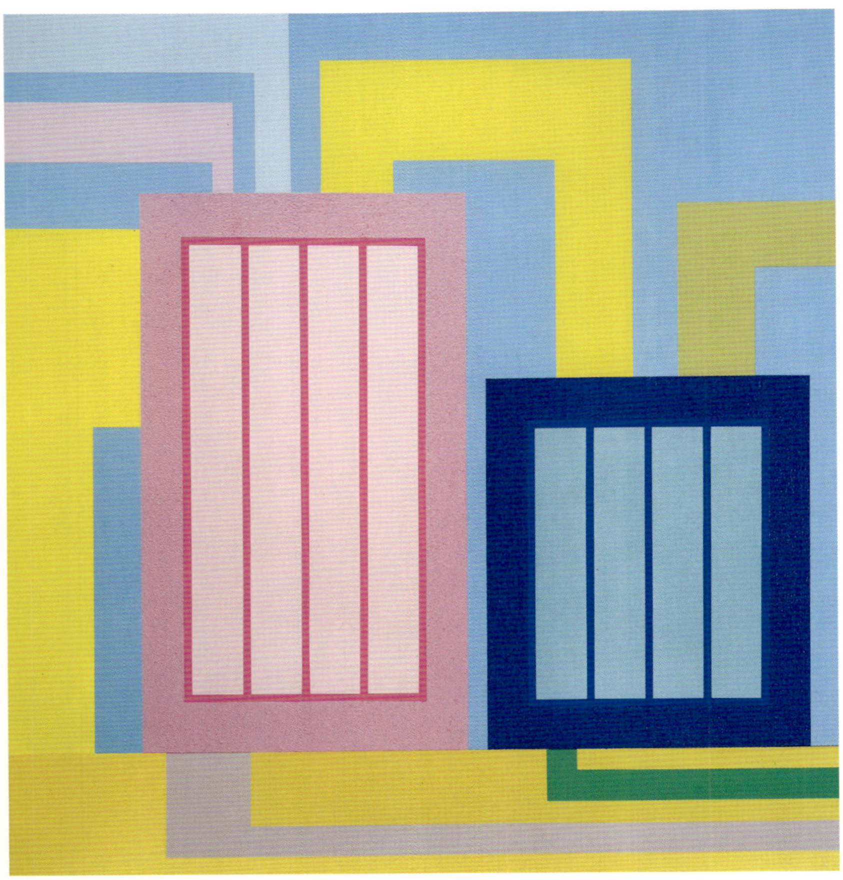

Optimizer, 1998
Acrylic and roll-a-text on canvas, 74 x 72 in (188 x 182.9 cm)

JAMES SIENA

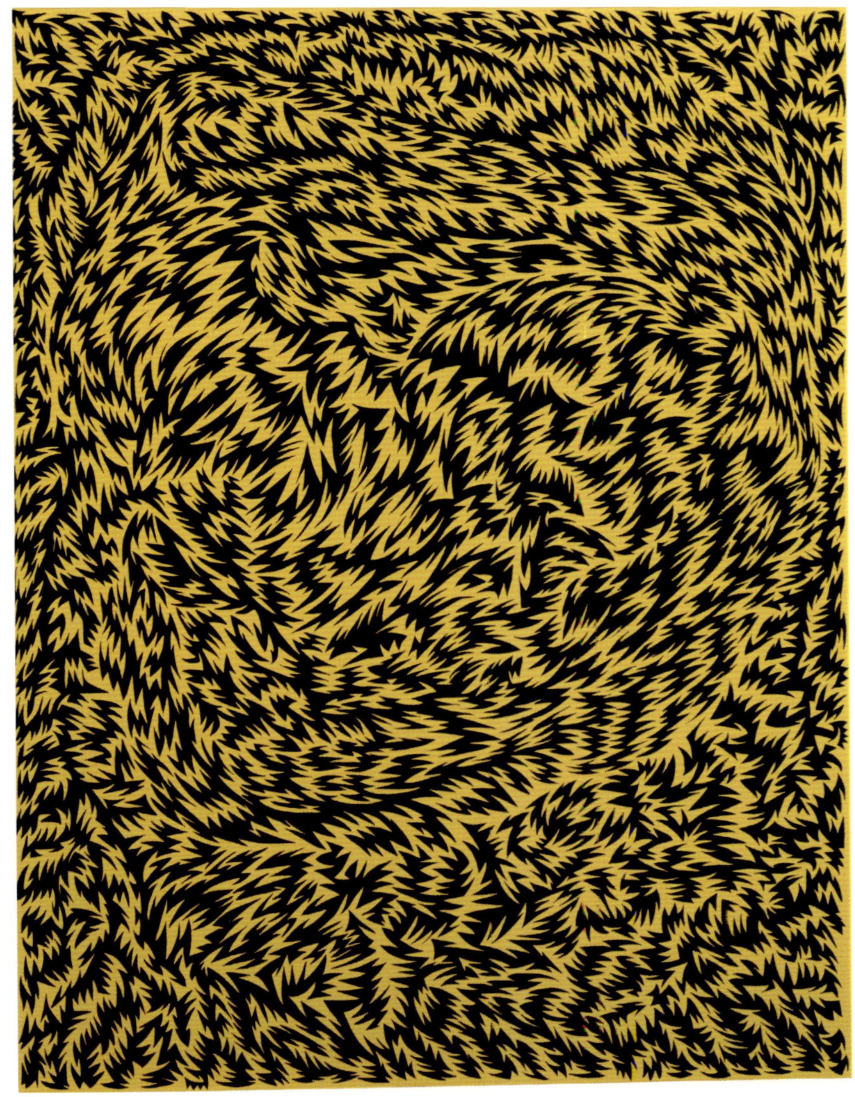

Untitled Yellow Black, 1991
Enamel on aluminum, 19 x 15 in (48.3 x 38.1 cm)

SEAN SCULLY

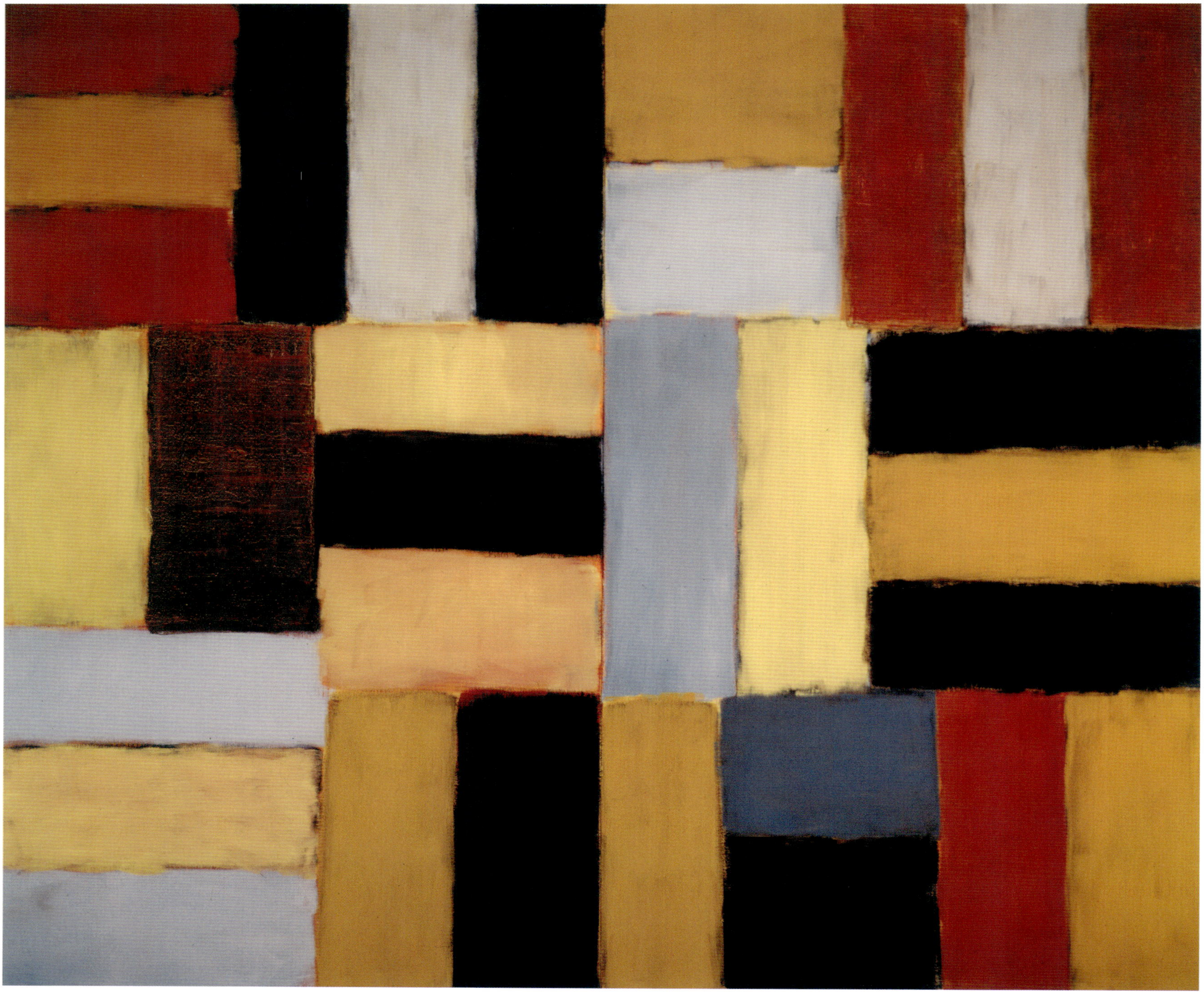

Wall of Light Fall, 2000
Oil on linen, 110 x 132 in (279.4 x 335.3 cm)

early Frank Stella, organic swirls, delicate lattice patterns that have an almost Islamic quality, and strangely distorted grids. Worlds apart from Halley's imprisoning geometry (which in fact includes bars that closely resemble prison bars), they suggest that rules can bring freedom as well as constraint.

Along with the grid, stripes were once a favored motif of formalists seeking to emphasize the flatness and objective shape of the canvas. And like the grid, they have acquired new meanings in the work of contemporary artists. Sean Scully, for instance, rejects the formalist notion that fields of regular stripes create intellectual order, suggesting instead that they illustrate messy reality. Scully takes his inspiration from life, from the stripes of gaily colored beach umbrellas, rows of pillars or barred windows, and the shadows that fall from stands of trees. Eschewing machine-like edges, Scully paints stripes with uneven edges that blend one into another. The compositions take on a crazy-quilt quality as patches of horizontal and vertical stripes of various colors and sizes butt up against each other. Some patches are piled up to have a three-dimensional relief quality. Others, though contained in a single canvas, are composed of swatches of grids that produce a discontinuous energy. Scully's muted colors come from nature—the rich tones of the earth, the shimmer of sea, the convergence of cloud and sky—imparting to the stripe a certain human and natural quality that seems light years away from the stark regularity of Minimalism. His *Wall of Light Fall*, 2000, is one in a series of works inspired by the fall of sunlight on Mayan stone walls. The notion of a "wall of light" is contradictory, of course, combining the material and the immaterial, and mirrors the work's oscillation between vertical bands of red and white that suggest both space and form.

Minimalist geometry takes another turn in the work of Al Held. Having begun his career as an Abstract Expressionist, Held soon veered off on the byway of geometric abstraction and spatial illusionism. Finding little of interest in the formalist celebration of flatness, he used the minimalist aesthetic of flatly painted, hard-edged geometric shapes to create careening compositions that employed every trick of Renaissance and Baroque perspective. His paintings are remarkably architectural, especially when they assume mural-size dimensions. In *See Through III*, 2002, undulating ribbons, volumetric cylinders and spheres, and patches of checkerboard patterns seem to float through a gravity-free zone. Some viewers have linked this checkerboard pattern to those seen in Renaissance floor patterns. Held's motifs often suggest bits of industrial debris or fragments of arcs, grids, or windows wrested from architectural structures. Theatrical shifts of light and dark pull the viewer into an unstable, ever-shifting space. Held, who worked in this ebullient mode from 1981 until his death in 2005, in many ways anticipated the strangely unnatural virtual space of digital design. But regardless of the digital look of his paintings, he continued to create them the old-fashioned way. Thus he deftly collapsed past and present—putting shapes and forms once derived from "eternal" geometry in the service of a mental space that only recently has been opened up by the evolution of advanced technology.

Minimalist geometry is literally enhanced by technology in the work of Liz Larner, who takes a mischievous approach to the once serious business of creating nonreferential, internally logical forms. The seriousness of geometric abstraction is undermined in works that involve deformations of the minimalist cube, for example. *Two or Three or Something*, 1999, is a wobbly linear structure made of steel and

AL HELD

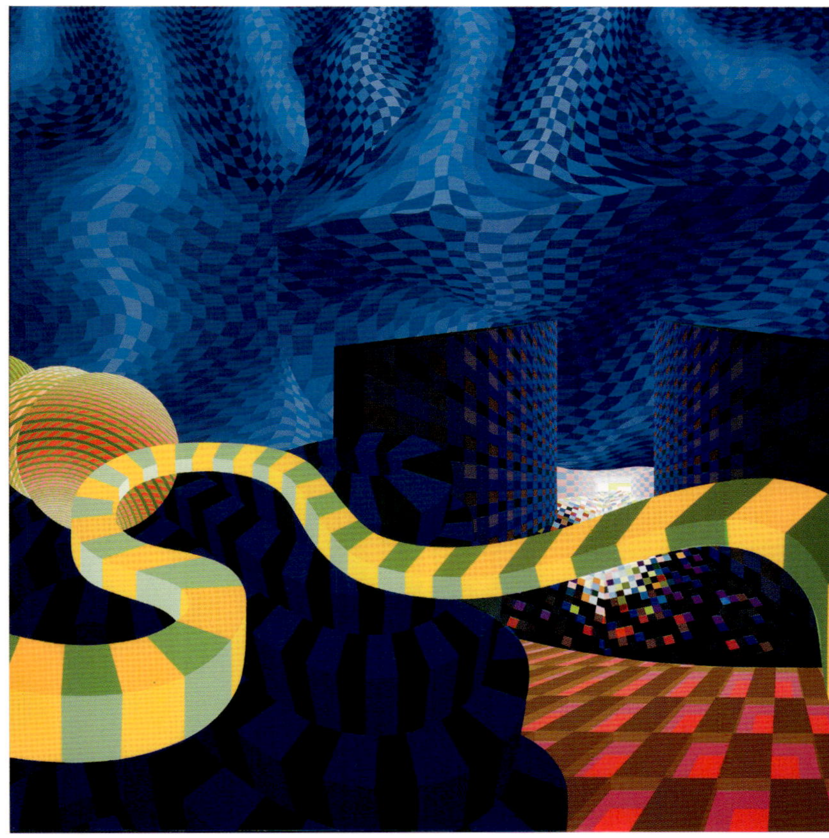

See Through III, 2002
Acrylic on canvas, 84 x 84 in (213.4 x 213.4 cm)

CHARLES RAY

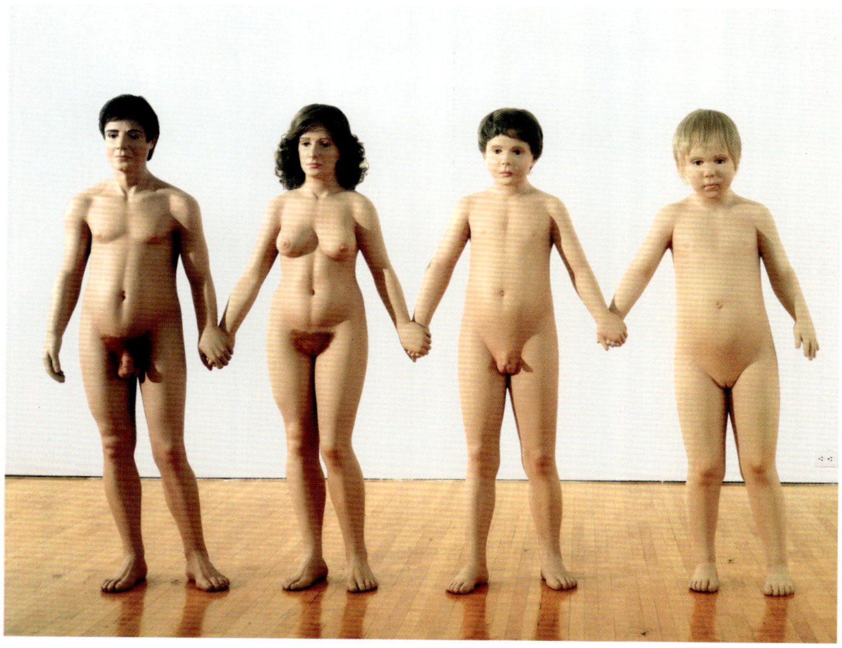

Family Romance, 1993
Mixed media, 54 x 96 x 24 in (137.2 x 243.9 x 61 cm)

mulberry paper that could, theoretically, be straightened and reshaped into the outlines of a cube. Larner also mocks Minimalism's emphasis on the object's interdependence with the surrounding space, for instance in *Corner Basher*, 1988, in which a ball and chain whipped the corner of a room into a ruin. Such works suggest the irreverence with which contemporary artists treat the pieties of modernist abstraction and demonstrate that the escape from metaphysics and the language of absolutes has opened up new expressive possibilities.

This is never clearer than in the work of Charles Ray, a figurative artist whose work is deeply informed by the principles of abstraction, and particularly Minimalism. Many of Ray's early works employ Minimalist cubes. *Memory of Moro*, 1978, for example, was a performance in which the artist extended his arm from a red cube while holding a red flag. (The piece was an homage to the Italian Premier Aldo Moro, who was kidnapped and murdered by Red Brigade terrorists that same year.) *Ink Box*, 1986, is a large, open-top black box filled to the brim with two hundred gallons of printer's ink. The shiny surface teases the viewer to touch it, which would wreak havoc on both the gallery floor and the unwitting participant. These early works took Michael Fried's suggestion that Minimalism is performative literally, incorporating references to the human body, or the promise of human interaction, into works that originate with Minimalist geometry. In several of Ray's later works, he flipped the equation: rather than expressing human factors in the ever-replicable cube, he turned human bodies into replications. *Family Romance*, 1993, for instance, was the first step. Sculptures of father, mother, toddler son, and infant daughter are all presented at the same height, beginning the fusion into serial sameness. And so geometric leads to organic and back again—a full circle of abstraction.

With its focus on the body and perception, the art of Charles Ray returns us to the "objective world" that the early abstractionists were determined to leave behind. But in presenting figurative works that pay homage to the principles of minimalist abstraction, his sculptures demonstrate how completely abstraction's once radical experiments have been absorbed and reinvented by contemporary artists. The revolution initiated by the likes of Mondrian and Kandinsky has yielded a generation of artists who feel completely comfortable with the language of abstraction but no longer feel the need to make absolutist distinctions between the visible and invisible or to choose between representation and abstraction. Instead, they embrace opposing tendencies as necessary tools for any exploration of a complex world.

LIZ LARNER

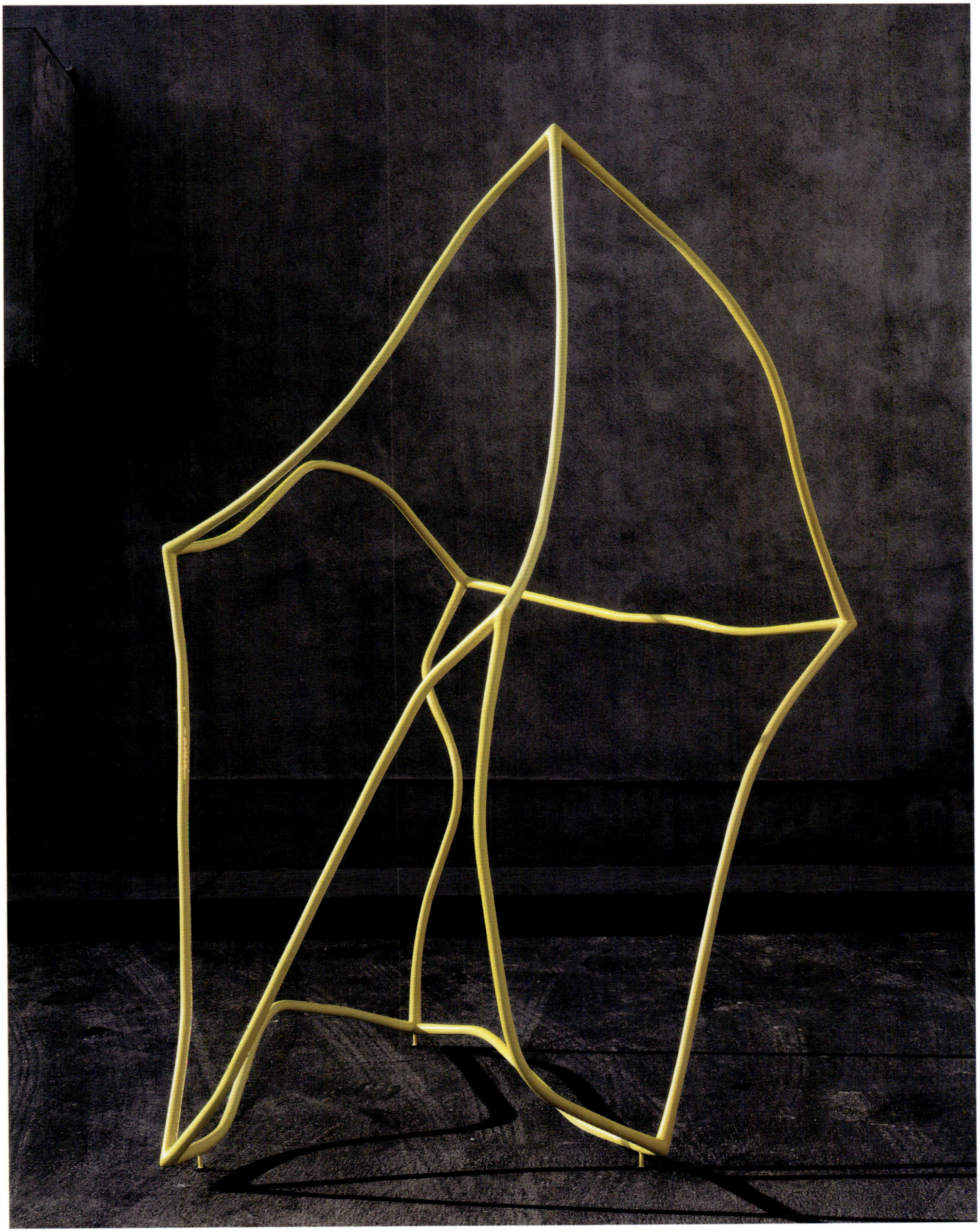

Two or Three or Something, 1999
Steel, mulberry paper, and watercolor, 100 x 80 x 68 in (254 x 203.2 x 172.7 cm)

ART & REPRESENTATION
THE FICTION OF REALISM

In his first-century masterwork *Natural History*, the Roman author Pliny the Elder tells the story of two Greek artists who conceived a competition to establish which was the better painter. To make their cases, each produced a startlingly realistic painting. The first artist presented a depiction of a cluster of grapes so convincing that birds came down from the sky and attempted to eat them. He turned triumphantly to his adversary and urged him to lift the curtain covering his canvas. In fact the curtain *was* the painting, or rather the painting a representation of a curtain, and so the second artist claimed victory. "You have fooled a bird," he crowed, "but I have fooled a fellow artist!"

This little tale resonates throughout the history of Western art, in which mimesis (imitation, mimicry, or representation of the visible world) has almost always played a central role. Notions about the value of mimesis go back to Aristotle, who argued in his *Poetics* (ca. 330 BCE) that art imitates our shared reality, and thus serves social and utilitarian functions in our process of learning about the world. This idea fell out of favor during the Middle Ages, when art was rendered in service to religion and was therefore subject to the rules of the invisible world of spirit rather than the visible world of matter. The diversion was relatively brief, however; with the birth of the Renaissance during the fifteenth century, the revival of classical philosophy, art, and literature brought with it a renewed interest in realism and representation. Painters were again judged by their skill in imitating the physical appearances of things in the world, a development that spurred the study of anatomy, perspective, and optics.

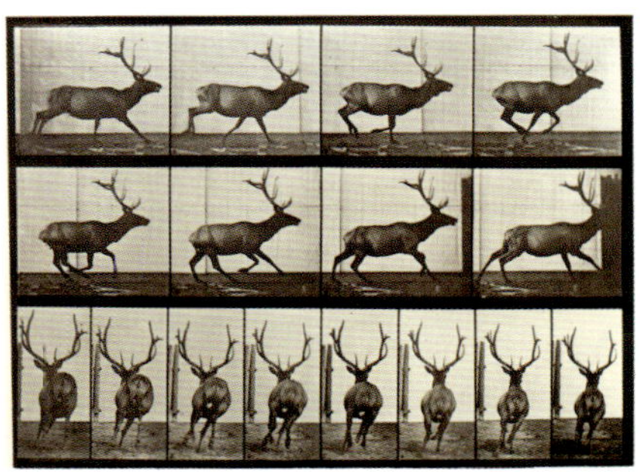

EADWEARD MUYBRIDGE
PLATE 695 FROM "ANIMAL LOCOMOTION"
1887
VINTAGE COLLOTYPE

In the centuries that followed, artists pursued ever more sophisticated means to fool the eye. In his *Death of the Virgin*, 1606, Caravaggio thrust the unwashed arm of the deceased Virgin Mary into the viewer's space. Tiepolo decorated the Baroque cathedral of the Kaisersaal in Würzburg, Germany, with faux columns and arches that blend seamlessly into representations of heavenly choirs drifting heavenward on painted clouds. Seventeenth-century Dutch masters such as Pieter Claesz and Willem van Aelst created incredibly lifelike still lifes whose dewy blossoms are kept forever fresh by glistening painted water droplets. This fixation on mimesis persisted until the advent of modernism in the late nineteenth century, whence commenced a series of movements—Impressionism, Post-Impressionism, Cubism, Constructivism, Expressionism, and so on—that all rejected the idea that artists should provide a mirror of nature.

Generally speaking, modern artists turned away from realism in favor of exploring more subjective modes of expression. But there is another curious and long-simmering rationale behind the rejection of realism, and it is revealed in Pliny's story. From one perspective, imitation can be construed as an effort to be *truthful* to the appearances of things in the world, but the second painter's triumph points to an element of *falsehood* in representation. The story raises the question: Is mimesis really about fostering visual trickery? And if so, is it immoral? In fact this very perspective preceded Aristotle's. Plato, Aristotle's teacher, argued in his *Republic* that the world that we experience through the senses is but a pale imitation of the "real" world of ideas and ideal forms, which we can only experience through our minds. As a result, for Plato, art that aims at recreating visual reality can never produce anything more than an imitation of an imitation. Hence, artists are essentially liars, and thus are summarily banished from his ideal Republic.

Plato's notion that the visible world is suspect or at least secondary returned to art in the early twentieth century, though with new conceptual underpinnings. Abstract painters such as Mondrian, Malevich, and Kandinsky—informed by new developments in particle physics and Freudian psychology—argued, like Plato, that the real is invisible to the naked eye. Hence, only abstraction could bring us close to the true essence of the universe, and only abstraction could be a harbinger of truth. This notion held great sway through the mid-twentieth century, and was only undone again with the postmodern revolution of the 1960s and '70s. This time it was not an Aristotelian belief in the relationship between art and reality that prompted the shift, but the postmodernist argument that there is no true essence of anything, no matter how invisible. Postmodernism maintained instead that all absolutes are mere fantasies in a world governed by relativism, ideology, and subjectivity. In the process of dismantling the modernist faith in absolutes, postmodernism returns to Plato's notion that everything we see is simply an imitation of an imitation. It simply does away with Plato's idea that somewhere out of reach there hovers some ideal and authentic "form" or essence to which our perceptible imitations refer. From the perspective of art, postmodernism then suggests that "realism" is no more (and no less) realistic than abstraction. Each is simply a representation of a reality that exists only in our minds.

The path from the comfortable certitude of Pliny's painters to this confusing state of unreal realities finds its crux in the nineteenth-century invention and development of photography. In his essay "The End of Art," philosopher and critic Arthur Danto argues that photography "solved" the problem that had faced artists since the Renaissance, namely how to create a convincing representation of the visible world through painting and sculpture. As a result, he believes, photography freed art to pursue a different set of goals involving ideology rather than representation.[1] This may be so, but all was not necessarily now clear-cut. By usurping the mimetic function of painting and sculpture, photography only complicated notions about what it means for an image to be "realistic." For instance, it soon became obvious that photography was not by definition a reflection of truth; it could be manipulated to produce false impressions. Cropping, scale shifts, double exposures, and altered negatives could be employed to change the meaning of a photographic image. Subtler manipulations proved just as effective: analyzing the political uses of photographic imagery, French theorist Roland Barthes suggested that a photograph, by itself, means nothing. Its meaning is subjective, shifting, and created by its specific social or cultural context.[2]

While Barthes admitted that photographs cannot satisfy a longing for "objective truth," he proposed that one thing gave it a tangible upper hand over all other art forms: its essential origin in outside reality. "Painting can feign reality without having seen it," he wrote in 1980. "But these references can be and are most often 'chimeras.' Contrary to these imitations, in Photography I can never deny that the thing has been there."[3] But even this partial confidence in a photograph's authenticity was short-lived. Contemporary photographers frequently enlist their art in the service of fiction, contriving elaborate imaginary scenes that might look entirely real. The digital revolution exacerbates the situation, making it possible to produce photographs with no ties to external reality. Entirely convincing settings, characters, and events can be created out of nothing more than a software imaging program.

The invention of photography has also set in motion radical changes in how we see. Painters have long translated the three dimensions of life onto the two-dimensional canvas, using conventions of Western art such as perspective and shadow. We like to think that these conventions are universal, natural, the realization of "real" sight, but widespread exposure to photography has forced us to recognize otherwise. The camera lens, unlike the naked eye, allows for selective focus, producing a distinct difference in detail between direct and peripheral vision. It also stops action, revealing the minutiae of a split second that are otherwise invisible. It wasn't until Eadweard Muybridge's photographic motion studies of the 1870s, for example, that we could "see" the movements made by running animals. To create his "Animal Locomotion" series (Plate 695, from 1887) for instance, Muybridge set up a row of cameras mechanically rigged to go off as a stag passed over wires connected to each camera, thereby revealing the incremental movements of its legs. More recently, time lapse photography allows us to "stop time" so that we can see how a drop of rain hits the surface of a pond or how plants twist and turn as they grow.

A number of artists incorporate photographic ways of seeing into their work. Vija Celmins, for example, creates meticulously realistic graphite drawings, etchings, paintings, and prints of such subjects as the rippling surface of the ocean, the pitted landscape of the moon, scatterings of small stones in the desert sand, the star-filled night sky, and translucent spider webs (*Web #10*, 2006). Her real subject, she insists, is not the real world, but the photographs of the scenes from which she makes her renderings. Complicating the notion of depicting photographs, which retain strong representational associations, she seeks out images that already have a high degree of abstraction. Her ocean images, for instance, have no horizon, but picture instead an apparently endless field of waves, while her night skies become black monochromes interrupted by tiny pinpricks of white. With intense precision, Celmins then renders the images even more abstract. Further, she deliberately undercuts any romantic interpretation of her otherwise evocative subjects by presenting them with cool objectivity, as if they were specimens observed under a microscope.

Chuck Close's efforts to replicate photographic realism by hand also led him to abstraction. Close is known for his enormous portrait paintings, each based on a small photograph of the subject's head, captured straight on and with a deliberately blank expression. Close transfers the photographic image to canvas using a rather mechanical mural method: drawing a grid on both the photograph and the canvas, he fills in each individual box on the canvas in correspondence with the source image. As a result, the conventions of photographic reproduction that usually go unnoticed become starkly visible: the details in the center of the image undergo extreme magnification—pores, stray hairs, a network of crow's feet, or a chipped tooth cannot be ignored—while the outer edges of the head and shoulders become soft and fuzzy. In the 1970s and '80s, when Close began working in this mode, viewers found this realism disconcerting, even monstrous. The paintings stood apart from the portrait tradition in their absolute refusal to seek the sitter's soul; instead, like the camera, they happily settled for the limitations of surface. Curiously, it is exactly the fidelity to the photographic image that makes them appear abstract. Up close they are just tiny brushstrokes and flecks of color that only resolve into a hyperreal image from a distance. In the 1990s, Close became suddenly paralyzed from the chest down, which forced him to change his working methods and consequently the kind of marks he placed inside the boxes of the grid. The units were now filled with looser, multicolored donuts, dots, and lozenges, making the paintings more abstract than ever, as in his *Self-Portrait*, 2004–5, though they still cohere from afar. Whether by turn of fate or by intent, Close's amoeba-like forms anticipated the pixels of the soon to be ubiquitous digital image.

One of the more eccentric takes on photo-realism appears in the work of Malcolm Morley, who since the 1960s has mingled photo-derived modes of representation and gestural painting in the same works. In *The Day of the Locust*, 1977, for instance, a painted copy of the yellow cover of the Los Angeles phone book is the backdrop for a scrambled collection of images including Red Cross helicopters, a Civil War battle scene, figures falling from ladders, and others climbing from a Trojan horse. Other paintings might include a carefully reproduced newspaper photograph of a battleship, or of a postcard of a beach scene, or of a model train, all surrounded by areas of expressionist brushstrokes. There are also apparently spontaneous watercolor paintings that in fact are meticulous recreations of earlier small-scale studies. Toward the end of the 1980s, Morley returned to his ships and planes, basing his representations on models observed through a camera obscura. More recently, he has been depicting sports scenes, car crashes, and collapsing buildings, with imagery derived mostly from photographs. Morley is often regarded both as a precursor of photo-realism and, in his later work, as a representative of the Neo-Expressionist movement. His association with two such supposedly antithetical movements and promiscuous mixing of styles and images highlights the artifice of all systems of representation.

Vik Muniz also mines the relationship between photographic imagery in the popular conscious and representational painting. He begins with familiar and iconic images—famous paintings, celebrity publicity shots, and historic news photographs—and "paints" them with materials such as cayenne pepper, peanut butter and jelly, sugar, and chads from a paper ballot. The relationship between subject and material is generally suggestive: Muniz recreated a photograph of Marilyn Monroe in diamonds, for instance, and a portrait of Sigmund Freud in chocolate syrup. His portrait of Don Quixote, *Don Quixote in his Study, after William Luke Price c. 1890 (from Rebus)*, 2004, is composed of an arrangement of plastic toys, in which the colors and shapes of army figures, wheels, and dolls operate like pointillist flecks of color to create a monumental image. These "paintings" are then photographed and presented in their new media. Like Close, Muniz is interested in perception—in how we "read" an image and what makes it realistic, or at least recognizable as an image. He also explores the illusionism of photography. When presented in their photographed form, his reproductions of the original image are often quite convincing—until we look closely and discover the shininess of the chocolate syrup or the glitter of the diamonds that comprise them. As the artist has remarked, "I don't want the viewer to believe in my images; I want him or her to experience the extent of his or her own belief in images—period."[4]

VIJA CELMINS

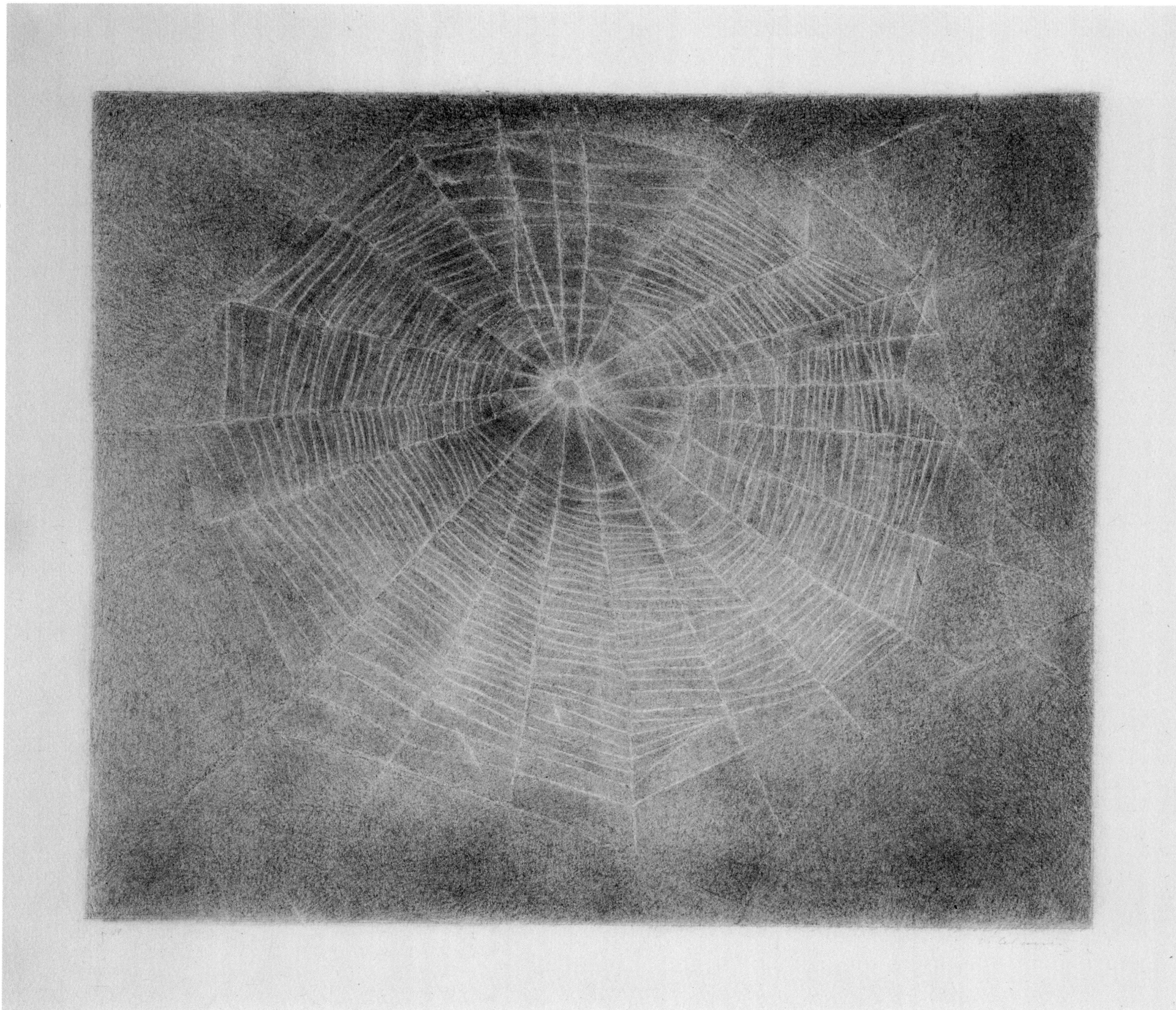

Web #10, 2006
Graphite and charcoal on paper, 19 1/4 x 22 1/2 in (49 x 57 cm)

CHUCK CLOSE

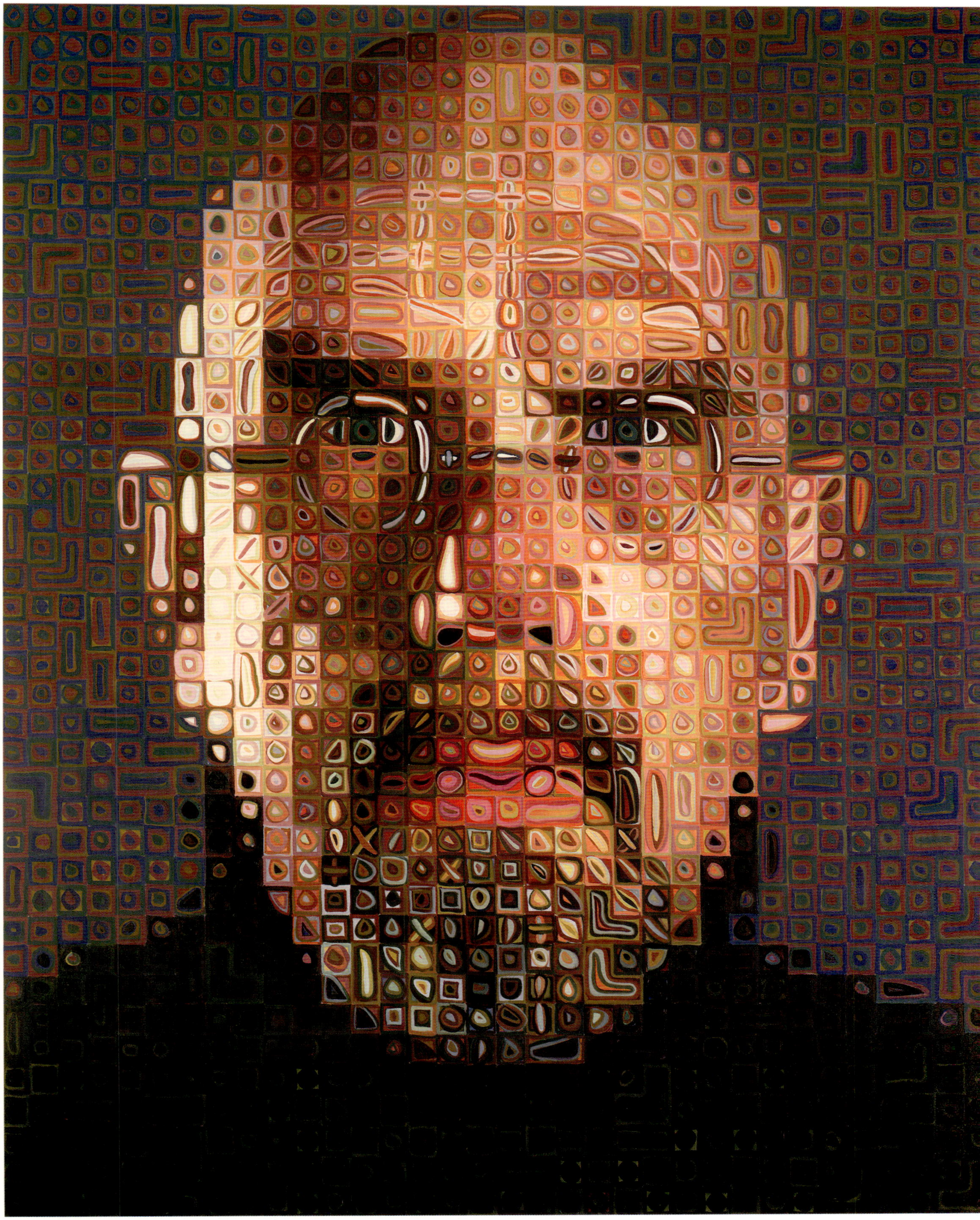

Self-Portrait, 2004–5
Oil on canvas, 102 x 84 1/2 in (259.1 x 214.6 cm)

VIK MUNIZ

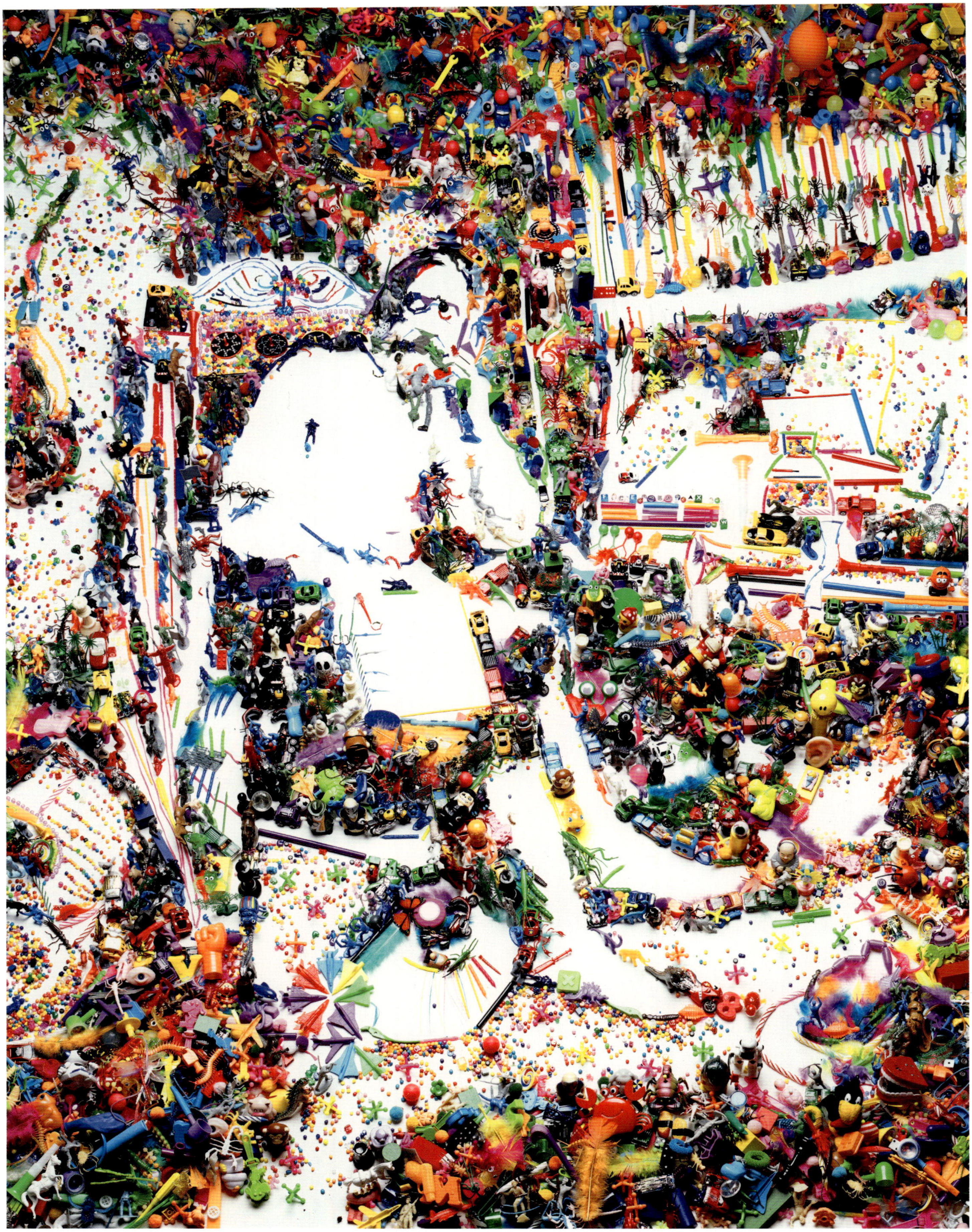

Don Quixote in his Study, after William Lake Price c. 1890 (from Rebus), 2004
Cibachrome print, 50 x 40 in (127 x 101.6 cm)

Gerhard Richter takes on both the realism of abstraction and the abstraction of realism in a self-consciously bipolar body of work. In a series of what he calls, generically, "Abstract Pictures," he creates strangely mechanical abstractions in which gestural marks reminiscent of Abstract Expressionism are laid over canvases in a contradictory, apparently automated fashion. (In fact, Richter has said that while some of what look like very large brushstrokes are applied with a squeegee, others are actually built up of many small strokes.) Richter also produces photo-based, photo-realist paintings that have a lush, painterly feel. Some are based on personal snapshots of his family or still lifes or the local countryside. Others draw from mass-media photographs—including series depicting murder victims, celebrities, and advertisements. In translating images from photographs into paint, Richter heightens contrast, and most importantly, blurs the imagery, creating the impression that the camera slipped or the negative was improperly developed. Critics have noted that these works have a dreamy, romantic feel. This may also be interpreted as nostalgia, as the paintings demonstrate the depletion of information and memory over time. The images are clearly based on photographs, which remain our culture's standard of "truth," but they seem on the verge of dissolution, as if they are being erased before our eyes. This is particularly the case in the remarkable series "October 18, 1977," 1988, fifteen paintings based on the life, and death, of Germany's notorious Baader-Meinhof gang, an imprisoned militant group whose members were found dead in their cells in 1977. The paintings depict blurry black-and-white images of their cells, their pre-prison personas, and their corpses, projecting a sense of mystery about who these figures were, why they did what they did, and how they died.

Luc Tuymans also uses a quasi-photographic mode to address the visual and psychological disappearance of information. Like Richter, Tuymans bases his muted, awkwardly brushed paintings on photographs that appear banal until one learns about their potent histories. A series of paintings of unremarkable courtyards and interiors turns out to depict the gas chambers and courtyard of a concentration camp. A series of dispassionate and abstracted paintings of an African leader decked out in ceremonial robes, an official portrait in western dress, a set of modernist building facades decked with flags, and a pair of hands holding the gold-capped teeth of an assassinated leader is a meditation on Belgian colonialism in the Congo and its chaotic and violent end forty years earlier, in 1960. In other paintings Tuymans gives equal weight (or lightness) to such obviously mundane subjects as wallpaper patterns and domestic interiors, as in *Lamp*, 1994. In his work, formal qualities of close-cropping, lack of detail, and a signature washed-out palette render the trivial and the momentous equally interesting and uninteresting, and equally distant from the kind of emotional engagement we traditionally associate with art. It is easy to recognize in these works a parallel to the leveling effect of the information explosion: the more images of horror we see, the less we feel.

A similar leveling takes place in the work of Elizabeth Peyton, though while Tuymans's work dances around larger issues of history and politics, Peyton confines her subjects and commentaries to entertainment culture and persona. Whether they depict her friends and acquaintances or glamorous celebrities, Peyton's small, sketch-like painted portraits all suggest a star-struck adolescent's clumsy drawings of her heroes and heroines copied from record-album covers and fanzines. Like

MALCOLM MORLEY

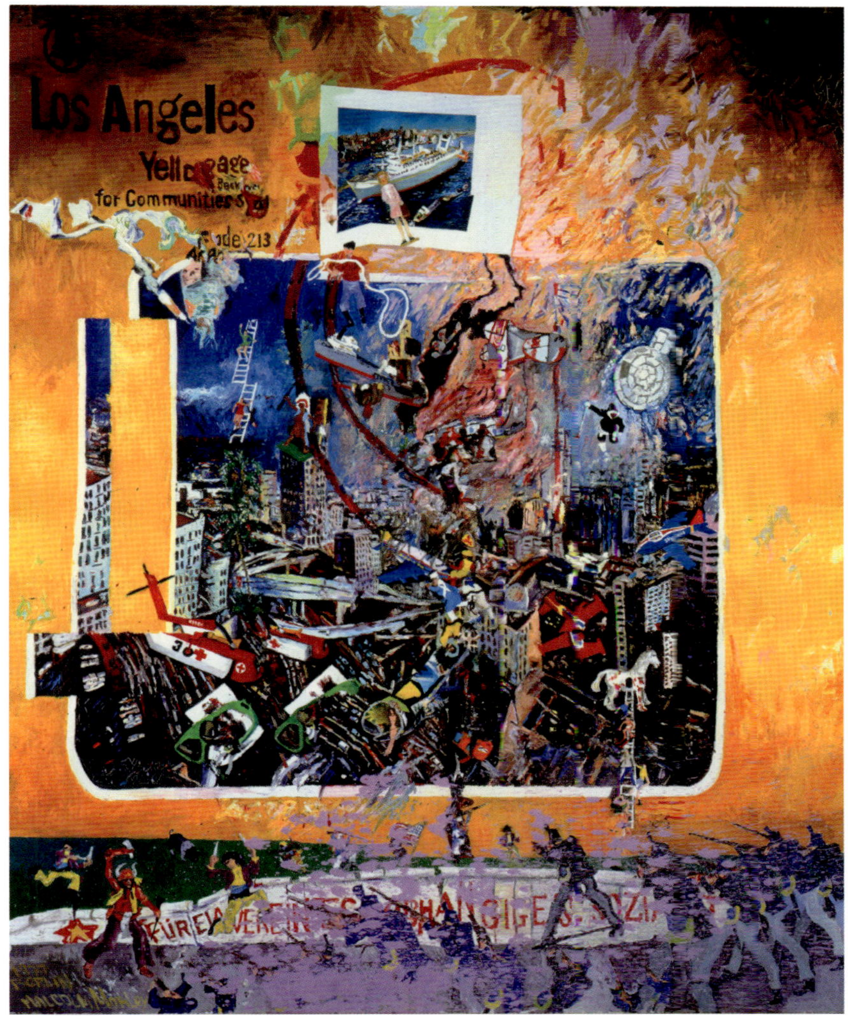

The Day of the Locust, 1977
Oil on canvas, 94 1/4 x 78 5/8 in (239.3 x 199.5 cm)
The Museum of Modern Art, New York

Tuymans, Peyton abstracts from photographic sources and uses flattened colors, exaggerated contrasts, and abrupt cropping that derive from a photographic way of seeing. Hipster heroes such as Kurt Cobain and Sid Vicious, slightly ridiculous luminaries such as the Queen Mother and Prince Harry, and Peyton's own art-world compatriots all are presented as pure surface, representatives of a world in which interiority has been eclipsed by the glare of the limelight. *Live to Ride (E.P.)*, 2003, for instance, is a self-portrait in which the artist/subject lounges in a Harley Davidson T-shirt. She leans slightly forward, with an inscrutable expression that gives little sense of emotional intensity or interior life.

Peter Doig, who uses snapshots, film stills, postcards, travel brochures, and album covers as the basis for vivid, dreamlike paintings, is another pointed revisionist of photographic originals. Unlike Tuymans and Peyton, however, Doig uses these sources to work his way back toward something like conventional painterly representation, presenting landscapes populated with lonely figures lost in vast expanses of sky, water, or land in strangely corroded surfaces and unnatural colors. In *100 Years Ago*, 2001, which is based on an Allman Brothers Band album cover, a bearded, long-haired figure sits in an orange canoe that slices across the entirety of the horizontal canvas. An island is visible in the distant background. Some critics have attributed the sense of melancholy and isolation in Doig's work to a childhood spent in rural Canada, but he also seems to share with artists like Tuymans and Peyton a sense of detachment and ennui—one that is amplified by the second-hand nature of photographic sources.

Just as painters like these draw on photography to distance their images from immediate experience, revealing the artifice at the heart of representation, certain photographers underscore the artifice of photography in a way that supports the postmodern notion that reality is all in our minds. These artists trade in the tension between photography's supposed truth-value and its actual status as a tool of the imagination. Jeff Wall, for instance, creates mural-size photographs that profoundly confound reality and illusion. Presented as huge transparencies set into light boxes, Wall's images are carefully staged vignettes into which individually photographed details are fused via digital means to form a nearly seamless whole. It has been said that Wall makes photographs not only in the style, but with the deliberation of a narrative history painter, and indeed his setup and shooting can take months. *Dead Troops Talk (A Vision After an Ambush of a Red Army Patrol, near Moqor, Afghanistan, Winter 1986)*, which appears to be a grisly war photograph, was actually created in the studio in 1992, and evidences such epic effort. It presents a complicated staged scene in which ashen, bloody "corpses" are revivified. The actors were photographed separately and digitally arranged in clusters, and even the rocky ravine in which they have been abandoned was built in the studio. Wall's works display a distinctive blend of painterly theatricality and photographic realism so that even at their most seemingly documentary (the artist calls his mode "near documentary") they retain an element of contrivance. Among his scenes are run-down urban neighborhoods, faceless corporate facades, and domestic interiors populated with glum characters that make for a subtle social commentary. The strange opacity of Wall's photographs suggest a world in which old social ties have been loosened or have disappeared altogether, in which old neighborhoods are remorselessly swallowed up by gentrification or decay.

James Casebere and Thomas Demand produce even more radically contrived

GERHARD RICHTER

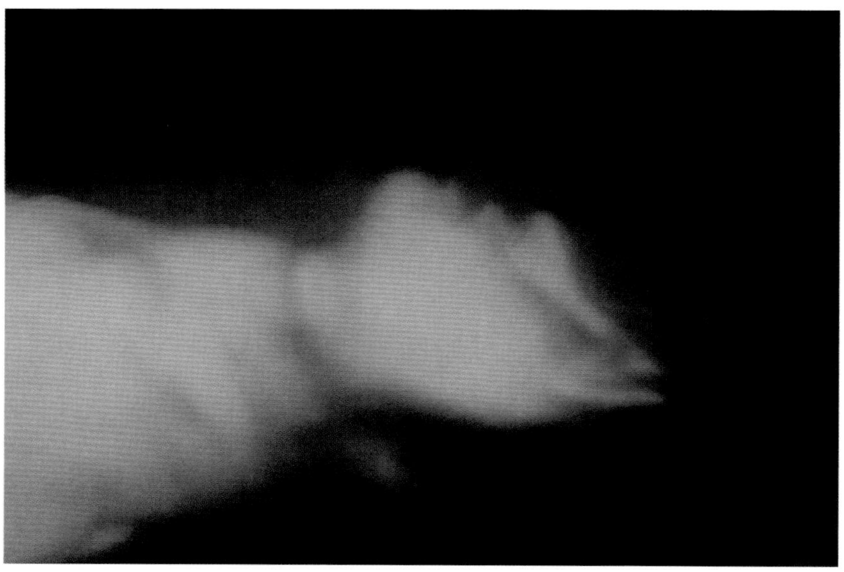

Dead (Tote), 1988
Oil on canvas, 13 3/4 x 15 1/2 in (35 x 40 cm)

LUC TUYMANS

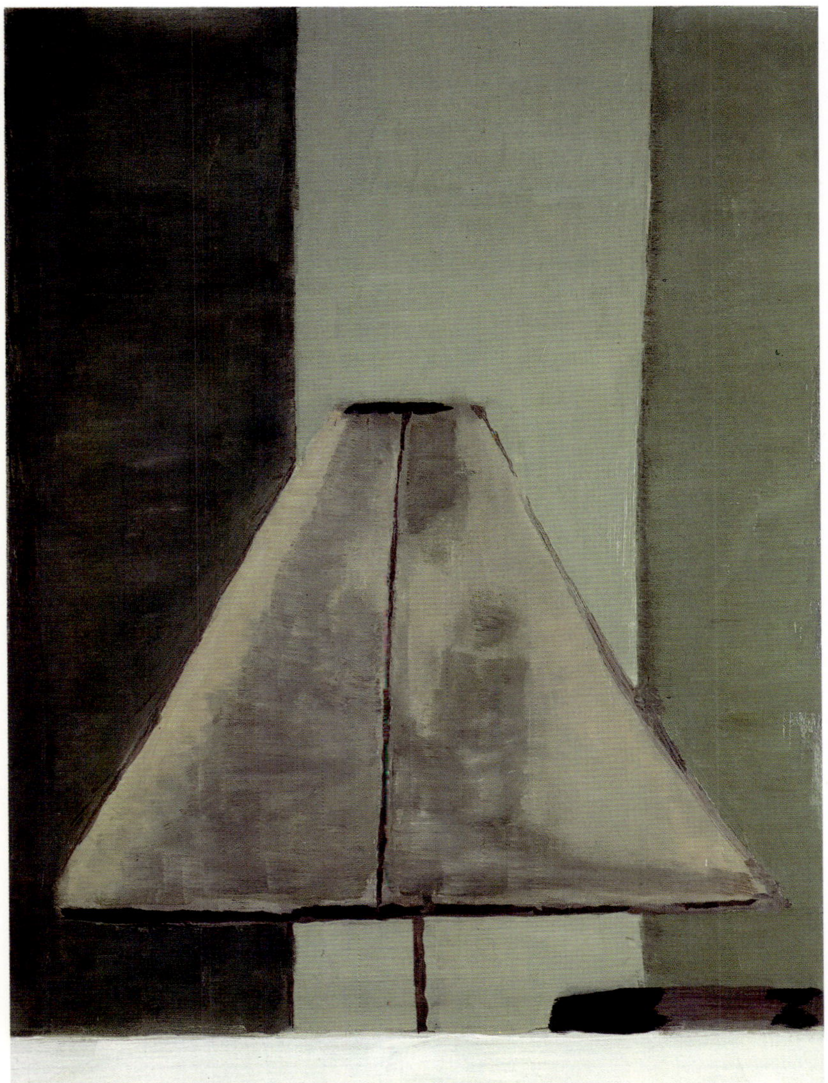

Lamp, 1994
Oil on canvas, 22 1/4 x 17 15/16 in (56.3 x 45.5 cm)

ELIZABETH PEYTON

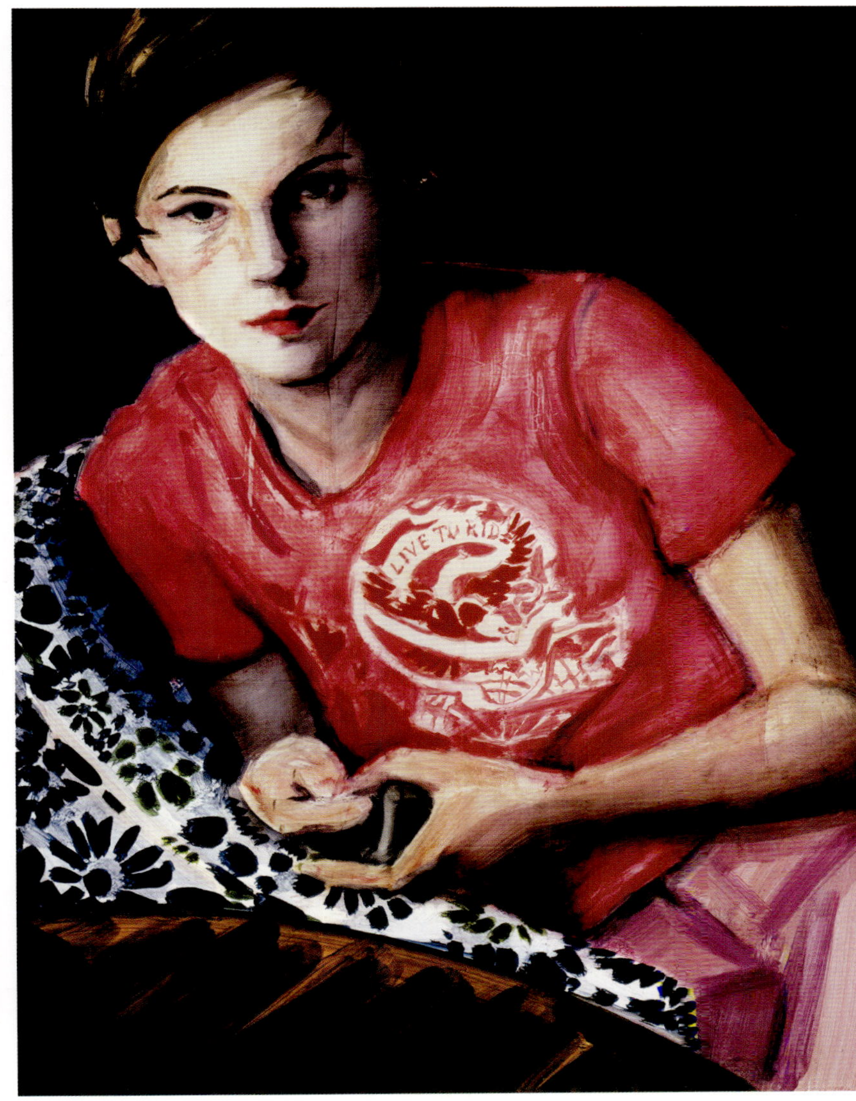

Live to Ride (E.P.), 2003
Oil on board, 15 x 12 in (38.1 x 30.5 cm)

JEFF WALL

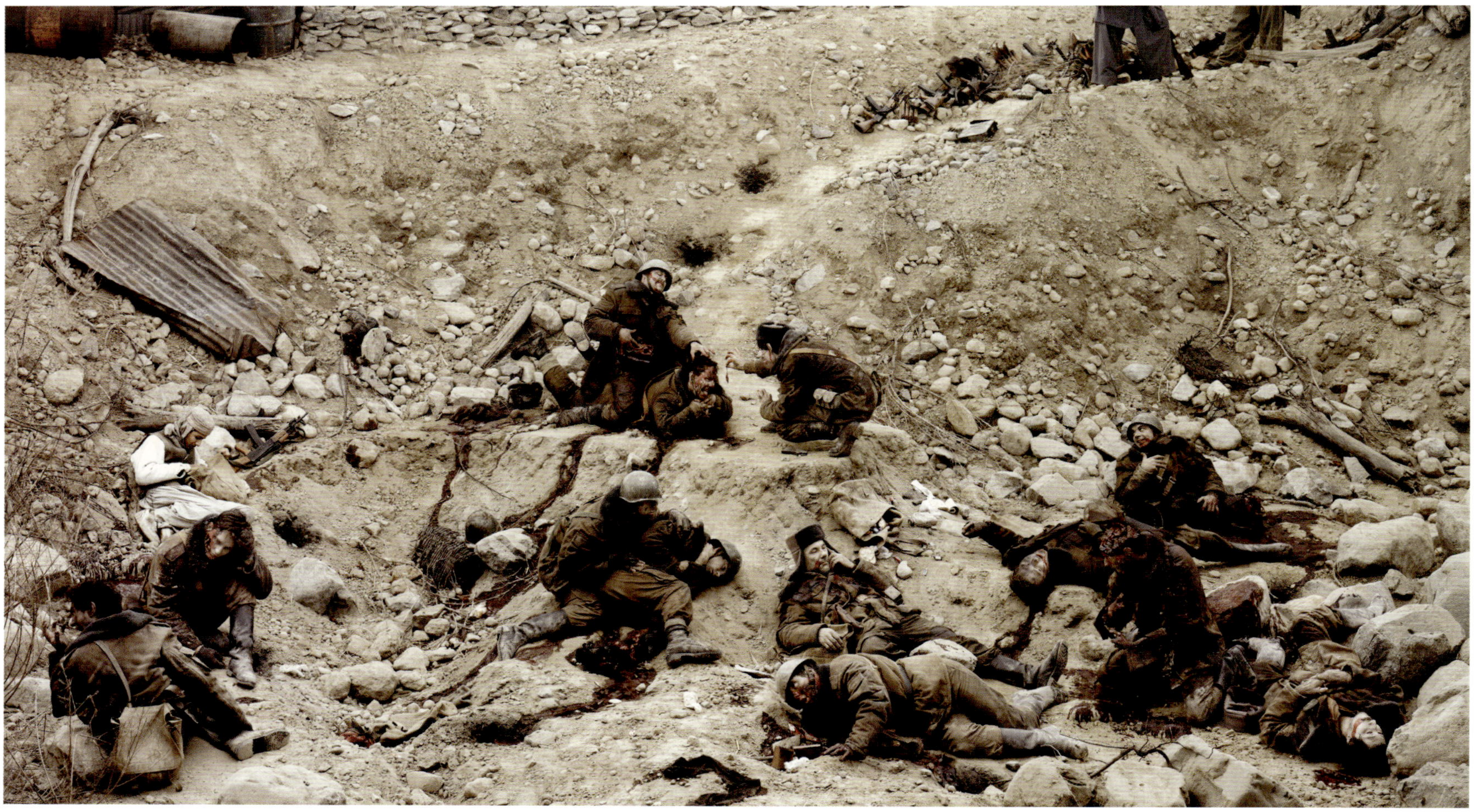

Dead Troops Talk (A Vision After an Ambush of a Red Army Patrol Near Moqor, Afganistan, Winter 1986), 1992
Transparency in lightbox, 90 1/6 x 164 1/6 in (229 x 417 cm)

PETER DOIG

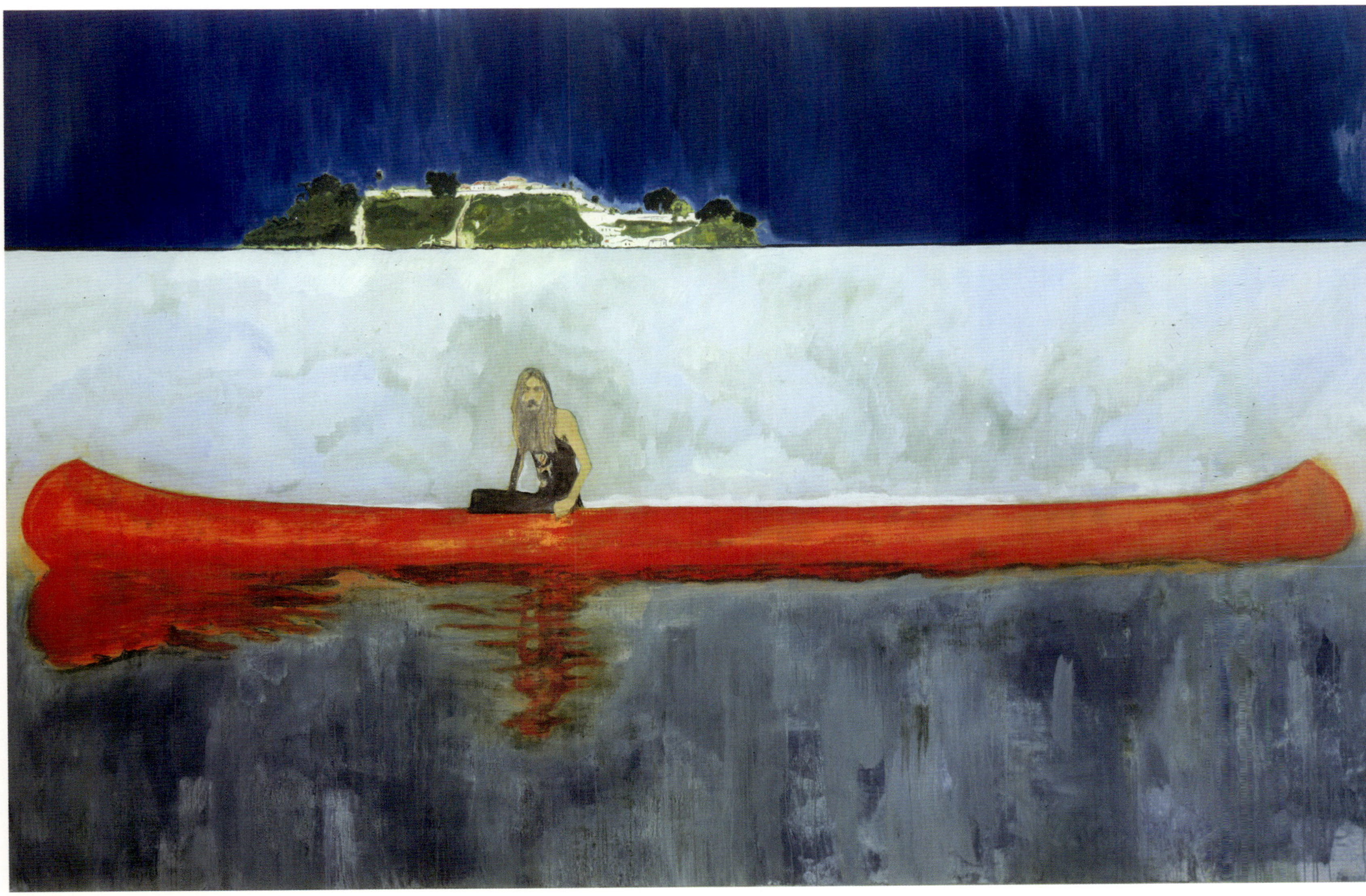

100 Years Ago, 2001
Oil on canvas, 94 1/2 x 141 3/4 in (240 x 360 cm)

JAMES CASEBERE

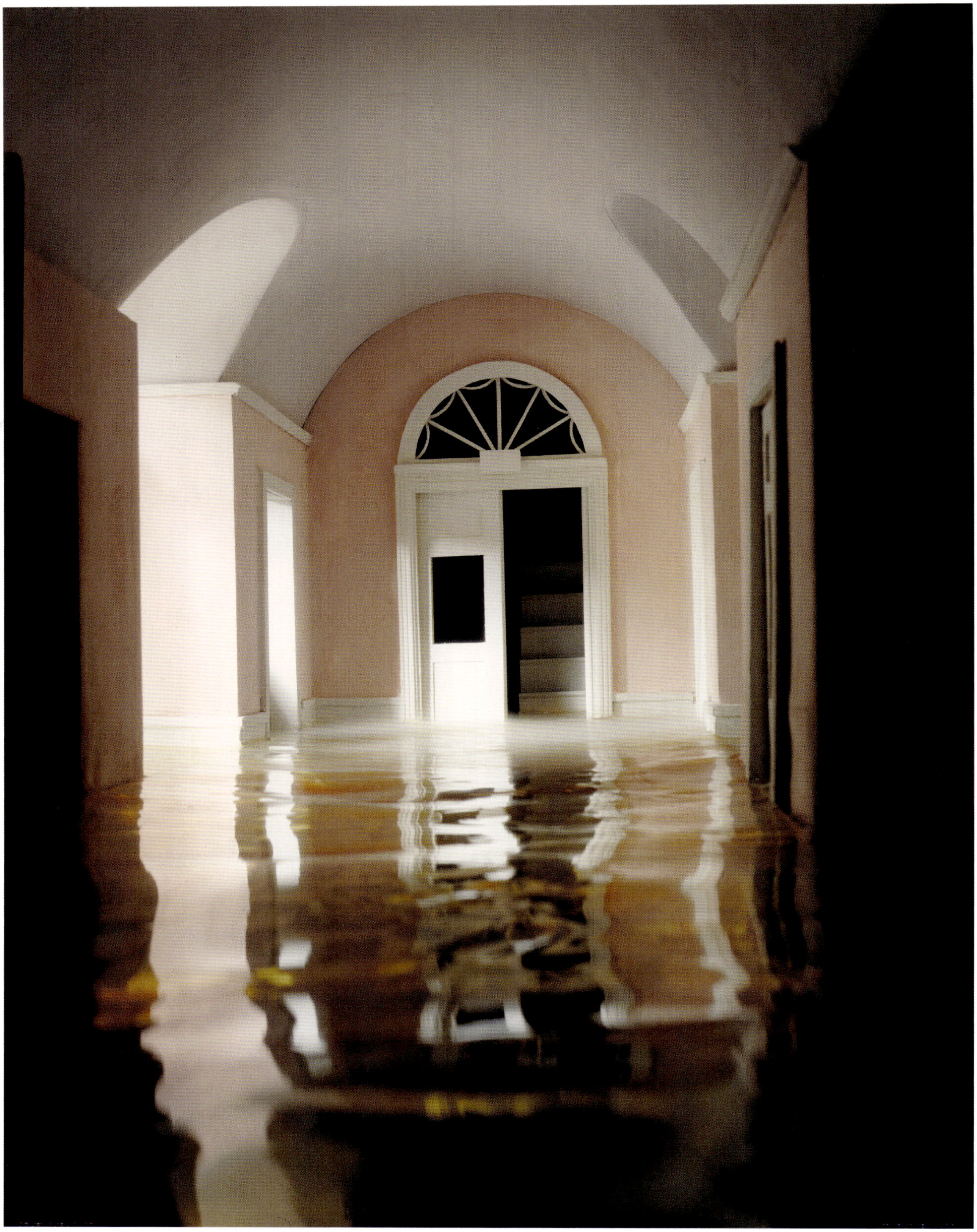

Pink Hallway #3, 2000
Cibachrome mounted on Plexiglas, dimensions variable

photography than Wall. Both create photographs of what appear to be architectural settings or interiors that on close study are clearly models, carefully constructed by the photographer to mimic the appearance of the real thing. Casebere presents photographs of miniature interiors modeled after real spaces. Sewer systems, institutional corridors, empty neoclassical living rooms, stark prisons, and monasteries are lovingly recreated, but there is always something a little off that gives the game away—light spills in from unlikely sources or doors and windows appear in unexpected locations, for example. In one series from 2001, interiors based on real and fictive locales including Thomas Jefferson's Monticello, the indigenous architecture of the Caribbean island of Nevis, and an imagined gallery space are stripped of furniture and flooded with water, suggesting an apocalyptic quality. *Pink Hallway #3*, 2000, shows a flooded corridor of a presitgious prep school in the U.S. Demand's equally desolate scenes frequently begin with found photographs of innocuous looking but historically significant interiors. Using paper and cardboard, he recreates such sites as Hitler's bunker, Jackson Pollock's studio, and Bill Gates's college dorm room. Titles rarely reveal the real-life site, which must be gleaned from gallery handouts or press releases. *Room (Zimmer)*, 1996, for instance, presents a disheveled space that, it turns out, is the hotel room where Scientology founder L. Ron Hubbard wrote *Dianetics*. These scenes are so finely constructed that they are almost convincing when blown up into large-scale color photographs. But again, as in Casebere's photographs, the seams begin to show: as we notice the texture of the paper that makes up the models, photography's ability to convince us that it offers a faithful transcription of the real world is turned against itself, as we simultaneously believe and disbelieve in its power.

Rather than make staged scenes seem real, photographer Philip-Lorca DiCorcia turns "real life" into a series of staged-looking tableaux. Superficially his work appears to belong to the "straight" documentary street photography tradition of Robert Frank or Garry Winogrand, but in fact DiCorcia manipulates lighting to crucial effect. For example, in the series "Streetwork," 1993–97, he shot photos of unknowing passersby on busy city sidewalks. Bright, strangely unnatural lighting, which was achieved by setting off supplemental flashes, highlights city dwellers' uniformly tense expressions and gestures. In another series, "Heads," 2000, DiCorcia zoomed in closer on these anonymous figures to create dramatic individual portraits. Setting up his camera under scaffolding in New York's Times Square, he installed a strobe light that was triggered when anyone stepped onto a certain section of the sidewalk. The flash of the strobe turned the surroundings black, and the unsuspecting subject is captured as if in a staged studio portrait. With such works DiCorcia demonstrates that documentary photography is not at all objective, but is rather a set of conventions that we have learned to read as denoting realism.

The conventions of documentary photography have been the lifelong subject of Bernd and Hilla Becher. For forty years the couple have used photography to explore the topology of vernacular industrial architecture, carefully documenting abandoned and often soon-to-be demolished water towers, smokestacks, blast furnaces, and grain elevators. In *Water Towers*, 1980, for example, they present these images in groups that reveal both similarities and dissimilarities in the subjects' forms. Their use of black-and-white photography, their placement of images in grids, and their concerted effort to minimize details of the edifices' surroundings are all techniques that emphasize documentary neutrality. Yet while the Bechers's work has a veneer

THOMAS DEMAND

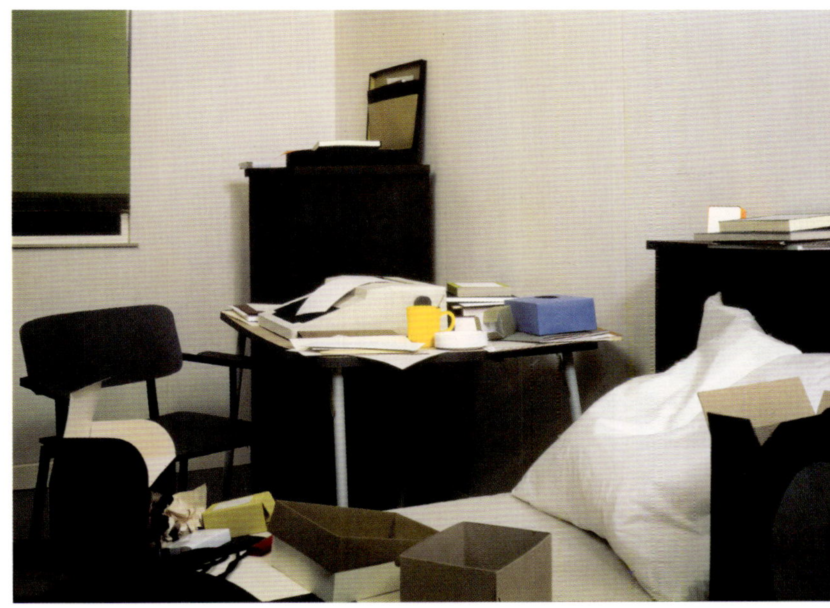

Room (Zimmer), 1996
Chromogenic print on photographic paper and Diasec, 67 3/4 x 91 3/8 in. (172.1 x 232 cm)
The Museum of Modern Art, New York

THOMAS RUFF

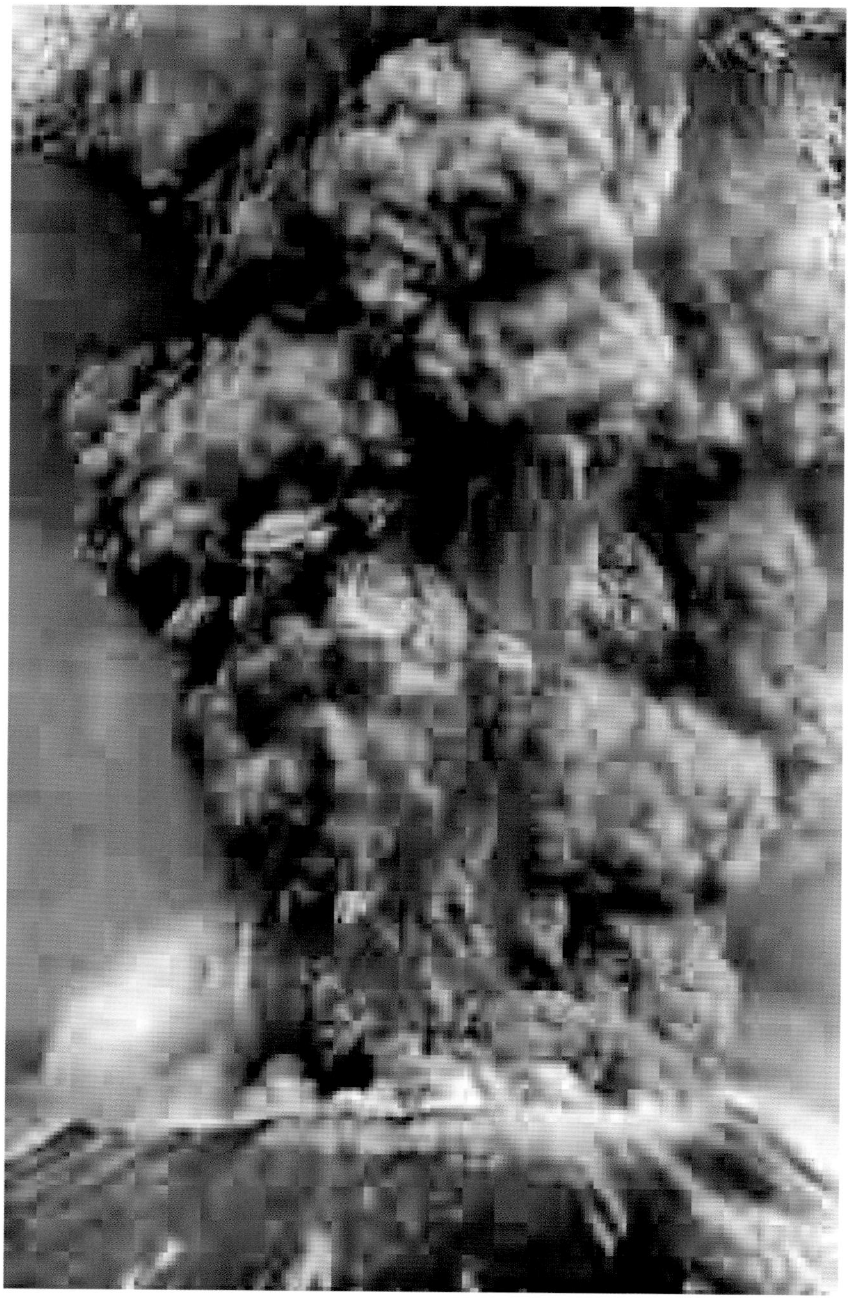

jpeg msh01, 2004
C-print with Diasec, 108 x 74 in (274.3 x 188 cm)

of scientific objectivity, their images exude an almost romantic sense of nostalgia. Their forms are surprisingly beautiful for buildings designed solely with function in mind, and they belong to a vanishing world. But despite these emotional tugs, the Bechers ultimately aim at a kind of objective truth. As Hilla Becher remarked in an interview, "For me, photography is by its very nature free of ideology. Photography with ideology falls to pieces."[5]

As professors since the mid-1970s at the Kunstakademie in Düsseldorf, the Bechers have influenced a whole generation of photographers. Among their former students is Thomas Ruff, for whom realism involves relinquishing all subjective decisions to the machine. Ruff is best known for his monumental color photographs of the expressionless faces of anonymous individuals. He has applied the same dispassionate approach to architectural exteriors and interiors, landscapes, and the night sky. Recently he has moved from pure photography to using digital imagery. Despite the change of approach, Ruff's clinical sensibility persists. One series, "Jpeg," 2004–2005, is composed of a selection of JPEG images culled from the Web to create a lexicon of contemporary history. Images of tourist destinations and disaster sites and reproductions of famous landscape paintings all receive the same treatment: enlarged to monumental scale, they are transformed into pixilated grids. Close up, the images dissolve into near abstraction as areas of shadows and light are broken down into mosaic-like patterns of tiny squares, while from a distance they resolve into a recognizable image. Often, as in *jpeg msh01*, 2004, which is based on a photograph of the eruption of Mount Saint Helens in Washington state, the source images depict natural or manmade disasters, so that the disintegration of the image mirrors the destructiveness of the event.

Like Ruff's, the work of Rineke Dijkstra has a detached, objective sensibility. Her photographs are cool, apparently dispassionate portraits of diverse individuals including matadors, young soldiers, club kids, and young mothers who have just given birth. Dijkstra is probably best known for her photographs of adolescents who stand awkwardly on the beach in their bathing suits and look directly at the camera. In *Kolobrzeg, Poland, July 26, 1992*, 1992, for example, a young girl stands diffidently in a pose that unconsciously mimics that of Botticelli's *Birth of Venus*. The clinical eye of the camera enhances our sense of the subjects' vulnerability, exposing their uncomfortable relationship to their own burgeoning sexuality. Dijkstra also has photographed a number of "continuous subjects," young men or women in life-changing situations whom she returns to periodically over several years. Among these subjects are a teenager serving in the French Foreign Legion, a young Bosnian refugee, and a young woman drafted into the Israeli army. Viewing these deadpan portraits of the same person over time, placed side by side, we see changes in attitude and physical appearance that hint at larger changes within. Here again, the supposed objectivity of photographic representation slides into subjectivity.

Wolfgang Tillmans takes on another familiar photographic genre—the amateur snapshot, deliberately imitating the washed-out color and apparently casual poses of family pictures and holiday snaps. His models have the self-consciousness of people put suddenly and unexpectedly before a camera lens in an intimate moment. In *Jochen taking a bath*, 1997, for instance, a young man is captured in a bathtub, his averted eyes indicating a certain sense of introspection. Tillmans photographs with what seems at times to be an indiscriminate and promiscuous glee. His subjects include nudes and sex scenes, bridges, rivers, night skies, abstract

BERND AND HILLA BECHER

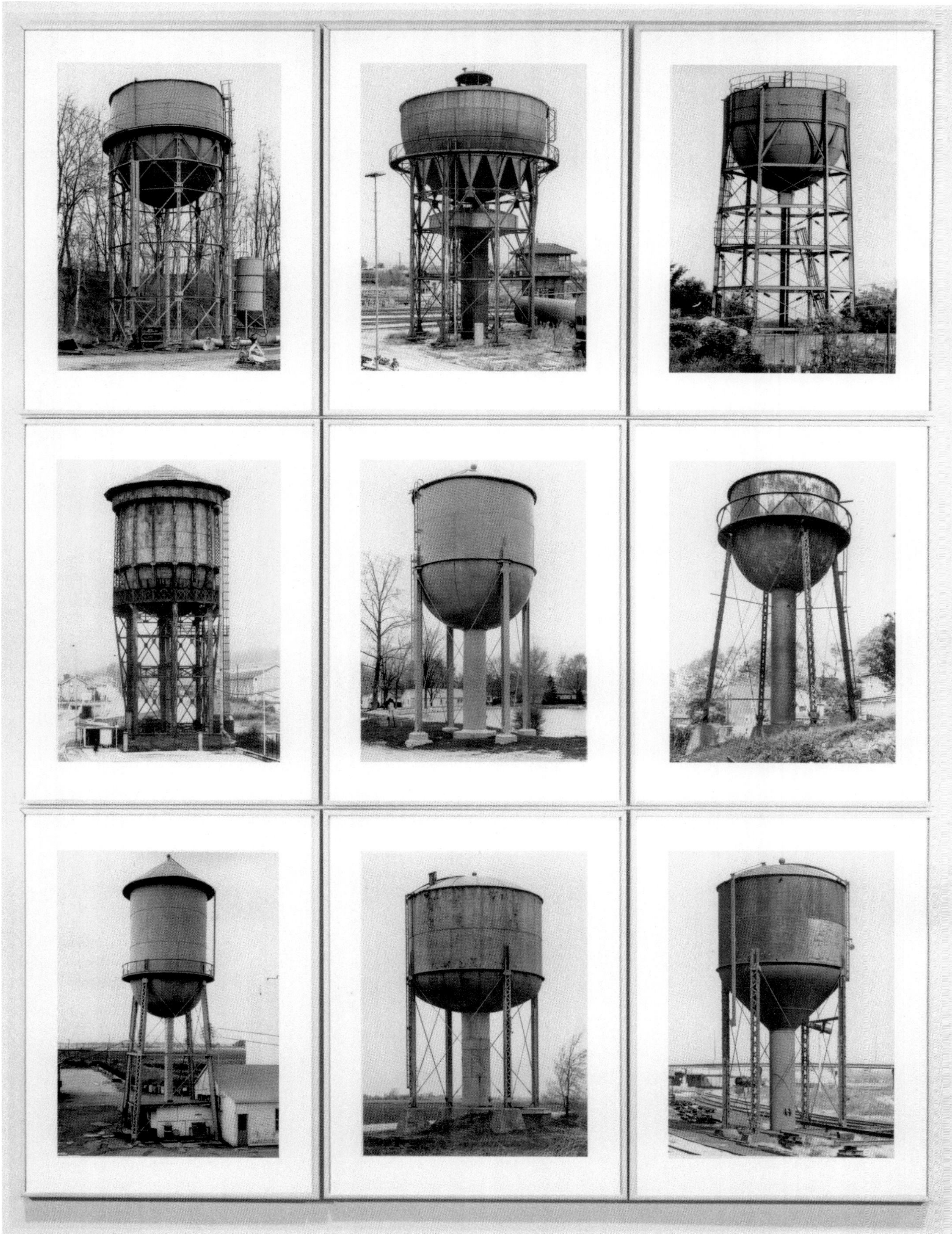

Water Towers, 1980
Black and white photographs mounted on board, 61 7/8 x 49 7/8 in (157.2 x 126.7 cm)
Solomon R. Guggenheim Museum, New York

PHILIP-LORCA DICORCIA

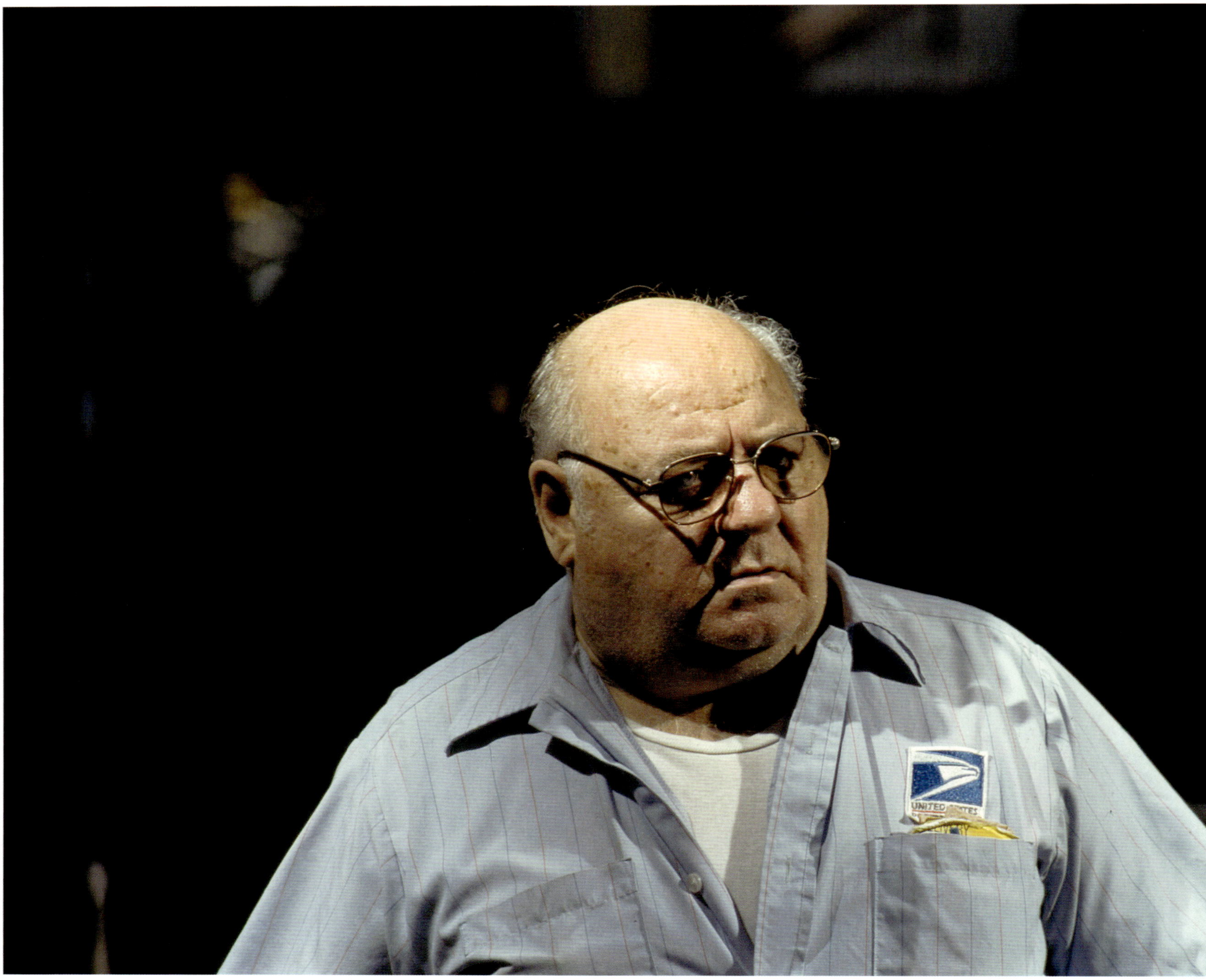

Head #9, 2000
Fujicolor Crystal Archive print paper, 48 x 60 in (121.9 x 152.4 cm)

RINEKE DIJKSTRA

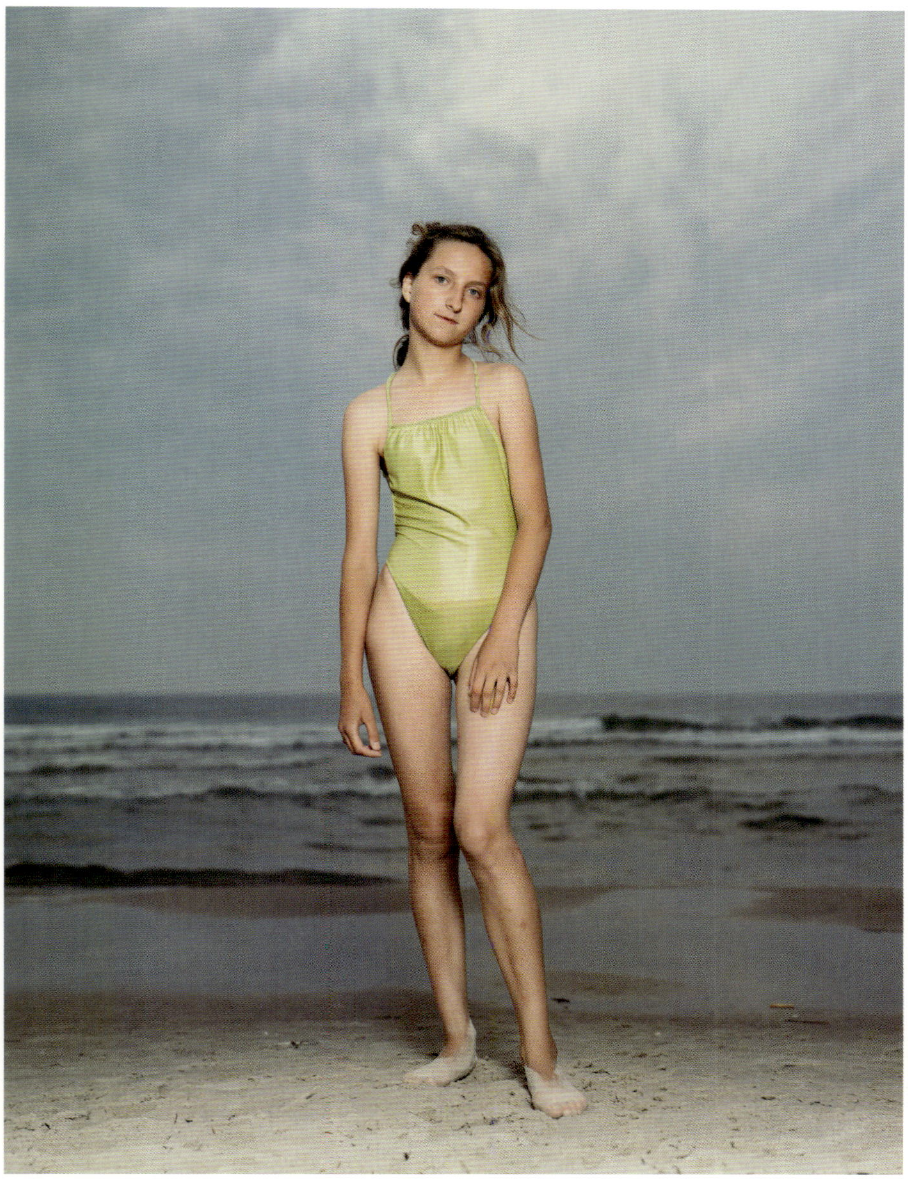

Kolobrzeg, Poland, July 26, 1992, 1992
C-print, 47 5/8 x 39 3/4 in (120.9 x 101 cm)

WOLFGANG TILLMANS

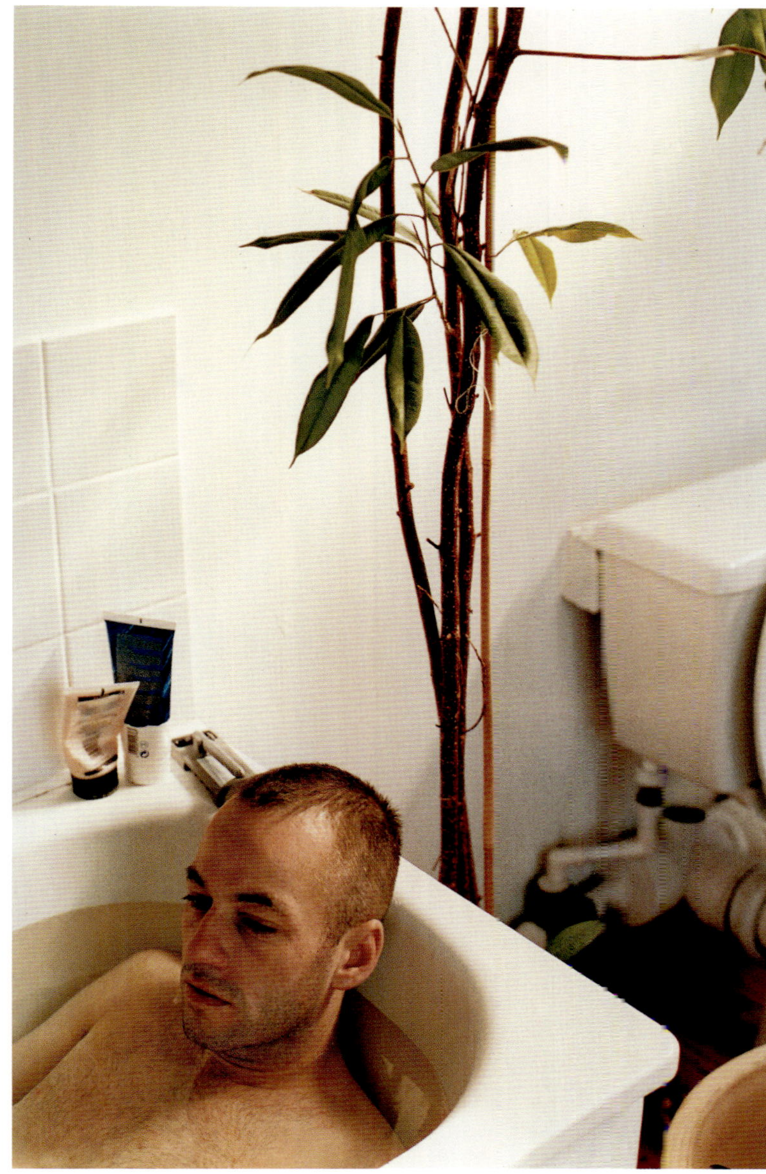

Jochen taking a bath, 1997
C-print, dimensions variable

light effects, celebrities, and nightclubs—a virtual glossary of the contemporary world. Off-handed composition and a deliberate lack of polish are joined by casual display—his photographs are printed in different sizes and tacked to the wall—in an outright denial of the aestheticism of "professional photography." With such unassuming strategies, Tillmans reinvigorates vernacular photography, providing an alternative to the high production values and theatricality frequently associated with art photography—though his romantic vision of life is of course as concocted as any.

The notion that realistic representations are as conditioned and constructed as any other version of the world led Roland Barthes to speculate that naturalism could serve as a cover for political or social ideologies. According to Barthes, myth his word for such false and self-serving constructions—"transforms history into Nature."[6] By this he meant that power relationships and the belief systems that support them can be made to seem part of the natural order and hence unassailable. The job of the artist, he believed, was to undermine these myths by revealing that there was nothing inevitable about the representational systems that sustained them.

This idea has been particularly relevant for artists who grew up under the weight of the Soviet bloc and have wrestled with Socialist Realism, an ideology-driven style or movement that claimed to represent the perfect worker's society. Vitaly Komar and Alexander Melamid grew up in Stalin's Russia and have said that the visual propaganda of that era has become inextricably mixed in their imaginations with their personal nostalgia for childhood. By the time they graduated from art school in the Soviet Union, "de-Stalinization" was in full swing, and the heroic mode of Socialist Realism was already a relic. During their early careers in the Soviet Union in the 1970s, they explored various conceptual strategies in which they commented more or less obliquely on the crumbling authority of the Soviet Empire. In 1977 they emigrated to the United States by way of Israel and found that in their new home they could take on the subject of Soviet propaganda more overtly. The duo gained widespread recognition for paintings that offer convincing imitations of the treacly sentimentality and grandiose heroicism that characterized the official art of the Stalin era, but always include an element of absurdity that is foreign to their models, effectively demolishing the mythology Socialist Realism was designed to promote. In *Double Self-Portrait as Young Pioneers*, 1982–83, a bust of Stalin, lit like a demigod, greets children dressed in Young Pioneer outfits who have the grown-up faces of the artists.

East Germany in the postwar era saw Communism grafted over Fascism, creating an isolated and deeply authoritarian state with its own version of Socialist Realism. But East Germany was also a breeding ground for a remarkable number of artistic rebels who emigrated to West Germany. These artists share a suspicion of authority of any sort. In their hands the politically directed realism of their East German years and the transcendent rhetoric of Western abstraction are equally dubious. Both, they suggest, are mere conventions designed to promote false consciousness and political quietude. Georg Baselitz, for example, emigrated to West Berlin in the mid-'60s and has undermined the conventions of both abstraction and realism simultaneously. His early, broadly brushed expressionist representations of loutish peasant figures in ruined landscapes over time began to fragment, as the figures seemed to tear themselves apart on the canvas. In 1969 Baselitz flipped the canvases upside down, and his figures have remained in this position ever since. A series of paintings of his wife Elke depicts her in various clothed and unclothed poses, apparently defying gravity as she hangs upside down from the top of the canvas, as in *Elke-weiblicher Akt I* (Elke-Female Nude I), 1974. This inversion prevents a literal reading of the image, but the presence of the figure also prevents the paintings from slipping into pure abstraction. Instead, they occupy a tenuous middle ground in which the tension between abstraction and representation is exacerbated by the disorientation of the image, challenging conventional viewing regimes, and metaphorically, ideological ones as well. Literally turned on its head, realism no longer serves as the confirmation of official verities, the purpose to which it was put in Soviet systems.

Sigmar Polke, like Baselitz an East German émigré, also undermines the idea of artistic coherence, by mixing modes of representation. Borrowing images from advertisements, news photos, children's book illustrations, and nineteenth-century engravings, he overlays paintings with Benday Dots (the screen pattern used in commercial printing), magnifies printing mistakes found in newspapers, and subjects his surfaces to chemical reactions by mixing solvents, toxins, and resins. The images Polke appropriates are always compromised in some way, and the intrusion of mechanical means of reproduction into the realm of painting allows him to question the veracity of documentary claims to truth. *Watchtower,* 1984, for instance, centers around an image of the very watchtower that stood at the border of a still-divided Germany. Stenciled over a decorative field of flowers and cross-hatches, it assumes a ghostly presence. Polke's various painterly marks have no more or less authenticity, and in fact are often themselves mechanically created. Despite a certain abstruseness that results from mixing so many systems of meaning, Polke manages to convey a breathtakingly heterogeneous vision of political and social chaos, which may justify the title of his 2003 exhibition at London's Tate Modern: "The History of Everything."

The presence in West Berlin of the rebellious Baselitz, Polke, and Richter (also an East German émigré) had a tremendous influence on younger artists during the 1980s. West Berlin attained legendary status as a center of wild and unrestrained artistic impulses in an era that bridged the twilight years of the Soviet Empire and the post–cold war era that followed the dismantling of the Berlin Wall in 1989. For artists it was a time of tremendous turmoil and freedom. This is reflected in the work of one of the stars of that period, Martin Kippenberger, a native West German who died in 1997 at the age of forty-three. In the spirit of Polke and Richter (as well as Francis Picabia, the flamboyant Surrealist who died in 1959 and was rediscovered and celebrated by younger artists in the 1980s), Kippenberger refused to adopt a specific discipline or to forge a signature style. He worked in a bewildering variety of media, including painting, installation, photography, book art, printmaking, sculpture, and performance.

The threads that run through Kippenberger's work are parody and anarchy. Many of his paintings are self-portraits that adamantly resist the self-mythologizing grandiosity common to that genre. The artist portrayed himself as a dissolute young man, features bloated by alcohol or bandaged after a fight in a night club, as a prematurely middle-aged man half-naked with a flabby torso (in *Untitled*, 1988, his lumpy body is suspended improbably by two balloons), and—when dying of cancer—in a pose borrowed from the dying soldiers in Géricault's 1819 masterpiece *The Raft of the "Medusa."* He also took on subjects that addressed the political and social currents of the twilight of the cold war. *Put your freedom in the corner, save*

VITALY KOMAR & ALEXANDER MELAMID

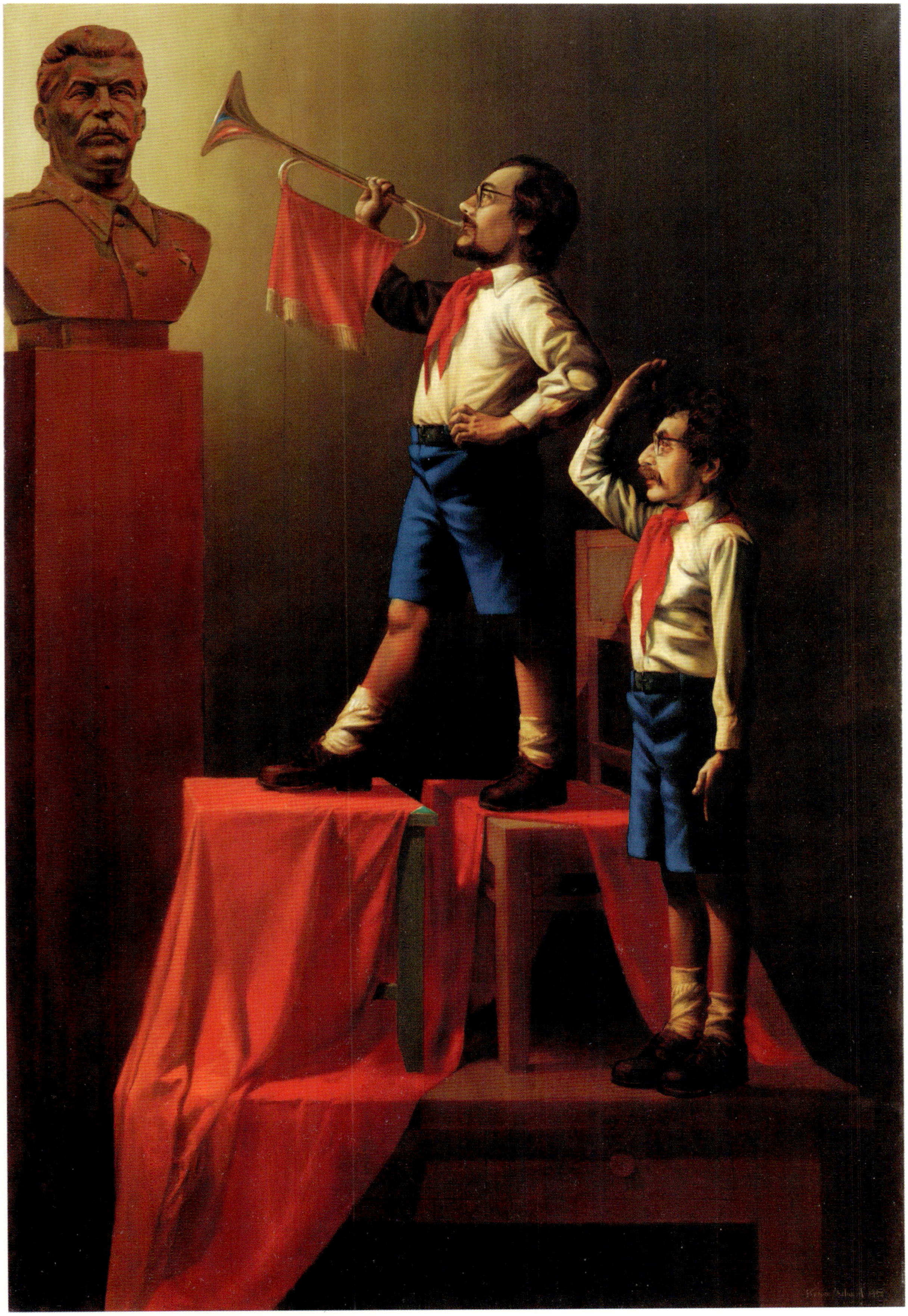

Double Self-Portrait as Young Pioneers, 1982–83
Oil on canvas, 72 x 50 in (182.9 x 127 cm)

SIGMAR POLKE

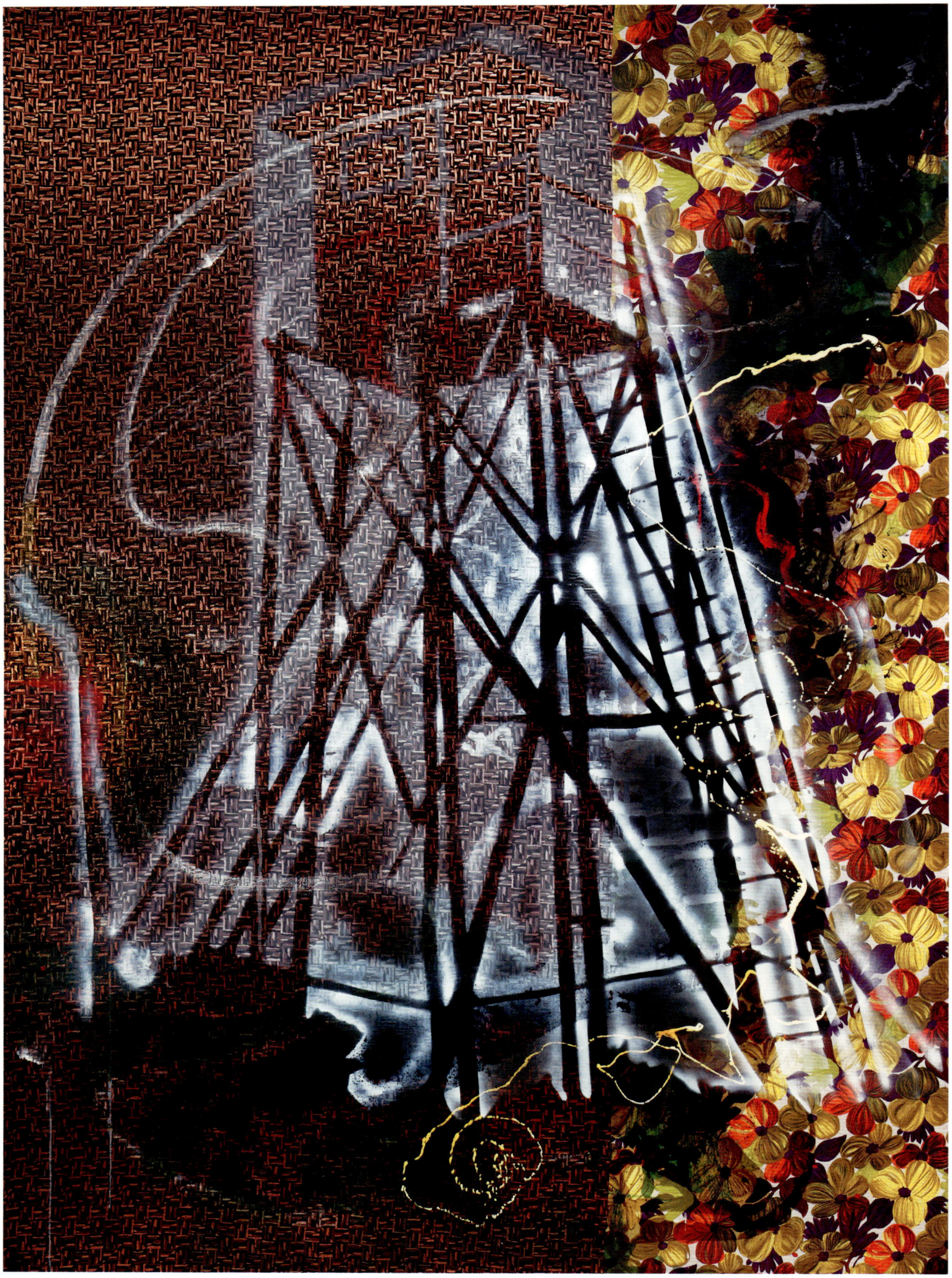

Watchtower, 1984
Synthetic polymer paints and dry pigment on fabric, 118 x 89 in (300 x 226 cm)
The Museum of Modern Art, New York

GEORG BASELITZ

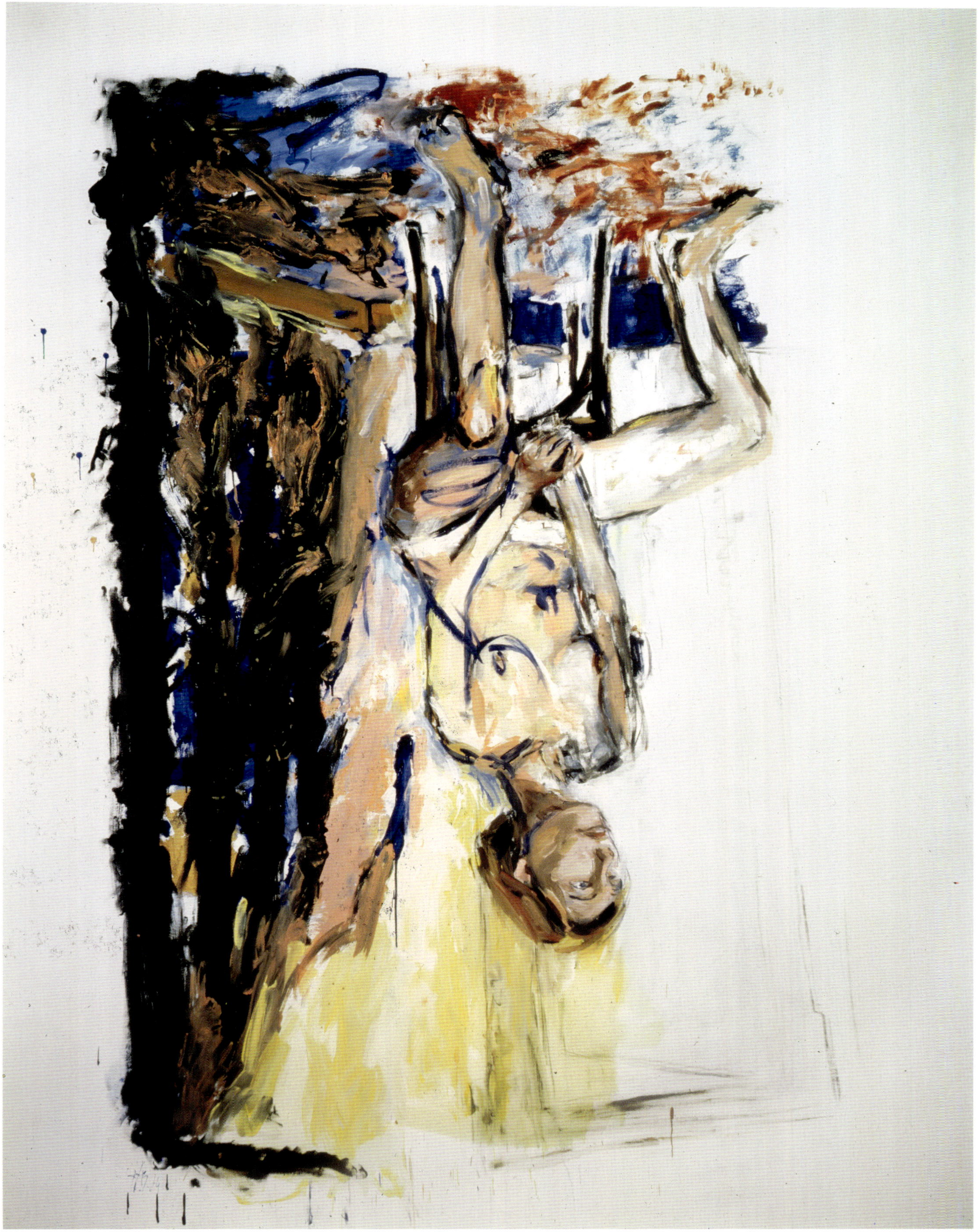

Elke-weiblicher Akt I (Elke-Female Nude I), 1974
Oil on canvas, 98 1/2 x 78 1/2 in (250.2 x 199.5 cm)

MARTIN KIPPENBERGER

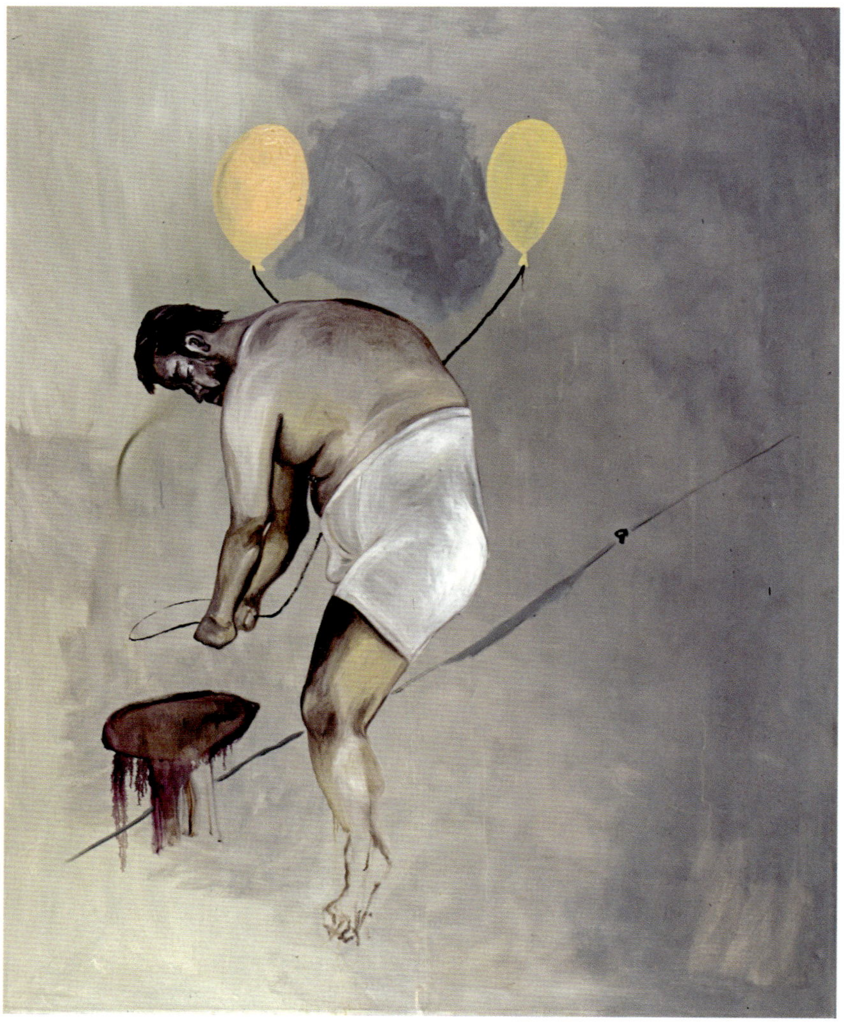

Untitled, 1988
Oil on canvas, 94 1/2 x 78 3/4 in (240 x 200 cm)

NEO RAUCH

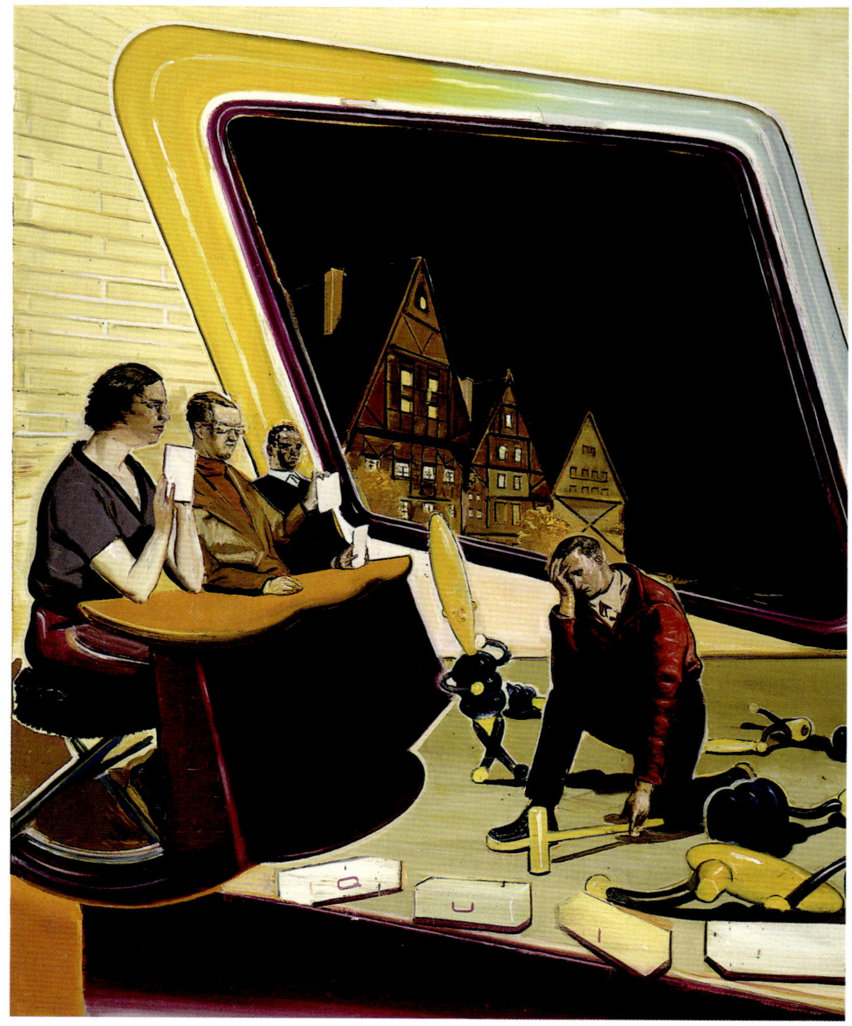

Quiz, 2002
Oil on canvas, 98 3/7 x 82 2/3 in (250 x 210 cm)

HANNE DARBOVEN

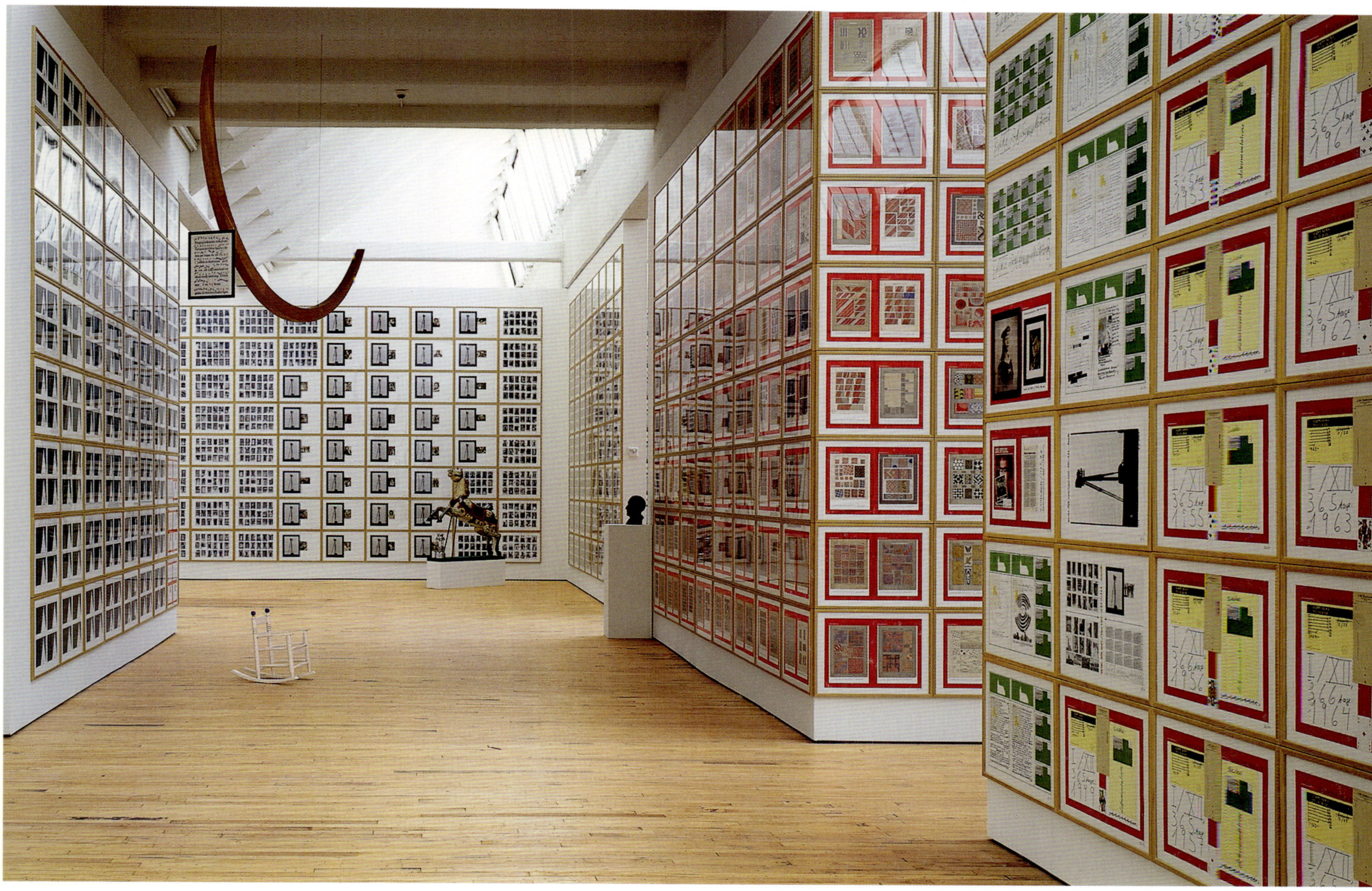

Kulturgeschichte (Cultural History) *1880–1983*, 1980–83
As installed at Dia Center for the Arts, New York, March 1996–June 1997

MATT MULLICAN

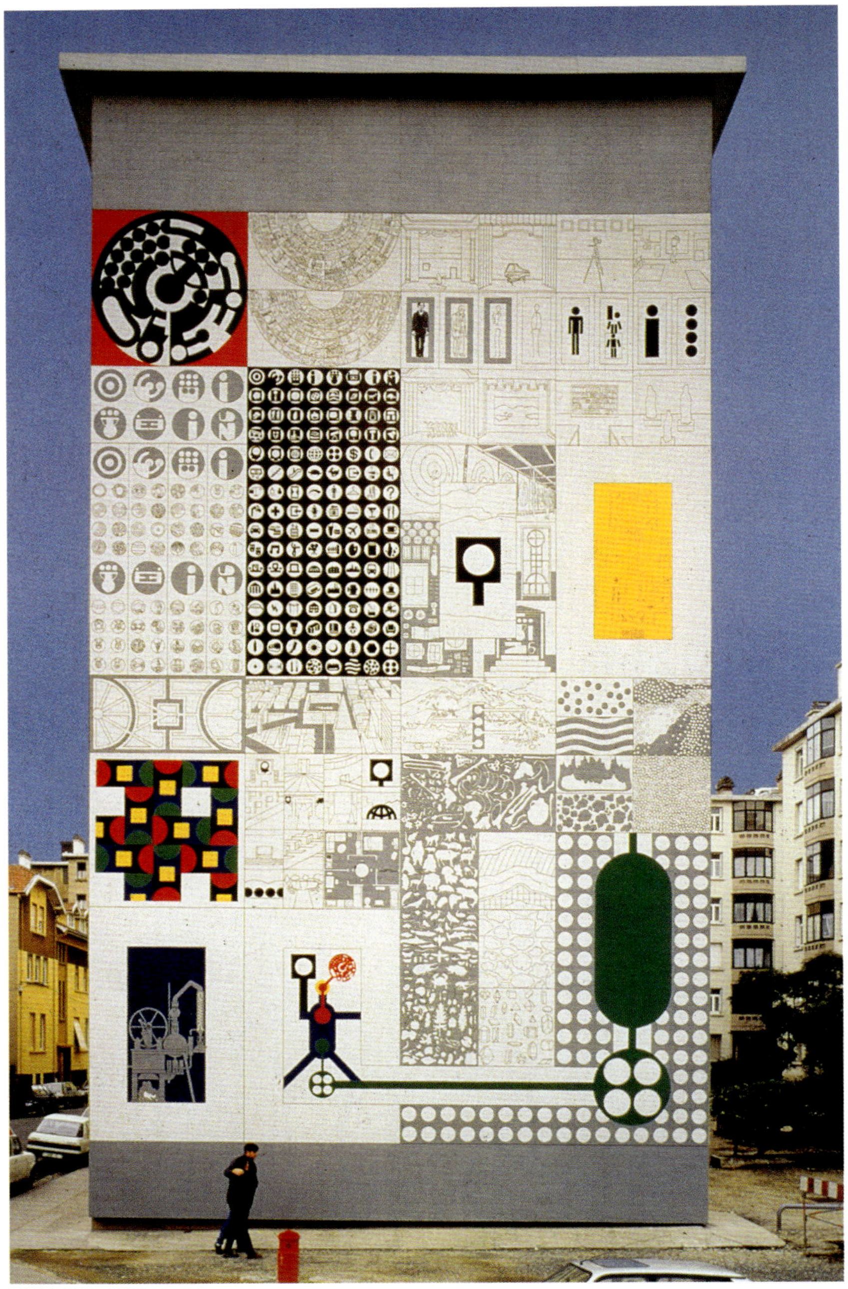

Untitled, 1993–94
Mural at Musée Urbain Tony Garnier, Lyon, France

it for a rainy day, 1990, recreates a section of the Berlin Wall, placed alongside a glued-together ceramic vase, symbolizing the reunification of a shattered Germany. Despite the seriousness of such topics, Kippenberger adopted a trickster stance that never allowed the viewer to be confident in the artist's intent.

Such willful instability is also a feature of a group of artists that emerged in the late 1990s from the city of Leipzig in Saxony. As students at the Leipzig School of Art, whose faculty consisted of practitioners of the official figurative style of the Soviet bloc, they absorbed and transformed the tenets of their training in strange and contradictory ways. The best-known member of this group is painter Neo Rauch. Like his compatriots, Rauch remains an aficionado of the strained figuration of his former teachers, but in his work it appears that Socialist Realism has undergone a strange mutation. His large tableaux, painted with a palette that favors drab hues of brown, green, and rust, suggest an East German version of *The Twilight Zone*, though Rauch has replaced the beleaguered shop girls, secretaries, and low-level corporate flacks of Rod Serling's '60s television classic with the proletarian heroes of Communist-era rhetoric—the school teacher, the butcher, the scientist, the gardener, the hiker, and so on. In *Quiz*, 2002, a group of what appear to be game-show contestants sit behind a desk in a sleek modernist room. Visible through a large window in the room is a row of quaint Bavarian-style houses. At their feet, in a pose which suggests exhaustion or perhaps remorse, is a man with a hammer surrounded by strange cartoon figures that he has apparently been dismantling. The relationships of figures in Rauch's work are unclear, and there is a slightly comic effect to the clueless way they go about their business in spatially and historically incoherent settings.

In the work of these artists we see how far we have come from the idea of art as straight mimesis. These works are figurative, full of images that we can recognize and identify, but the artists use them to reveal how artificial and even deliberately fraudulent these styles of representation can be, especially when adopted in the spirit of bad faith and political deception. Artists such as Close, Muniz, and DiCorcia suggest that all perception is conditioned by arbitrary conventions. In more sinister terms, artists such as Komar and Melamid, Polke, and Rauch point to the way representations can be manipulated toward ideological ends. In their view, powerful institutions, whether governmental or societal, can shape a population's sense of reality through representation. Does that mean that we must abandon all hope of understanding the world as it truly is? For another group of artists, topology, the study of types, offers a way out of this dilemma. In an approach that returns us in a backhanded way to Plato's invisible world of eternal forms and essences, they impose order on the chaotic world of unstable appearances by presenting images and objects that are meaningless outside of larger networks and relationships. Their works often have the quality of maps or charts, in which knowledge comes through an encyclopedic categorizing of things in the world.

This impulse, evident in the monumental photographic archive of the Bechers, as well as in Ruff's jpeg series and Tillmans's collection of everyday images of life, becomes even more wide-ranging in the hands of Hanne Darboven, who collects images, notations, marks, photographs, postcards, and even sculptural objects, then arranges and displays them in groups that suggest their relationships. One of her most comprehensive installations, *Kulturgeschichte* (Cultural History) *1880–1983*, 1980–83, requires an enormous gallery space with walls dividing the displays into distinct sections, each devoted to specific categories of culture. These include photographs of New York doorways circa 1980, film star pinups, art magazine covers devoted to contemporary artists, pages of cursive writing, drawings of textile patterns, and objects including a worn teddy bear, a giant crucifix, and a fake robot. The variety might at first seem encyclopedic. Ultimately, however, this collection of collections has an arbitrary quality, suggesting that any effort to produce an exhaustive representation of anything will ultimately come up short.

Matt Mullican, who has created a complicated lexicon of pictographs representing his effort to encompass at least one version of reality, seems intent on refuting this limitation. Mullican's pictographs are based on the kind of generic, universally understood symbols found in airports, restrooms, or on city street signs. But their apparent simplicity is deceptive. Taken together, they describe a complex cosmology in which one passes through various levels of awareness—of concrete things such as buildings and trees, scientific constructs such as subatomic particles, and on to human abstractions such as value systems, language, myth, science, and history. A color-coded system alludes to the location of each group of symbols in the hierarchy of consciousness, and they are presented in a variety of forms—posters, murals, prints, and online. *Untitled*, 1993–94, a hand-painted wall mural in Lyon, France, for instance, offers a compendium of his symbol system, which takes us visually through the stages, as Mullican sees them, of the evolution of human thought. Mullican's system is remarkably detailed and multilayered, but like Darboven, he hits a wall: even the most carefully constructed system of representation is still just that, a construction that necessarily excludes as much as it includes. His cosmology is finally highly subjective, telling us more about the content of one artist's mind than about the universe outside our heads.

This contingency is evident in another ambitious indexical project, Richter's *Atlas*, a monumental collection of found and artist-generated snapshots, newspaper and magazine clippings, pornographic images, photo-documentation of historical figures and events, and working sketches that the artist has been assembling since 1963. The artist originally envisioned *Atlas* as an archive of the source materials upon which his paintings are based, but as it grew, it became clear that *Atlas* also provides a picture, necessarily subjective and partial, of the period in which they were collected. Assembled without any overriding logic or principle beyond the artist's own interests, this compendium is not comprehensive of anything, yet through its sheer massiveness (over five thousand images and counting), it makes a promise of coherence that it simultaneously denies, reiterating the inescapable fact that any effort to create an objective representation of the world will inevitably fall short. While science and technology continue to operate on the assumption that there is a reality out there that exists independently of human subjectivity, art increasingly takes issue with that idea. In the postmodern era, "reality" has become as mutable as our minds.

GERHARD RICHTER

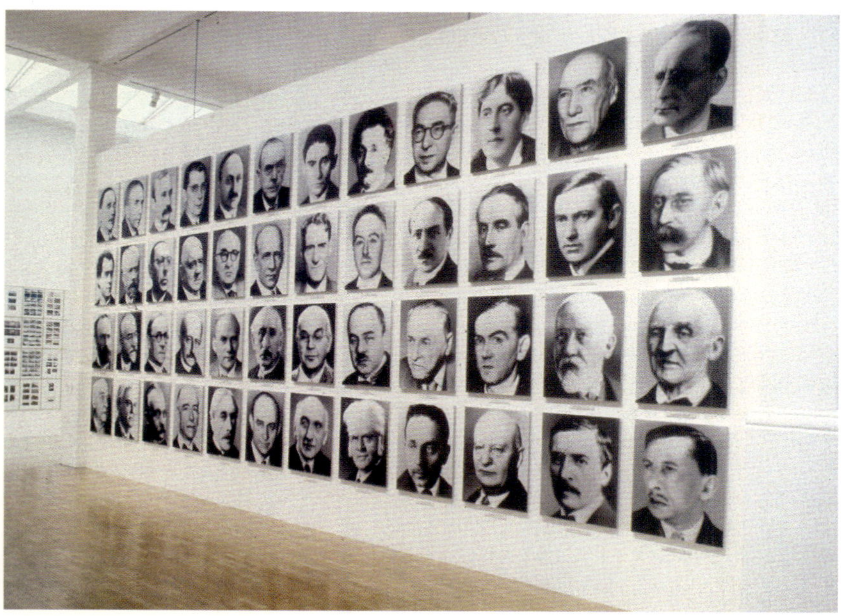

48 Portraits, 1971–72
48 photographs on Baryte paper between Plexiglas and aluminum board
27 1/4 x 21 1/4 in (69 x 54 cm) each
Detail from *Atlas*, as installed at Whitechapel Gallery, London, December 2003–March 2004

ART & NARRATIVE
POSTMODERN STORYTELLING

Historically, narrative has been a highly conspicuous feature of visual art. From the cave paintings of Lascaux and the murals on the walls of Pompeii to the raucous drinking scenes of the Dutch masters and the complicated battle portrayals of Delacroix, paintings have told stories. In the Middle Ages, paintings, stained glass windows, and elaborate sculptural tableaux on the surfaces of cathedrals told some of the most enduring stories of all—from the Bible. Later, during the Renaissance, the representations of religious scenes that had dominated art-making and patronage were accompanied, and at times eclipsed, by painting and sculpture that related the accomplishments of secular patrons. By the seventeenth century, sacred art was all but a side note, as History Painting, a species of visual narration that dealt with religious, mythological, historical, literary, or allegorical subjects, became the premiere genre of art. History Painters, fully endorsed by the academic establishment through the nineteenth century, frequently took on contemporary subjects, but depicted them using trappings, characters, and events borrowed from the classical world in order to give them greater moral or poetic weight.

Artists today continue to engage with narrative, for storytelling will always be a powerful engine for human expression. But contemporary narrative artists feel less compelled than did their History Painting forebears to focus primarily on the most dramatic or "newsworthy" event. Instead, they are free to concentrate on peripheral characters and background details and to follow the lead of great novelists, bearing in mind that the important thing is not so much the tale itself but how it is told. The stories of contemporary artists are extremely diverse in both subject and intent. Like History Painters of old, today's artists may take on grand subjects drawn from history and mythology, even to the extent of creating whole alternate universes. Or they may put a microscope on the intimacies of everyday life. Some narrative paintings and sculptures are instructive or designed to impart moral or ethical judgments. Others offer nothing more than pleasurable diversions like cheery Hollywood movies. In sum, today's narrative artists might create stories out of personal experience, history, past art and literature, popular culture, fantasy, or anything else they might dream up.

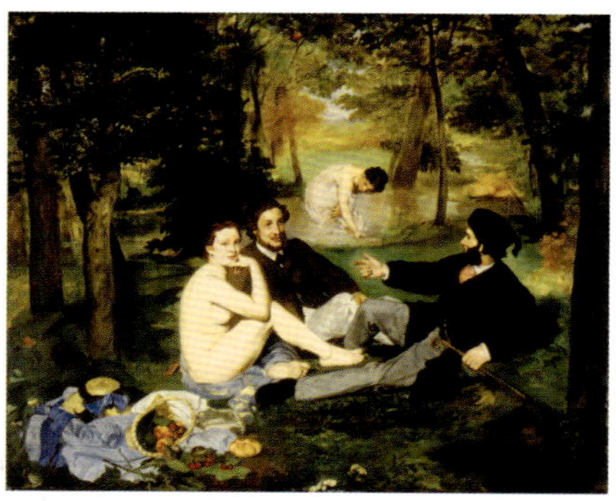

ÉDOUARD MANET
LE DÉJEUNER SUR L'HERBE
(LUNCHEON ON THE GRASS)
1863
OIL ON CANVAS
84 3/4 X 106 1/2 IN (215 X 271 CM)
MUSÉE D'ORSAY, PARIS

Despite its continued popularity, the narrative in art has undergone profound changes over the past century and a half. After holding sway over other genres for several centuries, the status of History Painting began to decline in the nineteenth century. English novelist William Makepeace Thackeray spoke for skeptics when in 1838 he described History Painting in the *London Times* as "pieces of canvas from twelve to thirty feet long, representing for the most part personages who never existed . . . performing actions that never occurred, and dressed in costumes they never could have worn." By the second half of the century, the modernist avant-garde blatantly disposed of pretensions to historical accuracy or reality. The French painter Édouard Manet, for instance, mocked the standards of academic painting by presenting a typical Renaissance pastorale but with a key difference: his 1863 *Le déjeuner sur l'herbe* (Luncheon on the Grass) features a female figure whose bare nakedness among clothed men and direct stare at the viewer make her seem sexually suggestive rather than innocently classical. Before him, in 1855, fellow Frenchman Gustave Courbet created a "real allegory"—*L'atelier du peintre* (The Studio of the Painter)—a self-portrait in the studio that included everyday figures from his life, a slumped figure on a cross, and a nude model, whose presence seems especially discordant, as rather than posing for him, she observes him as he paints a landscape in his studio that, given the four walls around them, can only exist in his imagination. In other words, Courbet pulled back the curtains on the artist's process, revealing how subjective artistic creation really is. The Impressionists diverged even further from so-called reality, suppressing storytelling in favor of attempts to replicate the perceptual experience of natural light and color. Such innovations demoted the storytelling impulse first by revealing its artifice and then by dispensing with it.

In the early twentieth century, the non-objective painting that led the avant-garde was stripped not only of narrative, but of representation altogether. And by the time we get to the mid-twentieth century, narrative was not only benignly neglected, but regarded as a noxious impurity to be purged from all art. Formalists regarded the History Painting tradition as visual art's wrong turn. By telling stories, it attempted to emulate literature, thus denying the essential nature of painting—as a purely optical experience. The notion that paintings should confine themselves solely to matters such as shape, color, and surface held powerful sway over the American art scene in the postwar era, and storytelling was for a time verboten. In the 1970s, with the rise of Pop Art, performance art, and feminist works like Judy Chicago's *The Dinner Party*, 1974–79 (which tells the stories of dozens of real and imaginary women's lives), all the supposedly extraneous narrative stuff that formalists tried to eradicate came rushing back into art, and has remained viable ever since. However, narrative has returned with a postmodern difference. Just as representation in contemporary art is now full of knowing allusions to its own artificiality, so too have artistic narratives become self-conscious, subtly signaling the viewer that the stories they tell may be biased, incomplete, or completely fictional. This tendency toward the elliptical and the inconclusive is not limited to the visual arts. It can also be observed in cinema, where even Hollywood, that bastion of conventional narrative, is occasionally infiltrated by strangely disjunctive films in which time runs backward as well as forward, narrators prove totally unreliable, and normal cause and effect no longer apply. Think of *Pulp Fiction* (1994), in which the scenes are scrambled chronologically, *Eternal Sunshine of the Spotless Mind* (2004), which progresses backward in time to reverse the process by which the protagonist's memory has been erased, or *Fight Club* (1999), in which it is revealed at the end of the movie that the narrator and his antagonist are one and the same.

A number of contemporary theorists have tried to describe this shift in the conception and presentation of narrative. Drawing on film and literature, literary critic Frederic Jameson invokes the idea of pastiche as a governing principle of the postmodern narrative, distinguishing it from old-fashioned parody in its lack of a clear referent. Parody, he argues, is a mocking imitation of an original style that is immediately identifiable. Examples here include Jon Stewart's *The Daily Show*, which is a clear send-up of conventional news programs, or the musical *Spamalot*, which is a take-off on *Camelot*. Pastiche is also an imitation, but its source is less obvious and its purpose less evident. It suggests something that seems familiar but no longer has a living presence in our lives. As an example of pastiche, Jameson cites the *Star Wars* epics, which are based in part on Buck Rogers–type Saturday afternoon serial movies from the 1930s to the '50s that will not be obvious referents for the saga's contemporary audiences but instead convey a generalized nostalgia and longing for a dimly sensed past. A Marxist, Jameson ties the shift from parody to pastiche to the psychological traumas and breakdown of coherence brought on by the economic and social upheavals of the post-industrial, late-capitalist world. Narratives characterized by pastiche are no longer about direct experience or the "real world," they are amalgams of vaguely remembered or misremembered fictions about the past. "In a world in which stylistic innovation is no longer possible, all that is left is to imitate dead styles, to speak through the masks and with the voices of the styles in the imaginary museum," he writes.[1]

Along similar lines, art critic Craig Owens describes the postmodern version of narrative as a form of allegory. In common parlance, allegory describes a work in which characters or events symbolically represent deeper meaning. Owens expands this definition, incorporating the notion of the palimpsest, which allows for infinite layering of meaning and recognizes that symbolic relationships are not simply one-to-one: "In allegorical structure, then, one text is *read through* another, however fragmentary, intermittent or chaotic their relationship may be; the paradigm for the allegorical work is thus the palimpsest."[2] The return of allegory perhaps comes as a surprise: it fell out of fashion in art with the demise of History Painting, whose use of nymphs and goddesses to represent everything from the spirit of the French Revolution to the wonders of electricity suggest how absurd the practice could become. Denounced as inauthentic during the modernist revolution, allegory has now returned as an essential feature of postmodernism. Marcel Duchamp's readymades, Robert Rauschenberg's collages, and Sherrie Levine's appropriations of photographs and modernist paintings are all based on the imposition of new meanings on borrowed images, objects, and narratives. But as Jameson's concept of pastiche suggests, the allegorical work's link to its source has been severed. Emptied of original meanings, Owens's allegory hangs by a thread—the new image or narrative has no direct relationship to the original source.

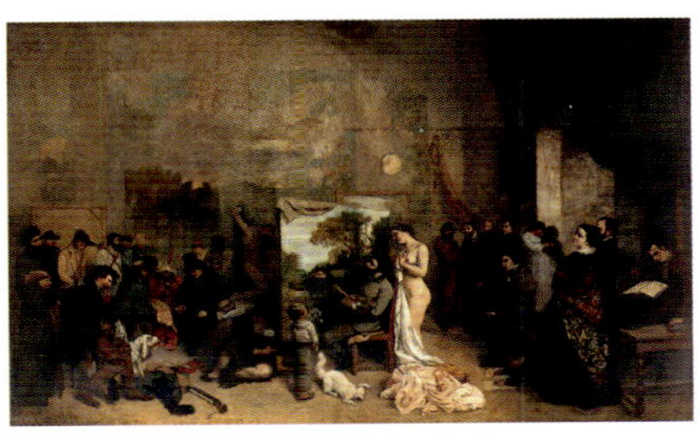

GUSTAVE COURBET
L'ATELIER DU PEINTRE
(THE STUDIO OF THE PAINTER)
1855
OIL ON CANVAS
142 1/4 X 235 5/8 IN (361 X 598 CM)
MUSÉE D'ORSAY, PARIS

For Owens and Jameson, these new developments led to works that are essentially illegible in any traditional sense. While Jameson sees this illegibility as a symptom of social breakdown, Owens's read is more salutary, regarding the postmodern artwork's "contingency, its insufficiency, [and] lack of transcendence"[3] as a bulwark against modernism's mythology of coherence. The French literary critic Roland Barthes, in turn, turns this analysis on its head. Acknowledging the apparent illegibility of the contemporary narrative, he finds a new principle of order by turning not to the creator's intentions or the work's relationship to some concrete reality, but to the actions of its receiver. In a highly influential essay from 1967 titled "The Death of the Author," Barthes takes issue with the conventional notion of an artwork as a repository of stable meanings deposited there by its creator. Instead, he insists, we must replace this idea of the intentional "work" with the concept of the interpretive "text." (He was writing about literature, but his ideas have been widely embraced and incorporated into thinking about contemporary art.) Barthes encourages us to consider the text as a web of ideas, images, and written passages that preexist the author and form the raw material for any new work of art. He describes the text as "a multi-dimensional space in which a variety of writings, none of them original, blend and clash. The text is a tissue of quotations drawn from the innumerable centers of culture."[4] Conceived in this way, no work of art or literature has a real author, if by that we mean a privileged figure who rises above this chaotic mix to create something new. Instead, Barthes suggests, whatever sense of coherence an artwork possesses comes not from the "author" but from the reader who engages with it and activates it. Barthes uses the metaphor of music to make his point, likening the text to a score that the performer brings to life.

These theories and tendencies emerge in the work of a range of contemporary artists who deliberately invoke the narrative tradition while undermining it at the same time. David Salle, for example, borrows from a number of low-brow narrative genres, including soft-core porn magazines, cartoons, advertising, paint-by-number pictures, and needlepoint designs. His paintings recall James Rosenquist's billboard-inspired Pop paintings in their fractured, collage-like compositions that refuse to cohere, and Alex Katz's deadpan portraits and landscapes, with their expressionless faces, flattened perspectives, and mechanical, almost photographic finish. Images are placed alongside or even on top of each other, suggesting, like Barthes, that it is up to the viewer to make sense of their relationships. *Byron's Reference to Wellington*, 1987, for example, is comprised of three distinct images cobbled together on one canvas to make a deliberately disjunctive whole. A brownish horizontal band on top presents a spread of dead fish that might have been borrowed from a Dutch still life; below, on one of two equal-size panels, is a kitschy illustration of a rustic eighteenth-century couple in paint-by-number style; on the other, a grisaille image of a young woman holding what looks like a crown of thorns. Though one might speculate that this is an allegorical story about death, other, more disparate images (a drawing of an ear, outlined tall ships) lay over these, further thwarting any attempt at forming a narrative. In the context of '80s art, such complicating strategies were read as a rejection of notions of artistic authenticity, individuality, and meaning. That Salle's amalgams of disparate images in different styles were are at times painted by different hands (the artist makes no secret of the fact that assistants work on his paintings) put such nihilistic readings in stark relief.

By imitating myriad precedents toward no evident narrative objective, Salle's work clearly illustrates Jameson's principle of pastiche. So does that of Cindy Sherman, an artist best known for creating carefully composed photographic tableaux that draw on such familiar genres as porn centerfolds, fashion photos,

Renaissance portrait painting, and film noir. Posing as the subjects who inhabit these genres, Sherman uses makeup, costumes, props, and prosthetic devices to transform herself into an ever more diverse and bizarre set of characters. She has impersonated femme fatales and wide-eyed career girls, pin-up models, hags, monsters, clowns, and sex dolls. Her photographs deliberately mimic certain genre conventions, but in the manner described by Jameson, there is always something slightly skewed, defamilarized, or incomplete about her imitation. His notion of pastiche is particularly relevant to her "Untitled Film Stills" series. Viewers often feel convinced that they have seen the film on which the photograph is based, but in fact, there is never a specific source. Instead, each of these black-and-white photographs simply mimics the style of European films and B movies of the '50s and '60s. For instance, in one of her many film stills, *Untitled Film Still #15*, 1978, she poses as a young woman in provocative clothing staring pensively out of a tenement window, evoking the familiar scenario of the small town girl forced to trade her virtue for survival in the big city. By the late 1970s, when Sherman was creating these images, such films were already a distant memory, and today they are even hazier.

Sherman's most elaborate excursion into the realm of pastiche can be found in her full-length feature film *Office Killer* (1997). The genre here under deconstruction is the horror flick, with its plot convention of unleashing a crazed killer on photogenic, feckless young people, its gratuitous gore, and its back-to-back thrills. Sherman sets her film in a publishing office. The killer, played by Carol Kane, is a mousy copyeditor who has been demoted to working from home in an office shakeup. She gets her revenge by murdering her co-workers one by one and installing their decaying corpses in her basement, where they become props in her ideal office fantasy. While the film parodies an already parodic genre, it becomes pastiche, freely combining gory elements from slasher films like *Nightmare on Elm Street* (1984) and *Scream* (1996) with depictions of repressed characters gone mad in the manner of *Carrie* (1976) and *Psycho* (1960). Sherman's use of a publishing office as a setting distances her film from the domestic environments of most horror movies. Further, *Office Killer* is self-reflexive: certain vignettes, as when a character played by Molly Ringwald sits pensively on a fire escape, deliberately echo some of Sherman's own photographs. Since Sherman first came to art world attention with a set of faux film stills, her creation of a movie that looks like it could have been the source of her previous works makes her whole enterprise seem marvelously circuitous—and, like other postmodern narratives, anti-chronological.

Sherman is not alone in employing pastiche to create dark and often apocalyptic visions of contemporary life. Gregory Crewdson draws on various genres to tell unsettling fictional tales about modern suburbia. The freeze-frame stillness of dramatic moments in his photographs recalls the History Painting tradition. And his subjects evoke Spielbergian Hollywood tropes in that ordinary people are always unexpectedly swept up by extraordinary forces. In Crewdson's carefully staged images, heavenly shafts of light descend on suburban backyards or burst up through the floorboards of split-level homes. People behave mysteriously. A woman floats Ophelia-like in her living room, which has been flooded and transformed into a reflecting pool. Another crouches on her knees amid a garden that has sprung up inside her house. A set of concentric rings appears in a vacant lot. A bird in a flower garden encounters a severed hand. Strange signs and phenomena

DAVID SALLE

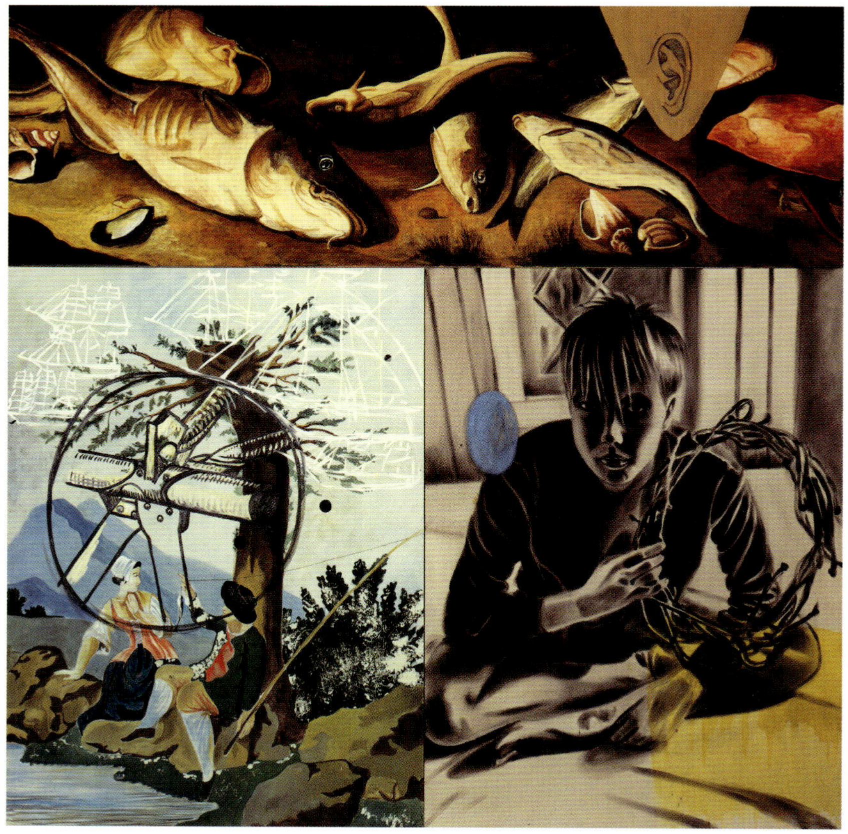

Byron's Reference to Wellington, 1987
Acrylic and oil on canvas, 156 x 126 in (396.2 x 320 cm)

envelop figures who seem numb or drugged. In *Untitled*, 1998, a light beams down out of the night sky to transfix a boy standing on a littered lawn, a six-pack of beer in his hand. Clearly, something creepy lurks within those neat ranch houses with tidy yards. We can't tell if these are dreams, fantasies, or apparitions, but they are so detailed that they become convincing photographic records of impossible events. They never explain themselves, but somehow read as outward expressions of an inner sense of anomie.

While Crewdson's reflections of a terrifying contemporary world are based in the present, Eleanor Antin revisits historic cataclysms and injustices to provide an allegorical reading of the present through the past. Since the early 1970s, Antin has been telling stories in films, photographs, and performances in which she assumes various fictional roles, among them an aging black ballerina named Eleanora Antinova, who worked with Sergei Diaghalev in the 1920s, and Eleanor Nightingale, an incarnation of the famous nurse, who discovers that patching up men to send them back to battle does nothing to solve the problem of war. Antin's 2001 series "The Last Days of Pompeii" tells the story of the decline and fall of ancient Rome in large-scale, lush photographs filled with costumed actors and clichéd props that suggest a Hollywood fantasy, costume dramas, and the absurdly overwrought depictions of Roman decadence in nineteenth-century History Paintings. Theatrical poses and symbolic details—a plate of half-eaten pomegranates signifying lust, a swaddled skull hinting at impending mortality—help tell the story. One image in the series, *The Golden Death*, presents a mountain of gold coins under which a group of inebriated aristocrats lie, apparently asphyxiated by their greed. The series as a whole progresses from scenes of insouciant hedonism to the expected tragic end, in which actors lie dead or dying among a welter of broken columns. While historically specific, "The Last Days of Pompeii" is so over the top that it is clearly not real history. Rather, it represents symbolically the unhappy fate of indulgent, self-absorbed societies that ignore warnings of imminent catastrophe.

Anna Gaskell's staged photographs share this sense of foreboding and anxiety, but conjure up a more private, psychosexual world. Gaskell, like the British magic realist painter Paula Rego, takes her inspiration from children's stories such as Lewis Carroll's *Alice in Wonderland* and Rudolf Erich Raspe's *The Surprising Adventures of Baron Munchausen*. Rather than restage these parables of female coming of age, Gaskell merely uses them as reference for isolated frames that tell a new, partial, inconclusive tale. In a 1996–97 series of photographs derived from *Alice in Wonderland* called "Wonder," adolescent girls dressed in blue pinafores find themselves confronted with both specific and abstract dangers, some of which seem to be purely mental, while others take the form of other children who tear at our protagonist's hair or loom over her supine body. Some of these images feature identically dressed twins suggestive of a split psyche, as the character cavorts suggestively, fights with, and in one image, resuscitates herself. Strange lighting, severe cropping, and claustrophobic spaces darken the relative air of innocence associated with the original tale.

Drawing freely on art history, film, and literature, the photographs of Crewdson, Antin, and Gaskell often offer too many or too few clues indicative of what's going on, exacerbating a sense of incoherence. They also emphasize their stories' incompleteness simply by virtue of being still, stop-action images. The viewer is thus left to attempt to fill in the story, to imagine what happened before each frame, and

CINDY SHERMAN

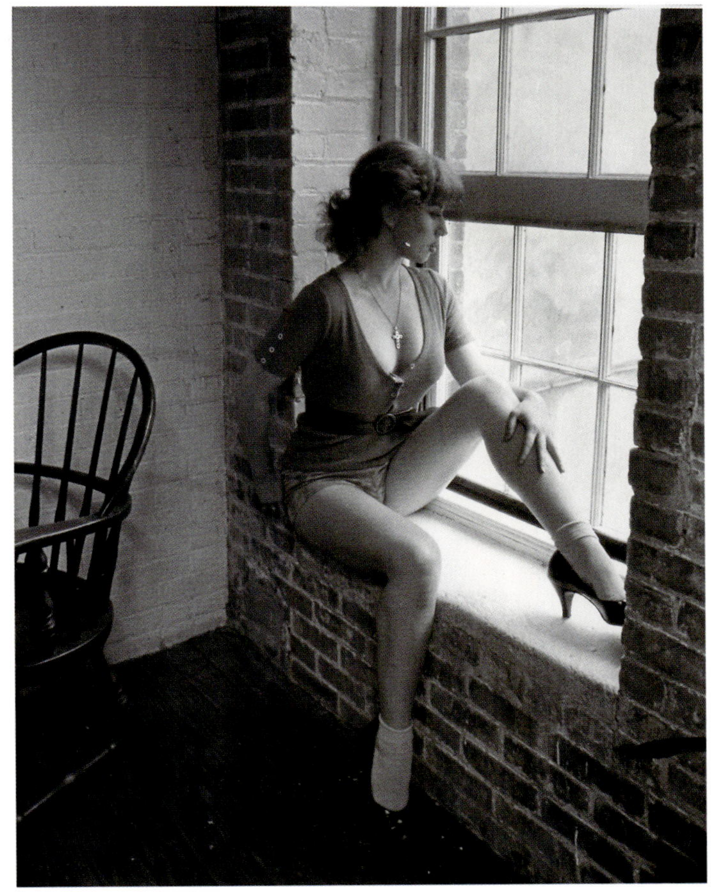

Untitled Film Still #15, 1978
Black and white photograph, 10 x 8 in (25.4 x 20.3 cm)

CINDY SHERMAN

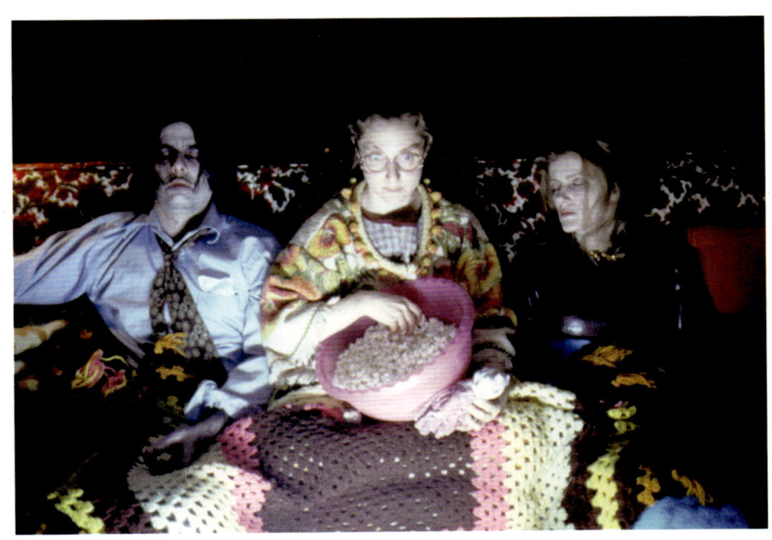

Office Killer, 1997
35mm film, 80 minutes 6 seconds

ELEANOR ANTIN

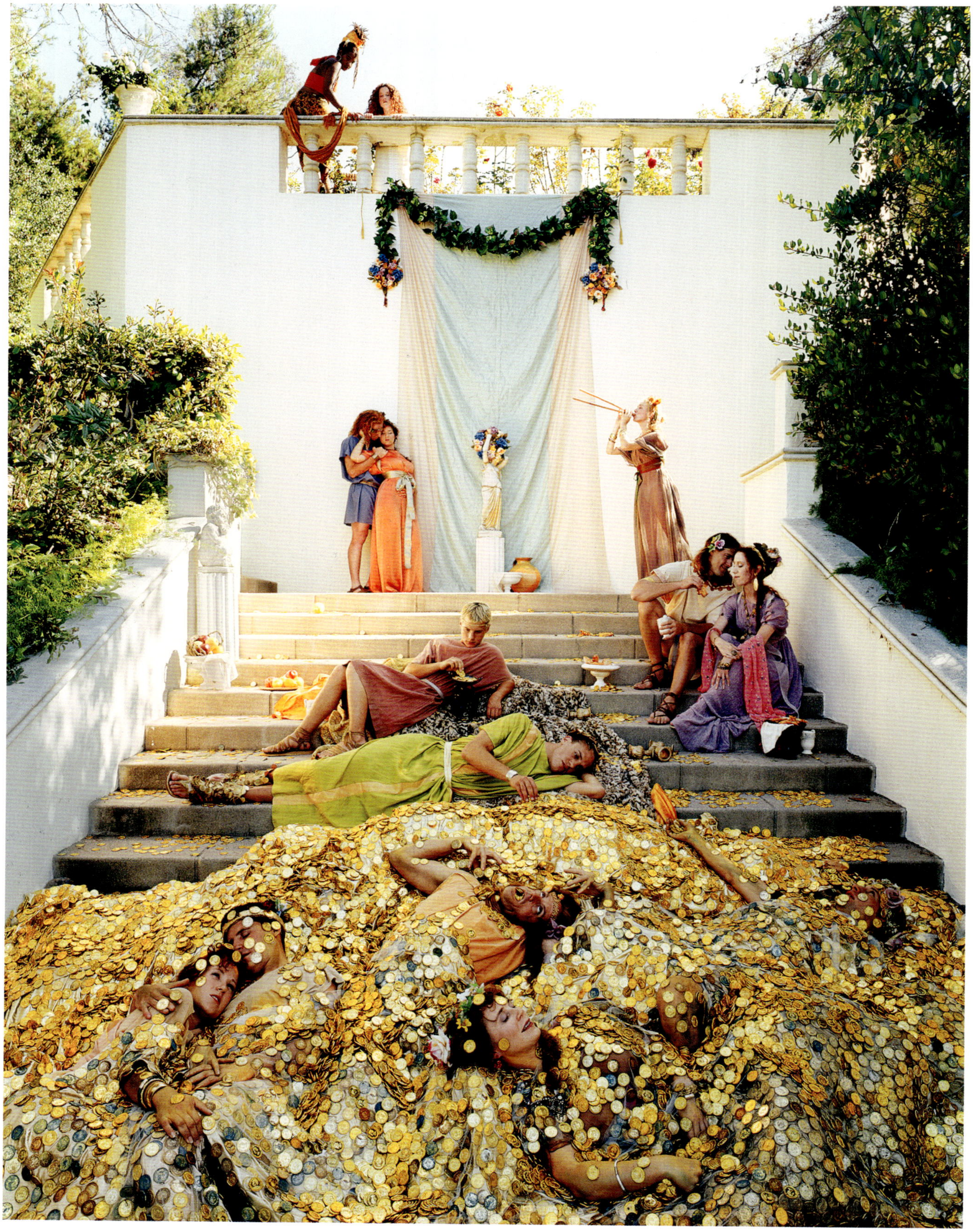

The Golden Death, from "The Last Days of Pompeii," 2001
C-print, 58 5/8 x 46 5/8 in (149 x 118.4 cm)

what might happen next. Postmodern storytellers who employ video and film, on the other hand, have the narrative tropes of time and continuity on their side, which only prompts them to use other means to fracture and fragment their narratives. Like practitioners of photographic pastiche, they often start with one or more particular genres—say, the horror movie, the Western, or the adventure film—then shuffle those genres' codes in ways that undermine the expected outcome.

One master of this approach is Isaac Julien, whose work addresses themes reflecting his life as a black gay man—what might be described as a kind of "double otherness." Julien creates disjointed, dream-like film narratives that mix documentary and fictional scenes, incorporate poetry, quotations, and multiple voices, and reference familiar Hollywood movies and genres. Often the artist projects his films on multiple screens, creating a rhythmic interplay as images and characters interact in various ways—at times flowing across several screens at once, at others separating or doubling to offer an almost cubistic sense of narrative progress. Rather than provide the clear narrative line that is the hallmark of popular film, Julien's stories are open-ended and ambiguous, allowing for multiple interpretations. For example, his 1999 film *The Long Road to Mazatlan* subverts the Western's sexual codes and clear distinctions between heroes and villains. The film centers on a pair of cowboys, one dressed in black and the other in white, who become involved in a dance of desire against a backdrop of desert landscapes and dusty Texas towns. In the course of the film there are references to such iconic works as Andy Warhol's 1968 film *Lonesome Cowboys*, 1968, David Hockney's paintings of swimmers and pools from the 1960s, and the famous "Are you talking to me?" scene from Martin Scorsese's 1976 film *Taxi Driver*.

Matthew Barney, who makes epic films and installations often consisting of props from the films, takes a far more idiosyncratic and enigmatic approach to storytelling. Barney's magnum opus is the seven-hour, five-part series *The Cremaster Cycle*, 1994–2002. The film's title refers to the muscle that raises and lowers the testicles. (When the testicles are raised in an embryo, the sexes are undifferentiated, and as such the film has been interpreted as a meditation on gender differentiation and, more generally, transformation.) Though each segment resembles a feature film both in length and visual polish, there are significant differences between *Cremaster* and what you see at the local multiplex. First, it is filled with outlandish characters and creatures that cross both gender and species lines. There is a cheetah-woman played by a beautiful amputee fitted with glass legs, a tap-dancing satyr, a bagpipe-playing Scot, a re-imagined Harry Houdini (played by Norman Mailer), and a tragic queen (played by Ursula Andress). The five parts make reference to everything from Busby Berkeley musicals and punk rock to obscure Masonic rituals and Gary Gilmore. The whole opus contains only twelve lines of dialogue, and the pace is also very different from standard Hollywood fare. Individual sequences are often drawn out to the point of tedium. One very long scene depicts a demolition derby inside the Chrysler Building in New York City, another an extended performance by Rockettes look-alikes on an Idaho football field. The film is full of dense symbolism and references to arcane legends, opera, popular culture, sports, Hollywood movies, and art films, a mix that makes for a highly ambitious and ambiguous narrative. At screenings of the whole cycle, audiences are often given crib sheets, which are only marginally helpful in deciphering meaning. That the films were produced and released out of order (4, 1, 5, 2, 3) only adds to the confusion.

GREGORY CREWDSON

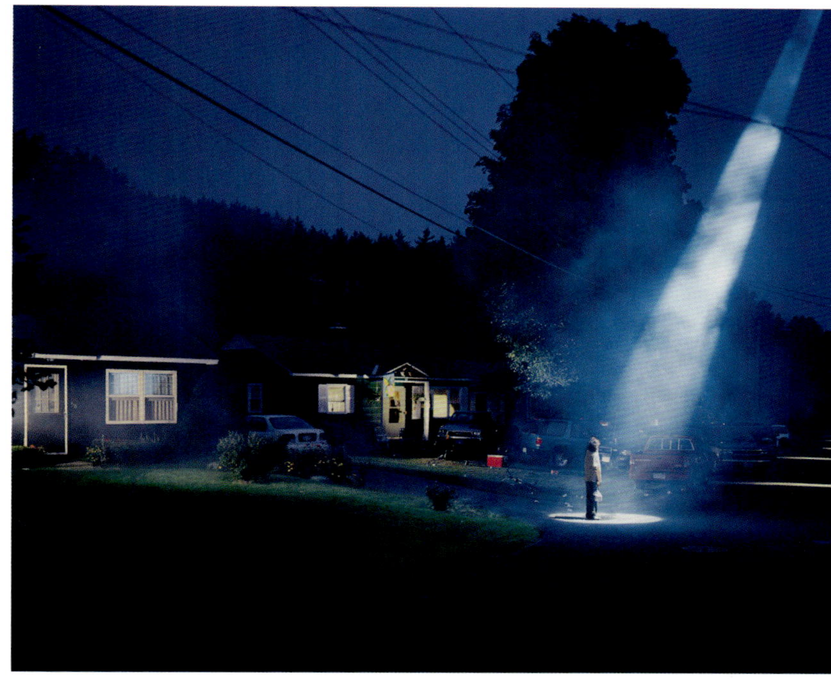

Untitled, 1998
Digital C-print, 50 x 60 in (127 x 152.4 cm)

ISAAC JULIEN

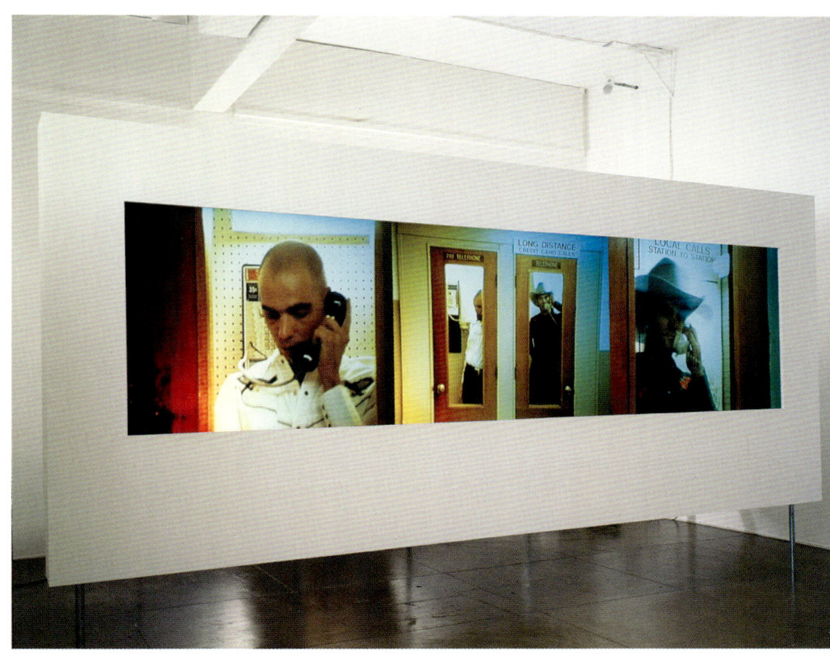

The Long Road to Mazatlan, 1999
Triple-screen rear-projection 16 mm sepia/color film, video transfer, sound, 20 minutes

MATTHEW BARNEY

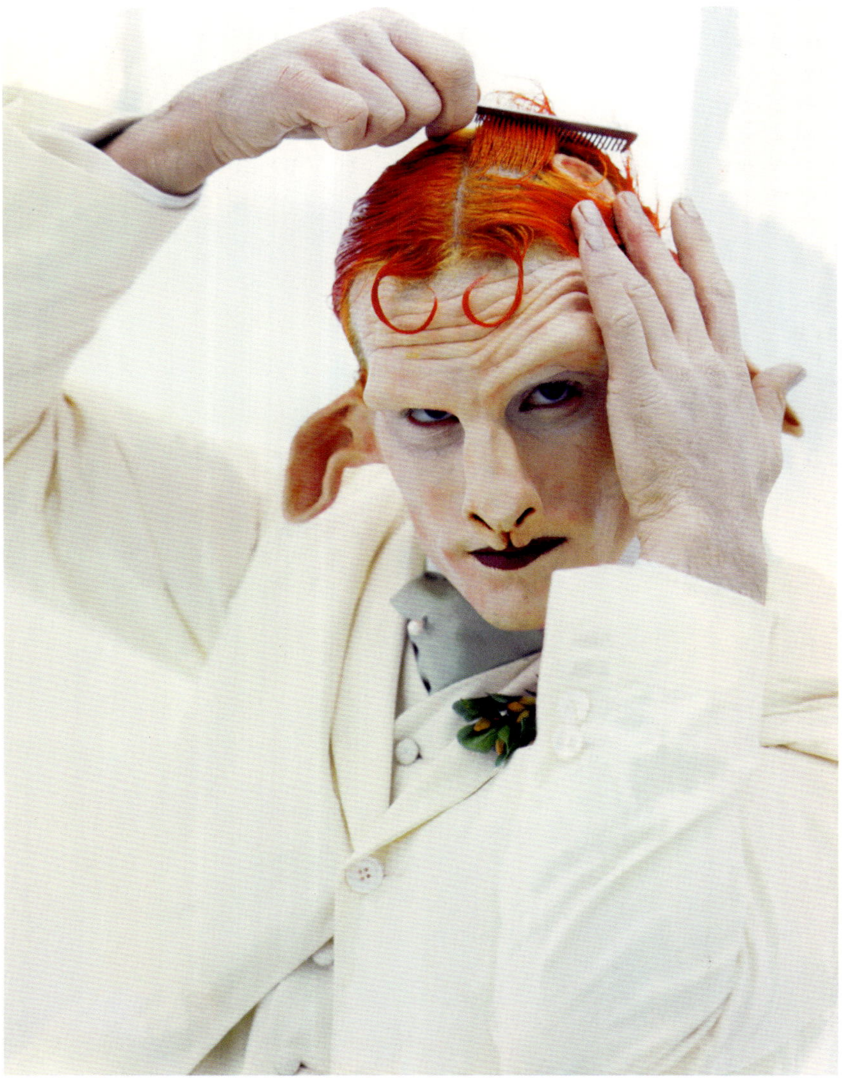

CREMASTER 4, 1994
Production still

In the end, *Cremaster* is a best taken as a surreal, poetic dream that seems to have something to do with the bending of gender, sexual liberation, and death.

Working at the opposite end of the time scale, Rodney Graham creates short, looped videos that simultaneously evoke and confound the conventions of film narrative. In these "circular featurettes," as Graham calls them, very little happens, and the end of the story blends more or less seamlessly into the beginning. His sources are sometimes musical, and often literary. For instance, *Vexation Island*, 1997, draws on Daniel Defoe's early eighteenth-century novel *Robinson Crusoe*. That book initiated the venerable convention of the shipwreck narrative, in which a modern individual is cast ashore in some island paradise and must relearn the most basic tasks of subsistence, or die. A fantasy of escape from civilization, the genre lives on in such contemporary forms as the Tom Hanks film *Cast Away* (2002) and the reality-TV show *Survivor*. Graham's lushly filmed version is only nine minutes long and presents only a peripheral incident in the Defoe book. A figure dressed like an eighteenth-century pirate lies prone on the beach, presumably shipwrecked. He awakens and is joined by a noisy parrot, which draws his attention to a coconut in a palm tree above. The man shakes the tree, causing the coconut to drop on his head, whereby he passes out again, thus returning to the state in which we first encountered him. Literally elliptical, Graham's version of the shipwreck story suggests not triumph over self and outside obstacles, but the futility of imagining escape.

Even more indeterminate are the film narratives of Aernout Mik. Projecting onto multiple screens and repeating certain sequences, he plays off the genre of television news journalism, presenting scenes of turmoil or disaster of the sort that frequently find their way to the nightly news. But instead of transmitting easily digestible facts and morals, Mik deliberately thwarts our expectations, providing no explanation for the chaos surrounding his characters, no climax in the action, and no emotional payoff. Further, he complicates what information he does provide. In *Refraction*, 2005, footage of the aftermath of a highway bus accident outside an unnamed European city is projected on three screens. At first it all looks very familiar—police and medics wandering about, the pile-up of cars and stalled motorists, some of whom have gotten out of their vehicles to peruse the wreckage. In time it becomes clear that something is missing, though, namely the victims or their physical remains, along with any evidence of another vehicle that might have been involved in the crash. When a shepherd and flock of sheep enter the scene, crossing the road and grazing amid relief workers who seem completely unaware of the interruption, we know we're watching a staged, imagined event. Though *Refraction* has all the earmarks of an objective news report of an accident scene, it reminds us that even an "eyewitness" account can be false.

Pierre Huyghe also withholds the emotional satisfaction audiences have come to expect, though in his case, from the movies. Huyghe's most compelling reinscription of a well-known film is his video *The Third Memory*, 1999. Here the same story—of a Brooklyn bank robbery gone wrong in 1972—is told three times: in archival television footage from the actual event, in a fictionalized film, and as enthusiastically recounted almost thirty years after the fact by one of the protagonists. Because the robbers took hostages and engaged in an eight-hour stand-off with police, the actual event was broadcast live on national television, interrupting coverage of Richard Nixon's nomination at the Republican

ANNA GASKELL

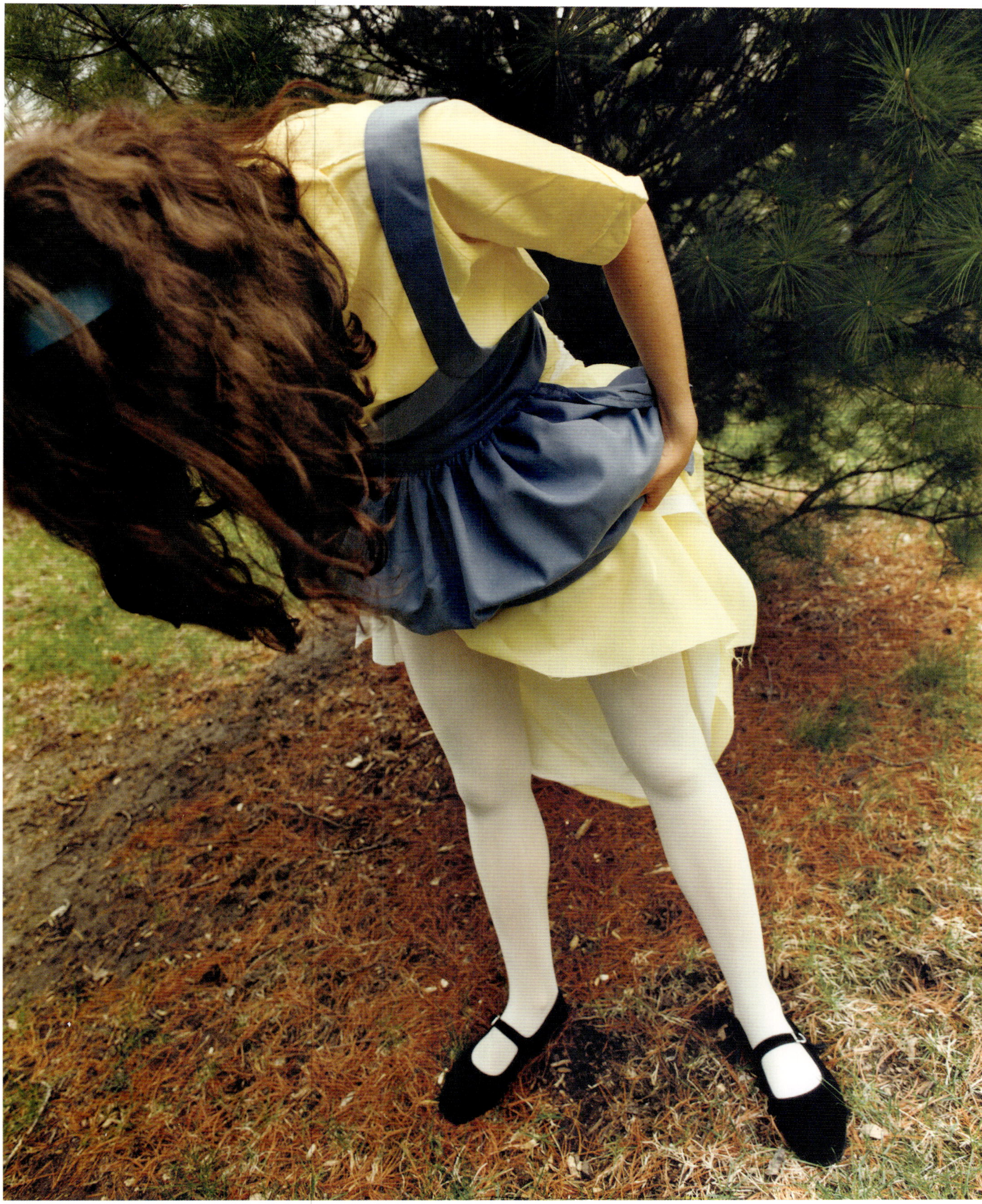

Untitled #16 (Wonder), 1996
Chromogenic print, 20 x 24 in (50.8 x 61 cm)

RODNEY GRAHAM

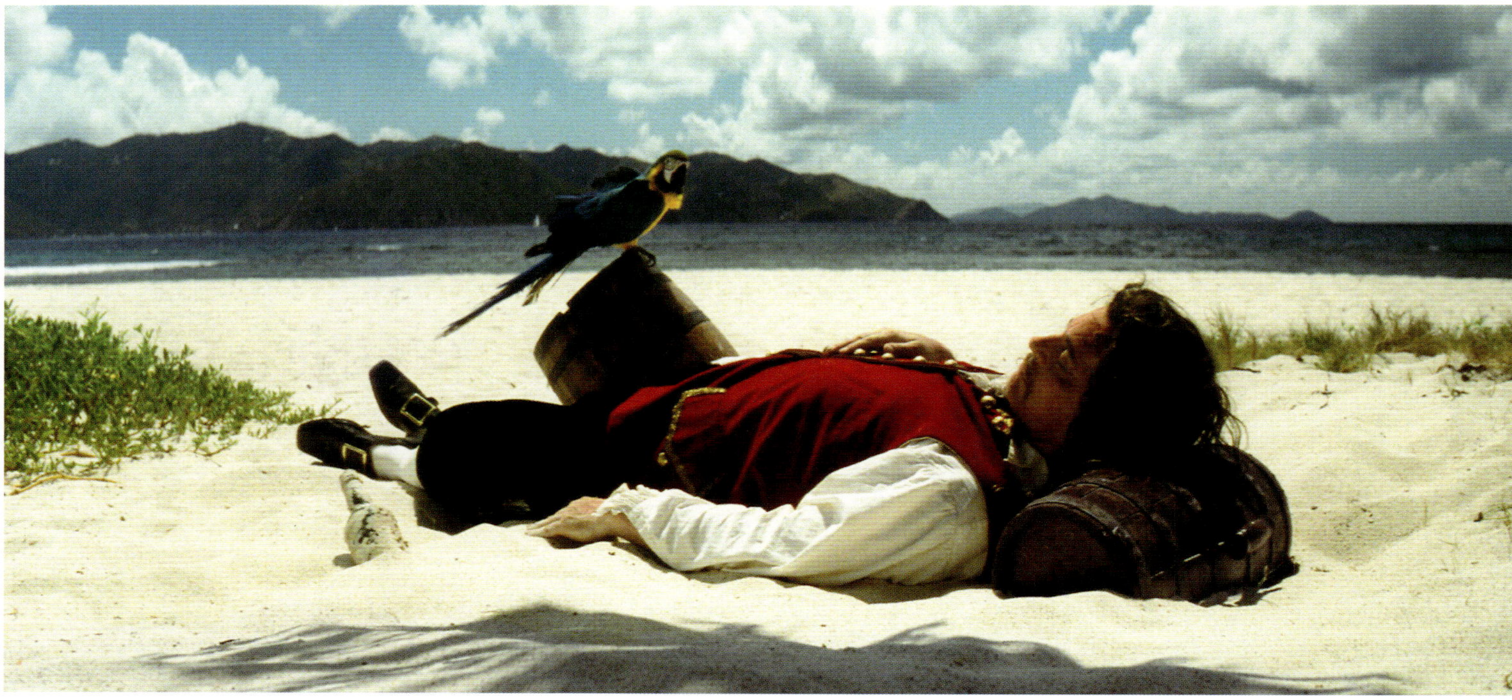

Vexation Island, 1997
Sony Superdata Video/Data Projector with Line Doubler, 10 minutes

STAN DOUGLAS

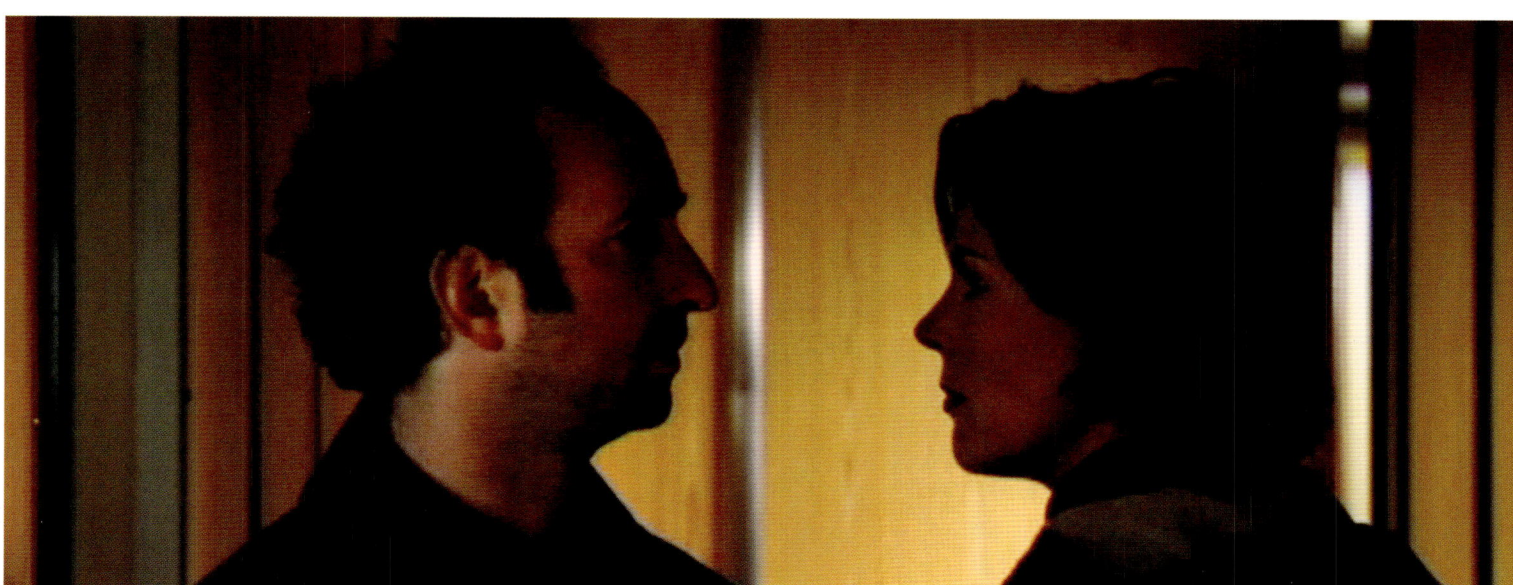

Journey Into Fear, 2001
DVD, 7 hours 40 minutes

AERNOUT MIK

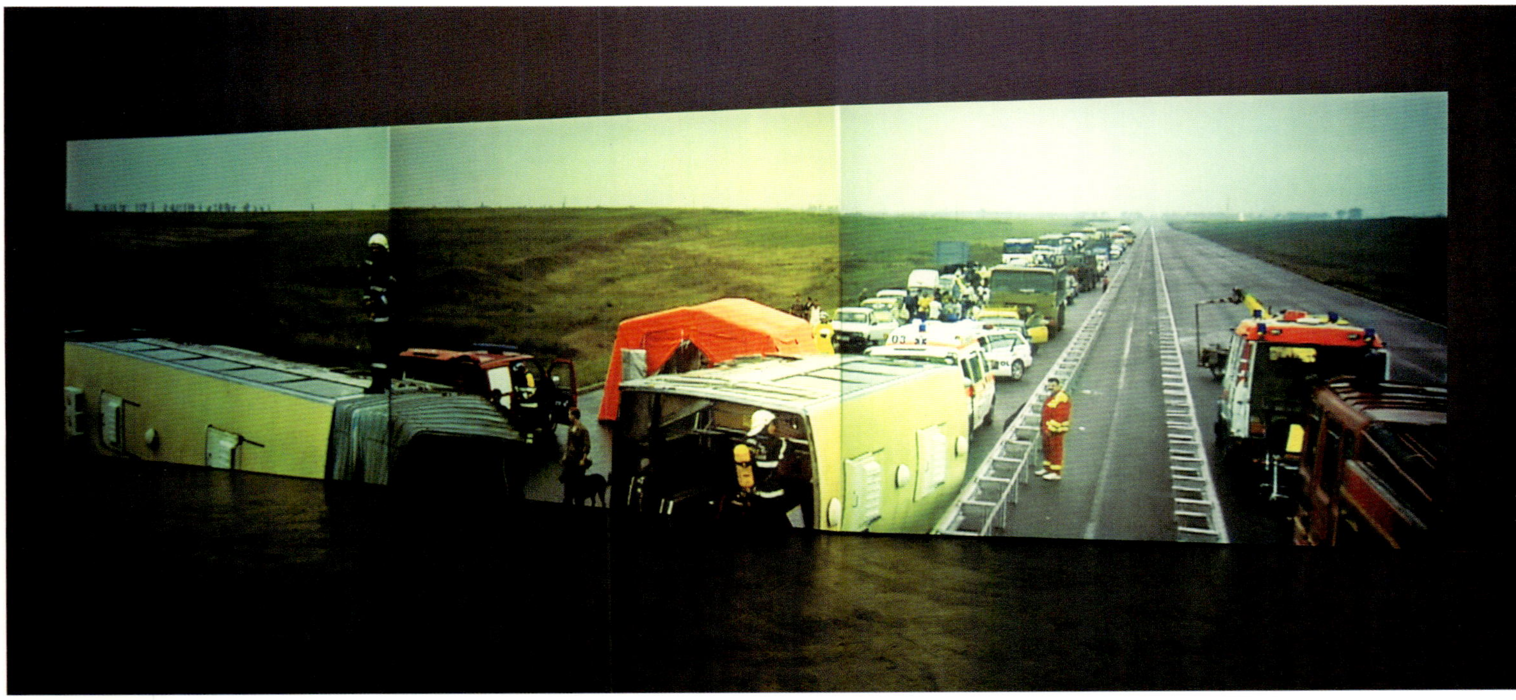

Refraction, 2005
Three-channel video installation, dimensions variable

PIERRE HUYGHE

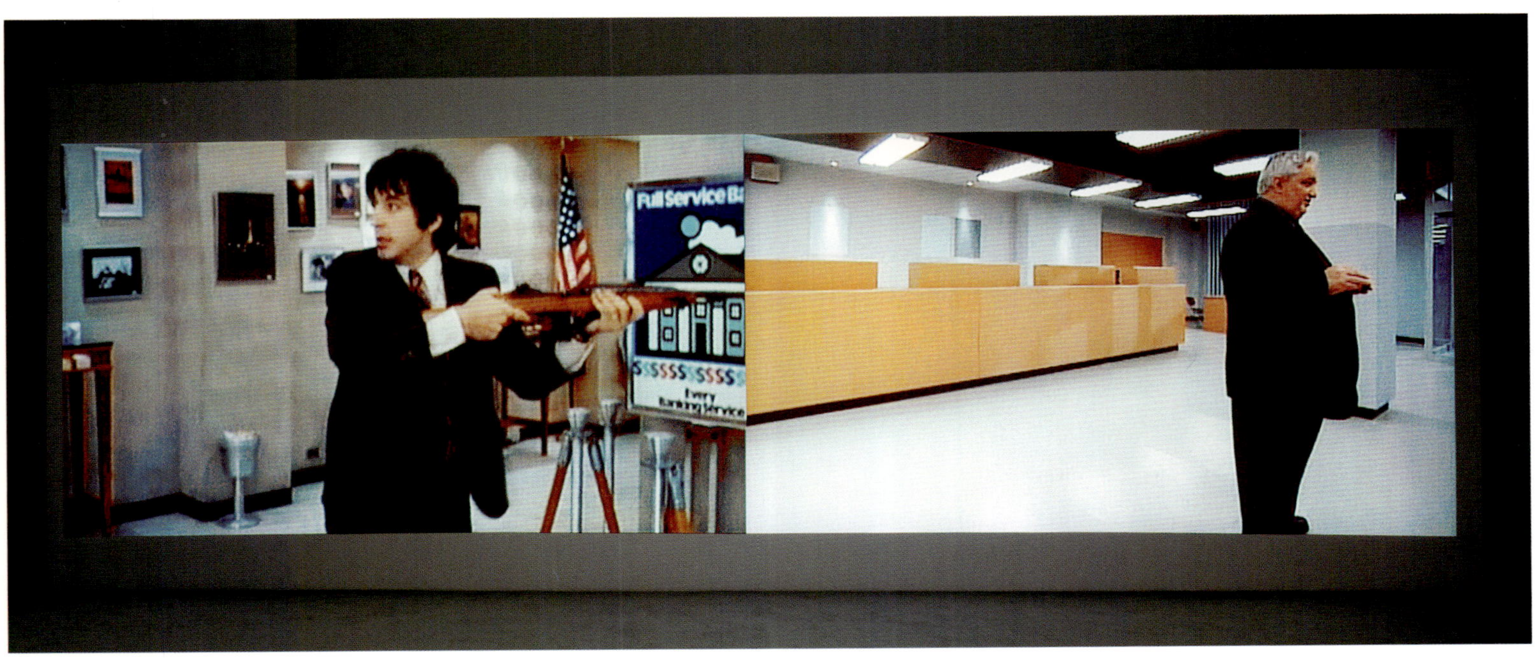

The Third Memory, 1999
Double projection, beta digital, video on monitor
9 minutes 46 seconds

CATHERINE SULLIVAN

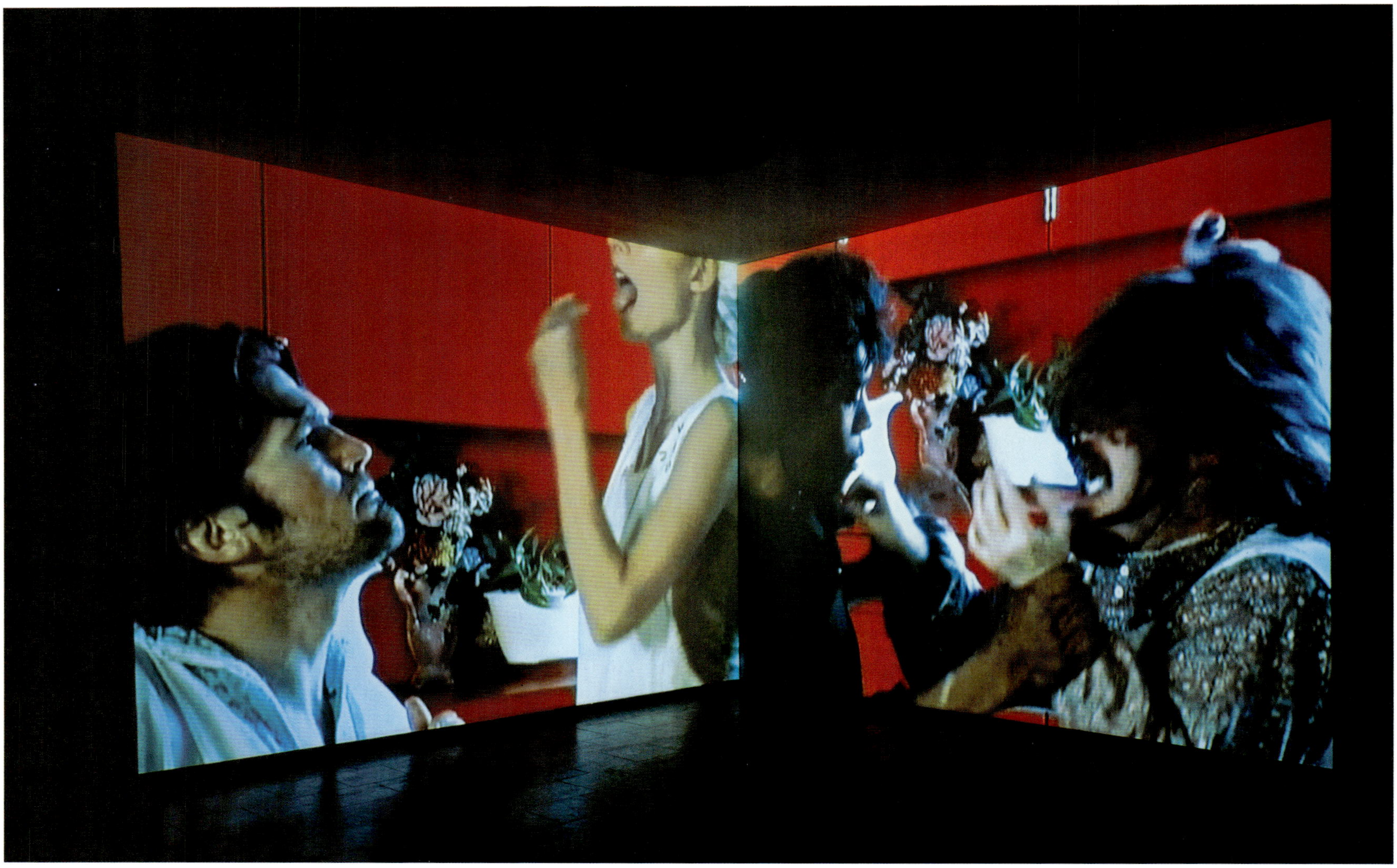

Gold Standard (hysteric, melancholic, degraded, refined), 2001
Two-channel color projection, 12 minutes 24 seconds

Convention. (The incident ended when police shot and killed one robber and captured the other.) The film version was *Dog Day Afternoon*, the highly acclaimed 1975 film by Sidney Lumet, starring Al Pacino. The later recollection is from the surviving robber, John Wojtowicz, who, released from prison, reenacts the robbery for Huyghe's camera on a set based on the movie set. Here, Wojtowicz embellishes the story and contradicts aspects of the original coverage of the crime, sometimes in keeping with Lumet's version, which has become the standard account of the event for most viewers and apparently even for Wojtowicz himself. Huyghe's three-part tale reveals how fictional our sense of fact can become in a media-saturated, Hollywood-spectacle age.

Video artist Stan Douglas also fractures our experience of fictional narratives and casts the truth in the shadow of doubt. His *Win, Place or Show*, 1998, is a double-screen video installation depicting an argument between a pair of dockworkers in a mock-up of a 1950s-era Vancouver housing development that was planned but never built. The narrative depicts the pair in an argument about a number of subjects (including horse racing, hence the title), which eventually comes to blows. The action unfolds in a repeating six-minute loop, but because it was filmed using twenty different cameras with clips spliced together by a computer operating in real time, the viewer eventually becomes aware that each telling is subtly different, due to the varied sequences of camera angles. Douglas takes the idea of multiple narratives in an aural direction in *Journey into Fear*, a 2001 video based on the 1943 film noir classic of the same name. Here, in another looped work, Douglas portrays two actors in an intense dialogue that unfolds in the cramped quarters of a container ship. Heightened emotion typical of a Hollywood thriller hints we're headed toward some dramatic denouement, but it soon becomes clear that the "plot" is actually going nowhere. The same fifteen-minute scene repeats over and over, though on close listen, it's apparent there are different dubbed voices in each loop. Using a computer to switch between various pre-recorded sets of dialogue, Douglas produced a film that could continue without repeating itself for 157 hours. With an unbroken sense of suspense that lacks any conventional resolution, Douglas suggests that we can't believe not only our eyes, but our ears as well.

Catherine Sullivan also presents multiple versions of the same narrative, often in both live and videotaped theater performances that highlight the distinctions between the two media and deconstruct the conventions by which actors convey theatrical illusions. Her ongoing preoccupation is with the conflation of the codes that govern both the actor's and the ordinary individual's behavior. Both, Sullivan suggests, are a stylized set of conventions that we learn to perform and interpret in specific ways. Like Huyghe and Douglas, Sullivan frequently re-choreographs and recreates specific scenes from popular films, interweaving them with other source material from theater, psychological studies, and literature. In *Gold Standard (hysteric, melancholic, degraded, refined)*, 2001, for example, Sullivan reworks a pivotal scene in Arthur Penn's 1962 movie *The Miracle Worker* in which Annie Sullivan tries to teach her young charge Helen Keller how to eat by herself. The scene is presented in multiple versions on side-by-side screens, each time with different actors whose race, age, and even gender vary along with their affects, which run the gamut in the work's subtitle. With such changes of identity and mood, the meaning of the scene constantly shifts, so that it may seem at one point a model of enlightened instruction and at another an exercise in sadism.

ILYA KABAKOV

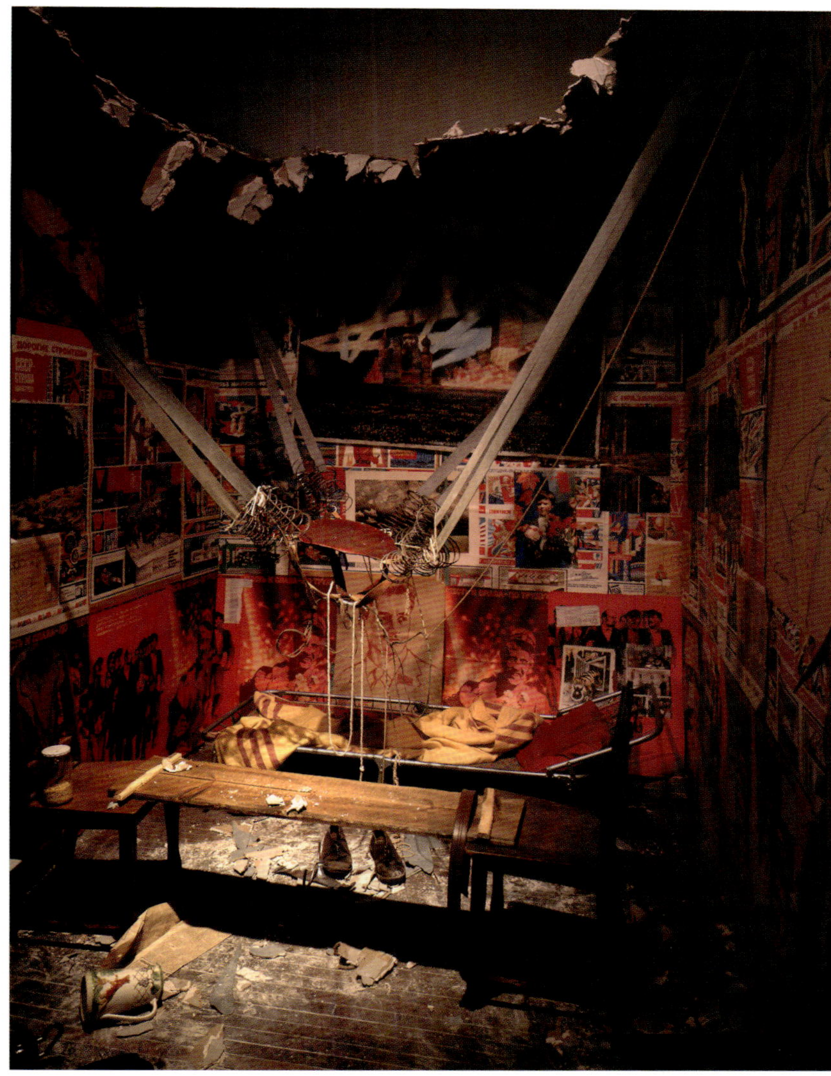

The Man Who Flew into Space from His Apartment, 1985–88
Installation with wood, board construction, room, furniture, found printed ephemera, household objects, dimensions variable
As installed at Ronald Feldman Fine Arts, New York, April–June 1988

Mutable, incoherent, and inconclusive narratives are often told by unreliable narrators, another convention of postmodern storytelling that undermines the very notion of authorship. Ilya Kabakov, who frequently works in collaboration with his wife, Emilia, is a master of unreliable narration. A child of the Stalin era, Kabakov was officially employed as a children's book illustrator in the Soviet Union while gaining clandestine fame among the artistic underground as one of the foremost "nonconformist" artists. His first works to appear in the West predated the fall of the Soviet empire and depict the drab, oppressive realities of Soviet life. But Kabakov has the soul of a novelist, rather than a reporter, so when he recreated an entire communal apartment in a 1988 gallery installation in New York, "Ten Characters," he peopled it with a fantastical group of residents who sought to escape their grim existence through obsessive and apparently pointless activities. A set of small rooms was filled with the personal effects of such characters as The Man Who Never Threw Anything Away, The Untalented Artist, and The Man Who Collects the Opinions of Others, their peculiar stories described in texts affixed near the entrance to each room. The most dramatic was *The Man Who Flew into Space from His Apartment*, which was covered with plaster dust from a gaping hole in his ceiling, through which, presumably, he had made his escape from Soviet reality.

Over time Kabakov has made installations conjuring other Soviet spaces: a public toilet where people line up to urinate without the luxury of a door, a provincial Soviet art museum with a leak in the ceiling, and an exposition hall in which citizens display projects for self-improvement. All of these works are accompanied by stories populated by a diverse set of characters from post-revolutionary Russia, where the dream of collectivity had degenerated into a nightmare of bureaucracy, authoritarianism, red tape, and lost hopes. These characters are based on believable types, but Kabakov is often both playful and elusive—one is never quite sure where he, the artist, stands in relationship to his inventions. In one elaborate installation, Kabakov literally fuses the two, devising a story about an early twentieth-century Russian artist and exhibiting his paintings, some of which are in fact reworkings of Kabakov's own early work. Another piece provides a rambling diary of the travails of Soviet life, purportedly written by the artist's mother, but then again possibly just a narrator of Kabakov's invention. As critics have suggested, this strategy of hiding one's own voice behind a screen of multiple personae and unreliable narrators may be Kabakov's response to growing up in a society in which personal expression could come at great cost.

Nedko Solakov is a generation younger than Kabakov, but he too grew up in the Soviet era and his work also exhibits a deep-seated skepticism toward authority and enforced belief. Solakov's installations scatter walls, floor, and ceiling with found and created objects, scrawled first-person commentary, drawings, maps, and faux newspaper reports. All of these disparate items are clearly invented and serve to document some absurdist premise, for example that the world is flat, or that a great collector of Western masterpieces lives in the artist's ancestral village in Africa in a hut without electricity (making it difficult for him to plug in his neon sculpture by Bruce Nauman). Like Kabakov, Solakov is not above fictionalizing himself. His elaborate installation *El Bulgaro*, 2000, purports to prove that the artist is related, by way of a seventeenth-century Spanish artist named El Bulgaro, to the lineage of Cervantes and El Greco. The case is bolstered by drawings,

NEDKO SOLAKOV

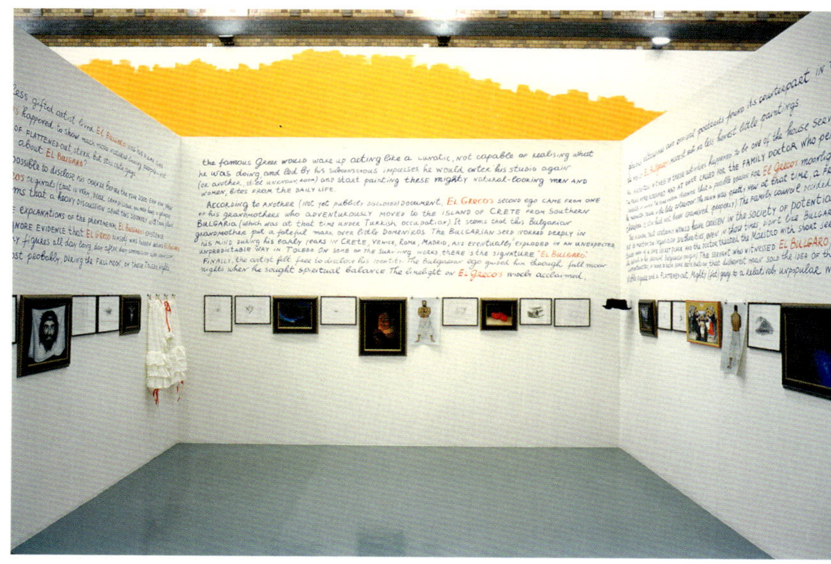

El Bulgaro, 2000
Complicated mixed media, texts, dimensions variable
The Ellipse Foundation Art Centre, Lisbon

EIJA-LIISA AHTILA

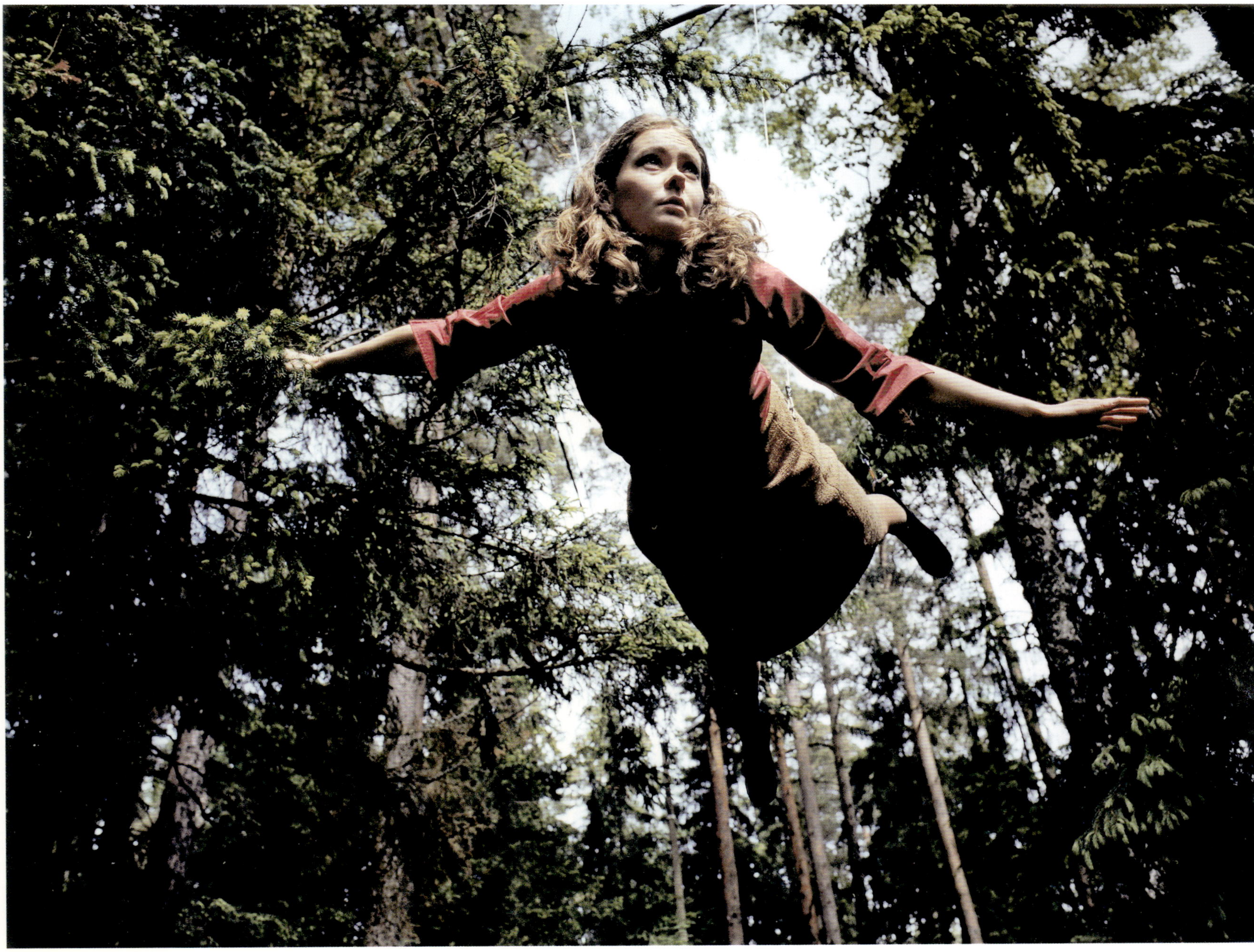

The House, 2002
DVD installation for 3 projections with sound, 14 minutes

TINA BARNEY

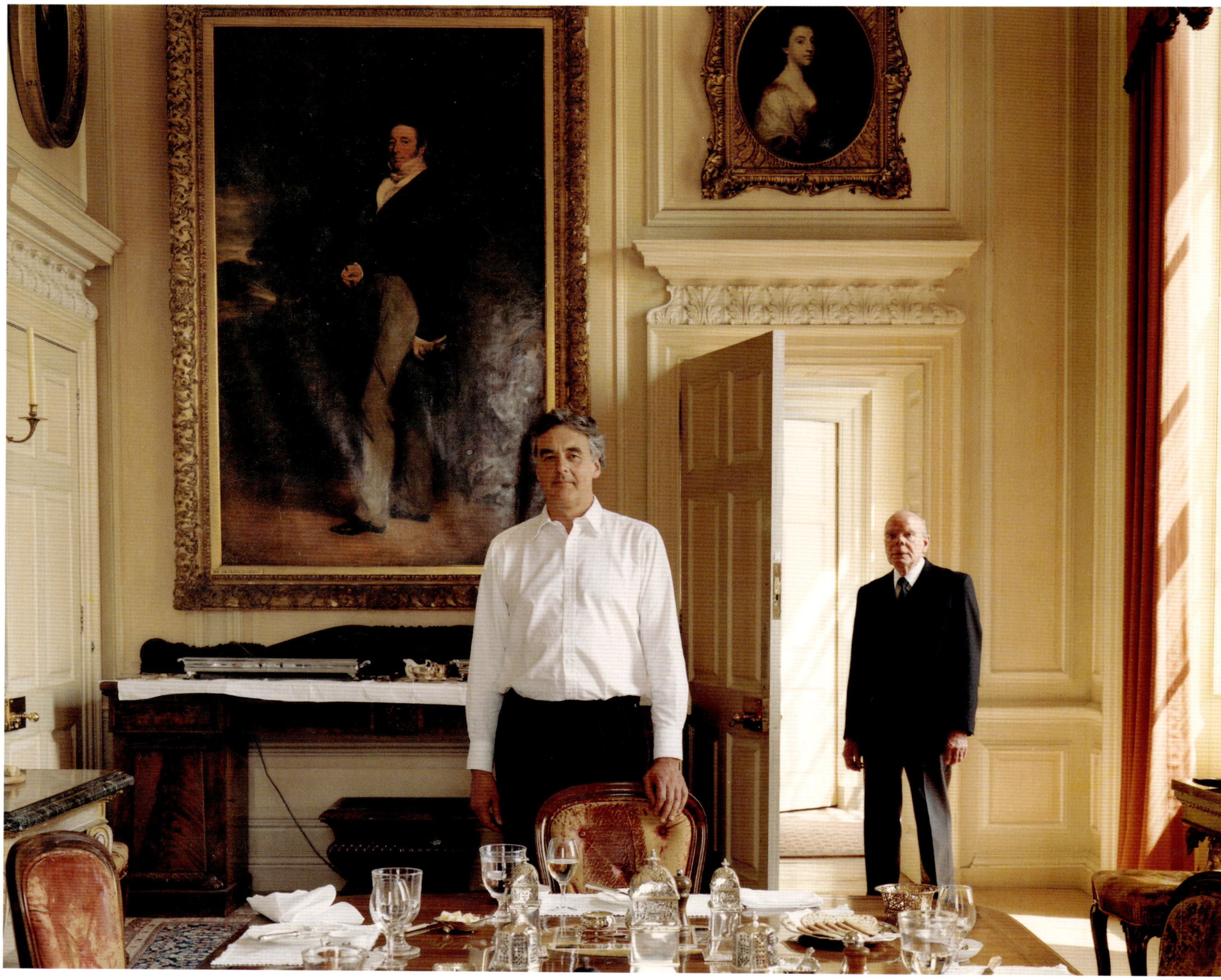

The Ancestor, 2001
Chromogenic color print, 48 x 60 in (121.9 x 152.4 cm)

supposedly by El Bulgaro himself, as well as by an anachronistic photo-portrait of this fictional character—in period garb but bearing the unmistakable features of Solakov. Rendering both himself and his character unreliable narrators at once, Solakov signals his distrust for the kind of authoritative or propagandistic voice that has long been identified with Soviet ideology.

While Kabakov and Solakov turn to the device of the unreliable narrator to suggest the madness of blind, unthinking adherence to a failed ideology, Eija-Liisa Ahtila uses it to express a literal kind of madness. Her videos and films present stories about apparently ordinary women (along with the occasional man) who are on the brink, or beyond the brink, of psychological breakdown. Presented on multiple screens, which reveal different perspectives and various information about the unfolding events, her narratives are constantly sliding between subjective and objective reality. Events in the mind are indistinguishable from events in the outside world, for instance, when, in *The House*, 2002, a cow saunters into the living room, or a car drives along the inside walls of a young woman's house. Similarly, in *The Wind*, 2002, a tearful female protagonist recounts her self-loathing while visitors, who may be real or just figments, appear in her house to torment her. Soon a cyclone sweeps through her home, upending everything and leaving the place in chaos. Is this a symbol of the external forces driving her mad, or does it come from within, representing a release of her anguished spirit? Despite the psychological nature of the trauma presented in Ahtila's films, there is nothing clinical or even deeply depressing about them. This is due in large part to the way events are presented—the fracturing effect of the multiple screens so aptly reflects the characters' crazy logic that events become almost plausible to the viewer, alleviating rather than creating disorientation.

In Gillian Wearing's work, the link between narrator and reality is severed in yet another way. Exploiting the confessional strain in human nature more compassionately than reality TV, Wearing invites her subjects to reveal or expose their innermost emotions or secrets, but always offers them a shield of some sort. Sometimes her subjects wear literal masks, as in *Trauma*, 2000, a video in which those who answered the artist's ad soliciting tales of childhood abuse or disturbance are outfitted with cheap plastic masks behind which to tell their stories. Other "shields" are the written signs expressing an individual's unspeakable thoughts in the series "Signs that say what you want them to say and not signs that say what someone else wants you to say," 1992–93. For this series of photographs, Wearing asked strangers to write whatever thought they wanted to express on placards and then took their portrait. Her subjects' smiling or impassive countenances belie such written sentiments as in *I'm Desperate*, or *Come back Mary, I love you*. In all of these works, the various shields become distancing devices, dramatizing the gap between surface perceptions and inner realities. By making literal the social mask, which hides a cauldron of roiling emotions, Wearing's works become metaphors for the uncertainty of all ordinary social encounters.

In other contemporary narratives, the conventional flow of the story is disrupted simply by the fact that the events are being recorded by the artist. Tina Barney creates large-format photographs of her family and friends in their homes, but these are not your everyday family-album snapshots. Barney and her subjects belong to America's Wasp aristocracy, and her images are fascinating in part because they reveal the domestic settings, attitudes, and rituals of a group that,

GILLIAN WEARING

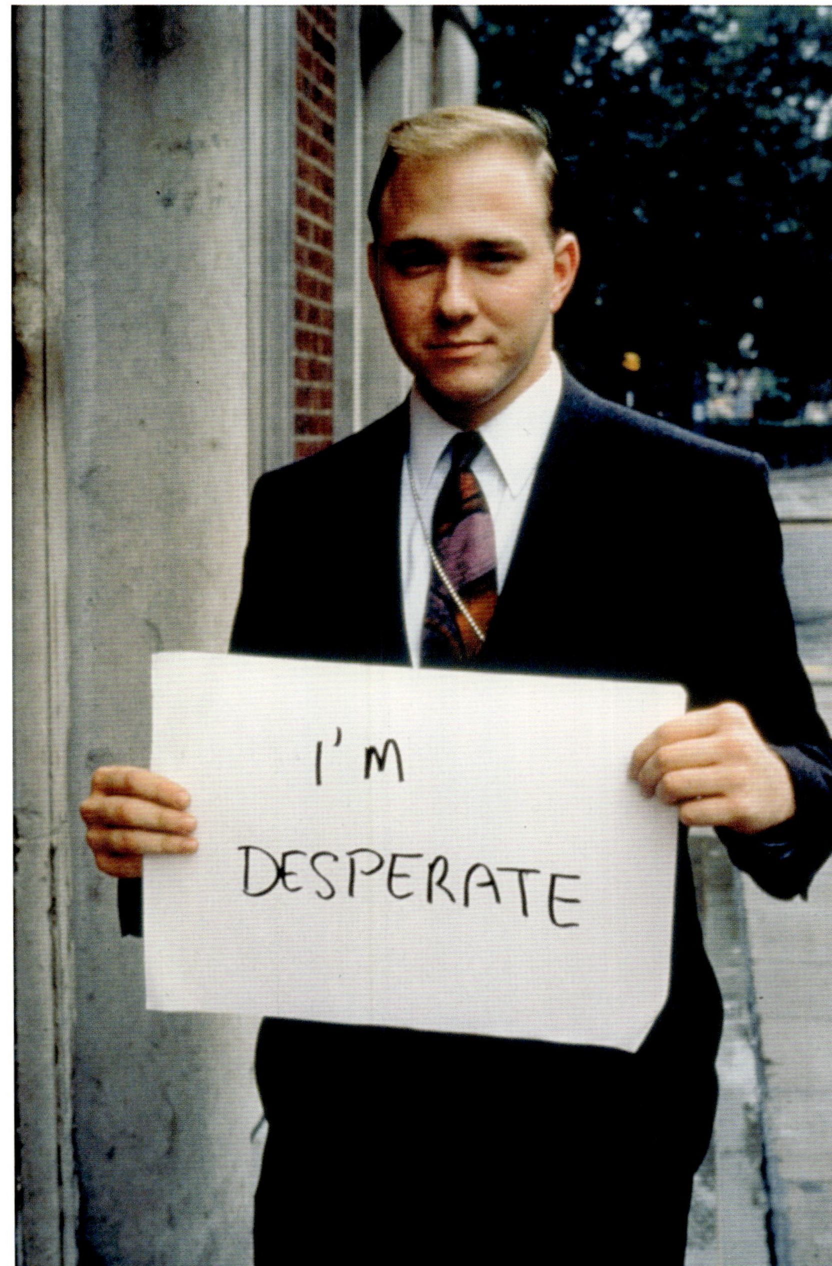

I'm Desperate, 1992–93
C-type print mounted on aluminum, 15 3/4 x 12 1/2 in (42 x 30 cm)

NAN GOLDIN

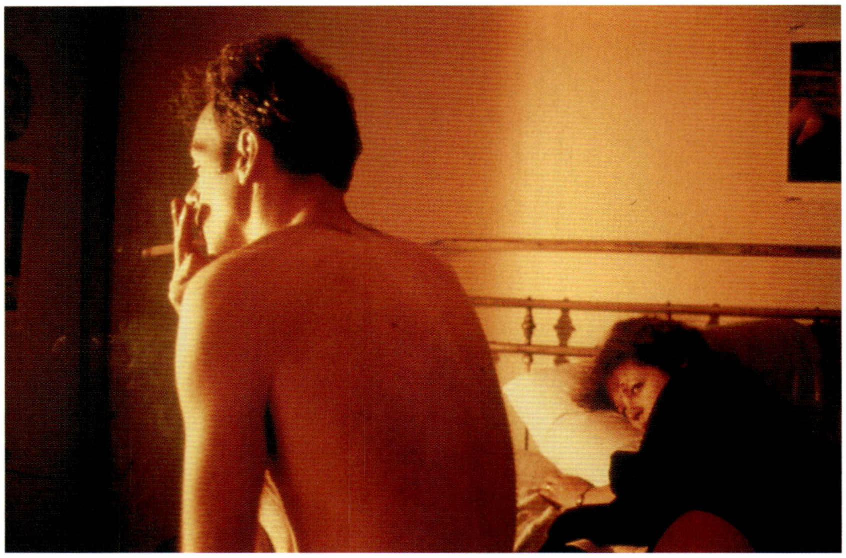

Nan and Brian in Bed, NYC, 1983
Cibachrome print, 30 x 40 in (76.2 x 101.6 cm)

NAN GOLDIN

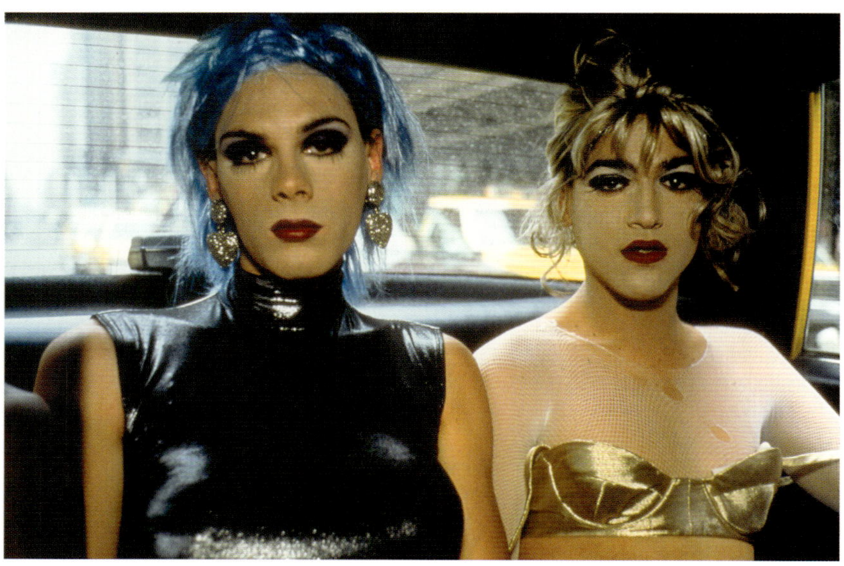

Misty and Jimmy Paulette in a Taxi, NYC, 1991
Cibachrome print, 30 x 40 in (76.2 x 101.6 cm)

stereotypically at least, combines emotional restraint with a deeply ingrained sense of privilege. In addition to the subjects themselves, details of décor—opulent window treatments, tasteful art collections, brass chandeliers, and manicured lawns—play important supporting roles, filling out the picture of private life among the wealthy. Barney's images are restagings of spontaneous poses; she waits for a resonant moment and then recreates it, sometimes immediately, though poses or even the disposition of furniture are often altered. The resulting mood is one of slight awkwardness, indicating the subjects' intense awareness of the camera's eye. In *The Ancestor*, 2001, for example, the dining room wall is dominated by a painting of a forebear posing stiffly in historical garb. Below the portrait, less formally dressed but no less stuffy, is the modern descendent standing before a beautifully set table. In the distance, standing by an open door, is the butler, a paragon of self-effacing alertness. Together, they suggest a world where the most average activities of everyday life become ritual.

In a similarly spontaneous-looking style, Nan Goldin photographs her own "family"—a self-selected one composed of artists, poets, musicians, transsexuals, drag queens, and other scruffy downtown-Manhattan bohemian types the artist befriended in the late 1970s and 1980s. *Misty and Jimmy Paulette in a Taxi, NYC*, 1991, for instance, captures a pair of drag queens in a reflective moment, elaborately dressed and made up yet not on stage. Beginning in 1980, Goldin began to organize her images and project them in an ever-changing epic slide show titled *The Ballad of Sexual Dependency*. She calls this work "the diary I let people read," and while it is far more coherent than many other artists' narratives, it is still loose and interpretive, accompanied by snatches of music from sources ranging from Kurt Weill and Maria Callas to James Brown, Screamin' Jay Hawkins, and Charles Aznavour. The overall theme is the pain inherent in interpersonal relationships, the tension between intimacy and autonomy, and the many-faceted nature of love and friendship. First shown as a diversion between sets at a punk club, *The Ballad of Sexual Dependency* is now a much-praised artwork.

Unlike Barney, Goldin does not pose her subjects. Instead she captures them in the most intimate poses—applying makeup before a drag performance, sobbing after a fight with a lover, even making love, sitting on the toilet, or shooting up. The intimacy is enhanced by the images' saturated color and the fact that most are shot indoors, with a flash, giving them a womb-like feel, removed from the light and air of the outside world. This is not to say that time stands still: in Goldin's work, subjects reappear over the years—we watch them age, exchange partners, and in some cases move from insouciant health to decline and death from AIDS. Goldin, too, appears in her photographs, as in *Nan and Brian in Bed, NYC*, 1983, and some of the most moving sequences present her struggles with an abusive relationship (we see her bruised face and watch it heal), her descent into drug addiction, and her recovery at a rehab center. Her images are so candid that one assumes Goldin's friends have lost all self-consciousness before her ubiquitous camera. One wonders, however, about the project's effects on Goldin herself, and how her own behavior may have been altered by her dual role as observer and observed.

Few artists have toyed as radically with the breakdown of barriers between artist and subject and so pressed the point of artist as observer as Sophie Calle, a French artist who has been described as a voyeur, an artist-stalker, and a photo-terrorist. Her works share not only narrative but scientific conventions—

SOPHIE CALLE

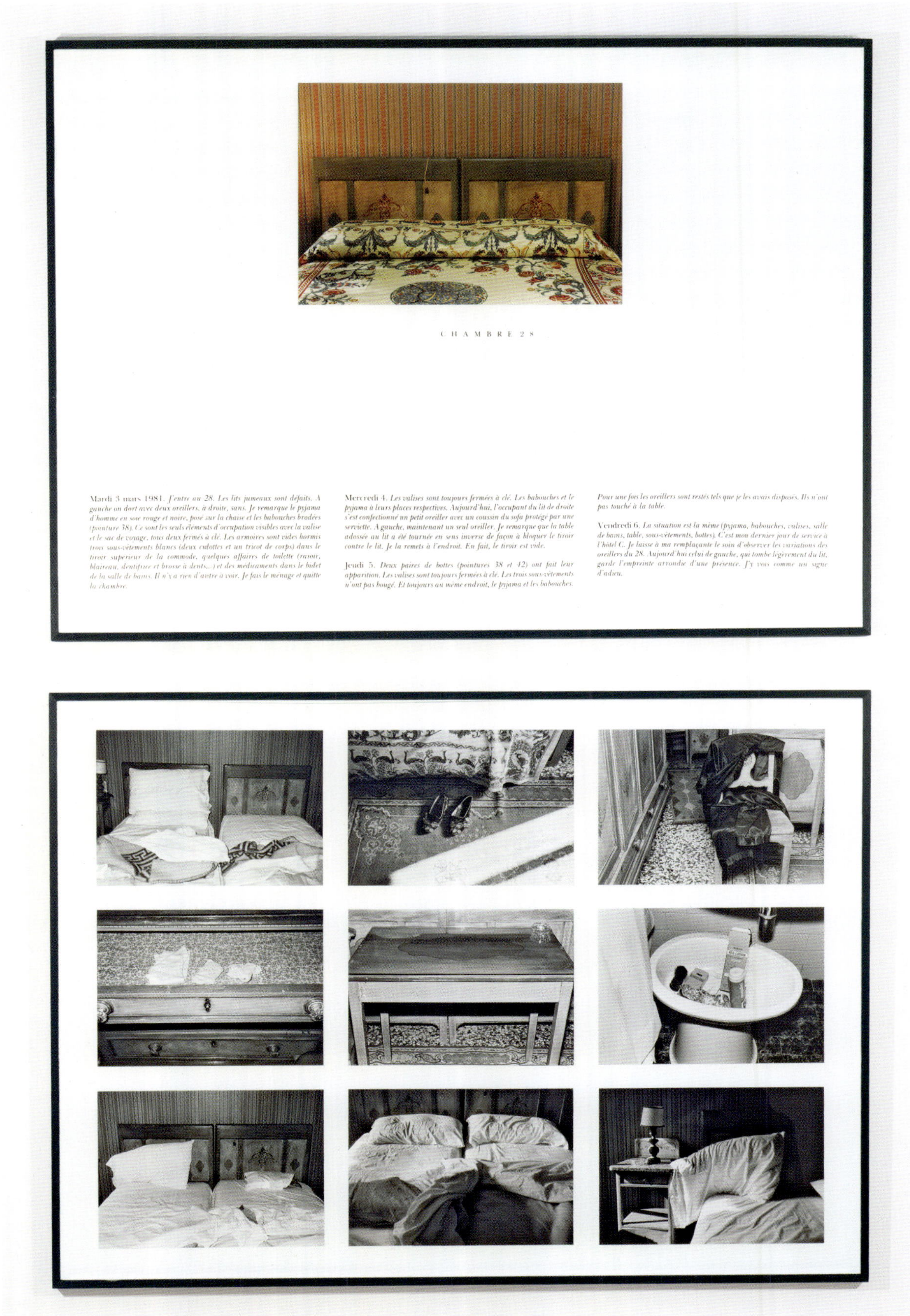

Chambre 28—3 Mars (Room 28—3 March), 1981
Color and black and white photographs, frames
40 1/4 x 56 in (102 x 142 cm)

she gathers data, often covertly, then, thrusting herself into provocative and even potentially dangerous case studies, watches to see how others will react. Calle's voyeuristic tendencies are the basis of "The Hotel," 1984, for which the artist took a job as a chambermaid so she could "spy" on guests. The resulting works are a combination of photographs and text, like *Chambre 28—3 Mars* (Room 28—3 March), 1981, that document her intrusions. She opened their suitcases, read their mail and diaries, took photographs of their beds and dirty laundry, and invented fanciful scenarios to explain the data she had uncovered. But perhaps her most intrusive surveillance work is found in "The Address Book," 1983, for which she photocopied the contents of an address book found on the street and then interviewed everyone in the book about the owner, a documentary filmmaker whom she had never met. She published these interviews serially in the French daily *Libération* for an entire month, at which point the owner of the address book wrote an angry letter to the publisher, demanding, unsuccessfully, that they publish a nude photograph of Calle he had unearthed. In short, Calle plays fast and loose with the line between fact and fiction, not only impacting but creating the very narratives she is recounting.

Artists who make the others active participants in the story of their work see through the logical consequences of Barthes's notion of the authorship of the viewer. Where Calle's participants are unwitting, those of Janet Cardiff, who often works with her husband, George Bures Miller, are fully cognizant of their essential role. Cardiff specializes in "audio walks" in which the "viewer" (the word doesn't quite fit here) is handed a set of headphones and sent off on an adventure led by a voice on a recorded tape. Cardiff sets her walks in specific settings—participants find themselves walking through a museum, a park, or a city street with an invisible friend who directs their path and whispers comments about the surroundings. Part of the charm of these works is the way in which they mix fact and fiction: the disembodied voice describes things we do see and things we don't see—a real landmark such as a door or a sculpture, for instance, or a supposed figure we are to follow, a bike apparently coming out of nowhere, a setting sun that may or may not be setting when we take our walk. Many of these walks are relatively eventless—we wander, notice things, and return to our starting point. But in the process we have been led to experience our surroundings much more consciously. One of Cardiff's most complete narratives is *The Muriel Lake Incident*, 1999, for which viewers wear headphones and peer into a diorama that situates them in the balcony of a movie theater. They hear sounds, some from the screen, some apparently from surrounding theater-goers, who at one point notice that a woman has come in late,

JANET CARDIFF

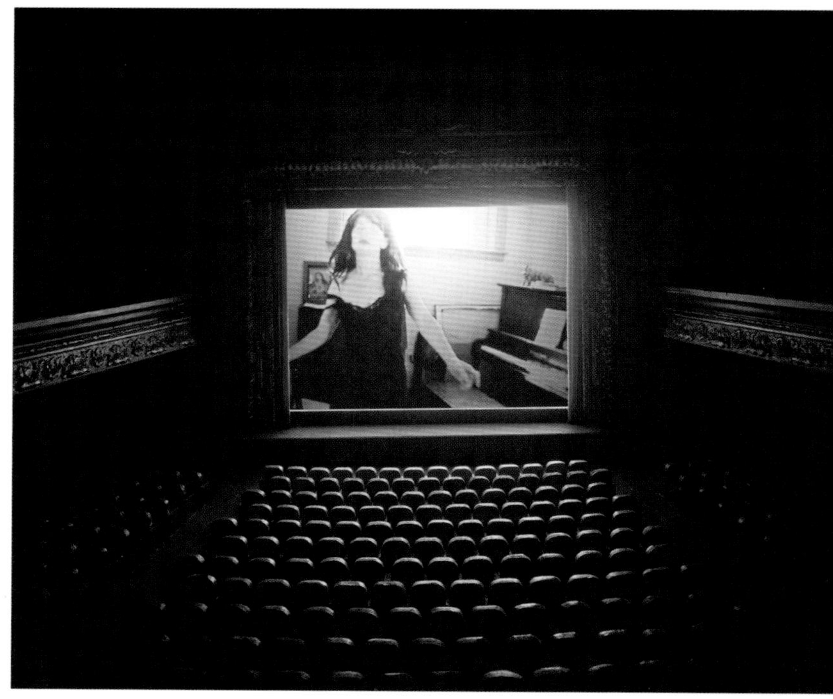

Muriel Lake Incident, 1999
Wood, audio, video projection, and steel
72 1/2 x 90 1/4 x 62 in (184.2 x 229.2 x 157.5 cm)

and so start to whisper. The woman says something about a suspicious character, then, suddenly there is the sound of the shot, of chaos and confusion in the theater, and viewers come to understand that they are part of (if not the makers of) their very own action picture.

Matthew Ritchie's epic tale of the rise and fall of some mythic civilization that may precede or come many eons after our own also relies on the viewer to play an essential part in the story. Since he first introduced *The Hard Way* in 1995, the narrative has grown in complexity, finding expression in the artist's voluminous writings, in digital form on his Web site, and in massive room-size installations in which painted, jigsaw puzzle-like versions of his characters, symbols, and cosmic landscapes swirl over walls, collect in piles on the floor, and invade the ceiling. In its various forms, Ritchie's narrative makes reference to everything from particle physics and theoretical mathematics to Genesis, pulp fiction, comic books, and game theory. Each installation deals with a group of properties or characteristics of the universe. For instance, his installation "Proposition Player," 2003, is, according to Ritchie, a rumination on gambling, quantum mechanics, and the elements of chance.[5] In short, Ritchie's cosmos is based on the creation myths of the Western world and centers around seven groups of seven characters who are also metaphysical principles or laws of physics. The epic begins with a gang of damaged celestial agents representing different parts of the human brain. Thrown from heaven, they fall to earth and shatter into segments across seven continents. These fragmentary creatures combine and recombine, making for an almost infinite set of possible narratives, which Ritchie pursues in his writings and installations. On his Web site, he tells the story in the overwrought language of pulp science fiction: "The boundaries between species were less clear then. What could be more exciting than sex with a creature whose every orifice was made to experience and give pleasure? Or a woman burning with a heatless crystal fire, whispering the secrets of eternity in to your shallow, mewling mind, each passage of flesh to flesh bringing more knowledge, more wisdom."[6]

The ambiguity here should come as a clue: Ritchie has produced not a clear narrative, but an allegory of creation that celebrates how art is born. And what makes his project most interesting is that the viewer, not the artist, is the ultimate creator. Given its multiple layers and tangled story lines, the only way to experience his work is to recreate it for oneself, following the threads of one's choice to create a narrative that is as viable as any other. What better illustration of Barthes's notion of the work as "a multi-dimensional space in which a variety of writings . . . blend and clash" than Ritchie's ever-proliferating universe?

MATTHEW RITCHIE

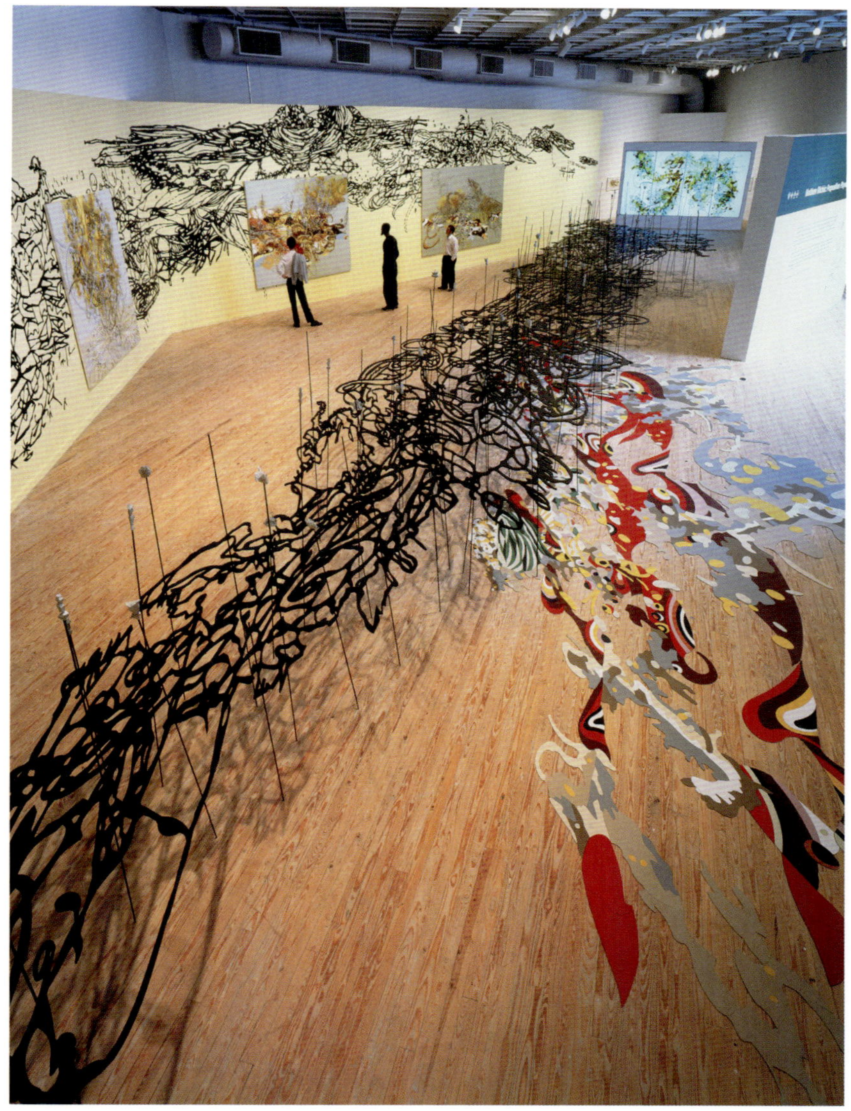

"Matthew Ritchie: Proposition Player," 2003
As installed at Contemporary Arts Museum Houston, Tex., December 2003–March 2004

ART & TIME

FROM REAL TIME TO REEL TIME

Andy Warhol's *Sleep* is a silent, black-and-white, six-hour film of a man sleeping. We see the man from several angles, and he breathes and shifts a bit, but otherwise nothing much happens—unless you count when he turns over in the middle of the film. (Rumor has it that at this point the audience at the first screening broke into applause.) Made in 1963, *Sleep* is an early exemplar of "real time" cinema, a filmmaking style or strategy in which the film unfolds in the same amount of time as the events it represents, lately made popular in cinema vérité, reality TV, and even a few Hollywood movies. (In the TV show *24*, for instance, each minute of airtime corresponds to a minute in the lives of the characters.) As in most examples of real time cinema, Warhol cheated with *Sleep*, creating an apparently seamless experience that in fact includes repeated loops, which only someone who watches the film closely from start to finish will notice.

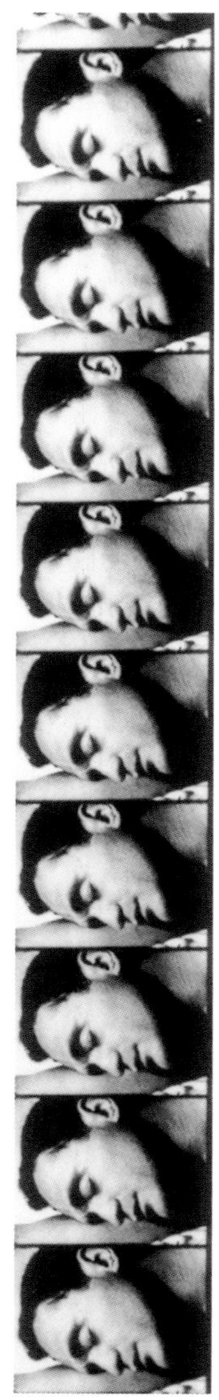

ANDY WARHOL
SLEEP
1963
BLACK AND WHITE, SILENT, 5 HOURS 21 MINUTES

"Real time" is one of those phrases so apparently self-evident that we rarely question it. But as Warhol's manipulation suggests, it is not as simple as it seems. Since the beginning of philosophical thought, the nature of time itself, and even its very existence, has been subject to debate. Aristotle questioned whether time exists independently of experience or whether consciousness brings it into existence. Augustine argued that time did not exist before God created it, and that therefore God alone exists in a state of eternity. (Scientists today follow a similar line of inquiry when they wonder whether time existed before the Big Bang.) Isaac Newton based his theory of mechanics on the belief that time and space exist independently of the events that happen in them. But other philosophers argued against the objective existence of time. Eighteenth-century skeptic George Berkeley went so far as to suggest that time, and the things that occur in it, are mental perceptions whose "reality" can never be proven. Buddhists maintain that time is an endlessly recurring circle and that we always end up where we began. Einstein's theory of relativity fuses space and time into a single entity. Twentieth-century philosopher Henri Bergson fused space and time in his notion of duration, describing "lived time" as the experience in which past and future merge into a continual present.

Such diverse and contradictory theories have worked their way from philosophy and science into every corner of modern life, particularly as technology has opened up radically new ways to experience time. Clocks divorced us from the seasonal and diurnal experience of time, breaking it up into measurable, repeating moments. This in turn led to mass production, in which tasks occur in a series of repeatable units. The hapless protagonist of Charlie Chaplin's 1936 classic film *Modern Times* comically illustrated the human consequences of this "progress" as he fell behind and was sucked up by the gears of the assembly-line machine. Photography, meanwhile, had made time literally visible. In the nineteenth century, Eadweard Muybridge's stop-action photographs allowed viewers to experience motion that had previously been too fast for the naked eye to see. His sequential images were a precursor to the invention of film, which ushered in a raft of new possibilities for the experience of time. In the 1920s Russian filmmakers such as Sergei Eisenstein played with distortion, strange camera angles, abrupt juxtapositions, and mirror reflections to dispel the illusion of linear time. Like Russian Constructivist artists such as Kazimir Malevich and Alexander Rodchenko, he believed his innovations had a political purpose: by jolting audiences out of their traditional understanding of time and space, he was helping to create radical new forms of consciousness in keeping with the radical reorganization of society within the new Soviet state. Simultaneously, Hollywood directors such as D. W. Griffith, working in the service of entertainment rather than politics, discovered the flashback, the split screen, the flash-forward, and slowed and accelerated motion.

Over a half century people came to take such cinematic ruptures—what might be called "reel time," for granted, so much so that it is clear how Warhol's use of "real time" in *Sleep* would be startling. During the late 1950s and '60s, others—avant-garde filmmakers, performance artists, and musicians—made likeminded works intended to wean people back into an experience of a pre-cinematic time. John Cage's *4'33"*, first "performed" by a pianist in 1952, consists of one or more musicians sitting in silence for a three-movement piece lasting four minutes and thirty three seconds, during which the audience is expected to renounce the usual surrender to the artist's imagination and instead pay attention to ambient sounds of the "real" audience and environment. Artists of the late 1960s and early '70s used nascent technologies such as the portable video recorder, surveillance cameras, and feedback systems to create heightened awareness of momentary positions in time and space. Often they did this by playing "real" and "reel" time against each other. Yoko Ono's *Sky TV*, 1966, collapses the two by using video monitors to show a live-feed, closed-circuit image of the sky outside the viewing space. Dan Graham, with his 1974 installation *Opposing Mirrors and Video Monitors on Time Delay*, situates audiences so that they simultaneously perceive themselves as reflections in a mirror in real time and as video images subject to a five-second delay. Bruce Nauman also created spaces outfitted with surveillance cameras and monitors that confuse temporal experience: *Live-Taped Video Corridor*, 1970, for example, prompts viewers to walk down a corridor toward a monitor that shows themselves from the back, apparently walking away. Works like these placed viewers simultaneously inside and outside the time unfolding on the monitor, sharpening their perception of their own physical and temporal coordinates.

Such efforts to get audiences to "be here now," as a popular admonition of the time had it, quickly ran up against the imperatives of commerce and technology. The quick cuts of MTV, the emergence of the "sound bite" as a key component of television news and advertising, and the triumph of the Hollywood action film all conspired to shorten the audience's attention span. The instant replay on sports channels and the pause, fast-forward, and replay buttons on the remote control gave us a sense that we could control the flow of time. Our entry into the cyber age continues to disrupt conventional notions of time and space. Advances in electronic communication make it possible to experience what video artist Bill Viola calls "parallel time," the sensation of existing simultaneously in one's body and in some far-flung locale, to be as aware of what is happening in a loft in New York City as in a street in Paris or a war zone in the Middle East. In cyberspace, time becomes completely elastic. Technology can make past and present coexist, erase the distinction between here and there, and even alter records of historical events and manipulate memory.

The tension between real time and reel time is in certain respects a replay of the age-old debate between objective and subjective understandings of time. The effort to hold onto real time, however elusive or problematic that entity might be, represents a belief that time has a concrete existence outside ourselves, and that we exist, and perhaps even come to be, within it. On the other hand, reel time recognizes that time is something we can manipulate and that, at least to a certain extent, it depends on us for its existence. This tension runs throughout the work of myriad contemporary artists—both those who work in time-based media and must confront the psychological and philosophical consequences of the manipulation of time, and those who make time the subject of their work.

Among contemporary artists, perhaps the most tenacious effort to hold on to real time is found in the work of On Kawara. Since the mid-1960s, Kawara has made over two thousand date paintings, which collectively make up the "Today Series," rectangular canvases in eight different sizes, on which the date is pristinely painted in white letters and numbers on a monochrome ground. Kawara follows a strict rule in creating these works—they must be started and completed on the day specified; if they aren't finished by midnight, they are thrown away. The finished works are stored in specially made boxes with a clipping from that day's newspaper in the city in which each was painted. (Kawara is a frequent traveler.) Containing the news of the day, the boxes are like time capsules, but the paintings themselves, which are often displayed without the box, contain no information about the date. If anything, they resemble calendar pages. Classic works of Conceptual art, the date paintings are at once severely restricted in their visual charms and full of imaginative possibilities for the mental time-traveler. They attempt to make time concrete and palpable, but in the end their emptiness serves to underscore the futility of any such attempt. Instead, the lived experience of time slips away, leaving only enigmatic traces in its wake.

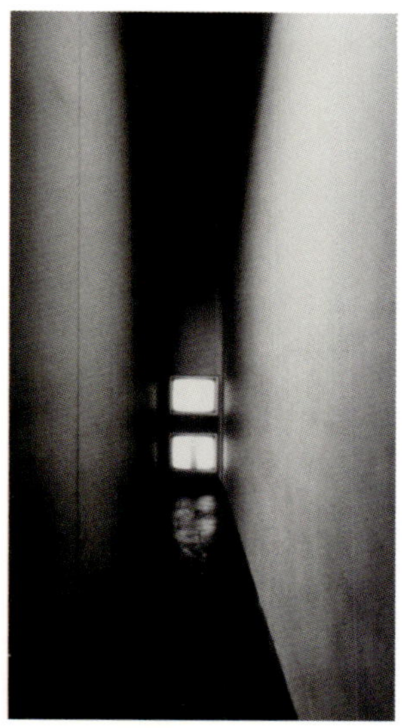

BRUCE NAUMAN
LIVE-TAPED VIDEO CORRIDOR
1970
WALLBOARD, VIDEO CAMERA, 2 VIDEO MONITORS, VIDEOTAPE PLAYER, VIDEOTAPE

A similarly quixotic attempt to create a visual representation of time appears in the art of Roman Opalka, who since 1965 has been at work on *OPALKA 1965/1-[infinity]*, a magnum opus consisting of hundreds of canvases filled with sequences of consecutive numbers that represent the artist's effort to count to infinity. In the early "Details," as he calls these paintings, the numbers, painted in white with a small brush, were set on a black field. In 1972, Opalka began adding incrementally more white to the black paint, calculating, correctly as it turned out, that around the year 2000 the ground would be as white as the numbers. Since then the numbers are visible only when the canvas is placed in slanting light. In a related continuing series that also dates back to 1965, the artist takes a photograph of himself at the end of each day. Placed together sequentially, these self-portraits form another record of the passage of time, this one marked on the artist's own aging face. Opalka plans to continue this project until his death.

While meditative works by artists like Opalka and Kawara attempt to stop time like a butterfly impaled on a pin, other artists' multimedia works combine everything from live action to video footage, film, music, closed-circuit television, and slide projections to revel in the fleeting, ever-changing nature of time. Joan Jonas has been refining this multi-prong approach since the late 1960s, creating performances and installations that draw on myth, ritual, literature, and history, all of which she presses into service to investigate the meanings of female identity. Among her signature elements are mirrors, which of course distort as much as they reveal, and masks, which allow for shifting personas. Over the years her works, which are presented variously as videos, performances, and installations, have become ever more elaborate. Critic Douglas Crimp has described the essential experience of Jonas's work as one of "de-synchronization," a word that gets at its spatial and temporal complexity.[1] Take for instance, *Lines in the Sand*, 2002, which was inspired by the epic poem "Helen in Egypt," written in the early 1950s by H.D. (Hilda Doolittle). Both the performance and the installation that Jonas created from this text suggest a world in which ordinary experiences of time and space have collapsed. There are spoken passages from H.D.'s text, projected photographs of her own grandmother's sojourn in Egypt in 1901, film clips of the kitschy recreation of Luxor, Egypt, in Las Vegas, and filmed and performed sequences in which Jonas dances, creates diagrams of ellipses and pyramids on a chalkboard, and literally draws a line in the sand. These fragments express the arc of history, mixing references to one of the oldest recorded civilizations with up-to-the-minute technological innovations from our own to create a tapestry of disparate moments.

Jonas's conjunction of pre-industrial and post-electronic consciousness is also a subtext in the work of the late Nam June Paik. Frequently dubbed "the father of video art," Paik, who died in 2006, spent his career subverting the advanced technology that makes modern communication—and his work—possible. Paik will forever be linked to television, despite (or perhaps because of) his vocal criticism of the ways in which that ubiquitous technology has shaped our consciousness. In 1969, in collaboration with video engineer Shuya Abe, he created the Paik-Abe Synthesizer, which distorts video images, turning them into dense, abstracted patterns that replicate the experience of a world in constant flux, in which the mind moves fluidly between "real life" and an incessant flow of electronic images, sounds, and "information." Thus, long before MTV, he explored the psychological and physical effects of artificially fragmented and accelerated visual imagery. As if to suggest how embedded this quintessentially contemporary experience is, Paik installed piles of flickering TV monitors in robots, architectural structures, and even arrangements of foliage. In *TV Garden*, 1974, a scattering of television monitors lay face up amid potted plants, offering an ironic critique of our relationship with nature today, which is seemingly more distanced than our connection with electronic media.

Paik's work explores how the mass media manipulate our sense of time, and hence our sense of self and world, an idea that has been taken up by younger artists of a generation that spends much of its time in the glow of various screens. Douglas

ON KAWARA

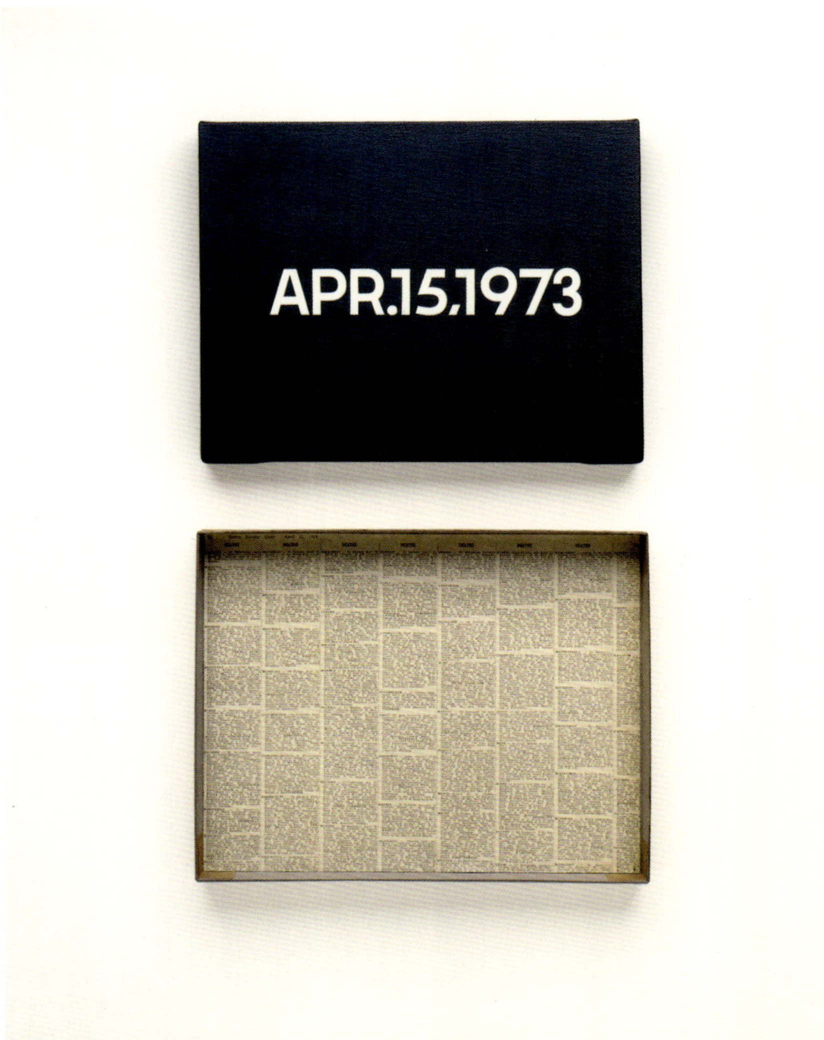

Apr. 15, 1973, 1973
Liquitex on canvas with handmade cardboard box, 10 x 13 in (25.5 x 33 cm)

ROMAN OPALKA

1965/1-∞, 1981
Acrylic on canvas, 75 5/8 x 53 1/8 in (192 x 135 cm)

NAM JUNE PAIK

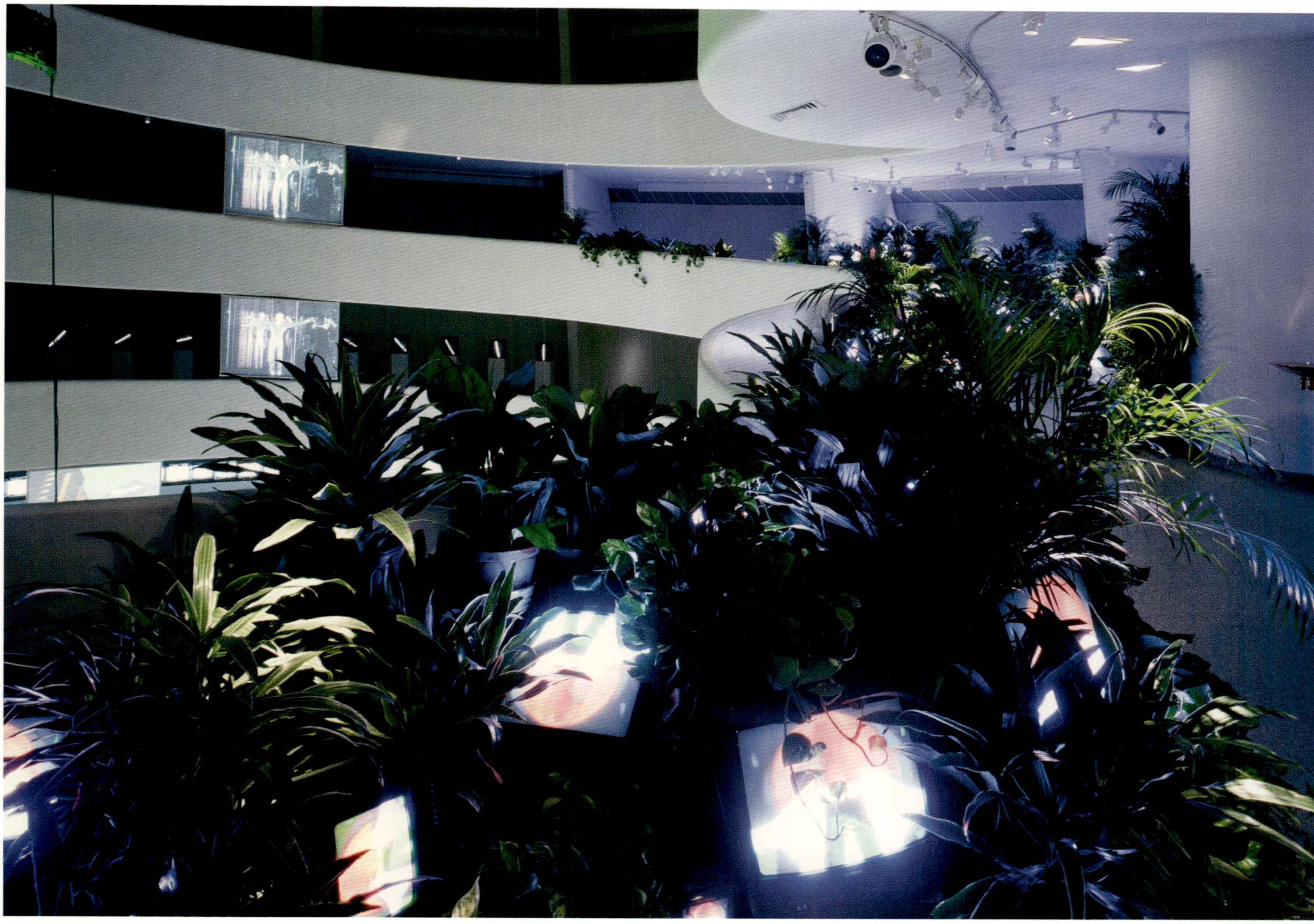

TV Garden, 1974
Video and audio installation with monitors and live plants
As installed at the Solomon R. Guggenheim Museum, New York, February–April 2000

JOAN JONAS

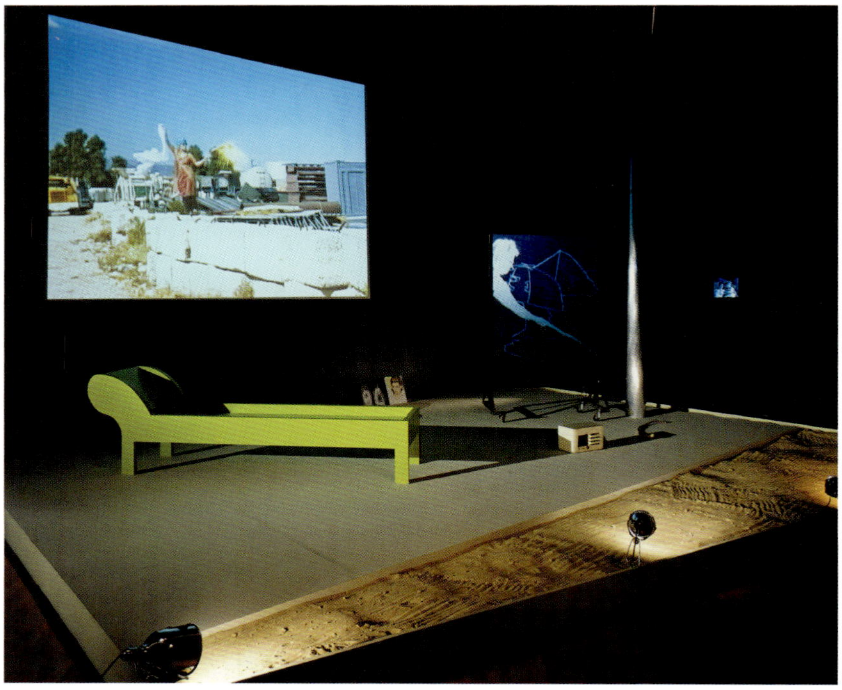

Lines in the Sand, 2002
Mixed media, dimensions variable
As installed at Queens Museum of Art, New York, December 2003–March 2004

DOUGLAS GORDON

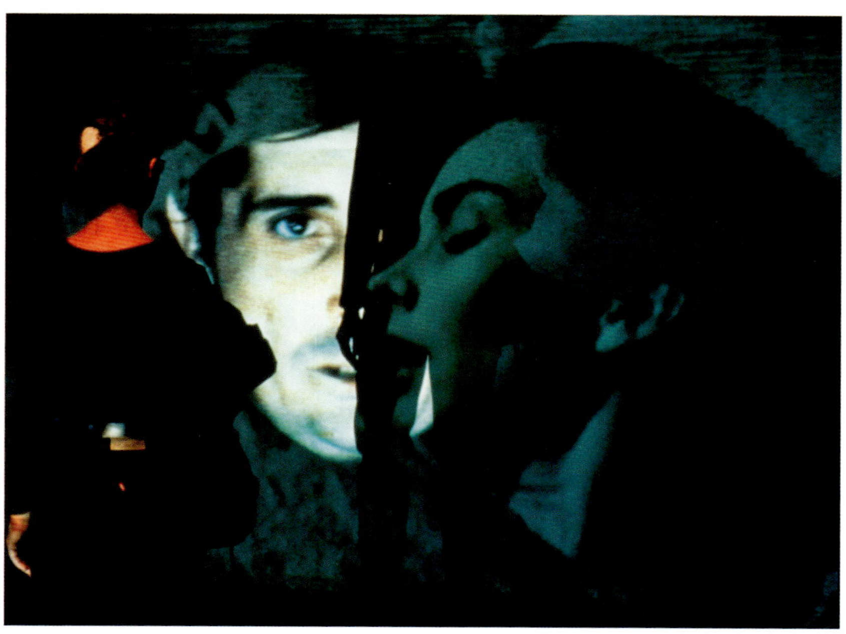

Between Darkness and Light (After William Blake), 1997
Double-projection video installation, 1 hour 47 minutes and 2 hours 35 minutes

Gordon, for instance, alters existing films, distorting reel time to mimic a real-life sense of psychological discomfort, incompleteness, and fragmentation. His *24-Hour Psycho*, 1993, is exactly that, a replay of Hitchcock's 1960 masterpiece projected at a few frames per second, so that the whole film consumes an entire day. In the process of extension, the story line disappears and the viewer is left with only microscopic and incoherent details. Gordon took his preoccupations to a more metaphysical plane with *Between Darkness and Light (after William Blake)*, 1997, which was originally installed in a pedestrian underpass in the German town of Muenster. On either side of a translucent screen he ran two films continuously, allowing chance to determine which scenes coincided at any moment. The films represent the sacred (*The Song of Bernadette*, from 1943) and the profane (*The Exorcist*, from 1973), and the dialogue between the two thus placed the viewer somewhere between heaven and hell and somewhere between several overlapping moments in real and reel time. In all of his work, Gordon disrupts our usual seamless enjoyment of Hollywood movies in order to expose the formulaic devices they use to entrance us. He makes it impossible to lose oneself in the action, constantly reminding us of the manipulations of reel time.

Christian Marclay's seven-minute video *Telephones*, 1995, takes a similar though more playful approach to warping time. Marclay, who is a musician as well as an artist, explores the disjuncture between time-based music and visual objects that exist in space, making sculpture out of such items as recording tape, vinyl records, album covers, and musical instruments, or producing sound works to be "viewed" in an art museum. For *Telephones* he applied the practice of music sampling to film, creating a humorous cinematic narrative made up of hundreds of clips from Hollywood movies that take us through the process of a telephone call—from the dialing to the first ring to hanging the receiver back on the hook. No full conversations take place, though we get many variations on characters saying "hello" and "goodbye" in attitudes that range from bored to amorous to histrionic. The result is an armature of an action filled with stylized gestures but emptied of all real content. But that emptiness hardly seems to matter—the work sweeps us along through a fractured then reconstructed fusion of cinematic conventions.

Paul Pfeiffer also exposes the conventions of reel time, presenting photographs and continuous loops of digitally altered soundless clips from sports broadcasts or Hollywood films that subject their stars to erasure, mechanical repetition, and various other indignities. His videos are mostly shown at minuscule scale, on tiny, six-inch monitors, and the results are disconcerting. In *The Pure Products Go Crazy*, 1998, Tom Cruise, in a looped clip from the 1983 movie *Risky Business*, seems to vibrate uncontrollably, face-down on a couch. *The Long Count (I Shook Up the World)*, 2000, plays and replays the third round of the 1964 boxing match between Sonny Liston and Cassius Clay, though the figures of Liston and Clay have been removed, leaving a pair of ghostlike presences that flicker across the surface. In a 2002 series of photographic works collectively titled *Four Horsemen of the Apocalypse*, a basketball player whose face and number have been digitally obscured attempts a jump shot on a court from which his fellow players have disappeared. In such works, with their bare trace of human presence, time no longer serves as the neutral medium in which individuals move and act. Instead it becomes an alien substance that operates independently of our perceptions.

Artists such as Gordon, Marclay, and Pfeiffer manipulate reel time to explode the temporal illusions embedded in conventional television or movies. Other artists use

CHRISTIAN MARCLAY

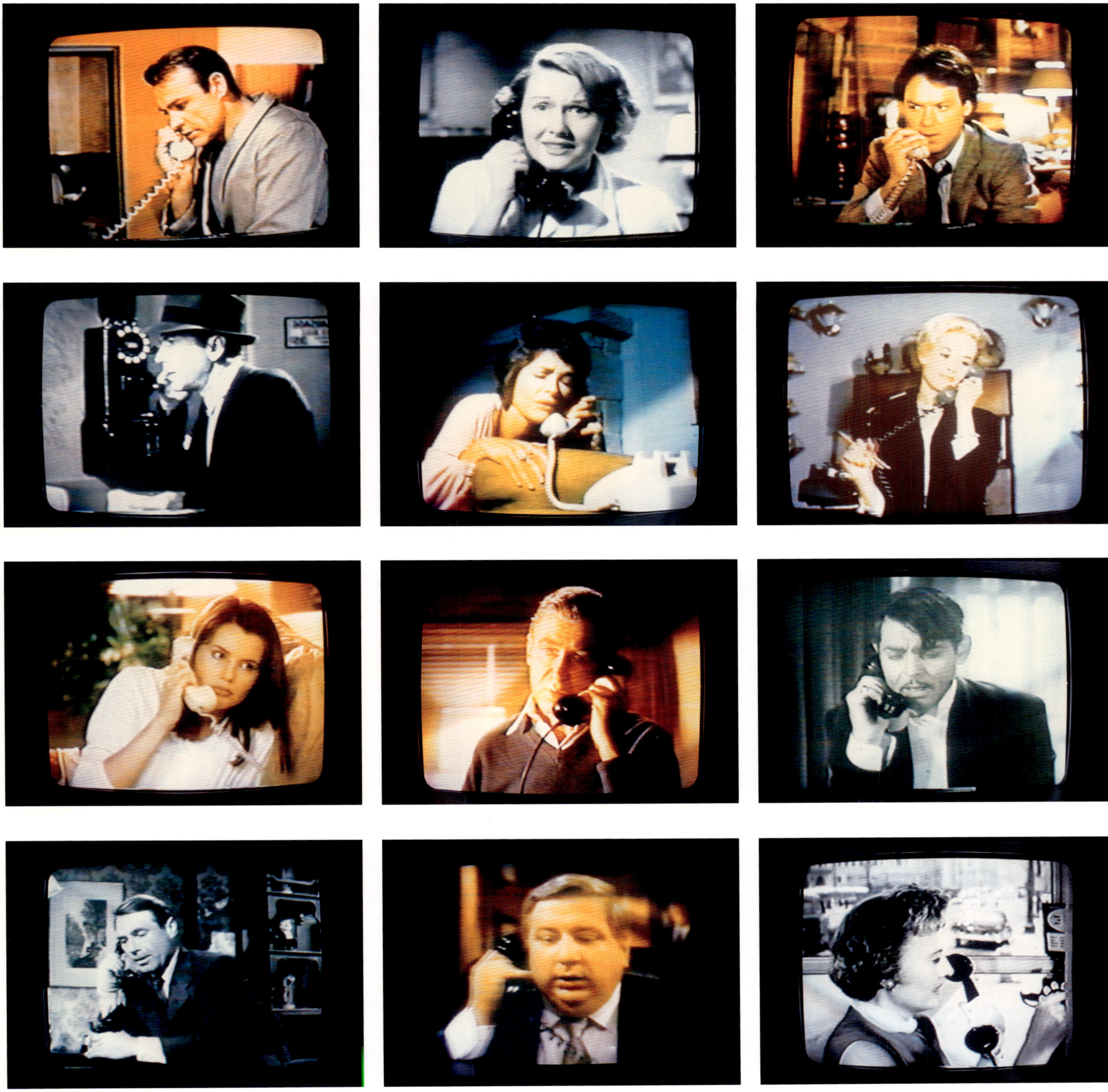

Telephones, 1995
Video stills, 7 minutes 30 seconds

PAUL PFEIFFER

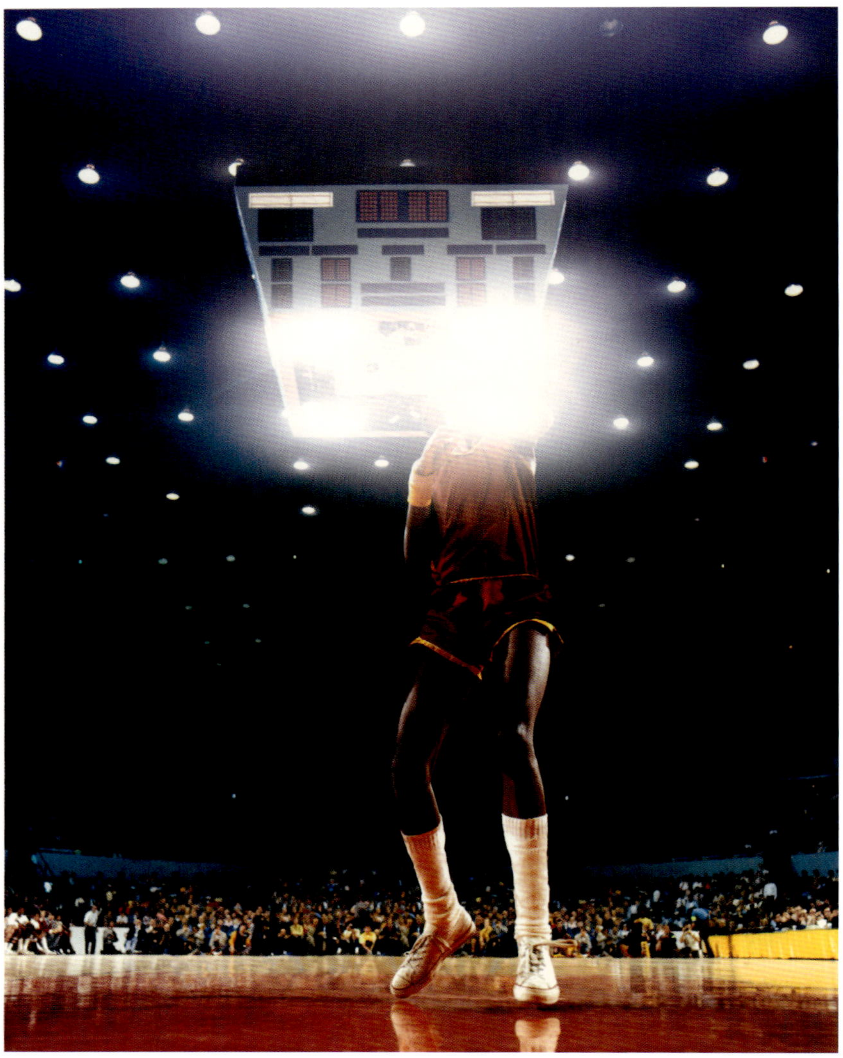

Four Horsemen of the Apocalypse (17), 2004
Digital Fugiflex print, dimensions variable

video toward opposite ends—to enhance or expand upon the meditative experience of high art, perhaps as an antidote to mediated experience. Eve Sussman's *89 Seconds at Alcázar*, 2004, a ten-minute video that animates Velázquez's famous seventeenth-century painting *Las Meninas*, brings the sense of time and movement implied in narrative paintings to life. The original painting is a portrait of the Spanish Princess Marguerite, portrayed along with several maids of honor and a pet dog; the artist, who is painting the portrait; a mirror whose reflection seems to place the king and queen at exactly the point at which we, the viewers, would be standing; and in the far distance, a mysterious figure exiting through a door at the back of the room. Sussman, who hired actors to play each role, puts all of these figures in motion, circling the camera around them to portray the moments up to and just after they would have taken the positions we see in Velázquez's painting. The video's fluid motion and deliberate choreography underline the notion that narrative painting is a frozen moment plucked from an unfolding drama, the temporal expanse of which exists only in the viewer's imagination.

Bill Viola also draws on the tradition of Western art, and a number of his works are also video re-creations of well-known paintings. *The Greeting*, 1995, for example, is a larger-than-life recreation of Italian Mannerist artist Jacopo da Pontormo's sixteenth-century masterpiece *Visitation*. Viola recreates the poses of Pontormo's tableau but updates the figures' clothing, so that it echoes Pontormo's costumes though without seeming anachronistic. But the biggest difference between the two versions of the scene is that Viola's is in motion: the women reach toward each other and embrace as a heavy wind stirs their flowing garments. The forty-five second action is projected in slow motion, stretched out to ten minutes, giving the scene the stately air of existing somehow outside of ordinary time, like many great works of art. This sense of strangely attenuated time appears again in Viola's 2002 video installation *Going Forth By Day*. Here Viola cites as an influence Giotto's frescoes for the Scrovegni Chapel in Padua, a fresco cycle that places the events of Christ's life from conception to resurrection into the time frame of mankind's existence from creation to the Last Judgment. Viola also aspires to this monumental sweep through time and space. He fills each wall of a darkened gallery with floor-to-ceiling image sequences that refer to the cycle of human life, each becoming a slow-moving allegorical narrative. For instance, our passage through life is suggested by an unhurried procession of people following a path through a forest. Death is represented by an old man who lies dying as a boat is prepared to take him to the next phase.

The stately dramatizations of Sussman and Viola unlock the imaginative time frozen within static narrative paintings. Photographer Hiroshi Sugimoto uses photography to return frozen tableaux to the flow of ordinary time. His black-and-white photographs of exotic animals in their native habitats appear to be the work of a remarkably lucky wildlife photographer. In fact, they depict dioramas at the Museum of Natural History in New York, and only the absolute perfection of the animals' poses gives away the story. In a similar fashion, Sugimoto's photographs of such figures as Henry VIII, Salvador Dalí, Winston Churchill, and Queen Victoria resemble staged studio portraits; an unnatural stillness reveals that they were in fact taken of the displays at Madame Tussaud's wax museum. In his ongoing "Theaters" series, begun in the mid-1970s, Sugimoto performs the opposite operation, arresting and condensing the time in a feature-length film into a single

EVE SUSSMAN AND THE RUFUS CORPORATION

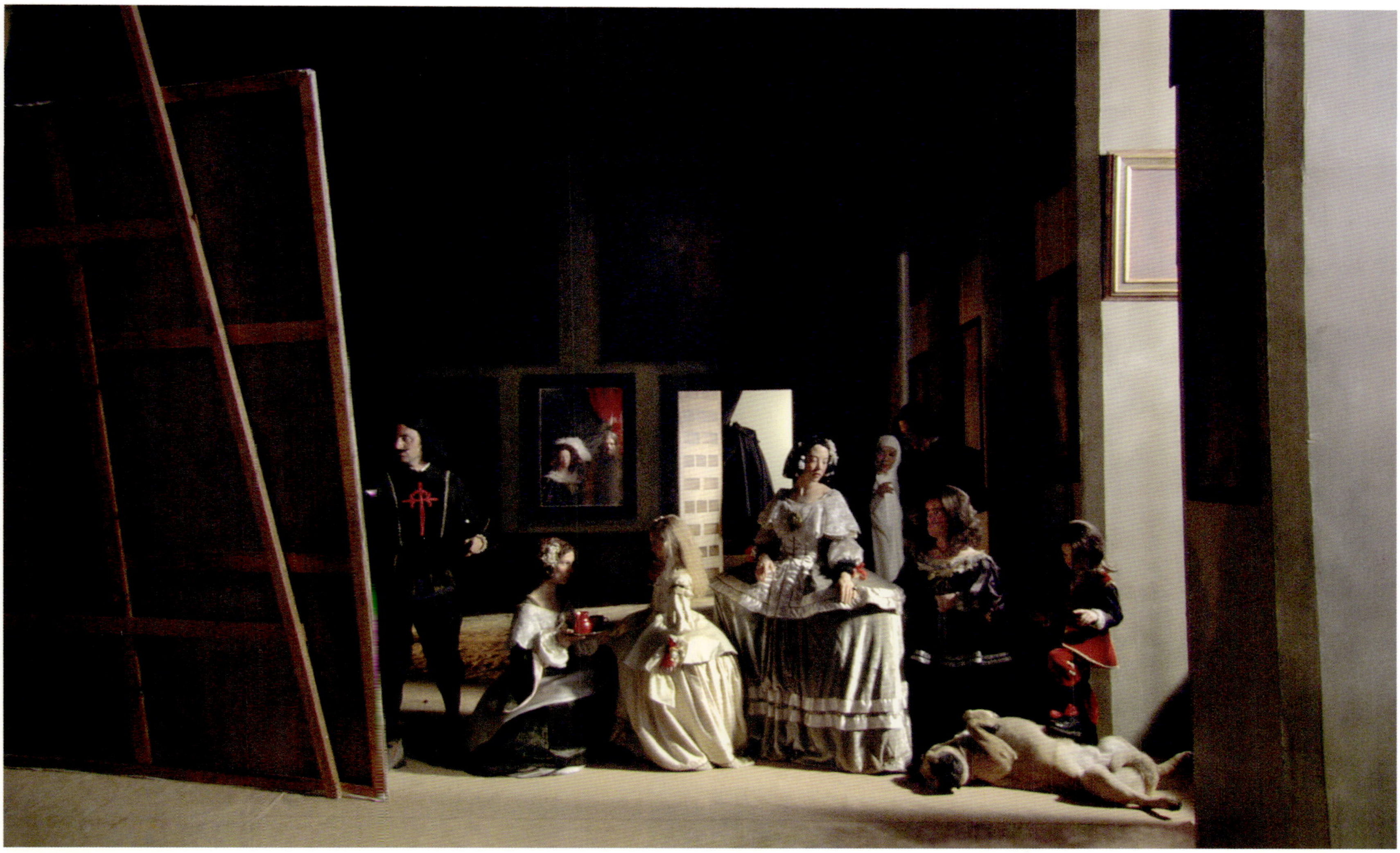

Dog Rolls, video still from *89 Seconds at Alcázar*, 2004
10 minutes

BILL VIOLA

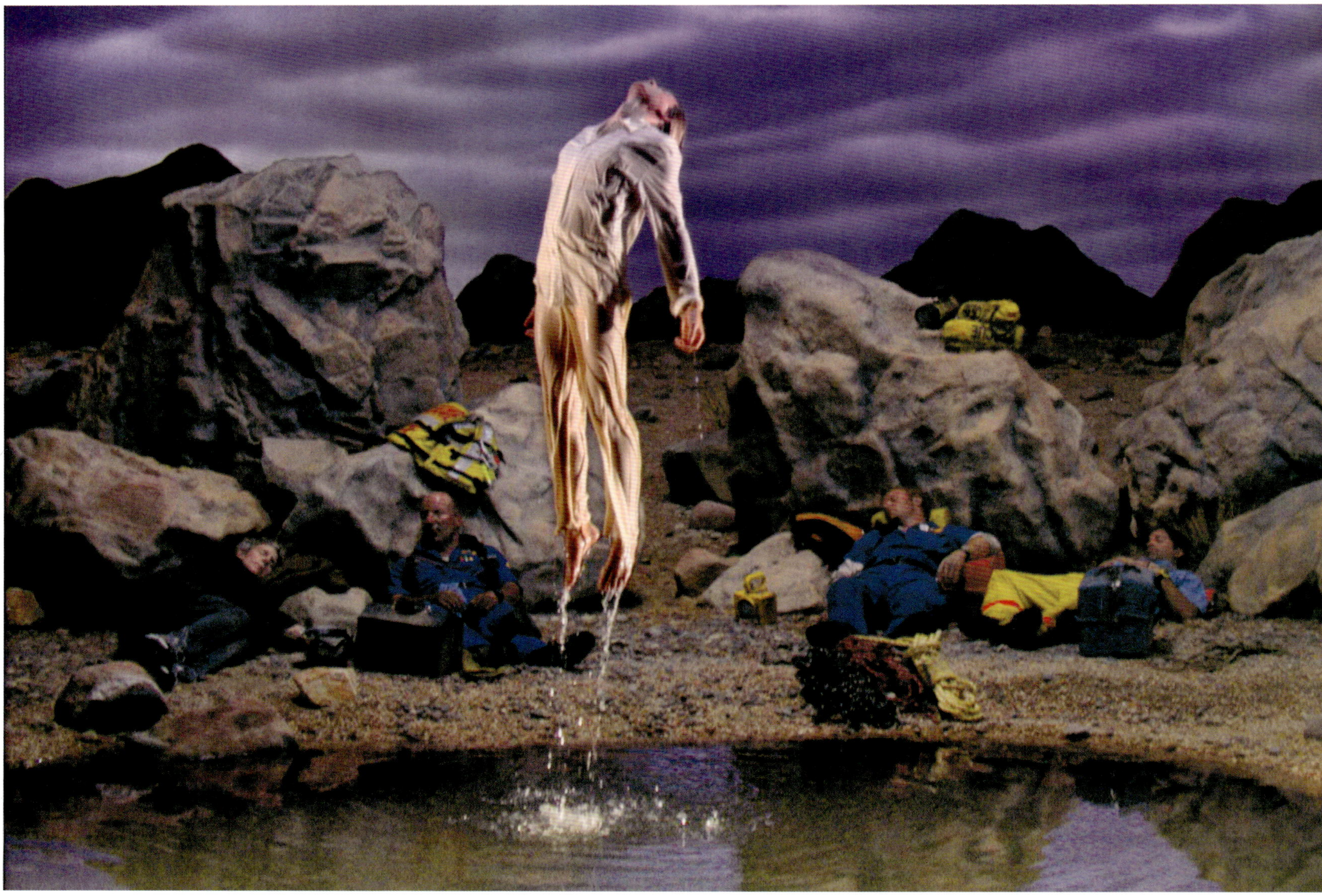

Going Forth By Day: First Light, 2002
Video/sound installation, five-part projected image cycle, each projection approx. 35 minutes

black-and-white frame. These photographs of the interiors of movie theaters capture ornate balconies and stages with eerily glowing, seemingly empty screens at their center. This apparent emptiness is in fact fullness, created by long exposures that last the duration of the film being shown, producing an effect that literally erases the movement and flux of ordinary life. Whether restoring or condensing time, Sugimoto uses the static nature of photography to create a tension between its stillness and the ever-mutating nature of the world it records.

David Hockney has also used photography to make fleeting time more palpable. Best known for his painted portraits and landscapes, Hockney began to explore the spatial complexities of his newly decorated home with a Polaroid camera in 1982. The result is a series of composite photo collages titled *My House, Montcalm Avenue* that provide a patched-together, panoramic view of the house and have a very different effect than a photograph taken from one vantage point at a single moment. Because the camera is moving, it reflects changes that take place in time. The light shifts from one sliver of imagery to another, figures who have moved reappear in different parts of the house. In the end Hockney gives us a vision of the scene that is close to the real experience of walking through space. So entranced was he by this effect that he has applied the technique to full-length Polaroid portraits of his friends, to scenes of the American West, and to views of Japanese gardens. In the process he updates Cubism, fracturing the picture plane into shards that reflect the fluid nature of human perception in time.

While many artists invent or evoke new senses of time, inviting viewers to experience them objectively, some create a space in which their audience is fully immersed in kaleidoscopic temporal flux. In the work of these artists, viewers are no longer outsiders peering into another world, they are plunged into the middle of the artwork, at times even taking on a performative role. They thus begin to experience Bergson's notion of "duration," in which time ceases to be experienced as a linear flow and instead becomes an all-encompassing present. For example, Pipilotti Rist's room-size video installations immerse us in a frenzied environment in which pop music, color, and moving images create a hypnotic world in which to explore sexuality, femininity, and fantasy. One of Rist's best-known works, *Ever Is Over All*, 1997, is a two-screen video installation that juxtaposes slowly roving images of red flowers with shots of a woman, played by Rist herself, dreamily walking down a city street as she smashes the windows of parked cars with an oversize metal flower. The accompanying sound track includes humming and birds chirping over a percussive beat. Like the flowers and the woman's flouncing blue dress, these aural elements speak of nature, beauty, and softness, all the stereotypical female attributes that the woman's destructive act contradicts.

In elaborate multi-screen video installations, Doug Aitken explores a similar immersion experience, in which he breaks down the typically linear structure of video and film to capture the contemporary perception of time as a fragmented, accelerated, and multi-layered experience. One of his best-known works, *Electric Earth*, 1999, uses not only multiple screens but also multiple rooms, each of which sweeps the viewer along into a different set of sensations. A lone protagonist, a young black man, wanders through a post-apocalyptic urban landscape. His image is projected on all the walls of each room as he moves with dance-like motions through empty parking lots, bedrooms, laundromats, and gas stations, which themselves seem to be vibrating and mutating. The work is full of blinking lights and abrupt and

HIROSHI SUGIMOTO

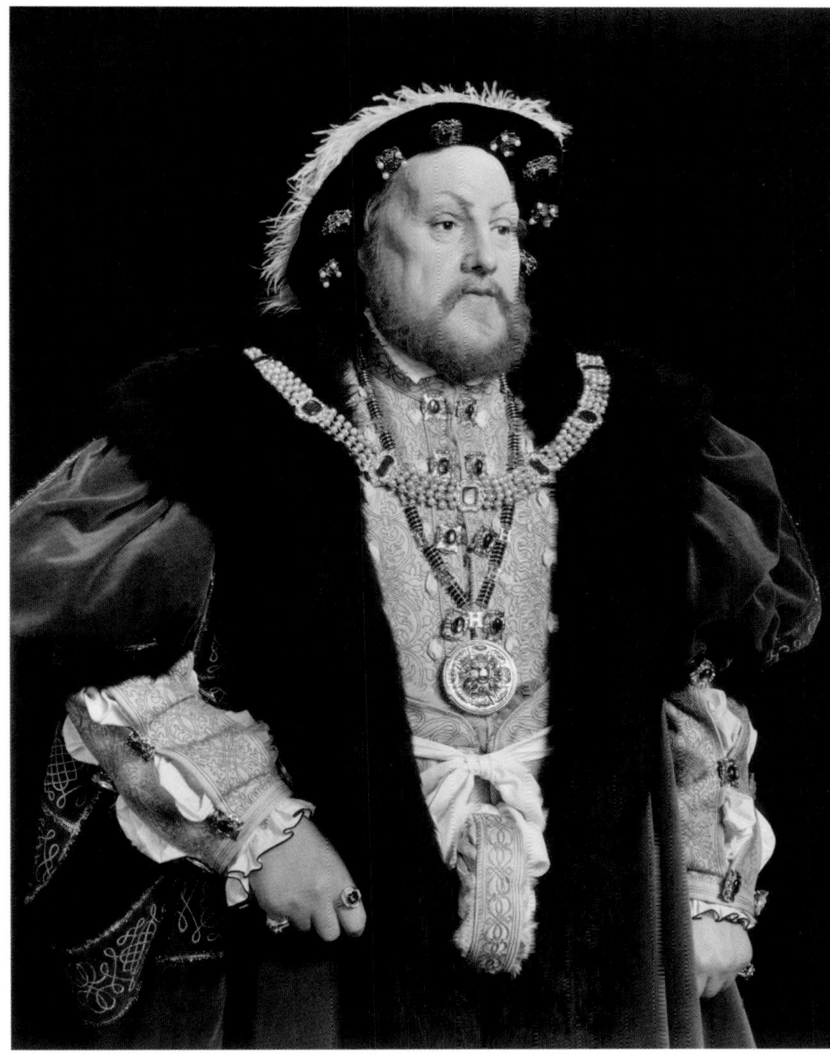

Henry VIII, 1999
Black and white photograph, 58 x 47 in (149 x 119 cm)

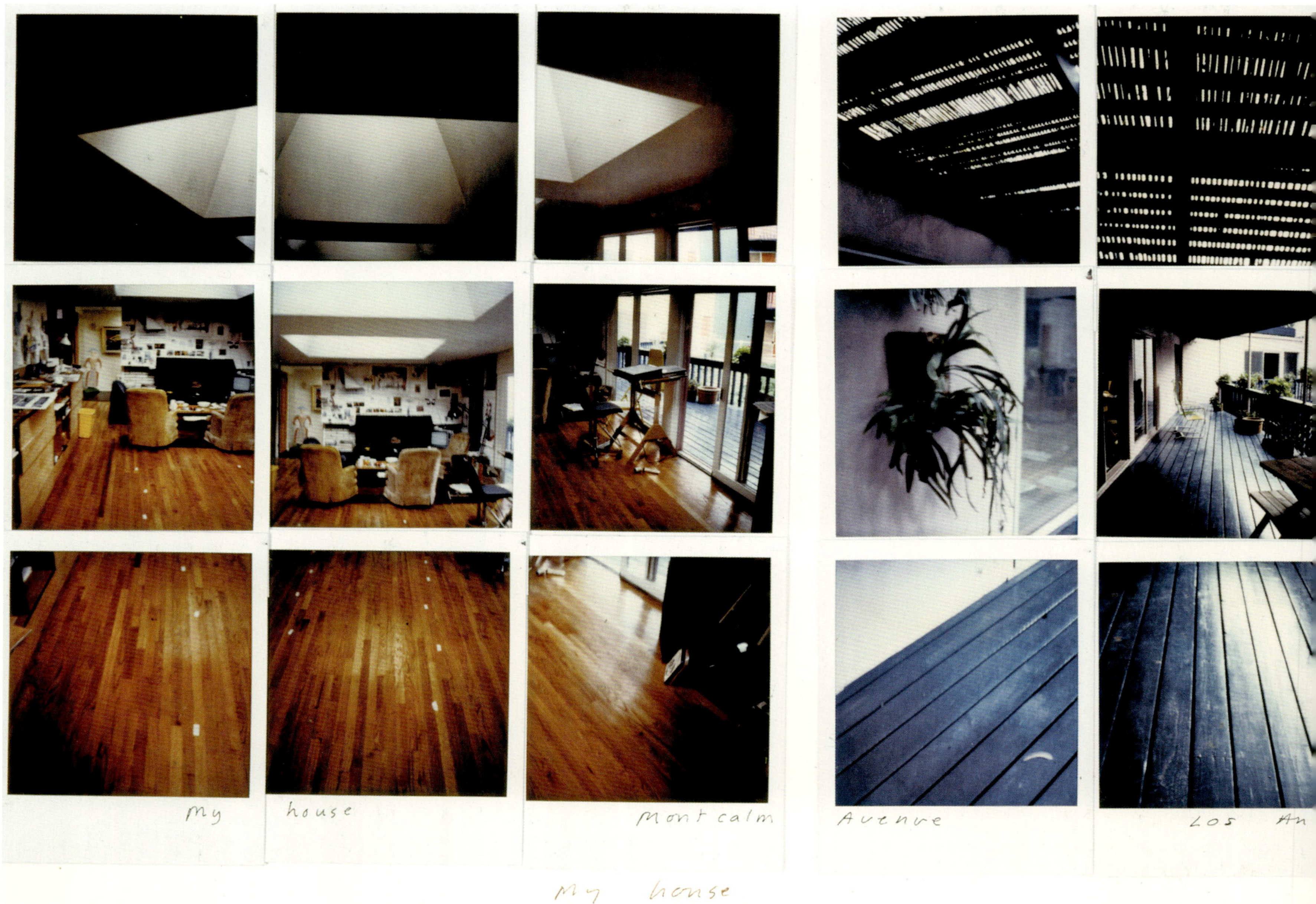
My house Montcalm Avenue Los An
My house

DAVID HOCKNEY

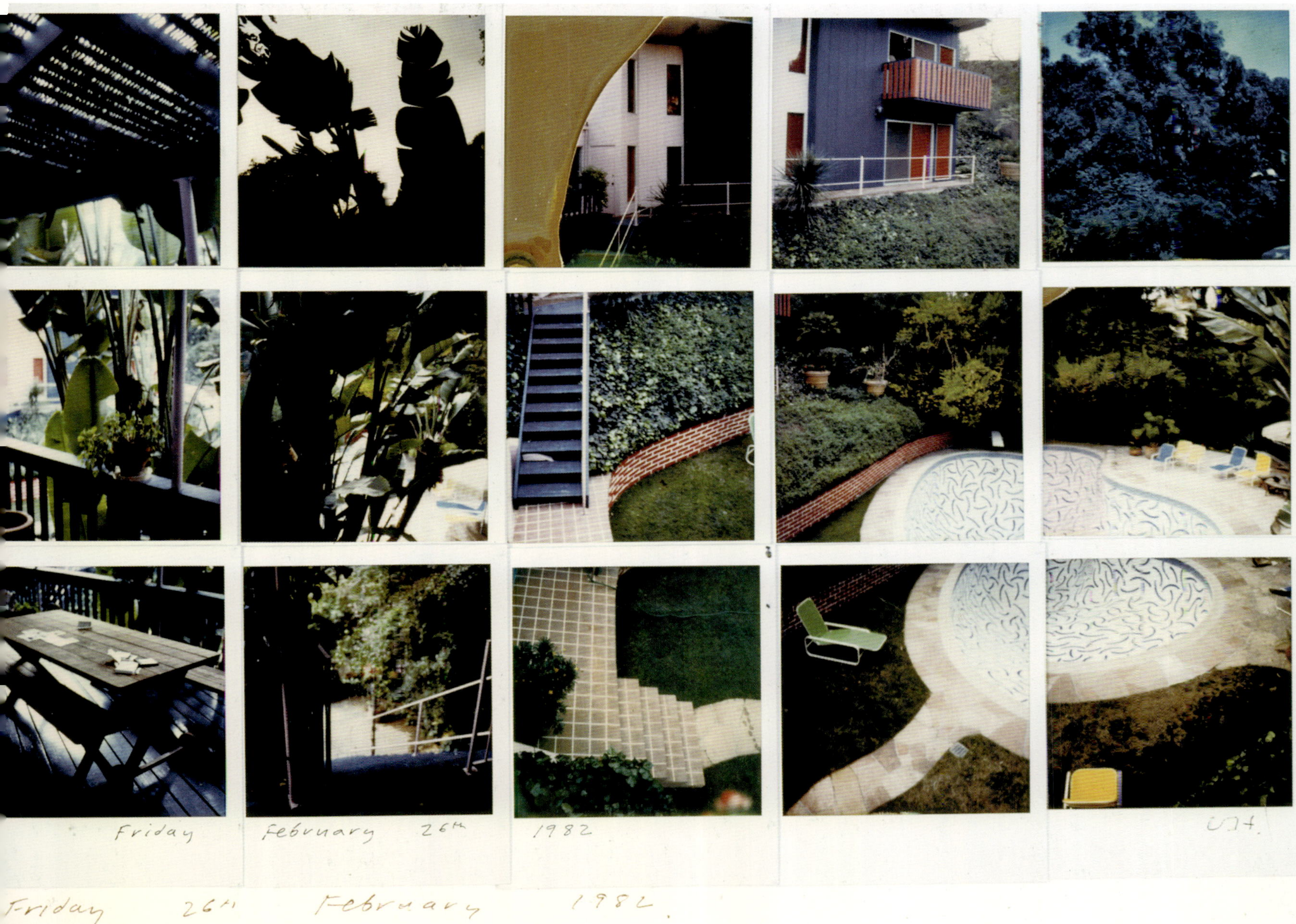

My House, Montcalm Avenue, Los Angeles, Friday, February 26th 1982, 1982
Composite Polaroid, 11 x 34 in (27.9 x 86.4 cm)

PIPILOTTI RIST

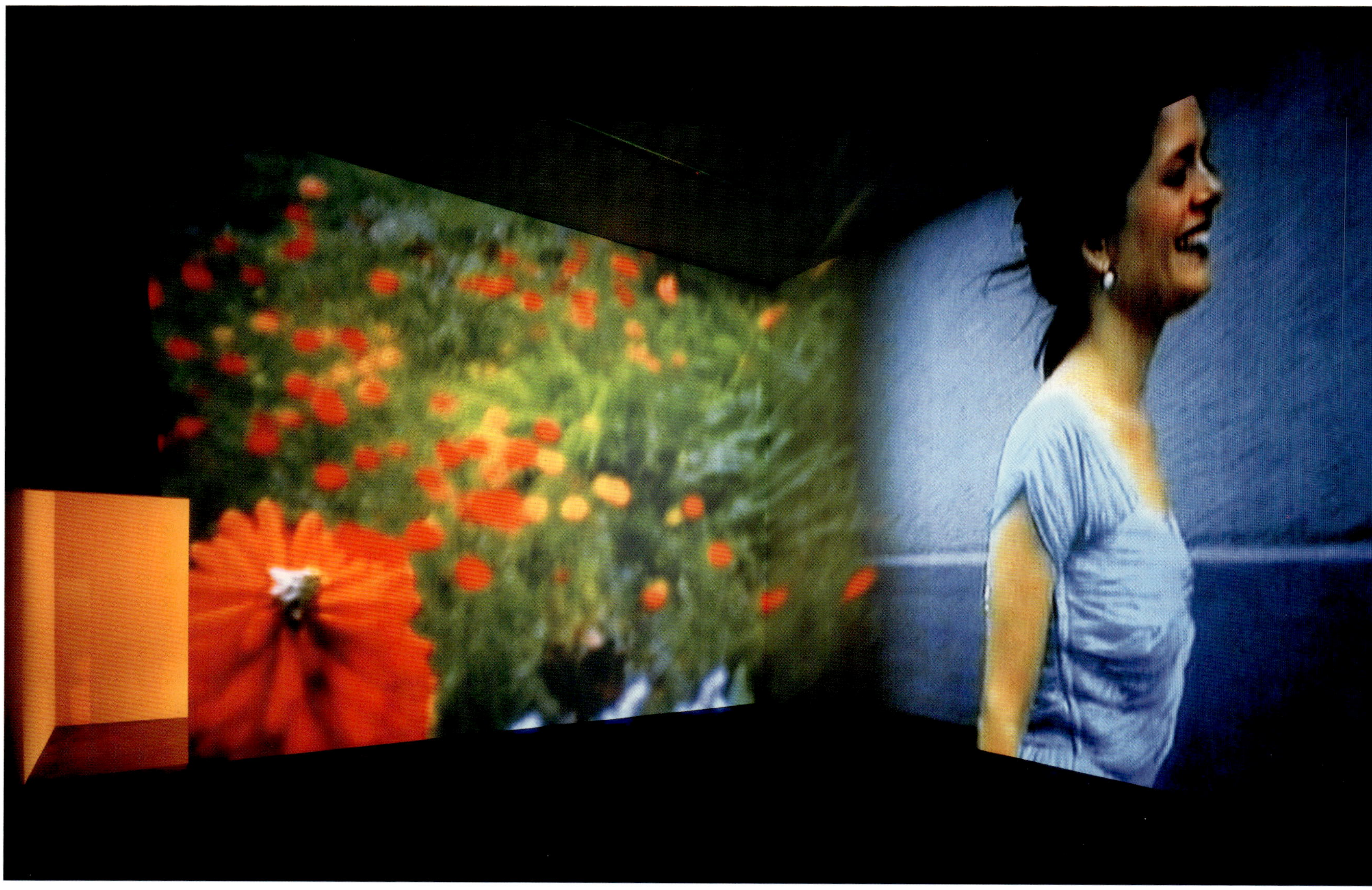

Ever Is Over All, 1997
2 laser disc players, 2 video projectors, 1 audio system, 2 laser discs
The Museum of Modern Art, New York

DOUG AITKEN

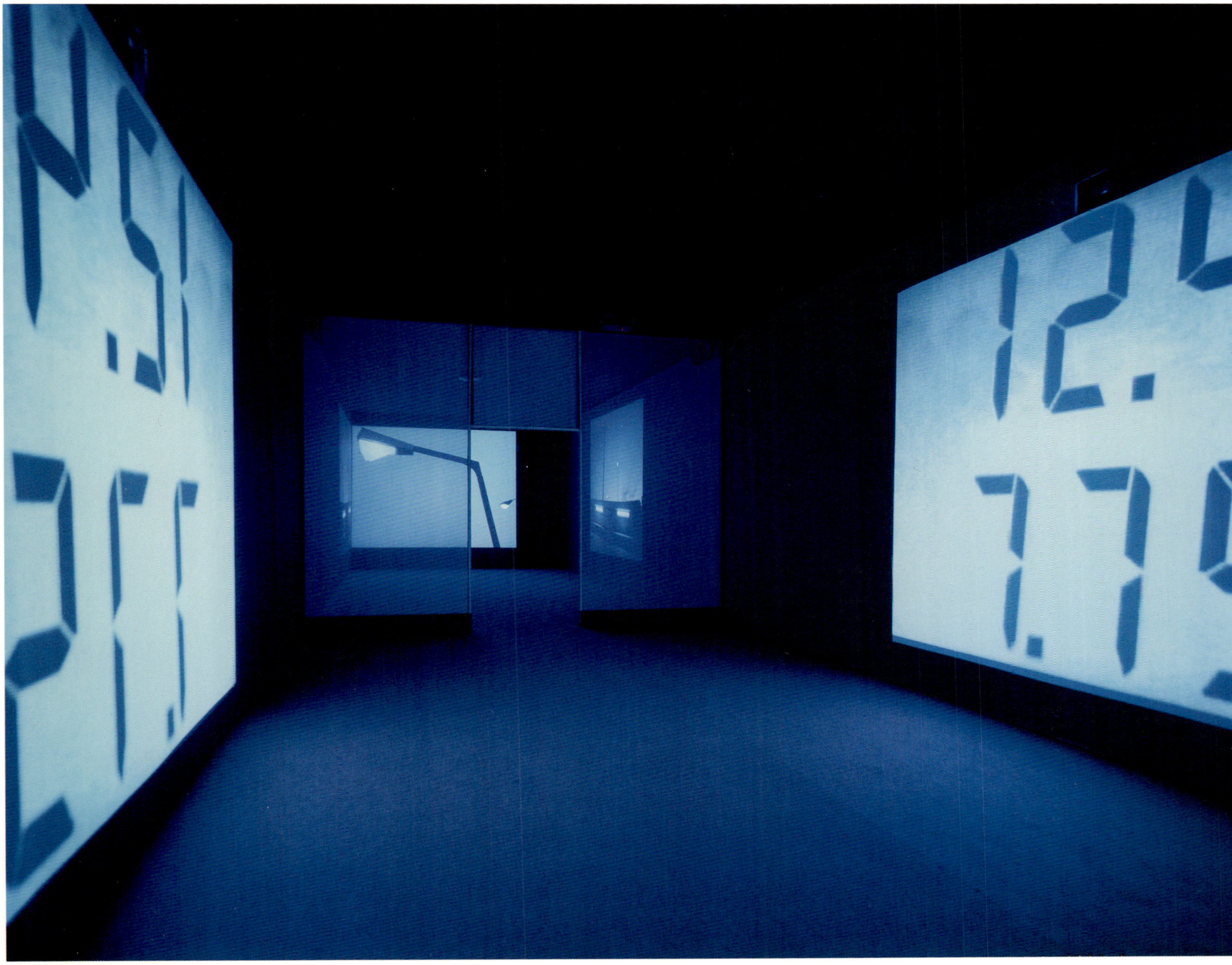

Electric Earth, 1999
8 laserdisc installation, dimensions variable
As installed at the 48th Venice Biennale, 1999

JEREMY BLAKE

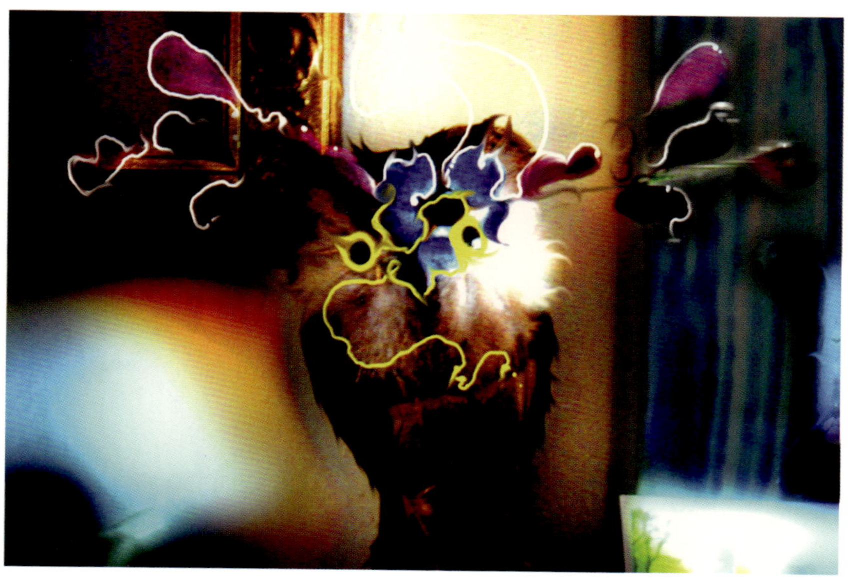

Reading Ossie Clark, 2003
DVD with sound for plasma or projection, 9-minute continuous loop

jittery camera sequences designed to disconnect viewers from any ordinary sense of time and place. A voice-over intones, "A lot of times I dance so fast that I become what's around me," a cryptic proclamation that is perhaps a key to the whole work. Aitken points out that the piece is intended to evoke the multi-scene quality of real experience: "Taking a walk can be an uncanny experience," he says. "Propelled by our legs we find rhythms and tempos. Our bodies move in cycles that are repetitious and machine-like. We lose track of thoughts. Time can slip away from us; it can stretch out or become condensed. Sometimes, the speed of our environment is out of sync with our perception of it. When this happens, it creates a kind of gray zone, a state of flux that fascinates me."[2]

The idea that time is not fixed, but rather is relative to the movements of body and mind, underlies the work of many contemporary artists. Jeremy Blake, who committed suicide in 2007 at the age of 35, took the notion a step beyond subjectivity, creating narratives that suggest that time is a function of our imagination and hence no more or less real than any other fantasy. His projected video *Winchester*, 2002, is filmed inside the mansion that the Winchester rifle heiress built with her inheritance to house the spirits of those whose lives were cut short by Winchester rifles. Blake evokes the past and the present simultaneously by mimicking the skips and scratches of weathered film, washing the screen periodically with swaths of pure color, and altering the speed of the film to create flickering presences that suggest the presence of ghosts. In *Reading Ossie Clark*, 2003, Blake recreates another kind of distorted sense of time and space—that of a psychedelic drug trip. His subject here is the mod-era fashion designer Ossie Clark, epitome of swinging London in the 1960s and '70s. The work combines narrated passages from Clark's posthumously published diaries (he was killed by a lover in 1996) with digitally altered, hand-painted abstractions, swatches of fabric designed by Clark, drifting smoke, and a soundtrack that recalls the trippy music of the period. The result is a hypnotic blend of sound and imagery that seduces the viewer into deep identification with the subject.

Stasi City, 1997, by Jane and Louise Wilson, also creates the sensation of infiltrating another psyche. Filmed in the abandoned headquarters of the East German secret police, this installation places the viewer between two screens showing related images that read like overlapping paths through the same space. The viewer becomes, in a sense, the eye of a moving camera. We travel through a labyrinth of vacant interrogation rooms, follow the motion of spinning reel-to-reel tape players, weave through rusting surveillance equipment, and pause over poignant remnants of office furniture. Occasionally there is a glimpse of a ghost-like human presence—a partial view of a woman riding an elevator, a figure levitating in an otherwise empty room. The motion is slow, dreamy, shrouding this once terrifying place with an aura of melancholy and nostalgia. There is, of course, an understated irony to this work. The Stasi served as the all-pervasive surveillance arm of the East German government. Its eyes were everywhere, and always led back to the nerve center in this once deeply guarded building. Now we become the eyes surveying those eyes, moving like ghosts ourselves through this ruined monument to absolute state control. By bringing us inside this once forbidden territory and letting us drift amid its ghosts and memories, the Wilsons seem to reverse the flow of time. The terrifying history of this place begins to reassert itself, pulling us along with it, so that we are eerily complicit with its denuded power.

JANE AND LOUISE WILSON

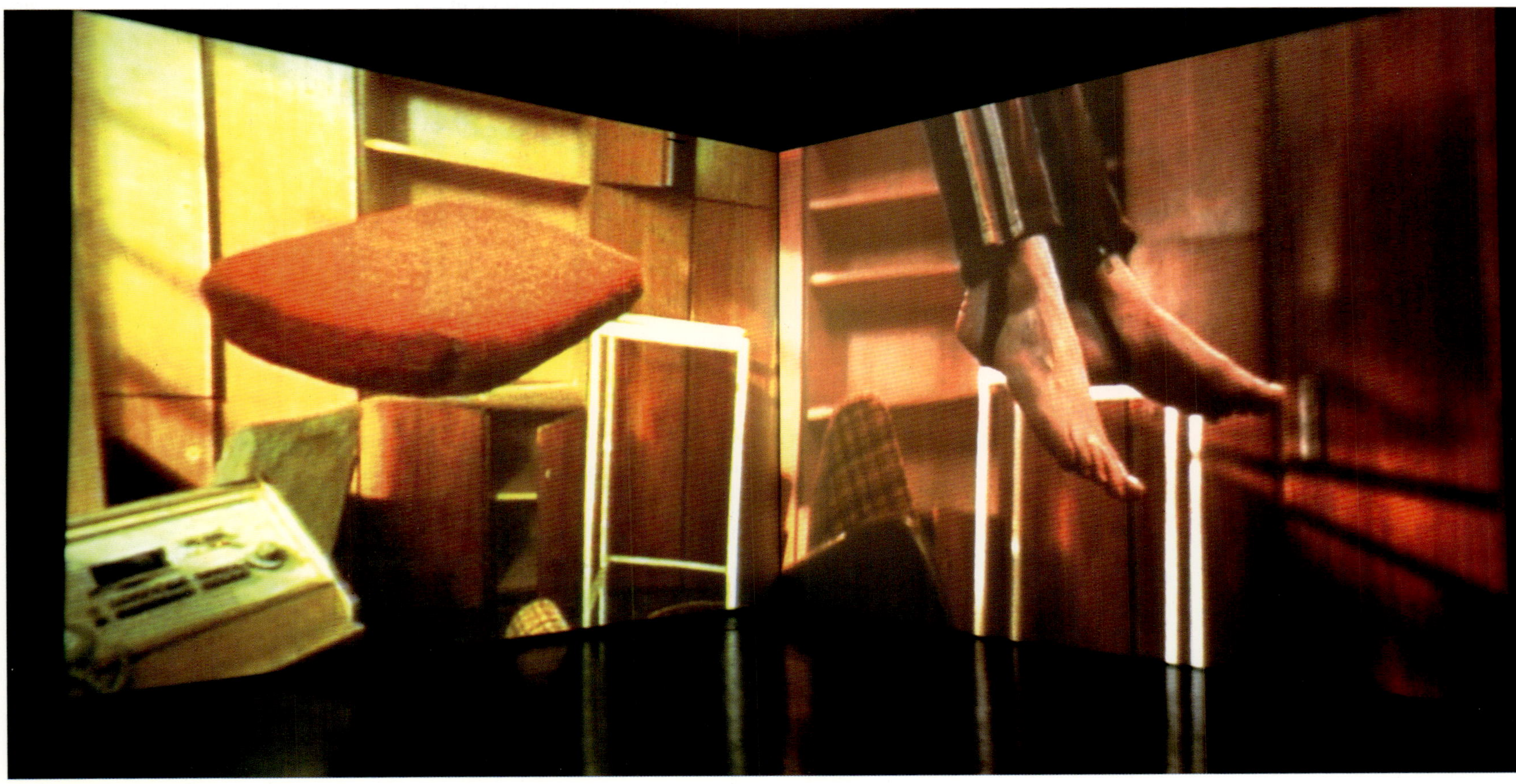

Stasi City, 1997
4-channel video installation, 5-minute loop

Sam Taylor-Wood implicates us in scenarios that take place in the present. Using multiple screens, she breaks down any sense of distinction between our coordinates in the viewing gallery and those of the scenes unfolding in projections on the wall. In *Travesty of a Mockery*, 1995, Taylor-Wood places the hapless viewer between two large screen projections depicting a young couple engaged in domestic warfare. The pair hurl abuse and physical objects at each other across the viewer's space, occasionally even crossing into the other's screen for some particularly nasty piece of vituperation. Taylor-Wood's 1999 installation *Third Party* is less threatening but just as immersive. The video, which documents a rather dreadful London party through which one circulates like a guest, plays across four walls and seven screens. What at first appears to be a random set of party vignettes—people drinking, a woman dancing, a couple cozying up—eventually resolves itself into a plot of sorts: a flirtation involving a would-be Lothario, a married woman, and her silently seething husband. The viewer is able to piece the story together while shifting views from screen to screen and finally becomes a part of the action when the man looks straight at the camera and asks, "What the fuck am I doing here?"

In Tony Oursler's work, the characters are more consistently in-your-face. Here, dolls, mannequins, disembodied heads, and other three-dimensional forms—enlivened by video projections of characters with faces or just jumbled configurations of eyes and mouths—directly address us with their woes. *Blue Husk*, 2001, for instance, an animated face delivering a stream-of-consciousness monologue, is projected onto a fiberglass sphere behind a hand-blown blue glass shell. Like many of Oursler's characters, this disembodied creature cajoles, complains, and screams, offering the viewer a very plausible approximation of being confined in a small room with a very unpleasant person. Video artist Bill Viola has described video installation as "sculpture with a mind."[3] It is hard to imagine a more apt description of Tony Oursler's creations and their expressions of irritation, lust, anguish, or desire. Despite the very obvious evidence of their low-tech genesis, it is difficult not to respond as if to another sentient being.

Rhythms of time take on political import in the work of Chantal Akerman. Since the early 1970s, Akerman has used film and video to draw our attention to subjects we might otherwise overlook. Her work often focuses on members of marginalized communities who have been bypassed by the electronic and consumer revolutions. In representing their lives, she deliberately decelerates time, creating a distinct rhythm that serves as a stark contrast to the frenzied pace of societies in the grip of modern technology. In *D'Est* (From the East), 1993, a video shot from the window of a slow-moving car during a journey from Germany to Russia, Akerman presents blank-faced men and women buried in winter coats and fur hats shivering as they queue up for food, buses, and trains or loiter in grim Soviet-era lobbies. Played in short-looped segments across twenty-four video monitors scattered throughout the gallery, the work underscores a sense of the futile circularity of lives lost to the minutiae of daily survival.

The multiple-monitor installation in *D'Est* erases viewers' sense of separateness from their immediate surroundings, and hence from the artificial time and space of the image itself. Gary Hill similarly erases distance by making the viewer move and interact with projected images. His remarkable interactive video *Tall Ships*, 1992, pushes the relationship between viewer and subject even further. To exprience this work, viewers walk along a ninety-foot darkened corridor lined with floor-to-ceiling projections of what initially appear to be distant figures representing a range of ages and types. By standing directly before one of these images, the viewer activates the figure, who walks forward until he or she is approximately life size. Each figure then stands in front of the viewer and seems to make eye contact, and after about ten seconds, turns and walks away. Here more than ever, the feeling that we have connected with another mind is inescapable—and disquieting—for it is they, rather than we, who make the decision to make and break the connection. In the darkness of the gallery, these apparently mindful creatures seem as real as, or perhaps even more real than we do, as Hill reverses the usual order of art viewing: the watcher becomes the watched.

This sense of being watched, a state the existential philosopher Jean-Paul Sartre called "being for others,"[4] has become an inescapable reality of contemporary life. George Orwell's prescient novel *1984* foresaw a future in which the daily actions of all citizens would be monitored by an invisible "Big Brother." In fact, with the emergence of reality TV, Webcams, and "CU see me" software, which makes it possible for people to place themselves under surveillance for an infinite Internet audience, and with the presence of surveillance cameras in locations as diverse as shopping malls, public parks, apartment building elevators, corporate lobbies, and movie theaters, it seems that everyone is watching everyone else. This leads to a sense of existing in multiple time frames—in one's own immediate reality and that of those whom one is watching or being watched by. A number of contemporary artists have adopted surveillance technology to capture the melding of reel time and real time that unedited and unmediated watching creates. There is, of course, nothing new about this approach—see Warhol's *Sleep*.

Like Warhol, Bruce Nauman redirects our attention to the minute events that occur when seemingly nothing is happening. Nauman's work since the 1970s has addressed everything from the limitations of language and the shape of empty space to the fragility of identity and the tyranny of communal consciousness. In 2001 he created a video installation titled *Mapping the Studio I (Fat Chance John Cage)*, which pays homage simultaneously to Warhol's *Sleep* and John Cage's *4'33"*. The work consists of a floor-to-ceiling surround-sound environment composed of seven wall projections that together present a nearly six-hour video recording of Nauman's studio at night. Though the work gives the impression of presenting a single night in the studio, like *Sleep*, it is a compilation, in this case of sequences filmed over many months. Also like *Sleep*, *Mapping the Studio* presents a narrative so uneventful that the importance of tiny events becomes magnified. Among those events, which are illuminated by a greenish infrared light, are incursions of mice and fluttering moths. Outside one hears dogs bark and a coyote howl in the distance. As in Cage's "silent" work, ambient and accidental sounds become part of the subject of the piece. The work invites the viewer to move through this virtual studio, much as an insomniac might wander the quiet house at night and succumb to a heightened awareness of the slow passage of time. *Mapping the Studio* recalls some of Nauman's earlier forays into the psychology of surveillance. But unlike earlier works, which turned on interactivity, here the viewer becomes only a voyeur, made aware of a world that is unfolding irrespective of his or her existence.

Tacita Dean also makes the viewer a neutral voyeur. Her video *Fernsehturm*, 2001, takes place in the revolving restaurant in the Fernsehturm television tower, which rises above the former East Berlin and offers a panoramic view of a city in the

SAM TAYLOR-WOOD

Third Party, 1999
Seven 16 mm film projections with sound, 10 minutes

TONY OURSLER

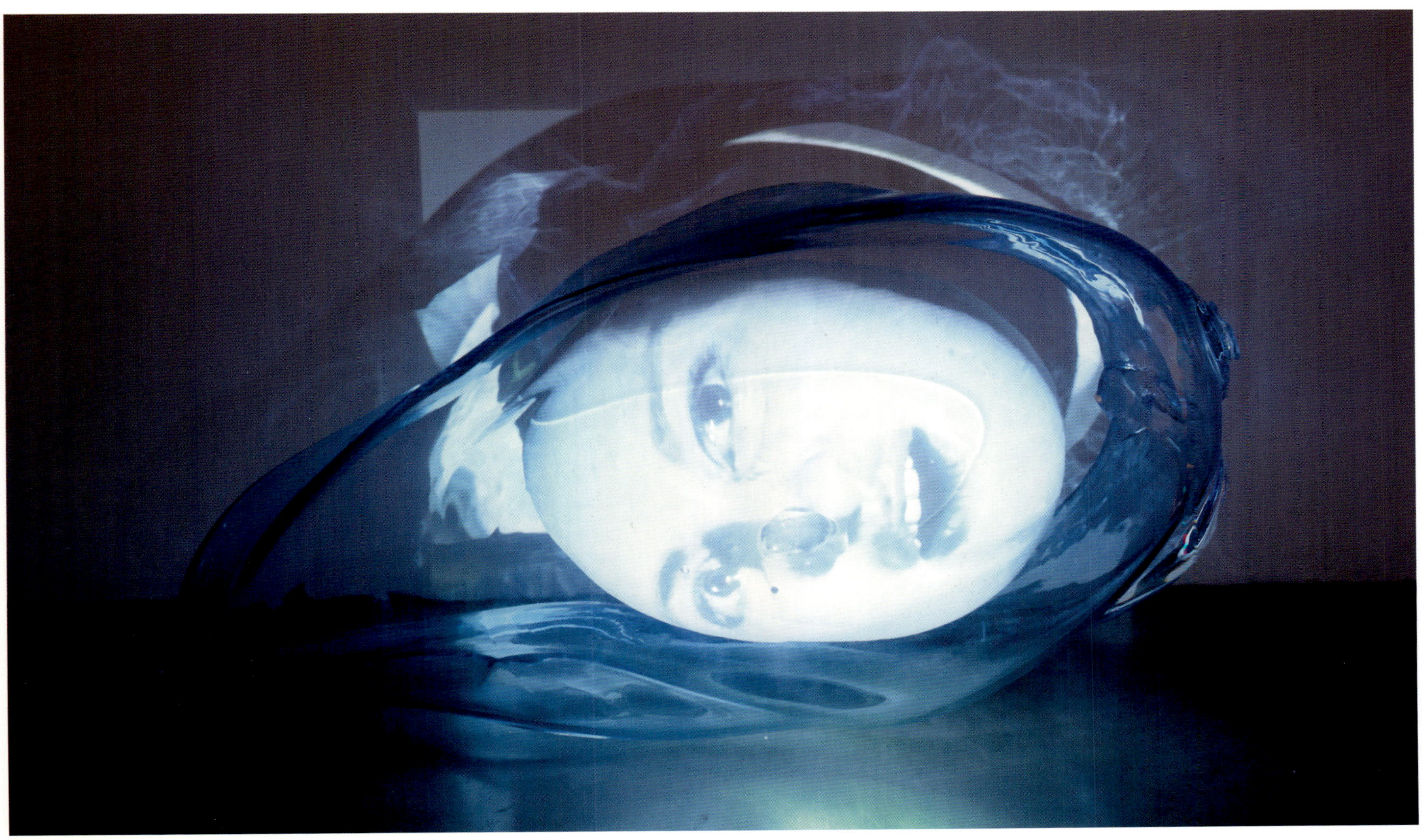

Blue Husk, 2001
Sony DPL CS2 projector, DVD player, DVD, glass, fiberglass sphere, performance by Tracy Leipold
Glass: 34 1/2 x 15 1/4 x 12 in (87.6 x 38.7 x 30.5 cm) fiberglass: 17 x 15 x 9 1/2 in (43.2 x 38.1 x 24.1 cm)

CHANTAL AKERMAN

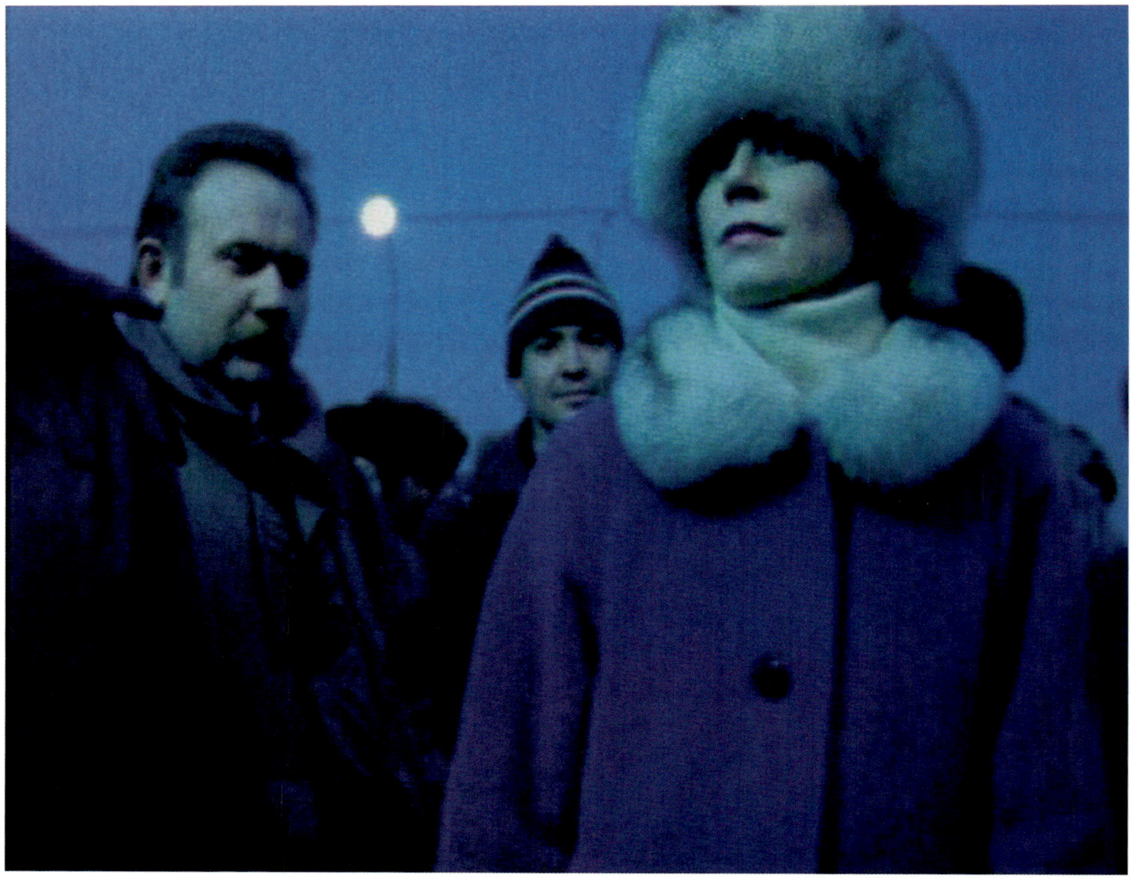

D'Est (From the East), 1993
35 mm documentary, color, 107 minutes

GARY HILL

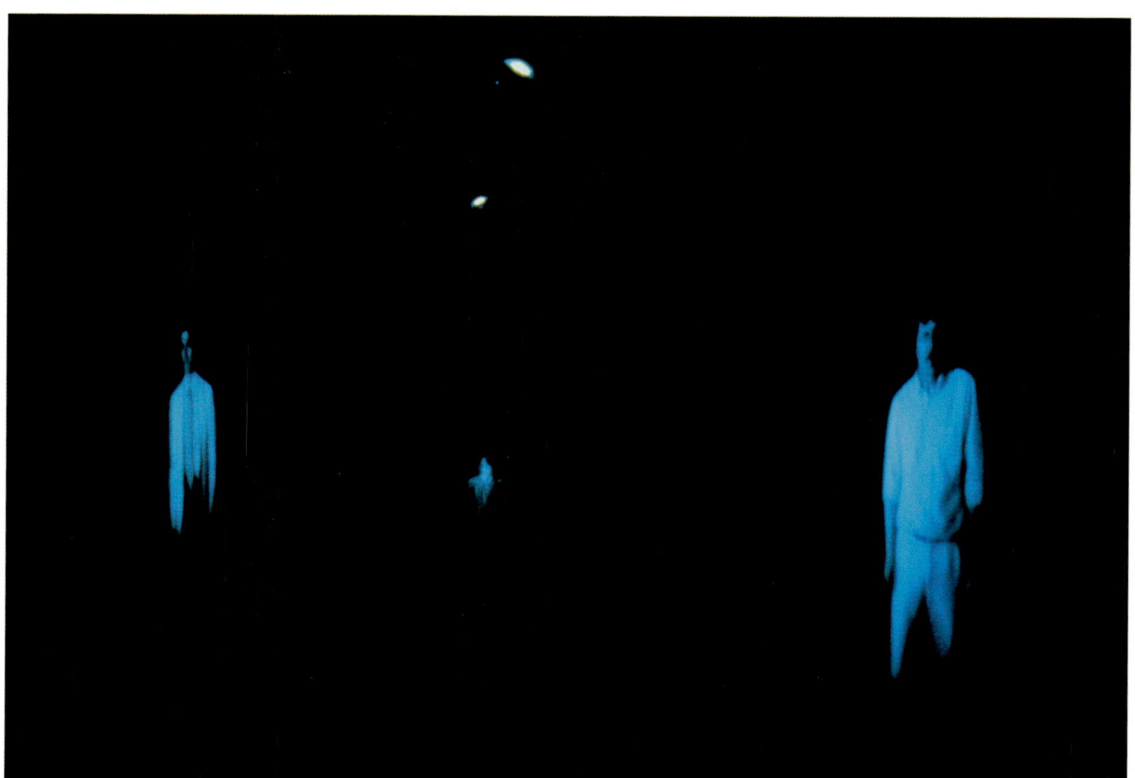

Tall Ships, 1992
16-channel video, black and white, silent

BRUCE NAUMAN

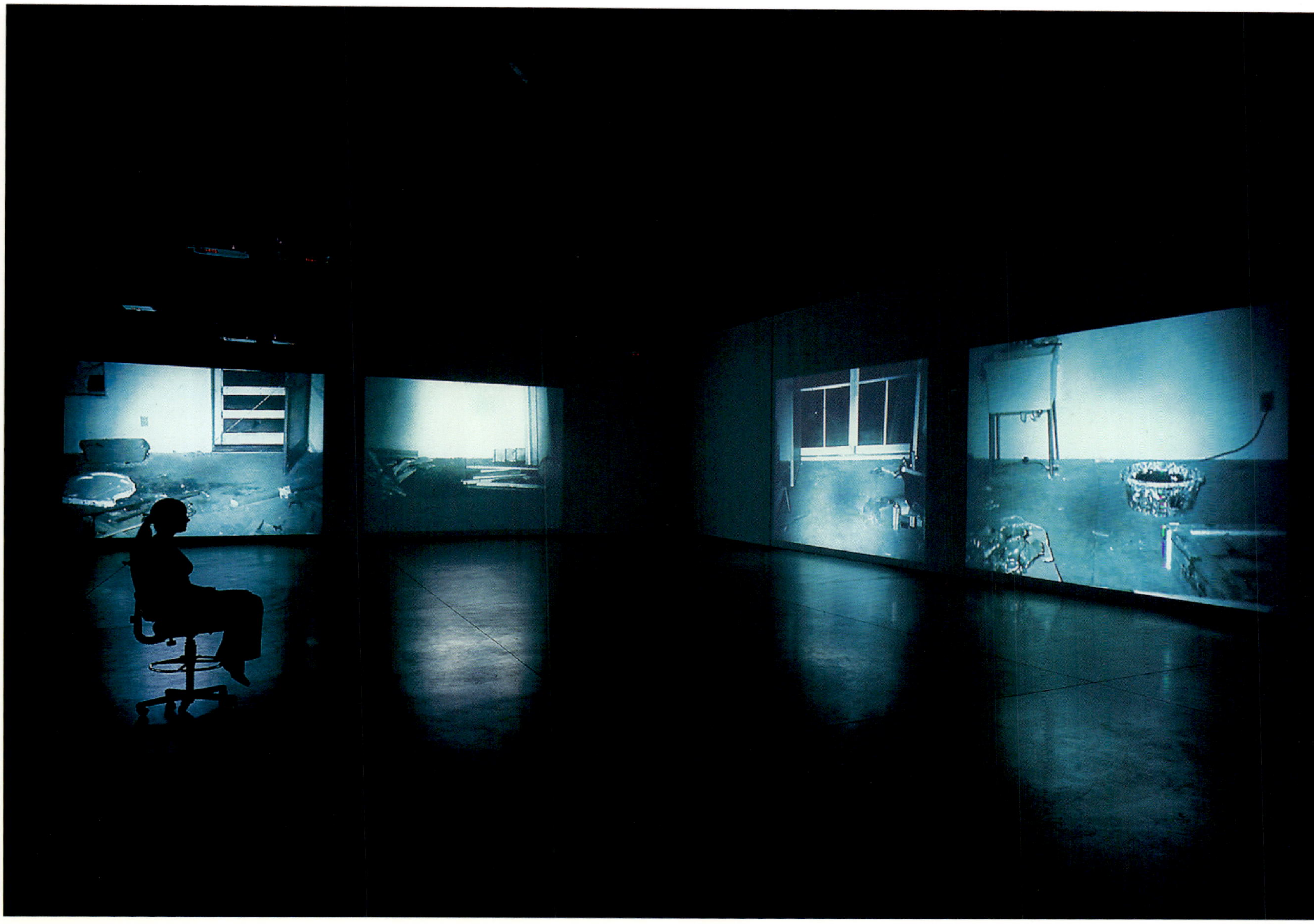

Mapping the Studio I (Fat Chance John Cage), 2001
Video installation with 7 DVDs, 7 DVD players, 7 projectors, 7 pairs of speakers, dimensions variable
As installed at Dia Center for the Arts, New York, January–June 2002

TACITA DEAN

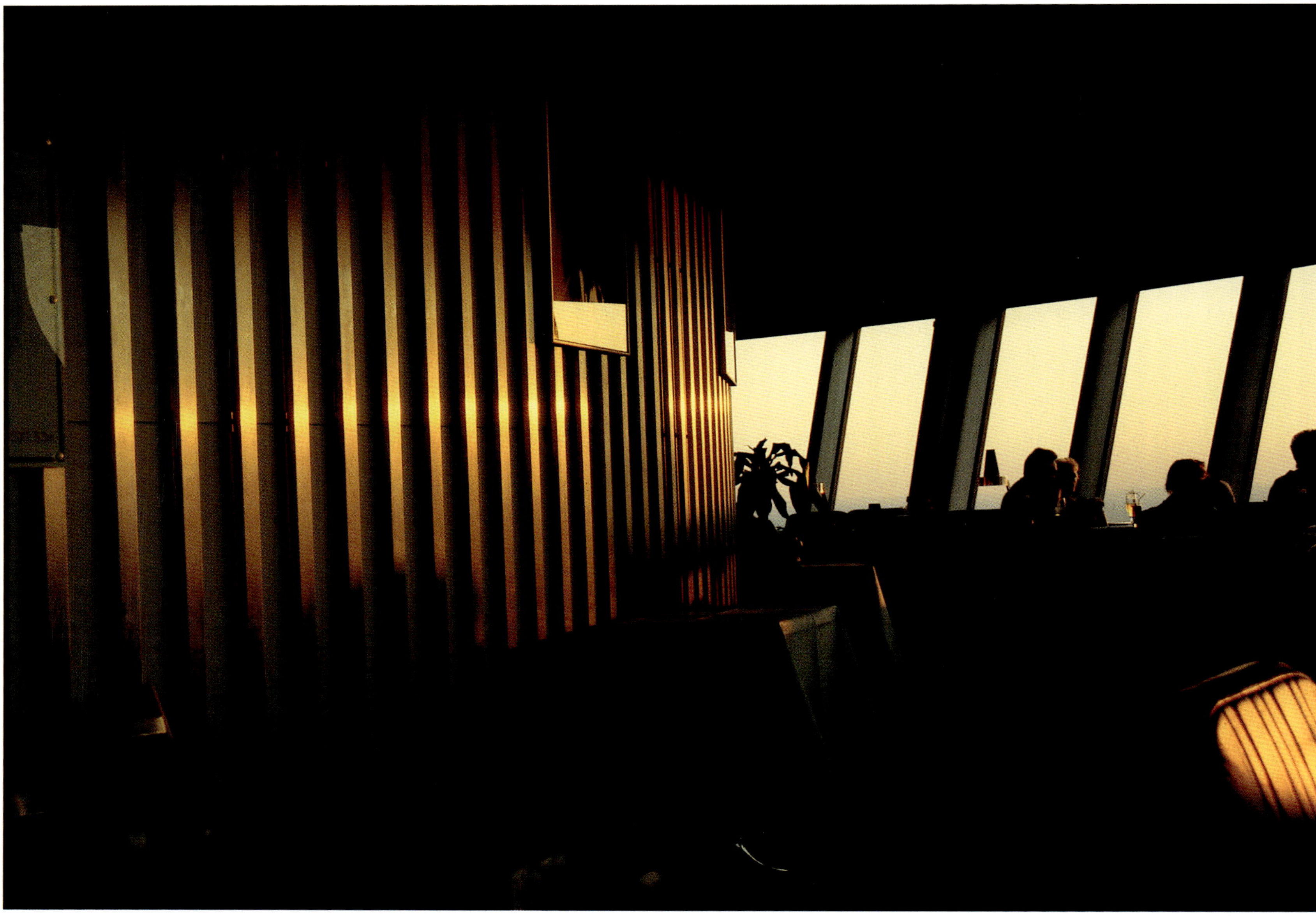

Fernsehturm, 2001
16 mm color anamorphic film with optical sound, 44 minutes

throes of enormous transformation. Dean is less concerned with Berlin, however, than with the comings and goings of the Berliners who visit the restaurant. Her video presents a wide-screen, mostly static view from a camera set inside the café. It begins with the staff's preparations for the evening shift. Waiters set the tables, then usher diners in and out, while customers eat and smoke. An organist arrives to entertain. As darkness descends, the windows lose their transparency and become mirrors reflecting the social rituals of the restaurant. This sense of the camera as witness to a slow eventlessness is even more pronounced in another of Dean's works. *Disappearance at Sea*, 1996, deals nominally with the true story of Donald Crowhurst, an amateur yachtsman whose hubristic attempt at a round-the-world journey ended with his drowning himself rather than face embarrassment at home. The ill-fated sailor is never explicitly referred to. Instead his disappearance becomes a metaphor for the disappearance of the light of day, which unfolds for the viewer in real time. As with *Fernsehturm*, we become one with the transition from day to night, reminded that this progression once formed the basic marker in the human understanding of time.

Wolfgang Staehle amplifies the sense of the all-seeing invisible eye, making it *far*-seeing. His installations bring live feeds of panoramic vistas from distant landscapes into the gallery, so that viewers can watch the slow unfolding of real-time events in distant locales. *Empire 24/7*, 2002, is a contemporary reworking of one of Warhol's pioneering real time films, *Empire*, in which he presented a view of the Empire State Building filmed with a single camera over eight consecutive hours from dusk to dawn on the night of June 25, 1964. Staehle's take was a Webcast of an around-the-clock view of the top third of the Empire State Building. The live feed was updated every four seconds so that the views seemed to lurch slightly, just as video surveillance transmissions do, giving them a slight air of unnaturalness that reminds us of our role as watchers.

In early September 2001, Staehle set up a tri-part Webcast, titled *2001*, in a New York gallery. He connected the gallery to three locales: a monastery on a hilltop near Stuttgart, Germany; the same TV tower Dean used in *Fernsehturm*; and Lower Manhattan, as seen from the South Williamsburg neighborhood of Brooklyn, across the East River. The idea here was to present simultaneous visions of near eventlessness, encouraging the viewer to focus on the micro-events of real life. As it happened, real life took an unexpected turn on September 11, and Staehle's camera became a witness to the collapse of the Twin Towers and smoldering aftereffects. Much has been written about the almost cinematic drama of this spectacle as it appeared on television screens around the world. But in the eye of Staehle's Webcam, this world-redefining event continued to unfold at a stately pace of four-second intervals. The piece offered a sobering reminder that however convinced we are that time is subjective and ever malleable, certain events reveal that time can also be brutally indifferent to the affairs of men.

WOLFGANG STAEHLE

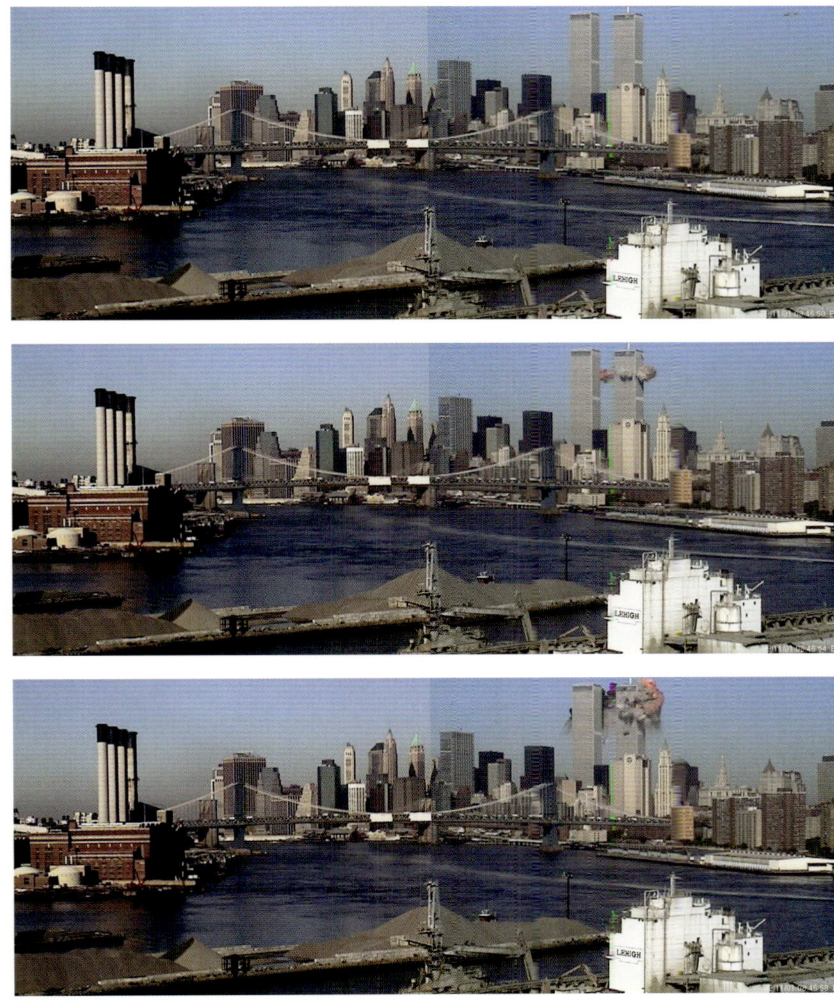

2001, 2001
Video projections, 24 x 9 ft (7.3 x 2.7 m) each

ART & NATURE AND TECHNOLOGY

REMAKING LAND AND BODY

From Mary Shelley's 1818 masterpiece *Frankenstein* to Hollywood sci-fi thrillers such as *Gattaca* (1997) and the *Matrix* trilogy (1999–2003), lurid fantasies about the dark underside of science and technology have pervaded popular culture. Often couched in moralistic terms, such imaginative works caution against the hubris of "playing God," and suggest that there will be dire consequences for individuals and for society as a whole if anyone seeks to alter the laws of nature. Judgment day most often comes in the (sometimes very near) future, but it always comes. In Margaret Atwood's 1986 novel *The Handmaid's Tale*, for instance, environmental pollution has rendered so many people sterile by the 1990s that an enslaved class of fertile women is maintained to serve as breeders for the infertile elite. In Ridley Scott's 1982 classic film *Blade Runner*, set in 2019, revolution simmers among the manufactured androids and replicants created to do humans' dirty work.

Back in the real world, such doomful sentiments run counter to the ever-accelerating pace of scientific and technological advancement, whose revolutionary discoveries have brought us space travel, the Internet, and modern medicine. Former fantasies—from cloning animals to in vitro fertilization to designer genes to genetic modification of food sources to ever more sophisticated robotic aids—have become reality. Some say these innovations will lead to a future in which disease is vanquished, labor is mechanized, human imperfections are eliminated, and hunger is a thing of the past. Others note that innovations have also brought us the atomic bomb, biological warfare, global warming, and the specter of human extinction. These clashing visions underscore the difficulties surrounding any effort to strike a balance between scientific and technological advances and social and ethical considerations. Either way, the future has become a complex territory in which the cosmic consequences of our choices will play out.

Artists have variously reflected the conundrum of progress versus imprudent ambition. Those of the Romantic era (from which Mary Shelley hails) went so far as to suggest that man is not the center of the universe, but rather a virus-like aberration that must be curtailed for the health of the planet. This suspicion of humanity can be found in the paintings of Thomas Cole, for instance, whose 1836 *The Course of Empire* chronicles the passage from a bucolic state of nature to the desolate ruins of a fallen civilization. Such dire portrayals offer a sharp contrast to the sunnier predictions of human progress espoused by modernist art movements such as Russian Constructivism, De Stijl, the Bauhaus, and Italian Futurism, all of which proposed visions of a new and rationally organized world based on the principles of industry. As the 1909 founding Futurist Manifesto feverishly put it: "We declare that the splendor of the world has been enriched by a new beauty: the beauty of speed. A racing automobile with its bonnet adorned with great tubes like serpents with explosive breath . . . a roaring motor car which seems to run on machine-gun fire, is more beautiful than the Victory of Samothrace."[1]

After a mid-century revival of interest in the handmade (in the form of the painterly gesture), the modernist love of technology surged again when in 1966 artists Robert Rauschenberg and Robert Whitman and engineers Billy Klüver and Fred Waldhauer founded Experiments in Art and Technology (also known as E.A.T.), a non-profit organization that catalyzed collaborations between hundreds of artists and engineers. Klüver, a research engineer with Bell Laboratories, had significant experience in the crossover of art and technology: he had lent the technical know-how to Jean Tinguely's *Homage to New York*, 1960, a self-destructing machine that was detonated in the garden of New York's Museum of Modern Art, and the heat-sealed Mylar to Andy Warhol's helium-filled *Silver Clouds*, 1966. E.A.T. initiated many projects, the most ambitious of which was the Pepsi Pavilion at Expo '70 in Osaka, for which more than sixty artists and engineers collaborated on a series of futuristic, interactive exhibits. E.A.T. also facilitated performances, with artists such as Yvonne Rainer, that blended dance and technology to extend the range of the body. Dancers might trip a wire that would set off lights, for instance, or a contact mike attached to a performer's throat would allow the audience to hear the modulations of her breath. These artists embraced new technologies fearlessly and optimistically, exploiting them but also giving back: in a few cases, the artists' innovations led to practical applications, as when sound captors concealed in the handles of tennis rackets in Rauschenberg's 1966 performance *Open Score* led to the invention of the wireless microphone.

By the 1980s, E.A.T.'s activities had slowed to a halt, as postmodernists began to reject its most basic celebratory premises. Rather than improving quality of life, postmodernists argued, technology and science had stripped away humanistic values like freedom, community, and progress by negating the very idea of the individual, creating a world in which both the human body and the environment could be reconstructed and manipulated through genetic engineering, monocultural farming, and insidious urban development. Notably, the postmodernists of the 1980s seemed almost indifferent to the political implications of a world in which nature and the body were mere tools of larger powers. Instead, they reflected on how nature, once considered the substrate of existence, had become nothing more than a comfortable illusion. As painter Peter Halley remarked, "The jungle ride at Disney World may in fact be more real to most people than the real jungle in the Amazon. . . . More and more people are becoming more comfortable in the simulated world than in the real one."[2]

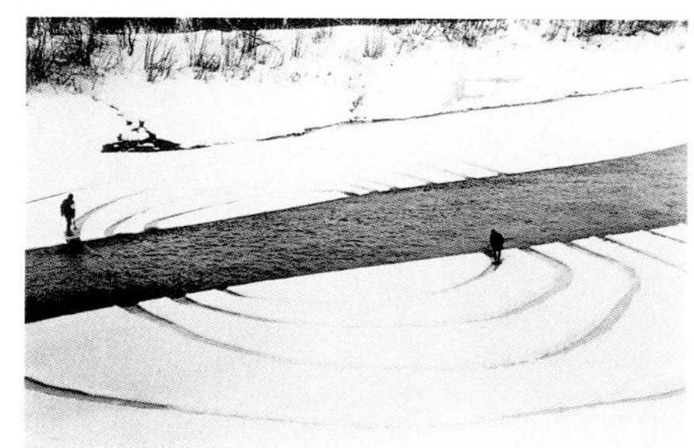

DENNIS OPPENHEIM
ANNUAL RINGS
1968
MIXED MEDIA, DIMENSIONS VARIABLE

The 1992 traveling exhibition "Post Human," which took its ominous title from a movement that imagines a future in which humans are "enhanced" beyond recognition, reflected on the corporeal side of things. It included the works of such artists as Jeff Wall, Cindy Sherman, Matthew Barney, and Damien Hirst, and purported to demonstrate that artifice had now eclipsed "nature" in everything from social life to biological growth. As the exhibition's curator, Jeffrey Deitch, explained his premise, "Human evolution may be entering a new phase that Charles Darwin never would have envisioned.... This new techno-evolutionary phase will bring us far beyond eugenics. Our children's generation could very well be the last generation of 'pure' humans."[3] With such intentionally provocative statements, postmodernists like Halley and Deitch seemed to suggest that the natural world and the human body were nothing more than artificial conceits to be altered and manipulated at will. But even as they were making these possibly tongue-in-cheek assessments, menacing developments such as the AIDS crisis and global warming made it clear there was indeed something "real" about the natural world and the human body that could not be so blithely dismissed.

Having moved through the distrustful escapism of the Romantic era, modernism's celebratory embrace of technological progress, and a decade or so of postmodernism's apparently flippant repudiation of humanism, artists today approach technology and science more cautiously. They recognize that these are tools that may be employed for good or ill upon our bodies and our natural environment. And in fact, the fate of these two essential entities is intertwined, for we are, as Pollock once said in a very different context, nature, and we separate ourselves from it at our peril. In keeping with this recognition, artists today sound warnings about the arrogant privileging of human desires over the well being of the natural world, and about reckless tinkering with the human body, whose outcome no one can predict. Most are aware that technology and science, like the evils in Pandora's Box, cannot be retrieved once they have been released upon the world, and thus often use their lessons to solve the very problems they have created.

This proactive approach is particularly evident in the work of artists in two particular areas of contemporary art: bio art and eco art, as they are often informally called. Bio art is primarily a byproduct of the tremendous advances made by science over the last twenty-five years in genetics, biotechnology, and genomics (the study of the entire genome). As techniques for altering genetic structures and redirecting the evolutionary process have become more widespread, so have concerns about the implications of these developments. Bio artists both experiment with the new technologies, often suggesting alternate applications and directions, and bring out the ethical issues that often seem so alien to "pure science." Such works began entering the mainstream art world with exhibitions like Mass MoCA's "Unnatural Science" and "Paradise Now: Picturing the Genetic Revolution," at Exit Art in New York, both 2000, which gathered groups of artists who use the new sciences as springboards for artistic explorations. Bio art's approach follows on the earlier phenomenon of eco art, which was first chronicled in *Art in the Land*, a 1983 book by artist Alan Sonfist, and first codified in the exhibition "Fragile Ecologies: Contemporary Artists' Interpretations and Solutions," organized by the Queens Museum of Art in 1992. Like bio art, eco art comes out of artists' concerns about the impact of human intervention in natural processes. It grows out of the Land Art movement of the late 1960s and early 1970s (though with several decisive differences), and thus warrants a brief detour through the mountains, lakes, and valleys of America.

Land Art was in part a reaction against the increasingly commercial nature of the art world of the 1960s. Artists moved out into the landscape to create works that could not be commodified, or in some cases, even easily visited. It was also a response to the nascent environmentalism of that period, sharing that movement's rejection of a human-centered world in favor of one that viewed mankind as one element in a larger ecosystem. For some artists, Land Art also converged with an interest in reconnecting with the nature-consciousness of primitive peoples. Ironically, when this desire took the form of massive earthworks based on the models of Stonehenge or the pyramids, it appeared to manifest a hubris and arrogance antithetical to the environmentalist credo of modesty in the face of nature. As a result, Land Art manifested itself in very different forms. At one end of the spectrum were quiet works like Dennis Oppenheim's *Annual Rings*, 1968, an early example of environmental Minimalism. For this work, Oppenheim simply shoveled the pattern of a tree's annual rings on a field of snow at the Canada-U.S.border. On the other were the massive earthmoving projects of artists like Michael Heizer and Robert Smithson. Smithson's 1970 *Spiral Jetty* is an enormous counter-clockwise coil of basalt rocks projecting from the shore 1,500 feet into the Great Salt Lake in Utah. James Turrell's *Roden Crater* is a multi-decade project that will transform a natural crater in the Arizona desert into a grand celestial observatory. Heizer's *Double Negative*, 1969, is a 1,500-foot-long, 50-foot-deep, 30-foot-wide gash cut into facing slopes of a Nevada mesa. Meanwhile, Heizer has been working since the early 1970s on *City*, a massive environmental sculpture in the Nevada desert that may well rival the lost cities of the ancient world. Designed eventually to occupy a space roughly equal to the National Mall in Washington, DC, it consists of a complex of structures inspired in part by Mississippian mounds, Mesoamerican ball courts and Pre-Colombian ritual sites.

Such ambitious projects drew fire from a faction of land artists who saw them as insults to nature. The British land artists, notably Richard Long and Hamish Fulton, chose instead a very light footprint, creating the most minimal interventions in the landscape. Long, for example, undertook solitary treks across unpopulated landscapes, documenting them in photographs and drawings. He limited his alterations to making piles, and circles and lines of stones, (like *A Line in Scotland, Cul Mor*, 1981), which he recreated in gallery settings. A younger adherent of this light touch, Andy Goldsworthy, creates ephemeral sculptures in the landscape using materials at hand. He has placed patterns on the forest floor composed of colorful autumn leaves, as in *Hole in leaves sinking, held underneath to a woven briar ring, keeping it afloat*, 1987, "painted" on stones with water, set preserved winter snowballs in a summer landscape, and made "sculptures" of cracked mud that will disappear with the first rain. After a brief "real" life, these fleeting gestures remain as art only in the artist's lush documentary photographs.

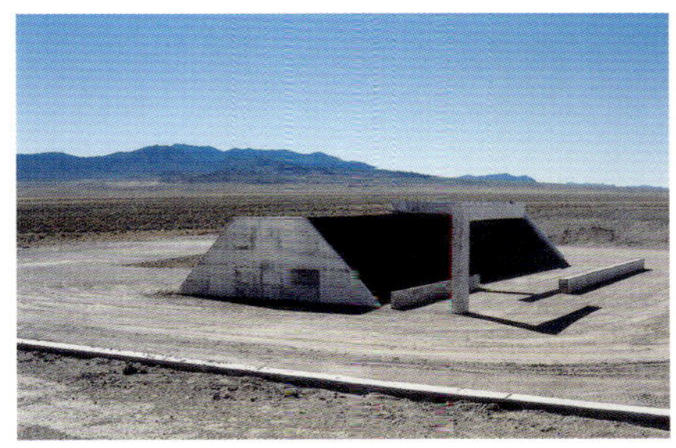

MICHAEL HEIZER
CITY: COMPLEX ONE
1972–76
CONCRETE, STEEL, COMPACTED EARTH
23 X 1200 X 521 FT (7 X 366 X 159 M)

Today's eco artists share their British forebears' humility in the face of nature's vastness, but their attitude is less benign. While they refuse the physical grandiosity of Smithson's work, they take a cue from his apocalyptic musings on entropy, in which he riffs on the second law of thermodynamics, which posits the irreversible decline of a system as it moves toward a state of equilibrium. "One's mind and the earth are in a constant state of erosion, mental rivers wear away abstract banks, brain waves undermine cliffs of thought, ideas decompose into stones of unknowing, and conceptual crystallizations break apart into deposits of gritty reason."[4] What this means in practical terms is that urban development and new technologies are inevitably accompanied by waste dumps and destruction. Smithson himself was fascinated with such sites, using them as locations for

ANDY GOLDSWORTHY

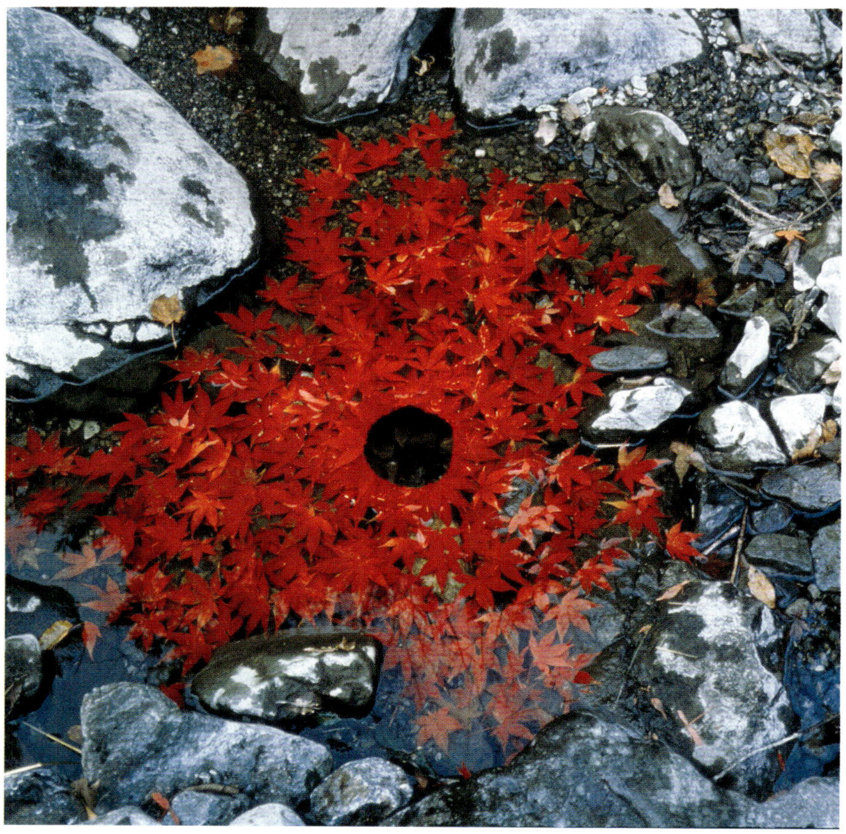

Hole in leaves sinking, held underneath to a woven briar ring, keeping it afloat, 1987
Cibachrome photograph, 24 x 24 in (61 x 61 cm)

RICHARD LONG

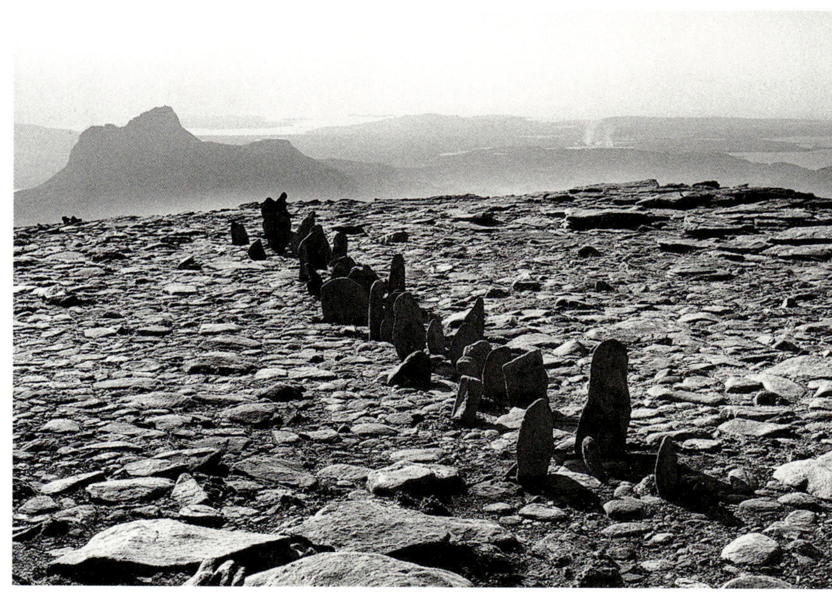

A Line in Scotland, Cul Mor, 1981
Black and white photograph

ALAN SONFIST

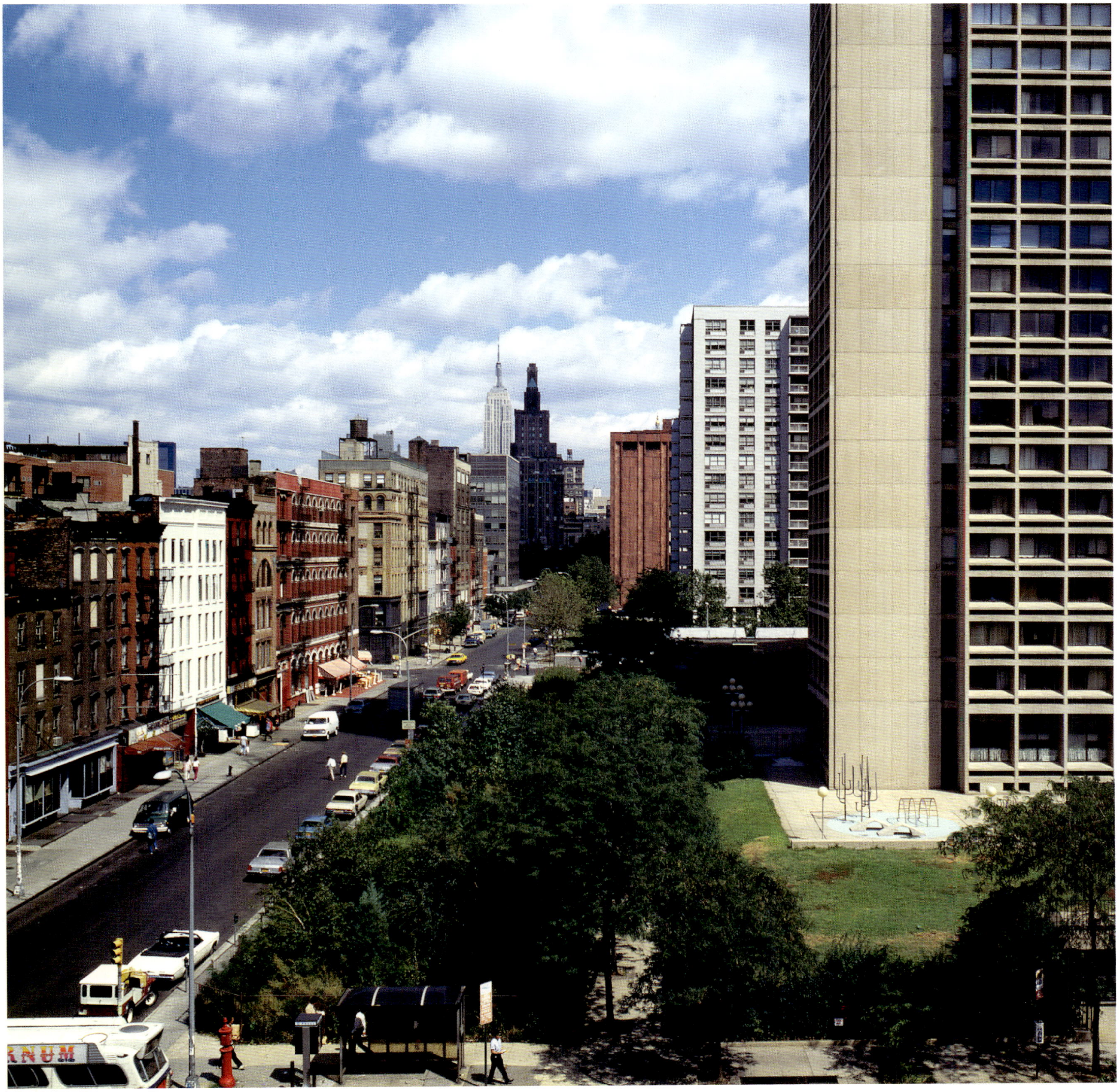

Time Landscape©, 1965–present
Indigenous trees, wildflowers, and grasses, 45 x 200 ft (14 x 61 m)
Installation at the corner of West Houston Street and LaGuardia Place, New York

MARK DION

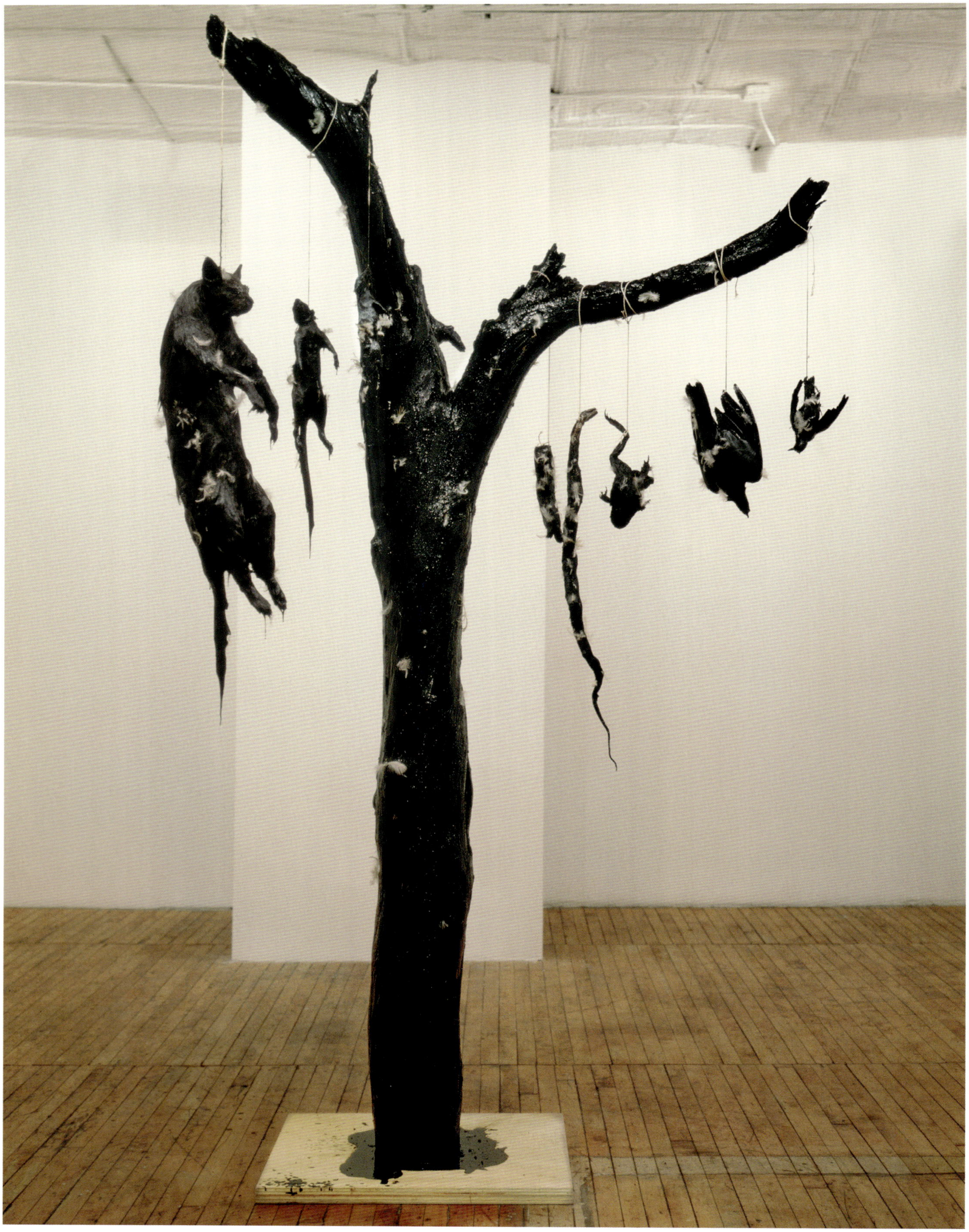

Tar and Feathers, 1996
Tree, wooden base, tar, feathers, various taxidermic animals, 102 x 39 5/8 in (259 x 101.6 cm)

MARY LUCIER

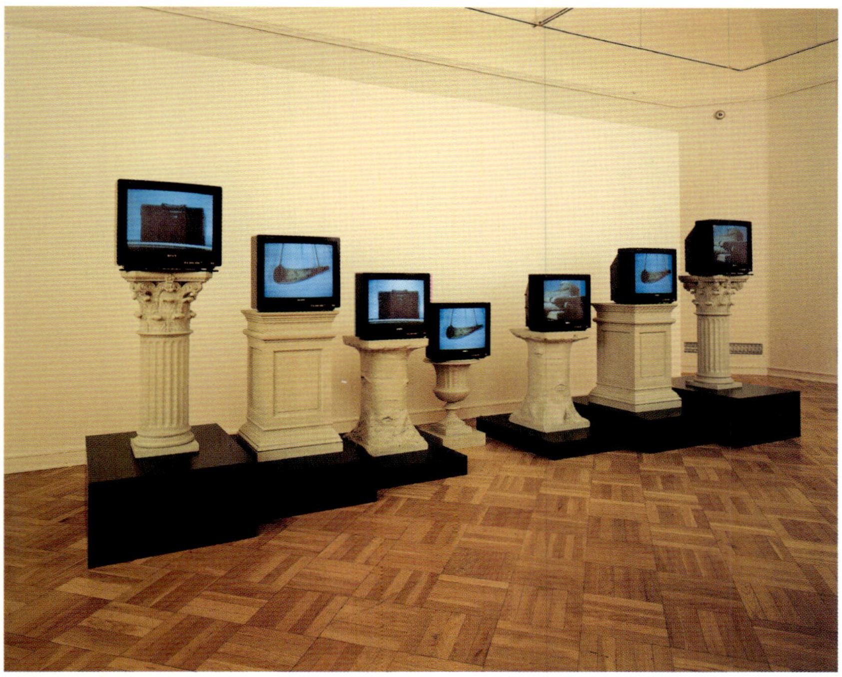

Wilderness, 1986
Video and mixed media, dimensions variable
As installed at the Henry Art Gallery, Seattle, July–September 1989

his work, and he declared that the industrial wastelands of the U.S. were the contemporary equal of the monuments of the ancient world. Today's eco artists, more wary of modernity's toll on natural ecosystems, subject Smithson's matter-of-fact acceptance of entropy to scrutiny, exploring the effects of urbanization, overpopulation, and technological development on the quality of human life and the natural world.

A seminal work that neatly addresses environmental concerns exactly as they relate to civilization is Alan Sonfist's *Time Landscape* ©, 1965–present, a nine thousand-square-foot urban forest planted on a once vacant lot in what has become one of the most desirable neighborhoods in downtown Manhattan. One of a series of the artist's "Time Landscapes," the piece not only "greens" the city, but recalls a time when the whole city was in fact green, for Sonfist planted seedlings of native species that grew here prior to European colonization. Subsequent "Time Landscapes," which Sonfist has created in cities throughout the United States and Europe, also incorporate reminders of a site's histories and ecologies. Like the time capsules that their title recalls, they offer an encapsulated glimpse of a long-vanished world, reminding us that where humanity once sought shelter from the savage wildness of nature, today nature must be sheltered from humankind.

Mary Lucier is another artist who has been meditating on progress, modernity, and nature since the 1970s, focusing particularly on the contradictions inherent in the pastoral ideal that underlies so much American art and literature. Her video installation *Wilderness*, 1986, visits interior and exterior locations associated with the nineteenth-century American Luminist and Hudson River School painters. Puncturing the idyll with emblems of industry and technology—among them a train, a bulldozer and a graffiti-scrawled wall—Lucier reminds us that the great pictorial celebrations of American wilderness were created while that wilderness was being systematically destroyed.

Like Lucier, whose work makes a case for responsible stewardship of the earth, Mark Dion is also concerned with ethics in ecology. His work often borrows from the conventions of museum display, that seemingly neutral framework for reconsidering our relationship to the natural world. By and large, his conclusions do not reflect well on our collective decisions. *Museum of Poison (Biocide Hall)*, 2001, is an installation of vitrines stocked with the packaging for chemicals used to eradicate pests from home, garden, and farm. Displayed in this way, they begin to resemble artifacts of an ancient lost civilization, slyly reminding us that overuse of such substances may lead us in the same direction. *Tar and Feathers*, 1996, presents the tarred remains of a taxidermied rat, cat, and pigeon, among other creatures, hanging from a tree. These are among the few species that can thrive in urban environments. Dion also explores the non-organic detritus of urban life. He excavated the site of the redesigned Museum of Modern Art in New York, for example, then displayed architectural debris as if it were the precious relics of ancient civilizations. With such archaeologically oriented works, Dion ruminates on the impact of civilization on the natural world and the chances for the future coexistence of humans and animals.

Sophie Ristelhueber gathers evidence of landscapes that have been subjected to more intentionally and immediately destructive human activities. Much of her work centers on territories ravaged by war, though she has also taken photographs of scarred and wounded bodies, drawing a parallel, like Lucier, between the vulnerability of both the landscape and the human body to human intervention.

SOPHIE RISTELHUEBER

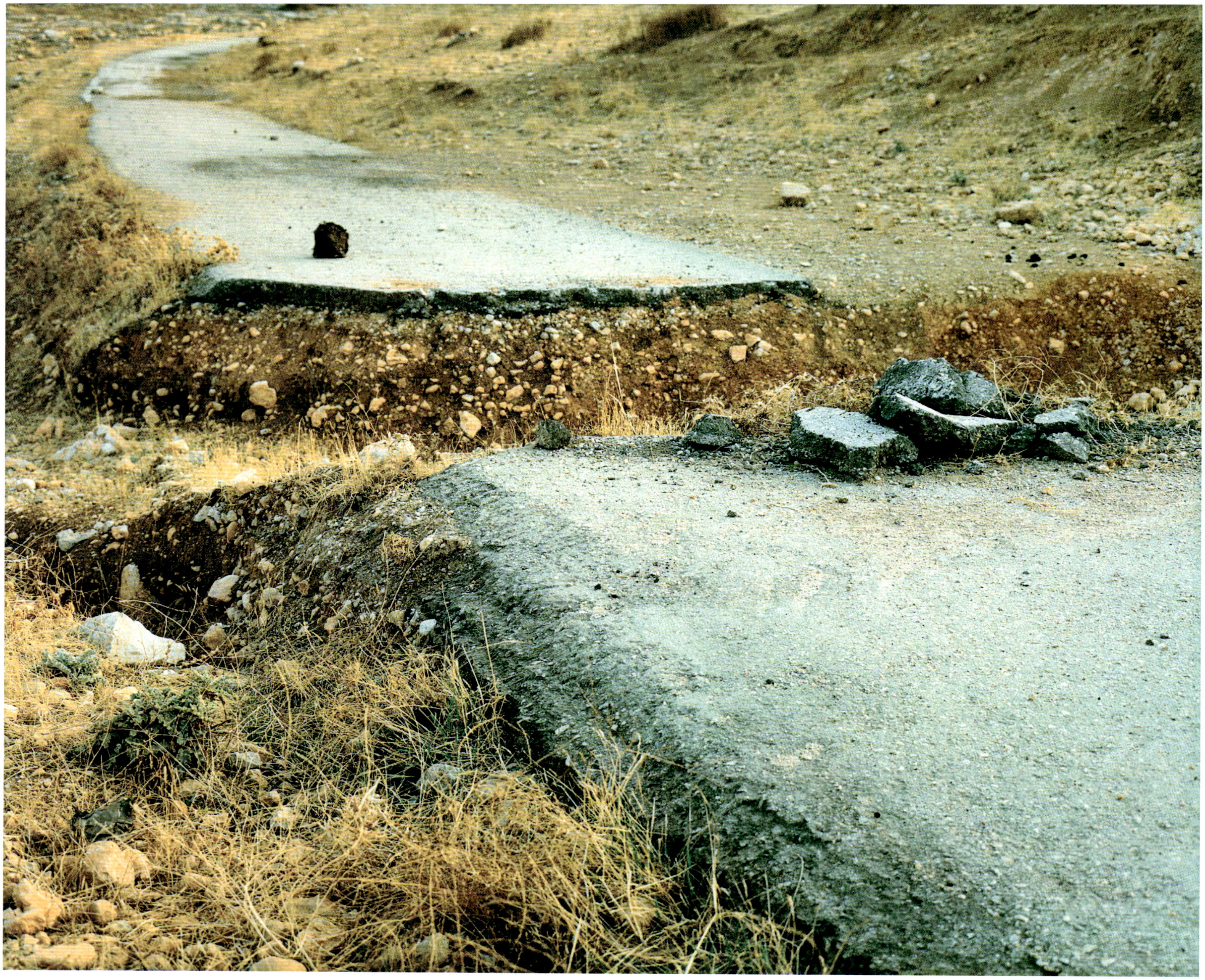

WB (#6), 2006
C-print, 47 1/4 x 59 in (120 x 150 cm)

Ristelhueber focuses on poignant and telling details. Her photographs of Beirut in the aftermath of civil war reveal the devastation of that conflict through details like a bullet-riddled street sign, while photographs of the thin blankets discarded by the retreating Iraqi army, or a tin cup half-filled with desert, reveal the traces of the 1992 Gulf War in the sands of Kuwait. Aerial photographs of the Kuwait desert reveal the larger-scale destruction war hails upon the earth. Her 2004 series "WB" reveals how the West Bank of the Jordan River has been reduced to a wasteland by the Israeli occupation. Here the camera lingers over roads that have been rendered useless by trenches, piles of rocks, and concrete blocks. In these, as in all Ristelhueber's photographs, figures rarely appear. Instead, landscapes appear alien, at times almost lunar, pitted with trenches, tank tracks, and bomb craters, emptied of human habitation and lost to the mindless destruction of war.

Works by artists such as Lucier, Dion, and Ristelhueber have an elegiac quality. Other eco art strikes a more hopeful note, exploring ways to address the problems that so-called progress creates by looking at them through a hybrid art-science lens. Sometimes this work is barely recognizable as art, but neither does it function inside the ordinary parameters of science and land use. Instead it suggests a new paradigm that eschews end products and established formats in favor of experimentation. Among the preeminent practitioners in this cross-disciplinary vein are Newton and Helen Mayer Harrison, a husband-and-wife artist team who have worked together, and with scientists and urban planners, since the 1970s. Focusing on cleaning up polluted watersheds and restoring biodiversity, the Harrisons produce proposals that combine ecological and economic analysis to challenge conventional thinking about flood control, irrigation, and forestry. The Harrisons work internationally, traveling to coal mines in the former East Germany, the banks of the Sava River in the former Yugoslavia, the farms of middle England, and the rain forests of the Pacific Northwest. "Peninsula Europe," 2001, an exhibition consisting of maps, photos, and sound installations, proposes a re-imagining of European borders from discrete nations to an ecological whole. Seeing themselves first and foremost as instigators, they measure success not by whether their proposals come to fruition, but by how effectively they insert their ideas into political and social debates to provoke a process of incremental change they call "conversational drift."

An equally unconventional approach toward art and the politics of the environment appears in the work of Mierle Laderman Ukeles. In her thirty years as the official if unsalaried artist-in-residence of the New York City Department of Sanitation, Ukeles has produced performance, installation, and public works projects that seek to alter public perceptions about the meaning and significance of garbage. Her work replaces the simple notion of "waste" with one of "maintenance," encouraging a view of the city as a complex organism whose interwoven systems of consumption, production, circulation, and disposal are all inescapable, and in which garbage is a natural byproduct of normal functioning. One of her first works in her official role was *Touch Sanitation*, 1978–84, in which she shook hands with all 8,500 of New York's sanitation workers, acquainting herself with an essential piece of the sanitation system. Subsequent works have included *The New York City Art Parade*, 1983, in which she choreographed an elaborate parade of garbage trucks, weaving them through the city streets as if they were ballet dancers. She also covered a garbage truck in mirrors (*The Social Mirror*, 1983), for use by the sanitation workers who followed parades as the cleanup crew. More recently, she has focused on landfill

NEWTON HARRISON AND HELEN MAYER HARRISON

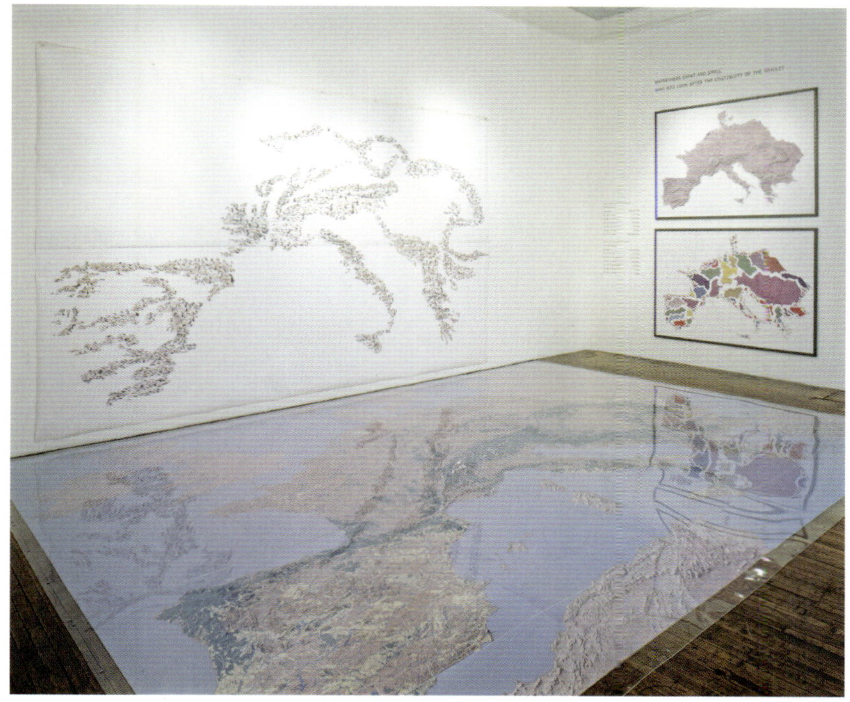

"Peninsula Europe," 2001
As installed at Ronald Feldman Fine Arts, New York, April–May 2003

MIERLE LADERMAN UKELES

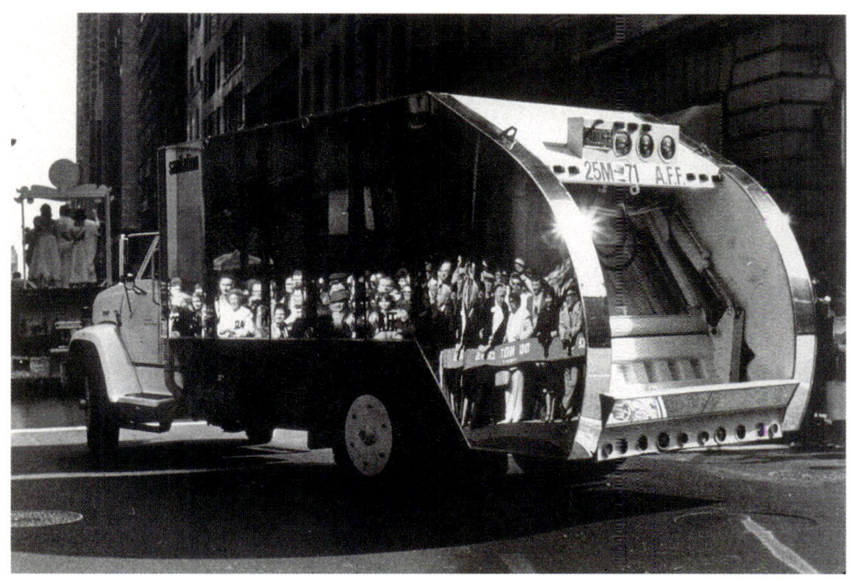

The Social Mirror, 1983
Performance, New York

MEL CHIN (WITH DR. RUFUS CHANEY)

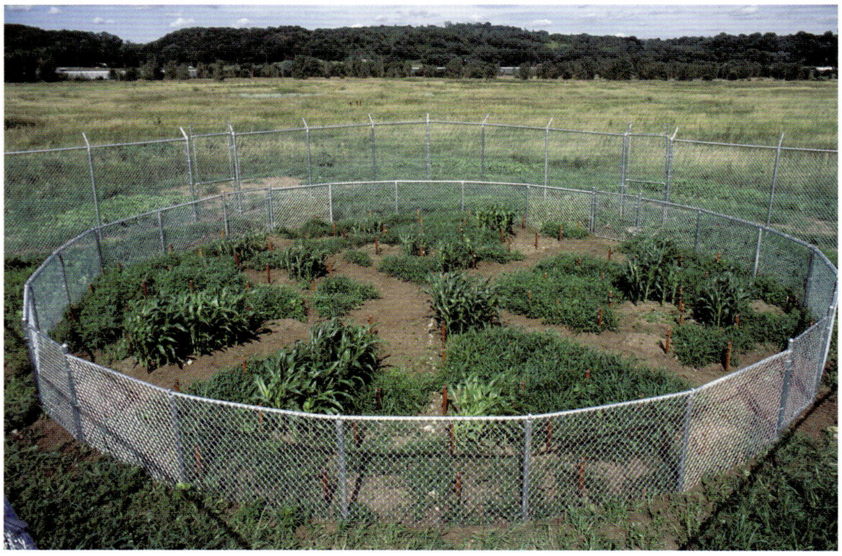

Revival Field, 1990
Installation at Pig's Eye Landfill, St. Paul, Minn.

STEVEN ROWELL FOR THE CENTER FOR LAND USE INTERPRETATION

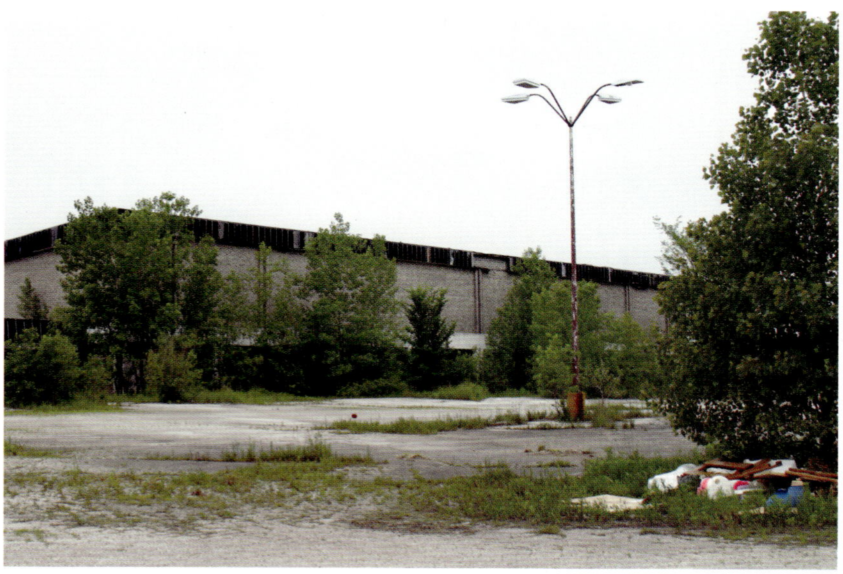

Dixie Square Mall #18, June 11, 2003, 2003
Digital photograph, 8 x 12 in (20.3 x 30.5 cm)

reclamation. In 1989, the New York City Department of Cultural Affairs appointed her as the official artist of Fresh Kills, the Staten Island landfill that contains a half century's worth of New York City's garbage, relying on her to help transform it from an eyesore into a community asset. Ukeles attends meetings with architects, engineers, and environmentalists, working to create public awareness through exhibitions that demonstrate the complex process by which a landfill is sealed, how the garbage decomposes, and how the groundwater is purified.

Mel Chin also works to restore sites in collaboration with experts, in particular with Rufus Chaney, an agronomist with the U.S. Department of Agriculture, with whom Chin has explored the idea that land contaminated by toxic metals might be cleansed by sowing "hyper-accumulating" plants, which absorb metal from the soil. Not only would this purify the land, the metals would then be harvested and recycled, defraying the costs of restoration. The project, ongoing since 1990, is called *Revival Field*, and it showed signs of feasibility when tested on a toxic-waste site outside Minneapolis, Minnesota. Chin has subsequently installed *Revival Fields* at other toxic sites around the world. Ecology is only one of Chin's preoccupations as an artist. Among his other projects was a collaboration with software engineers that resulted in *KNOWMAD*, 1999, a video game based on the rug patterns of nomadic peoples facing persecution. Among his works, however, *Revival Field* is the only one whose status as art has been questioned. In 1990 the NEA grant that eventually funded it was initially rescinded on the grounds that the project did not constitute "art." After an outcry from artists and art administrators as well as the NEA panelists who had awarded Chin the grant, the NEA director relented and the money was released. This brouhaha underlines the persistent resistance toward art that veers too close to science. In defense, Chin has noted that the process of "carving" away pollution is akin to the sculptor chiseling away at marble to bring out the hidden form within.[5]

A younger generation of eco artists draws on new communications systems to both investigate environmental issues and, perhaps, mobilize action to solve them. Under the directorship of founder Matthew Coolidge, the Center for Land Use Interpretation (CLUI) is located in a small office in Los Angeles, but expands its reach both physically and through the Internet in a proliferating set of activities that includes research, exhibitions, lectures, and artist residencies. The organization's overarching aim is to analyze how land is used and misused in the service of economic development and global politics. Its programs have addressed chemical weapons incinerators, pit mines, aerospace complexes, counter-terrorism facilities, and hydroelectric power plants. Its online database maps significant U.S. land uses around transportation, water, culture, industry, nuclear waste, and the military, allowing visitors to track the often invisible functions of the American landscape. The center also organizes exhibitions, such as "The Best Dead Mall in America" in 2003, a photographic documentation of the Dixie Square Mall in suburban Chicago, and the following year, "A View into the Pipe," which documented an excavation of Los Angeles's main sewer pipe, offering a rare glimpse of the inner workings of the metropolis. With such works, CLUI lives up to its name, conceiving activism as a diffusion of information much like the Harrisons' conversational drift.

Jennifer Allora and Guillermo Calzadilla have been working together since 1995 on projects that address the utilization of a particular swath of land—their home, Puerto Rico. Much of their work revolves around the island's status as an

ALLORA & CALZADILLA

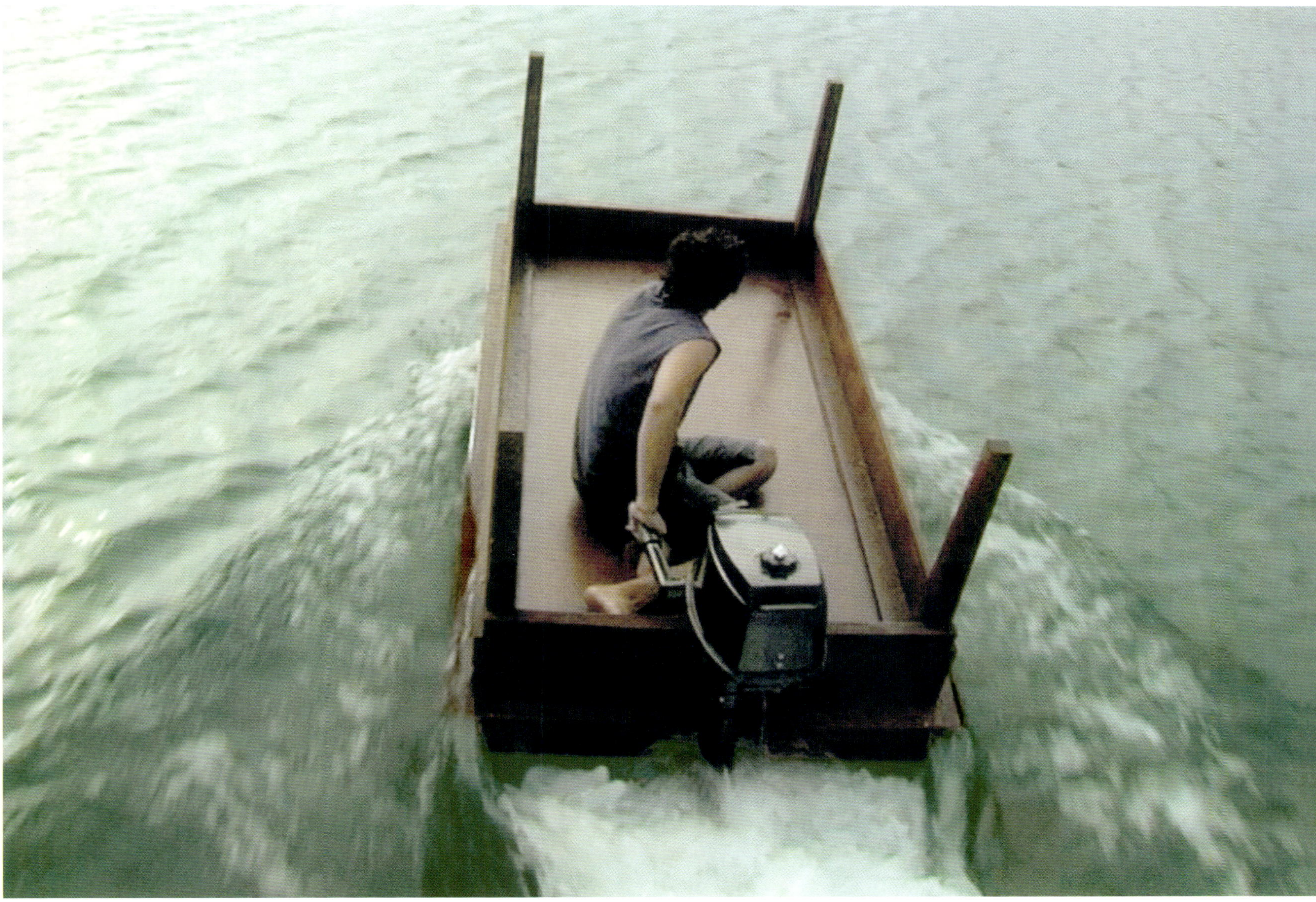

Under Discussion, 2005
Single-screen video projection, color, dimensions variable

unincorporated territory of the United States and the political, social, and ecological conundrums that relationship creates. One particular focus has been Vieques, an island off the shore of Puerto Rico that U.S. military and NATO forces used for sixty years for naval maneuvers, bombing practice, and testing napalm and germ and chemical warfare agents. In 2001 Allora and Calzadilla joined the fight to close the Vieques military base with *Landmark*, a multi-part project that includes photographs of sand marked by footprints containing messages, maps, and icons suggesting alternative uses for the site. The imprints were courtesy the artists, who provided activist demonstrators with rubber soles to be attached to their shoes during civil disobedience actions on the island. In 2003, bowing to pressure, the U.S. government finally relinquished Vieques to civil ownership.

Since the military base's closing, Allora and Calzadilla have remained vigilant in their concern for the island: among the remaining issues are whether the island's indigenous people displaced by the military will reclaim it, and whether the planned transformation of the naval grounds into a wildlife refuge will simply mask health dangers lingering from toxic chemicals absorbed over decades of bombing exercises. *Under Discussion*, 2005, a video reflecting on these lingering concerns, follows an activist as he navigates a makeshift boat along the Vieques coast. The boat, it turns out, is a motorized upturned conference table, a symbol of frustrations around negotiating the island's future. The image is not only symbolic, however—the artists intend to provoke real change. "Of course it's absurd," they have said of the boat, "but maybe the absurdity of a seafaring table will mobilize discussion, taking the debate in new directions."[6]

Just as eco artists warn us about the threat of technological "advancement" for the land, bio artists caution its impact on the body. The activist artist collective Critical Art Ensemble (CAE), for instance, has been criticizing genetic engineering for a decade, appropriating and displaying its methods in order to reveal its dependence on politics, corporate profits, and hidden agendas far removed from the public good. *Flesh Machine*, 1997, allowed viewers to go through actual genetic screening and then "assess the potential value of their bodies as commodities, and hence their place in the new genetic market economy."[7] But CAE's best-known piece, or almost piece, is one that was never shown. In 2004 one of its members, Steven Kurtz, was investigated by the Joint Terrorism Task Force for possible intent to engage in biological terrorism. Summoned to Kurtz's house when his wife suffered a fatal heart attack, police searched his studio and confiscated suspicious-looking petri dishes filled with bacteria, along with all of the artist's teaching notes, books, and computer. Far from plotting to unleash some devastating new biological plague on an unsuspecting world, Kurtz was in fact cultivating bacteria that could be found in a high school science lab—for use in an interactive artwork investigating the genetic modification of food. Kurtz's case had yet to be resolved at the time of this writing.

Natalie Jeremijenko, armed with training in biochemistry, physics, neuroscience, and mechanical engineering, creates provocative and often humorous works that underscore the dangers of adhering unthinkingly to new technologies and the negligence of government science labs and biotech companies that ignore ecological concerns in their rush to apply genetic engineering. Her works employ the apparatus of scientific experiments or trade-show demonstrations. For instance, she has taken existing technology for mechanical dogs and upgraded it so that her canine robots

NATALIE JEREMIJENKO

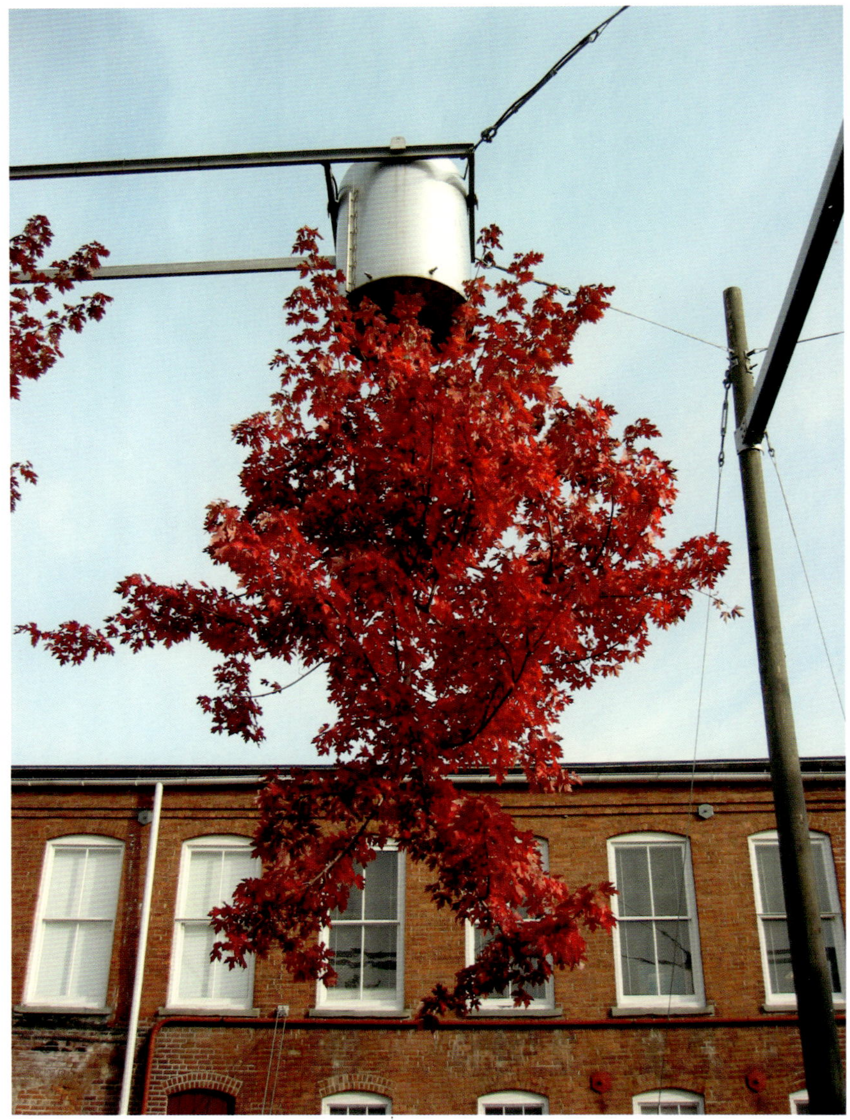

Tree Logic, 1999
Six flame maple trees, eight 35-inch telephone poles, stainless steel planters and armature, aircraft cable, drip irrigation system
Installation at MASS MoCA, North Adams, Mass., 1999–present

CRITICAL ART ENSEMBLE

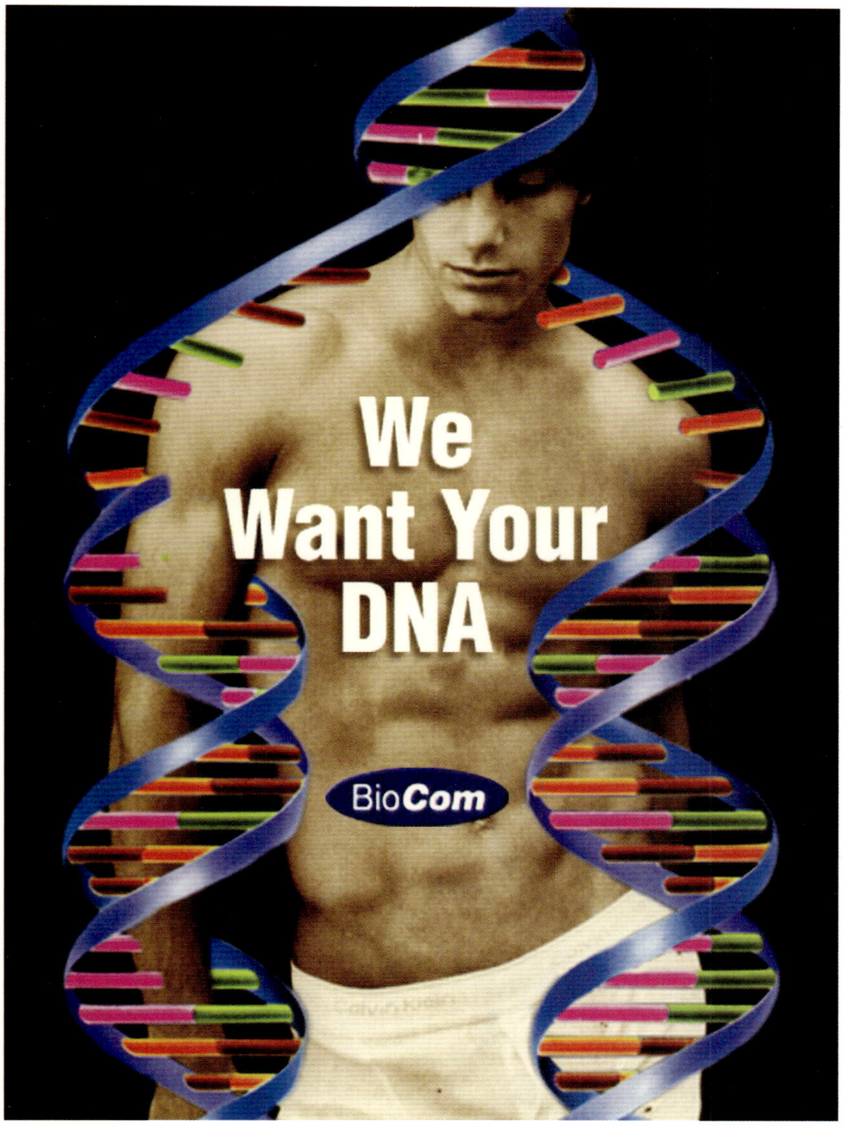

Flesh Machine, 1997
Digital website collage

CHRISTINE BORLAND

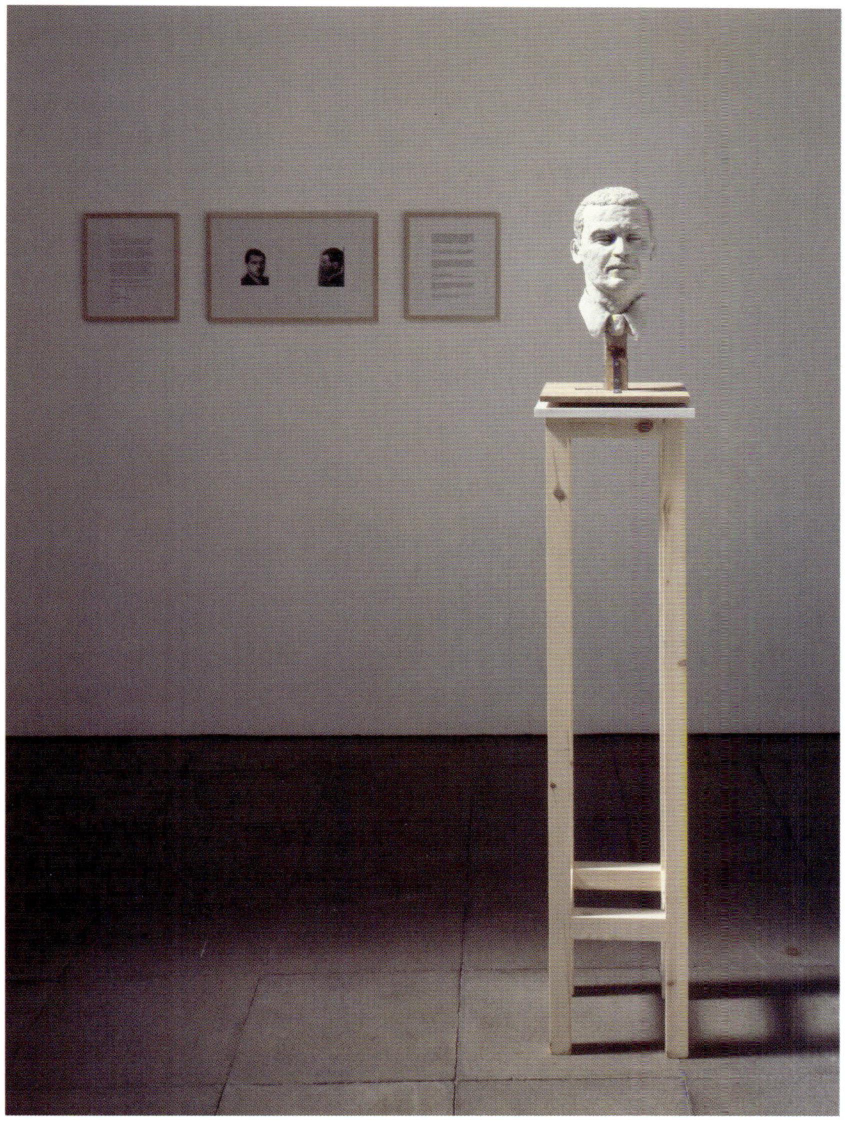

L'Homme Double, 1997
Clay, steel, wood, acrylic, documents, and photographs
Each stand with bust 67 x 12 5/8 x 12 5/8 in (170 x 32 x 32 cm)
Sammlung Migros Museum für Gegenwartskunst, Zürich

can sniff out concentrations of toxic vapors at contaminated industrial sites. For *Tree Logic*, 1999, she inverted six live trees and suspended them from a truss. They continued to grow, though bending toward the sun, resulting in shapes that were scientifically rational but visually bizarre. In both of these works, the trees can be seen as metaphorical surrogates for humans, who are equally subject to the laws of nature, even in unnatural circumstances.

Christine Borland addresses one such unnatural twisting of the laws of human nature—eugenics, the selective breeding of humans to emphasize traits deemed desirable—in formally exquisite objects and installations that question our use of science in the service of human perfection. *L'Homme Double*, 1997, for instance, was inspired by Borland's interest in the notorious Doctor Joseph Mengele, who ran the Nazis' eugenics experiments and whose personal charm and handsome appearance were said to have captivated even the victims of his torture. For this work, Borland asked six academic portrait sculptors to make clay busts based on a fuzzy photograph of Mengele, which are then displayed with a set of written descriptions by and photographs of Auschwitz survivors. The resulting objects vary in detail, but all share the soulless banality of academic sculpture. Thus they provide a striking illustration of the homogeneity that the Nazis sought in both art and their genetically pure German physiognomy. In other works, Borland examines the link between illness and genetics, the implications of genetic testing, the historic use of plants to induce abortion, and the fate of individuality in a science-driven culture. With such works, she delicately draws us into ethical meditations on the use of science, natural processes, and technology for ends that are not always beneficent.

Jim Sanborn also brings home the destructive consequences of science on humanity, and at a far larger scale. *Critical Assembly*, 1998–2003, is an installation of original equipment used to develop the atomic bomb in Los Alamos during the 1940s. Sanborn gathered these raw materials by scouring retirement homes and placing want ads in New Mexico newspapers seeking former Manhattan Project lab workers, many of whom had bought equipment sold off as surplus in the 1950s. As presented in an exhibition at the Corcoran Gallery in Washington, D.C., Sanborn's artifacts of destruction, some authentic and some refabricated, took on ambiguous meanings. On one hand, they were eerily beautiful, resembling pieces of modernist sculpture, and on the other they were haunted by their destructive mission. Polished metal assemblages, metal bowls, clicking Geiger counters, gray graphite cubes, and paraffin bricks were transformed into monuments of an antiquated but still functional technology, which, Sanborn made clear, could be reactivated with the insertion of a chunk of active plutonium. *Critical Assembly* raises troubling questions about science's devotion to the pursuit of knowledge for its own sake, especially when the consequences may be dire for humanity. It also evokes a period and an environment in which the creation of weapons of mass destruction was deemed politically justifiable, casting light on contemporary arguments about power, terror, and the proper uses of our technological and military might.

Alongside artists who explore the extension of human power through technology in the form of genetic engineering, eugenics, and the bomb are those who address the new science of cybernetics. Donna Haraway, one of the foremost theorists of the field, defines the cyborg, the product of cybernetics, as "a hybrid of machine and organism."[8] The intersection between the mechanical and the human can go both ways: attributing human qualities to machines, as in the 2001 Spielberg film *A.I.*, or transforming and extending human powers through mechanical means, be they prosthetic limbs, brain-computer interfaces, or even performance-enhancing drugs. Such investigations have a long history, dating back to Leonardo da Vinci's flying machines and the eighteenth-century automatons that played musical instruments, walked, sang, and played chess. A contemporary manifestation is AIBO, Sony's robot dog that barks, fetches, and even plays soccer on command. Given the allure and the repercussions of altering our very selves, it is not surprising that artists who have taken up the possibilities of cybernetics exhibit approaches that range from the fanciful to the unsettling.

Leonardo's contemporary heir is Panamarenko, who has spent some forty years creating all manner of flying machines, as well as submarines, cars, and even a motorized parachute. Living as he does in an era when air and even space travel are part of our everyday reality, Panamarenko is more interested in the fantasies that flight elicits than in the actual functionality of his gravity-defying machines. He draws on primitive technologies whose inner workings are completely transparent, lending his works something of the spirit of high-school science projects, unfazed by the fact that they rarely work. His monumental *Aeromodeller*, 1971, is a huge, inflated, but non-functional blimp made of nylon fabric and attached to a gondola. Equally ambitious and equally non-functional is his *Raven's Variable Matrix*, 2000, a flying machine that resembles a cross between an ergonomic bike and a glider outfitted with giant, dragonfly-like wings. With its chainsaw motor and bicycle wheels, and bungee cords where a seatbelt should be, the work wears its functional futility on its sleeve. *Archaeopterix III*, 1990, also presents an amalgam of technological gadgetry, this time to simulate both the appearance and the flight technique of a pre-Jurassic bird. A graduate of the Happenings of the 1960s, Panamarenko shares that era's playful approach to performance and technology.

Panamarenko's enthusiasm for flight finds its next-generation match in the work of Paul Ramirez Jonas, who creates tongue-in-cheek replicas of the apparatus of early space exploration or air travel. For *Box Kite*, 1993, the artist recreated turn-of-the-century kites resembling the Wright Brothers' flying gliders and equipped each with a disposable camera that he triggered to take pictures of the earth from the air. In the resulting images, the artist is often visible, though just barely, at the other end of the kite string. *Men on the Moon, Tranquility*, 1990–present, is a four-part project that takes on the magic of space flight as Ramirez Jonas records the transmitted conversations between Buzz Aldrin and Neil Armstrong during twenty-three hours of the Apollo 11 moon mission. In a conflation of historical technologies, the artist used a replica of Edison's first 1879 phonograph to record these sounds onto hundreds of grooved wax cylinders. Ramirez Jonas has also created earthbound works. "50 State Summits," begun in 2002, when (and if) completed will present a series of photographs of the artist mounting the highest point in every state and waving a flag that reads "OPEN." Recalling the triumphant achievements of the great explorers, the piece reminds us of a pre-steroids time, when old-fashioned, unaugmented bodies could still be winners.

Panamarenko and Ramirez Jonas's enthusiasm for mechanically enhanced bodies is atypical. More often, artists who explore the intersection between human and mechanical power imbue their work with a sense of wariness and warning. Rebecca Horn began her career making prosthetic devices that turn human bodies into strange animal avatars. In the 1970 performance *Unicorn*, she had a nude young

JIM SANBORN

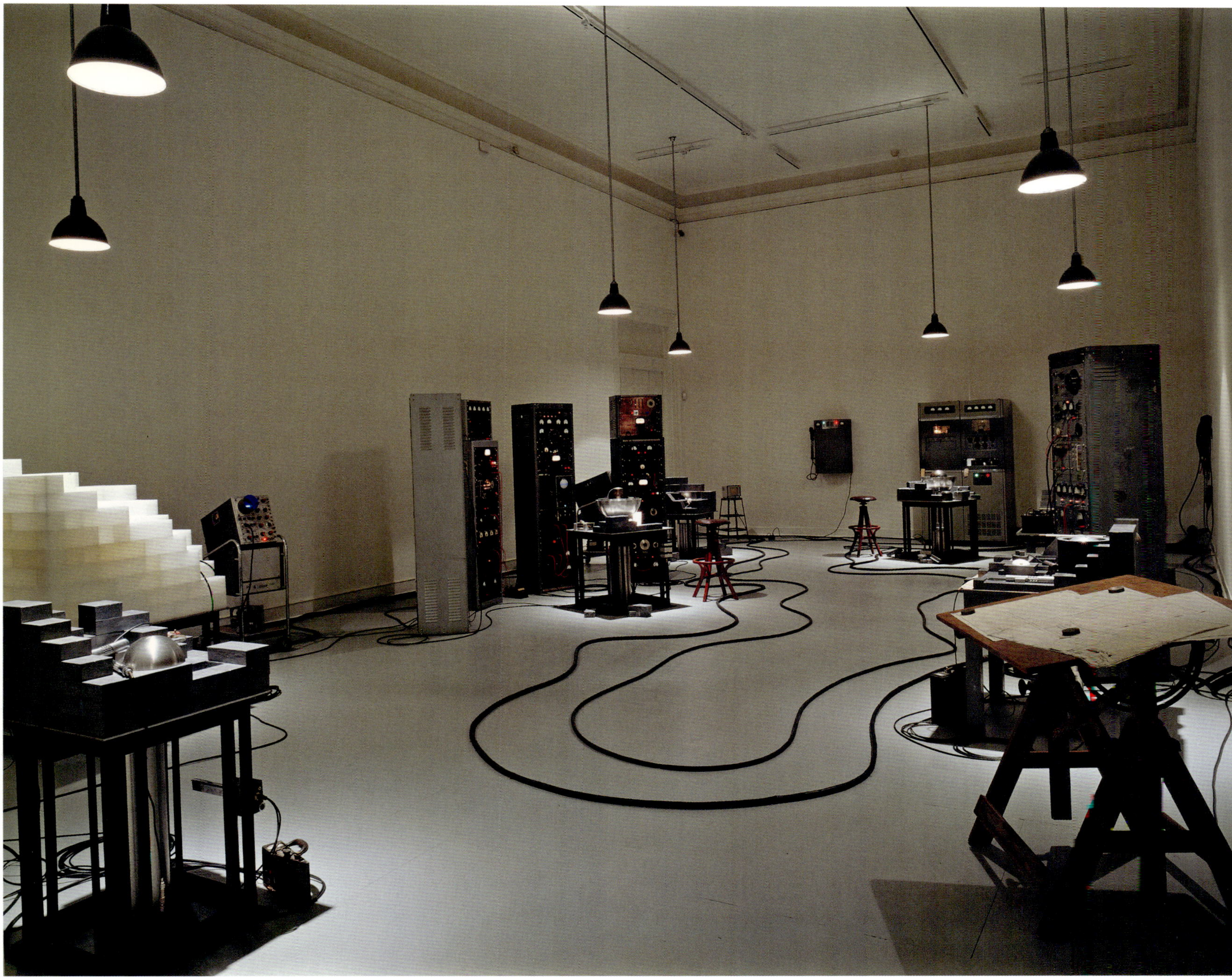

Critical Assembly: Laboratory Environment for the Assembly of the Trinity Device, c. 1945, 1998–2003
Aluminum, brass, gold-, silver- and nickel-plated brass, lead, stainless steel, boron-impregnated plastic, detector probes, Geiger-Muller (G-M) counters, simulated hydraulic lifts, alpha-detector, tungsten carbide, paraffin blocks, deuterium gas cylinder, graphite, wire, and sound, dimensions variable
As installed at the Corcoran Gallery of Art, Washington, D.C., November 2003–January 2004

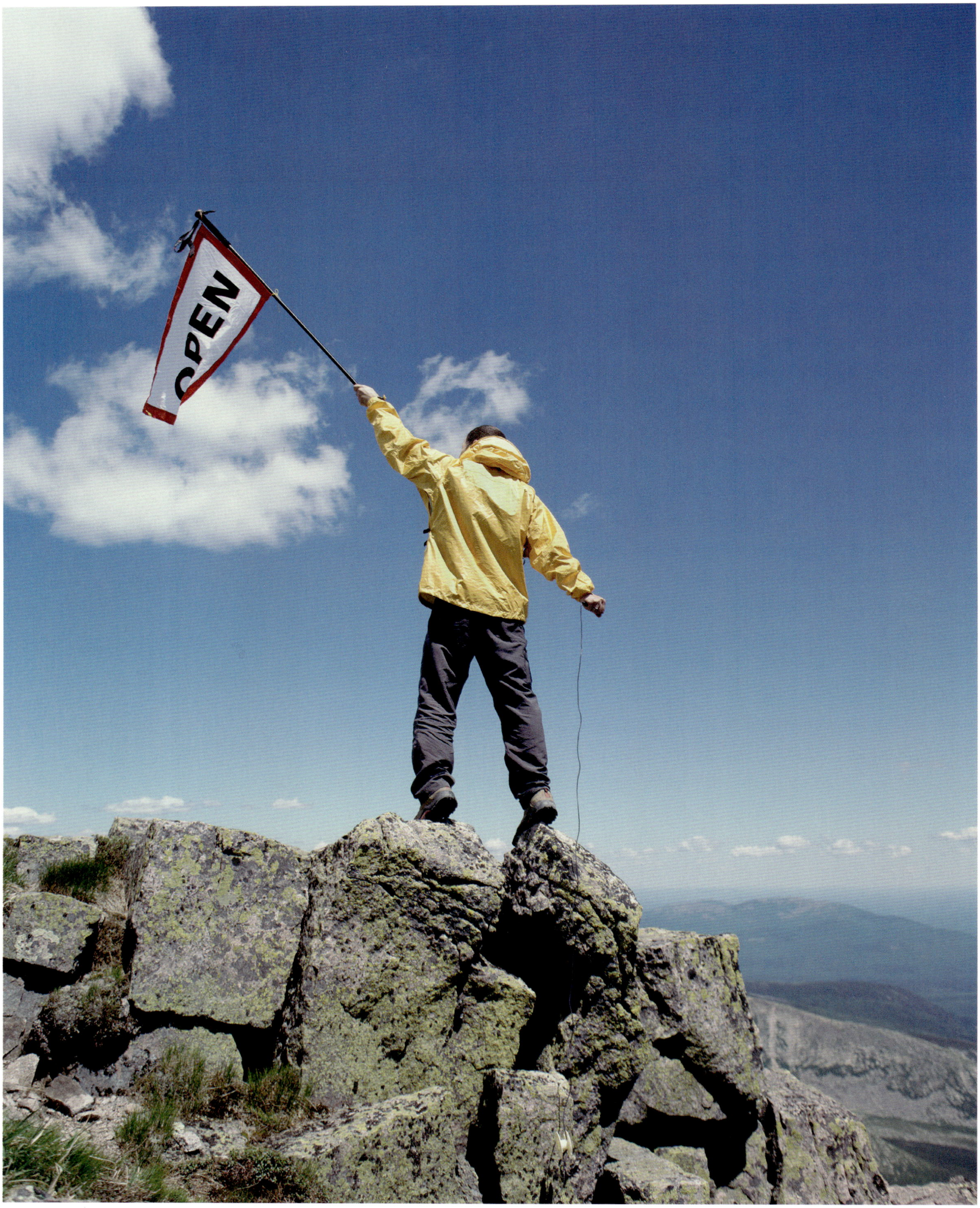

50 State Summits, Maine, Mount Katahdin, 2002
C-print, 24 x 19 1/2 in (61 x 49.5 cm)

PANAMARENKO

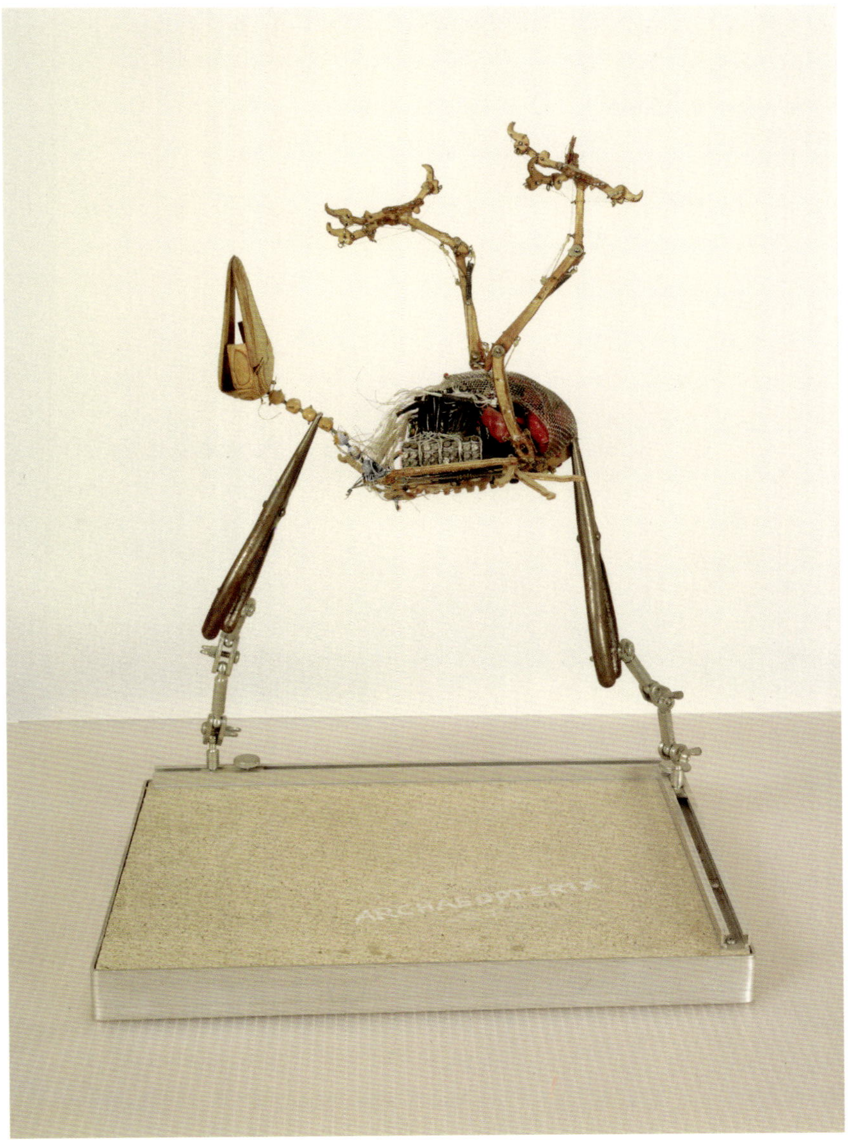

Archaeopteryx III, 1990
Wood, glue, strings, and electronic chips
17 x 11 1/2 x 8 in (43.2 x 29.2 x 20.3 cm), base 9 3/4 x 13 x 1 in (24.8 x 33 x 2.5 cm)

REBECCA HORN

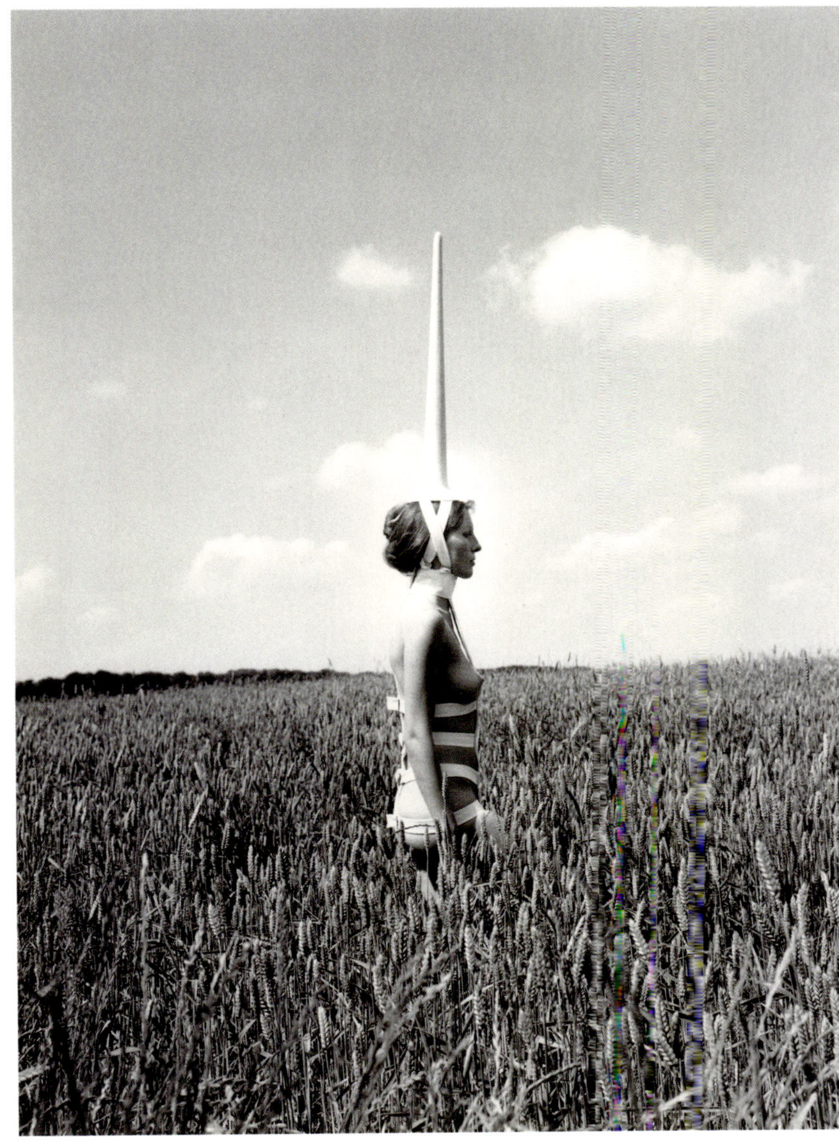

Unicorn, 1970
Fabric, wood, dimensions variable

LEE BUL

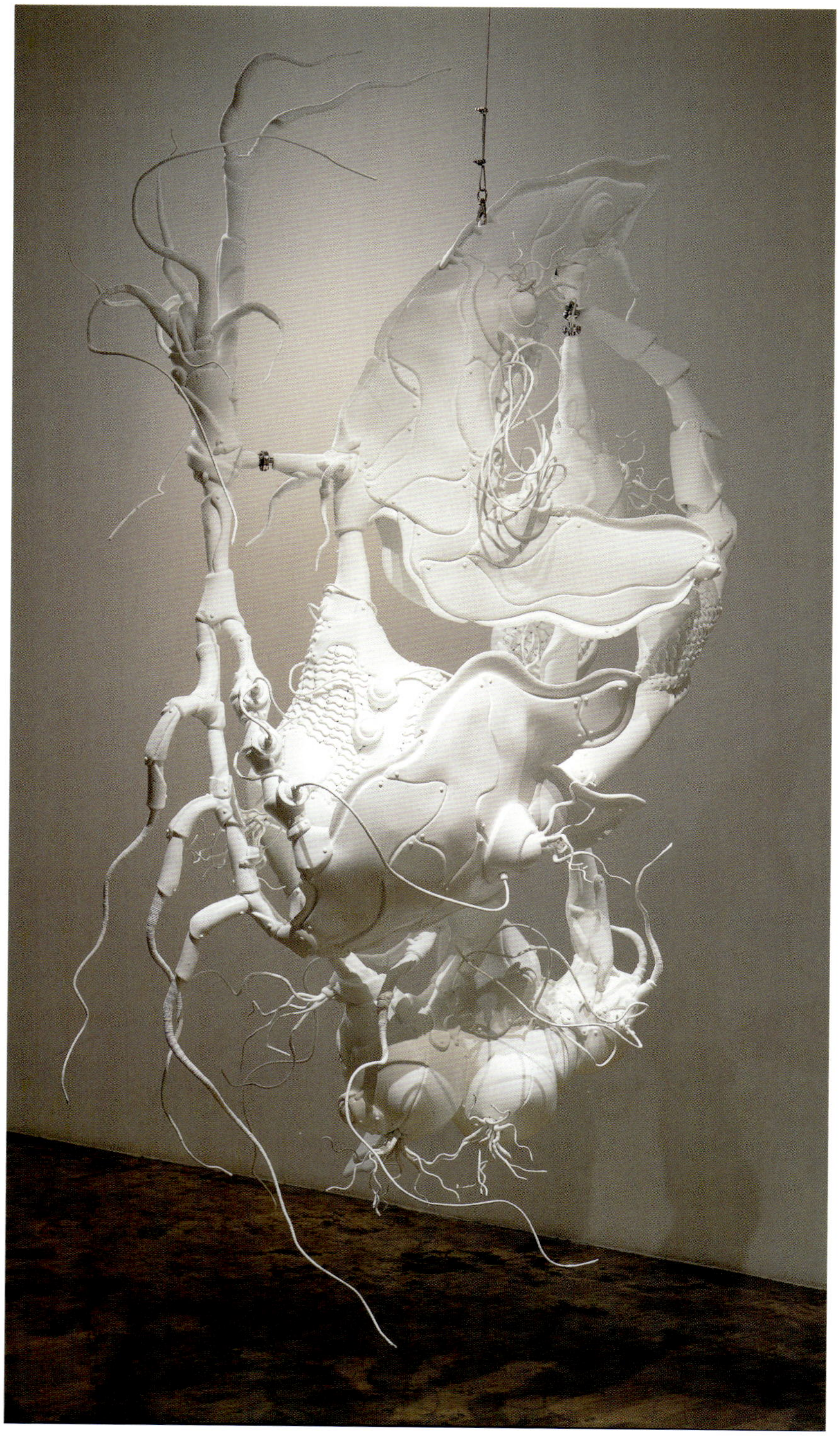

Chrysalis, 2000
Hand-cut polyurethane panels on aluminum armature, polyurethane coating
106 1/4 x 61 7/8 x 47 1/4 in (270 x 157 x 120 cm)
Fukuoka Asian Art Museum, Japan

woman wear a tall horn-shaped headdress and walk through a field. In more recent works, the physical human body has disappeared from Horn's work, but it remains psychologically present in kinetic sculptures that snap, flail, and pound away like malevolent spirits, sometimes flinging pigment against the wall or scattering ashes on the floor. Certain works suggest frustrated or funny sexual congress. *Kiss of the Rhinoceros*, 1989, for instance, is composed of a pair of curved steel arms that periodically rise and "hug" before delivering a brief zap of electricity, then fall back away to inertia. Others threaten death or destruction. All of these works are dysfunctional, recalling the Romantic era's abhorrence of the machine.

Lee Bul's take on the relationship between bodies and machines is equally unsettling, and also has a feminist spin. Her earliest works, from the early 1990s, consisted of her wearing costumes that transformed her body into a mutant creature, replete with soft organs, grotesque, hyper-sexualized body parts, and viscera. These were followed, in the late 1990s, by a series of cyborg sculptures made from silicone and white porcelain and suspended from the ceiling. Headless and missing limbs, they lacked individual identity, but even in armor-like shells the bodies were unmistakably female. Exaggeratedly small waists and oversized busts and buttocks suggested stereotypical male fantasies of a world in which female energy is potentially monstrous and also necessarily curtailed. Other works, like *Chrysalis*, 2000, are more insect-like, with floating feelers that reach out threateningly. And Lee has lately begun melding body and machine in a series of karaoke pods with names like *Anthem*, 2000 and *Live Forever*, 2001—lavishly upholstered, phallic-shaped capsules for one, equipped with a set of karaoke tapes of popular songs, which the inhabitant is invited to play. Lee's karaoke pods offer a curious reversal of the usually social karaoke experience, suggesting something more akin to an isolation chamber and pointing to the social detachment that so often results from modern mechanized entertainment, making us machine-like in behavior if not form.

Roxy Paine also blurs the line between human, nature, and machine, creating mechanical means for performing human actions, for example the creation of artworks. Paine's *PMU (Painting Manufacture Unit)*, 1999–2000, is a computer-programmed apparatus that paints canvases in an ironic send-up of the rhetoric of individuality that surrounds modernist abstraction. *SCUMAK*, 1998, performs the same operation for sculpture, mechanically producing blobs of plastic. Paine also brings machine-like precision to creating replicas of natural objects. For *Bluff*, he set a life-size stainless steel tree in Central Park as part of the 2002 Whitney Biennial. He has also lovingly recreated fields of poisonous mushrooms or garden weeds, giving them names like *Psilocybe Cubensis Field*, 1997, and *Weed Choked Garden*, 2005, and placing them incongruously in pristine white gallery spaces. By turning plants that are generally considered dangers or pests into art objects, Paine asks that we reconsider our assumptions about the uses and abuses of the natural world. All of his works turn on the inherent conflict between the human desire to control our surroundings and the serendipity of nature, which resists any such efforts.

While Horn and Lee play on our fears of humans becoming overly machine-like, Paine and Wim Delvoye offer glimpses of the possibility that machines may take on human characteristics. In Delvoye's *Cloaca Turbo*, 2003, the specific human functions under consideration are eating, digesting, and excreting. *Cloaca* is a monumental, biologically-correct machine designed to be fed twice a day with a restaurant-supplied meal. Over the course of two hours—in a process visible to

ROXY PAINE

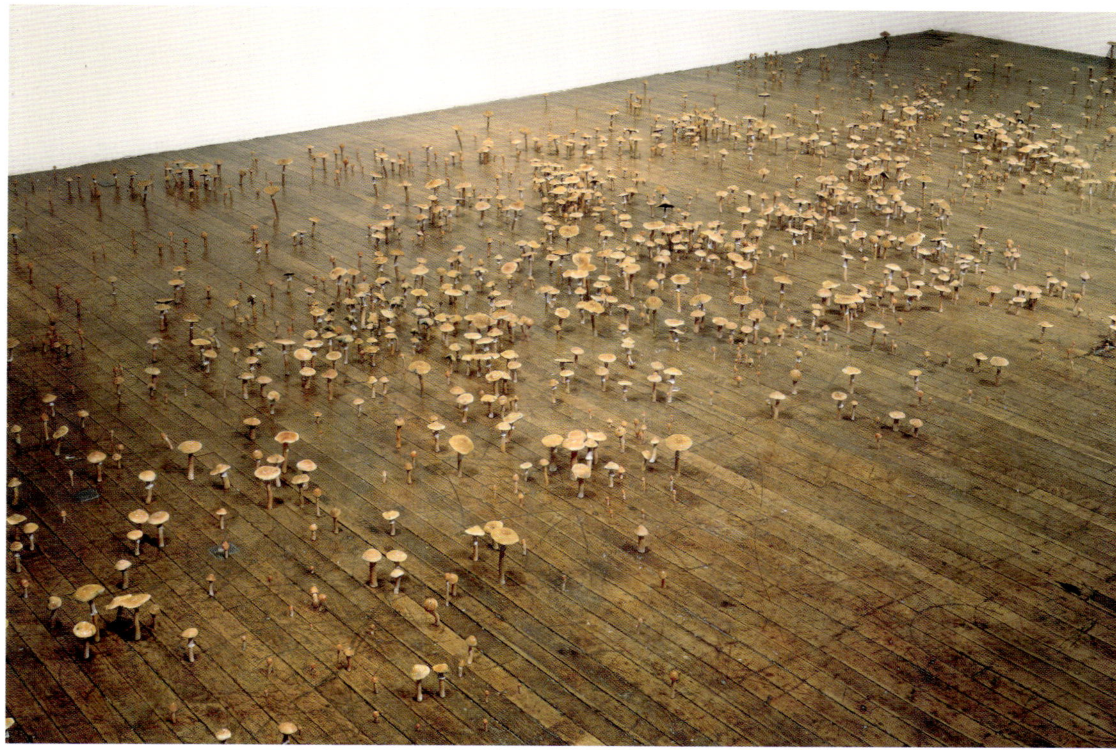

Psilocybe Cubensis Field, 1997
2200 polymer mushrooms with lacquer and oil paint
4 1/2 x 328 x 222 in (11.4 x 833.1 x 563.9 cm)

ROXY PAINE

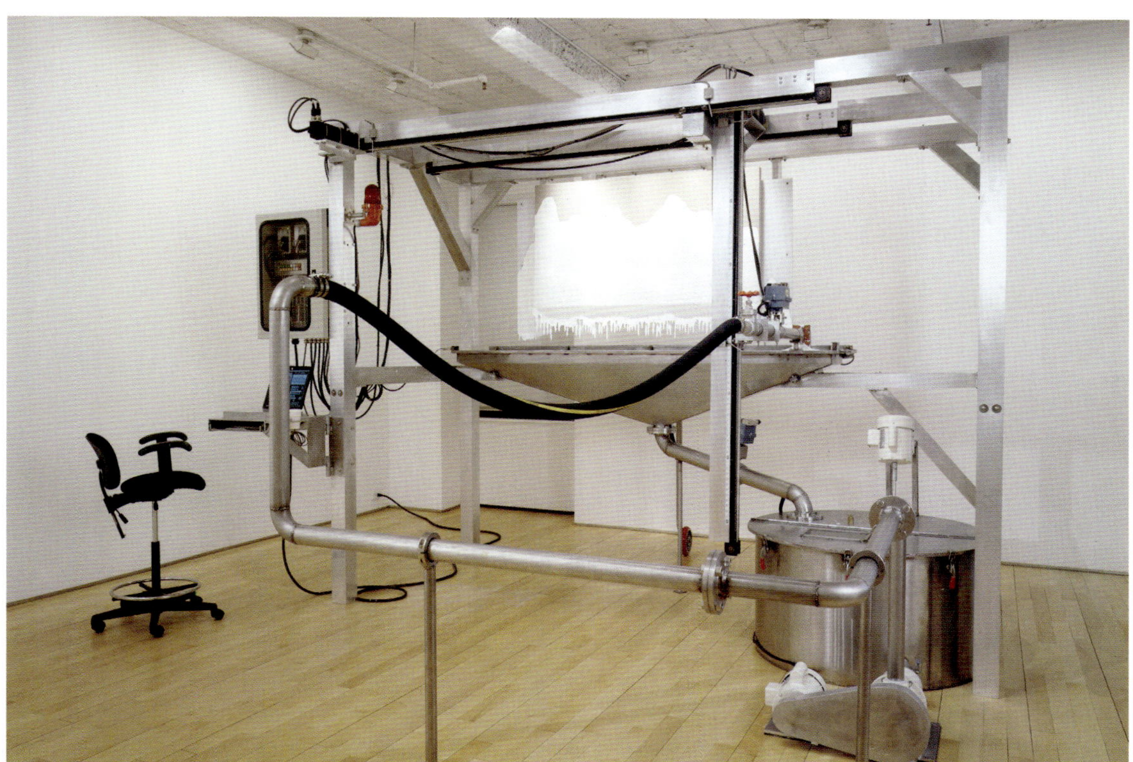

PMU (Painting Manufacture Unit), 1999–2000
Aluminum, stainless steel, computer, electronics, relays, custom software, acrylic, servo motors, valves, pump, precision track, glass, and rubber, 110 x 157 x 176 in (279.4 x 398.8 x 447 cm)

WIM DELVOYE

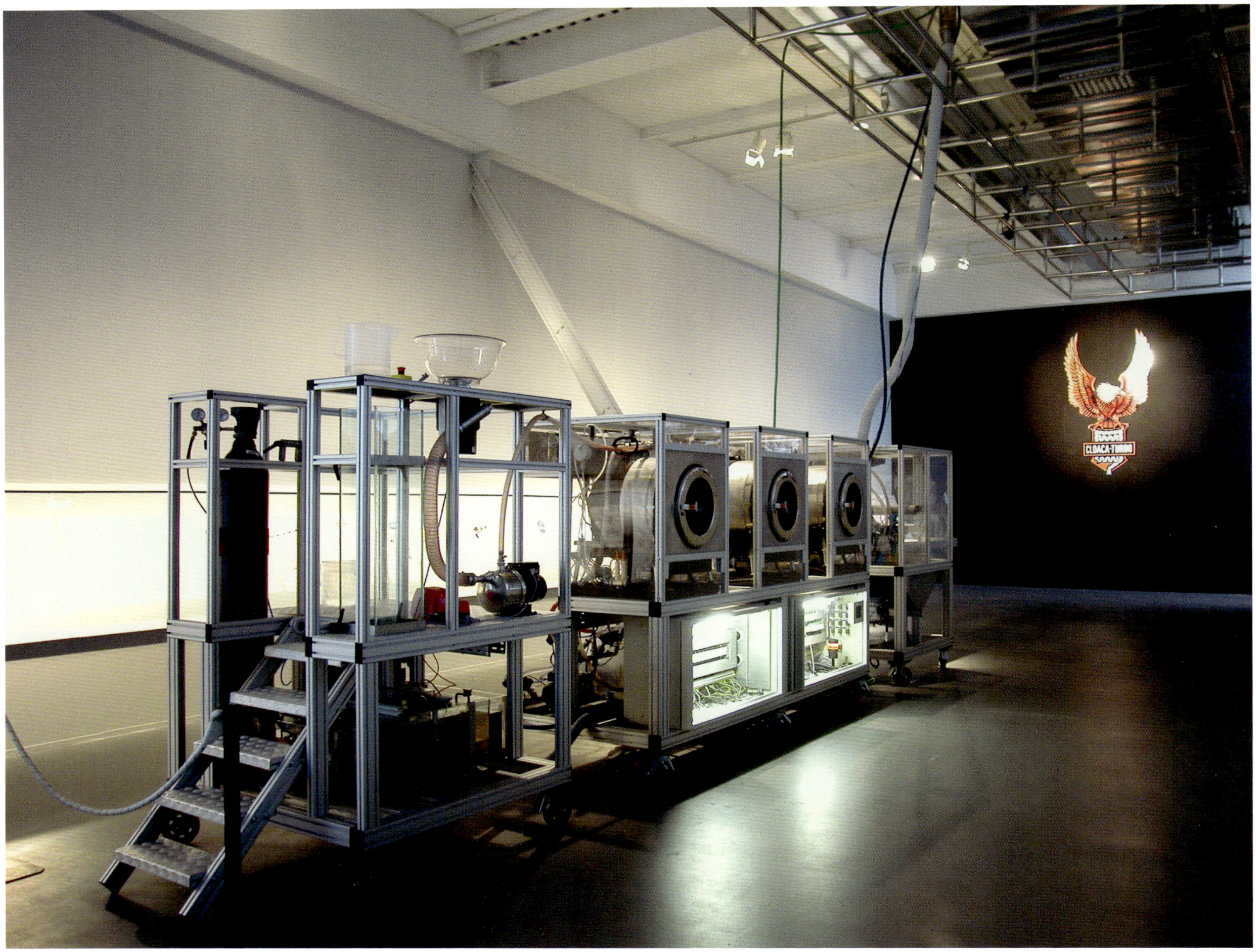

Cloaca Turbo, 2003
Mixed media, 78 3/4 x 325 1/4 x 50 3/8 in (200 x 826 x 128 cm)

viewers who watch its transparent functions—the food passes through a series of glass containers, in which it is broken down by the same acids and microorganisms found in the human stomach. Finally, with enviable regularity, it excretes the solid remains onto a slowly revolving metal disc. *Cloaca* has a mad-scientist quality, full of funnels, glass jars, plastic tubes, pumps, wires, and stainless steel stands. And, in fact, it is the product of eight years of collaboration with a team of experts in the fields of gastroenterology, computer technology, and plumbing. Unlike more conventional experiments in cybernetics, which tend to focus on reproducing our higher powers, Delvoye labors to make a machine that performs one of the most basic bodily functions.

As any student of popular culture would recognize, the human merger with machines represents one of our deepest fears about technology. Another fear is fear of ourselves—our own propensity to interfere with "natural processes" through relatively benign practices such as plastic surgery, organ transplants, and selective breeding of farm animals and pets to more problematic pursuits such as cloning, genetic manipulation, and cryogenics, pursuits that raise questions that go to the heart of what it means to be human. Theologians and philosophers have pondered such questions of ethics and identity for centuries, delving into the relationship between matter and spirit. Are we our bodies? Are we our minds? Our souls? Are we our emotions? Our memories? Our genetic structures? Whichever the answer, when these entities are "unnaturally" altered, we question not only personal identity but also whether there is a point beyond which we cease being human altogether.

Such questions have also provided artists with a fertile field of play. Nancy Burson, for example, has developed sophisticated computer software programs that alter human faces—revealing how any individual might age or appear if they belonged to a different race or gender. These transformations have real-world implications. Burson's most famous work involves the "aging" of the face of Etan Patz, who disappeared in Manhattan in 1979 at the age of six, to reveal what he might look like years later. Though this didn't turn up the missing boy, Burson's software has been used by the FBI in a number of other missing children cases. On a lighter note, Burson has also created composite portraits, morphing together the faces of a group of movie stars to present a tabloid version of ideal beauty, or the features of Hitler, Mussolini, Khomeini, Stalin, and Mao to creates a portrait of the ultimate dictator. *First and Second Beauty Composites*, 1982, presents two sets of blended faces. The first combines Bette Davis, Audrey Hepburn, Grace Kelly, Sophia Loren, and Marilyn Monroe and the second is a morphing of Jane Fonda, Jacqueline Bisset, Diane Keaton, Brooke Shields, and Meryl Streep. Oddly, rather than providing an idealized image of physical perfection, these composites end up looking generic and creepy.

Burson's composite photographs find an eerie counterpart in the work of performance artist Orlan, who has managed to become a composite herself in a series titled "The Reincarnation of Saint Orlan." These minutely documented (and in one case internationally televised) surgical "performances" allow us to bear witness as Orlan turns her own body into a medium for sculpture. Between 1990 and 1993 Orlan undertook nine operations to alter her features, using as a template specific details chosen from famous Renaissance and post-Renaissance paintings of idealized females. While this project has sometimes been erroneously described as an effort to recreate the ideal of Western beauty in her own body, in fact Orlan

NANCY BURSON

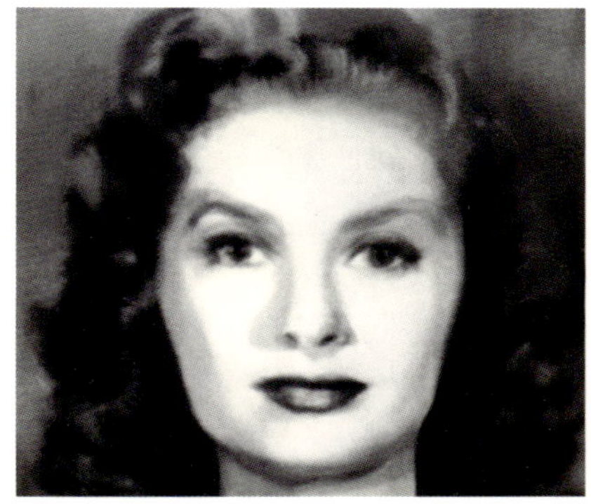

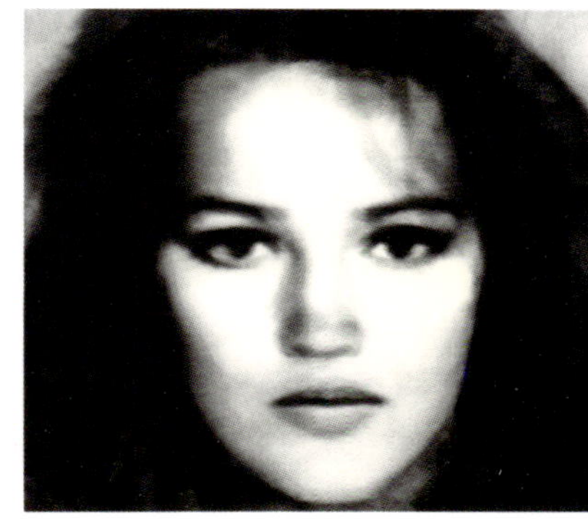

First and Second Beauty Composites, 1982
Gelatin silver prints, 7 3/4 x 8 3/4 in (19.7 x 22.2 cm)

NANCY BURSON

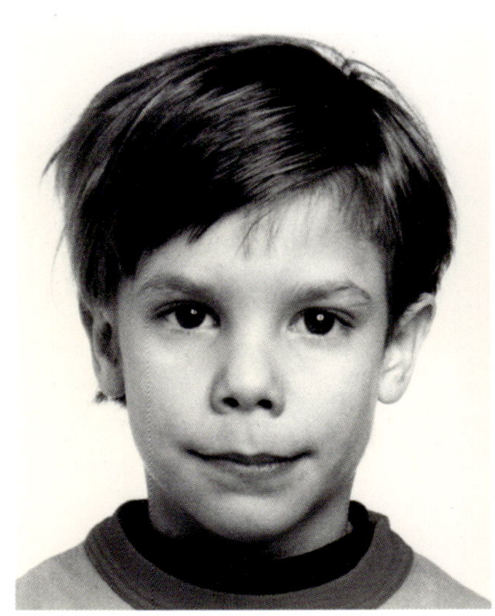

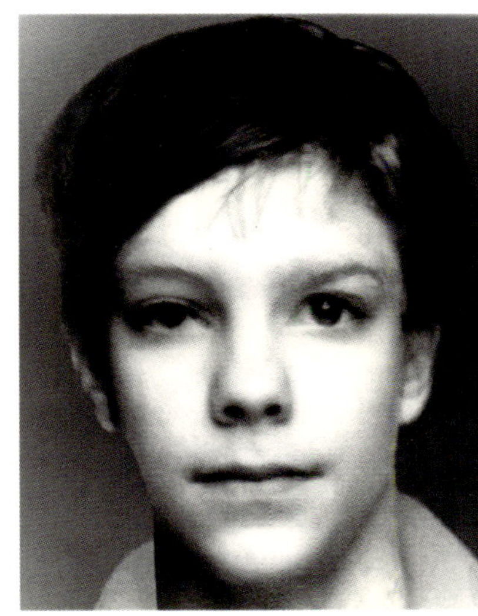

Etan Patz Update, 1984
Gelatin silver prints, 8 1/2 x 8 1/2 in (21.6 x 21.6 cm)

ANTHONY AZIZ & SAMMY CUCHER

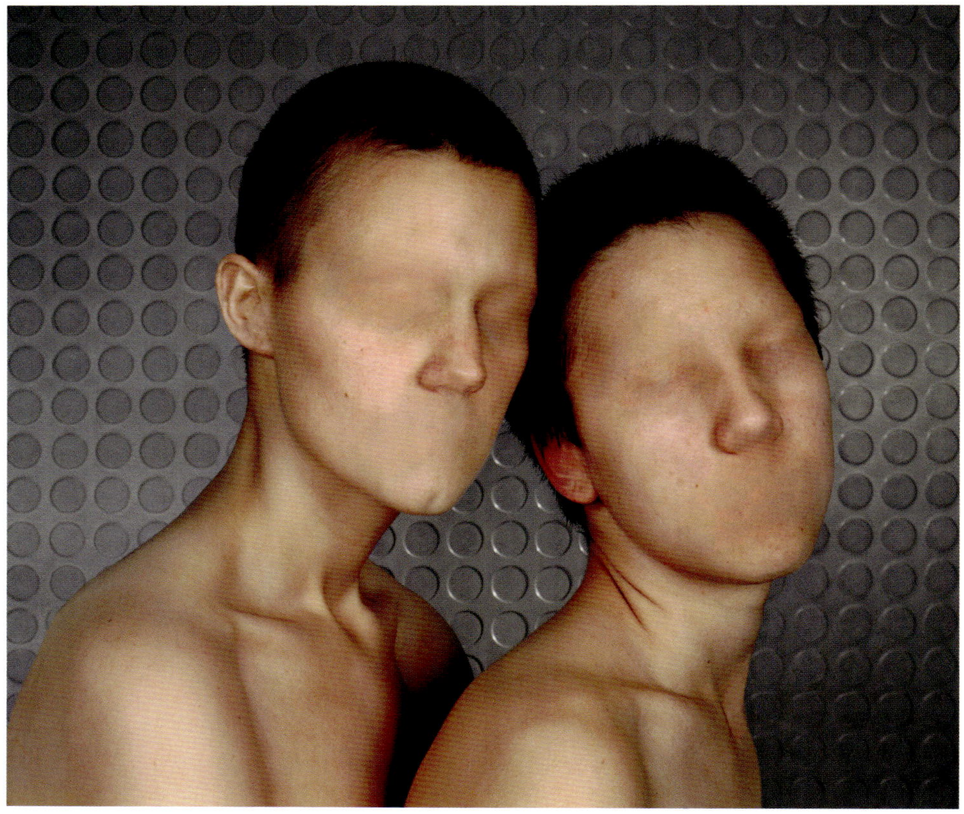

Pam and Kim, from the "Dystopia" series, 1994–95
C-print, 50 x 40 in (127 x 101.6 cm)

PATRICIA PICCININI

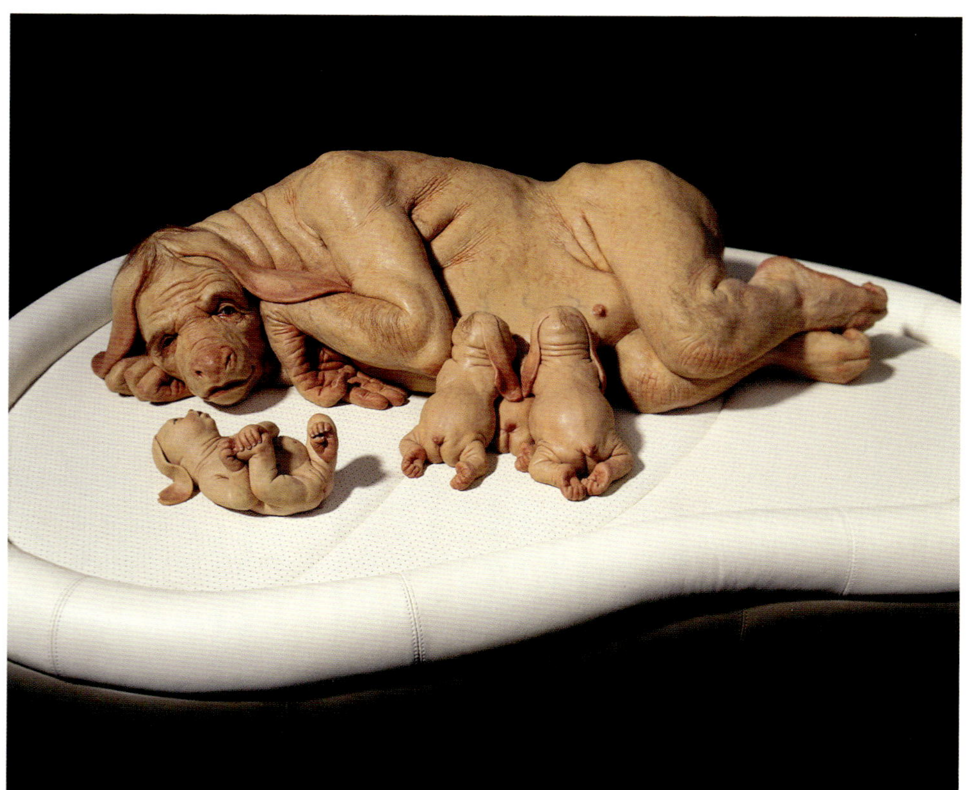

Young Family, 2002
Silicone, polyurethane, leather, human hair, dimensions variable

notes that she chose each model (among them Boucher's *Europa*, Leonardo's *Mona Lisa*, Botticelli's *Venus* and Gérôme's *Psyche*) for her history rather than her beauty. To emphasize her disinterest in conventional standards of beauty, for her last operation Orlan inserted silicon bumps in her forehead, suggesting budding horns. In a complementary body of work, "Self-Hybridations," begun in 1998, Orlan digitally transforms her face by morphing its image with the distorted features of pre-Columbian and African sculptures. Orlan's unmistakable eyes peer from faces sporting elongated necks and noses, strange protuberances, flattened foreheads, elaborate ornamental markings, and helmet-like hair arrangements. The results are oddly futuristic and primitive at the same time, suggesting some new breed of human drawn from the whole of mankind's genetic store.

Hints of genetic mutation and bio-engineering also haunt the work of artist team Anthony Aziz and Sammy Cucher, who use digital technology to create images of human bodies that seem in the process of losing all individual differentiation or have melded with architecture. The 1992 series "Faith, Honor, and Beauty" comprises photographs of magnificent human nudes who have no genitalia, nipples, or belly buttons. The figures stand in triumphant postures, holding "attributes" in the medieval sense—symbols that attest to their status as soldiers, athletes, or mothers. In the context of these images, their subtractions seem less like deficiencies than indications of their having somehow transcended old-fashioned biological imperatives. Less exultant are the figures in the duo's "Dystopia" series, 1994–95, digitally altered photographs of faces from which features are all but erased as smooth skin covers the hole where a mouth or eyes ought to be. In "Interiors," 1998–2000, the human form has disappeared altogether, replaced by generic interiors that appear to be composed of human skin, complete with freckles, spots, pores, and hair follicles: the ultimate body building fusion.

The consequences of perhaps not-too-distant cellular experiments are also the subject of Patricia Piccinini's meticulously realistic sculpted creatures that reflect the possible horrific results of our manipulation of the genetic code. These range from designer babies, or *LUMPS (Lifeform with Unevolved Mutant Properties)*, 1994–95, intelligent, disease-resistant, but otherwise weirdly unformed and definitely uncuddly, to a mouse with a human ear attached to its back (based on an actual experiment with tissue engineering) to a pair of little boys representing prematurely aging "failed clones," like Dolly, the world's first cloned sheep. *Young Family*, 2002, composed of acrylic, silicone, human hair, and leather, presents an utterly convincing, if strange, pink-skinned creature nursing her young pups. Resembling a pig with her floppy ears and wrinkled snout, her legs and arms appear human, and her expression of maternal anxiety all the more so, suggesting there is no longer a definitive boundary between human and animal. Beyond its fascination, Piccinini's work is designed to make us pause and ask how far we are willing to go in our effort to "perfect" the human genome. Where do we draw the line between eradicating genes associated with hereditary diseases and creating designer humans? And when genetic experiments fail, who will bear the consequences?

Alexis Rockman presents similarly disturbing fantasies about mutant animal species. Drawing on the illustrative techniques of natural history museums, he creates a world full of monstrous insects, hybrid animals, and impossibly mutated creatures engaged in an endless cycle of copulation, mutual destruction, death, and decay. In meticulously painted tableaux, Rockman includes such unnatural

ORLAN

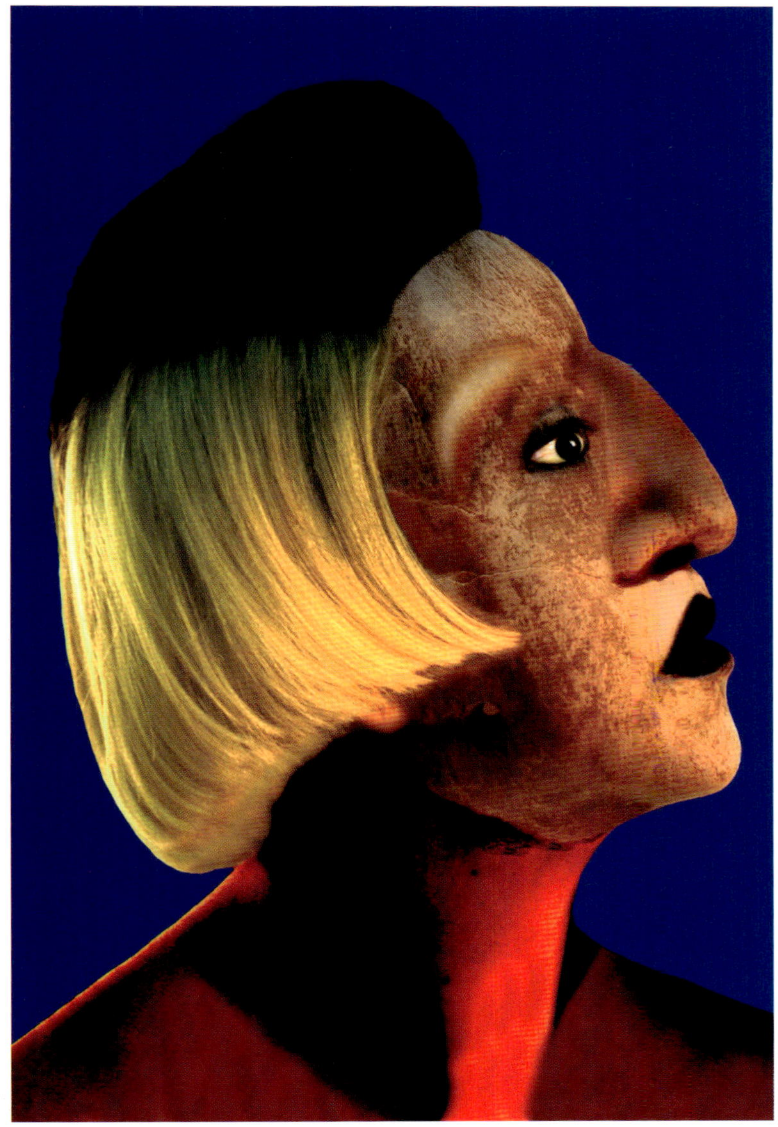

Refiguration/Self-Hybridization Pre-Columbian N°38, 1998
Cibachrome print, 63 1/2 x 42 1/2 in (161.3 x 108 cm)

ALEXIS ROCKMAN

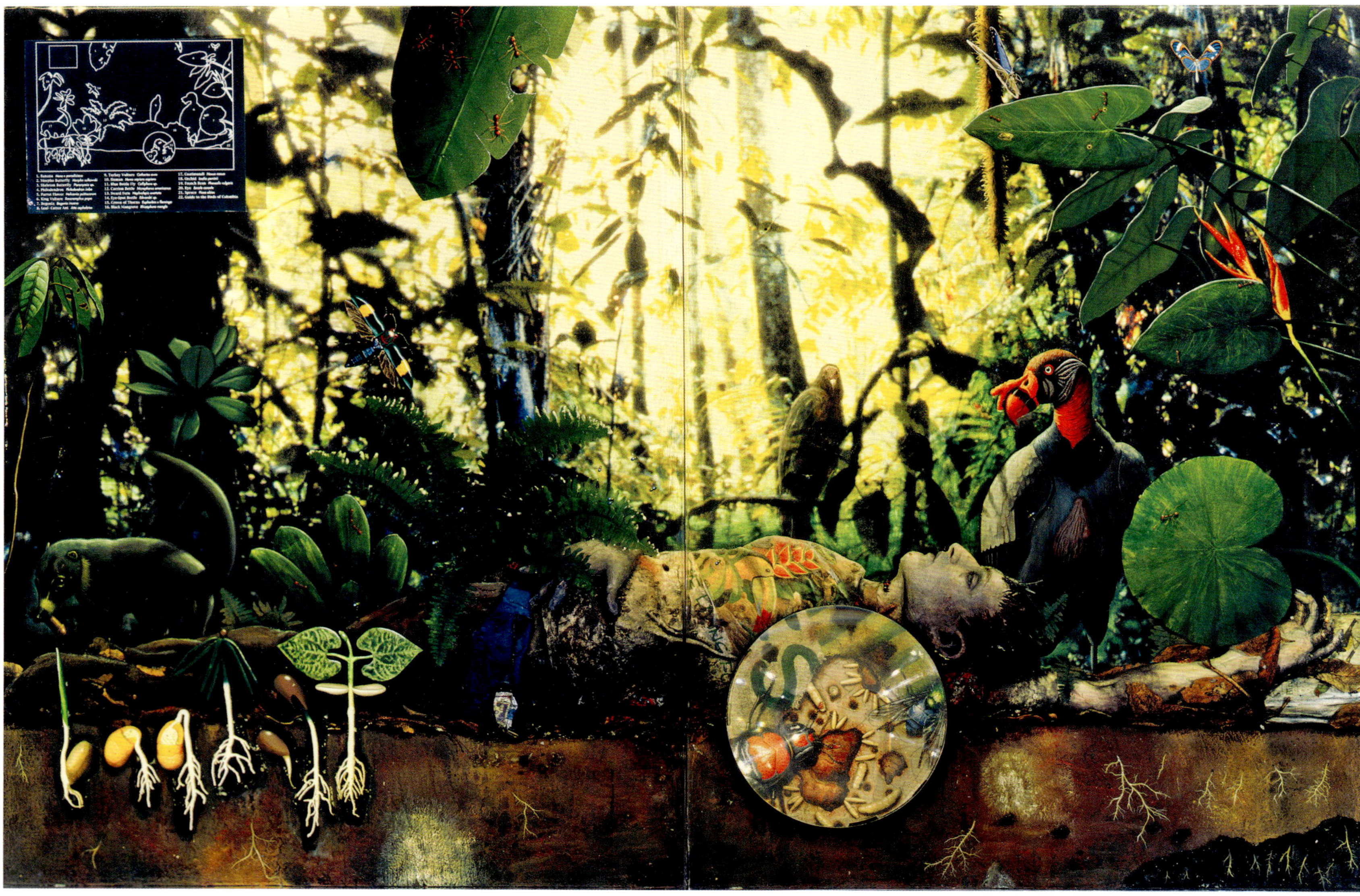

The Ecotourist, 1997
Envirotex, digitized photograph, artificial plants, carved Styrofoam, acrylic and oil paints, botanical models, plasticine, synthetic hair, latex rubber, clothing, nylon waist pouch, book jacket, metal wedding ring, Fresnel lens, rice, plastic taxidermied human eyeball, leaves, empty pack of Camel cigarettes on 2 gessoed wood panels
56 x 88 x 5 in (142.2 x 223.5 x 12.7 cm)

phenomena as winged, antlered, and bird-clawed rabbits, marsupials with metal bird beaks riveted on, the inter-species coupling of mice and squirrels, square tomatoes, dairy cows with tiny heads and giant udders, meat-eating plants, and parasitic fungi. His paintings often present cross-sections that reveal a nether world beneath the earth's surface, or even behind the wood paneling of a suburban home, where species feed on each other or dwell in murk created by spills of oil, garbage, and other human-made debris. In *The Ecotourist*, 1997, he has even inserted a self-portrait as a decaying corpse. Whether his bizarre hybrids or deformed creatures have emerged as the product of ecological disaster, nuclear radiation, or bad agricultural policies, Rockman's vision of nature is anti-romantic to the extreme. While humorous, his scenes reveal a future of destruction unleashed by unwitting human intervention.

Trumping all, Eduardo Kac has moved beyond the representation of genetic modification to the real thing. Pioneering what he calls "transgenic art," Kac comes unsettlingly close to the ambitions of Shelley's Dr. Frankenstein. In *Genesis*, 1999, he translates a biblical quote first into Morse code and then into the language of DNA, then makes this sequence into an actual gene by stringing the DNA bases together. Inserted into living E. coli bacteria, the sequence results in an organism that mutates when activated by ultraviolet light. The biblical phrase Kac used is often cited to justify human attempts to dominate nature: "Let man have dominion over the fish of the sea, and over the fowl of the air, and over every living thing that moves over the earth." Even more "God-like" is Kac's *GFP Bunny*, 2000, also known as Alba, a living albino rabbit with jellyfish DNA so it will glow green under ultraviolet light. Alba's chemistry quite closely mirrors that of Glofish, a commercially produced fish used in environmental water-quality studies that glows green or red when exposed to certain chemicals and industrial pollutants. But Alba has no such functional purpose, she is merely the product of the artist's imagination.

Thus Kac raises the question: Should we do things simply because we can? Evoking debates over the ethical limits of science and technology, he functions in a middle-ground between the "dominionism" of the biblical phrase and the despair of the nineteenth-century Romantics. Considering the impact of "progress" on the natural landscape and the human (and non-human) body, artists today critique science and technology in full recognition that, as products of nature ourselves, we are bound by natural laws that may be bent but never broken.

EDUARDO KAC

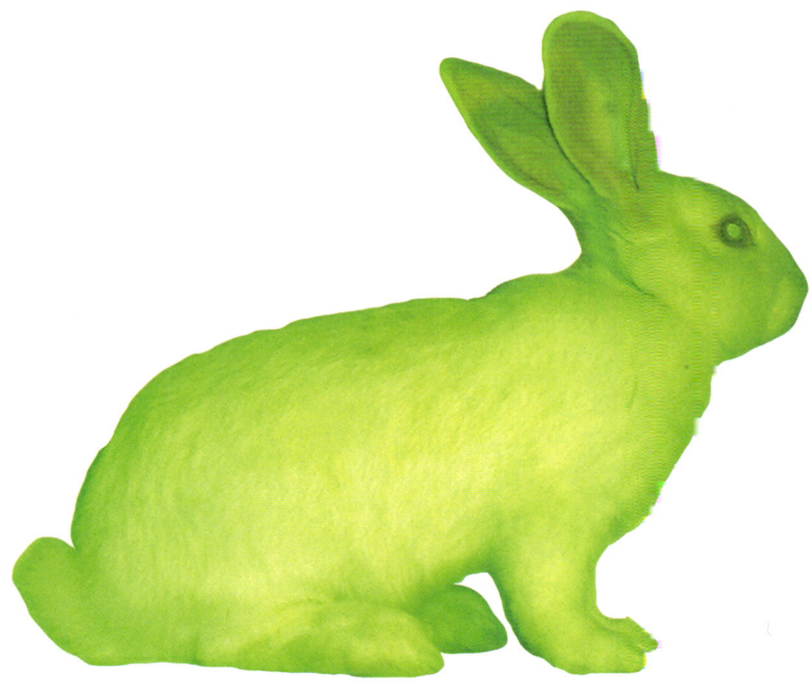

GFP Bunny, 2000
Alba, the fluorescent bunny

ART & DEFORMATION

CELEBRATING HUMAN IMPERFECTION

The exaltation of idealized human bodies was once considered the artist's highest calling. Think of the taut physique of Michelangelo's *David*, the softly rounded curves of *Venus de Milo*, or Titian's supple *Venus of Urbino*. Today, artistic celebrations of bodily perfection are likely to be dismissed as old-fashioned or ideologically suspect. There are many reasons for this dramatic shift. The rise of abstraction among the avant-garde precipitated a temporary demise of the figurative all together. Later, feminist critique of the "male gaze" made the unexamined idealization (or objectification) of female beauty dubious. And performance art has shifted attention from the body as subject to the body as instrument or art material. The rejection of idealized bodies in art has happened right alongside society's increasing demand for physical perfection, an obsession that is expressed in myriad advertisements and products of pop culture.

Artists today, in reaction to these impossible standards, are often representing not beautiful bodies but ordinary, imperfect ones, and sometimes even downright ugly or mutant ones. But media hype around beauty alone can't explain contemporary artists' fascination with deformed, mangled, and even dead and decaying bodies. Nor does it explain why artists are so willing to highlight bodily secretions and functions normally shunned in polite company. In place of *Venus de Milo*, contemporary art serves up the still life photographs of Joel-Peter Witkin, which feature arrangements of rotting corpses and body parts; the catsup, chocolate syrup, and mayonnaise drenched characters in Paul McCarthy's mini-dramas; and the wart-covered hags of Cindy Sherman. Whether presented in graphic photographs, through sensuously surfaced paintings, as humorously offensive performances, or in strangely distorted figural sculptures, works such as these challenge all of our conventional assumptions about order and beauty in art.

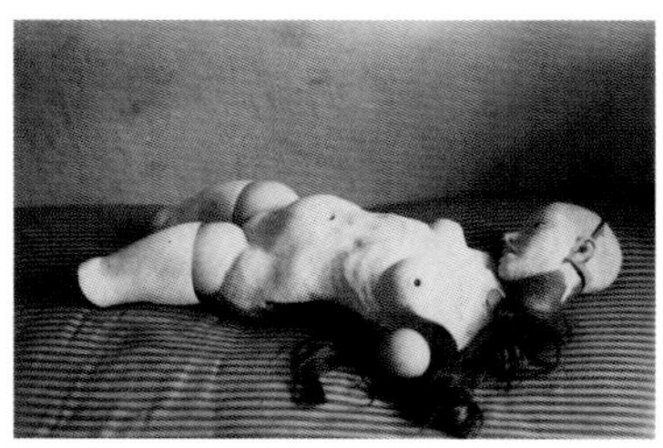

HANS BELLMER
LA POUPÉE (DOLL)
1934
VINTAGE GELATIN SILVER PRINT
2 1/2 X 3 5/8 IN (6.3 X 9.2 CM)

Among the primary terms used to describe this tendency to blight the body in contemporary art are the *grotesque,* the *carnivalesque*, *abjection*, and *informe* (from the French, meaning formless), each of which has its own particular set of meanings and characteristics. The *grotesque*, for example, can be traced back, in location and in etymology, to the walls of Roman grottoes, where Renaissance scholars discovered highly ornamental frescoes depicting fantastical chimeras. Artists then, newly liberated from the heavy hand of the medieval church, saw griffins, satyrs, and centaurs as celebrations of the free play of the imagination. Over time, however, the vernacular meaning of the word *grotesque* has come to describe that which is distasteful, abhorrent, or ugly—perjorative judgments that evidence the discomfort we feel when categories are breached and the normal order of nature overturned. As art historian Frances Connelly notes, "The grotesque is defined by what it does to boundaries, transgressing, merging, overflowing, destabilizing them. Put more bluntly, the grotesque is a boundary creature."[1] The term *carnivalesque* is more recent but the concept it embodies stretches back to the Middle Ages. The word first appeared in 1940 in the writings of Russian literary critic Mikhail Bakhtin, in his groundbreaking study of the sixteenth-century French writer François Rabelais.[2] Bakhtin traces the carnivalesque to the folk culture of the medieval carnival, describing how such celebrations allowed the peasantry to turn the tables on the civil and religious authorities who ordinarily held them in strict control. On carnival days, all hierarchies and official orders were suspended, temporarily replaced by a liberating chaos in which priests and rulers were impersonated, mocked, and generally portrayed in the worst possible light. Further, the relations of body and soul were reversed, and such functions as breaking wind, defecating, and copulation were put on public display.

The term *abjection* has come into vogue in recent years to describe a similarly uninhibited tendency in contemporary artists and writers who employ such taboo materials as dirt, hair, excrement, dead animals, menstrual blood, and rotting food, and such taboo subjects as castration, dismemberment, incest, and bestiality as a way of confronting often unmentionable aspects of gender and sexuality. In the early 1980s theorist Julia Kristeva identified abjection as a horrified reaction (often brought on by witnessing a corpse, vomit, or other signs of our own materiality) to the loss of a sense of self. In modern art and literature, she describes it as "What disturbs identity, system, order. What does not respect borders, positions and rules, the in between, the ambiguous, the composite."[3] This borderless place is described as well in the notion of the *informe*, which art historians Rosalind Krauss and Yve-Alain Bois made the subject of an influential 1996 exhibition at the Centre Georges Pompidou, in Paris. Invoking French writer Georges Bataille's call for the destruction of aesthetic ideals of harmony and unity via the disruptive forces of eroticism and the unconscious, the exhibition and surrounding theory suggests that the avant-garde had transgressed binary classifications such as figure and ground, self and other, and male and female to the point that such categories have collapsed altogether.[4]

These four terms, all of which are essential to theoretical discussions of contemporary art, share a focus on impurity, border states, mutations, hybridization, and the irrational. Art in this vein involves breaching boundaries that are usually viewed as sacrosanct: life and death, good and evil, spirit and flesh, creation and destruction, human and animal, and organic and inorganic matter. It may emerge from a dual place as well, mingling dream or imagination with prosaic waking reality. This is of course the basis for the Surrealist movement, which fed off the instability of dream images in loosing the underlying psychosexual anxieties of the modern age. Images of sexual activity, often of a deliberately perverse nature, are common in these works, as are scatological references. The Italian artist Piero Manzoni, for instance, once produced ninety cans of "artist's shit" to be sold at the same price per gram as gold.

Works that express these qualities materialize variously in images of deformed bodies, which have an impressive aesthetic lineage. Among those who have contributed are Hieronymus Bosch, Pieter Bruegel the Elder, Francisco Goya, the seventeenth-century Mannerists, who deliberately exaggerated and distorted details of human anatomy, and nineteenth-century Romantic artists like Eugéne Delacroix and Théodore Géricault, whose depictions of death, madness, and disease subverted academic classicism. In the modern era, precursors of the current embrace of deformation include George Grosz, who created savagely satirical drawings of Germany's bourgeois society between the two world wars, and Hans Bellmer, who manipulated life-size pubescent dolls and photographed them, creating dismembered, fragmented, and sexualized images of the female body. These made their first appearance in 1934 in the Surrealist journal *Minotaure*, in the form of eighteen photographs of a mannequin made of wood, flax fiber, plaster, and glue, and collectively titled "La Poupée (Doll): Variations on the Montage of an Articulated Minor." Such modernist deformation has often taken on a political cast as a reaction against the obsession with physical perfection that has been a hallmark of repressive regimes. Under the Soviet regime, for example, artists were enlisted to portray idealized full-bodied peasant girls and muscle-bound young farm hands, while in Nazi Germany officially sanctioned paintings and sculptures depicted blond paragons of sexless athleticism. In the Soviet Union, artists who failed to produce sufficiently uplifting depictions of noble Russian-ness found their careers abruptly curtailed, while in Nazi Germany their counterparts were denounced as "degenerate" and forced to escape the country or risk death in concentration camps.

In contemporary art the political aspect of deformative representation is relatively muted, though it still seeks to disrupt established orders represented by the sexist patriarchy, repressive governments, political correctness, puritanism, and official culture. Though it may not always be obvious, the disruptions of deformation perform an important service: by presenting grotesque or abject representations of self and world, they subvert idealized representations and bring us closer to the truth of being human. While valuable, no one said this truth is easy, and probably nowhere is the disruption of established norms more distressing than when it is applied to the human body. Instinctively projecting ourselves onto figural representations, we internalize the mutations, fragmentations, and realignments of the painted and sculpted human form, which may be one reason the Nazis found the distortions of modern art so unnerving. In the wake of World War II, representations of distorted and deformed bodies became a frequent subject in art. Willem de Kooning's "Women" paintings of the early 1950s, for instance, pictured monstrous women with enormous breasts and fierce eyes baring carnivorous teeth outlined by blood red lips. Among de Kooning's inspirations were the concurrent figural sculptures of Alberto Giacometti, who, like de Kooning, distorted the human figure almost to the point of abstraction. Giacometti's figures are elongated, wraith-like creatures in stiff poses common to ancient Egyptian or Cycladic sculpture. Their rough surfaces and extreme attenuation suggest bodies that have been eaten away, leaving behind only the barest suggestion of sentient humanity.

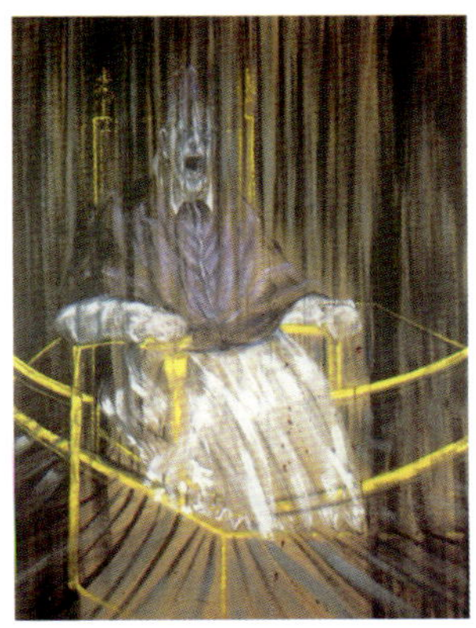

FRANCIS BACON
STUDY AFTER VELAZQUEZ'S PORTRAIT OF POPE INNOCENT X
1953
OIL ON CANVAS
60 1/4 X 46 1/2 IN
(153 X 118 CM)

The psychic wounds inflicted by the horrors of World War II are also evident in the art of Francis Bacon, whose paintings from the 1950s include reworkings of traditional religious themes that express a sense of the breakdown of civilization and lament the failure of religion to provide an effective moral compass. *Study after Velázquez's Portrait of Pope Innocent X*, 1953, reinvents Velázquez's 1650 portrait, but in Bacon's version a shower of vertical brushstrokes imprisons the figure in his gold throne, his mouth open in a silent scream. Bacon also appropriated Crucifixion imagery, but his figures surrounding the cross are transformed into monsters possessed of little more than gaping mouths; even his studies of hanging beef carcasses appear more human. Until his death in 1992, Bacon returned repeatedly to depictions of deformed and monstrous human bodies, sometimes conjoined in sexual embraces that might also be death struggles.

From the perspective of contemporary art, the most influential purveyor of deformation may have been Philip Guston, who late in life turned from Abstract Expressionism to cartoonish paintings of body parts and anthropomorphic objects. Guston's willingness to jettison the pieties of Abstract Expressionism created great consternation among his Abstract Expressionist colleagues, who saw his move as a betrayal of their common values. However, it also made him a hero among younger artists, who saw in his late work permission to subvert good taste and formal decorum in an embrace of the grotesque. His paintings feature floating heads half submerged in water, giant eyeballs resting on the horizon like rising (or setting) suns, and dissolute smokers and drinkers glumly contemplating their lives from the safety of their beds, as in the aptly titled *Painting, Smoking, Eating*, 1973. In this and many works, body parts and other objects—shoes, feet, irons, severed limbs, brushes, nails, books, cigarette butts—are piled or scattered over bleak landscapes.

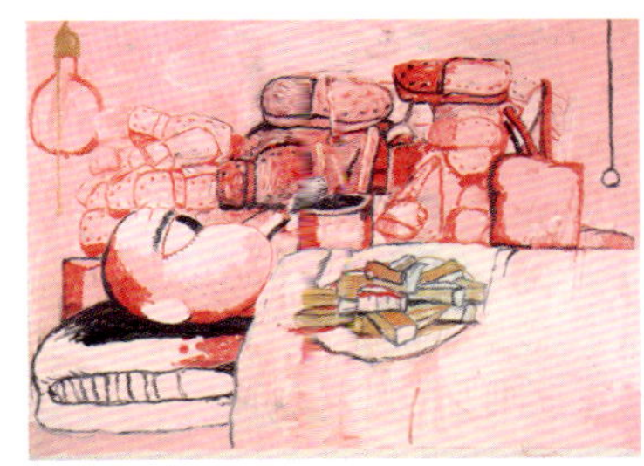

PHILIP GUSTON
PAINTING, SMOKING, EATING
1973
77 1/2 X 103 1/2 IN
(196.9 X 262.9 CM
STEDELIJK MUSEUM, AMSTERDAM

Louise Bourgeois, whose disturbing sculptures, drawings, and installations reflect a vision of nature gone awry, is, like Guston, very influential among younger contemporary artists, and also influenced by trauma. Her sculptures—which are realized in a wide variety of media, including bronze, marble, latex, stuffed fabric, plaster, and steel—present sphinxes with multiple breasts, cave-like lairs filled with pods or balls, abstract masses of phallic protrusions, and giant female spiders guarding their eggs. Some works address unstable domesticity. Female bodies fuse with houses, which subsume their heads but leave their naked bodies exposed, and prison cells confine girlish dresses and upholstered chairs. (The dresses are from Bourgeois' own childhood, which, she has related, was marked by psychosexual damage.) While she invents all sorts of deformed bodies, Bourgeois expresses the female body in particular as a fragmented, incomplete, and unstable entity. *Untitled*, 2001, for instance, is a fabric sculpture in which the truncated lower body of a female form with an exposed vagina is topped with what might be a pile of eviscerated organs. Some commentators have linked Bourgeois's warped representations to so-called female hysteria, a discredited nineteenth-century diagnosis for women's psychological breakdowns, which were thought to be caused by a "wandering womb" that brought on involuntary convulsions. In her work "hysteria" becomes a metaphor for conflicted female consciousness, and the body becomes an instrument that speaks its inner traumas.

Japanese artist Yayoi Kusama's work has also been linked to childhood trauma. Growing up in postwar Japan, where women's roles were extremely constricted, she had hallucinations in which she or her surroundings dissolved into fields of nets or dots. As a young woman she moved to New York in hopes of gaining a measure of creative and personal freedom. By the 1960s she had become something of a media sensation, playing the role of a Japanese love goddess in public performances in which she sometimes appeared painted with psychedelic polka dots, as in *Self-Obliteration by Dots*, 1968. In the early 1970s Kusama suffered a mental breakdown and returned to Japan, where she has lived in a sanatorium since 1974, creating paintings and sculptures that speak in various ways of the experience of feeling disoriented or invisible. Obsessive repetition of dots and organic and often phallic motifs are her signature; organized in undulating grids or webs, they create a delirious pictorial space. Kusama has also created a series of mirrored rooms that reflect the viewer's image infinitely, thus removing any sense of stable identity. Having rejected both the role of traditional Japanese woman and that of Western sex fetish, Kusama finds freedom in invisibility, making her body multiply, fracture, and disintegrate until it is no longer recognizable.

The deformed body is less overtly personal and more political in the work of Magdalena Abakanowicz. The child of Polish aristocrats who were forced to flee their home outside Warsaw in 1939, Abakanowicz grew up in Gdansk under Communist rule, concealing her family background. Her hollow, husk-like figural sculptures express a sense of alienation that has been tied to this early trauma. Headless, sometimes armless, they are realized in roughly textured bronze or stiffened burlap that wrinkles like dry skin, as in *Coexistence*, 2002. Sometimes they are arrayed in crowds that accentuate their loss of individuality, seeming less like people than thickets of trees. Some figures stand alone, balanced on plinths or wheels. Others are veritably *informe* shells, with only a gentle curve evoking a human back. Abakanowicz has said that these creatures were inspired by her experience of the cruelty of crowds in Communist Poland, where an ideology of group solidarity could become a cover for the evasion of individual responsibility. But over the years, as her figures have become more fragmented and her nearly identical throngs have given way more and more to individual characteristics, their apparent inhumanity has become leavened with a sense of vulnerability. One is always aware that the solid exteriors house hollow cores, and that their apparent strength may be nothing but an illusion.

Thomas Schütte likewise brings a social and political context to his eclectic oeuvre, remaking the figure and the portrait in ways that undermine any pretensions toward human nobility and the conventions of heroics. Monumental clay heads are scored so that they resemble flayed skulls; crudely modeled male wax figures posed like war hero statues in a village square are roped together in a way that is anything but honorific. Schütte also makes large photographs of small wax heads with distorted features that accentuate their weird sepulchral nature. The piquantly titled *United Enemies*, 1993, a series of two-headed creatures wrapped in fabric and bound with ropes, has been interpreted as a comment on the uncomfortable reunion of East and West Germany. Men are not the only targets of Schütte's satire. His elephantine bronze women are crude approximations of the nudes of sculptors such as Henry Moore and Aristide Maillol. With such works, Schütte takes up the

LOUISE BOURGEOIS

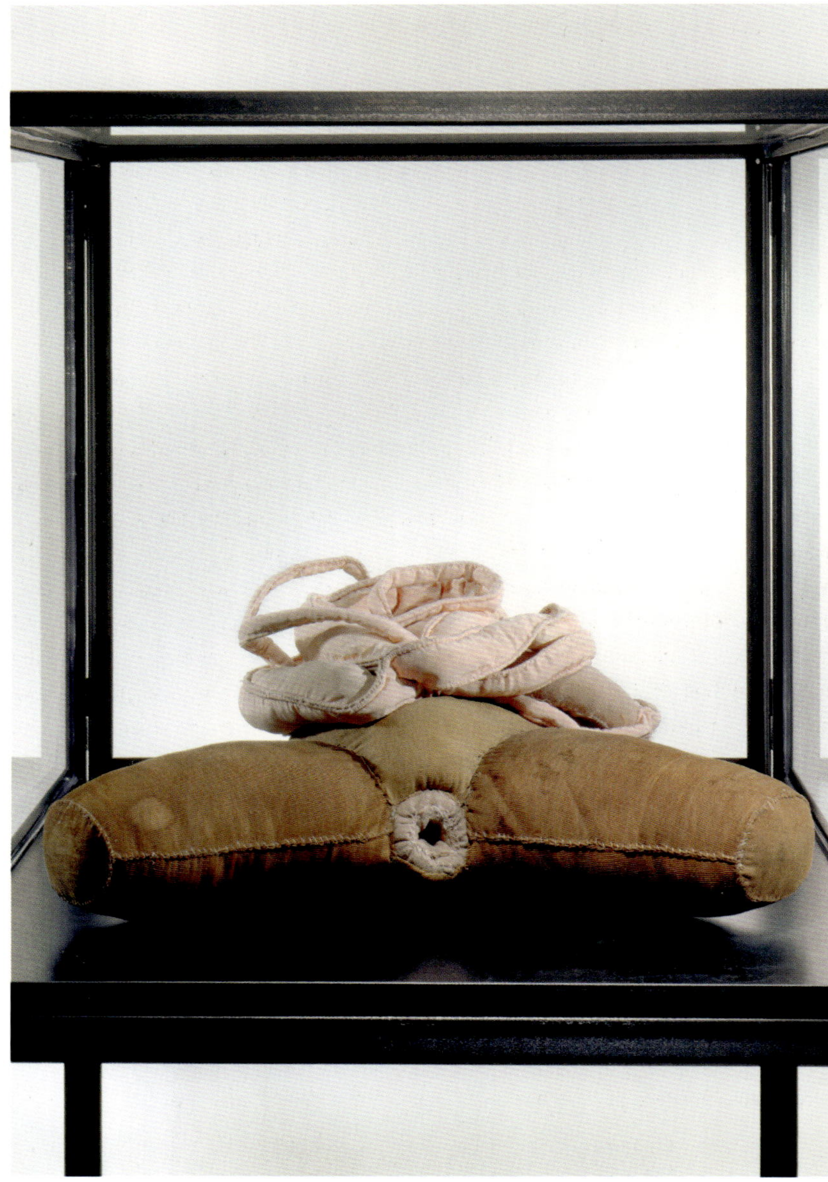

Untitled, 2001
Fabric and steel, 69 x 33 x 33 in (175.3 x 83.8 x 83.8 cm)

figurative tradition to replace illusions of grandeur with those that suggest the indignity, cruelty, and stupidity of the human condition.

Wangechi Mutu addresses the politics of post-colonial fantasy, employing the language of the grotesque in figurative personages collaged from photographs clipped from fashion and porn magazines, books about African art, and the pages of *National Geographic*. The latter source, which has long fetishized "exotic," bare-breasted African women with ritual scars, face markings, and bone jewelry, is a particularly loaded source. In Mutu's hands, these ornamental elements are mingled with images that hint of the ravages of disease and female mutilation. The resulting personages are at once frightening and alluring, evoking a celebration of the goddess cult. In *My Mountain, My Wind*, 2005, for instance, a female figure whose pose suggests the studied elegance of a fashion model is created from cutouts of lips, eyes, beads, and ambiguous body parts. One eye is set within what looks like the open jaw of a frightening beast, while her skull sports a topknot composed of a smaller figure pushing through a tangle of foliage. The strange mix of recognizably human elements in the collage only serves to emphasize the figure's distance from conventional Western standards of beauty and femininity.

Psychological trauma caused by war, sexism, mental illness, bad politics, and colonialism is not the only impetus for reflecting and projecting the deformed body. Some artists approach figural deformations with insouciance. John Currin, for instance, paints sumptuous portraits that deliberately draw on art historical precedents with a slightly unsavory pedigree. He might apply the figural distortions and exaggerations of styles like seventeenth-century Mannerism or early twentieth-century American Regionalism, say, or nineteenth-century academic painting or fifteenth-century northern Renaissance realism to contemporary scenes and characters. His subjects' impossibly round breasts and strangely skinny limbs recall paintings of Eve by Lucas Cranach, while his absurdly elongated necks and torsos evoke the Italian Mannerist Parmigianino. At times he plays on the exaggerated wholesomeness of American realists such as Grant Wood, Andrew Wyeth, and most explicitly Norman Rockwell, whose folksy caricatures of bean-pole boys and button-nosed, buxom girls presented an idealized version of middle-America to his postwar fans. There are also nods to '50s-era pin-up girls whose hugely oversized breasts burst out of tight sweaters and to that era's fashion photography where, by contrast, elegance was defined as a slenderness that verged on the skeletal. Other works veer into the explicitly pornographic. Always, Currin walks a fine line between bad taste and camp, injecting something new into something old. *Homemade Pasta*, 1999, for example, presents a cozy kitchen scene in which a pair of cooks hovers over a homemade pasta machine. It could be one of Norman Rockwell's *Life* magazine covers but for the fact that the domestic partners here appear to be a gay male couple. Here Currin's distortions may contain a social message. The figures' oversized heads and slightly exaggerated features give them a child-like gentleness that seems deliberately at odds with heartland fears of homosexuality and gay marriage.

The work of Dana Schutz is also permeated with edgy humor and references to paintings past, setting figures within cozy domestic settings or vast landscapes that recall the pastorals of Henri Rousseau or the Impressionists. *Civil Planning*, 2004, for example, clearly owes something to Manet's *Déjeuner sur l'herbe* of 1863. This picnic, however, is surrounded by scattered arms and legs, a weird purple monster, and a

YAYOI KUSAMA

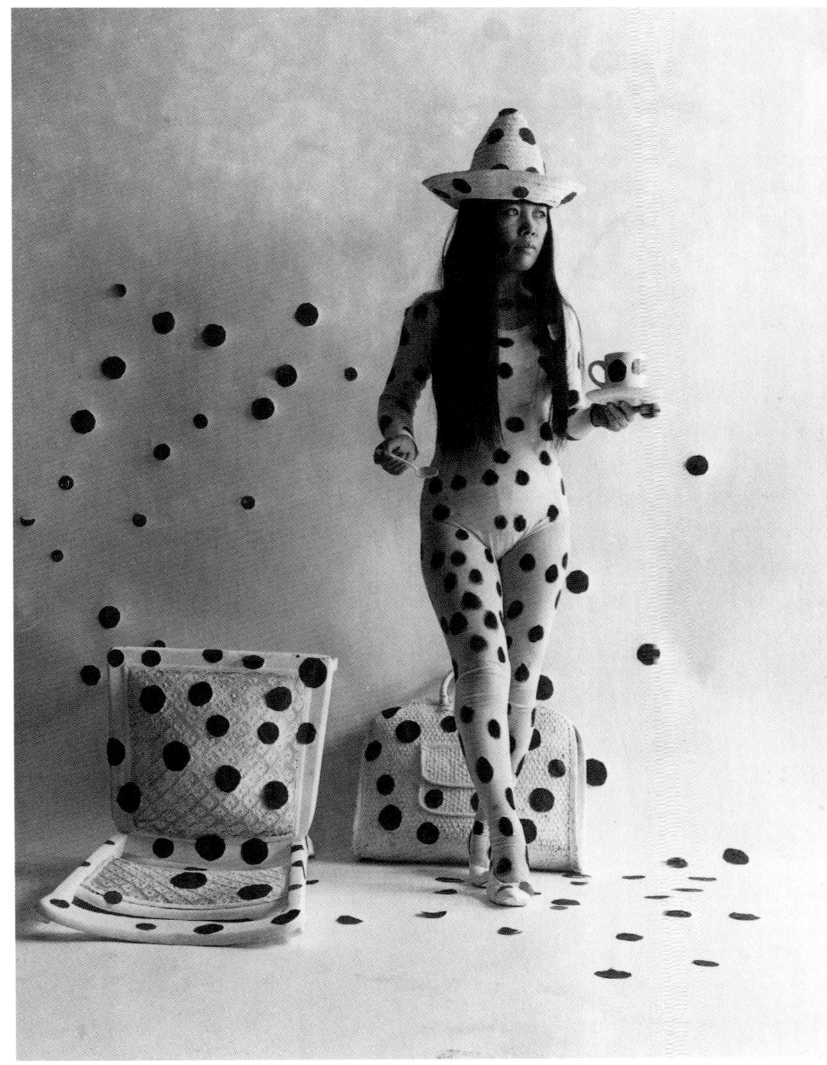

Self-Obliteration by Dots, 1968
Performance, documented with black and white photograph

MAGDALENA ABAKANOWICZ

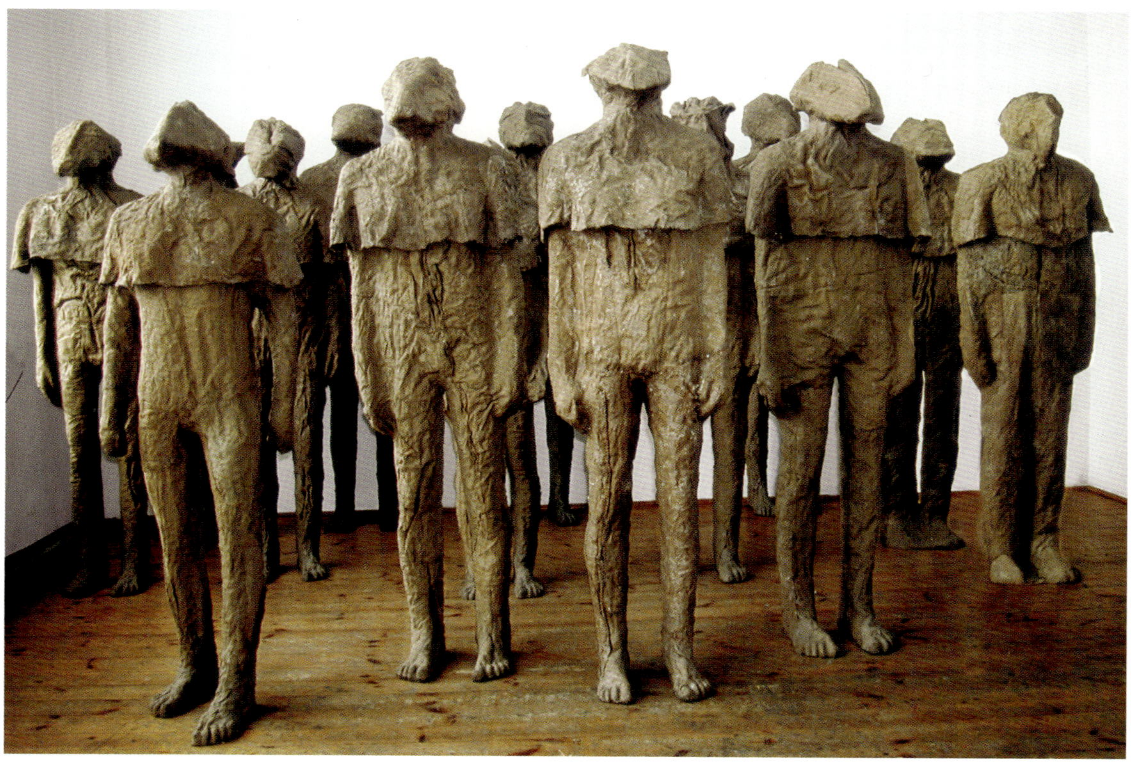

Coexistance, 2002
14 figures made of burlap

THOMAS SCHÜTTE

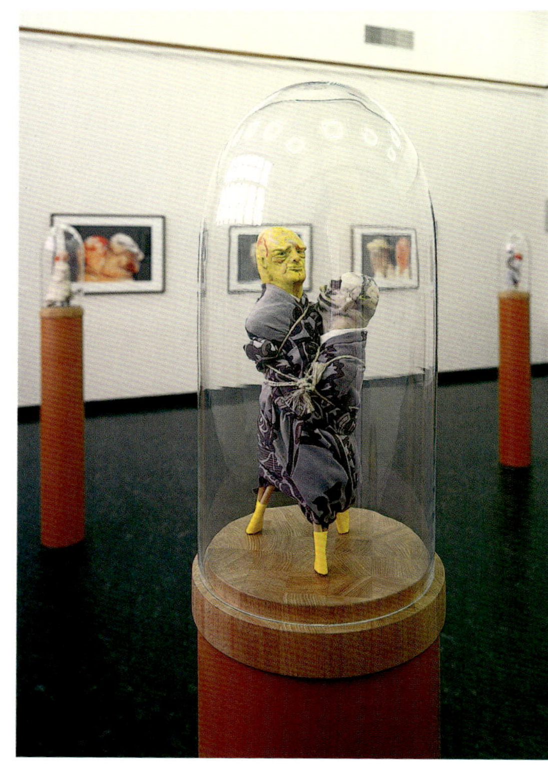

United Enemies, 1993
Suite of 3 sets of figures, mixed media, Sculpey, fabric, glass
27 1/8 x 39 in (69 x 99 cm) each

WANGECHI MUTU

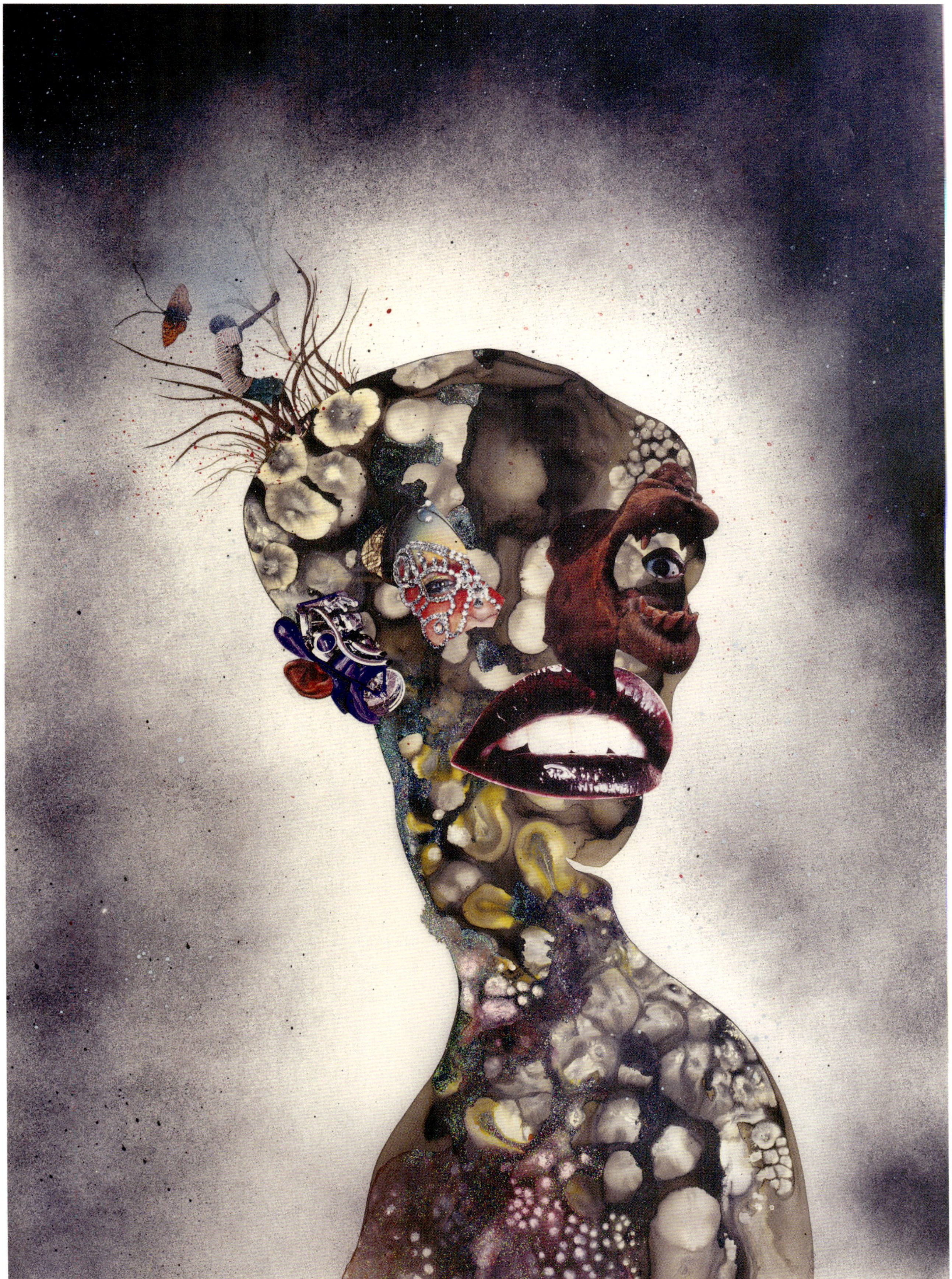

My Mountain, My Wind, 2005
Ink, acrylic, collage, and contact paper on Mylar, 37 x 28 in (14.6 x 11 cm)

JOHN CURRIN

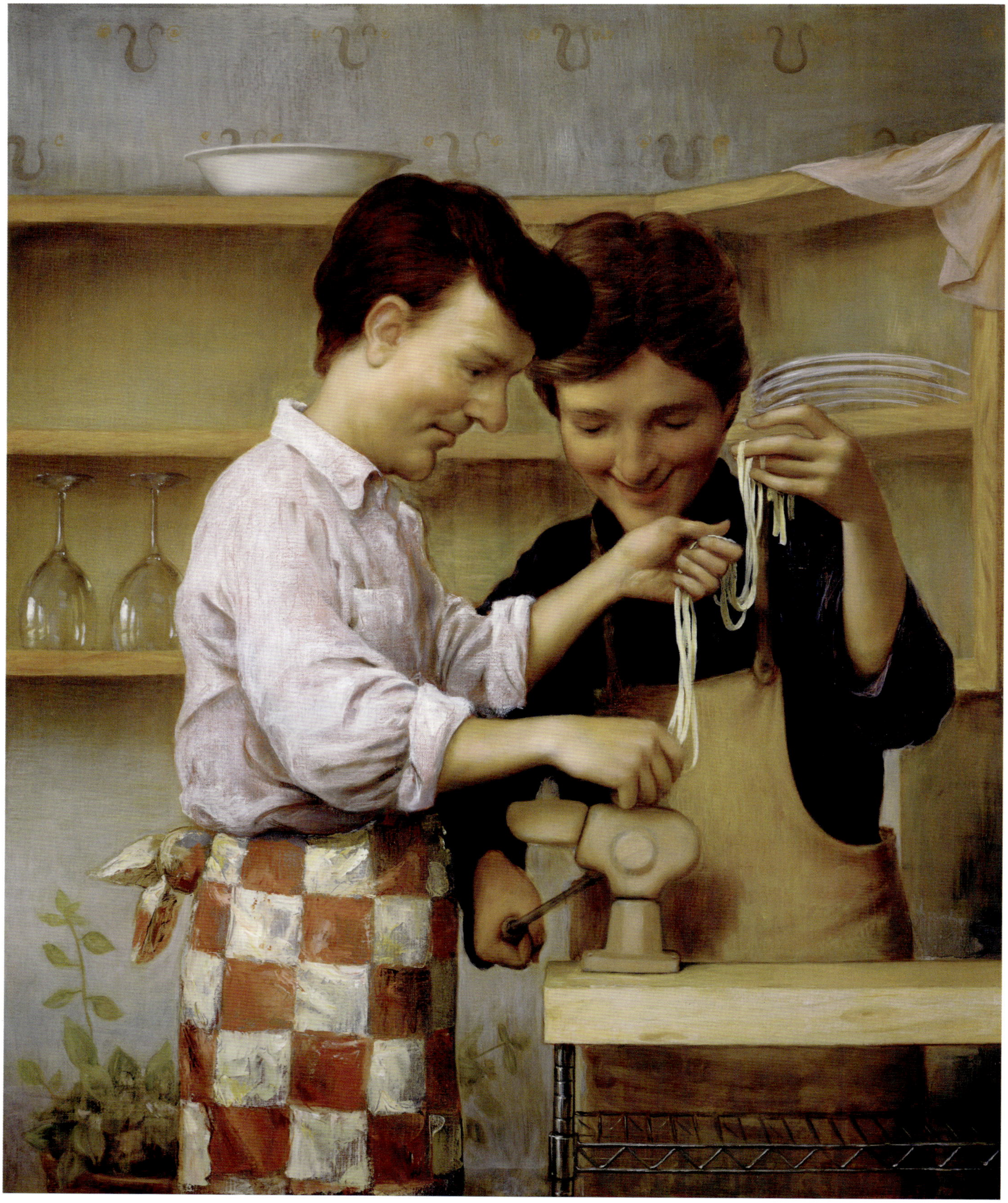

Homemade Pasta, 1999
Oil on canvas, 50 x 42 in (127 x 107 cm)

little background vignette of a naked crowd dragging a body. In other of Schutz's paintings, figures explode, devour themselves, or sort through one another's body parts. The artist's loose painting style lends a mood of chaos and dissolution, but also of exuberance, to her work. Broad swaths of paint in vibrant colors butt up against each other or invade other forms so that at times it is difficult to distinguish objects and figures. One gets the sense of a world in flux, driven by unstoppable forces, shredding the body to pieces in a way that feels perhaps as exhilarating as it does terrifying. Thus Schutz's works reflect a vision of the world that is simultaneously dystopian and oddly hopeful. She has remarked, "I embrace the area between which the subject is composed and decomposing, formed and formless, inanimate and alive."[5] However dreadful things may be at the moment, she seems to be saying, they are always changing, regenerating, and mutating.

Unlike artists of an older generation, who presented mutant and deformed bodies as visible manifestations of inner demons, unresolved sexual conflicts, or cries of anguish against the dehumanizing forces of the modern world, artists like Currin and Schutz are clearly having some fun. Though certainly more repulsive, the work of brothers Jake and Dinos Chapman also seems more interested in entertainment than existential angst. The Chapmans create life-size sculptures of mutant children composed of abnormal arrangements of limbs, heads, orifices, and sexual organs. The individual parts of these figures are as perfect as any to be found on sex dolls or department store mannequins, right down to the luxurious manes of lustrous blond and brown hair. Here, however, the familiarity ends. The Chapmans' creatures have penis noses, appendages sprouting in odd places, and heads that are perforated with anus-like apertures. They prance about in forests, entangle their multiple organs and orifices in comical orgies, or fully fuse into many-headed and many-limbed mutants, as in *Zygotic Acceleration, Biogenetic De-sublimated Libidinal Model*, 1995.

Ron Mueck, who also makes unabashedly crowd-pleasing deformed bodies, is often compared to the late Duane Hanson, whose hyper-realistic sculptures of pudgy tourists and suburban housewives are audience favorites. Hanson's works are celebrated for their remarkable verisimilitude—they are easily mistaken for real people. Mueck's figures, sculpted from fiberglass, resin, and silicone, are equally given to painstaking detail, down to open pores, moles, and crenellated flesh, but they could never be mistaken for real people, given their scale. *Pregnant Woman*, 2002, stands commandingly naked and eight feet tall. *Boy*, 2001, is even more monumental: it measures twice her height, but as it is crouching, it would likely stand at some thirty feet. While these works initially inspire awe at their meticulous craft, there are also psychological resonances to be found: often the weak are made strong by growing and the strong weak by shrinking. One of Mueck's most powerful works is *Dead Dad*, 1996–97, in which the subject lies naked, ashen, and withered on the ground at about two thirds actual scale, emphasizing an already strong sense of pathos. Mueck sculpted *Dead Dad* as an effigy of his late father. While the work harks to the postmortem casts and photographs that Victorians made to remember the dead, it differs from them in its resolute acceptance of the physical reality of death and the changes it works upon the body.

Cindy Sherman, whose black-and-white faux film stills of the 1970s are discussed in Chapter 5, has continued to pose as her own subject, but has moved on to darker impulses since the mid-'80s. While her scenes of terror and gore are so fake as to

DANA SCHUTZ

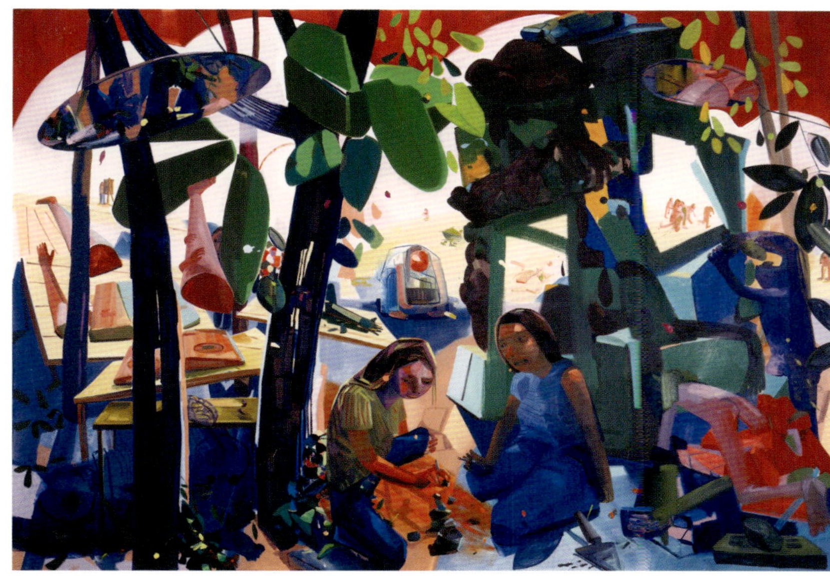

Civil Planning, 2004
Oil on canvas, 9 ft 6 in x 14 ft (2.9 x 4.3 m)

JAKE AND DINOS CHAPMAN

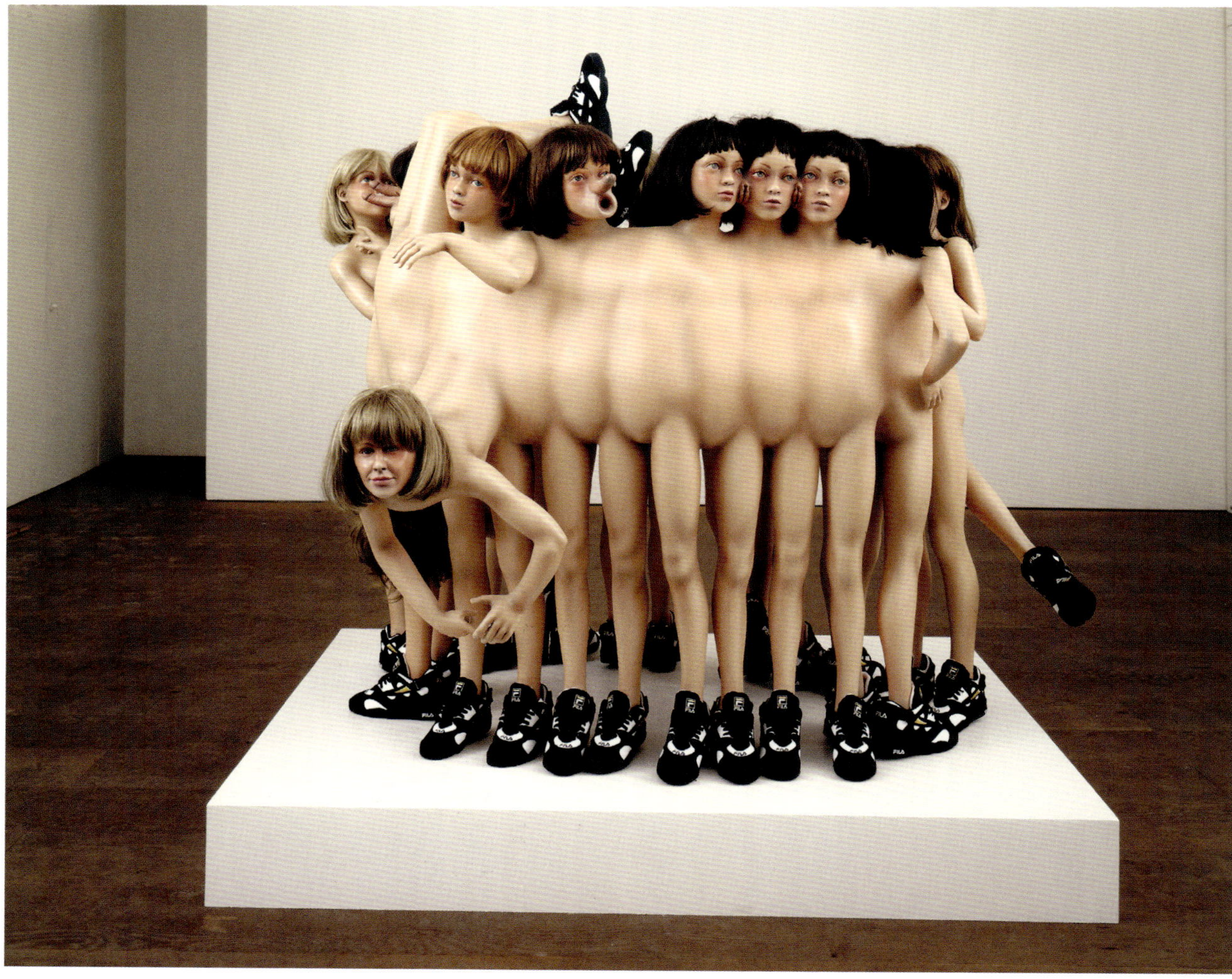

Zygotic Acceleration, Biogenetic De-sublimated Libidinal Model (enlarged x 1000), 1995
Mixed media, 58 7/8 x 70 1/2 x 54 7/8 in (150 x 180 x 140 cm)

RON MUECK

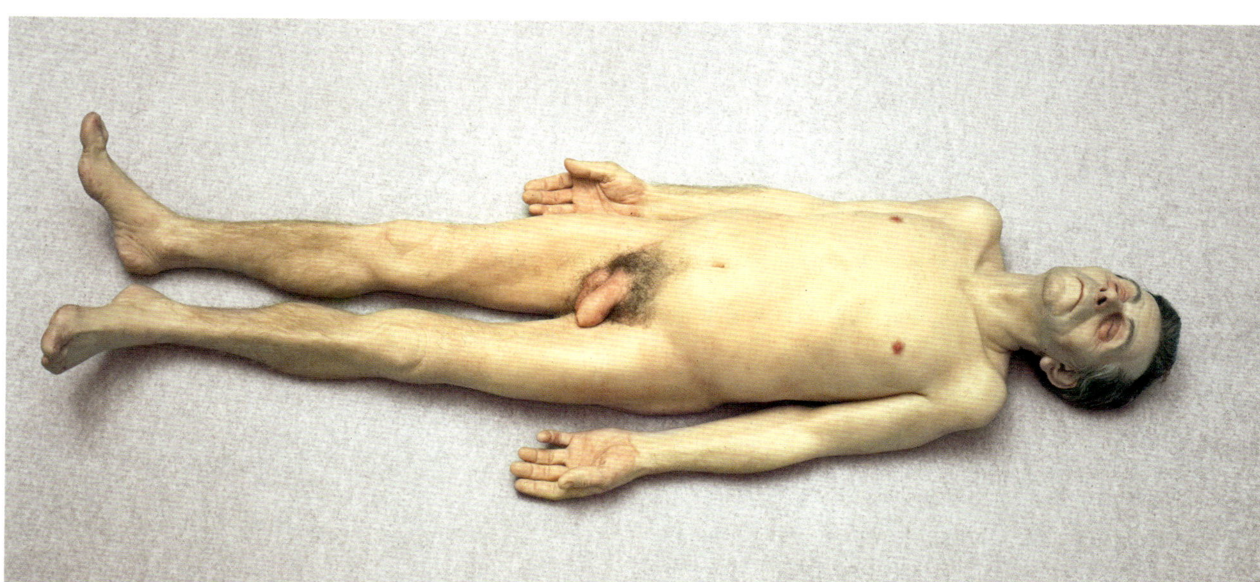

Dead Dad, 1996–97
Mixed media, 7 7/8 x 40 1/6 x 15 in (20 x 102 x 38 cm)

be funny, in the end they are more disturbing than the work of Currin, Schutz, the Chapmans, and Mueck. Sherman's most controversial series, "Sex Pictures," 1992, features explicitly sexual photographs—like *Untitled #258*—of dolls that recall those of Hans Bellmer. Sherman rarely appears here; rather, the focus is on the aftermath of clearly terrible acts. One work features a naked doll lying helpless on the ground in a scenario suggestive of a rape scene. Another embodies the ultimate logic of pornography, presenting an odalisque composed of little more than a hag head and a giant vagina. Such works are simultaneously repulsive and riveting. Their power lies in their ability to touch our deepest fears, which include losing control of our bodies and succumbing to the irrational, and to offer the possibility of catharsis.

Sherman's photographs recall Mikhail Bakhtin's carnivalesque, providing a release valve through which to purge and ideally move on to renewal. A particular means to this end is to subvert authority through invocation of the abject, by transgressing decorum and blatantly flaunting bodily substances that are most often kept to oneself. Paul McCarthy, best known for his motorized sculptures and lavish multimedia installations, does just this, attacking some of the most sacred cows of mass culture. In both live and video performances, McCarthy often uses viscous substances—ketchup, mayonnaise, Vaseline, or chocolate—as substitutes for blood, sperm, and excrement, deploying them in domestic settings to suggest force-feeding, incest, sexual humiliation, and the general degradation of the all-American dysfunctional family. Even when sex and defecation (which seem inextricably linked in these works) are not explicitly evoked, McCarthy's narratives defile all manner of authority. Often the agent of destruction is a deranged doppelgänger of a symbol of innocence from McCarthy's 1960s childhood—among them Ronald McDonald, Mickey Mouse, Howdy Doody, and even *MAD* magazine's emblem of good-natured idiocy, Alfred E. Newman, who in *Bossy Burger*, 1991, is a demented chef flinging ketchup around the actual set of the sitcom *Family Affair*. Excepting perhaps the latter childhood hero, these products of media culture are of course designed to inculcate children with consumerist values. Their new role as purveyors of onanism, mutilation, and general mayhem signals McCarthy's rebellion.

Mike Kelley, who has referred to his work as "propaganda gone wrong," has also made an assault on the sentimental mythology of childhood a primary theme. Comic books, Saturday morning cartoons, stuffed animals, and children's fantasies are the vessels through which we come face to face with adolescent sexual desires, murderous rages, and scatological fixations. Like McCarthy, Kelley works in a variety of forms. These include drawings of steaming excrement and splattered mucus and snot, sculptures fashioned from dingy, threadbare stuffed animals salvaged from thrift stores and sewn together to resemble disemboweled inner organs or metasticizing cells, and performances that degrade symbols of religious, political, or artistic worship. His stuffed-animal works, in particular, are strangely affecting. *More Love Hours Than Can Ever be Repaid*, 1987, for example, is a wall work composed of dozens of homemade crocheted rabbits, yarn dolls, gingham creatures, and sock monkeys. With his poetic title, Kelley suggests the callousness with which children (and by extension, adults) discard items that once received their all-encompassing attention.

Kelley and McCarthy occasionally collaborate on performances and videos, doubling their exuberantly disgusting assaults on convention. In their 1992

CINDY SHERMAN

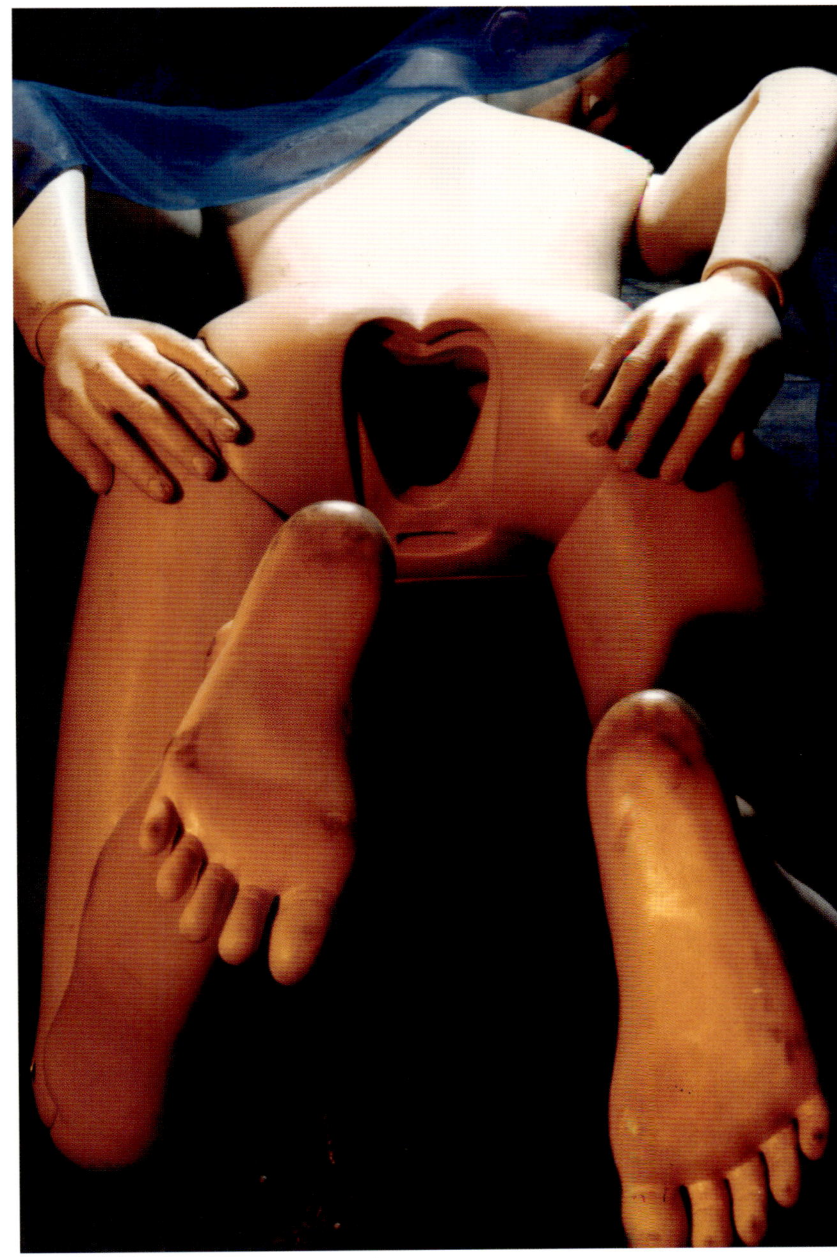

Untitled #258, 1992
Color photograph and color print, 68 x 45 in (172.7 x 114.3 cm)

MIKE KELLEY AND PAUL MCCARTHY

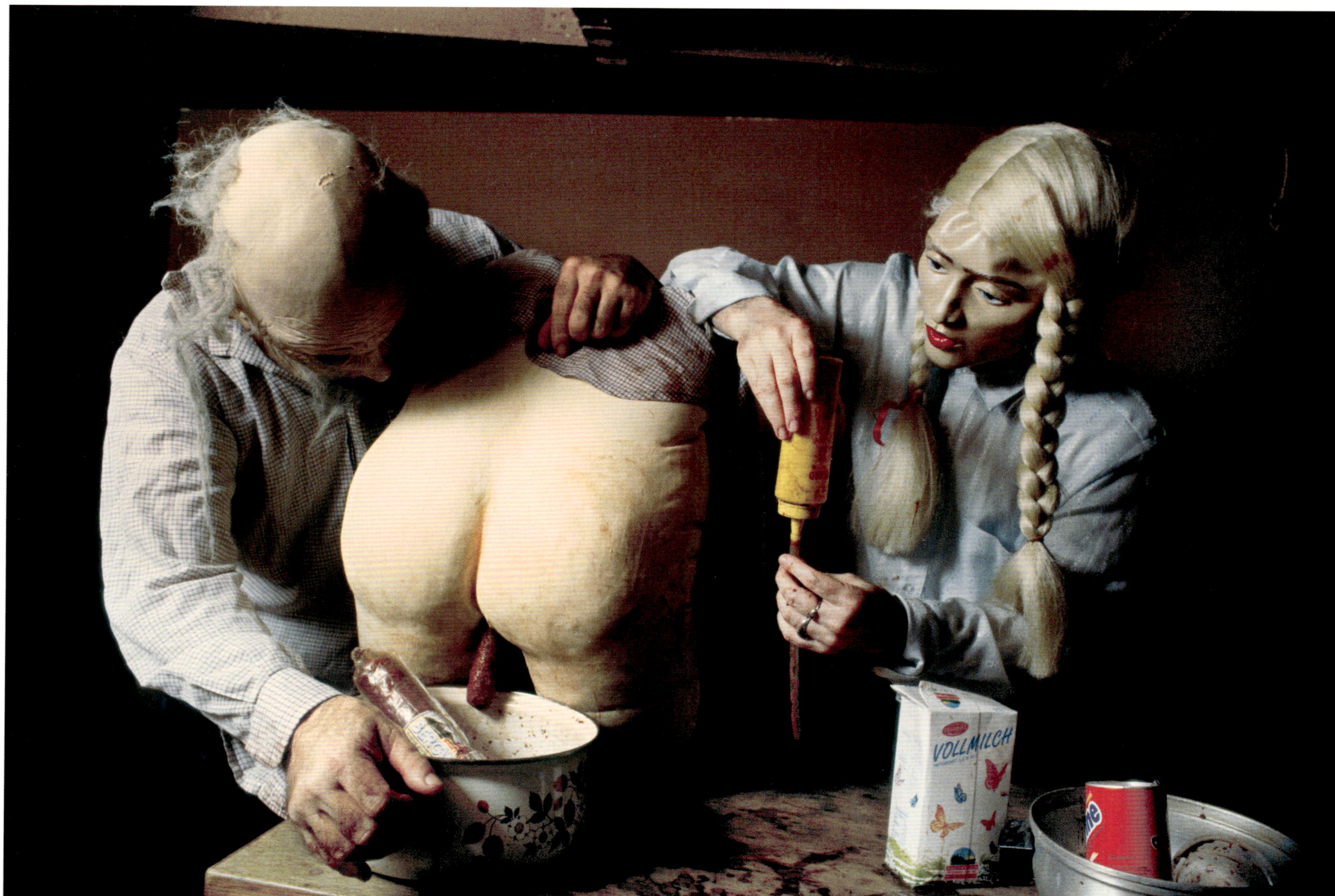

Heidi: Midlife Crisis Trauma Center, 1992
Installation and video, wood, assorted found objects, foam bodies, and paintings, dimensions variable

MIKE KELLEY

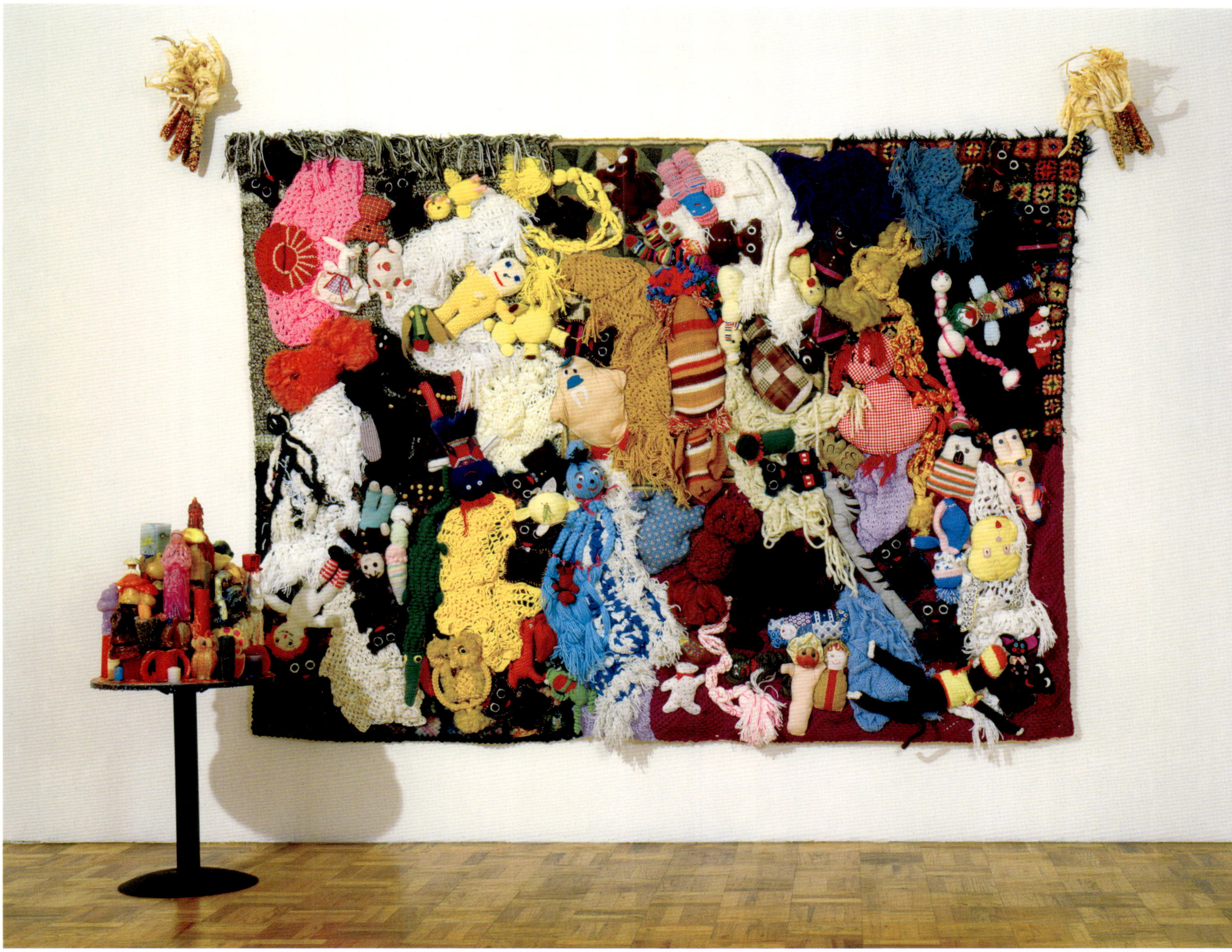

More Love Hours Than Can Ever Be Repaid, 1987
Handmade stuffed animals and afghans sewn on canvas backing
96 x 127 x 6 in (243.8 x 322.6 x 15.2 cm)
In the foreground is *The Wages of Sin*, 1987

KIKI SMITH

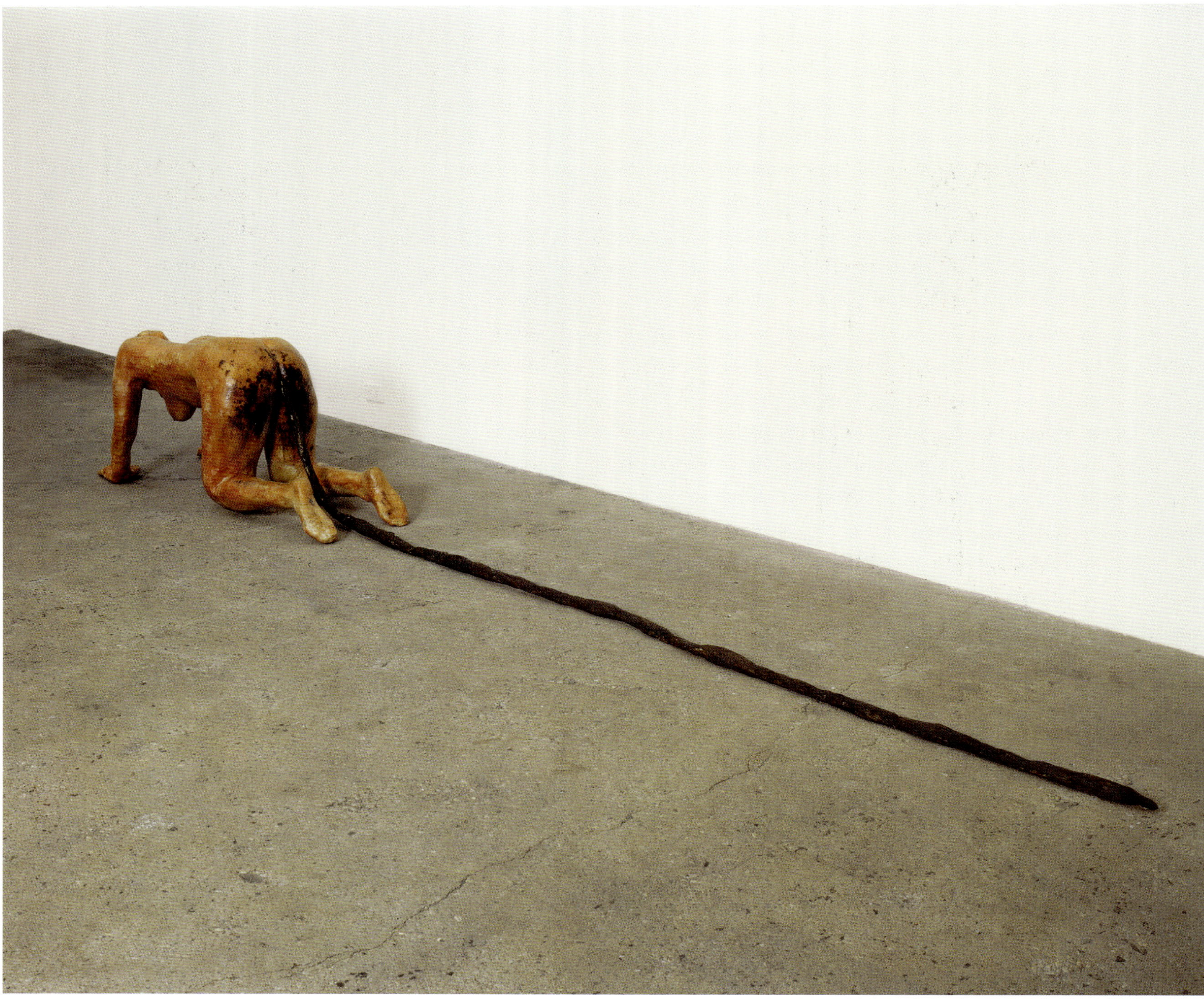

Tail, 1992
Wax, pigment, and papier-mâché
13 ft 4 in x 1 ft 11 in x 1 ft 11 in (4.1 x .6 x .6 m)

installation and video work *Heidi: Midlife Crisis Trauma Center and Negative Media-Engram Abreaction Release Zone*, 1992, they turn Heidi, the classic story's innocent schoolgirl from the Alps, into a depraved Lolita with a lusty, pedophile grandfather. Exposing the underbelly of virtue, the artists challenge a peculiarly American utopian mindset, undermining every kind of cherished conviction, including religious beliefs, family values, patriotism, artistic standards, and social norms of good and evil, reminding us that there is no escape from our animal natures. In an intriguing twist on an already twisted tale, younger artists Sue de Beer and Laura Parnes have created a sequel to McCarthy and Kelley's *Heidi*, calling it *Heidi 2*, 2000, the "unauthorized sequel." Their narrative jumps forward in time, portraying the Swiss miss as a mother with a daughter, also named Heidi, of her own. Presented in a domestic environment filled with Nerf furniture, life-size action figures, plastic mannequins, and masks of teen idol Leonardo DiCaprio, the video presents a mother-daughter relationship rife with oedipal tensions, sexual competition, and lessons that would never be approved by the American Psychiatric Association. It ends with a scene in which the mother tears open Heidi 2's stomach in order to insert a television monitor into her intestines.

Whereas McCarthy, Kelley, de Beer, and Parnes assault the forces of rationality and authority by lavishly celebrating the brutish and the bestial, other artists explore the animal side of human nature with relative reserve. Drawing on feminist perspective, they make reference to bodily fluids, waste, and viscera as a means of rethinking Western culture's traditional equation of woman and nature. From their viewpoint, nature is not, as the old dualism has it, the opposite of culture, reason, and male spheres of influence. Instead it is another form of knowing. Hence, when their work turns inward to the body as material substance and biological process, they are less interested in generating a feeling of disgust than in exposing a mode of experience that is often subsumed or undervalued.

In Kiki Smith's work, for instance, the body serves as a means of understanding our place in the world. For many years it was her principal subject. Working in a variety of media ranging from sculpture, installation, drawings, and prints, Smith has explored the pure physical beauty of the human body. She has created exquisite glass stomachs and sperm, red-stained paper "skin," rolled-paper umbilical cords, terra cotta rib cages, ceramic hearts, and bronze uteruses. From early recreations of internal organs and systems, she has moved outward toward representations of skin, muscles, and finally, the entire human body. Smith's work is in one sense the quintessential expression of the stereotypical "feminine" sensibility. Deeply concerned with issues of beauty and decoration, she employs materials traditionally associated with women's crafts—glass, paper, wax, fabric, and lace, along with more "masculine" substances such as bronze and pewter. However, these are not conventional representations of beauty or the body. Her birds are scattered over the ground, dead of some mysterious disease. Her doilies double as human cells or orifices. The nudes lean against the wall with patterned fabric intestines spilling from their guts or dangle in midair as breast milk, blood, and semen run down their legs. In one particularly disturbing work titled *Tail*, 1992, a naked female figure on all fours excretes a long trail of feces. Smith makes the state of the body a marker for psychological states—her images of abjection reveal human fragility, while her melded creatures remind us that there is no comfortable division between mind and body or between the human and natural worlds.

SUE DE BEER AND LAURA PARNES

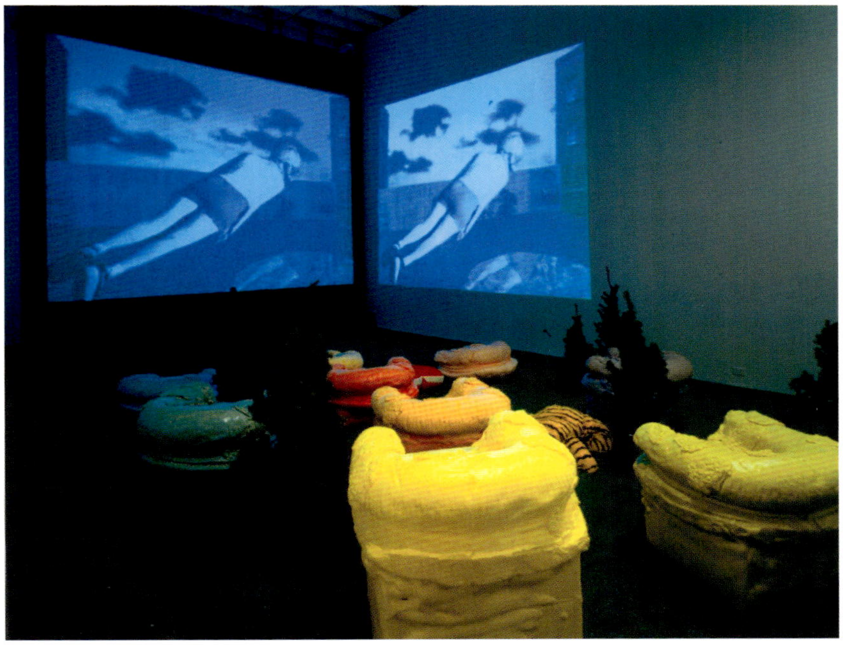

Heidi 2, 2000
Mixed media, dimensions variable
As installed at Deitch Projects, New York, January–February 2000

Beauty and disgust also mingle in the work of Rona Pondick, which is deeply indebted to such Surrealists as René Magritte and Salvador Dalí. Pondick creates strange and disturbing sculptural fusions—breast-like bottles, piles of cast ears growing from clumps of paper pulp, heaps of small balls outfitted with yellowed and sometimes chattering teeth, and weird shiny stainless steel creatures that merge the artist's head or limbs with parts of monkeys, dogs, foxes, marmots, or cougars. *Fox*, 1999, presents a cast of Pondick's head attached to the body of a fox. The oversized head rests on the floor, seemingly pulling the lithe animal toward the ground as it bears the physical and metaphorical weight of human consciousness. Pondick's mutants point inward, suggesting manifestations of internal psychological conflicts. Some of these works seem to allude to the consequences of abandoning oneself to one's appetites, others to the conquest of our supposedly more refined sensibilities by an animal self.

Annette Messager works with mutant forms as well, employing diverse media, including photographs, found objects, drawings, taxidermied animals, and handmade dolls, and presenting them in accumulations—they may be impaled on spikes in the middle of the gallery, hanging in clusters on the wall, or suspended from the ceiling. While full of pathos, the work often has an air of black humor, as in *Articulés-Désarticulés* (Articulated-Dislocated), 2002, in which pulleys raise and lower soft sculptures of dolls and body parts from the ceiling in an unmistakable and carnivalesque parody of sexual activity. On the floor, other organic forms lie inert, apparently spent. Messager's materials and techniques (which include knitting, embroidery, and sewing) are drawn from the domestic and stereotypically feminine sphere, but express contrastingly desecrated subjects, once again upsetting the feminine/masculine dichotomy.

Like Smith and Messager, Petah Coyne traffics in expressions of femininity. She builds sculptures around clusters of artificial flowers, lace, hair, birds, ribbons, and plaster figurines of the Virgin Mary, but removes them from their normal decorative functions. Covered with wax, tar, or horse hair, they are transformed into symbolic objects that are at once vital and elegiac. Coyne's sculptures are full of such deliberate contradictions. Materials that evoke living flesh play off others that suggest cinders and ashes. The purity of white wax and plaster is a stark foil to the black sand, wax, and tar that conjure up associations of death and decay. Objects resembling pods and roots evoke natural life forms, but they are suspended from the ceiling like severed trophies. Stuffed birds reference the freedom of flight, but they are encrusted with wax and frozen in amorphous lumps like artifacts preserved in mounds of cooled lava. *Untitled #820 (MIT Peacocks)*, 1992–2001, embodies all these contradictions. This white wax sculpture hangs from the ceiling by a chain wrapped with white satin. Bows and flowers are partially submerged in the ungainly wax form, while swooping peacock feathers attached to doves conjure an impossible dream of entrapment and escape. Despite, or perhaps because of their strangeness, works like these have an undeniably organic quality; in fact, Coyne calls them her "girls" in homage to the complex internal states they represent.

Helen Chadwick, who died prematurely of a heart attack at the age of forty-three, expressed internal states quite literally. Chadwick began her career creating performances and photographic tableaux that used her own nude body, much in the manner of Carolee Schneemann and Hannah Wilke. Eventually she moved on to making photographs in which she used various materials as surrogates for the body

ANNETTE MESSAGER

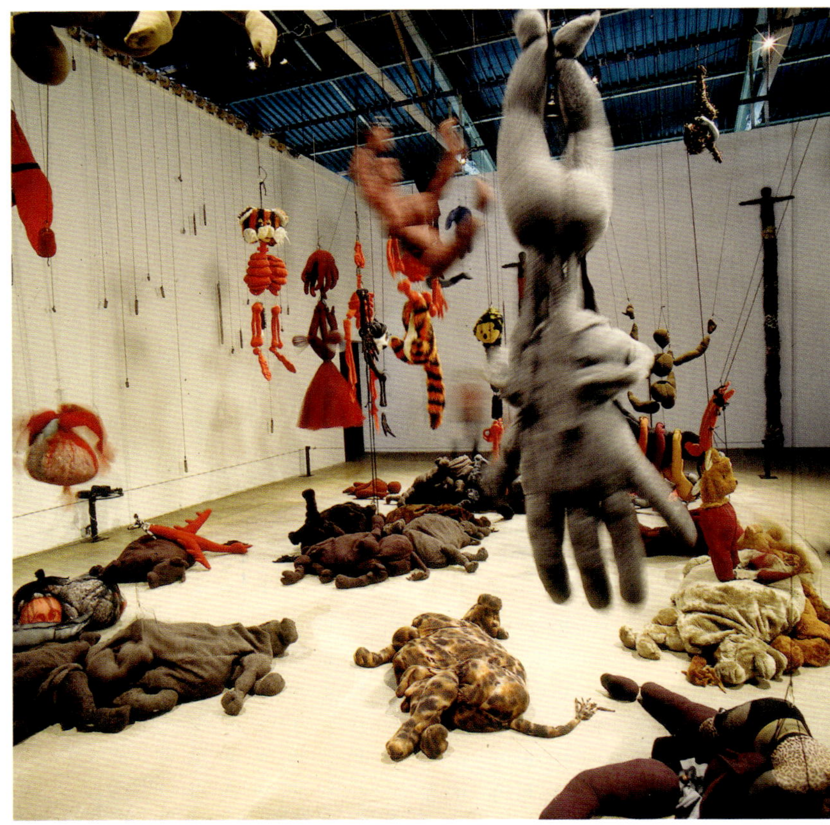

Articulés-Désarticulés (Articulated-Dislocated), 2002
Computerized automatons in fabric, electric motors, wood, and ropes
23 ft x 49 ft 2 in x 39 ft 4 in (7 x 15 x 12 m)
As installed at Documenta 11, Kassel, Germany, 2002
Centre National d'Art et de Culture Georges Pompidou, Paris

PETAH COYNE

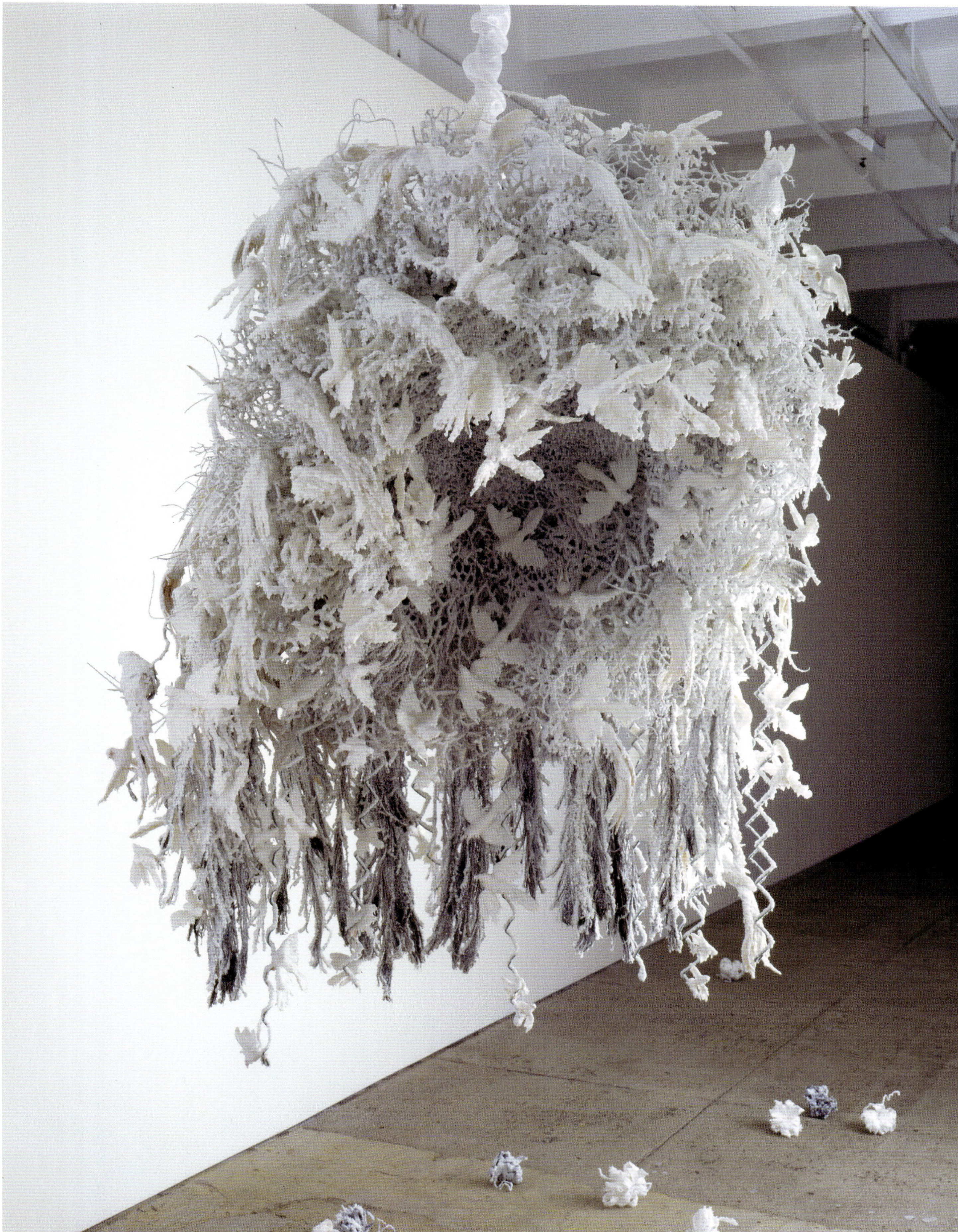

Untitled #820 (MIT Peacocks), 1992–2001
Mixed media, 83 x 70 x 75 in (210.8 x 177.8 x 190.5 cm)

RONA PONDICK

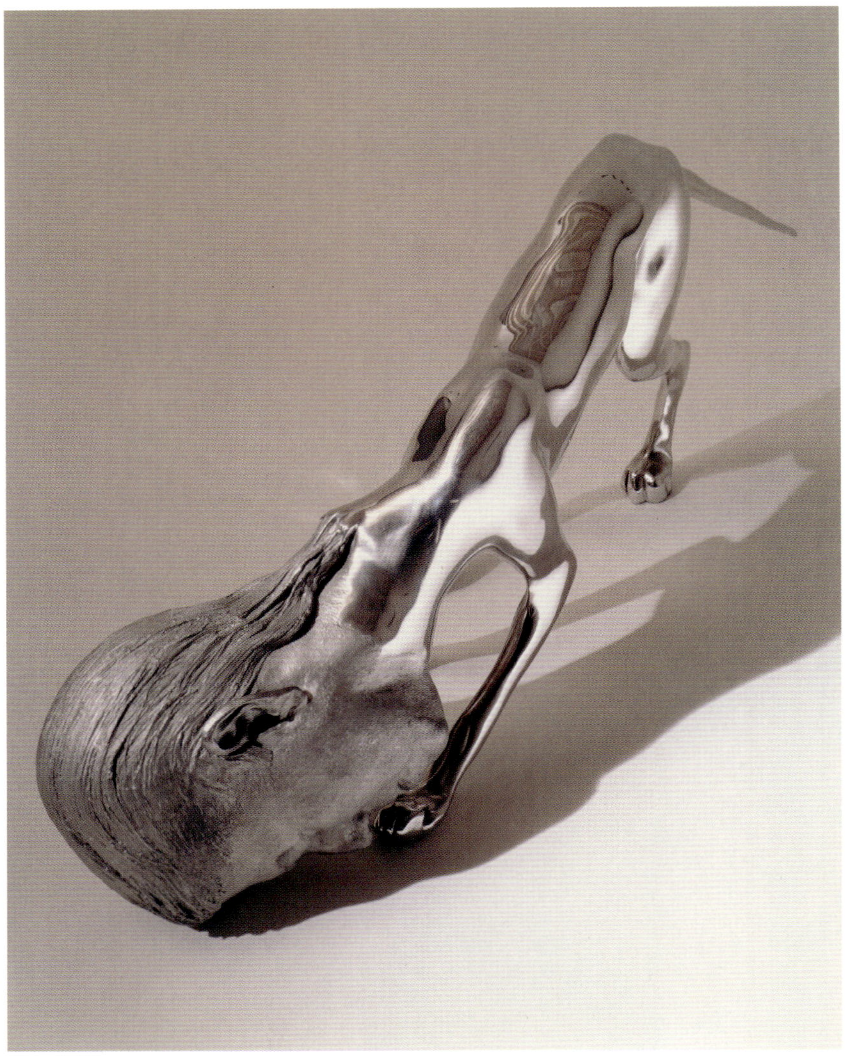

Fox, 1998–99
Stainless steel, 37 x 9 x 14 in (94 x 23 x 36 cm)

and body fluids. For the series of photographs "Meat Abstracts," 1989, Chadwick nestled light bulbs on animal organs that she arranged like still lifes on expanses of velvet or suede, giving them an almost religious aura. The glistening chunks of red animal flesh served as a metaphor for the visceral human body. This combination of elegant presentation and unsettling materials is also a hallmark of works such as *Piss Flowers*, 1991, consisting of white-lacquered bronze casts of the physical impressions created when Chadwick and her partner urinated in the snow. Without the graphic title, these delicate sculptures could pass for petal-like eruptions of white coral. With such works, Chadwick prettified distinctly unladylike subjects to challenge audiences to question their socially inculcated responses toward completely natural bodily functions.

Smith, Messager, Coyne, and Chadwick deliberately blur boundaries and mingle opposites to defy arbitrary cultural taboos and proscriptions surrounding the female body. There is probably no aspect of human life more fraught with rules and regulations than death, which is of course the ultimate boundary. In all cultures and historical periods, dead bodies and their representations are enmeshed in elaborate systems of religious and social control. In our own time, death is surrounded by contradictions. Representations of death are as common in the movies as they are absent from daily life. War photographers often find themselves in a moral quandary about how graphically to present the toll of war. Yet filmmakers constantly outdo each other in manufacturing gore and viscera. An anecdote cited in Plato's *Republic* 2,400 years ago sums up this timeless pull between attraction and repulsion. According to this story, a man named Leonides found himself struggling against his desire to see the corpses of executed criminals outside the walls of Athens. When finally he could not resist, he rushed to the execution spot and cried to his errant eyes, "There, ye wretches, take your fill of the fine spectacle."[6]

The impulse toward deformation often centers on the distortion, fragmentation, and evisceration of the human body. But deformative border crossing can also run between high and low art or realism and abstraction. One need only be reminded of the furor that surrounded Philip Guston's late work to realize that a refusal to honor established formal categories can count as rank betrayal. Today Guston's influence is felt in the work of a number of painters who deliberately subvert the rules of formal and thematic decorum, either by seeming to mock the tropes of formalist abstraction by melding them with cartoon imagery, by slipping pornographic motifs into works that seem derived from more decorous traditions, or by dispensing with all distinctions between media, styles of representation, or format that have traditionally been used to impose some kind of order on contemporary art. In their hands, the impulse toward deformation yields works that are deliberately, and often humorously, hard to categorize.

Among the heirs to Guston's legacy is Carroll Dunham, whose early works in the 1980s hovered between abstraction and representation. Painting on pieces of wood, he let the knots and grain suggest organic forms that he then incorporated into his compositions, combining drips and gestural marks with bulbous forms suggesting internal organs, penises, and nascent hammer-headed creatures. By the mid-1990s these incipient beings had blossomed into full-fledged characters. Giant blocky heads drawn with a thick cartoon-style line sprout multiple orifices, their massive faces flaunting lips that might be mouths or genitals. Protruding growths suggest both fingers and penises. Painted in garish tones of florescent

HELEN CHADWICK

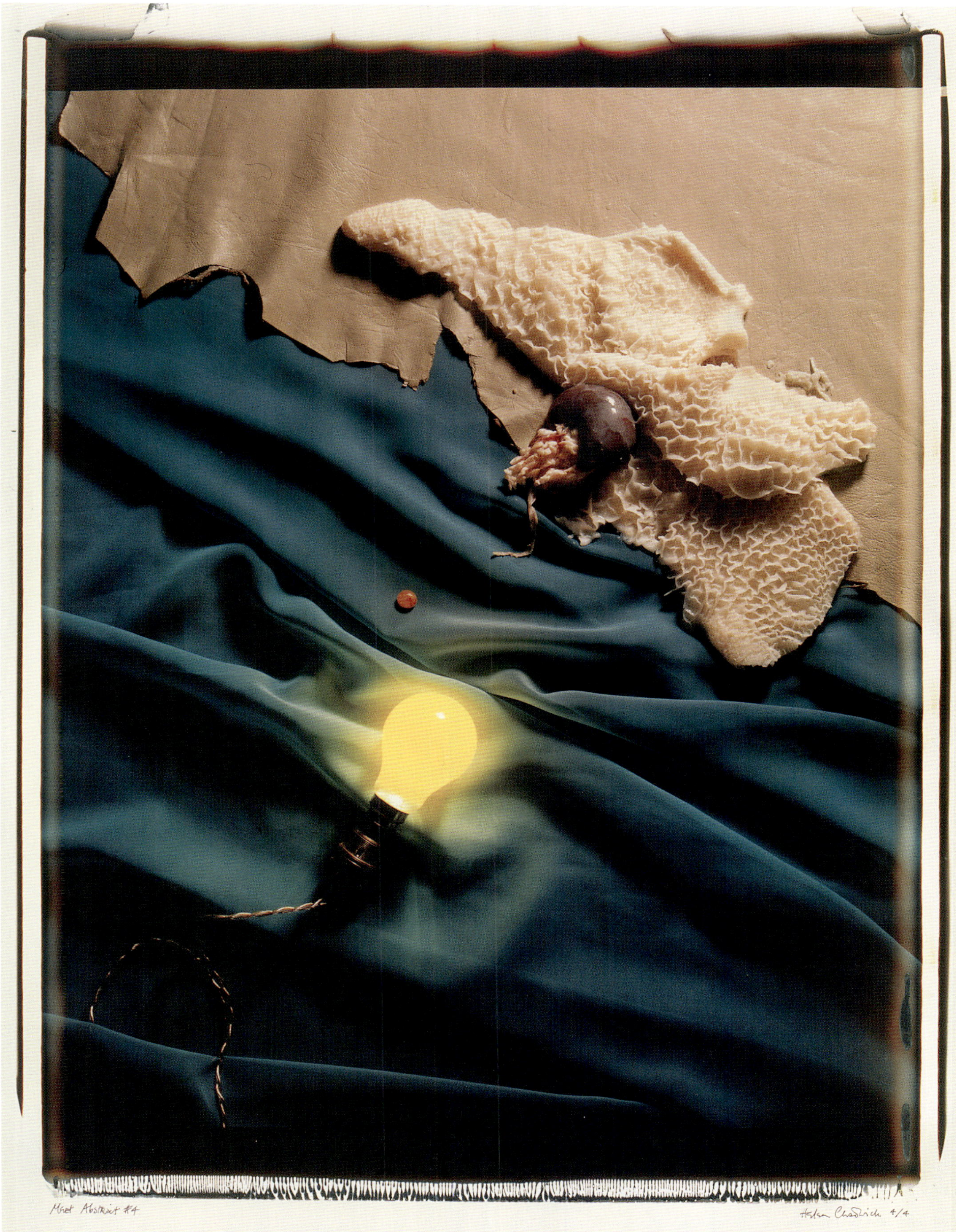

Meat Abstract #4, 1989
Polaroid and silk mat, 31 7/8 x 28 in (81 x 71 cm)

CARROLL DUNHAM

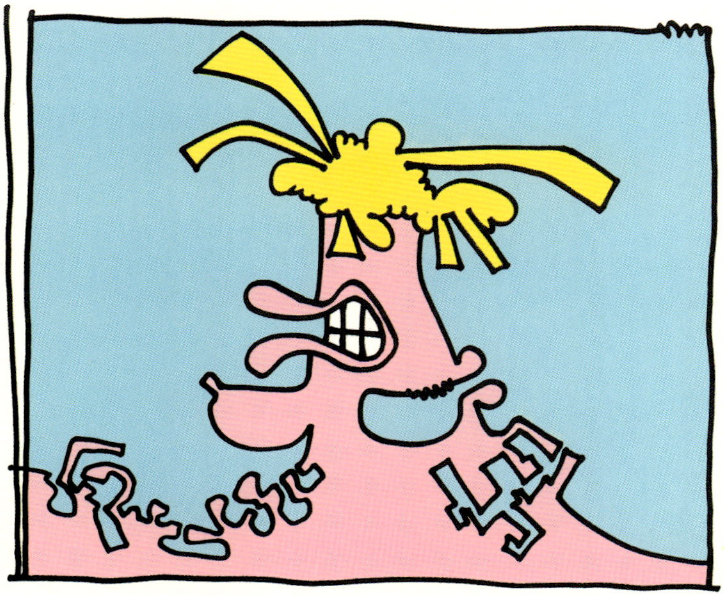

Female Portraits, 2000
One of thirteen lithographs, 13 x 17 in (33 x 43.2 cm)

PETER SAUL

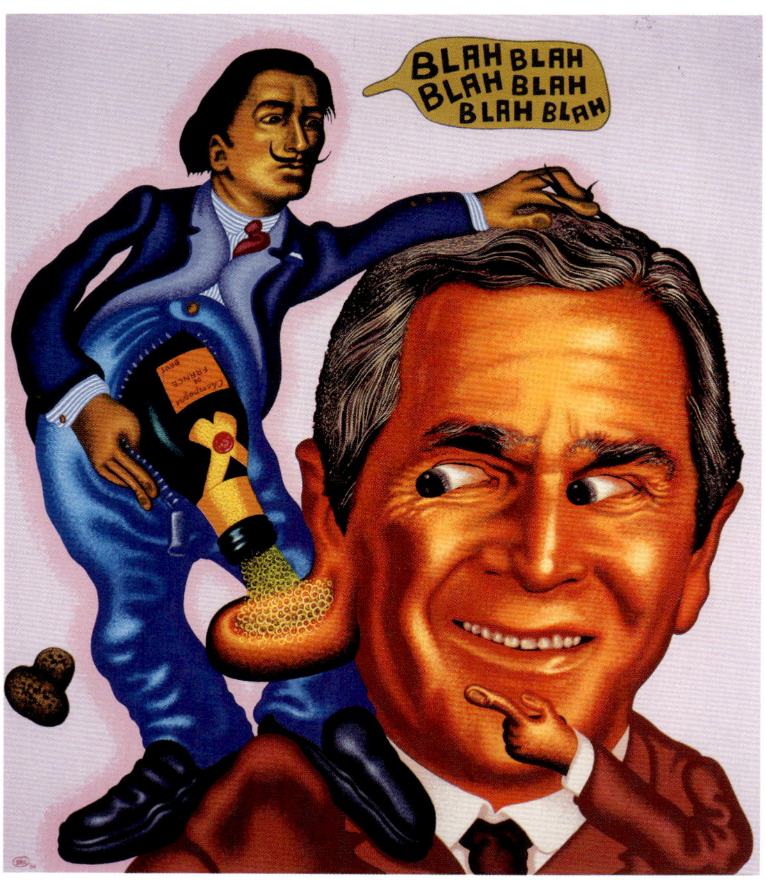

Dali Advises the President, 2004
Acrylic on canvas, 74 x 66 in (188 x 167.6 cm)

green, lavender, bright red, deep yellow, and peacock blue, these creatures erupt with painted Styrofoam balls that cluster like giant pimples or malignant growths. They face off aggressively, pull guns on each other, brandish knives, or simply grin malevolently. They often defy gender roles. In *Female Portraits*, 2000, for instance, a toothy creature topped with a blob of yellow seems the embodiment of male aggression; it can be identified as female only by its pink hue and a vaguely breast-like swelling just below the neck. With figures like these—mutant, hybrid, overcome by base instincts and mindless desire—Dunham creates a carnivalesque vision of humanity on the brink of self-destruction.

Cartoon style takes on an even more biting edge in the work of Peter Saul, whose influences include underground comics, *MAD* magazine, and the surrealism of Dalí. Since the mid-1960s Saul has adopted a garish, careening style to satirize everything from postwar suburbia to art-world formalism, American militarism, and government corruption. In paintings that parody the distortions of the surrealists, figures, cars, and buildings stretch and snap like taffy, landscapes billow and pulsate, and characters, some anonymous and some clearly recognizable from the real worlds of art and politics, spew out bubbles of acerbic text. They also discharge sprays of vomit or excrement, sprout fingers or penises in place of noses, bend in rubbery contortions that may bring their feet up over their heads, and engage in polymorphous and at times pornographic sexual activity as body parts literally melt into each other. Saul's works can be sharply satirical and searingly political. In some, businessmen and women curl provocatively around dollar bills and dollar signs. Orgies of sex and gluttony become metaphors for corruption. During the Vietnam War, Saul frequently introduced corpulent figures representing the generals and politicians who were wreaking havoc on Vietnamese farmers and country people. He has also taken aim at supposedly sacrosanct institutions. More recently, Saul has featured George W. Bush in equally critical terms, as in *Dalí Advises the President*, 2004, an apparent commentary on the fizzy emptiness of political dialogue, in which a diminutive Salvador Dalí whispers sweet nothings while pouring champagne into the ear of a sneering George W. Bush. Works such as these exemplify deformation's subversive potential as a tool for social and political critique.

Lari Pittman also combines a dazzling array of stylistic quotations and polymorphous sexual images to create visual cacophony while challenging societal conventions about sex and gender. His sources include everything from wallpaper patterns to Victorian children's books. Grotesque images of fecundity, coiling plants, sex organs, insects, and birds jostle against notational devices such as targets, flow chart arrows, architectural schema, and punctuation marks. *A Decorated Chronology of Insistence and Resignation, Untitled #9*, 1992–93, suggests the passage of a long-nosed Pinocchio through a field of doilies, feces, and human orifices, along a path marked by signs that take him from an initial hopeful "HEY!" to the final oblivion of "R.I.P." Pittman depicts a state of incessant flux, in which references to sex symbolize metamorphosis. Embryos sprout penises, penises become dance-hall girls, and hermaphroditic owls wear bras and Jockey shorts. It's as if the whole world were in the process of copulating with itself. But despite the frenzy, the use of stylized images borrowed from earlier phases of American pop culture lends these works a surprising modesty. An air of childlike innocence is suggested, oddly enough, in Victorian silhouettes of men ejaculating or in pornographic phrases spelled out in looping italics. But there are also references

LARI PITTMAN

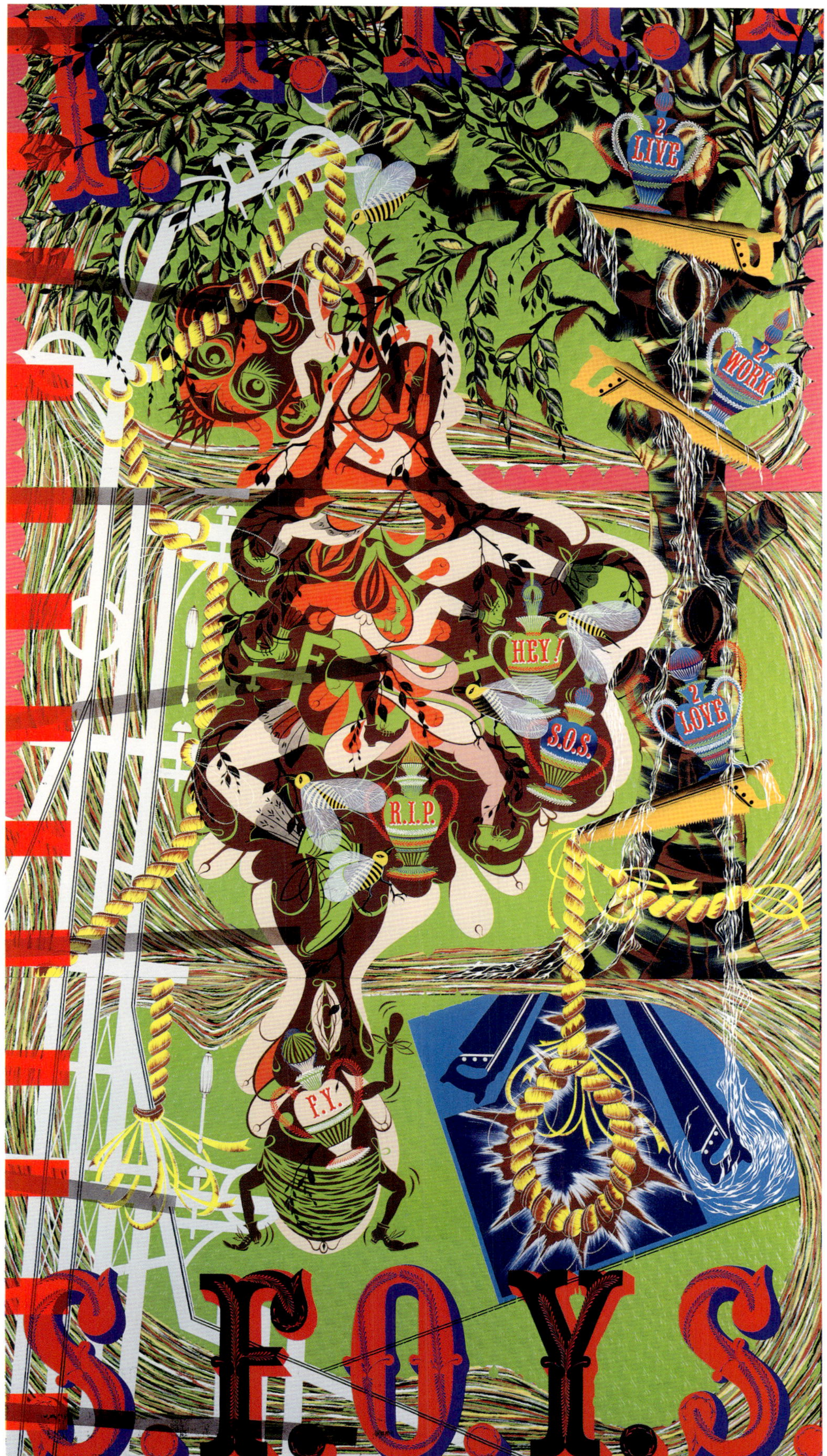

A Decorated Chronology of Insistence and Resignation, Untitled #9, 1992–93
Acrylic and enamel on three mahogany panels, 14 x 8 ft (4.3 x 2.4 m)

FABIAN MARCACCIO

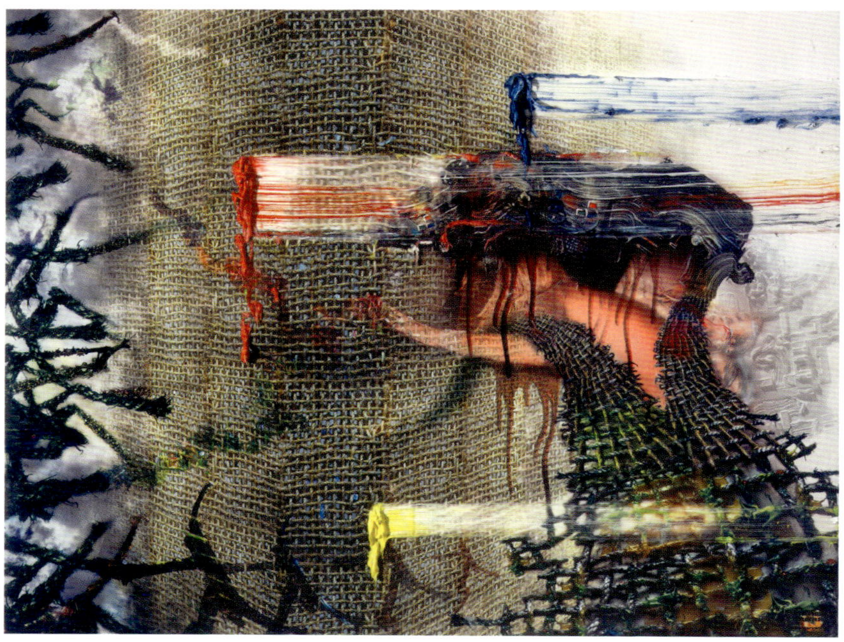

Content Vertigo Paintant, 2001
Mixed media on canvas, 71 3/8 x 95 1/8 in (182.8 x 243.8 cm)

to darker forces—nooses, guns, hooks, and shackles, suggesting that creation and destruction are at work in the world in equal force.

Fabian Marcaccio brings an exaggerated machismo to works that exist between abstraction and representation, frequently working on a mural-size scale that threatens to overwhelm the space in which his pieces are installed. Reflecting the deformative nature of his works, Marcaccio refers to them as "paintants," a conflation of the words painting and mutant. They consist of digital imagery printed directly onto the canvas, carefully painted realist images, and cast and poured silicone, which is sometimes overpainted with gestural brushstrokes. It is often difficult to discern what is a "genuine" brushstroke and what has been enhanced with silicon texture, or where the "real" surface of the canvas ends and a virtual representation of canvas begins. Marcaccio also allows the edges of images to meld into each other, which complements the indeterminacy of the transgressive imagery itself. This may include depictions of entrails, men in military fatigues, nudes done up as guerilla fighters, alluring mangled body parts, as well as close-up digital reproductions of woven materials. *Content Vertigo Paintant*, 2001, melds a gun and a female nude. In all, Marcaccio reveals the aggressive side of abstraction, particularly as practiced by the Abstract Expressionists. In a parody of the notion of "action painting," a term coined by critic Harold Rosenberg, he has even built a *Paintant Robot*, 2002, which shoots paint pellets around the gallery from an air gun.

These heirs of Guston suggest the aggressive side of deformation, in which the breakdown of categories is largely a destructive act, meant to destabilize social, formal, and political conventions at once. But deformation also has a reconstructive side, as can be seen in the work of the late Elizabeth Murray. Here again, the elastic space and movement of cartoons (the artist has cited Disney as an important influence) provide an underlying source. However, in Murray's hands cartoons are transformed into near abstractions of objects from everyday life. Schematic drawings of cups, chairs, tables, and books lope across organically shaped canvases. Body fragments, especially mouths, ears, fingers and other sensory parts, intertwine with domestic décor, leaving no distinction between animate and inanimate objects. In *Arm-Ear*, 1993, for instance, a central red chair is perforated by a sausage-like cable that connects to schematic ears. Perhaps these belong to an absent listener. Or perhaps the whole ensemble is becoming some kind of musical instrument itself. The structures of Murray's three-dimensional paintings are as fluid and open as the images themselves. Sometimes the edge of the canvas follows the contour of the images, and sometimes it deliberately breaks it up, so that the eye has to jump across an expanse of white wall or over another layer of canvas to complete the form—contributing our own reconstructive act.

With her generative gestures, Murray demonstrates that deformation is a many-sided tool. It may celebrate chaos and destruction, but it also addresses the equally untidy processes of birth, growth, and creation. Our contemporary fascination with works that celebrate the breakdown of established orders grows from a recognition that there is beauty in change, decay, and regeneration. Humans, no less than other creatures, are part of the cycle of life and death. In the end, order and deformation are two sides of the same coin, and together they bring forth the world that we know. Out of the destruction of the old comes the possibility of the new.

ELIZABETH MURRAY

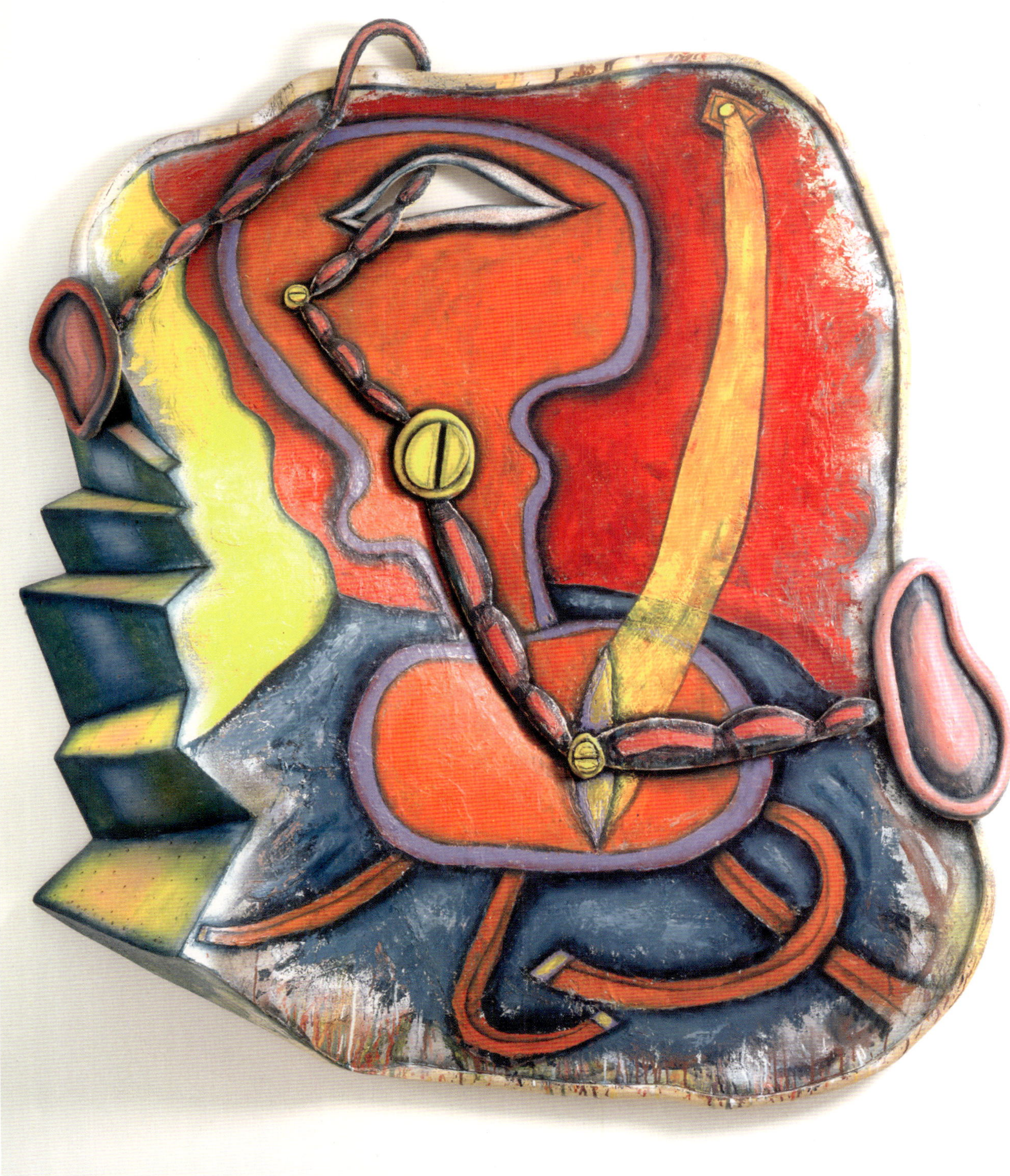

Arm-Ear, 1993
Oil on canvas mounted on bentwood
74 x 71 x 12 in (188 x 180.3 x 30.5 cm)
Newark Musem, N.J.

ART & THE BODY

FROM OBJECT TO SUBJECT

In 1989 Barbara Kruger created a graphic work that declared "Your body is a battleground." She was referring to the gender wars, but the history of contemporary painting, sculpture, performance, and body art suggests that her statement has much wider ramifications. The body, long a *subject* of art, became a frequent and conscious *medium* of Western art beginning in the 1950s.[1] Ever since, it has been embroiled in conflicts and controversies that have flowed over into the realms of politics, religion, and law, touching off clashes over social mores, gender definitions, and community standards. The forms that body-based performance art takes are remarkably varied. Performers throughout the world have found the human body to be an unusually versatile instrument that can be used to celebrate human sexuality, express private traumas, or explode gender and racial stereotypes. From the mid-1950s up through the 1970s, body-based performance art established itself in countries as diverse as Japan, Austria, Brazil, and France. In the United States, the birth of performance art is often linked to the publication of a series of photographs taken by Hans Namuth in 1950 of Jackson Pollock in the throes of creative frenzy. Caught in the act of dancing over his canvases as he spilled and spattered them with paint, Pollock embodied the notion of "action painting." It was only a short leap to the "living brushes" of Yves Klein, who in the early 1960s covered nude models with blue paint, and had their bodies pressed or dragged along canvases on the floor. In a contemporaneous "action," Italian artist Piero Manzoni created living sculptures by signing the backs or arms of his models.

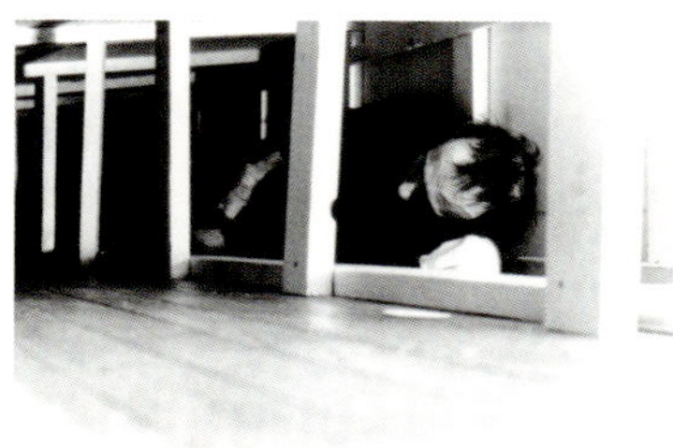

VITO ACCONCI
SEEDBED
1972
BLACK & WHITE PHOTO ENLARGEMENT
95 1/2 X 62 X 1 IN
(242.6 X 157.5 X 2.5 CM)

Pollock was also an important influence on Allan Kaprow, father of the Happening. Originally a rehearsed and scripted set of actions, Happenings evolved into improvisational events that involved the audience. Like action painting, they broke down the traditional separation of the artist and the art object, but Happenings merged the two to produce works that existed only as ephemeral creations. This idea had widespread effects, ranging from the interactive performances and kinetic sculptures of Hélio Oiticica and Lygia Clark (see also chapter 16) to the experiments of the Japanese Gutai artists, who explored the limits of art by, for instance, rolling naked in a pile of mud or painting canvases with their feet. Elsewhere, performance and body art took a darker turn in the work of "endurance artists" such as Chris Burden, who nailed himself to a Volkswagen, or Vito Acconci, who hid under a gallery floor and audibly masturbated in *Seedbed*, 1972. Articulating fantasies about the viewers walking above, he set up a deliberately uncomfortable situation in which viewers were forced to consider their relationship to the unseen artist. In a similar spirit, Gina Pane cut her face with razor blades and walked over broken glass. But even these confrontational actions pale beside the works of such notable Viennese "Actionists" as Hermann Nitsch and Arnulf Rainer, who repeatedly clashed with police during performances that included public masturbation, self-mutilation, and animal slaughter. Founded in 1957, Hermann Nitsch's Orgies-Mysteries Theater (or OMT) moved to a permanent home in 1971 in a castle in Prinzendorf, Austria, purchased by the artist for the presentation of ritualistic performances involving animal carcasses, entrails, and blood.

The history of body and performance art is especially closely entwined with the feminist art movement of the 1970s. As part of an effort to challenge restrictive definitions of female sexuality, feminist artists actively exhibited their own naked bodies in performances designed to undermine the passive, pin-up connotations of female nudity. Often these actions took a transgressive turn, as when Valie Export cut the crotch out of her jeans and paraded through a pornographic movie theater, or when Charlotte Moorman was arrested for playing the cello topless in a performance with Nam June Paik. Perhaps the two most influential women body artists are Carolee Schneemann and Marina Abramovic. Both came of age in the 1970s and have continued to pursue body-based performance art, but their uses of their bodies are in some ways diametrically opposed. Much of Schneemann's work celebrates pleasure, while Abramovic focuses on self-mastery in the face of daunting and often painful physical tasks.

Among Schneemann's classic works are her 1964 performance *Meat Joy*, in essence a Dionysian revel in which scantily clad men and women rolled around amid plucked chickens, fish, and buckets of paint. Other works from this time were equally sexual. In *Fuses*, 1965, Schneemann and a longtime lover had sex in public. For *Interior Scroll*, 1975, a naked Schneemann extracted a long paper strip from her vagina and read from it a witty response to critics of her work. More recently, Schneemann has addressed mortality and memory and harked back to the archaic rituals that preceded the Western mind/body split. Her recent works tend to take the form of installation rather than performance, but they still have a performative aspect. *Mortal Coils*, 1994–95, for example, commemorates fifteen of the artist's friends who had recently died, flashing slide projections of their absent faces on the walls while coils of rope suspended from a ceiling-mounted apparatus endlessly turn.

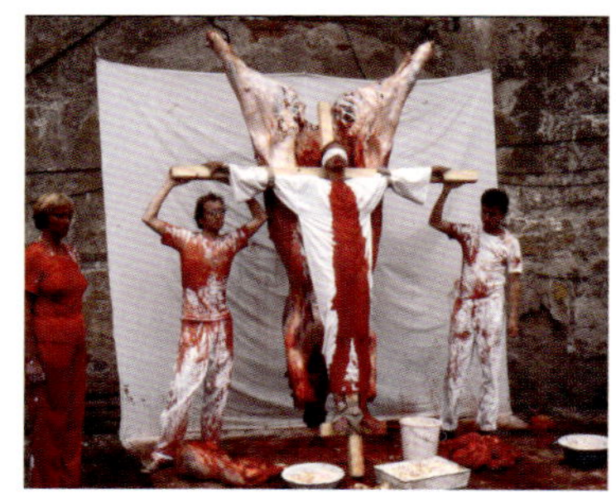

HERMANN NITSCH
80TH ACTION: ORGIES-MYSTERIES THEATER
1984
SCHLOSS PRINZENDORF, AUSTRIA

Schneemann's unabashed pleasure in her own body and delight in unfettered sexuality offer an alternative to the iconoclasm and asceticism of other feminist models. Abramovic, by contrast, uses her body in ways that accentuate self-control, physical endurance, and risk. In the 1970s, she worked with a male partner, Ulay, who was also her lover. They became known for acts of unsettling violence or self-laceration. In performances that can now be experienced through grainy documentary videos, they slap each other with increasing vehemence, or scream at each other in very close quarters. For the pair's last performance, in 1989, they walked the length of the Great Wall of China, each starting from an opposite end. By the time they met in the middle, their relationship and their performance partnership were over. Since then, Abramovic has continued a solo exploration of themes of endurance and self-discipline. Often her works take the form of physical trials. For *The House with the Ocean View*, 2002, she lived for twelve days without eating, speaking, reading, or writing, but fully exposed in a specially built loft "house" installed in a

MARINA ABRAMOVIC

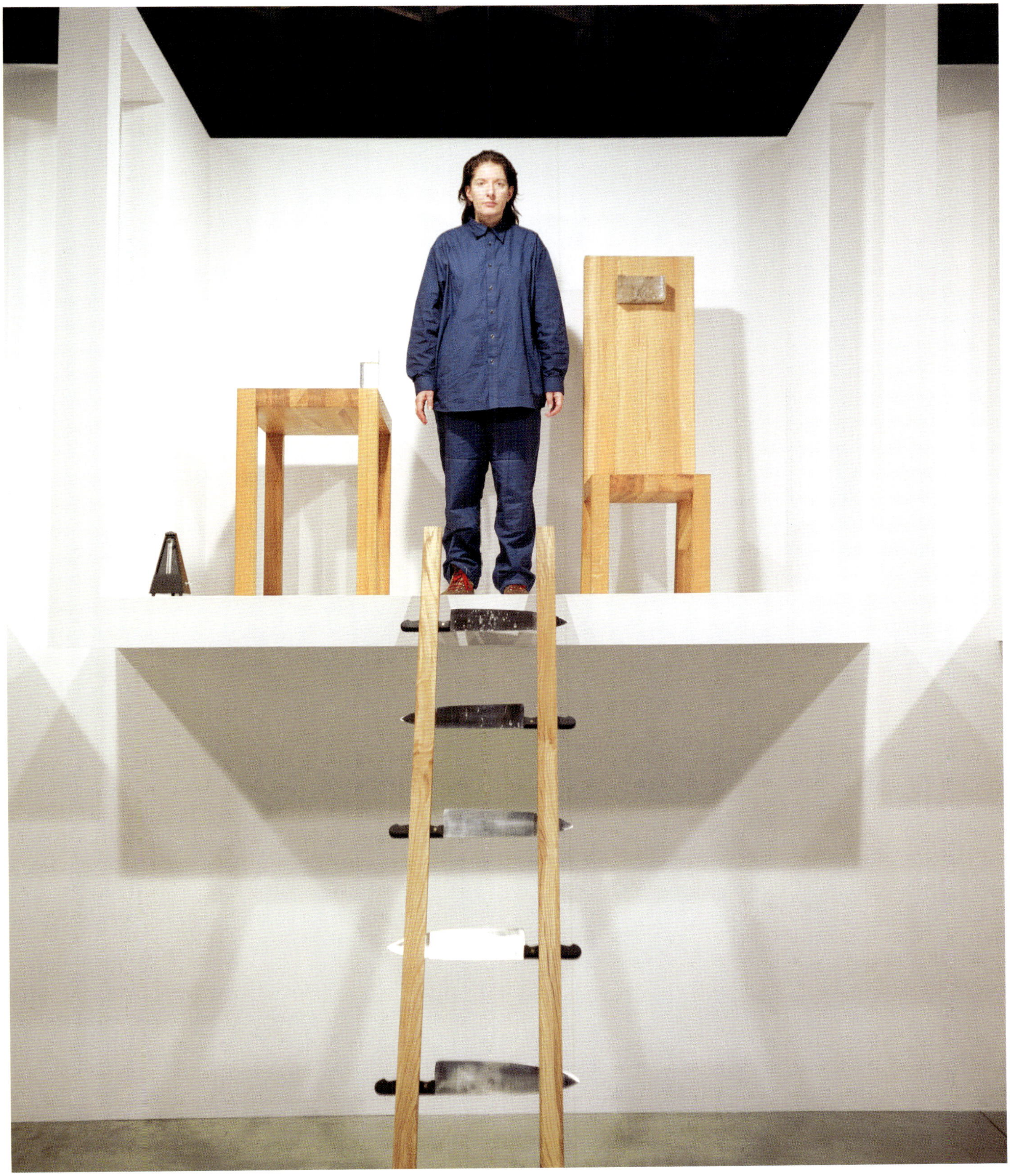

The House with the Ocean View, 2002
Performance, Sean Kelly Gallery, New York, November 2002

CAROLEE SCHNEEMANN

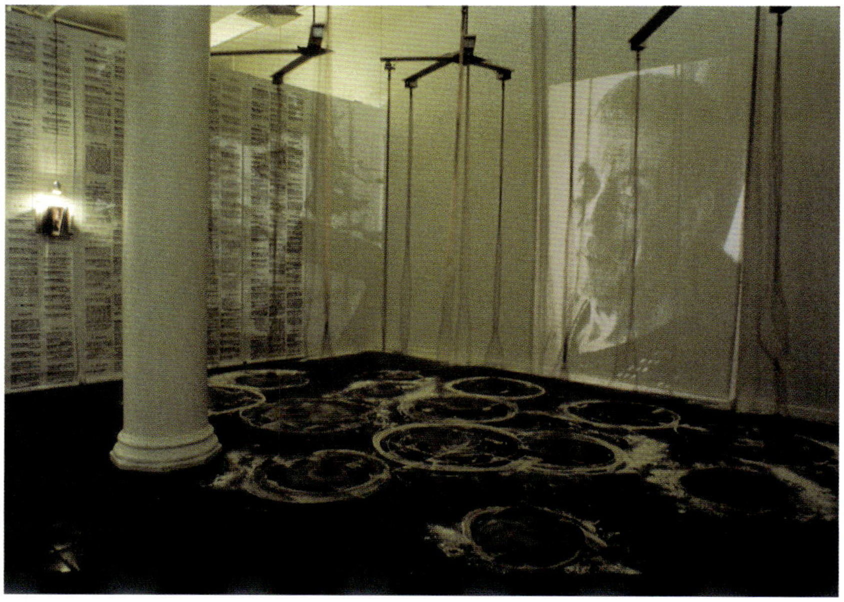

Mortal Coils, 1994–95
Multimedia installation, 4 slide projector units with motorized mirror systems, 17 motorized manila ropes, suspended and revolving from ceiling units, and "In Memorium" wall scroll text

JANINE ANTONI

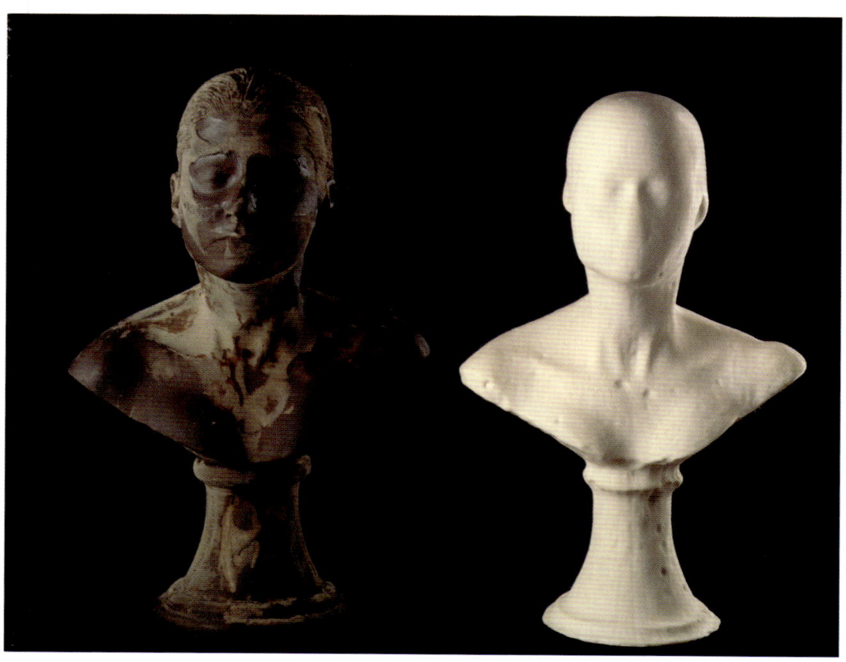

Lick and Lather, 1993–94
Two busts: one chocolate and one soap, two pedestals
24 x 16 x 13 in (61 x 40.6 x 33 cm)

Chelsea gallery in New York. It was a work whose challenges were as much mental as physical, likened by critics to a religious acolyte's self-imposed ordeal.

In their very different ways, Abramovic and Schneemann create a path to mental transcendence through corporeal action, a strategy that younger "body artists" have picked up. Janine Antoni, in particular, has extended Abramovic's concerns with endurance and self-control. Antoni creates objects as well as actions, but all of her works have a performative quality. In one early work, *Loving Care*, 1993, she puts a female spin on the macho energy of Abstract Expressionism by painting the floor with her long hair dipped in hair dye. Among her best-known works is *Lick and Lather*, 1993–94, in which she creates sculptures out of blocks of chocolate or lard, shaping them by chewing or licking the chocolate and by washing herself with the lard. Antoni's works suggest specific metaphoric associations. Her interest in lard and chocolate, for instance, is a cyclical one that relates to the human body's systems. Chocolate, when ingested, returns to the body as fat, while lard is the fat used to create soap that washes the body. In essence Antoni dissolves the distance between herself and the materials of her work.

Tania Bruguera's work is more confrontational. Citing Ana Mendieta (see chapter 11) and Abramovic as sources of inspiration, Bruguera creates performances, installations, and videos that use bodies as instruments to explore social, political, and religious restraints. Many of Bruguera's early works employ blood and animal parts in ways that recall both the pre-Columbian spiritual traditions of her native country and the violations perpetrated on individuals and groups by colonial and current political authorities. For *el peso de la culpa* (the burden of guilt), a performance at the 1997 Havana Biennial, Bruguera slung a butchered lamb around her neck and ate Cuban soil mixed with water in homage to the native Cubans who did the same to commit ritual suicide in defiance of the Spanish conquistadors. Other works involve architectural settings that place the viewer in uncomfortable and even unbearable situations. At Documenta 11 in 2002, Bruguera's audiences were thrust into a room lit with blinding spotlights. Outside, one heard the relentless, amplified sound of a live performer endlessly stomping, stopping, and cocking a rifle. With such works Bruguera provokes the senses while evoking the conflict between individual and state. She reminds us that freedom, liberty, and self-determination are not abstract ideals, but achievements that write their effects on our physical bodies.

The influence of '70s-era body art is not limited to artists from Western countries. Surprisingly, one of its strongest recent manifestations has been among a group of artists in mainland China who began to explore performance art in the early 1990s. Among the leaders of this movement are Zhang Huan and Ma Liuming. Working without official sanction, they set up an art colony in a rural area they dubbed "Beijing East Village" in homage to the anti-establishment ethos of the 1980s New York art scene, and they drew on limited information about Western performance art to create works that addressed their own situation. Both engaged their unclothed bodies in their performances, but their goals were quite different.

Echoing Abramovic, among others, Zhang Huan set up situations in which he had to endure physical or mental pain. In *12 Square Meters*, 1994, for example, he covered himself with honey and sat for hours in a public toilet while flies covered his skin. He has since left China and adapted his performances to a Western context. Often these touch on the dilemma of the nomadic immigrant, who is never quite at home anywhere. In *My America (Hard to Acclimatize)*, 1999, a performance at the Seattle

TANIA BRUGUERA

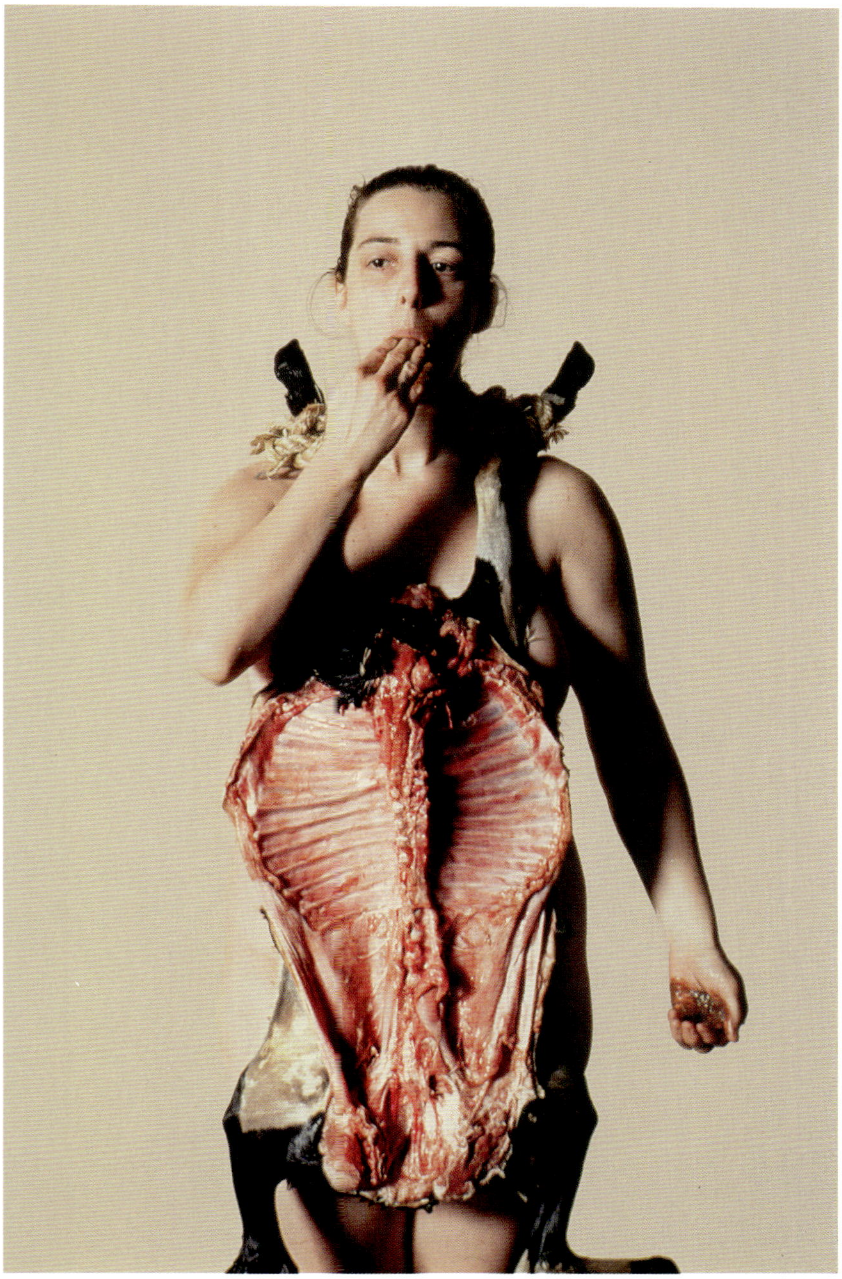

el peso de la culpa (the burden of guilt), 1997
Decapitated lamb, rope, water, salt, and Cuban soil, dimensions variable

Art Museum, he lead a group of naked Americans through a set of ritual actions that culminated with their pelting him with food as he sat passively in a chair. The sight of this mob turning on the expressionless artist was both comic and unsettling, dramatizing Zhang's sense that he could never fully belong in this alien world.

By contrast, Ma Liuming uses nakedness and his feminine face to explore sexual ambiguity and the porous line between male and female, playing a character named Fen-Ma Liuming. (The addition of the feminine sounding Fen to the artist's otherwise masculine name emphasizes the mixing of genders.) With makeup, Ma's face resembles that of a beautiful woman, while his unclothed body is unmistakably male. Echoing Abramovic and Ulay in *Fen-Ma Liuming Walks the Great Wall*, 1998, he traverses the Great Wall of China in character. While Fen-Ma Liuming raises issues around homosexuality and feminism for Western audiences, the artist declares himself more interested in the exploration of mental and emotional states of being. For instance, he notes that he frequently uses fish as a metaphor for the state of innocence and sexlessness of the fetus immersed in the maternal body. Similarly, his use of nudity, which may be read in China as sexual provocation, is for Ma a demonstration of gender ambiguity.[2]

Performance art suggests the transgressive potential of the body as an art medium. Artists like Bruguera employ performance to challenge the political powers that be. Abramovic and Antoni use body-based performance art to gain control of their own subjectivity. Someone like Zhang might use it to dramatize the individual's alienation from society. The subversive use of the body in art is not confined to performance, however. In the 1960s, feminist artists and critics began to re-evaluate the use of the body as subject matter and to react against sexist assumptions embedded in traditional artistic representations of the female body. Reflecting the same experimental ethos that inspired the performance art of the 1960s and '70s, they were galvanized to rewrite the history of Western art and to examine the political implications of the body's representation in painting and sculpture.

The feminist analysis of figurative representation drew on several key ideas. The first, outlined by art historian Kenneth Clark in a series of lectures given in 1953 at the National Gallery in Washington, D.C., revolved around the distinction between the "naked" and the "nude." "To be naked," Clark maintained, "is to be deprived of our clothes, and the word implies some of the embarrassment most of us feel in that condition. The word 'nude,' on the other hand, carries, in educated usage, no uncomfortable overtone. The vague image it projects into the mind is not of a huddled and defenseless body, but of a balanced, prosperous, and confident body: the body re-formed."[3] This distinction allowed art connoisseurs in the pre-feminist era to separate artistic delectation from prurience. On one side were the refined sensibilities of the aesthete, for whom statues or paintings of nude women could be read as allegories, symbols, or tributes to their own impeccable taste. On the other were those degraded individuals for whom nakedness was associated with lust, desire, or embarrassing physical functions.

By the 1960s, however, this neat distinction was becoming muddied. Feminist art historians such as Linda Nochlin, Griselda Pollock, Carol Duncan, and Ann Sutherland Harris began to wonder why the female nude had been the quintessential motif of post-Renaissance art. They examined the subliminal messages conveyed by nubile flesh served up as coquettish allegories of virtue, justice, and truth. And they asked why men and women are represented so differently in the work of the Old

ZHANG HUAN

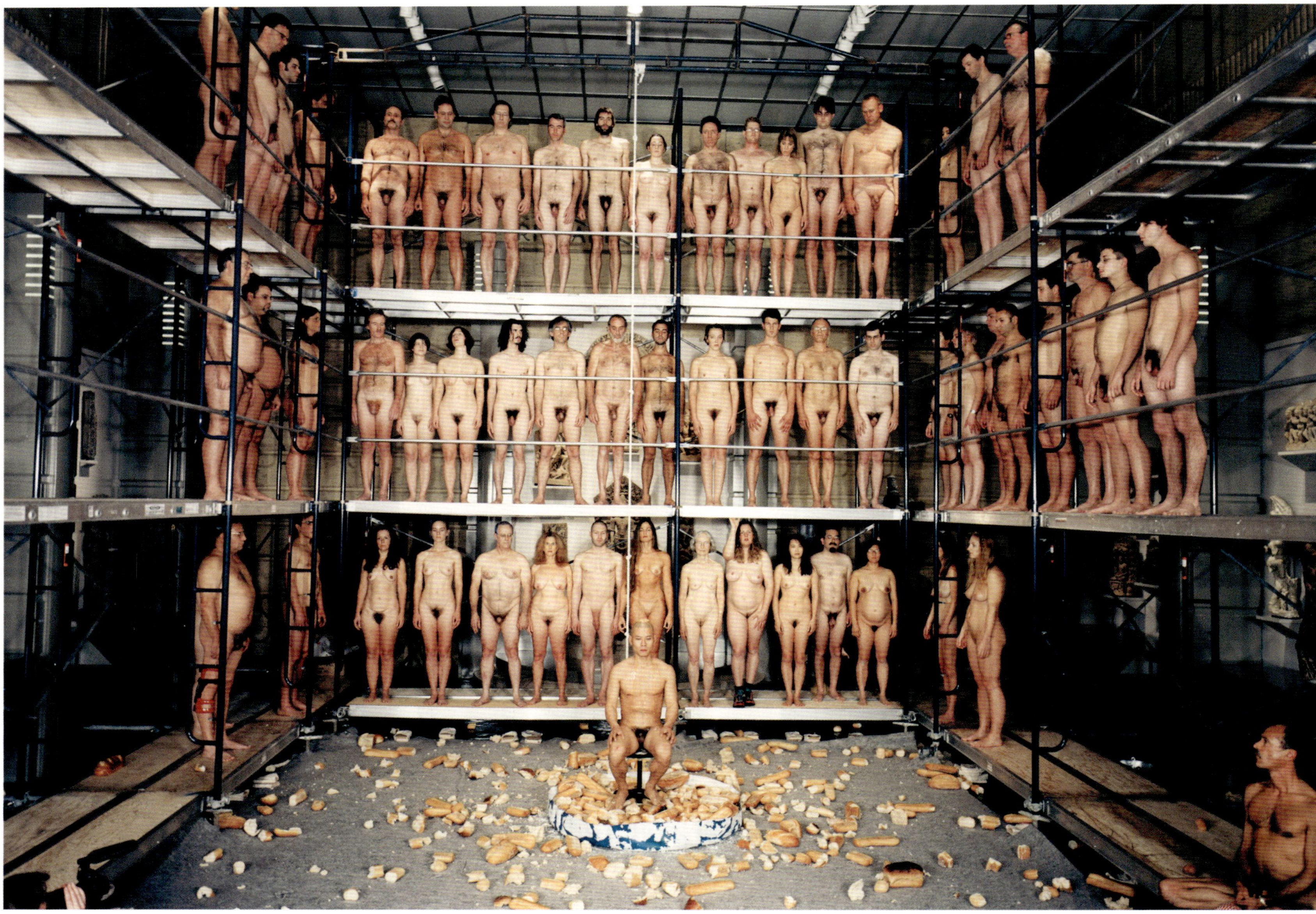

My America (Hard to Acclimatize), 1999
Performance, Seattle Art Museum, Wash., November 1999

MA LIUMING

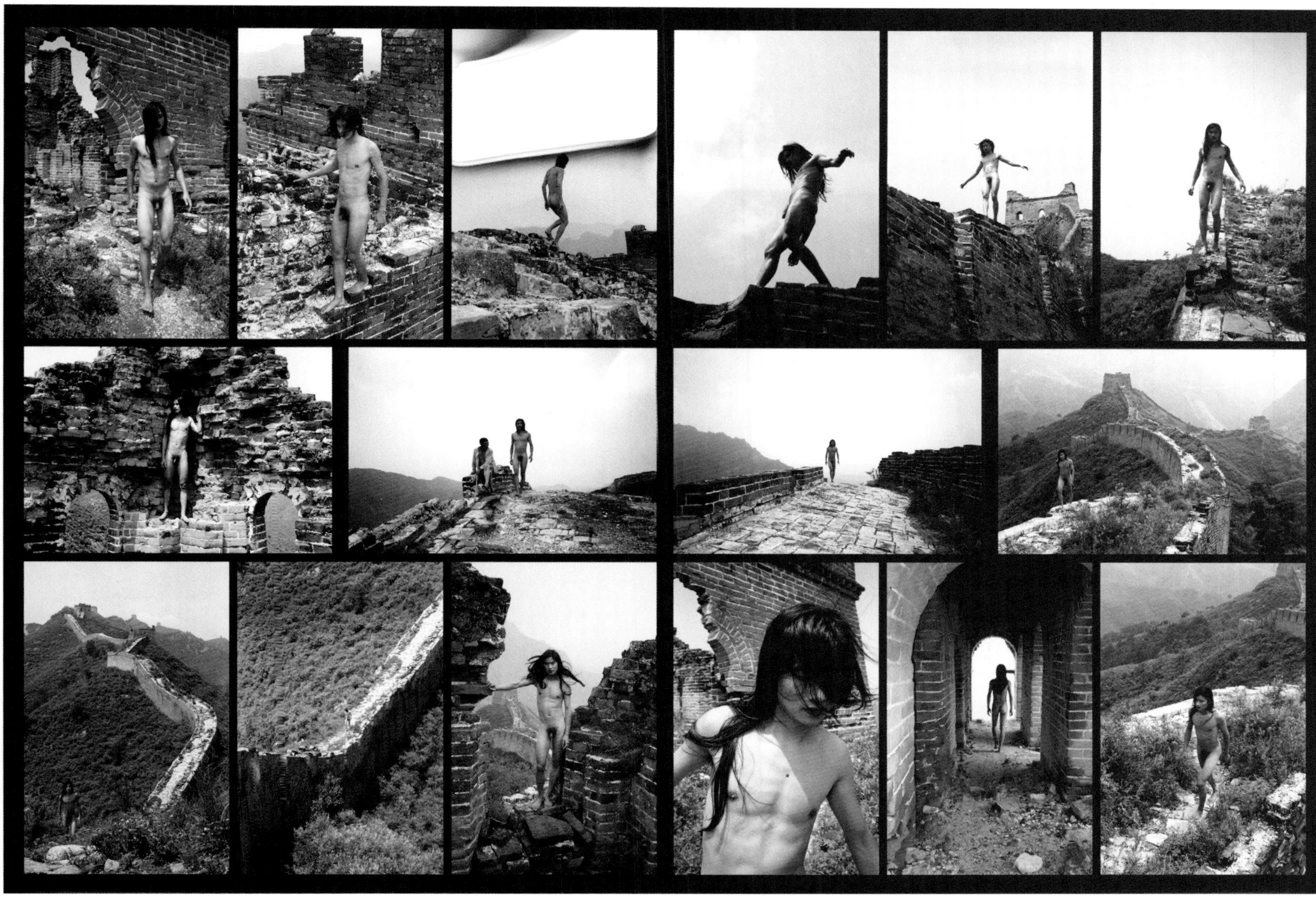

Fen-Ma Liuming Walks the Great Wall, 1998
Photographic documentation of a performance

Masters and their followers.[4] Marxist critic John Berger provided one answer. In art, as in advertising, Berger noted, "Men act and women appear. Men look at women. Women watch themselves being looked at."[5] From this insight has grown a massive literature. Using tools drawn from psychoanalysis, Marxist theory, film criticism, and post-structuralism, feminists have analyzed the way in which Western art replicates the unequal relationships already embedded in Western culture.

One of the most influential of these critiques is theorist Laura Mulvey's 1975 essay "Visual Pleasure and Narrative Cinema," in which she argues that Hollywood cinema is structured around the "male gaze."[6] By this she means that cinema assumes the existence of a male spectator, who transforms women into fetishes either of the feared yet desired phallic mother, or of the castrated woman whom man must subjugate to regain his lost mastery over the world. Extended to painting and sculpture, this notion has been used to explain not only the popularity of the female nude throughout Western art history, but also the particular ways in which the nude is presented. For instance, as Berger points out, whatever the ostensible subject of traditional paintings of the female nude, these naked ladies tend to be arranged in poses that accentuate their accessibility to the unseen and presumably male viewer. By extension, then, the female nude has become one of Western art's most popular subjects because it flatters men by reinforcing their dominance while relegating women to the rule of fantasy objects.

Feminist artists have responded to this series of insights in a variety of ways. Some, like Barbara Kruger, Mary Kelly (see chapter 10), and Jenny Holzer (see chapter 15), eschewed representations of the female body altogether, exploring instead a deliberately non-sensual aesthetic that favored text over image. Other women artists have argued that the problem is not with depiction of the female body in itself, but with who is doing the presenting. Hence they attempt to replace the male gaze with a female one. One pioneer of this approach is Joan Semmel, who in the 1970s created a series of paintings depicting her own and her lover's naked bodies literally from the female perspective, capturing the scene as she viewed it from her reclining position, as in *Touch*, 1977. At about the same time Sylvia Sleigh began to paint male nudes in poses that deliberately mimicked those of the luscious odalisques and flirtatious Venuses of the Old Masters. Her *Turkish Bath*, 1973, is based on an 1862 painting by Ingres with the same name and depicts a group of naked men (all recognizable to contemporary audiences as art critics of the time) lounging in a bathhouse. Hannah Wilke was known in the '70s for performances in which she cavorted nude in front of the camera, daring the viewer to regard her as a passive fantasy object. Later, when she was dying of lymphoma, Wilke presented equally unflinching images, this time of her disease-ravaged body, in a series of photographs entitled *Intra-Venus*, 1993. No longer presenting the ideal feminine image, these photographs display a swollen and bruised body, deformed by cancer treatment. For her and her peers, depicting the nude became a way to assert control over society's attitudes toward sexuality, gender relationships, and ideals of physical beauty.

Over the last thirty years, the nude has not disappeared from art, as some of its feminist critics had originally hoped. However, it has been thoroughly reworked by both male and female artists in ways that depart sharply from traditional formulas. For example, one of the most celebrated painters of the nude today is Lucian Freud, whose figures could not be further from the alabaster virgins and voluptuous temptresses favored by artists like Titian and Ingres. Instead, many are big and

JOAN SEMMEL

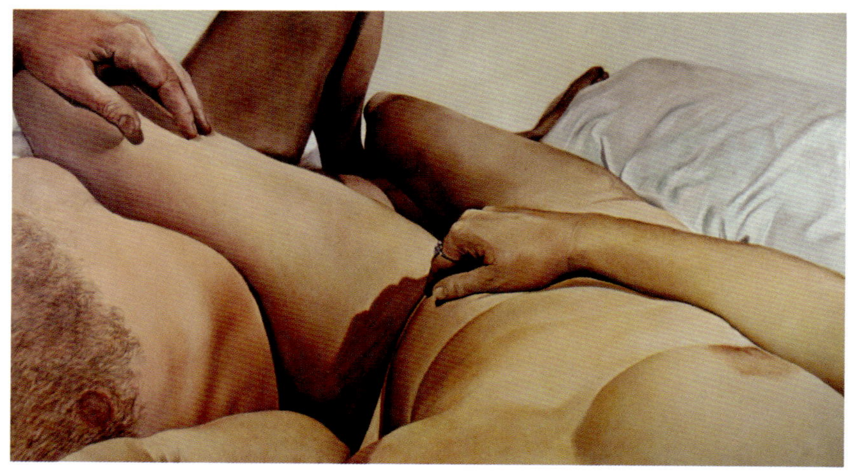

Touch, 1977
Oil on canvas, 54 x 106 in (137.2 x 269.2 cm)

blowsy, painted with broad strokes of paint that bring out rolls of fat, dimpled skin, and blotchy complexions. These mountains of flesh might be termed grotesque but for the sheer exuberance of paint handling that the artist displays. Other figures present unmistakable signs of age—hipbones protruding out of shrinking flesh, strange cavities that hollow out cheeks or thighs, and huge calloused feet that thrust awkwardly toward the viewer. The subjects squat, sprawl, or sag in bare rooms and inhospitable studio settings. They often seem equally male and female, as emphasized by a series of paintings of the late cross-dressing performance artist Leigh Bowery. What they are not is seductive and sexually enticing. In this, Freud's figures seem like textbook cases in the self-conscious nakedness that Kenneth Clark opposed to the idealized and aestheticized "nude."

Jenny Saville is often described as a student of Freud's because, like him, she presents lusciously painted figures that border on the grotesque. Unlike Freud's, however, Saville's subjects lack individuality, and often seem on the verge of losing their humanity altogether. (In fact, some works depict corpses, with bruised and swollen faces.) Her paintings feature almost exclusively female subjects, bodies spread out like landscapes, creating a play between the generative capacities of nature and woman. Their monumental scale, tight focus, and thickly loaded brushstrokes blur the distinction between body and landscape. Similarly blurred at times are certain gender distinctions. In *Matrix*, 1999, female genitals splayed in the foreground and topped with massive breasts are attached to a close-cropped head whose stubbled face seems unmistakably male.

Saville often uses her own body, distorted beyond recognition, as a model. In a similar mode of varying the idealized nude, John Coplans turned his own aging body into art. Coplans, who died in 2003, came late to photography, after a career as a critic, editor, painter, curator, and museum director. In 1984, at the age of sixty-four, he entered the ring as a photographer whose sole subject was his own nude body. Coplans's works deliberately subvert the conventions of the artistic nude. The camera lingers over every imperfection of the artist's sagging flesh, zeroing in on matted body hair, ripples of fat, and hills and valleys of untoned muscle. In some photographs, the close examination of rolling flesh mimics the gentle folds of landscape. In others, his belly and nipples become a cosmic animal face. Coplans conceals his identity, cropping his head and face out of the picture, which allows for a level of abstraction. Some works, like *Frieze, No. 4, Three Panels*, 1994, in which the body is represented three times over, are broken up into further abstracting grids. Many images focus just on hands, fingers, elbows, or feet, turning them into abstractions that bring to mind everything from tiny animals to female genitalia. Coplans often imitates the poses of the headless, fractured figures on Hellenic reliefs. But instead of aspiring to the Hellenic ideal of masculine perfection, his photographs convey the pull of gravity on aging flesh. He presents himself as a warrior of a sort whose adversary is not other soldiers but time itself.

In interviews, Coplans noted more than once how much he hated the classical perfection of the bodies in the photographs by Robert Mapplethorpe, who in a sense approached the issue of the nude from a completely opposite direction. While Coplans made his body into an abstraction that resembled various non-corporeal objects, Mapplethorpe sexualized his images of flowers, fruit, and vases, so that they exuded the same aura of decadence and desire as his famous (some would say infamous) nudes. Though he produced a small number of female nudes, most

SYLVIA SLEIGH

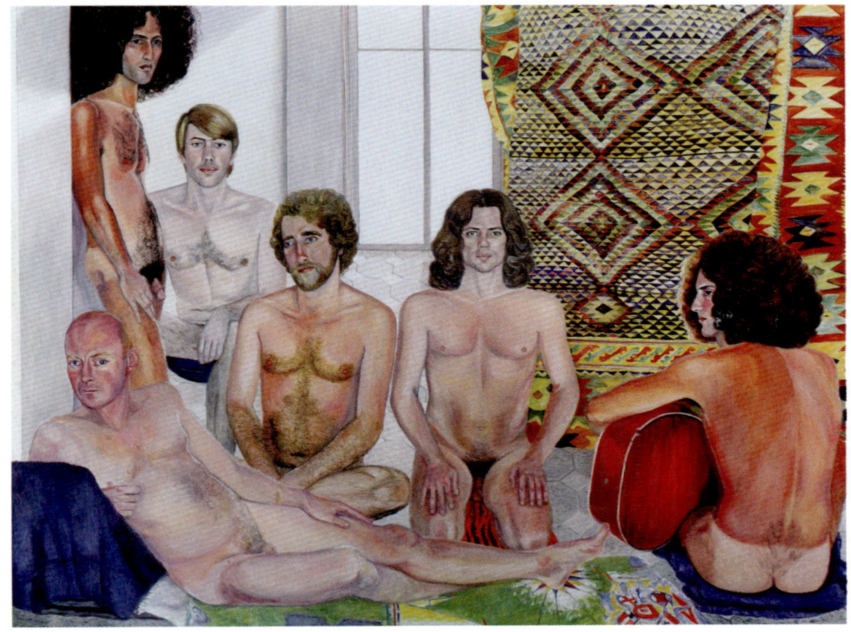

The Turkish Bath, 1973
Oil on canvas, 76 x 102 in (193 x 259.1 cm)
The David and Alfred Smart Museum of Art, The University of Chicago

HANNAH WILKE (WITH DONALD GODDARD)

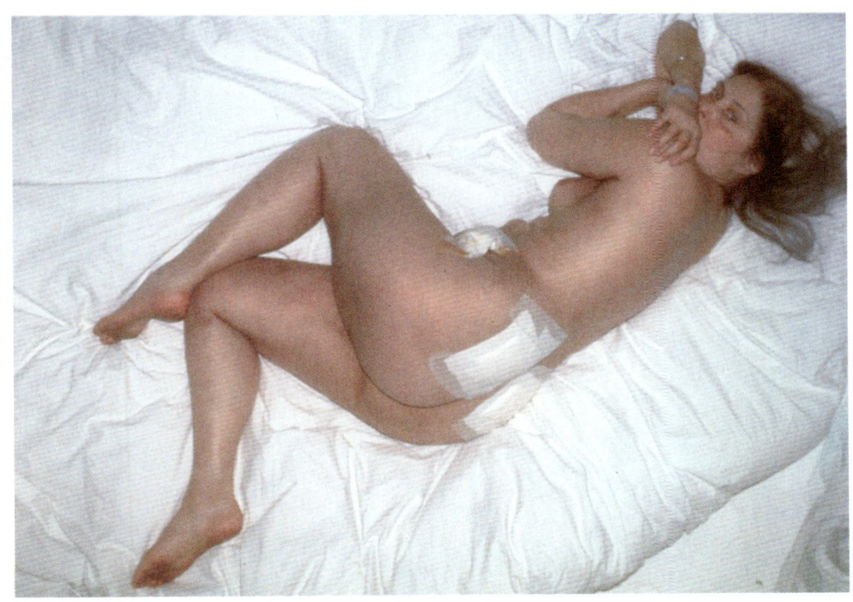

Intra-Venus, 1993
Chromagenic supergloss photograph, 48 x 72 in (121 x 182 cm)

LUCIAN FREUD

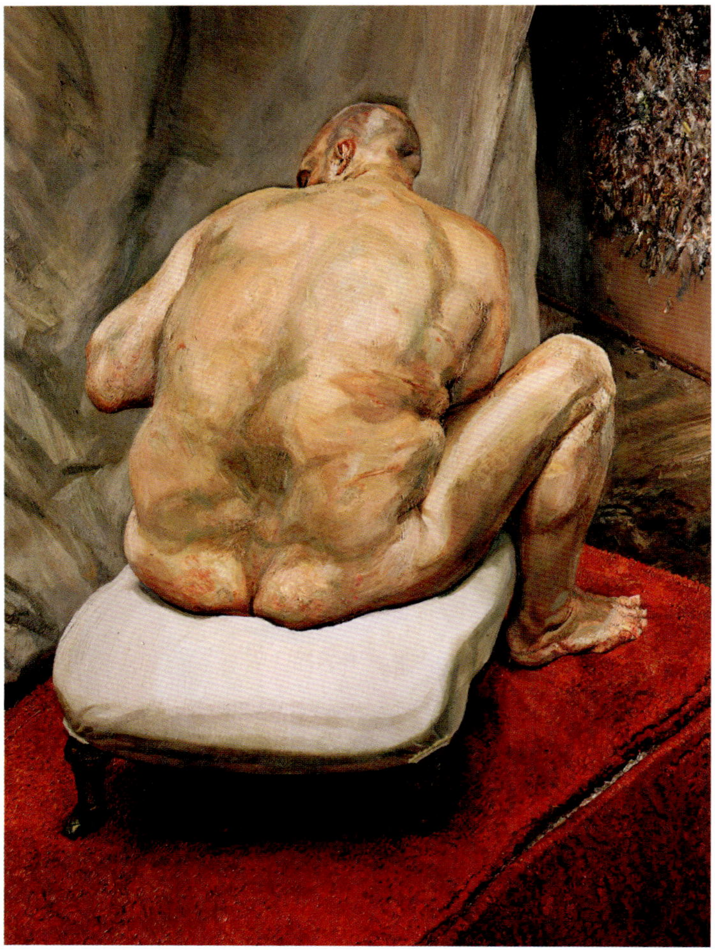

Back View (Leigh Bowery), 1992
Oil on canvas, 72 x 54 in (183 x 137.2 cm)

JENNY SAVILLE

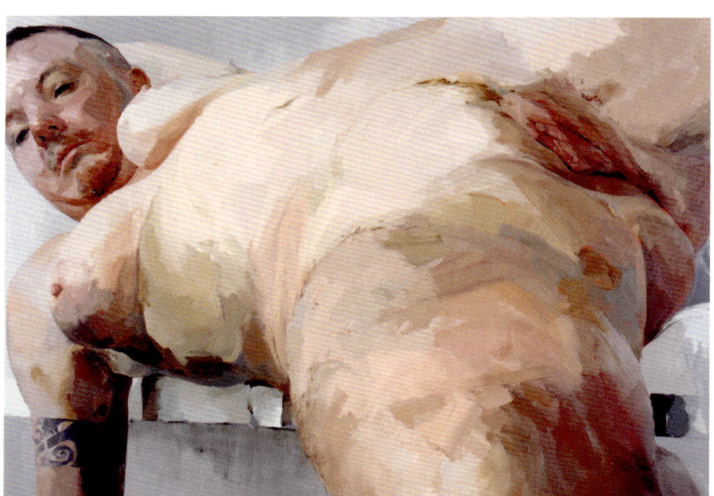

Matrix, 1999
Oil on canvas, 84 x 120 in (213.4 x 304.8 cm)

of which depicted the body builder Lisa Lyon, Mapplethorpe is best known for his seductively lit photographs of well-built and well-endowed young white and African American men. In some cases his subjects are presented in poses that recall the seductive presentation of traditional female nudes. In others they deliberately recall the stances, lighting, and physical perfection of Old Master depictions of Catholic saints. In a series titled "X Portfolio," 1978, they solemnly portray various sado-masochistic rituals common to the gay subculture to which Mapplethorpe belonged—a man's fist disappears up another's man's anus, for instance, or one man urinates into another's mouth.

These latter works sparked enormous controversy when they were shown as part of a traveling retrospective that toured the country after Mapplethorpe's death from AIDS in 1989. Critics of the National Endowment for the Arts, which had contributed a small amount to the exhibition, pointed to Mapplethorpe's works as evidence of the funding agency's support of pornography. Political pressure led to the cancellation of the exhibition at one venue and the indictment of a museum director for "pandering pornography" at another. Regardless of such moralistic assessments, the photographs in the "X Portfolio," like Mapplethorpe's less controversial figure studies, clearly focus on physical perfection, presenting a provocative, sexually enticing, *male* nude. In other words, Mapplethorpe's sexualized figures break the mold: they are presented as the product of the male homosexual gaze. From this perspective, supporters have argued that they are as radical a subversion of the dominant male heterosexual gaze as are feminist works devoted to the exploration of female desire. At the same time, Mapplethorpe's critics have argued that his photographs exploit their subjects in a manner reminiscent of the worst perpetrators of the male gaze, citing in particular Mapplethorpe's frequent use of prodigiously endowed black men as models in his photographs. *Man in the Polyester Suit*, 1980, for example, focuses on a black model's sizeable penis emerging from the open fly of his pants. In *Thomas,* 1987, a toned, nude black man is enclosed within a circle, frozen in an idealized athletic pose, as if his arms and legs were spokes of a wheel. Such images, critics argue, reinforce stereotypes about black male sexual prowess while turning the subjects into dehumanized sexual objects.

Glenn Ligon has addressed this very question in his own work. Ligon, who is black and gay, engages issues around slavery, the suppression of minority voices, and the uneasy status of the homosexual African American male. In the early 1990s he created an extended series of photographs and texts that ask whether the depiction of black men in Mapplethorpe's work bravely exposes socially unacceptable desires or serves as a degrading gay counterpart to traditional pornographic representations of women. Ligon's work, *Notes on the Margin of the Black Book*, 1991–93, began as precisely that—a set of private margin notations on his copy of a compilation of Mapplethorpe's photographs of black men. In its final state, Ligon's piece takes the form of an elegantly framed set of images from Mapplethorpe's book interspersed with framed texts expressing the views—ranging from righteous outrage to grateful recognition of a kindred spirit—of a diverse group of commentators, including artists, politicians, Christians, gay theorists, and drag queens. The work thus becomes an open-ended dialogue on the larger social meanings of Mapplethorpe's work, and on the implications of the public presentation of private fantasy.

Mapplethorpe's photographs, and Ligon's response to them, highlight difficult questions about the power of representation and society's proper role in regulating

JOHN COPLANS

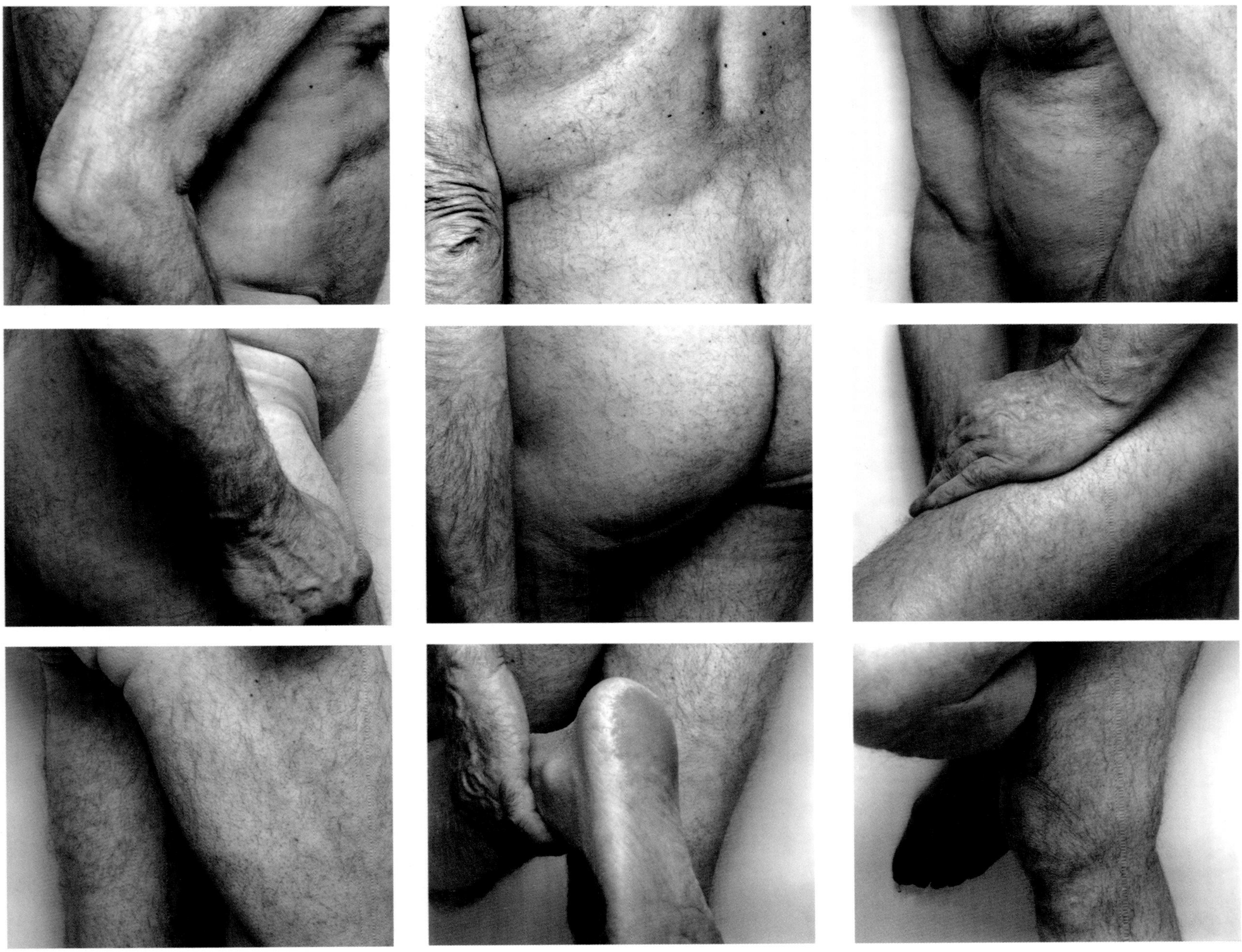

Frieze, No. 4, Three Panels, 1994
Gelatin silver prints, 78 x 102 in (198.1 x 259.1 cm)

ROBERT MAPPLETHORPE

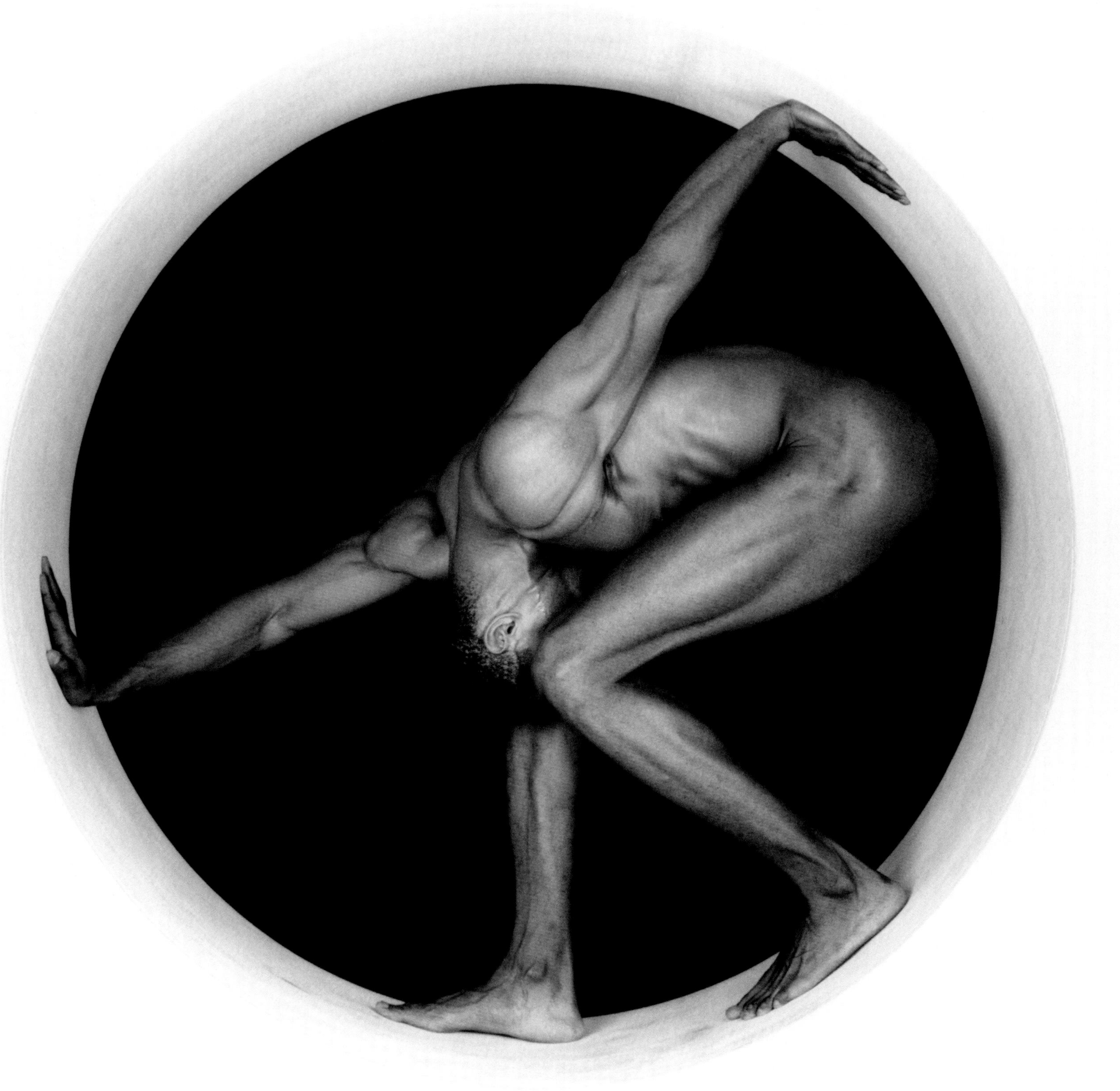

Thomas, 1987
Gelatin silver print, 18 7/8 x 18 7/8 in (47.9 x 47.9 cm)

GLENN LIGON

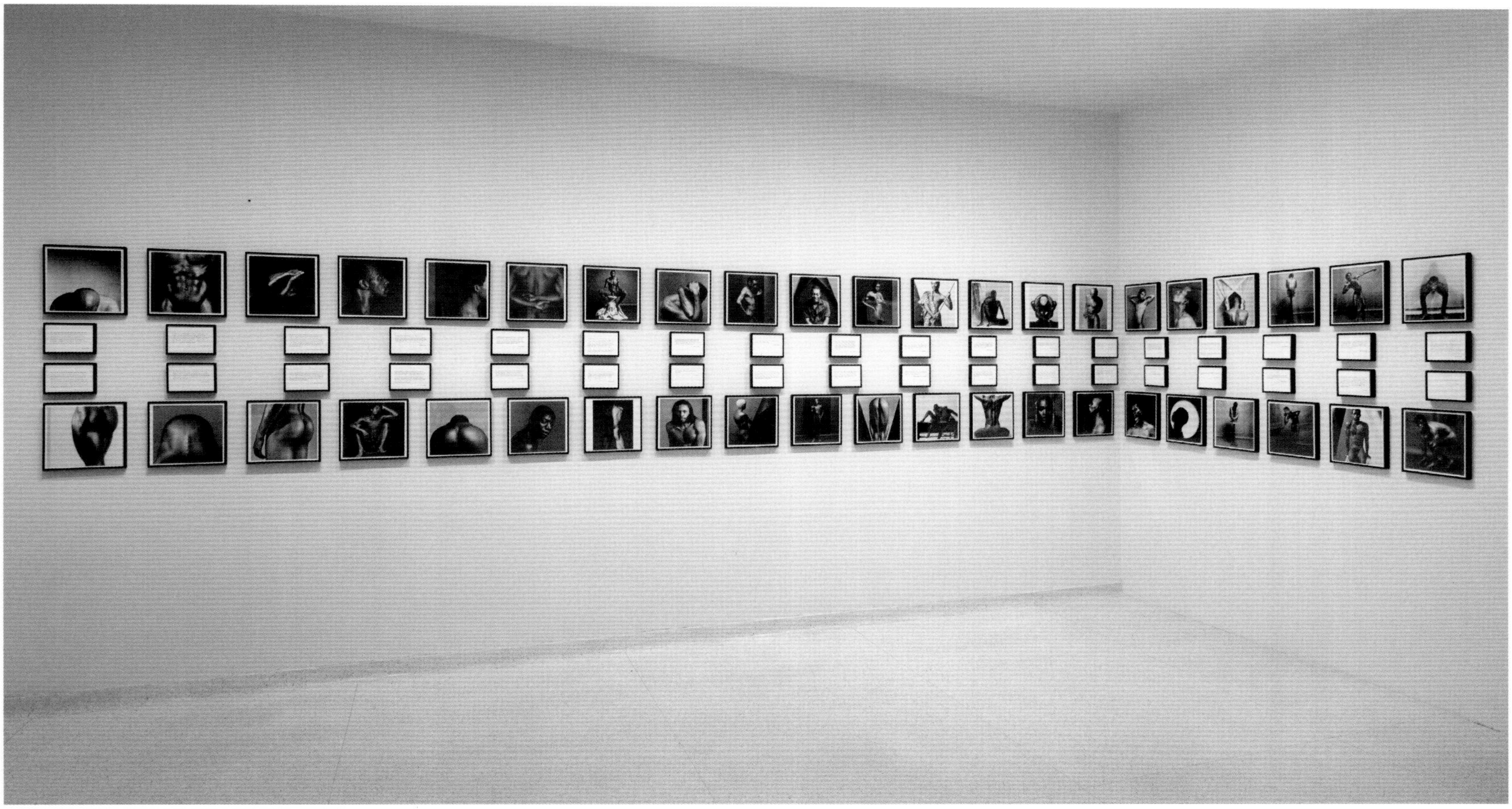

Notes on the Margin of the Black Book, 1991–93
91 offset prints and 78 text pages
Each print 11 1/2 x 11 1/2 in (29.2 x 29.2 cm), each text 5 1/4 x 7 1/4 in (13.3 x 18.4 cm)
Solomon R. Guggenheim Museum, New York

it. These questions emerge in the art of other contemporary artists who use pornography as a source or motif. Interestingly, many of the artists who draw on pornography are female. While they may find it easier to mine this material because their gender deflects charges that they are simply reinforcing the male gaze, these artists have not been immune to criticism. Within the feminist community, there is often a split between older women artists whose mission has been to undermine degrading stereotypes and younger women who seem to embrace them. Nonetheless, these "bad girls," as they have been dubbed, turn out to have an equally subversive agenda, in which pornography serves as a tool of social critique. The works of these artists—whether male or female—are not pornographic in any strict sense of the word; rather, they borrow from pornography to provoke reflection on social values, sexual mores, and the essential nature of desire and pleasure. While acknowledging that pornography may reinforce unsavory and degrading stereotypes, they argue that it also has the potential to destabilize rigid and oppressive social conventions.

Nobuyoshi Araki, best known for his photographs of erotic scenes from Tokyo's famous Red Light District, has often been compared to Mapplethorpe for applying the stylistic conventions of commercial photography to pornographic subjects. He presents naked or nearly naked young women in scenes of fetishistic bondage—bound and suspended with ropes, smeared with blood-colored paint, or sprawled on the beds of Japanese "love hotels." Despite these photographs' superficial resemblance to Western pornography, they are in fact deeply Japanese. Araki draws on the tradition of Edo-period shunga woodblock prints, which depict remarkably explicit sex acts in the decorative graphic style of the day. He also plays on the sexual obsessions that lurk just below the surface of Japan's apparently puritanical society. *Untitled (Kaori)*, 2004, for instance, presents a beautiful woman lying on the ground with her kimono hiked up to reveal her genitals, while a lizard looks on, peering over her thigh, in an erotic fantasy image that merges the demure and the wanton.

Among the group of western artists who flirt with pornography is Eric Fischl, who gained attention in the mid-1980s with a group of figurative paintings that insinuate an undertone of corruption and decadence in the upper middle-class suburban lifestyle. Lifting the curtain on the American dream, Fischl produced suggestive images that hinted at incest, pedophilia, rape, and other sexual perversities playing out in suburban living rooms and bedrooms, and even on relatively exposed backyard patios. In these paintings, adolescent boys furtively masturbate in plastic swimming pools, adults expose themselves in sexually provocative poses to young boys (as in *Bad Boy*, 1981, in which a boy watches a naked, splay-legged woman while simultaneously stealing from her purse), and entire families disrobe as a prelude to scenarios that seem decidedly less than innocent. These works gained Fischl a notoriety that none of his subsequent work has matched, though later works show a more nuanced sense of sexual psychology. Turning his attention to everyday adult sexual behavior, Fischl has presented sexual partners in a variety of intimate poses that suggest foreplay, sex, and its aftermath. Yet rather than desire, the figures tend to display attitudes ranging from alienation and boredom to disgust. In *Bedroom Scene #7: After the Tantrum, Unholy News*, 2004, for instance, the figures are surrounded by strewn flowers and broken crockery, evidence of a fight. Turning from the voyeuristic preoccupation of traditional paintings of the voluptuous female nude, *Krefeld Project, Sunroom, Scene #1*, 2002, leaves the woman clothed but exposes her male partner in all his overweight, imperfect nakedness. In such works, Fischl uses the language of sexual congress common to conventional pornography not to incite desire, but to suggest certain truths about the over-hyped nature of our contemporary dreams of sexual ecstasy and satisfaction.

Since the early 1990s, Lisa Yuskavage, perhaps the quintessential "bad girl," has been creating paintings of nubile waifs with exaggeratedly large breasts and pointed nipples like those in *Playboy* cartoons. Turning the tables on the male gaze, her works offer raunchy, titillating, and unabashedly pre-feminist depictions of female sexuality. Instead of rejecting male fantasies about women as sexual objects, Yuskavage makes these fantasies her own, investing them with a very female sensibility. Among Yuskavage's recurring subjects is budding female sexuality. Works like *Day*, 1999–2000, present barely pubescent girls who fondle their swelling breasts with evident pleasure. In other paintings, Yuskavage presents pregnant women whose swelling bellies mime the luscious roundness of fruit scattered nearby. These figures are lovingly painted in layers of translucent oil paint that give their skin and surrounds a luminous glow. But Yuskavage's lush brushwork cannot camouflage the fact that these voluptuous figures have more in common with romance-novel cover art than with "high-art" nineteenth-century odalisques. Her paintings' settings and details often play on the clichéd conventions of soft-core eroticism, among them glowing sunsets, flowers, pillows, satin-lined interiors, filmy lingerie, cherry nipples, absurdly exaggerated breasts, buttocks, and hips, and dreamy faraway expressions. Yet somehow Yuskavage's figures retain a sense of self-possession that removes them from the realm of pure fantasy object. They are self-consciously kitschy to the point of parody and thus offer a double-edged guilty pleasure: the viewer is alternately drawn to and unsettled by these exaggerated representations of sexuality. In the end, Yuskavage's work suggests that the pleasure we feel in art is not so different from that of pornography. Both forms of representation can appeal to our carnal instincts.

This duality is also at the heart of the work of Cecily Brown. Brown's large-scale paintings depict orgy scenes in which figures couple and uncouple, penises rise and explode, and bodies mingle promiscuously as if in a state of continual metamorphosis. Even the colors have an erotic intensity: Pompeii reds, cheeky pink and orange, and gold broken up with accents of blue, white, and green that recall the burnished flesh in paintings by Rubens or Titian. However, unlike Yuskavage's portraits, Brown's paintings are near abstractions. The figures are partially or almost completely masked by slathered paint and gestural marks. In *Guys and Dolls*, 1997–98, for instance, we see what seems to be an aerial view of a field of sprawling naked bodies, but they are broken up into patterns and swirling strokes that make it difficult to tell where one body ends and another begins. These energetic scenes might almost be mistaken for late Abstract Expressionist compositions: there are echoes of the slashing brushstrokes of Willem de Kooning, the meaty flesh of Chaim Soutine, and the dissolving forms of Francis Bacon. The disjuncture between the voluptuous hedonism of pornography and the sexual energy and machismo of Abstract Expressionism makes for a wry double vision. Flipping the trope of Victorian sculptors shaping nubile flesh to represent high-minded abstractions, Brown reduces Abstract Expressionism to an explosion of sexualized masculine potency.

Egyptian-born artist Ghada Amer also turns the tables on Abstract Expressionism. In her embroidered canvases, colorful abstract fields of twisting thread only partially conceal delicately embroidered line drawings below. The over layer of threads and

NOBUYOSHI ARAKI

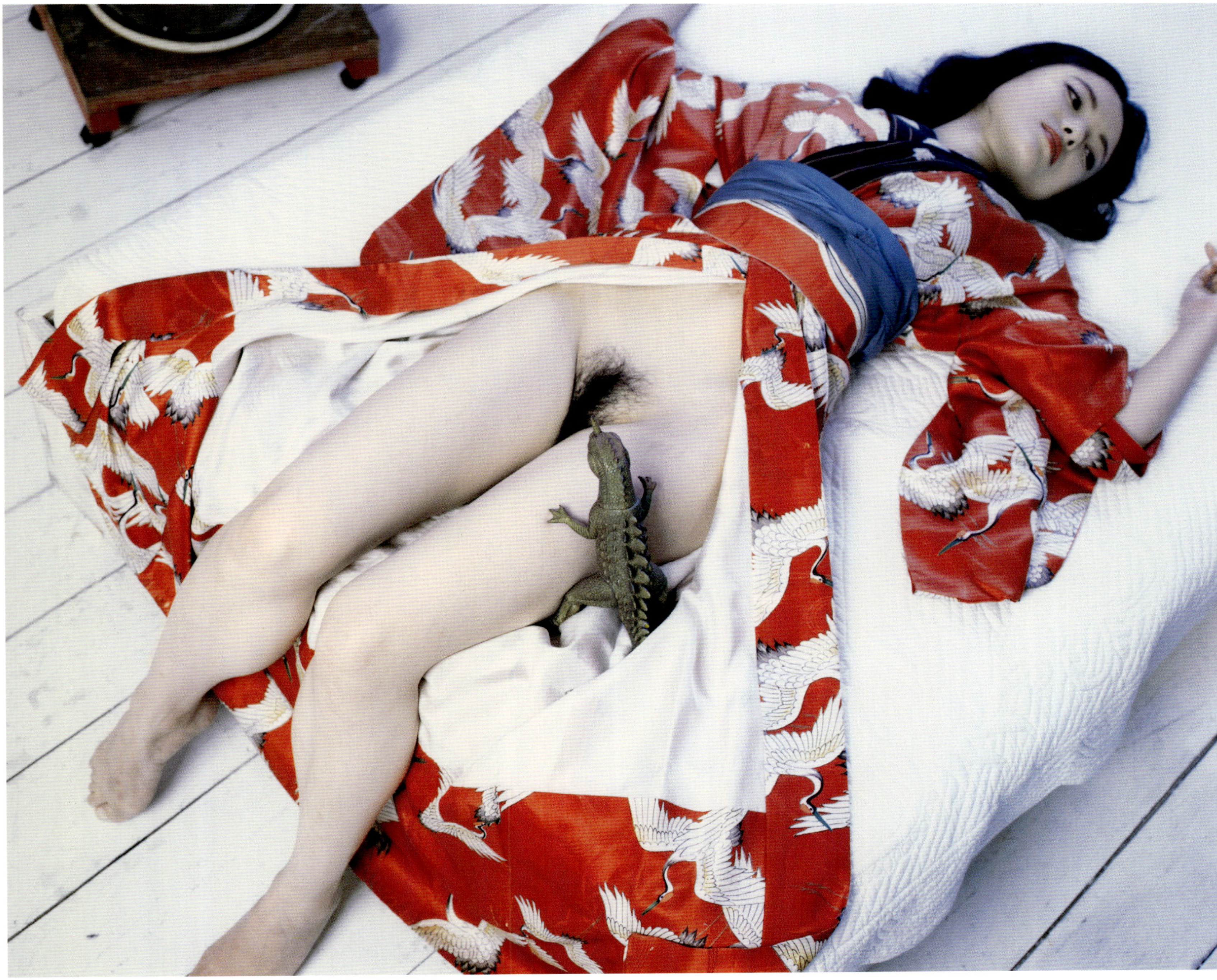

Untitled (Kaori), 2004
C-type print, 15 3/4 x 19 1/2 in (39.8 x 49.7 cm)

ERIC FISCHL

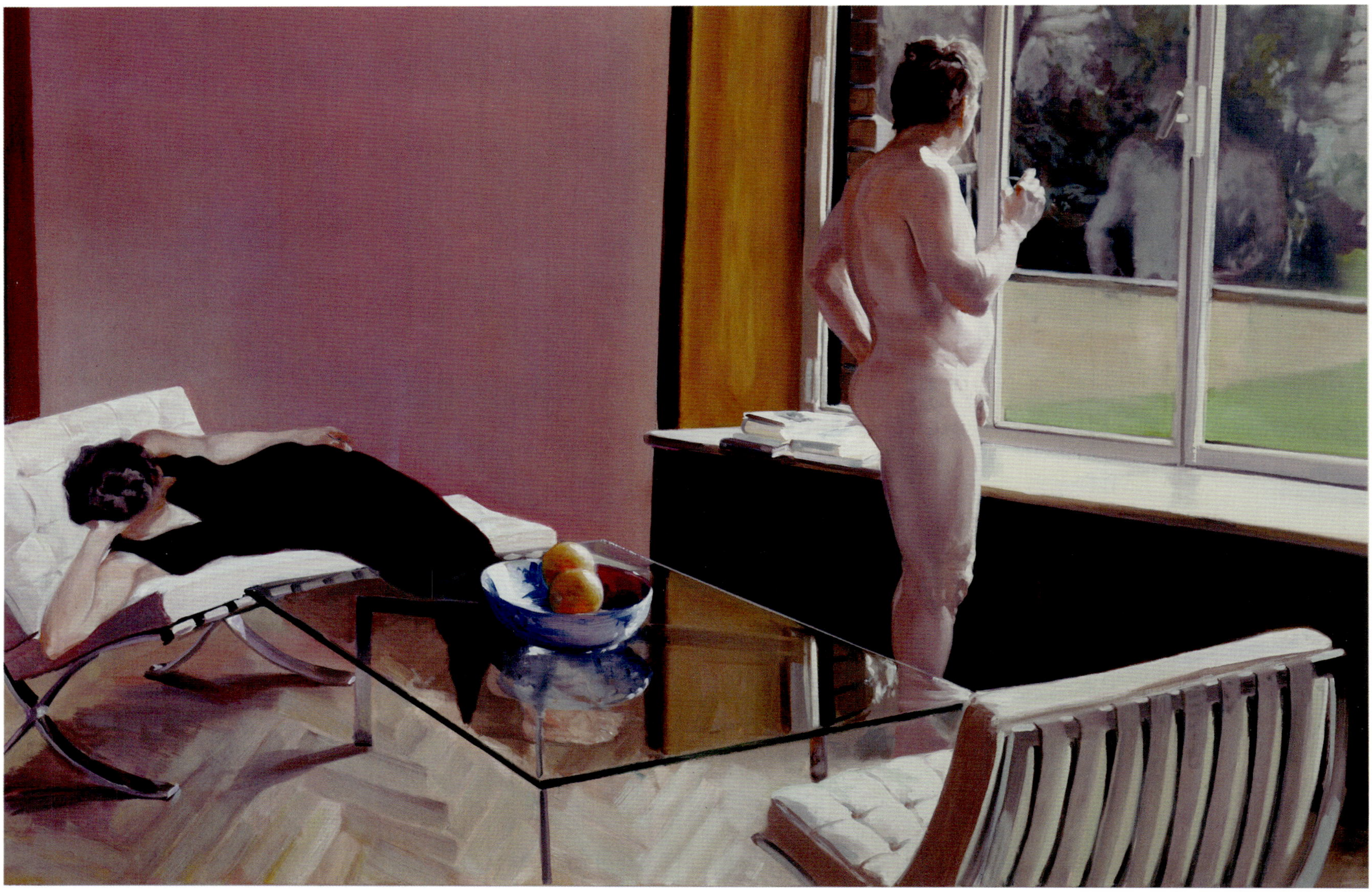

Krefeld Project, Sunroom, Scene #1, 2002
Oil on linen, 78 x 120 in (198.1 x 304.8 cm)

LISA YUSKAVAGE

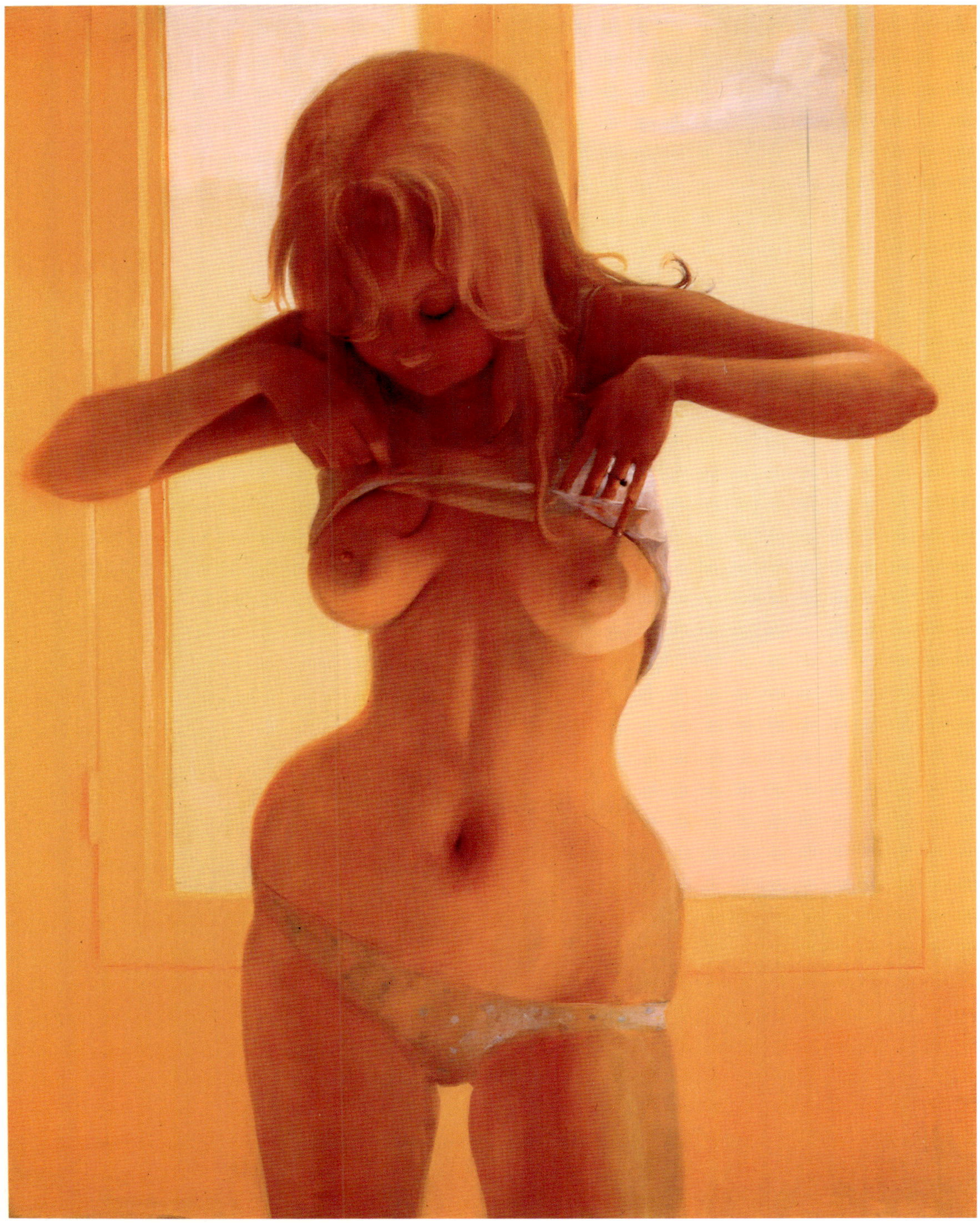

Day, 1999–2000
Oil on linen, 77 x 62 in (195.6 x 157.5 cm)

tiny stitches consciously emulates the drips, spatters, and loops of Jackson Pollock, but by employing a traditional female craft, Amer feminizes the ejaculatory drips and aggressive brush strokes that have given Abstract Expressionism its aura of machismo. The half-hidden images beneath expand the transformation. Borrowed from a variety of sources, they include scenes from porn magazines and from stories like *Snow White* and *Sleeping Beauty* that promote coercive messages about submissive femininity. *Red Strokes on Raw Canvas*, 2004, for instance, presents a set of red gestural marks that float over skeins of tangled lines. Closer inspection reveals these lines to describe barely distinguishable representations of naked women pleasuring themselves. Critics have frequently discussed Amer's works in the context of the Muslim veil, noting the artist's Egyptian heritage. In this light the images masked within these "painted" embroideries can be seen as an expression of resistance to the suppression of women's rights and sexuality under Islamic regimes. However, the artist has argued that such readings are overly narrow. Instead she insists that her subject is a general rejection of worldwide taboos against the expression of female sexual pleasure.

Yuskavage, Brown, and Amer focus on the mixed messages surrounding femininity, desire, and pleasure in contemporary culture. For African American women artists this situation is complicated by the ugly history of slavery and racism, which amounts to a double oppression. For example, the lingering effects of white fantasies about the voracious sexuality of black women, a mythology born when black slaves both threatened and titillated their "civilized" white owners, is a particularly charged subject. Legacies like these have prompted African American women artists to deal with bodies and sexuality differently, as they seek to illuminate what it means to be a black female in a predominately white, patriarchal society.

Kara Walker creates dramatic murals that appear to perpetuate the most offensive slave-era stereotypes of pickaninnies, minstrels, and slap-happy slaves. Female figures in particular are frequently arranged in sexually demeaning, disturbing poses. Walker presents these scenarios as silhouette cutouts that deliberately echo such sources as Victorian portrait silhouettes and Mother Goose illustrations. This format creates a peculiar disconnect between the nasty content of the images and their associatively benign mode of presentation. Walker presents lynchings, beatings, and rapes with disconcerting insouciance. In *Danse de la Nubienne Nouveaux*, 1998, for instance, a young slave girl hurtles toward a cannibal's pot with the exuberance of a circus performer. Other works emphasize sexual stereotypes of the prodigiously equipped African male, or of the African woman with enormous buttocks. Yet instead of horror or outrage, the images exude an oddly childlike fascination with mayhem, anarchy, and scatology. One gets a sense of a world in which all barriers of civilized action have been lifted, leaving behind only the grossest and most degrading animal instincts. As an African American, Walker is free to explore these images in a way that a white artist might not be. In her hands, hateful stereotypes provide fertile ground for considering the ways images become instruments of control.

Walker's work suggests that the African American body is captive to systems of oppression, a subject that also infuses the art of Lorna Simpson. Simpson first became known in the 1980s for works that combine brief texts with deliberately flat and uninflected photographs of black women in shapeless black shifts. These "anti-portraits" depict only their subject's backs and are usually presented as serial images. Accompanying texts are often little more than a phrase or common cliché such as "black as coal" or "pretty as a picture," which deliberately tell us nothing about the woman in the photograph, suggesting the social invisibility of black women in American society. In *Guarded Conditions*, 1989, the repeated image of a black woman seen from the back with her hands clenched behind her is accompanied by alternating texts reading "sex attacks" and "skin attacks," suggesting the double vulnerability of African American women. In later works, Simpson has focused on specific body details that allude to the African American experience. In particular she has presented coolly clinical depictions of arrangements of black hair, a subject that has inspired a surprisingly large amount of academic literature concerning hair as a status symbol in African American identity. In other works, Simpson alludes to the female body by focusing on such objects as high-heeled shoes. Here the emphasis is on the elaborate artifices women embrace in the name of femininity. Occasionally, the body disappears altogether, existing only as a potent absence in mysterious alleyways and street scenes. The body returns in videos such as *Corridor*, 2003, which was filmed on location in a seventeenth-century and a modernist house. This two-channel projection presents narratives focusing on the same young black woman in period and contemporary dress carrying out everyday tasks appropriate to the era of the two houses. Together they suggest that while times have changed, gender conventions have not.

Renee Cox creates works that present the triumphant black female body. Cox is a woman of Jamaican descent who uses her own often naked body in photographic tableaux celebrating female power and eroticism. Taking on the persona of her comic-strip alter ego Raje, she depicts herself as Wonder Woman's Black Amazon sister. In humorous poster-size photographs, Raje does battle with Western stereotypes of African American women. Provocatively dressed in a revealing Jamaican tricolor super-heroine outfit, she has liberated Aunt Jemima and Uncle Ben from their slave-based identities, snarled Times Square traffic to prevent taxis from speeding away from African American customers, and challenged Nazis, the Ku Klux Klan, and other groups implicated in racism against her people. Cox has also created a number of pieces that reexamine traditional artistic and religious themes from a black woman's perspective. *Cousins at Pussy Pond*, 2001, recasts Manet's iconic *Le Déjeuner sur l'herbe*, this time with Cox as the central, nude figure, with her male picnic companions transformed into African tribesmen.

Ellen Gallagher, who is also African American, depicts body parts and the objects associated with them to explore the peculiar "double otherness" of the black female. In the late 1990s she produced a series of apparently abstract paintings that, on close examination, revealed that the lines running horizontally through the canvases were actually strings of cartoonish drawings of bulbous lips and eyes. These partial caricatures reference the minstrel shows of the nineteenth and early twentieth century, which revolved around stereotypes of blacks as lazy, comic buffoons with exaggerated features. More recent works contain collaged imagery drawn from mid-century magazine advertisements directed at African American women that dramatize the demands placed on women, particularly black women, to conform to specific ideals of beauty. Gallagher's monumental *Negro a Day*, 2004–5, for instance, is composed of collages based on ads from *Ebony*, *Our World*, and *Black Digest* from the 1930s through the 1970s. The artist snipped out details, rearranged blocks of texts, and added brightly colored plasticine sculpted in the form of masks or hair.

CECILY BROWN

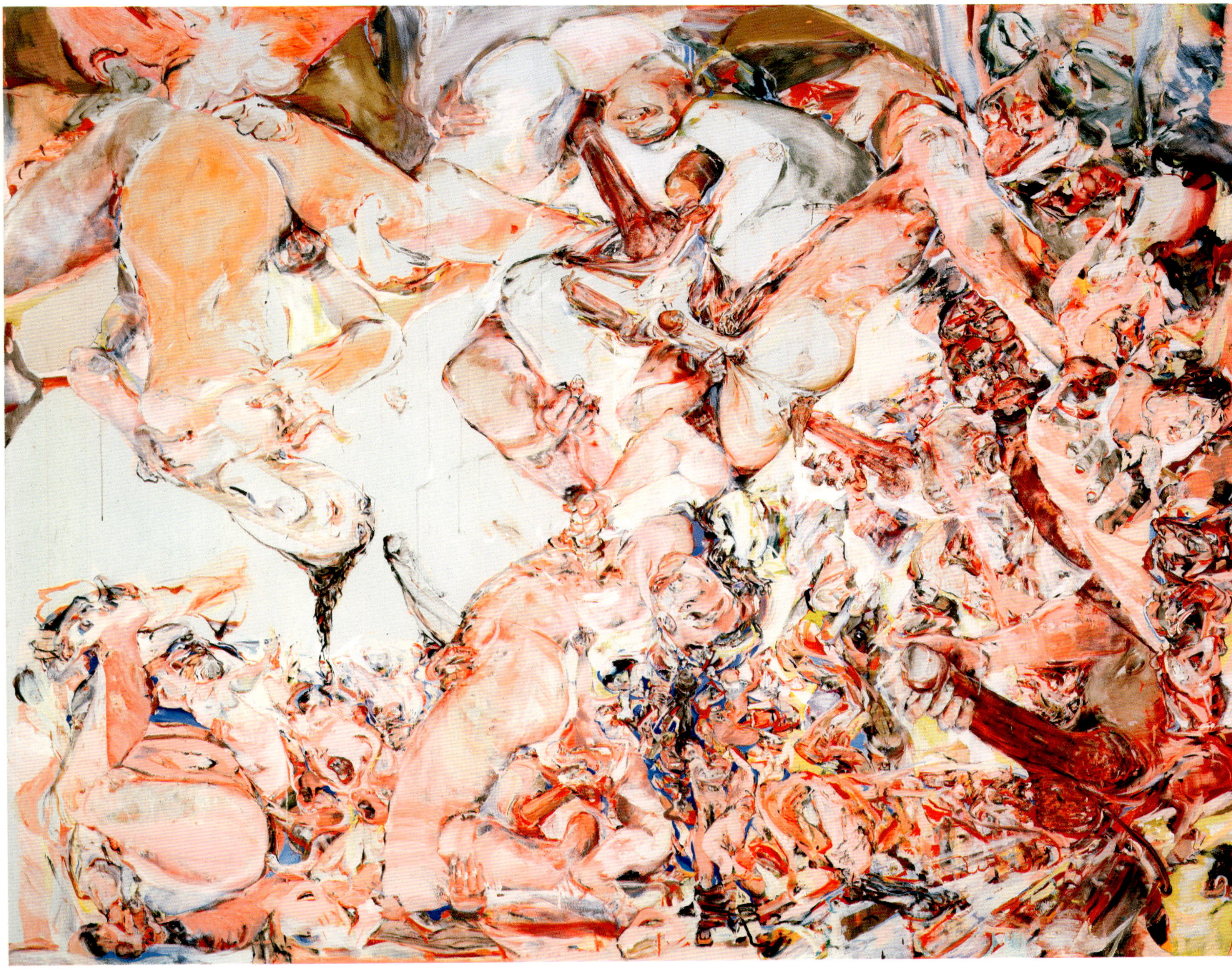

Guys and Dolls, 1997–98
Oil on linen, 76 x 98 in (193 x 248.9 cm)

GHADA AMER

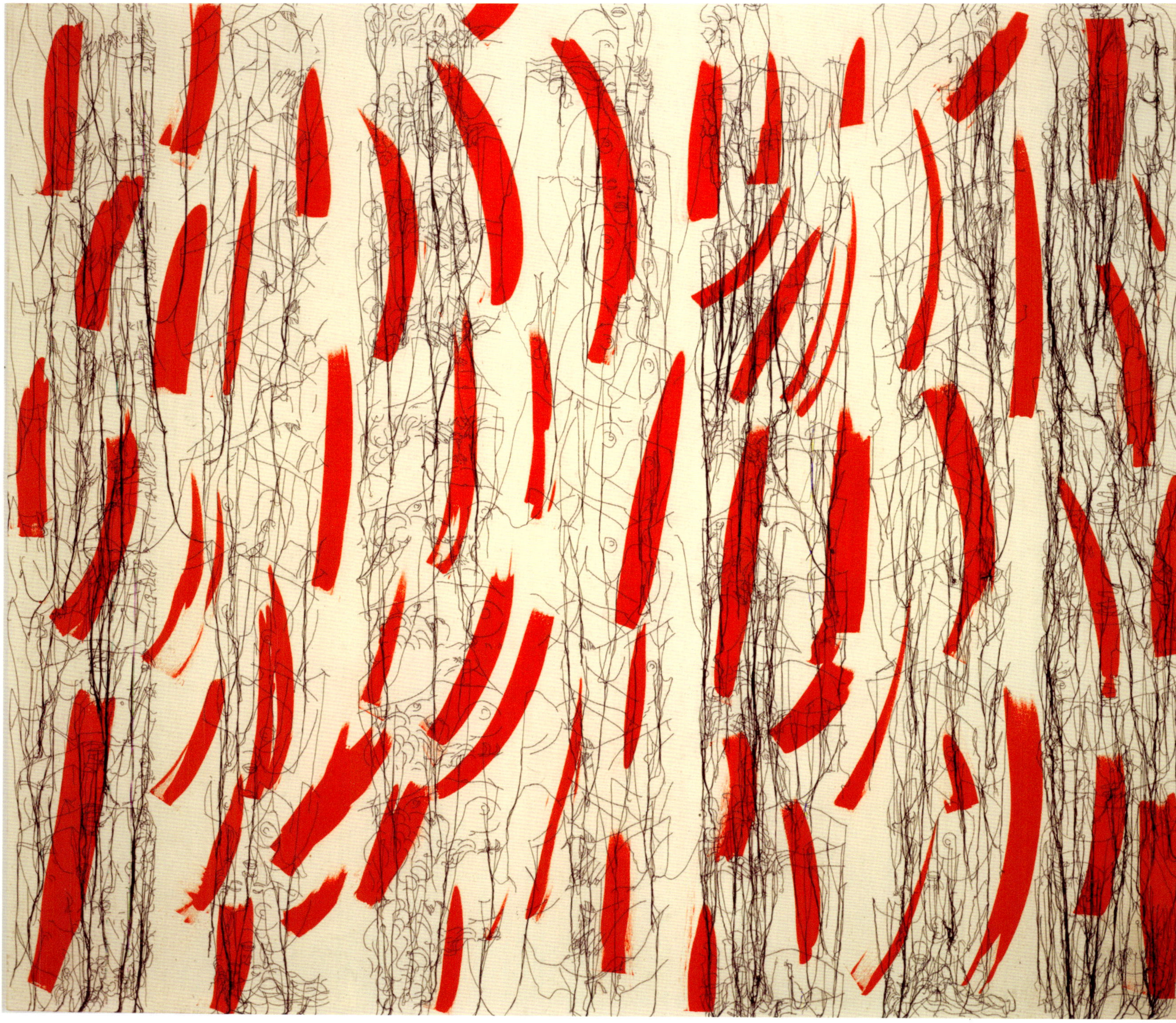

Red Strokes on Raw Canvas, 2004
Acrylic, embroidery, and gel medium on canvas
72 x 84 in (182.9 x 213.4 cm)

KARA WALKER

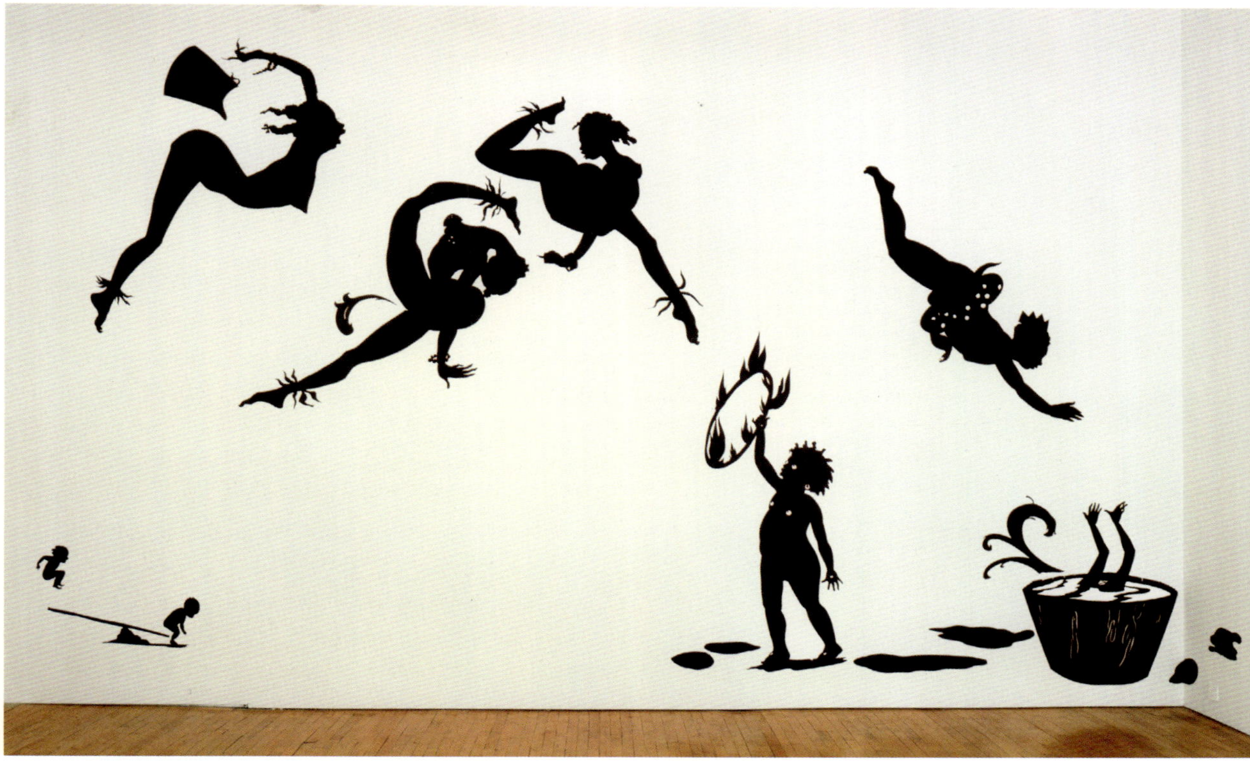

Danse de la Nubienne Nouveaux, 1998
Cut paper and adhesive on wall, 10 x 20 ft (3 x 6.1 m)

LORNA SIMPSON

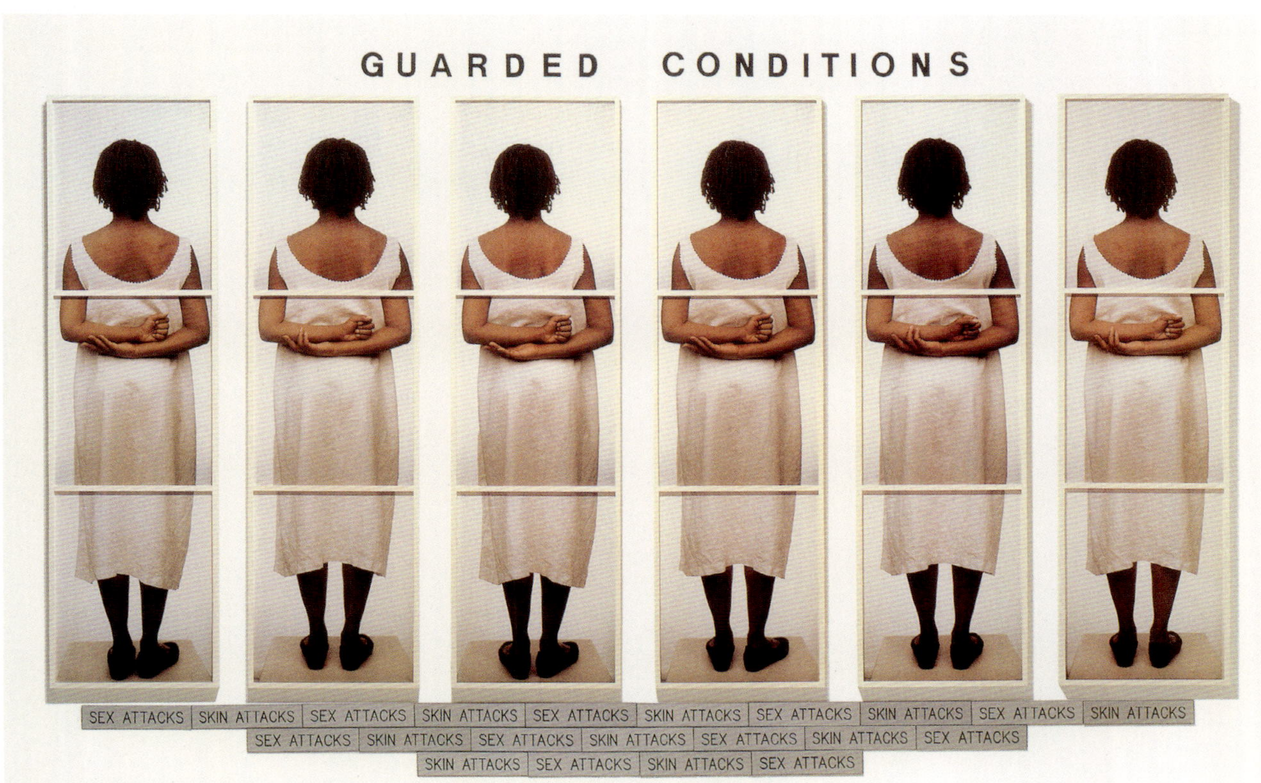

Guarded Conditions, 1989
18 color Polaroids, 21 plastic plaques, plastic letters, 91 x 131 in (231 x 333 cm)

RENEE COX

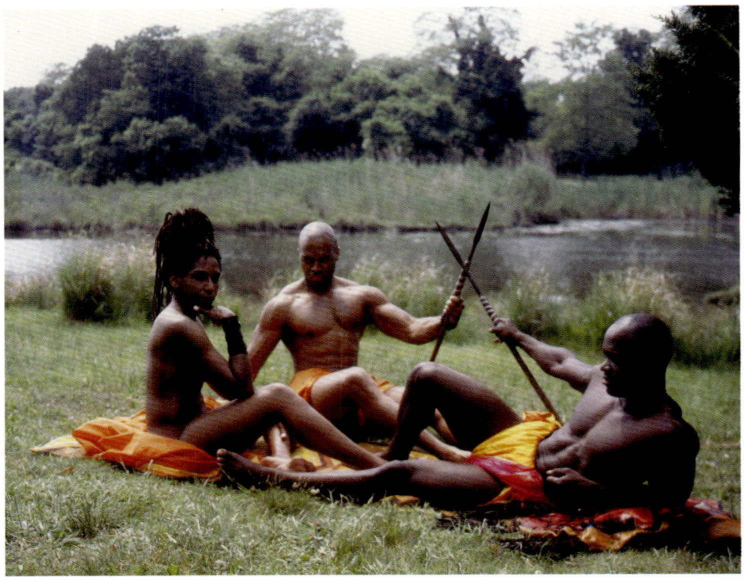

Cousins at Pussy Pond, 2001
Archival digital C-print mounted on aluminum, dimensions variable

ELLEN GALLAGHER

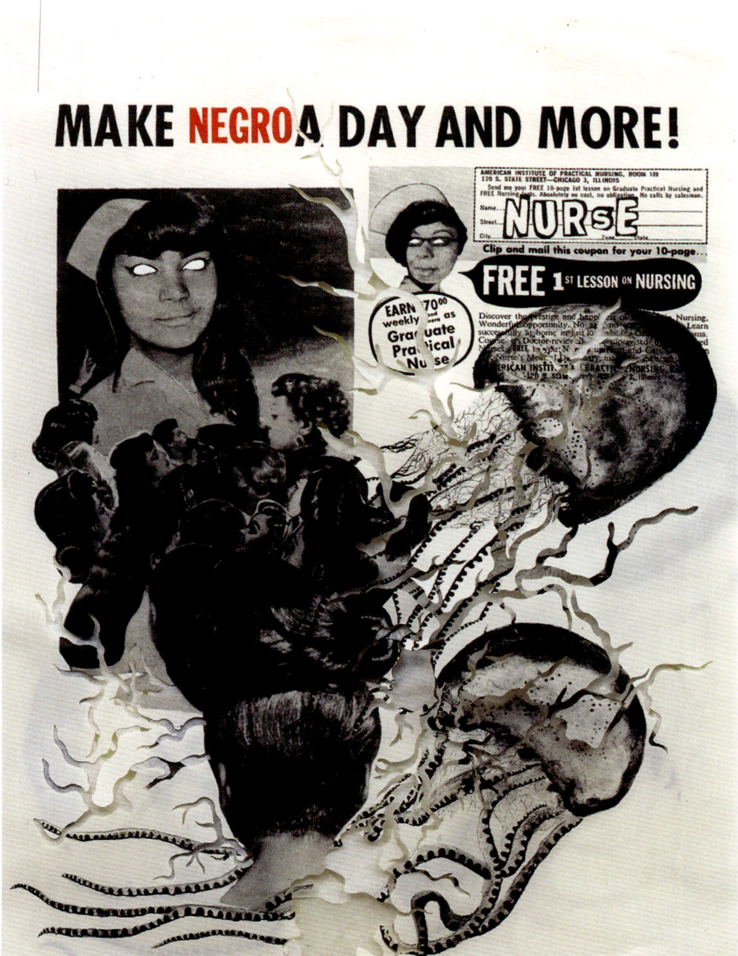

Negro a Day, 2004–5
Photogravure, aquatint, gouache, and laser cutting in four sheets
Edition of twenty, with unique gouache, 13 x 10 in (33 x 25.4 cm)

The results underscore magazine readers' anxieties about dark or bad skin or kinky hair, as revealed by ads for skin whiteners, wigs, and hair straighteners. Gallagher also calls attention to the marketing language attached to these products, including references to synthetic fibers such as afrilon and afrylic, and wigs with names like Nu-Nile, Kongolene, and Freedom Puff. Her alterations of these raw materials accentuate the African American woman's sense of otherness, turning black wig models, entertainers, and characters into newly minted androids, aliens, and chimeras existing somewhere between fact and fantasy.

Marlene Dumas, a white native of South Africa who witnessed the apartheid era firsthand, creates gestural, distorted figurative paintings rendered in thin layers of sepia-toned paint that bleed into each other or seep across the canvas like stains. This stylistic device gives the images a sense of urgency, but there is also a generalized quality about them, derived from their sources in photographs taken by the artist, or culled from newspapers, magazines, and film archives. Like Walker and Cox, Dumas flirts with social taboos. One of her series is based on photographs of strippers and prostitutes in the act of plying their trade. Other works present mixed-race and possibly same-sex couples in the throes of sexual intercourse—a particularly incendiary subject in apartheid South Africa. Others deal with childbirth or death—the two poles of human life whose physical manifestations tend to be swept from public view. Even Dumas's depictions of children are unsettling. Her small boys and girls are hollow-eyed and merciless looking, a reminder that even children growing up in a racist regime are not innocent of its effects. A 1993 painting titled *Over Lyken Lopen*, which means "over dead bodies," presents a naked five-year-old girl straddling the body of a man, staring warily at the viewer, and hiding an arm behind her back. An odd combination of vulnerability and aggression radiates from her, along with a sexual power that should not be hers for some time to come.

Taken together, Dumas's paintings suggest that the body is inevitably enmeshed with political and social realities. At times a battleground in the struggle between the individual and society, the body can also serve as a site for self-testing and self-discovery. As an art material that requires no special expense or expertise, it is remarkably democratic, available to artists in even the most remote and economically deprived areas. As a subject, it remains fertile and accessible. In the end, body art is extraordinarily effective in reflecting our common humanity.

MARLENE DUMAS

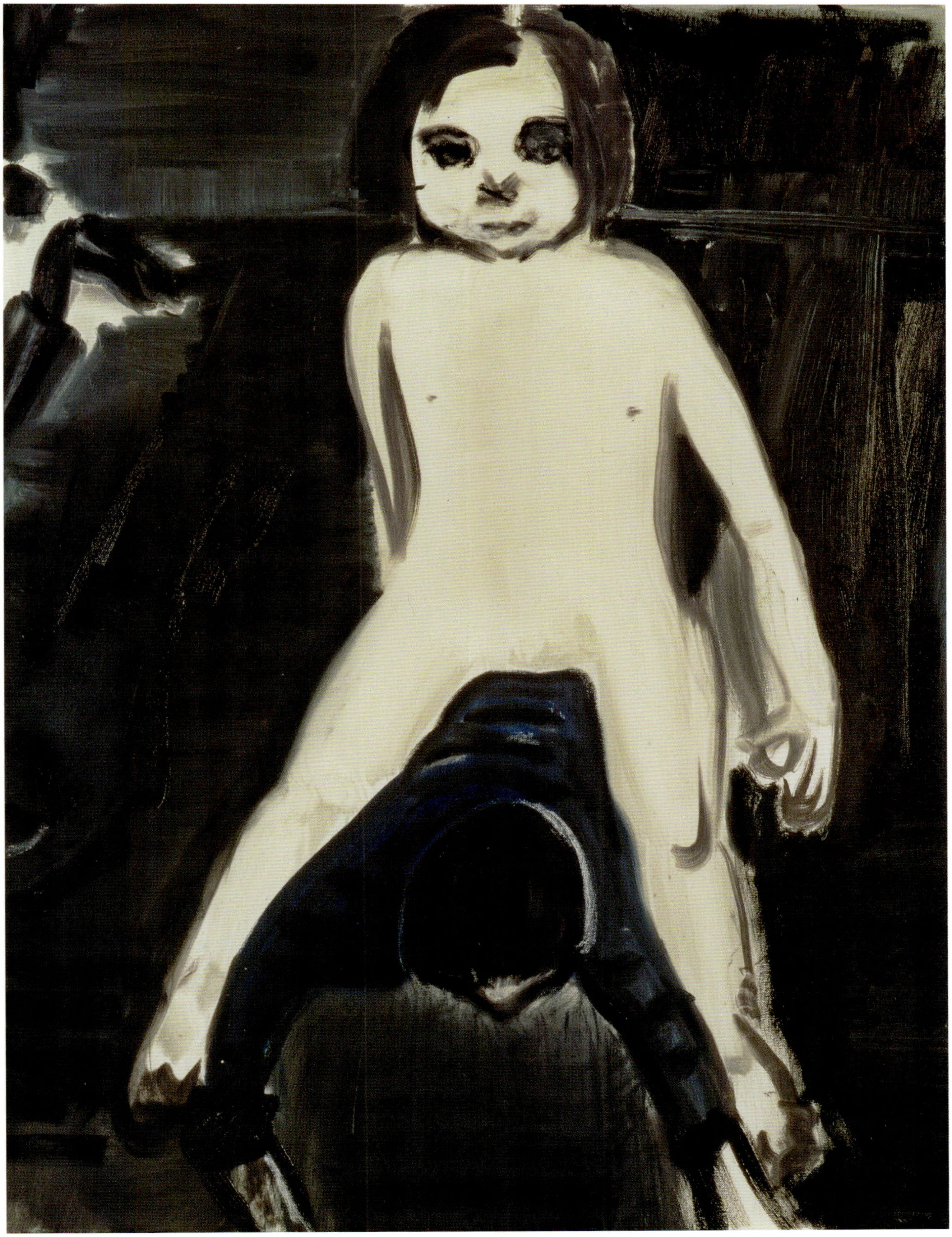

Over Lyken Lopen, 1993
Oil on canvas, 35 1/2 x 27 1/2 in (90 x 70 cm)

ART & IDENTITY

THE RISE OF THE HYBRID SELF

In the wake of the heated 1988 American presidential campaign season, a sculpture appeared in a parking lot kitty-corner from the National Portrait Gallery in Washington, D.C. It was a billboard-size metal cutout painted with an image of the Reverend Jesse Jackson, who had lost his bid for the Democratic nomination to Michael Dukakis. Though still quite recognizable, Jackson's visage had undergone significant alterations. The famous African American preacher and politician was portrayed as a white-skinned, blue-eyed blond. Painted like graffiti across the sculpture were the words "How Ya Like Me Now?" This work was part of an exhibition for the Washington Project for the Arts, a small alternative arts organization, but its role in that show was short lived: before the installers could complete their work, a group of African American men knocked the piece down with a sledgehammer and proceeded to pummel it (it later took on another life, displayed indoors surrounded by sledgehammers and an American flag). It quickly became apparent that the vandals read the work as a piece of blatant racism denigrating the first black man to run for President. In fact, the author of the work, David Hammons, himself African American, stated in interviews that his intention was to expose the racism of the white establishment and thumb his nose at the all-white subjects commemorated nearby in the National Portrait Gallery. Thus, in unexpected ways, this work raised intriguing issues about the relationship between identity and art. Specifically, it graphically demonstrated the inadequacy of modernist assumptions about the universality of art and the irrelevance of particulars like the artist's—or the spectator's—race, sex, and ethnicity. Indeed, in the case of *How Ya Like Me Now?* the artist's race was crucial to any interpretation of the work, and the work's meaning was dependent on the social and political context in which it was created.

At the time, this was no small revelation. During the 1980s, as debates around "political correctness," "multiculturalism," and "identity politics" roiled the art world, guardians of the old-fashioned notion of "quality" (including critics Hilton Kramer and Robert Hughes) argued that nothing less than the integrity of art was under attack. Attempting to shield high culture from the polluting force of politics, they asserted that artistic judgment, unclouded by prejudice or ignorance, reflects an indisputable consensus. Thus, art that proclaimed its allegiance to specific political or social positions, or that was designed to appeal to specific audiences, was by definition inferior. The adversaries of these latter-day modernists, the multiculturalists, countered that such arguments for a shared canon of masterpieces were simply tools of oppression, meant to confine artistic production to a small circle of white European or American males. What the "quality" faction pointed to as universal standards of taste, multiculturalists like Lucy Lippard, Maurice Berger, and bell hooks saw as a mass of prejudices exclusive to a narrow-minded elite. Denouncing "Eurocentricism," they demanded that the art world open itself to artists from groups and backgrounds that had previously been swept to the margins.

Today it is clear that the multiculturalists have won. By any calculation—be it the roster of artists in international biennials, the makeup of art gallery stables, the artists whose work is sold at auction and collected by museums and individuals—race, ethnicity, gender, and sexuality barriers have been breached, if not completely overthrown. This new diversity has many origins, among them heightened tolerance and understanding (not to mention that only a thick-skinned curator would mount an exhibition consisting only of white European or American males). Nonetheless, a strange thing happened on the way to a multicultural art world. The notion of "identity art" came under attack even within diverse factions of the art world. Viewing it as an oversimplification that reduced artists to a biographical fact—their skin color, ethnicity, gender, or sexual preference—theorists began to posit the idea that identity, no less than the discredited idea of universal taste, was a social construct. They found support for this idea in postmodern theory, which holds that the self has no stable core, but is rather an illusion cobbled together from our internalized motley collection of media images, social messages, and manipulated desires. This illusion does not hold: it ultimately produces a sense of incoherence amid the ceaseless movement of people, goods, and electronic messages across geographic and psychic borders that prompted its formation in the first place.

Thus today we find ourselves in a double bind, both obsessed with identity and haunted by the fear that it doesn't really exist. Take, for instance, the issue of race. In a forum organized in 1985 for the publication *Critical Inquiry*, Henry Louis Gates, Jr., Chair of Harvard's Afro-American Studies Department, posed the question "Does Race Exist?"[1] Somewhat surprisingly, considering how frequently the term is bandied about, he argued that it does not. Gates pointed out that there is no basis in science for absolute distinctions on the basis of race. Instead, he suggested, "racial" categories are arbitrarily applied to distinguish groups that may have wildly different cultures, belief systems, and economic interests. Once institutionalized, this categorization then becomes a construct—and the basis for differential treatment. Similar theories have arisen around gender identity, though of course gender has a firmer basis in biology than does race. Nonetheless, its social and political status has been equally contentious, and the rise of feminist consciousness parallels the rise of the civil rights movement, not to mention many other fights for equality: each follows a pattern of embrace, rejection, and finally a more nuanced understanding of identity association. These phases, which may overlap and recur from one movement and one individual to the next, are also reflected in art that emphasizes identity, either by celebrating, questioning, or recognizing it as something that is ultimately and always hybrid.

In the art world, the embracing phase was born with the feminist art movement, which began in the late 1960s as feminist scholars began to question long-held assumptions about genius, greatness, and maleness in art. In a highly influential essay published in 1971, art historian Linda Nochlin asked: "Why have there been no great women artists?"[2] She answered the question by refusing to take her own bait, instead arguing that the paucity of women in the "canon" could be traced to institutional, educational, and economic barriers rather than innate inferiority. This argument opened the door to a whole range of feminist approaches to art history and art-making. Feminist scholars unearthed unknown women artists, recounted the obstacles to their success, and questioned the way the game was played. Meanwhile, feminist artists refused to play the old game, rejecting the "gender-neutral" ideal of modernist abstraction to instead explore aspects of women's personal experience thus far declared off limits to serious art. Some, such as Joyce Kozloff, based their paintings on the decorative patterns of non-Western cultures. Others, such as Faith Ringgold, incorporated craft traditions like quilting into work that addressed her own history and that of her African American ancestors. Miriam Schapiro invented a format she called *femmage*, collage paintings using lace, aprons, embroidered handkerchiefs, and other "feminine"

DAVID HAMMONS

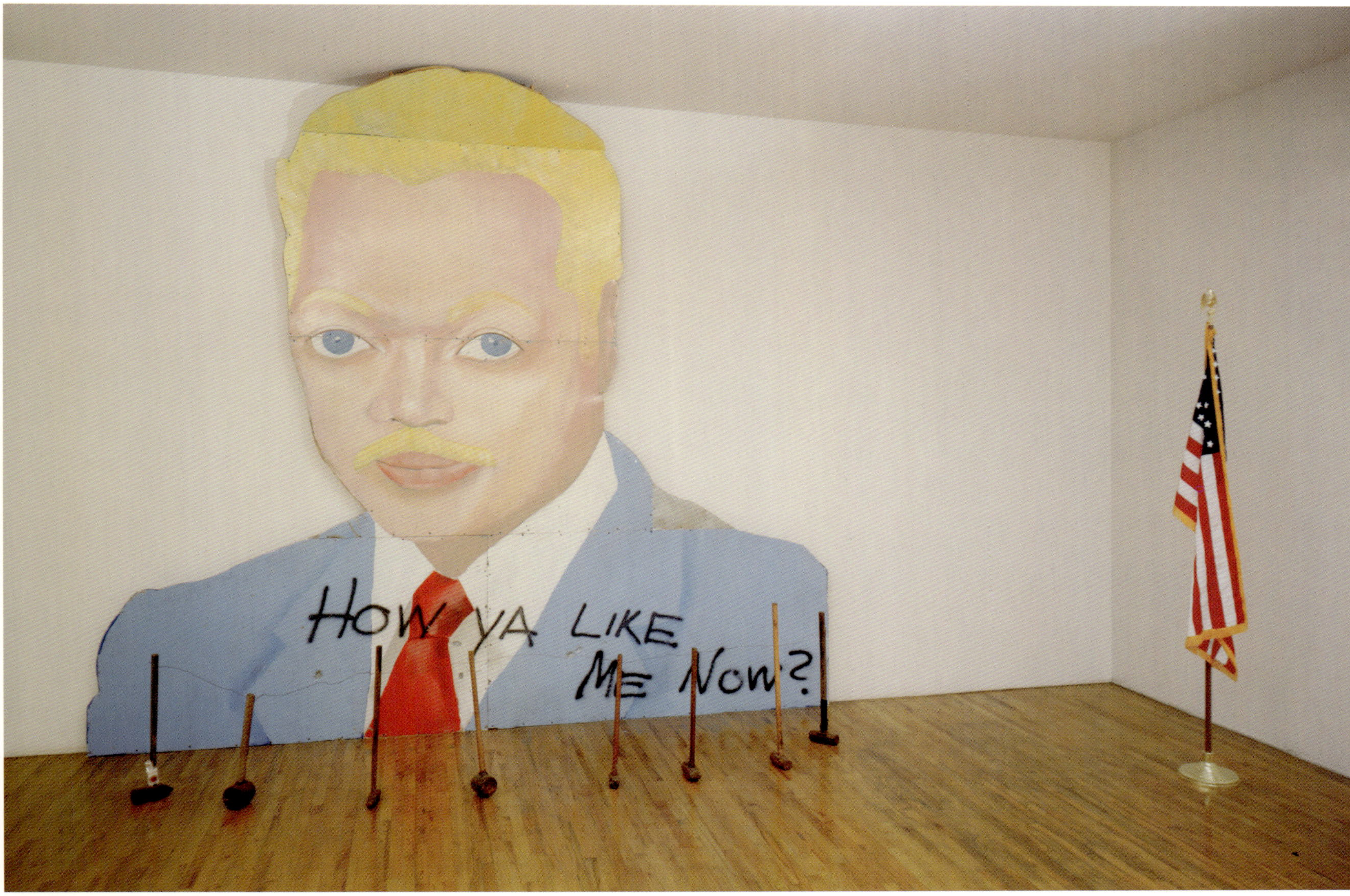

How Ya Like Me now?, 1988
Tin, plywood, sledgehammers, paint, and American flag, 12 x 18 ft (3.7 x 5.5 m)

KERRY JAMES MARSHALL

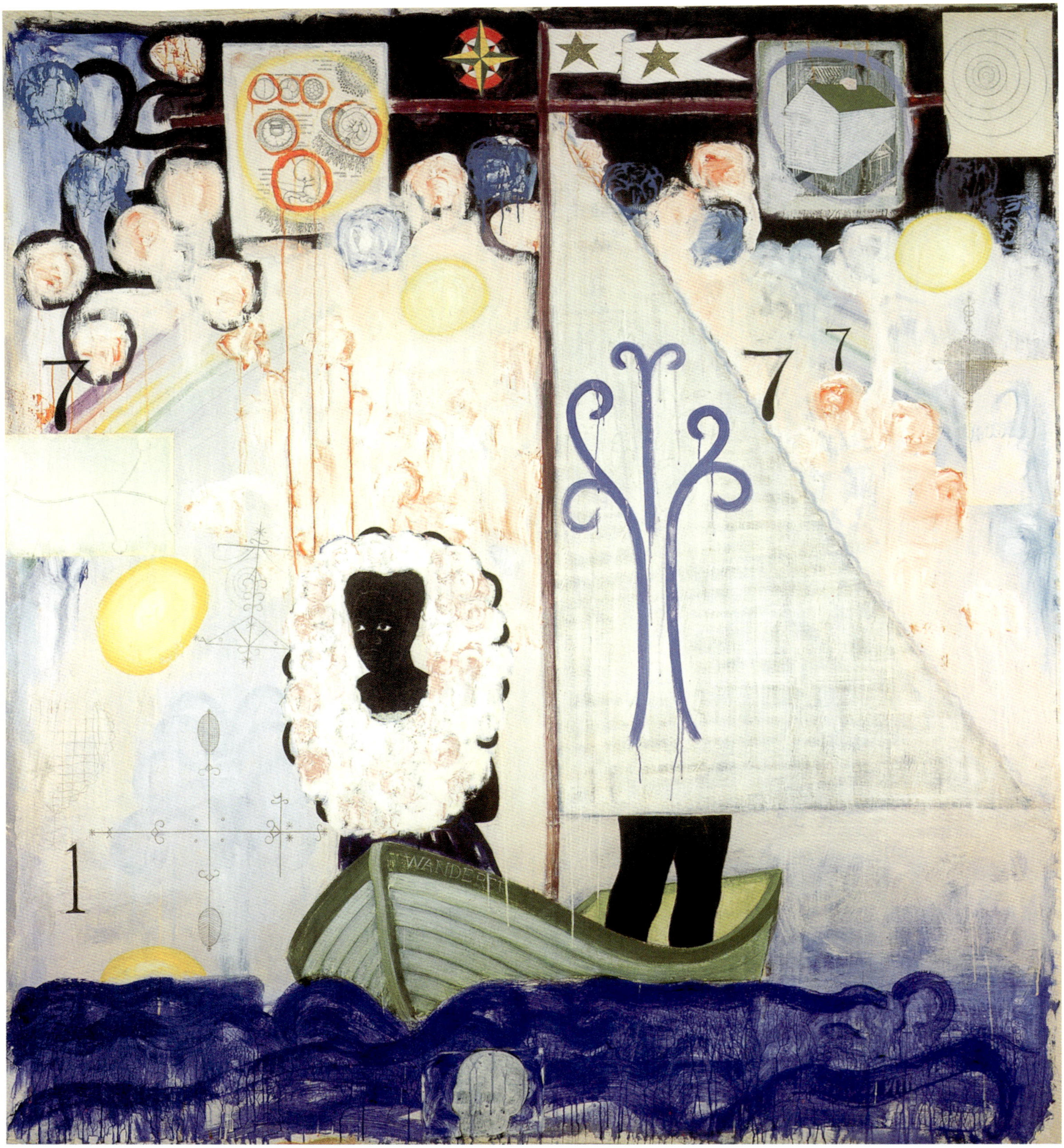

Voyager, 1992
Acrylic and collage on canvas, 85 x 85 in (215.9 x 215.9 cm)

materials. Meanwhile, feminist critic Lucy Lippard and others began to catalogue what might be called intrinsically female imagery—seeing the explosion of autobiography, for instance, as a sign of women artists liberating themselves from male standards of objectivity.[3]

Judy Chicago's *Dinner Party*, 1974–79, a watershed work of the feminist art movement, is a monumental installation consisting of a triangular table set with thirty-nine ceramic plates and embroidered runners that celebrate great women of myth and history—from a figure dubbed "Primordial Goddess" through the Greek poet Sappho, medieval writer Hildegard of Bingen, Queen Elizabeth I, and suffragette Susan B. Anthony up to more recent figures like Virginia Woolf and Georgia O'Keeffe. Inscribed on the tile floor under the table are the names of 999 other venerable women. While paying homage to undersung female contributions to history, *The Dinner Party* is also a celebration of crafts associated with women, and it honors the female body and sexuality: each of the plates, tailored to its particular guest, has a vaginal form, which becomes more dimensional and explicit as one moves forward in history around the table. Despite its controversial genital imagery and its reputedly "essentialist," or biologically determinist, approach to feminism, *The Dinner Party* remains an icon of feminist art, dazzling for its ambition and audacity. Further, it catalyzed the introduction of other identity issues, such as ethnicity and sexual orientation, into art and art discourse. For the first time, significant numbers of African American artists began to be recognized as important mainstream artists, gay theorists applied the lessons of feminist art to exploring a "queer" sensibility, and multiculturalism introduced artists from "minority" backgrounds to larger audiences.[4] These changes were not just a matter of increasing the numbers of previously excluded groups: they revolutionized the way in which art was interpreted, judged, and valued. In particular, artists began to reexamine how history is written and how it might be rewritten to include the experiences and contributions of marginalized groups.

JUDY CHICAGO

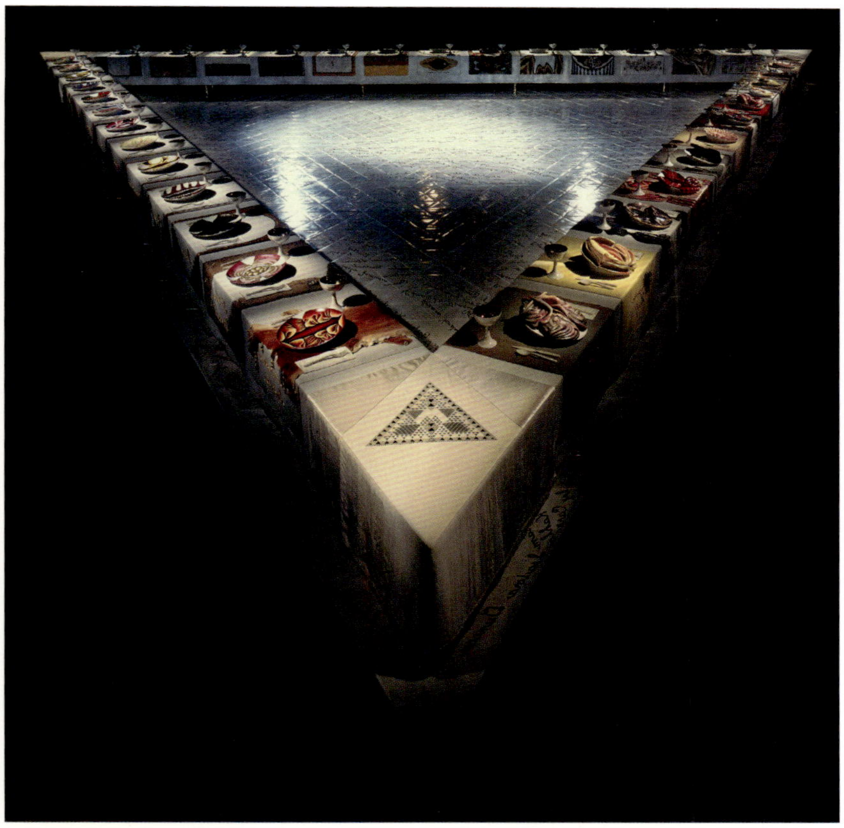

The Dinner Party, 1974–79
Mixed media, ceramic, porcelain, and textile, 48 x 42 x 3 ft (14.6 x 12.8 x .9 m)
Brooklyn Museum, New York

Kerry James Marshall uses the conventions of history painting to unearth and dramatize the hidden history and present realities of African American life. His monumental figurative paintings are often set in domestic interiors that suggest the homes of poor and working-class African Americans, sometimes in specific places such as the South Side of Chicago. Texts, diagrams, and paraphrases of folk art—representations of blue birds, garlands of flowers, and the like—deliberately contradict the squalor of the settings. The series "Lost Boys," 1993, consists of stylized, folk art-style portraits of young incarcerated black men. The title is a rueful play on the willfully escapist boys of J. M. Barrie's *Peter Pan*. Some paintings pay homage to the leaders, heroes, and victims of the civil rights movement, with African American angels standing sentinel in contemporary living rooms, mourning the fallen. Yet other paintings present allegories of African and African American history. *Voyager*, 1992, for instance, depicts a couple in a small boat surrounded by a complex network of symbols that refer to the cycles of life and death. The dominant image of the ship is double-edged—on one hand, it presents a powerful symbol of migration and spiritual search, but for the African man and woman on its deck, it also suggests the journey into slavery. (Indeed, Marshall modeled his ship after the luxury schooner *Wanderer*, which was outfitted to transfer slaves to Georgia in 1848, a few years before the outbreak of the Civil War.) That the woman sits, equipped with a flotation life-ring of sorts, while the standing man is hidden behind the triangle of the sail, gives the work a distinctly poignant tone, as if his identity were disappearing into his future life as a slave.

Pepón Osorio also seeks to illuminate the experiences of marginalized groups, specifically Puerto Ricans in America. His installations are characterized by an overload of kitsch—plastic toys, Puerto Rican flags, and tourist and religious tchotchkes—that immerse us in narratives about the social realities of life in Latino communities. *Badge of Honor*, 1995, is presented in a pair of adjacent rooms, one a Latin teenager's bedroom, the other a prison cell. On videos installed in each room we see a father in prison talking to his son. As the dialogue unfolds, the viewer becomes aware of the son's resentment of his father's absence, as well as the father's guilt and desire to impart useful advice. The complexity of their relationship is revealed and it is no surprise to learn that these characters are in fact, not actors, but real people in real-life situations. Osorio further melds fact and fiction in *Face to Face*, 2004, which he made after a three-year volunteer residency at Philadelphia's Department of Human Services. This work reconstructs the department's actual offices, complete with desks, computer terminals, and piles of paper work, and includes a video of one actual client, a mother narrating the harrowing story of her suicidal son. Such works reveal the way in which racism, poverty, and social and personal dysfunction combine to define and limit the lives of those outside the "mainstream" culture.

Shirin Neshat, an Iranian photographer and video artist who left her native country just before the 1979 revolution, gives voice to women silenced by Iran's Islamic fundamentalist society. In video installations such as *Turbulent*, 1998, and *Rapture*, 1999, she places the viewer in the crossfire between two screens on opposite sides of the room. One presents the private, highly secluded world of veiled women while the other offers a glimpse of the boisterous public world of men. By separating men and women in this way, Neshat allows the viewer to see what no Iranian ever can—simultaneous views of these two carefully segregated worlds. At times the figures on the two screens seem to be responding to each other, as in *Turbulent* when a popular male singer, belting out a love song to a noisy crowd of men in western dress, is watched silently from the opposite wall by a woman in a black chador. When he finishes his performance, he turns and watches her as she sings a guttural wordless lament to an empty room. Similarly, in *Rapture* men and women pursue a pair of very different activities on opposite sides of the room. The men move frenetically around a fortress on the sea, performing various rituals, while the women, filing slowly across the sand, launch a boat that will take some of them into an indefinite future. Most recently, Neshat has been creating a more conventional feature-length narrative film based on the novel *Women Without Men* by the Iranian novelist Shahrnush Parsipur. The film, like the book, follows five Iranian women from different classes during the U.S.-assisted coup d'état that replaced Iran's first democratically elected government with the Shah. While each woman's story touches on this political upheaval, each also deals with human dilemmas, like fertility and madness, to which we can all relate to some extent.

It's not surprising that many artists who represent marginalized identities tell stories to bring these identities to life, but some artists eschew narrative and instead explore identity by appropriating and manipulating materials associated with specific cultures. Chris Ofili, a British-born artist of Nigerian heritage, examines the intermingling of Western and African influences in contemporary pop culture by combining references to hip-hop, soul, and rap, "blaxploitation" movies of the 1970s, Britain's history of racism, and African modes of decoration to create dazzling, glitter-encrusted, Op Art–inspired paintings. Among Ofili's recurring motifs are portraits of real and imaginary people, patterns of colored dots inspired by ancient cave paintings in Zimbabwe, and balls of elephant dung studded with rhinestones or map pins, which often serve as bases for the paintings, like the ball-and-claw feet on old furniture. Such dung was responsible for a famous controversy around Ofili's *Holy Virgin Mary*, 1996 (see chapter 11), whose display Mayor Giuliani of New York protested, calling it a sign of disrespect to the iconic figure of the Catholic religion. (In fact the dung was not intended as a symbol of defilement; it serves as a fuel and building material in Africa.) Ofili's other subjects have included real-life heroes of black culture such as Miles Davis, James Brown, and Cassius Clay, an invented superhero named Captain Shit, who sports an Afro hairdo and outrageous 1970s-style funk suits in *The Adoration of Captain Shit and the Legend of the Blackstars*, 1998, and Doreen Lawrence, mother of a young black man murdered by a gang of white youths in London in 1993. Thus Ofili celebrates both African and African diasporic identity. And even when he targets the darker undercurrents of racism and exploitation, all the seductions of these works are inescapable.

David Hammons also frequently uses found or recovered objects associated with the reality and the clichés of "blackness" in his work. He has created sculptures out of cotton plants, gold chains, black hair, cheap whisky bottles, and basketballs. In *Flying Carpet*, 1990, he used fish hooks to attach fried chicken wings to a Persian carpet. But Hammons has also created works that have no obvious link to his racial identity, some of which assault the authority and commercialism of the art world. In 1983 he famously sold snowballs on a street corner in Harlem. In 2002, for a piece titled *Concerto in Black and Blue*, he "installed" a show in a cavernous warehouse space by turning off the lights and providing visitors with tiny blue flashlights with which to make their way through an otherwise dark and empty gallery. Periodically Hammons takes a hiatus from the art world altogether, professing a greater interest in the action of "the street." Such gestures suggest that Hammons is interested less in fitting into the art world's preexisting structure than in challenging and changing it. His unwillingness to be pigeonholed as an African American artist points to the great drawback of identity-based art. With the assertion of identity comes the risk of being ghettoized.

In the world of theory, this contradiction has been staged as a standoff between the "essentialists," who seek a stable definition of identity, and the "deconstructionists," who regard identity as a social construct that can be manipulated for political and social ends. By the mid-1990s the indiscriminate embrace of "identity art" by curators and critics (and, to a much lesser degree, collectors) had created a backlash. It was derided (unfairly, some thought) as "victim art," which gained its impact and notoriety solely from its makers' complaints against society. Commentators argued that "difference" and "otherness" had become commodities in themselves, fetishized by curators and critics for their own professional ends. Even worse, critics of a deconstructive bent began to dissect these concepts to unearth their hidden biases. "Otherness," they pointed out, created a false binary. It could exist only in relationship to something that is assumed to be somehow more complete, stable, and "authentic." Similarly, "difference" implies difference from something—it can't exist in itself. Thus, critics argued, these concepts actually reinforce the hierarchies they claim to undermine. To be "other" is to be considered less than the male or less

PEPÓN OSORIO

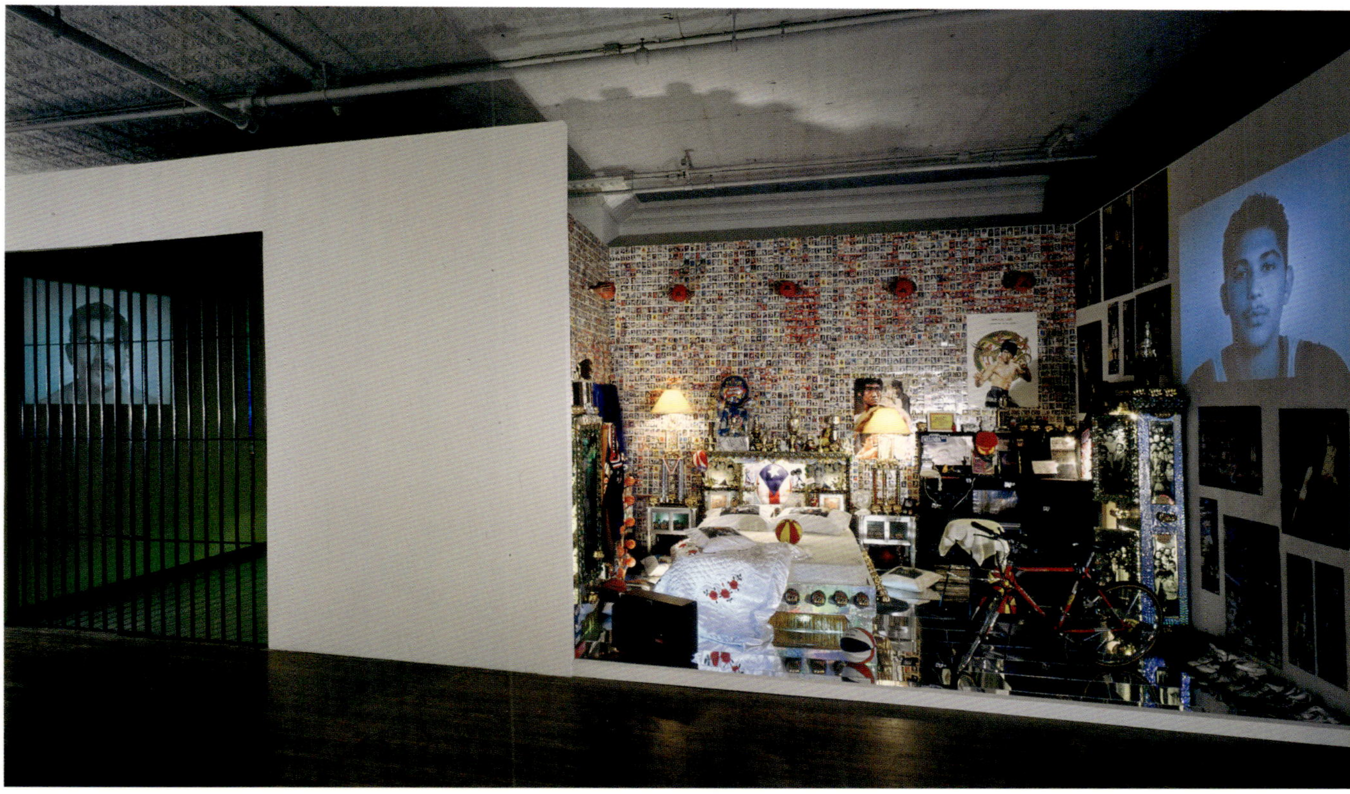

Badge of Honor, 1995
Mixed media and video installation, 12 ft x 26 ft 10 in x 12 ft (3.7 x 8.2 x 3.7 m)
As installed at Ronald Feldman Fine Arts, New York, April–June 1996

SHIRIN NESHAT

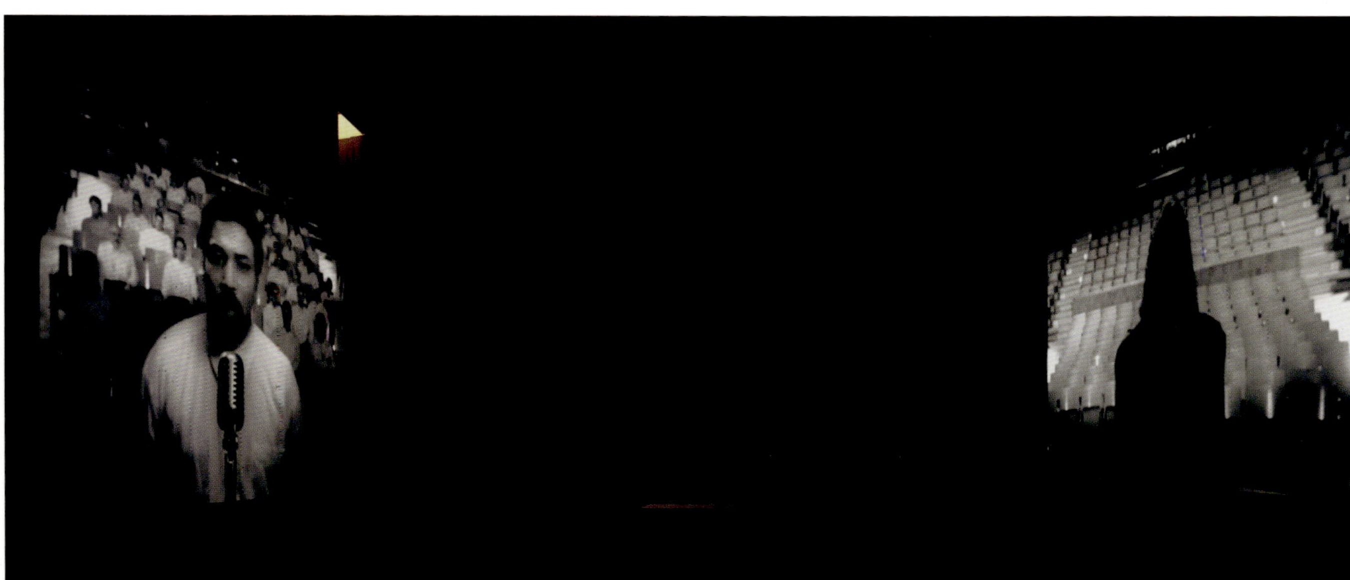

Turbulent, 1998
Video and sound installation, two simultaneous projections, black and white, 10 minutes, projected image 9 x 12 ft (2.7 x 3.7 m)
As installed at MUSAC (Museo de Arte Contemporáneo de Castilla y León), Spain, September–December 2005

CHRIS OFILI

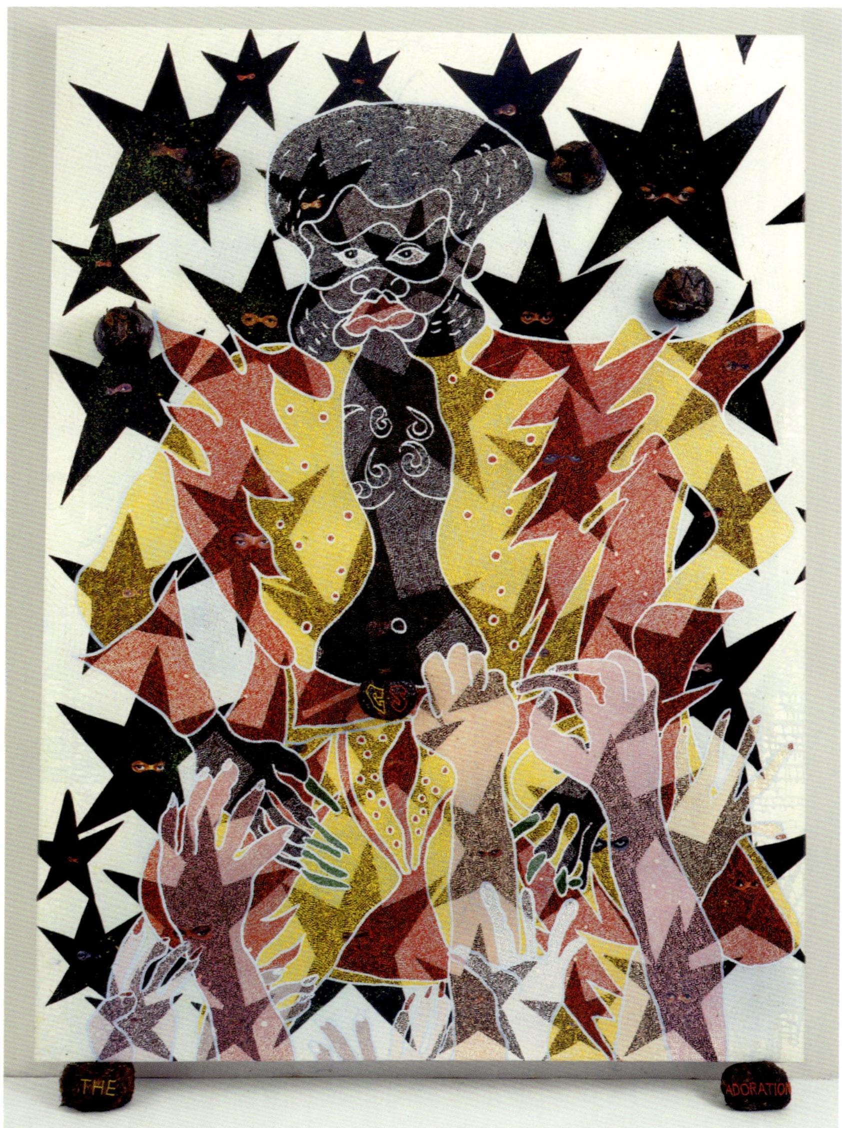

The Adoration of Captain Shit and the Legend of the Blackstars, 1998
Acrylic, oil, resin, paper collage, glitter, map pins, and elephant dung on canvas
96 x 72 in (243.8 x 182.8 cm)

than the individual of white European heritage, to be no more than a sideshow in the grand narrative of world history.

Among the few critics to find a middle ground in this debate is Trinh T. Minh-ha, who has recommended that the false dualism of majority and minority be replaced by a more fluid vision of identity. In her words, there is "A Third World in every First World/A First World in every Third World/And vice versa." Elaborating on this serpentine logic, she writes, "otherness and sameness are more useful when they are viewed not in terms of dualities or conflicts but in terms of degrees and movements within the same concept, or better, in terms of differences both within and between entities."[5] In other words, the false superiority and universality of mainstream culture is best attacked by positing the instability of all identity, revealing that whiteness, masculinity, and European heritage are no more and no less problematic than any other "marginal" identity. As a result, the key issue then turns out to be not identity itself, but how identities are represented.

This argument that all areas are gray is the crux of Adrian Piper's critique of the notion of race. An artist and a professional philosopher, Piper is of one-sixteenth African ancestry, and though she appears to be "white," she identifies herself as African American. In her work, which includes performance, installation, video, collage and philosophic argument, Piper uses her own experience as one who easily passes for white to question the validity of race as a fixed category and to undermine racial stereotypes. In the video installation *Cornered*, 1988, she relentlessly lectures her viewer to expose the prejudices that maintain the fiction of black and white. Dressed as a television newscaster reporting the news across the barricade of an upturned table, she asserts her blackness, despite her visual whiteness, and attacks a stereotypical viewer's presumed assumptions about his or her own potential "whiteness" and "blackness." With such works Piper suggests how race has become encoded in the American experience, and how "blackness" and "whiteness" are arbitrary categories that have little to do with visual discrimination and everything to do with learned biases.

The feminist version of the critique of identity has similarly taken aim at stereotypes of masculinity and femininity, seeking to undermine these categories' "naturalness" by discovering their origins in culture or psychology. Barbara Kruger, whose graphic, poster-like works juxtaposing pithy texts and grainy photographic images were everywhere in the 1980s (see chapter 9), designed her messages to subvert media conventions about gender, consumption, and power. Her texts assumed the authoritative tone of advertising, but Kruger subtly manipulated the "voice," reversing the expected order, in which a dominant male speaks to a submissive female, so that the woman addressed the men about the conditions of her inequality. The attitudes suggested by the texts ranged from submission to defiance, as in "We have been ordered not to move," or "We won't play nature to your culture." Many of these graphic compositions ended up on consumer products such as T-shirts, shopping bags, and matchbooks, traveling full circle back into the world from which they had sprung. Perhaps her best-known work, which has been reproduced on shopping bags, suggests a helpless acquiescence to the demands of commodity capitalism, declaring, "I shop therefore I am." In the late '90s, Kruger began to present large-scale installations, in which sound and images overwhelm the viewer with ranting public messages. She has also created room-scale video installations like *Twelve*, 2004, in which actors speaking her dialogue play out dismal power games in

DAVID HAMMONS

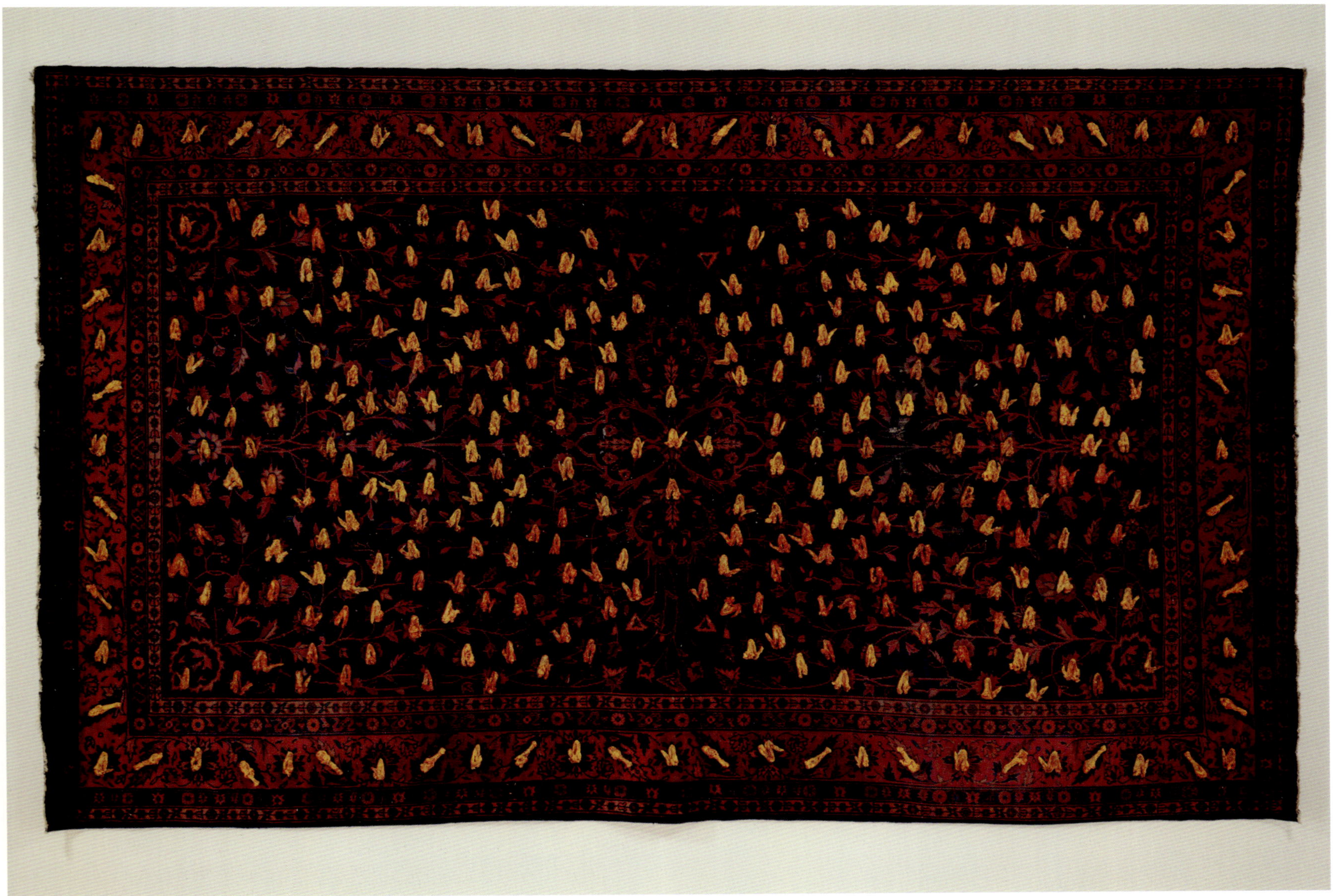

Flying Carpet, 1990
Persian rug, wire, and fried chicken
9 ft 5 in x 15 ft 5 in x 4 in (2.9 m x 4.7 m x 10.2 cm)

ADRIAN PIPER

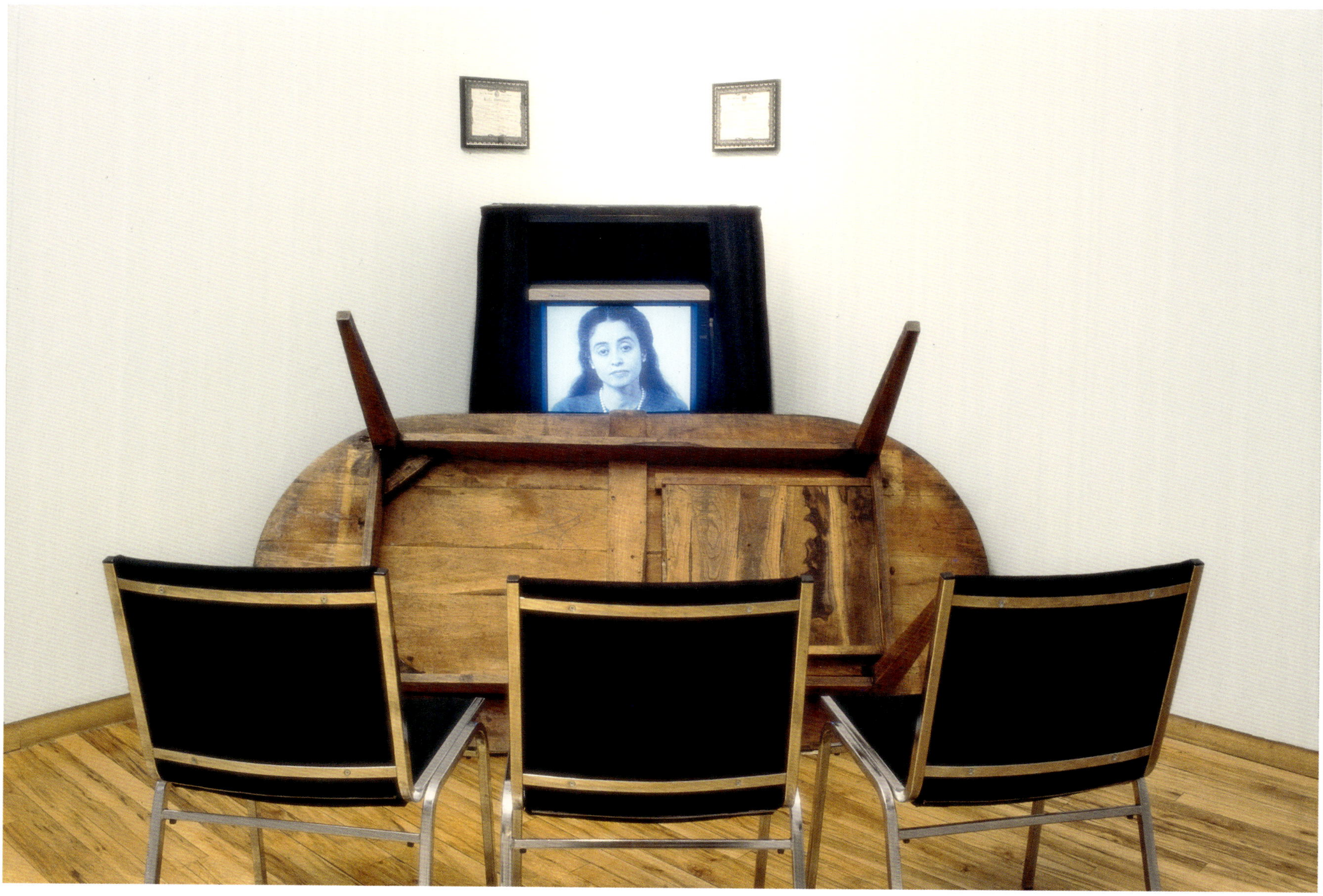

Cornered, 1988
Single-channel video installation, video tape, monitor, two birth certificates, table, chairs, 16 minutes 20 seconds
Museum of Contemporary Art, Chicago

BARBARA KRUGER

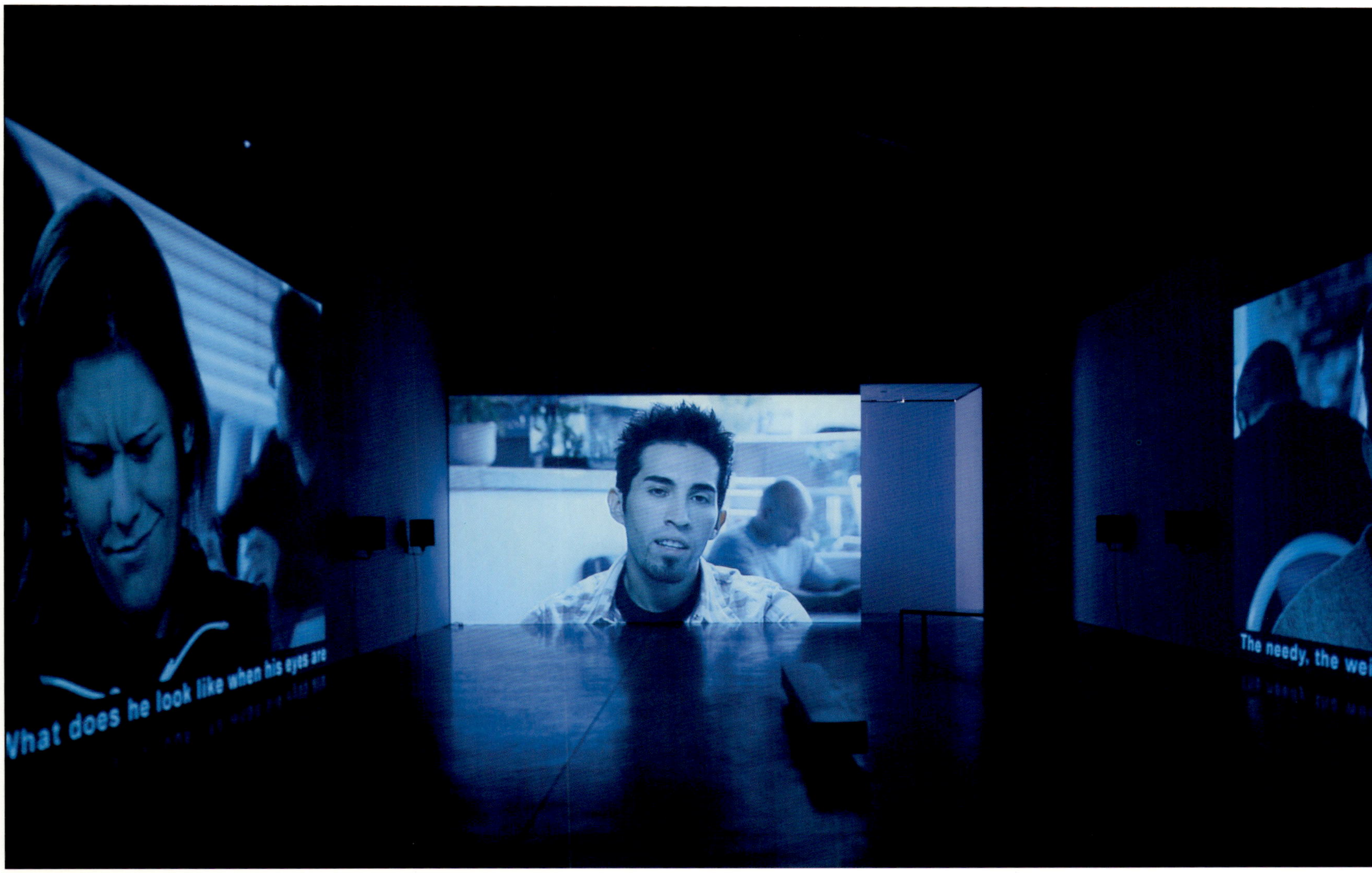

Twelve, 2004
Four-screen digital video installation, 12 minutes
As installed at Mary Boone Gallery, New York, March 2004

ROBERT COLESCOTT

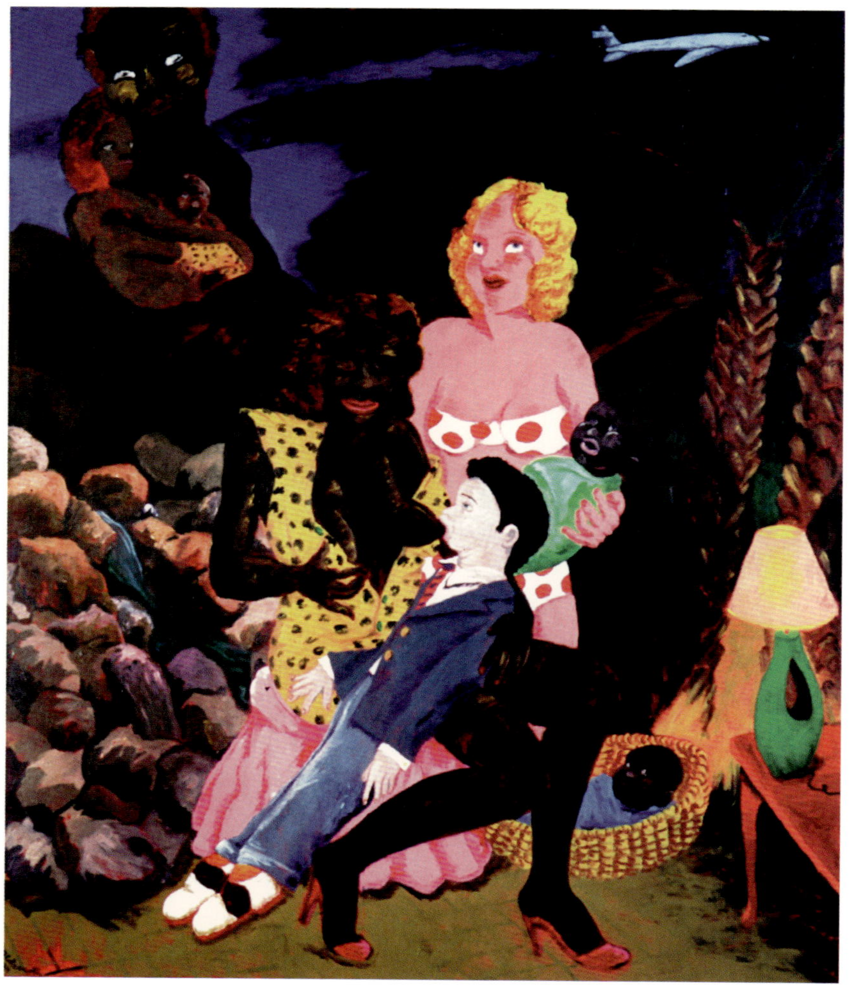

The Original, 1983
Acrylic on canvas, 84 x 72 in (213.4 x 182.9 cm)

stereotypical scenes at the family dinner table or high school lunchroom. Whether her subject is consumerism or interpersonal relationships, Kruger's work provides an ominous sense that our very identities are nothing but raw materials for forces beyond our control.

Mary Kelly takes a more abstract and theoretical approach to the question of identity, proposing that the culture that creates us is a text to be decoded. Drawing on the theories of French psychoanalyst Jacques Lacan, she explores how gender identity is constructed through a series of psychological traumas and identifications. Kelly's best-known work is *Post-Partum Document*, 1973–79, a six-part, 165-piece document of the first six years of her son's life that encompasses the minutiae of infanthood, incorporating diagrams, annotated letters, stained nappys, the child's drawings, feeding charts, and analyses of the child's first utterances. Unlike the conventional scrapbook, Kelly's document interrogates the Lacanian account of the child's process of socialization, testing Lacan's hypothesis about the replacement of the infant's sense of undifferentiated wholeness (the "imaginary") with the less satisfying but more realistic realm of the "symbolic," in which the individual is aware of his separateness and hence able to enter into social relationships. In other works Kelly has used a similarly conceptual mode to examine the changes inflicted on a woman's self-image by the process of aging and the creation of ethnic identity in an Albanian war orphan left for dead and rescued by the Serbs. Like Kruger, Kelly focuses on the involuntary forces that shape our sense of self, whether social, political, or psychological.

While artists such as Piper, Kruger, and Kelly use theory and psychology to undermine fixed notions of identity, other artists attack the subject with humor. African American painter Robert Colescott has spent his career satirizing stereotypes of black life and history. He remains best known for a series of paintings created in the 1970s that reworked famous history paintings in insidious ways, like his offering for the American Bicentennial celebrations in 1976, *George Washington Carver Crossing the Delaware*, 1975. Adopting a composition roughly based on the 1851 painting by Emanuel Gottlieb Leutze, which is known to every schoolchild, Colescott substituted the African American peanut innovator for the father of the country and filled the boat with a motley collection of racist caricatures, among them a shoeshine boy, a banjo player, and a bare-bottomed mammy. More recently, Colescott has turned to broader satires, mixing black and white characters in raucously cartoonish paintings that present scenarios involving interracial sex, racial discord, and violence and deliberately evoke white fantasies about the shiftlessness, sexual voracity, and cunning subservience of African Americans. In *The Original*, 1983, for instance, a white boy suckles at the breast of a black woman while a blond woman in a bikini looks on holding a black baby, playing out cultural taboos around interracial coupling, while also riffing on pernicious assumptions about black fertility. Despite his apparent intention to skewer stereotypes, Colescott has occasionally come under fire for perpetuating denigrating images of African Americans. His relentlessly un-politically correct work raises the question: Does the presentation of viscous racial stereotypes undermine or reinforce them? Colescott argues that humor, that great identity equalizer, is the most powerful weapon against fear and prejudice.

This tactic reappears in the work of Michael Ray Charles, who traffics in what is sometimes referred to as negrophilia—the demeaning figurines, posters, and paintings of bug-eyed, watermelon-mouthed "darkies" that were once ubiquitous

MARY KELLY

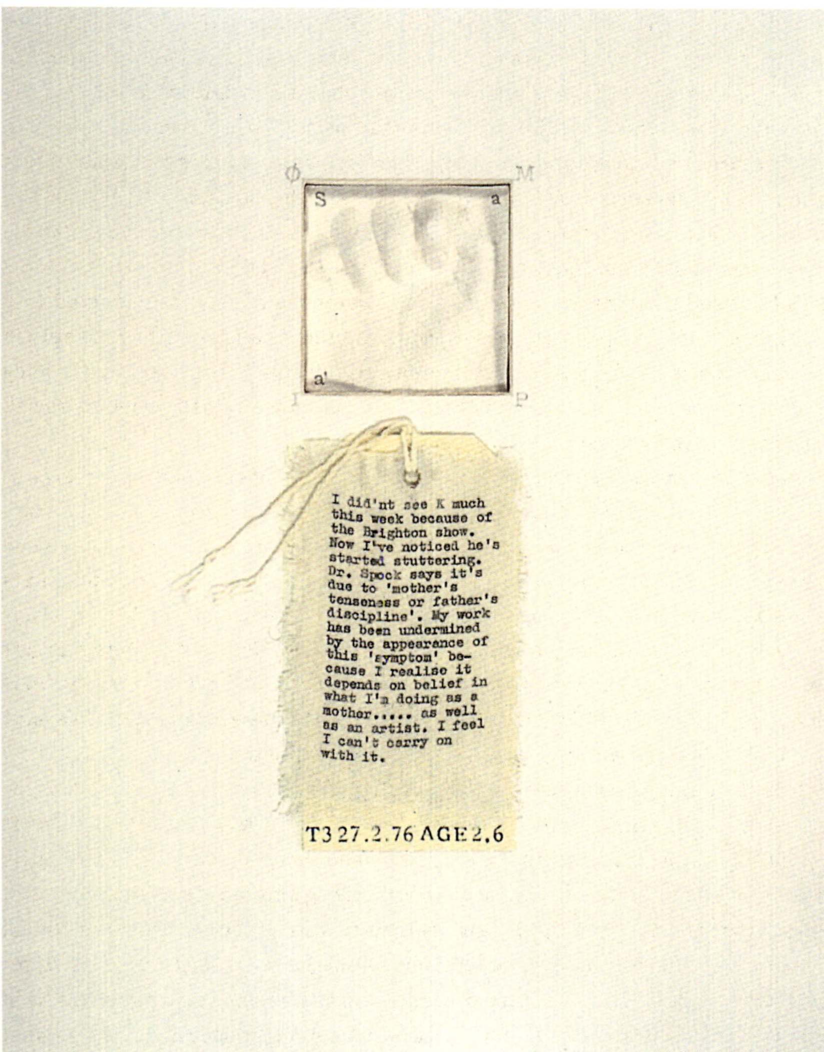

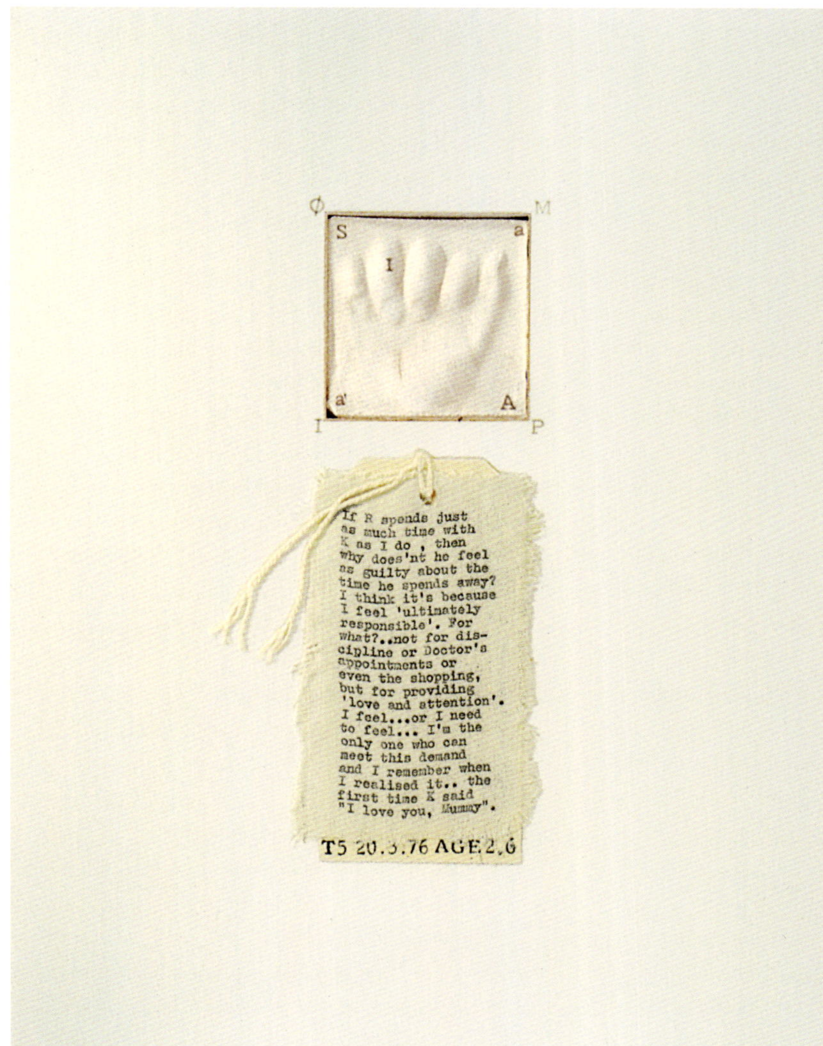

Post-Partum Document: Documentation IV, Transitional Objects, Diary and Diagram, 1976
Perspex units, white card, body/hand imprint in clay, plaster of Paris, cotton fabric, and string
11 x 14 in (28 x 35.5 cm)
Kunsthaus Zürich

in American culture. Charles, who has a background in commercial art, revives such marketing icons as Sambo, Aunt Jemima, and Uncle Ben as well as a collection of far more unsavory types once held up as creatures of ridicule, and presents them in newly "antiqued" paintings that suggest faded circus posters or peeling wooden signs. His subjects are often entertainers or athletes, the two stable professions stereotypically available to African Americans, and occasionally they morph somewhere between people and monkeys. Evoking the casual cruelty of such images, Charles suggests that even in our supposedly more enlightened times, racist attitudes still linger just below the surface. *(Forever Free) The Constant Gardener*, 2006, offers a graphic image of this reality. Surrounded by symbols of American patriotism, a Ku Klux Klansman sits in front of the houseplant he has apparently nurtured, which consists of a stack of anguished African American heads sprouting leafless branches. More a tumor than a verdant shoot, this growth reminds us of the mortal toll that racism has enacted on some of America's people.

Gay stereotypes, too, can be undermined by satire, as in the work of Nayland Blake or Cary Leibowitz, aka CandyAss. In performances, installations, and photographs, Blake has adopted the bunny rabbit as a symbol of clichés about homosexual male promiscuity (and, in a reference to Uncle Remus/Brer Rabbit stories, of his biracial background). This humorous character appears in a variety of formats in his work—as child-size bunnies strung up by their ears, as a costume worn by the artist as he haplessly attempts to perform a two-step routine, or as an oversized costume displayed on its own. *The Big One*, 2003, for instance, presents a fluffy, white rabbit suit some sixteen feet in length that sprawls on the floor like an enormous animal-skin rug. Lying supine on the floor, this giant-size suit is simultaneously humorous, cuddly, and oddly threatening. Leibowitz's work turns simultaneously on his gay and Jewish identity. In works with texts such as "Do these pants make me look Jewish?" or a series of paintings for a show entitled "Gain! Wait! Now!," 2001, Leibowitz presents a loser persona that deliberately undercuts the image of the straight, macho male artist, using humor as a defense against double identity marginalization. The latter installation featured a pyramid of umbrella stands, which might also be seen as garbage cans, each decorated with an embarrassing bar mitzvah photograph of the overweight artist wearing his 1970s-era white bar mitzvah suit.

Despite being a majority ethnic group in the United States (if "group" can describe such a diverse population), Hispanics, too, remain among the marginalized. Mexican-born performance artist Guillermo Gómez-Peña adopts a variety of invented identities designed to tweak the Anglo audience's discomfort with the idea of Latin culture. Asked to participate in the Edge '92 Biennial, organized in commemoration of the quincentennial of Columbus's voyage to the New World in Madrid, Spain, he enlisted artist and critic Coco Fusco to join him in a performance titled *Two Undiscovered Amerindians Visit Madrid*. The pair, costumed as gorgeously painted old Hollywood-style "natives," took up residence in an elaborately decorated cage and responded mutely as guides earnestly explained their antics and culture to members of the biennial audience. In 1998 Gómez-Peña posed as "Jacques Fromage du Merde," a "noted French ethnographer" who in a fictional interview for a call-in radio show presented a pair of "live Mexican cyborgs" designed to realize all the audience's deepest fears about immigration, Latin culture, and "otherness" in general. The "cyborgs" extolled drug dealing, sexual predation, urban violence, and

NAYLAND BLAKE

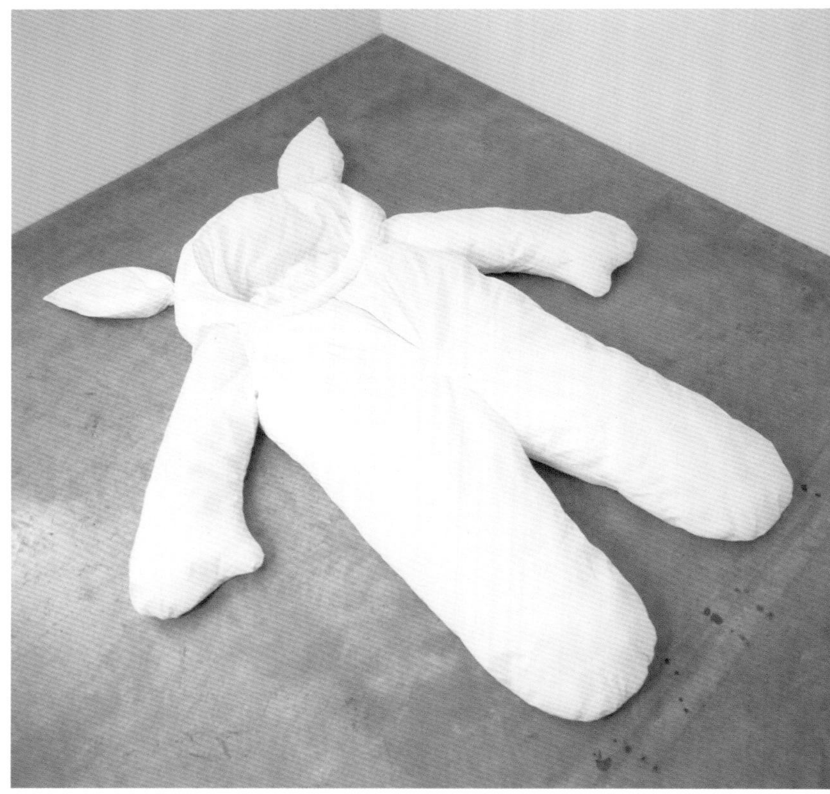

The Big One, 2003
White nylon, 16 ft x 15 ft x 6 in (4.9 m x 4.6 m x 15.2 cm)

MICHAEL RAY CHARLES

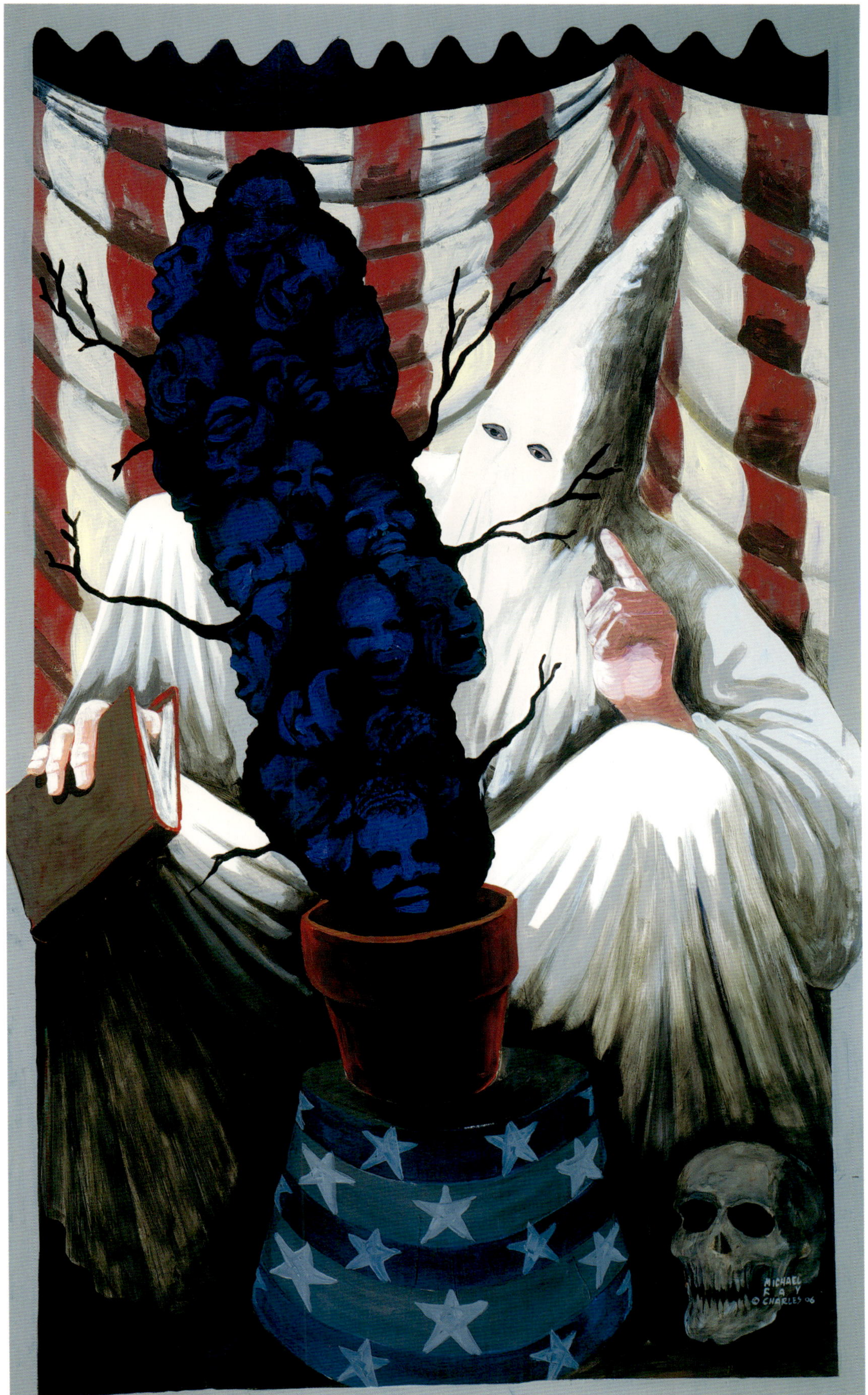

(Forever Free) The Constant Gardener, 2006
Acrylic latex and copper penny on paper, 99 x 60 in (252 x 152 cm)

CARY LEIBOWITZ

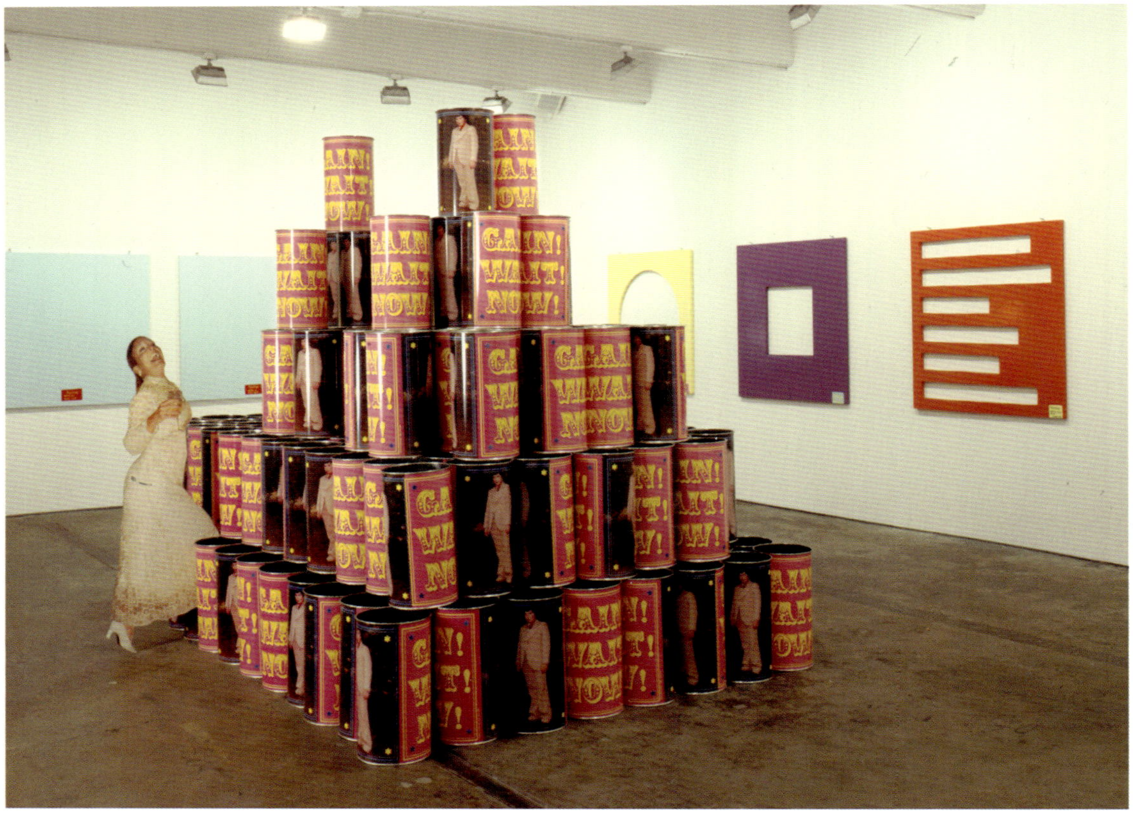

"Gain! Wait! Now!," 2001
As installed at Andrew Kreps Gallery, New York, November–December 2001

GUILLERMO GÓMEZ-PEÑA AND COCO FUSCO

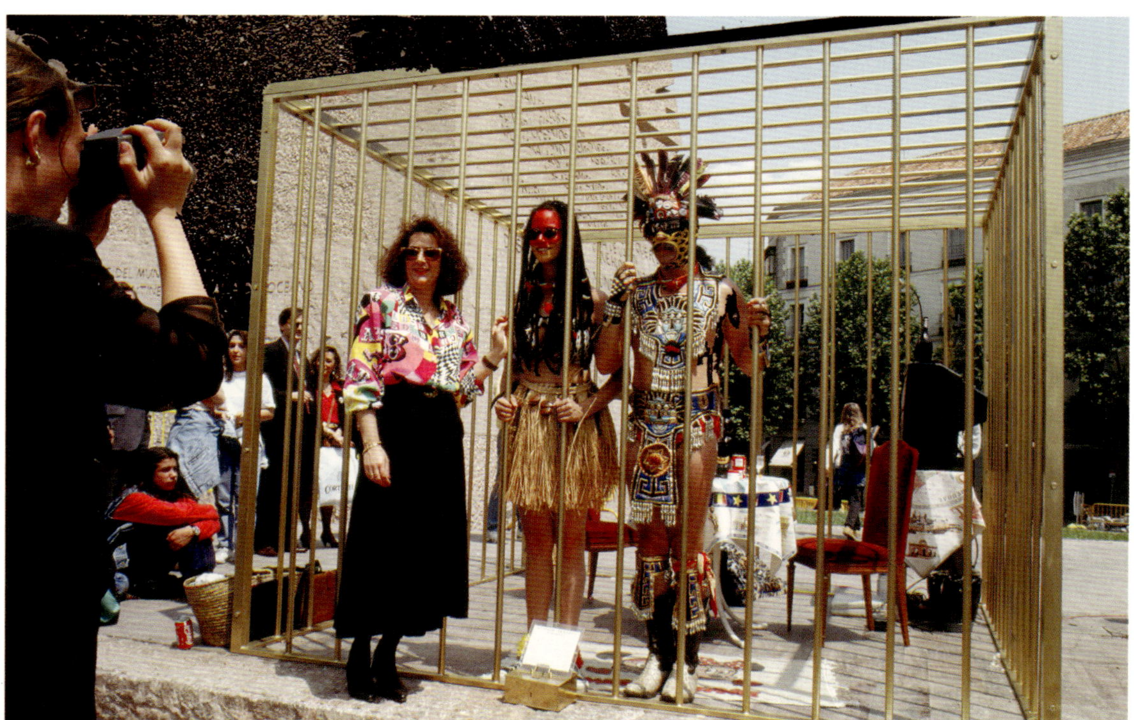

Two Undiscovered Amerindians Visit Madrid, 1992
Performance, Plaza de Colón, Madrid

activities associated with "illegals." Here humor trespassed into the realm of the absurd, which isn't to say that some listeners might not have been fooled.

Jimmie Durham, a political activist and artist of Cherokee descent, approaches the identity paradoxes of Native Americans, for whom issues of sovereignty, authenticity, and cultural erasure are ever present. In some works, he spoofs ethnographic clichés by which Native Americans have been presented in natural history museums. In others, he replicates an indigenous aesthetic based on tribal traditions, using animal skulls, shells, feathers, and fur, as well as contemporary objects such as discarded car parts, hardware, and plastic toys. In yet other works, Durham mixes these two approaches. In a series of drawings with attached objects titled "Six Authentic Things," 1989, for instance, he presents fake Indian artifacts as if they were "real." (Of course, the fact that Durham is a "real" Native American returns some measure of authenticity.) The exhibition, "On Loan from the Museum of the American Indian," 1985, similarly satirizes the fetishization of otherness, presenting artifacts of modern life, among them toothbrushes and family photos, used by contemporary Native Americans. The exhibit included *Types of Arrows*, which displays three different arrows with the mockingly obvious labels of "tiny," "wavy," and "short and fat." In mischievous works like these, Durham models himself on the figure of the Coyote, the Native American embodiment of the trickster, the destructive force that ultimately leads to higher consciousness.

Challenging stereotypes to reveal the ambiguity of identity is a political strategy in that it undermines the sort of conventional thinking that reinforces race-, gender-, and ethnicity-based inequality. But identity politics has also spurred some artists to direct political action, particularly within the gay community, where homophobia and lagging responses to the AIDS crisis have cost lives.[6] In the early 1980s, agitprop groups such as General Idea and Gran Fury emerged to battle the invisibility of AIDS outside the gay community. General Idea was the invention of three Canadian artists, Jorge Zontal, Felix Partz, and AA Bronson, who adopted the tools of advertising, marketing, and public address to get their message heard. Their most brilliant stroke was a reinscription of Pop artist Robert Indiana's famous LOVE logo in 1987. General Idea reworked this graphic word/image, substituting the letters of the word AIDS for Indiana's innocuous LOVE and printing it on posters, billboards, tchotchkes, electronic images, lottery tickets, and stamps, which were widely distributed through museums and shops. They also appropriated other modernist art works for their own purposes. For instance, they parodied Yves Klein's blue-slathered female models by using three blue-painted stuffed French poodles as "living paintbrushes," and created mass-produced glass dildos as companions to Duchamp's 1954 *Wedge of Chastity*. As the AIDS crisis grew more urgent (claiming Zontal and Partz in 1994), the parodies did, too. The group's 1992 installation *Magic Bullet* featured 1,500 helium-filled, capsule-shaped Mylar balloons, which recalled both Andy Warhol's silvery pillows of 1966 and the anti-HIV drug AZT.

Gran Fury, an offshoot of ACT UP, an activist group that emerged in the late 1980s to raise awareness around AIDS, also exploited existing media channels to convey messages about AIDS and gay rights. Taking its name from the car favored by the New York Police Department, Gran Fury consisted of a shifting group of artists who worked together from 1988 until 1994, creating posters, billboards, and other projects that wittily drew attention to the AIDS crisis and to public attitudes about homosexuality. One of their most successful projects began as a series of posters

JIMMIE DURHAM

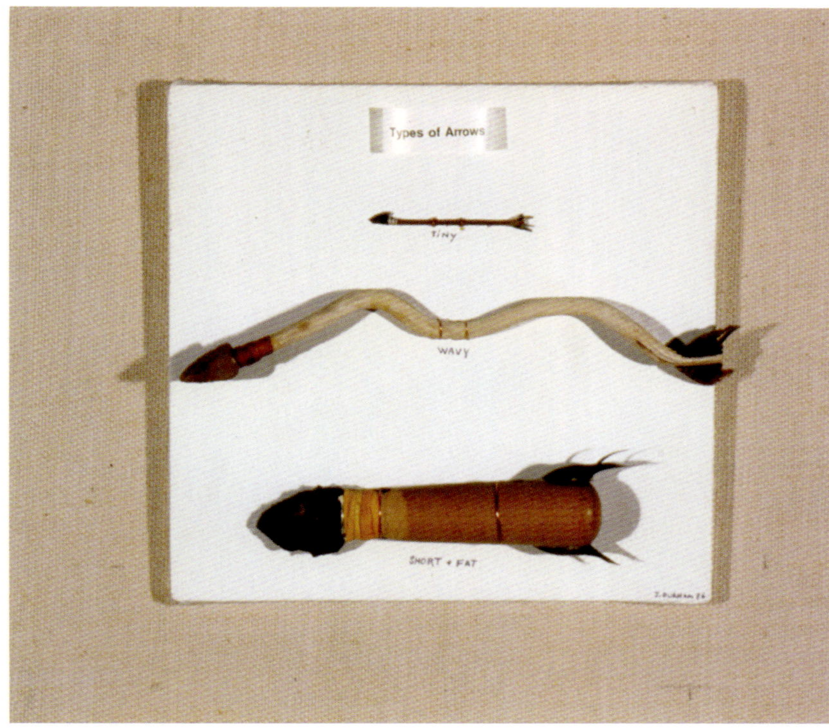

Types of Arrows, 1985
Mixed media, 14 x 21 1/2 x 2 in (35.6 x 54.6 x 5.1 cm)

GENERAL IDEA

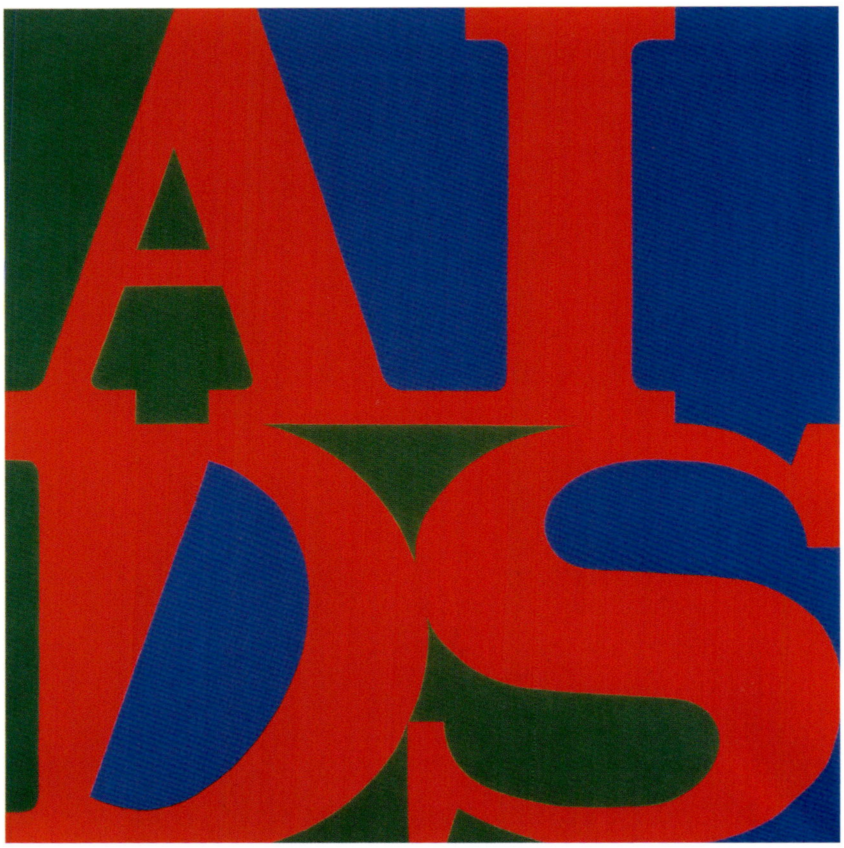

AIDS, 1987
Acrylic on canvas, 72 x 72 in (182.9 x 182.9 cm)

plastered on buses and subway platforms in San Francisco, Chicago, New York, and Washington, D.C. It featured pairs of attractive same-sex and heterosexual couples kissing under the logo "Kissing Doesn't Kill: Greed and Indifference Do." Designed to resemble familiar clothing industry campaigns, the posters used Madison Avenue techniques for subversive purposes.

Applying an activist approach to Latino identity issues, artists Elizabeth Sisco, Louis Hock, and David Avalos, a San Diego-based artist collective, create "actions" that expose contradictions between their border community's attitudes toward illegal aliens and its economic dependence on them. In 1988 they installed a set of bus posters that juxtaposed images of hotel workers with the greeting "Welcome to America's Finest Tourist Plantation." Another project, *America's Finest?*, 1990, consisted of ads posted on bus benches throughout the city that criticized the increasing use of deadly force by San Diego police officers. Perhaps most subversive of all, when the collective received a $4,500 grant from the National Endowment for the Arts in 1993, they gave the money away in $10 bills to 450 undocumented workers along the U.S./Mexico border. Titling the action *Arte Reembolso/Art Rebate*, they envisioned it as a rebate to the illegal immigrants who do the city's menial labor but receive no benefit from the taxes they pay. Because this work, like much activist work, took place in the public arena, it provoked heated discussion in the local media. It also prompted the NEA to revoke part of the grant, creating even more publicity, which of course, only aided the group's cause.

HOCK E AYE VI Edgar Heap of Birds, an artist of Cheyenne and Arapaho descent, creates activist public artworks that provoke viewers to recognize the tragic history of America's indigenous peoples. Borrowing from Conceptual art, he has placed signs along highways "welcoming" present-day inhabitants of the United States to places they think of as their own homes. Printed in the same colors and type as conventional highway markers, these signs, which bear such lines as "Purchased? Stolen? Reclaimed?," raise questions about the true ownership of the American landscape. Commissioned to create a permanent public artwork by the Denver Art Museum in 1996, Heap of Birds made *Wheel*, a monumental piece based on the Big Horn Medicine Wheel created centuries ago by the Cheyenne Indians in northern Wyoming's Big Horn Mountains. Updating this ritual object, which consists of twenty-eight rows of stones radiating from a central cairn to an encircling stone rim, Heap of Birds produced ten porcelain-enameled steel towers aligned in a grassy circle in such a way that one of the vectors cutting across the piece corresponds to the sunrise and sunset of the summer solstice. With this gesture, he went some way toward restoring a forgotten history.

Finally, a number of artists have rebelled against the limitations of identity-based art by embracing hybridity, by recognizing that the notion of stable identity is nothing more than a comforting myth in a world where mobility, intermarriage, shifting roles, and continually renegotiated borders ensure that no one has claim to racial, ethnic, or even gender purity. The reality, more confusing, but ultimately more satisfying, is that we all exist within multiple worlds and that our sense of self is created by the mixture of many identities. It is this state of affairs that the novelist Salman Rushdie celebrates in *The Satanic Verses* when he asks: "How does a newness come into the world? How is it born? Of what fusions, translations, conjoinings is it made? How does it survive, extreme and dangerous as it is?"[7] As Rushdie suggests, hybridity is destabilizing, but it is also regenerative.

GRAN FURY

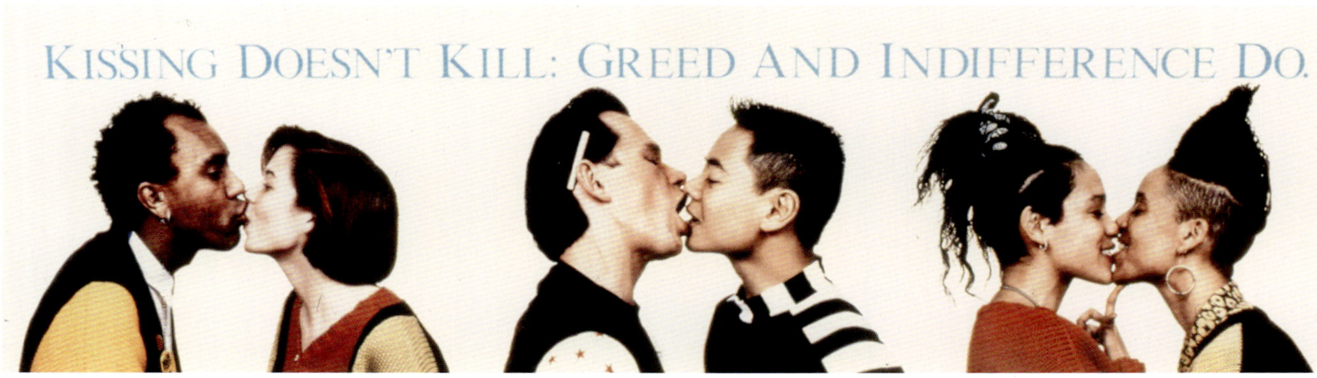

Kissing Doesn't Kill: Greed and Indifference Do, 1989
Bus poster

ELIZABETH SISCO, LOUIS HOCK, AND DAVID AVALOS

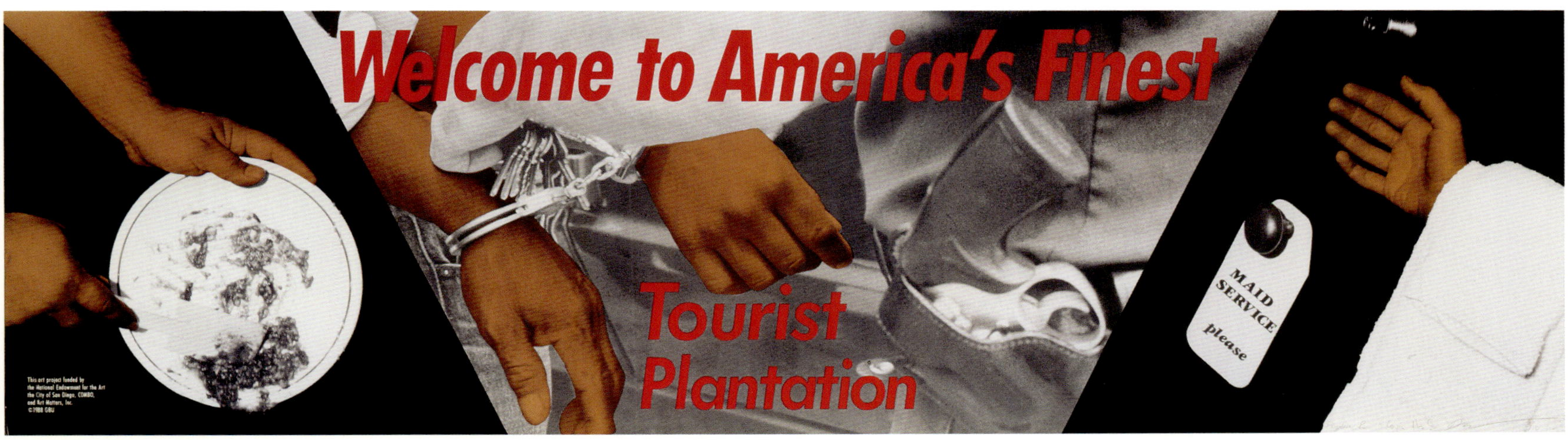

Welcome to America's Finest Tourist Plantation, 1988
Poster on rear of San Diego Transit buses, three-color silkscreen on vinyl, 21 x 72 in (53.3 x 182.9)

HOCK E AYE VI EDGAR HEAP OF BIRDS

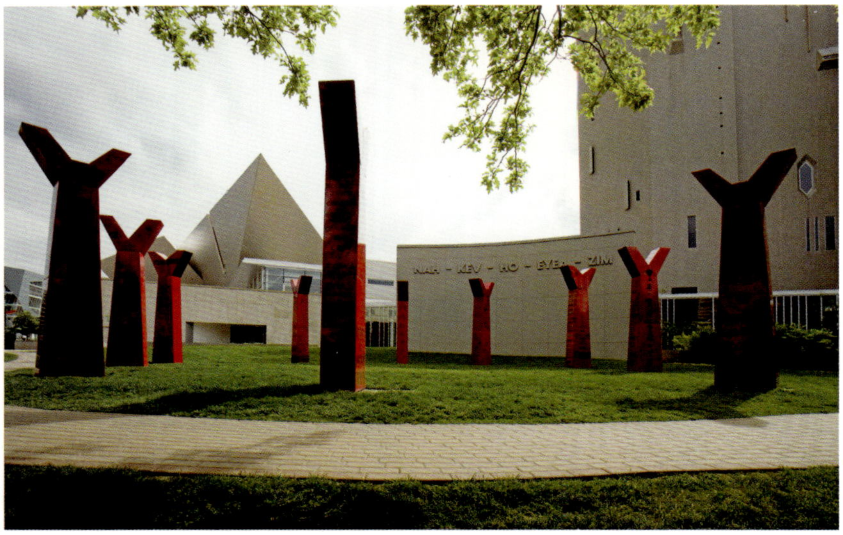

Wheel, 1997–2005
Ten standing forms fabricated in porcelain-coated panels on steel over a galvanized metal framework
Denver Art Museum

ANDREA ROBBINS AND MAX BECHER

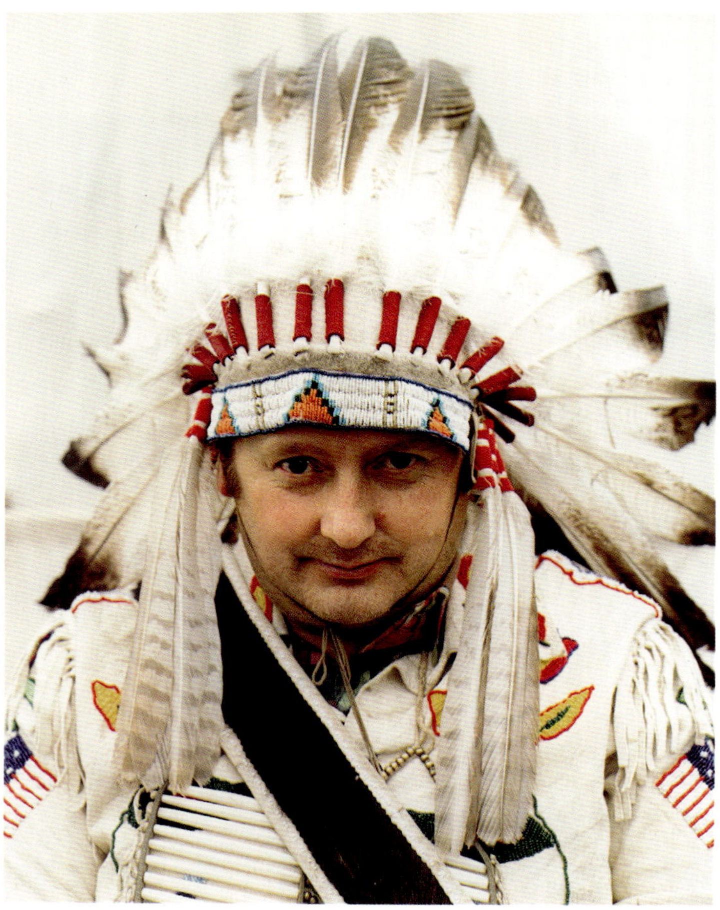

German Indians: Chief, 1998
Chromogenic print, 30 x 25 3/4 in (76.2 x 65.4 cm)

Artists explore hybridity from a number of perspectives, observing it in others, embracing it in themselves. Andrea Robbins and Max Becher, for example, have created a series of photographs of "German Indians," or rather Germans who dress up as and emulate Native Americans. Why this strange hybrid? Generations of Germans grew up reading the romanticized Wild West fantasies of novelist Karl May, and this German writer's birthday is the occasion for full-dress powwows in various parts of Germany. Participants come wearing face paint and ceremonial robes. Robbins and Becher's photographs capture the oddity of blond, blue-eyed "Indians" eating with plastic utensils or engaging in war dances for crowds of tourists. Other works by this artist team document cultural transpositions of buildings. They have photographed American-style strip malls in the French countryside, Dutch windmills in Michigan, highly incongruous colonial German buildings in the Namibian desert, the London Bridge lovingly reconstructed in Lake Havasu, Arizona, and the installation of a full-scale replica of Stonehenge in Washington State. Whether human or architectural, Robbins and Becher's cross-global hybrids speak to the allure of the other, and to making that other one's own.

Yasumasa Morimura enacts his own hybrid transformations, assuming new personas in photographic self-portraits as media and art-world icons. Made up with uncanny realism to resemble Hollywood film stars in their most famous roles, celebrated artists such as Frida Kahlo, and the subjects of Western art masterpieces, Morimura, who is slender with fine features, crosses both racial and gender lines. In *Futago*, 1988, he recreates Manet's *Olympia*. However, there are a number of subtle changes, including the addition of overtly Japanese fabrics on the courtesan's bed and the substitution of Manet's feline with a black ceramic "beckoning cat" of the sort used in Japanese business establishments to welcome visitors. The most dramatic change is in the persona of Olympia and her black maid, both played by the artist. Morimura has also photographed himself as Rita Hayworth in her notorious nude portrait, Marilyn Monroe famously pushing down her wind-swept skirt in *The Seven-Year Itch*, and Faye Dunaway posing coquettishly as the gangster moll from *Bonnie and Clyde*. Morimura's fascination with these subjects is in part a function of his history. As a child growing up in postwar Japan, he was inundated with the images and products of American popular culture. As such, his work reflects an identity formed through virtual contact with an idealized distant world. He recreates his fantasies not to debunk them, but to pay what seems to be the sincerest homage, in the process giving back to the West a fractured, Asianized version of its most cherished fictions.

Nikki S. Lee treks even further into the world of hybrid masquerade in a series of projects in which she infiltrates various subcultures, mimicking the dress, gestures, and lifestyle of their members and having someone take a picture of her as an indistinguishable part of the group. A slight Korean woman, Lee is chameleon-like, transforming herself into figures as diverse as an exotic dancer, an East Village punk, a dowdy retiree, a redneck southerner, a drag queen, a Wall Street yuppie, and a skateboarding kid. In *The Ohio Project*, 1999, for instance, she becomes a bleached-blond trailer-park denizen. Here she struts with body builders, poses in the door of her trailer and nestles next to an unkempt man who lovingly brandishes his rifle beneath a poster of the Confederate Flag. While her transformations are often remarkable, the most intriguing aspect of Lee's work is the way in which she operates like a mole, entering into disparate milieus in which she is accepted by "authentic" members

YASUMASA MORIMURA

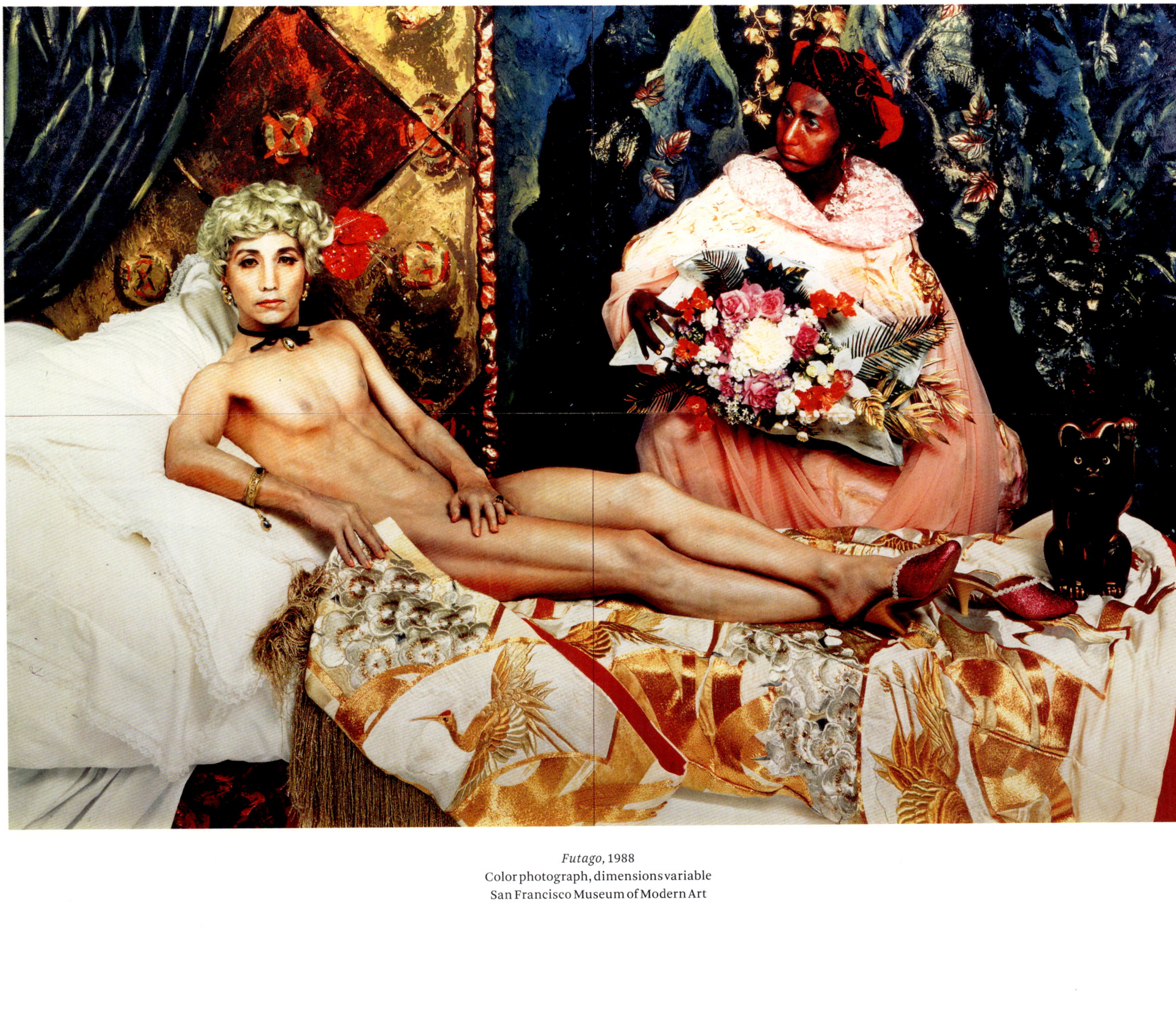

Futago, 1988
Color photograph, dimensions variable
San Francisco Museum of Modern Art

of the tribe. The resulting images, which have the look of casual snapshots, are a far cry from Morimura's slick art photographs. They seem more like anthropological documents of the so-called exotic cultures existing right in our midst.

In performances and videos, Tamy Ben-Tor also assumes a variety of personas, but she does so with a still more political purpose. Ben-Tor creates outrageous characters whose rants reveal some of the ugliest prejudices in the contemporary world. Among the characters she has created for performance are a Nazi-type youth who beats a tambourine and rages about American culture, capitalism, and cappuccino; a racist Scandinavian academic; and a grande dame who congratulates herself on her sympathy for the poor of Marrakech and India. In Ben-Tor's video *Women Talk About Adolf Hitler*, 2004, she takes on Holocaust denial and revisionism with a pantheon of female characters who alternately try to understand and excuse Hitler, confess a secret attraction to him, and condemn him. The final character in the video is a young woman who dons a Hitler mustache and caresses Hitler's portrait. Ben-Tor's hybrid feat is less about convincing transformation than about confronting her audience with unsympathetic characters who embody attitudes and realities it might prefer to ignore.

Kutlug Ataman creates documentary-style video installations that feature telling portraits of real, highly idiosyncratic individuals. He, like many of the other artists in this chapter, focuses on the margins of society, but the people he memorializes refuse to be reduced to types. His subjects are as diverse as they are eccentric: they are real-world hybrids. One is Semiha Berskoy, an eighty-seven-year-old Turkish diva who over the course of an eight-hour film vamps, acts out opera scenes, discusses her life, talks to her mother who is personified by a partially clothed mannequin, and seems to be unable to make clear distinctions anymore between real life, fantasy, and the stage. A 2002 work, *1 + 1 = 1*, presents a Turkish Cypriot woman who speaks to the viewer on two facing screens about the psychological and political costs of her double identity. The double identity is mirrored in the structure of the work, as she appears on two facing screens, wearing the same clothes and sitting at the same table, but telling different parts of her story in each one. Thus as the title suggests, her two ethnic identities make a single whole, though one that is not without contradictions and complexities.

Speaking of his attitude toward identity, Ataman has said, "I do not think identity belongs to the individual. Identity is like a jacket. People you never see will make it and you wear it. Identity is something other than you, outside of you. It's a question of perception. You can be aware of it and manipulate it, play with it, amplify it, or mask it for infinite reasons."[8] In the end, identity is like a reflection in still water—it is only clearly visible until you reach out and try to grasp it in your hand.

TAMY BEN-TOR

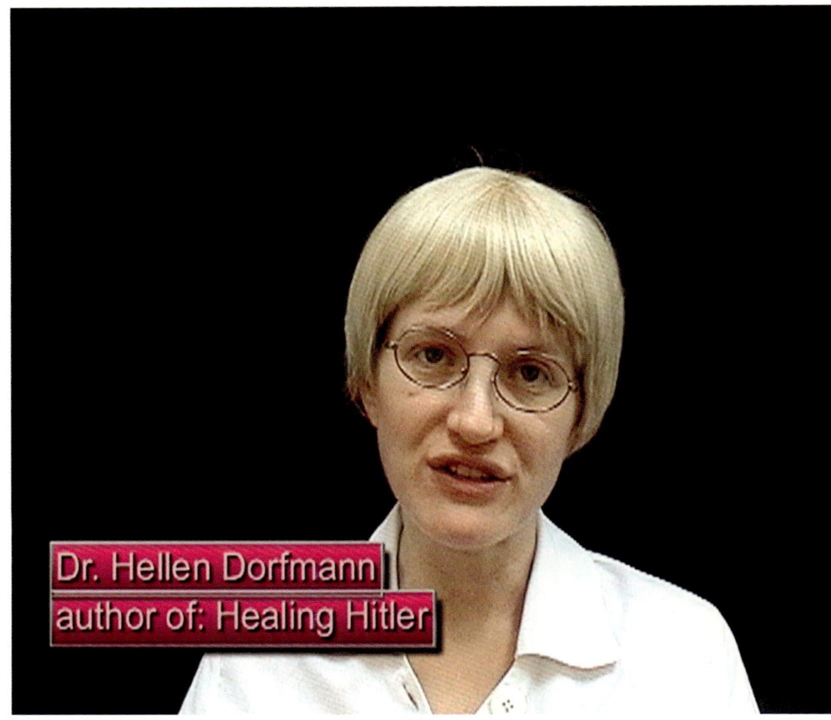

Women Talk About Adolf Hitler, 2004
DVD, 7 minutes 40 seconds

KUTLUG ATAMAN

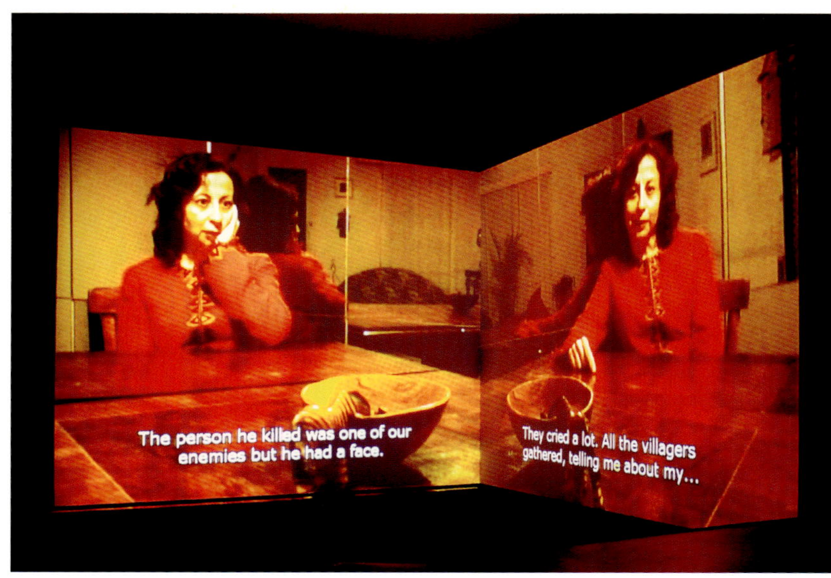

1+1=1, 2002
Two-screen video installation, 2 DVDs, each approx. 50 minutes

NIKKI S. LEE

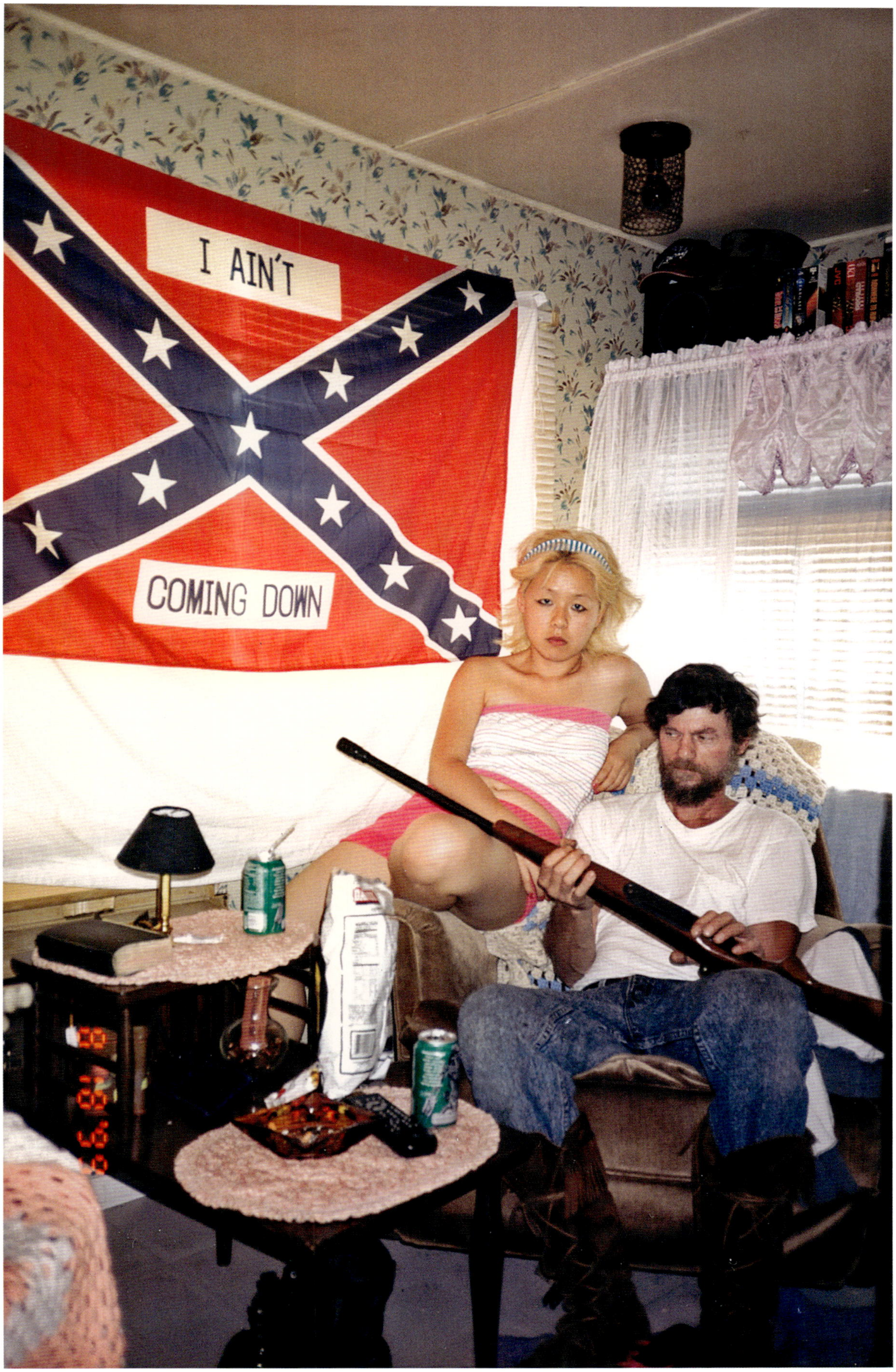

The Ohio Project (7), 1999
Fujiflex C-print, 40 x 30 in (101.6 x 76.2 cm)

ART & SPIRITUALITY

REDISCOVERING TRANSCENDENCE

Throughout much of Western history, art and religion have been thoroughly entwined. Under the patronage of the Catholic Church, medieval and Renaissance artists such as Giotto, Fra Angelico, Michelangelo, and Raphael gave visual form to Church teachings, in the process creating some of the most enduring masterpieces of Western art. Without Christianity, we would not have the remarkable sculptures and stained glass windows that are the glory of Chartres Cathedral, Giotto's Arena Chapel fresco cycle in Padua, or Michelangelo's Sistine Chapel paintings. Nor is great religious art confined to the West. Before Leonardo's *Last Supper*, there were the Buddhist stupas of Tibet, Indonesia, India, and Thailand; the Mayan pyramids of Teotihuacán; and African tribal fertility figures and fetishes. It wasn't until after the Reformation, with the rise of the mercantile class, the nationalization of Christianity, and the secularization of culture, that art production in the Western world extracted itself from religion, though artists continued to draw on biblical characters and narratives as part of a common cultural heritage.

Religious imagery persisted, that is, until the birth of modernism in the late nineteenth century, when the alliance between Western art and organized religion came entirely undone. With the emergence of pan-European avant-garde movements that promised to sweep away old habits and traditions, early modernists identified organized religion with the reactionary and authoritarian forces that were everywhere being overthrown. Distancing themselves from orthodox religious beliefs, they nonetheless retained a rhetoric of transcendence and spirituality, creating a vision of art as a sacred practice unto itself. In his influential 1910 essay "Concerning the Spiritual in Art," Wassily Kandinsky wrote of art's "deep roots of mystical inner thought," thus displacing the experience of spirituality from religion to the realm of individual feeling.[1] Other artists, including Piet Mondrian, Kasimir Malevich, Arthur Dove, and Marsden Hartley, fell under the sway of Theosophy, a non-theist philosophy that drew on Hindu and Buddhist teachings and encouraged its acolytes to seek truth through individual revelation, universal brotherhood, and spiritual ecstasy.

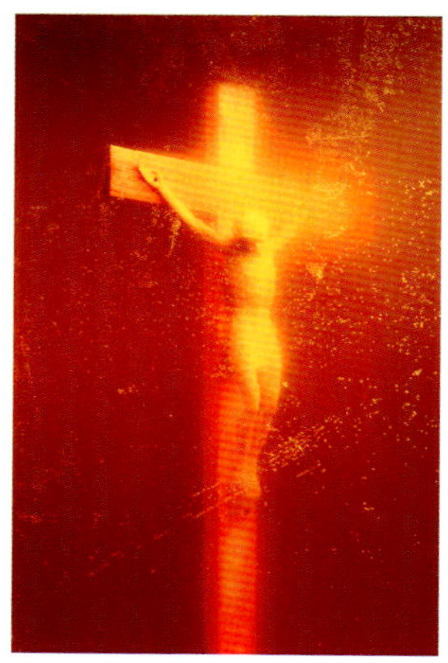

ANDRES SERRANO
PISS CHRIST
1987
95 1/2 X 62 X 1 IN
(242.6 X 157.5 X 2.5 CM)

The decoupling of spirituality from established religion freed avant-gardists in several catalytic ways. No longer beholden to an established faith and its accompanying representation, they could choose their subject matter, or even no particular subject matter at all. They could continue to revere great artists of the past while focusing on the formal properties rather than the religious content of their work. (Both of which led to abstraction.) And they could embrace the exquisite distortion of African art on its own terms, regardless of its ritual function (which led quite specifically to Cubism). By the post-World War II era, the separation of religious form from subject matter had progressed to the point that an artist's religious beliefs could be irrelevant to the nature of a commission. One result of this was Houston's Rothko Chapel, a meditative space created by Catholic clients to house the paintings of Mark Rothko, a Jewish artist, and designed to provide a non-sectarian sanctuary. Another series of works which crossed religious borders were a set of abstract paintings created from 1958–1964 by Jewish artist Barnett Newman to represent the Stations of the Cross. By the time Joseph Beuys took up a form of shamanism in the 1960s, advocating a return to animistic, pre-Western forms of ritual—for instance lecturing to a dead hare and sharing a cage with a wild coyote—the cleansing of any taint of religion from spiritually based art was complete.

As abstract spirituality has replaced religion in modern and contemporary art, art world insiders and outside observers alike have tended to assume that art and religion have become natural antagonists. For instance, in 1979 critic Rosalind Krauss noted the emergence of an "absolute rift" between art and religion following the desacralization of art in the nineteenth century.[2] This so-called rift seemed especially apparent in the 1980s and '90s, when a series of controversies exploded in the American art world. First there was Andres Serrano's *Piss Christ*, 1987, a photograph of a dime-store crucifix immersed in urine, which became the centerpiece in a political controversy over government funding for the arts, a lightning rod for conservative criticism, and for some, the ultimate expression of contemporary art's decadence and irreligiosity. In 1999 there was the Chris Ofili controversy over his *Holy Virgin Mary*, 1996, at the Brooklyn Museum, mentioned in Chapter 10. A year later the Brooklyn Museum came under censure again for including Renee Cox's *Yo Mama's Last Supper*, 1996–2001, a revised version of Leonardo's masterpiece featuring African American apostles and a female, bare-breasted Christ. In 2001, a young Chicana artist named Alma Lopez came under fire during a show at the Museum of International Folk Art in Santa Fe, New Mexico, for depicting the Virgin of Guadalupe as a modern-day woman wearing a bikini of roses.

Each of these controversies had different causes and consequences, but all turned on the belief that the artists appropriating religious symbols were doing so to express their enmity to religion, and were thus denigrating faith. In fact, the situation is far more nuanced. Each of the artists accused of sacrilege have themselves professed a personal relationship with religion, and none were mocking believers. (Indeed, Ofili and Lopez are practicing Catholics.) Strangely, not only conservatives and the religious right interpreted their works as mockeries of religion; art critics, curators, and other art insiders did too, even when the artists in question rejected that notion. Such critical presumptions have led some artists who address religion affirmatively to mask their themes, while others have openly expressed devotion. And of course some artists do engage religious themes specifically to challenge organized religion. In any case, if one looks at the range of contemporary art that incorporates spirituality, it becomes clear that the art-religion split has been greatly exaggerated. Artists have continued to draw on religious sources and spiritual beliefs in the face of indifference and even resistance from the art establishment for reasons that take us back to the traditional relationship between art and religion. In diverse cultures and across the centuries, art has drawn on metaphors and images to give form to invisible forces. It has served to articulate the ultimate questions: Why are we here? What is the meaning of life, of death? Is there anything beyond the world we know? Do unseen forces guide the actions of mankind and the upheavals of nature? What is good and what is evil? These questions are too powerful and too essential to be abandoned by contemporary art.[3]

CHRIS OFILI

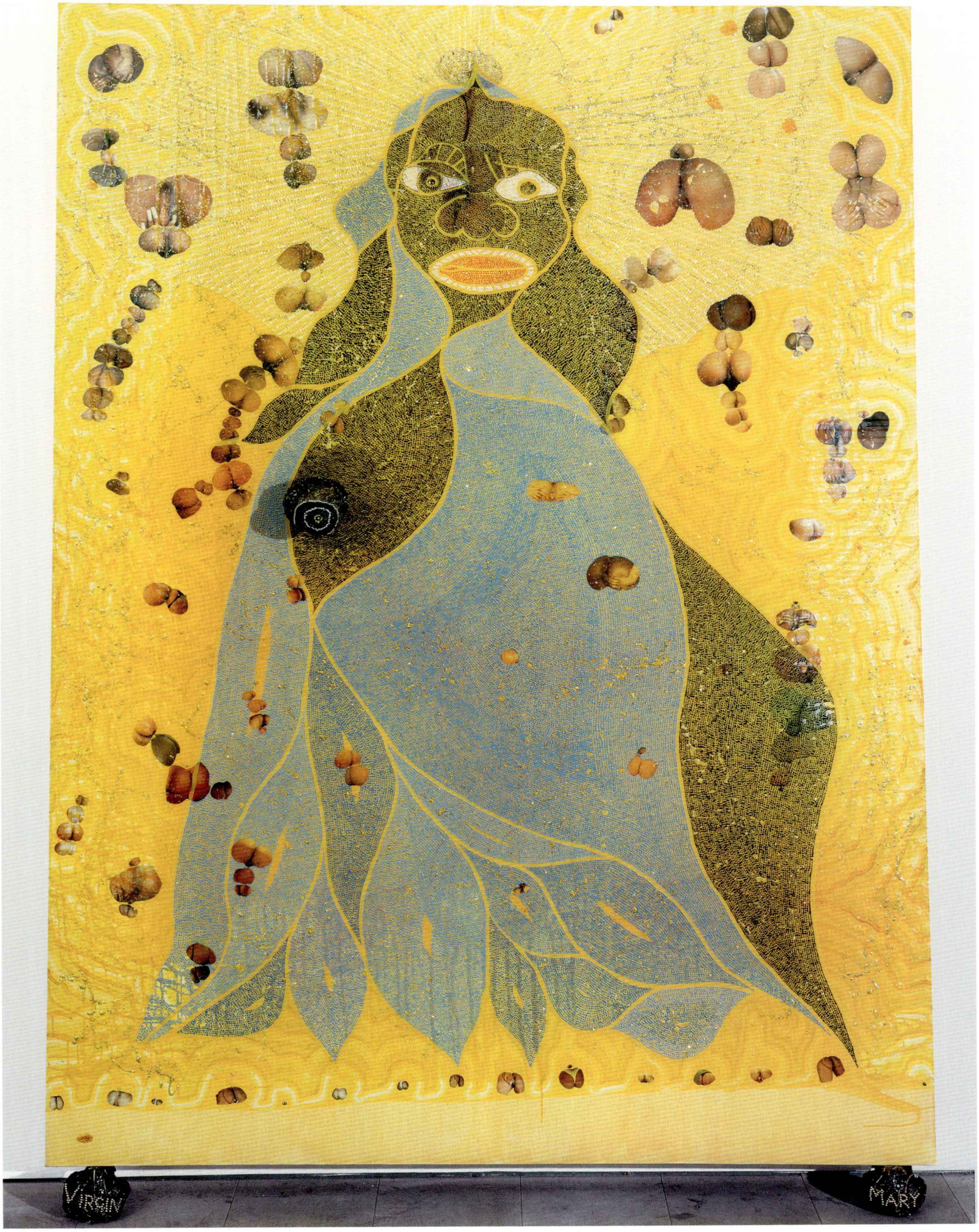

The Holy Virgin Mary, 1996
Acrylic, oil, resin, paper collage, glitter, map pins, and elephant dung on canvas
96 x 72 in (243.8 x 182.8 cm)

ANDRES SERRANO

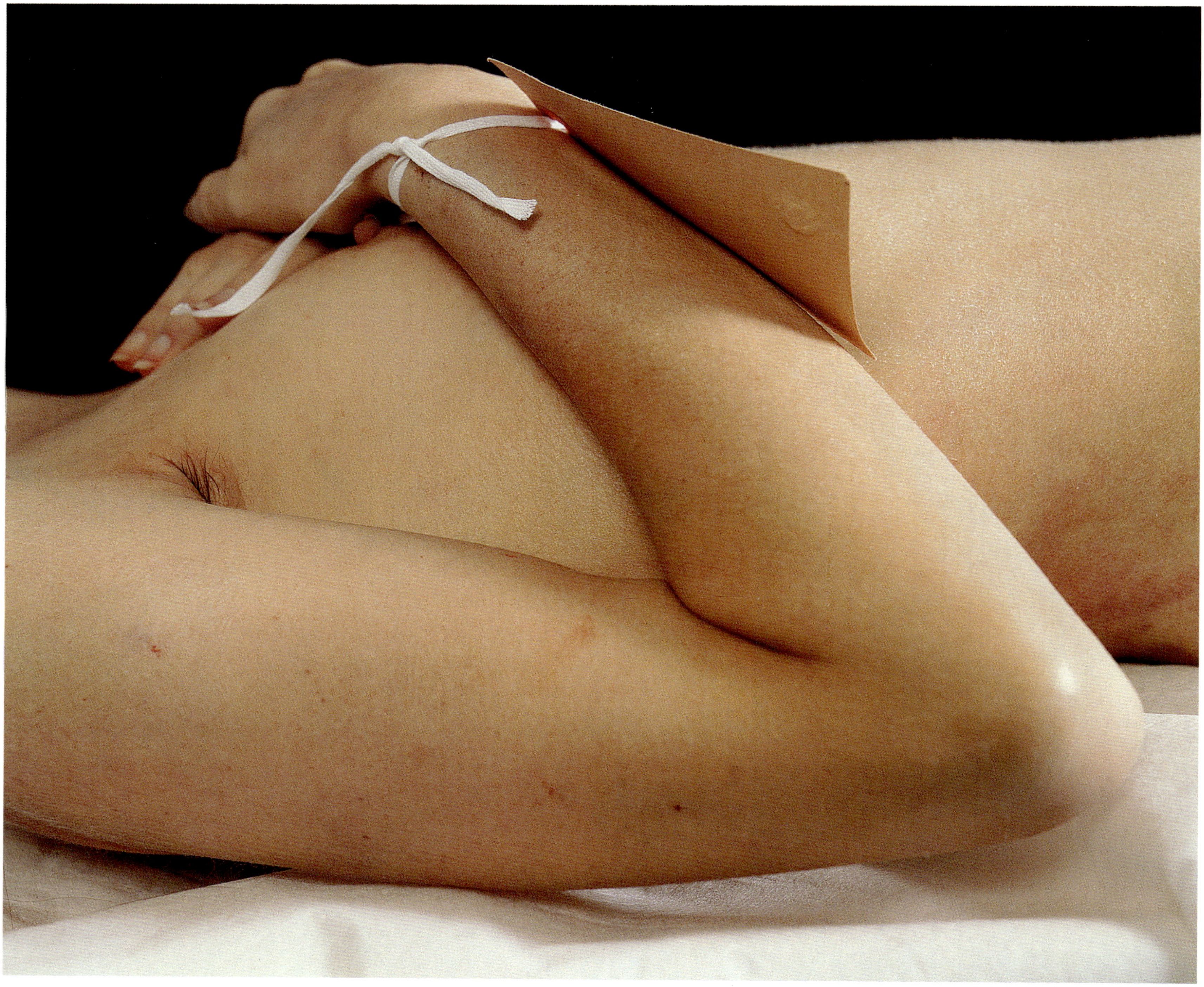

The Morgue (AIDS Related Death II), 1992
Cibachrome, silicone, Plexiglas, wood frame, 49 x 60 in (124.5 x 152.5 cm)

Established religions today seldom extend the kind of patronage that yielded the Sistine Chapel or the Arena Chapel frescoes, and of course contemporary artists rarely serve religion directly through the creation of liturgical imagery and the illustration of sacred texts. They do, however, draw on the visual and literary symbolism of religion for their own, more private expressive ends. Despite its intentionally provocative title, Serrano's *Piss Christ* was inspired by the seductions of traditional Catholic art. It was one of a series of photographs in which religious artifacts were photographed through fluids, among them blood, milk, and water, to create a visual aura of unearthly beauty; they represent the blood of Christ, the milk of the Virgin and, somewhat more obscurely, the semen of God as the elements through which the miracle of Christ's incarnation made human redemption possible. Serrano, who was raised Catholic, frequently employs references to canonical religious paintings, appropriating their compositions, lighting, and sensuous color to bring a sense of otherworldly presence to contemporary subjects. For example, his "Morgue" series of 1992 presents carefully lit and cropped images of bodies laid out in a morgue. Each got there as a result of a violent and unexpected death, but in Serrano's hands the bodies are transformed to evoke such religious motifs as the Nativity and the Deposition of Christ. Together, they speak to one of Serrano's larger purposes: nothing less than a serious and respectful exploration of the relationship of body and soul as presented in religious art.

Kiki Smith is also from a Catholic background and also draws on religious symbolism, though she does so more critically, using traditional representations of the Virgin Mary and female saints to suggest that Catholicism promotes contradictory messages about womanhood. *Virgin Mary*, 1993, is a wax female figure with its skin removed and with outstretched arms, suggesting the cost of submission to God's will. Another sculpture, *Mary Magdalene*, 1994, riffs on the Renaissance artist Donatello's sculpture of the same name from 1455, but while Donatello depicted the legendary former prostitute in her later years as a gaunt, half-crazed hermit in the desert, Smith covered her naked body not with animal skins but with a layer of body hair, and restored her former sensuality by making her voluptuous. Thus Smith suggests her own unwillingness, as a contemporary woman, to accept Christianity's traditional opposition of piety and sexuality.

Female religious icons also appear in the work of artist Mariko Mori, who populates her installations, video, and photography with Pop-inflected representations of Shinto goddesses and Buddhist saints. Mori first came to international recognition with a series of staged photographs in which she spoofed the rigid roles laid out for women in contemporary Japanese society, appearing herself as cyber princess, Shinto goddess, geisha, and Japanese everywoman. In time, Mori's works have become technically dazzling, as she experiments with digital imaging, virtual reality, and other special effects that often offset ancient, anti-materialist forms of spirituality. In the video *Pureland*, 1998, the artist, in a peach-colored kimono, floats in the sky while cartoon musicians swoop by, Jetson-style. Mori's melding of Shinto-Buddhist spirituality and cyber reality peaks in *Wave UFO*, 1999–2002, a giant white pod that was installed in the glass atrium of a midtown Manhattan office building. Visitors who ventured inside were hooked up to electrodes that monitored their brainwaves and generated a light show that was part interactive bio-feedback and part pre-programmed graphic animation. While embedded in kitsch, the aim of Mori's work is not satirical but sincere, suggesting that the sensory overload of

ALMA LOPEZ

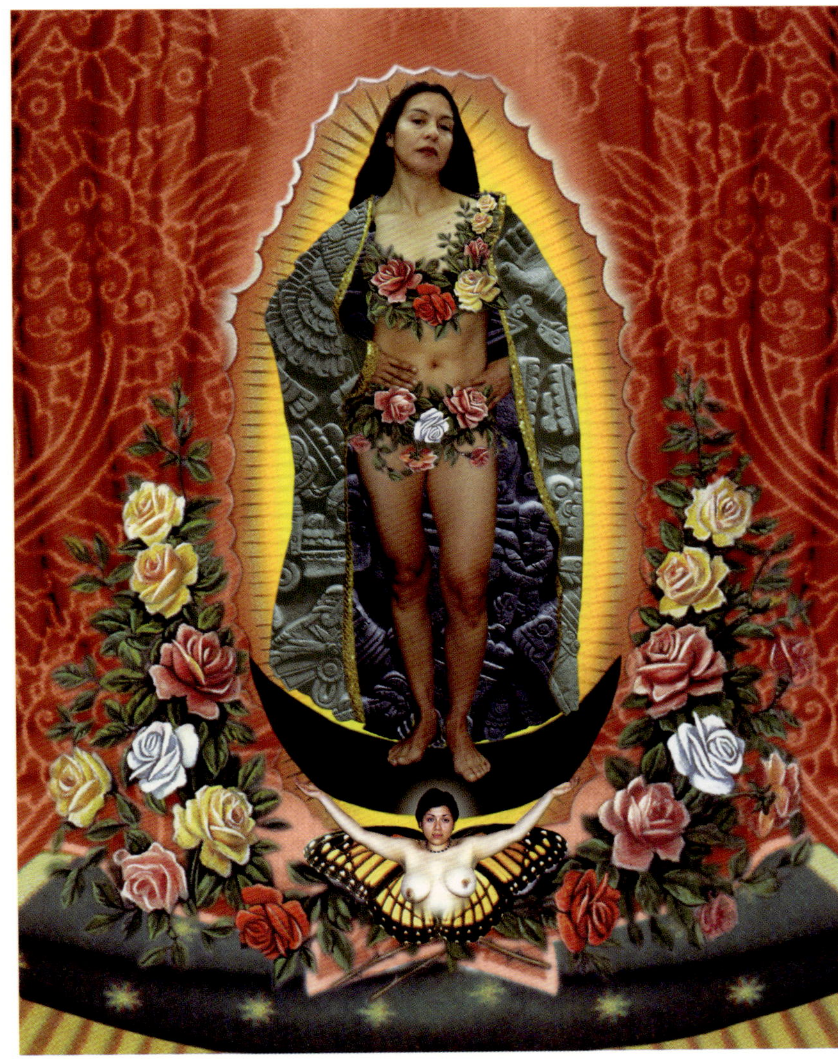

Our Lady, 1999
Iris print on canvas, 14 x 17 in (35.6 x 43.2 cm)

KIKI SMITH

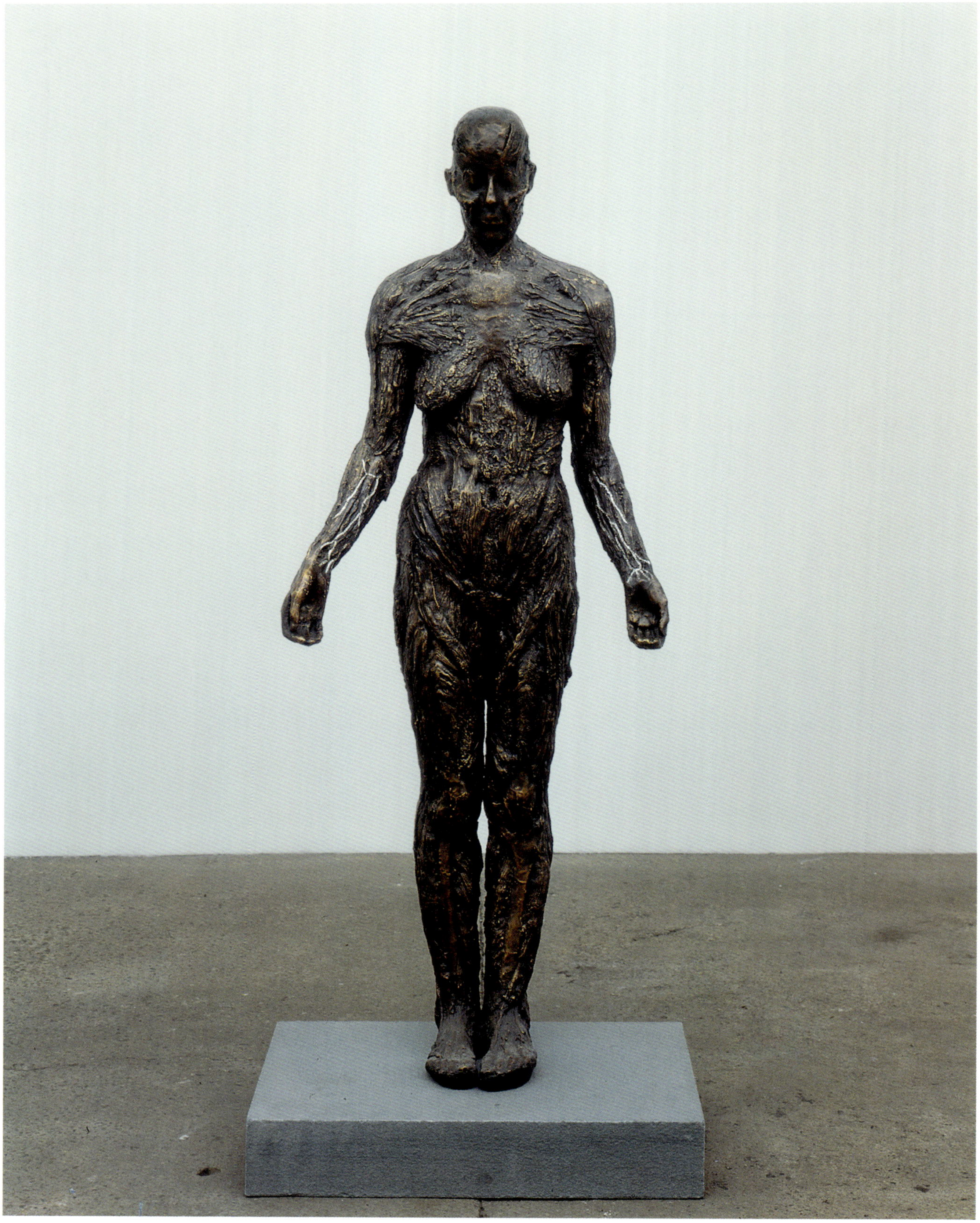

Virgin Mary, 1993
Bronze and silver inlay, life-size

MARIKO MORI

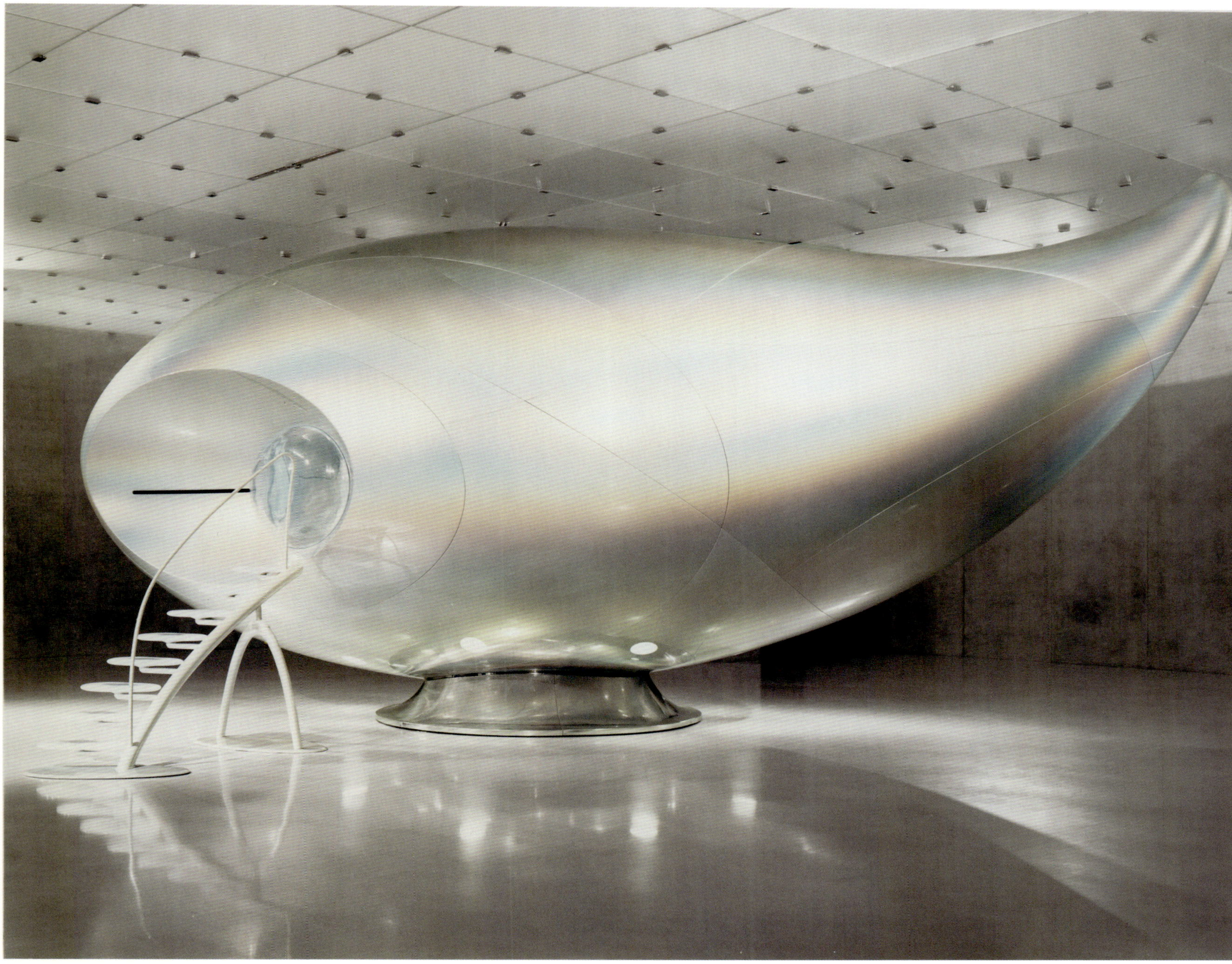

Wave UFO, 1999–2002
Brainwave interface, vision dome, projector, computer system, fiberglass, Technogel®, acrylic, carbon fiber, aluminum, magnesium
16 ft x 36 ft 10 in x 17 ft 2 in (4.9 x 11.3 x 5.3 m)

SHAHZIA SIKANDER

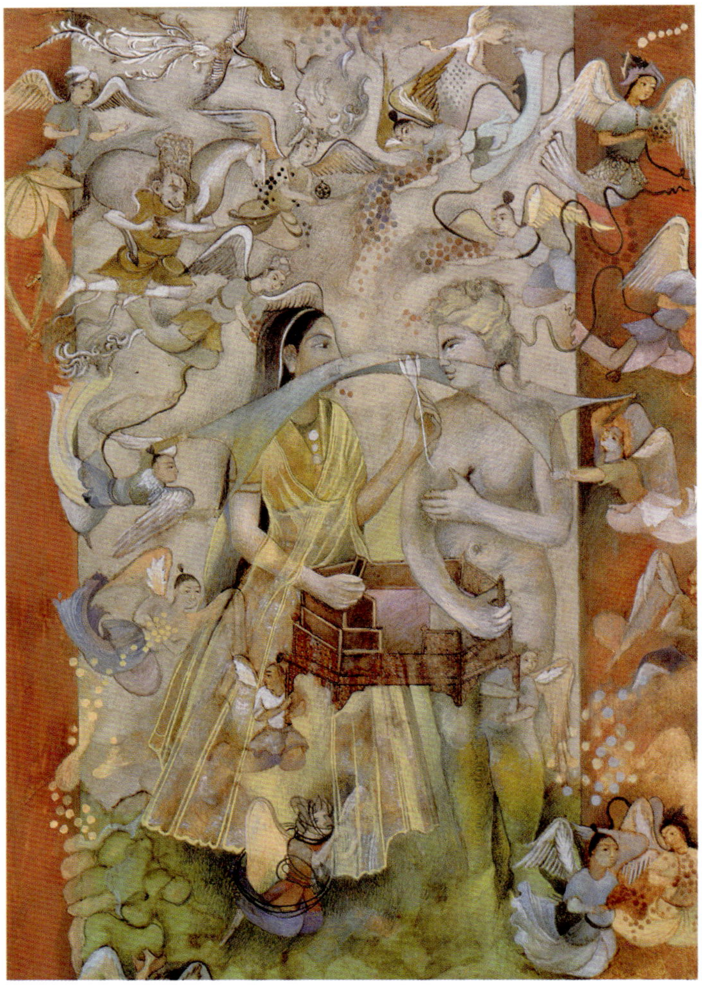

Sly Offering, 2001
Vegetable color, dry pigment, watercolor, tea, and ink on hand-prepared wasli paper
8 1/8 x 5 in (20.6 x 12.7 cm)

TRENTON DOYLE HANCOCK

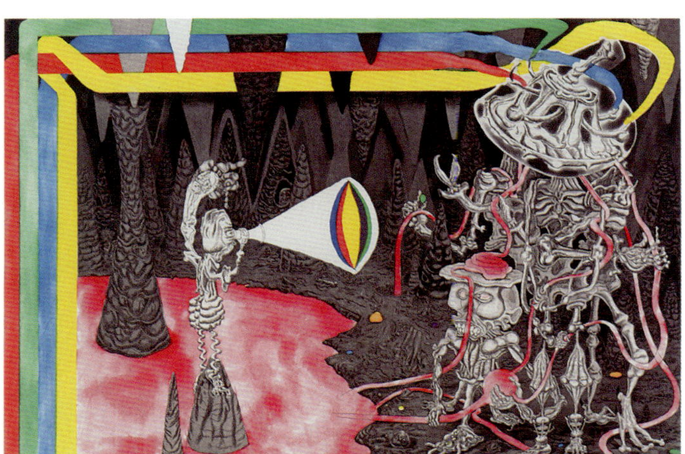

The Ossified Theosophied (Harmony), 2005
Color etching, 25 x 19 1/2 in (63.5 x 49.5 cm)

modern technology might transport viewers to a state of universal consciousness and enlightenment.

Shahzia Sikander also incorporates religious iconography into her work. Drawing on her intensive study of traditional South Asian miniature painting techniques, she combines the practices of Hindu Rajput and Muslim Mughal painting (already a hybrid), with motifs borrowed from Western Renaissance art. Her compositions, rendered in the manuscript-page scale and format of traditional miniatures, are layered and seductive like their precedents, but on close viewing, anomalies emerge. Mythical beasts, naked women in translucent veils, Hindu goddesses, and snatches of landscape are dismantled and remixed in a way that parallels Sikander's own identity as an artist displaced from her native Pakistan to the United States. In *Entanglement*, 2001, a pair of snake-bodied figures is imprisoned behind a pair of guns with twisted barrels. In *Sly Offering*, 2001, a woman in a sari and a Western nude face off beneath a host of Asian angels. Sikander has also combined digital animation with her paintings, creating kaleidoscopic arrangements of slowly changing images, texts, and symbols superimposed over traditional-looking compositions. With such works she simultaneously follows and breaks the rules of the miniature tradition, suggesting that art, tradition, identity, and spirituality are all subject to processes of change.

Trenton Doyle Hancock, whose stepfather was a Baptist minister, grew up immersed in the rhetoric of the biblical Book of Revelation, which recounts the final rebellion of Satan against God at Armageddon and culminates in the second coming of Christ and the dispatch of the just and unjust to their eternal rewards. Not surprisingly, given the potency of this saga, Hancock has appropriated its spirit in his work. His ongoing untitled chronicle, which he began in 1998, is an invented narrative that recounts the epic battle between what Hancock calls the Mounds, who combine characteristics of trees, animals, and humans and represent nature and sensuality, and the more humanoid Vegans, who live underground and are vegetarian, puritanical, color blind, and bent on world domination. This narrative, ongoing since 2000, has yielded an all-encompassing universe played out in paintings that splash across the walls of entire rooms and combine various drawing styles, bits of fake black-and-white fur or fabric, and narrative text with graphic punch. Words curl in explosive spirals over surrealist landscapes or figures, interweave with images to become almost abstract patterns, or hover like captions, retelling the apocalyptic tale from the artist's own evangelical Christian upbringing—updated, reimagined, and as powerful as ever. *The Ossified Theosiphied (Harmony)*, 2005, depicts a pivotal moment in the story, when a Vegan minister proposes to tame his unruly people by introducing them to color via a "Miracle Machine," a development that reflects the notion that optical pleasure (clearly a metaphor for art) may have a redemptive function.

Mark Wallinger, who was raised in the tradition of the Church of England, also represents biblical texts, though he steers clear of the realms of fantasy and imagination. For him, everyday life supplies adequate material for meditations on heaven, hell, death, and belief rendered in video, photography, sculpture, and installation. One of Wallinger's best-known works, *Ecce Homo*, 1999, represents Christ just prior to the Crucifixion as a contemporary young man in a loin cloth wearing a barbed wire crown. Installed on a plinth in Trafalgar Square, it was a resonant contrast to the nearby monument to Lord Nelson, enduring emblem

MARK WALLINGER

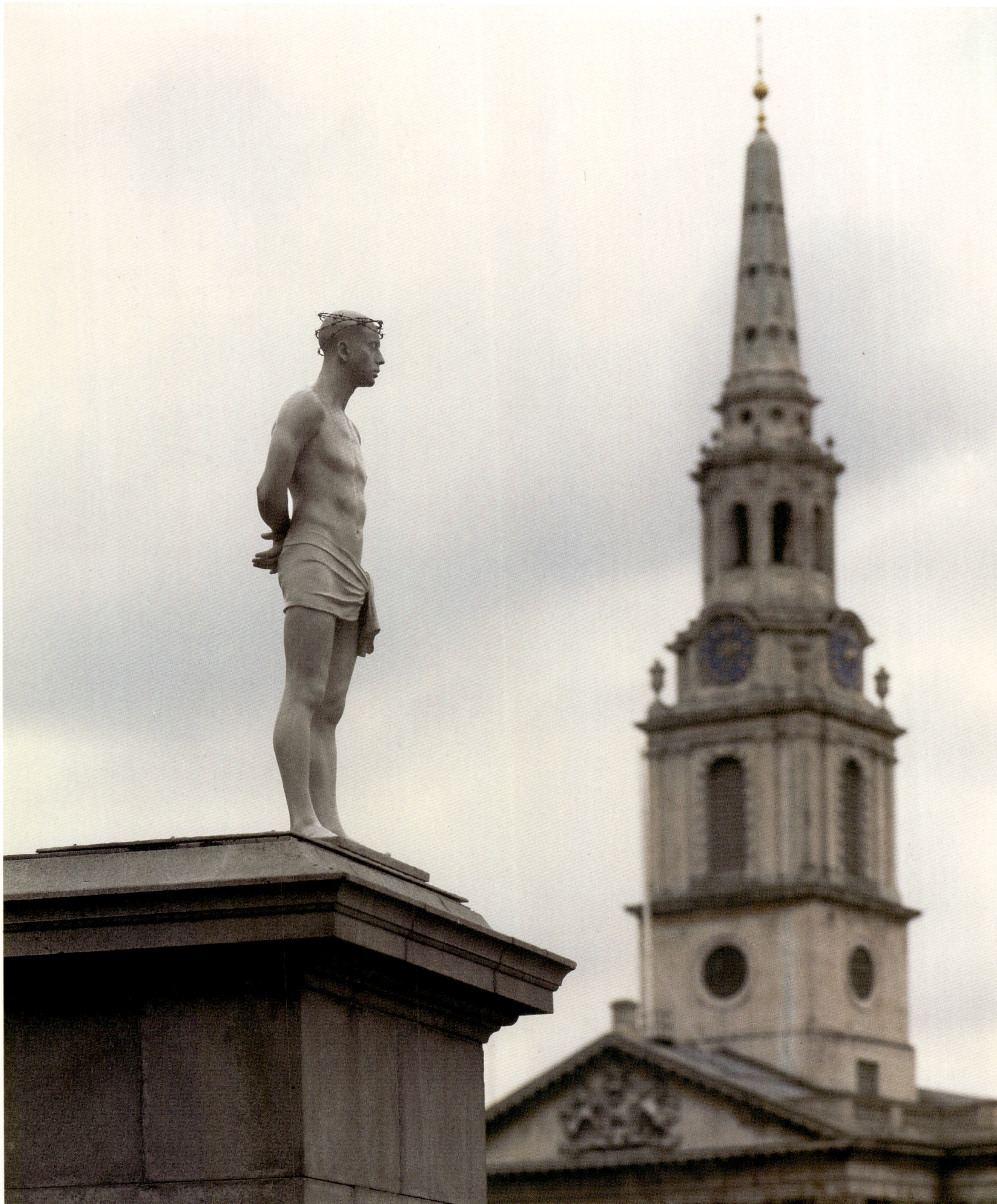

Ecce Homo, 1999
White marbleised resin, gold leaf, barbed wire, 71 3/4 in (182 cm) high
As installed at Trafalgar Square, London, July 1999–February 2000

R. B. KITAJ

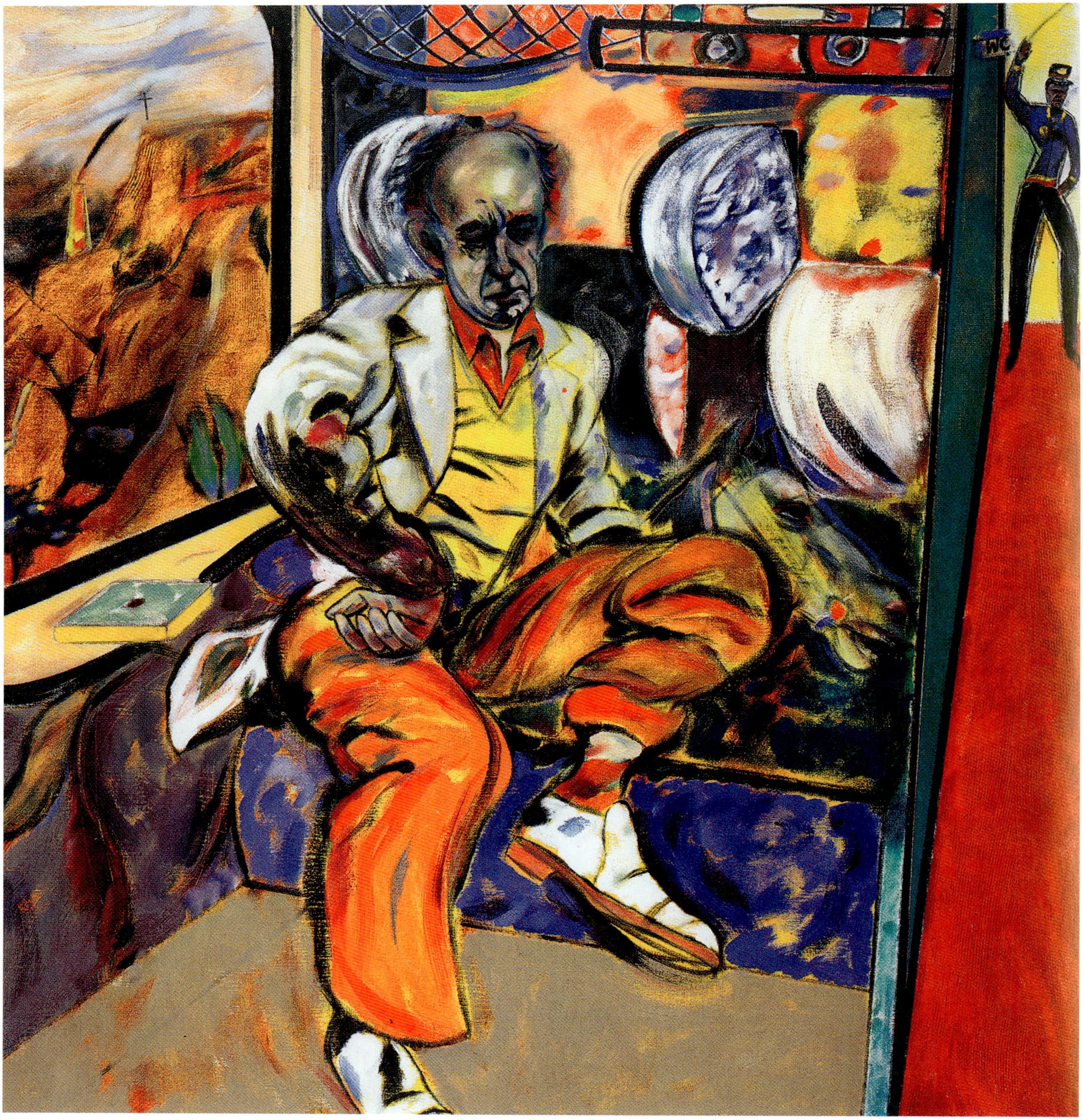

The Jewish Rider, 1984–85
Oil and black chalk on canvas, 60 x 60 in (152.4 x 152.4 cm)
Scottish National Gallery of Modern Art, Edinburgh

of British seapower and nationalism. Wallinger has also adopted an alter ego, a character named Blind Faith. As his name suggests, Blind Faith is sightless. He has a white cane and sunglasses, and wears a white shirt and black tie. In the 1997 video *Angel*, he speaks a garbled reversed version of the opening five verses of the Book of John as he walks backward up the down escalator at London's Islington tube station. On adjacent escalators, commuters go up and down normally, but Blind Faith's orientation makes them appear to be facing the wrong way. When Blind Faith completes his recitation, he turns around, walks up the elevator, and disappears from view, like some prophet briefly touching down in contemporary urban life.

As these examples show, contemporary artists engaging Christian, Buddhist, Hindu, and Muslim traditions have a wealth of visual references from which to draw. Art in a Jewish religious tradition, which forbids the creation of images of God, has tended to be more abstract and symbolic. Another factor that enters into representations of Jewish spirituality is the complexity of Jewish identity. Are Jews members of a common religion, ethnic group, nation, or set of cultural traditions? Depending on the individual, the answer might be all or none of the above. R. B. Kitaj expresses the many facets of modern Jewish consciousness in paintings whose kaleidoscopic imagery is realized in eclectic styles drawing from expressionism, Cubism, Surrealism, primitivism, and realism. His diverse themes range from his own sexuality to twentieth-century politics. Some works include symbols of transport and imprisonment, among them trains, chimneys, suitcases, and ladders, that allude to the rise of fascism and the Jewish experience of the Holocaust. In *If Not, Not*, 1975–76, which contains an image of the Auschwitz gatehouse, the reference is explicit. In other works, like *The Jewish Rider*, 1984–85, it is more subtle: a figure in contemporary clothes rides on a train in relative comfort, but a cross and a smokestack in the landscape outside the window and an authoritarian looking train conductor in the background allude to the trains that took Jews to concentration camps and to their deaths. Regardless of the passage of time and the diversity of Jewish identification, the legacy of the Holocaust lurks in some of Kitaj's most potent work.

Archie Rand, a fan of comic strips and graphic novels—whose illustrators, he has noted, are disproportionately Jewish—has created a contemporary equivalent of traditional Jewish storytelling in his paintings. His 2002 cycle *The Nineteen Diaspora Paintings*, for example, tells biblical stories in a loose graphic style with bubbles of text hovering over the characters. The stories are familiar but combined with contemporary references: in *Cain and Abel*, Cain is led away from the scene of his brother's murder by burly cops, as a police photographer records the scene. Solomon appears in the guise of a construction worker building his temple, while the prophet Elijah rises to heaven in a spaceship. Another cycle, *The Eighteen: Blessings at the Heart of Jewish Worship*, 1998, dispenses with imagery, each painting conveying through abstract colors and patterns the emotional meaning of one of the eighteen blessings spoken during daily services at the temple. Similarly, Rand's *Chapter Paintings*, 1989, combine pop culture images with traditional Jewish symbols to explicate each of the divisions of the Torah. With all of these works, Rand speaks to the modern world, revitalizing the sense of moral urgency in parables that might otherwise seem like mere conventions from eras past.

Helène Aylon also mines the Jewish literary tradition, but she does so to challenge women's exclusion from certain parts of Jewish ritual and to counter patriarchal

ARCHIE RAND

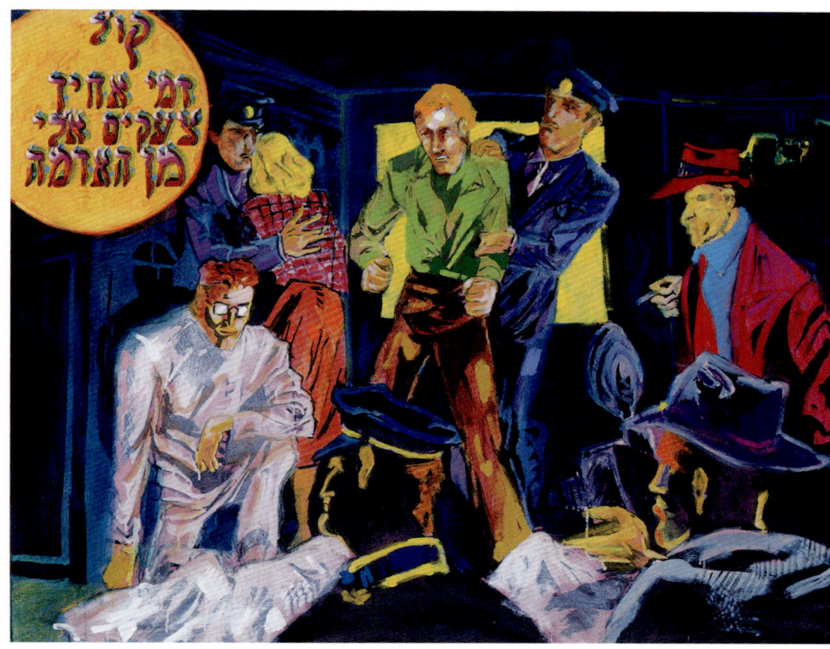

Cain and Abel, 2002
Acrylic on fabric, 48 x 64 in (121.9 x 162.6 cm)

messages embedded in the Torah. For Aylon, who was raised Orthodox and married a rabbi while still in her teens, the Jewish tradition at times coheres into a suffocating system whose orthodoxies must be challenged in the name of gender equality. Her text-based work reflects the Jews' status as "people of the book," and in fact her reexamination of sacred texts from a feminist point of view is very much in keeping with the Jewish tradition of midrash, or biblical commentary, which has engaged Jewish scholars for millennia. In her installation of the five books of the Torah, *The Liberation of G-d*, 1990–96 (the missing "o" is in keeping with the Jewish prohibition against naming God), Aylon has included a video in which she makes marks in those books highlighting the phrases that underscore assumptions, rituals, and laws that denigrate women. In a text that accompanies *The Liberation of G-d*, she argues that these injustices are not inherent in her religion, noting, "I look into the passages / where patriarchal attitudes / have been projected onto / G-d / as though man / has the right to have / dominion / even over / G-d." Instead her work proposes to perform a *tikkun*, or a healing, to repair the damage these errors have done to Jews' relationship with the Divine.

Grisha Bruskin grew up in Soviet Russia, where Jews were forbidden from practicing their religion, but were stigmatized nonetheless. Later in life, the artist studied Judaism, and while living in Soviet Russia and, more recently, in the United States, he has created work based on Jewish and Soviet myth, both of which have their sacred writings, their holy relics, their messianic missions, and their chosen people. Bruskin's 1984 series "Alefbet" developed out of his reading of the Kabbalah, the Jewish philosophy based on a mystical interpretation of Scripture. The series consists of paintings and sculptures of figures in traditional Jewish garb, each equipped with an "attribute" in the manner of Russian icons. The attributes, which traditionally identify the role or status of the figure, are given a twist here. They come out of Jewish tradition or folklore, but are not confined to traditional meanings. For instance, in *Vision*, 1998–99, a figure with two oversized eyes suggests the ability to see into the future; in another, animal masks on human figures reflect on the Second Commandment's interdiction against human representation. While "Alefbet" expresses the liberating potential of Jewish mythology, "Birth of the Hero," 1985–88, takes on the stultifying dishonesty of Soviet myth: the celebratory clichés are personified in painted bronze or stainless steel statues of blank-faced Soviet types—the soldier, the young pioneer, the worker, the athlete. As in "Alefbet," each figure displays an attribute, many of which underline the absurdity of official Soviet creed. Here, attributes include elements like small fighter planes or replicas of Lenin's mausoleum. Taken together, these two series suggest the two sides of myth, one a source for self-exploration and discovery, and the other an authoritarian system of citizenry control.

The duality expressed in Bruskin's two series is representative of a conflict that often infuses the work of contemporary artists coming from a Judeo-Christian tradition, who have inherited the supposed opposition between contemporary art and religion. By contrast, for artists working in other spiritual traditions, art is and always has been a vital element in religious worship and spiritual exploration, with no modernist breach along the way. The late Montien Boonma, for instance, was a practicing Buddhist, and his works employ materials and objects used in Buddhist ritual, melding them with natural forms and Buddhist architecture. Some of his sculptures were based on Buddhist alms bowls, "painted" with healing herbs and

HELÈNE AYLON

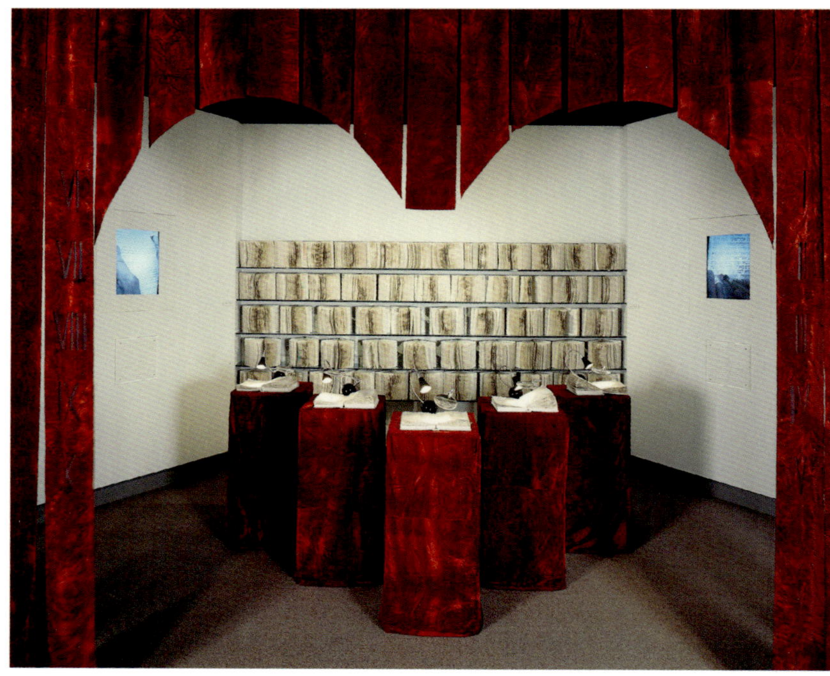

The Liberation of G-d, 1990–96
As installed at the Jewish Museum, New York, 1996

enclosed in temple-like stacks of hundreds of ceramic temple bells. In other works, Boonma, who died of cancer in 2000, addressed the unreality of suffering and the continuity of life through reincarnation. His *House of Hope*, 1997, is a meditative space entered by ascending a set of simple wooden stairs, then passing through thousands of cascading strands of Buddhist prayer beads made of herbal medicines. *Melting Void: Molds for the Mind*, 1999, is also interactive and meditative. Built from fragments of molds used to cast a sculpture of the Buddha's head, these giant propped-up helmets invite the viewer to stand inside and be enveloped by darkness, as the noise and clutter of daily life momentarily melt away. Through such works, Boonma created spaces that seemed to exist outside of ordinary space and time.

Like Buddhism, the hybrid religions born of the fusion of African, pre-Columbian, and Christian traditions have continuity on their side. José Bedia is an initiate of Palo Monte, an Afro-Cuban religion that draws equally on Kongo rituals and the New World experience of slavery endured by the religion's founders. Bedia has combined his knowledge of Palo Monte, which honors the trees of the forest as revered spirits, with a study of the rituals of the Lakota Indians of North Dakota to create sculptures, drawings, and installations that are deeply spiritual and seethingly political, celebrating pantheism and resistance to colonial intrusion. A recurring figure in Bedia's work is Sarabanda, a legendary black man who worked on the railroad and defended the people of Cuba. At the Institute of Contemporary Art in Philadelphia in 1994, in an installation titled *De Donde Vengo* (Where I'm Coming From), Bedia installed a huge flying figure of Sarabanda over an old Cadillac's six-cylinder engine "planted" with branches, evoking Palo Monte talismans of good fortune and virility. A 1992 installation titled *Brevisima relación de la destrucción de las Indias* (A brief history of the destruction of the Americas) protested the widespread celebrations of the 500th anniversary of Christopher Columbus's "discovery" of America. The installation included a section titled "The arrival of Christ," in which three animal pelts were nailed to a wall in a counter-crucifixion commemorating the genocide of the native peoples by the Christian conquerors. With such works, Bedia uses the visual language of ritual to suggest the historic and contemporary melding of religion and politics.

Ana Mendieta's work also incorporates pre-Columbian and Afro-Cuban beliefs. Mendieta, who died in 1985 after a fatal fall from her window, used her own body in works designed to explore the boundaries between the worlds of matter and spirit. Mendieta moved from Cuba to Iowa in 1961 at the age of thirteen under the auspices of Operation Peter Pan, a program organized by the American Catholic Church to remove children from Castro's Cuba. This traumatic separation from her parents and her native country permanently marked her consciousness and became a subtext for much of her art. Influenced early on by the ritualistic performance art of Bruce Nauman, Carolee Schneemann, and Vito Acconci, Mendieta visited Mexico in 1973, which sparked an interest in her Cuban heritage. Subsequently she began to incorporate references to Spanish Colonial Catholicism, Afro-Cuban practices like Santería, Abakua, and Palo Monte, and the nature worship of indigenous Caribbean religions into her work. Mendieta is best known for her "Siluetas," a series of works in which she merged her body with nature, either literally, by laying naked in various landscapes—sometimes covered with mud, grass, or flowers, as in *Imagen de Yagul* (Image of Yagul), 1973—or figuratively, by creating surrogates for her body out of flowers, rocks, blood, twigs, earth, or fire. Though later commentators saw in these

GRISHA BRUSKIN

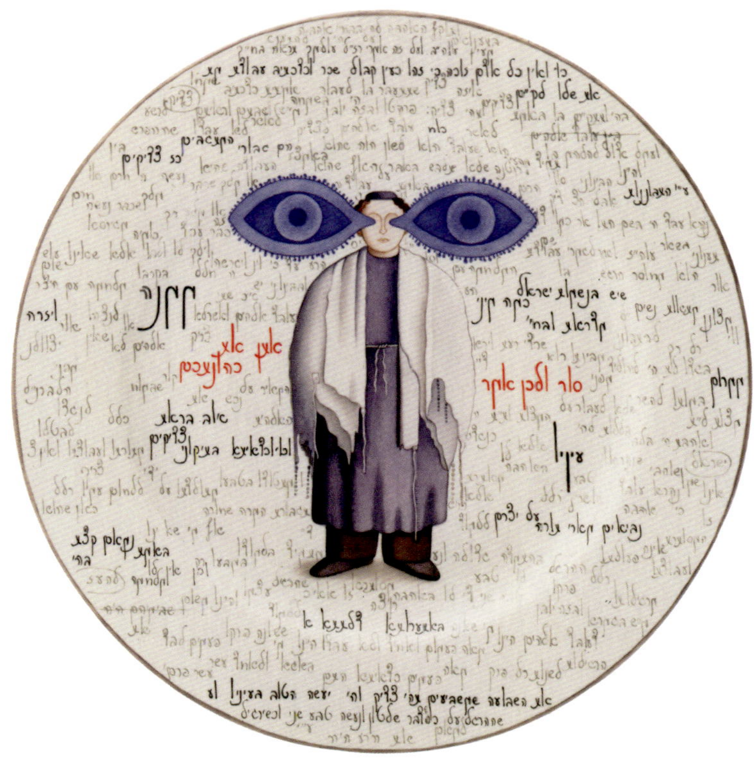

Vision, 1998–99
Hand-painted porcelain, 14 in (35.6 cm) diameter

MONTIEN BOONMA

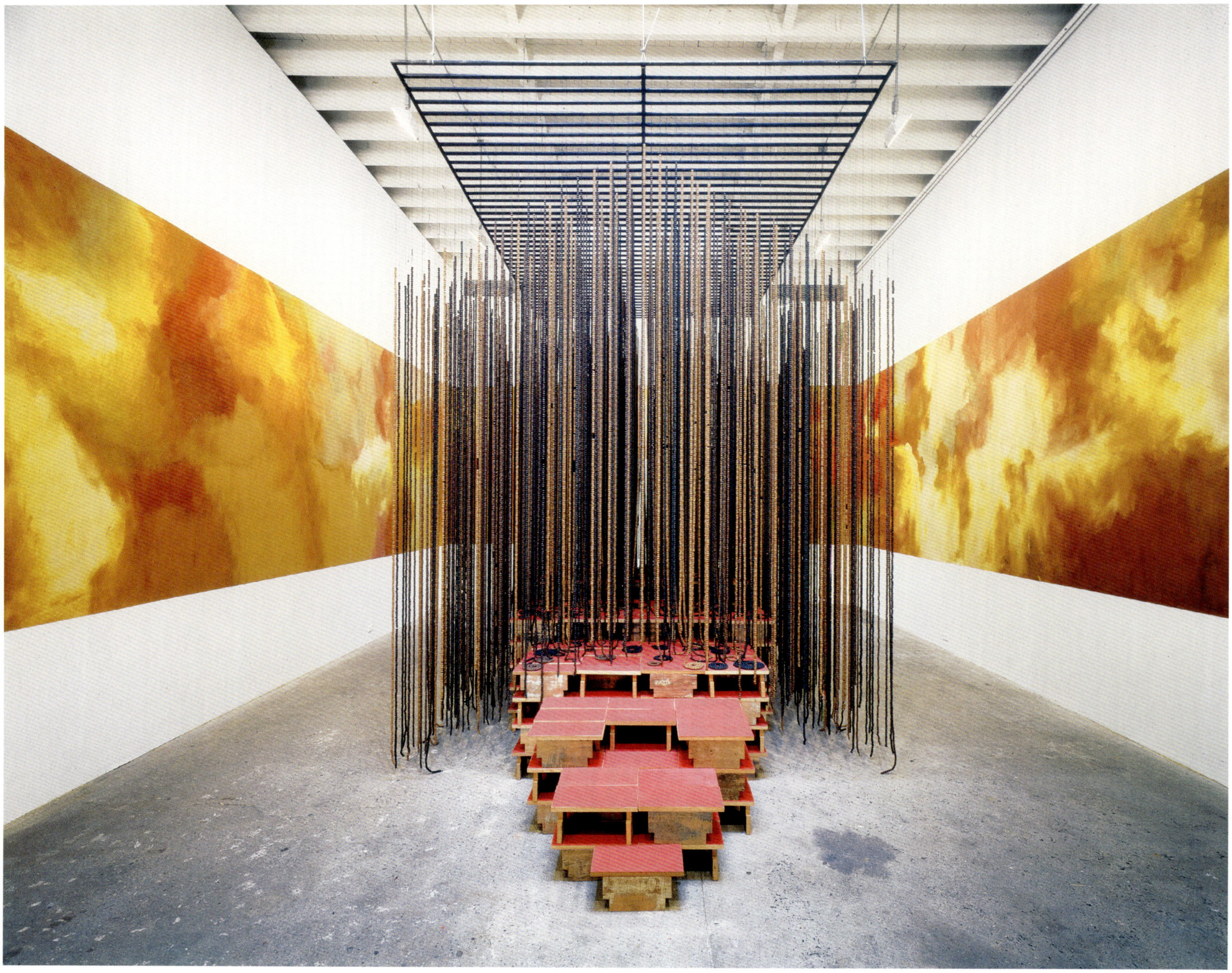

House of Hope, 1997
Steel grill, herbs, Chinese medications

JOSÉ BEDIA

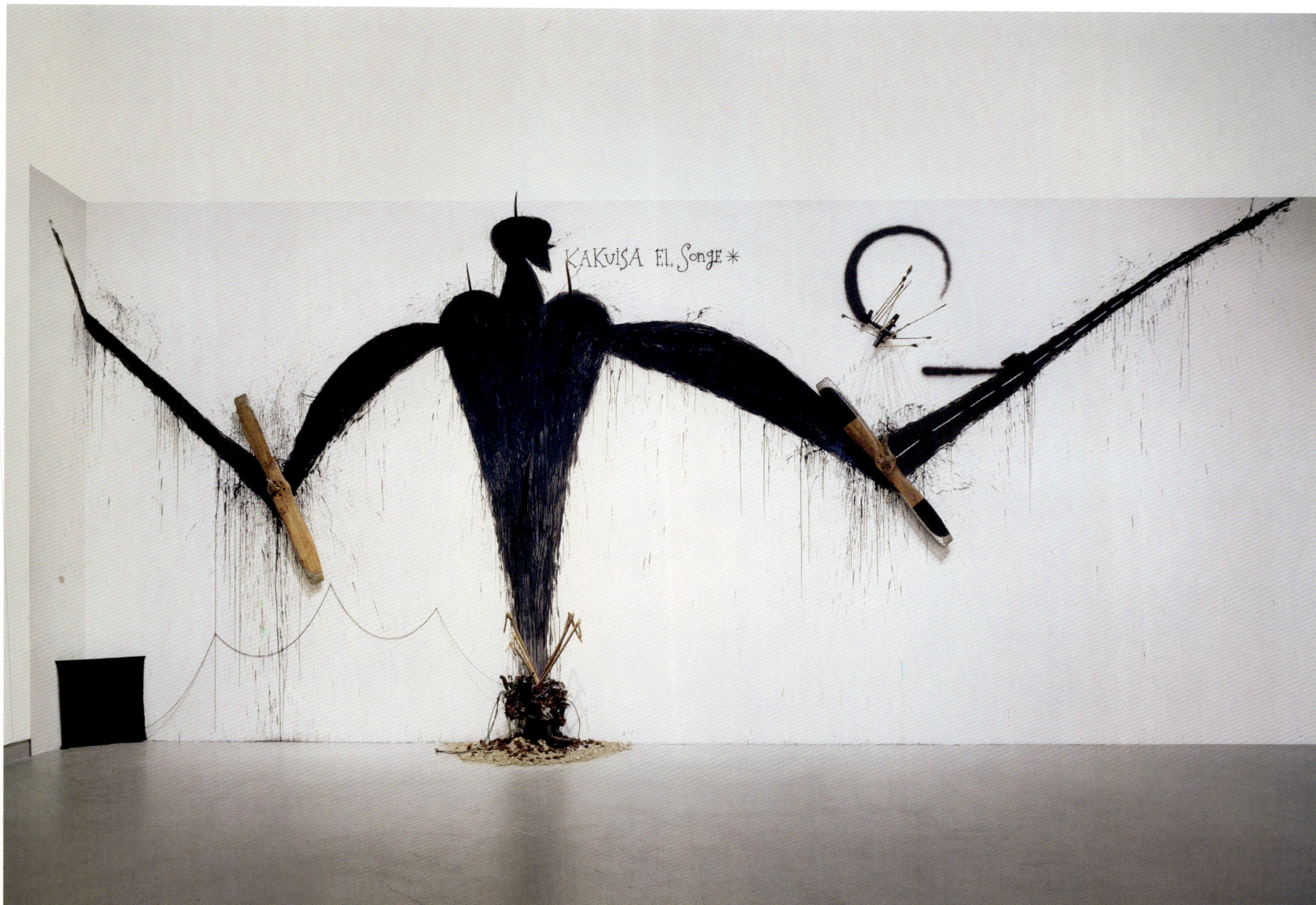

De Donde Vengo (Where I'm Coming From), 1994
Mixed media

ALISON SAAR

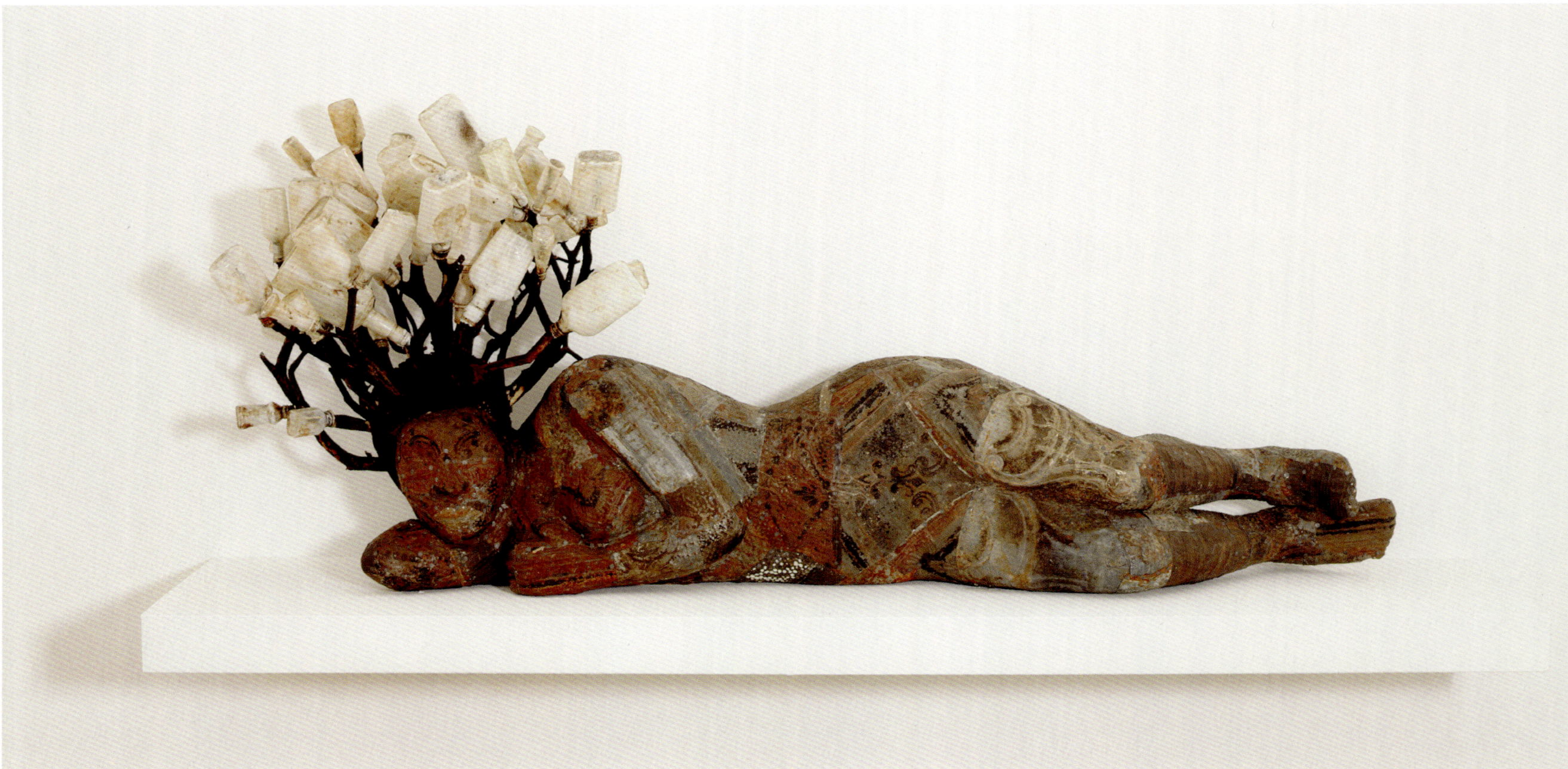

Compton Nocturne, 1999
Wood, ceiling tin, bottles, 28 x 78 x 22 in (71 x 198 x 56 cm)

CHRISTIAN JANKOWSKI

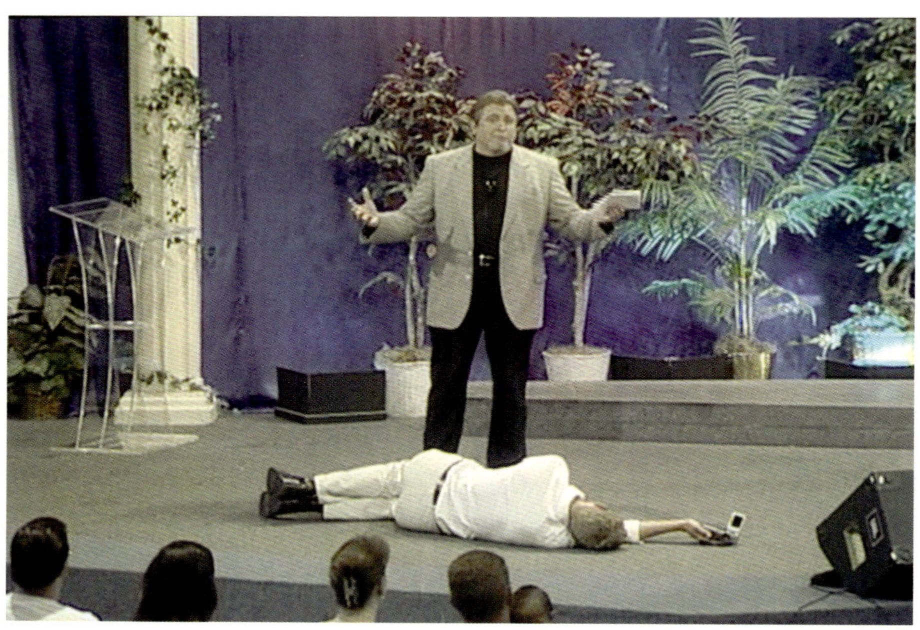

The Holy Artwork, 2001
DVD, 16 minutes

works a preoccupation with death, the artist herself affiliated the "Siluetas" with wombs as well as graves. Mendieta's animist leanings clearly reinforced her sense of the cyclical nature of life, in which death is a beginning as well as an end.

Hybrid spirituality appears not only in Latin America but also in the religious traditions of the American South, where elements of Christianity and residual African shamanism meld. Alison Saar creates sculptures that touch on the practice of "conjure," or the summoning of spirits and forces for either benevolent or malevolent purposes. Like the folk artists who inspire her, Saar uses found materials that radiate a sense of history and spirit, attaching ceiling tin, nails, plastic flowers, votive candles, and discarded license plates to roughly carved wood figures. One recurring element is the blackened skillet, on which Saar paints black women's faces, turning these emblems of domestic labor into monuments to the women who used them. Sometimes Saar's sculptures explicitly reference African antecedents, as in *Love Zombie*, 1988, a robust female figure outfitted with a nail-embedded compartment in her chest and resembling Kongo *nkisi* fetish figures. *Compton Nocturne*, 1999, presents a reclining wood figure with hair made of dark roots or branches that form a sort of bottle tree, an African American totem created to ward off evil spirits. Such works, modern-day fetishes, reinvest contemporary life with ancient principles.

For many artists, such as Boonma and Mendieta, religious traditions serve as vehicles for personal spiritual exploration. Others are drawn to the communal, participatory, performative side of religious worship that is particularly evident in the tradition of Christian evangelism, with its call-and-response chanting, trance-like dancing, and occasional snake handling expressing faith for followers who are filled with the spirit. While his film and video work has taken inspiration from Hollywood movies, horror films, and the art world itself, Christian Jankowski's video *The Holy Artwork*, 2001, makes Evangelism its very subject. Jankowski worked with televangelist Pastor Peter Spencer, who presides over the Harvest Fellowship Church in Texas, to create a broadcast sermon that likens the transcendence of art to that of prayer. As the preacher exhorts his live and television audience to accept the sacred nature of art, the artist comes up to the stage and collapses at the preacher's feet, mimicking believers so overcome with the spirit that they lose consciousness. Speaking over the artist's prone body, the preacher continues his sermon: "It took Christian falling down, no longer becoming the center of attention, to make this a great piece of art." The service ends as a Gospel chorus sings a hymn of praise to God while the phone number for donations appears at the bottom of the screen. *The Holy Artwork* hovers between absurdity, suggesting an ironic send-up of modernist rhetoric about art's quasi-religious nature, and genuine belief, as this rhetoric seems completely acceptable to the religious believers to whom it is addressed.

The Reverend Ethan Acres, a practicing evangelical minister and an artist, uses art to bring people to God in a more purely earnest spirit. An Alabama native, Acres spent his adolescence preaching in Baptist congregations before going on to get an M.F.A. from the University of Nevada and an honorary doctor of divinity over the Internet from the World Christianship Ministries. Since the 1990s, Reverend Acres has been creating religiously inspired performances with a flair for audience enticement (let's "put the *fun* back in fundamentalism," he says). He operates a chapel on wheels—a camper trailer refitted with a baptismal font, neon under-carriage, and stained-glass windows—performs marriages and exorcisms, and gives

ANA MENDIETA

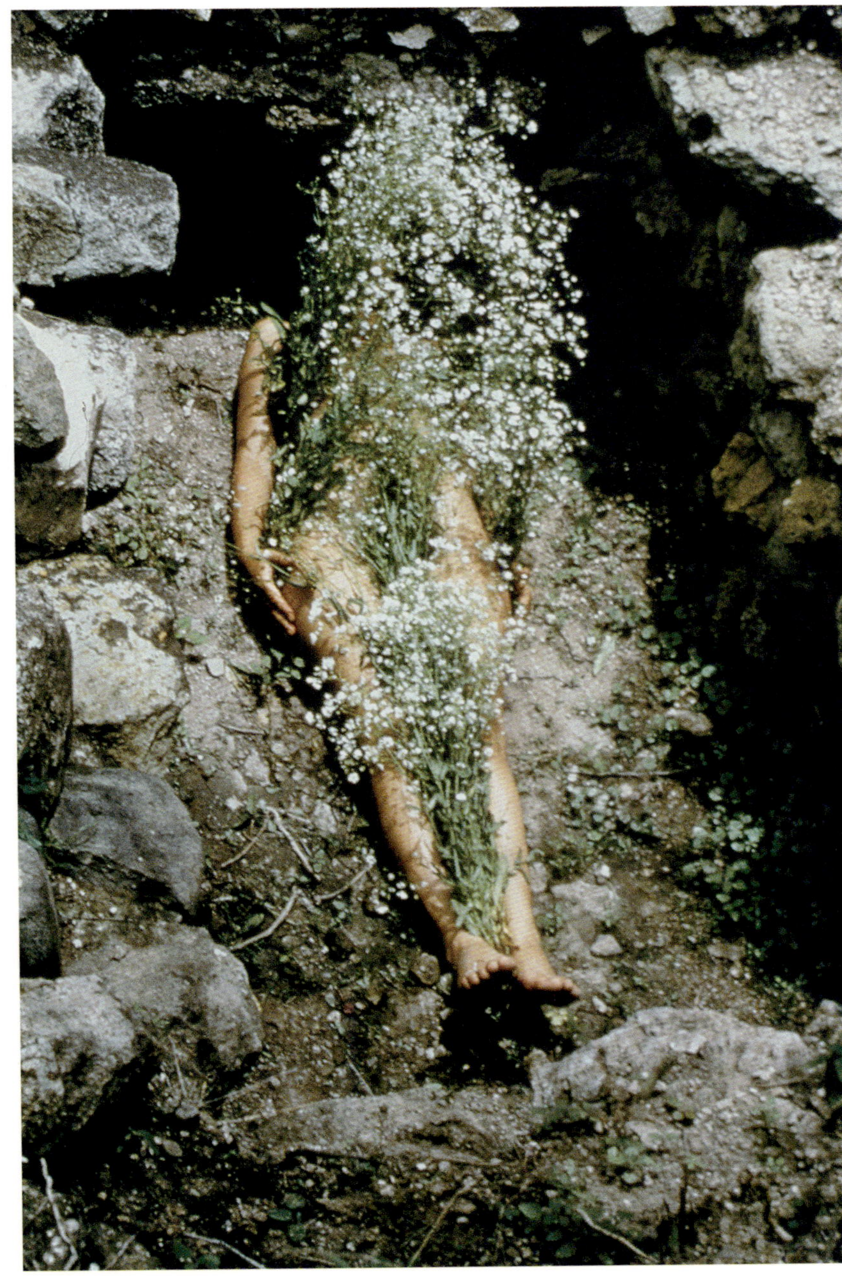

Imagen de Yagul (Image of Yagul), 1973
Lifetime color photograph, 20 x 13 1/4 in (50.8 x 33.7 cm)

REVEREND ETHAN ACRES

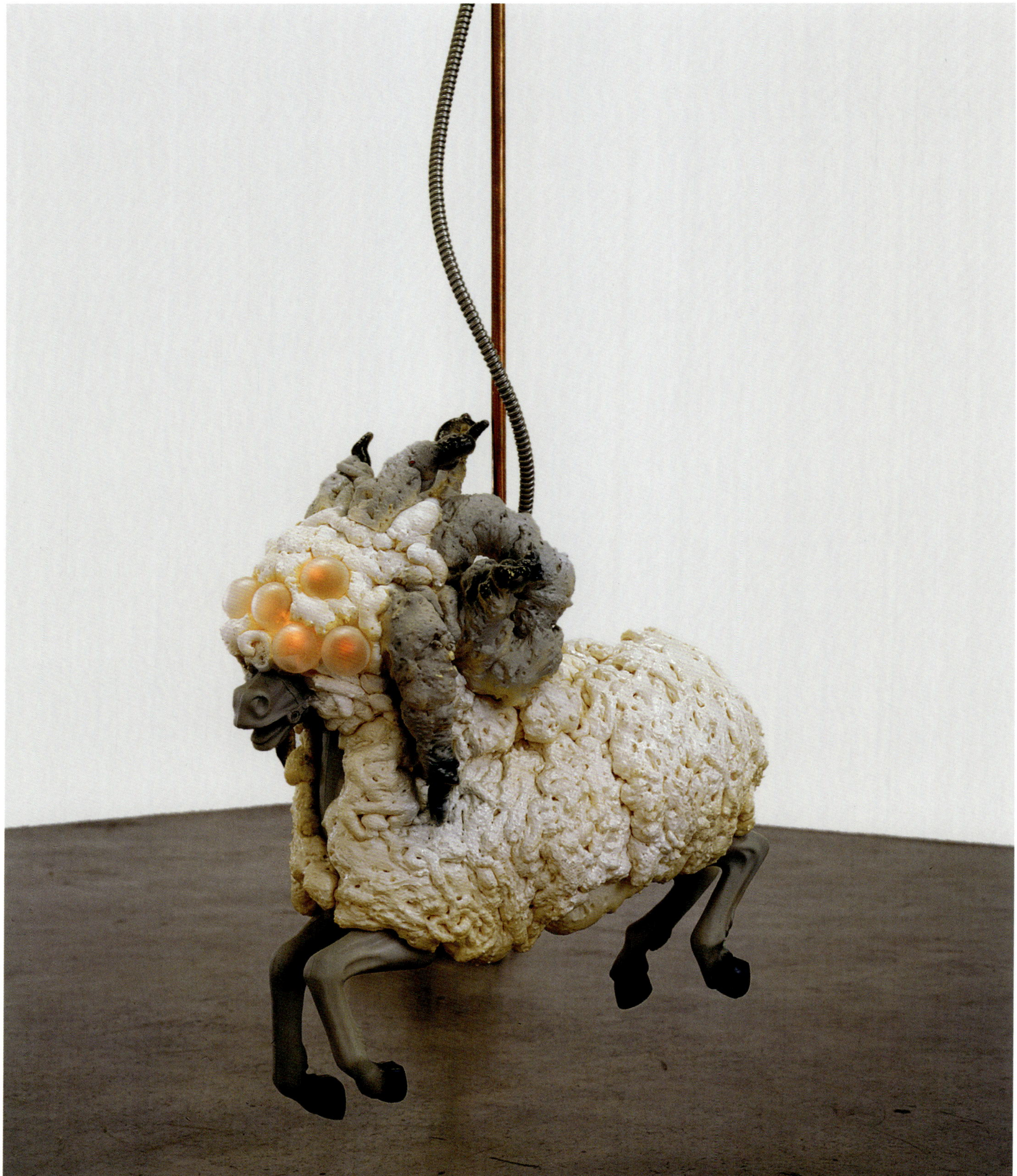

Lamb of God, 1996
Mixed media, 36 x 36 x 18 in (91.4 x 91.4 x 45.7 cm)

sermons that draw on pop culture, explore the devil's modern-day temptations, and promise a peculiarly showbiz style of redemption. His comically uplifting message also appears in sculptures created from found and low-tech materials that depict biblical allegories and parables, and in still photos that seem to present miraculous events. *Lamb of God*, 1996, is a life-size rocking horse, suspended overhead, revolving like a carousel figure, and outfitted with glowing plastic eyeballs that turn it into the fearsome Lamb of the Book of Revelation.

Performance artist Ron Athey takes a more critical approach to the evangelical tradition. Raised by his grandmother and aunt to be a minister in what he describes as an "underground Pentecostal church" that featured faith healing, speaking in tongues, stigmata, and dances in the spirit, Athey is now an HIV-positive gay man covered with tribal tattoos. Athey draws on his background, combining it with ritualistic symbolism from tales of Christ's Passion and the trials of the saints, in performance works dealing with his internal conflicts and the psychological and social toll of AIDS. The artist is active in the S&M subculture, and elements of those activities also appear in his art. His performances have such titles as *Martyrs and Saints*, 1992, and *Deliverance*, 1998, and include onstage piercings, mummification, flagellation, and bloodletting. He notes a special fondness for Saint Sebastian, an officer in the Roman army who was ordered executed by bows and arrows for offering aid to persecuted Christians. In a performance titled *Sebastian Suspended 1999 No. 9*, 2006, his pierced and tattooed body is suspended by chain from scaffolding. Athey also recalls Christ's agonies by donning a literal crown of thorns. The artist argues that his works ultimately serve as an exorcism of the self-hatred acquired in his early Pentecostal years. He finds masochistic play transformative and cathartic, and his performances are designed to reenact both positive and negative aspects of his early experiences.[4]

James Lee Byars took a more personal though no less showman-like approach to life as a spiritual quest. The artist, who died of cancer in 1997, incorporated aspects of Conceptual art, Minimalism, and Fluxus performance into his unorthodox work. Dressing like a magician, in a gold suit and top hat, and confining his work to the colors black, red, white, and gold, he did not distinguish between art, life, and spiritual practice, but rather transformed it all into campy ritual. Critic John Perreault described him as a Zen mystic crossed with a dandy.[5] Among the sensual objects he produced were gold orbs; "books" fashioned from marble and limestone; wall murals of paper crescents, stars, circles, and towers based on ceremonial Japanese origami; and glass spheres arranged on the floor in the form of alchemical symbols. *The Angel*, 1989, consists of 125 delicate blown-glass spheres arranged in four curves that have the evanescence of bubbles, as if they might burst at any moment. In 1994 Byars created a performance and installation titled *The Death of James Lee Byars*, in which he reclined in a gold casket wearing a gold lamé suit in a room whose walls were lined with gold leaf, as if to turn himself into a religious relic.

Byars's art, with its focus on and fetishization of the mortal body, reflects a tendency often found in art inspired by religion: a tension between the world of matter, with its temptations, distractions, and unavoidable desires, and the realm of spirit. In Western traditions in particular, body and spirit are often regarded as opposing forces, and spiritual growth requires struggling to subdue the body. Asian traditions such as Hinduism, Buddhism, and Sufism, by contrast, tend to

RON ATHEY

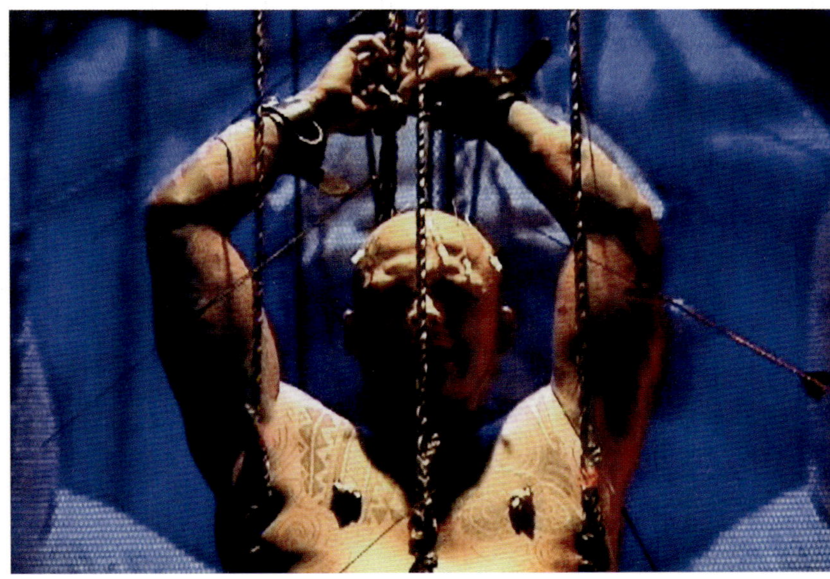

Sebastian Suspended 1999 No. 9, 2006
C-print from video still, edition 1 of 15, 6 x 8 in (15.2 x 20.3 cm)

JAMES LEE BYARS

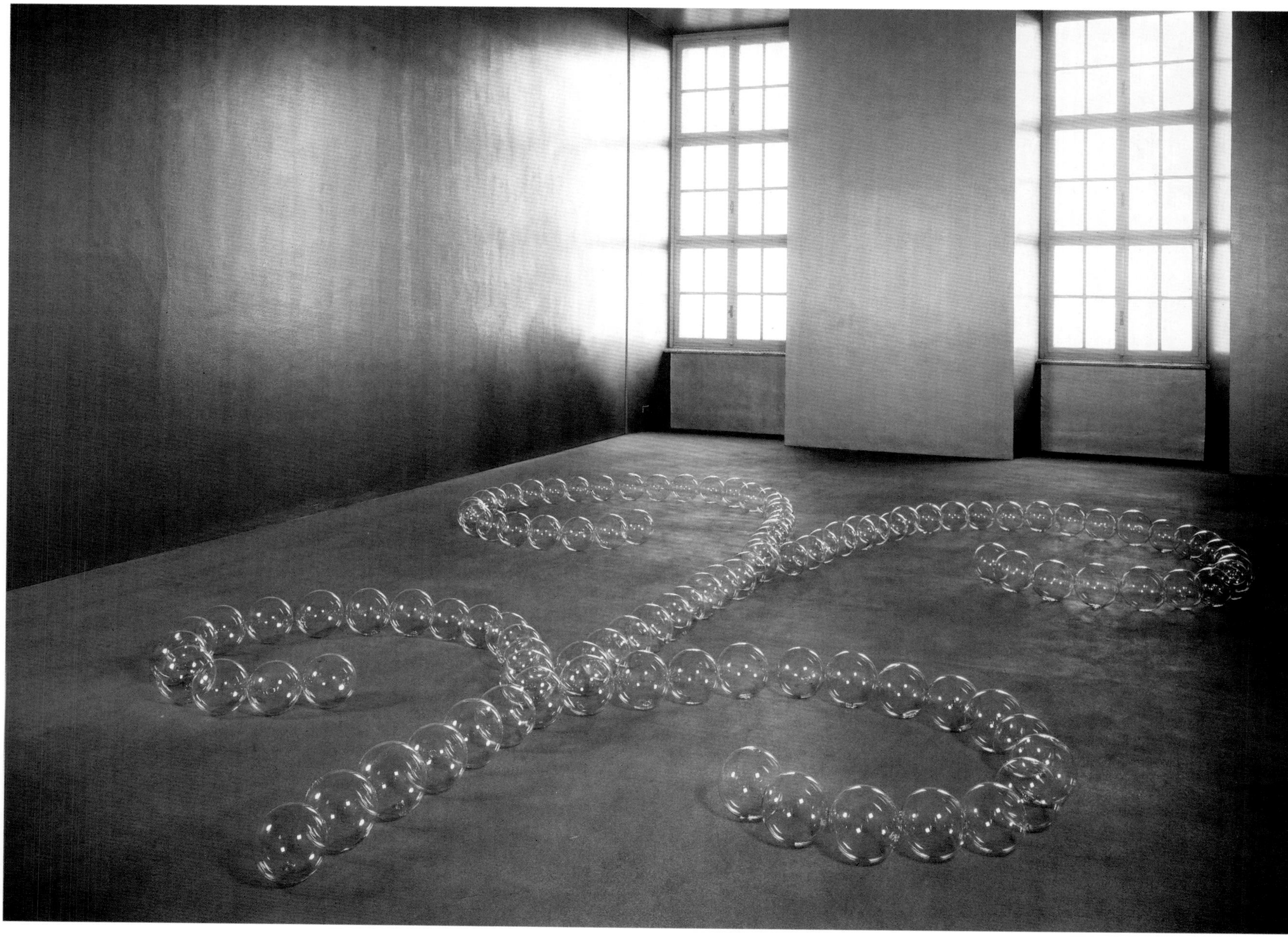

The Angel, 1989
125 glass spheres, 7 in (20 cm) diameter

regard the body as an illusion and instead promise spiritual transformation though purification and transcendence of worldly desires. In the past several decades, Eastern spiritual traditions have attracted strong followings among artists and other seekers frustrated with Western culture's materialism, dualism, and rationalism. In the 1960s and '70s artists such as John Cage, writers such as Allen Ginsberg and Robert Pirsig, and LSD gurus like Timothy Leary and Richard Alpert turned to Zen Buddhism as an escape from political and social turmoil. Meanwhile, more recently, artists from Asian cultures operating in a global environment have found themselves equally susceptible to Western influences. The rise of Christianity in Korea, for instance, or the embrace of consumerism in Japan, has affected traditional modes of belief and religious practice. The cultural cross-currents have given way to a more generalized sense of spirituality that contains Eastern and Western elements.

Curiously, Eastern practices like Zen, Hinduism, and Sufism mesh surprisingly well with developments in Western art over the last thirty years. The reductive aesthetic of Minimalism, the perceptual experiments of Post-Minimalism, and Conceptualism's dematerialized objects provide a visual language that syncs with spiritually-altered states of consciousness. This synchronicity is evident, for instance, in the work of Shirazeh Houshiary, who creates work that draws on her Sufi beliefs but is very much in keeping with the visual language of contemporary Western art. Sufism is an esoteric branch of Islam that centers on the quest for self-knowledge and proposes the fundamental unity of the physical and spiritual realms. Houshiary notes that her sculpture, drawing, and installations are dedicated to "unveiling the invisible." To this end, she uses the formal language of Minimalism, with its cubes, cylinders, and squares, but in her hands, these forms become containers of energy. The sculpture *Breath II*, 2004–5, for instance, is a glazed brick tower in the shape of a double helix that issues sounds drawn from the major religions: the Islamic call to prayer, a Jewish song, the exhalations of Buddhist monks, and a chant by the twelfth-century Christian mystic Hildegard of Bingen. The title of the work suggests its intention, which is to create a sense of a living, breathing entity.

Minimalist geometry is similarly transformed in the work of Anish Kapoor. The child of an irreligious Hindu and an Iraqi Jew, Kapoor embraced Buddhism in his adulthood, and since the 1980s, he has worked with light and perception to create an experience of emptiness that is, paradoxically, full of energy. Kapoor builds large-scale pristine sculptural forms with concave indentations coated with fields of rich, velvety pigment in colors ranging from deep blue to butterfly yellow. The pigment absorbs the light, so that when a viewer stands directly before these works, it is impossible to detect their depth. Instead they seem at once flat and infinitely deep. Other works employ curved stainless steel, which creates reflections that distort the surrounding space while incorporating the viewer into the work. One of the most dramatic of these is *Cloud Gate*, 2004, a 110-ton elliptically shaped sculpture of reflective stainless steel inspired by the form of a drop of mercury. Critics have connected Kapoor's work to the Buddhist concept of the void, a state of consciousness that exists outside of the material world, suggesting that they might even allow viewers to "touch" the void.

Mysticism and modernism also meet in the work of Wolfgang Laib, a master of ephemeral materials who fashions pollen, beeswax, milk, and rice into simple geometric forms that draw simultaneously on Buddhism, Hinduism, and Minimalism.

SHIRAZEH HOUSHIARY & PIP HORNE

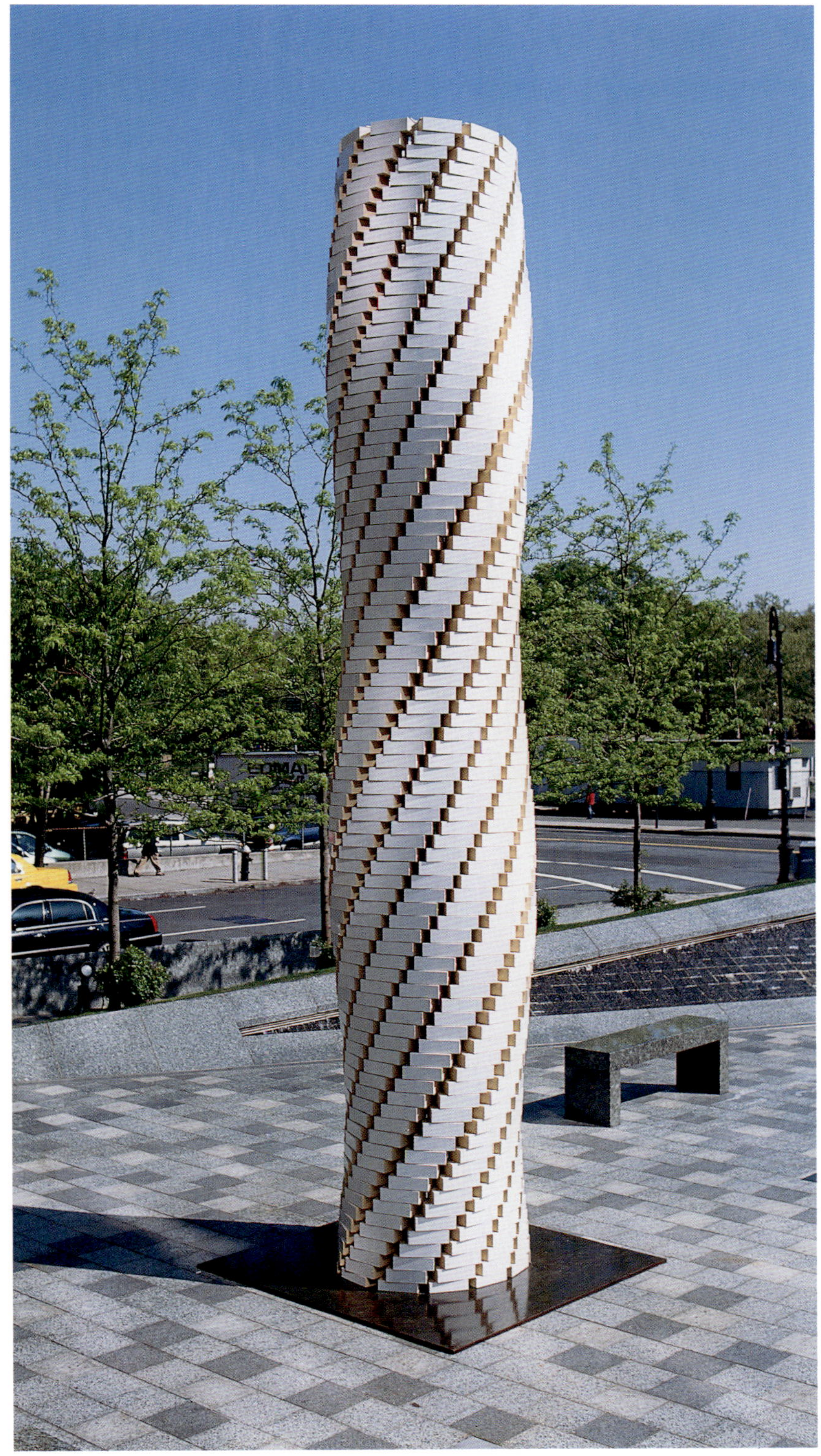

Breath II, 2004–5
Limestone bricks and audio equipment, 21 ft 4 in x 3 ft 11 in x 3 ft 3 in (6.5 x 1.2 x 1 m)
As installed at the Ritz-Carlton Hotel, Battery Park, New York, May 2004–April 2005

ANISH KAPOOR

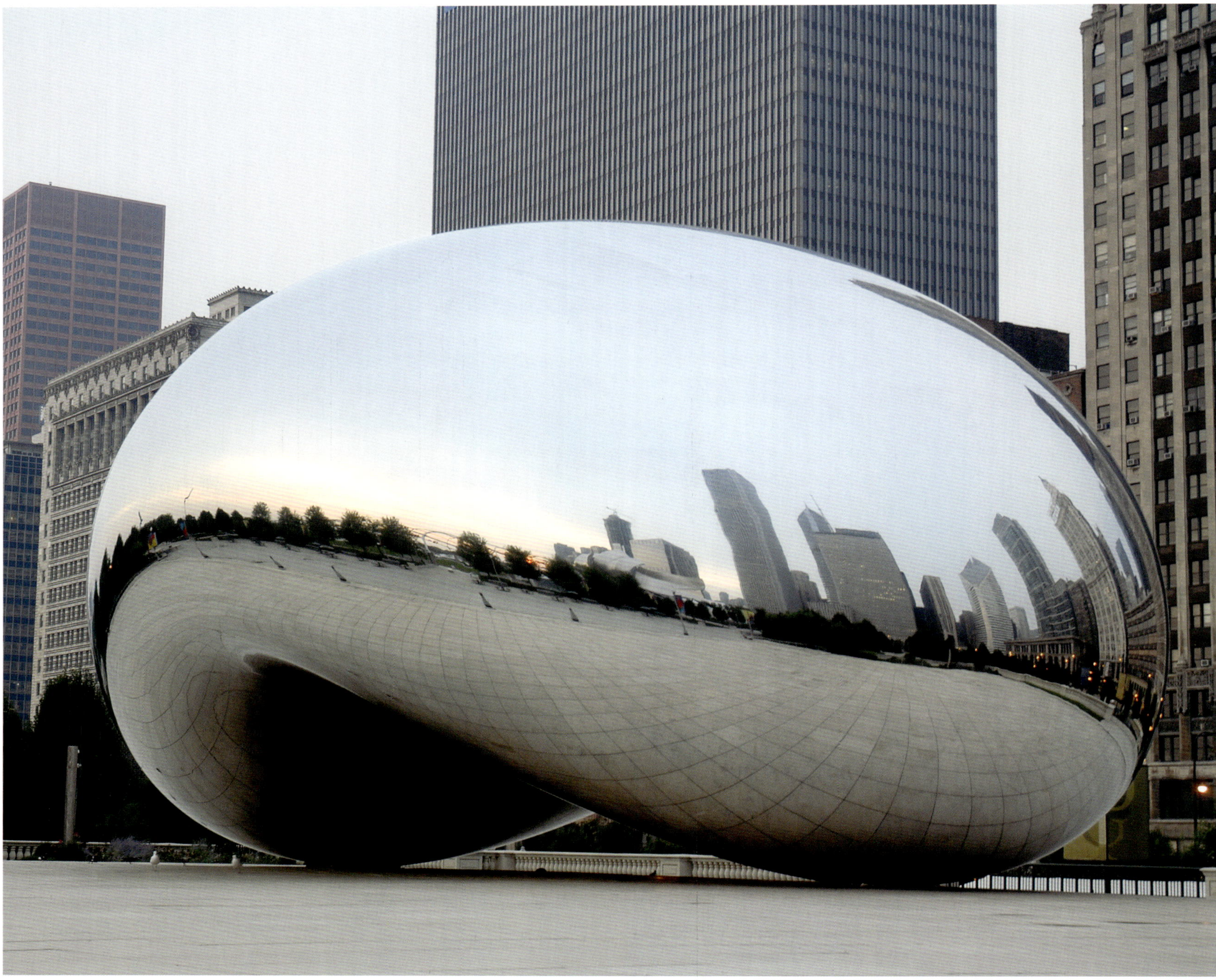

Cloud Gate, 2004
Stainless steel, 66 x 33 ft (20.1 x 10.1 m)
Millennium Park, Chicago

Laib's signature squares of yellow pollen, painstakingly gathered from dandelions, buttercups, and other plants, are laid directly on the floor, daring the viewer to sneeze or otherwise disrupt them. In this they resemble Tibetan mandalas, which are created from intricate patterns of colored sand only to be swept away and discarded after their period of meditative use. *The Five Mountains Not to Climb On*, 1984, consists of five small cone-shaped mounds of golden hazelnut pollen arranged on the floor. The work's title at once spoofs their vulnerability and also suggests the potential for a mental scale shift. Other, larger structures, which may take the form of ziggurats or walk-in rooms, are built from blocks of creamy yellow beeswax. Such works have an almost palpable aroma, which is especially powerful inside the enclosures. Often compared to Joseph Beuys, Laib likewise engages in a search for universal spirituality through a language of natural materials, but Laib is less concerned with the social aspects of art. Instead he provides meditative spaces and objects that function as a door to alternate realities.

Michael Joo draws on his Korean background to incorporate shamanistic elements into investigations of identity, history, and science. He also employs the tropes of Conceptual art to suggest a more holistic alternative to the Western tendency to separate mind and body, nature and culture. In some works he parodies the Western obsession with scientific reason, applying experiments using residues of the human body, among them tears, urine, and sweat, to "prove" various racial stereotypes. *Saltiness of Greatness*, 1992, for example, consists of four stacks of compressed salt supposedly representing the lifetime output of energy by four famous Asians—Genghis Khan, Tokyo Rose, Mao Zedong, and Bruce Lee. Other works propose to soften Western rationalism with magical thinking. One of Joo's most poetic works is *Salt Transfer Cycle*, 1993–95, which addresses the human embrace of the cycles of nature. This video/performance piece has three parts. In the first we see documentation of Joo's "swim" through 2,000 pounds of MSG, the artificial salty substance associated with Asian cooking. In the second part, he performs a parody of evolution in the Great Salt Lake in Utah as he progresses from swimming to an upright posture, emerging from the lake covered with salt like some strange arctic creature. In the last segment, he films himself sitting naked and salt-covered in a salt lick in the northern mountains of South Korea. As he sits motionless, wild elk come and lick his body, suggesting his oneness with nature.

Olafur Eliasson's work, while not overtly spiritual, reflects a generalized concern with consciousness. Eliasson takes his cue from the space in which he is to install a piece and transforms it through subtle, or not so subtle, alterations of light, color, sound, and temperature. For *Your Now Is My Surroundings*, a 2000 installation in a New York gallery, Eliasson removed glass from the skylight, built a ramp below it, and mirrored the walls from eye level to the edges of the skylight. In the resulting space, disembodied heads of visitors mingled with reflected and actual images of the sky. For one of his most ambitious works, *The Weather Project*, 2003–4, Eliasson transformed the monumental Turbine Hall of the Tate Gallery London by lighting it with an artificial sun powered by hundreds of yellow monofilament bulbs. He completed the effect of a cold, sunny winter day by pumping the space with a light fog. Such works, with their perception-altering effects, extend the contemporary search for alternate forms of consciousness while dispensing with any direct link to traditional spiritualities or belief systems.

WOLFGANG LAIB

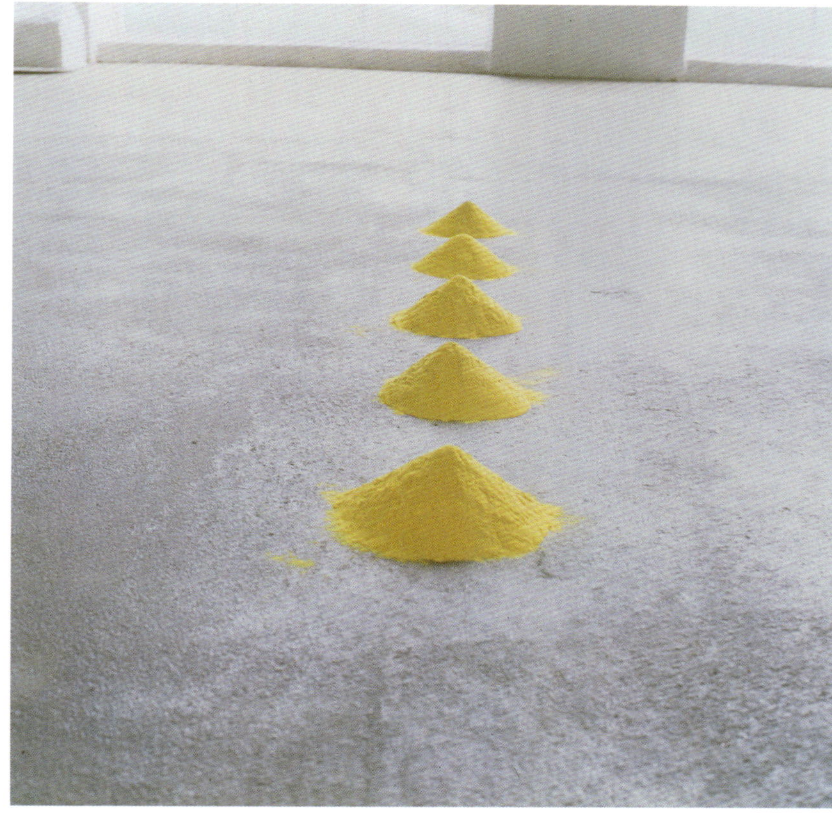

The Five Mountains Not to Climb On, 1984
Pollen from hazelnut, 2 3/4 in (7 cm) high

MICHAEL JOO

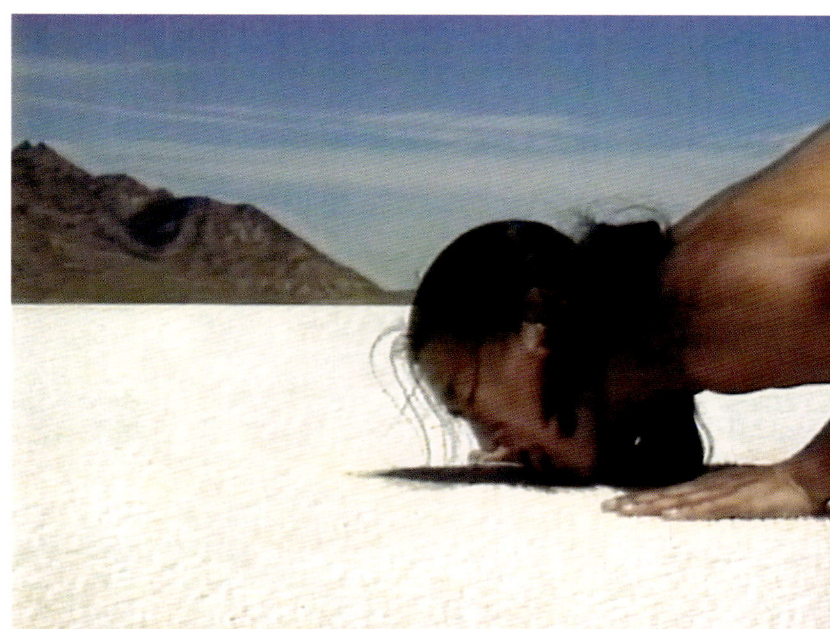

Salt Transfer Cycle, 1993–95
Video still

FRED TOMASELLI

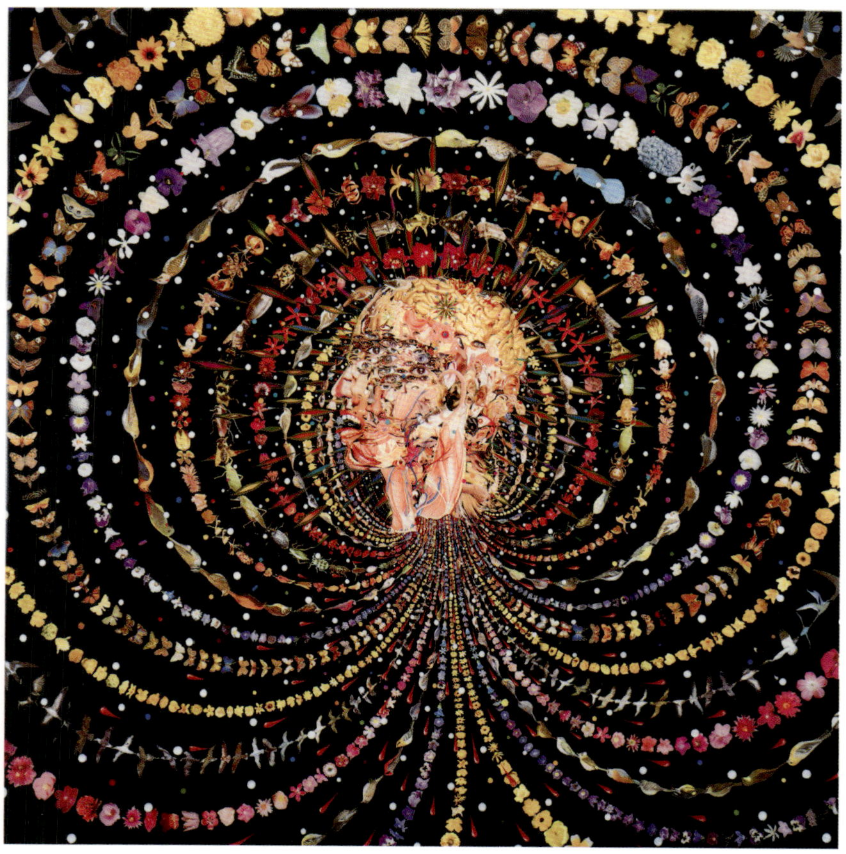

Breathing Head, 2002
Leaves, photocollage, acrylic, gouache, resin on wood panel, 60 x 60 in (152.4 x 152.4 cm)

Artists such as Houshiary, Kapoor, Laib, and, less explicitly, Eliasson, attempt to escape the constraints of the material world through perceptually induced spirituality. Fred Tomaselli, a product of the 1970s counterculture, mingles the New Age fascination with Eastern spiritualities with an homage to the mind-altering properties of hallucinatory drugs. Referencing sources ranging from psychedelic rock album covers and posters to Navaho rug designs, Tantric paintings, and Islamic decoration, Tomaselli creates intensely decorative collage paintings, many of which contain actual legal and illegal drugs, sealed under layers of transparent resin. Embedded marijuana leaves, tablets, pills, and capsules, as well as insects, pressed flowers, and cutouts from fashion magazines become decorative elements in compositions that suggest exploding galaxies, mandalas, oscillating sound waves, and impossibly dense jungle landscapes. The collages are both visually stunning and humorous. They are full of discordant details—birds with human eyes clipped from fashion magazines, forests of trees fashioned from marijuana leaves—that suggest such themes as the conflict between nature and culture or between society and technology. *Breathing Head*, 2002, offers a particularly graphic image of the idea of consciousness expansion. At the center of this collage is a head, composed of many eyes and flesh-colored cutouts, which becomes the center of a vortex of radiating lines composed of strings of real leaves and collaged images of butterflies, birds, and flowers.

In sum, Tomaselli takes on the utopian yearnings of our time, presenting them with a mixture of affection and irony. Turning the age-old quest for spiritual transcendence on its head, he suggests that Eden is nothing more than a pharmacological fantasy, and reminds us that the spiritual dimension of contemporary art can take many forms. Freed from filling the role of proselytizers for established religions, Tomaselli and other contemporary artists who make spirituality their theme revitalize the most ancient of artistic inspirations in surprising ways. Contrary to critical assertions about the inherent incompatibility of art and religion, their partnership turns out to provide a basis for myriad explorations of life, mortality, consciousness, and spirit.

OLAFUR ELIASSON

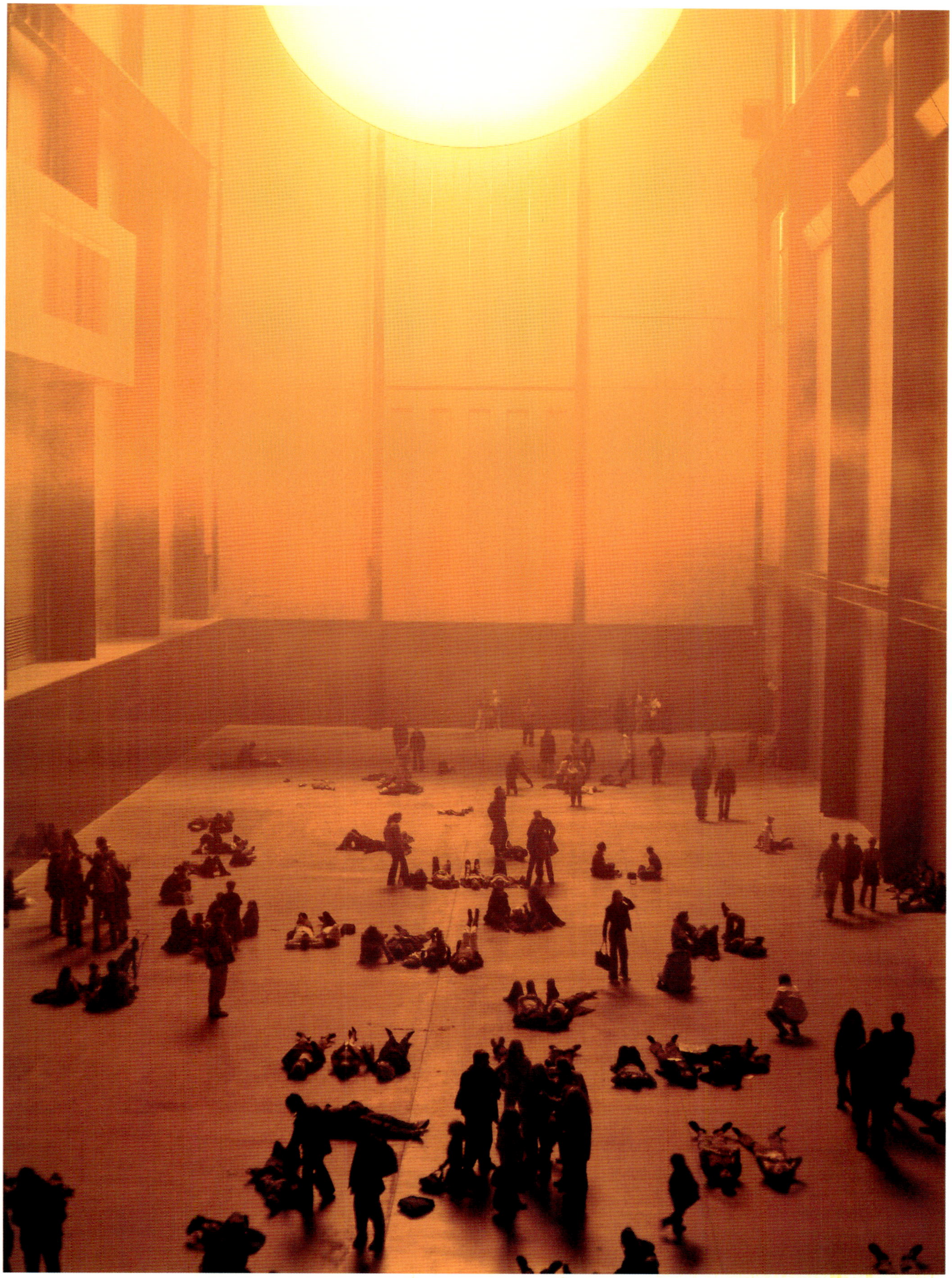

The Weather Project, 2003–4
Mono-frequency light, panel, fog machine, mirrored foil, steel
87 ft 7 in x 73 ft 2 in x 11 ft 1/2 in (26.7 x 22.3 x 155.4 m)
As installed at the Turbine Hall, Tate, London

ART & GLOBALISM

NEGOTIATING A BORDERLESS WORLD

In 1984 it was still possible for an institution as prominent as the Museum of Modern Art in New York to install an exhibition of work by 169 mostly white, mostly male artists from the United States and Europe, and dub it an "International Survey of Recent Painting and Sculpture." (The paltry showing of women, fourteen in all, kicked off a protest that led to the founding of the Guerrilla Girls; see chapter 15.) Now such a roster would be dismissed as insultingly Eurocentric and hopelessly provincial, as any international exhibition worth discussing today includes artists from every continent and from dozens of countries. A watershed moment: the 2002 edition of Documenta, the mammoth international exhibition mounted every five years in Kassel, Germany, each time under the directorship of a different international curator. In that year, for the first time in its half-century history, Documenta was organized by a non-white curator, Nigerian-born Okwui Enwezor, who not only gave special emphasis to artists from countries that Documenta had historically overlooked, including Korea, Chile, Croatia, Lebanon, India, South Africa, Senegal, Cuba, Iran, and China, but preceded the exhibition with several discussions, dubbed "platforms," that were held in locales as far flung as Lagos, St. Lucia, and New Delhi. Of course Enwezor's project was not without precedent, and its model of global expanse has become only more pronounced. The past decade or so has seen a remarkable proliferation of international biennials and cultural festivals bringing new art to and from such once marginalized centers as Gwangju, Havana, Istanbul, Shanghai, Dakar, and Cairo.

This proliferation is one face of a multifaceted phenomenon generally referred to as globalism, a product of the cold war's end, which opened up borders long blocked by the Iron Curtain. It is also the effect of such technological developments as the fax machine, the Internet, and the satellite feed, which have made instantaneous communication across the globe not only possible but commonplace. Few developments in contemporary times have had such far-reaching effects, or have engendered greater disagreement. Globalism's proponents see it as a counter balance to the destructive nationalisms of the last century. They laud it for opening up new markets, catalyzing unprecedented economic opportunities in underdeveloped countries, and creating new models for political and cultural exchange that cut across all geographic and political boundaries. One of globalism's most vociferous advocates is *New York Times* columnist Thomas Friedman, who argues in his book *The World Is Flat* that a convergence of technology and geopolitical developments has broken down the barriers to international competition that once favored the United States and Europe over such emerging powerhouses as India and China.[1] Then there are the critics, who contend that globalism has in fact increased the disparity between rich and poor nations, and between the rich and poor within nations. Chief among these critics is Noam Chomsky, the linguist and political activist who has long argued in his many books that globalism, along with institutions such as the International Monetary Fund and the World Bank, instituted in the wake of World War II to regulate the world economy, are simply ploys to cement the privileges of the dominant corporate elite. In this view, the centralization of money and power are deeply undemocratic, shifting resources, jobs, and capital away from the needs of individuals to serve the interests of multinational corporations, generating intense poverty and unrest among globalism's "losers."

In the cultural world as well, the advance of globalism is not perceived as uniformly positive or negative either. International biennials, some have argued, reveal the diversity of cultural expression around the world while creating prospects for artists from the farthest reaches of the globe. But as it opens up borders and opportunities, globalism can also favor cultural synthesis over local cultures and traditions. It levels some barriers, only to erect others. Thus, within the art world, globalism has had mixed effects. The decentered art world leads some artists to abandon the notion of cultural difference in the service of a kind of stylistic "esperanto" that is uniformly legible to the art cognoscenti. Other artists, resisting this trend, are moved to fetishize ethnic and national identities in an effort to protect the "brand" they represent. It is thus not always clear whether the world is developing a truly global culture or whether globalism is just a code word for the Westernization of non-Western cultures. Some critics charge that globalization enforces homogenization, while others argue that it reinforces the value of local concerns, histories, and identities.

Perhaps no artist better expresses the unstable quality of current geopolitical realities than Alighiero e Boetti, the late Italian artist who in 1972 chose to insert the Italian conjunction *e* ("and") into his name to reflect a sense of multiple identity. Boetti is associated with Arte Povera, the Italian art movement that challenged the fetishization of the art object by making art from deliberately ephemeral and unorthodox materials. Boetti's work as a whole is characterized by a fascination with systems of order and classification, resulting in disparate works that include an embroidery project purporting to list "the thousand longest rivers in the world," copies of 144 title pages of magazines from 1988, stacked pages of calendar months, and embroidered grids that transform numbers into symbols. Boetti is best known for his embroidered maps of the world, produced between 1971 and 1992, in which each country is designated by sections of its national flag. The maps are riotously beautiful, full of stars, stripes, and other abstracted emblems by which nations choose to represent themselves. Taken together, this series of maps also charts the changing course of geopolitics, as nations appear and disappear, the Soviet empire dissipates, and borders shift, seemingly in a constant state of flux. In La *mappa del mondo* (The map of the world), 1984, for instance, an enormous swath of Eastern Europe and Asia bears the crimson color of the Soviet flag. Thus Boetti's series illustrates the unreliability of maps as ordering systems of the world. Adding to this sense of geopolitical unrest is the fact that the embroidery itself was by Afghan women refugees who were exiled to Pakistan when the Soviets invaded their country.

Boetti's maps point to globalism's dual impact in the contemporary art world. On one hand it provides the backdrop against which artists work and within whose confines they define themselves. And on the other it provides subject matter, especially for artists critical of the art and political establishments' tendency to extol globalism as an unalloyed good. Artists who assume roles as both products and observers of the new global reality are often in a unique position to comment on its implications. They do so with a variety of tactics, ranging from demonstrating globalism's effects on real people to analyzing the abstract forces of the globalization of markets and political systems to considering the dehumanizing nature of the mass psychology that characterizes global society. While critiquing globalism, some artists also find ways to exploit systems of global exchange and communication for their own purposes. Yet others reflect on their own changing status within a globalized universe. For some this means an examination of post-colonial realities, for others

ALIGHIERO E BOETTI

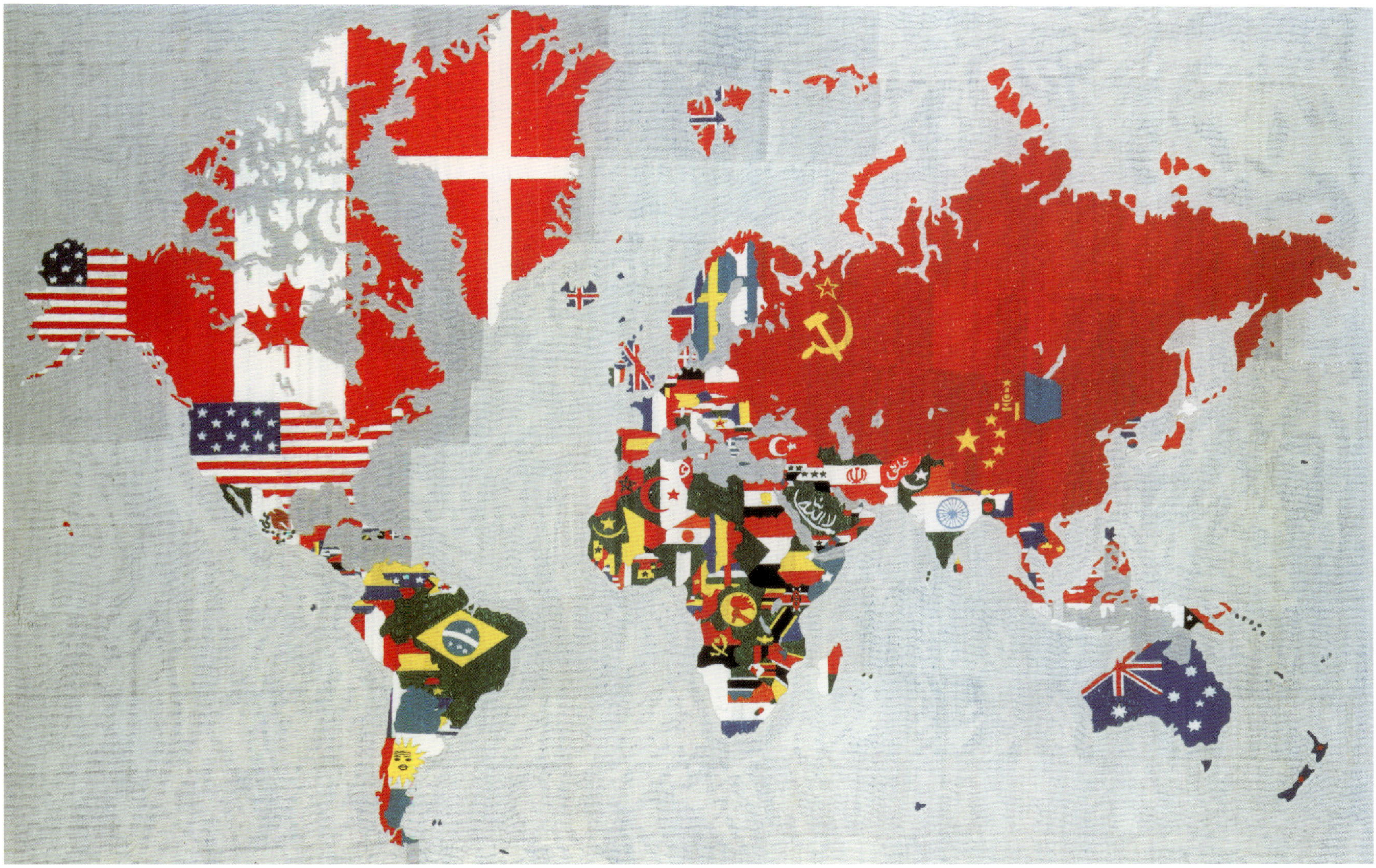

La mappa del mondo (The map of the world), 1984
Embroidered fabric mounted on board

ALLAN SEKULA

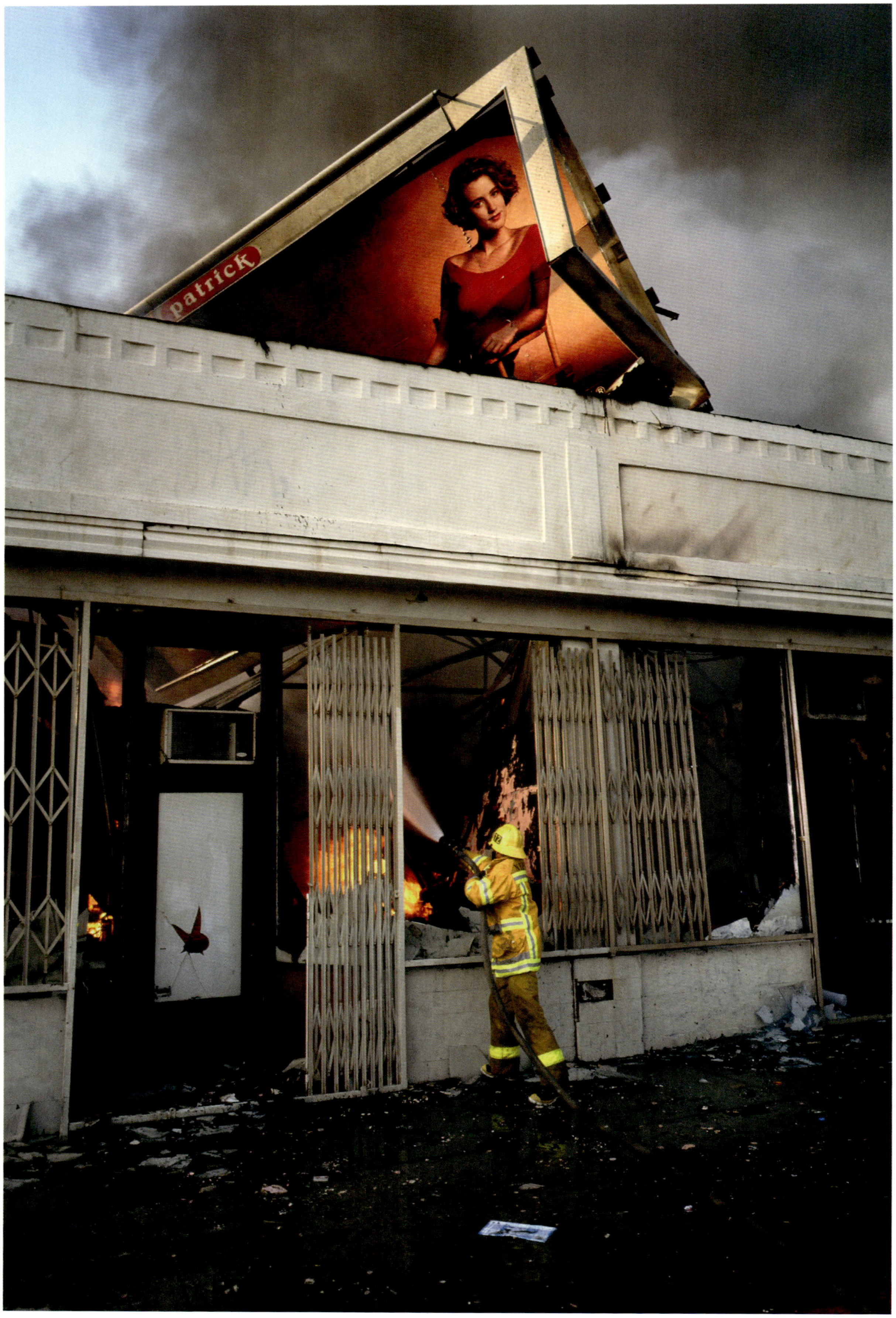

Koreatown, April 1992, from "Fish Story," 1989–2005
Silver dye-bleach print, 40 x 30 in (101.6 x 76.2 cm)

a reflection on their own condition as global nomads. For all of these artists, the ambiguous legacy of globalism yields a new understanding of the individual's place in the world.

Allan Sekula, for example, casts a sweeping light on the environmental and social effects of globalism by focusing on its implications for specific places or groups. Sekula, a photographer and a writer, works in a mode akin to documentary journalism. His books and installations combine photographs with written commentary and may incorporate captions, historical anecdotes, literary allusions, and exposition. Sekula has been drawn in particular to coastlines as places where issues of economic interdependence are revealed, exploring, for example, the economic devastation unleashed by the closing of shipyards in England and Scotland, or the aftermath of an oil spill on the northern coast of Spain. One of Sekula's most ambitious works is "Fish Story," 1989–2005, which comprises over a hundred color photographs, dozens of text panels, and slide projections. The outcome of Sekula's six-year transoceanic exploration of port cities and the shipping trade, "Fish Story" touches on subjects as diverse as seventeenth-century Dutch maritime painting, nineteenth-century naval strategy, Jules Verne's Captain Nemo (whose wealth derived from a sunken Spanish galleon), and the emergence of the shipping container as a symbol of the standardization of contemporary commerce. Combined, Sekula's vast amount of visual and written material creates a picture of a changing world in which modern trade, though still dependent on the sea, has dramatically been transformed. He suggests how concrete relationships between sailor, dockworker, and manufacturer have been superseded by the more abstract movements of the stock market and the flow of international capital and how, in the process, traditional lifestyles have disappeared as port cities have become impoverished and peripheral.

Like Sekula, Alfredo Jaar seeks out real-world situations that illuminate larger issues. *Geography=War*, 1991, took Jaar to a remote village on the coast of Nigeria that serves as the final resting place for piles of toxic waste discarded by Italian tankers. There he photographed impoverished children playing in the waste dumps and scavenging for salable debris, which became the basis for a series of installations. Through artful arrangements of photographs and mirrors or mirror-like surfaces, Jaar made the images visible only as reflections. In one installation, the photos are reflected from an overhead light box onto water-filled metal barrels. In another, mirrors placed against the wall capture the partially obscured images contained in light boxes set in front of them so that the fragmented images from Nigeria mingle with the viewer's mirrored image, creating doubled reflections that point to our complicity in the process by which First World detritus becomes Third World treasure. Framing and presentation are crucial in Jaar's work, leading to his presenting his subjects as fully conscious individuals rather than as faceless victims of impersonal global forces.

Mark Lombardi was less interested in the fate of individuals per se than in representing the flow of global capital between powerful players, financial institutions, political organizations, and governments. The artist, who died in 2000, undertook exhaustive research into such events as the U.S. Savings and Loan scandal or into the links between the Vatican Bank, the Mafia, and the illegal transport of firearms, for instance, then transformed his information into delicately drawn diagrams that bring to mind a combination of family trees or flow charts and

ALFREDO JAAR

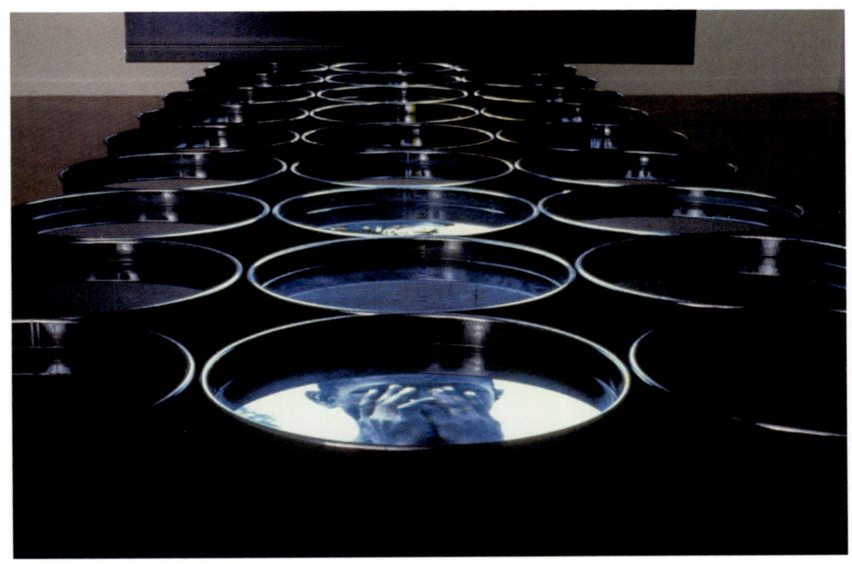

Geography=War, 1991
Double-sided light boxes with color transparencies, framed mirrors
4 x 28 x 12 ft (1.2 x 8.5 x 3.7 m)

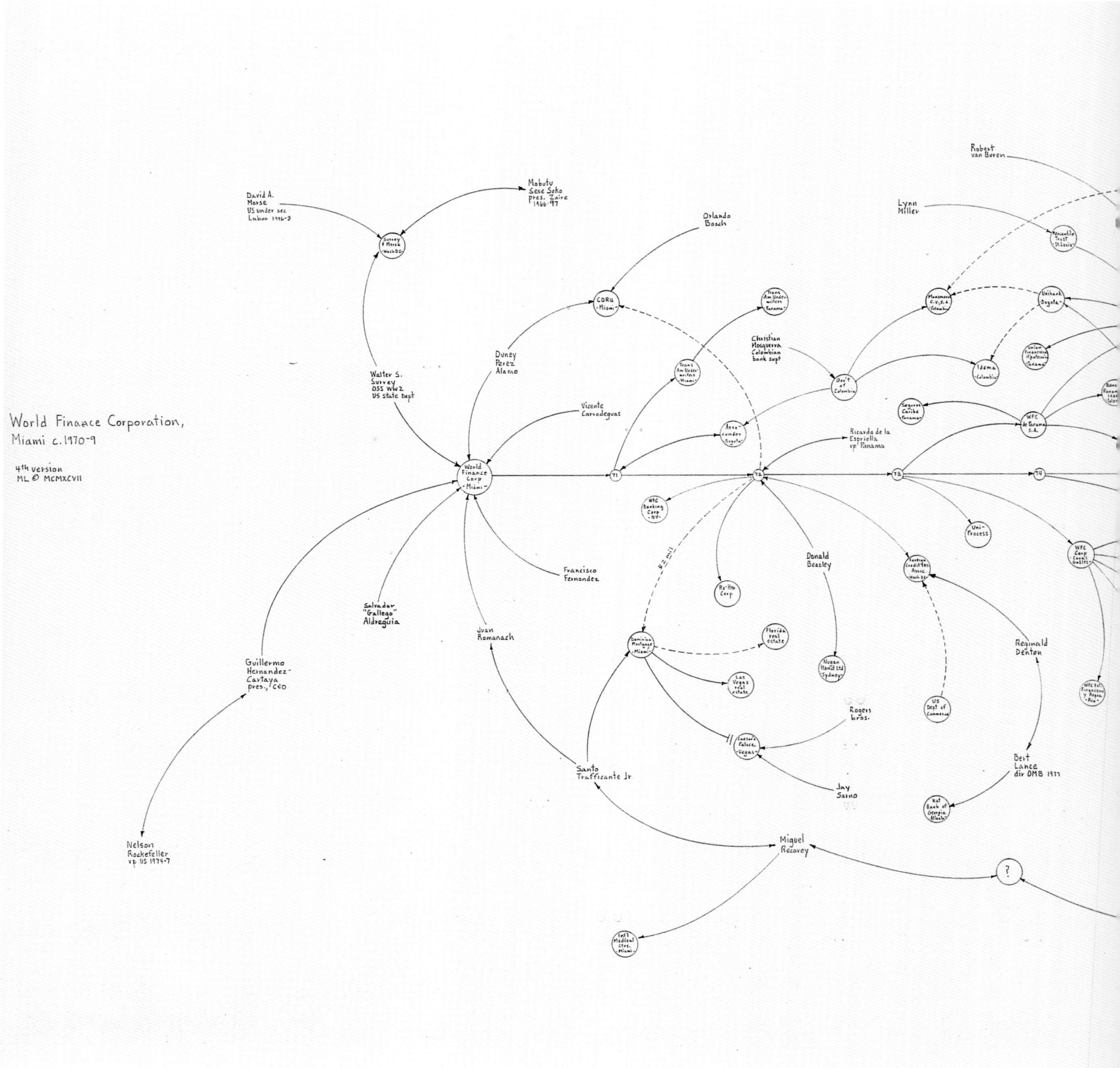

World Finaace Corporation,
Miami c.1970-9
4th version
ML © MCMXCVII
David A. Morse US under sec Labor 1946-9
Mobutu Sese Seko pres. Zaire 1966-97
Surrey & Morse -Wash DC-
Walter S. Surrey OSS WW2 US state dept
Duney Perez Alamo
Orlando Bosch
CORU -Miami-
Vicente Carrodeguas
World Finance Corp -Miami-
Francisco Fernandez
Salvador "Gallego" Aldreguia
Juan Romanach
Guillermo Hernandez-Cartaya pres., CEO
Nelson Rockefeller vp US 1974-7
71
72
73
74
Trans Am Underwriters -Miami-
Trans Am Underwriters -Panama-
Aeracondor -Bogota-
WFC Banking Corp -NY-
Christian Mosquerra Colombian bank supt
Gov't of Colombia
Ricardo de la Espriella vp Panama
#2 mil
Ra-Hen Corp
Donald Beazley
Dominion Mortgage -Miami-
Florida real estate
Las Vegas real estate
Nugan Hand Ltd -Sydney-
Caesar's Palace -Vegas-
Rogers bros.
Jay Sarno
Santo Trafficante Jr
Miguel Recarey
Int'l Medical Ctrs. -Miami-
Robert van Buren
Lynn Miller
Mercantile Trust -St.Louis-
Unibank -Bogota-
Idema -Colombia-
Seguros Caribe -Panama-
WFC de Panama S.A.
Uni-Process
WFC Corp -Coral Gables-
US Dept of Commerce
Reginald Denton
Bert Lance dir OMB 1977
Nat Bank of Georgia -Atlanta-
?

MARK LOMBARDI

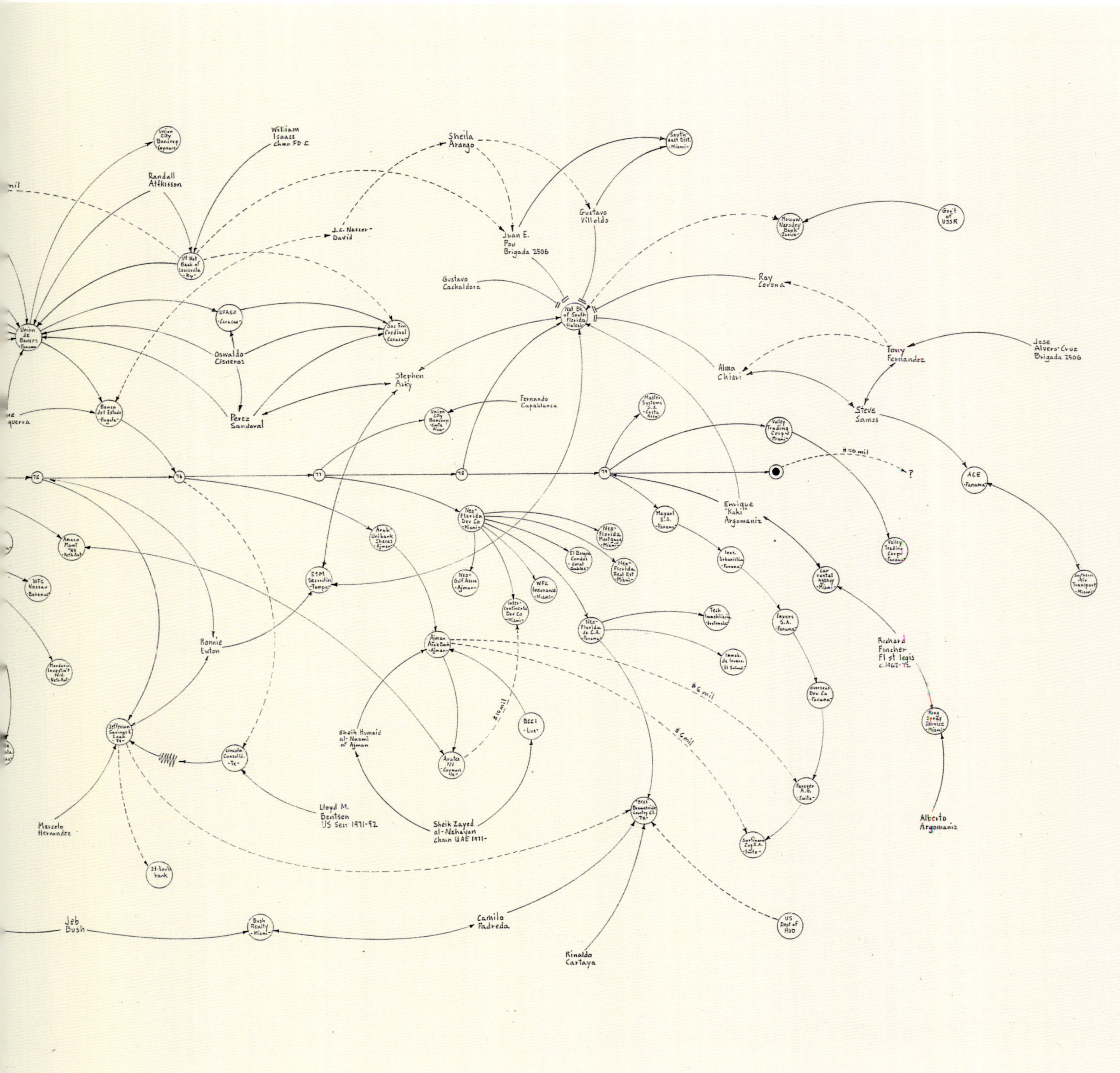

World Finance Corporation, Miami, c. 1970–79 (4th Version), 1997–2000
Graphite on paper, 29 5/8 x 59 1/8 in (75.2 x 150.4 cm)

the conceptual renderings of Sol LeWitt. One diagram shows how Iraq was armed in the 1980s through a secret scheme involving the top levels of the administrations of Ronald Reagan and the elder George Bush, Margaret Thatcher, and Italy's largest bank. Another, *World Finance Corporation, Miami, c. 1970–79 (4th Version)*, 1997–2000, follows the major financial scandal in which $50 million was "lost" at the hands of the Corporation's founder, who had ties to the CIA, the Mafia, Fidel Castro, and Colombian drug lords. Following a code of Lombardi's own making, these events and relationships become fields of circles and solid and broken lines, which spread like spider webs over the paper, enmeshing the names of organizations and individuals in often surprising interconnections. Lines converge on certain centers or nodes that formally provide visual resting points and conceptually represent key figures at the center of apparently unrelated entities. The information, drawn from publicly available sources, maps out a world in which money serves as the connective thread, entangling us all in an invisible network of influence peddling and finanicial and political manipulation.

Julie Mehretu has also developed a personal abstract language to represent the maelstrom of global exchange. While some of her formal elements—floating triangles, arcing lines, explosive vectors—recall the celebratory dynamism of early modernists like Kandinsky, Mondrian and the Futurists, the commotion she charts is worlds away from theirs. Mehretu presents her vision in large, layered drawings based on maps, diagrams, architectural forms, and urban planning grids overlaid with clouds of abstract marks and lines that create a sense of overwhelming energy. Despite their intense vitality, these pulsing webs of motion are fraught with a sense of inhumanity or estrangement, as the implication of human presence is reduced to little more than a tiny speck tossed about by larger forces. While some works suggest vortexes swallowing up any physical or mental structures that come near, others, like *Dispersion*, 2002, are centrifugal. Here whiplash lines, small colorful rectangles, and dense scribbles are blasted apart, leaving a void in the center of the composition that might allude to both a bursting stock market bubble and to the hole in the ground after the attacks of 9/11 (an association that is strengthened by the image of a blue airplane piercing the flying rubble). In the bigger picture, Mehretu's project suggests the postmodern unraveling of every certainty that ever produced our confidence in the future.

Like Mehretu, Andreas Gursky suggests the alienation of the individual amid the forces of globalism. His large-scale photographs present sweeping panoramas drawn from the worlds of international commerce, finance, and entertainment that are often digitally manipulated to heighten color, superimpose varied perspectives, or repeat certain details to eerily unnatural effect. Gursky's subjects include store shelves stacked with countless pairs of running shoes, apparently endless bands of empty balconies wrapping the interior atriums of generic business hotels, and a bird's-eye view of a huge crowd at a rave, all waving their hands in the air. Rampant consumerism, soulless emptiness, and prescribed crowd behavior, respectively, are at the heart of these images, all of which, despite their vivid details, make humans appear, again, small and inconsequential. This is so even when the individuals are global power brokers, as in the diptych *Hauptversammlung* (Stockholders' Meeting), 2001, in which digital manipulation and layering have created a strange group portrait of the boards of directors of various German corporations. Rows of small figures sit behind floating tables that hover above a vast sea of heads set against a strangely dissonant Alpine backdrop. Inscribed above their heads, like messengers from some unseen Olympus, are the logos of the corporations each represents, conveying the real source of the tiny figures' authority. Here, and in all of Gursky's views into the world, formal regularity creates a coercive geometry that becomes a visual metaphor for the invisible constraints that finance, urban development, and technology place on human life.

Expressions of homogenization and alienation appear in the work of the late Juan Muñoz, who made figurative sculptures, some of which were inspired in part by the ceramic tomb sculptures of third-century warriors excavated in Xi'an, China. Muñoz created a number of theatrical installations featuring what he called his "Chinese statues." These variously sized but otherwise clone-like figurative works—some are dwarfs, some are puppets, some are life-size, yet others emerge from bulbous bases—have vaguely Asian features, shaved heads, and sinister smiles that seem to mock the viewer or enjoy a secret bit of deviltry. They peer down from balconies, line up on sets of bleachers, lurk in corridors, or peer at themselves in mirrors. In *Towards the Corner*, 1998, seven near life-size figures are assembled on a bench, laughing. Whether the viewer is in on the joke or serving as its butt is an open question. Muñoz uses uniformity to suggest a sense of threat, but his creations seem to have a distinct, if unknowable, inner life. They gather in what the artist called "conversation pieces," but their mystery speaks to the essential alienation that persists even amid global communication's promise of interconnectedness.

The pathology of the crowd is equally in evidence in the works of Antony Gormley, who creates fields of figures wrought of such materials as terra cotta, steel, bronze, and lead. Sometimes his work consists of crowds of tiny figures so numerous (40,000 in *European Field*, 1994, for instance), that they take over entire rooms, forbidding the viewer anything but visual access. When realized on a larger scale, Gormley's figures take on particular characteristics, standing around in poses that might suggest dejection, submission, or indifference. Some curl up in fetal positions, as in *Critical Mass*, 1995; others slump against the wall. Some figures are solid, while others are composed of matrixes of stainless steel bars. Whatever their effect, they have a generic quality, as if literally taken from a mold or lifted from the screen of some digital design program, while conveying a sense of being coerced, confined, or otherwise bereft of personal control. Gormley's early work consisted of abstracted cast-lead figures whose seams showed, suggesting that they had been pieced together through some mass production process.

The individual is diminished further still in the work of Michal Rovner, who works in video projections and still photography to create images of leaderless and faceless crowds moving aimlessly through bleak and undifferentiated landscapes. Cipher-like, they take the form of blurry silhouettes that shuffle, pace, or file across the screen in hypnotically slow motion. Observers have compared the groups of figures to swarms of insects, bees in a hive, or flocks of birds. Such metaphoric associations are enhanced by the contexts in which Rovner projects her images. For the exhibition "in stone," 2004, she superimposed the figures on cracked stone tablets, as in the work *Degel*. Here they became hieroglyphic, each one a trembling mark in an otherwise mute written language. Though not didactically political, Rovner's crowds express a vision of nightmarish conformism, pointing to the process by which not only globalism but also fascism and blind nationalism can influence group consciousness to obliterate individual will or desire.

JULIE MEHRETU

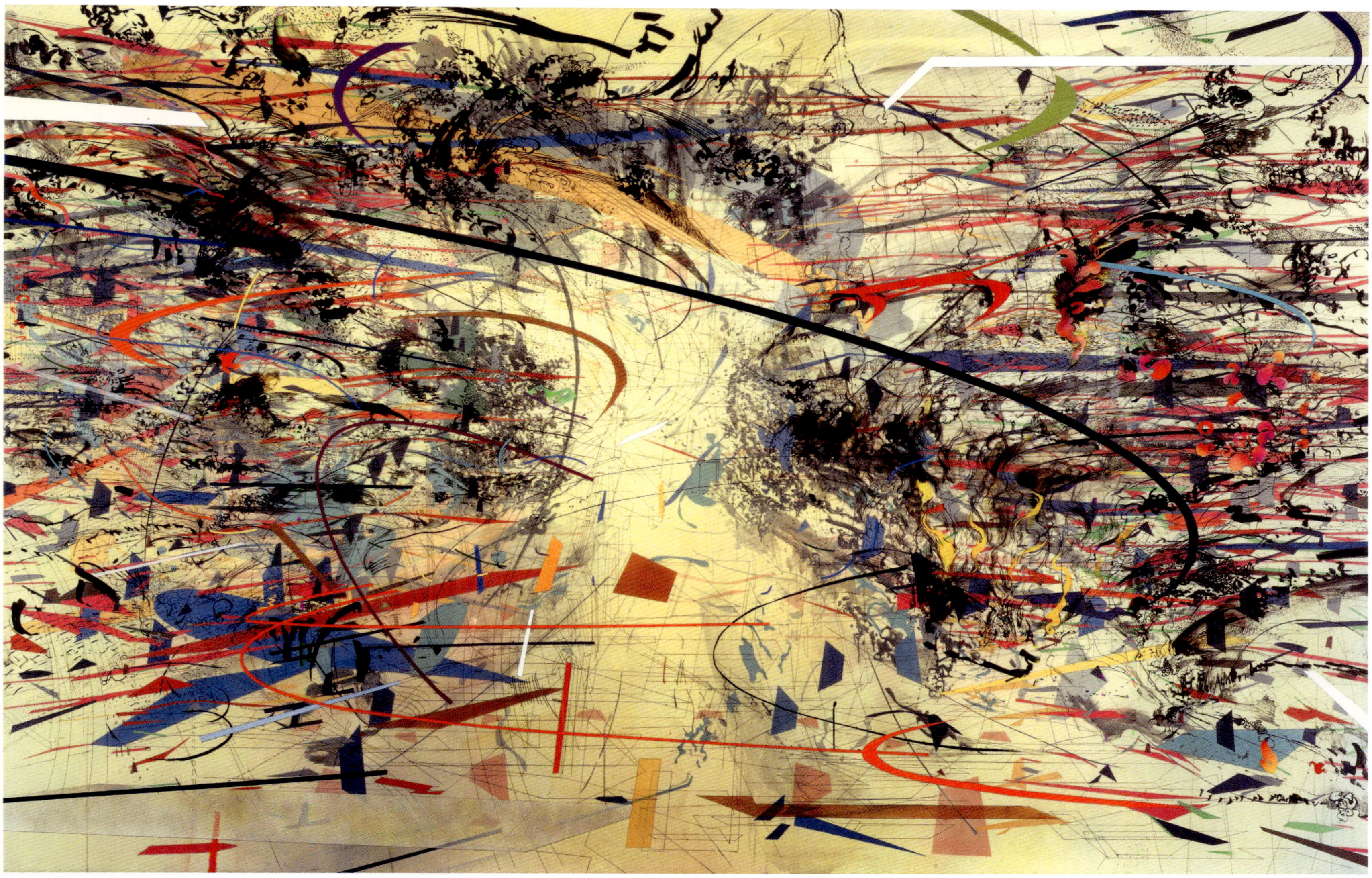

Dispersion, 2002
Ink and acrylic on canvas, 90 x 144 in (228.6 x 365.8 cm)

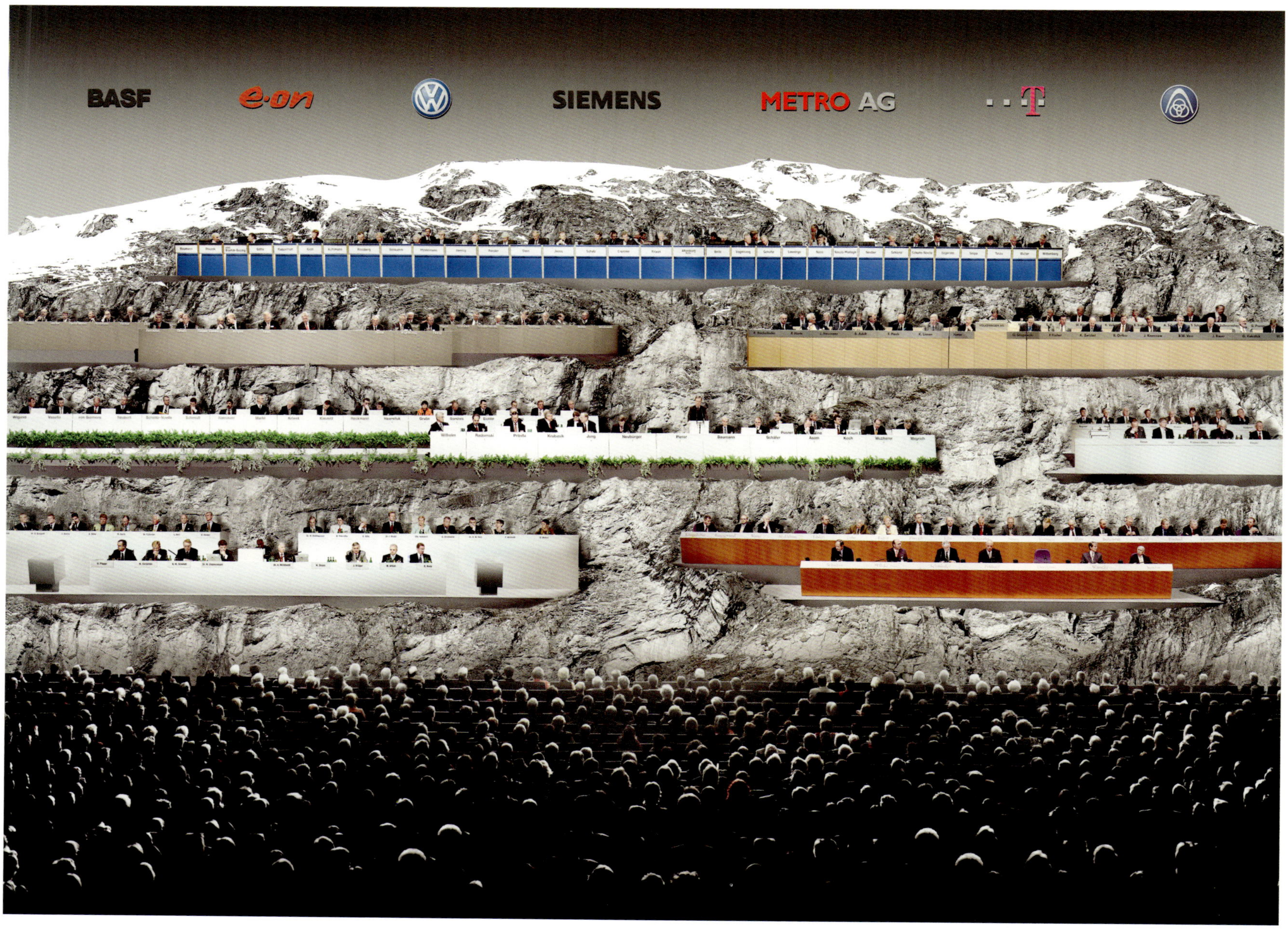
BASF
e·on
SIEMENS
METRO AG

ANDREAS GURSKY

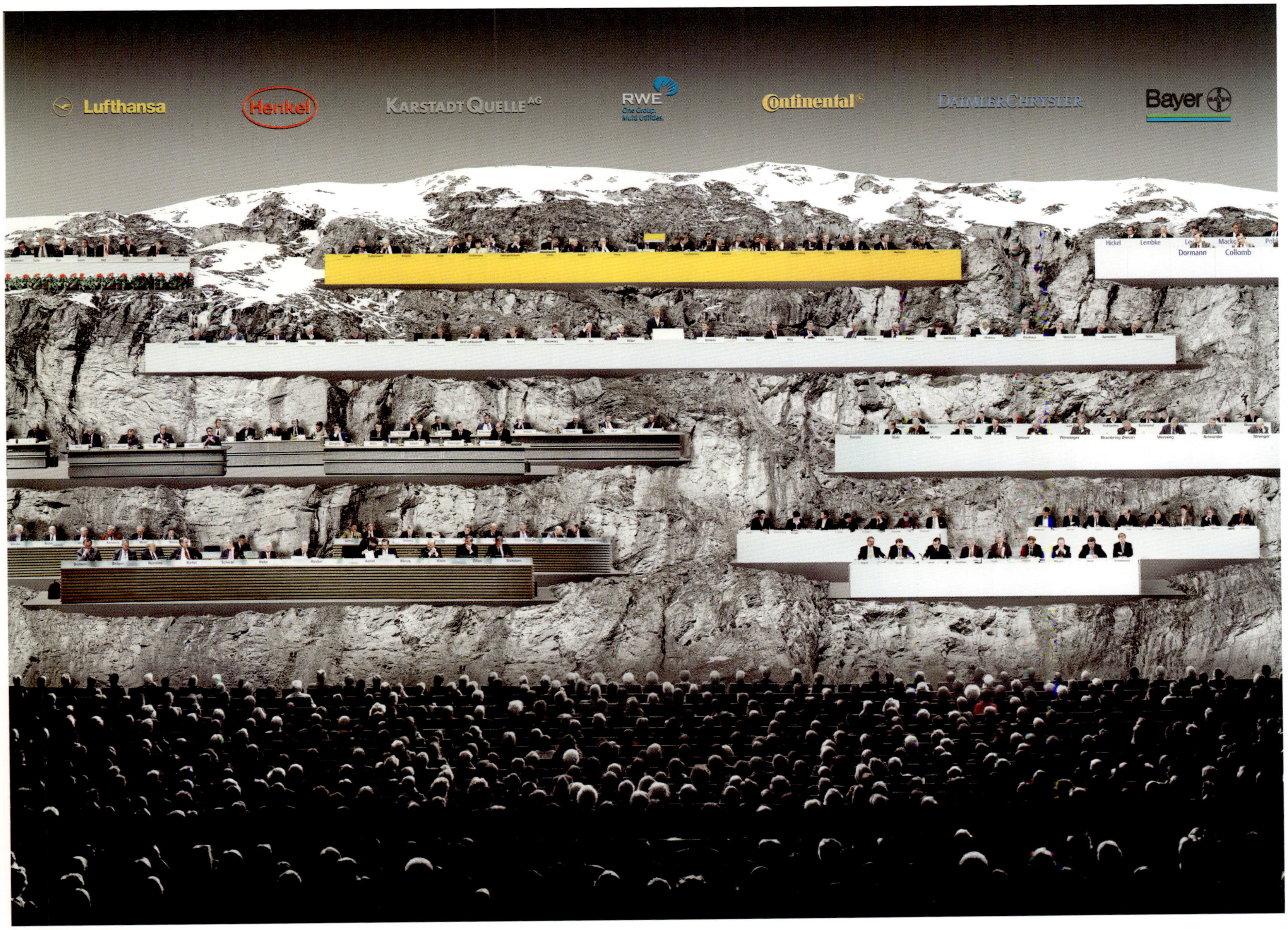

Hauptversammlung (Stockholders' Meeting), 2001
Diptych, C-print, 81 x 120 in (205.7 x 304.8 cm)

JUAN MUÑOZ

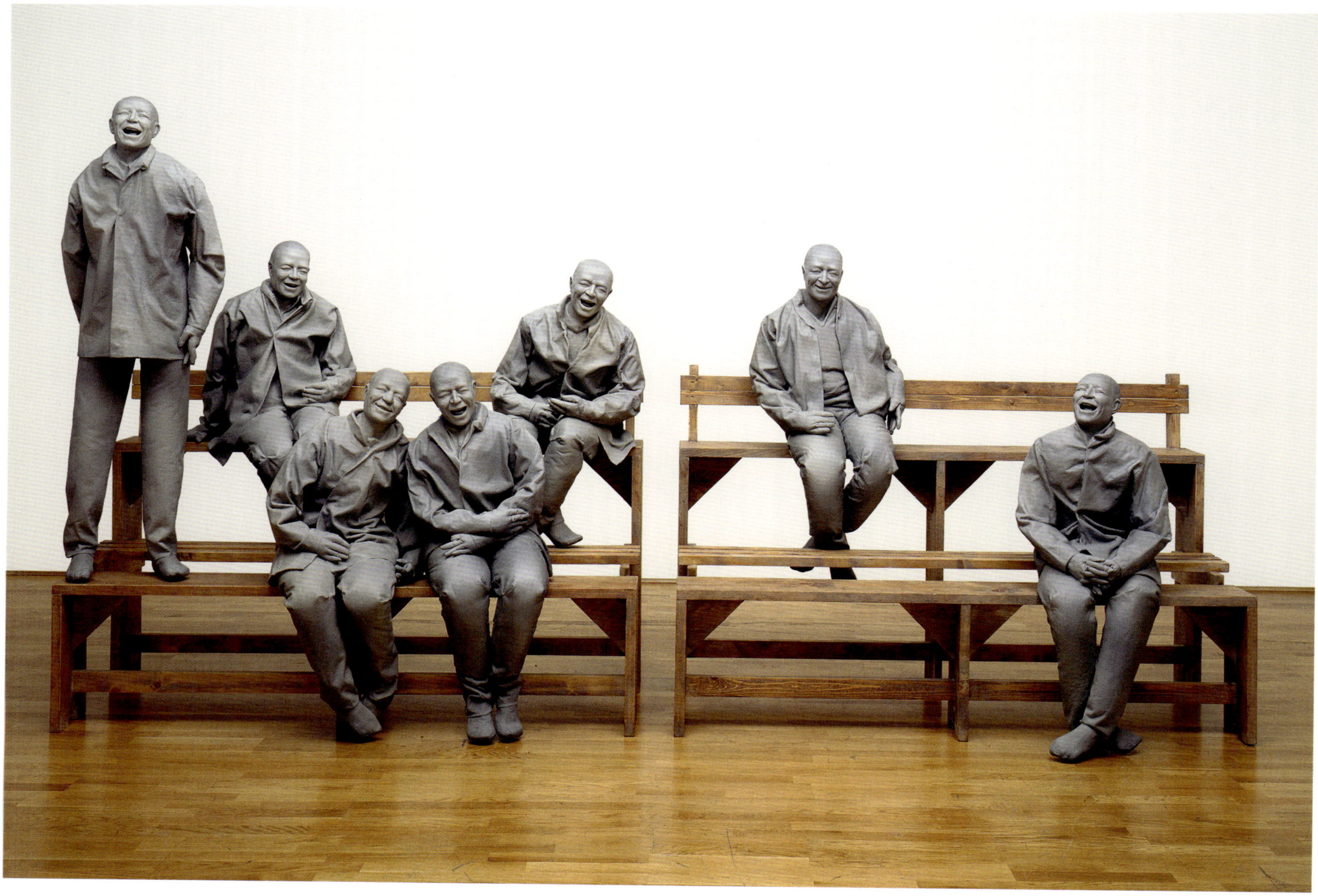

Towards the Corner, 1998
Resin, mixed media, wood grandstand, 78 1/2 x 130 x 44 1/2 in (199.4 x 330 x 113 cm)

ANTONY GORMLEY

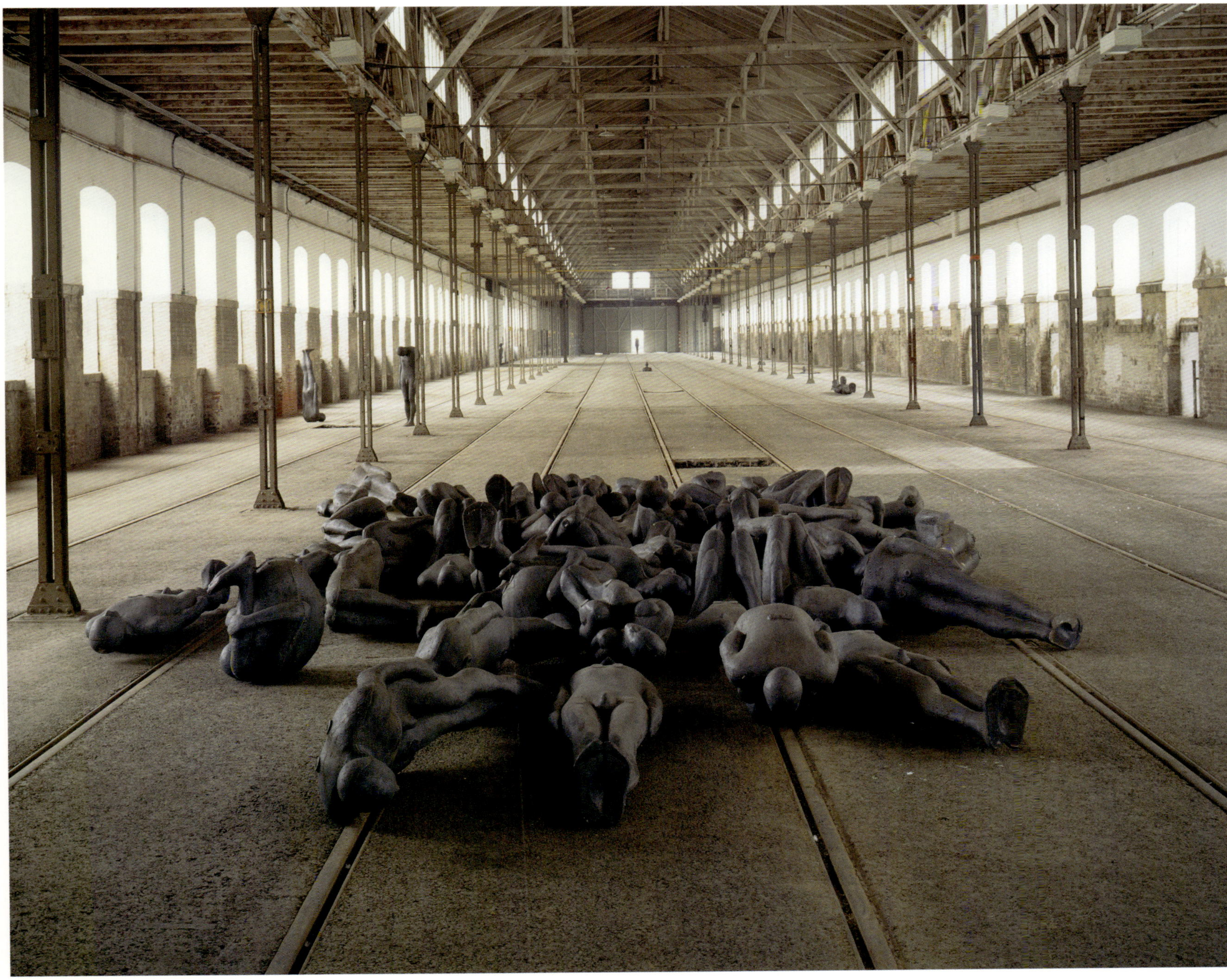

Critical Mass, 1995
Cast iron, 60 life-size body forms
As installed at Remise Museum, Vienna, October–November 1995

A more optimistic take on the indistinguishable crowd appears in some of the work of Do-Ho Suh, who suggests the strength of collective action in such works as *Floor*, 1997–2000, where visitors are invited to walk on a thick plate of glass held a few feet above the ground by the thousands of tiny plastic figures visible beneath it. Other works exhibit a less sanguine view of the crowd. *Who Am We?*, 2000, consists of thousands of tiny faces from the artist's high school yearbook printed in rows, on large sheets of wallpaper. From a distance, details blur, suggesting the subsuming of the individual into the mass. Taking a different tack, Suh's *Seoul Home/L.A. Home/New York Home/Baltimore Home/London Home/Seattle Home*, 1999, describes another effect of globalism: the rootlessness of the nomadic individual. Modeled after his parents' house in Seoul, this ethereal life-size sculpture sewn of celadon silk can be folded up and transported from "home" to "home." Which is exactly what Suh has done, in fact, naming it after all of the cities in which it has been exhibited.

Where Suh begins to suggest a hopeful side to globalism, artists such as Eugenio Dittborn and Cildo Meireles demonstrate how its byproducts might directly right societal wrongs, in particular how communication systems might subvert oppressive governments. Dittborn began making his "airmail paintings" in 1984, during the reign of the Chilean dictator General Augusto Pinochet, whose highly repressive military government kept Chileans largely isolated from the rest of the world. Collages of painted and photo-silkscreened images transferred to light cloth and sewn onto a sturdier cloth backdrop, the airmail paintings can be folded into rectangles and easily shipped in international airmail packages. When displayed in galleries, they are unfolded and tacked on the wall, along with the envelopes in which they were mailed, presenting a record of their travels around the world and dramatizing the way in which art might circumvent censorship at home. The images in his paintings are varied, but many refer to troubling circumstances. They may include mug shots of Chilean women criminals from the 1930s, faces drawn by schizophrenics in a Chilean psychiatric hospital, representations of ancient mummies that were frozen in the Andes, images of mass graves found in northern Chile, pages from Chilean newspapers, and bits of writing, some appropriated, some written by Dittborn himself. *To Return (RTM), Airmail Painting No. 103*, 1993, represents the return of the personal effects or actual remains of travelers who never make it home alive. With such images and narratives, Dittborn casts a spotlight on questions of exile, loss, and frustrated dreams, mirroring his own sense of being an outsider to the larger world of international culture and political freedom—and offering a glimmer of hope for an alternative.

Like Dittborn, Meireles has responded to the abuses of a military dictatorship by transforming art into a medium of subversion, though in his native Brazil. And he too took advantage of pre-existing circulation systems to disseminate messages that would undermine the authorities. In 1970, at the height of the dictatorship, he created his *Inserções em Circuitos Ideologicos: Projeto Coca-Cola* (Insertions into Ideological Circuits: Coca-Cola Project), for instance. For this work, Meireles inscribed a set of politically provocative messages onto Coca-Cola bottles that were then returned to circulation through a recycling program. When the bottles were empty, these inscriptions—which included phrases such as "Yankee Go Home" (a commentary on the economic infiltration of Brazil's economy by U.S. corporations like Coca-Cola)—were nearly invisible. Only when the bottles were refilled with soda and returned to stores were they readable. This piece came out of an earlier "insertion," for which he stamped American and Brazilian banknotes with similar messages and again returned them to circulation. After a series of government threats and canceled exhibitions, Meireles left Brazil for the United States, where he created poetic, participatory installation works using elements from everyday life, among them coins, clocks, and measuring sticks, as well as excrement and combustible natural gas (the latter released into a room outfitted with a burning candle), to create environments that suggest the dangers of enforced ideologies.

Information circulation in the global age is also essential to the work of Walid Raad, though in a very different way. Raad, who works under the name of his fictional foundation, The Atlas Group, presents documentation of politically charged scenarios that, though believable, are completely fictitious. Drawing on the already unstable political situation of the Middle East, frequently referring specifically to the Lebanese civil war that ravaged his native country from 1975 to 1991, Raad explores how history gets written and codified in works that take the form of fabricated photographic, textual, or video archives. *Hostage: The Bachar Tapes*, 2001, for example, inserts an unknown (invented) Lebanese hostage named Souheil Bachar into the real history of the Lebanese hostage crisis, during which real figures such as Terry Anderson and Terry Waite were held by Islamic militants in Beirut for seven years. Supposed archival video footage along with after-the-fact interviews with Bachar chronicle the indignities he endured at the hands of the other hostages. *My Neck Is Thinner than a Hair*, 2001, is presented as a notebook, kept by the fictitious Lebanese historian Dr. Fadl Fakhouri, that purports to document the makes of the cars used in every car bombing in Lebanon during the civil war. These invented scenarios play on the kind of data historians use to construct history, reminding us how unreliable such reports actually are and that even in a world of instantaneous communication and global dissemination of information, "truth" remains dubious, vulnerable to manipulation.

Questions of historical veracity have another kind of resonance in postcolonial countries, where the values, customs, language, and institutions imposed on colonized populations were not easily shed after colonial powers relinquished their hold. (Neither were the ethnic divisions and nationalist hatreds fueled by years of subjugation.)[2] After the departure of European, American, and Japanese powers in Africa, the Americas, and Asia, it often became difficult for those left behind to sort out the authenticity of their own identities. Instead, as theorists like Homi Bhabha and Gayatri Chakravorty Spivak have pointed out, inhabitants of postcolonial societies have a tendency to internalize the representations imposed on them by the departed occupiers. As a result, questions of authenticity and identity become extremely difficult to parse. Is it possible to return to native traditions that had been irrevocably altered or even destroyed during the years of colonial rule? Or is it preferable to adopt the colonizer's visual and cultural language and thus be able to speak to global powers on their own terms? These questions are not confined only to the colonized. Colonizers as well must contend with how their cultures have been influenced by decades or, in some cases, centuries, of occupation. One need look no further than contemporary England or France to see how the customs, cultural traditions and political tensions of immigrants from former colonies are reshaping life in these former Empires.

Joyce Kozloff, a pioneering feminist artist, has in recent years turned her attention to maps as a tool for understanding the complex dynamics of colonial and

MICHAL ROVNER

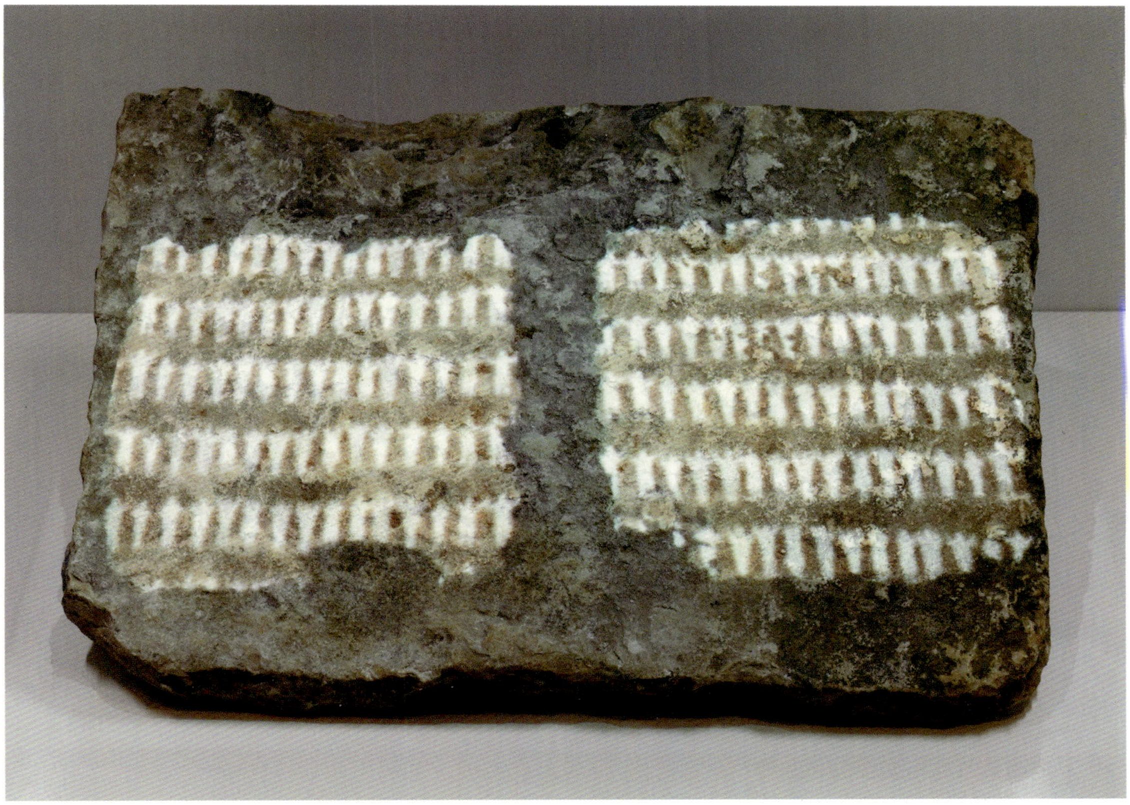

Degel, 2004
Steel vitrine with glass, stone, and DVD video projection
57 1/8 x 32 x 20 in (145.1 x 81.3 x 50.8 cm)

DO-HO SUH

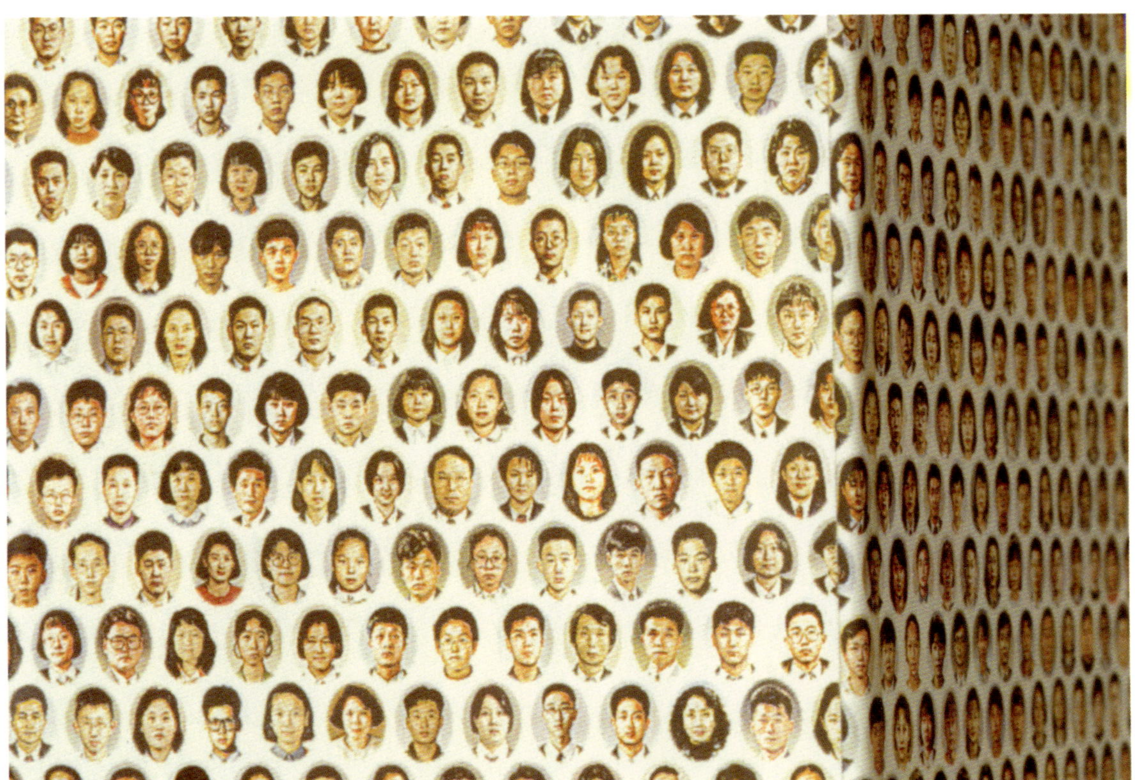

Who Am We?, 2000
Four-color offset print on paper, each sheet 24 x 36 in (61 x 91.4 cm)

EUGENIO DITTBORN

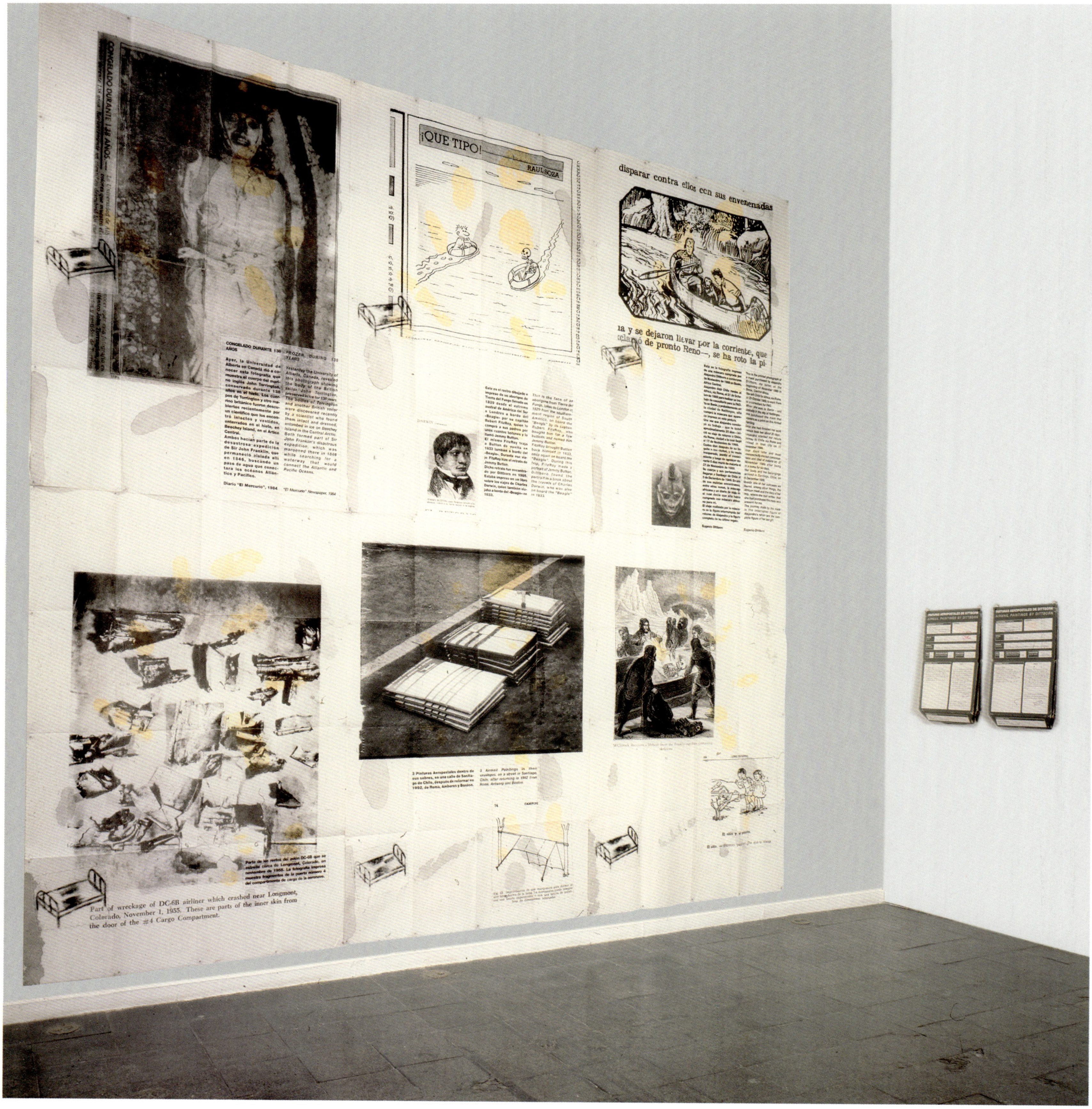

To Return (RTM), Airmail Painting No. 103, 1993
Paint, stitching, photo silkscreen, and charcoal on 6 sections of non-woven fabric
165 1/2 x 165 1/2 in (420 x 420 cm)

CILDO MEIRELES

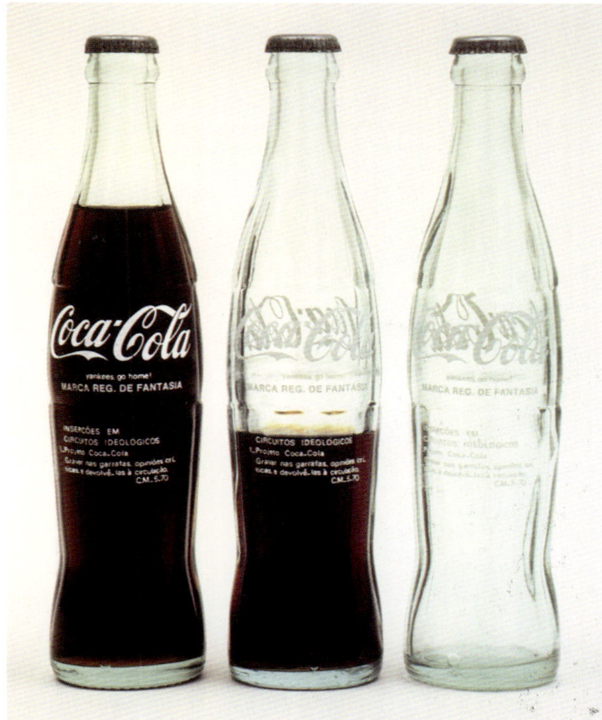

Inserções em Circuitos Ideologicos: Projeto Coca-Cola
(Insertions into Ideological Circuits: Coca-Cola Project), 1970
Coca-Cola bottles, transferred text, 7 in (18 cm) high
Tate, Britain

THE ATLAS GROUP (WALID RAAD)

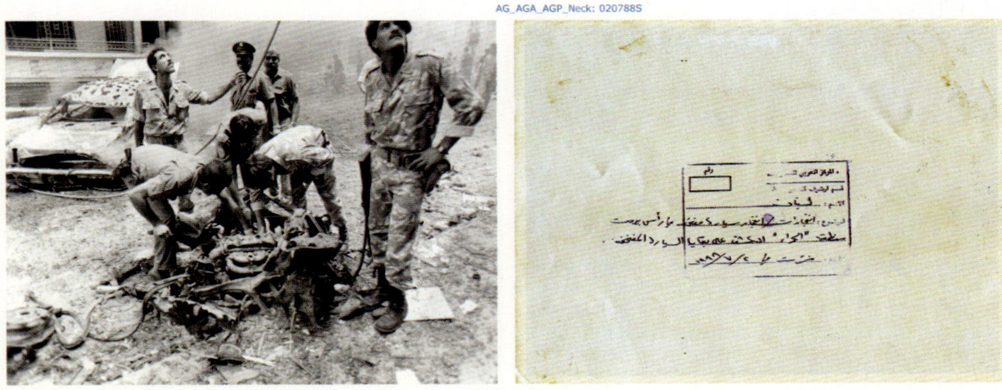

My Neck is Thinner than a Hair: Engines (2 July 1988 Arab Documentation Center), 2001
Color photograph, 9 1/2 x 13 2/5 in (24 x 34 cm)

JOYCE KOZLOFF

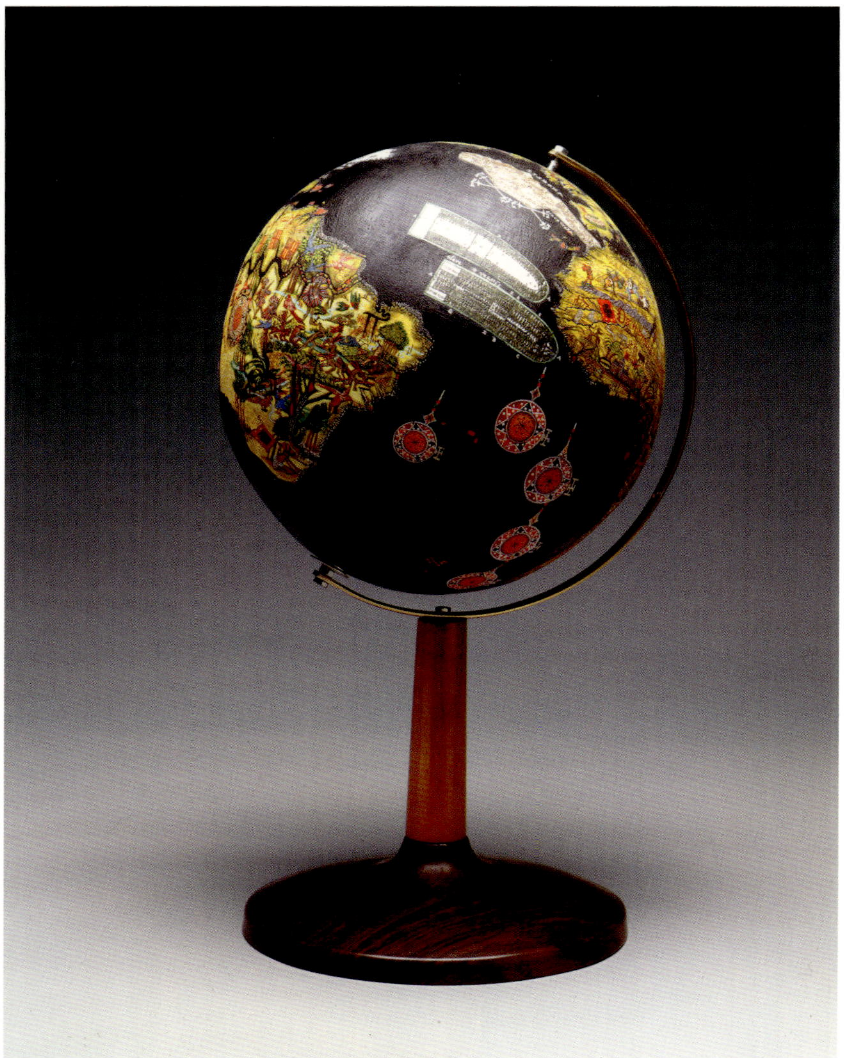

La Conquista, 1999
Watercolor, plastic, and rope on cardboard, wood and metal base
40 in (101.6 cm) circumference

postcolonial societies. In her hands, maps are revealed to be documents that embody not geographical truth but the often narrow perspectives of explorers, colonizers, traders, and conquerors. As a result, maps embody the psychology of domination, the seductions of power, and the fallacies of the patriarchal, Western version of history. In seductive tapestry-like paintings and sculptures Kozloff fragments, reshuffles, alters, and recreates maps from many sources. These may include cosmological and nautical charts, antique maps, topographical maps, and nineteenth-century real estate maps. By liberally altering colors, overlaying map sections with related historical images, outlining and dividing the maps with decorative borders, and overlapping unrelated maps, she amplifies the hidden assumptions embedded in these artifacts. For example, *La Conquista*, 1999, is a large, standard-issue globe whose surface has been covered with a thin layer of plaster to suggest a fresco. It incorporates elements from a variety of maps and charts dating from the sixteenth through eighteenth century. As the title suggests, this work is a meditation on the conquest of the Americas. Much of it is laced with a sense of tragedy—diagrams of slave ships, views of slave ports, drawings of indigenous peoples as exotic savages, and most poignantly, a map of Tenochtitlan, capital of the Aztec empire, sent home by the Spanish conquistador Hernando Cortés as record of the city he was about to destroy. Kozloff has painted the sea black, perhaps a gesture of mourning for the destructive impulses that she alludes to here. *La Conquista* is part of "Knowledge," 1999, a series of map-related pieces that suggest the paradoxes inherent in the process of globalization, which both brings the salutary spread of scientific and technical information and allows that information to be put to insidious purposes.

Yinka Shonibare, MBE (Member of the Order of the British Empire), in a similar vein, explores the contradictory fallout of the European colonization of Africa. He is best known for dramatic tableaux of headless mannequin figures dressed in Victorian-style European costumes whose authenticity is undermined by the batik-patterned cloth out of which they are fashioned. As it turns out, the history of Shonibare's West African textiles exemplifies one of the paradoxes of colonialism. Initially produced by English manufacturers in the late nineteenth century for the Indonesian market, the fabrics failed there but were taken up in West Africa, where they are now perceived and embraced as genuine products of indigenous design. The mixed history of these fabrics complements the activities that the headless figures undertake. Though they are draped in pseudo-African batik, they pursue activities associated with the British ruling class: fox hunting, posing stiffly on the grounds of their country estates, and even, in *Gallantry and Criminal Conversation*, 2002, engaging in an insouciant orgy in the shadow of their carriages. Through such narrative reinvention and identity hybridization, Shonibare reflects on the continuing impact of colonial thinking. In his works we glimpse both the desire of the dominators to appropriate "otherness" for themselves and the longing of the dominated to adopt the lifestyles of their oppressors.

The unresolved nature of colonial influence is even more graphically demonstrated in the work of Zwelethu Mthethwa, who brings us into the post-apartheid shantytowns outside Cape Town, depicting residents in their quarters using the time-honored style of portrait photography. More striking than the subjects, however, is how inventively they have used the detritus of consumer culture to create home environments. As immigrants from rural townships who came

YINKA SHONIBARE, MBE

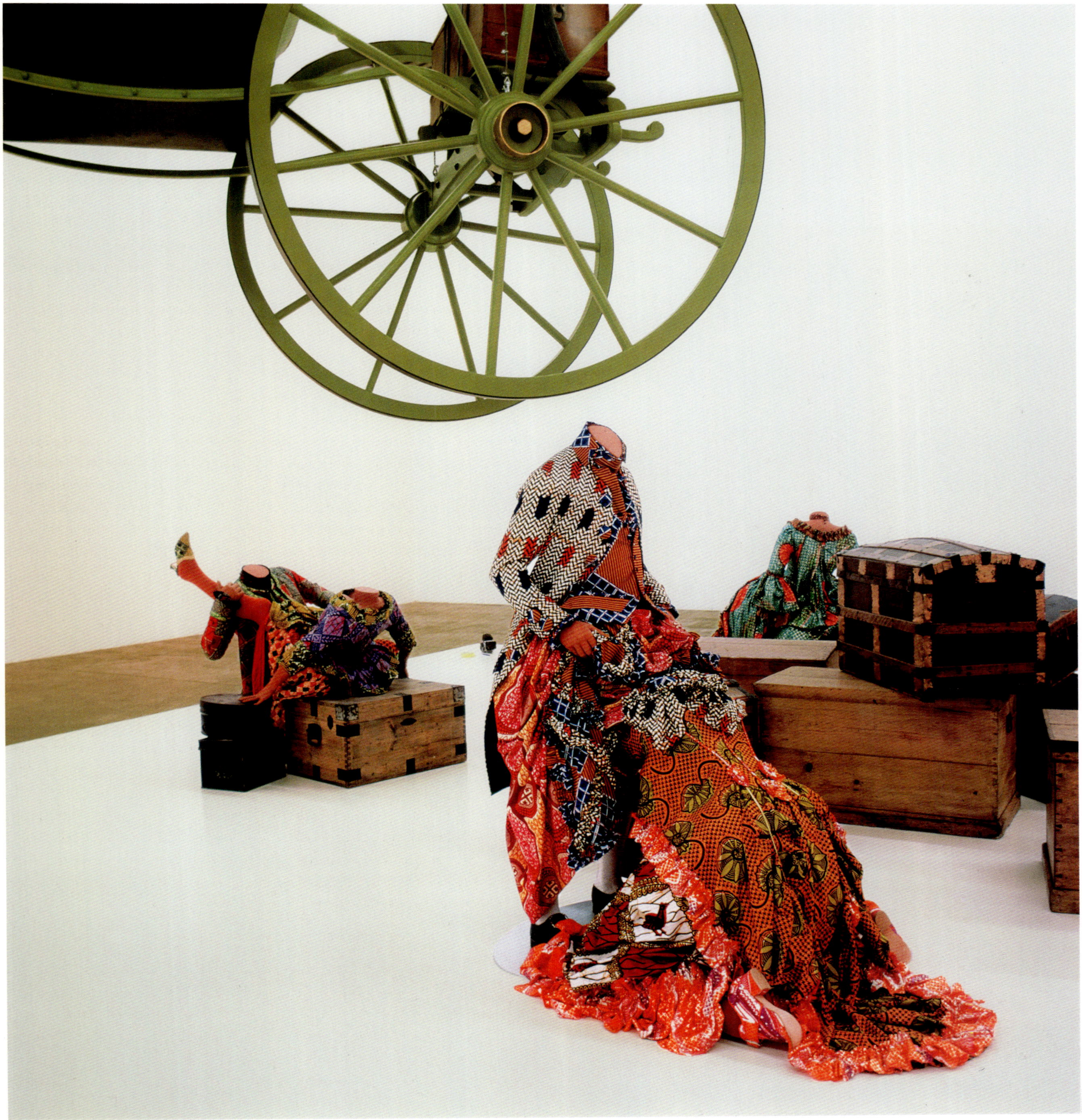

Gallantry and Criminal Conversation, 2002
11 life-size fiberglass mannequins, various metal and wood cases, Dutch wax-printed cotton, leather, wood, steel carriage
Carriage approx. 6 ft 8 in x 8 ft 4 in x 15 ft 5 in (2 x 2.5 x 4.7 m); plinth 29 ft 7 in x 29 ft 7 in x 5 in (9 m x 9 m x 13 cm)

MANUEL OCAMPO

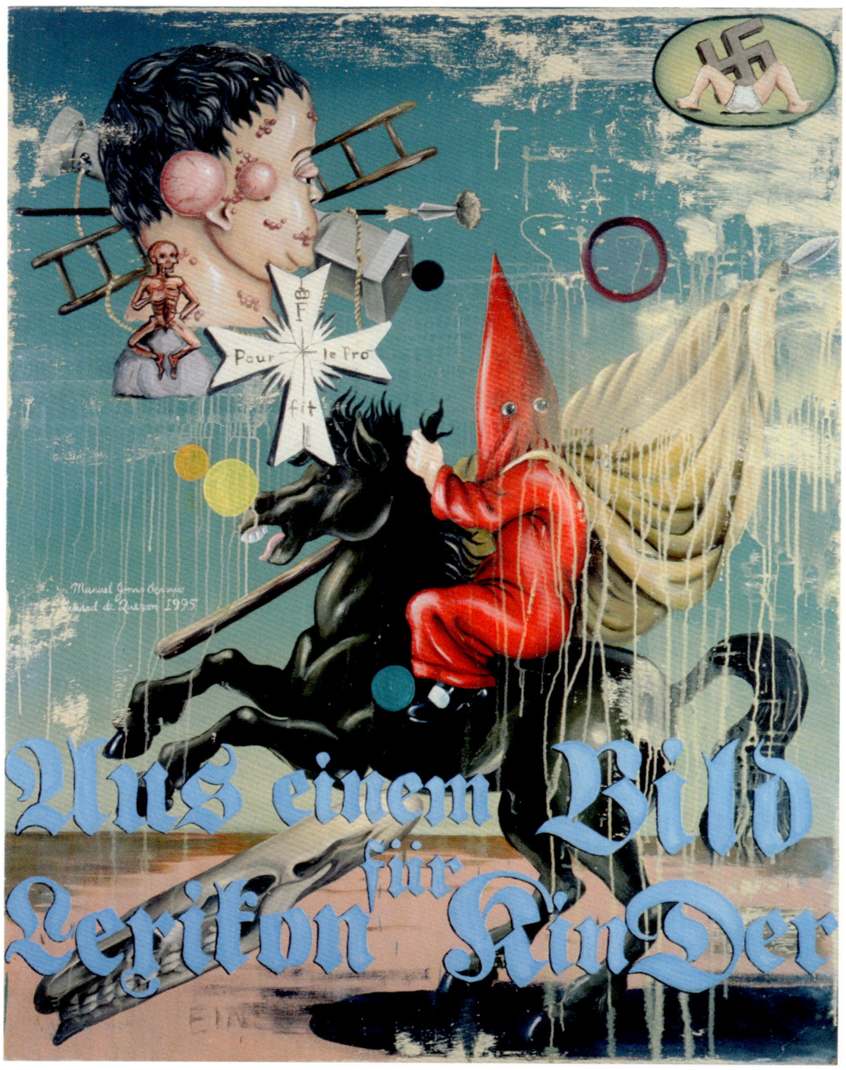

From a Children's Picture Dictionary, 1995
Oil on canvas, 60 x 48 in (152.4 x 122 cm)

to the big city in search of work, they fill their tiny rooms with makeshift furniture and ornamentation—a stack of suitcases does double-duty as a table, walls are papered from floor to ceiling with advertisements torn from newspaper circulars or pages from glossy magazines, often featuring seductive models or celebrities who seem to come from another universe. In one untitled work from 2000, for instance, a young woman poses in her neat but humble home, surrounded by carefully hung plastic buckets and colorful wallpaper made of magazine pages. The figures in all of these photographs exhibit the quiet, composed dignity typical of formal portrait subjects, and as such become paradoxical testaments to their ambiguous status amid the dislocations brought about by globalism and postcolonial upheaval.

For Manuel Ocampo the oppression of colonialism is tied in with the outsized influence of the Catholic Church on his native Philippines. One legacy of the Spanish conquest of the Philippines is a popular culture rife with Catholic ritual and imagery (to which Ocampo contributed as a young artist when he painted "colonial-era" devotional paintings for a thriving market in fake religious imagery). Another legacy is the perceived alignment between Catholic officials and the country's political and economic elite. Ocampo's paintings draw from the traditions of political cartoons, Philippine folk paintings, and popular tourist art, and flirt with all sorts of inflammatory material, including pornography, sacrilege, scatology, and racist imagery. A single canvas may present a frenzied amalgam of colonial religious imagery, ironic and often scathingly satiric texts, and mixtures of ecclesiastical and political symbols that reflect the artist's anger at the misuse of authority and the hypocrisy of the powerful. At times, Ocampo's paintings ape the florid excess of the Spanish Baroque as filtered through the brushes of poorly schooled colonial painters. In the process, they mix the sacred and profane in ways that are simultaneously humorous and transgressive. Recurring images include swastikas, profusely bleeding images of crucified Jesus, fragmented bodies, crosses formed by the intersection of painting stretchers or weapons, and emaciated peasants and the gluttonous fat cats who prey on them. The dark imagery of *From a Children's Picture Dictionary*, 1995, for example, belies the innocence of the title. This apocalyptic scene centers on a hooded figure whose allegiance is ambiguous. He may represent a Christian penitent, a Klansman, or even one of the Horsemen of the Apocalypse. He is surrounded by symbols of death, evil, and strife, including an anamorphic skull floating beneath the horse's feet, a Nazi swastika, a skeletal figure in front of a disturbingly diseased head, as well as a Greek cross. Religion here clearly offers no solace.

Like Shonibare, Ocampo undermines the residue of colonial thinking by adopting and subverting the official visual language of the colonial power. In a related strategy, Tracey Moffatt plays with the notion of "Orientalism," a term that the late literary theorist Edward Said used to describe the West's tendency to deal with "otherness" by feminizing and exoticizing it.[3] Moffatt, who is of Australian aboriginal descent, embraces that otherness to suggest its coercive nature. Some of her work draws on the appalling official policies regarding aborigines that persisted in Australia into the 1960s. The fate of aboriginal children taken forcibly from their parents to be raised by white families forms the background for her film *Night Cries: A Rural Tragedy*, 1989, an homage to the 1955 feature film *Jedda*, by Australian filmmaker Charles Chauvel. Both films suggest the cruelty of the policy, but while Chauvel's ends with the death of the aboriginal daughter, *Night Cries* imagines her dreary life

ZWELETHU MTHETHWA

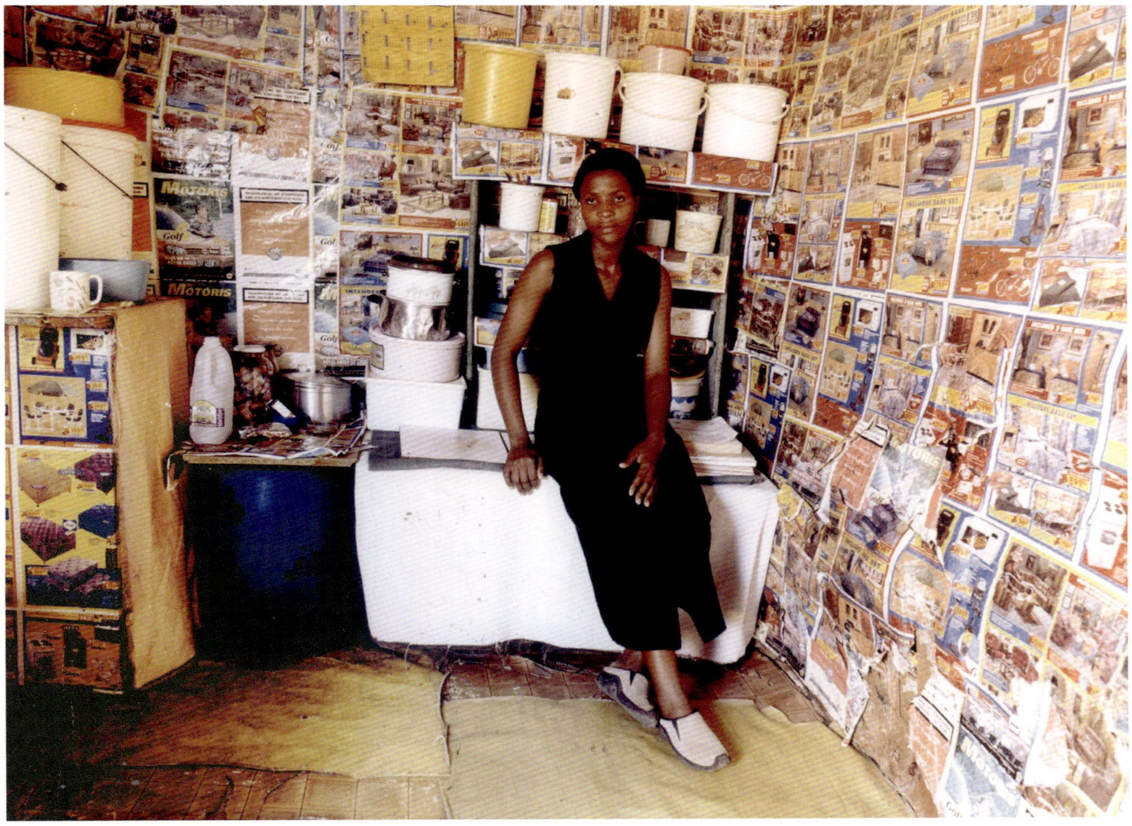

Untitled, 2000
C-print, 70 1/2 x 95 in (179.1 x 241.3 cm)

TRACEY MOFFATT

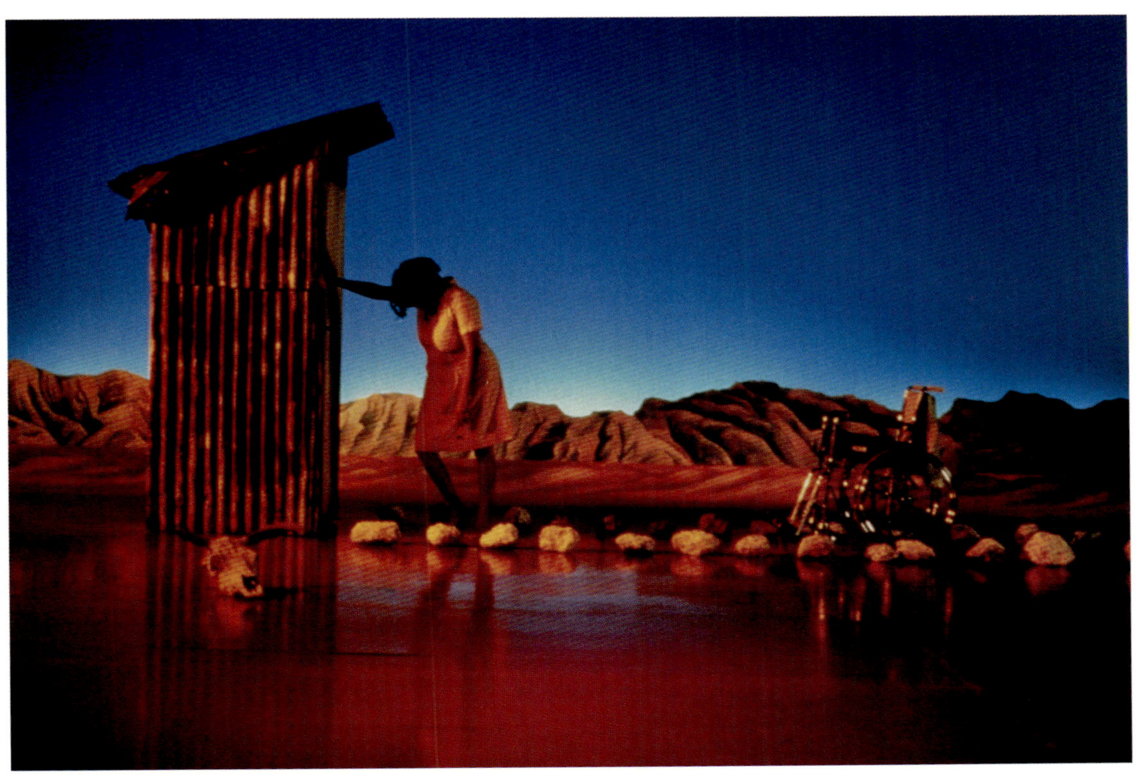

Night Cries: A Rural Tragedy, 1989
35 mm film, Dolby sound, screening format DVD, 17 minutes

spent in servitude to the elderly woman who adopted her. Thus the film exposes the thoughtless cruelty of a policy developed by social reformers determined to bring "civilization" to the untamed "savages" of the Australian outback.

Among artists taking aim at the colonial legacy, Yukinori Yanagi speaks as a citizen of a country that has yet to officially acknowledge the full impact of its imperial policies, and some of his works specifically address the legacy of Japan's wartime ambitions and resounding defeat at the end of World War II. Yanagi remakes Japanese symbols of power in ways that undermine their potency, for instance arranging toys to create an image of the national flag of Japan, or recreating the Imperial Chrysanthemum Crest, symbol of the Japanese emperor, in neon or carpeting. One version of a crest includes a quote by the Japanese novelist Yukio Mishima: "When did the emperor become an ordinary human being?" This question poignantly suggests how confused the defeated Japanese were when forced by American conquerors to repudiate the emperor's divinity, for it was the doctrine of his divinity that had justified the war. Yanagi's best-known works refute the notion of the nation state, reflecting the spectacular costs of his own country's forays into militant nationalism. His *World Flag Ant Farm*, first presented in 1990 and recreated since then, is a live ant farm with one side of its sealed plastic box open for viewing. Ants tunnel through fields of colored sand arranged to depict the flags of the countries of the world, and their meandering paths blur the sharp edges of these symbols of national hegemony until finally they become almost unreadable. Yanagi has also designed ant farms in the shape of U.S. or Japanese currency, which can be read either as a statement about the corrosive power of capitalism, represented here by diligently toiling worker ants, or as a herald of the inevitable collapse of artificial national boundaries—both of which, of course, are aspects of globalism.

Lothar Baumgarten presents an outsider's view of colonial power struggles. One of his recurring subjects is the history of the native tribes of the Amazon, with whom he lived for a few years in the 1970s, and whose numbers and way of life have been nearly decimated by the encroachment of "civilization." In installations that draw on the strategies of Conceptual art, Baumgarten reminds us that a culture without a written language or "Western" sense of time is easily redefined by invaders. For one of his best-known works, *America: Invention*, 1993, he took over the entire Frank Lloyd Wright-designed rotunda of New York's Guggenheim Museum and inscribed its curving walls with the names of vanished or diminished tribes. Because the tribes lack a written language, many of the names were simply transcriptions of lingual sounds made by Western explorers and anthropologists. Thus they illustrate the process by which a colonizing power literally names the peoples it subjugates. One section of the museum wall was reserved for words that described the effects of European contact on the Amazonian tribes—among them "exploited," "decimated," "classified," and "baptized." Of course there is a certain irony in Baumgarten's sympathy for the oppressed. Though he condemns the colonizers for silencing them, he is equally unable to give the tribes a voice, and in the end is also reduced to speaking of them in the language of the conquerors.

Artists such as Baumgarten raise the issue of self-representation, asking who speaks for various groups and how history shapes a sense of identity. These questions are especially pressing for artists who exist between places—who, either by choice or by force, have left their native countries to reside elsewhere. Whether they see themselves as nomads, immigrants, or exiles, many remain haunted by a sense

YUKINORI YANAGI

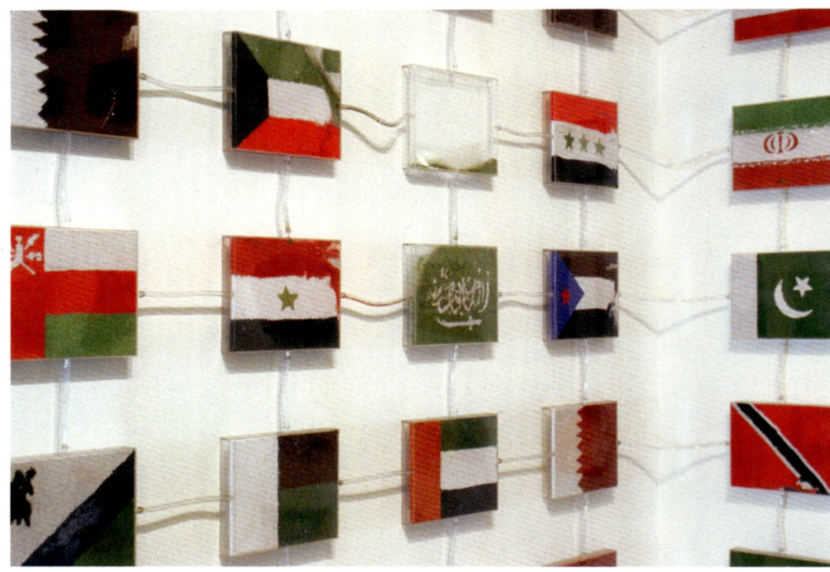

The World Flag Ant Farm (detail: *Persian Gulf*), 1990
Ants, colored sand, 180 plastic boxes and plastic tubes, each box 10 x 12 in (24 x 30 cm)
Naoshima Contemporary Art Museum, Benesse House, Kagawa, Japan

LOTHAR BAUMGARTEN

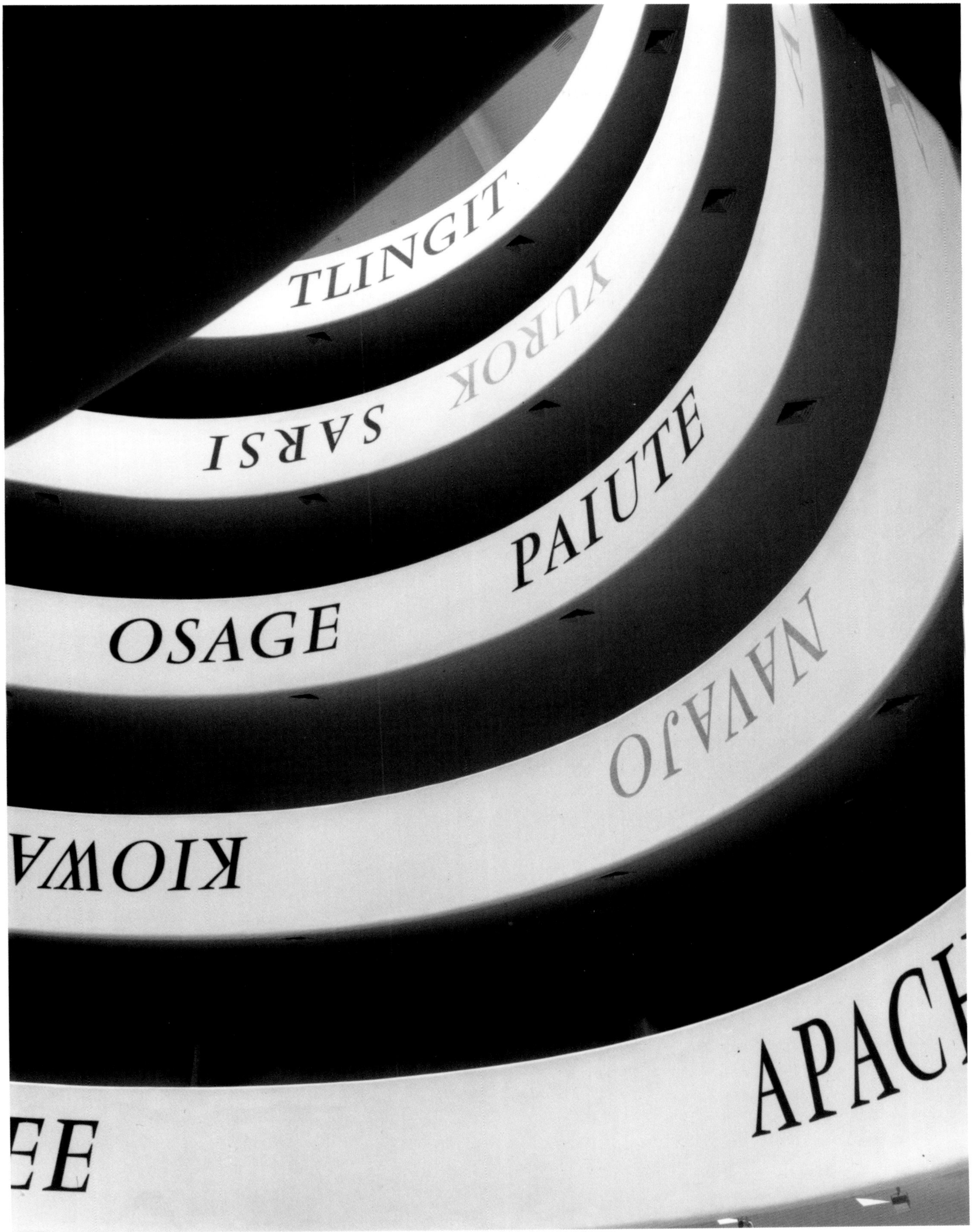

America: Invention, 1993
As installed at the Solomon R. Guggenheim Museum, New York, January–March 1993

of dislocation. Ethnographer James Clifford suggests one way in which displaced people might cope with this reality. He argues that we must abandon the notion of "culture" as some kind of fixed entity, and instead embrace the notion of "cultures," which are always in a state of disintegration, recreation, and renegotiation. He argues against the "salvage paradigm," in which cultural influence is a one-sided process flowing from the more- to the less-developed societies to suggest a multi-directional influence, noting, "Many traditions, languages, cosmologies, and values are lost, some literally murdered, but much has simultaneously been invented and revived in complex oppositional contexts."[4] In other words, culture must be seen as a two-way street, and the disruptions suffered by displaced people can serve as tools for change and reinvention.

The late Chen Zhen transformed this experience of nomadism into art. A Chinese-born artist who suffered the chaos of the Chinese Cultural Revolution during his adolescence, Chen went on in the 1980s to become one of the leaders of the Chinese avant-garde. In 1986 he moved to Paris, where he began to create object-based installations that used humor to reflect the experiences of living between two very different cultural worlds. In *Daily Incantations*, 1996, Chen transformed Chinese chamber pots into a semblance of the Buddhist bells that for centuries have called worshippers to prayer. Wafting from the "bells" were recorded sounds evocative of the strangely bifurcated China of Chen's childhood—the rhythmic scouring of chamber pots mingled with recitation of passages from Mao's *Red Book*. In the center of the installation, modernity intruded in the form of a giant ball of discarded TVs, radios, amplifiers, speakers, and other outdated electronic equipment held together by a tangle of electronic wires. The work served as a case study in cultural difference, juxtaposing physical and industrial waste while playing off Buddhist spirituality against both Western materialism and Communist indoctrination.

Chen referred to the condition of living between cultures as "transexperience." He presented a hybrid visual language, which, if not completely legible to all viewers, could still be understood and enjoyed on some level by all. A similar mix of references to traditional and modern cultures appears in the work of Cai Guo-Qiang. In *Cry Dragon/Cry Wolf: The Ark of Genghis Khan*, 1996, for instance, a fanciful boat made of logs and inflated sheepskins is ineffectually powered by a brace of Toyota engines. Other works draw on feng shui, calligraphy, herbal medicine, and Chinese funerary customs, and are often infused with an undercurrent of humor, as when Cai invited Westerners and Asians to come together in the herb-infused water of *Cultural Melting Bath*, 1997, at the Queens Museum of Art in New York. This literal take on the melting pot materializes the blurring of lines that once separated tribes, nations, and individuals, a lesson inscribed in Cai's own history as an artist raised in China who left for Japan and now lives in New York. Cai is best known for an ongoing series of signature works involving controlled explosions of gunpowder and fireworks that draw lines in the earth or transient patterns in the sky. Some yield "drawings" created by careful manipulation to form burn patterns or traces of smoke that resemble Chinese ink paintings. These works, collectively titled "Projects for Extraterrestrials," are addressed to alien life forms that will observe the light they generate millions of years hence. Taking a step beyond globalism, they suggest that we are all outsiders, emphasizing our precarious hold on this planet.

Xu Bing also reimagines traditional Chinese forms, employing the visual and symbolic aspects of the calligraphy of his native China to suggest a situation in which such communication is aborted or deliberately thwarted. His *Book from the Sky*, 1987–2001, is a breathtakingly labor-intensive work that consists of hundreds of open books laid like a carpet on the floor beneath a canopy of strips of uncut book pages. Both canopy and books are covered with texts that appear to be written in Chinese characters but are in fact composed of pseudo-Chinese characters that anyone versed in the language will recognize as gibberish. For this project, Xu invented over four-thousand counterfeit pictographs, which he carved onto wood blocks to be printed onto innumerable sheets of paper. This non-language recalls the effects of a computer virus that scrambles and drains meaning out of transmitted messages. In the context of Chinese history, the work suggests both the subtle erosion of language affected through propaganda and the fact that the cultural revolution severed China from its literary traditions. Xu reinvents calligraphy from the opposite perspective in a series of works devoted to his "New English Calligraphy (NEC)." Presented in the form of posters, books, and an installation set up to look like a classroom, "NEC" is a set of marks resembling ink strokes of the sort constituting Chinese characters. In fact, they are combined to denote the letters of the Roman alphabet. With a bit of practice, the Western viewer begins to discern that what appears to be unreadable Chinese script is highly stylized English text. "NEC" cuts two ways. By demonstrating how English speakers exoticize their encounters with the "other," Xu comments sardonically on the difficulties inherent in any cross-cultural communication. On a more hopeful note, he may also be suggesting that our differences are not so great as they appear.

Wenda Gu's creation of a linguistic esperanto is more purely optimistic. For a series of works ongoing since 1993 titled "United Nations," Gu builds architectural spaces that resemble teahouses, temples, and national monuments, their walls defined by swaths of porous scrim interwoven with bits of human hair collected from barbershops around the world. Blond, brunette, and red locks are shaped into letters and characters that mimic various Eastern and Western languages. As in Xu's pseudo-calligraphy, these look authentic, but here Gu seems to evoke not negative cross-cultural misunderstanding and bias but a celebration of the linguistic chop suey emerging from the fusion of cultures and languages in the global community. Gu's work looks ahead to a utopian moment when all humankind's debilitating differences will be erased.

Kimsooja, who comes from a nomadic tradition in which all of one's possessions were designed to be folded up and taken away, recalls Chen's "transexperience" in both her heritage and her current experience as a woman living between her Korean past and her Western present. Her sculpture and installation works are combined with or accompanied by performances in which she appears as an alter ego known variously as Needle Woman, Mirror Woman, or Beggar Woman. In the video *A Needle Woman*, 1999–2001, Kimsooja sits impassively, her back to the camera, in front of a variety of bustling streets—in Cairo, Delhi, Lagos, London, Mexico City, New York, Shanghai, and Tokyo—becoming a kind of motionless center, a cosmic outsider, existing in another time and consciousness apart from the world around her. *A Mirror Woman: The Ground of Nowhere*, 2003, a sixty-foot-high vertical cylinder of white fabric, was installed in the lobby of Honolulu's colonial-era City Hall, whose atrium roof Kimsooja arranged to have reopened. Sealing off all but the opening to the sky directly above the fabric column, she placed a mirror floor on the ground at the column's center, so that visitors who stepped inside found themselves

CHEN ZHEN

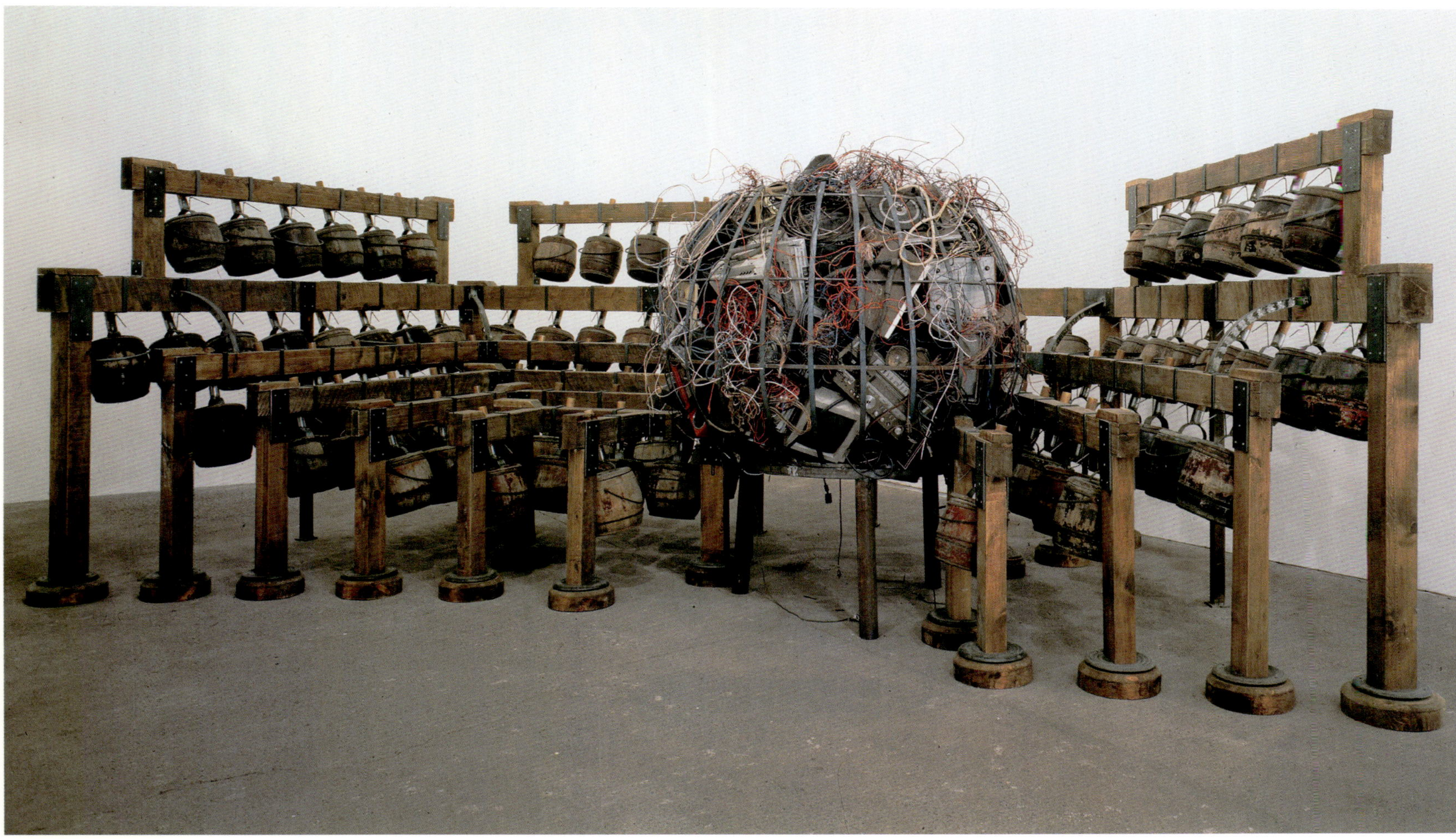

Daily Incantations, 1996
Wood, metal, Chinese chamber pots, electric wires, residue of electrical and electronic objects, sound system
90 5/8 x 27 3/8 x 137 7/8 in (230 x 700 x 350 cm)

CAI GUO-QIANG

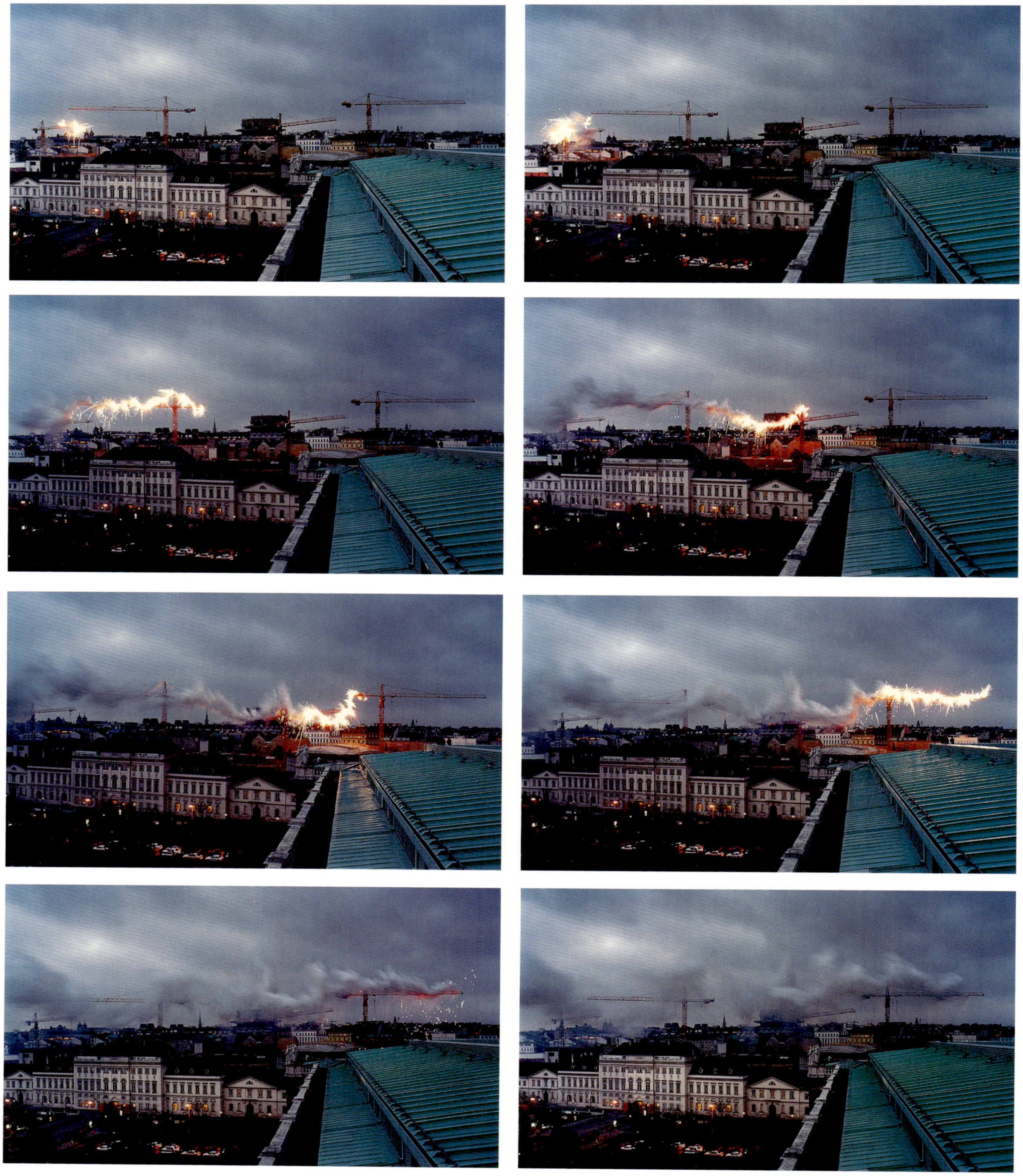

Dragon Sight Sees Vienna: Project for Extraterrestrials No. 32, 1999
6 lbs 13 oz (15 kg) gunpowder, 1,969 ft (600 m) gunpowder fuse, construction cranes
15 seconds, 4:30 p.m., 6 November 1999, Museumsquartier, Vienna

XU BING

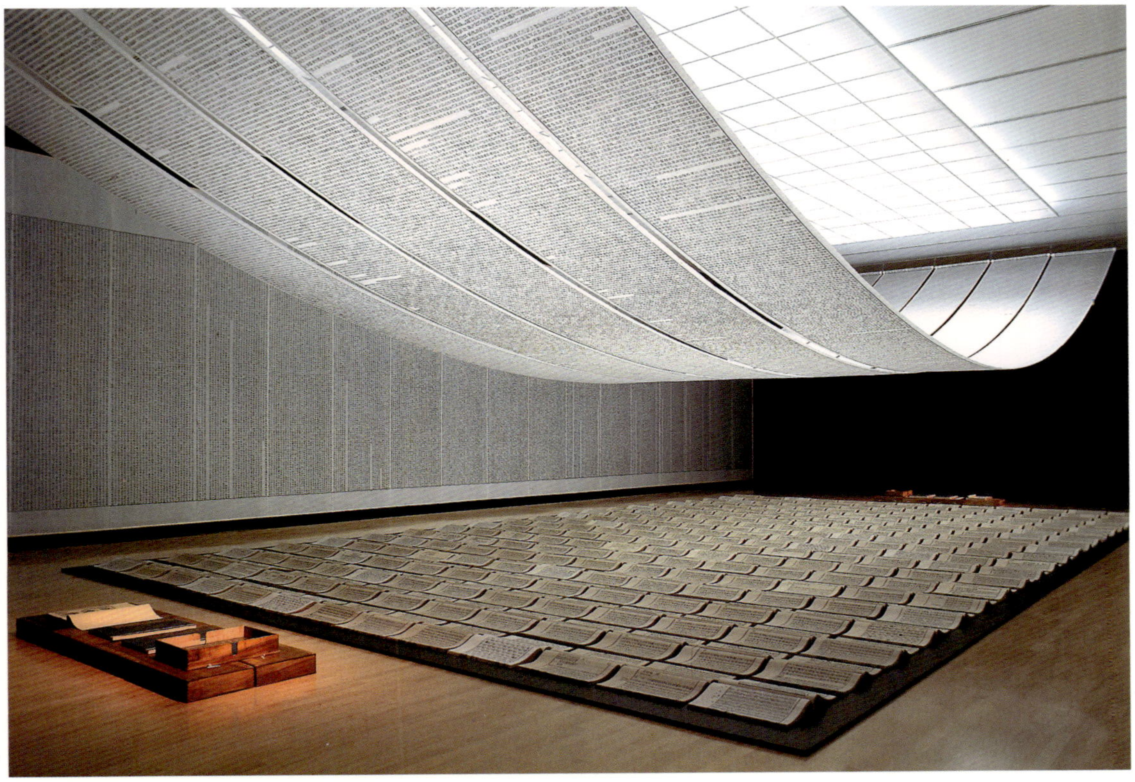

Book from the Sky, 1987–2001
Hand-printed books and scrolls printed from wood blocks inscribed with "false" characters
As installed at the National Gallery of Canada, Ottawa, 1988

WENDA GU

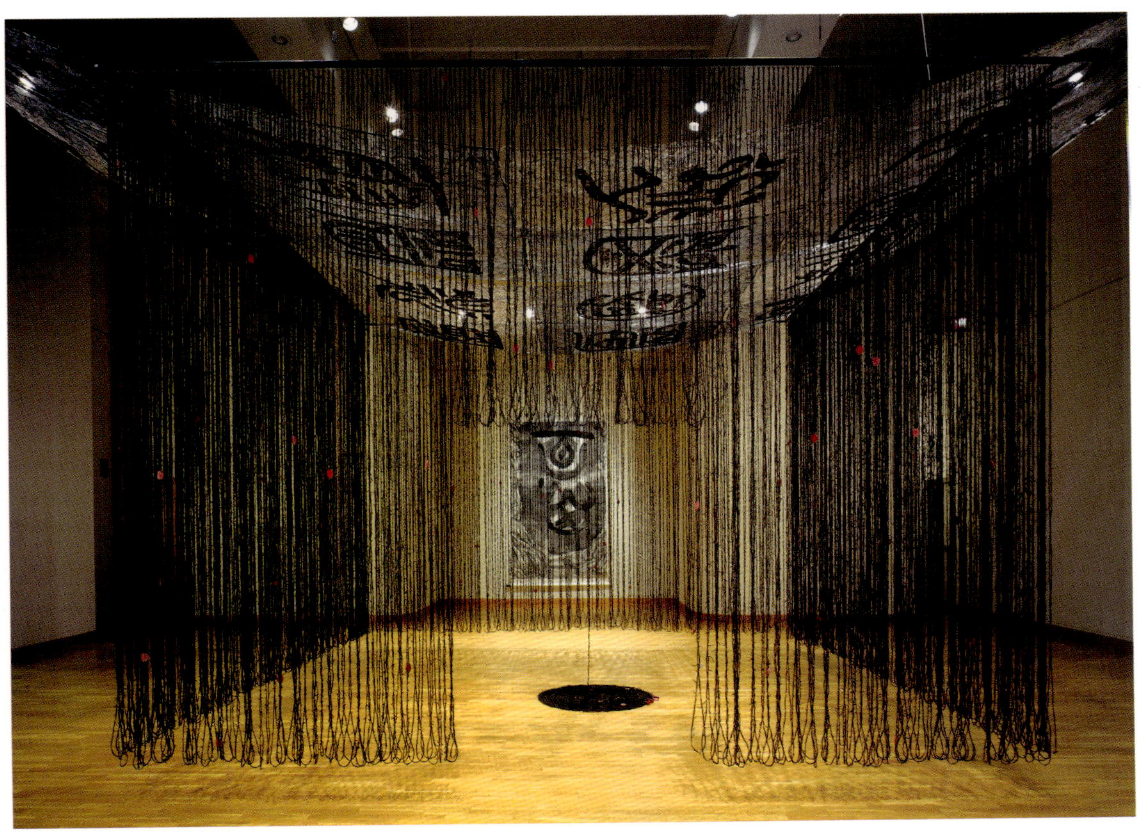

united nations – united 7561 kilometers, 2002
Hair, glue, and rope, 16,404 ft (5000 m) of human braids from 4,698 miles (7561 km) of human hair with rubber stamps of 191 nations of the world
As installed at Bates College Museum of Art, Maine, June–October 2004

EMILY JACIR

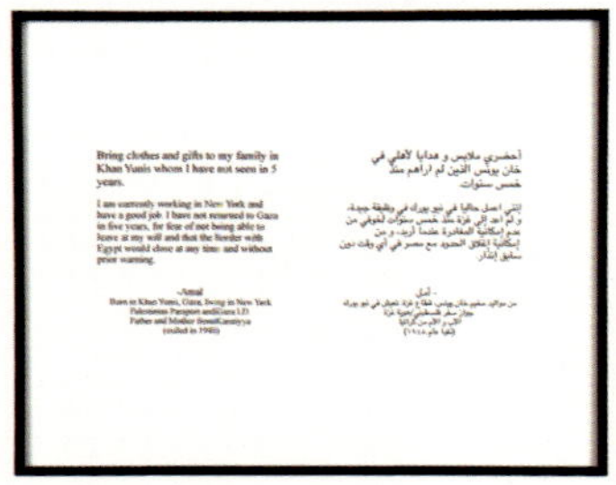

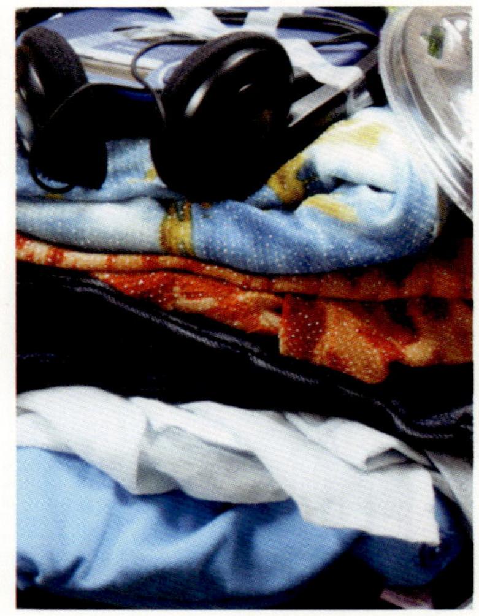

Where We Come From (Amal), 2001–3
32 framed laser prints and C-prints mounted on cintra board
text: 9 1/2 x 11 1/2 in (24 x 29 cm); photograph: 20 x 16 in (50.9 x 40.6 cm)

KCHO

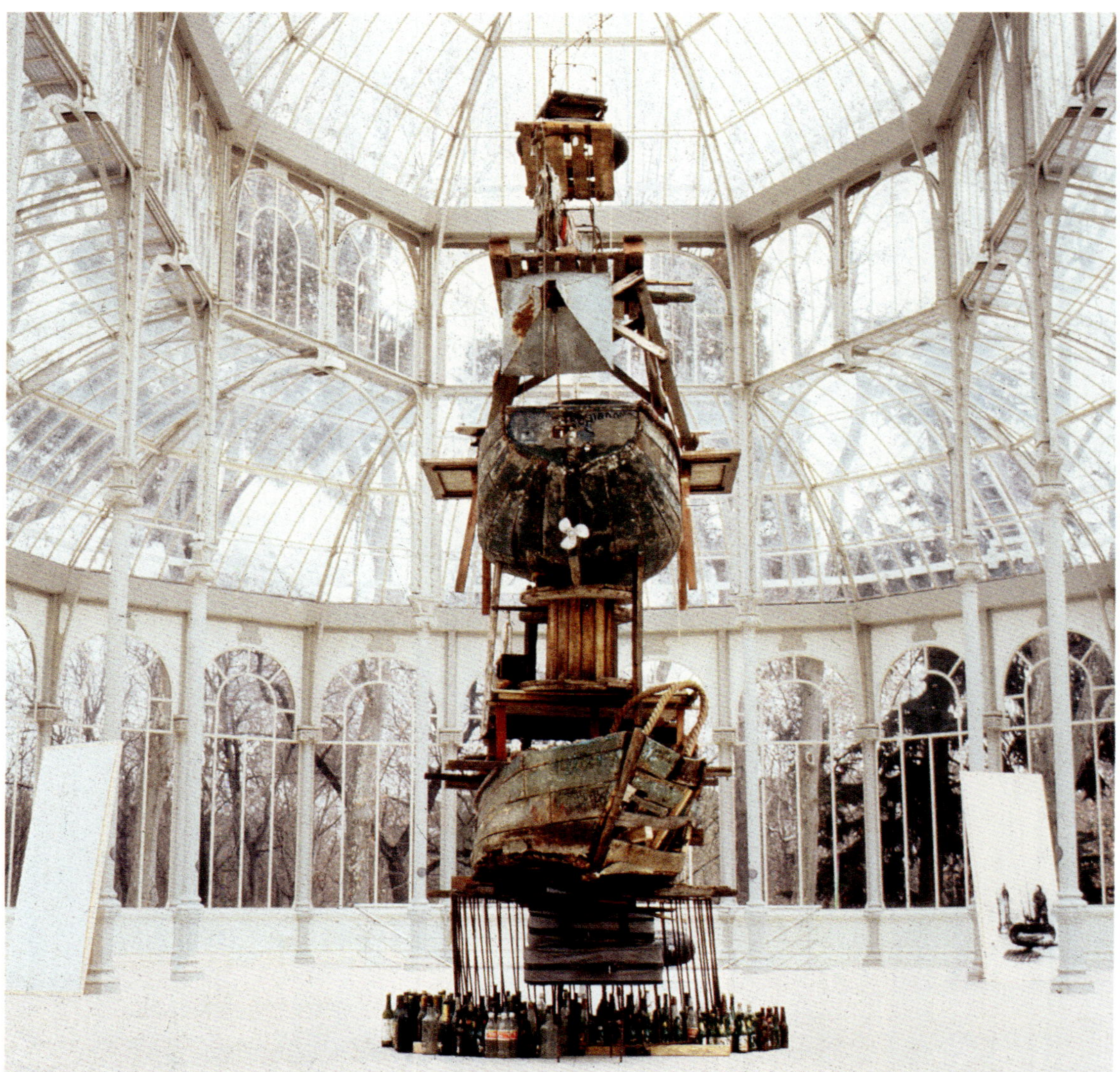

In My Mind, 1995–97
Mixed media, approx. 26 x 16 x 10 ft (8 x 5 x 3 m)
As installed at Palacio De Cristal, Madrid, 2000

standing on a piece of sky. Meanwhile, the fabric swayed gently in the breeze, creating a seemingly living, breathing space. Clouds drifting above and reflected below suggested, paradoxically, the feeling of rolling on an open sea. As part of an arts festival celebrating Korean immigration to the United States, *A Mirror Woman* referenced the immigrant's sense of destabilized identity, but it also provided a universal experience of merging with earth and sky.

While globe-trotting artists express the insecurity of the nomadic life and the contradictions of hybrid identity, there are many people in the world who are unable to cross borders and move freely. Emily Jacir makes this point poignantly in her series *Where We Come From*, 2001–3. Jacir, an artist of Palestinian ancestry, took advantage of her American passport to travel through her homeland, fulfilling simple requests from Palestinians with no such access. Asking what favors she could do for them, she received a surprising variety of requests. Some appeals were seemingly mundane. "Walk the streets of Nazareth," one petitioner asked. "Do something normal in Haifa," entreated another. A man living in a restricted area asked Jacir to pay his phone bill at the Israeli Post Office from which he was barred; another asked her to go on a date with a Palestinian girl he had only spoken to. Jacir carried out her petitioners' requests to the best of her abilities and reported back to them. The work she created from this odyssey consists of text explaining the requests and documentation of her efforts to fulfill them. By avoiding the polemics that surround the Israeli-Palestinian conflict, she presents the situation as a narrative of inaccessible foods and haunts, of separated families, of graves not visited, and insurmountable obstacles to ordinary activities. She lifts the conflict from the abstract realm of geopolitics to reveal its effects on the everyday lives of ordinary people.

Freedom of movement also appears as an impossible fantasy in the work of Kcho (Alexis Leyva Machado). Able to leave his native country of Cuba only with great difficulty, he constructs sculptures out of the instruments and accessories of travel. Boats are a frequent subject, representing the primary means of illegal escape from this island nation. Kcho has constructed boats out of open books (mostly textbooks and Marxist tracts), jury-rigged them out of clamps and bent wood, set them on "oceans" composed of beer bottles, outfitted them with inner tubes and propellers, and filled their skeletal frames with bicycles or piled them with luggage. For the 1997 Havana Biennial Kcho created a towering installation entitled *In My Mind*, 1995–97, consisting of wooden boats precariously stacked with bottles underneath.

In Kcho's work, the boat is considerably more than just a means of transportation. It becomes a symbol of mental and physical freedom. As such, it points to one of the most positive aspects of globalism. Whatever its effects in realigning large-scale balances of political and economic power, for individuals the opening of borders and erasing of psychological and physical divisions can prove truly liberating. No matter how complex globalism is, the greatest gift it might give the world is the freedom to dream.

KIMSOOJA

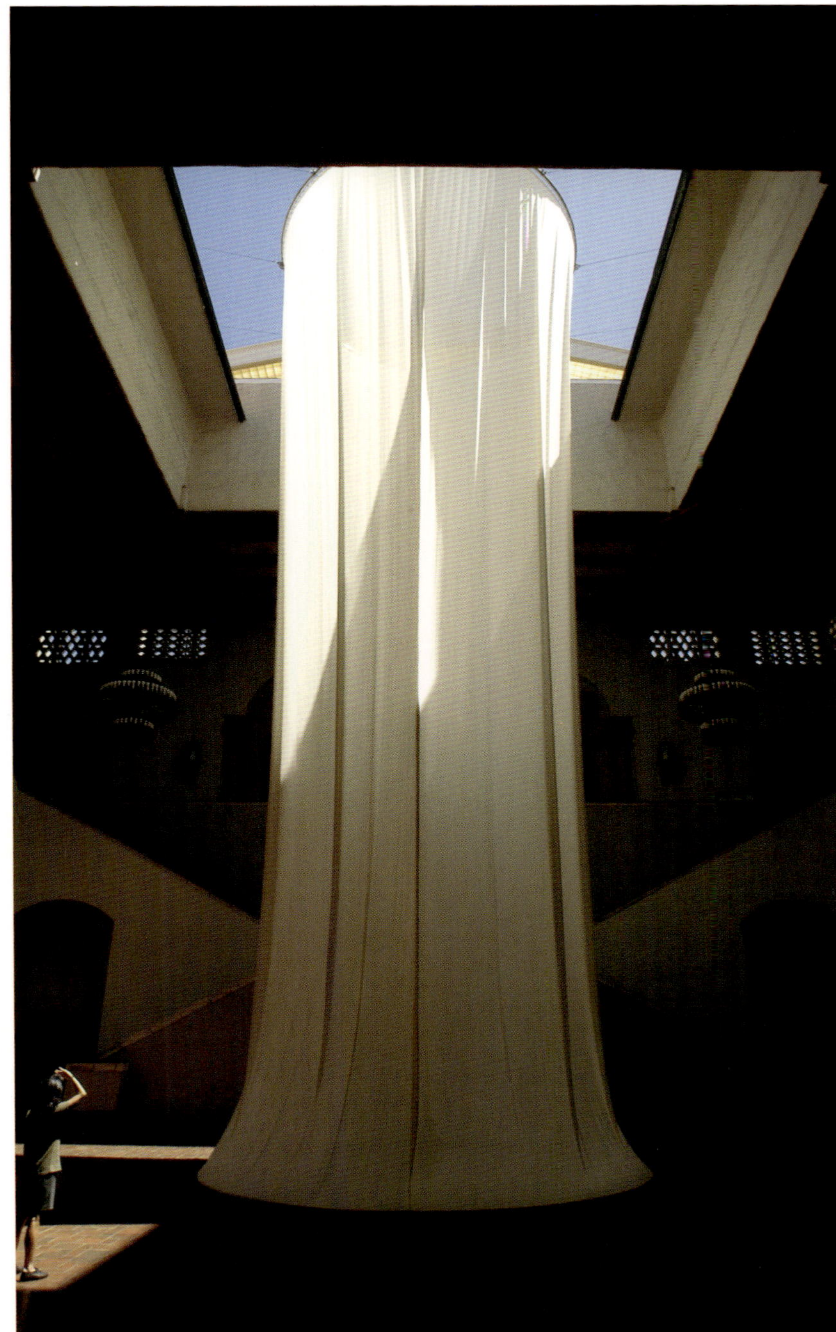

A Mirror Woman: The Ground of Nowhere, 2003
Aluminum ring, fine gauze cotton, mirror, wood, 57 x 21 ft (17.4 x 6.4 m)
As installed at Honolulu City Hall, Hawaii, September–October 2003

ART & ARCHITECTURE
THE UTOPIAN FALLACY

By some standards architecture is the most conservative of the arts, and for very particular reasons: buildings depend for their realization on concentrations of wealth, and they are intended to stand the test of time, so their creators tend to stick with conventions. Strange, then, that at the dawn of the modern age architecture was one of the chief incubators of revolutionary ideas about the reconstitution of society. Visionary architects as diverse as Adolf Loos (who famously equated ornament with crime[1]), Le Corbusier (who proposed that a "house is a machine for living in"[2]), International Style proponents Ludwig Mies van der Rohe and Philip Johnson, American lovers of democracy Frank Lloyd Wright and Louis Sullivan, and Bauhaus founder Walter Gropius all adhered to the idea that perfection in the built environment would lead to the perfection of its inhabitants, expressing absolute faith in the potential of architecture and design to act as agents of social transformation. Such utopian notions were among the driving forces of modernity. They were also one of its great delusions. The early twentieth century gave birth to a plethora of architectural movements born of a belief that properly harnessing technology and mass production could finally produce a rational, egalitarian, and hygienic social order. Today this faith lies in shambles, blown apart as much by the devolution of the modernist ideals of efficiency, rationality, and functionalism into dehumanizing exercises in corporate standardization as by the dystopian consequences of the sinister social experiments conducted under the aegis of Fascism and Communism.

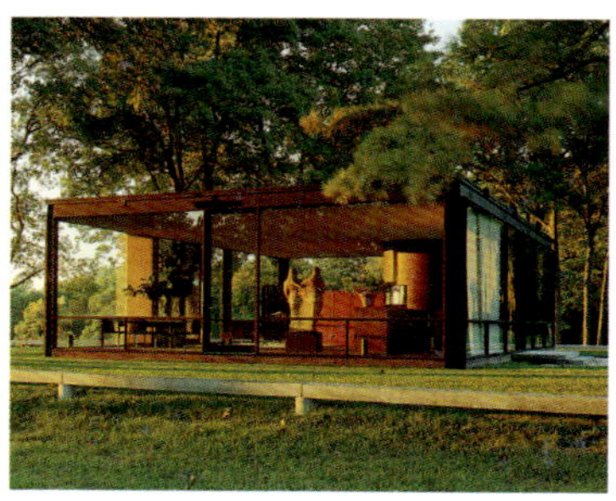

PHILIP JOHNSON
GLASS HOUSE
1949-50
NEW CANAAN, CONNECTICUT

The failure of the utopian impulse in architecture has freed the architect from the role of social visionary. Most architects operate less as benevolent social planners than as narrowly defined engineers charged with realizing a project within the restrictions of budget, zoning, and safety laws. When they do have the opportunity to stretch their imaginations, architects generally do so in the context of commissions for singular buildings that are less likely to change the world than to raise their own and their patrons' artistic profiles. These commissions have spawned a raft of architectural projects that reject rationality for fantasy, disharmony, and references to the eclectic history of architecture. Museum buildings, in particular, have provided architects with showcases of this sort. Frank Gehry's Guggenheim Bilbao in Spain, for instance, is a cubistic arrangement of curves and planes in glinting titanium steel that gives no hint of its function or interior configuration. Santiago Calatrava's addition to the Milwaukee Art Museum in the United States is topped by a two-hundred-foot angled mast attached to cables meant to evoke the soaring architecture of suspension bridges.

Interestingly, the dreams and failures of modernist architecture, while largely constraining architects, have invigorated contemporary artists. Artists today have forgotten neither the allure nor the dangers of early modernism's revolutionary ideals, and many realize that architecture can provide a visual and philosophical language for addressing the contradictions of contemporary life. Architecturally inclined artists today find in architecture a medium through which they can critique contemporary living and working environments, evaluate the lingering impact of modernism's notions of progress and rationality, and investigate the implications of the postmodern embrace of consumer capitalism. Artists who straddle the line between art and architecture examine the ways in which people today do and might live. They put forth their own visionary proposals, which range from the sublime to the ridiculous, encompassing everything from rethinking whole cities to designing toilets. They also issue warnings about the hubris involved in grand schemes that fail to account for the realities of human psychology, social hierarchies, and political conflict. They ask us to consider how architecture can enhance or dispel a sense of common good and public life. In a few cases, they even propose that architecture might still serve as a catalyst for social change.

A number of contemporary artists have taken on the contradictions inherent in modernist architecture's valorization of "transparency," an aesthetic sparked by the merging of industrial engineering and visionary architecture in the first third of the twentieth century. Transparency took various forms, among them the functionalist "glass box," which incorporated steel frames, reinforced concrete, and plate glass, and the gleaming glass-and-steel skyscrapers that have come to symbolize the modern urban skyline, made possible by the invention of the non load-bearing wall. One icon of this genre is Mies's Seagram Building in New York, 1954–58, with its streamlined contour and formal purity. Another is Philip Johnson's Glass House, 1949–50, whose walls and open floor plan erase any concept of privacy. The Glass House was praised for its physical clarity and its tendency to melt into the surrounding landscape. But its open floor plan also anticipated the depersonalized open cubicles and glass walls of the contemporary corporate office space.

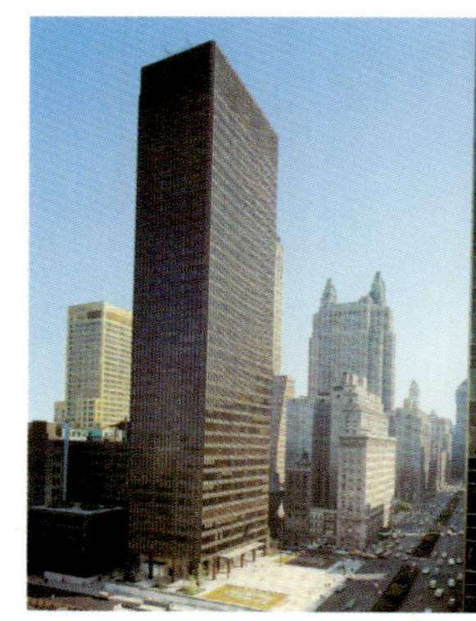

LUDWIG MIES VAN DER ROHE
SEAGRAM BUILDING
1954-58
NEW YORK

A subversive attitude toward modernist architecture's claims to rationality, functionality, and permanence characterized the work of Gordon Matta-Clark, a student of architecture in the late 1960s who during his short lifetime (he died of cancer in 1978 at the age of thirty-five) created a series of works that remain touchstones for artists interested in debunking modernism's exalted aspirations. Matta-Clark literally dismantled architectural space in works that used houses and buildings that were abandoned or slated for demolition as their raw materials. He transformed these structures into environmental sculptures through a series of "building cuts," slicing a building in half, cutting slits or holes in roofs and walls that opened up vistas to other rooms and to the outside world, and removing whole facades so that interior private spaces were exposed to public view. These works had a limited lifespan, and in fact they exist today only in drawings, photographs, films, and other documentation. *Splitting*, 1974, is a collage of photographs he took of one of his best-known building cuts—a two-story house in New Jersey that he split down the middle. For *Fake Estates*, which began in 1972 and was never completed, Matta-Clark appropriated micro-plots between lots, otherwise useless spaces created by irregularities in New York City's zoning process. Purchasing these

GORDON MATTA-CLARK

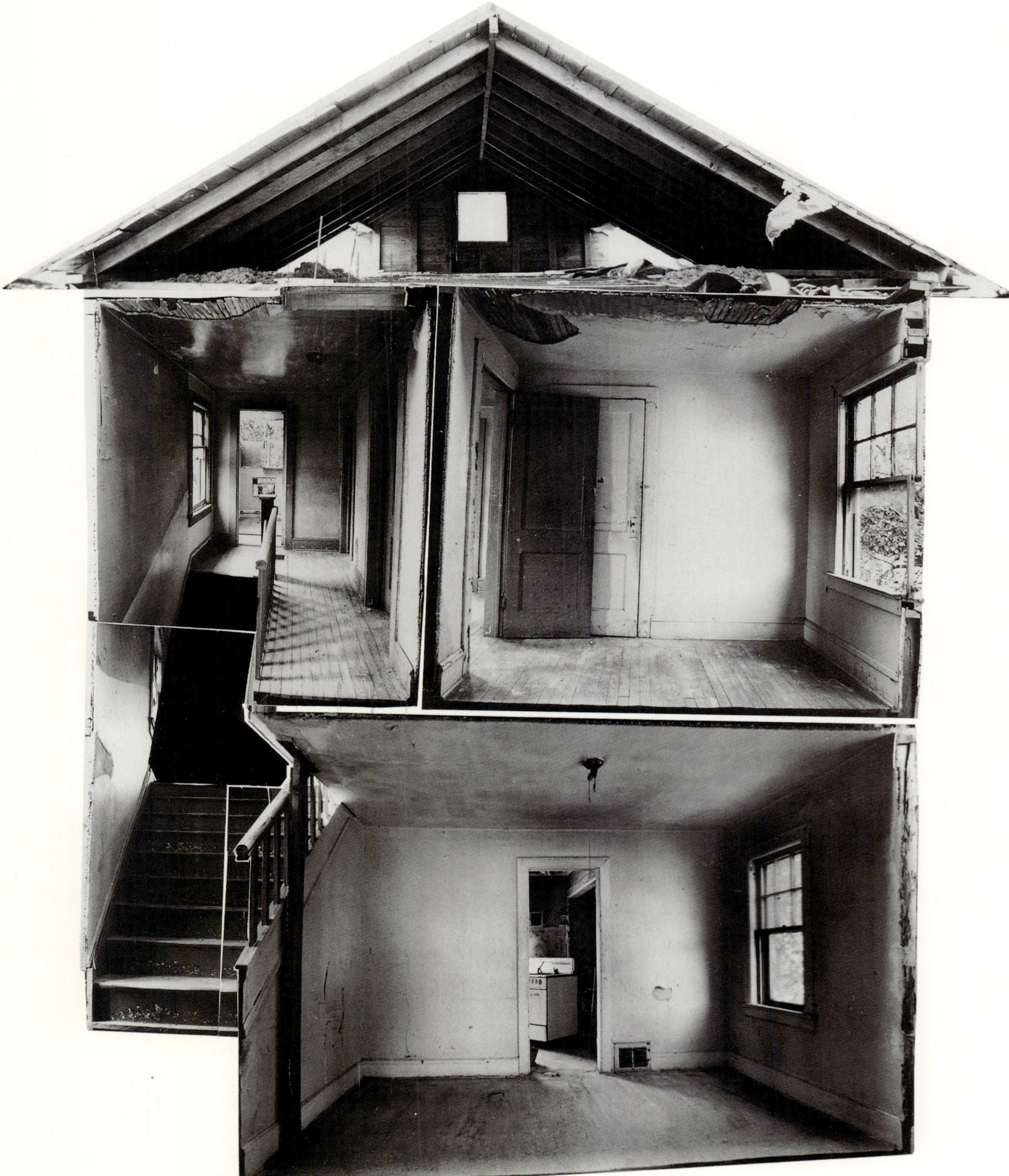

Splitting, 1974
Collaged black and white photograph on cardboard
32 1/2 x 27 3/4 in (82.6 x 70.5 cm)

RACHEL WHITEREAD

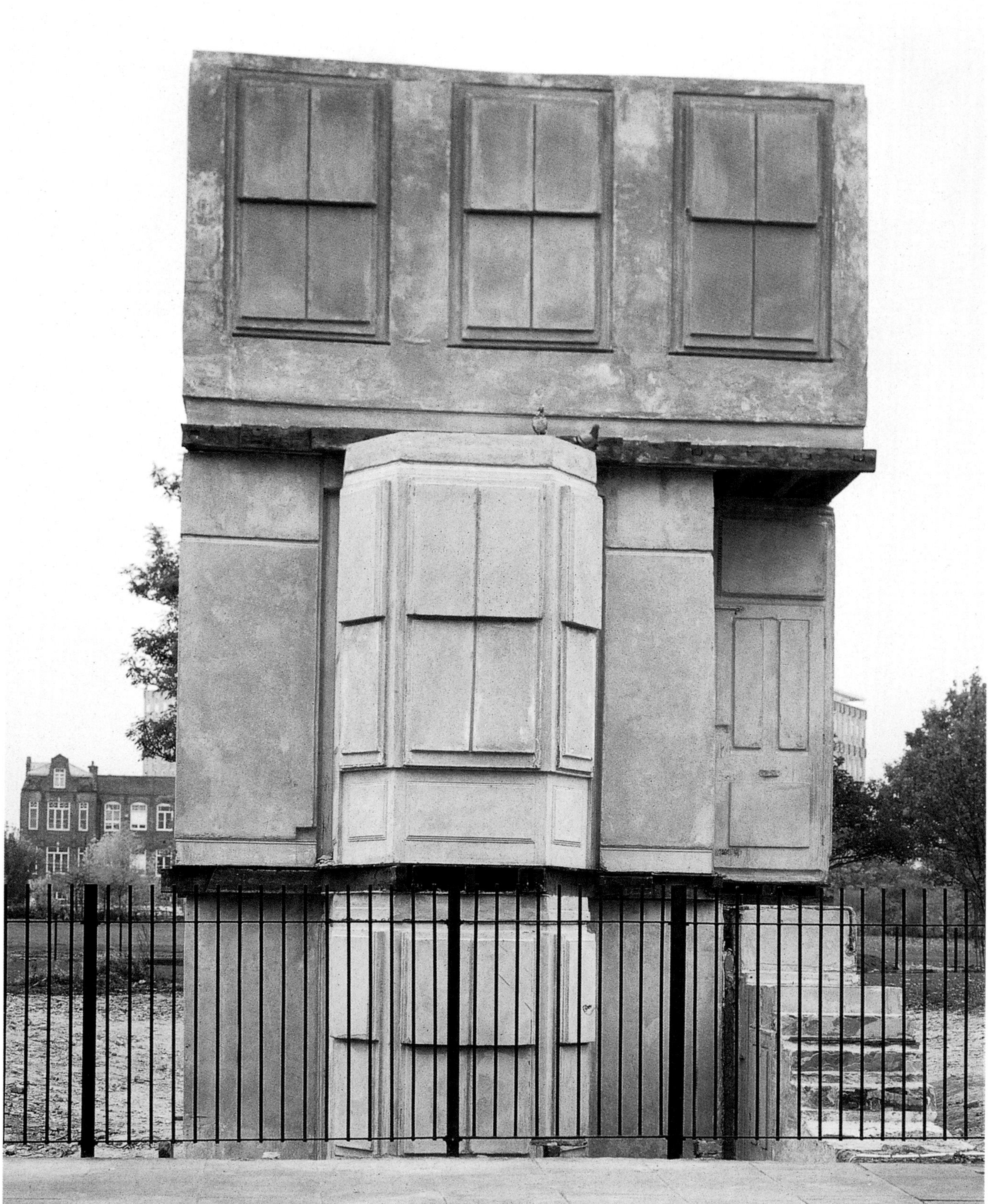

Untitled (House), 1993
Building materials and plaster, approx. 32 ft 6 in (10 m) high
193 Grove Road, London E3, demolished 11 January 1994

tiny plots with the intention of auctioning them off, Matta-Clark drew attention to the metaphoric potential of spaces in between. Matta-Clark's interest in demolition, ruin, and architectural fragments (his term for such forms of deconstructed architecture was "anarchitecture," as in anarchy-plus-architecture) is reflected in contemporary sculpture and photography, including the work of artists discussed elsewhere in this book, such as Jessica Stockholder or Bernd and Hilla Becher. Among contemporary architects, a kinship is particularly evident in a series of projects created in the 1970s by James Wines's firm SITE Environmental Design for Best Products, which physically deconstructed the conventional retail showroom. In one of these buildings, the brick veneer of the facade was peeled away, revealing the blank wall below, while others were characterized by unfinished edges that resembled newly created modernist ruins, already in an advanced state of decay.

Like that of Matta-Clark, Rachel Whiteread has used architectural spaces slated for demolition as raw material. Some of her works are essentially casts of empty space, made by pouring liquid concrete, plaster, rubber, or resin around real objects, into rooms, and even into whole buildings. The casts make space solid, creating strange objects lined with indentations marking the location of bookcases, cabinets, windowsills, and doors. These sculptures bear some resemblance to Minimalist works in their blocky, functionalist geometry, but they also convey poignant echoes of a former life. Despite their physical density, they have something of the quality of phantoms, as implied by the title *Ghost*, 1990, Whiteread's cast of a living room complete with a reverse relief of its fireplace, molding, and windows. *House*, 1993, her best-known and most controversial sculpture, was a full-scale cast of the interior of a condemned, three-story Victorian terraced row house in London's East End. After heated debate among the press and the public about the status of *House* as a work of art, it was bulldozed in 1994. Whiteread's smaller-scale casts also present artifacts of an earlier time. They include the interiors of hot-water bottles, the spaces beneath beds or the legs of kitchen chairs and tables, the insides of bathtubs and wardrobes, and the gaps around the spines of books in a library. Because she chooses domestic objects and spaces with a previous life, Whiteread's sculptures are imbued with a poignant vulnerability. They encapsulate the transience of memory, childhood, and security in a world subject to unceasing change.

Daniel Buren also works with preexisting architectural sites, both celebrating and subverting architecture's authority by emblazoning public buildings, museums, and other "privileged sites" with striped banners and panels that echo the utilitarian striped cloth found everywhere in France—on shirts and cabanas, for instance. Through these interventions, Buren has stated, he intends to return art and architecture to the people. But the actual effect can be quite different. One of his most famous works, *Les Deux Plateaux*, 1985–86, a permanent installation at Paris's Palais-Royal, the seventeenth-century palace of Cardinal de Richelieu, generated a great deal of controversy among the public it was meant to liberate. This installation of striped pillars of varying heights fills the grand courtyard of an historic institution. The juxtaposition of crisp modernist geometry with classical colonnades is deliberately jarring, recalling early modernism's goal to reject the past and dispense with the dead weight of history.

The social and psychological effect of architecture is a recurring theme in the work of Dan Graham, who since the 1970s has worked in video, photography, performance, and installation, as well as theoretical writings, often employing

DANIEL BUREN

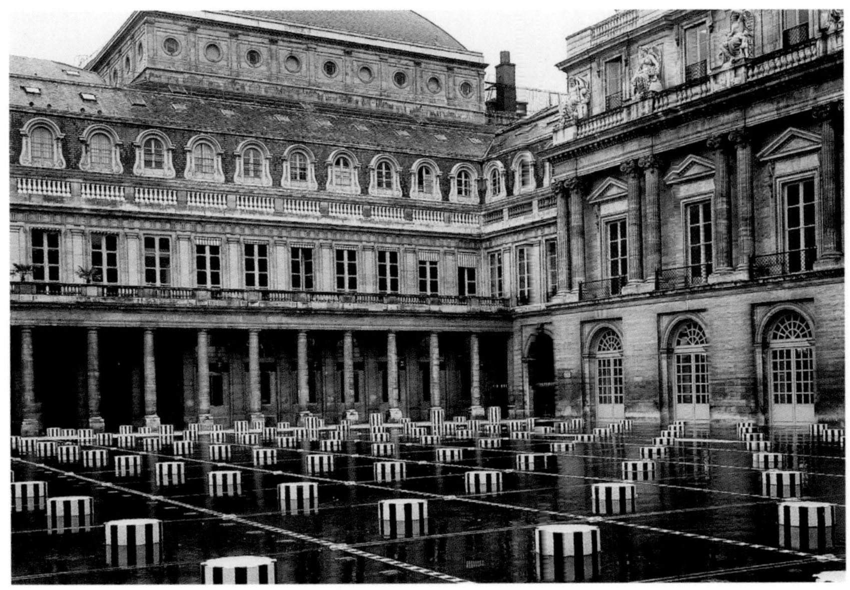

Photo-souvenir: *Les Deux Plateaux*, 1985–86
Cement, marble, stone, galvanized steel, water, electricity
9,840 square ft (3,000 square m)
Work in situ, main courtyard, Palais-Royal, Paris

MONICA BONVICINI

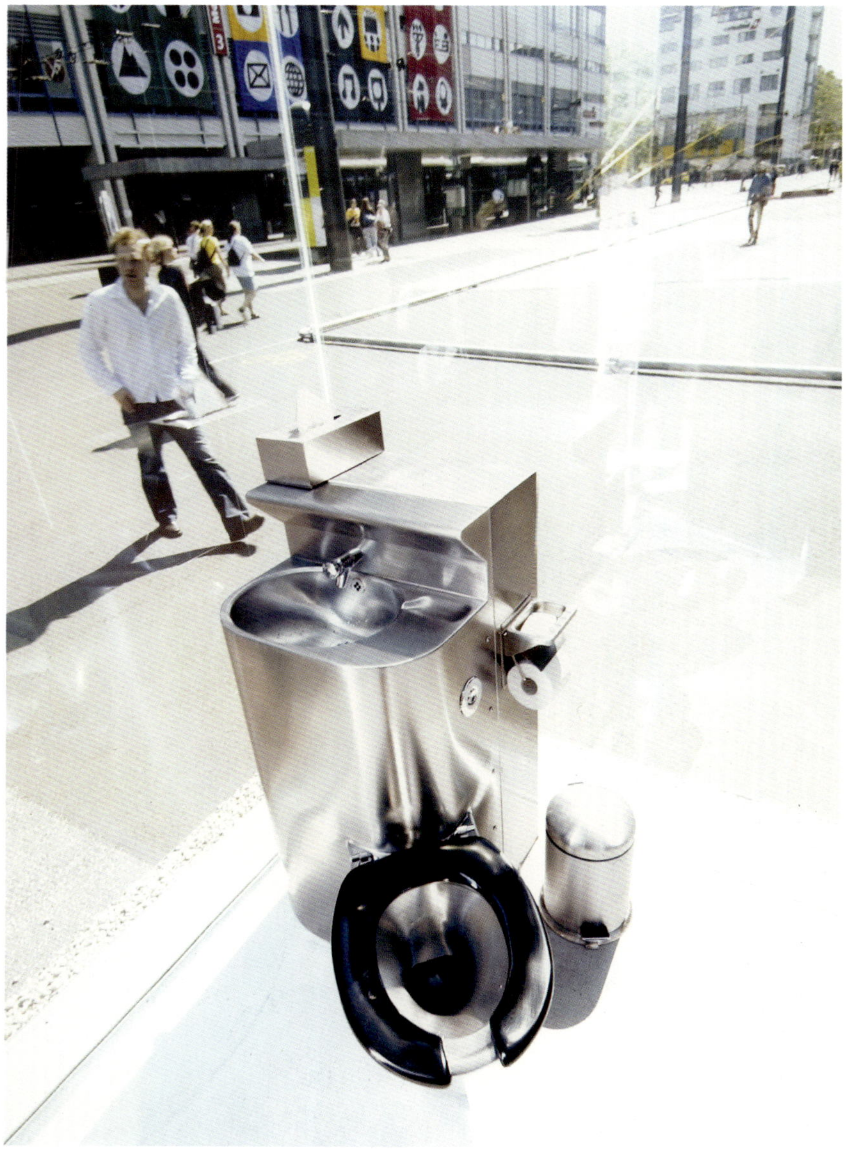

Don't Miss a Sec, 2003–4
Two-way mirror structure, stainless steel, toilet unit, concrete floor, aluminium, fluorescent lights
98 1/2 in x 55 1/8 x 74 3/4 in (250 x 140 x 190 cm)
As installed at Art Basel, Switzerland, June 2004

two-way mirrors and video feedback to suggest the complexities of our interactions with art, architecture, and each other. *Cinema*, 1981, for instance, is a model for a movie theater constructed of two-way mirror glass, which may be reflective or transparent depending on the relative amount of light inside and out. In Graham's cinema, the usual film experience, in which the lowering of the lights allows each viewer to enter a private cocoon, is subverted, making audience members as aware of their fellow viewers and the passersby outside as they are of the film itself. Graham's series of "pavilions," which he has been constructing since the late 1970s, represent his most sustained examination of the psychology of modernist architecture. These two-way-glass minimalist structures are placed in parks or on urban rooftops, where viewers experience them differently, depending on the naturally changing light and shadows. On sunny days, the glass walls of the pavilion are transparent from the outside but mirror-like from within. When the natural light is dimmer, the opposite conditions prevail. In a nod to the modernist fixation on transparency, the pavilions destabilize the viewer's sense of what is public and private, visible and invisible, inside and outside. But they also subtly undermine the autonomy and clean-machine aesthetic of the so-called glass-box building by reintroducing reflections and the unpredictable effects of nature.

Two-way glass functions similarly in Monica Bonvicini's reinvention of the public toilet. *Don't Miss a Sec*, 2003–4, is a glass-enclosed loo that plays off the notion of the panopticon, a prison design first conceived by eighteenth-century British philosopher and social reformer Jeremy Bentham, who proposed that prisoners could be better controlled if they were always in view of a central guardhouse. Bonvicini's toilet, which was installed in a London public square that once housed a penitentiary, and in which Bentham had proposed installing a panopticon guardhouse, contains all of the normal accoutrements of a public toilet, including a stainless steel WC unit, sink, soap, paper, and even reading material. Because it is made of two-way reflective glass, users can see the outside world, while passersby only glimpse their own reflected images. Despite the actual privacy, the transparency from inside creates a perceived breakdown of public and private space. In other works, Bonvicini extends her investigation into the coercive aspects of modernist architecture exemplified by Brutalist structures such as Le Corbusier's monastic and little-loved design for Unité d'Habitation, a mid-century housing project in Marseilles that was the prototype for the standardized public housing projects so ubiquitous in the second half of the twentieth century. Bonvicini's *Stairway to Hell*, created for the 2003 Istanbul Biennial, united two floors of an industrial exhibition space via a gleaming metallic staircase that was suspended from chains and topped with glass walls cracked with bullet holes.

Liam Gillick, who has referred to his architecturally inspired works as a "post-utopian" vision of the future, suggests that the modernist belief in behavior control through the organization of space manifests itself today in the dictates of the corporate sphere.[3] His visual vocabulary of brightly colored Plexiglas sheets arranged in grid-patterned screens on aluminum frames deliberately echoes Donald Judd's "primary structures" and the clean geometry of the International Style. These structures, however, are designed as parodies of corporate office environments. Gillick's titles point to their critical intentions. Take, for instance, *Assessment Think Tank*, 1997, which consists of a Plexiglas box that might have come from a showroom of modular units designed to be customized for individual clients and situations.

DAN GRAHAM

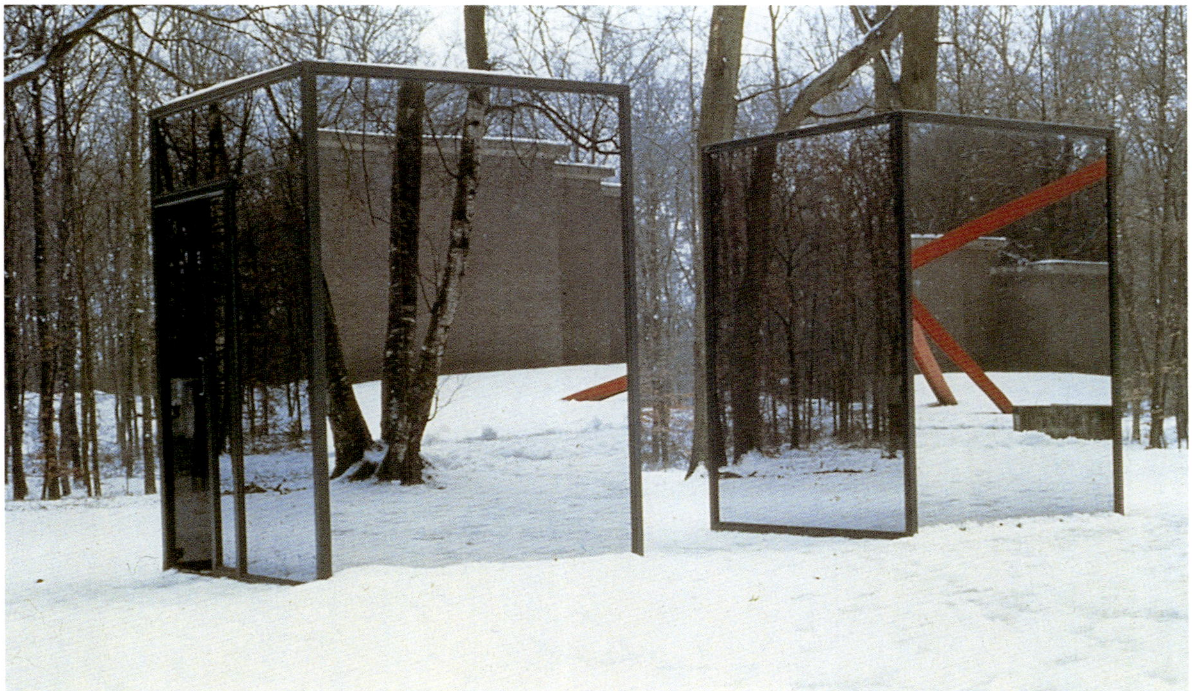

Two Adjacent Pavilions, 1978–82
Two-way mirror, glass, steel, 98 7/8 x 73 1/4 x 73 1/4 in (251 x 186 x 186 cm)
As installed at Documenta 7, Kassel, Germany, 1982

LIAM GILLICK

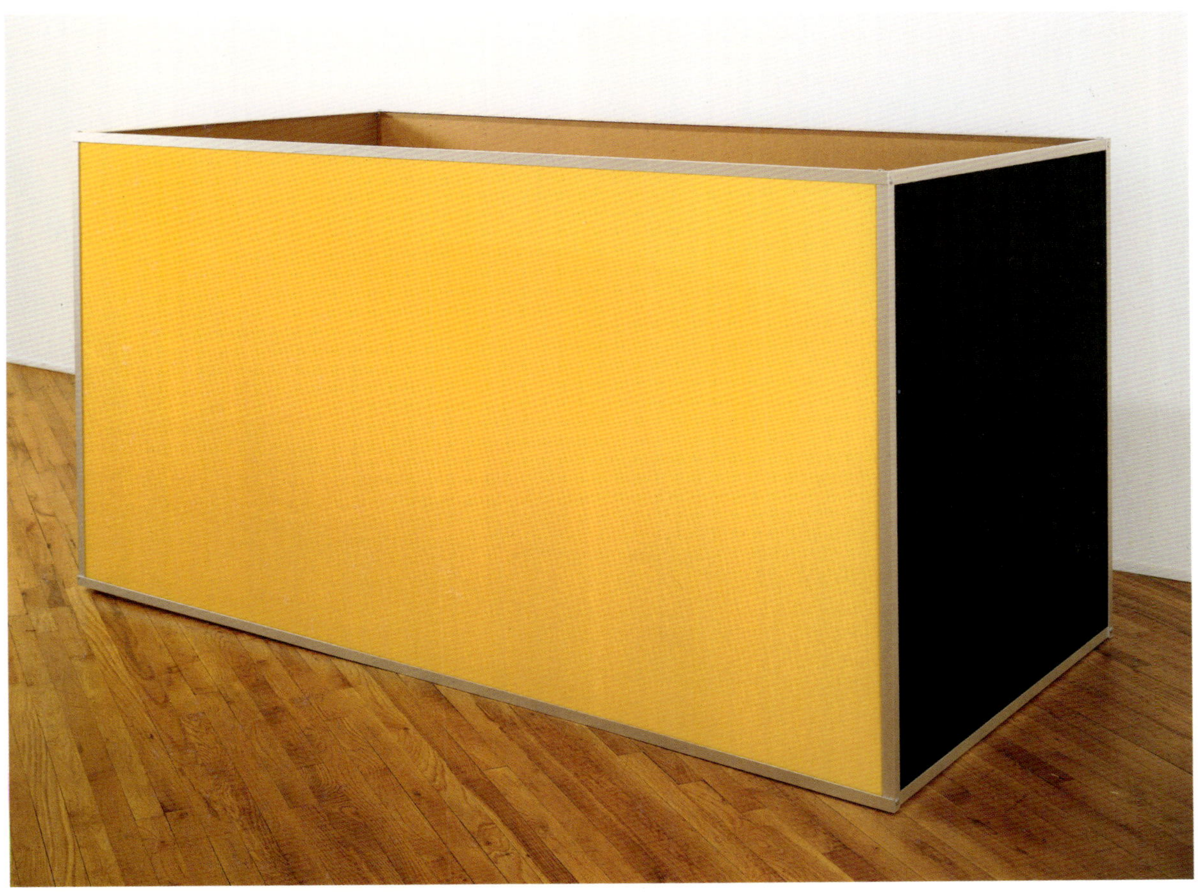

Assessment Think Tank, 1997
Anodized aluminum, Plexiglas, 94 1/2 x 47 1/4 x 47 1/4 in (240 x 120 x 120cm)

DENNIS ADAMS

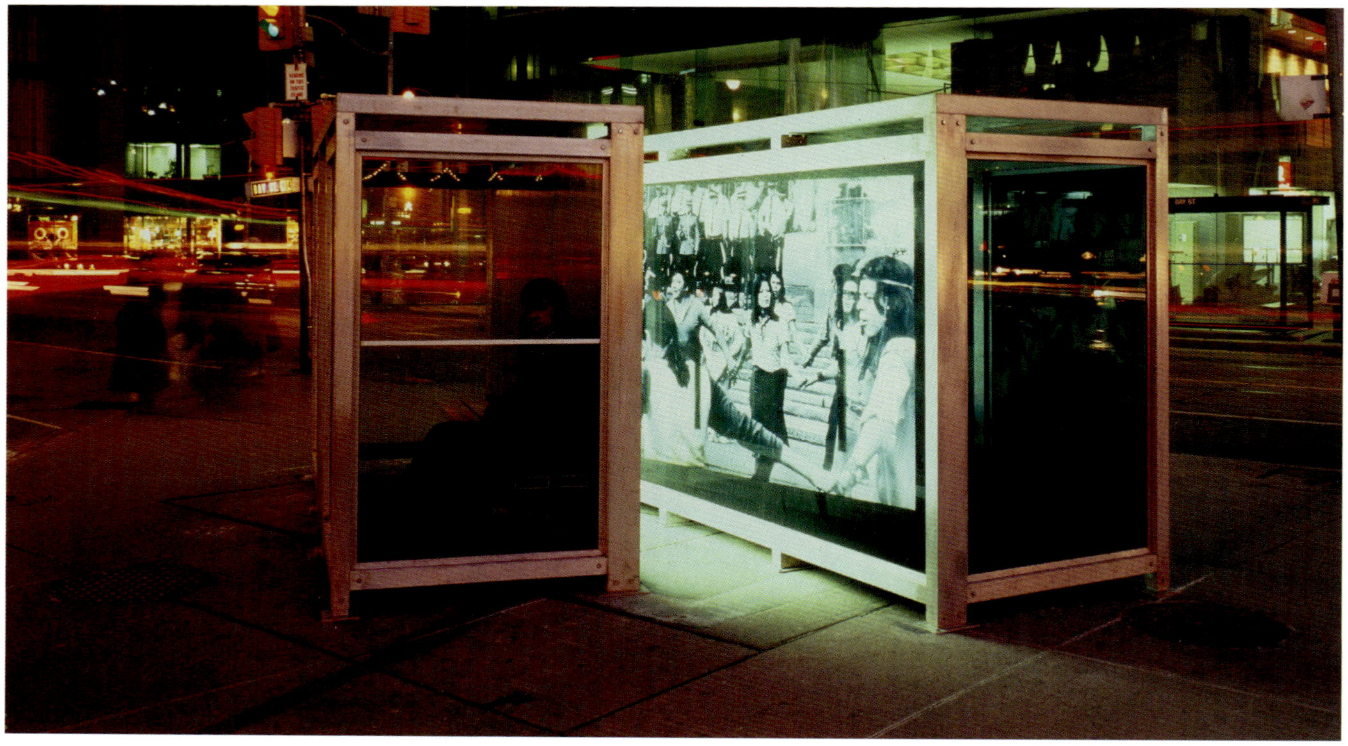

Bus Shelter VIII, 1988
Mixed media, each shelter 86 x 144 x 53 in (218.4 x 365.8 x 134.6 cm)

IÑIGO MANGLANO-OVALLE

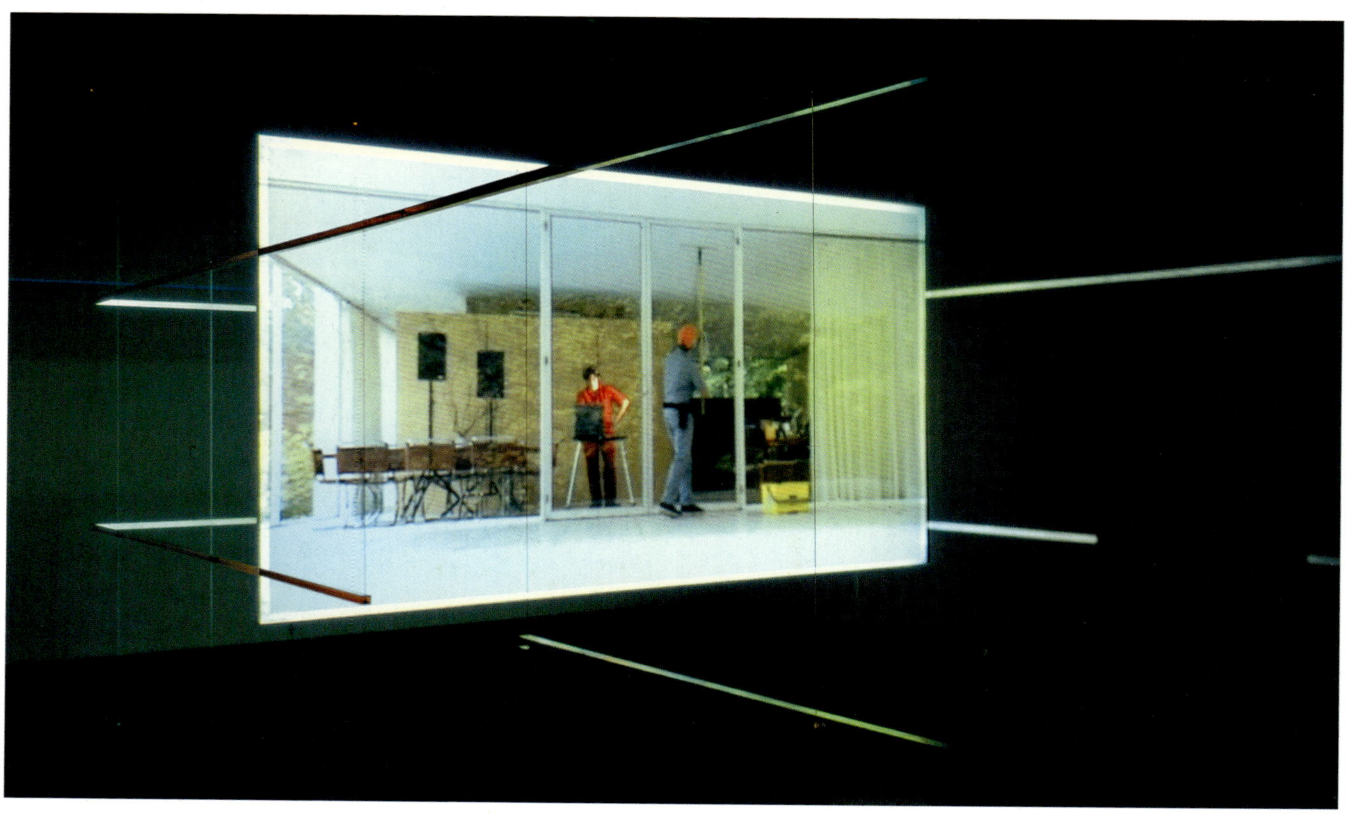

Le Baiser/The Kiss, 2000
Multi-channel video installation and projection, CD audio recording, and mixed media, dimensions variable

Local Discussion Screen, 2001–2, appropriates the soundproof barriers set up around corporate offices (and suggests a sculptural version of a Mondrian painting). Each of these titles, and the objects they describe, suggest a need for communication of a sort often in short supply in corporate settings.

Dennis Adams uses the language of modernist architecture to demonstrate how modern societies suppress unpleasant realities or memories. Adams's earliest works in this vein, created in the 1980s, are constructivist bus shelters that house not slick fashion advertisements but lightbox-mounted photographs referencing such troubling subjects as homelessness or the claims of native Canadians in Montreal. *Bus Shelter VIII*, 1988, shows a protest by native Canadians outside the Parliament building in Ottawa. Adams extended the reminders of social ills and unresolved conflict to the form of the shelters as well, using two-way mirrored glass and skewed seating and dividers to create fractured and inaccessible spaces that undermine functionality. For a 1991 exhibition at the Museum of Modern Art in New York, Adams restaged a 1942 MoMA exhibition titled "Road to Victory," which celebrated America's participation in World War II. In Adams's version, installed at the time of the first Gulf War, photographs of the original "Road to Victory" from the MoMA archive were placed in mirrored vitrines so that they were visible only as reflections. Beyond the row of vitrines was a glossy black wall on which ghostly reflections of soldiers in the Saudi Arabian desert could be seen. By presenting these images in conjunction, and in such a way that viewers could see them only indirectly, at a distinct remove, Adams emphasized the fleeting nature of historical memory.

Isa Genzken's architecturally inspired sculptures employ the sleek geometric forms and industrial materials associated with architects such as Mies and Johnson, but with various suggestions of disintegration. *New Buildings for Berlin*, 2004, for instance, offers ideas toward rebuilding a city divided and devastated by the cold war. In an apparent rebuke to the frenzy of high-end architectural designs that had been proposed, these sculptures consist simply of sheets of colored glass propped against each other. Genzken's works resemble eroding high-rises, and are often combined with adhesive tape, plastic, and such kitsch readymades as plastic eagles and feather boas. When topped with tableaux of toy soldiers or fake flowers they become unsettling. The artist's attitude toward architectural modernism might be summed up by the title of *Fuck the Bauhaus*, 2000, which undermined modernist rationality by festooning boxy architectural structures with plastic toys, garbage bags, and other bits of flotsam and jetsam.

Iñigo Manglano-Ovalle also looks askance at the seductions of modernist architecture. In *Le Baiser/The Kiss*, 2000, a video installation in which the artist plays a window washer cleaning the vast facade of Mies's Farnsworth House, the structure of the installation itself, with its video screens held by thin polished aluminum bars and suspended from the ceiling by taut wires, mimics the aesthetic of industrial functionalism underlying this International Style house. The video opens on the Farnsworth House in its sylvan Illinois setting, then moves closer until we see a workman busily drawing his squeegee across its panes of glass. Inside the house we glimpse another figure, who is wearing a headset and apparently oblivious to the maintenance worker on the other side of the glass. The work thus comments on modernist architecture's obsession with transparency, both celebrating the sheer beauty of the house and suggesting that formal openness does not obliterate the class divide.

ISA GENZKEN

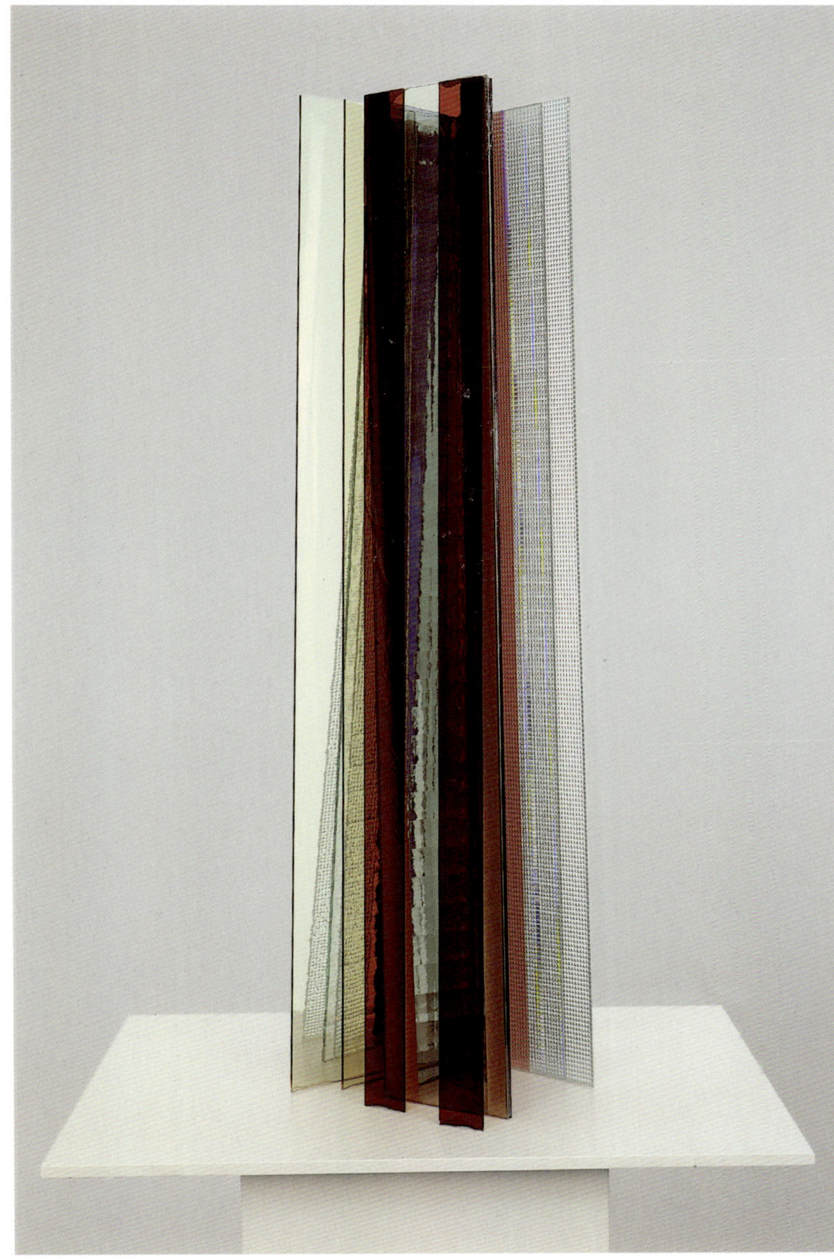

New Buildings for Berlin, 2004
Glass, adhesive tape, silicone, wood
89 x 23 1/2 x 17 3/4 in (226 x 60 x 45 cm)

ELIZABETH DILLER AND RICARDO SCOFIDIO

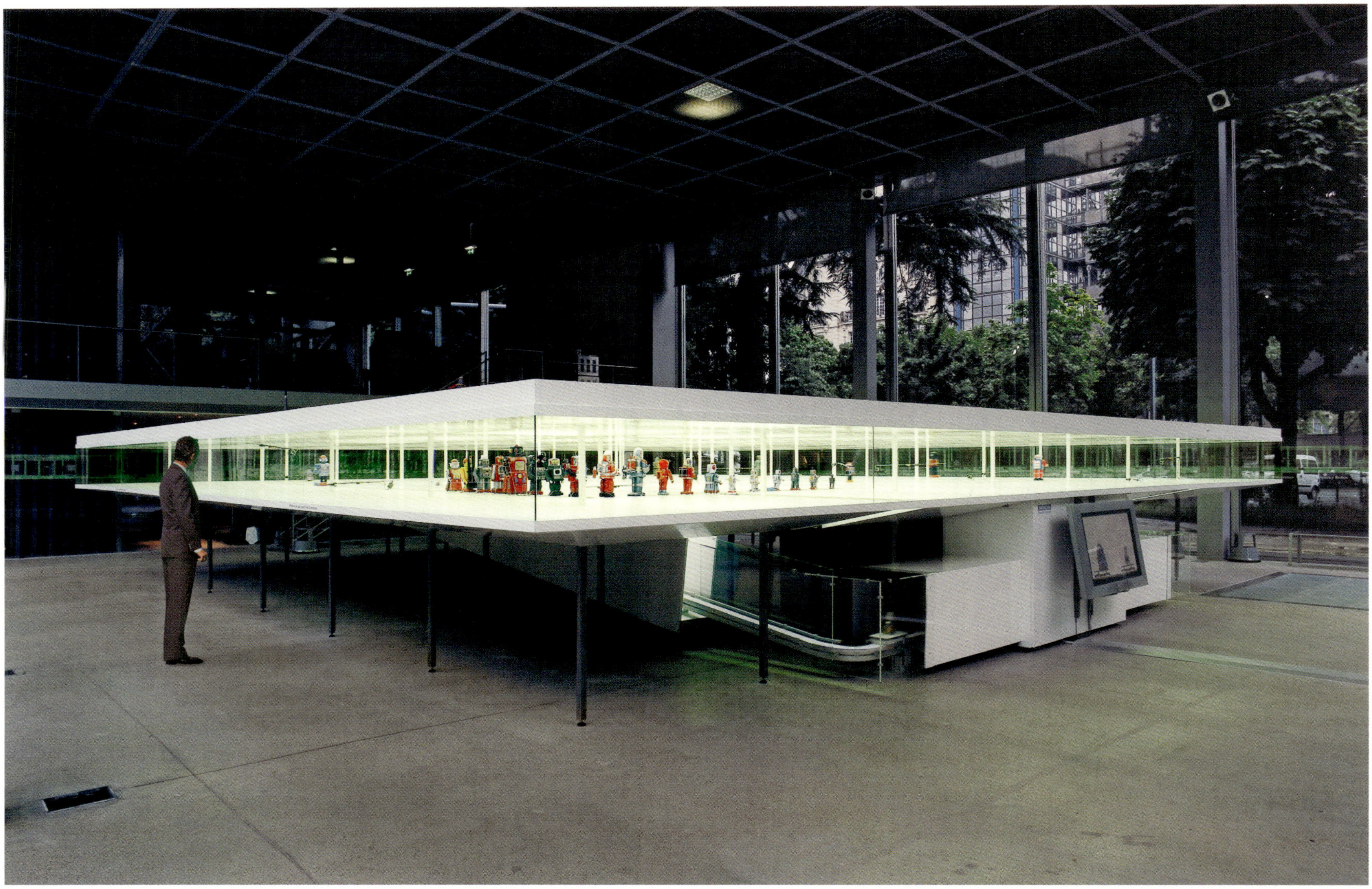

Master/Slave, 1999
Mixed media, 33 x 33 x 1 1/2 ft (10 x 10 x .5 m)

One particular way in which the logic of modernist transparency plays out in contemporary life is in the use and proliferation of surveillance, a subject of interest to Elizabeth Diller and Ricardo Scofidio. Architects who are equally at home in the world of art, Diller and Scofidio work in a variety of forms, from temporary interventions into existing architectural structures to unrealized architectural models to fully realized architectural structures. Among their frequent motifs is the surveillance camera, which, along with computer-assisted videos and robots, suggests the peculiar intermingling of public and private experience in contemporary American society. For their renovation of Brasserie, a New York restaurant on the ground floor of Mies van der Rohe's Seagram Building, for instance, Diller and Scofidio inserted surveillance cameras that transmitted images of people entering the restaurant onto screens above the bar, allowing patrons to become at once watcher and watched. Other works highlight the relationship between surveillance and control. *Master/Slave*, 1999, is an elaborate installation featuring a collection of small Japanese robots that have been installed single file along a three-hundred-foot-long conveyor belt. Moving endlessly within a glass vitrine that evokes the stark interior of the classic modernist office building, they are captured by surveillance cameras that transmit images of their passage to nearby video monitors. Periodically the robots drop out of sight, where they are scanned by an X-ray machine that puts their inner workings on display. Thus the work describes in disconcerting detail how the elaborate surveillance systems that now pervade almost every public space might one day be privy to not only our outer movements but to our internal selves as well.

Whereas some artists address the implied threats of modernist architecture by embodying its transparent, corporate, classist, Big Brotherish conventions, others propose contrasting architectural approaches. Vito Acconci, for example, replaces Le Corbusier's mechanistic notion that a house is a "machine for living" with an organic model, in which buildings seem to operate almost like living creatures. Acconci's aesthetic grows out of his earlier career as one of the innovators of body art, an amalgam of practices that fostered psychic and physical confrontations between real bodies and the surrounding environment. Acconci's 1994 redesign of the facade of the Storefront for Art and Architecture in New York, a collaboration with architect Steven Holl, melded the interior and exterior space of this narrow storefront exhibition space. Outfitted with hinges, perforated openings in the facade can be rotated, opened, and closed, so that the exterior wall is an ever mutable, permeable skin weaving together street and interior. Since founding the design-oriented Acconci Studio in 1988, the artist has created many such functional yet playful designs for parks, gardens, lobby interiors, and transportation hubs. Incorporating fence-like walls that are at once solid and transparent, roofs that arc like splashes of liquid, and shapes that seem on the verge of metamorphosis, these designs deliberately subvert severe modernist approaches to space and structure.

Tadashi Kawamata also uses organic metaphor to undermine modernist rationality, creating chaotic wooden structures that attach themselves to existing buildings and seem to proliferate like viruses, or like scaffolding run amok. Over the years Kawamata's "host" buildings have included an abandoned hospital, a functioning bridge, a war-ravaged church, museums, commercial shops, and even a nightclub. For his *Toronto Project: Colonial Tavern Park*, 1989, for instance, the artist filled the gap between a pair of unoccupied neoclassical bank buildings with

ACCONCI STUDIO
(VITO ACCONCI, LUIS VERA, AND STEVEN HOLL)

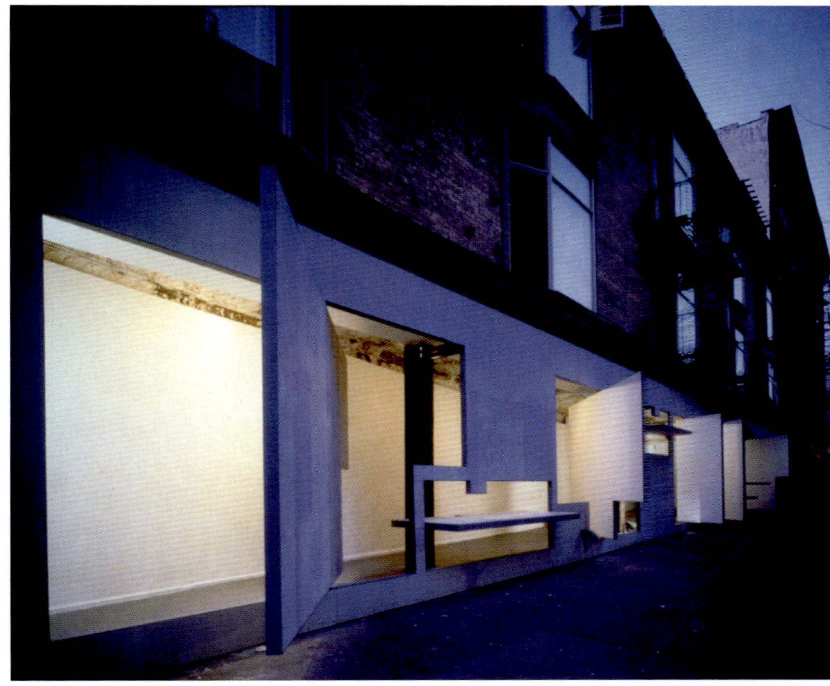

Facade, Storefront for Art and Architecture, 1993
Supraboard, plaster, steel, hinges, light
9 x 100 x 14 ft (2.7 x 30.5 x 4.3 m)
97 Kenmare Street, New York

TADASHI KAWAMATA

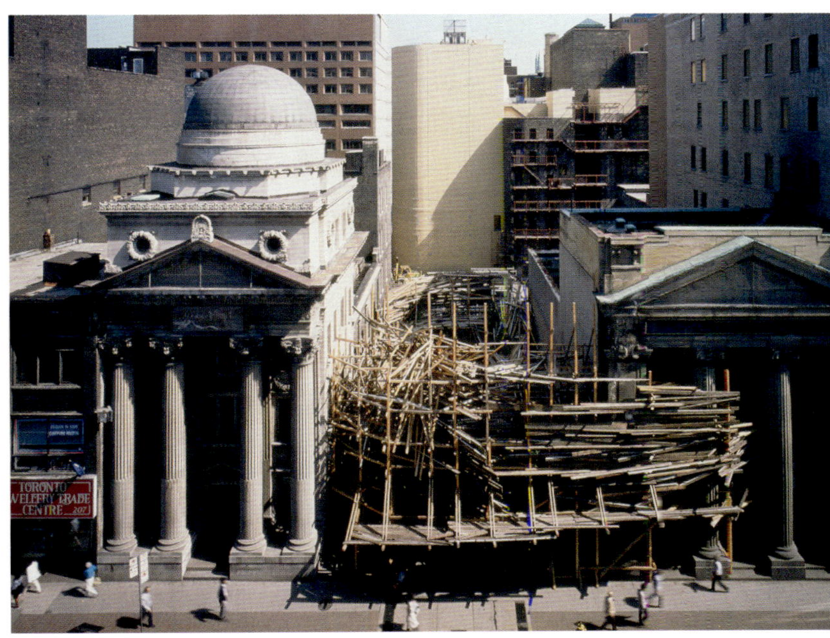

Toronto Project: Colonial Tavern Park, 1989
Mixed media
As installed on Yonge Street, Toronto, June–September 1989

BEN LANGLANDS AND NIKKI BELL

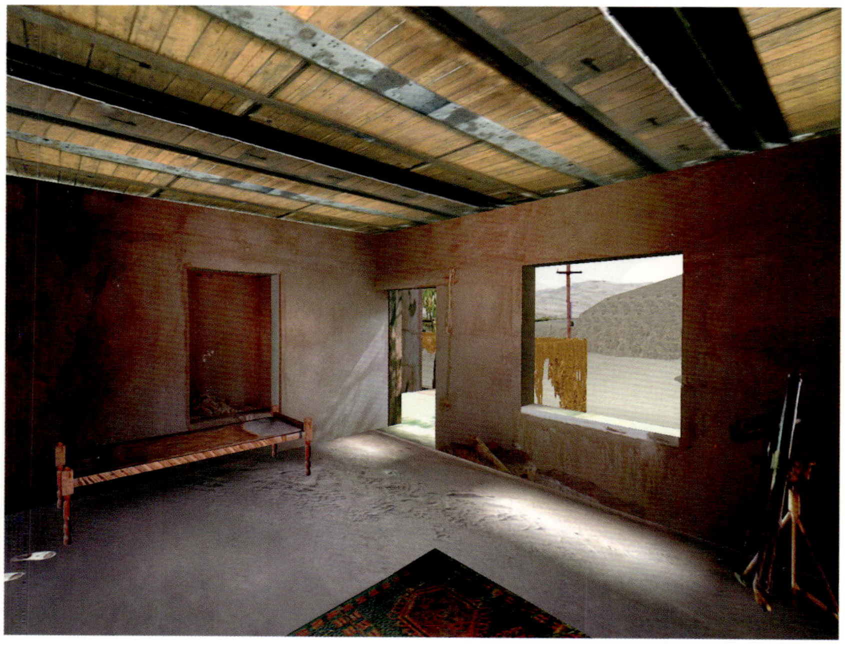

The House of Osama bin Laden, 2003
Interactive digital animation and projection

MARJETICA POTRČ

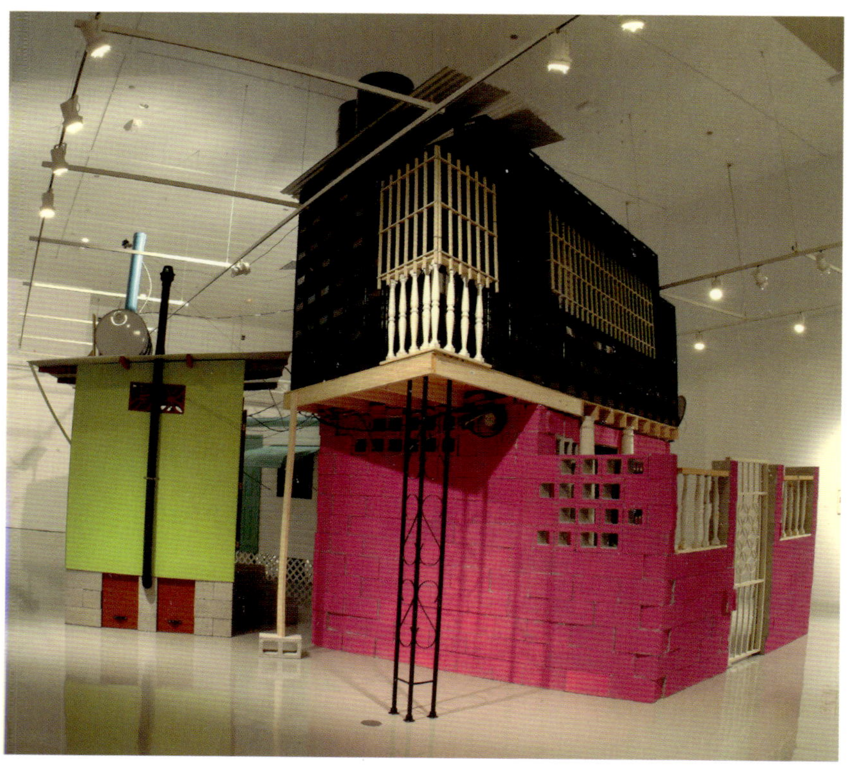

Urgent Architecture, 2003
Building materials, energy and communication infrastructure, dimensions variable
As installed at Palm Beach Institute of Contemporary Art, Fla., 2003–4

a bridge of timber splinters that seemed on the verge of engulfing their once placid facades. In most cases, the artist's projects are temporary additions to the urban landscape. In fact, Kawamata considers the process of construction and demolition to be as important as the completed structure. Associations stirred by these works are many—their resemblance to scaffolding makes them seem like a comment on the burgeoning urban development that turns so many city neighborhoods into construction sites. On the other hand, their makeshift construction points toward the kind of unofficial, ad hoc structures that spring up like kudzu on the peripheries of developing cities and provide provisional housing for migrant workers and refugees from rural poverty. At the same time, the organic metaphor of the virus, which Kawamata uses quite deliberately, suggests a vision of urban growth that is mindless, unstoppable, and quite possibly pernicious to human life.

Not all architecturally oriented art takes the form of three-dimensional structures. Ben Langlands and Nikki Bell use digital technology and the language of Conceptual art to investigate the political meanings of architecture. The team's most striking exploration of this theme is *The House of Osama bin Laden*, 2003, in which video-game technology is used to present a virtual tour of the now empty building in Daruntah, Afghanistan, that served as bin Laden's home for a brief period in the 1990s. Like standard video games, the piece is interactive: viewers manipulate a joystick to slide in and out of the compound or to traverse bleak, crumbling concrete structures surrounded by pocked earth and the remains of rusty vehicles. They can also go inside the house and navigate empty rooms, storage cupboards, and bunkers. Like Diller and Scofidio, Langlands and Bell exploit the voyeuristic potential of technology, but here the stakes are eerily dangerous (we're peering into the private world of a villain) and thoroughly safe (it's just a video game, after all). With this work, a politically charged architectural structure becomes as real to viewers as virtual reality will allow.

Benjamin Edwards also turns to digital technology and a two-dimensional surface to probe architecture's underlying meanings. His paintings explore what he refers to as "capitalist utopias" and are created using the same kind of new technologies that are transforming the American landscape. They incorporate satellite maps, blueprints, corporate logos, and abstracted images digitally distilled from the artist's own snapshots of corporate headquarters, suburban parking lots, megastores, and other emblems of the anonymity and social dispersion that characterize contemporary American life. These are arranged on canvas and superimposed with brightly colored painted rectangles, squares, and ovals. The paintings offer schematic representations of a futuristic urban space that, thanks to the logos and elements from real locales, are oddly familiar. They reflect a way of seeing and organizing space that would be possible only in the digital era. *Immersion*, 2004, for instance, offers a sweeping aerial panorama full of floating planes of color and abstract geometric symbols that, in homage to Renaissance perspective, seem to be rushing toward a single point in the far distance. Whether we are gliding over a plaza, a highway, or a parking lot is not clear, and in fact, Edwards seems to be suggesting that such real world distinctions hardly matter to a disembodied postmodern consciousness.

If architectural modernism has ultimately failed in its self-proclaimed utopian aspirations, as Edwards's works suggest, some artists still hope that architecture might be an engine of social change. Marjetica Potrč has observed the barrios of

BENJAMIN EDWARDS

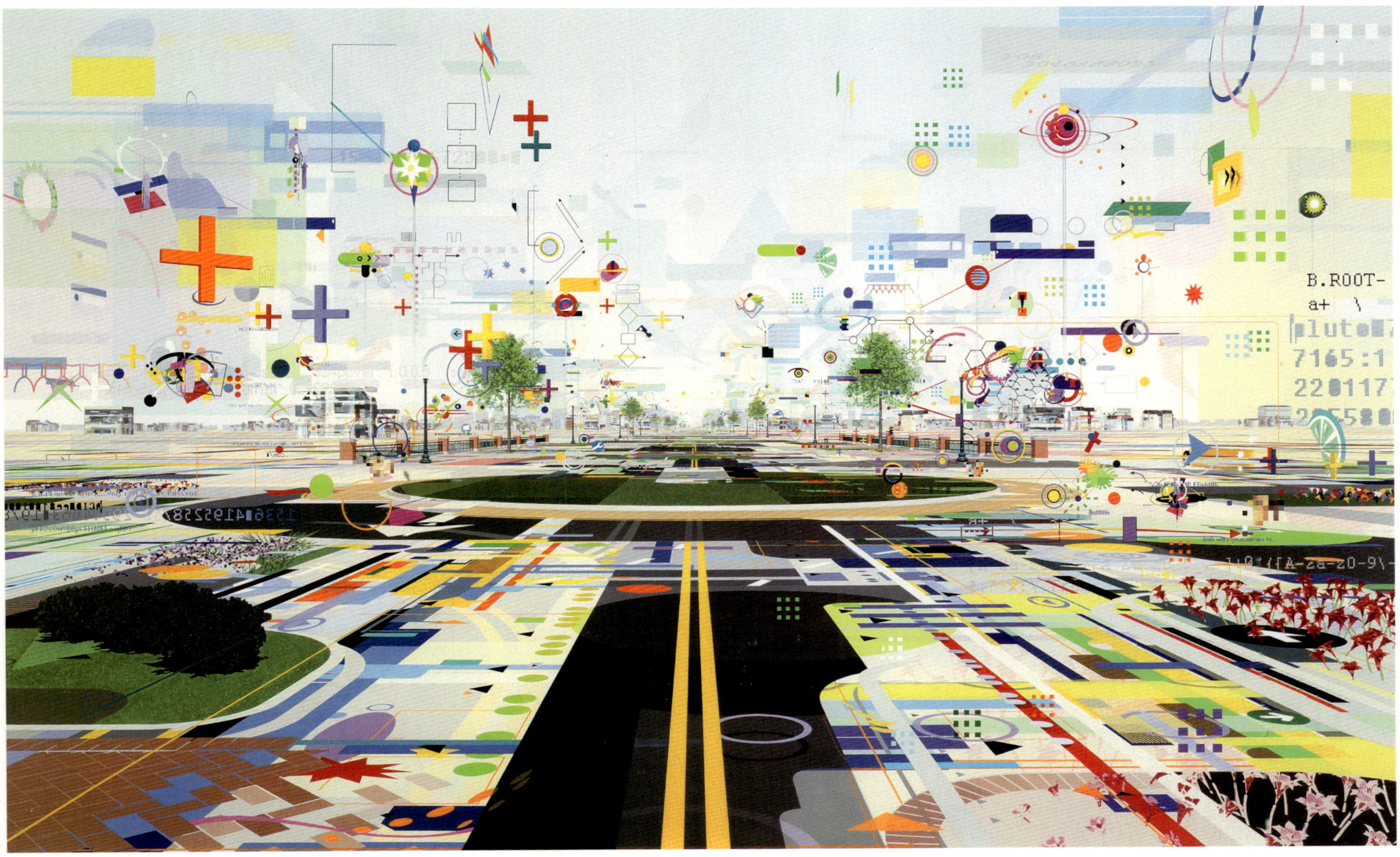

Immersion, 2004
Acrylic, texture media, and landscaping foam on canvas
75 x 125 in (190.5 x 317.5 cm)

SIAH ARMAJANI

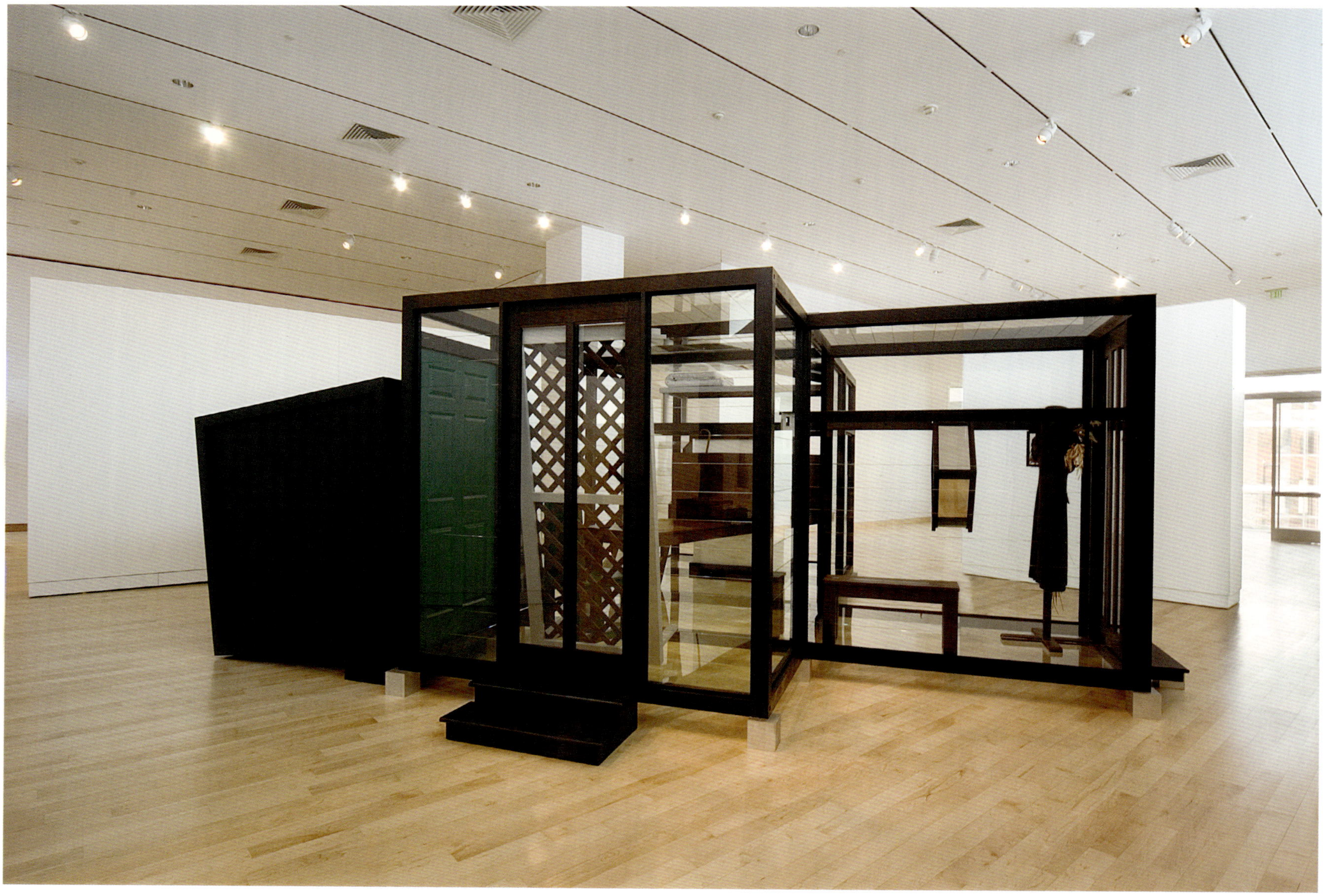

Emerson's Parlor, 2006
Laminated wood, glass, plywood, metal bed frames, mattress and pillow, white and black paint, wool, straw, black felt curtain, diamond-shaped mirror, coat, and hat, 22 x 20 x 10 ft (6.7 x 6.1 x 3 m)
Madison Museum of Contemporary Art, Wis.

Caracas, townships in South Africa, gypsy settlements in Belfast, and refugee housing in Ljubljana, and posits that these urban environments have been shaped by a series of battles for territory waged by inhabitants of what she calls the "formal city," who benefit from laws, zoning, and official planning, and those of the "informal city" who, being propertyless, must take what they can get. Loosely reflecting evolutionary theory, the artist's proposals suggest that cities take shape through selective adaptation as various organisms fight for survival. Some of Potrč's works take the form of sculptures that incorporate the structures of the "informal city." A large architectural installation for *Urgent Architecture*, her 2003–4 exhibition at the Palm Beach Institute of Contemporary Art in Florida, for example, resembled a Cubist sculpture and was composed of forms culled from a shack in Caracas, houses in Palestinian and Israeli settlements in the West Bank, and a mobile home in Florida, each evidencing the ingenuity of their makers. Potrč also creates functional structures intended for use in the real world—for instance, a dry toilet that collects waste for fertilizer, created in collaboration with Israeli architect Liyat Esakov and designed to service those in rural communities who lack access to city services like running water. Finally, Potrč articulates her sculptural and humanitarian ideas in photo essays and wall drawings that address how amenities are apportioned among marginal populations.

Bodys Isek Kingelez also overlooks the pathologies of architectural modernism, finding its promises of progress and prosperity still seductive, if not fully convincing. The artist's fantastical cityscape sculptures are constructed of such recycled materials as corrugated cardboard, bottle caps, brightly colored paper, and tinfoil. Displayed on tabletops like demented architectural models, they oscillate between the real and the imagined, with spires and skyscrapers melding details of modernist buildings in such cities as New York and Paris with fanciful arches, spirals, and curlicues. In these works elements culled from modernist and postmodernist architecture—the cantilevered balconies of high-rise apartment buildings, the scalloped tops of Art Deco skyscrapers, and the coiling ramps of parking garages—are transformed into playful constructions that seem to resemble party favors more than real urban environments. *Ville fantôme*, 1996, is an idealized version of the artist's native Kinshasa, with the urban decay replaced by shiny office towers and riotously colorful buildings. Kingelez's sculptures also contain representations of all of the amenities that progressive architects mandate for their ideal cities, among them spacious parks, wide highways, and inviting plazas. Although his exuberant cities exist only in the imagination, the use of real recycled materials suggests the implications of globalism, reminding us that in developing countries first-world waste often serves as third-world building material.

Siah Armajani also finds inspiration in the humble forms and materials of vernacular architecture. In a spirit not unlike that of Frank Lloyd Wright, who grounded his designs both in the American landscape and in its precepts of participatory democracy, Armajani has devoted his life to constructing formal analogs to democratic concepts. To his models of bridges, gazebos, and meeting rooms, which serve as utilitarian places of communication and social connection, he adds homey elements such as wagon wheels, lattice fences, and wooden gables that evoke small-town America. Armajani's sculptures often incorporate quotes from writers who embody traditional American ideals, among them Ralph Waldo Emerson, Herman Melville, and Walt Whitman. *Emerson's Parlor*, 2006, is a sculptural

BODYS ISEK KINGELEZ

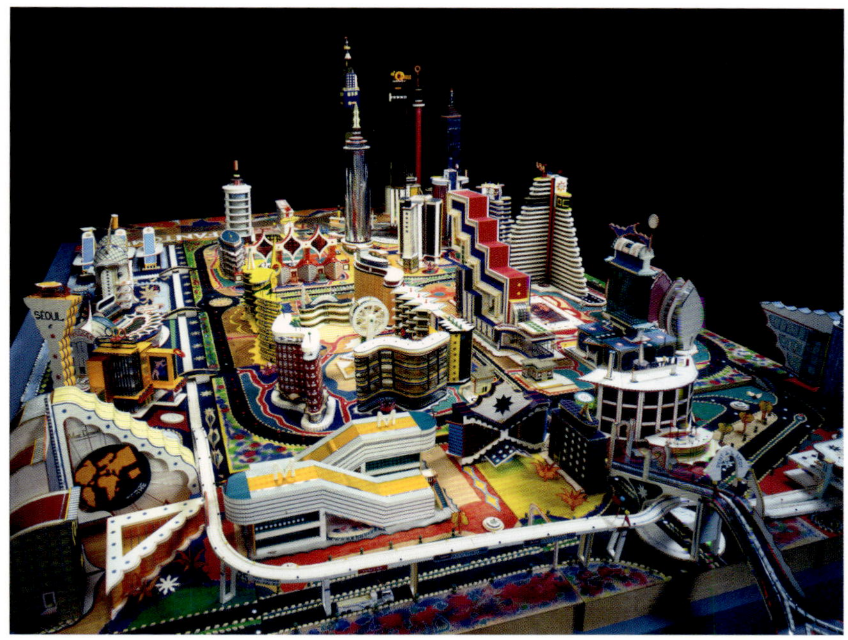

Ville fantôme, 1996
Paper, plastic, and cardboard
3 ft 11 in x 18 ft 8 in x 7 ft 10 in (1.2 x 5.7 x 2.4 m)

installation that pays homage to one of Armajani's heroes, containing elements specific to Emerson's life, including a white house and a wooden coffin, which refer to the death of Emerson's first wife, Ellen, from tuberculosis. While Armajani's works look back to an earlier and arguably simpler America, he is not trading in nostalgia in the manner of Celebration, Disney's planned community in Florida, or exercises in "new urbanism" based on fantasies of a so-called real America of the past. Instead, there is always an edge to his work, which challenges us to adopt principles of self-discipline, community participation, and intellectual honesty. Armajani's real target is the depersonalized corporatization of the American landscape, which manifests itself as much in strip malls and giant discount stores as in the densely packed skyscrapers of contemporary cities. Using the language of architecture, Armajani urges us to think more critically about how we live.

Frank Lloyd Wright's melding of aesthetics, architecture, art, utopian impulse, and social philosophy took its ultimate form in his Taliesin School of Architecture, a compound in the Arizona desert where to this day students live, work, and learn together while sharing tasks communally. This vision is reflected in the philosophy and productions of Rural Studio, a school and studio located in rural Hale County, Alabama, founded in 1991 by the late Samuel Mockbee, an architect and fifth-generation southerner. Also influenced by the turn-of-the-century Arts and Crafts Workshop of William Morris, Rural Studio promises to mend social and economic rifts through good design. Here, architecture students from nearby Auburn University live together and hone their skills by building houses and community buildings for the residents of this poverty-stricken rural county. Students and clients learn from each other while proving that good design needn't be prohibitively expensive. Rural Studio projects combine a funky southern vernacular style with elements of high modernism, using materials that are largely scavenged or donated. Thus old tires become insulation, a car windshield becomes a house window, and hay bales covered with stucco form sturdy walls. Other structural and ornamental ingredients include bottles, carpet yarn, catfish netting, and chicken wire. *Yancey Chapel,* 1994–95, for instance, has walls made of tires filled with sand, reinforced with rebar and covered with stucco; it is topped by a pitched roof made from scavenged metal shingles and meant to suggest the look of a caved-in barn. Hale County is the location of many of the Depression-era photos featured in *Let Us Now Praise Famous Men*, the 1941 book by photographer Walker Evans and writer James Agee, so it had a distinct place in America's cultural history before the arrival of the Rural Studio. Now it serves as a laboratory for ways in which architecture can alleviate and perhaps even reverse the ills documented in that book.

Joep van Lieshout, founder of Atelier van Lieshout, also reimagines community through architecture, but he takes a more sardonic view of the communal. In 2001 van Lieshout founded AVL-Ville, a one-year experiment in survivalist living sited in Rotterdam and set up as a free state, complete with its own flag, constitution, and currency. AVL-Ville had a hospital, an organic farm, an art school, and group housing, as well as workshops for making weapons, bombs, alcohol, and medicine. Citizens lived in refurbished shipping containers and were expected to support themselves by producing objects on commission, such as bicycle shelters, study cells, and portable toilets. As a model for living, it thus combined the commune and the company town. More recently van Lieshout has turned to more dystopian schemes, creating detailed outlines for planned communities that resemble robotic societies in which rationality and efficiency have run amok more than rural retreats. In his fictional community "The Technocrat," which is illustrated in his installation *Mini-Technocrat*, 2004, residents sleep on wooden bunks and undertake useless jobs like filing away at tree trunks. Fed ample cheap food so that they will produce large amounts of excrement that is transformed into cooking fuel by a biogas digester, they are kept happy with alcohol produced in a distillery outfitted with two hoses—one to supply the alcohol to their mouths, the other to carry away their waste. Here, architecture is inseparable from the coercive structures of a totalitarian society, providing a physical model for the restriction of mental freedom.

Andrea Zittel also lives out the ideals of autonomy while replicating corporate structures, though her outlook is possibly more optimistic. The artist's Web site describes her A-Z Enterprise, a real and conceptual project, as encompassing "all aspects of day to day living. Home furniture, clothing, [and] food all become the sites of investigation in an ongoing endeavor to better understand human nature and the social construction of needs."[4] Zittel's creations mix utopian ideals and old-fashioned do-it-yourself ingenuity. They include compact living units that can be folded up and hauled away on wheels, like small U-Haul trailers. Inside one finds cabinets combining sink, shower, bathtub, and medicine cabinet, dining tables with recessed holes for glasses and dishes, and comforters that can serve as coats, blankets, carpets, curtains, or, when stacked, beds and seating. Unlike van Lieshout, Zittel seems uninterested in communal life. Her living units accommodate only a single resident, and are ill equipped for even an occasional guest. *A-Z Management and Maintenance Unit Model 003*, 1992, was designed to sit within the artists' tiny Brooklyn apartment. Using only sixty of the available two hundred square feet, it nevertheless allows for all of the necessary functions of life, including eating, sleeping, cleaning, and storage.

The mobility of Zittel's units offers the possibility of escape but also eschews any possibility of putting down roots. Thus they tap into the frontier mentality that characterized the American psyche in the early days of the nation and persists in the current population's relentless movement. Though Zittel's mobile units are presented with the pretense of seriousness as solutions to the problems of contemporary life, they also satirize the fantasies of the rugged survivalists who declare themselves independent of larger social structures. At the same time, they serve as ominous reminders that war and environmental disaster may one day turn us all into involuntary survivalists.

Absalon also produced housing units for one. His "cellules," white-painted units suggesting a cross between an igloo, a monastic cell, and a space capsule, were intended for the artist's private use, and would accommodate both his physical and his mental being. Like Zittel's mobile units, Absalon's structures are premised on the conviction that mobility is a necessary condition of personal freedom. He hoped to erect these structures in various cities around the world, so he could retreat safely within them no matter where he traveled, but he was able to complete only six wood and cardboard models before his death in 1993. Roughly all the same size, each of these models assumes a different shape. Likewise, the contents are the same, but configured differently—cupboards, bed, desk, stools, shelving, and bathroom and kitchen facilities are all realized in geometric forms that bring to mind Minimalist sculpture. Absalon's structures present a striking contrast to the open units preferred by Zittel; his are closed, with only narrow perforations for doors and

SAMUEL MOCKBEE AND RURAL STUDIO

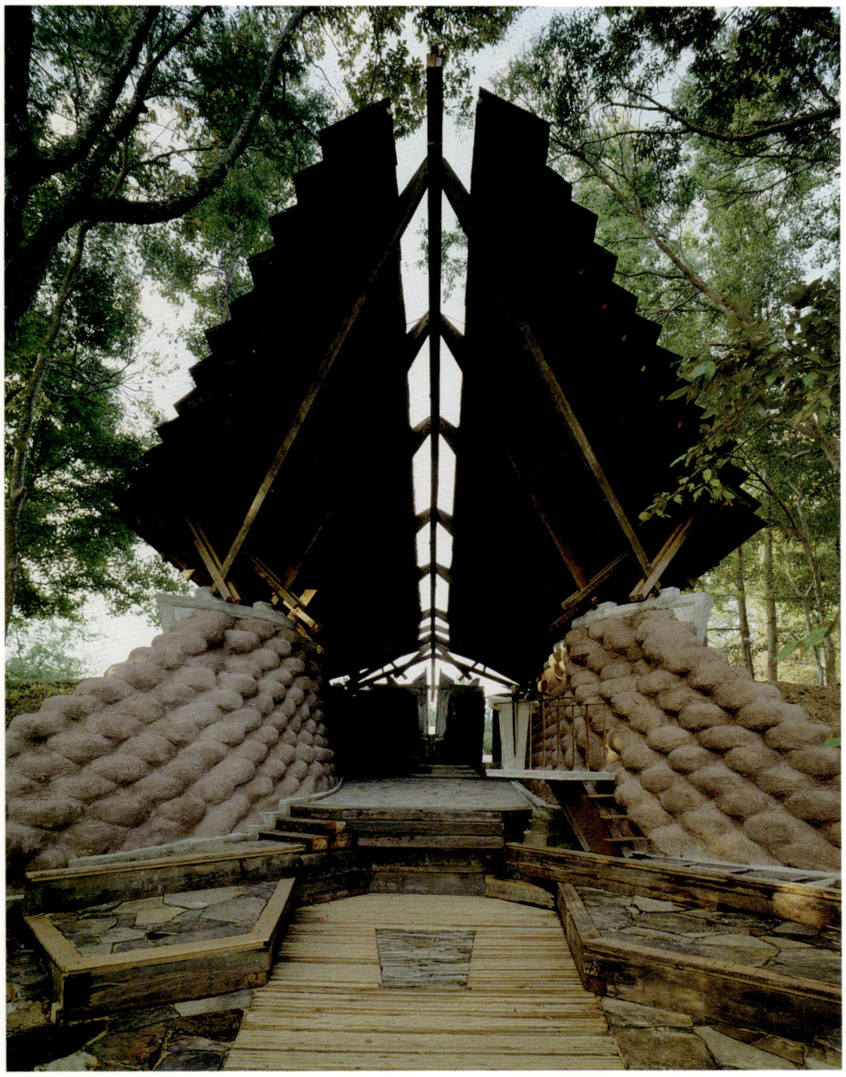

Yancey Chapel, 1994–95
Sawyerville, Alabama

ATELIER VAN LIESHOUT (JOEP VAN LIESHOUT)

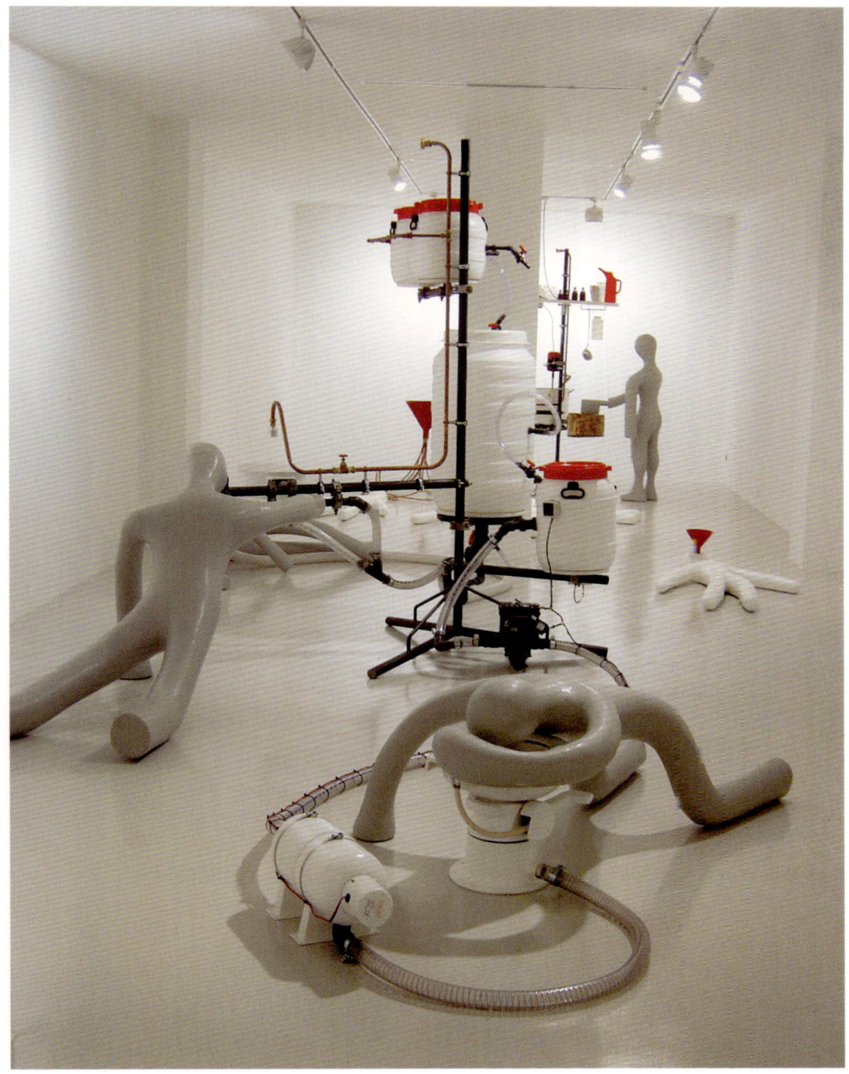

Mini Technocrat, 2004
Fiberglass, PU foam, wood, PVC,
steel, barrels, and tubes, dimensions variable

ANDREA ZITTEL

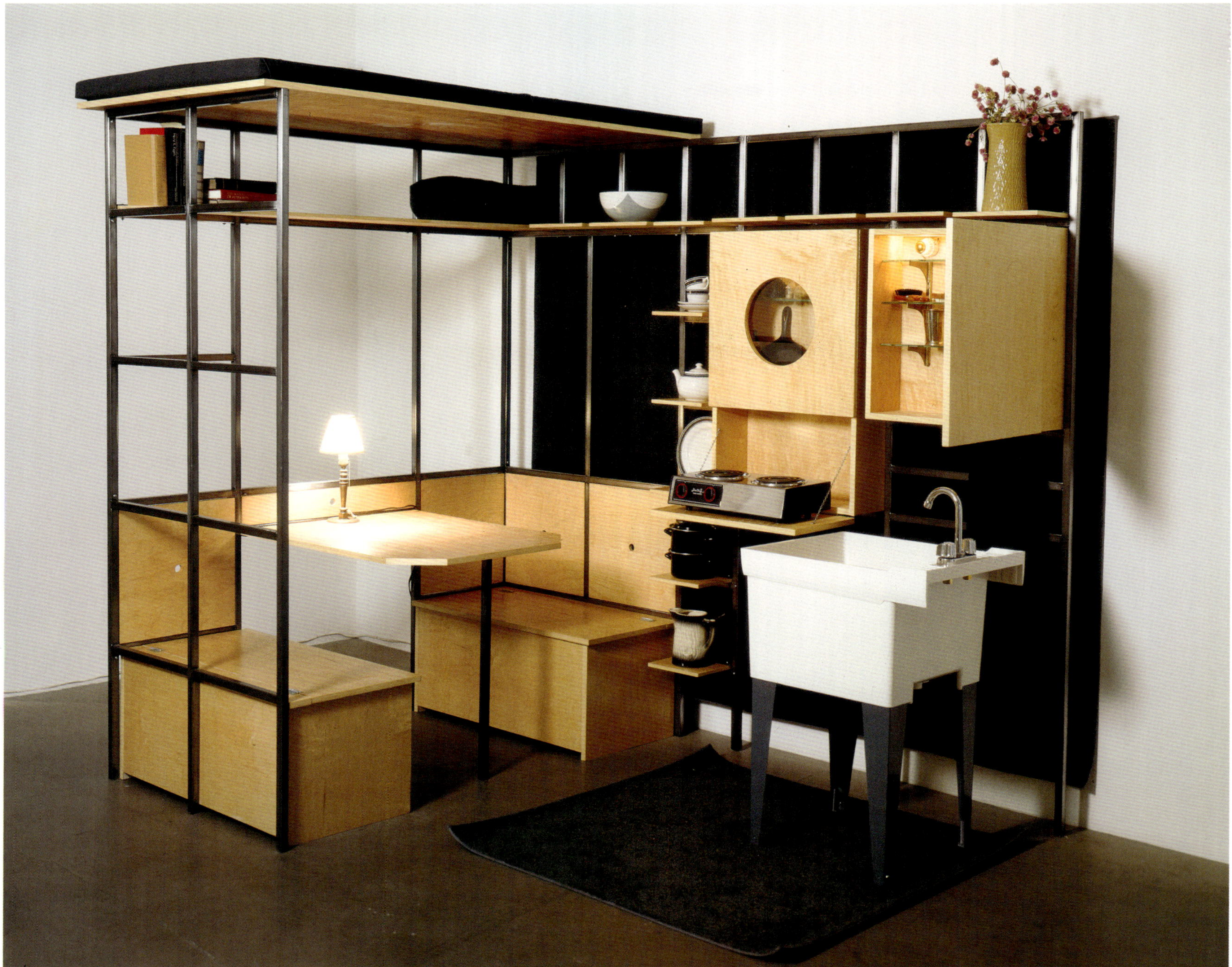

A-Z Management and Maintenance Unit Model 003, 1992
Steel, wood, carpet, plastic sink, glass, mirror
86 x 94 x 68 in (218.4 x 238.8 x 172.7 cm)

ABSALON

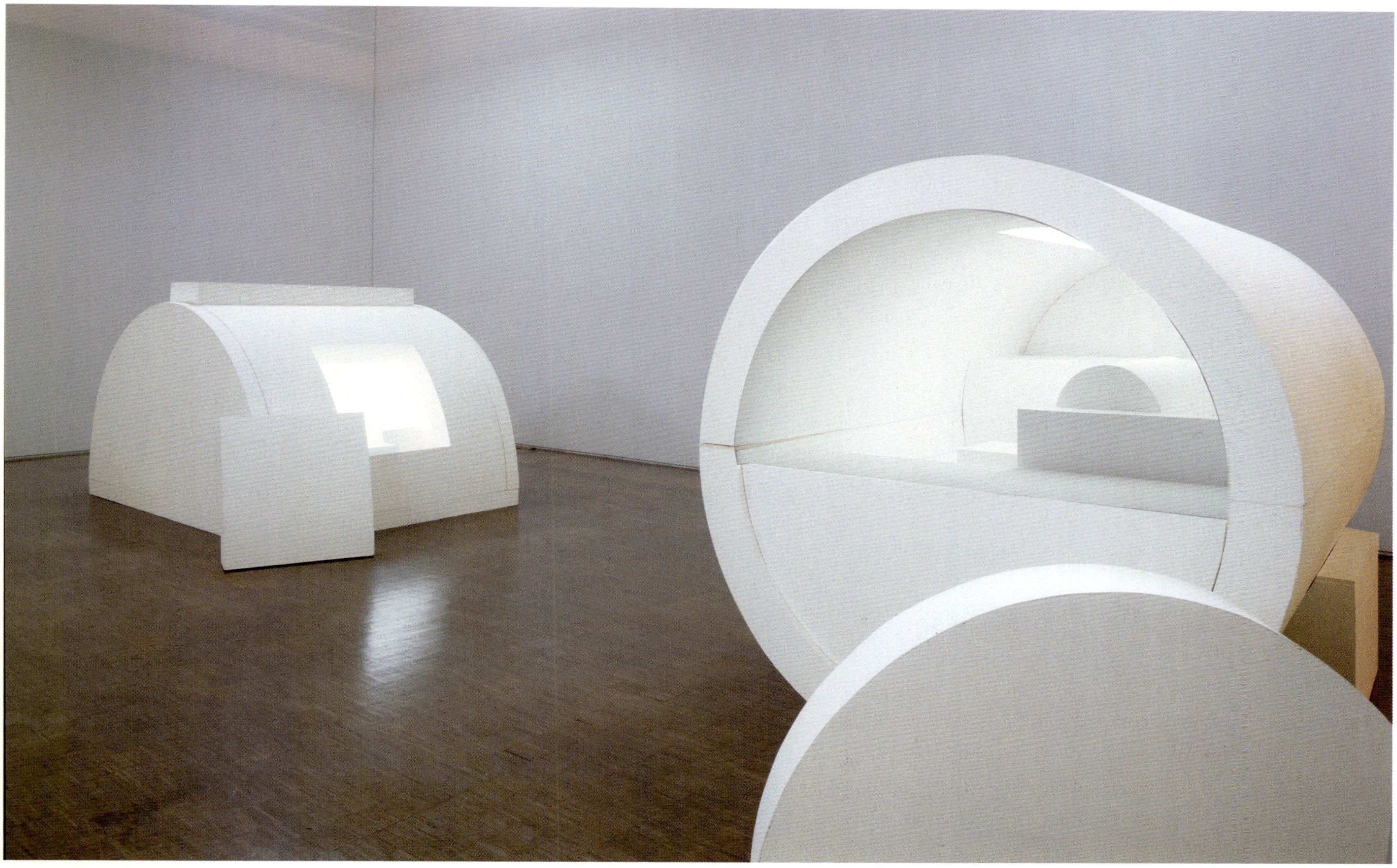

Cellule n°4, 1990
Wood, cardboard, white paint, 70 7/8 x 98 3/8 x 59 in (180 x 250 x 150 cm)
CAPC (Musée d'art contemporain), Bordeaux, France

LOS CARPINTEROS

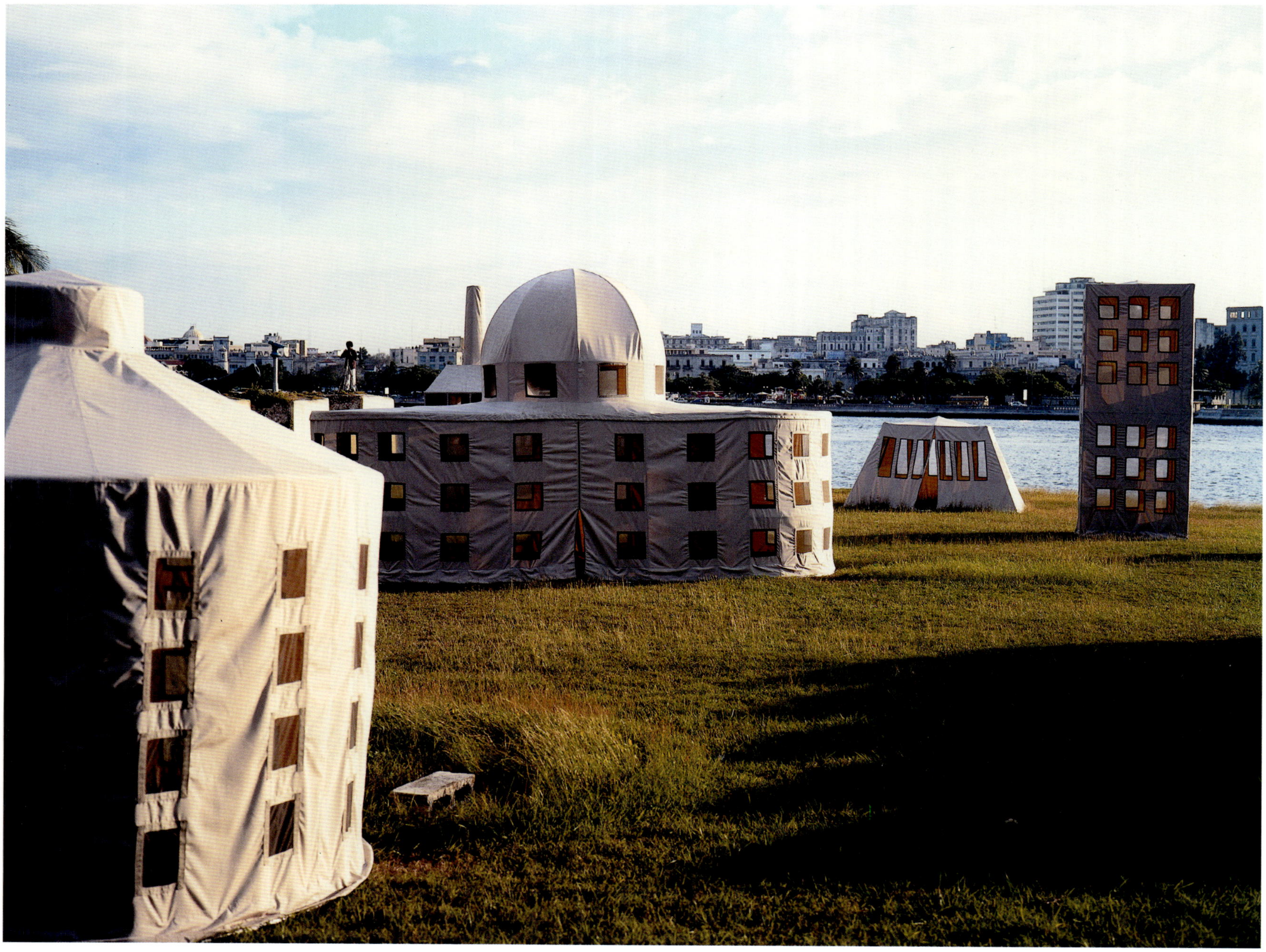

Ciudad Transportable (Transportable City), 2000
Ten tents, aluminum, and nylon

windows, lending them a hermetic, protective quality. The effect of living in them, one imagines, would be akin to being suspended in a sensory deprivation chamber.

The collective Los Carpinteros (The Carpenters), which was formed in 1991 and disbanded in 2003, created whole portable cities designed to subvert the illusion of permanence and stability favored by traditional architects and urban planners. *Ciudad Transportable* (Transportable City), 2000, consists of ten nylon and aluminum tents that recreate buildings (among them a church, a school, a lighthouse, a prison, a factory, a military barracks, and a domed capital) that the artists view as the essential components of any city. The installation was originally built for an exhibition in the artists' native Havana, then transported to other international exhibitions. The tents' lightweight, transportable structure is implicitly essential for Cuban artists, for whom international travel is often impossible—the art can go where the artists cannot—and also suggests refugee camps. Similarly critical of architectural conventions is a series of works by Los Carpinteros that transform buildings and functional objects—among them the Russian Embassy in Havana, a water tank, a grenade, and a coffee pot—into well-crafted chests of drawers. These works draw attention to the relationship between architecture and furniture design, both of which modernists employed in their pursuit of social transformation. In the hands of Los Carpinteros, such aspirations take on an absurdist quality, as the social values embedded in such structures and objects quickly lose their larger meanings when transformed into semblences of functional objects.

Franz West further complicates modernism's convictions about the relationship between design and ideology with his deliberately awkward, barely functional furniture/sculptures that are as misshapen as lumps of papier-mâché and plaster, the very materials from which they are, in fact, frequently fashioned. West's other favored materials include wood, foam, gauze, and duct tape, with which he has created spiderweb-like metal-and-foam chaise lounges, modular chairs overhung with a lamp-like sculpture that prevents those seated from seeing each other, and colorful tables and chairs. Such works could not diverge further from the vaunted rationality and functionality of modernist design. Rather than adapt themselves to human needs, as most utilitarian objects do, they seem to have a life of their own that humans can share only by relinquishing all normal expectations of comfort and ease. One of West's most ambitious projects, installed temporarily in 2004 by the Public Art Fund in the plaza at New York's Lincoln Center, comprised strange, sickly colored, tube-like aluminum sculptures, including *Double Ring*, that resembled nothing so much as looping bits of human intestine. Despite their uninviting appearance, the public happily sat on and climbed over these works. Thus they replaced narrow modernist notions of functionality with a more expansive, playful approach to questions of utility.

Simon Starling also targets modernist design. One of his most ambitious projects, *Inverted Retrograde Theme, USA (House for a Songbird)*, 2002, combines two systems of modernist creation—composer Arnold Schoenberg's twelve-tone system and architect Simon Schmiderer's prefab concrete housing. The latter, used for public housing projects in Puerto Rico in the 1960s, exemplifies the practical failure of much modernist design. Schmiderer's open plan proved counter-productive to residents' security needs; they were forced to cover their large windows with steel grills. In Starling's reworking of this project, two scale models of the modular buildings are presented as mirror images and turned upside down, an homage to the

FRANZ WEST

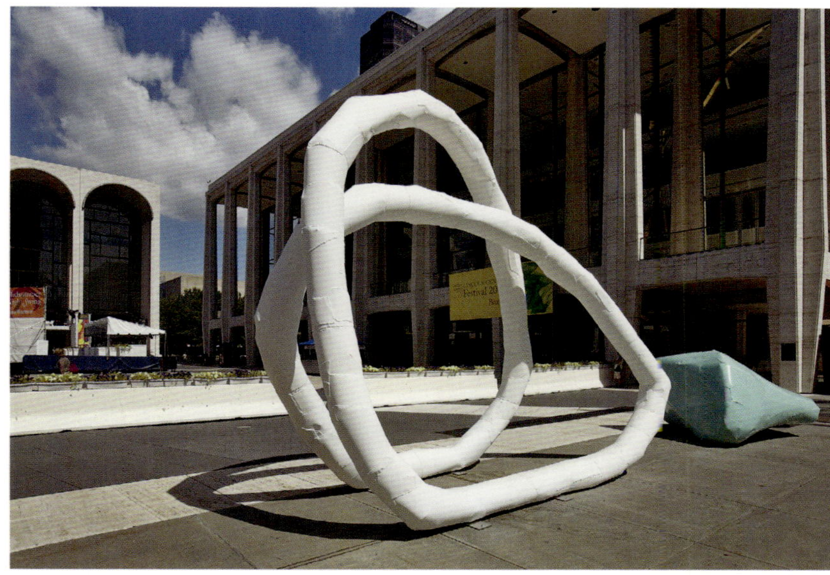

Double Ring, 2004
Lacquered aluminum, 13 ft 8 in x 16 ft x 5 ft 11 in (4.2 x 4.9 x 1.8 m)
As installed at Lincoln Center, New York, July–August 2004

SIMON STARLING

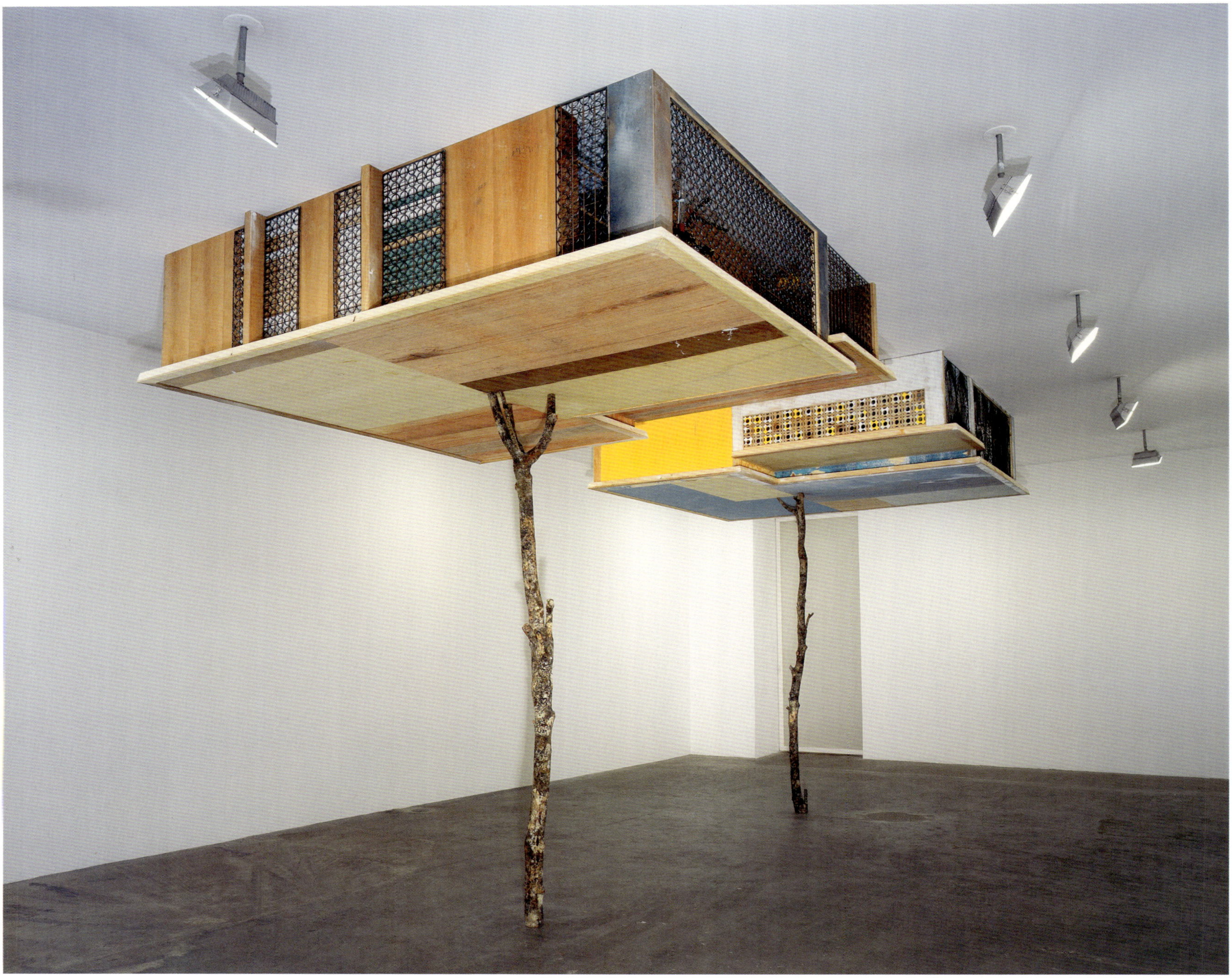

Inverted Retrograde Theme, USA (House for a Songbird), 2002
Wood, iron, mahogany, and birds
133 x 122 x 140 in (337.8 x 309.9 x 355.6 cm)

inversion of sounds in Schoenberg's system and a reflection of the dysfunctionality of the design. Reinforcing the real human effects of poor design, Starling inserted live parakeets into the housing project models, evoking the caged entrapment of its residents.

Jorge Pardo creates architectural interiors that draw on design styles that have only recently become unfashionable, using colored Plexiglas, tile, and plywood to evoke the late-modernist decor of the 1960s, '70s, and '80s. The artist's lamps, for instance, wrought in organic shapes and a yellow-beige, red-brown, and blue palette, recall the era's "flower power" style and in the process completely blur the line between "high art" and functional design. For *Project*, 2000, his redesign of the lobby of the Dia Center for the Arts in New York, Pardo swathed the floors and columns in ceramic tiles of orange, gold, lemon, pale blue, and lime. These colors tie together areas with diverse uses, including the reception area, the ticketing facility, the seating area, and the bookstore, thus synchronizing the non-art functions of the institution. In this candy color–coordinated space Pardo also installed a full-scale model of a Volkswagen Beetle. Fabricated in brown clay, the car was clearly useless, thus paying perverse homage to the myth of functionality, replacing it with a well-developed sense of the absurd.

Modernist architects and designers foresaw a future in which life might be improved through a more rational organization of the spaces and structures in which it takes place. Today's dreams of utopia are infused with everything from cautious sincerity to doubt to irony to outright disdain. Even when artists dare to imagine a better world, their efforts to create it tend to be couched in terms of individual rather than societal change. As a result, a movement devoted resolutely to looking ahead is now a poignant piece of history. But to say that its dreams are dead is not to say that they had no impact. They have simply mutated into iterations that would have been unimaginable to their optimistic progenitors.

JORGE PARDO

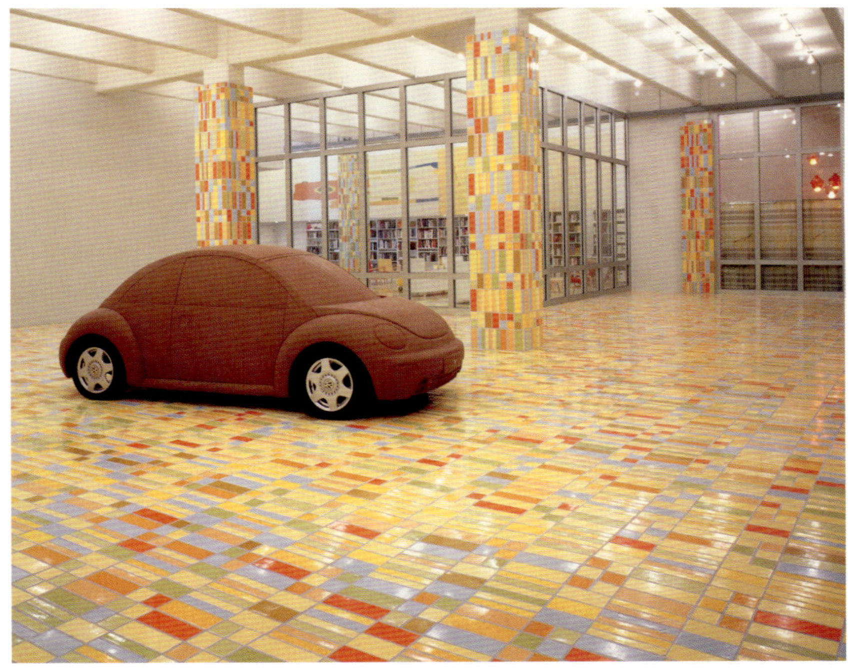

Project, 2000
Lobby, bookshop, gallery, 108 x 108 ft (32.9 x 32.9 m) overall
As installed at Dia Center for the Arts, New York, September 2000–June 2001

ART & ITS INSTITUTIONS

ART REFLECTS ON ITSELF

The notion that art should provide a window on the world has been well established at least since the mid-fifteenth century, when Leon Battista Alberti laid out the principles for representing space through the system of one-point perspective. Conceiving the picture plane as a stage on which objects were arranged in diminishing scale, the artist drew the eye into the painting and hence away from any of the distracting apparatus that might have dispelled the illusion. In a humorous work from 1982, painter Mark Tansey spoofed the progress of the modernist revolution that did away with this age-old conception of art. Titled *A Short History of Modernist Painting*, the large-scale triptych depicts the evolution away from painterly illusion in three stages. The first panel shows a woman in a garden hat hosing down a suburban window—shorthand for eradicating the notion of the painting as a representational window on the world. In the second panel a man butts his head against a concrete wall—a reference to the rise of formalism and its insistence on reducing painting to a flat surface. In the final panel, a chicken gravely regards itself in a mirror—an allusion to the self-referentiality of art whose subject has become itself. In addition to offering a distilled lesson in modern art history, Tansey's painting exemplifies how some contemporary artists focus on the institutional frame of art, examining systems of historicism, patronage, presentation, distribution, and evaluation with much the same criticality as critics and art historians. Increasingly, these institutional systems and those who carry them out—art's curators, critics, dealers, collectors, patrons, and funders, all of whose agendas may be quite different from those of the artists they champion—have been satirized, analyzed, and subverted. When artists explore the art system, they often reveal hidden tensions, inequities, and hypocrisies that illuminate the functions of art in contemporary society.

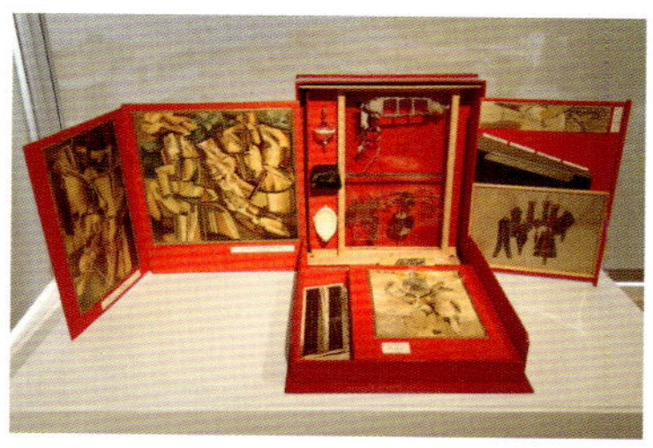

MARCEL DUCHAMP
BOITE SERIES F
1966
75 COPIES, 68 ITEMS
16 1/4 X 152 X 3 7/8 IN
(41.5 X 38.5 X 9.9 CM)

Among the most comprehensive attempts to expose the complex interrelationships within the institutional art world is Antoni Muntadas's video installation *Between the Frames: The Forum*, 1983–93. Based on a series of video interviews the artist recorded over several years, the piece is made up of sections titled "The Dealers," "The Galleries," "The Collectors," "The Museums," "The Docents," "The Critics," "The Media," and "Epilogue," in which the artists finally speak. In the installation, each section of interviews is presented in a different cell-like room. By dividing up the art world into categories, Muntadas presents a topology of the art system—along with none-too-subtle critique. The interviews with collectors, for instance, are intercut with scenes of frenetic trading on the Tokyo Stock Exchange, while the dealers are sardonically accompanied by images of the fully computerized Vancouver sky train, which runs along pre-programmed tracks without the benefit of a driver. The interviews themselves suggest that the members of these groups regard their place in the system very differently, without the cynicism implicit in the video clips. Dealers, for example, avoid a crassly economic view of their role, describing themselves as educators, risk takers, catalysts, and intellectuals. Similarly, collectors present themselves not just as investors but as patrons and philanthropists. Museum professionals are divided over whether their job is to preserve the heritage of the distant or recent past or to create a place for cultural provocation. Critics argue about whether they are more or less important than artists. The artists express a grave discomfort with the use of art as a form of financial and social leverage. Taken as a whole, this "forum" blasts apart any sense of the art world as a monolithic entity, simultaneously destroying romantic notions of the artwork as an autonomous object that stands apart from the messy realities of the everyday world. Ultimately it suggests that an artwork's interpretation depends less on the intentions of the artist than on the way it is absorbed and positioned by the art system.

Between the Frames is a prime example of what is known as "institutional critique," a strategy by which artists make a clear-eyed assessment of their place in the art world. One progenitor of this approach was Marcel Duchamp, whose readymades suggested that it is not the object in itself but rather the context in which it is seen that determines whether or not something is considered art. Duchamp further articulated this idea with his *Boîte-en-valise*, a simple leather suitcase filled with tiny reproductions of some of the artist's most famous works. Created first in 1941, then in multiples, with postcard reproductions standing in for the original art works, this piece extended Duchamp's critique of the preciousness of the individual art object by suggesting that even their repository, the museum, could be mass produced. In an ironic aftereffect that perfectly reflects Duchamp's stance, existing examples of his suitcase museum are now highly prized art objects.

In the 1960s and '70s Conceptual artists took up Duchamp's challenge to the object-value of art, presenting a radical redefinition of art as pure idea, stripped free of any material (or marketable) form. Art & Language, a group of British artists who were early proponents of Conceptual art, promoted this introspective version of art through densely layered theoretical writings as well as lists and indexes illustrating their belief that the analysis of art should replace the art object. American artist Joseph Kosuth, who eventually joined Art & Language, was pursuing similar ideas on the other side of the Atlantic. Among his best-known works of the 1960s is his "One in Three" series, in which three versions of an ordinary item, such as a clock or a chair—the actual object, a photo of the same object, and its dictionary definition—are presented side by side, as if to question which is the "real" object after all. Along similar lines, Lawrence Weiner created artworks that were simply verbal descriptions painted on the wall, such as *Many Colored Objects Placed Side By Side To Form A Row Of Many Colored Objects*, 1979. These pieces suggested that the work of art could exist solely as an idea in the viewer's mind and that no matter how the "objects" were presented—in form or in words—their essence would carry on.

In the view of the Conceptual artists, the valorization of the art object was a vestige of outmoded, romantic ideas about the autonomy, universality, and eternal beauty of art. Such sentimental myths, they believed, had elevated art into an unnatural realm, producing a false separation between art and life. This critique led inevitably to a focus on the institutions that had generated this false consciousness (museums, for instance). Conceptualists believed that it was the artist's job to expose art's dependence on the framework in which it was presented, and they did their job via a variety of impudent interventions. For instance, when asked to participate in the Museum of Modern Art's 1970 exhibition "Information," Vito Acconci redirected his personal mail to the museum and arranged to have the guards hold it for him until he came by to pick it up in a "performance" of his dependence called *Service Area*. Other artists sought to undermine the gallery system by sending out invitations to shows that didn't exist or consisted simply of a locked and empty gallery. Still others created deliberately circular works. For his "Measurement" series of the late 1960s, Mel Bochner used black tape and Letraset to create large-scale diagrams of the rooms in which they were installed, so that work was nothing more than a schema of the work. Michael Asher made the system literally transparent, removing the wall separating a gallery's display area from its office in an effort to unmask its hidden business operations.

Works like these undermined the idea of art as autonomous object, but they did so in a spirit of intellectual and philosophical detachment. Conceptual artists presented works that resembled nothing so much as pseudo-scientific experiments undertaken to see how far art could be divested of material substance and special claims before it disappeared altogether. But there is a direct, practical side to this issue as well. In a world in which galleries battle for fashionable artists whose works sell for tens and even hundreds of thousands of dollars, collectors regard art as an investment on a par with real estate, and art fairs have become the locus for art feeding frenzies, romantic fantasies about the artist's outsider status run up squarely against fact. While today's art market is hotter than ever, Clement Greenberg analyzed the roots of this economic reality as early as 1939, in an essay proclaiming that the avant-garde is always connected to the ruling class by, in the critic's memorable phrase, "an umbilical cord of gold."[1] In other words, artists' very sustenance depends on attracting purchases by the elite, a cold reality that sets up an unavoidable clash between the myth of avant-garde artists' radical freedom and the reality of their entanglement in a world of status, investment, and money.

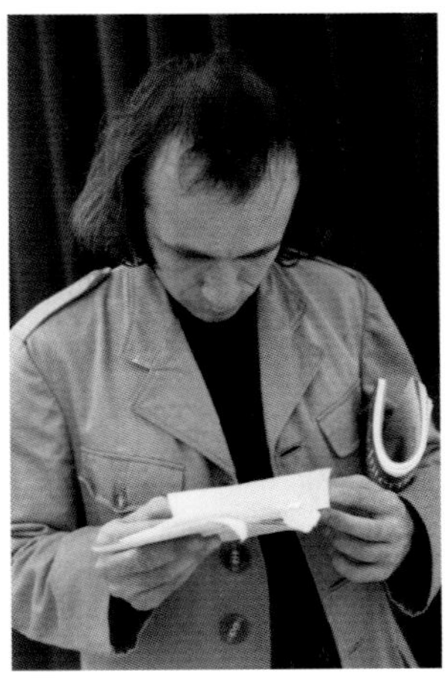

VITO ACCONCI
SERVICE AREA
1970
ACTIVITY, 3 MONTHS, VARYING DAYS, VARYING TIMES EACH DAY, INSTALLATION AT THE MUSEUM OF MODERN ART, NEW YORK

In spite of these pressures, active resistance to the art system has a healthy pedigree. Artists have taken aim particularly at museums, those lofty establishments that serve as gatekeepers, deciding which artists will go down in art history and which will not. Back at the dawn of modernism, for instance, the Futurists, in their dismissal of all things traditional, announced in one of their many manifestos: "We will destroy the museums, libraries, academies of every land, will fight moralism, feminism, every opportunistic or utilitarian cowardice."[2] In a more mournful spirit that suggested how the institution can wring the lifeblood out of artists' progeny, the critic and theorist Theodor Adorno opined, "Museums are the family sepulchers of works of Art."[3] In his novel *Utz*, whose protagonist is an obsessive collector of Meissen figures, Bruce Chatwin suggests a method of revivification: "Ideally museums should be looted every fifty years, and their collections returned to circulation."[4]

The response of artists to the problems of museums include the creation of faux museum exhibitions in which to display objects that, by virtue of their absurdity, inappropriateness, or scale, would never find their way into a real museum exhibition. The disconnect between convincing presentation and unlikely objects illuminates the means by which museums convey a sense of truth, meaning, and historical continuity. One of the most influential models for the faux museum exhibition was the late Marcel Broodthaers's short-lived "Musée d'Art Moderne." Beginning in 1968, Broodthaers opened different departments of this nineteenth century–style "museum" in various cities and cultural institutions and for various lengths of time. Among the "departments" were the "Documentary Section," which existed for a single day and consisted of a sculpture of a museum carved out of sand on a beach. His "Nineteenth Century Section" featured empty fine-art crates bearing stenciled instructions such as "Keep dry" and "Handle with care," which were displayed alongside postcard reproductions of famous nineteenth-century French paintings. In 1972 he abandoned the project, fearing that his fictive museum was too closely approximating the real thing.

Hans Haacke has used the tools of Conceptual art to produce a scathing attack on what he has called "the consciousness industry." In the 1960s Haacke was known for kinetic artworks that explored the properties of natural elements and phenomena, among them air, water, wind, and condensation. He incorporated these into installations to create what he called "Real Time Systems," in which observers could view subtle changes. But it was Haacke's application of the idea of the "Real Time System" to the socio-political realm that set him on the path for which he is now best known. In 1971, invited to mount a retrospective at the Guggenheim Museum in New York, Haacke proposed among his works one titled *Shapolsky et al. Manhattan Real Estate Holdings, A Real Time Social System, as of May 1, 1971*. The piece consisted of photographs, charts, and diagrams documenting the holdings of one of the city's major real estate families, most of whose properties, as the photographs revealed, were in slum neighborhoods. After Haacke's show was cancelled by the Guggenheim's director shortly before its opening, a mythology that persists to this day came to surround *Shapolsky et al.*, namely, that the exhibition was canceled because Haacke revealed the unsavory financial dealings of one of the Guggenheim's board members. In fact the cancellation inspired Haacke to create *Solomon R. Guggenheim Museum Board of Trustees*, 1974, which outlined the corporate affiliations of Guggenheim board members. But for *Shapolsky et al.*, the rationale for cancellation was more sweeping: this "real time system" simply would have brought a too-ugly reality of the urban economy into the rarified space of the museum.

In critiquing systems of patronage, Haacke invented a new set of tools for investigating art's place within culture, and other artists interested in how the burgeoning art market has altered basic assumptions about how art is made, seen, and understood have followed his lead. The art of "commodity critique" arose in the 1980s as a response to a reinvigorated art market. Shaking off the gloom of the economically depressed 1970s, the '80s were marked by a high-flying economy, a fashionable passion for art collecting, and new attention to audience share by market-savvy museum professionals. Artists began to confront the possibility of achieving real financial success. Dealers and collectors emerged as media celebrities. Art prices became the subject of public debate. Favored artists found themselves with long waiting lists of buyers who wanted them to continue producing whatever it was that had first brought them notice. In this super-heated atmosphere, artists began

MARK TANSEY

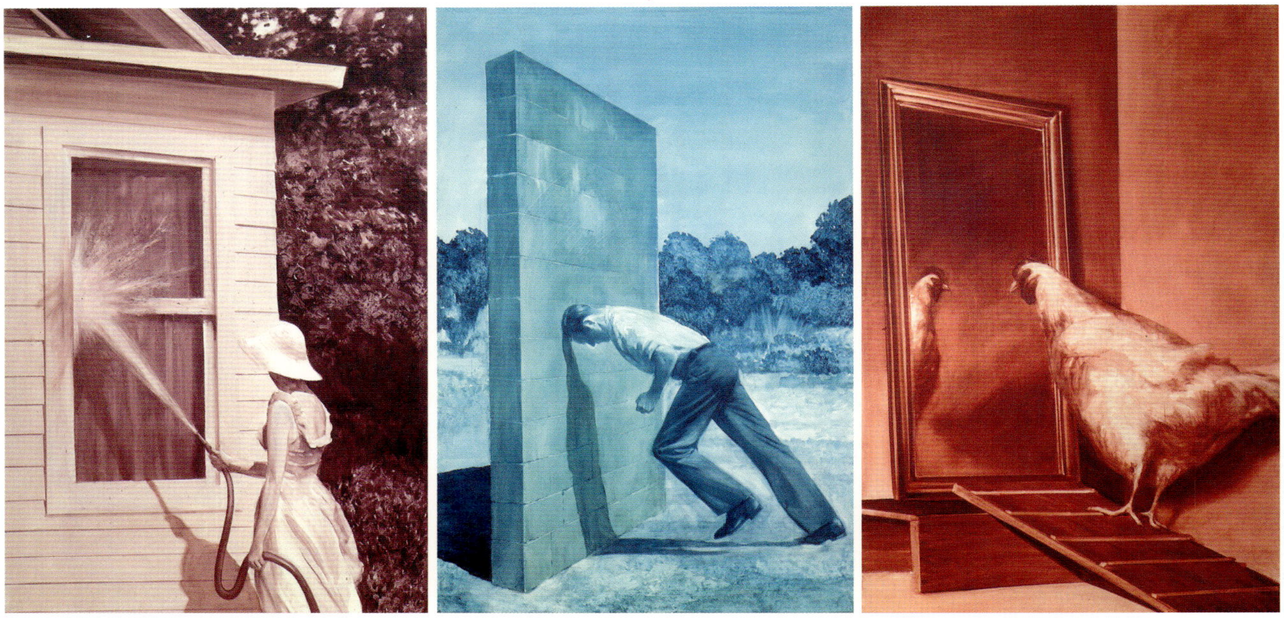

A Short History of Modernist Painting, 1982
Triptych, oil on canvas, each panel 58 x 40 in (147.3 x 101.6 cm)

LOUISE LAWLER

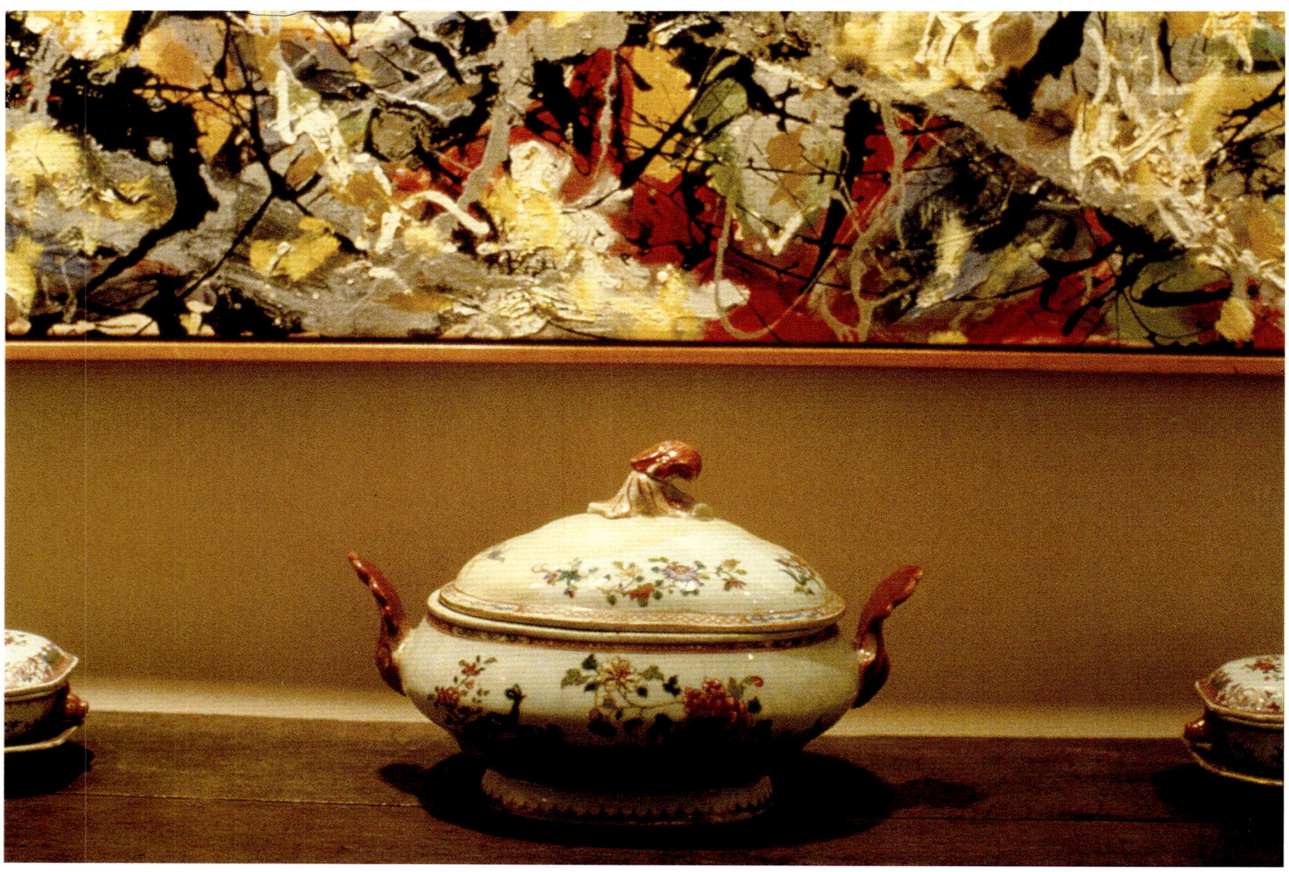

Pollock and Tureen (Arranged by Mr. and Mrs. Burton Tremaine, Connecticut), 1984
Cibachrome, 16 x 20 in (40.6 x 50.8 cm)

to examine their own roles as producers of goods for a luxury market. They turned their attention to the activities of galleries, collectors, and dealers, accompanying their investigations with coy admissions of their own inevitable complicity in the market system. Drawing on a group of favored French post-structuralist theorists, artists celebrated the impossibility of escape from this compromised situation.[5] Artist Barbara Kruger embraced the commercial side of art, noting, "I wanted them [my art works] to enter the marketplace because I began to understand that outside the marketplace there is nothing—not a piece of lint, a cardigan, a human being."[6] Artist Jeff Koons put it even more flatly: "The market is the critic now."[7]

The 1980s art of commodity critique was rife with paradox—artists saw themselves as covert agents, infiltrating the art market and the collector's home with works that secretly laid waste to all the values that well-heeled art patrons held dear. Yet as collectors became ever more powerful, joining museum boards and advising funding agencies, it was questionable who was being manipulated by whom. Much of the work in this vein mocked its own pretensions to high art—Jeff Koons's exquisite and expensive recreations of tchotckes, for instance, which sold for hundreds of times their dime-store values. Louise Lawler presented a more nuanced take on the complex ties between taste, patronage systems, and art. Her in situ photographs depict other artists' artworks on collector's walls, in museum storerooms and gallery exhibitions, and at art auctions. Rather than zooming in on the work itself in the manner of standard art documentation, Lawler's views show art in context, undermining the illusion of autonomy that so much of the art-world apparatus has been designed to support. The images in her photographs are often partial or fragmented—we glimpse the reflection of a Frank Stella work on a polished wooden floor or a sliver of a Jasper Johns painting next to its wall label in an auction house. *Pollock and Tureen (Arranged by Mr. and Mrs. Burton Tremaine, Connecticut)*, 1984, presents the lower half of a Jackson Pollock painting hanging above a domestic sideboard. Often Lawler's tableaux present typically unseen and informal spaces. One series shows plastic-draped plaster casts of classical sculptures jumbled together in a corner of a museum storeroom, and another, racks, easels, pedestals, and podiums in an art-free auction room. Lawler's photographs are often accompanied by texts that function not as explanations but rather as added layers of ambiguity. Even the titles of her shows are tantalizingly inconclusive. A 1998 exhibition, which featured photographs of Andy Warhol's *Silver Clouds*, was ethereally titled "Something About Time and Space But I'm Not Sure What It Is"—which seems to underscore her presentation of "great" works of art as rather humble and incidental.

By the early 1990s, the art market had temporarily slowed, commodity critique was out of fashion, and artists were dusting off discredited notions like authenticity, sincerity, and originality. Nonetheless, their uneasiness with the institutions surrounding art remained palpable. The '90s marked the beginning of the ongoing era of museum expansion, global markets, art fairs, and international biennials. Terms like "cultural diplomacy" and "cultural tourism" entered the lexicon, indicating that art would now be viewed as a tool of political expansion and international development. In keeping with this new climate, museum staffs began to abandon old models like the library, church, and archive and to mimic institutions more like the shopping mall, the entertainment center, and the multinational corporation. As museums have expanded their interest in contemporary art, they have begun to move

ANTONI MUNTADAS

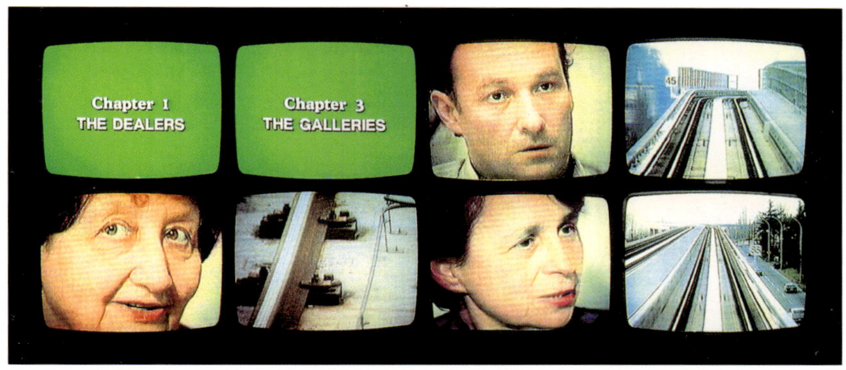

Between the Frames: The Forum, 1983–1993
Installation, including architecture, video, lighting and furniture, dimensions variable

well beyond their old role as presenters of cultural artifacts. Through commissions, celebrations of mid-career and emerging artists, and special exhibitions devoted to contemporary themes, they are increasingly in a position to influence what artists choose to make. At the same time, contemporary artists drawing on Conceptual art and the pointed tactics of predecessors such as Haacke and Lawler have developed an array of strategies aimed at deconstructing museum practices. Some artists dig into museum collections, creating arrangements of objects that underscore the social and political agendas underlying patterns of patronage and collection. Others deflate curatorial pretensions with pseudo-exhibitions that mock the practices of that profession. Artists may appropriate and reinvent the apparatus by which art is presented to the public. Or they may document the ways in which art is presented, thereby revealing the artifice at work in supposedly "neutral" presentations of art and other museum artifacts.

Interestingly, this process of critique is not entirely one-sided. Some museums have welcomed artists' interventions, mounting shows with titles such as "Museum as Muse" (Museum of Modern Art in New York, 1999) or "The End(s) of the Museum" (Tàpies Foundation in Barcelona, 1995). These shows, and others like them, invite artists to conceive museum exhibitions about the museum exhibition, examining the underlying assumptions that surround their cooperative activity. An increasingly popular curatorial strategy is to invite artists to rummage through museum collections and organize exhibitions that expose hidden agendas, neglected gems, or gaps in the collection. One of the most influential models for this kind of show was "Mining the Museum," curated by Fred Wilson at the Maryland Historical Society in 1992. Sorting through the museum's storerooms, Wilson found (and didn't find) items revealing the institution's long-standing failure to address the contributions of African Americans to the state's history, which he then placed in the galleries in provocative juxtapositions. One gallery, for example, contained a set of pedestals supporting busts of famous white luminaries with no historical relationship to Maryland. Next to them Wilson placed a set of empty pedestals, celebrating in absentia notable black Marylanders whose busts are not in the Society's collection. "Mining the Museum" was not Wilson's first or last foray into institutional critique. Among other notable works is *Guarded View*, 1991, a row of headless dark-skinned mannequins dressed in the guard uniforms of New York's major museums that remind us that African Americans are more likely to be seen in a museum on security detail than as either audience or artists.

FRED WILSON

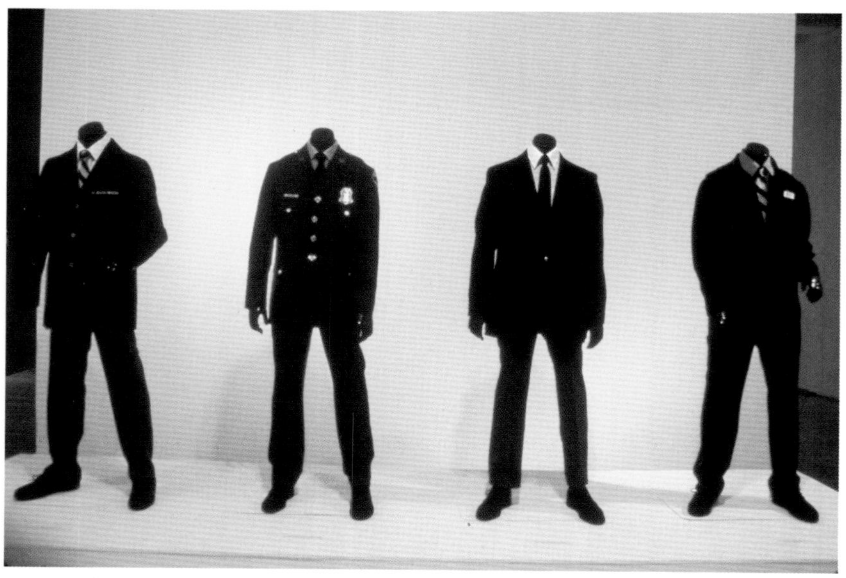

Guarded View, 1991
4 mannequins with museum guard uniforms
6 ft 3 in x 4 ft x 13 ft 10 in (1.9 x 1.2 x 4.2 m) overall

Two years before "Mining the Museum," Joseph Kosuth used materials from the storage room of the Brooklyn Museum to create an equally provocative exhibition. This show appeared at the height of the "culture wars," which pitted avant-garde artists such as Karen Finley, Andres Serrano, and Robert Mapplethorpe against politicians anxious to use the purported obscenity of their works to close down government funding of the arts. Kosuth's show, "The Play of the Unmentionable," was an impassioned plea against censorship of art and literature that took over the museum's spacious lobby, covering the walls with a tapestry of artworks and texts representing a multifaceted argument in favor of freedom of expression. Excerpts from the writings of figures as diverse as Oscar Wilde, Adolf Hitler, and Jean-Jacques Rousseau were juxtaposed with works from the collection that had at some point in their history been deemed politically, religiously, or sexually objectionable. By means of his selections and careful juxtapositions, Kosuth revealed the impact of fashion

JOSEPH KOSUTH

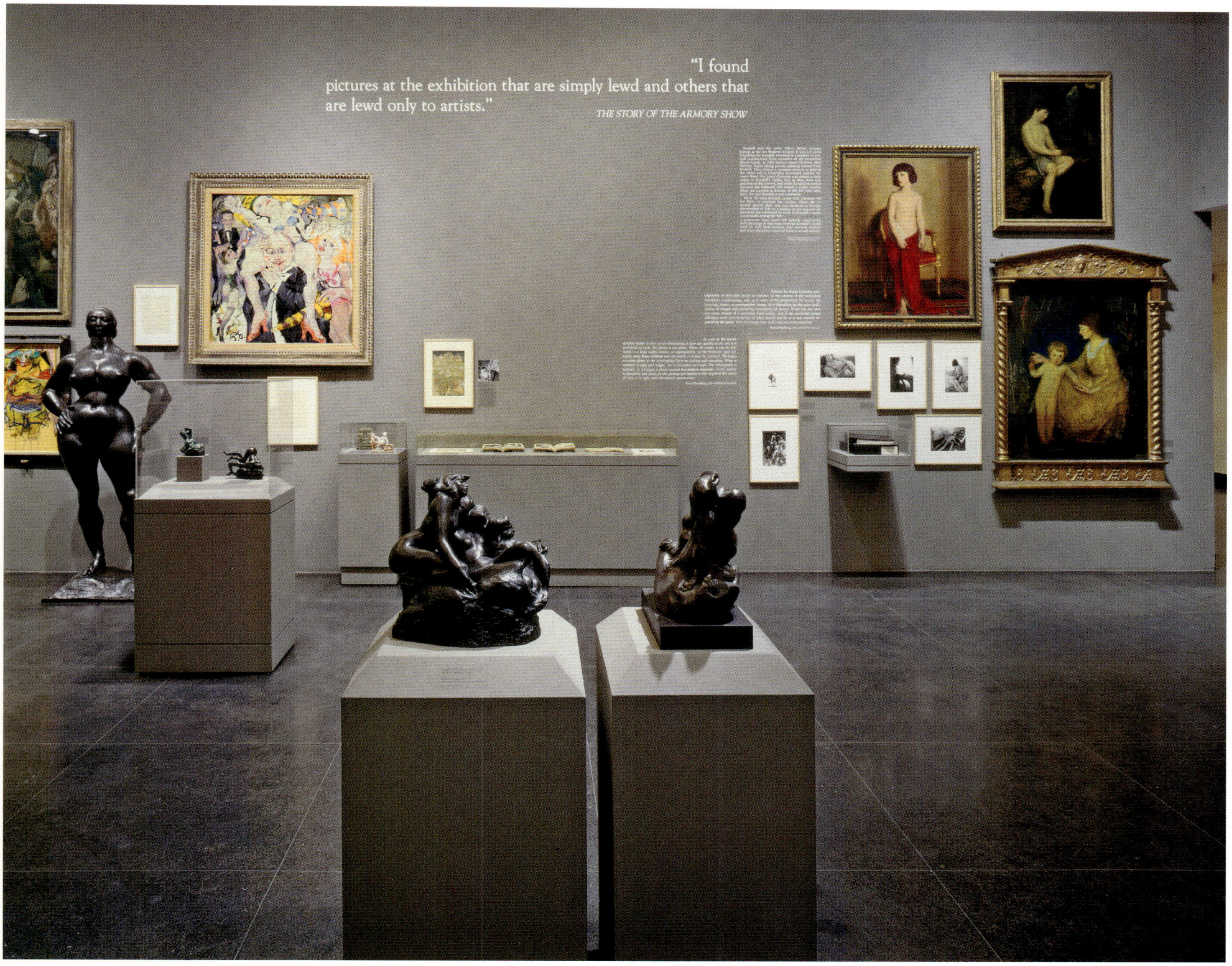

"The Play of the Unmentionable," 1990
As installed at the Brooklyn Museum, New York, September–December 1990

and politics on censorship, as works that would appear unobjectionable in one era became threatening in another. Bauhaus furniture, for instance, was suppressed by the Nazis, while erotic Shunga prints from Japan, considered perfectly acceptable in the eighteenth century when they were created, would now be deemed pornographic. Kosuth also included contemporaneous texts critical of the 1913 Armory Show in New York, which introduced avant-garde European art to the American public to much derision, thus revealing that condemnations of now iconic artworks were expressed in language very similar to that of present-day arbiters of aesthetics and morality. Due to the great public interest in censorship at that time, the exhibition enjoyed record attendance and widespread media coverage, insinuating itself into the larger political debate about the social purposes of art.

When Marcel Broodthaers created his "Musée d'Art Moderne," he seemed to suggest that the presentation and preservation of actual art is only a secondary aspect of museology, which first and foremost exists simply to support its own activities. In a likeminded spirit, Maurizio Cattelan and curator Jens Hoffmann staged a faux biennial in 1999 that had all the elements of a real biennial, except the art. Press releases were sent out, photographers hired, and a roster of well-known international artists were invited to attend the 6th Caribbean Biennial in St. Kitts, an island in the West Indies, for seven days, during which they were promised dialogues, panel discussions, interactions with local audiences, and "reciprocal confrontations." In fact they participated in what turned out to be a week of drinking, partying, and sun worshiping, all culminating in an unplanned hurricane. The "curators'" point—that art has become all but irrelevant amid the wave of much-publicized international art events—was loud and clear.

Similar ironies surround Barbara Bloom's 1989 installation *The Reign of Narcissism*, which takes on the genre of the private museum, like that in the London home of nineteenth-century architect Sir John Soane or in the Italian villa and monument to infamous poet and fascist Gabriele d'Annunzio. Bloom's installation is a circular room designed to suggest a Victorian parlor, complete with mirrors, upholstered chairs, elegant architectural moldings, portrait busts on column-like pedestals, and cases containing watermarked porcelain cups, cameos, stationery, chocolates, and books. The kicker here is that all of these items feature the artist's own name or likeness, so that the whole museum becomes a monument to herself. Her installation *The Seven Deadly Sins*, 1988, hints at a relationship between aesthetic pleasure and depravity. Here we find an elegant, museum-like setting with period chairs and paintings representing each of the seven sins, suggesting that the art museum experience is a guilty pleasure to be indulged in at a cost to our moral well-being.

The private museum provides Joan Fontcuberta with grist for another kind of commentary. A trickster whose artworks generally contain some element of fiction, Fontcuberta "curated" a 1995 exhibition in Barcelona titled "The Artist and the Photographer" that consisted of a series of installations of photo-based works purportedly by Pablo Picasso, Antoni Tàpies, and Joan Miró—*From Joan Miró's Suite Destino: "Assaig per a triple salt mortal" (Attempt at a triple somersault), 1963*, 1995—each of whom is a Barcelona native honored with a private museum in that city. The installations were accompanied by exhibition catalogues complete with exegesis, reproductions, and historical documentation of the works, but were, in fact, all counterfeits by Fontcuberta. In the absence of any indication that this project was a hoax, visitors tended to take it at face value, demonstrating how the apparatus surrounding an exhibition is all that is needed to confer authenticity on the art. In a similar mode, Fontcuberta has created works that suggest how journalism, science, and religion also play on our willingness to suspend disbelief. Among his convincing fictions are projects documenting the life of a Russian cosmonaut erased from history by the Soviet bureaucracy, a monastery near the Russian border with Finland whose acolytes are trained in the arts of making miracles, and a misconstructed advanced weapon system supposedly circling the earth.

Christian Boltanski has also explored how modes of display imbue simple objects with layers of meaning. In installations such as *Inventory of the Man of Barcelona*, 1995; *Inventory of the Man of New York*, 1998; and *Inventory of Objects Belonging to a Young Woman of Charleston*, 1991, he presents collections of the everyday possessions of anonymous individuals in vitrines placed alongside more conventional displays. Carefully labeled in the most orthodox museum style, the prosaic reading lamps, card tables, knickknacks, shoes, umbrellas, and gloves become invested with new meanings as we try to decipher the character and history of their fictitious owners. In installations with series titles like "The Archives" and "Monument," to which he has frequently returned over the years, Boltanski takes the opposite approach. Rather than present "inventories" of objects to represent an absent person, he presents people directly, in photographic portraits, yet they too remain only apparently identifiable. Boltanski's photographs of anonymous young children from the pre- and postwar period are displayed in darkened rooms, frequently lit by candles or single light bulbs in a manner reminiscent of religious shrines. Though viewers are given no details about the identity of the subjects (often Boltanski does not have that information himself)—as in *Archive Dead Swiss*, 1990—they tend to read these installations as a remembrance, often assuming that Boltanski has created a memorial to the victims of the Holocaust. Thus the artist reminds us how impressionable we viewers are—that the way in which objects are displayed thoroughly determines how we will perceive them.

Susan Hiller's project *From the Freud Museum*, 1991–97, explores a similar associative phenomenon. In a set of museum-style conservation boxes, she presents carefully labeled arrangements of personal objects and mementos that are deliberately eclectic: one box contains a photocopy of a Mayan calendar, glyphs, numerals, names of days, and modern obsidian blades, while another houses an image of Annie Oakley and a pair of cow-shaped milk pitchers. The installation was first presented in an exhibition at Freud's last home, now a London museum, where Freud's own collection of strange and wonderful objects, including eighteenth- and nineteenth-century painted country furniture and Egyptian, Greek, Roman, and Oriental antiquities, is on display. Freud's psychoanalysis theorized the existence of an unconscious woven together from fragmented memories, dreams, and desires that on excavation reveal some understanding of the self. Hiller's boxes, with their apparently random assortment of contents, promise a parallel revelation, as if one might find meaning in them given enough analytical attention. Whether that meaning will be "true," or just a creation of our own minds, and whether these are one and the same, are of course other questions altogether.

Perhaps the most extensive and ambiguous application of museological techniques to unconventional materials can be found in the Museum of Jurassic Technology, a complex artist's project founded in an unassuming storefront on Venice Boulevard in Los Angeles's Culver City neighborhood in 1989. Conceived by

MAURIZIO CATTELAN

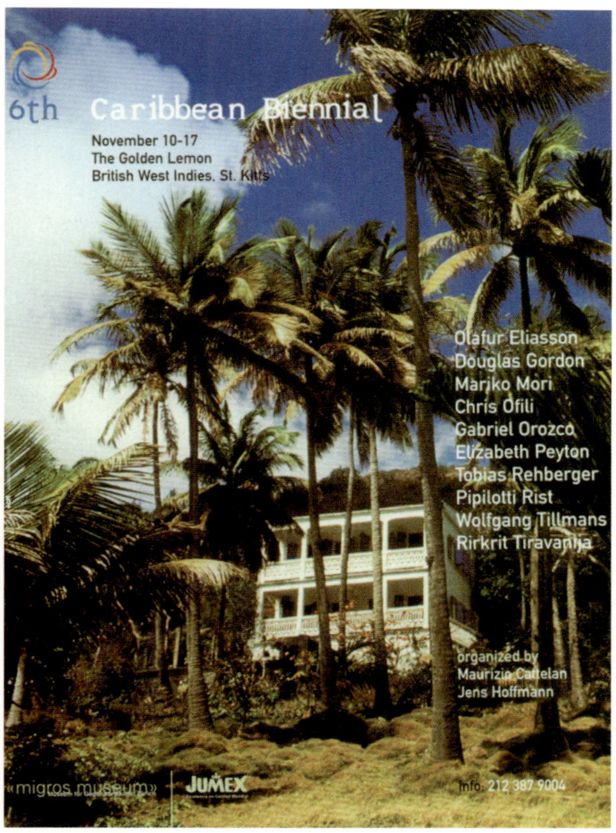

Poster for the "6th Caribbean Biennial," St. Kitts, 1999
Offset litho, dimensions variable

BARBARA BLOOM

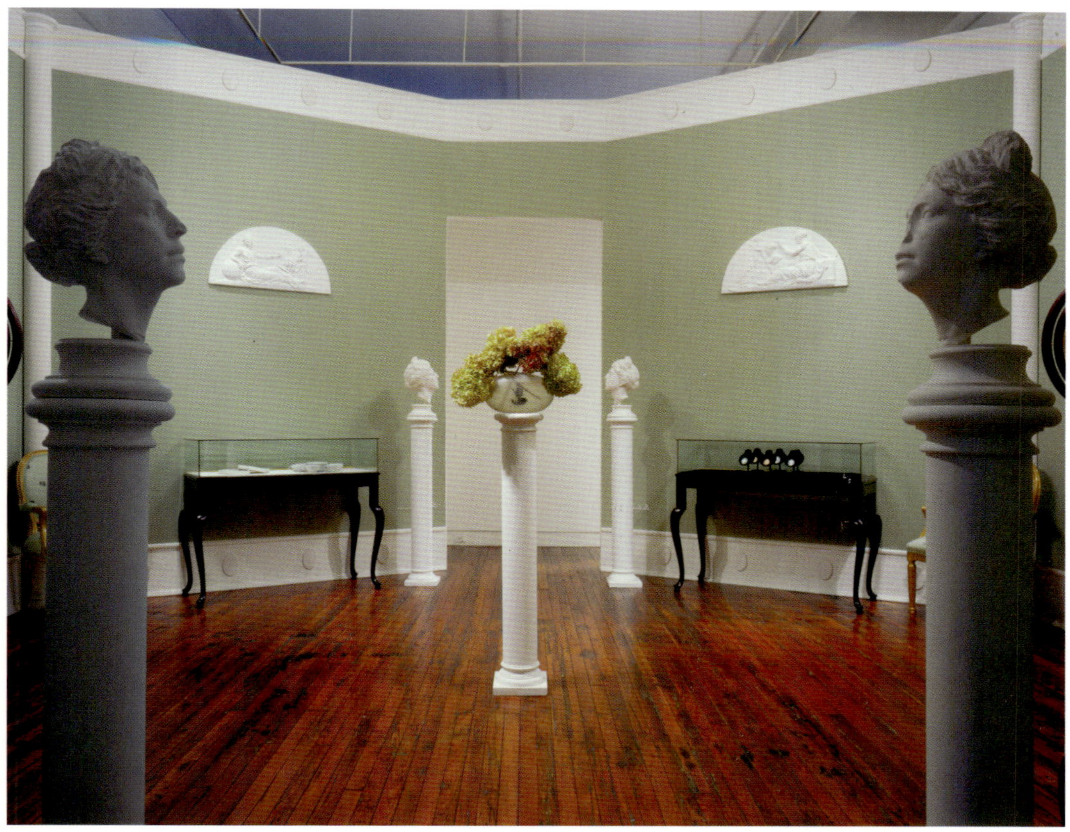

The Reign of Narcissism, 1989
Mixed media, dimensions variable
Museum of Contemporary Art, Los Angeles

JOAN FONTCUBERTA

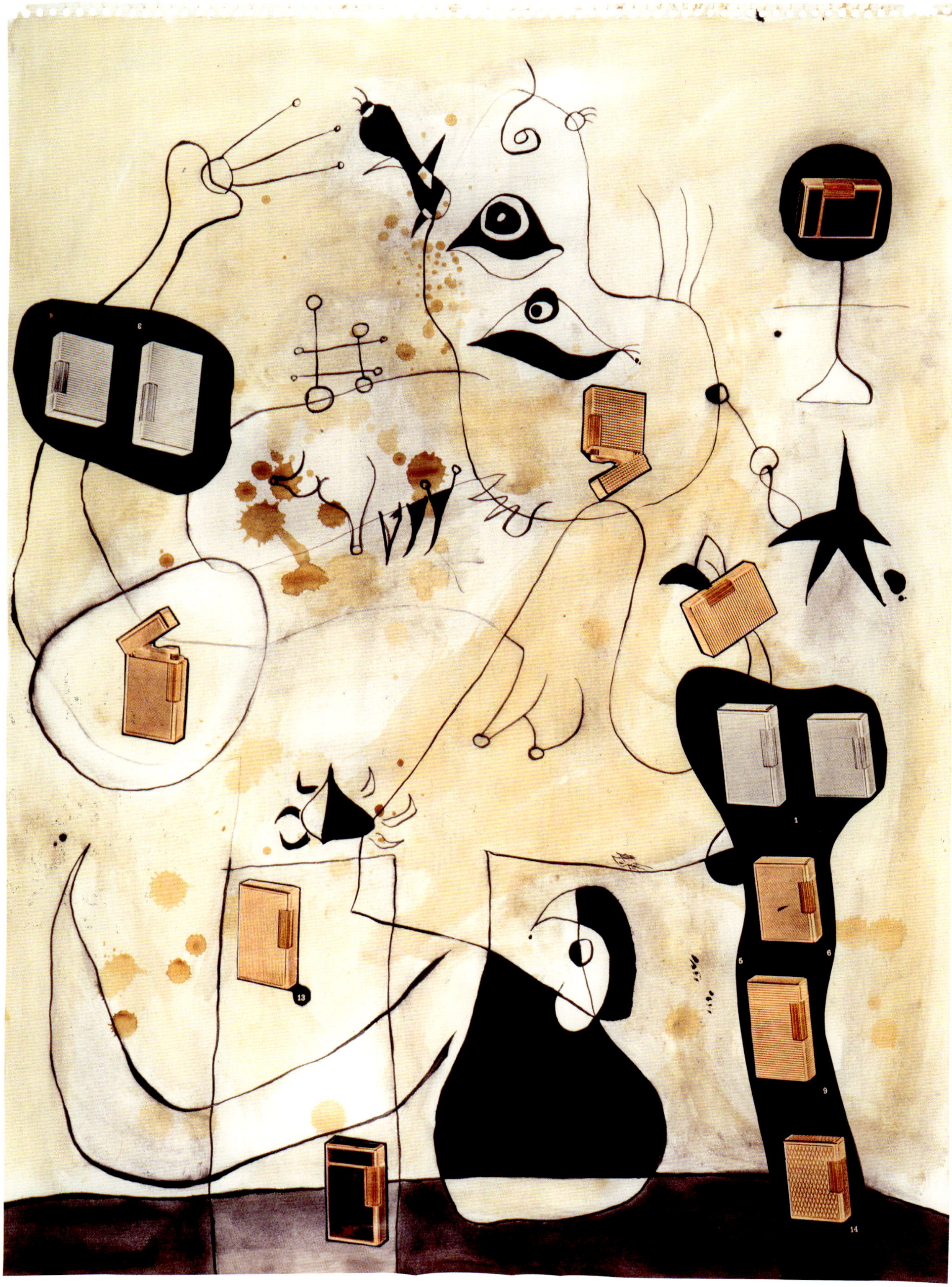

From Joan Miró's Suite Destino: "Assaig per a triple salt mortal" (Attempt at a triple somersault), 1963, 1995
Pencil, ink, and collage, 26 1/2 x 18 in (67 x 46 cm)

CHRISTIAN BOLTANSKI

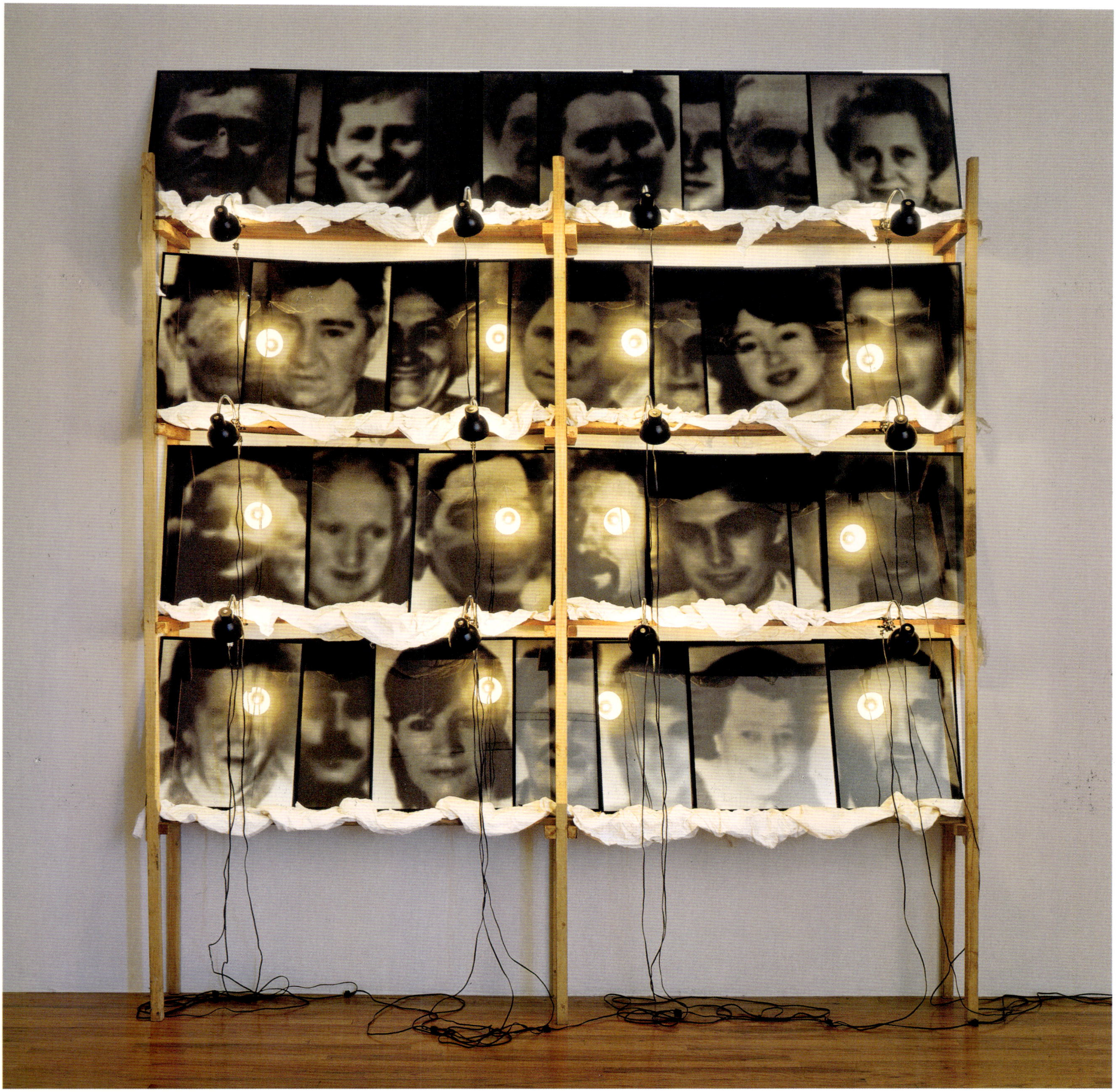

Archive Dead Swiss, 1990
Photographs, lamps, white linen, wooden shelves
128 x 110 1/2 x 22 1/2 in (325.1 x 280.7 x 57.2 cm)

SUSAN HILLER

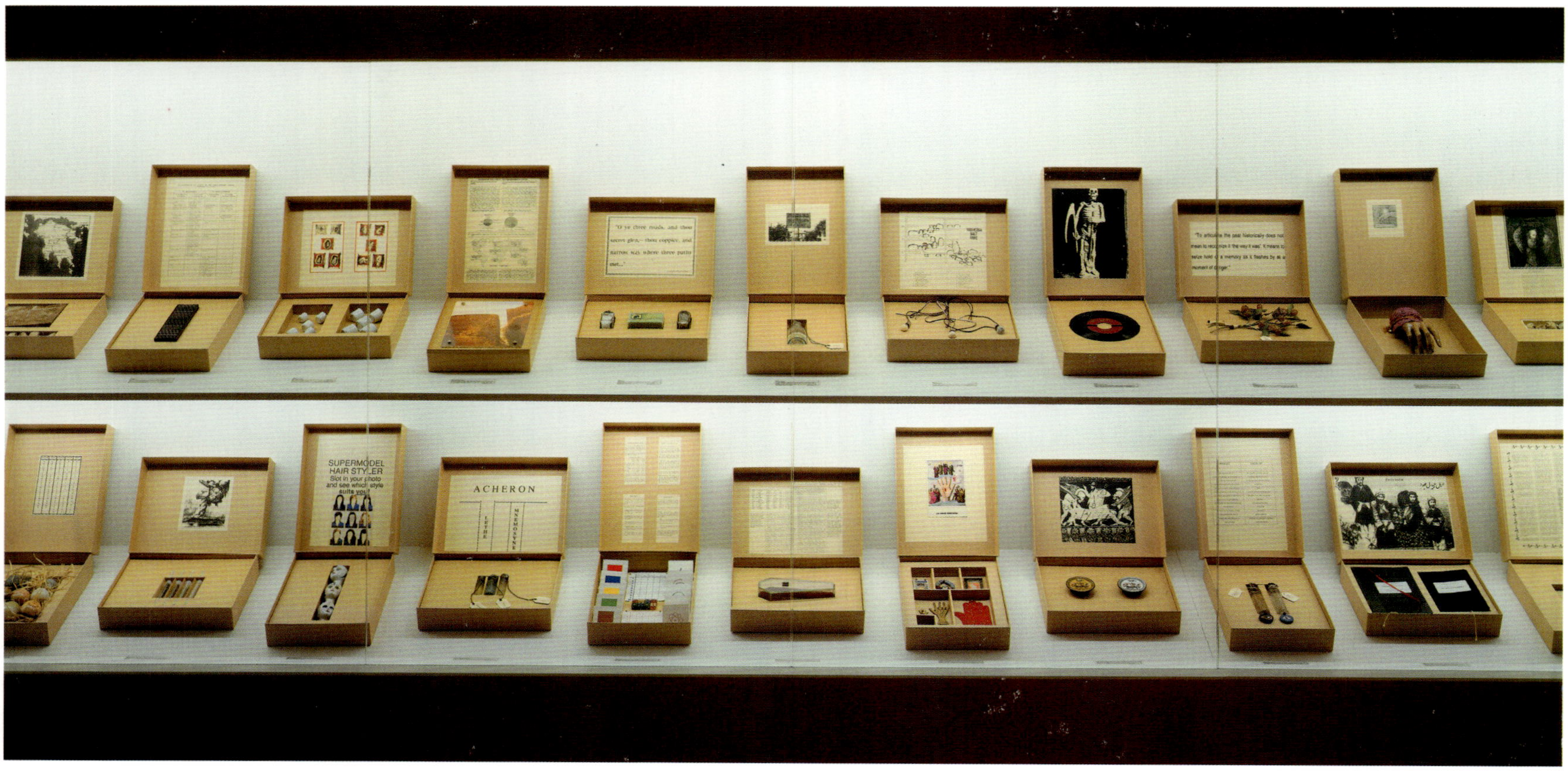

From the Freud Museum, 1991–97
Vitrine installation including artifacts, notes, customized cardboard boxes, dimensions variable

"curator" David Wilson, the museum's perplexing identity begins with its name, which couples two contradictory ideas—"Jurassic," a geologic era dating back over a hundred million years, and "technology," surely a more recent concept. The contents of the museum are not dinosaur bones and computer chips, as one might guess. Rather, the museum is based on the Renaissance *Wunderkammer* or cabinet of curiosities, into which collectors placed strange and exotic objects from around the world with quirky regard for scientific categories and systems of organization. Wilson's displays are scattered throughout a dimly lit warren of rooms and accompanied by textual explanations that often mystify rather than explain. Subjects range from the plausible to the fantastic. There's *Pope John Paul II*, 1987, a micro-miniature portrait of the former pope carved from a single human hair and placed in the eye of a needle; a presentation of the life cycle of the Cameroonian stink ant; a magnetic fortune-telling machine crafted by a seventeenth-century Jesuit; and a horn that allegedly once was attached to a woman's head. Whether any of these objects or their origin stories are real or not is indiscernible. Is the Museum of Jurassic Technology a spoof, a critique, or a serious exercise in museology? Even its most ardent fans seem unable to make up their minds on this point. Essayist Lawrence Weschler, who wrote a book about the museum, argues that it is a species of conceptual art.[8] Curator Ralph Rugoff describes it as a prime example of "museum as metaphor," arguing that "this museum isn't merely a model of something else—it's a technology for altering habitual ways of seeing and thinking."[9] Indeed, one emerges from the museum less convinced of having learned something new than of having had a remarkable art experience.

Where some artists question conventions of museology by inserting fake (or, as in the case of the Museum of Jurassic Technology, possibly fake) exhibitions into museum galleries, Guillaume Bijl critiques the elitism of the museum by placing real-life, prosaic, populist displays inside its doors. Bijl's installations mimic displays devoted to leisure, entertainment, and shopping, realizing his facsimiles with disconcerting verisimilitude. In 2002 he installed *"Your Supermarket"* in the Tate Gallery in Liverpool as part of a group show devoted to the theme of art and shopping. This functioning market was regularly restocked by Tesco Supermarket employees. Unpurchased crates of fruit and vegetables, sandwiches, and carry-out meals were later taken from the museum to Salvation Army hostels and children's homes in the area. Among Bijl's other real-world recreations within spaces conventionally devoted to art are a driving school, a fitness studio, and a psychiatric hospital. The effect of these works, which the artist refers to as "composition trouvé," or found compositions, is to suggest the relative lack of social significance of art as compared with materials and activities that serve society's basic needs and desires.

Pawel Althamer also intermingles "real life" and institutional space. For the performance/installation *Blokers*, 2004, Althamer transported a group of teenagers from a Polish suburb to a museum in the beautiful Dutch city of Maastricht, where they contributed a tapestry of graffiti to the museum's vestibule. For kids from a dreary neighborhood, Maastricht's museum represented what Althamer called a version of "paradise." In 2003 Althamer presented an "exhibition" in an upscale gallery in Berlin's fashionable Mitte district, returning the space to its prior dilapidated condition, from before the area had been gentrified. In these works, Althamer blurs the distinction between the messy realm of ordinary life and the fantasy of aesthetic purity suggested by "white box" museum and gallery spaces.

HAGOP SANDALJIAN AND
THE MUSEUM OF JURASSIC TECHNOLOGY

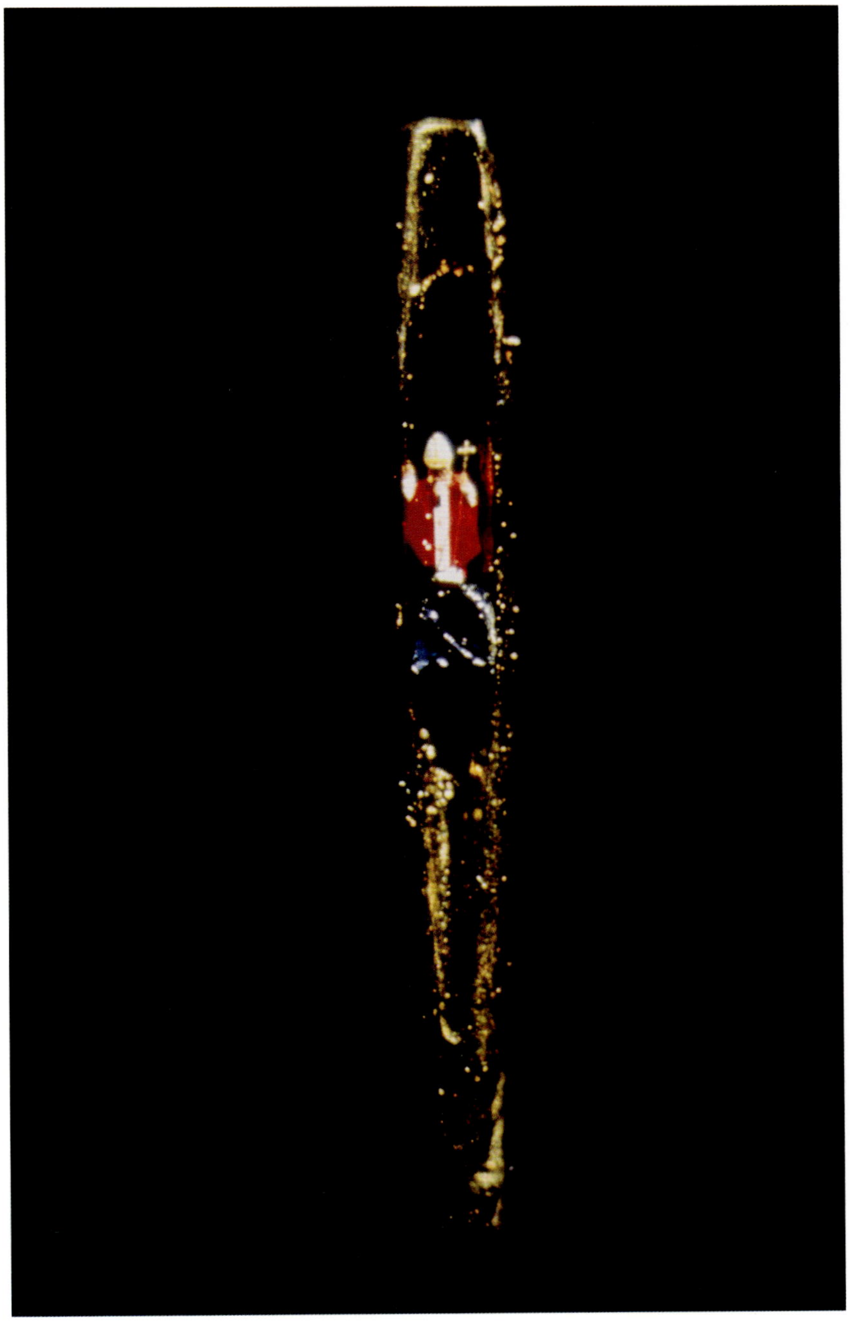

Pope John Paul II, 1987
Human hair, dust, paint, sewing needle, microscopic size

GUILLAUME BIJL

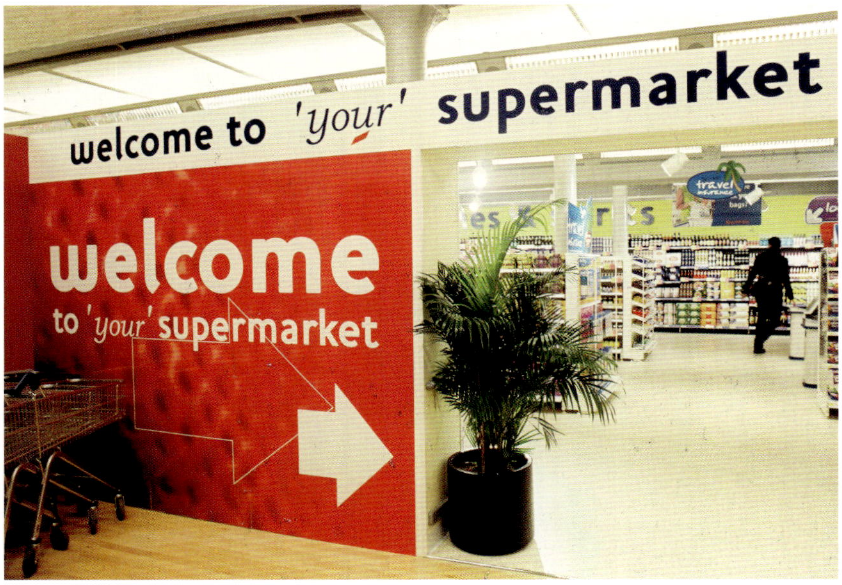

"Your Supermarket," 2002
Mixed Media, dimensions variable
As installed at Tate Liverpool, December 2002–March 2003

PAWEL ALTHAMER

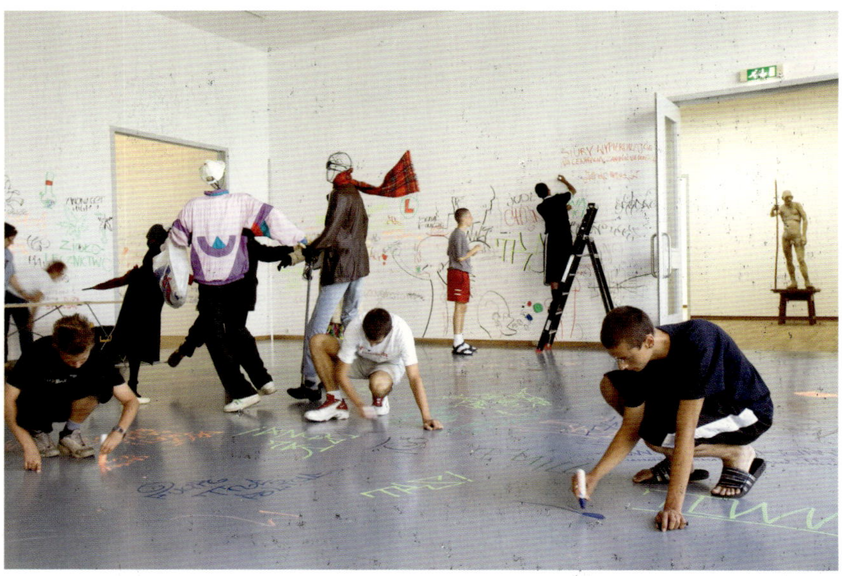

Blokers, 2004
Performance, DVD, 24 minutes
Bonnefantenmuseum, Maastricht, Netherlands

Whereas some artists explore the way in which our perception of objects is conditioned by presentation, others dispense with the object altogether and instead draw viewers' attention to the educational, security, and architectural apparatus surrounding the museum or gallery exhibition. Performance artist Andrea Fraser takes on the gallery talk. In its pure form, the live, guided talk is meant to authoritatively explain an exhibition. By contrast, Fraser, though dressed in a prim suit that identifies her as a museum volunteer, meanders into matters rarely broached by the conventional museum lecturer, straying off into a discussion of her social connections, the design of the drinking fountain, or patronage opportunities available for those who want the gift shop to bear their name. In *Welcome to the Wadsworth*, 1991, she impersonates an artist taking a group of visitors through the Wadsworth Atheneum Museum of Art in Hartford, Connecticut, during which she quotes from local politicians, Hartford residents, and museum literature, choosing statements that underscore tensions between community and institution. In related performances she satirizes representatives of the contemporary art world. For *Kunst muss hangen* (Art Must Hang), 2001, she impersonated German artist Martin Kippenberger delivering a drunken lecture at an art club in Berlin. For her most notorious performance, an untitled 2003 work, Fraser auctioned herself off as a sexual partner to a collector on the condition that their encounter be videotaped and displayed as art. Beneath the satire and shock of Fraser's performances is a deep consciousness of the inextricable links between money, celebrity, and social status in the dysfunctional family that is the contemporary art world.

Addressing another stand-by of museum education, Janet Cardiff and George Bures Miller have reinvented the museum audio guide. Typically, these guides—tape recordings available for rental at the entrance of a blockbuster exhibition—are meant to illuminate the works and general theme of the show. Museums often go to great lengths, even commissioning celebrity readers, to make them both entertaining and authoritative. By contrast, Cardiff and Miller take the viewer on a highly personal tour that may ignore the artwork altogether and instead comment on a passerby, the view out a window, some obscure feature of the museum's architecture, or a "personnel only" door that leads to the museum's inner workings. Cardiff's *In Real Time*, 1999, for instance, offers a tour of the Carnegie Library of Pittsburgh, Pennsylvania. Following along with a fifteen-minute video appearing on a hand-held screen, the viewer is guided through offices and stacks while hearing a disorienting story that blends music and elements of science fiction with the "real life" world he or she is traversing. Hence, rather than illuminating the exhibition, these diversionary guides lead viewers to focus more intently on the environment and the operations of the museum itself.

Behind-the-scenes museum security is an ongoing subject for Julia Scher, who in addition to being an artist is a bonded security professional with her own company, Security by Julia. Scher creates museum and gallery installations that employ real security equipment and simulate the look of real security offices. In Scher's paranoid world, cameras, monitors, soothing recorded voices, and office desks manned by people wearing the company's signature pink security uniforms surround viewers who gradually realize that they are both the subject and the object of surveillance as they watch themselves, or watch others watching them. Recordings of a soothing female voice may exhort viewers with contradictory messages such as "Don't worry" and "Please do not leave until the sensors have completely absorbed you." In some works the surveillance is live, though its purposes are often subverted. *Superdesk*, 1993, is a corporate-style reception desk turned around so its normally hidden back is exposed to visitors. Further undermining the receptionist's authority is the fact that visitors are invited to photograph themselves, rather than be photographed by gate-keeping security guards. Scher's installations often contain a sexual and even sado-masochistic undercurrent. One work offers visitors "cleavage tongs and buttock analysis tongs," and another consists of a bed with video monitors and security cameras attached to its four posts. Overall, Scher evokes the security-crazed consciousness that pervades not only museums, but so much of our public life, suggesting how easily people surrender their privacy to technological systems in exchange for promises of personal and public safety.

Kate Ericson and Mel Ziegler, who worked as a team until Ericson's death in 1995, investigated still other aspects of the exhibition apparatus. In a series of exhaustively researched works created for the Museum of Modern Art in New York, they focused on such arcana as the shades of white paint used to cover exhibition walls, and the names of the workers who created the museum's track-lighting systems, window panes, and gallery furniture. *MoMA Whites*, 1990, presents jars containing the minutely varied shades of white paint used at MoMA, each emblazoned with the name of the hue. Some whites, the artists discovered, were standard industrial offerings, with generic names such as "Decorator White." Others were created to satisfy the desires of particular curators, whose names they then acquired. "McShine White," for example, was the preferred shade of curator Kynaston McShine. For *Signature Piece*, 1988, also devised for MoMA, Ericson and Ziegler silk-screened the signatures of otherwise uncelebrated "creators" next to the industrial fixtures that they had produced. In exposing evidence of decision-making and human labor in the museum, Ericson and Ziegler's works dispel the apparent neutrality and anonymity of the institutional setting. This strategy extended to other institutions as well: the pair investigated and catalogued paint hues used in public housing, brand names of bar soaps, and the marketably nostalgia-tinged appellations of prefabricated suburban house models, revealing the hidden realities of branding and class structure.

The art of institutional critique also extends to the art audience. In his large-scale color photographs of museum interiors, Thomas Struth suggests how the popularization of the museum experience is playing out for the crowds who flock to see famous collections or blockbuster exhibitions. Struth's lush images depict such famous museums as the Louvre in Paris, the Metropolitan Museum of Art in New York, and the Pergamon Museum in Berlin, as well as cathedrals, pagodas, and other architectural monuments that serve as major tourist sites. In his *Louvre 4, Paris 1989*, 1989, the focus is as much on the visitors milling around in front of Géricault's *Raft of the "Medusa"* as on the masterpiece itself. Such photographs also highlight the scale of the galleries, in which viewers are often dwarfed by the art, opulent frames, beautiful terrazzo floors, and vaulted ceilings, which seem designed to cultivate a sense of awe and reverence that is quite at odds with the ordinary garb and behavior of the mere mortals who actually inhabit these spaces. Thus Struth's work raises questions about how institutions shape and manipulate our experience of art, suggesting that the elitism of museums is in fact a hidden agenda meant to keep the experience lofty and seductive—and perhaps forever inaccessible.

Photographer Candida Höfer also captures the opulent interiors of museums, libraries, theaters, and picture galleries, but her images are of deteriorating spaces,

ANDREA FRASER

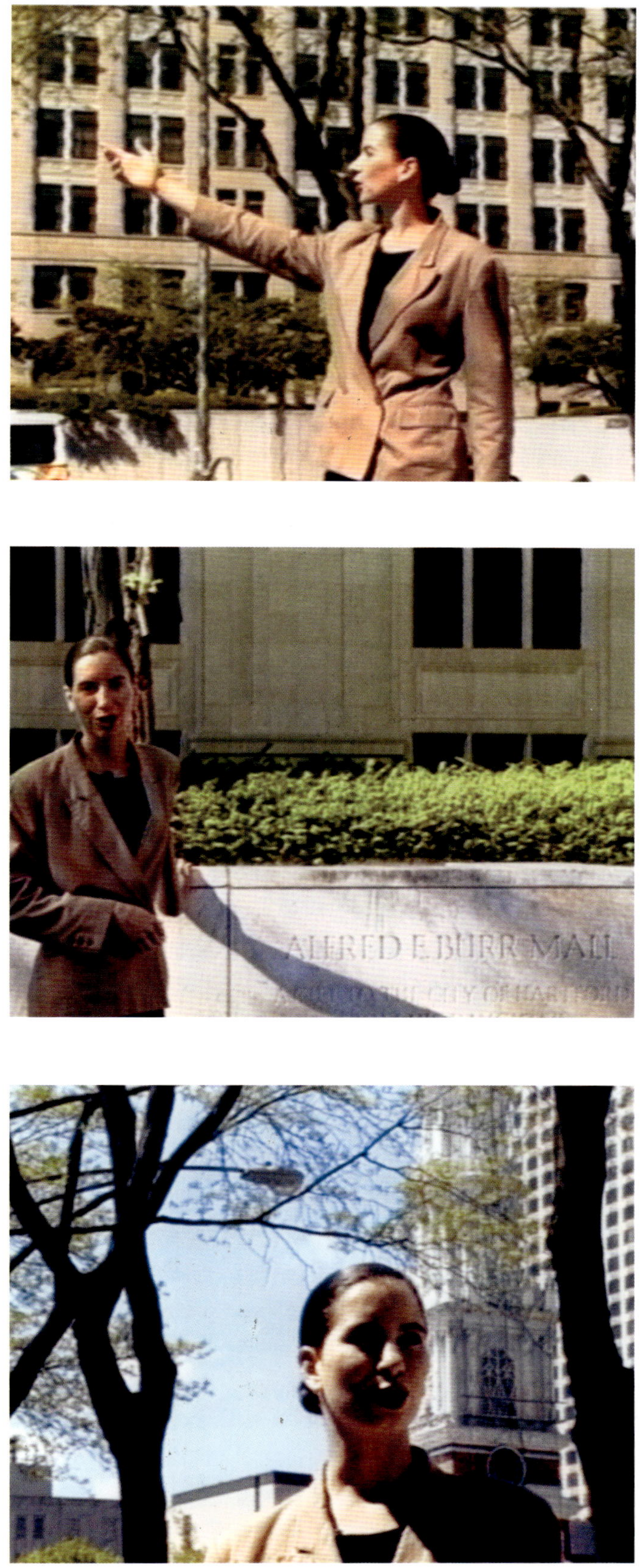

Welcome to the Wadsworth, 1991
Performance and videotape, 25 minutes

JANET CARDIFF

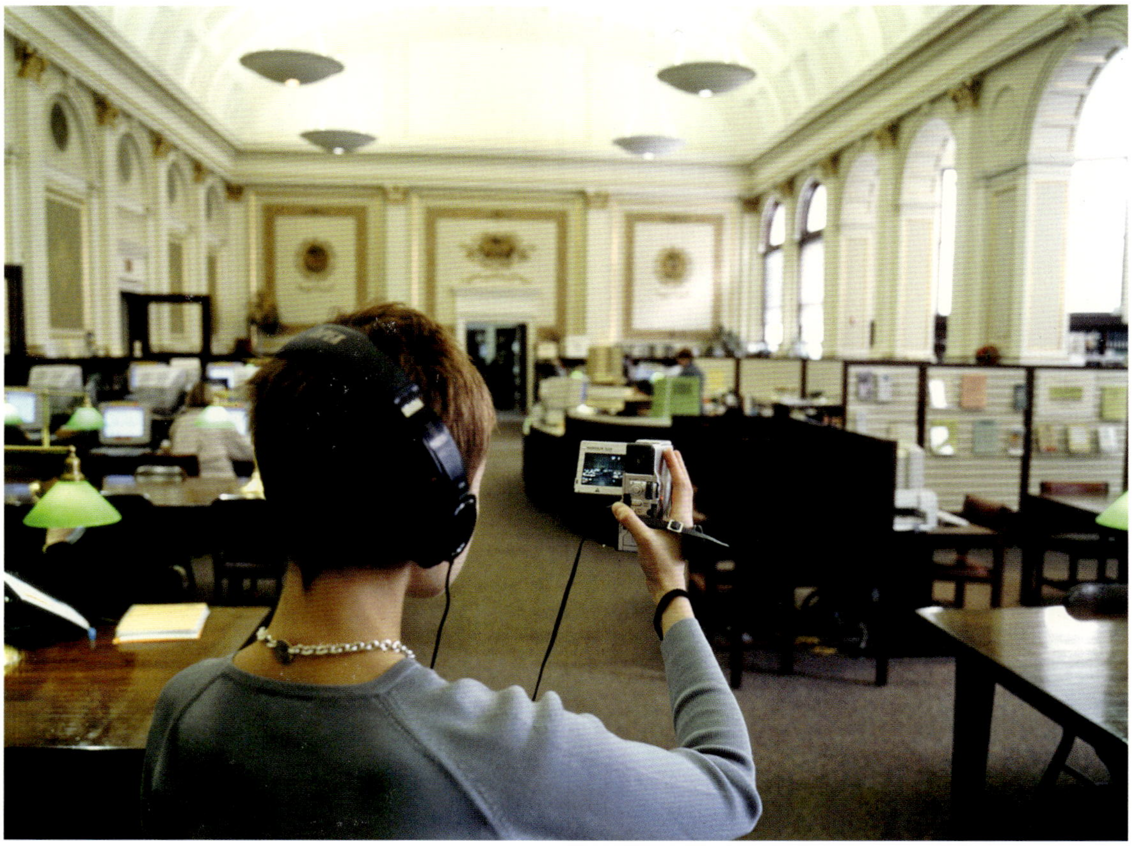

In Real Time, 1999
Audio and video walk at Carnegie Library of Pittsburgh, Pa.

JULIA SCHER

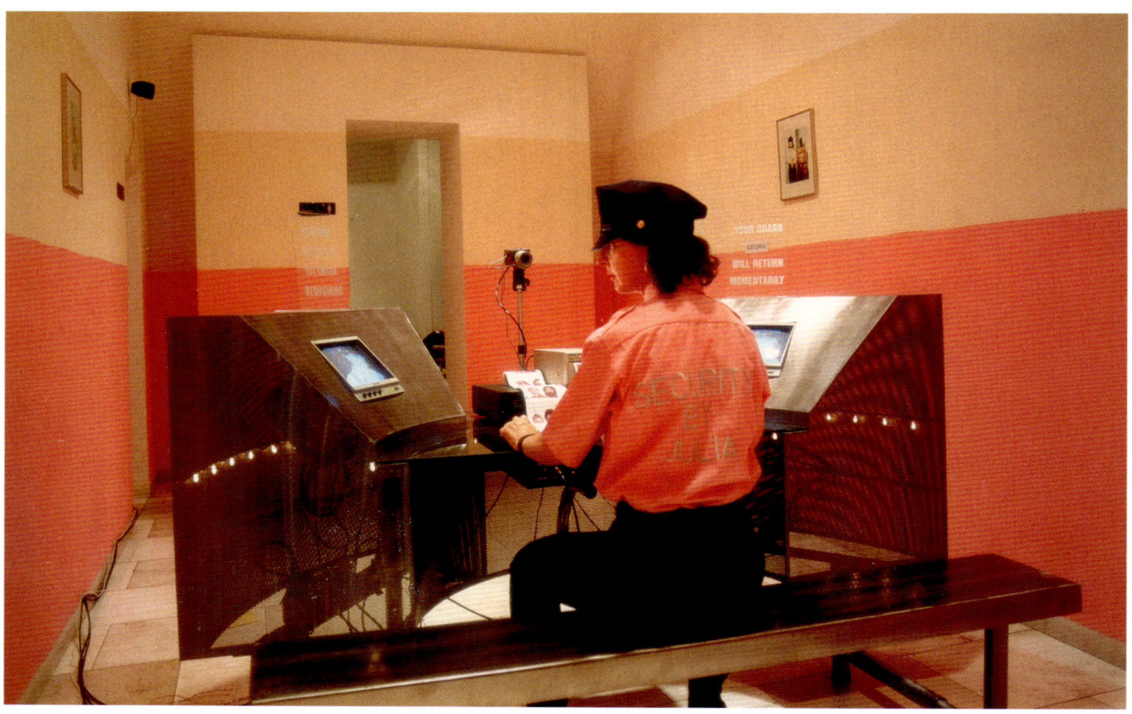

Superdesk, 1993
Mixed media installation, dimensions variable

KATE ERICSON AND MEL ZIEGLER

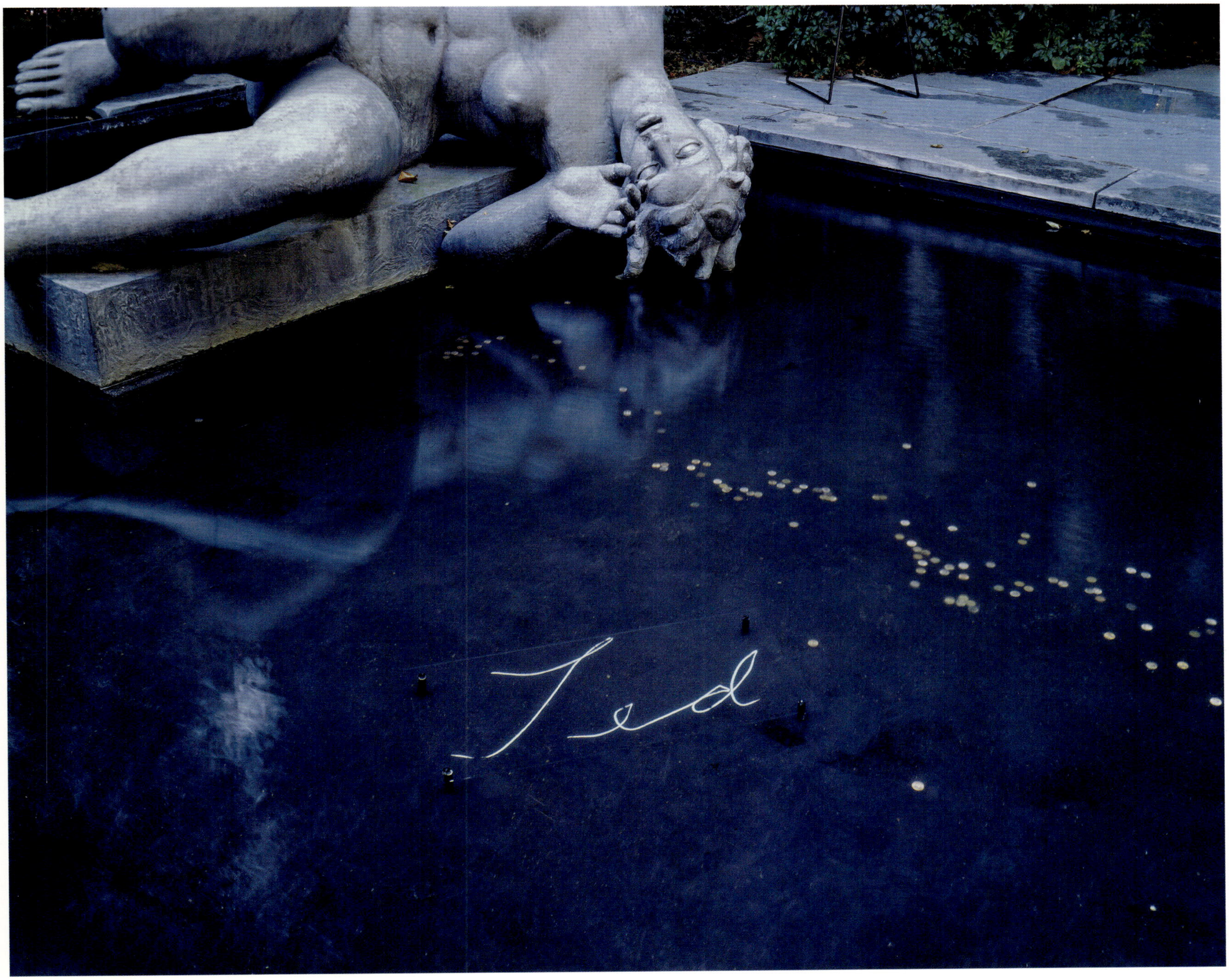

Signature Piece, 1988
Silkscreened acrylic
As installed at The Museum of Modern Art, New York, October–November 1988

CANDIDA HÖFER

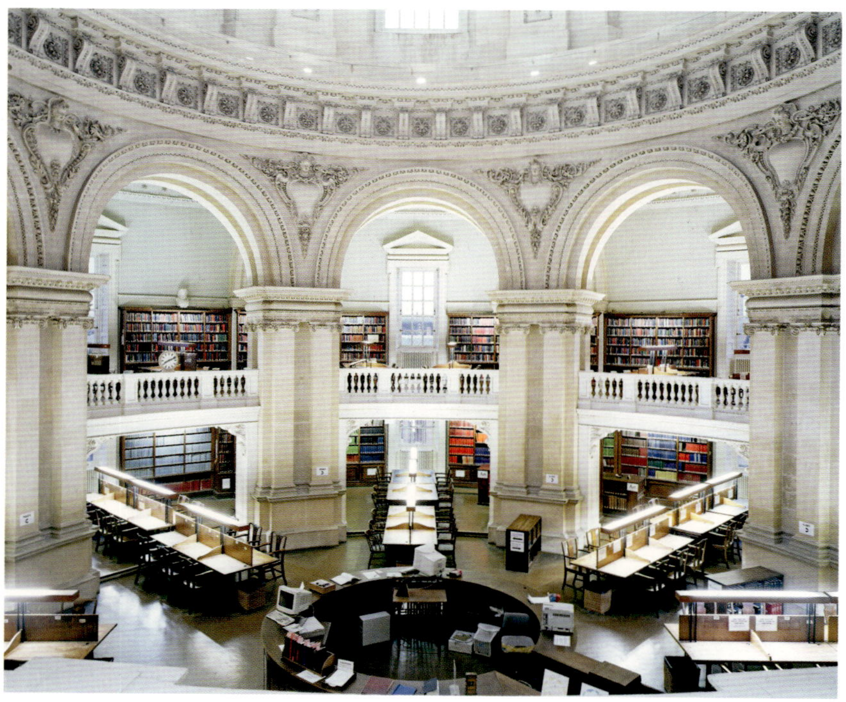

Radcliffe Camera Oxford, 2004
C-print, 59 7/8 x 73 5/8 in (152 x 187 cm)

and devoid of human presence. As a result, we focus entirely on their discolored gilt moldings, faded draperies, and peeling architectural reliefs. Crafted long ago for the pleasure of an aristocratic few, these details call to mind a gentry in decline, an impression heightened by the presence in some images of stanchions, information signs, and other markers of the public role of these once-private enclaves. For instance, in *Radcliffe Camera Oxford*, 2004, the grand sweep of the Baroque rotunda is curiously at odds with the workaday quality of the study workstations, computers, and information desk arranged in a radiating pattern on the floor below. Other works provide a view into barren museum back rooms or stark institutional lobbies and lounges filled with cheap industrial chairs and folding tables. A student of the Bechers, Höfer combines their mode of dispassionate observation with an air of melancholy—the absence of people leaches out any sense of vitality. We are reminded of critics of the museum who argue that these institutions are the sepulchers of art.

Höfer's depictions of empty and fraying museums recall the moment when museums were temples to art, and libraries were revered collections of the finest thoughts of humankind—a moment now firmly in the past. In its place is a realization that art and ideas remain alive precisely because they can't be separated from the flux of life. For better or for worse, as artists involved in institutional critique demonstrate, the frame is as important today as the material it enshrines. All the institutions of art—including artists themselves—are subject to the same economic, social, and political forces that shape the everyday world outside their doors.

THOMAS STRUTH

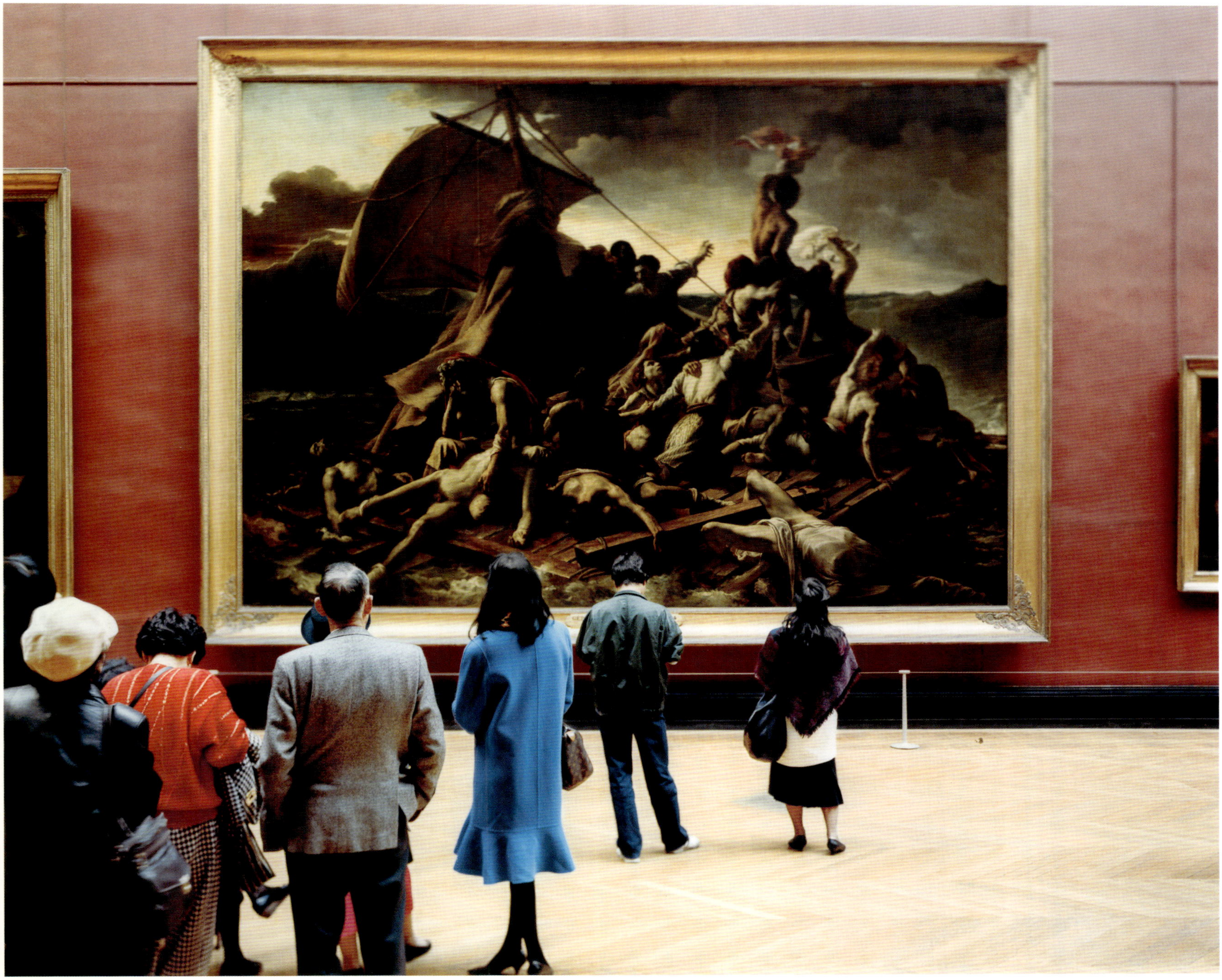

Louvre 4, Paris 1989, 1989
C-print mounted on Plexiglas, or color photography on Perspex, 73 5/8 x 83 in (187 x 211 cm)

ART & POLITICS

THE RHETORIC OF DISSENT

When nineteenth-century French writer and critic Théophile Gautier made the phrase "*l'art pour l'art*" ("art for art's sake") a rallying cry for aesthetes opposing any didactic function of art, he honed in on a conflict long at the heart of artistic production. Should artists steer clear of politics on the theory that engagement with social issues stifles the "pure" nature of art? Or can they rightfully infuse their art with ideology to suggest new models for thought and action? Art history provides a rich supply of paradigms for politically engaged art, ranging from the monumental history paintings of Jacques-Louis David to the bitingly satiric *Los Caprichos* of Francisco Goya. But it is also replete with resolutely apolitical art—the charmingly erotic confections of Jean-Honoré Fragonard, for example, or the ermine-wrapped socialites who beam from the canvases of John Singer Sargent.

At the dawn of the twentieth century, modernists asserted their commitment to provoking change through art by calling themselves the "avant-garde," a military metaphor that matched their intent to charge forth in battle against an oppressive and outmoded ancien régime. Still, it was not always clear whether some avant-garde movements, such as Fauvism, advocated persuasive engagement with the world or rather withdrawal from its corruption to a place where ideals could go unsullied. In the early twentieth century, art movements such as Russian Constructivism, de Stijl, and the Bauhaus chose engagement, proposing to bring about utopian societies by making intensely rational art. The spectacular failure of those utopian dreams unleashed a darker, more active strain of politically oriented art that aimed to expose the corruption and injustices of real societies. One of the great masterpieces of political art is Picasso's *Guernica*, 1937, which depicts the Nazi German bombing of Guernica, Spain during the Spanish Civil War. This searing painting has long since transcended its origins, and resonates across time and place as a cry of pain against the pointless suffering inflicted on the helpless victims of war. In Germany between World Wars I and II, artists George Grosz, Otto Dix, and Max Beckmann critiqued the corruption of Weimar society with satirical paintings of overfed bureaucrats, mercenary prostitutes, and heartless industrialists. During the same period Mexican muralists Diego Rivera, David Alfaro Siqueiros, and José Clemente Orozco promoted revolutionary nationalism in monumental public murals that depicted the sweep of history—from the century-old oppression of peasants and workers to the hoped-for socialist utopia of the future. During the 1930s and '40s, American artists such as Thomas Hart Benton, Jacob Lawrence, and Ben Shahn explored the shining promise of American democracy and the struggles of workers and social reformers who fought to hold America to its standards.

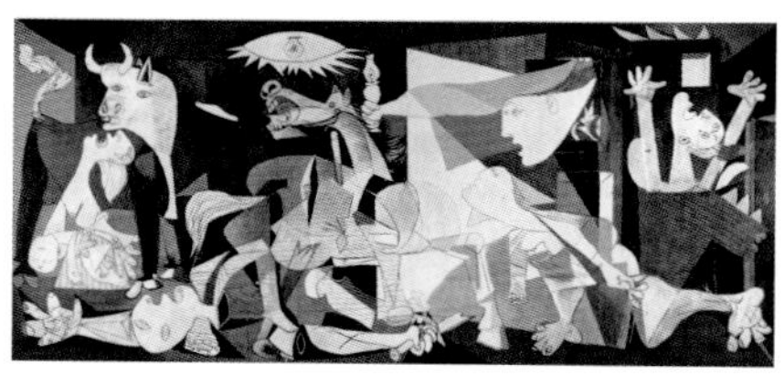

PICASSO
GUERNICA
1937
OIL ON CANVAS
11 FT 6 IN X 25 FT 6 IN (3.5 X 7.8 M)
MUSEO NACIONAL CENTRO DE ARTE REINA SOFIA, MADRID, SPAIN

By mid-century, the sorry chronicle of war and oppression in the twentieth century drove some artists *away* from political engagement. Turning inward, they argued that art should create a space for personal, rather than universal, freedom. This view reached full expression among the Abstract Expressionists, who espoused a philosophy of radical individualism and autonomy in which the corrupting influence of politics played no part. Contrary to such protestations, art historians have demonstrated that detachment did not guarantee disengagement. In the 1970s, Max Kozloff and Eva Cockcroft published groundbreaking articles revealing that Abstract Expressionist art was a player in cold war politics.[1] Specifically, in the 1950s, the work of artists such as Jackson Pollock, Mark Rothko, and Barnett Newman, however unwitting they may have been, was exported overseas by the CIA in a series of exhibitions of contemporary American art designed to illustrate the superiority of American democracy over Soviet-style Communism. In this formulation, Soviet social realism represented a totalitarian regime that forced artists to become agents of the propaganda machine, while Abstract Expressionism, with its distinctive, improvisational marks, symbolized the freedom of action afforded citizens of America's democracy.

The debate over the role of politics in art continues today in conflicts between defenders of "quality" and proponents of "critique." In the former camp are critics such as Robert Hughes and Hilton Kramer, who decry the debasement of high culture rendered by one-dimensional "message art." In a popular book published in 1993, Hughes denounced the "culture of complaint," by which he meant political artists' apparent tendency to assume a mantle of victimhood and to interpret the world through their own frustrations. Hughes was taking aim in particular at the surge of "identity art" that emerged in the 1980s as the art world admitted women, minorities, and gay artists.[2] Similarly, in the 1980s Kramer became a spokesperson for the return to standards of quality in art, dismissing much of what had gone on in the preceding decades as the "revenge of the philistines."[3] In recent years, Kramer has seemed to see himself as the successor to mid-century critic Clement Greenberg, who argued against the intrusion of "external" concerns such as narrative, politics, and biography into the creation and evaluation of art. Like Greenberg, critics such as Kramer and Hughes view themselves as champions of a vision of art that is pure, free of partisan bickering, and expressive of the highest achievements of humanity.

On the other side of the ring are the proponents of "cultural critique," theorists such as Benjamin Buchloh and Hal Foster who have espoused an "anti-aesthetic" stance, taking aim at the cultivation of pleasure and the appreciation of beauty that are at the heart of Kramer and Hughes's definitions of "quality." For Buchloh and Foster and their ilk, such values represent a kind of moral rot that must be countered by a principled dissection of the illusions and false seductions of artistic representation.[4] In place of the mainstays of conventional art appreciation—a belief in the artist's originality, the possibility of genuine self-expression, the conviction that art is a special kind of endeavor—they offer critical analysis that reveals how aesthetic pleasure serves the interests of an authoritarian political, economic, and social apparatus. Thus while Kramer and Hughes gravitate toward painters and sculptors engaged in aesthetic explorations of old-fashioned notions like beauty, these cultural critics celebrate artists who, for instance, appropriate media images to expose their pervasive manipulation, underscore the commodity nature of art, or reveal their own complicity in systems of political and psychic oppression.

Between these black-and-white views lies a gray area in which the dichotomy between quality and critique is far less absolute. Here, artists adopt a variety of strategies to address the complexities of the political world. Borrowing from the classical art of rhetoric, they explore modes of persuasion that engage the audience's emotions and intellect. They may exploit visual languages drawn from art history, mass media, and popular culture, and new technologies that are opening up unprecedented channels of communication. For some it is enough to bear witness to the injustices and horrors of our times, while others take an activist stance, encouraging viewers to become participants in political or social actions. Politically oriented artists also engage various kinds of audiences, from the art-savvy to the general public. Within these approaches, concern for aesthetics and critique is often equal, suggesting that beauty may in fact be a powerful tool in the rhetorician's arsenal.

Certainly questions of aesthetics were very much on the mind of Leon Golub, one of the best-known political artists of the second half of the twentieth century. Golub, who died in 2005, drew on paradigms from art history, looking for inspiration in everything from classical Roman wall paintings and Greek sculptural reliefs to nineteenth-century history painting and twentieth-century graffiti. Having come of age in the era of Abstract Expressionism, Golub nonetheless refused to abandon figuration and realism. In the 1970s his disgust with the Vietnam War pushed him away from classically inspired expressions of masculine power toward more topical references. *Vietnam II,* 1973, for instance, draws on newspaper photos to create an image that illustrates the literal and psychological gulf between a cluster of armed, combat-ready U.S. soldiers and a group of frightened Vietnamese villagers. In the 1980s these subjects led, in turn, to his "Mercenaries" and "Interrogations" series, paintings based on news reports and documentary photographs of the brutality of right-wing death squads in Latin America. These works, which remain Golub's best known, explore the darkest aspects of the human will to power. They feature groups of figures usually presented from a low vantage point so that they tower over the viewer. Clusters of merciless mercenaries brandish guns, casually smoke cigarettes, and, as one title has it, "horse around" over their helpless prisoners. In *Interrogations (II),* 1981, casually dressed interrogators take a break to smoke a cigarette and chat around a naked and hooded figure tied to a chair. Here, as in other works from this series, some of the figures seem to catch our eye, as if to implicate us in their unsavory activities. While the outfits of the figures—T-shirts, camouflage pants, military vests—locate them in the present, other aspects of the paintings give them a more timeless quality. Backgrounds tend to be dark red, an echo of the murals of Pompeii, while the compositions themselves invoke the flattened space of Roman friezes. The surfaces of the paintings, meanwhile, are as tortured as the cowering victims. Golub frequently scraped his canvases with a meat cleaver to create a visual corollary to violation.

Golub's paintings veer between the immediacy of the newspapers from which his subjects were sometimes drawn and a sense of ancient and eternal tragedy. A similar balancing act appears in the Abu Ghraib paintings by Fernando Botero. Botero is best known for his highly mannered, popular paintings and sculptures of corpulent figures and nudes. In 2004 he took on a much darker subject in a series of paintings based on published accounts of torture at the Abu Ghraib prison in Iraq. While they present details familiar from news reports—the bras and panties prisoners were forced to don, the snarling dogs, the combat boots and latex gloves worn by the guards—these paintings also contain deliberate echoes of traditional Christian iconography. Bound and hooded figures assume poses that bring to mind medieval and Renaissance paintings of Christ and the trials and tortures of the

LEON GOLUB

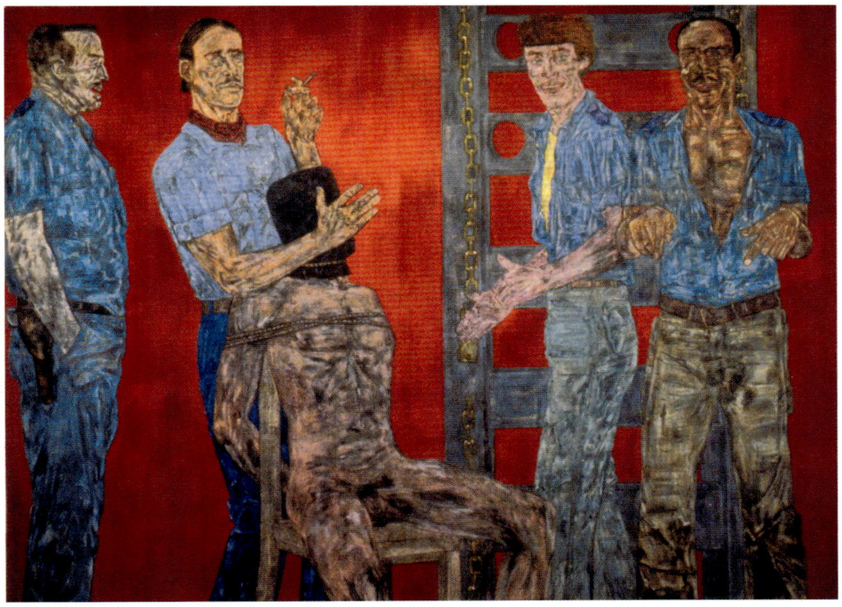

Interrogations (II), 1981
Acrylic on canvas, 120 x 168 in (304.8 x 426.7 cm)
The Art Institute of Chicago

NANCY SPERO

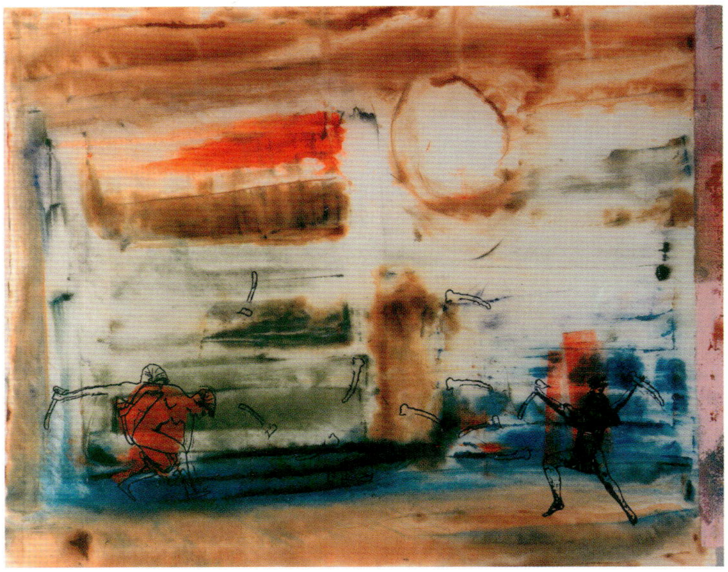

Azur, 2002, detail
Handprinting and printed collage on paper, 39 panels
2 x 277 ft (.6 x 84.4 m)

JÖRG IMMENDORFFF

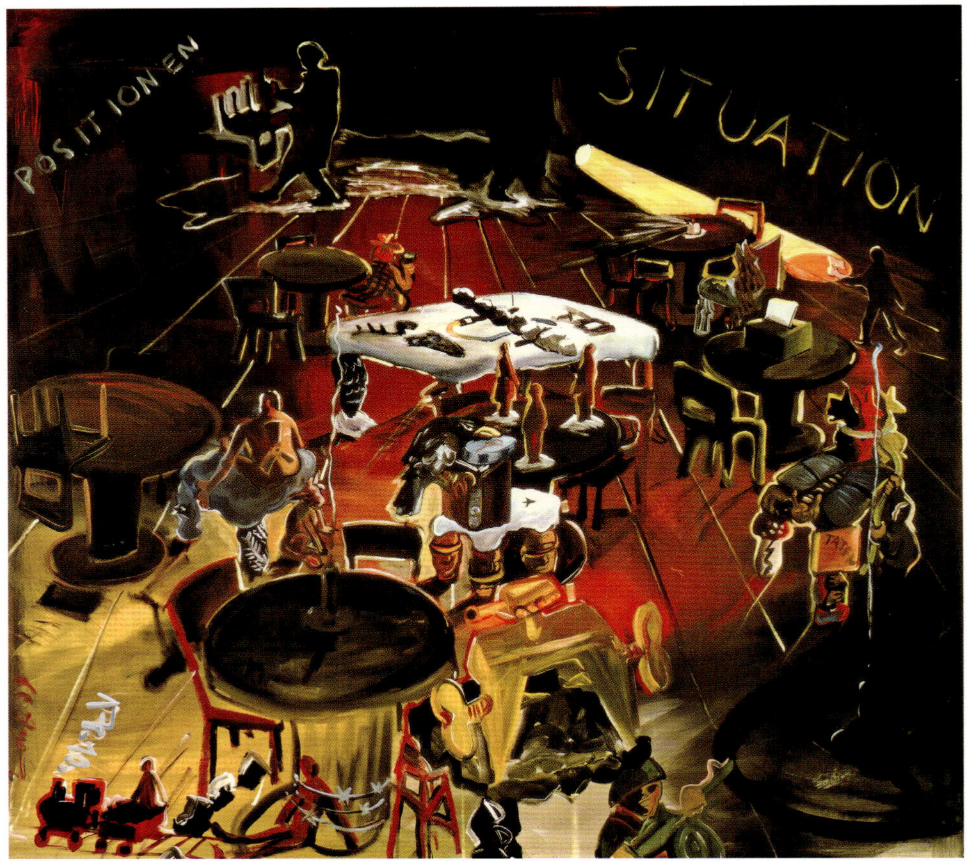

Café Deutschland, 1979
Acrylic on canvas, 110 1/4 x 137 3/4 in (280 x 350 cm)

saints. They also recall Golub's "Mercenaries" series, but while Golub focused on the twisted psychology of the torturers, Botero seems more interested in the prisoners, whose bodies are marked and distorted by physical abuse. Other than a disembodied hand or foot, the torturers are largely absent in these works. Psychologically and symbolically, they are represented by prison dogs that resemble the hounds of hell more than the standard-issue German shepherds familiar from the photographs at Abu Ghraib. *Abu Ghraib 45*, 2005, a particularly horrifying image from this series, depicts a dog mauling the back of a bound and supine prisoner whose white T-shirt is stained with a spreading pool of blood. Despite bearing witness to such specific events, these works transcend them, touching on such universal themes as the gratuitous cruelty of captors to their captives and the capacity of one human to strip away all vestiges of dignity from another.

Nancy Spero also draws on traditional imagery, and like those of Golub (to whom she was long married) and Botero, her paintings are permeated with a sense of outrage and sorrow. But in contrast to the raw, explosive energy that characterizes their work, Spero's paintings are delicate and fugitive, their images stenciled, stamped, collaged, or traced onto transparent papers that unfurl across the wall like Chinese scrolls. *Azur*, 2002, is an enormous, three-tiered collage that wraps around the four walls of the gallery and features a large cast of female characters including acrobats, dancers, divers, victims, avengers, and warriors. Spero's compositions are fugue-like, as similar images repeat, multiply, merge, and fade away across an ever-shifting backdrop. Drawing images from archeology, mass media, history, and fantasy, her work explores archetypes of female power and vulnerability. A single painting may contain images as diverse as the screaming head of Marianne, icon of the French Revolution; a fearsome, snake-crowned Medusa; fertility cult figures; the German Valkyries; Greek Maenads; the arching body of the Egyptian sky goddess Nut; contemporary women in bondage regalia; and a smattering of real people, including the young Queen Elizabeth and the female martyrs of the German resistance group The White Rose. While not exactly narrative, this interplay of images suggests the everlasting links between sex, power, and violence.

Pervasive psychic violence is also a theme of Jörg Immendorff's panoramic paintings. Born into postwar Germany, Immendorff explores the fraught nature of a nation haunted by its actions in World War II and literally broken in half by the division that followed. He draws in part on the prewar German art of Grosz, Beckmann, and Dix, whose portrayals of the decadence and social inequality of Weimar Germany forecast the cataclysm that was to follow. Immendorff's best-known works, his "Café Deutschland" paintings of the late 1970s and 1980s, are set in a cavernous, dimly lit café crammed with figures and symbols from Germany's present and past. One may find Erich Honecker, president of what was then East Germany, fellow artist A. R. Penck, Karl Marx, a swooping German eagle with knife-like talons, nude couples dancing with abandon, or swastikas sculpted of ice, attesting to a frozen history. The artist, too, often appears, drinking with friends, participating in the festivities, or passed out on a table within a careening interior that defies the stable perspective of Renaissance space. In contrast to the frenzied activity in some of these paintings, in *Café Deutschland*, 1979, the bar is almost emptied out and the German eagle lies slumped over a slab of ice. This nightmarish world suggests a metaphor for the artist's psyche, weighed down by an unspeakable history and a brutally divided country.

FERNANDO BOTERO

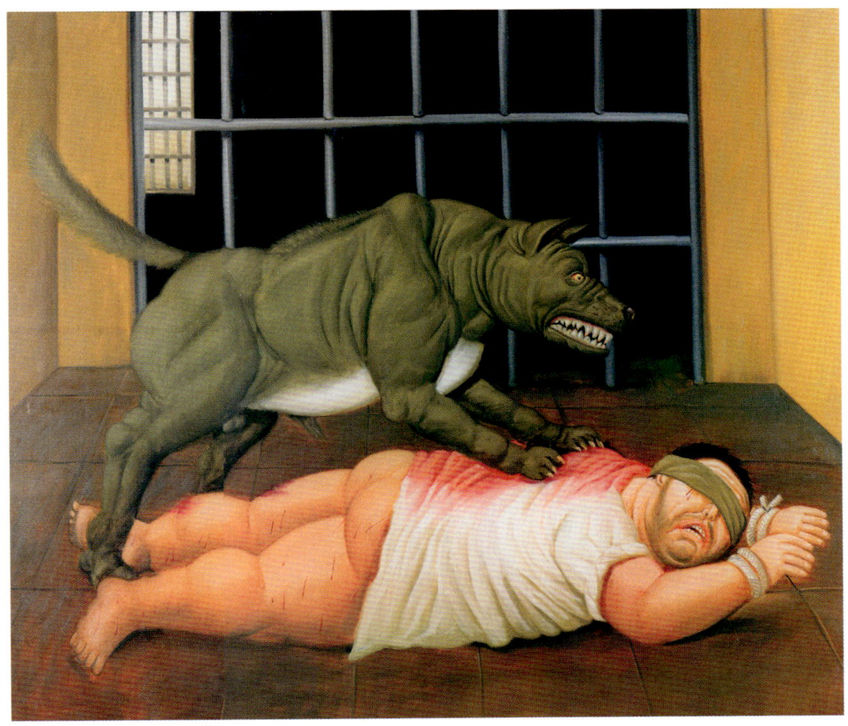

Abu Ghraib 45, 2005
Oil on canvas, 65 3/8 x 78 3/4 in (166 x 200 cm)

ANSELM KIEFER

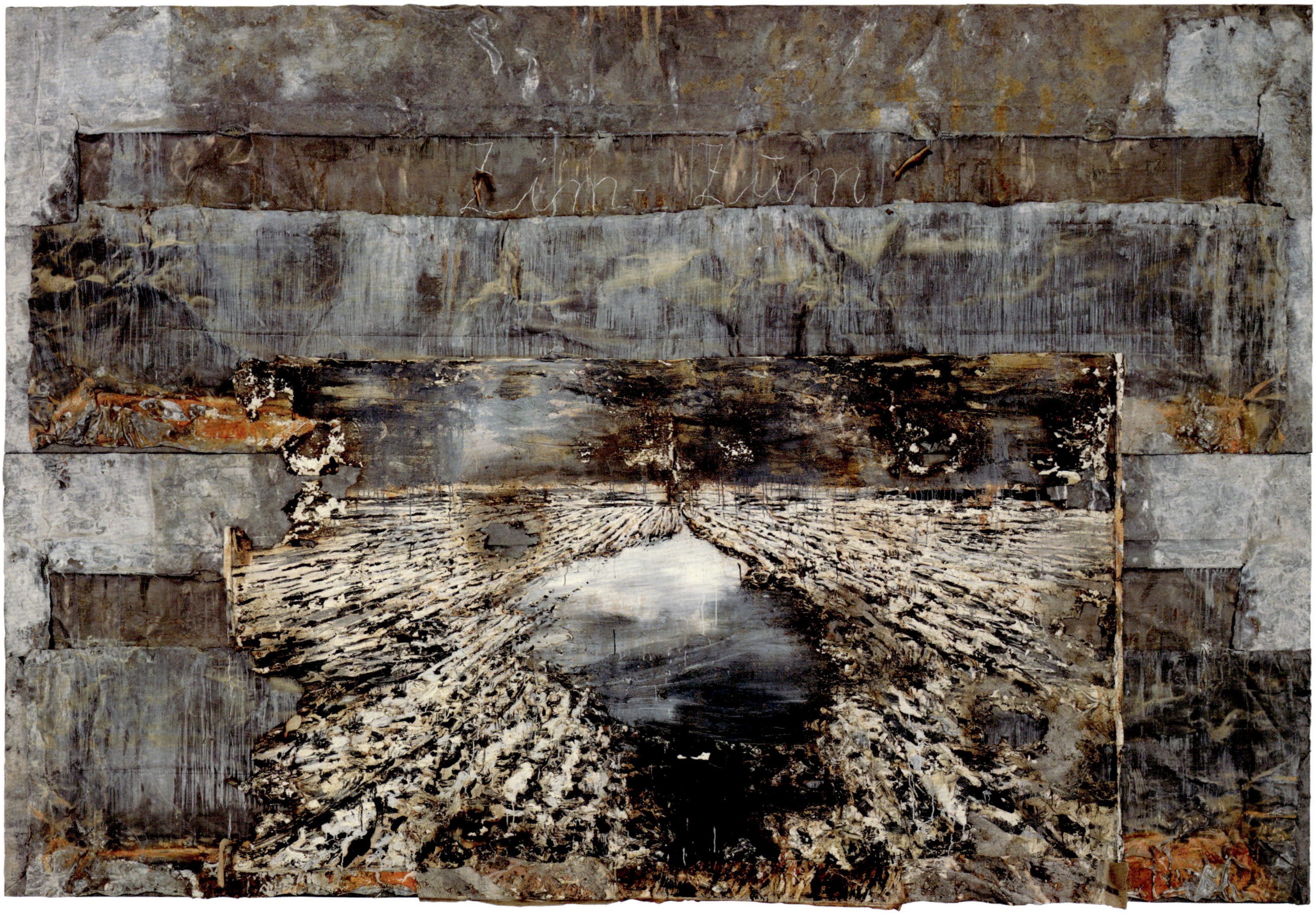

Zim Zum, 1990
Oil crayon, ashes and canvas on lead, 12 ft 6 in x 18 ft 4 in (3.8 x 5.6 m)
National Gallery of Art, Washington, D.C.

Anselm Kiefer also addresses the complexities of postwar German identity, in enormous and ambitious paintings that invoke the heroic spirit of German Romanticism, which dissipated with its repudiation in the wake of the Nazi defeat. Borrowing also from Nordic, Greek, Egyptian, early Christian, and Jewish mythology, along with Teutonic mysticism, Kiefer creates works that combine references to both German guilt and idealism, expressing an ambiguous stance that alternates between disgust with history and an apparent desire to vault back to a supposedly purer time. This conflict between idealism and reality is inscribed onto the surface of the works. Swaths of thick paint interspersed with encrusted tufts of straw, clay, sand, fragmented photographs, and splashes of molten lead force the eye to jump between the physical materials on the surface and the illusion of the image, deliberately undermining pictorial depth. Kiefer's paintings are often dominated by architectural structures—factory buildings, brick chimneys that unmistakably allude to the ovens of the concentration camps, pyramids, and underground chambers. Or they may present the aftermath of some catastrophe, depicting scorched earth, abandoned railroad tracks (another Holocaust reference), or wasted fields. The title of his work *Zim Zum*, 1990, is from the Kabbalah, a Jewish mystical theology, and refers to the breath of God that allowed for both the creation of the world and the introduction of evil. A scorched landscape, composed of textured, torn, and wrinkled sheets of lead covered with paint, crayon, sand, dust, and ash, suggests the destructive consequences of mankind's will to power.

William Kentridge bears witness to the psychological trauma created by another broken political system, South Africa's former policy of racial apartheid. In video animations made from drawings whose dynamic style brings to mind the work of such German Expressionists as Käthe Kollwitz and Max Beckmann, he creates episodic narratives in which mental events—the return of repressed memories, nightmares, the pain of loss, or the rush of sexual desire—have as much weight as real events. Kentridge's animation technique lends to the feeling of constant flux: he films a set of continuously changing drawings altered with additions and erasures whose traces remain on the paper support. In this surrealistic world, a cat may morph into a telephone, or a puff of cigarette smoke may become the vapor trail of a fighter plane. The stories Kentridge tells, in which personal tragedy is often inseparable from societal oppression, are equally fluid. Two recurring characters lend continuity: the lonely industrialist Soho Eckstein, and Felix Teitelbaum, who embodies the sensual, life-affirming impulses that Soho has all but squelched. The relationship between these two is ambiguous; sometimes they seem like alter egos, sometimes, as when Felix seduces Soho's wife, adversaries. Along with such personal details, most of the works also evoke the brutality of apartheid. In *Johannesburg, 2nd Greatest City After Paris*, 1989, workers stand listlessly in an endless line while Soho dines magnificently. In *History of the Main Complaint*, 1996, Soho lies attached to tubes in a hospital, haunted by the memory of a black man run down by a car. *In Mine*, 1991, Soho's coffee press becomes a drill boring into the depths of a mine where workers sleep on wooden planks. As such moments emerge, merge, and disappear from the paper on which they are drawn, Kentridge provides a powerful metaphor for the erasure and manipulation of historical memory.

Artists such as Golub, Spero, and Kiefer draw on well-established, grand traditions of Western art to provide a visual language for exploring large-scale human disasters such as war. Other politically oriented artists have turned to

WILLIAM KENTRIDGE

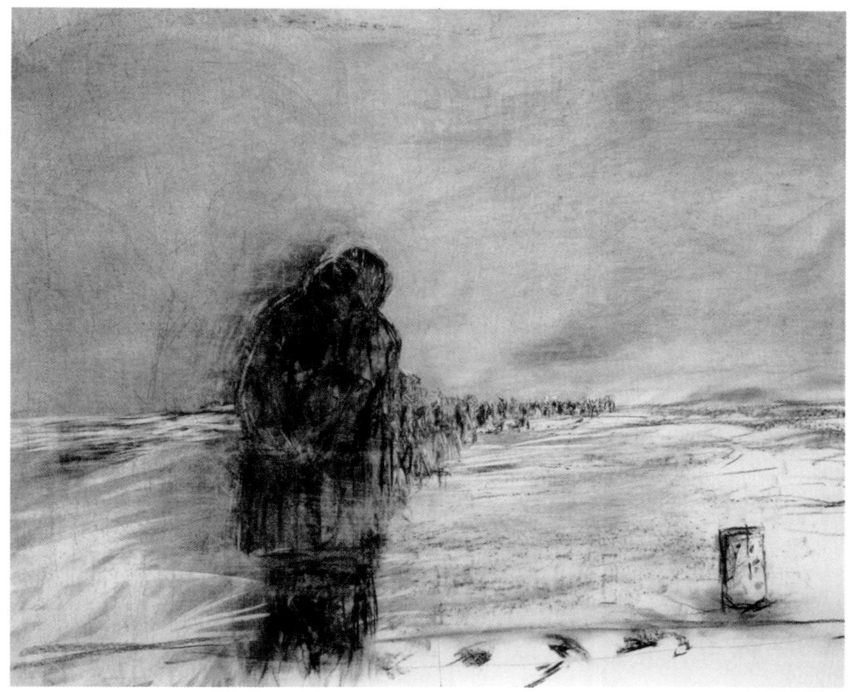

Johannesburg, 2nd Greatest City after Paris, 1989
Charcoal on paper, 36 1/4 x 51 1/8 in (92 x 130 cm)

another precedent, mining the subversive veins of popular imagery to comment on particular contemporary societal ills, such as religious hypocrisy, AIDS, and urban violence. The artistic ancestors in this case include such eighteenth- and nineteenth-century caricaturists as William Hogarth, James Gillray, Honoré Daumier, and José Guadalupe Posada. Another important precursor is Francisco Goya, whose cycle of etchings *Los Caprichos*, begun at the tail end of the eighteenth century, mocked the follies and vices of Spanish society with references to witchcraft, nightmares, and the supernatural. More recent sources include activist underground comics, Japanese manga, political cartoons, and the mass-produced broadsides, prints, and posters that serve as vehicles for populist debate.

Traditions of caricature from both East and West have inspired Masami Teraoka, who moved to the United States from Japan in 1961. Teraoka initially gained attention for his gently parodic paintings in the style of Japanese woodblock prints that dealt with such typically American foibles as consumerism, sex, fast food, and tourism. Since 1992, however, he has traded this Japanese style for historical motifs that evoke the grim pageantry of the Spanish Inquisition, the dark revelry of Hieronymus Bosch, and the searing satire of Goya's *Caprichos*. Teraoka's primary theme is the hypocrisy of religious and political authorities who indulge in lust and crime while sanctimoniously condemning the lesser infractions of those over whom they have power. His mural-like paintings contain medieval landscapes, Gothic arches, robed inquisitors, and images of corpses crawling out of reopened graves. *Virtual Inquisition/The Pope of Thong*, 2003, indicts the Church hierarchy for its obsession with women's sexuality at the expense of their physical well-being. The painting is dominated by a papal figure in an opulent gold vestment in a passionate embrace with a seductress entwined with an octopus. To one side a stripped and bound pregnant woman hangs by her feet. Together the two females represent the clichés that limit women to the roles of mother or whore. Teraoka's themes are not all traditional. Contemporary touches include computer keyboards and laptops in the hands of scarlet-clad clergy, microphones that poke and prod at writhing figures, computer mice that float about, tethered by cords that bind nubile women, and London's distinctive red telephone booths, which double as confessionals. Such imagery seems to suggest that technology has instigated new and insidious forms of torture.

David Wojnarowicz, who died in 1992 of AIDS, also expressed disgust for the hypocrisy and sanctimony of the powers that be. His art, particularly that made after his diagnosis, was a cry of rage at the indifference of religious and government institutions to the AIDS epidemic. Whether working in painting, photography, performance, or film, Wojnarowicz created a very personal vocabulary drawn from an eclectic range of sources. His collage-like paintings combine painted cartoon images, stream-of-consciousness texts, bits of maps, and fragments of pornographic photographs, pieced together to create surrealistic tapestries whose meanings lie in their associations. Wojnarowicz divided reality into what he referred to in his voluminous writings as the pre-industrial "World" of authentic feeling and experience and the "Pre-Invented World" of technology, science, language, law, official history, and coercive social structures into which we are born. The split between the two reflects the split between nature and culture, between the spiritual and material worlds. In *Excavating the Temples of the New Gods*, 1986, Wojnarowicz suggests the two sides. Among the symbols of the false idols of culture found here

MASAMI TERAOKA

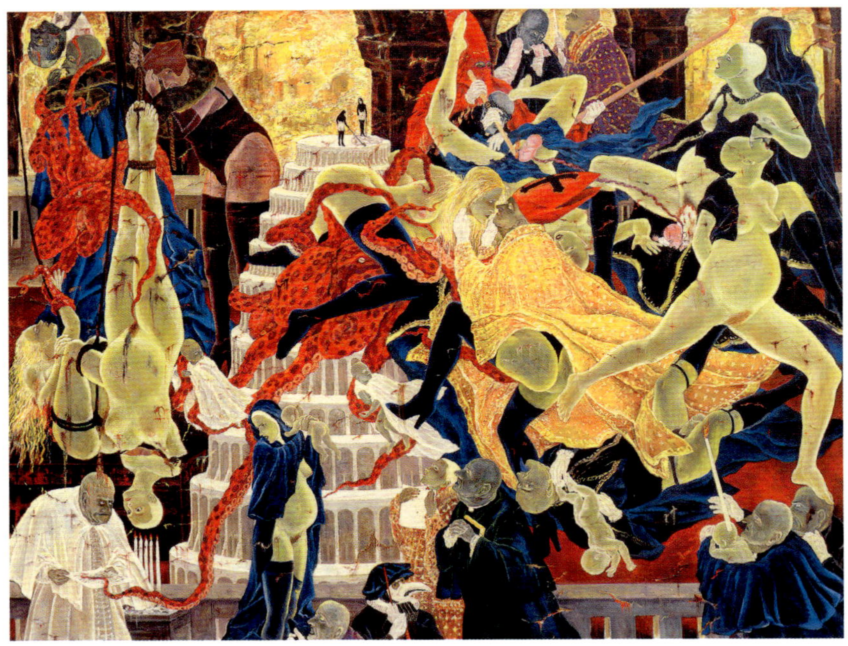

Virtual Inquisition/The Pope of Thong, 2003
Oil on canvas, 77 1/2 x 100 1/2 in (196.9 x 255.3 cm)

are factory chimneys, a field of five-dollar bills, a map delineating arbitrary national borders, and a giant animal-like form created of machine parts, old tires, abandoned cars, and other detritus of industrial society. But all is not lost, the painting seems to suggest: signs of optimism appear in the form of ritualistic personages representing genuine spirituality.

Where Wojnarowicz offers glimmers of hope among ruin, Enrique Chagoya presents a deceptively friendly veneer behind which political supremacy and cultural dominance lurk. In Chagoya's hands Western cartoon characters such as Mickey Mouse, Superman, and the Seven Dwarfs represent a self-serving and misguided colonial impulse. Frequently joined by figures borrowed from pre-Columbian and colonial religious art, they enact satirical tableaux that underscore the venality and destructiveness of American power and religious authority. In *Their Freedom of Expression . . . The Recovery of Their Economy*, 1984, for instance, Chagoya comments on American imperialism in the context of the culture wars by depicting Ronald Reagan as a wizened Mickey Mouse in the company of a miniature Henry Kissinger in the same guise. The former is midway through scrawling one dictate ("Russkies and Cubans out of Central Ame . . ."), while the latter adds his two cents: "By the way, keep art out of politi . . ." Chagoya works in a variety of media, among them drawings, monotypes, etchings, and paintings. Sometimes he superimposes his own imagery over reproductions of vintage European prints, symbolically reclaiming the voice of the indigenous peoples who are often stereotyped in these depictions. Other works parody pre-Columbian codices, transforming books created by the Mayans to record their history into artifacts that might have been left by clueless colonizers attempting to classify civilizations they did not understand.

Paul Chan's animated cartoons also offer a remarkable stew of cultural references, ranging from rap to Samuel Beckett to Henry Darger to Goya. Created in a deliberately low-tech style of digital rendering resembling early video games or retro cartoons like *South Park*, Chan's works are generally presented as large-scale, double-sided projections. Their stories are ambiguous, but they are filled with indelible set pieces. *My Birds . . . Trash . . . The Future*, 2004, is a seventeen-minute digital video set in a barren landscape dominated by a single dead tree that recalls the setting for Beckett's existential drama *Waiting for Godot*. A flock of mangy birds inhabit the tree, which becomes a backdrop for characters including a naked and shivering Pier Paolo Pasolini, the murdered Italian filmmaker, and Biggie Smalls, the rapper killed in a drive-by shooting. There is also a windstorm of flying papers generated by a Microsoft screen-graphic program, an invasion of hunters and copulating refugees, and a tableau of bodies hanging from the tree that recalls the more gruesome images in Goya's series "Disasters of War." *1st ~~Light~~*, 2005, an animation of falling objects projected onto the floor, is equally mournful, its tower-like shaft of light and cascading bicycles and bodies clearly alluding to the tragedy of September 11. Despite such poignancy and power, Chan, an openly devout activist, has noted repeatedly in interviews that he keeps his politics separate from his art. Drawing such a distinct line between the two suggests that there are tensions and complexities in making politically engaged art.

Artists such as Teraoka, Wojnarowicz, Chagoya, and Chan use the vocabulary of cartoon and caricature to deflate the omnipotent and present the atrocities of contemporary society in a new light. Part of the power of their work comes from the transposition of popular imagery into a high-art context. By contrast, Art

DAVID WOJNAROWICZ

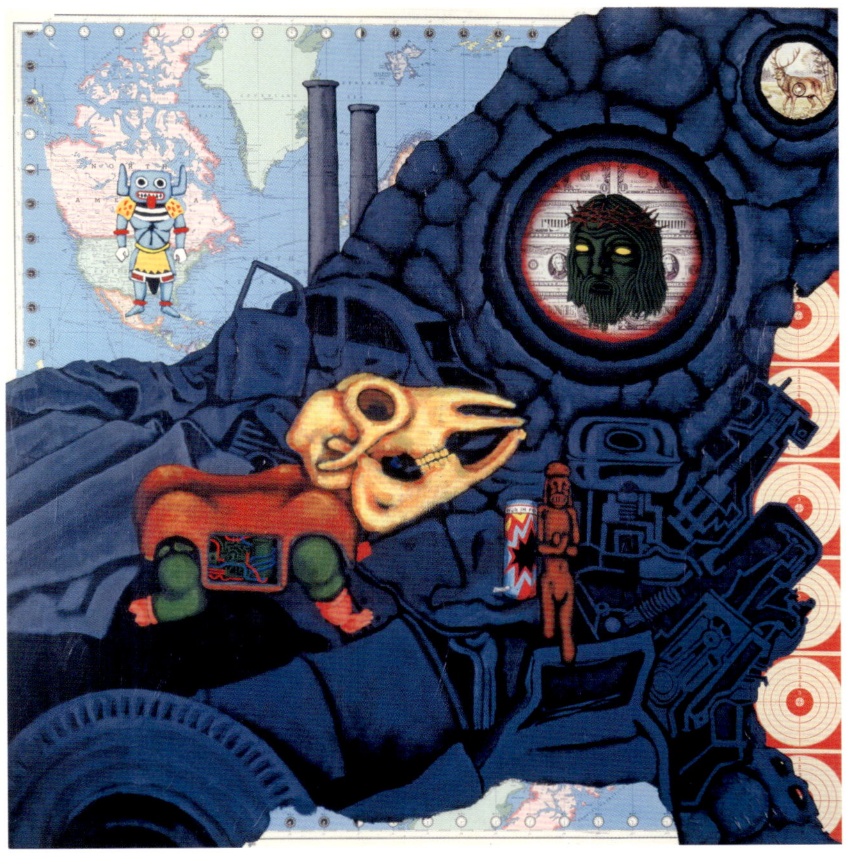

Excavating the Temples of the New Gods, 1986
Acrylic and collage on Masonite, 48 x 48 in (121.9 x 121.9 cm)

ENRIQUE CHAGOYA

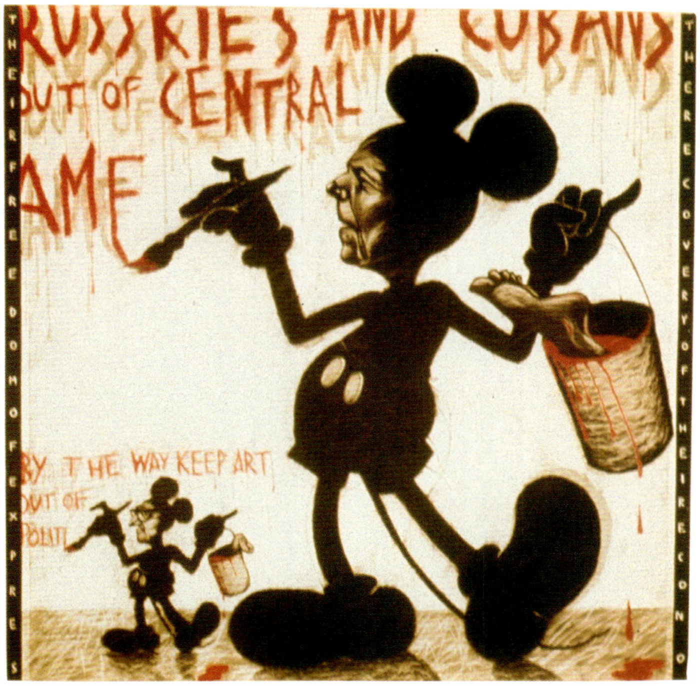

Their Freedom of Expression...The Recovery of Their Economy, 1984
Charcoal and pastel on paper, 80 x 80 in (203.2 x 203.2 cm)
San Jose Museum of Art, Calif.

ART SPIEGELMAN

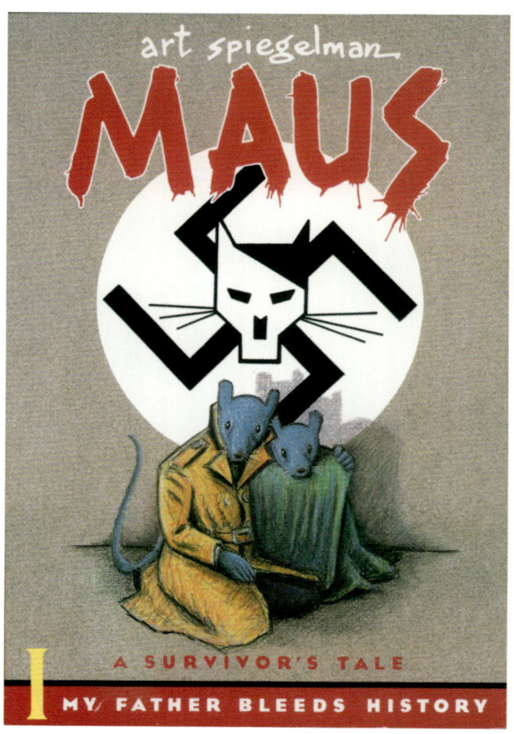

Maus: A Survivor's Tale, 1992
Book cover

Spiegelman and Sue Coe bring the breadth and seriousness of high art back into the popular genres that have inspired so many politically concerned artists. Spiegelman injects complex social and political commentary into the medium of the alternative comic book. Though his work has appeared in major museum exhibitions, including a solo show at the Museum of Modern Art in New York, he has operated largely outside the art world proper. His graphic narratives appear in *RAW*, the graphic magazine he created with his wife, Françoise Mouly, in the 1980s, in full-size "graphic novels," and in the pages of publications such as the *New Yorker*. His best-known work, for which he won a Pulitzer Prize in 1992, is the two-volume graphic novel *Maus: A Survivor's Tale*, which recounts his father's experiences of the Holocaust. The scenes constantly shift back and forth from the present day, in which we follow Spiegelman as he attempts to work out his relationship with his emotionally damaged father, to the past, in which we see his father's life in Poland in the run-up to the war and his fierce efforts to survive in the Auschwitz concentration camp. Spiegelman suggests the universality of this conflict between oppressors and victims by depicting Jews as mice and Nazis as cats.

The work of Sue Coe is also as likely to be found in mass-media and alternative publications as in conventional art settings. Drawing on such predecessors as Daumier, Kollwitz, Grosz, and 1930s political photomontage artist John Heartfield, Coe has cultivated a dramatic illustrational style that underscores the horror of the injustices she depicts. Mostly rendered in black and white, with deep shadows and distorted perspectives, her graphic images focus on the human cost of such social maladies as war, rape, homelessness, hunger, AIDS, and racism. Coe also extends her sympathies to the animal kingdom in works that point to the vulnerability and unnecessary suffering of animals in slaughterhouses and scientific laboratories. Many of her works have been published in book form. *How to Commit Suicide in South Africa*, published in 1983, refers ironically to the apartheid government's claims that activists who died in its custody had killed themselves. Mixing hallucinogenic images of a violent interrogation with facts and figures about the history and human toll of apartheid, the book became an organizing tool for students and activists supporting the American boycott against investment in South African stock. More recently, Coe's books *Porkopolis* and *Dead Meat* have been adopted by the animal rights movement. Such works demonstrate Coe's commitment to using art as an activist tool.

Among artists who turn for inspiration to the mass media, borrowing the rhetorical devices of advertising, public service announcements, and news reports to prompt a more critical approach to information, Martha Rosler is a pioneer. Two of her series of collages, separated by over thirty years, emphasize the way in which media reports of violence and destruction overseas are neutralized for audiences back home. "Bringing the War Home: House Beautiful," 1967–72, was created at the time of the Vietnam War, then updated in 2004 to comment on the Iraq war. The original version consists of collaged images of burned, wounded, and napalmed children or slaughtered soldiers superimposed onto the windows and interiors of picture-perfect suburban homes. The 2004 version incorporates into generously appointed domestic interiors images from the Iraq war of amputee veterans, soldiers in desert garb, and the flaming sky of "shock and awe." Juxtaposing the domestic fantasies of shelter magazines with horrific images from a faraway war, Rosler exposes the compartmentalized consciousness that allows life to continue uninterrupted

PAUL CHAN

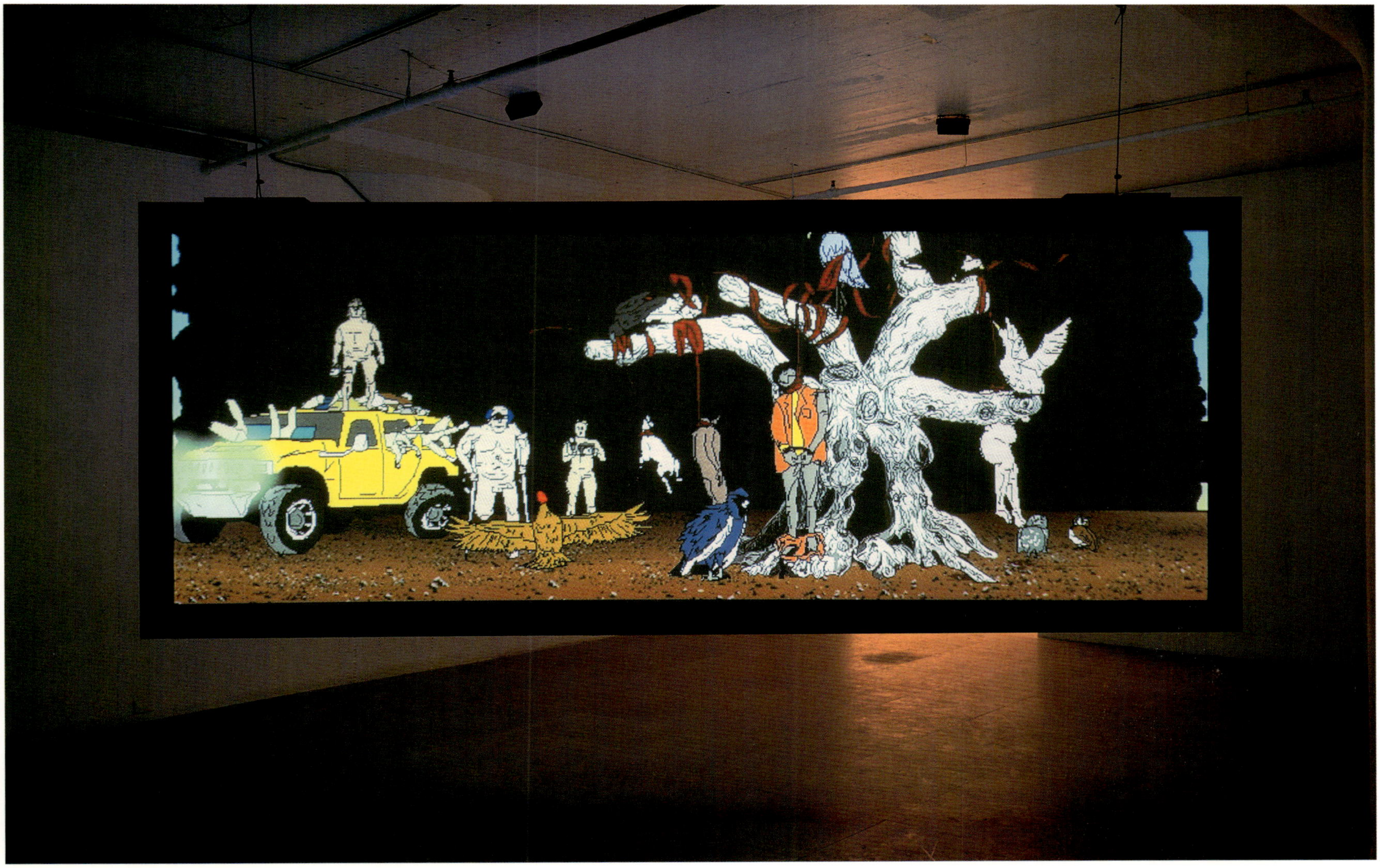

My Birds... Trash... The Future, 2004
Two channel digital projection installation, dimensions variable

SUE COE

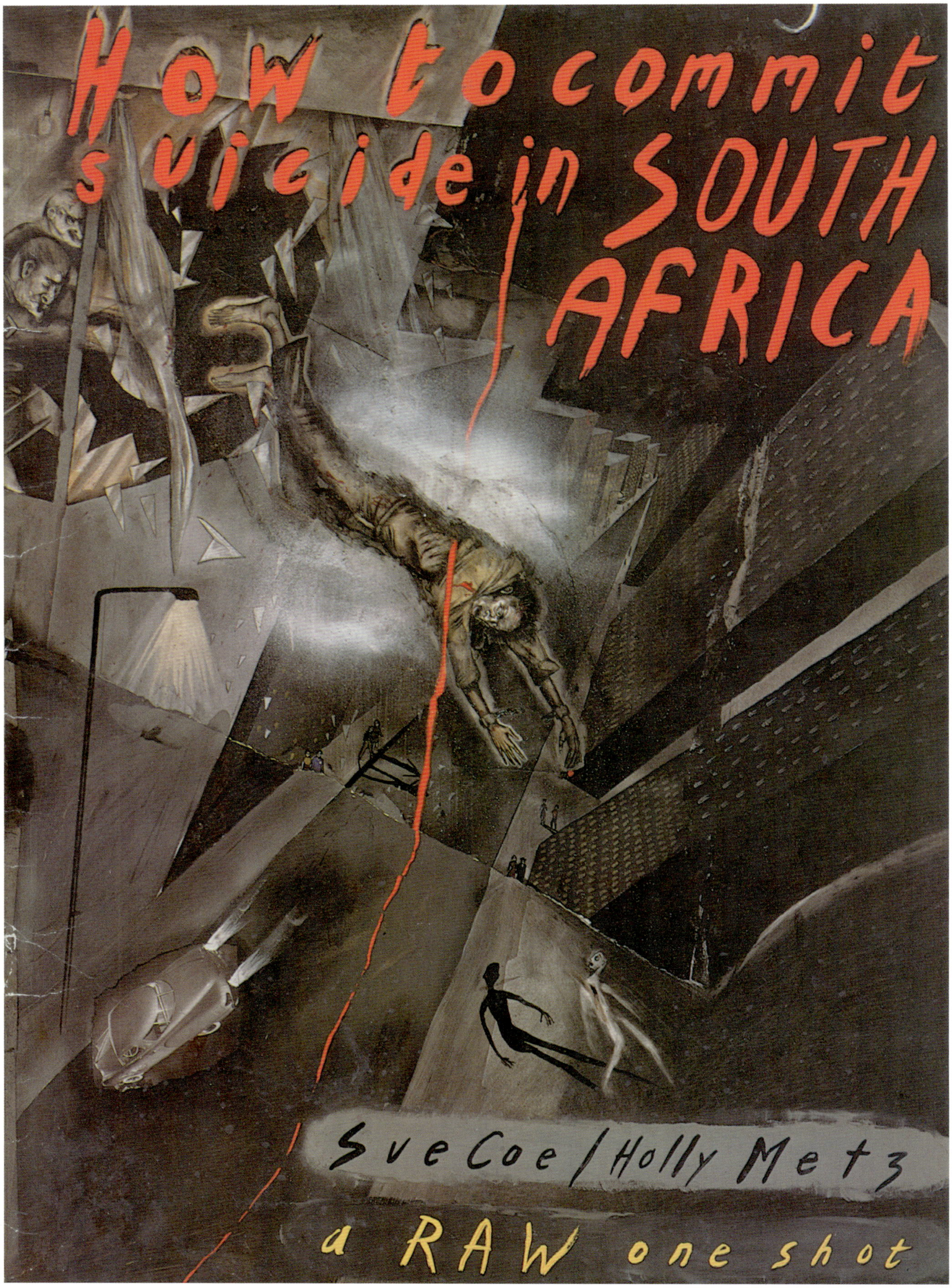

How to Commit Suicide in South Africa, 1983
Book cover

MARTHA ROSLER

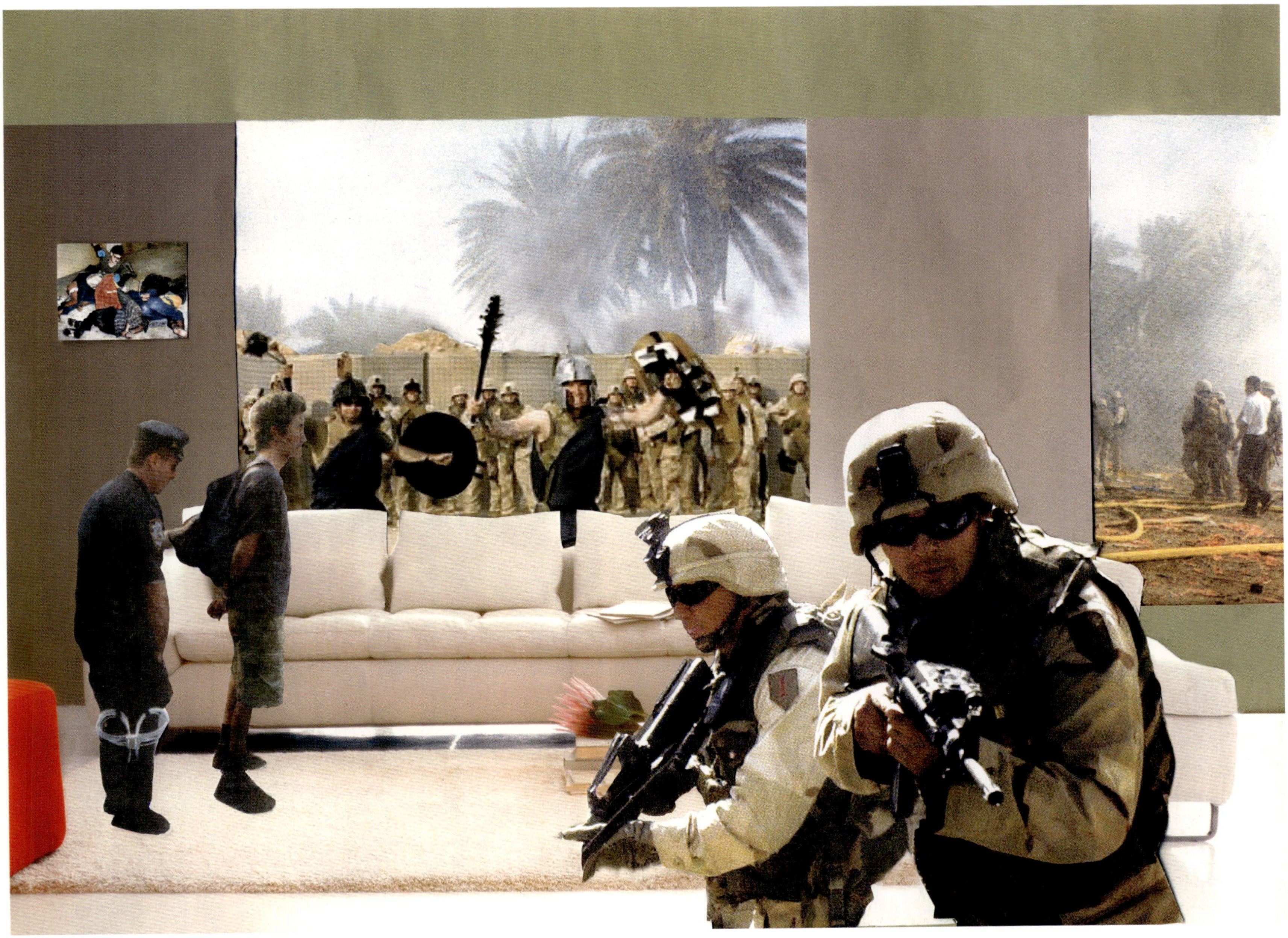

Gladiators, from "Bringing the War Home: House Beautiful," 2004
Photomontage, 20 x 24 in (50.8 x 61 cm)

despite news reports of unimaginable horrors elsewhere, making it impossible for viewers to persist with their easy dismissal of unpleasant realities. Rosler's videos, photo essays, installations, performances, and texts have addressed not only the lulling deceptiveness of the mass media, but its penetration into every corner of contemporary life, as well as the privatization of formerly public spheres of activity such as urban planning, cultural funding, and political campaigns. Homelessness, poverty, and women's equality have also been key subjects in Rosler's seminal political works.

Such eclecticism of media and subject also mark the work of Group Material, a shifting collective of activist artists who operated in New York from the late 1970s until 1997. Several members, among them Julie Ault and Doug Ashford, formed the ongoing core of the group, while others collaborated at one point or another, among them Andres Serrano, Felix Gonzalez-Torres, and Tim Rollins. In both its organization and the kinds of projects it undertook, Group Material promoted the idea of a participatory democracy, treating culture as a collaborative process in which no distinction is made between artists and non-artists. Similarly, no distinction was made between fine art and mass media. Group Material's exhibitions included the artifacts of high and low culture and invited contributions by artists, activists, and community members. The group had no "home," but rather operated like nomads, installing shows in disparate places, from museum walls to posters on the sides of buses. In particular, group members were interested in forcing "elitist" art institutions to open their doors to a more diverse constituency and a more engaged set of political and social causes. Invited to participate in the 1991 Whitney Biennial, rather than promoting their own careers and points of view, Group Material installed work by other artists, from Leon Golub to LeRoy Neiman (an artist with a wide popular audience but virtually no admirers in the established art world), along with artifacts from the "real world," including magazine articles and loaves of Wonder Bread. The salon-style installation was among the group's "AIDS Timelines," a series begun in 1989 that mapped out a chronology of responses to the crisis by artists, political leaders, and grassroots organizations, and sought to reveal the government's indifference to the disease. With such works, Group Material tore down the barriers between art and politics, bringing an activist consciousness into the heart of the art world.

Group Material took its name from a work by Conrad Atkinson, a leading political artist since the 1960s. Atkinson grew up in an impoverished mining region in northern England, and he brings an underdog's perspective to issues of power, nationalism, immigration policy, and industrially-caused disease. Like his progeny, Group Material, he resists assuming a signature style. He borrows from both popular culture and so-called low art and seeks out non-art venues for his works, among them union halls, subway stations, public buses, and newspapers. Recently he has turned his attention to landmines, recreating them in porcelain and emblazoning them with such iconic images as the English "Willow Pattern," Albrecht Dürer's *Praying Hands*, or the Madonna—as in *Landmine (Madonna and Child with St. John the Baptist)*, 1996—chillingly melding beautiful craftsmanship with the devastating power of actual landmines. "Strike at Brannans," a 1972 exhibition of Atkinson's work at London's Institute of Contemporary Arts, was an early model of the mobilization of media for social change. The exhibition addressed a contemporaneous workers' strike at a thermometer factory, presenting information

GROUP MATERIAL

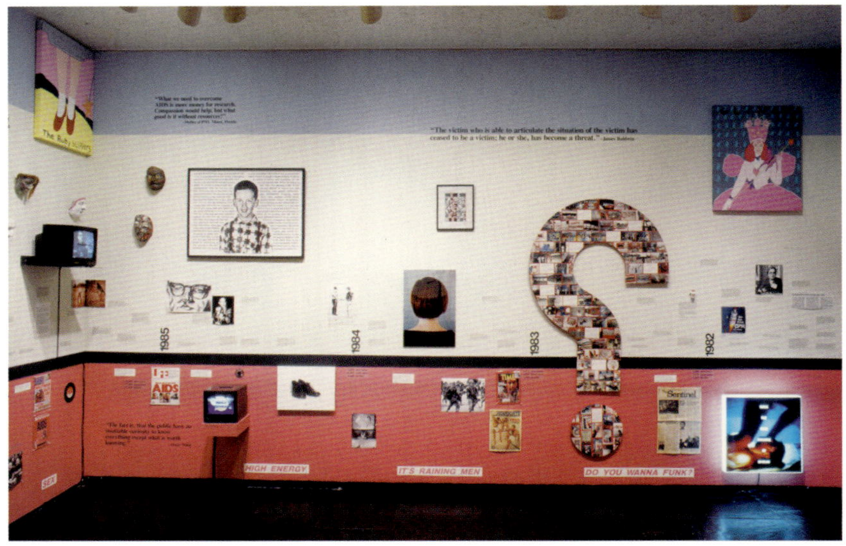

AIDS Timeline, 1991
Mixed media, dimensions variable
As installed at the Whitney Biennial, Whitney Museum of American Art, New York, 1991

CONRAD ATKINSON

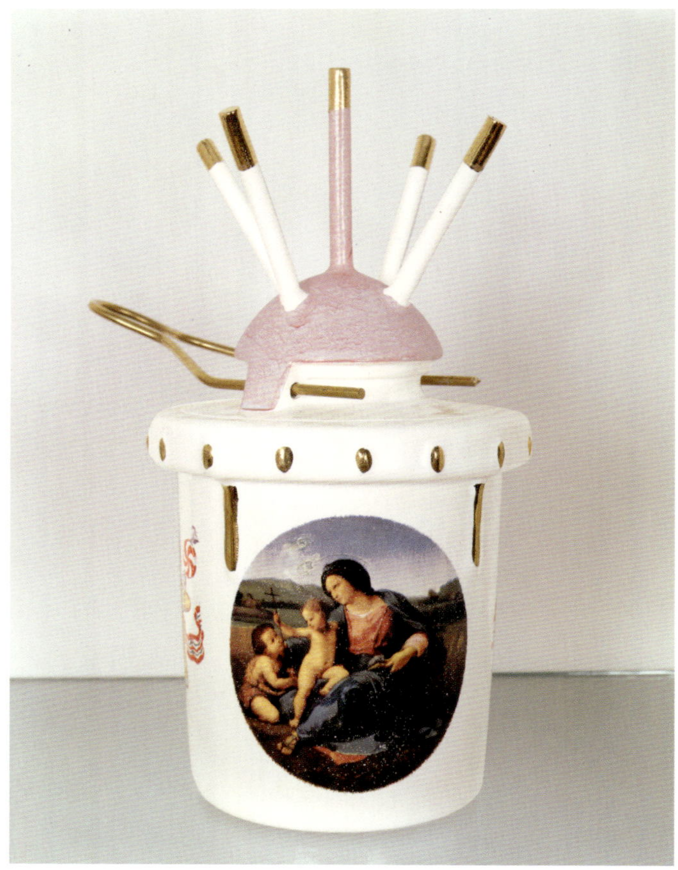

Landmine (Madonna and Child with St. John the Baptist), 1996
Glaze transfer with hand painting on Biscuitware, 9 x 5 x 5.5 in (22.9 x 12.7 x 14 cm)

on the strike including tapes, letters, video, photographs, police documents, newspaper clippings, and a reproduction of the company's 1927 charter, wrought in gold, with the strikers' signatures overprinted in blood-like red. It had real repercussions: the installation generated national publicity for the strikers, who ultimately unionized in London. Further, Atkinson gave money made from selling prints specially created for the show to the strikers' families.

In the decades since Atkinson's watershed show, artists have become increasingly conversant with the mechanisms by which information, entertainment, advertising messages, and propaganda are disseminated to a broad public. Now they not only incorporate those forms but appropriate, emulate, and mix them to "jam" the system or to substitute other, unsanctioned messages. Marcel Odenbach, for example, delves into newsreel film archives of twentieth-century horrors and tragedies, mixing the materials he finds there with snippets of vintage commercials, segments from classic Hollywood films, and contemporary footage, all overlaid with soundtracks that incorporate everything from the music of Bach to movie scores. The resulting videos are kaleidoscopic accounts of the carnage of war and the enduring presence of racial prejudice, political cruelty, and conspicuous consumption. These are not narratives in any conventional sense, but rather tapestries of sound and image that suggest the way ordinary life is invaded by memories and images of past and present horrors. Odenbach often uses multiple video monitors to accentuate a sense of fragmented reality. In his video installation *Eine Faust in der Tasche Machen (Make a Fist in the Pocket)*, 1994, one wall features a large projection that mixes idyllic scenes of Thai life with violent images of skinheads in Germany. On the opposite wall are monitors offering archival footage of the international uprisings, demonstrations, and government reprisals that dominated world news in 1968. Interspersed are clips of Nazi book burnings and clacking typewriters. Thus the viewer, caught in the middle, is invited to contemplate the unhealthy relationship between political violence and the media that reports and sometimes aggravates it.

Jenny Holzer appropriates both the slogan-like one-liners and the physical apparatus of advertising and mass media, particularly LED electronic-sign technology, in her subversions. Holzer began her career in the late 1970s in New York, where she anonymously wheat-pasted posters with her signature "Truisms"—trite, presumptuous statements on a variety of subjects—on walls throughout Manhattan. Playing off the urban audience's immersion in constant messages, she soon turned to LED, moving-type signage, which, whether outdoors or in museums—like her 1989 installation at the Guggenheim in New York, *Various Texts*—recalls the visual cacophony of Times Square or the news-feed updates that run beneath talking heads. In a quieter mode, she has incised her messages on park benches or sarcophagi. Holzer's "Truisms" offer a mix of contradictory social, political, and psychological positions. One series from 1977 contained such disparate remarks as "Abuse Of Power Should Come As No Surprise," "An Elite Is Inevitable," "Any Surplus Is Immoral," and "Money Creates Taste." A much reproduced statement from Holzer's "Survival Series," 1983–85, displayed on posters and on the Times Square Spectacolor billboard, pleaded "Protect Me From What I Want." Such disjointed litanies deliberately imitate and undermine the authoritative, even propagandistic tone of advertisements, public service announcements, and so-called opinion leaders, encouraging viewers to question these stealthy, often disembodied voices.

MARCEL ODENBACH

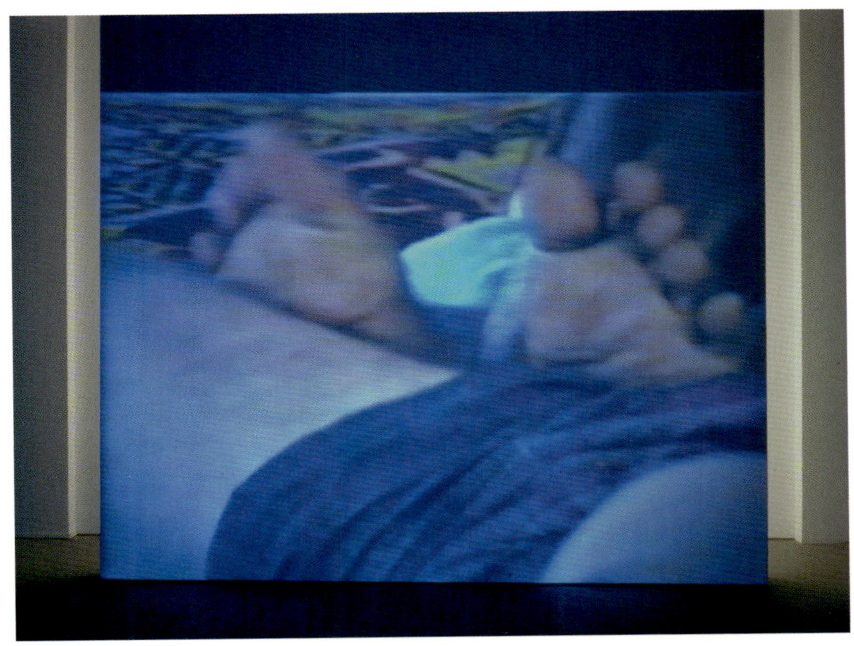

Eine Faust in der Tasche machen (Make a Fist in the Pocket), 1994
Video installation, 8 videotapes

JENNY HOLZER

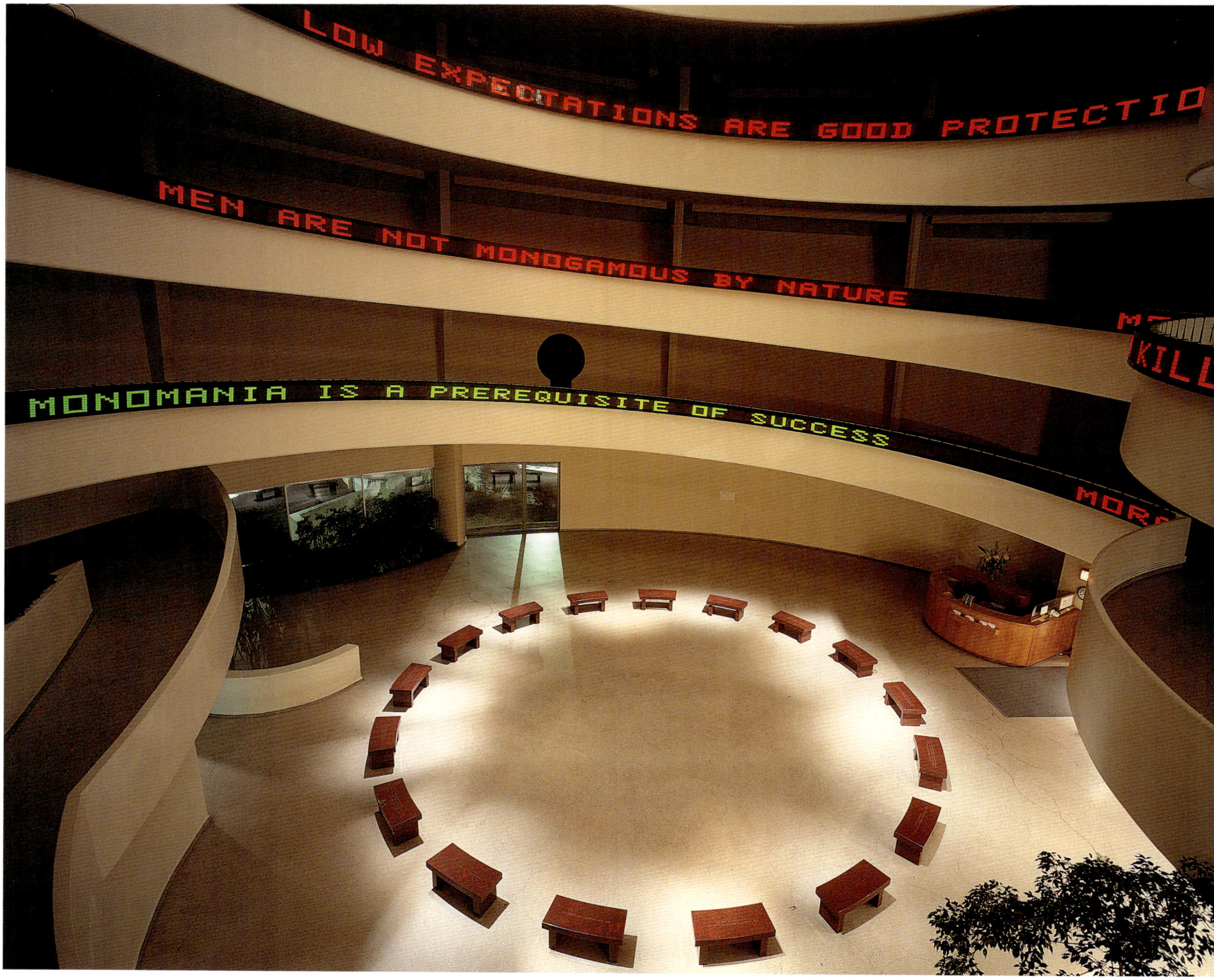

Various Texts, 1989
Extended helical tricolor LED signboard, 17 Indian Red granite benches
Sign length 513 ft (156.5 m); benches 42 x 18 x 17 in (106.7 x 45.7 x 43.2 cm) each
As installed at the Solomon R. Guggenheim Museum, New York, 1989–90

The advent of the Internet poses new possibilities for politically active artists. A contemporary version of the newsreel and the populist broadside or pamphlet, the Internet allows for the expression of uncensored, unofficial views, opinion, and political dialogue. Given its broad reach, it also has proved a useful tool for artists seeking an audience outside conventional art-world settings. The collective Yes Men uses Web sites and other media outlets to interfere with the messages of mainstream corporate entities. In 2000 they set up a mock Web site that claimed to represent the World Trade Organization and solicited speaking engagements at various international conferences. Masquerading as real WTO representatives, Yes Men members gave lectures designed to point up the absurdity of various World Trade policies. For instance, they maintained that the U.S. Civil War was unnecessary, because slave labor is now available throughout the underdeveloped world. They also proposed that democratic elections be replaced with Internet sales of votes. In 2002 the Yes Men purported to represent Dow Chemical, which refused to accept responsibility in the 1984 chemical spill at its newly purchased subsidiary's Union Carbide factory in Bhopal, India, which cost the lives or health of hundreds of thousands of local residents. The ruse culminated in a broadcast interview with the BBC on the twentieth anniversary of the disaster. Posing as a Union Carbide spokesperson, one of the Yes Men offered the company's apology for the accident and promised a multi-billion dollar compensation package for the victims. Following the broadcast, Dow's share price fell 4.2 percent in twenty-three minutes, wiping $2 billion off its market value, and forcing the real company to issue an immediate disclaimer.

The Guerrilla Girls, a group of women artists so named for their subversive tactics and for the gorilla masks they don to preserve their anonymity, took their message to the street, another aptly public location for political art. The group formed in 1984 in response to the scarcity of women artists in museums and major galleries, particularly in the Museum of Modern Art's "International Survey of Recent Painting and Sculpture," in which only 19 among 169 artists were women. Wearing their trademark gorilla masks and short skirts, the Guerrilla Girls attacked the anti-female bias of the art world with a combination of theatrics, humor, and incisive critique, surreptitiously plastering the walls of SoHo, then the center of New York's art scene, with graphic posters offering statistics on the dismal representation of women and "others" in major museums, galleries, and art magazines. No one was immune, not even fellow artists. One poster asked: "What do these artists have in common?" It then listed artists' names and answered: "They allow their work to be shown in galleries that show no more than 10 percent women artists or none at all." Another queried rhetorically: "Do women have to be naked to get into the Met. Museum?" Publicly shaming the powerful proved highly effective, as individuals and institutions scrambled to improve their ratings. Meanwhile, the Guerrilla Girls have become celebrities in their own right, invited to give lectures, appear on television, and be interviewed for mass-circulation publications—all in their gorilla masks, of course.

Like Holzer and the Guerrilla Girls, Krzysztof Wodiczko turns the street into a stage, using pre-existing structures as a template for his concerns. Wodiczko remains best known for projecting loaded photographic images on the facades of corporate and government buildings during the 1980s. Through the juxtaposition of image and architecture, he dramatized the hidden values embodied in these heroic-

YES MEN

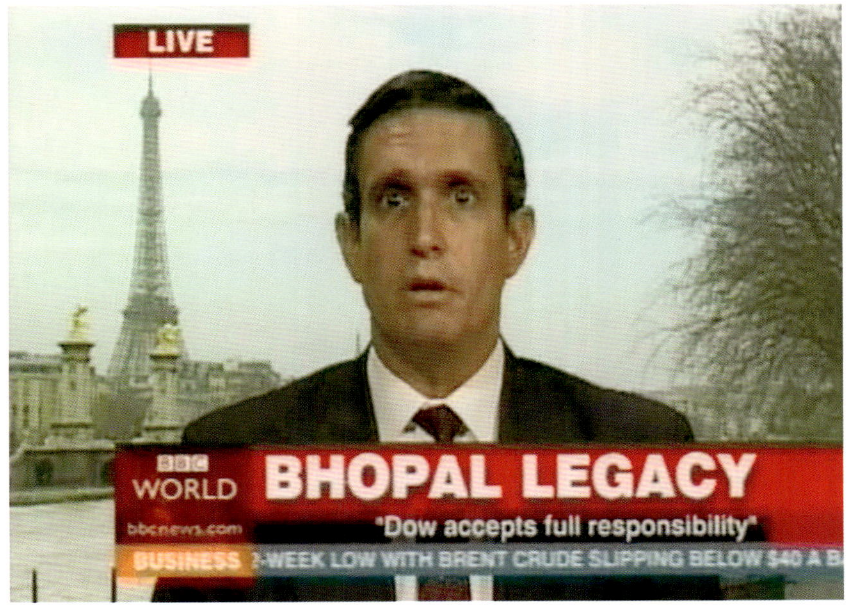

Yes Men Score a Hit for Bhopal, 2002
Television broadcast

GUERRILLA GIRLS

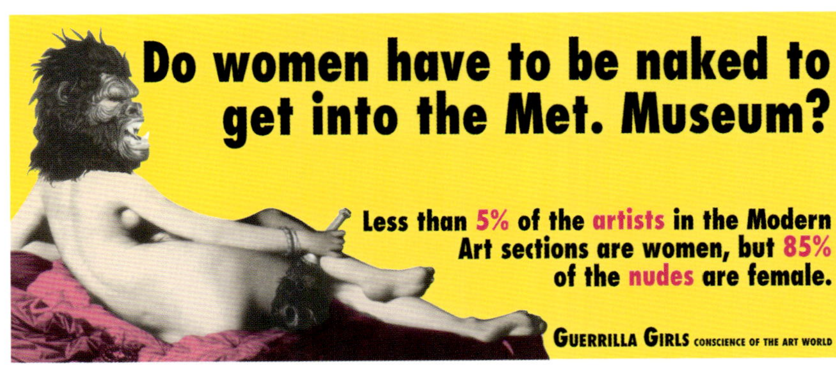

Do women have to be naked to get into the Met. Museum?, 1989
Poster, 11 x 28 in (27.9 x 71.1 cm)

KRZYSZTOF WODICZKO

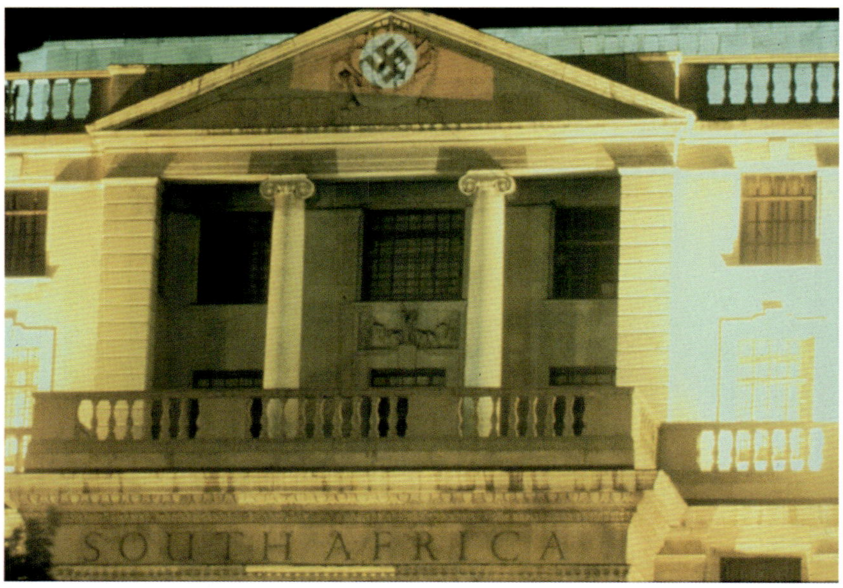

Projection, South Africa House, London, 1985
Projected for two hours, Trafalgar Square, London,
August 1985

JIM COSTANZO (FOR REPOHISTORY)

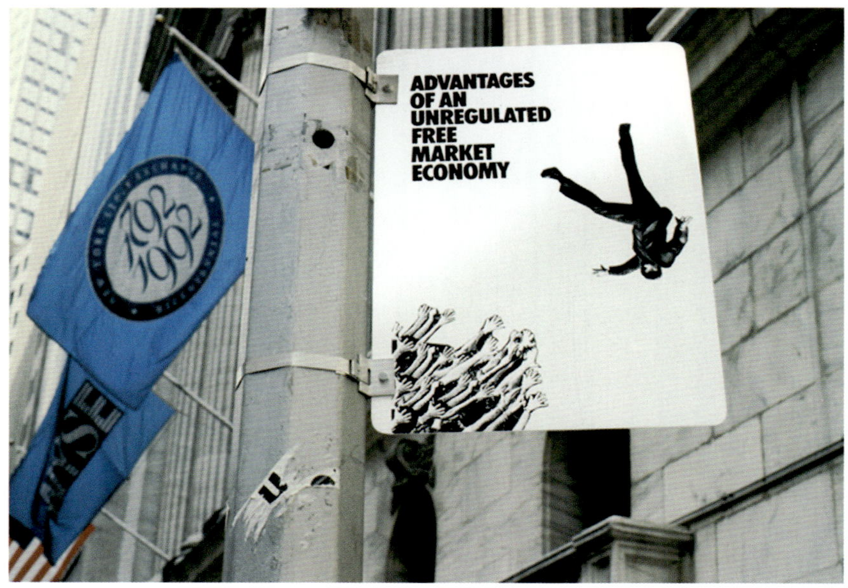

Lower Manhattan Sign Project, Sign #14, 1992
Mixed media, 24 x 18 x 1/8 in (61 x 45.8 x .3 cm)

looking structures. For example, by projecting an image of a bank of microphones, flanked by hands holding a gun and a candle, on Washington, D.C.'s Hirshhorn Museum at the time of the 1988 presidential election, he highlighted the contrasting political options of peace or war. In his *Astor Building*, 1984, he superimposed chains and padlocks over a high-rent New York apartment building, suggesting how gentrification makes housing prohibitively expensive for the ordinary city resident. In most cases, Wodiczko received official permission to conduct these interventions. One unsanctioned projection, which lasted very briefly given its incendiary message, involved the juxtaposition of a swastika over the South African Embassy in London in 1985, at the height of the apartheid era. Wodiczko has since moved on to create more-or-less functional street artifacts that suggest, with sly absurdity, how victims of social and economic inequalities might empower themselves. His "Homeless Vehicles," 1987–89, look like shopping carts, but they ingeniously unfold to provide their homeless owners with compartments in which to sleep, wash up, and store refundable recyclables. Thus these simple carts ostensibly turn invisible and impoverished members of society into self-sufficient, independent entrepreneurs.

The street is also the primary canvas for a group of New York–based artists and writers who came together in the late 1980s under the name REPOhistory. In keeping with their name (REPOhistory is shorthand for repossessing history), the group's avowed mission is to unearth lost or forgotten past events and combine them with current politics. Their work tends to be site-specific and information based. *Lower Manhattan Sign Project*, 1992, for instance, consisted of street signs that mimicked the Chamber of Commerce–style historical markers typically found in tourist districts, but their versions highlighted the overlooked political and social struggles of minorities and others who have drawn the short straw. Reflective of REPOhistory's emphasis on democracy and participation, each sign was designed by a different artist in a different style, and chronicled such events as strikes, incidents of police brutality, and public interest lawsuits over housing discrimination. *Sign #14*, by Jim Constanzo, was placed near the New York Stock Exchange. It recalled the rash of suicides that followed the 1929 market crash with an image of a falling figure and text memorializing the individual brokers who died not by their own fault, but due to a systemic failure brought on by the deregulation of the economy.

The projects of artists and groups such as Holzer, Wodiczko, Guerrilla Girls, and REPOhistory often consist of temporary interventions into the shared spaces of urban life. They are, in other words, among the work known as public art. Public art ranges from the banal—what Claes Oldenburg once referred to unflatteringly as "the turd in the plaza"—to projects that actively engage the specific history, community needs, or cultural memory of a particular population or neighborhood. While public art has a long history, going back to the pyramids of Egypt and the once ubiquitous equestrian statues in town squares, its recent form has been shaped by debates over the "ownership" of public space, conflicts between public and private interests, and the degree to which the desires and needs of local communities should determine the public planning process.

A seismic event in the evolution of thinking about public art occurred in 1989, when public outcry led to the removal of Richard Serra's *Tilted Arc* from Federal Plaza in downtown Manhattan. *Tilted Arc*, commissioned by the U.S. Government's Percent for Art program in 1981, was a 120-foot-long curtain of steel placed diagonally across the plaza. Almost from the beginning, office workers in the two buildings fronting the plaza complained that the sculpture cut off their access and views, cast deep shadows on what was already a rather bleak square, and was simply a magnet for graffiti. In 1988, when a movement formed to remove *Tilted Arc*, artists and art professionals turned out in force to defend the work, and Serra himself rather infamously announced: "Art is not supposed to be democratic. It is not for the people."[5] In late 1989, following massive community protests, public hearings, and a rash of finger pointing across the art/public divide, the work was unceremoniously torn down and its pieces placed in what has turned out to be permanent storage.

The uproar wasn't quite over then. *Tilted Arc* initiated a radical reconsideration on the part of both artists and government administrators about the meaning of public art. In particular, the debacle contributed to a new understanding of the idea of site-specificity, a concept that had emerged in the mid-1960s as part of artists' rejection of modernism's philosophy of the autonomy of the art object. As applied to public art, it referred to the notion that a work's meaning and even its existence as art depended on its relationship to its surroundings. The *Tilted Arc* controversy clinched this idea, as Serra and his supporters argued that the sculpture was inseparable from its setting and thus its removal equaled nothing less than its destruction. Others argued that the physical properties of the site could not be the only criterion in placing public art. In fact, they noted, the problem with *Tilted Arc* was that it responded only to the surrounding architecture and ignored the function of the plaza, the work's audience, and its symbolic role as an emblem of government power. In the wake of these debates, the idea of site-specificity came to incorporate not only formal concerns, but also the work's relationship to the site's history, its uses, and the demands of its multiple constituencies, which dovetailed with discussions in the urban planning sphere about how the public square can reshape citizens' sense of themselves as thoughtful and responsible individuals.

The story of Maya Lin's 1982 Vietnam Veterans Memorial progresses along similar lines—engendering great controversy—but has a very different ending. Like *Tilted Arc*, the Vietnam Veterans Memorial is, in essence, a long, minimalist wall. Stretching across the lawn of the Mall in Washington, D.C., it consists of a pair of black granite slabs, each 246 feet long, set ten feet below grade on a hillside, and installed so that they meet at a right angle at the lowest point in the grade. Incised in the slabs are the names of all of the American soldiers who died in the Vietnam War. Visitors walking the length of the memorial to search out specific names are literally drawn down into the earth as the wall of names grows to tower over their heads. Thus, while the memorial invites viewers to honor the memory of the fallen warriors, it eschews the triumphal quality that so often accompanies traditional war memorials. In this, it reflects the ambivalence that still surrounds the Vietnam War decades after the American withdrawal in 1975. In keeping with the war's difficult history, Lin designed the memorial to resemble a symbolic wound in the land, providing a metaphor for the psychic wound inflicted by the war on the nation's consciousness. Her decision to honor the individual casualties, rather than the war itself, was revolutionary at the time. Lin was still an undergraduate student at Yale University's School of Architecture when she submitted the winning design for an architectural competition. Veterans' groups objected to its abstraction, demanding a more conventional memorial. (In response to their demands, a figurative group

MAYA LIN

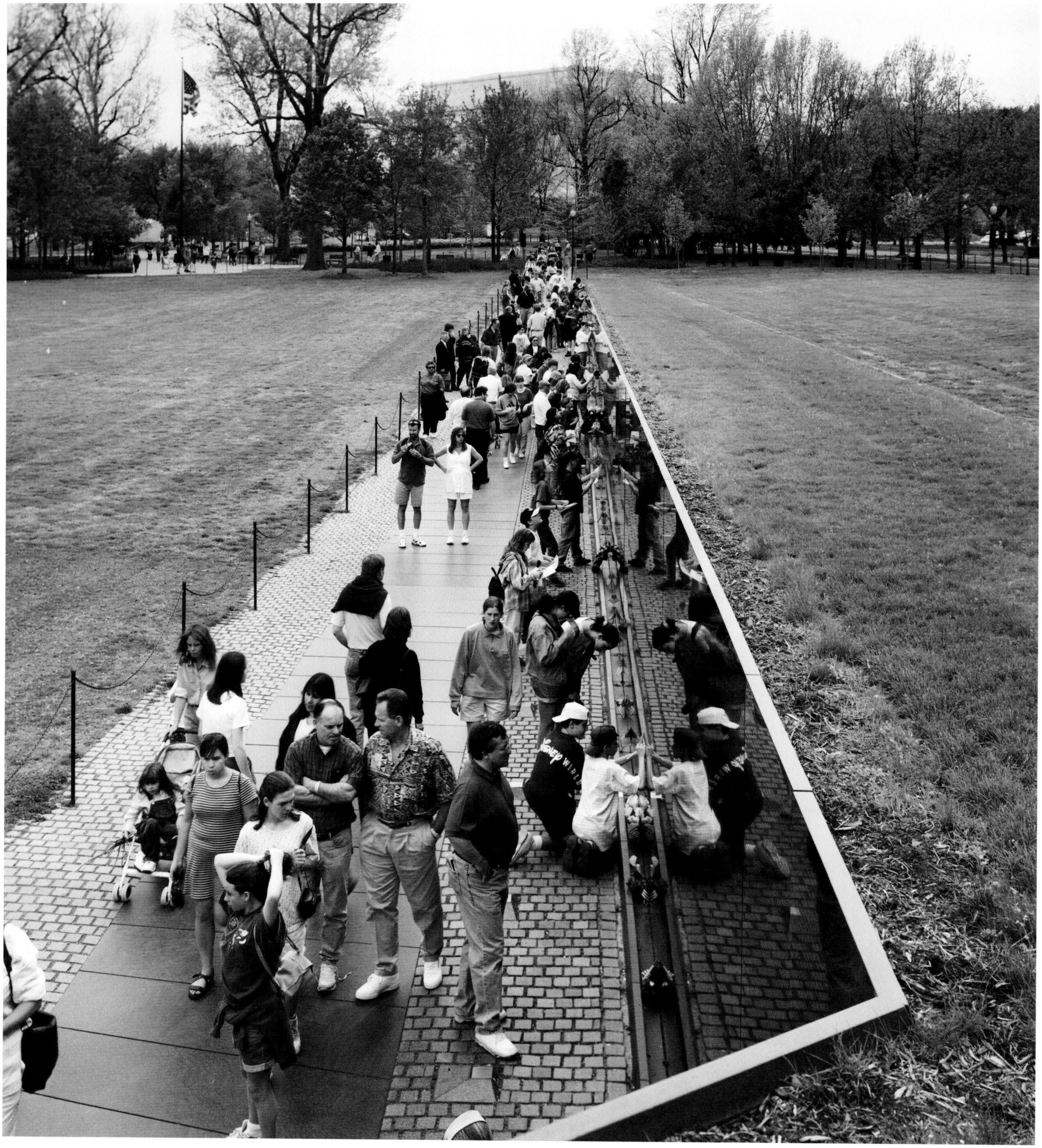

Vietnam Veterans Memorial, 1982
Polished black granite, length 493 1/2 ft (150.4 m), height varies between 8 in (20.3 cm) and 120 in (304.8 cm)
Constitution Gardens, Washington, D.C.

RICHARD SERRA

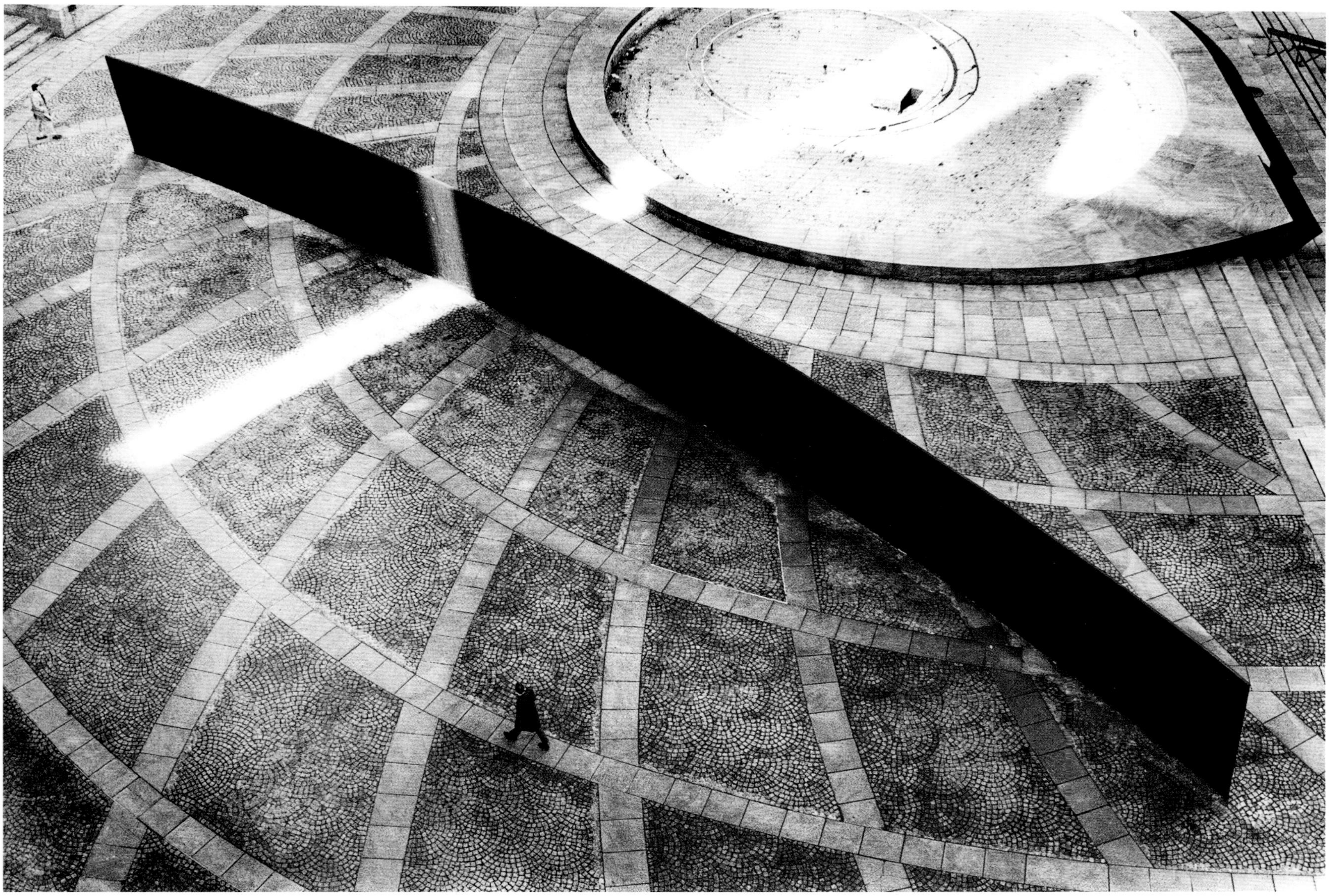

Tilted Arc, 1981
Cor-Ten steel, 12 x 120 ft (3.7 x 36.5 m)
Federal Plaza, New York, destroyed 15 March 1989

GUNTER DEMNIG

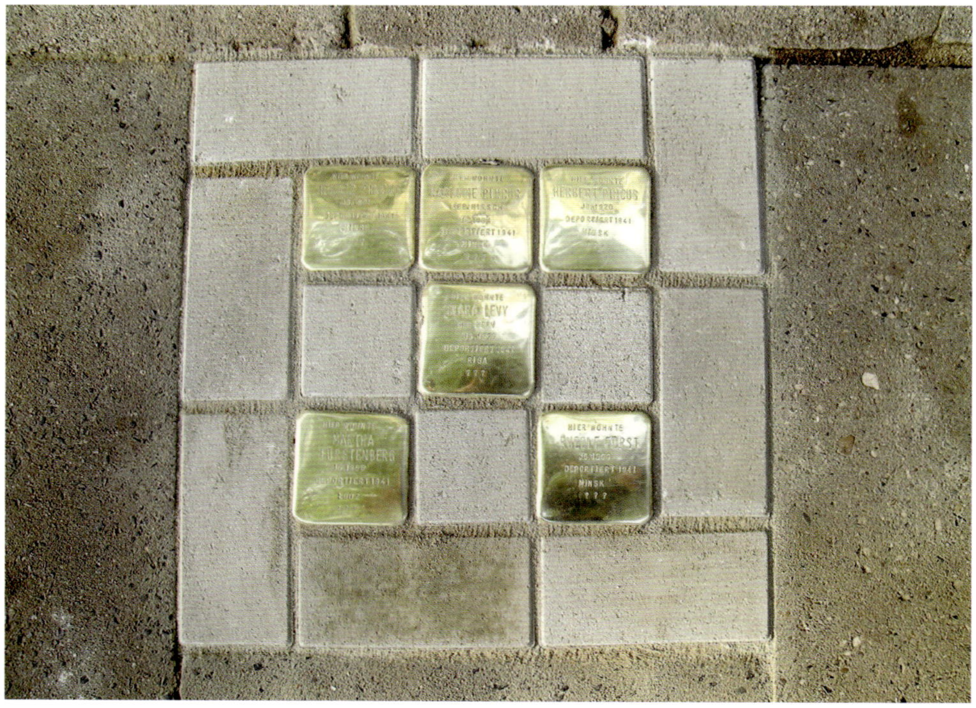

Stolpersteine (Stumbling Blocks), 1993–2007
Paving stones covered with engraved brass plates, dimensions variable

JOCHEN GERZ AND ESTHER SHALEV GERZ

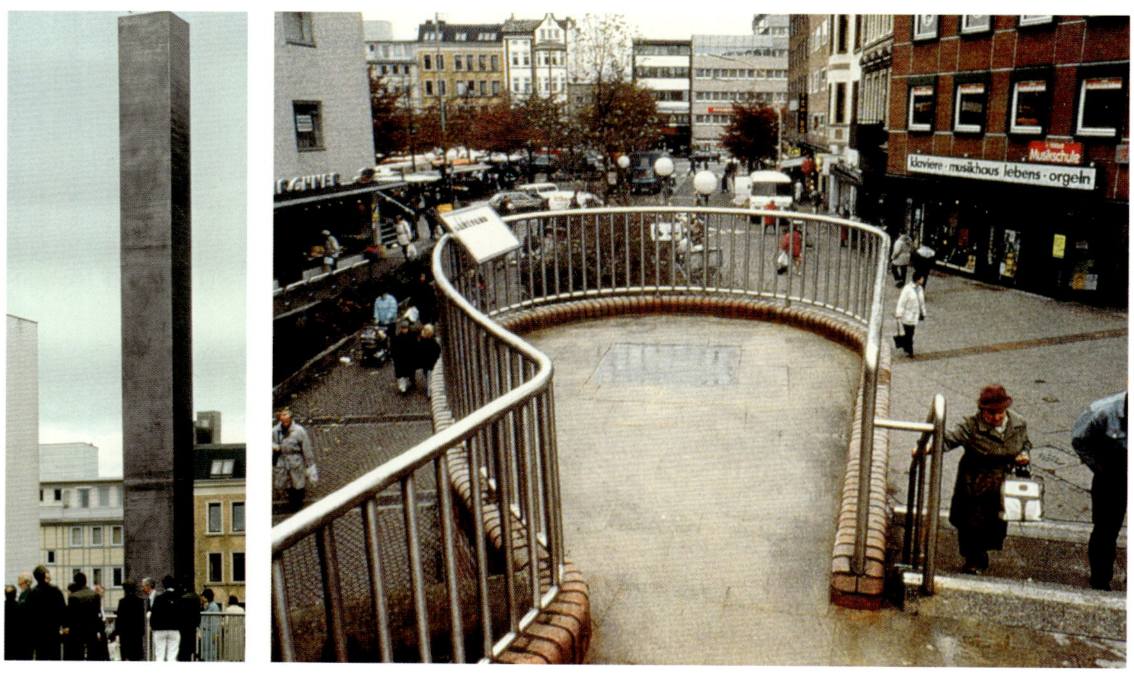

Mahnmal gegen den Faschismus (The Monument Against Fascism), 1986–93
Aluminum structure with a lead sheet cover weighing 7 tons
3 ft 3 in x 3 ft 3 in x 39 ft 4 in (1 x 1 x 12 m)
As installed in Harburg, Germany, 1986 (left) and 1993 (right)

HOUSTON CONWILL, ESTELLA CONWILL MAJOZO, AND JOSEPH DEPACE

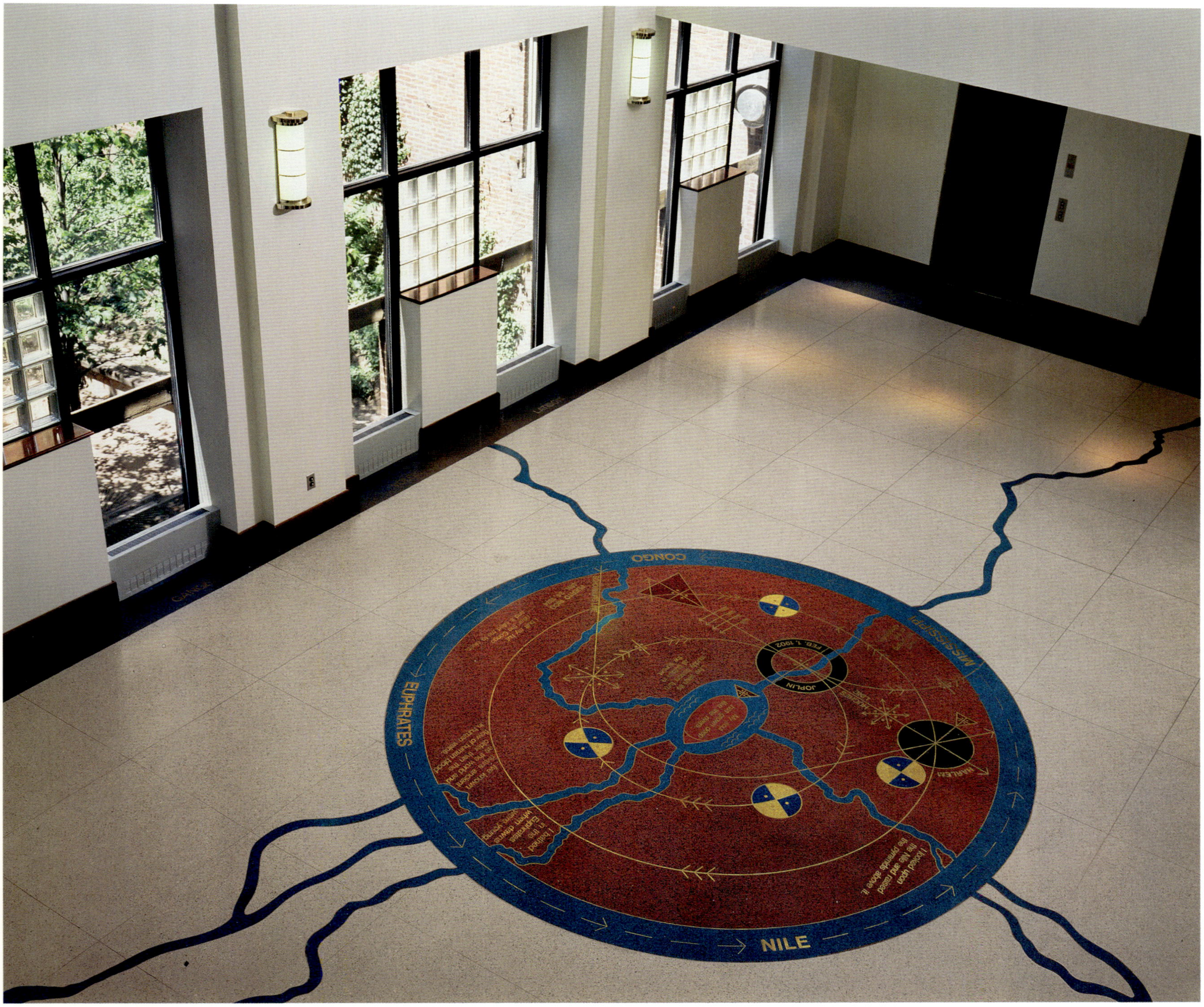

Rivers, 1991
Brass and terrazzo floor, 20 x 40 ft (6.1 x 12.2 m), cosmogram 12 ft (3.7 m)
Installation at the Schomburg Center for Research in Black Culture, New York

sculpture was installed not far from Lin's memorial.) But over time, even they have been won over by the simplicity of the memorial and its respectful treatment of the dead and those who come to mourn them. As a result, the memorial has come to be lauded as a model for public monuments. Today, it is one of the most visited sites on the Mall.[6]

The Vietnam Veterans Memorial suggests one way in which public art can address contentious historical events, and its impact can be felt in the conception of recent memorials to the Holocaust. In Germany, in particular, the Holocaust seems to have almost as many meanings as there are citizens. Questions swirl around its memory. Who should be honored? Who should be held responsible? Can any physical structure contain the immensity of this catastrophe?[7]

Unsurprisingly, given the complexity of this history, official memorial proposals tend to generate bitter controversy; several artists, however, working informally, have managed to capture both the horror and the larger implications of the Holocaust by reaching out to the public in innovative ways. Since 1993 German artist Gunter Demnig has embedded brass plaques bearing the names of thousands of Holocaust victims on cobblestones laid in the streets of the German towns and cities where they lived. Demnig calls these stones, which rise slightly above the regular paving, "Stolpersteine" (Stumbling Blocks), a name that emphasizes the way they interrupt the process by which unpleasant memories and histories are smoothed over by time. Locations for the stones are researched by schoolchildren and patrons, and the modest cost (about $100 U.S. per stone) is covered by private sponsorship. Dispersed, modest in scale, and designed for private contemplation, Demnig's stones self-consciously avoid the monumentalism associated with fascism (and most memorial monuments), in the process suggesting that the best way to avoid paralyzing debates about the meaning of historical events is to skirt official channels altogether.

Another successful "anti-monument" to the Holocaust is one created by German artist Jochen Gerz. Working with his wife, Esther Shalev Gerz, in 1986, he created *Mahnmal gegen den Faschismus* (The Monument Against Fascism), in Harburg, Germany, consisting of a forty-foot pillar set in a plaza in a suburban mall. Passersby were invited to engrave their names on the object, and as a section became covered with signatures the pillar was lowered into the ground, until eventually the whole thing had been buried. This process took seven years, and when it was over, only the memory of the vanishing monument and its sentiments remained. In Saarbrücken, Germany, Gerz created an equally self-immolating anti-monument. Enlisting students in his studio art class, he stealthily uprooted cobblestones from Saarbrücken Schloss, the town square in front of the building that served as Gestapo headquarters during Hitler's rein. The students temporarily replaced these stones with similar ones, then engraved on the original cobblestones the 2,160 names of the locations of abandoned or demolished Jewish cemeteries. These were then restored to the square, placed with the names on the underside. When Gerz publicly announced the guerrilla action, visitors flocked to the square to search in vain for the invisible names. Thus, the memorial itself existed, like the missing cemeteries, only in memory.

Equally as difficult to memorialize as the Holocaust is slavery in America. The artist team of Houston Conwill, Estella Conwill Majozo, and Joseph DePace have taken a community-sensitive approach to site-specificity in their memorials to this dark aspect of history. In what might be seen as a deliberate counter to Richard Serra's formidable wall of steel, they invite passersby to walk over their "cosmograms," circular diagrams embedded in the floors of public lobbies and rotundas. In form, these images draw on the slave tradition of the cakewalk, a late-nineteenth-century ballroom dance whose origins lie in the "ring-shout" worship performances given by plantation slaves for their owner's amusement. In subject, they frequently focus on forgotten or overlooked aspects of a site's African and African American history. They also refer to Congolese cosmograms, which represent the place where the worlds of the living and the dead intersect. *Rivers*, 1991, which is installed at the Schomburg Center for Research in Black Culture in the Harlem neighborhood of New York City, is inspired by the Langston Hughes poem "The Negro Speaks of Rivers," and is located on the floor of the Center over the spot where Hughes's ashes are interred. It incorporates abstract Congolese symbols and verses from the Hughes poem and takes the form of a mandala: its outer edge is inscribed with the names of the four great rivers of the African diaspora; other terrazzo lines represent rivers, meandering through the cosmogram and across the floor of the rotunda, as if drawing life and energy from its center. Thus, in keeping with the idea of the cosmogram as a connection between worlds, *Rivers* ties together past and present, nature and culture, and the realms of spirit and everyday life, while inviting audiences to become part of the history it represents.

A more recent event that has stirred mixed emotions around public memorials is 9/11, and the rebuilding on the site of the World Trade Center in New York. In the years since the terrorist attacks, conflicting sentiments have dogged efforts to create a permanent memorial to the victims of this calamity. But a temporary memorial installed for thirty-two days in spring 2002 captured the combination of sorrow and yearning that New Yorkers felt in the dark months after the attack. This work was the creation of artists Julian LaVerdiere and Paul Myoda (who conceived of the project) and a team of designers. Titled *Tribute in Light*, it was exactly that—two shafts of light created by eighty-eight searchlights that rose in the night sky above Manhattan from the exact site of the fallen towers. This ghostly spectacle served both as a farewell, filling the yawning gap in the city's skyline, and as a symbol of hope, expressing the belief that out of the darkness, light would return again.

Tribute in Light occupies one end of the spectrum of art devoted to politics. Golub's dark visions inhabit the other. Together they point to the diversity and potential of politically oriented art. From despair to hope, from private ruminations to public celebrations, from reworkings of traditional art forms to an embrace of new technologies and new modes of public address, contemporary art in the political mode helps us make sense of the confusions, traumas, and promise of the world.

JULIAN LAVERDIERE AND PAUL MYODA

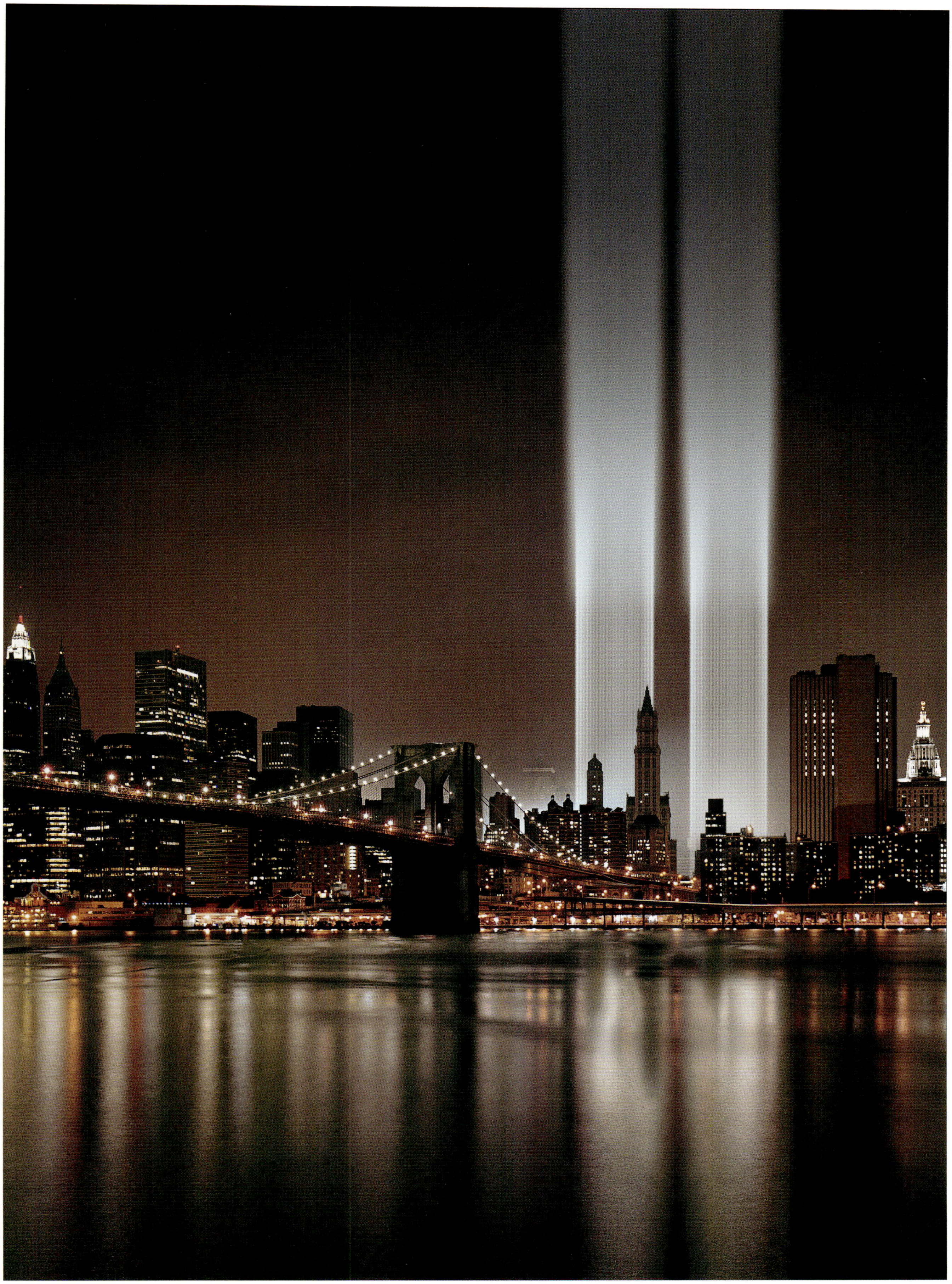

Tribute in Light, 2001
Digital concept rendering

ART & AUDIENCE
REINVENTING THE VIEWER

One of the sacred tenets of the formalist version of modernism was the virtue of disinterested contemplation. In an analogy drawn from the then cutting-edge technology of wireless communication, the early twentieth-century British critic Roger Fry maintained that the artist should be thought of as the transmitter, the art object the medium, and the spectator the receiver of the meaning of a work of art. In essence, the viewer's task was simply to clear away any messy static inhibiting clear reception of the artist's ideas. By the second half of the twentieth century, however, developments both inside and outside the art world began systematically demolishing this article of faith. Minimalism, for example, which seemed on one hand to be the logical extension of formalism's reductive impulse, nonetheless elevated the role of the viewer, who in a sense "completed" the work of art by physically interacting with it. As we have seen, this state of affairs so troubled formalist critic Michael Fried that in 1967, in his essay "Art and Objecthood," he demanded a return of art from this depraved state of "theatricality" to one of "presentness," in which the artwork would again be a self-contained object whose existence is in no way altered or compromised by the presence of the viewer.[1] But Fried's battle was a losing one, as artists throughout the world began to adopt ideas about viewer participation from literary theory, specifically from Roland Barthes's 1968 essay "The Death of the Author," which maintained that the real "author" of any piece of writing was in fact the reader who brought it to life.[2] Even before the publication of this highly influential essay, German scholar Hans Robert Jauss had articulated an important prelude to its premise. His "reception theory" held that the reader/viewer does not passively receive a text, but actively "negotiates" with it to reach an interpretation based on his or her cultural background and personal experiences.[3]

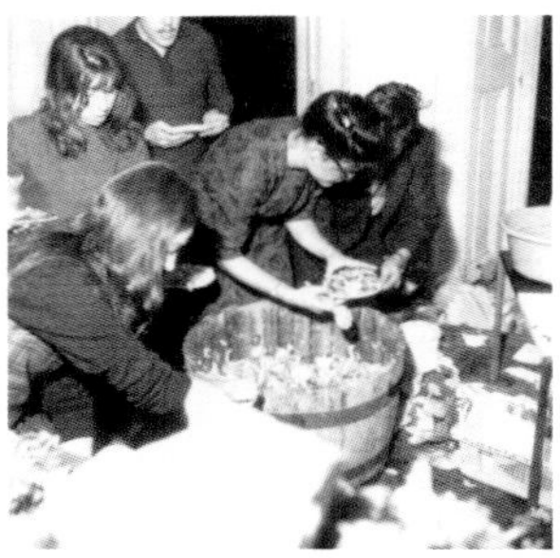

ALISON KNOWLES
PROPOSITION #2: MAKE A SALAD
1962
INSTITUTE OF CONTEMPORARY ARTS, LONDON, OCTOBER 1962

A decade before all of this, an entire art movement coalesced in Europe around another theorist, Guy Debord, author of the 1967 text *The Society of the Spectacle*, which remains influential to this day.[4] Anticipating the notion of "hyper-reality" proposed by Jean Baudrillard in the 1980s, Debord argued that capitalist society had moved from a focus on production to a focus on consumption, in the process perfecting tools to manipulate the masses and transform them into mindless, passive consumers of its goods. These ideas reflected his involvement with the Situationist International (SI), a movement founded in 1957 by Debord and a pan-European group of avant-garde artists devoted to creating revolutionary "situations" designed to shake the viewer's passive acceptance of the role of non-thinking spectator. In practice this involved such actions as appropriating images and texts from the mass media, distributing leaflets, and participating in occupations and student strikes. The SI was active into the early 1970s, and their radical redefinition of the relationship between art and its audience was inspirational in an era of great political and social turmoil, as artists began to experiment with ways to use art to break down what many saw as oppressive power structures.

A more gently anarchic philosophy lay behind such contemporaneous movements as Happenings and Fluxus. The father of the Happening was the late Allan Kaprow, who conceived improvisational performances and events in which the audience's participation was key. Kaprow supplied the place, objects, or props, and perhaps some general guidelines for action, and the rest was up to the audience. Situations defined as Happenings ranged from people being invited to move things around in a furnished room, to gather in the street and all fall down at a specified signal, or to go out into the streets and scavenge for debris. Fluxus, a movement whose leaders included George Maciunas, Wolf Vostell, and Nam June Paik, was similarly freeform. Opposed to the strident ambitions of the Situationists, Fluxus emphasized ephemeral actions and playful interventions into the processes of daily life. Often their works were little more than one-liners, sight gags, or sound events. Under the aegis of Fluxus, for example, Paik spontaneously interrupted his own piano performance to leap into the audience and cut off John Cage's tie, artist Alison Knowles gave a performance in which she came on stage, made a salad, and exited, and Yoko Ono directed an audience to watch the sun until it became square.

Over the past decade the participatory aspect of art has reemerged as "relational aesthetics," a term French critic Nicholas Bourriaud coined in 1997.[5] Bourriaud identified a tendency in the work of various contemporary artists that stresses interaction, interpersonal connection, and the notion of art as a gift. Relational aesthetics describes work by artists who go beyond the idea that an artwork requires completion by the viewer. Instead, the viewers (now more accurately termed participants) and their interactions may actually become the artwork. Bourriaud sees a political significance in this tendency, as artists circumvent capitalist modes of exchange in favor of actions that emphasize collaboration and communication, such as sharing a meal, taking home a piece of an artwork, conversations between strangers, or working with local communities. Such activities, he argues, strengthen bonds that have been weakened by the market economy's emphasis on individuality and consumption. Interestingly, they also dismantle all of the normal mechanisms for gauging the quality and value of an artwork.

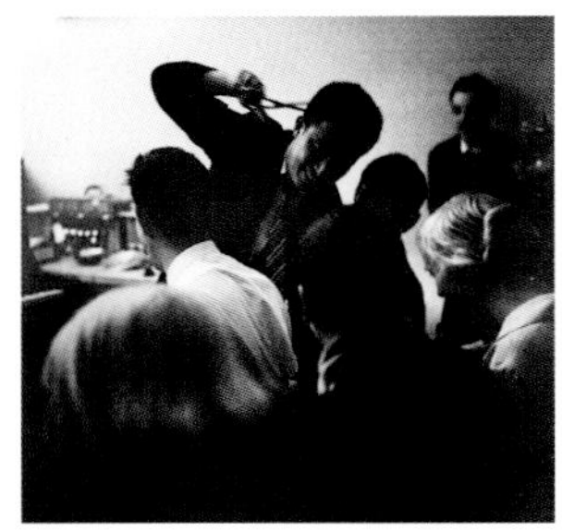

NAM JUNE PAIK
ÉTUDE FOR PIANOFORTE
1960
PERFORMANCE OF THE ARTIST CUTTING OFF JOHN CAGE'S TIE

Among the most important precedents for recent manifestations of participatory art are the works of the late artists Lygia Clark and Hélio Oiticica, who in the 1960s and '70s developed a radically audience-based art against the backdrop of Brazil's increasingly repressive military regime. Both of these artists were originally influenced by Brazil's Constructivist movement of the 1950s, but quickly moved beyond geometric paintings and sculptures to works that engaged the audience's full body and senses. Clark's trajectory began with her first expressions of interactivity, a series of "Bichos" (Animals) from the early 1960s (hinged metal plates that the viewer could manipulate to create various shapes). Her 1963 sculpture *O dentro é o fora* (The inside is the outside) is based on a Möbius strip and allows viewers to physically experience the continuity between inside and outside. Such formal interactive works were followed by Clark's "Propositions," easily replicable props made to be used by the audience. *Stone and Air*, 1966, for example, involved the participant breathing into a plastic bag that held a stone. From these works, Clark progressed to creating wearable hoods, masks, goggles, gloves, and suits meant to alter and extend one's relationship to the outside world. Her final works (Clark died in 1988) are a series of "Relational Objects" made of simple materials such as shells, water, sand, Styrofoam, fabric, and nylon stockings, meant to activate the body's latent memory and aid in emotional healing.

Oiticica, who died in 1980, also found his way from Constructivism to participatory art, but his works often have more political implications. In his early work, like Clark, he subverted the objecthood of conventional sculpture, presenting painted wood constructions that were suspended away from the wall, so that viewers were required to circle around them. From there, he proceeded through a series of increasingly interactive works. Among his best-known works are his "Parangolés" (slang for a situation of sudden confusion or excitement), 1964–79—wearable creations based on colorful Brazilian Samba capes worn by dancers in ritual performances, some of which were emblazoned with anti-authoritarian, inflammatory statements like "I Am Possessed," "I Embody Revolt," and "From Adversity We Live." Oiticica's late works included rooms filled with natural elements such as water, sand, pebbles, straw, and plants or, alternatively, with cultural artifacts such as videos, photographic images, and pop music. Viewers were invited to enter and enjoy themselves in any way they wished.

Among the descendants of Oiticica and Clark is Erwin Wurm, who mixes a bit of Monty Python in with his relational art. His performative "sculptures" are often nothing more than photographs of someone performing an action like sticking out his tongue, videos of people apparently in mortal battle with their clothes, or sets of props and instructions (for example, a set of balls and the directive to "lie on the balls—no part of your body should touch the ground"). Wurm's "Instructions for Idleness," 2001, is like a rule book for anti-social and self-humiliating actions, consisting of a series of photographs of the artist following such commands as "take naps on the office toilet" and "stay in your pyjamas all day." It is not clear how many "viewers" of this work also took up these particular challenges as anything more than a participatory thought experiment.

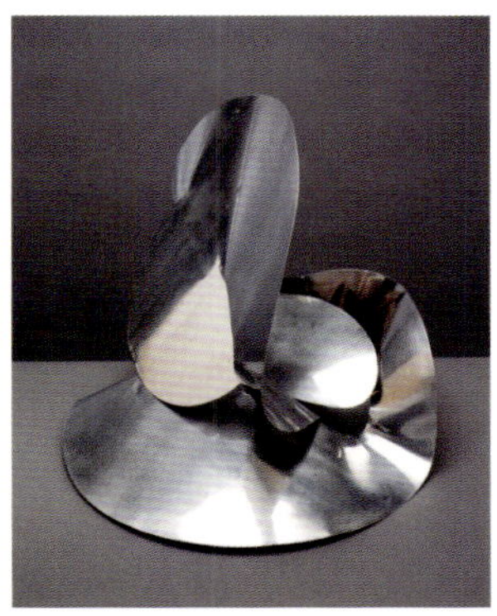

LYGIA CLARK
O DENTRO É O FORA
(THE INSIDE IS THE OUTSIDE)
1963
STAINLESS STEEL ASSEMBLAGE
14 X 18 X 15 IN
(35.5 X 45.7 X 38.1 CM)

Carsten Höller provides spectators with visceral experiences that produce a childlike sense of release and in the process break down utilitarian ways of thinking. Among Höller's creations are long, dark, winding passageways that lead into light-filled rooms. *Upside Down Mushroom Room,* 2000, ends in a chamber filled with giant revolving mushrooms that seem to be growing downward from the ceiling. One model for Höller's work is the carnival ride, which requires that participants master their anxiety to gain catharsis. In 2006 Höller made this connection explicit by installing sculptures at Mass MoCA in the United States that were based on carnival rides from his childhood. Even when his works do not involve actual motion, the idea of travel is implied. *The New World Race,* 1999, for instance, transformed the Moderna Museet in Stockholm into a racetrack, with lanes on the floor and a set of unlikely vehicles (including a bathtub and a pair of child's lederhosen held aloft by a flock of stuffed seagulls) installed for the imaginary competition. Other works involve flying machines or tube-like slides that carry viewers from one floor of a building to another. Despite the echoes of childhood playgrounds, the slides are designed as prototypes for transportation in an imaginary futuristic society, suggesting that Höller has aims that go beyond mere entertainment.

Even more cathartic (on the part of the artist anyway) are the performance/installations of John Bock, who has cited the influence of Kaprow's Happenings and a pantheon of art world and theatrical figures ranging from Joseph Beuys, the Viennese Actionists, Bertolt Brecht, and Salvador Dalí to such pop culture icons as Alice Cooper, Dean Martin, and Elvis. His works, which appear to be wildly spontaneous, are in fact loosely scripted, and instigate a barely contained chaos that frequently involves other artists and often spills out into the audience. His performances take place on jury-rigged stages and theatrical contraptions featuring rickety scaffolding, tunnels, towers, and chutes, and use props like live frogs, fruit and vegetables, shaving cream, and exploding paint balls. Bock wears outlandish costumes, sometimes with enormous heads stuffed with cotton wool. Often he gives "lectures" that are in fact frenzied and often incoherent monologues touching on psychology, economics, politics, art history, and popular culture. *8 ½ x 11—mit Schisslaveng* (Off the Cuff), 2006, invited viewers to climb to the roof of a New York gallery via a specially installed spiral staircase, where they found a collection of makeshift objects composed of wood planks, rolls of carpet, pipes, and other utilitarian materials out in the open. Whether one took this as a climax or an anti-climax, it was certainly an unexpected situation in which normal art world rules didn't seem to apply.

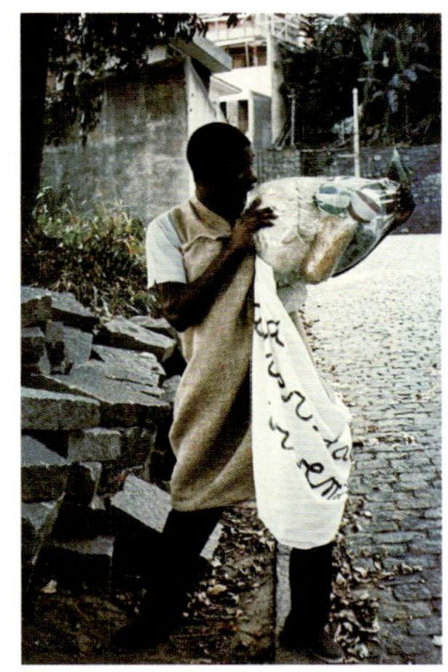

HÉLIO OITICICA
PARANGOLÉ P16 CAPE 12,
"FROM ADVERSITY WE LIVE"
1964
BURLAP, COTTON FABRIC,
PLASTIC, WOODEN SHAVING
DIMENSIONS VARIABLE

Harrell Fletcher creates temporary works that encourage ordinary people to tap into their creative impulses. *The Sound We Make Together,* a 2003 project presented at DiverseWorks, an alternative space in Houston, Texas, included video footage of local groups who were invited to practice their regular recreational activities in the gallery. Among the participants were a Baptist choir, a meditation class, and a break-dance team. Fletcher has also made use of the Web as a gathering place with *Learning to Love You More*, an ongoing project since 2002 for which participants are given assignments and the results are posted online for public consumption. The assignments include instructions such as "interview someone who has experienced war" or "describe your ideal government." The thousands of responses on the project's Web site attest to the desire of non-artists to express themselves to a virtual community.

Philippe Parreno also acts as an impresario of participation, using art to bring other artists and creators together. In 1999 he joined with fellow artist Pierre Huyghe to buy the rights to a generic Japanese cartoon figure they named Ann Lee. The artists then gave her traits and various voices and assembled designers and animators who brought Ann Lee to life in several films, the first of which was called *Anywhere Out of the World*, 2000. For the overall three-year project, titled *No*

CARSTEN HÖLLER

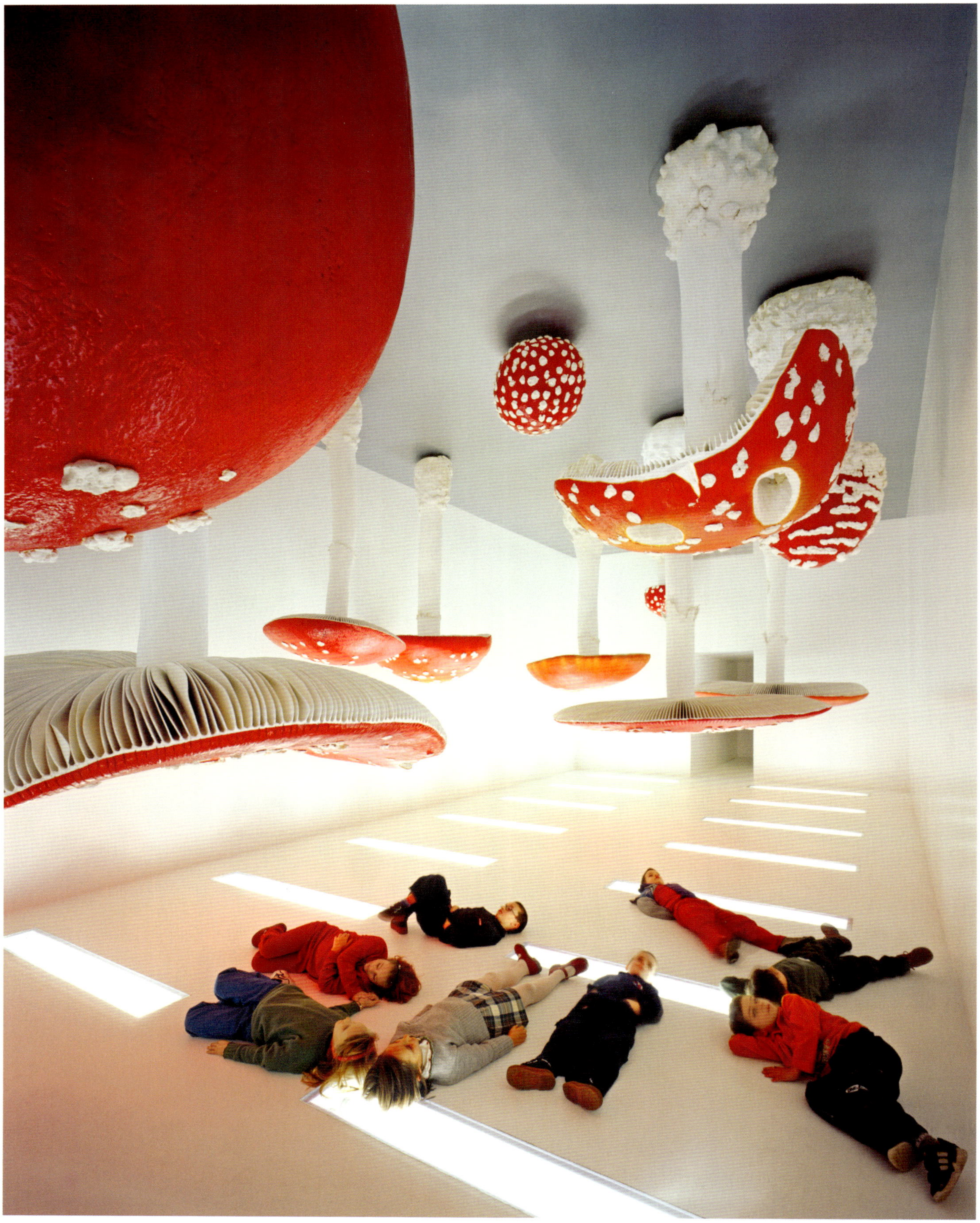

Upside Down Mushroom Room, 2000
Polystyrol, polyester, wood, color, metal, metal constructions, electric motors, plasterboard, neon light, glass, acrylic painting, iron structure,
14 ft 7 in x 19 ft 6 in x 40 ft 7 in (4.5 x 6 x 12.5 m)
As installed at Fondazione Prada, Milan, November 2000–January 2001

ERWIN WURM

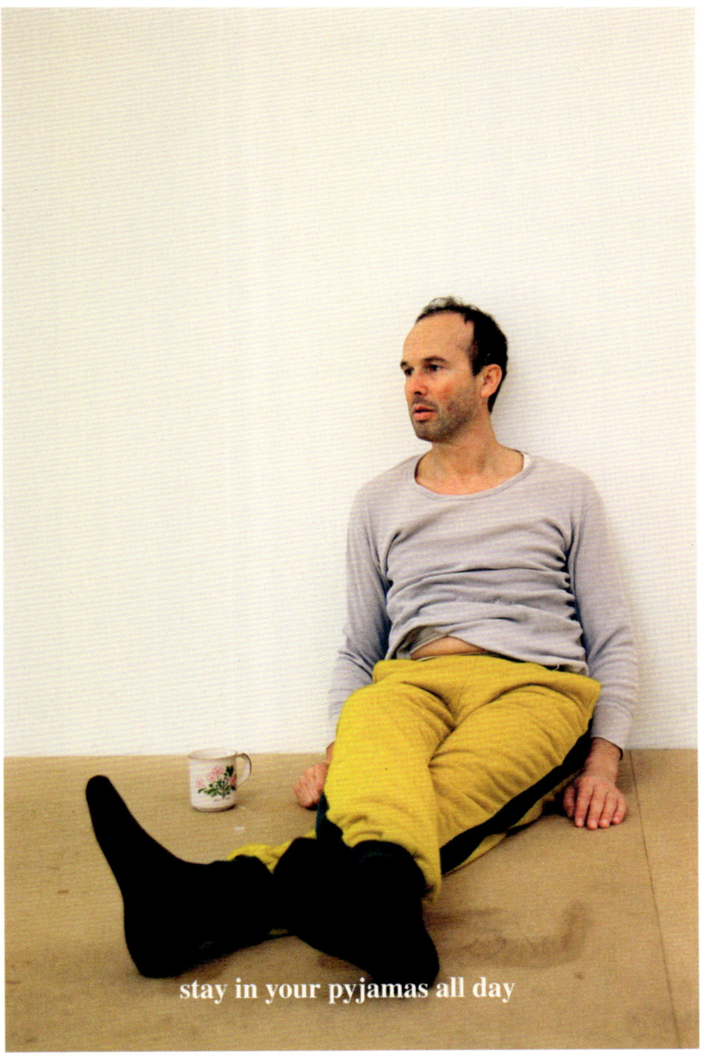

Stay in Your Pyjamas All Day, 2001
C-print on aluminum, 25 5/8 x 17 in (65 x 43 cm)

JOHN BOCK

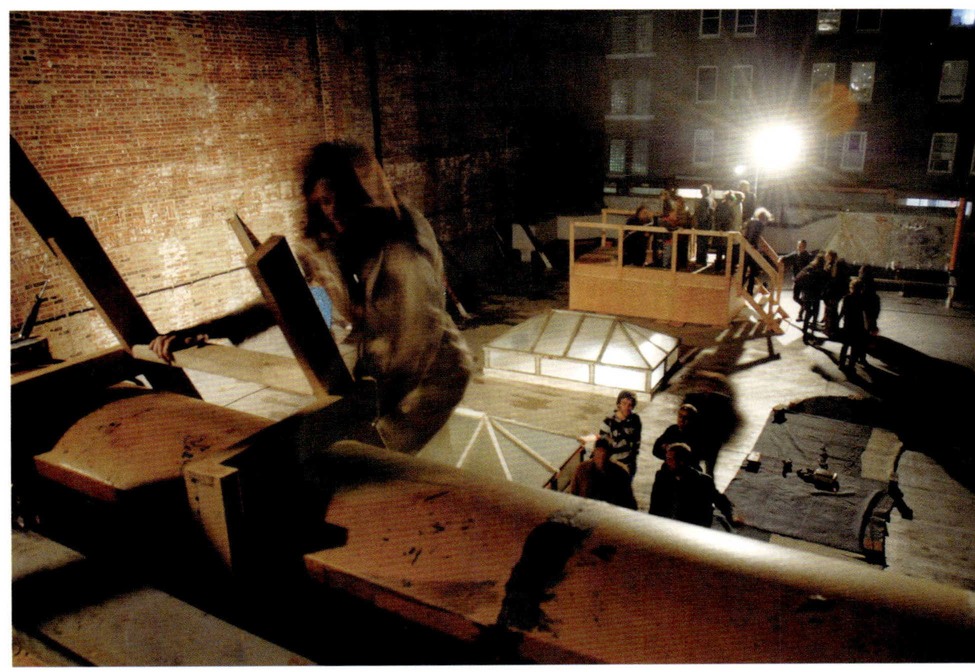

8 ½ x 11—mit Schisslaveng (Off the Cuff), 2006
Spiral staircase, sculptural elements atop gallery, DVD
As installed at the Anton Kern Gallery, New York, October–November 2006

HARRELL FLETCHER

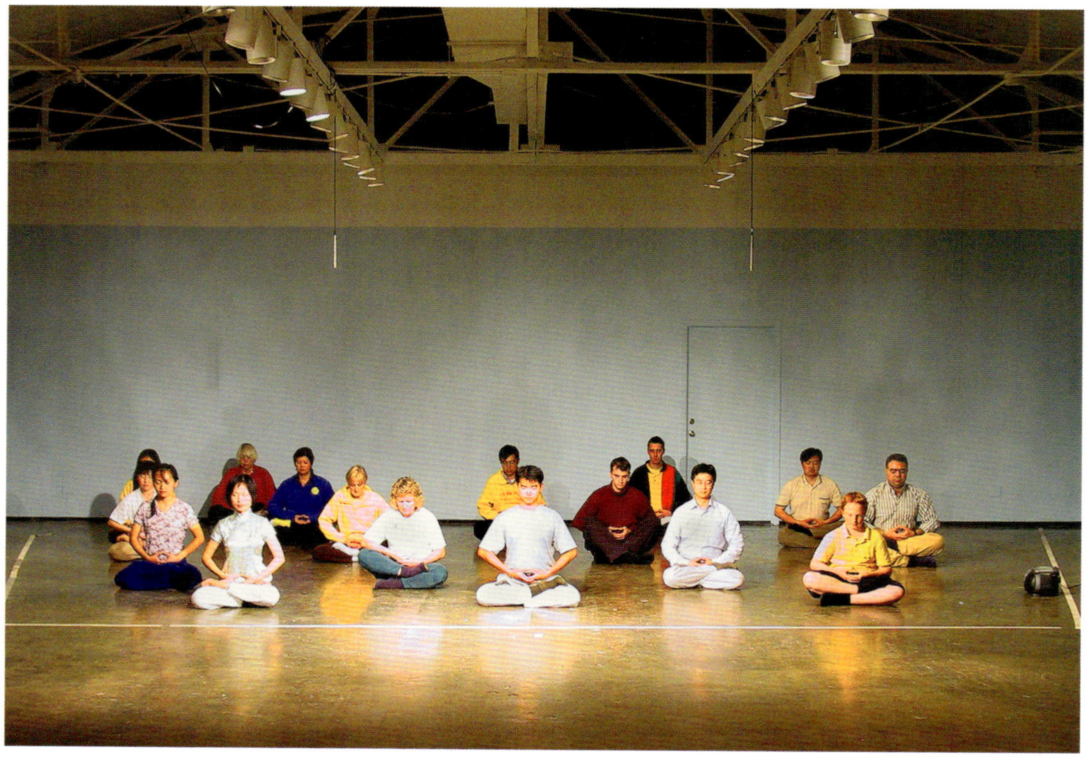

The Sound We Make Together, 2003
Video of a performance at DiverseWorks, Houston, Tex.
36 minutes 15 seconds

PHILIPPE PARRENO

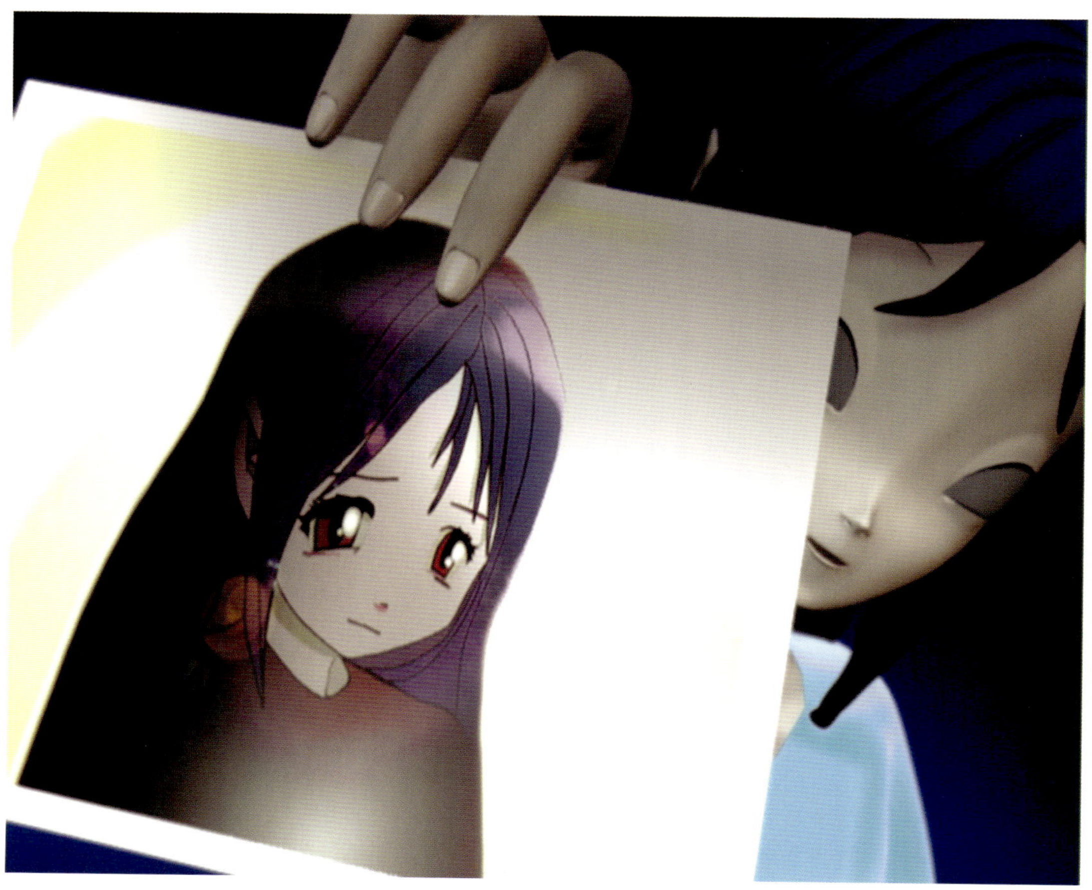

Anywhere Out of the World, 2000
3D animation movie transferred onto DVD, Dolby Digital surround sound,
blue carpet, poster, 4 minutes

Ghost, Just a Shell, they invited several other artists to "animate" Ann Lee in their own ways, further multiplying the personalities of this once lifeless creature. For another enigmatic collaborative work, Parreno invited a group of artists to a party the night before his own gallery opening. At this "pre-party," they were invited to participate in various absurdist activities, such as putting on wigs and having their fake hair cut, or donning boots and having Italian phrases carved into the soles. The next day, at the actual opening, the guests were gone, the gallery was empty, and only memories (and an audio tape) of the preceding night's frivolities remained. With such works, Parreno declares a complete lack of interest in such traditional markers of artistic creativity as authorship or the creation of unique objects. Instead, his art is the communal activity that surrounds it.

Members of the art collective Gelitin—Ali Janka, Florian Reither, Tobias Urban, and Wolfgang Gantner—have worked together since 1995 on all manner of collaborative and participatory projects. They include a hand-operated elevator consisting of three men hoisting visitors to the roof of a three-story building, a human birthday cake composed of a tangle of naked bodies sprouting candles from their fingers, toes, and orifices, and a giant pink straw-stuffed bunny that sprawls on a remote alpine hill in Austria. *Tantamounter 24/7*, which the artists presented in 2005 at a New York gallery, is likely their most labor-intensive participatory work yet. For this project, the four members of the group and two collaborators ensconced themselves for a week in a large wooden box outfitted with rudimentary plumbing, a kitchen, food, and a warehouse-worth of junk, raw materials, and tools. They remained inside, hidden from the public, who were invited to bring objects to the gallery and drop them into a slot on top of the box. Out of sight, Gelitin made a copy of the item out of whatever materials they had on hand, and when finished, ejected both the original and replica. An expensive camera came out with a cardboard double, while a take-out container of sushi was duplicated as an artful arrangement of leftovers from their lunch. A small child inserted into the machine remained there for three hours and was expelled with her "replica," nine Elmo dolls. The "tantamounter" was thus a take on the Xerox machine, though its copies were three-dimensional, of course, and far more ingenious, offering a playful tribute to craftsmanship and the notion of originality.

Ann Hamilton creates collective labor experiences for more political purposes, presenting a vision of America that reflects its democratic impulses. Her installations, which are often set in cavernous old warehouses or factory buildings, frequently involve massive accumulations of materials that must be prepared by a legion of volunteers. *indigo blue*, 1991, was created in Charleston, South Carolina, as part of "Places with a Past," a public art project for which artists were asked to create in situ works that addressed aspects of the area's rich history. Hamilton's title referred to the natural dye that was once a part of the city's economy and is associated with the uniforms of blue-collar workers. She collected seven tons of such uniforms, and had each shirt and pair of pants carefully folded and piled in thecenter of a large industrial space. Thus the clothes themselves and the unseen hands that folded them paid homage to the little-celebrated history of manual labor in America. Lending further weight to the piece, an attendant stationed in the space for the duration of the exhibition was charged with erasing the pages of old blue-cloth-covered military manuals, suggesting the replacement of conventional versions of history with reminders of the lives of the ordinarily unsung citizens whose hidden activities make things work.

GELITIN

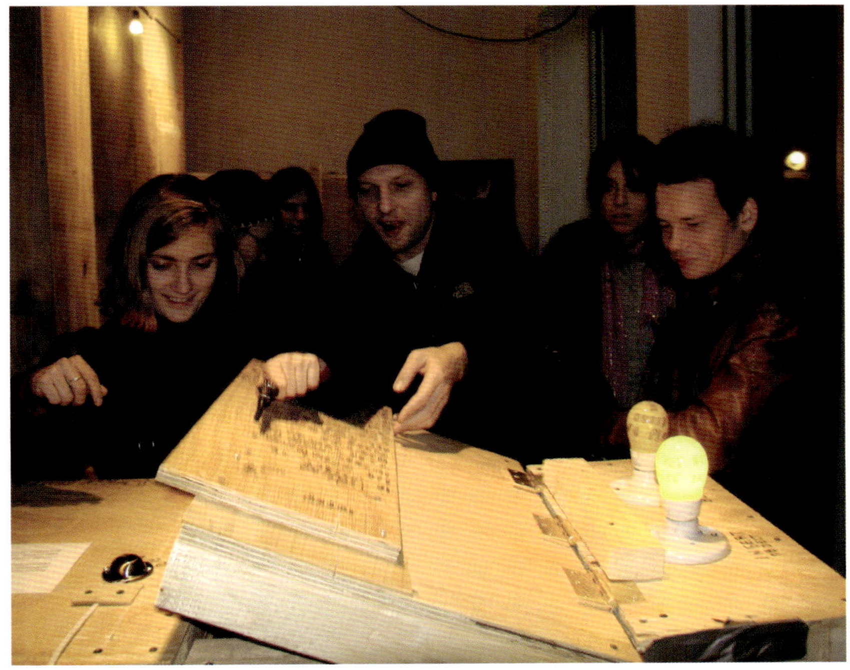

Tantamounter 24/7, 2005
Mixed media, dimensions variable
Installation and performance at Leo Koenig Gallery, New York, November 2005

ANN HAMILTON

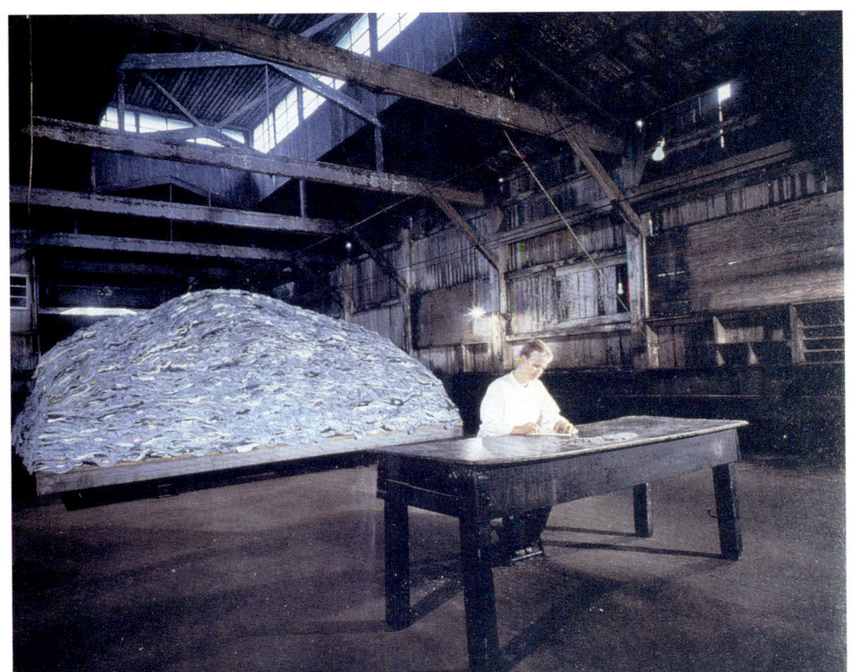

indigo blue, 1991
48,000 blue pants and shirts, dimensions variable

Thomas Hirschhorn's participatory works are also politically charged. His large-scale environments—composed of throwaway materials such as cardboard, plywood, cellophane, packing tape, and aluminum foil—allude to history, philosophy, and contemporary politics. Crammed with heterogeneous printed media, among them statistical charts, reproductions of magazine and newspaper images, video clips, and books, most of them affixed, apparently at random, to the walls, Hirschhorn's installations act as monuments to his cultural heroes, though always with a subversive twist. One of the most elaborate of these works was his *Bataille Monument*, created for the exhibition Documenta 11 in 2002. A mid-twentieth-century French writer who explored the links between eroticism, religion, and transgression and advocated the realization of transcendence through excess, Georges Bataille is an unusual subject for an urban monument. Hirschhorn further deviated from the monument tradition by situating this work in a low-income Turkish neighborhood in Kassel, Documenta's home city. To create the monument, really more of a gathering place, Hirschhorn enlisted the help of young people from the area. After they assisted in the construction of makeshift shacks, they were paid to man them for the duration of the show. The shacks were used in a variety of ways—as a library of books related to Bataille, a workshop, a snack bar, and a television studio that was open to neighborhood youths. Ultimately, this work erased the boundaries between the local residents and the high-art audience of visitors to Kassel, as well as between art, education, politics, and community work. Thus *Bataille Monument* was a fitting tribute to a thinker unwilling, much like Hirschhorn himself, to abide by conventional distinctions.

For Hirschhorn, as for other artists inspired by Situationism, participatory art functions as a social or political provocation. This is particularly so for artists drawn to street performance, which reconfigures the relationship between individual and environment, demanding that spectators respond to the spectacles placed in their path—unless, as is sometimes the case, they are unaware of them. Vito Acconci's 1969 *Following Piece* is one precedent in this vein. For this work, the artist simply followed random individuals on the street until they entered into private spaces. Yoko Ono performed a more confrontational variation on this work that same year, enlisting a camera crew to follow a woman who may or may not have been complicit through the streets of London and eventually into her apartment. Titled *Rape*, the piece played on the sense of violation inherent in the breaching of individual privacy, even in public places. Equally provocative was Austrian artist Valie Export's *Tapp und Tastkino* (Tap and Touch Cinema), 1968, for which she made herself an object of display by donning a small, curtained box on her naked torso, inviting passersby to stick their fingers in behind the curtain. Finally, there were the street performances of Adrian Piper from the early 1970s, in which she transformed herself in odd or repellent ways—walking around with a "WET PAINT" sign, for example, or talking to herself in the subway with a plastic bag in her mouth. William Pope.L also uses street performance as a mode of consciousness raising, often adopting the persona of a homeless person who accosts people to combat his social invisibility. Pope.L is best known for his "crawls," performances in which he drags himself along city streets, pulling himself forward on his belly like a soldier crawling through the jungle. On one such crawl, still ongoing, he is covering the twenty-two miles of the "Great White Way" in Manhattan that stretches along Broadway from Wall Street to Harlem. Dressed in a Superman costume, with a

THOMAS HIRSCHHORN

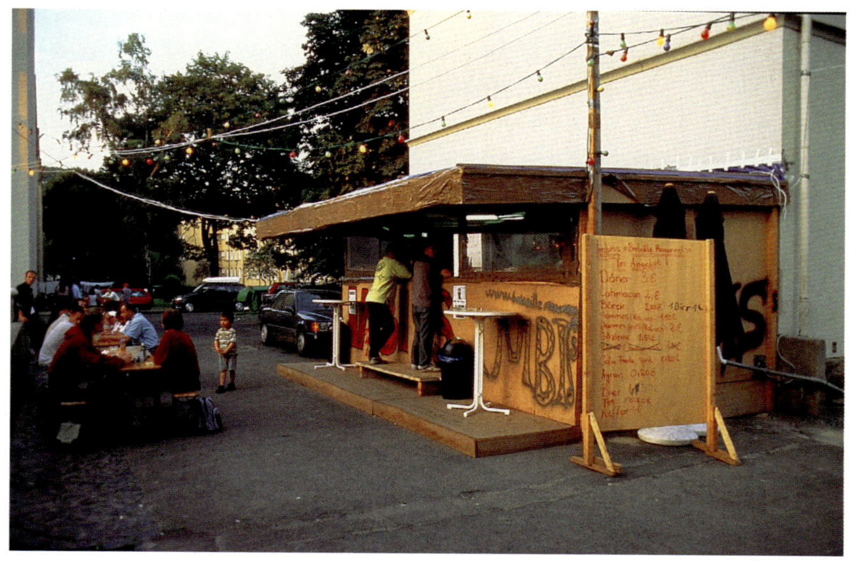

Bataille Monument, 2002
Mixed media
As installed at Documenta 11, Kassel, Germany, 2002

skateboard strapped to his back for quick escape, he appeared to remain oblivious to the stares, comments, and astonishment of passersby, as he focused on his strenuous, nonsensical mission. In such works, Pope.L, an African American, plays on racial and economic stereotypes while also toying with his spectators' sense of political correctness. He generates discomfort by exploiting the ambiguity of his position—spectators are never sure whether he is indeed a deranged street person or simply an actor playing that role. Occasionally this confusion has led viewers to intervene, as when an observer (himself African American) began to berate first the white cameraman who was recording the crawl, and then the artist himself, calling him "a disgrace to your race" before summoning the police.

The urban traversal appears in a quieter guise in Francis Alÿs's work. Alÿs undertakes "*paseos*," or strolls, through Mexico City neighborhoods, accompanied by various accoutrements that transform the walks into metaphoric journeys. One of his first paseos was *The Collector*, 1991–92, in which he pulled a magnetic toy on wheels through the streets of Mexico City. Along the way bits of metal attached themselves to the toy, thus representing the random accumulation of experience. For onlookers Alÿs's inexplicable actions focus attention on the ephemeral nature of urban life and their own status as simply another fleeting imprint on its surface. Not all of Alÿs's works are solitary. In 2002, for a performance called *When Faith Moves Mountains*, Alÿs enlisted five hundred volunteers who, equipped with shovels, moved a giant sand dune outside Lima, Peru, four inches from its original position. The title of the work underscores its quixotic nature: Alÿs spoofed the monumental earth moving projects of land artists like Robert Smithson and Michael Heizer while also focusing attention on the landless inhabitants of the settlements in the city's outskirts, who require much more than faith to survive.

The performances of Vanessa Beecroft—highly dramatic, static spectacles set in lavish interiors—are what one might call anti-street. Beecroft orchestrates large groups of naked or near-naked female models who stand around in poses that echo the hauteur of high-fashion photo shoots. Wearing stiletto heels, bikini bottoms, or at times nothing at all, they hold these poses for up to three hours at a time for an audience that is invited to observe but not to interact with them. By and large these performances have occurred in museum settings, where they take on the character of a perverse art opening in which the art objects are immobile human beings. In *VB 46*, 2001, a nude woman with a strip of dyed-red pubic hair circled twenty motionless blond nude models sporting pale body makeup and pubic waxes. The audience stood cautiously on the sidelines. A variation on this theme involves uniformed U.S. Navy Seals arranged in equally stylized military formations. From one perspective, the effect is quite different—the men are clothed and anything but exposed and vulnerable. But they exhibit the same degree of physical control and almost inhuman stasis as the female models. Thus they have a similar effect of reducing viewers to the role of voyeur while inculcating a sense of personal inadequacy in the face of the performers' physical and behavioral perfection.

Much more generous in spirit is a strain of participatory art that views the artwork as a gift. A particularly touching expression of this idea appears in the work of Felix Gonzalez-Torres, who died of AIDS in 1996. Gonzalez-Torres's spare installations employed unremarkable objects to present poetic commentaries on the politics of AIDS, the seductions of homoerotic desire, and a personal sense of loss. A number of works were inspired by the life and death of his lover, Ross Laycock. *Untitled*

WILLIAM POPE.L

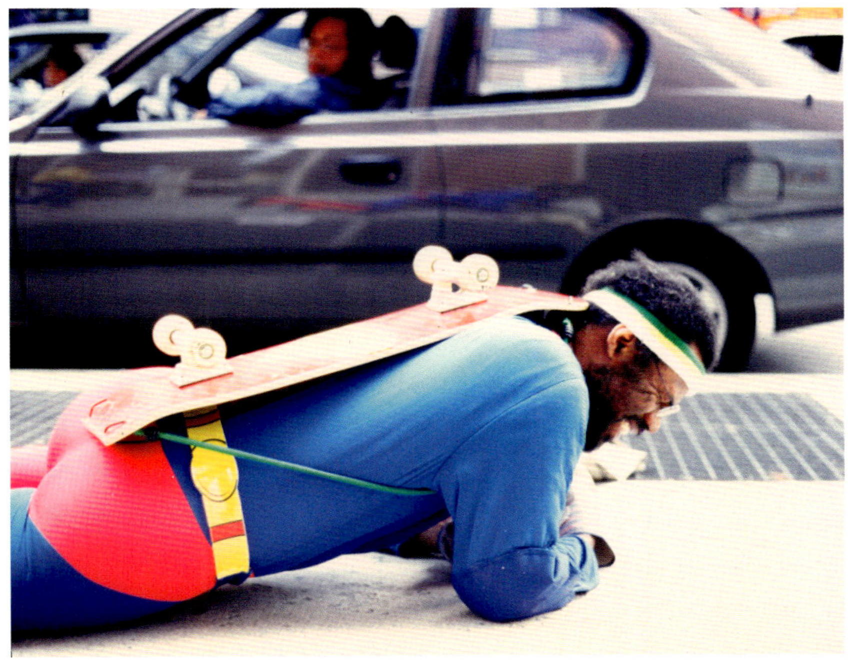

The Great White Way, 22 miles, 9 years, 1 street, 2001–ongoing
Performance, New York

FRANCIS ALŸS

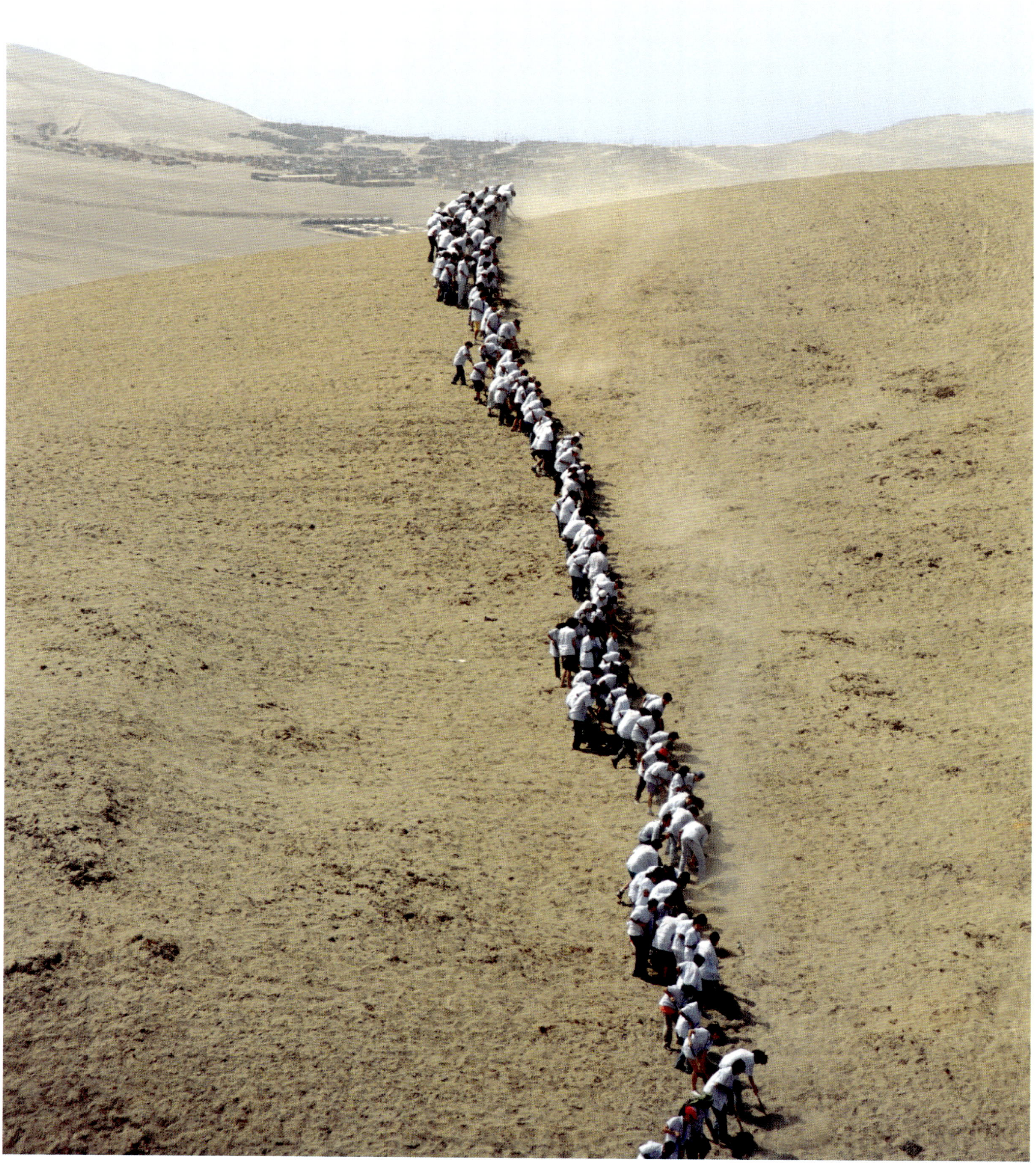

When Faith Moves Mountains, 2002
In collaboration with Cuauhtémoc Medina and Rafael Ortega
Photographic documentation of an event, Lima, Peru

VANESSA BEECROFT

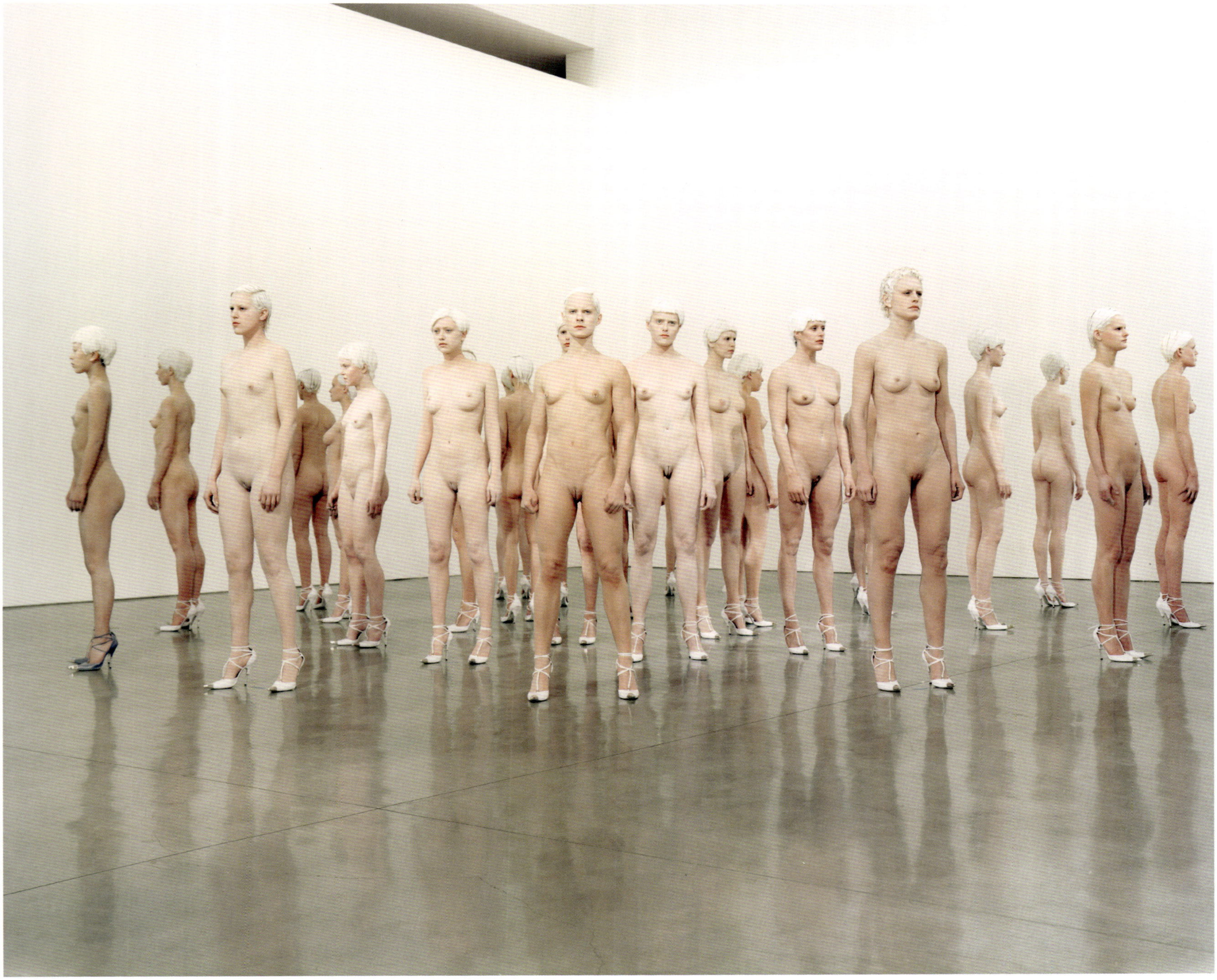

vb46.017 Los Angeles, 2001
Photographic documentation of a performance

(Perfect Lovers), 1991, consisted of a pair of battery-operated clocks on a wall. Initially ticking away in comfortable companionship, they eventually fell out of sync until one wound down and stopped, a harbinger of death. Among Gonzalez-Torres's best-known works were his "spills," mounds of colorfully wrapped candies piled on the floor of gallery and museum installations. In a gesture that defied conventions about the preciousness of art and its "please do not touch" status in institutional settings, the artist invited viewers to take a piece home, and when the piles became too small, galleries would replenish them. Like the bulbs and clocks, the candies had metaphoric meanings. The sprightly *"Untitled" (USA Today)*, 1990, was composed of candies in shiny red, white, and blue wrappings to reflect the reflexive patriotism favored by that newspaper's constituency. More poignant were the silver candies of *"Untitled" (Placebo)*, 1991; first exhibited just after Laycock's death, the title alludes to the futility of his long medical treatment. The weight of the pile, including replenishments, was equal to the combined weight of the two lovers. Gonzalez-Torres also produced stacks of posters that exhibition visitors were invited to take; their images, such as clouds, were largely poetic, again reflecting Gonzalez-Torres's meditations on mortality and love.

Rirkrit Tiravanija's projects also invite viewers to partake in gifts—specifically of food and drink. Inspired in part by his own grandmother, a restaurateur in Bangkok, Tiravanija is best known for performances in which he sets up shop in a gallery space for the duration of the exhibition as a cook and host. He brings a wok, cooking pots, noodles, and vegetables, and creates spicy Thai dishes that are served to anyone who happens to visit, turning openings in particular into festive eateries with beer, food, and great amounts of sociability. When the show is over, nothing is left that might conventionally be called art—the garbage is taken away, the pots and pans are removed to be used again. For one such meal, *Untitled (Pad See-ew)*, first created for friends in 1990 and then recreated as a performance at the San Francisco Museum of Modern Art in 2002, the artist made a favorite noodle dish from his native Thailand. Tiravanija has also installed a recording studio in a museum, set up a replica of his apartment in a gallery for use by visitors, and constructed a party shack in an exhibition space, complete with instruments available for use by any visiting musicians. In these and other works, Tiravanija explores ways to eliminate the distinction between art and life. When describing the materials or ingredients he uses for his projects, he often includes "lots of people."

Lee Mingwei also focuses on the human interaction that characterizes relational aesthetics, but his work often relies on individual encounters in gallery or museum settings he has outfitted for that purpose. For *Sleeping Project*, 1999, he set up a pair of beds in a gallery and invited individuals chosen by lottery to join him for sleepovers. For *Tourist Project*, 2002, he asked individuals to give him tours of their favorite city neighborhood. In other works, Mingwei has enlisted others as primary participants. For *The Letter Writing Project*, 1998, Lee attempted to reconnect visitors with absent, deceased, or estranged loved ones by providing an intimate enclosure in which they were invited to write letters to significant people in their lives. Writers were given the choice of leaving the letters open in the booth for others to read, or sealing them and giving them to the artist to post. In the end, Lee collected more than nine thousand letters, testimony to the audience's longing to connect.

Surasi Kusolwong practices a more impersonal form of exchange that suggests the marketplace more than the intimate meeting. Referencing the traditional

FELIX GONZALEZ-TORRES

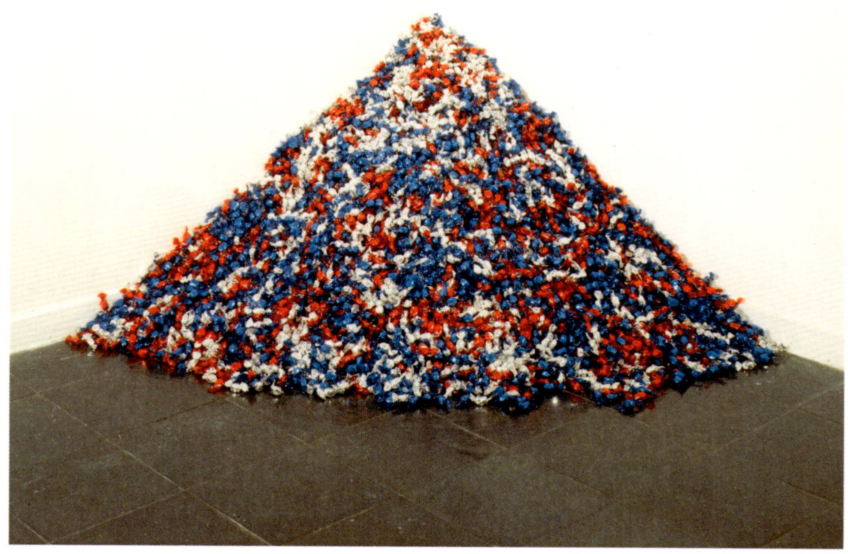

"Untitled" (USA Today), 1990
Candies, individually wrapped in red, silver, and blue cellophane, endless supply
Overall dimensions vary with installation, ideal weight 300 lbs (136 kg)

Asian market, in which everything from spices to old clothes to electronic gadgets are spread out for purchase, Kusolwong gathers the mass-produced products common to these settings and arranges them in carefully color-coordinated displays. The titles of these performances emphasize the artist's lack of interest in profit: *1000 Lire Market* (*La vita continua*), 2001, is an outdoor market he set up in San Gimignano, Italy. *Pay Less for the Best,* 2001, took place in Milwaukee, Wisconsin, and *Everything the Same Price*, 2001, was presented in Geneva, Switzerland. Museum visitors are invited to choose any item—plastic sand buckets, knit hats, gardening tools, and all sorts of utilitarian and decorative objects—and exchange a dollar for it. These installations spoof the ubiquitous dollar stores filled with items manufactured in Asia, but they are also meditations on the meaning of value, use, and commercial exchange.

The transfer of authority from artist to viewer has many repercussions. On one hand, it can be argued that it does away with the traditional aesthetic criteria by which art is normally judged. If a work of art depends for its completion on external events and the actions of outside spectators, it is hard to apply notions of originality, creativity, or intentionality to it. From another perspective, the transformation of the viewer into a participant radically redefines the definition of the artist, opening up the possibility that anyone and everyone is an artist. This was the gospel of Joseph Beuys, an advocate of what he called "social sculpture," a concept that grew out of his conviction that the ultimate purpose of art is the democratic transformation of human society. Beuys's utopian view held that artworks should be instruments of private and social change. He explored this idea in both personal performances that tested his own limits (as when he locked himself in a gallery for three days with a live coyote so as to better connect with his animal nature), and in larger orchestrated communal projects. *7000 Oaks*, his 1982 project for Documenta 7, for example, called for the planting of seven thousand oak trees in Kassel. The result was a five-year, massive mobilization of members of Beuys's Free International University, resulting in the reforestation of a town that had been largely denuded of trees by postwar development. Each sapling was paired with a basalt column of stone about four feet tall, which would represent the creative efforts of both the individual and the collective, and which the tree would eventually greatly overshadow.

Agnes Denes also enlists collaborators to create large-scale environmental works whose location and configuration dramatize the need to reconcile nature and culture. Her earliest work in this vein was the 1982 *Wheatfield: A Confrontation*, in which the participatory aspect was largely symbolic as she pitted urban and rural land uses against each other. She planted a field of golden wheat on a future construction site under the shadow of the World Trade Center in New York, then harvested it at the end of the season. The return, however brief, of a bit of prime urban real estate to its agricultural past underlined the conflict between human greed and human need. More recent permanent interventions, such as *Tree Mountain—A Living Time Capsule—11,000 People, 11,000 Trees, 400 Years*, have employed small armies of collaborators. *Tree Mountain* was first conceived in 1982 and completed in the Pinsiö gravel pits in Ylöjärvi, Finland, in 1996. This work involved eleven thousand people planting eleven thousand trees in a spiraling pattern derived both from abstract mathematics and natural patterns, such as those found in the center of a sunflower. *Tree Mountain* is designed to hold back the erosion of the land, which provides a home for wildlife, and to create a symbolic model for the productive

RIRKRIT TIRAVANIJA

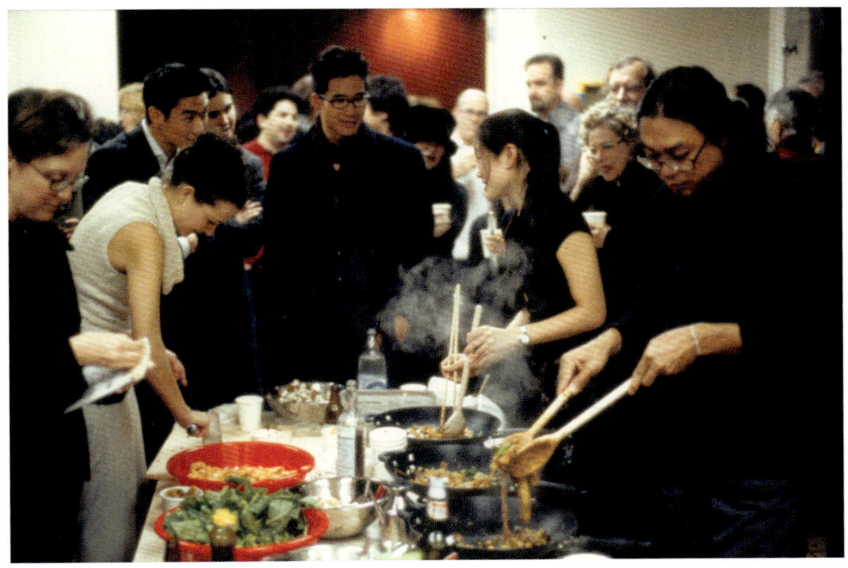

Untitled (Pad See-ew), 1990/2002
Performance at the San Francisco Museum of Modern Art, February 2002

LEE MINGWEI

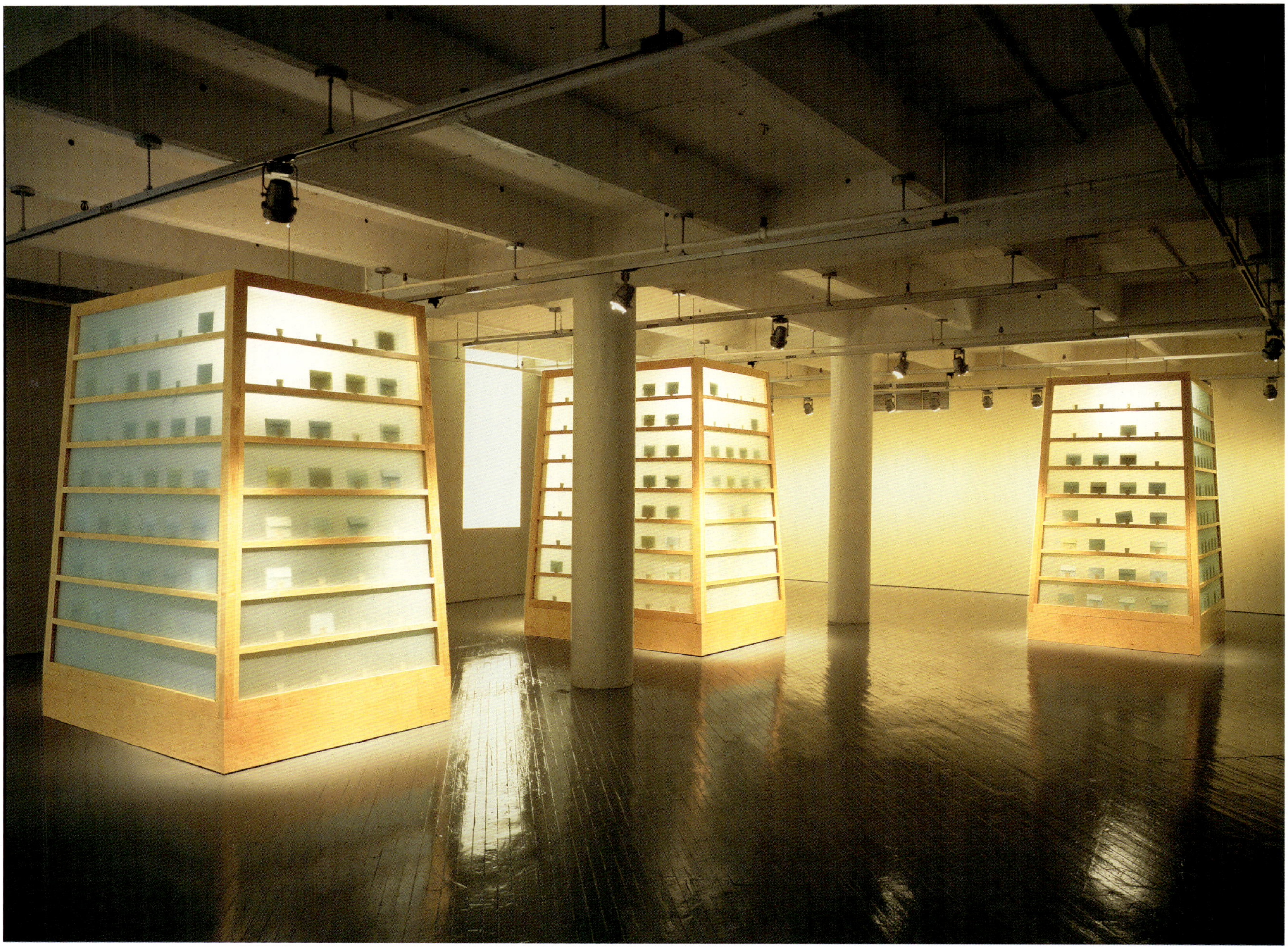

The Letter-Writing Project, 1998
Wood and glass, three booths, 114 x 67 x 91 in (289.6 x 170.2 x 231.1 cm) each
Whitney Museum of American Art, New-York, and the YAGEO Art Foundation, Taipei

SURASI KUSOLWONG

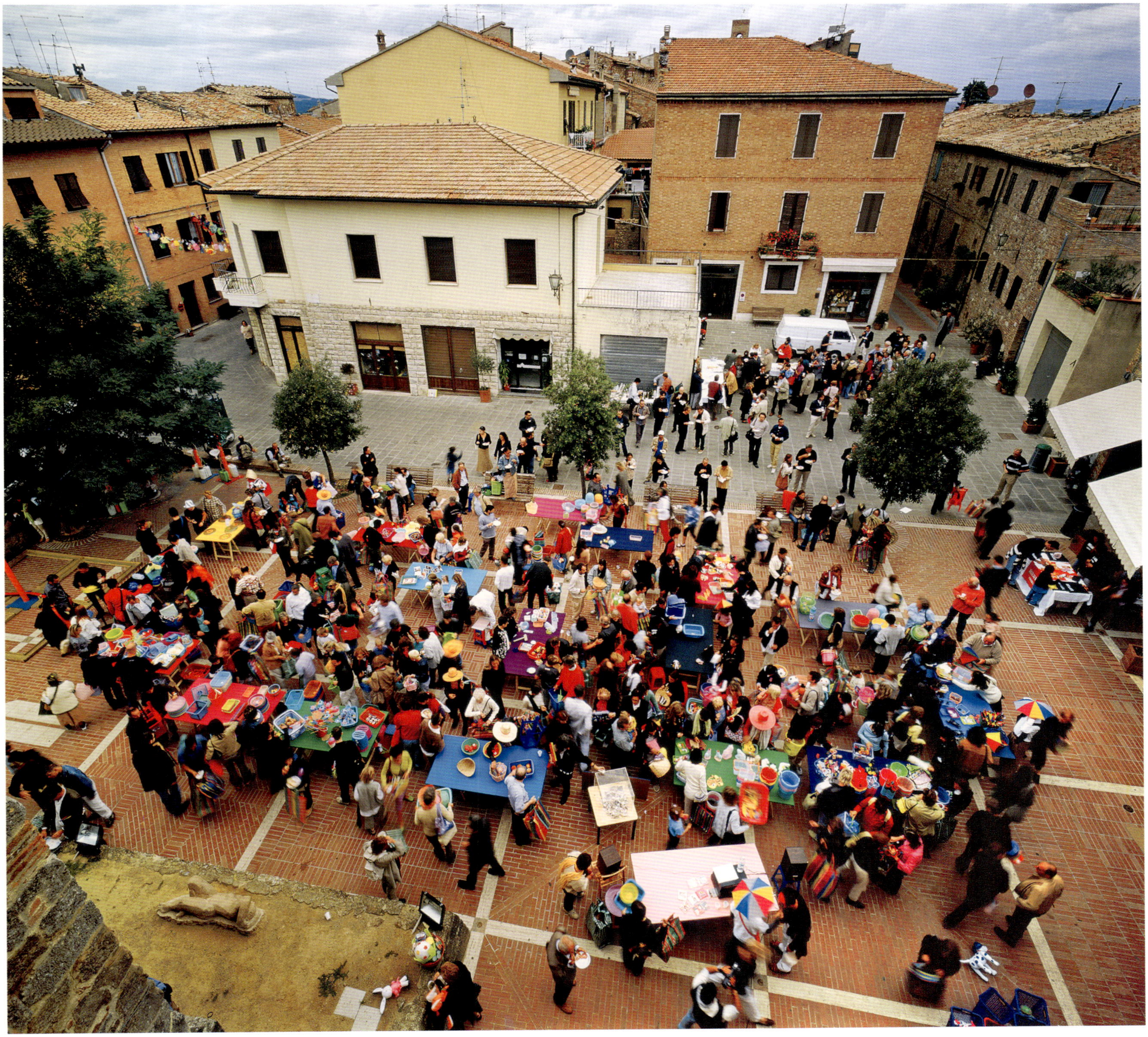

1000 Lire Market (La vita continua), 2001
Mixed media, variable dimensions

AGNES DENES

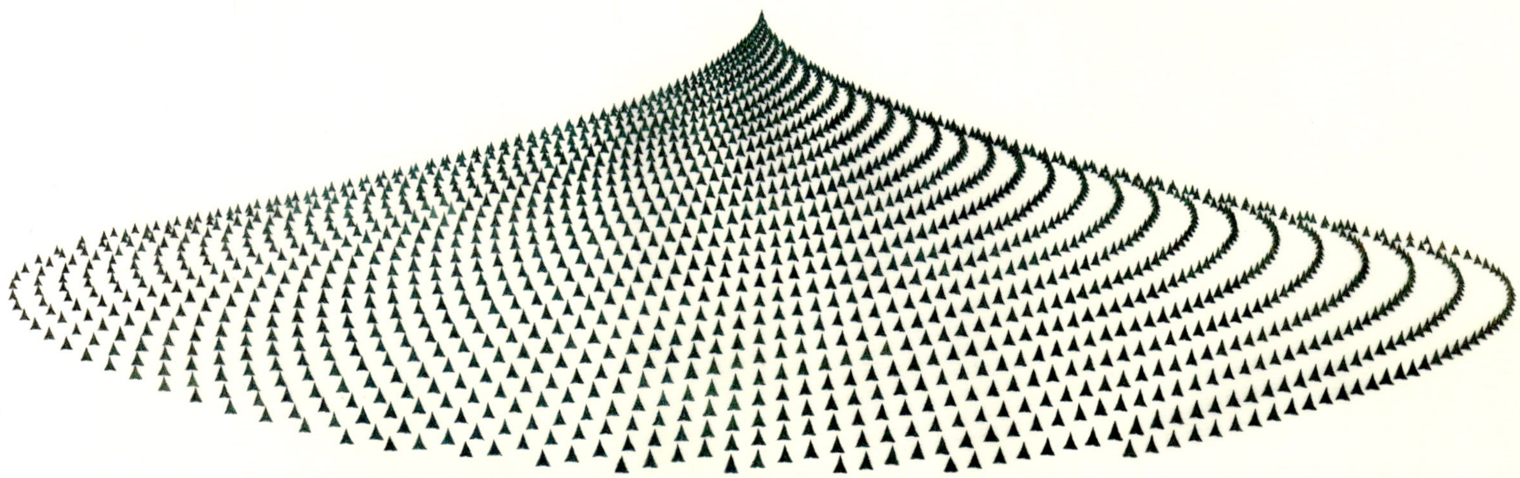

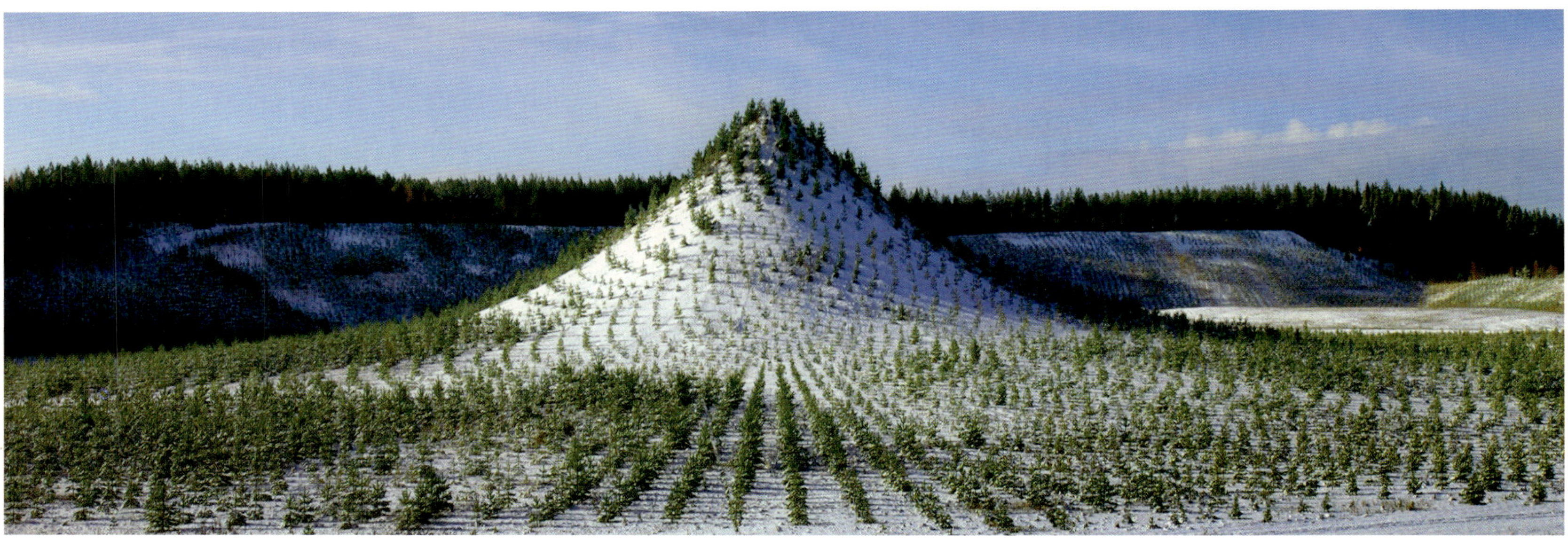

Tree Mountain—A Living Time Capsule—11,000 People, 11,000 Trees, 400 Years, 1982–96
Original concept drawing, 1982 (top): metallic ink and gouache on mylar, 33 7/8 x 96 in (86 x 244 cm); winter view, 2004 (bottom)
Ylöjärvi, Finland

interaction of interconnected individuals. It also represents an ongoing commitment from the volunteers who remain behind after the artist has left to tend to the new environments.

Christo and Jeanne-Claude, a husband-and-wife team whose large-scale, high-visibility projects engage large numbers of participants and bring art to a mass audience, offer a related model for communal art. Working with an army of local volunteers, they undertake temporary transformations of urban and rural environments. One of their first such works was *Running Fence 1972–76*, a twenty-four-mile curtain of yellow fabric cutting across the hills of northern California. They have also wrapped the Reichstag in Berlin in a white shroud, installed over a thousand blue umbrellas in a landscape outside Tokyo, swathed eleven islands off the coast of Miami in pink fabric, and inscribed New York's Central Park with hundreds of "gates" hung with orange fabric. At their best, the pair's projects have a monumental, magical, and whimsical quality. But equally important is the process by which these projects come into being: Christo and Jeanne-Claude work with local authorities, raise the millions needed to implement their projects, enlist volunteers, and galvanize local press. Given the intricacy of the negotiations required to secure permission and to carry out these projects, they are often years in the making. *The Gates, Central Park, New York City, 1979–2005*, for instance, took a full quarter-century to be realized from initial concept to fruition.

A similar mix of aesthetics, participation, political savvy, long-term planning, and networking underlies the work of Kristin Jones and Andrew Ginzel. *Mnemonics*, an ambitious project that occupied them from 1989 to 1992, was created as a city-sponsored artwork for Stuyvesant High School in downtown Manhattan. The school, founded in 1904, has a remarkable history, having been home to numerous Nobel Prize–winning scientists and performers such as James Cagney, Thelonius Monk, and Tim Robbins. For their installation, which would both incorporate aspects of the school's history and suggest its connections to the larger world, the artists inserted over four hundred hollow glass blocks into the school's walls and filled them with evocative objects. Some objects are artifacts from Lower Manhattan; others, gathered from embassies and consulates, are from around the world—a vessel of melted snow from Mount Fuji or a fragment of the Great Wall of China, for example. Yet others are memorabilia solicited from alumni. Some of the blocks were left open, to be filled by successive graduating classes. Thus, many people were involved in the creation of *Mnemonics*, and more will be involved in its continued upkeep as it fulfills its promise as a large-scale, ever-growing collective memetic device.

Tim Rollins, a founding member of Group Material who went on to adapt that collective's activist principles to the field of art education, also works with students as collaborators. As a high school teacher in the South Bronx section of New York City in the early 1980s, Rollins devised after-school workshops in which at-risk and struggling students would create collective artworks that explored the relationship between their own life situations and the stories of great literature. This grew into an independent educational program called the Art and Knowledge Workshop, whose participants Rollins christened Kids of Survival, or K.O.S. Under Rollins's tutelage, K.O.S. has produced remarkably sophisticated artworks based on such books as Nathaniel Hawthorne's *The Scarlet Letter*, George Orwell's *Animal Farm*, Franz Kafka's *Amerika*, Ralph Ellison's *Invisible Man*, and Malcolm X's autobiography. Rollins introduces the students to cultural productions ranging from Renaissance

JOSEPH BEUYS

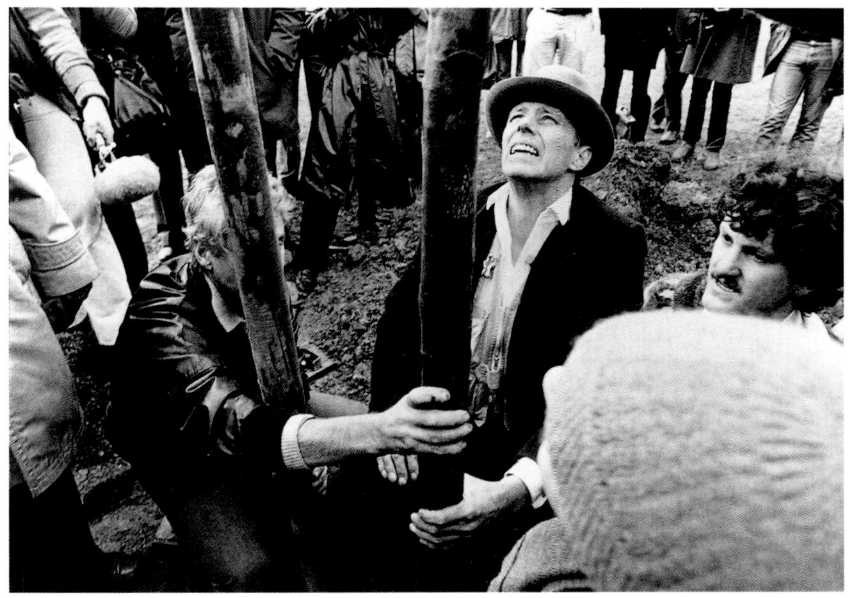

7000 Oaks, 1982
7,000 granite blocks, 7,000 holm oak trees
Action, Documenta 7, Friedrichsplatz, Kassel, Germany, 1982

CHRISTO AND JEANNE-CLAUDE

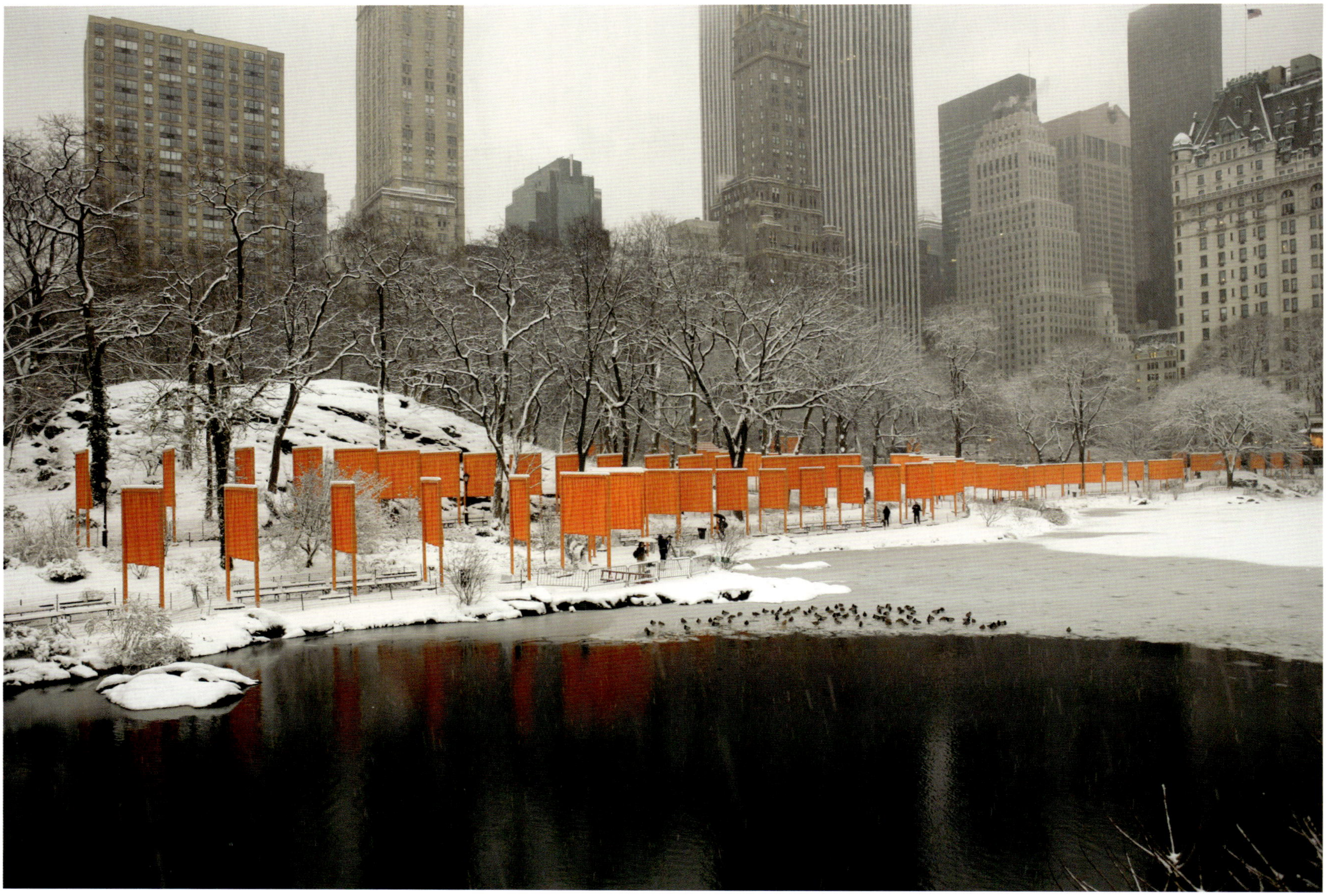

The Gates, Central Park, New York City, 1979–2005, 2005
As installed in Central Park, New York, February 2005

art to comic strips, the styles of which are integrated into their paintings, which are executed on the very pages of the books that inspired them. Though the projects often result in gallery-scale artworks, K.O.S. has occasionally done large public works. *Amerika—For the People of Bathgate*, 1988, is a mural painted on the side of a school on Bathgate Avenue in the South Bronx. Like other works in the "Amerika" series, this one presents an intertwined network of golden trumpets whose shapes are inspired by everything from Walt Disney to Hieronymus Bosch. In the mid-1980s, the art market discovered the paintings of K.O.S., which have sold at times for great sums. Rollins and K.O.S. put the money earned back into the project, using it to finance travel, stipends, and an educational fund for K.O.S. members. As the original members have grown up, many have used the money to become the first college graduates in their families. Today Rollins continues to operate K.O.S. as a national and international outreach program to young people, presenting workshops at art centers, alternative high schools, and community youth programs.

Sculptor John Ahearn also engages the South Bronx community in making his participatory work. A resident of this embattled area of New York from 1979 to 1995, Ahearn gained visibility both in the neighborhood and in the larger art world for his plaster and bronze sculptures of local residents. Working in collaboration with Rigoberto Torres, Ahearn cast his figures directly from his subjects during casting sessions that often turned into block parties. The final casts, painted to create a striking semblance of life, were made in multiple copies, one of which was given to the sitter. Finished as full or partial body casts, the figures in the sculptures often included identifying attributes, such as a favorite T-shirt, a pet, or an item suggesting the sitter's job (auto mechanic, housewife, student, and so on). Some of the casts have been incorporated into three-dimensional murals placed on Bronx buildings, such as *Homage to the People of the Bronx, Double Dutch at Kelly Street I*, 1981–82, which depicts four neighborhood girls jumping rope. Such works form a celebratory portrait of a neighborhood of individuals.

A spirit of community activism also inspired Rick Lowe to establish Project Row Houses, a broadly conceived art and social services organization founded in 1993 in one of the poorest African American neighborhoods in Houston, Texas. Working collaboratively with a team of artists, architects, administrators, and community members, Lowe has transformed twenty-two abandoned "shotgun" houses (built by freed men in the South after the Civil War) into low-income homes, artists' residencies, offices, galleries, workshop spaces, and transitional housing for single teenage mothers who receive training in child care and job skills. In the houses dedicated to art, photography, and literary projects, invited artists spend six months creating installations that address the history and cultural issues of the surrounding community and involve community members in the creation of the works. Among the artist projects is Whitfield Lovell's *Echo*, 1996, wall drawings from early twentieth-century studio portrait photographs of African Americans. Lowe's unique approach to community arts programming is catching on: in the past few years, he has been invited to advise in the creation of similar projects in other cities around the United States.

The Living Museum, founded in 1983 by Bolek Greczynski and Dr. Janos Marton, engages a particularly exceptional art community. Grenczynski, who died in 1995, was a native of Poland who directed avant-garde theater productions and art actions before coming to the United States. Marton, the son of a dissident Hungarian economist, is an artist and psychologist. Together, they created a workshop and

KRISTIN JONES AND ANDREW GINZEL

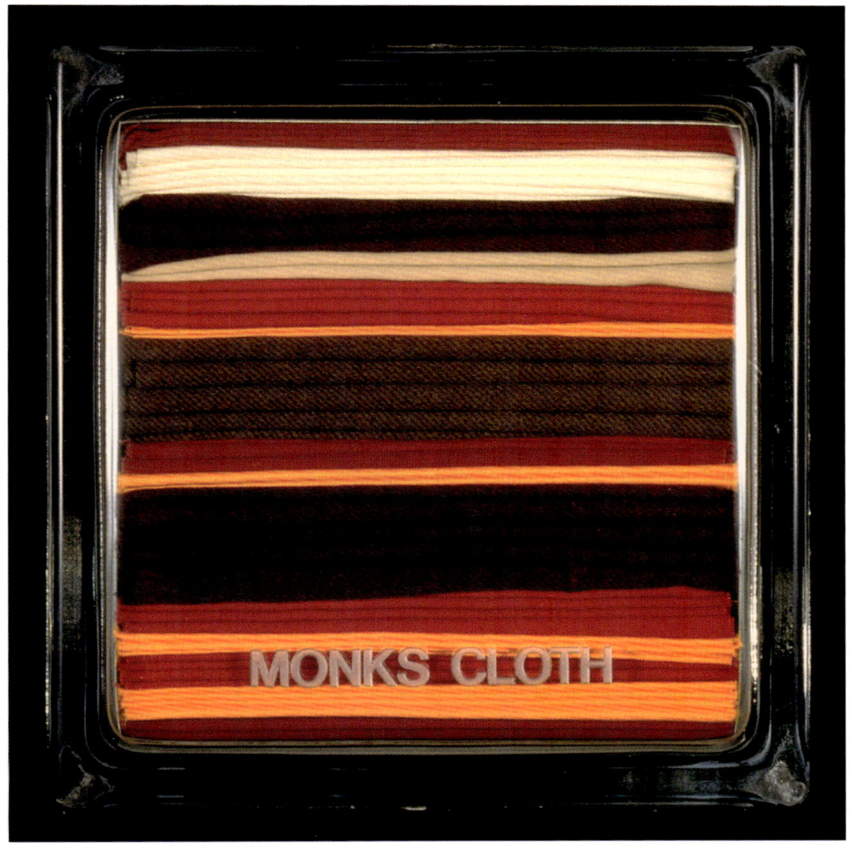

Mnemonics (detail), 1992
400 glass blocks, each with collected artifacts
Each block 8 x 8 x 4 in (20.3 x 20.3 x 10.1 cm)

TIM ROLLINS + K.O.S.

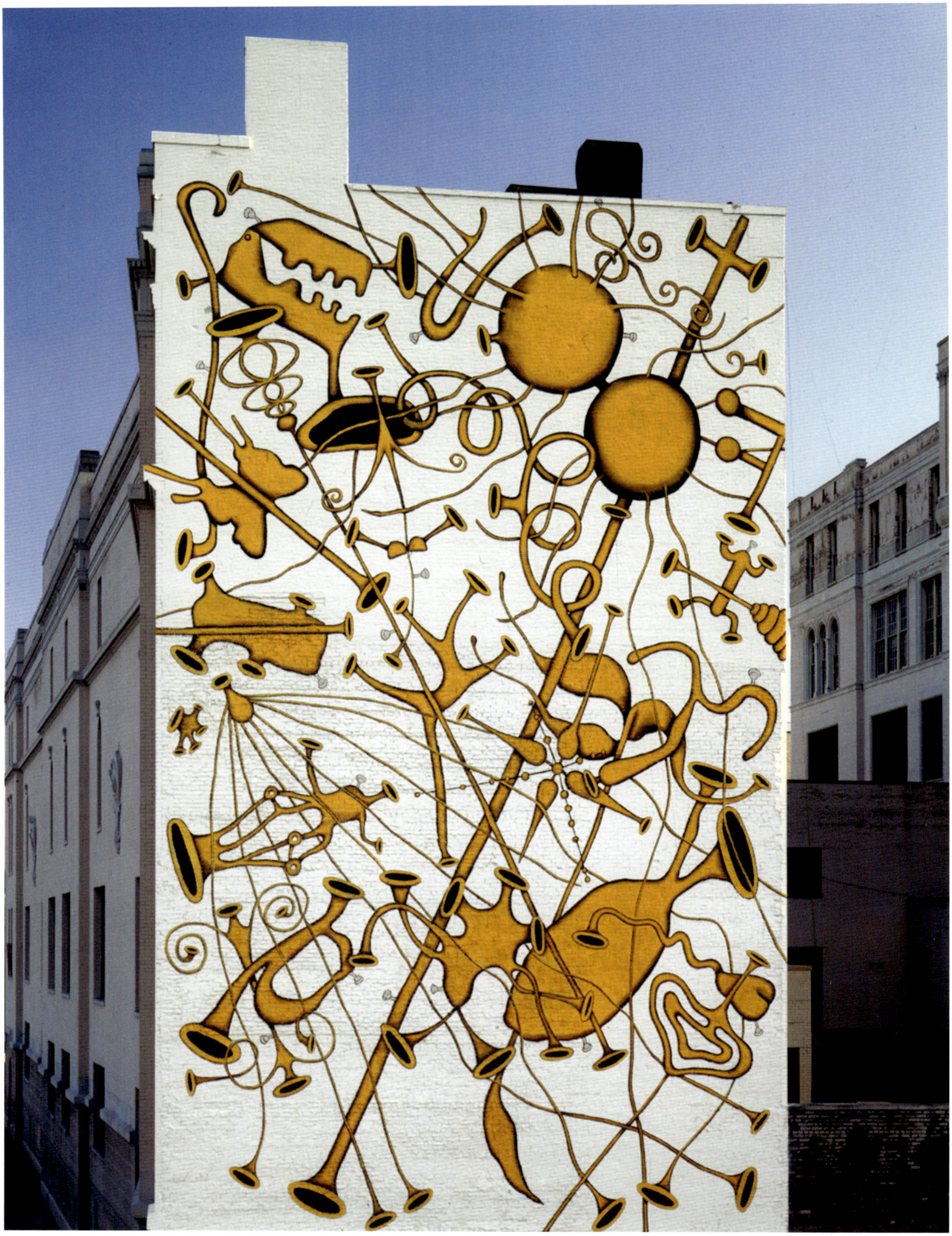

Amerika - For The People of Bathgate, 1988
Enamel paint, 35 x 55 ft (10.7 x 16.8 m)
Mural at 1701 Fulton Avenue, Bronx, New York

JOHN AHEARN

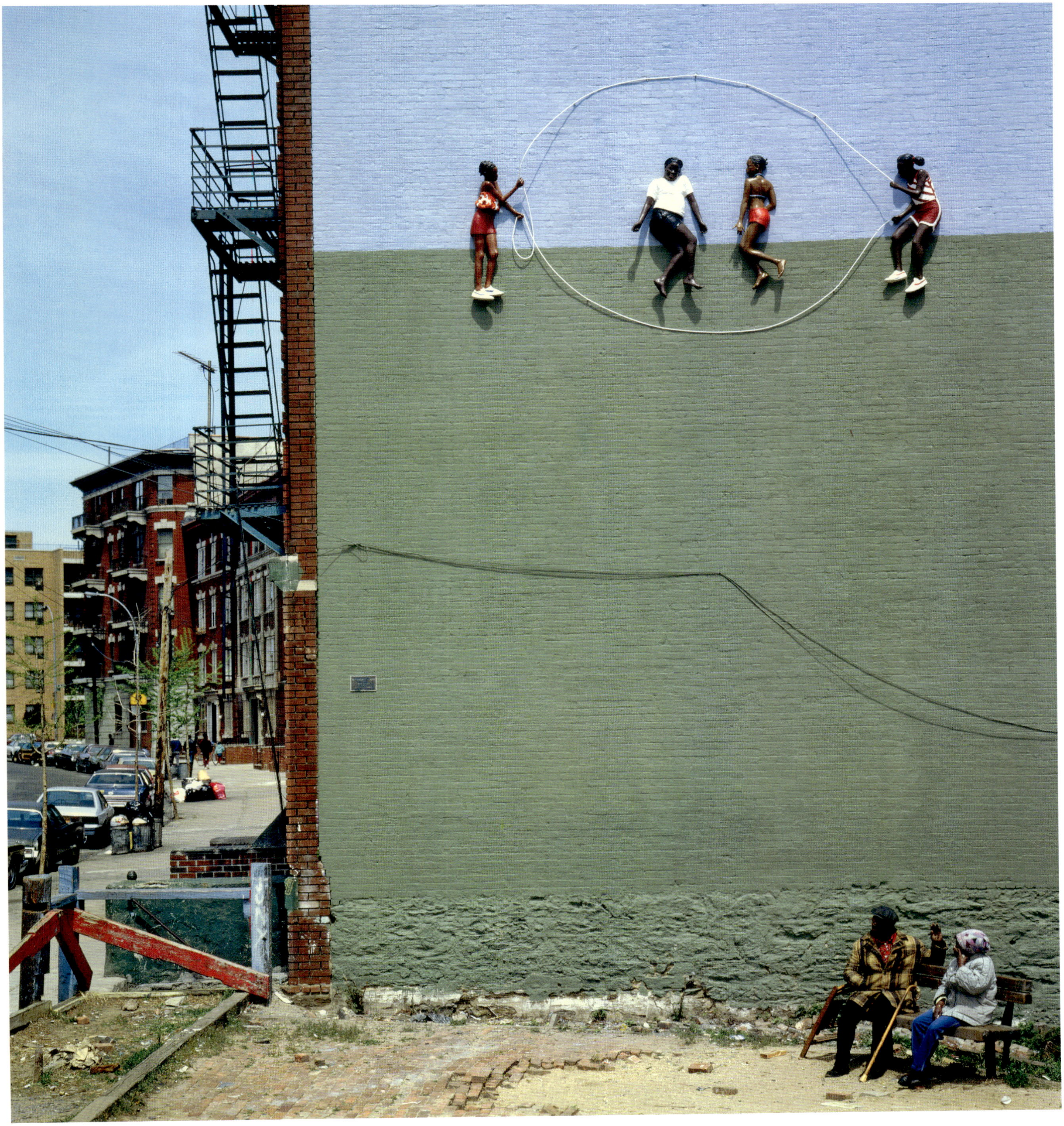

Homage to the People of the Bronx, Double Dutch at Kelly Street I, 1981–82
Cast fiberglass, oil, cable, each figure 54 x 54 x 12 in (137.2 x 137.2 x 30.5 cm)

WHITFIELD LOVELL

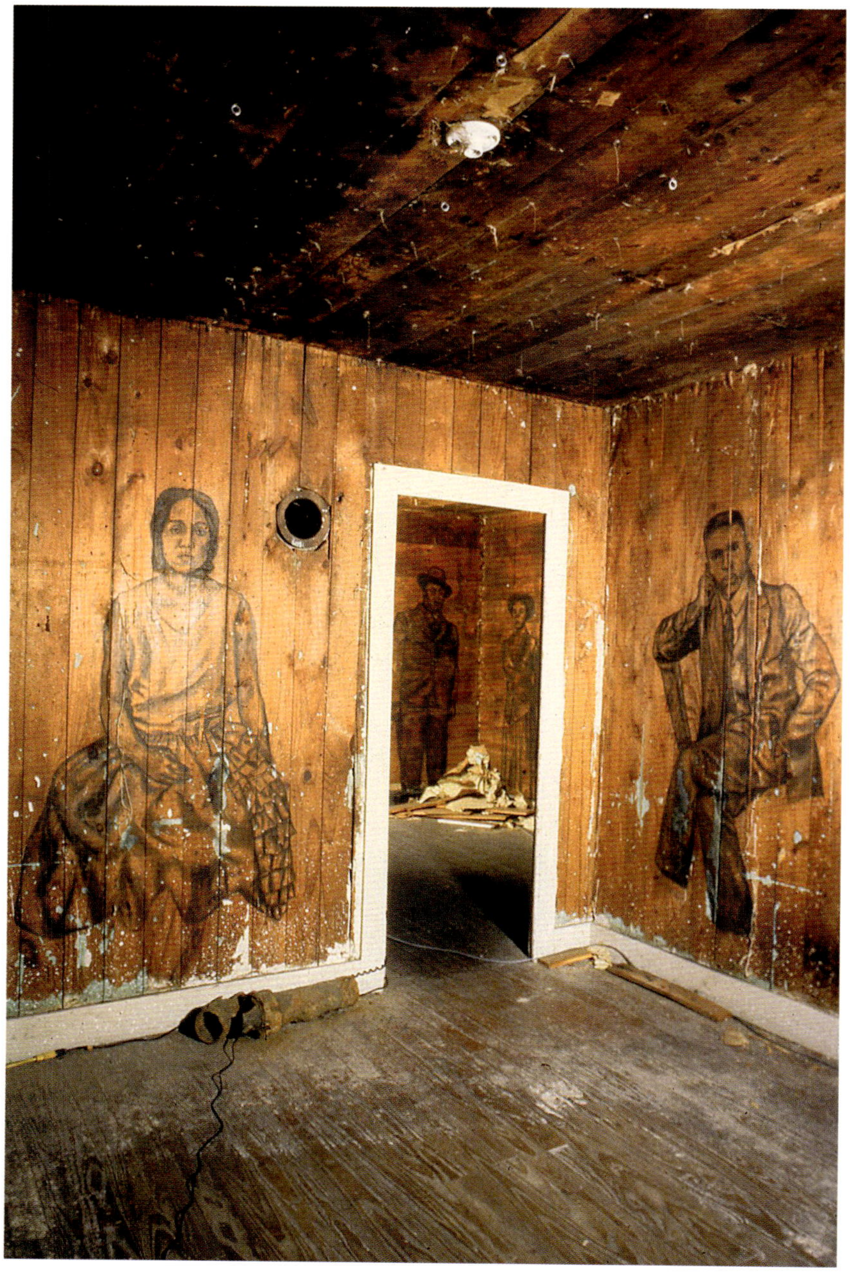

Echo, 1996
Charcoal on wood
Project Row Houses, Houston, Tex.

gallery in the Creedmoor Psychiatric Center in Queens, New York, for a group of artists-in-residence who are also patients at the hospital. Despite the fact that patients' diagnoses include schizophrenia and other forms of psychosis, the project refuses to consider their art-making as simply a form of therapy or as a diagnostic tool. Taking into account the complex relationship between creativity and mental illness, the artist-patients are encouraged to tap parts of their consciousness that more conventional psychiatric regimens might rather suppress. Dr. Marton, who still leads the project, works with artist-patients to create multifaceted works that are exhibited in The Living Museum's public gallery (a huge abandoned building that formerly housed the psychiatric center's main kitchen), filled with art made by patients over the past twenty-odd years. There are also a series of rooms, such as the Church Room, the Hospital Room and the Seclusion Room, which are filled with objects that relate to these essential elements of human social life. Some works are rendered in highly personal styles, others clearly reference Expressionism or Conceptualism; the materials range from paint and cardboard to found objects such as matchbooks, bibles (donated by a religious charity), and domestic appliances. In other words, the work displays all of the diversity of contemporary art and attests to Beuys's notion that artistic potential resides in every individual.

Participatory art is a direct challenge to cherished assumptions about the meaning of art, its function in society, and the special nature of the artist's calling. But in their place, it poses a set of models for the melding of art and life and opens up exciting new possibilities for artists seeking a more significant role in contemporary culture. Where is art going? How will it be different in the future? Of all the myriad forces at work unmaking and remaking art today, none may ultimately be more momentous than the democratization of art through participation.

DR. JANOS MARTON AND THE LIVING MUSEUM

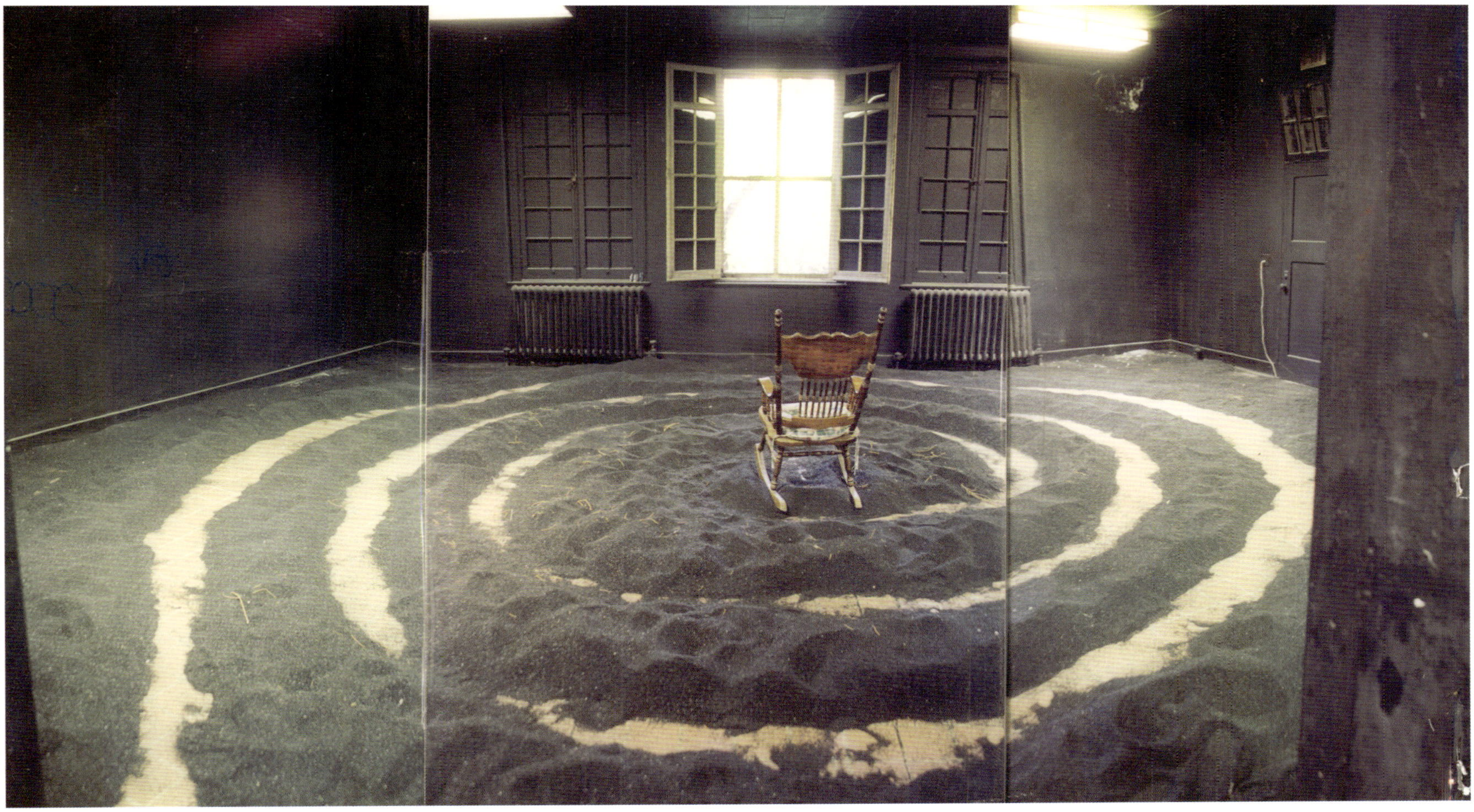

Seclusion Room, 2002
Volcanic sand on terra cotta floor, dimensions variable

NOTES

INTRODUCTION

1. Alfred H. Barr, Jr., flowchart, reproduced on the jacket of the original edition of his CUBISM AND ABSTRACT ART (New York: Museum of Modern Art, 1936).
2. Clement Greenberg, "Avant-Garde and Kitsch" and "Towards a Newer Laocoon," in POLLOCK AND AFTER: THE CRITICAL DEBATE, ed. Francis Frascina (New York: Harper and Row, 1985), 21–33 and 35–46. Originally published in PARTISAN REVIEW 6 (Fall 1939) and 7 (July–August 1940).
3. Michael Fried, "Art and Objecthood," ARTFORUM 5 (June 1967): 12–23.
4. Arthur Danto, "Bad Aesthetic Times," in ENCOUNTERS AND REFLECTIONS: ART IN THE HISTORICAL PRESENT (New York: Farrar, Straus and Giroux, 1986), 297–312.
5. Linda Nochlin, "Why Have There Been No Great Women Artists?" in WOMEN, ART, AND POWER AND OTHER ESSAYS (New York: Harper and Row, 1988), 145–78. Originally published in ARTNEWS 69 (January 1971), 22–39 and 67–71.
6. Jean-François Lyotard, THE POSTMODERN CONDITION: A REPORT ON KNOWLEDGE (Minneapolis: University of Minnesota Press, 1984).

ART & POPULAR CULTURE

1. Greenberg, "Avant-Garde and Kitsch," 25.
2. Andy Warhol, Kasper König, Pontus Hulten, and Olle Granath, eds., ANDY WARHOL (Stockholm: Moderna Museet, 1968), 14.
3. Calvin Tomkins, "The Prankster," NEW YORKER, October 4, 2004, 56.
4. Andy Warhol, THE PHILOSOPHY OF ANDY WARHOL: FROM A TO B AND BACK AGAIN (New York: Harcourt Brace Jovanovich, 1975), 91.
5. Marshall McLuhan and Quentin Fiore, THE MEDIUM IS THE MASSAGE (New York: Bantam, 1967). In the title to McLuhan's best-known book the last word of his dictum was changed by a typesetter's typo, and he decided to keep the alteration.
6. Jean Baudrillard, "Simulacra and Simulations," in JEAN BAUDRILLARD: SELECTED WRITINGS, ed. Mark Poster (Stanford, Calif.: Stanford University Press, 1988), 166–84.
7. Warhol, König, et al., ANDY WARHOL, 10.
8. Coosje van Bruggen, JOHN BALDESSARI (New York: Rizzoli, 1990), 35.
9. "Doug Aitken talks to Ed Ruscha," FRIEZE (June/July 2004): 102.
10. Andy Warhol and Pat Hackett, POPISM: THE WARHOL '60S (New York: Harcourt Brace Jovanovich, 1980), 3.
11. Andy Warhol, AMERICA (New York: Harper and Row, 1985), 8.

ART & THE QUOTIDIAN OBJECT

1. Marcel Duchamp, "Apropos of the Readymade," in SALT CELLAR: THE WRITINGS OF MARCEL DUCHAMP, ed. Michel Sanouillet and Elmer Peterson (New York: Da Capo Press, 1973), 141.
2. Arthur Danto, THE TRANSFIGURATION OF THE COMMONPLACE: A PHILOSOPHY OF ART (Cambridge, Mass.: Harvard University Press, 1981).
3. Walter Benjamin, "The Work of Art in the Age of Mechanical Reproduction," in ILLUMINATIONS, trans. Harry Zohn, ed. Hannah Arendt (New York: Schocken Books, 1969), 217–59.
4. Hilton Kramer, "Duchamp and His Legacy," NEW CRITERION 14 (October 1995).
5. Haim Steinbach, quoted in "'80s Then: Haim Steinbach talks to Tim Griffin," ARTFORUM 41 (April 2003): 230.
6. Mark Van de Walle, "Jessica Stockholder," ARTFORUM 34 (April 1996): 78.
7. Sarah Sze, quoted in Eleanor Heartney, "The Return of the Red Brick Alternative," ART IN AMERICA 86 (January 1998): 63.
8. Daniel Birnbaum, "Jason Rhoades Talks about His Impala Project," ARTFORUM 37 (September 1998): 135.

ART & ABSTRACTION

1. Quoted in Mark Rosenthal, ABSTRACTION IN THE TWENTIETH CENTURY: TOTAL RISK, FREEDOM, DISCIPLINE (New York: Solomon R. Guggenheim Museum, 1996), 37.
2. Quoted in Charlotte Douglas, "The First All-Russian Congress of Poets of the Future," in SWANS OF OTHER WORLDS: KAZIMIR MALEVICH AND THE ORIGINS OF ABSTRACTION IN RUSSIA (Ann Arbor, Mich.: UMI Research Press, 1980), 36.
3. Rosenthal, ABSTRACTION IN THE TWENTIETH CENTURY, 37.
4. Wassily Kandinsky, CONCERNING THE SPIRITUAL IN ART (1912; repr., New York: Wittenborn, 1966), 54.
5. Arthur Dove, letter to Arthur Jerome Eddy (October 3, 1913), quoted in Rosenthal, ABSTRACTION IN THE TWENTIETH CENTURY, 263.
6. Barbara Rose, "ABC Art," ART IN AMERICA 53 (October/November 1965): 58.
7. Fried, "Art and Objecthood."
8. Robert Ryman, "On Painting," lecture delivered at the Solomon R. Guggenheim Museum, New York, January 9, 1991, reprinted in Christel Sauer and Urs Rassmuller, ROBERT RYMAN (Paris: Espace d'Art Contemporain; Schaffhausen, Switzerland: Hallen für Neue Kunst, 1991), 59.
9. Bridget Riley, "The Experience of Painting," in THE EYE'S MIND: BRIDGET RILEY, COLLECTED WRITINGS, 1965–1999, ed. Robert Kudielka (London: Thames and Hudson, 1999), 122.
10. Frank Stella, WORKING SPACE (Cambridge, Mass.: William Stout Architectural Press, 1986).
11. Rosalind E. Krauss, "Grids," in THE ORIGINALITY OF THE AVANT-GARDE AND OTHER MODERNIST MYTHS (Cambridge, Mass.: MIT Press, 1985), 9.
12. Sol LeWitt, "Paragraphs on Conceptual Art," in CONCEPTUAL ART: A CRITICAL ANTHOLOGY, ed. Alexander Alberro and Blake Stimson (Cambridge, Mass.: MIT Press, 1999), 12. Originally published in ARTFORUM 5 (Summer 1967): 79–83.

ART & REPRESENTATION

1. Arthur Danto, "The End of Art," in THE DEATH OF ART, ed. Berel Lang (New York: Haven, 1984), 5–35.
2. Roland Barthes, "Myth Today," in A BARTHES READER, ed. Susan Sontag (London: Jonathan Cape, 1982), 93–149.
3. Roland Barthes, CAMERA LUCIDA (New York: Hill and Wang, 1981), 76.
4. Vik Muniz, quoted in Peter Galassi, "Natura Pix," in VIK MUNIZ (Paris: Centre National de la Photographie, Caisse des depôt et consignations, et Galerie Xippas, 1999). Reproduced online at www.vikmuniz.net.
5. Hilla Becher, quoted in Ulf Erdmann Ziegler, "The Bechers' Industrial Lexicon," ART IN AMERICA 90 (June 2002): 142.
6. Barthes, "Myth Today," 116.

ART & NARRATIVE

1. Frederic Jameson, "Postmodernism and Consumer Society," in THE ANTI-AESTHETIC: ESSAYS ON POSTMODERN CULTURE, ed. Hal Foster (Port Townsend, Wash.: Bay Press, 1983), 115.
2. Craig Owens, "The Allegorical Impulse: Toward a Theory of Postmodernism," in ART AFTER MODERNISM: RETHINKING REPRESENTATION, ed. Brian Wallis (New York: New Museum of Contemporary Art; Boston, David R. Godine, 1984), 204.
3. Ibid., 235.
4. Roland Barthes, "The Death of the Author," in Barthes, IMAGE, MUSIC, TEXT, ed. and trans. Stephen Heath (New York: Hill and Wang, 1977), 145.
5. Matthew Ritchie, "The Hard Way," www.adaweb.com/influx/hardway.

ART & TIME

1. Douglas Crimp, "De-synchronization in Joan Jonas's Performances," in JOAN JONAS: SCRIPTS AND DESCRIPTIONS, 1968–1982, ed. Crimp (Berkeley, Calif.: University Art Museum Berkeley; Eindhoven, the Netherlands: Stedelijk van Abbemuseum, 1983), 8.
2. Saul Anton, "A Thousand Words: Doug Aitken," ARTFORUM 38 (May 2000): 161.
3. David Ross, Bill Viola, and Peter Sellars, BILL VIOLA (Paris: Flammarion, 1997), 22.
4. Jean-Paul Sartre, BEING AND NOTHINGNESS, trans. Hazel E. Barnes (New York: Simon and Schuster, 1993).

ART & NATURE AND TECHNOLOGY

1. F. T. Marinetti, "The Foundation and Manifesto of Futurism," 1909, repr. in THEORIES OF MODERN ART, ed. Herschel B. Chipp (Berkeley and Los Angeles: University of California Press, 1968), 286.
2. Peter Halley, in "Criticism to Complicity," roundtable discussion moderated by Peter Nagy, FLASH ART, no. 129 (Summer 1986): 46.
3. Jeffrey Deitch, POST HUMAN (New York: Jeffrey Deitch, 1992), 29.
4. Robert Smithson, "A Sedimentation of the Mind: Earth Projects," in ROBERT SMITHSON: THE COLLECTED WRITINGS, ed. Jack Flam (Berkeley and Los Angeles: University of California Press, 1996), 82.
5. Mel Chin, quoted on ART:21 (ART IN THE TWENTY-FIRST CENTURY), PBS, September 2001, www.pbs.org/art21/artists/chin/clip2.html.
6. Hans-Ulrich Obrist, "1000 Words: Allora and Calzadilla," ARTFORUM 43 (March 2005): 205.
7. Gregg Bordowitz, "Tactics Inside and Out: Critical Art Ensemble," ARTFORUM 43 (September 2004): 214.
8. Donna Haraway, "A Cyborg Manifesto: Science, Technology, and Socialist-Feminism in the Late Twentieth Century," in SIMIANS, CYBORGS AND WOMEN: THE REINVENTION OF NATURE (New York: Routledge, 1991), 149.

ART & DEFORMATION

1. Frances S. Connelly, MODERN ART AND THE GROTESQUE (Cambridge: Cambridge University Press, 2003).
2. Mikhail Bakhtin, RABELAIS AND HIS WORLD, trans. Helene Iswolsky (Cambridge, Mass.: MIT Press, 1968).
3. Julia Kristeva, POWERS OF HORROR: AN ESSAY ON ABJECTION, trans. Leon S. Roudiez (New York: Columbia University Press, 1982), 4.
4. Yve-Alain Bois and Rosalind E. Krauss, FORMLESS: A USER'S GUIDE (New York: Zone Books, 2000).
5. Artist's statement, 2004.
6. PLATO: THE COLLECTED DIALOGUES, trans. Paul Shorey, ed. Edith Hamilton and Huntington Cairns (Princeton, N.J.: Princeton University Press, 1961), 682.

ART & THE BODY

1. See RoseLee Goldberg, PERFORMANCE ART: FROM FUTURISM TO THE PRESENT (London: Thames and Hudson, 1979), and LIVE ART SINCE THE '60S (London: Thames and Hudson, 2004); Paul Schimmel, OUT OF ACTIONS: BETWEEN PERFORMANCE AND THE OBJECT, 1949–79 (Los Angeles: Museum of Contemporary Art, 1988); and Amelia Jones, BODY ART / PERFORMING THE SUBJECT (Minneapolis: University of Minnesota Press, 1998).
2. Qian Zhijian, "Performing Bodies: Zhang Huan, Ma Liuming, and Performance Art in China," ART JOURNAL 58 (Summer 1999): 60–81.
3. Kenneth Clark, THE NUDE: A STUDY IN IDEAL FORM (London: Bollingen, 1972), 3. Based on a series of 1953 lectures at the National Gallery, Washington, D.C.; originally published in 1956.
4. See Griselda Pollock, VISIONS AND DIFFERENCE: FEMININITY, FEMINISM AND THE HISTORIES OF ART (London: Routledge and Kegan Paul, 1988); Nochlin, WOMEN, ART, AND POWER; and Ann Sutherland Harris and Linda Nochlin, WOMEN ARTISTS, 1550–1950 (New York: Random House, 1976).
5. John Berger, WAYS OF SEEING (London: British Broadcasting Corporation; Harmondsworth, England: Penguin, 1972), 47.
6. Laura Mulvey, "Visual Pleasure and Narrative Cinema," repr. in Wallis, ed., ART AFTER MODERNISM, 361–73.

ART & IDENTITY

1. Henry Louis Gates, "Introduction: Writing 'Race' and the Difference It Makes," repr. in RACE, WRITING AND DIFFERENCE, ed. Gates (Chicago: University of Chicago Press, 1985).
2. Nochlin, "Why Have There Been No Great Women Artists?" 22–39.
3. See especially Lucy R. Lippard, "What Is Female Imagery?" In FROM THE CENTER: FEMINIST ESSAYS ON WOMEN'S ART (New York: E. P. Dutton, 1976).
4. The groundbreaking texts on multiculturalism were Lucy R. Lippard, MIXED BLESSINGS: NEW ART IN A MULTICULTURAL AMERICA (New York: Pantheon, 1990), and Thelma Golden, David Deitcher, and Guillermo Gómez-Peña, THE DECADE SHOW: FRAMEWORKS OF IDENTITY IN THE 1980S (New York: New Museum of Contemporary Art, 1990). An early theorization of queer theory appears in Eve Kosofsky, EPISTEMOLOGY OF THE CLOSET (Berkeley and Los Angeles: University of California Press, 1990).
5. Trinh T. Minh-Ha, "Of Other Peoples: Beyond the 'Salvage Paradigm,' " in DISCUSSIONS IN CONTEMPORARY CULTURE, NO. 1, ed. Hal Foster (Seattle: Bay Press, 1987), 139–40.
6. See Douglas Crimp, ed., AIDS: CULTURAL ANALYSIS, CULTURAL ACTIVISM (Cambridge, Mass.: MIT Press, 1988).

7. Salman Rushdie, THE SATANIC VERSES (New York: Picador, 1988), 8.
8. Quoted in Ana Fingel Honigman, "What the Structure Defines: An Interview with Kutlug Ataman," ART JOURNAL 63 (Spring 2004): 82.

ART & SPIRITUALITY

1. Kandinsky, CONCERNING THE SPIRITUAL IN ART, 53. See also Maurice Tuchman, THE SPIRITUAL IN ART: ABSTRACT PAINTING, 1890–1985 (Los Angeles: Los Angeles County Museum of Art, 1986).
2. Rosalind Krauss, "Grids," 1980, repr. in Krauss, THE ORIGINALITY OF THE AVANT-GARDE AND OTHER MODERNIST MYTHS (Cambridge, Mass.: MIT Press, 1985), 12.
3. Publications addressing contemporary art and religion include THE VISUAL CULTURE OF AMERICAN RELIGIONS, ed. David Morgan and Sally M. Promey (Berkeley and Los Angeles: University of California Press, 2001); James Elkins, ON THE STRANGE PLACE OF RELIGION IN CONTEMPORARY ART (New York: Routledge, 2004); and the author's own POSTMODERN HERETICS: THE CATHOLIC IMAGINATION IN CONTEMPORARY ART (New York: Midmarch Arts Press, 2004).
4. Ron Athey, "Interview with Jurij V. Krpan," VIRUS, no. 10 (January 1997). Reprinted in English at www.undo.net.
5. John Perreault, "Artopia," ARTSJOURNAL Weblog, December 6, 2004, www.artsjournal.com/artopia/2004/12/james_lee_byars_at_the_whitney.html.

ART & GLOBALISM

1. Thomas Friedman, THE WORLD IS FLAT: A BRIEF HISTORY OF THE TWENTY-FIRST CENTURY (New York: Farrar, Straus and Giroux, 2004).
2. See Robert J. C. Young, POSTCOLONIALISM: A VERY SHORT INTRODUCTION (Oxford: Oxford University Press, 2001).
3. Edward Said, ORIENTALISM (New York: Vintage, 1979).
4. James Clifford, THE PREDICAMENT OF CULTURE: TWENTIETH CENTURY ETHNOGRAPHY, LITERATURE AND ART (Cambridge, Mass.: Harvard University Press, 1988), 16.

ART & ARCHITECTURE

1. See Adolf Loos, "Ornament and Crime," in ADOLF LOOS, SPOKEN INTO THE VOID: COLLECTED ESSAYS, 1897–1900, trans. Jane O. Newman and John H. Smith (Cambridge, Mass.: MIT Press, 1982).
2. Le Corbusier, TOWARDS A NEW ARCHITECTURE (New York: Dover, 1985), ix.
3. Liam Gillick, in an interview with Anthony Spira, Whitechapel Art Gallery, May 2003, www.whitechapel.org/content.php?page_id=511.
4. See www.zittel.org.

ART & ITS INSTITUTIONS

1. Clement Greenberg, "Avant-Garde and Kitsch," 24.
2. Marinetti, "Founding and Manifesto of Futurism," 1909, repr. in MARINETTI: SELECTED WRITINGS, ed. R. W. Flint, trans. R. W. Flint and Arthur Coppotelli (New York: Farrar, Straus and Giroux, 1972), 42.
3. Theodor W. Adorno, "Valery Proust Museum," in PRISMS, trans. Samuel and Shierry Weber (Cambridge, Mass.: MIT Press, 1997), 175.
4. Bruce Chatwin, UTZ (New York: Penguin, 1988), 20.
5. Though artists of the 1980s were reading Roland Barthes, Jacques Derrida, and Michel Foucault, the most influential theoretical writer of the time was Jean Baudrillard, whose essay "Simulacra and Simulations" became a sacred text for the commodity critics. See Jean Baudrillard: SELECTED WRITINGS, 166–184.
6. Barbara Kruger, quoted in Carol Squires, "Diversionary (Syn)tactics: Barbara Kruger Has Her Way with Words," ARTNEWS 86 (February 1987): 80.
7. Jeff Koons, quoted in Nagy, mod., "Criticism to Complicity," 47.
8. Lawrence Weschler, MR. WILSON'S CABINET OF WONDER: PRONGED ANTS, HORNED HUMANS, MICE ON TOAST, AND OTHER MARVELS OF JURASSIC TECHNOLOGY (New York: Pantheon, 1995).
9. Ralph Rugoff, "Beyond Belief: The Museum as Metaphor," in VISUAL DISPLAY: CULTURE BEYOND APPEARANCES, ed. Lynne Cook and Peter Wollen (Seattle: Bay Press, 1995), 69.

ART & POLITICS

1. Max Kozloff, "American Painting during the Cold War," ARTFORUM 11 (May 1973): 43–54; and Eva Cockcroft, "Abstract Expressionism, Weapon of the Cold War," ARTFORUM 12 (June 1974): 39–41. Both reprinted in Frascina, ed., POLLOCK AND AFTER.
2. Robert Hughes, THE CULTURE OF COMPLAINT: THE FRAYING OF AMERICA (New York: Oxford University Press, 1993).
3. Hilton Kramer, THE REVENGE OF THE PHILISTINES: ART AND CULTURE, 1972–1984 (New York: Simon and Schuster, 1985).
4. Foster, ed., THE ANTI-AESTHETIC; and Wallis, ed., ART AFTER MODERNISM.
5. Richard Serra, quoted on PBS Web site accompanying "Culture Shock," www.pbs.org/wgbh/cultureshock.
6. Charles L. Griswold, "The Vietnam Veterans Memorial and the Washington Mall: Philosophical Thoughts on Political Iconology," in ART AND THE PUBLIC SPHERE, ed. W. J. T. Mitchell (Chicago: University of Chicago Press, 1990), 79–111.
7. James E. Young, "The Counter Monument: Memory against Itself in Germany Today," in Mitchell, ART AND THE PUBLIC SPHERE, 49–78.

ART & AUDIENCE

1. Fried, "Art and Objecthood."
2. Barthes, "The Death of the Author."
3. Hans Robert Jauss, 1967 lecture at the University of Constance, Germany, published as TOWARD AN AESTHETIC OF RECEPTION (Minneapolis: University of Minnesota Press, 1982).
4. Guy Debord, THE SOCIETY OF THE SPECTACLE, trans. Donald Nicholson-Smith (London: Rebel Press / AIM, 1987).
5. Nicholas Bourriaud, RELATIONAL AESTHETICS (Paris: Presses du Reel, 2003).

CHRONOLOGY

1977

"Pictures," an exhibition of work by Troy Brauntuch, Jack Goldstein, Sherrie Levine, Robert Longo, and Philip Smith, at Artists Space, New York, signals new direction in art, as does founding of COLAB (Collaborative Projects, Inc.), a loosely organized collective of artists who came together to organize underground exhibitions, film screenings, performances, and concerts. Opening of the Centre Georges Pompidou, Paris. Kasper König's Skulptur Projekte debuts in Muenster, Germany.

1978

Apple computer is introduced. Important exhibitions include: "Bad Painting," curated by Marcia Tucker, New Museum of Contemporary Art, New York; "New Image Painting," curated by Richard Marshall, Whitney Museum of American Art, New York.

1979

Iranian Revolution. The Shah flees and the Ayatollah Khomeini assumes power. Iranian students storm the U.S. embassy and hold 52 hostages for 444 days. The Soviets invade Afghanistan. Margaret Thatcher becomes British Prime Minister, a post she will hold until 1990. Jerry Falwell founds the Moral Majority in the U.S. Group Material, an influential art collective, and Fashion Moda, an important Bronx-based alternative space, are founded in New York. In Italy, the 1979 Venice Biennale is directed by Giovanni Carandente.

1980

Ronald Reagan is elected U.S. President and remains in office until 1988. CNN is launched as the first all-news network. Saddam Hussein launches war against Iran. In New York, the "Times Square Art Show," a sprawling exhibition, hung in a decrepit former bus depot and massage parlor off Times Square and organized by Fashion Moda and COLAB, signals emergence of new generation of artists, including Jenny Holzer, David Hammons, Charlie and John Ahearn, Jean-Michel Basquiat, Keith Haring, and Kiki Smith. Inaugural exhibition of ABC No Ric is "The Real Estate Show," which takes place in an abandoned East Side tenement. Jasper Johns's Three Flags sells for over $1 million, a first for a living artist. Metro Pictures Gallery, with a stable that includes Robert Longo, Sherrie Levine, Richard Prince, and Cindy Sherman, opens in SoHo.

1981

The AIDS crisis emerges. Polish government crushes the Solidarity movement. Prince Charles and Diana Spencer marry. Gracie Mansion Gallery opens in director Gracie Mansion's bathroom in her East Village apartment, serving as harbinger of the shortlived but highly influential East Village art scene. Soon to follow are Fun Gallery, Civilian Warfare, and Nature Morte. German Neo-Expressionist painters are exhibited in numerous New York galleries. Important exhibitions include: "A New Spirit in Painting," curated by Nicholas Serota, Norman Rosenthal, and Christos Joachimides, Royal Academy of Arts, London; "Westkunst: Contemporary Art since 1939," curated by Kasper König, Museen der Stadt, Cologne; "New York/New Wave," curated by Diego Cortez, P.S. 1 Center for Contemporary Art, New York; "Not Just for Laughs: The Art of Subversion," curated by Marcia Tucker, New Museum Of Contemporary Art, New York.

1982

Maya Lin's Vietnam Memorial is unveiled in Washington, D.C., and after initial protests becomes a model for public memorials. Leonid Brezhnev, General Secretary of the U.S.S.R., dies; Yuri Andropov takes over. Important exhibitions include: "Zeitgeist," curated by Norman Rosenthal and Christos Joachimides, Martin-Gropius-Bau, Berlin; "Transavantguardia Italia/America," curated by Achille Bonito Oliva, Galleria Civica, Modena, Italy; "Italian Art Now: An American Perspective," curated by Diane Waldman, The Solomon R. Guggenheim Museum, New York; "Art and the Media: A Fatal Attraction," curated by Thomas Lawson et al., Chicago Renaissance Society; "Extended Sensibilities: Homosexual Presence in Contemporary Art," curated by Dan Cameron, New Museum of Contemporary Art, New York; "Image Scavengers," Institute of Contemporary Art, Philadelphia, Pa.; "Post-Minimalism," Aldrich Museum of Contemporary Art, Ridgefield, Conn. The 1982 Venice Biennale is directed by Gian Alberto Dell'Acqua and Documenta 7 is directed by Rudi Fuchs.

1983

U.S. Embassy is bombed in Beirut, killing 40 people. New York's East Village art scene takes off, with dozens of galleries opening in tiny storefronts in this grimy neighborhood. Important exhibitions include "The New Art," organized by Michael Compton, Tate Gallery, London; "Science Fiction," curated by Peter Halley, John Weber Gallery, New York; "Post Graffiti," Sidney Janis Gallery, New York; "Expressions: New Art from Germany," St. Louis Art Museum, Mo.; "Sound and Vision: oday's Music," New Museum of Contemporary Art, New York; "Recent British Video," curated by Stuart Marshall, The Kitchen, New York.

1984

Indira Gandhi is assassinated. Chemical disaster in Bhopal, India, kills thousands. Reagan is re-elected U.S. President in landslide election. Congress cuts off aid to Nicaragua, and illegal guns sales start to fund the contras. "'Primitivism' in 20th Century Art: Affinity of the Tribal and the Modern," curated by Kirk Varnedoe and William Rubin for the Museum of Modern Art, New York, kicks off a heated debate over the long cherished assumptions about the superiority and universality of Western Modernist art. This debate is most fully expressed in a remarkable exchange of letters in Artforum between critic Thomas McEvilley and the exhibition curators. Similarly controversial is the Museum of Modern Art's "An International Survey of Recent Painting and Sculpture," curated by Kynaston McShine, MoMA, New York, which includes only 19 women among its 169 artists. Other important exhibitions include: "The Hard Won Image," curated by Richard Morphet, Tate Gallery, London; "Blam! The Explosion of Pop, Minimalism, and Performance," organized by Barbara Haskell, Whitney Museum of American Art, New York; "New Hand Painted Dreams: Contemporary Surrealism," Barbara Gladstone Gallery, New York; "Von Hier Aus," curated by Kasper König, Messegelände, Düsseldorf; "Art and Ideology," curated by Benjamin Buchloh, Donald Kuspit, Lucy Lippard, Nilda Peraz, and Lowery Sims, New Museum of Contemporary Art, New York; "Content: A Contemporary Focus 1974-84," curated by Howard N. Fox, Miranda McClintic, and Phyllis Rosenzweig, Hirshhorn Museum and Sculpture Garden, Washington, D.C. The 1984 Venice Biennale is directed by Paolo Portoghesi, and the first Havana Biennale is held. The first Turner Prize is won by Malcolm Morley.

1985

Mikhail Gorbachev assumes power in the U.S.S.R. The Guerrilla Girls are founded in response to the poor showing of women and minorities in New York galleries and museums. Anonymous members of the group begin appearing at art events in gorilla masks and plastering posters around SoHo citing the dismal statistics for women artists. Charles Saatchi founds The Saatchi Gallery in London. Important exhibitions include: "L'Amour Fou: Photography and Surrealism," curated by Rosalind Krauss and Jane Livingston, Corcoran Gallery of Art, Washington, D.C.; "Les Immatériaux," curated by Jean-François Lyotard, Centre Georges Pompidou, Paris; "The Knot: Arte Povera," curated by Germano Celant, P.S. 1 Contemporary Art Center, New York; "The Art of Memory/The Loss of History," curated by William Olander, New Museum of Contemporary Art, New York; "The European Iceberg: Creativity in Germany and Italy Today," curated by Germano Celant, Art Gallery of Ontario, Toronto; "Difference: On Representation and Sexuality," Kate Linker and Jane Weinstock, New Museum of Contemporary Art, New York. Howard Hodgkin wins the Turner Prize.

1986

Joseph Beuys dies. Chernobyl nuclear disaster occurs. Iran-Contra scandal emerges. In New York, "Neo-Geo" comes into fashion as a term describing geometric abstraction in works by such artists as Peter Halley, Jeff Koons, Ashley Bickerton, and Meyer Vaisman. These artists are featured in a much-discussed show at Sonnabend Gallery, New York. Other important exhibitions include: "The Spiritual in Art: 1890–1985," curated by Maurice Tuchman, Los Angeles County Museum of Art; "Endgame: Reference and Simulation in Recent Painting and Sculpture," curated by Elisabeth Sussman, David Joselit, and Bob Riley, Institute of Contemporary Art, Boston; "Tokyo: Form and Spirit," curated by Martin and Mildred Friedman, Walker Art Center, Minneapolis, Minn.; "Vienna 1900: Art, Architecture and Design," curated by Kirk Varnedoe, The Museum of Modern Art, New York; "The Machine Age in America, 1918–1941," curated by Dianne Pilgrim and Richard Guy Wilson, Brooklyn Museum, New York; "Damaged Goods: Desire and the Economy of the Object," curated by Brian Wallis, New Museum of Contemporary Art, New York; "Chambre d'amis," curated by Jan Hoet, a series of installations placed in private homes in Ghent, Belgium; "Art and Its Double," curated by Dan Cameron, Fundacio Caixa de Pensions, Barcelona; "Japon des avant gardes, 1910–1970," Centre Georges Pompidou, Paris. The 1986 Venice Biennale is directed by Paolo Portoghesi. Gilbert and George win the Turner Prize.

1987

Act Up is founded at the Lesbian and Gay Community Center in New York to combat indifference to AIDS crisis. Andy Warhol dies. The Public Art Fund in New York begins "Messages to the Public," a program in which texts by artists such as Nancy Dwyer, Jenny Holzer, and Alfredo Jaar are displayed on the Spectacolor Board in Times Square. The AIDS Memorial Quilt is displayed on the Washington Mall. New York's East Village art scene dissipates as galleries close or move to SoHo. On October 19, the U.S. stock market crashes, and the market loses 22% of its value in one day. Important exhibitions include: "American Women Artists 1830–1930," curated by Eleanor Tufts for the inaugural exhibition of the National Museum of Women in the Arts, Washington, D.C.; "Recent British Sculpture," curated by Mary Jane Jacob and Graham Beal, Museum of Contemporary Art, Chicago; "Berlinart 1961–1987," curated by Kynaston McShine, The Museum of Modern Art, New York; "Contemporary Hispanic Art in the United States," curated by Jane Livingston and John Beardsley, The Museum of Fine Arts, Houston, Tex.; "Art of the Fantastic: Latin American Art 1920–1987," curated by Hollister Sturges and Holliday T. Day, Indianapolis Museum of Art, Ind.; "Fashion and Surrealism," curated by Harold Koda, Richard Martin, and Laura Sindarbrand, Fashion Institute of Technology, New York: "Contemporary Art from Central Europe," curated by Dieter Reonte, Museum Moderne Kunst, Vienna; "New York Art Now," Saatchi Gallery, London. Documenta 8 is directed by Manfred Schneckenburger. The second installment of Kasper König's Skulptur Projekte opens in Muenster, Germany. Richard Deacon wins the Turner Prize.

1988

George H. W. Bush is elected President of the United States. Soviets leave Afghanistan. Pan Am Flight 103 explodes over Lockerbie, Scotland; Libyan terrorists are suspected of planting the bomb. "Freeze," curated by Damien Hirst for the London Docklands Development Corporation and Olympia and York, signals the emergence of the Young British Artists (YBAs). Other important exhibitions include: "Utopia Post Utopia," curated by Elizabeth Sussman and David Joselit, Institute of Contemporary Art, Boston; "Democracy: A Four-Part Exhibition," a series of installations and public discussions organized by Group Material and Gary Garrels, DIA Art Foundation, New York; "Deconstructivist Architecture," curated by Philip Johnson and Mark Wigley, The Museum of Modern Art, New York; "The Latin American Spirit: Art and Artists in the United States," curated by Luis Cancel, Bronx Museum of the Arts, New York; "Refigured Painting: The German Image," curated by Thomas Krens, Michael Govan, and Joseph Thompson, The Solomon R. Guggenheim Museum, New York, and Williams College Museum of Art, Williamstown, Mass. The 1988 Venice Biennale is directed by Giovanni Carandente. Tony Cragg wins the Turner Prize.

1989

Berlin Wall is demolished. Thousands are killed when a student protest in Tianannmen Square in Beijing is put down by the army. Iranian leader Ayatollah Ali Khomeini issues a fatwa against writer Salman Rushdie. The ruptured tanker Exxon Valdez sends 11 million gallons of crude oil into Alaska's Prince William Sound. Auction records are broken with the $82.5 million sale of van Gogh's Portrait of Dr. Gachet. Richard Serra's Tilted Arc is removed from Federal Plaza in New York City after a nine-year battle. The U.S. Senate castigates the National Endowment for the Arts (NEA) over a small grant awarded to Andres Serrano for a show that includes his Piss Christ. The Corcoran Gallery of Art cancels a retrospective exhibition of work by Robert Mapplethorpe because of fears of government reprisals. Controversy also whirls around the exhibition "Witnesses: Against Our Vanishing," curated by Nan Goldin for Artists Space, New York, because of an incendiary catalog essay by David Wojnarowicz. Important exhibitions include: "A Forest of Signs: Art in the Crisis of Representation," curated by Ann Goldstein and Mary Jane Jacob, Museum of Contemporary Art, Los Angeles;

"Against Nature: Japanese Art in the 1980s," curated by Thomas Sokolowski, Kathy Halbreich, Shinji Kohmoto, and Fumio Nanjo, Grey Art Gallery, New York, and MIT List Visual Arts Center, Cambridge, Mass.; "Strange Attractors: Signs of Chaos," curated by Laura Trippi, New Museum of Contemporary Art, New York; "Situationists 1957–72," curated by Peter Wollen and Mark Francis, Centre Georges Pompidou, Paris, and Institute of Contemporary Arts, London; "Image World: Art and Media Culture," curated by Marvin Heiferman, Whitney Museum of American Art, New York; "Making Their Mark: Women Artists Move into the Mainstream, 1970–1985," curated by Randy Rosen, Cincinnati Art Museum, Ohio; "If You Lived Here: The City in Art, Theory and Social Activism," project conceived by Martha Rosler, DIA Art Foundation, New York; "Magiciens de la terre," Centre Georges Pompidou and la Grande Halle de la Villete, Paris. Richard Long wins the Turner Prize.

1990

Iraq invades Kuwait. East and West Germany are reunited. Margaret Thatcher resigns as British Prime Minister. The NEA rescinds grants to the "NEA Four" (Karen Finley, Holly Hughes, John Flick, and Tim Miller), igniting a legal battle that eventually ends up in the Supreme Court of the United States. Dennis Barrie, director of the Contemporary Arts Center Ohio, is put on trial for "pandering obscenity" in exhibiting the Mapplethorpe retrospective. Important exhibitions include: "High and Low: Modern Art and Popular Culture," curated by Kirk Varnedoe and Adam Gopnik, The Museum of Modern Art, New York; "The Decade Show: Frameworks of Identity in the 1980s," curated by Julia P. Herzberg, Laura Trippi, Gary Sangster, and Sharon Patton, New Museum of Contemporary Art, New York, Museum of Contemporary Hispanic Art, New York, and Studio Museum of Harlem, New York; "The Play of the Unmentionable," curated by Joseph Kosuth, in the lobby of the Brooklyn Museum, New York; "Post-Minimalism: American Sculptures 1965–75," curated by Richard Armstrong and Richard Marshall, Whitney Museum of Contemporary Art, New York; "Between Spring and Summer: Soviet Conceptual Art in the Era of Late Communism," curated by David Ross, Institute of Contemporary Art, Boston; "Artificial Nature," curated by Jeffrey Deitch, Deste Foundation for Contemporary Art, Athens. The 1990 Venice Biennale is directed by Giovanni Carandente. The Turner Prize is not awarded this year.

1991

U.S. leads a coalition in Operation Desert Storm to expel Iraq from Kuwait; South Africa repeals apartheid. Boris Yeltsin presides over dissolution of the Soviet Union. Important exhibitions include: "Places with a Past: New Site-Specific Art," curated by Mary Jane Jacob for the Spoleto Festival, Charleston, S.C.; "Degenerate Art: The Fate of the Avant Garde in Nazi Germany," curated by Stephanie Barron, Los Angeles County Museum of Art; "The Interrupted Life," curated by France Morin, New Museum of Contemporary Art, New York; "DisLocations," curated by Robert Storr, The Museum of Modern Art, New York; "The West as America: Reinterpreting Images of the Frontier, 1820–1920," curated by William Truettner, National Museum of American Art, Washington, D.C.; "Metropolis," curated by Norman Rosenthal and Christos Joachimides, Martin-Gropius-Bau, Berlin; "Passages de l'image," curated by Christine van Assche, Catherine David, and Raymond Bellour, Centre Georges Pompidou, Paris. Anish Kapoor wins the Turner Prize.

1992

Bill Clinton is elected U.S. President and will remain in office for eight years. Riots erupt in Los Angeles over Rodney King verdict. Bosnia and Herzegovina secede from Yugoslavia, beginning the Bosnian War, which will rage until 1995. Important exhibitions include: "Helter Skelter: L.A. Art in the Nineties," curated by Paul Schimmel, Museum of Contemporary Art, Los Angeles; "Post Human," curated by Jeffrey Deitch for the Musée d'Art Contemporain, Lausanne, Switzerland; "Young British Artists," organized by the Saatchi Gallery, London; "Fragile Ecologies: Contemporary Artists' Interpretations and Solutions," organized by the Queens Museum of Art, New York; "Parallel Visions: Modern Artists and Outsider Art," curated by Maurice Tuchman and Carol S. Eliel, Los Angeles County Museum of Art; "The Great Utopia: Art of the Russian and Soviet Avant Garde 1915–32," organized by the Solomon R. Guggenheim Museum, New York, the Soviet Ministry of Culture, and Frankfurt's Schirn Kunsthalle; "On Site," 18 room-sized installations at a soon to be demolished armory organized by the Museum of Contemporary Art, Chicago; "Hand Painted Pop: The Formative years, 1955–62," curated by Paul Schimmel and Donna DeSalvo, Museum of Contemporary Art, Los Angeles. Documenta 9 is directed by Jan Hoet. Grenville Davey wins the Turner Prize.

1993

Muslim fundamentalists try to destroy the World Trade Center in New York. PLO leader Yasser Arafat and Israeli Prime Minister Yitzhak Rabin sign a peace accord. North American Free Trade Agreement eliminates trade tariffs between Mexico, the U.S., and Canada. The European Treaty is ratified. Important shows include the "1993 Biennial Exhibition," the notorious "political biennial," curated by Elizabeth Sussman, Whitney Museum of American Art, New York; "American Art in the Twentieth Century: Paintings and Sculpture 1913–1993," curated by Christos M. Joachimides and Norman Rosenthal, Royal Academy of Arts, London; "Rolywholyover: A Circus," curated by John Cage and Julie Laza, Museum of Contemporary Art, Los Angeles; "Face of the Gods: Art and Altars of the Black Atlantic World," curated by Robert Farris Thompson, Museum for African Art, New York; "Stalin's Choice: Soviet Socialist Realism 1932–56," curated by Alanna Heiss, Joseph Backstein, Katherine Becker, Zdenka Gabalova, and Peter Wollin, P.S. 1 Contemporary Art Center, New York; "In the Spirit of Fluxus," curated by Elizabeth Armstrong and Joan Rothfuss, Walker Art Center, Minneapolis, Minn.; "Latin American Artists of the Twentieth Century," curated by Waldo Rasmussen, The Museum of Modern Art, New York. The 1993 Venice Biennale is directed by Achille Bonito Oliva. The First Asia Pacific Triennial is held in Queensland, Australia. This is the first such show to focus on Asia and the Pacific. Rachel Whiteread wins the Turner Prize.

1994

Civil war rages in Rwanda. IRA peace talks result in a cease-fire. Investigation of Whitewater scandal begins. Nelson Mandela is elected president of South Africa. Russians attack Chechnya. Important exhibitions include: "Japanese Art after 1945: Scream against the Sky," curated by Alexandra Monroe, The Solomon R. Guggenheim Museum, New York; "Black Male: Representations of Masculinity in Contemporary American Art," curated by Thelma Golden, Whitney Museum of

American Art, New York; "Asia/America: Issues of Identity in Contemporary Art," curated by Margo Machida and Vishakha Desai, The Asia Society, New York; "The Italian Metamorphosis, 1943–1968," curated by Germano Celant, The Solomon R. Guggenheim Museum, New York; "Bad Girls," curated by Marcia Tucker, New Museum of Contemporary Art, New York; "L'Hiver de l'Amour," curated by Olivier Zahm and Elein Fleiss, ARC Musée d'Art Moderne de la Ville de Paris. The First Shanghai Biennial is held, as is the First Gramercy International Art Fair, which eventually evolves into the New York Armory Show. Antony Gormley wins the Turner Prize.

1995

The Federal Building in Oklahoma City is bombed. Nerve gas attack in Tokyo subway kills eight and injures thousands. Bosnia and Croatia sign a peace treaty. Important exhibitions include: "Culture in Action," a community-based public art exhibition curated by Mary Jane Jacob, Sculpture Chicago; "Masculin-Feminin: Le Sexe de l'art," curated by Marie-Laure Bernadac and Bernard Marcade, Centre Georges Pompidou, Paris; "Recent Art from East Central Europe," curated by Laura Hoptman, Museum of Contemporary Art, Chicago; "Russian Jewish Artists, 1890–1990," curated by Susan Tumarkin Goodman, Jewish Museum, New York; "Reconsidering the Object of Art, 1965-75," curated by Ann Goldstein and Anne Rorimer, Museum of Contemporary Art, Los Angeles; "Gulag to Glasnost: Nonconformist Art for the Soviet Union," curated by Alla Rosenfled and Jeffrey Weschler, Jane Voorhes Zimmerli Art Museum, Rutgers, N.J.; "Video Spaces," curated by Barbara London, The Museum of Modern Art, New York; "'Brilliant': New Art from London," curated by Richard Flood, Walker Art Center, Minneapolis Minn.; "Beat Culture and the New America, 1950–1965," curated by Lisa Phillips, John Handhardt, Ray Careny, and Steven Watson, Whitney Museum of American Art, New York; "Too Jewish: Challenging Traditional Identities," curated by Norman Kleeblatt, Jewish Museum, New York; "In a Different Light," curated by Nayland Blake and Lawrence Rinder, University of California Berkeley Art Museum & Pacific Film Archive. The 1995 Venice Biennale is directed by Jean Clair, the exhibition's first non-Italian director. The first Gwangju Biennial and the first Johannesburg Biennial take place. Damien Hirst wins the Turner Prize.

1996

The Unabomber, Theodore Kaczynski, is arrested in Montana. Important exhibitions include: "Making Mischief: Dada Invades New York," curated by Francis M. Naumann, Whitney Museum of American Art, New York; "Counterculture: Alternative Information from the Underground Press to the Internet," curated by Brian Wallis, Exit Art, New York; "Cultural Economies: Histories from the Alternative Arts Movement," curated by Julie Ault, Drawing Center, New York; "Contemporary Art in Asia: Traditions/Tensions," curated by Apinan Poshyananda, Asia Society, New York; "L'Informe: Mode d'emploi," curated by Rosalind Krauss, Meyer Schapiro, and Yve-Alain Bois, Centre Georges Pompidou, Paris; "Negotiating Rapture: The Power of Art to Transform Lives," curated by Richard Francis and Sophia Shaw, Museum of Contemporary Art, Chicago. The first edition of Manifesta, the roving European Biennial, opens in Rotterdam. Douglas Gordon wins the Turner Prize.

1997

Tony Blair becomes British Prime Minister, a post he will hold until 2007. Princess Diana dies in a car crash. Hong Kong is handed over to China. The Guggenheim Bilbao opens. Important exhibitions include: "Cities on the Move," curated by Hou Hanru and Hans Ulrich Obrist, Vienna Secession; "Minimalia: An Italian Vision in 20th-Century Art," curated by Achille Bonito Oliva, Venice Biennale; "Objects of Desire: The Modern Still Life," curated by Margit Rowell, The Museum of Modern Art, New York; "Women and Abstract Expressionism: Painting and Sculpture, 1945–59," curated by Joan Marter, Sidney Mishkin Gallery at Baruch College, New York; "Apocalyptic Wallpaper," curated by Donna DeSalvo and Annetta Massie, Wexner Center for the Arts, Columbus, Ohio; "Exiles and Emigrés: The Flight of European Artists from Hitler," curated byStephanie Barron, Los Angeles County Museum of Art; "Amours," curated by Philippe Sollers, Fondation Cartier, Paris; "L'autre," curated by Harold Szeemann, Lyon Biennale d'Art Contemporain, France; "Art/Fashion," curated by Germano Celant, Ingrid Sischy, and Pandora Tabatbai Asbaghi for the Solomon R. Guggenheim Museum as an expanded version of their show at the 1996 Biennale di Firenze; "Sensation: Young British Artists from the Saatchi Collection," curated by Norman Rosenthal and Charles Saatchi, Royal Academy of Arts, London. The 1997 Venice Biennale is directed by Germano Celant. Documenta 10 is directed by Catherine David, the first woman commissioner of this event. The third installment of Kasper König's Skulptur Projekte opens in Muenster, Germany. Gillian Wearing wins the Turner Prize.

1998

President Clinton is impeached by the U.S. Congress. A historic peace agreement brings peace to Northern Ireland. Important exhibitions include: "Inside Out: New Chinese Art," curated by Gao Mingliu, San Francisco Museum of Modern Art and the Asia Society, New York; "China: 5000 Years," curated by Sherman Lee and Julia Andrews with the assistance of the PRC Ministry of Culture, The Solomon R. Guggenheim Museum, New York; "Out of Actions: Between Performance and the Object, 1949–79," curated by Paul Schimmel, Museum of Contemporary Art, Los Angeles; "The Art of The Motorcycle," curated by Thomas Krens, The Solomon R. Guggenheim Museum, New York; "The American Lawn: Surface of Everyday Life," curated by Beatriz Colomina, Elizabeth Diller, Alessandra Pone, Ricardo Scofidio, Georges Teyssot, and Mark Wigley, Centre Canadien d'Architecture, Montreal; "Years of Sculpture: From the Pedestal to the Pixel," curated by Richard Flood, Walker Art Center, Minneapolis, Minn.; "Support/Surfaces Years," curated by Daniel Abadie, Jeu de Paume, Paris. The first Berlin Biennale is held. Chris Ofili wins the Turner Prize.

1999

Protests against World Trade Organization shut down the city of Seattle. Two students kill twelve in a shooting at Columbine High School in Littleton, Colo. "Sensation" sparks controversy when it comes to the Brooklyn Museum and New York Mayor Rudolph Giuliani condemns Chris Ofili's Holy Virgin Mary, 1996, as "sick stuff." The Museum of Modern Art and P.S. 1 Center for Contemporary Art merge. The Museum of Modern Art initiates a year and a half long series of collection exhibitions prior to its closing for renovation. Other important exhibitions include:

"The Museum as Muse: Artists Reflect," curated by Kynaston McShine, The Museum of Modern Art, New York; "Global Conceptualism: Points of Origin, 1950s–1980s," curated by Jane Farver and a team of international curators, Queens Museum of Art, New York; "The American Century, 1900–2000," curated by Barbara Haskell and Lisa Phillips, Whitney Museum of American Art, New York; "The Un-Private House," curated by Terence Riley, The Museum of Modern Art, New York; "Contemporary Art from Cuba," curated by Marilyn Zeitlin, Independent Curators Inc.; "Regarding Beauty," curated by Neal Benezra and Olga Viso, Hirshhorn Museum, Washington, D.C.; "Examining Pictures: Exhibiting Paintings," curated by Judith Nesbitt and Francesco Bonami, Whitechapel Art Gallery, London; "Abracadabra: International Contemporary Art," curated by Catherine Grenier, Tate Gallery, London; "Gutai," curated by Daniel Abadie, Jeu de Paume, Paris. The 1999 Venice Biennale is directed by Harold Szeemann. The First Liverpool Biennial of Contemporary Art is held. Steve McQueen wins the Turner Prize.

2000

Reformists win control of the Iranian parliament for the first time since the 1979 Islamic revolution. A nationwide uprising overthrows Serbian president Slobodan Milosevic. George W. Bush becomes U.S. President in a contested election. The Tate Modern opens in London with a thematic organization of its collection. The Centre Georges Pompidou in Paris reopens after two years of renovation. Important exhibitions include: "1900: Art at the Crossroads,' curated by Robert Rosenblum, The Solomon R. Guggenheim Museum, New York and the Royal Academy of Arts, London; "Made in California: 1900–2000," curated by Stephanie Barron, Los Angeles County Museum of Art; "Utopia: The Search for the Ideal Society in the Western World," curated by Roland Schaer, New York Public Library and the Bibliothèque Nationale, Paris; "Apocalypse: Beauty and Horror in Contemporary Art," curated by Norman Rosenthal, Royal Academy of Arts, London; "Unnatural Science," curated by Laura Heron, Mass MoCA, North Adams, Mass.; "Paradise Now: Picturing the Genetic Revolution," curated by Marvin Heiferman and Carole Kismaric, Exit Art, New York; "Hip Hop Nation: Roots, Rhythms and Rage," curated by KevinPowell, Brooklyn Museum, New York; "The Greenhouse Effect," curated by Lisa Corrin and Ralph Rugoff, Serpentine Gallery, London, and the Natural History Museum, London; "Encounters: New Art from Old," curated by Richard Morphet, National Gallery of Art, London; "Superflat," curated by Takashi Murakami, Shibuya Parco Gallery, Tokyo; "Re-Play: Beginnings of International Media Art in Austria," curated by Sabine Breitwieser and Heidi Grundmann, Generali Foundation, Vienna. Wolfgang Tillmans wins the Turner Prize.

2001

The U.S. pulls out of Kyoto Protocols. Massive protests erupt in Genoa on occasion of G8 summit meeting. On September 11, two terrorist-piloted airplanes crash into World Trade Towers in New York. Another plane crashes into the Pentagon in Washington, D.C., and a fourth crashes in rural Pennsylvania. Total death toll is 2,973. In retaliation, U.S. and coalition attack Taliban-held Afganistan. The U.S. Patriot Act is signed into law by Congress 45 days after the attacks. Important exhibitions include: "Century City: Art and Culture in the Modern Metropolis, Paris, Vienna, Moscow, Rio de Janeiro, Lagos, Tokyo, New York and Bombay," curated by various curators, Tate Modern, London; "Bitstreams," curated by Lawrence Rinder, Whitney Museum of American Art, New York; "The Short Century: Independence and Liberation Movements in Africa 1945–1994," curated by Okwui Enwezor, Museum Villa Stuck, Munich, in cooperation with House of World Cultures, Berlin; "Mies in Berlin," curated by Terence Riley, The Museum of Modern Art, New York; "Freestyle," curated by Thelma Golden, Studio Museum in Harlem, New York; "Art on the Edge of the Law," curated by Jessica Hough and Richard Klein, Adrich Museum, Ridgefield, Conn.; "Beau Monde: Toward a Redeemed Cosmopolitanism," curated by Dave Hickey, Site, Sante Fe, N.Mex.; "Zero to Infinity: Arte Povera 1962–1972," curated by Frances Morris and Richard Flood, Tate Modern, London, and Walker Art Center, Minneapolis, Minn.; "010101: The Art of Technological Times," curated by Aaron Betsky, San Francisco Museum of Modern Art. The 2001 Venice Biennale is directed by Harold Szeemann. Martin Creed wins the Turner Prize.

2002

President Bush declares Iraq, Iran, and North Korea to be the "axis of evil." The Nationalist Front Party candidate Jean-Marie le Pen comes in second in French presidential elections. India is rocked with Hindu-Muslim violence. The Palais de Tokyo, a massive new interdisciplinary art space, opens in Paris. Important exhibitions include: "Mirroring Evil: Nazi Imagery/Recent Art," curated by Norman Kleeblatt, Jewish Museum, New York; "La Révolution Surréaliste," curated by Victoria Combalía, Centre Georges Pompidou, Paris; "Drawing Now: Eight Propositions," curated by Laura Hoptman, The Museum of Modern Art, New York; "Gene(sis): Contemporary Art Explores Human Genomics," curated by Robin Held, Henry Art Gallery, Seattle; "Mexico City: An Exhibition about the Exchange Rates of Bodies and Values," curated by Klaus Biesenbach, P.S. 1 Contemporary Art Center, New York; "Game On," curated by Conrad Bodman and Lucien King, Barbican Gallery, London; "Cher Peintre," curated by Alison M. Gingeras, Sabine Folie, and Blazenka Perica, Centre Georges Pompidou, Paris. The first Art Basel Miami art fair is held in Miami, Fla. Documenta 11 is organized by Okwui Enwezor, the first non-white, non-European to curate this event. Keith Tyson wins the Turner Prize.

2003

The Iraq War begins. Baghdad falls, followed by widespread looting. Saddam Hussein is captured in Iraq. Dolly the sheep becomes the first successfully cloned mammal. The space shuttle Columbia explodes. War breaks out in Darfur, Sudan. DIA Beacon opens in Beacon, N.Y. Important exhibitions include: "Contemporary African Diaspora," curated by Laurie Ann Farrell, Museum for African Art, New York; "The American Effect," curated by Lawrence Rinder, Whitney Museum of American Art, New York; "Cuba on the Verge," curated by Terry McCoy, International Center for Photography, New York; "Images of the Grotesque," curated by Gabriel Pérez-Barreiro, Jack S. Blanton Museum of Art, Austin, Tex.; "Only Skin Deep: Changing Visions of the American Self," curated by Coco Fusco and Brian Wallis, International Center of Photography, New York; "Yanomami: Spirit of the Forest," curated by Bruce Albert and Davi Kopenawa, Fondation Cartier, Paris. The first Frieze Art Fair is held in London. The 2003 Venice Biennale is directed by Francesco Bonami. Grayson Perry wins the Turner Prize.

2004

Madrid commuter trains are bombed by terrorists, killing 191. Fighting continues in Iraq. The U.S. National Security Advisor, Condoleezza Rice, admits that the intelligence on Iraq's weapons of mass destruction may have been wrong. The Abu Ghraib prisoner abuse scandal emerges. George W. Bush is elected to a second term as U.S. President. An earthquake-triggered tsunami engulfs coast of Indonesia. Yasser Arafat, Chairman of the Palestinian Liberation Organization, dies. The Museum of Modern Art, New York, reopens in Manhattan. Important exhibitions include: "Inverted Utopias: Avant-Garde Art in Latin America," curated by Mari Carmen Ramirez and Hector Olea, International Center for the Arts of the Americas at the Museum of Fine Arts, Houston, Tex. "East Village USA," curated by Dan Cameron, New Museum of Contemporary Art, New York; "Extreme Abstraction," curated by Louis Crachos and Claire Schnieder, Albright Knox Art Gallery, Buffalo, N.Y.; "Beyond Geometry: Experiments in Form, 1940-1970," curated by Lynn Zelevansky, Los Angeles County Museum of Art; "Between Past and Future: New Photography from China," curated by Chris Phillips and Wu Hung, International Center of Photography, New York; "The Interventionists: Art in the Social Sphere," curated by Nato Thompson, Mass MoCA, North Adams, Mass.; "Art of the Garden," curated by Nicholas Alfrey, Stephen Daniels, Mary Holock, Martin Postle, and Ben Tufnell, Tate Britain, London; "The Beauty of Failure/The Failure of Beauty," curated by Harold Szeeman, Fundacio Joan Miró, Barcelona; "Africa Remix," curated by Simon Njami, Museum Kunst Palast, Düsseldorf. Jeremy Deller wins the Turner Prize.

2005

London Underground bombed by terrorists, killing 52 and wounding 700. Riots in French suburbs fan fear of immigrants. Hurricane Katrina slams into U.S. Gulf coast; levees are breached in New Orleans, and Bush administration comes under fire for inadequate response. The first free elections in fifty years are held in Iraq. Christo and Jeanne Claude's The Gates takes over New York's Central Park. Important exhibitions include: "Little Boy: The Arts of Japan's Exploding Subculture," curated by Takashi Murakami for the Japan Society, New York; "The Triumph of Painting," curated by Charles Saatchi, Saatchi Gallery, London; "Double Consciousness: Black Conceptual Art since 1970," curated by Valerie Cassel, Contemporary Art Museum, Houston, Tex.; "The Disappeared," curated by Laurel Reuter, North Dakota Museum of Art; "Ecstasy: In and About Altered States," curated by Paul Schimmel, Museum of Contemporary Art, Los Angeles; "Remote Viewing: Invented Worlds in Recent Painting and Drawing," curated by Elisabeth Sussman, Whitney Museum of American Art, New York; "Open Systems: Rethinking Art c. 1970," curated by Donna DeSalvo, Tate Modern, London; "Back to Black–Art, Cinema and the Racial Imaginary," curated by Patrine Archer-Straw, David A. Bailey, and Richard Powell, Whitechapel Gallery, London; "Summer of Love: Art of the Psychedelic Era," curated by Christoph Grunenberg, Tate Liverpool, London; "Populism," curated by Lars Bang Larsen, Christina Ricupero, and Nicholas Schafhausen, Frankfurter Kunstverein, Frankfurt. The 2005 Venice Biennale is directed by Maria de Corral and Rosa Martinez. The first Moscow Biennale of Contemporary Art is held. Simon Starling wins the Turner Prize.

2006

Insurgent attacks escalate in Iraq. Israel launches attack on Hezbollah. Iran announces that it has successfully enriched uranium. Violent demonstrations erupt across the Muslim world over publication of Danish cartoons. Saddam Hussein is hanged in Baghdad. Important exhibitions include: "Energy/Experimentation: Black Artists and Abstraction, 1964–1980," curated by Kellie Jones, Studio Museum of Harlem, New York; "Tropicalia: A Revolution in Brazilian Culture," curated by Carlos Basualdo, Barbican Art Gallery, London; "Art for a Change, Los Angeles in Paris, 1955–85," Centre Georges Pompidou, Paris; "AngloMania: Tradition and Transgression in British Fashion," curated by Andrew Bolton and Harold Korda, Metropolitan Museum of Art, New York; "Graffiti," curated by Charlotta Kotik, Brooklyn Museum, New York; "High Times, Hard Times: New York Painting, 1967–75," curated by Katy Siegel, Independent Curators Inc; "Undercover Surrealism: Picasso, Miró, Masson, and the Vision of Georges Bataille," curated by Dawn Ades, Simon Baker, and Fiona Bradley, The Hayward Gallery, London. The first Singapore Biennale is held. Tomma Abts wins the Turner Prize.

2007

Protestants and Catholics form a unity government in Ireland. Tony Blair steps down as British Prime Minister. Scientists confirm global warming. Conservative candidate Nicolas Sarkozy defeats Socialist candidate Ségolène Royal in French presidential elections. Important exhibitions include: "Global Feminisms," curated by Maura Reilly and Linda Nochlin, Brooklyn Museum, New York, on the occasion of inauguration of the Sackler Center for Feminist Art and the permanent re-installation of Judy Chicago's Dinner Party (1974–79); "Wack! Art and the Feminist Revolution," curated by Connie Butler, Museum of Contemporary Art, Los Angeles; "The Happiness of Objects," curated by Sarina Basta, Sculpture Center, New York; "Foto: Modernity in Central Europe, 1918–1945," curated by Matthew Witkovsky, National Gallery of Art, Washington, D.C.; "Escultura Social: A New Generation of Art from Mexico City," curated by Julie Rodriguez Widholm, Museum of Contemporary Art, Chicago; "Black Light/White Noise: Sound and Light in Contemporary Art," curated by Valerie Cassel Oliver, Contemporary Arts Museum, Houston, Tex.; "Panic Attack! Art in the Punk Years," curated by Mark Sladen and Ariella Yedgar, Barbican Art Center, London; "Made in Germany," curated by Stephan Berg, Velt Gomer, and Ulrich Krempel, Sprengel Museum Hannover, Kestnergesellschaft, Kunstverein Hannover, Germany. The 2007 Venice Biennale is directed by Robert Storr, the first American to hold that post. Documenta 12 is directed by Roger M. Buergel. The fourth installment of Kaspar König's Skulptur Projekte opens in Muenster, Germany.

LIST OF ARTISTS

ABAKANOWICZ, MAGDALENA b. 1930 Falenty, Poland
ABRAMOVIC, MARINA b. 1946 Belgrade, Yugoslavia
ABSALON b. 1964 Ashod, Israel; d. 1993 Paris, France
ABTS, TOMMA b. 1967 Kiel, Germany
ACCONCI, VITO b. 1940 New York, N.Y., USA
ACRES, REVEREND ETHAN b. 1970 Fort Payne, Ala.
ADAMS, DENNIS b. 1948 Des Moines, Iowa, USA
AHEARN, JOHN b. 1951 Binghamton, N.Y., USA
AHTILA, EIJA-LISA b. 1959 Hämeenlinna, Finland
AITKEN, DOUG b. 1968 Redondo Beach, Calif. USA
AKERMAN, CHANTAL b. 1950 Brussels, Belgium
ALIGHIERO E BOETTI. SEE **BOETTI, ALIGHIERO E**
ALLORA, JENNIFER b. 1974 Philadelphia, Pa. USA
ALTHAMER, PAWEL b. 1967 Warsaw, Poland
ALŸS, FRANCIS b. 1959 Antwerp, Belgium
AMER, GHADA b. 1963 Cairo, Egypt
ANTIN, ELEANOR b. 1935 New York, N.Y., USA
ANTONI, JANINE b. 1964 Freeport, Bahamas
APFELBAUM, POLLY b. 1955 Abington, Pa., USA
ARAKI, NOBUYOSHI b. 1940 Tokyo, Japan
ARMAJANI, SIAH b. 1939 Tehran, Iran
ATAMAN, KUTLUG b. 1961 Istanbul, Turkey
ATHEY, RON b. 1961 Groton, Conn., USA
ATKINSON, CONRAD b. 1940 Cumbria, UK
AVALOS, DAVID b. 1947 San Diego, Calif., USA
AYLON, HELÉNE b. 1931 New York, N.Y., USA
AZIZ, ANTHONY b. 1961, Lunenberg, Mass. USA
BACON, FRANCIS b. 1910 Dublin, Ireland; d. 1992 Madrid, Spain
BALDESSARI, JOHN b. 1931 National City, Calif., USA
BARNEY, MATTHEW b. 1967 San Francisco, Calif., USA
BARNEY, TINA b. 1945 New York, N.Y., USA
BASELITZ, GEORG b. 1938 Deutschbaselitz, Germany
BASQUIAT, JEAN-MICHEL b. 1960 New York, N.Y., USA d. 1988 New York, N.Y., USA
BAUMGARTEN, LOTHAR b. 1944 Rheinsberg, Germany
BECHER, BERND b. 1931 Siegen, Germany
BECHER, HILLA b. 1934 Potsdam, Germany
BECHER, MAX b. 1964 Düsseldorf, Germany
BEDIA, JOSÉ b. 1959 Havana, Cuba
BEECROFT, VANESSA b. 1969 Genoa, Italy
BELL, NIKKI b. 1959 London, UK
BELLMER, HANS b. 1902 Kattowicz, Poland d. 1975 Paris, France
BEN-TOR, TAMY b. 1975 Jerusalem, Israel
BEUYS, JOSEPH b. 1921 Krefeld, Germany; d. 1986 Düsseldorf, Germany
BICKERTON, ASHLEY b. 1959 Barbados
BIJL, GUILLAUME b. 1946 Antwerp, Belgium
BLAKE, JEREMY b. 1971 Fort Sill, Okla., USA; d. 2007 New York, N.Y., USA
BLAKE, NAYLAND b. 1960 New York, N.Y., USA
BLECKNER, ROSS b. 1949 New York, N.Y., USA
BLOOM, BARBARA b. 1951 Los Angeles, Calif., USA
BOCK, JOHN b. 1965 Gribbohn, Germany
BOETTI, ALIGHIERO E b. 1940 Turin, Italy; d. 1994 Rome, Italy
BOLTANSKI, CHRISTIAN b. 1945 Paris, France
BONVICINI, MONICA b. 1965 Venedig, Italy
BOONMA, MONTIEN b. 1953 Bangkok, Thailand
BORLAND, CHRISTINE b. 1965 Darvel, UK
BOTERO, FERNANDO b. 1932 Medellin, Colombia
BOURGEOIS, LOUISE b. 1911 Paris, France
BROWN, CECILY b. 1969 London, UK
BRUGUERA, TANIA b. 1968 Havana, Cuba
BRUSKIN, GRISHA b. 1945 Moscow, Russia
BUREN, DANIEL b. 1938 Boulogne-Billancourt, France
BURSON, NANCY b. 1948 Saint Louis, Mo., USA
BURTON, RICHMOND b. 1960 Talladega, Ala., USA
BYARS, JAMES LEE b. 1932 Detroit, Mich., USA; d. 1997 Cairo, Egypt
CAI GUO-QIANG b. 1957 Guanzhou City, China
CALLE, SOPHIE b. 1953 Paris, France
CALZADILLA, GUILLERMO b. 1971 Havana, Cuba
CARDIFF, JANET b. 1957 Brussels, Ont., Canada
CASEBERE, JAMES b. 1953 Lansing, Mich., USA
CATTELAN, MAURIZIO b. 1960 Padua, Italy
CELMINS, VIJA b. 1938 Riga, Latvia
CENTER FOR LAND USE INTERPRETATION founded 1994, Oakland, Calif., USA
CHADWICK, HELEN b. 1953 Croydon, UK; d. 1996 London, UK
CHAGOYA, ENRIQUE b. 1953 Mexico City, Mexico
CHAN, PAUL b. 1973 Hong Kong
CHAPMAN, DINOS b. 1962 London, UK
CHAPMAN, JAKE b. 1966 Cheltenham, UK
CHARLES, MICHAEL RAY b. 1967 Lafayette, La., USA
CHEN ZHEN b. 1955 Shanghai, China; d. 2000 Paris, France
CHICAGO, JUDY b. 1939 Chicago, Ill., USA
CHIN, MEL b. 1951 Houston, Tex., USA
CHRISTO & JEANNE-CLAUDE: Christo b. 1935 Gabrovo, Bulgaria; Jeanne-Claude b. 1935 Casablanca, Morocco
CLARK, LYGIA b. 1920 Belo Horizonte, Brazil; d. 1988 Rio de Janeiro, Brazil
CLOSE, CHUCK b. 1940 Monroe, Wash., USA
COE, SUE b. 1951 Tamworth, UK
COLESCOTT, ROBERT b. 1925 Oakland, Calif., USA
CONWILL, HOUSTON b. 1947 Louisville, Ky., USA
COPLANS, JOHN b. 1920 London, UK; d. 2003 New York, N.Y., USA
COURBET, GUSTAVE b. 1819 Ornans, France; d. 1877 La Tour du Peilz, Switzerland
COSTANZO, JIM (REPOHISTORY) b. 1958 Morristown, N.J., USA
COX, RENEE b. 1958 New York, N.Y., USA
COYNE, PETAH b. 1953 Oklahoma City, Okla., USA
CRAGG, TONY b. 1949 Liverpool, UK
CREWDSON, GREGORY b. 1962 New York, N.Y., USA
CRITICAL ART ENSEMBLE founded 1987 Tallahassee, Fla., USA
CUCHER, SAMMY b. 1958 Lima, Peru
CURRIN, JOHN b. 1962 Boulder, Colo., USA
DARBOVEN, HANNE b. 1941 Munich, Germany
DEACON, RICHARD b. 1949 Bangor, UK
DEAN, TACITA b. 1965 Canterbury, UK
DE BEER, SUE b. 1973 Tarrytown, N.Y., USA
DELVOYE, WIM b. 1965 Wervik, Belgium
DEMAND, THOMAS b. 1964 Munich, Germany
DEMNIG, GUNTER b. 1947 Berlin, Germany
DENES, AGNES b. 1938 Budapest, Hungary
DEPACE, JOSEPH b. 1954 New York, N.Y., USA
DICORCIA, PHILIP-LORCA b. 1953 Hartford, Conn., USA
DIJKSTRA, RINEKE b. 1959 Sittard, The Netherlands
DILLER, ELIZABETH b. 1954 Lodz, Poland
DION, MARK b. 1961 New Bedford, Mass., USA
DITTBORN, EUGENIO b. 1941 Santiago, Chile
DOIG, PETER b. 1959 Edinburgh, UK
DONOVAN, TARA b. 1969 New York, N.Y., USA
DOUGLAS, STAN b. 1960 Vancouver, B.C., Canada
DUCHAMP, MARCEL b. 1887 Blainville Crevon, France d. 1968 Neuilly-sur-Seine, France
DUMAS, MARLENE b. 1953 Cape Town, South Africa
DUNHAM, CARROLL b. 1949 Old Lyme, Conn., USA
DURHAM, JIMMIE b. 1940 Washington, Ark., USA
EDWARDS, BENJAMIN b. 1970 Iowa City, Iowa, USA
ELIASSON, OLAFUR b. 1967 Copenhagen, Denmark
EMIN, TRACEY b. 1963 London, UK
ERICSON, KATE b. 1955 New York, N.Y., USA; d. 1995 New York, N.Y., USA
ESSENHIGH, INKA b. 1969 Belfonte, Pa., USA
FISCHL, ERIC b. 1948 New York, N.Y., USA
FISCHLI, PETER, b. 1952 Zurich, Switzerland
FLETCHER, HARRELL b. 1967 Santa Maria, Calif., USA

FLEURY, SYLVIE b. 1961 Geneva, Switzerland
FONTCUBERTA, JOAN b. 1955 Barcelona, Spain
FÖRG, GÜNTHER b. 1952 Füssen, Germany
FRASER, ANDREA b. 1965 Billings, Mont., USA
FREUD, LUCIAN b. 1922 Berlin, Germany
FRIEDMAN, TOM b. 1965 Saint Louis, Mo., USA
FRITSCH, KATHARINA b. 1956 Hamburg, Germany
FRIZE, BERNARD b. 1949 St Mandé, France
FUSCO, COCO b. 1960 New York, N.Y., USA
GALLAGHER, ELLEN b. 1965 Providence, R.I., USA
GASKELL, ANNA b. 1969 Des Moines, Iowa, USA
GELITIN founded Vienna, Austria
GENERAL IDEA founded 1969 Toronto, Ont., Canada
GENZKEN, ISA b. 1948 Bad Oldesloe, Germany
GERZ, JOCHEN b. 1940 Berlin, Germany
GILBERT AND GEORGE: Gilbert b. 1943 San Martino, Italy; George b. 1942 Devon, UK
GILLICK, LIAM b. 1984 Aylesbury, UK
GINZEL, ANDREW b. 1954 Chicago, Ill., USA
GOLDIN, NAN b. 1953 Washington, D.C., USA
GOLDSWORTHY, ANDY b. 1956 Cheshire, UK
GOLUB, LEON b. 1922 Chicago, Ill., USA; d. 2004 New York, N.Y., USA
GÓMEZ-PEÑA, GUILLERMO b. 1955 Mexico City, Mexico
GONZALEZ-TORRES, FELIX b. 1957 Guaimaro, Cuba; d. 1996 New York, N.Y., USA
GORDON, DOUGLAS b. 1966 Glasgow, UK
GORMLEY, ANTONY b. 1950 London, UK
GRAHAM, DAN b. 1942 Urbana, Ill., USA
GRAHAM, RODNEY b. 1949 Vancouver, B.C., Canada
GRAN FURY founded 1988 New York, N.Y., USA
GROUP MATERIAL founded 1979 New York, N.Y., USA
GU, WENDA b. 1955 Shanghai, China
GUERRILLA GIRLS active mid-1980s to mid-1990s
GURSKY, ANDREAS b. 1955 Leipzig, Germany
GUSTON, PHILIP b. 1913 Montreal, Que., Canada; d. 1980 Woodstock, N.Y., USA
HALLEY, PETER b. 1953 New York, N.Y., USA
HAMILTON, ANN b. 1956 Lima, Ohio, USA
HAMMONS, DAVID b. 1943 Springfield, Ill., USA
HANCOCK, TRENTON DOYLE b. 1974 Oklahoma City, Okla., USA
HARING, KEITH b. 1958 Kutztown, Pa.; d. 1990 New York, N.Y., USA
HARRISON, HELEN MAYER b. 1929 New York, N.Y., USA
HARRISON, NEWTON b. 1932 New York, N.Y., USA
HARRISON, RACHEL b. 1966 New York, N.Y., USA
HATOUM, MONA b. 1952 Beirut, Lebanon
HEILMANN, MARY b. 1940 San Francisco, Calif., USA
HEIZER, MICHAEL b. 1944 Berkeley, Calif., USA
HELD, AL b. 1928 Brooklyn, N.Y., USA; d. 2005 Todi, Italy
HILL, GARY b. 1951 Santa Monica, Calif., USA
HILLER, SUSAN b. 1940 Tallahassee, Fla., USA
HIRSCHHORN, THOMAS b. 1957 Bern, Switzerland
HIRST, DAMIEN b. 1965 Bristol, UK
HOCK E AYE VI EDGAR HEAP OF BIRDS b. 1954 Wichita, Kans., USA
HOCK, LOUIS b. 1948 Los Angeles, Calif., USA
HOCKNEY, DAVID b. 1937 Bradford, UK
HÖFER, CANDIDA b. 1944 Eberswalde, Germany
HÖLLER, CARSTEN b. 1961 Brussels, Belgium
HOLZER, JENNY b. 1950 Gallipolis, Ohio, USA
HORN, REBECCA b. 1944 Michelstadt, Germany
HORNE, PIP b. 1951 Birmingham, UK
HOUSHIARY, SHIRAZEH b. 1955 Shiraz, Iran
HUYGHE, PIERRE b. 1962 Paris, France
IMMENDORFF, JÖRG b. 1945 Bleckede, Germany; d. 2007 Düsseldorf, Germany
JAAR, ALFREDO b. 1956 Santiago, Chile
JACIR, EMILY b. 1970 Jerusalem, Israel
JANKOWSKI, CHRISTIAN b. 1968 Göttingen, Germany
JERIMIJENKO, NATALIE b. 1966 Mackay, Australia
JOHNSON, PHILIP b. 1906 Cleveland, Ohio, USA; d. 2005 New Canaan, Conn., USA
JONAS, JOAN b. 1936 New York, N.Y., USA
JONES, KRISTIN b. 1956 Washington, D.C., USA
JONES, RONALD b. 1952 Falls Church, Va., USA
JOO, MICHAEL b. 1966 Ithaca, N.Y., USA
JUDD, DONALD b. 1928 Excelsior Springs, Mo., USA d. 1994 New York, N.Y., USA
JULIEN, ISAAC b. 1960 London, UK
KABAKOV, ILYA b. 1933 Dniepropetrovsk, Russia
KAC, EDUARDO b. 1962 Rio de Janeiro, Brazil
KANDINSKY, WASSILY b. 1866 Moscow, Russia; d. 1944 Neuilly-sur-Seine, France
KAPOOR, ANISH b. 1954 Bombay, India
KAWAMATA, TADESHI b. 1953 Hokkaido, Japan
KAWARA, ON b. 1933 Kariya, Japan
KCHO (ALEXIS LEYVA MACHADO) b. 1970 Isla de la Juventud, Cuba
KELLEY, MIKE b. 1954 Detroit, Mich., USA
KELLY, ELLSWORTH b. 1923 Newburgh, N.Y., USA
KELLY, MARY b. 1941 Minneapolis, Minn., USA
KENTRIDGE, WILLIAM b. 1959 Johannesburg, South Africa
KIEFER, ANSELM b. 1945 Donaueschingen, Germany
KILGALLEN, MARGARET b. 1967 Washington, D.C., USA d. 2001 San Francisco, Calif., USA
KIMSOOJA b. 1957 Taegu, Korea
KINGELEZ, BODYS ISEK b. 1948 Kimbenbele, Zaire
KIPPENBERGER, MARTIN b. 1953 Dortmund, Germany d. 1997 Vienna, Austria
KITAJ, R.B. b. 1932 Chagrin Falls, Ohio, USA
KNOWLES, ALISON b. 1933 New York, N.Y., USA
KOMAR, VITALY b. 1943 Moscow, Russia
KOONS, JEFF b. 1955 York, Pa., USA
KOSUTH, JOSEPH b. 1943 Toledo, Ohio, USA
KOZLOFF, JOYCE b. 1942 Somerville, N.J., USA
KRUGER, BARBARA b. 1943 Newark, N.J., USA
KUSAMA, YAYOI b. 1941 Matsumoto City, Japan
KUSOLWONG, SURASI b. 1965 Ayuthaya, Thailand
LAIB, WOLFGANG b. 1950 Metzingen, Germany
LANGLANDS, BEN b. 1955 London, UK
LARNER, LIZ b. 1960 Sacramento, Calif., USA
LAVERDIERE, JULIAN b. 1971 Hadley, N.Y., USA
LAWLER, LOUISE b. 1947 Bronxville, N.Y., USA
LEDRAY, CHARLES b. 1960 Seattle, Wash., USA
LEE BUL b. 1964 Yongwol, Korea
LEE MINGWEI b. 1964 Taipei, Taiwan
LEE, NIKKI S. b. 1970 Kye-Chang, Korea
LEIBOWITZ, CARY b. 1963 New York, N.Y, USA
LEIRNER, JAC b. 1961 São Paulo, Brazil
LEVINE, SHERRIE b. 1947 Hazleton, Pa., USA
LEWITT, SOL b. 1928 Hartford, Conn., USA; d. 2007 New York, N.Y., USA
LIESHOUT, JOEP VAN b. 1963 Ravenstein, The Netherlands
LIGON, GLENN b. 1960 Bronx, N.Y., USA
LIN, MAYA b. 1959 Athens, Ohio, USA
LIVING MUSEUM. **SEE MARTON, DR. JANOS**
LOMBARDI, MARK b. 1951 Syracuse, N.Y., USA d. 2000 Brooklyn, N.Y., USA
LONG, RICHARD b. 1945 Bristol, UK
LONGO, ROBERT b. 1953 Brooklyn, N.Y., USA
LOPEZ, ALMA b. 1966 Sinaloa, Mexico
LOS CARPINTEROS founded 1994 Cuba
LOU, LIZA b. 1969 New York, N.Y., USA
LOVELL, WHITFIELD b. 1959 Bronx, N.Y., USA
LOWE, RICK b. 1961 Eufaula, Ala., USA
LUCAS, SARAH b. 1962 London, UK
LUCIER, MARY b. 1944 Bucyrus, Ohio, USA
MAJOZO, ESTELLA CONWILL b. 1949 Louisville, Ky., USA
MALEVICH, KAZIMIR b. 1878 Kiev, Ukraine; d. 1935

Leningrad, Russia

MA LIUMING b. 1969 Huangshi, China

MANET, ÉDOUARD b. 1832 Paris, France; d. 1883 Paris, France

MANGLANO-OVALLE, IÑIGO b. 1961 Madrid, Spain

MANGOLD, ROBERT b. 1937 North Tonawanda, N.Y., USA

MAPPLETHORPE, ROBERT b. 1946 Queens, N.Y., USA d. 1989 New York, N.Y., USA

MARCACCIO, FABIAN b. 1963 Rosario de Santa Fe, Argentina

MARCLAY, CHRISTIAN b. 1955 San Rafael, Calif., USA

MARDEN, BRICE b. 1938 Bronxville, N.Y., USA

MARSHALL, KERRY JAMES b. 1955 Birmingham, Ala., USA

MARTIN, AGNES b. 1912 Maklin, Sask., Canada; d. 2004 Taos, N.Mex., USA

MARTON, DR. JANOS (THE LIVING MUSEUM) b. 1949 Budapest, Hungary

MATTA-CLARK, GORDON b. 1942 New York, N.Y., USA; d. 1978 New York, N.Y., USA

MCCARTHY, PAUL b. 1945 Salt Lake City, Utah, USA

MCCOLLUM, ALLAN b. 1944 Los Angeles, Calif., USA

MCELHENY, JOSIAH b. 1966 Boston, Mass., USA

MCGEE, BARRY b. 1966 San Francisco, Calif., USA

MEHRETU, JULIE b. 1970 Addis Ababa, Ethiopia

MEIRELES, CILDO b. 1948 Rio de Janeiro, Brazil

MELAMID, ALEXANDER b. 1946 Moscow, Russia

MENDIETA, ANA b. 1948 Havana, Cuba; d. 1985 New York, N.Y., USA

MESSAGER, ANNETTE b. 1943 Berck, France

MIES VAN DER ROHE, LUDWIG b. 1886 Aachen, Germany; d. 1969 Chicago, Ill., USA

MIK, AERNOUT b. 1962 Groningen, The Netherlands

MOCKBEE, SAMUEL (RURAL STUDIO) b. 1941 Meridian, Miss., USA; d. 2001 Jackson, Miss., USA

MOFFATT, TRACEY b. 1960 Brisbane, Australia

MONDRIAN, PIET b. 1872 Amersfoort, The Netherlands d. 1944 New York, N.Y., USA

MORI, MARIKO b. 1967 Tokyo, Japan

MORIMURA, YASUMASA b. 1951 Osaka, Japan

MORLEY, MALCOLM b. 1931 London, UK

MORRIS, SARAH b. 1967 London, UK

MTHETHWA, ZWELETHU b. 1960 Durban, South Africa

MUECK, RON b. 1958 Melbourne, Australia

MULLICAN, MATT b. 1951 Santa Monica, Calif., USA

MUNIZ, VIK b. 1961 São Paulo, Brazil

MUÑOZ, JUAN b. 1953 Madrid, Spain; d. 2001 Ibiza, Spain

MUNTADAS, ANTONI b. 1942 Barcelona, Spain

MURAKAMI, TAKASHI b. 1962 Tokyo, Japan

MURRAY, ELIZABETH b. 1940 Chicago, Ill.; d. 2007 Washington County, N.Y.

MUSEUM OF JURASSIC TECHNOLOGY founded 1988 Culver City, Calif., USA

MUTU, WANGECHI b. 1972 Nairobi, Kenya

MUYBRIDGE, EADWEARD b. 1830 Kingston, UK; d. 1904 Kingston, UK

NAUMAN, BRUCE b. 1941 Fort Wayne, Ind., USA

NESHAT, SHIRIN b. 1957 Qazvin, Iran

NITSCH, HERMANN b. 1938 Vienna, Austria

NOZKOWSKI, THOMAS b. 1944 Teaneck, N.J., USA

OCAMPO, MANUEL b. 1965 Quezon City, Philippines

ODENBACH, MARCEL b. 1953 Cologne, Germany

OFILI, CHRIS b. 1968 Manchester, UK

OITICICA, HÉLIO b. 1937 Rio de Janeiro, Brazil; d. 1980 Rio de Janeiro, Brazil

OPALKA, ROMAN b. 1931 Hocquincourt, France

ORLAN b. 1947 Saint-Étienne, France

OROZCO, GABRIEL b. 1961 Jalapa, Mexico

OSORIO, PEPÓN b. 1955 Santurce, Puerto Rico

OURSLER, TONY b. 1957 New York, N.Y., USA

PAIK, NAM JUNE b. 1932 Seoul, Korea; d. 2006 Miami, Fla., USA

PAINE, ROXY b. 1966 New York, N.Y., USA

PANAMARENKO b. 1949 Antwerp, Belgium

PARDO, JORGE b. 1963 Havana, Cuba

PARKER, CORNELIA b. 1956 Cheshire, UK

PARNES, LAURA b. 1968 Buffalo, N.Y., USA

PARRENO, PHILIPPE b. 1964 Oran, Algeria

PETTIBON, RAYMOND b. 1957 Tucson, Ariz., USA

PEYTON, ELIZABETH b. 1965 Danbury, Conn., USA

PFAFF, JUDY b. 1946 London, UK

PFEIFFER, PAUL b. 1966 Honolulu, Hawaii, USA

PICASSO, PABLO b. 1881 Malaga, Spain; d. 1973 Mougins, France

PICCININI, PATRICIA b. 1965 Freetown, Sierra Leone

PIPER, ADRIAN b. 1948 New York, N.Y., USA

PITTMAN, LARI b. 1952 Los Angeles, Calif., USA

POLKE, SIGMAR b. 1941 Oels (now Olesnica), Poland

PONDICK, RONA b. 1952 Brooklyn, N.Y., USA

POPE.L, WILLIAM b. 1955 Newark, N.J., USA

POTRČ, MARJETICA b. 1953 Ljubljana, Yugoslavia

PRINCE, RICHARD b. 1949 Panama Canal Zone, Panama

PURYEAR, MARTIN b. 1941 Chicago, Ill., USA

RAAD, WALID (THE ATLAS GROUP) b. 1967 Chbanieh, Lebanon

RAMIREZ JONAS, PAUL b. 1965 Pomona, Calif., USA

RAND, ARCHIE b. 1949 Chicago, Ill., USA

RAUCH, NEO b. 1960 Leipzig, Germany

RAY, CHARLES b. 1953 Chicago, Ill., USA

REED, DAVID b. 1946 San Diego, Calif., USA

REPOHISTORY founded 1989 New York, N.Y., USA

RHOADES, JASON b. 1965 Newcastle, Calif., USA; d. 2006 Los Angeles, Calif. USA

RICHTER, GERHARD b. 1932 Dresden, Germany

RILEY, BRIDGET b. 1931 London, UK

RIST, PIPILOTTI b. 1962 Schweizer Rheintal, Switzerland

RISTELHUEBER, SOPHIE b. 1949 Paris, France

RITCHIE, MATTHEW b. 1964 London, UK

ROBBINS, ANDREA b. 1963 Boston, Mass., USA

ROBLETO, DARIO b. 1972 San Antonio, Tex., USA

ROCKMAN, ALEXIS b. 1962 New York, N.Y., USA

ROLLINS, TIM b. 1955 Pittsfield, Maine, USA

ROSENQUIST, JAMES b. 1933 Grand Forks, N.Dak., USA

ROSLER, MARTHA b. 1943 Brooklyn, N.Y., USA

ROVNER, MICHAL b. 1957 Tel Aviv, Israel

ROWELL, STEVEN b. 1969 Houston, Tex., USA

RUFF, THOMAS b. 1958 Zell, Germany

RUSCHA, ED b. 1937 Omaha, Nebr., USA

RYMAN, ROBERT b. 1930 Nashville, Tenn., USA

SAAR, ALISON b. 1956 Los Angeles, Calif., USA

SACHS, TOM b. 1966 New York, N.Y., USA

SALCEDO, DORIS b. 1958 Bogotá, Colombia

SALLE, DAVID b. 1952 Norman, Okla., USA

SANBORN, JIM b. 1945 Washington, D.C., USA

SANDALJIAN, HAGOP b. 1931 Alexandria, Egypt

SAUL, PETER b. 1934 San Francisco, Calif., USA

SAVILLE, JENNY b. 1970 Cambridge, UK

SCHAPIRO, MIRIAM b. 1923 Toronto, Ont., Canada

SCHER, JULIA b. 1954 Hollywood, Calif., USA

SCHNABEL, JULIAN b. 1951 New York, N.Y., USA

SCHNEEMANN, CAROLEE b. 1939 Fox Chase, Pa., USA

SCHÜTTE, THOMAS b. 1954 Oldenburg, Germany

SCHUTZ, DANA b. 1976 Livonia, Mich., USA

SCOFIDIO, RICARDO b. 1935 New York, N.Y., USA

SCULLY, SEAN b. 1945 Dublin, Ireland

SEKULA, ALLAN b. 1951 Erie, Pa., USA

SEMMEL, JOAN b. 1932 New York, N.Y., USA

SERRA, RICHARD b. 1939 San Francisco, Calif., USA

SERRANO, ANDRES b. 1950 New York, N.Y., USA

SHALEV-GERZ, ESTHER b. 1948 Vilnius, Lithuania

SHERMAN, CINDY b. 1954 Glen Ridge, N.J., USA

SHONIBARE, YINKA (MBE) b. 1962 London, UK

SIENA, JAMES b. 1957 Oceanside, Calif., USA

SIKANDER, SHAHZIA b. 1969 Lahore, Pakistan
SIMPSON, LORNA b. 1960 Brooklyn, N.Y., USA
SISCO, ELIZABETH b. 1954 Cheverly, Md., USA
SLEIGH, SYLVIA b. 1916 Llandudno, UK
SLOMINSKI, ANDRES b. 1959 Meppen, Germany
SMITH, KIKI b. 1954 Nuremburg, Germany
SOLAKOV, NEDKO b. 1957 Cherven Briag, Bulgaria
SONFIST, ALAN b. 1946 New York, N.Y., USA
SPERO, NANCY b. 1926 Cleveland, Ohio, USA
SPIEGELMAN, ART b. 1948 Stockholm, Sweden
STAEHLE, WOLFGANG b. 1950 Stuttgart, Germany
STARLING, SIMON b. 1967 Epsom, UK
STEINBACH, HAIM b. 1944 Rechovot, Israel
STELLA, FRANK b. 1936 Malden, Mass., USA
STOCKHOLDER, JESSICA b. 1959 Seattle, Wash., USA
STRUTH, THOMAS b. 1954 Geldern, Germany
SUGIMOTO, HIROSHI b. 1948 Tokyo, Japan
SUH, DO-HO b. 1962 Seoul, Korea
SULLIVAN, CATHERINE b. 1968 Los Angeles, Calif., USA
SUSSMAN, EVE b. 1961 London, UK
SZE, SARAH b. 1969 Boston, Mass., USA
TAAFFE, PHILIP b. 1955 Elizabeth, N.J., USA
TANSEY, MARK b. 1949 San José, Calif., USA
TAYLOR-WOOD, SAM b. 1967 London, UK
TERAOKA, MASAMI b. 1936 Onomichi, Japan
TILLMANS, WOLFGANG b. 1968 Remscheid, Germany
TIRAVANIJA, RIRKRIT b. 1961 Buenos Aires, Argentina
TOMASELLI, FRED b. 1956 Santa Monica, Calif., USA
TUYMANS, LUC b. 1958 Mortsel, Belgium
UKELES, MIERLE LADERMAN b. 1939 Denver, Colo., USA
VIOLA, BILL b. 1951 New York, N.Y., USA
WALKER, KARA b. 1969 Stockton, Calif., USA
WALL, JEFF b. 1946 Vancouver, B.C., Canada
WALLINGER, MARK b. 1959 Chigwell, UK
WARHOL, ANDY b. 1928 Pittsburgh, Pa., USA d. 1987 New York, N.Y., USA
WEARING, GILLIAN b. 1963 Birmingham, UK
WEISS, DAVID b. 1946 Zurich, Switzerland
WEST, FRANZ b. 1947 Vienna, Austria
WHITEREAD, RACHEL b. 1963 London, UK
WILKE, HANNAH b. 1940 New York, N.Y., USA; d. 1993 New York, N.Y., USA
WILSON, FRED b. 1954 New York, N.Y., USA
WILSON, JANE b. 1967 Newcastle upon Tyne, UK
WILSON, LOUISE b. 1967 Newcastle upon Tyne, UK
WINTERS, TERRY b. 1949 Brooklyn, N.Y., USA
WODICZKO, KRZYSZTOF b. 1943 Warsaw, Poland
WOJNAROWICZ, DAVID b. 1954 Redbank, N.Y., USA d. 1992 New York, N.Y., USA
WURM, ERWIN b. 1954 Bruck, Austria
XU BING, b. 1955 Chongqing, China
YANAGI, YUKINORI b. 1959 Fukuoka, Japan
YES MEN founded 2000
YUSKAVAGE, LISA b. 1962 Philadelphia, Pa., USA
ZHANG HUAN b. 1965 An Yang, China
ZIEGLER, MEL b. 1956 Campbelltown, Pa., USA
ZITTEL, ANDREA b. 1965 Escondido, Calif., USA

BIBLIOGRAPHY

INTRODUCTION

BURGIN, VICTOR. *The End of Art Theory: Criticism and Postmodernity*. London: Macmillan, 1986.

DANTO, ARTHUR. "Approaching the End of Art." In *The State of the Art*, 202–18. New York: Prentice Hall, 1987.

———. "Bad Aesthetic Times." In *Encounters and Reflections: Art in the Historical Present*, 297–312. New York: Farrar, Straus and Giroux, 1986.

FINEBERG, JONATHAN. *Art since 1940: Strategies of Being*. Englewood Cliffs, N.J.: Prentice Hall, 1995.

FOSTER, HAL, *Recodings: Art, Spectacle, Cultural Politics*. Port Townsend, Wash.: Bay Press, 1985.

———. *The Return of the Real: The Avant-Garde at the End of the Century*. Cambridge, Mass.: MIT Press, 1996.

———. ed. *The Anti-Aesthetic: Essays on Postmodern Culture*. Port Townsend, Wash.: Bay Press, 1983.

FOSTER, HAL, ROSALIND KRAUSS, YVE-ALAIN BOIS, AND BENJAMIN BUCHLOH. *Art since 1900: Modernism, Antimodernism, Postmodernism*. London: Thames and Hudson, 2005.

FRIED, MICHAEL. "Art and Objecthood." *Artforum* 5 (June 1967): 12–23.

GREENBERG, CLEMENT. "Avant-Garde and Kitsch" and "Towards a Newer Laocoon." In *Pollock and After: The Critical Debate*, edited by Francis Frascina, 21–33, 35–46. New York: Harper and Row, 1985. Originally published in *Partisan Review* 6 (Fall 1939) and 7 (July–August 1940).

LEUNG, SIMON. *Theory in Contemporary Art since 1985*. Malden, Mass.: Blackwell, 2004.

LYOTARD, JEAN-FRANÇOIS. *The Postmodern Condition: A Report on Knowledge*. Translated by Geoff Bennington and Brian Massumi. Minneapolis: University of Minnesota Press, 1984.

NAIRNE, SANDY. *State of the Art: Ideas and Images in the 1980s*. In collaboration with Geoff Dunlop and John Wyver. London: Chatto and Windus, 1987.

NOCHLIN, LINDA. "Why Have There Been No Great Women Artists?" In *Women, Art, and Power and Other Essays*, 145–78. New York: Harper and Row, 1988. Originally published in *ARTnews* 69 (January 1971).

SANDLER, IRVING. *Art of the Postmodern Era*. New York: HarperCollins, 1996.

WALLIS, BRIAN, ed. *Art after Modernism: Rethinking Representation*. New York: New Museum of Contemporary Art; Boston: David R. Godine, 1984.

ART & POPULAR CULTURE

BAUDRILLARD, JEAN. "Simulacra and Simulations." In *Jean Baudrillard: Selected Writings*, edited by Mark Poster, 166–84. Stanford, Calif.: Stanford University Press, 1988.

FRANCIS, MARK, AND HAL FOSTER. *Pop.* London: Phaidon Press, 2005.

GRUNENBERG, CHRISTOPH, AND THOMAS KELLEIN, eds. *Shopping: A Century of Art and Consumer Culture.* Ostfildern, Germany: Hatje Cantz, 2003.

GUINS, RAIFORD, AND OMAYRA ZARAGOZA CRUZ. *Popular Culture: A Reader.* Thousand Oaks, Calif.: Sage, 2005.

MADOFF, STEVEN HENRY, ed. *Pop Art: A Critical History.* Documents of Twentieth-Century Art. Berkeley and Los Angeles: University of California Press, 1997.

MCLUHAN, MARSHALL, AND QUENTIN FIORE. *The Medium Is the Massage.* New York: Bantam, 1967.

VARNEDOE, KIRK, AND ADAM GOPNIK. *Modern Art and Popular Culture: Readings in High and Low.* New York: Harry N. Abrams, 1990.

WARHOL, ANDY. *The Philosophy of Andy Warhol: From A to B and Back Again.* New York: Harcourt Brace Jovanovich, 1975.

WARHOL, ANDY, AND PAT HACKETT. *POPism: The Warhol '60s.* New York: Harcourt Brace Jovanovich, 1980.

WARHOL, ANDY, KASPER KÖNIG, PONTUS HULTEN, AND OLLE GRANATH, eds. *Andy Warhol.* Stockholm: Moderna Museet, 1968.

ART & THE QUOTIDIAN OBJECT

BENJAMIN, WALTER. "The Work of Art in the Age of Mechanical Reproduction." In *Illuminations*, translated by Harry Zohn, edited by Hannah Arendt, 217–59. New York: Schocken, 1969.

BUSKIRK, MARTHA. *The Contingent Object of Contemporary Art.* Cambridge, Mass.: MIT Press, 2005.

BUSKIRK, MARTHA, AND MIGNON NIXON, eds. *The Duchamp Effect.* Cambridge, Mass.: MIT Press, 1996.

CABANNE, PIERRE. *Dialogues with Marcel Duchamp.* New York: Da Capo Press, 1987.

DANTO, ARTHUR. *The Transfiguration of the Commonplace: A Philosophy of Art.* Cambridge, Mass.: Harvard University Press, 1981.

DUCHAMP, MARCEL. *Salt Cellar: The Writings of Marcel Duchamp.* Edited by Michel Sanouillet and Elmer Peterson. New York: Da Capo Press, 1973.

KRAMER, HILTON. "Duchamp and His Legacy." *New Criterion* 14 (October 1995).

MOLESWORTH, HELEN, "Work Avoidance: The Everyday Life of Marcel Duchamp's Readymades." *Art Journal* 57 (Winter 1998).

———. ed. *Part Object Part Sculpture.* Columbus, Ohio: Wexner Center for the Arts; University Park: Pennsylvania State University Press, 2005.

ROSENTHAL, MARK. *Understanding Installation Art: From Duchamp to Holzer.* New York: Prestel, 2003.

ART & ABSTRACTION

COLPITT, FRANCES, ed. *Abstract Art in the Late Twentieth Century.* Contemporary Artists and their Critics. London: Cambridge University Press, 2005.

GOODING, MEL. *Abstract Art.* London: Tate Gallery, 2001.

GREENBERG, CLEMENT. "Towards a Newer Laocoon." In *Pollock and After: The Critical Debate*, edited by Francis Frascina. New York: Harper and Row, 1985. Originally published in *Partisan Review* 7 (July–August 1940).

FRIED, MICHAEL. "Art and Objecthood." *Artforum* 5 (June 1967): 12–23.

HALLEY, PETER. *Collected Essays, 1981–87.* Zurich: Bruno Bischofberger Gallery, 1988.

KANDINSKY, WASSILY. *Concerning the Spiritual in Art.* 1912. Reprint, New York: Wittenborn, 1966.

KRAUSS, ROSALIND. "Grids." 1980. Reprinted in *The Originality of the Avant-Garde and Other Modernist Myths.* Cambridge, Mass.: MIT Press, 1985.

MEYER, JAMES. *Minimalism.* London: Phaidon Press, 2000.

ROSENTHAL, MARK. *Abstraction in the Twentieth Century: Total Risk, Freedom, Discipline.* New York: Solomon R. Guggenheim Museum, 1996.

ROSE, BARBARA. "ABC Art." *Art in America* 53 (October/November 1865): 57–69.

SCHAPIRO, MEYER. "The Nature of Abstract Art." In *Modern Art: 19th and 20th Centuries.* New York: George Braziller, 1982.

STELLA, FRANK. *Working Space.* Cambridge, Mass.: William Stout Architectural Press, 1986.

VARNEDOE, KIRK. *Pictures of Nothing: Abstract Art since Pollock.* A. W. Mellon Lectures in the Fine Arts. Princeton, N.J.: Princeton University Press, 2006.

ART & REPRESENTATION

BARTHES, ROLAND. *Camera Lucida.* New York: Hill and Wang, 1981.

———. "Myth Today." In *A Barthes Reader*, edited by Susan Sontag, 93–149. London: Jonathan Cape, 1982.

BENJAMIN, WALTER. *Illuminations.* Translated by Harry Zohn. New York: Schocken, 1969.

DANTO, ARTHUR. "The End of Art." In *The Death of Art*, edited by Berel Lang. New York: Haven, 1984.

FOSTER, HAL. *The Return of the Real: The Avant-Garde at the End of the Century.* Cambridge, Mass.: MIT Press, 1996.

HALLEY, PETER. *Collected Essays, 1981–87.* Zurich: Bruno Bischofberger Gallery, 1988.

HEARTNEY, ELEANOR. *Postmodernism.* London: Tate, 2002.

KUSPIT, DONALD. *The End of Art.* Cambridge, England: Cambridge University Press, 2005.

KRAUSS, ROSALIND. *The Originality of the Avant-Garde and Other Modernist Myths.* Cambridge, Mass.: MIT Press, 1986.

LAWSON, THOMAS. "Last Exit: Painting." Reprinted in *Art after Modernism: Rethinking Representation,* edited by Brian Wallis, 153–65. New York: New Museum of Contemporary Art; Boston: David R. Godine, 1984.

OWENS, CRAIG. *Beyond Recognition: Representation, Power, and Culture.* Berkeley and Los Angeles: University of California Press, 1994.

ART & NARRATIVE

BARTHES, ROLAND. "The Death of the Author." In *Image, Music, Text*, edited and translated by Stephen Heath. New York: Hill and Wang, 1977.

BERGER, ARTHUR ASA. *Narratives in Popular Culture, Media, and Everyday Life.* Thousand Oaks, Calif.: Sage, 2002.

BURNHAM, PATRICIA M., AND LUCRETIA HOOVER GIESE, eds. *Redefining American History Painting.* New York: Cambridge University Press, 1995.

CURRIE, MARK. *Postmodern Narrative Theory.* New York: St. Martin's Press, 1998.

GREEN, DAVID, AND PETER SEDDON, eds. *History Painting Reassessed.* Manchester, England: Manchester University Press, 2000.

GREENBERG, CLEMENT. "Towards a Newer Laocoon." In *Pollock and After: The Critical Debate*, edited by Francis Frascina. New York: Harper and Row, 1985. Originally published in *Partisan Review* 7 (July–August 1940).

JAMESON, FREDERIC. "Postmodernism and Consumer Society." In *The Anti-Aesthetic: Essays on Postmodern Culture*, edited by Hal Foster. Port Townsend, Wash.: Bay Press, 1983.

OWENS, CRAIG. "The Allegorical Impulse: Toward a Theory of Postmodernism." In *Art after Modernism:*

Rethinking Representation, edited by Brian Wallis. New York: New Museum of Contemporary Art; Boston: David R. Godine, 1984.

ART & TIME

CAPPELLAZZO, AMY, ADRIANO PEDROSA, AND PETER WOLLEN. *Making Time: Considering Time as a Material.* Los Angeles: Palm Beach Institute of Contemporary Art, 2000.

GERE, CHARLIE. *Art, Time and Technology.* Culture Machine. Oxford: Berg, 2006.

HALL, DOUG, AND SALLY JO FIFER, eds. *Illuminating Video: An Essential Guide to Video Art*. New York: Aperture, 2005.

JENKINS, HENRY. *Convergence Culture: Where Old and New Media Collide.* New York: New York University Press, 2006.

JONES, CAROLINE A., ed. *Sensorium: Embodied Experience, Technology, and Contemporary Art*. Cambridge, Mass.: MIT Press, 2006.

KERN, STEPHEN. *The Culture of Time and Space, 1880–1918*. Cambridge, Mass.: Harvard University Press, 1983.

MORGAN, JESSICA, AND GREGOR MUIR. *Time Zones/Recent Film and Video*. London: Tate, 2004.

RUSH, MICHAEL. *New Media in Late 20th-Century Art*. London: Thames and Hudson, 1999.

———. *Video Art.* London: Thames and Hudson, 2003.

SARTRE, JEAN-PAUL. *Being and Nothingness.* New York: Simon and Schuster, 1993.

ART & NATURE AND TECHNOLOGY

ANKER, SUZANNE, AND DOROTHY NELKIN. *The Molecular Gaze: Art in the Genetic Age.* Cold Spring Harbor Laboratory Press Series on Genomics, Bioethics, and Public Policy. Cold Spring Harbor, N.Y.: Cold Spring Harbor Laboratory Press, 2004.

BENDER, GRETCHEN. *Culture on the Brink: Ideologies of Technology.* Discussions in Contemporary Culture 9. New York: New Press, 1998.

DEITCH, JEFFREY. *PostHuman.* New York: Jeffrey Deitch, 1992.

FLAMM, JACK, ed. *Robert Smithson: The Collected Writings*. Berkeley and Los Angeles: University of California Press, 1996.

HARAWAY, DONNA. "A Cyborg Manifesto: Science, Technology, and Socialist-Feminism in the Late Twentieth Century." In *Simians, Cyborgs and Women: The Reinvention of Nature*. New York: Routledge, 1991.

HAYLES, N. KATHERINE. *How We Became Posthuman: Virtual Bodies in Cybernetics, Literature, and Informatics*. Chicago: University of Chicago Press, 1999.

"INSIDE OUT: ARTS NEW TERRAIN." SPECIAL ISSUE, *Artforum* 44 (Summer 2005).

JONES, CAROLINE. *Machine in the Studio.* Chicago: University of Chicago Press, 1996.

KASTNER, JEFFREY, AND BRIAN WALLIS, eds. *Land and Environmental Art.* New York: Phaidon, 2005.

LEVIN, THOMAS Y., URSULA FROHNE, AND PETER WEIBEL, eds. *CTRL[SPACE]: Rhetorics of Surveillance from Bentham to Big Brother.* Cambridge, Mass.: MIT Press; Karlsruhe: WKM, 2002.

MALEN, LENORE, ELLEN K. LEVY, AND BERTA M. SICHEL, eds. "Contemporary Art and the Genetic Code." Special issue, *Art Journal* 55 (Spring 1996).

MARINETTI, F. T. "The Foundation and Manifesto of Futurism." 1909. Reprinted in *Theories of Modern Art*, edited by Herschel B. Chipp. Berkeley and Los Angeles: University of California Press, 1968.

MATILSKY, BARBARA. *Fragile Ecologies*. New York: Rizzoli, 1992.

PENNY, SIMON. *Critical Issues in Electronic Media.* SUNY Series in Film History and Theory. Albany: State University of New York Press, 1995.

SMITH, STEPHANIE, AND VICTOR MARGOLIN, eds. *Beyond Green: Toward a Sustainable Art*. Chicago: Smart Museum of Art; New York: Independent Curators International, 2005.

SPAID, SUE. *Ecovention: Current Art to Transform Ecologies*. Cincinnati: Contemporary Arts Center, 2002.

ART & DEFORMATION

ADAMS, JAMES LUTHER, AND WILSON YATES, eds. *The Grotesque in Art and Literature: Theological Reflections.* Grand Rapids, Mich.: William B. Eerdmans, 1997.

BAKHTIN, MIKHAIL. *Rabelais and His World*. Translated by Helene Iswolsky. Cambridge, Mass.: MIT Press, 1968.

BOIS, YVE-ALAIN, AND ROSALIND E. KRAUSS. *Formless: A User's Guide*. New York: Zone Books, 2000.

CONNELLY, FRANCES S. *Modern Art and the Grotesque.* Cambridge: Cambridge University Press, 2003.

KORT, PAMELA, ed. *Comic Grotesque: Wit and Mockery in German Art, 1870–1940*. New York: Neue Galerie; Munich: Prestel, 2004.

KRISTEVA, JULIA. *Powers of Horror: An Essay on Abjection*. Translated by Leon S. Roudiez. New York: Columbia University Press, 1982.

STORR, ROBERT. *Disparities and Deformations: Our Grotesque.* Santa Fe, N.Mex.: Site Sante Fe, 2004.

ART & THE BODY

BERGER, JOHN *Ways of Seeing*. London: British Broadcasting Corporation; Harmondsworth, England: Penguin, 1972.

BRAND, PEG ZEGLIN, ed. *Beauty Matters*. Bloomington: Indiana University Press, 2000.

CLARK, KENNETH. *The Nude: A Study in Ideal Form*. London: Bollingen, 1972. Based on a series of 1953 lectures at the National Gallery, Washington, D.C.; first published in 1956.

GOLDBERG, ROSELEE. *Performance: Live Art since the '60s*. London: Thames and Hudson, 2004.

———. *Performance Art: From Futurism to the Present*. London: Thames and Hudson, 2001.

HARRIS, ANN SUTHERLAND, AND LINDA NOCHLIN. *Women Artists, 1550–1950*. New York: Random House, 1976.

JONES, AMELIA. *Body Art / Performing the Subject*. Minneapolis: University of Minnesota Press, 1998.

———, ed. *The Feminism and Visual Culture Reader*. New York: Routledge, 2002.

KIM, YU YEON. *Translated Acts: Performance and Body Art From East Asia, 1990–2001.* New York: Queens Museum of Art, 2001.

MULVEY, LAURA. "Visual Pleasure and Narrative Cinema." Reprinted in Brian Wallis, *Art after Modernism: Rethinking Representation*, 361–73. New York: New Museum of Contemporary Art; Boston: David R. Godine, 1984.

NOCHLIN, LINDA. *Women, Art, and Power and Other Essays*. New York: Harper and Row, 1988.

O'DELL, KATHY. *Contract with the Skin: Masochism, Performance Art, and the 1970s.* Minneapolis: University of Minnesota Press, 1998.

POLLOCK, GRISELDA. *Visions and Difference: Femininity, Feminism and the Histories of Art.* London: Routledge and Kegan Paul, 1988.

SCHIMMEL, PAUL. *Out of Actions: Between Performance and the Object, 1949–79*. Los Angeles: Museum of Contemporary Art, 1988.

WAR, TRACEY, AND AMELIA JONES. *The Artist's Body*. London: Phaidon Press, 2000.

ART & IDENTITY

BERGER, MAURICE, ed. *White: Whiteness and Race in Contemporary Art*. Baltimore: Center for Art and Visual Culture, UMBC, 2003.

CRIMP, DOUGLAS, ed. *AIDS: Cultural Analysis, Cultural Activism*. Cambridge, Mass.: MIT Press, 1988.

FUSCO, COCO, AND BRIAN WALLIS. *Only Skin Deep: Changing Visions of the American Self*. New York: Harry N. Abrams, 2003.

GATES, HENRY LOUIS, ed. *Race, Writing and Difference*. Chicago: University of Chicago Press, 1985.

GOLDEN, THELMA, DAVID DEITCHER, AND GUILLERMO GÓMEZ-PEÑA. *The Decade Show: Frameworks of Identity in the 1980s*. New York: New Museum of Contemporary Art, 1990.

KLEEBLATT, NORMAN L., ed. *Too Jewish: Challenging Traditional Identities*. New York: Jewish Museum; New Brunswick, N.J.: Rutgers University Press, 1996.

KOSOFSKY, EVE. *Epistemology of the Closet*. Berkeley and Los Angeles: University of California Press, 1990.

LIPPARD, LUCY R. *From the Center: Feminist Essays on Women's Art*. New York: E. P. Dutton, 1976.

———. *Mixed Blessings: New Art in a Multicultural America*. New York: Pantheon, 1990.

MCEVILLEY, THOMAS. *Art and Otherness: Crisis in Cultural Identity*. New York: McPherson, 1995.

MEYER, RICHARD. *Outlaw Representation: Censorship and Homosexuality in Twentieth-Century American Art*. Boston: Beacon, 2004.

RAMIREZ, MARI CARMEN. *Beyond the Fantastic: Contemporary Criticism from Latin America*. London: inIVA; Cambridge, Mass.: MIT Press, 1995.

ART & SPIRITUALITY

ARTHURS, ALBERTA, AND GLENN WALLACH, eds. *Crossroads: Art and Religion in American Life*. New York: New Press, 2001.

BAAS, JACQUELYNN, AND MARY JANE JACOB. *Buddha Mind in Contemporary Art*. Berkeley and Los Angeles: University of California Press, 2004.

BAIGELL, MATTHEW. *Jewish Art in America: An Introduction*. New York: Rowman and Littlefield, 2006.

ECKART, CHRISTIAN, HARRY PHILBRICK, AND OSVALDO ROMBERG, eds. *Faith: The Impact of Judeo-Christian Religion on Art of the Millennium*. Ridgefield, Conn.: Aldrich Museum of Art, 1999.

ELKINS, JAMES. *On the Strange Place of Religion in Contemporary Art*. New York: Routledge, 2004.

HEARTNEY, ELEANOR. *Postmodern Heretics: The Catholic Imagination in Contemporary Art*. New York: Midmarch Arts Press, 2004.

HELLER, ENA GIUERSCU, ed. *Reluctant Partners: Art and Religion in Dialogue*. New York: American Bible Society, 2004.

JULIUS, ANTHONY. *Idolizing Pictures: Idolatry, Iconoclasm and Jewish Art*. London: Thames and Hudson, 2000.

MORGAN, DAVID. *The Sacred Gaze: Religious Visual Culture in Theory and Practice*. Berkeley and Los Angeles: University of California Press, 2005.

MORGAN, DAVID, AND SALLY M. PROMEY, eds. *The Visual Culture of American Religions*. Berkeley and Los Angeles: University of California Press, 2001.

PLATE, S. BRENT, ed. *Religion, Art, and Visual Culture: A Cross-Cultural Reader*. New York: Palgrave, 2002.

POOLE, JENNIFER, AND SARAH WYATT, eds. *The Invisible Thread: Buddhist Spirit in Contemporary Art*. New York: Snug Harbor Cultural Center, 2004.

TUCHMAN, MAURICE. *The Spiritual in Art: Abstract Painting, 1890–1985*. Los Angeles: Los Angeles County Museum of Art, 1986.

KANDINSKY, WASSILY. *Concerning the Spiritual in Art*. 1912. Reprint, New York: Wittenborn, 1966.

ART & GLOBALISM

BHABHA, HOMI. *The Location of Culture*. London: Routledge, 2004.

BLAZWICK, IWONA, ed. *Century City: Art and Culture in the Modern Metropolis*. London: Tate, 2001.

CLIFFORD, JAMES. *The Predicament of Culture: Twentieth Century Ethnography, Literature and Art*. Cambridge, Mass.: Harvard University Press, 1988.

FERGUSON, RUSSELL, MARTHA GEVER, TRINH T. MINH-HA, AND CORNEL WEST. *Out There: Marginalization and Contemporary Culture*. Cambridge, Mass.: MIT Press, 1992.

FRIEDMAN, THOMAS. *The World Is Flat: A Brief History of the Twenty-first Century*. New York: Farrar, Straus and Giroux, 2004.

GRIFFIN, TIM, AND JAMES MEYER. "Global Tendencies: Globalism and the Large Scale Exhibition." *Artforum* 42 (November 2001): 152–63.

MERCER, KOBENA, ed. *Cosmopolitan Modernisms*. Annotating Art's Histories: Cross-Cultural Perspectives in the Visual Arts. Cambridge, Mass.: MIT Press, 2004.

MOSQUERA, GERARDO, AND JEAN FISHER, eds. *Over Here: International Perspectives on Art and Culture*. Documentary Sources in Contemporary Art. Cambridge, Mass.: MIT Press, 2007.

SAID, EDWARD. *Orientalism*. New York: Vintage, 1979.

TRINH, T. MINH-HA, *Woman, Native, Other: Writing Postcoloniality and Feminism*. Bloomington: Indiana University Press, 1989.

YOUNG, ROBERT J. C. *Postcolonialism: A Very Short Introduction*. Oxford: Oxford University Press, 2001.

ART & ARCHITECTURE

BASUALDO, CARLOS, AND REINALDO LADDAGA. "Rules of Engagement: From Toilets in Caracas to New Media in New Delhi." *Artforum* 42 (March 2004).

BINGHAM, NEIL. *Fantasy Architecture, 1500-2036*. London: Hayward Gallery Publishing, 2004.

CELANT, GERMANO, ed. *Architecture and Arts, 1900–2004*. Milan: Skira, 2004.

GRAHAM, DAN. *Rock My Religion: Writings and Projects, 1965–1990*. Cambridge, Mass.: MIT Press, 1993.

HITCHCOCK, HENRY RUSSELL, AND PHILIP JOHNSON. *The International Style*. New York: W. W. Norton, 1997.

JENCKS, CHARLES. *Language of Post-Modern Architecture*. New York: Rizzoli, 1991.

JODIDIO, PHILIP. *Architecture: Art*. New York: Prestel, 2005.

KRUFT, HANNO-WALTER. *A History of Architectural Theory*. New York: Princeton Architectural Press, 1994.

LE CORBUSIER. *Towards a New Architecture*. New York: Dover, 1985.

LEFEBVRE, HENRI. "From the Production of Space." 1974. In *Architecture Theory since 1968*, edited by K. Michael Hayes, 179. Cambridge, Mass.: MIT Press, 2000.

LOOS, ADOLF. "Ornament and Crime." In *Adolf Loos, Spoken into the Void: Collected Essays 1897–1900*, translated by Jane O. Newman and John H. Smith. Cambridge, Mass.: MIT Press, 1982.

MUMFORD, LEWIS, ed. *Roots of Contemporary American Architecture*. New York: Dover, 1952.

VENTURI, ROBERT. *Learning from Las Vegas*. Cambridge, Mass.: MIT Press, 1977.

ART & ITS INSTITUTIONS

CARRIER, DAVID. *Museum Skepticism: A History of the Display of Art in Public Galleries*. Durham, N.C.: Duke University Press, 2006.

CRIMP, DOUGLAS. *On the Museum's Ruins*. Cambridge, Mass.:

MIT Press, 1995.

DAVIS, DOUGLAS. "The Museum of the Third Kind." *Art in America* 93 (June–July 2005).

DUBIN, STEVEN. *Displays of Power: Memory and Amnesia in the American Museum*. New York: New York University Press, 1999.

DUNCAN, CAROL. *Civilizing Rituals: Inside Public Art Museums.* Critical Studies in the History and Theory of Art. New York: Routledge, 1995.

FRASER, ANDREA. "From the Critique of Institutions to an Institution of Critique." *Artforum* 44 (September 2005): 278–83.

GREENBERG, REESA, BRUCE FERGUSON, AND SANDY NAIRNE, eds. *Thinking about Exhibitions*. New York: Routledge, 1996.

MCSHINE, KYNASTON. *The Museum as Muse: Artists Reflect*. New York: Museum of Modern Art, 1999.

MÖNTMANN, NINA, ed. *Art and Its Institutions: Current Conflicts, Critique and Collaborations*. London: Black Dog, 2006.

POLLOCK, GRISELDA, AND JOYCE ZEMANS, eds. *Museums after Modernism: Strategies of Engagement.* New Interventions in Art History. Malden, Mass.: Blackwell, 2007.

STANISZEWSKI, MARY ANNE. *The Power of Display: A History of Exhibition Installations at the Museum of Modern Art*. Cambridge, Mass.: MIT Press, 1998.

WALLACH, ALAN. *Exhibiting Contradiction: Essays on the Art Museum in the United States.* Boston: University of Massachusetts Press, 1998.

WESCHLER, LAWRENCE. *Mr. Wilson's Cabinet of Wonder: Pronged Ants, Horned Humans, Mice on Toast, and Other Marvels of Jurassic Technology*. New York: Vintage, 1996.

ART & POLITICS

AULT, JULIE. *Alternative New York, 1965–85*. Minneapolis: University of Minnesota Press, 2003.

BECKER, CAROL. *The Subversive Imagination: The Artist, Society and Social Responsibility.* New York: Routledge, 1994.

BOLTON, RICHARD, ed. *Culture Wars: Documents from the Recent Controversies in the Arts*. New York: New Press, 1992.

BORER, ALAIN. *The Essential Joseph Beuys*. Cambridge, Mass.: MIT Press, 1997.

COCKCROFT, EVA. "Abstract Expressionism, Weapon of the Cold War." *Artforum* 12 (June 1974): 39–41. Reprinted in *Pollock and After: The Critical Debate*, edited by Francis Frascina. New York: Harper and Row, 1985.

DUBIN, STEVEN C. *Arresting Images: Impolitic Art and Uncivil Actions*. New York: Routledge, 1994.

FINKELPEARL, TOM, ed. *Dialogues in Public Art*. Cambridge, Mass.: MIT Press, 2001.

FOSTER, HAL, ed. *The Anti-Aesthetic: Essays on Postmodern Culture*. Port Townsend, Wash.: Bay Press, 1983.

HEARTNEY, ELEANOR. *Defending Complexity: Art, Politics and the New World Order*. Lenox, Mass.: Hard Press, 2006.

HUGHES, ROBERT. *The Culture of Complaint: The Fraying of America*. New York: Oxford University Press, 1993.

KESTER, GRANT, ed. *Art, Activism, and Oppositionality: Essays from Afterimage*. Durham, N.C.: Duke University Press, 1998.

KOZLOFF, MAX. "American Painting during the Cold War." *Artforum* 11 (May 1973): 43–54. Reprinted in *Pollock and After: The Critical Debate*, edited by Francis Frascina. New York: Harper and Row, 1985.

KRAMER, HILTON. *The Revenge of the Philistines: Art and Culture, 1972–1984*. New York: Simon and Schuster, 1985.

MITCHELL, W. J. T., ed. *Art and the Public Sphere*. Chicago: University of Chicago Press, 1990.

SENIE, HARRIET F. *Contemporary Public Sculpture: Tradition, Transformation and Controversy.* New York: Oxford University Press, 1992.

SENIE, HARRIET F., AND SALLY WEBSTER, eds. *Critical Issues in Public Art: Content, Context and Controversy.* New York: HarperCollins, 1992.

WALLIS, BRIAN, MARIANNE WEEMS, AND PHILIP YENAWINE, eds. *Art Matters: How the Culture Wars Changed America*. New York: New York University Press, 1999.

ART & AUDIENCE

BISHOP, CLAIRE. *Participation.* Documents of Contemporary Art. Cambridge, Mass.: MIT Press, 2006.

BRENSON, MICHAEL, EVA M. OLSON, AND MARY JANE JACOB. *Culture in Action: A Public Art Program of Sculpture Chicago*. Seattle: Bay Press, 1995.

BORER, ALAIN, ed. *The Essential Joseph Beuys*. Cambridge, Mass.: MIT Press, 1997.

BOURRIAUD, NICHOLAS. *Relational Aesthetics*. Paris: Le Presses du Réel, 2003.

DEBORD, GUY. *The Society of the Spectacle*. Translated by Donald Nicholson-Smith. London: Rebel Press/AIM, 1987.

FELSHIN, NINA, ed. *But Is It Art: The Spirit of Art as Activism.* Seattle: Bay Press, 1995.

JAUSS, HANS ROBERT. *Toward an Aesthetic of Reception.* Translated by Timothy Bahti. Introduction by Paul de Man. Minneapolis: University of Minnesota Press, 1982. Published version of a lecture given at the University of Constance, Germany, in 1967.

KESTER, GRANT. *Conversation Pieces: Community and Communication in Modern Art*. Berkeley and Los Angeles: University of California Press, 2004.

KWON, MIWON. *One Place after Another: Site Specific Art and Locational Identity*. Cambridge, Mass.: MIT Press, 2004.

LACY, SUZANNE, ed. *Mapping the Terrain: New Genre Public Art.* Seattle: Bay Press, 1995.

THOMPSON, NATO, AND GREGORY SHOLETTE, eds. *The Interventionists: Users' Manual for the Creative Disruption of Everyday Life*. Cambridge, Mass.: MIT Press, 2006.

PICTURE CREDITS

All works are in private collections or the artist's collection unless otherwise stated. All works © the artists or their estates.

Abbreviations: t=top, b=bottom, (l)=left, r=right

© The artists/Courtesy 303 Gallery, New York: 29, 75(l), 107, 130t, 157, 159
Courtesy Acquavella Galleries, Inc.: 226t
Courtesy George Adams Gallery, New York and Gallery Paule Anglim, San Francisco: 374t
Courtesy Chris Ofili, Afroco: 248, 267
Courtesy Alexander and Bonin, New York/ Photo: Muammer Yanmaz: 56; Photo: Dieter Schwerdtle: 57; Photo: Jorge Brantmayer: 306; Photo: Ivan Dalla Tana: 411
Courtesy Arndt & Partner, Berlin and Zurich, Photo Vegar Moen: 134
© The Robert Mapplethorpe Foundation/Courtesy Art + Commerce: 228
ArtPace, San Antonio/Photo: Riley Robinson: 280b
Art Resource, New York: 69, 83
Erich Lessing/Art Resource, New York: 366
© and courtesy the artist: 17, 86, 151, 154-55, 165, 171, 174, 179(l), 183r, 187, 188t, 191, 220t, 221, 222, 224, 259b, 269, 276, 310, 312, 330, 353r, 363, 381t; 386b; 392(l), 392r, 396t, 406, 409
Courtesy the artist/Photo: Kira Perov: 152, Photo: Rhee Jae-yong: 184; Photo: Grahm Baring: 188b; Photo: James Wildman: 334; Photo: Dirk Pauwels: 358t; Photo: Paul Mellaart: 358b; Photo: Claudio Oiticica: 393r; Photo: Wolfgang Volz: 408
Courtesy Associazione Arte Continua, San Gimignano, Italia/Photo: Attilio Maranzano: 405
Courtesy Baldessari Studio and Marian Goodman Gallery, New York: 24
Courtesy Bates College Museum of Art, Lewiston, Maine/Photo: Luc Demers: 317b
© The artists/Courtesy Peter Blum Gallery, New York: 75r, 319
© The artist/Courtesy Marianne Boesky Gallery, New York: 48t
© 2003 Takashi Murakami/Kaikai KiKi Ltd., Co. All rights reserved/Courtesy Marianne Boesky Gallery: 34
Courtesy the artist and Tanya Bonakdar Gallery, New York: 172
Courtesy the artist, Tanya Bonakdar Gallery, New York, and Neugerriemschneider, Berlin: 289
Courtesy Mary Boone Gallery, New York: 251
© 2002 Zindman/Fremont, New York/Courtesy Mary Boone Gallery, New York: 42, 89(l), 232
Photo Zindman/Fremont, New York/Courtesy Mary Boone Gallery, New York: 81b, 124
Courtesy Janet Borden, Inc.: 136
Photo: Jack E. Boucher: 384
Courtesy the Eli and Edythe L. Broad Collection, Santa Monica: 18r; Photo: Douglas M. Park Studio, Los Angeles: 78t
Courtesy the artists and Gavin Brown's enterprise, New York: 103r, 403
Photo: Sherman Bryce: 387
Center for Land Use Interpretation Photographic Archive: 176b
© The Helen Chadwick Estate/Leeds Museums & Galleries (Henry Moore Institute Archive): 211
© The artists/Courtesy Cheim & Read, New York: 82t, 196
Courtesy the artist and Catharine Clark Gallery, San Francisco: 372
Courtesy James Cohan Gallery, New York: 185, 202b, 272b, 238, 309
© The artist/Consult Overseas LTD (Lebanon): 307b
Paula Cooper Gallery, New York: 149, 266
© Walker Evans Archive, The Metropolitan Museum of Art/Courtesy Paula Cooper Gallery, New York: 45t
© The John Coplans Trust: 227
Courtesy the artist and Corvi-Mora, London: 327b
© Cotthem Gallery, Belgium: 255
Courtesy Galerie Crone, Berlin/Photo: Javier Campo, Madrid: 379
Courtesy Galerie Chantal Crousel/Photo: Florian Kleinefenn: 339
© The artists/Courtesy D'Amelio Terras, New York: 52, 85b
© D.B.: 325
Courtesy DC Moore Gallery, New York: 308, 412
Courtesy Deitch Projects, New York: 33, 278; Photo: Tom Powel Imaging: 207
Courtesy Deitch Projects/The Dakis Joannou Collection, Athens/Photo: Tom Powel: 315
Courtesy Deitch Projects/© Kunsthaus Bregenz/ Photo: Markus Tretter: 271
© Denver Art Museum: 260t
Dia Art Foundation, New York: 117
Courtesy Dia Center for the Arts/Photo: Bill Jacobson: 63
Photo: Thomas R. DuBrock/Collection of Julie Kinzelman and Christopher Tribble, Houston, Tex.: 53
Ezra Stoller © Esto: 322r
Courtesy Etherton Gallery, Ariz., and Dawson Gallery, Los Angeles: 96
© 1983 Sue Coe/Courtesy Galerie St. Etienne, New York: 376
REPOhistory Archive, Fales Library & Special Collections, New York University: 382r
Courtesy Patricia Faure Gallery, Santa Monica, Calif.: 282
Courtesy the artist and Feigen Contemporary, New York: 158
© The artists/Courtesy Ronald Feldman Fine Arts, New York: 126, 133, 175t, 175b; Photo: D. James Dee: 113; Photo: Alan Zindman: 183(l); Photo: Dennis Cowley: 247t; Photo: Zindman/Fremont: 378b
© The artists/Courtesy Zach Feuer Gallery, New York: 182, 262t; Photo: Oren Slor: 201
© The artist/Courtesy Galleria Emi Fontana, Milan: 326
Raymond Fogre Ltd. Fine Art Services: 81t
Photo: Uta Franke: 386t
© The artists/Courtesy Gagosian Gallery, New York: 54(l), 148b, 226b, 235, 238b, 348t; Photo: Robert McKeever: 200, 236
Courtesy General Idea (AA Bronson, New York/ Toronto): 258
Courtesy Gallery Laure Genillard, London: 35
© The artists/Courtesy Gladstone Gallery, New York: 26, 51, 162b, 218(l), 247b; Photo: Michael James O'Brien: 128
© Nan Goldin: 138
© The artists/Courtesy Marian Goodman Gallery, New York: 23, 47t, 58, 102, 104, 111(l), 131b, 162t, 198r, 208, 313, 353(l), 370; Photo: Cathy Carver, New York: 355
© Crystal Eye Ltd., Helsinki/Courtesy Marian Goodman Gallery, New York and Paris/Photo: Marja-Leena Hukkanen: 135
Gran Fury Records, Manuscripts and Archives Division, The New York Public Library, Astor, Lenox and Tilden Foundations: 259t
Courtesy Greenberg Van Doren Gallery, New York: 333
© The artist/Greene Naftali Gallery, New York: 27r, 375
Courtesy greengrassi, London: 82b
Courtesy the artist and Christopher Grimes Gallery: 294
Courtesy Group Material/Photo © 1991 Ken Schles: 378t
© The artist/Courtesy www.guerrillagirls.com: 381b
© The Solomon R. Guggenheim Foundation, New York/Photo: Ellen Labenski: 147
Courtesy Solomon R. Guggenheim Museum, New York: 62; Gift of the Bohen Foundation, 2001: 229
© The Estate of Philip Guston/Courtesy McKee Gallery, New York: 195r
Courtesy the artist and Haines Gallery, San Francisco: 170(l)
Courtesy Glenn Halvorson for the Walker Art Center, Minneapolis, Minn.: 176t
Printed by Hamilton Press, Venice, Calif./ Courtesy the artist: 25
Galerie Peter Herrmann, Berlin: 335
Rhona Hoffman Gallery, Chicago: 367
© Timothy Hursley: 337(l)
Courtesy In Situ, Paris: 340
Courtesy J. Johnson Gallery, Jacksonville Beach, Fla.: 91
Courtesy the artist and Casey Kaplan, New York: 342
© Kawamata and on the table/Organized by Mercer Union/Photo: Peter McCallum: 331b
© The artists/Courtesy Sean Kelly Gallery, New York. Used with permission: 106, 237b, 397b; Photo: Steven P. Harris: 219; Photo: Ken Schles: 351
Courtesy the artist and Kent Gallery, NYC: 328t
Courtesy the artist and Anton Kern Gallery/ Photo: Tom Powel Imaging: 287b; Photo: Jan Windszus: 395r
Phyllis Kind Gallery, New York: 280t
Estate Martin Kippenberger/Galerie Gisela Capitain, Cologne: 116(l)
Courtesy Leo Koenig, Inc., New York: 190, 397t
© Jeff Koons: 19, 20, 43
Balthazar Korab Ltd.: 322(l)
Courtesy Andrew Kreps Gallery: 256t
Courtesy Galerie Krinzinger, Vienna: 395(l)
© Yayoi Kusama/Photo: Hal Reif: 197
Courtesy the artist and Yvon Lambert, New York and Paris: 129
Courtesy Yvon Lambert, New York and Paris/ Photo: David Allison: 148t
Julia LaVerdiere and Paul Myoda © 2001/With support from Creative Time and the Municipal Art Society: 389
Courtesy the artist and Lehman Maupin Gallery, New York: 262b
© The artists/Courtesy Galerie Lelong, New York: 90, 209, 295, 368(l), 382(l)
© Estate of Ana Mendieta/Collection Galerie Lelong, New York: 281
Lennon, Weinberg, Inc., New York: 173
Courtesy Lisson Gallery, London: 177
© The artist/List Visual Arts Center, MIT/ Photo: Charles Mayer: 349
Courtesy the artist and Lombard-Feid Projects, New York/Photo: Will Brown: 404
Courtesy The Luggage Store, San Francisco: 32b
Courtesy the artists and Luhring Augustine Gallery, New York: 127t, 140, 156, 220b, 261, 360t
Galerie Mai, Zurich: 118
© The artists/Courtesy Matthew Marks Gallery, New York: 48b, 71, 76, 254, 300-301
© The artists/Courtesy Marlborough Gallery, New York: 274, 369; Photo: Artur Starewicz: 198(l)
Courtesy Mass MoCA, North Adams, Mass./ Installation made possible by the Sterling & Francine Clark Art Institute, Williamstown, Mass./Photo: Doug Bartow, 2002: 178
Courtesy the artists and Lehmann Maupin Gallery, New York: 305b; Photo: CharlieSamuels.com: 285
© The artists/Courtesy Lehmann Maupin Gallery, New York, and Sonnabend Gallery, New York: 18(l)
Courtesy Paul McCarthy Studio: 204
© Vija Celmins, Courtesy McKee Gallery, New York: 98
© The artists/Courtesy Metro Pictures, New York: 27(l), 50, 125t, 161b, 203, 348b
© Grisha Bruskin/Courtesy Meyerovich Gallery, San Francisco: 277
Courtesy the artist and Robert Miller Gallery, New York: 238t
© Miramax Film Corp.: 125b,
Courtesy Victoria Miro Gallery, London: 105
© The artist/Courtesy Victoria Miro Gallery, London, commissioned and produced by Artpace, San Antonio, Tex.: 127b
© The artists/Courtesy Mitchell-Innes & Nash, New York: 47b, 377
© Mark Morosee Photography: 393(l)
© Adrian Piper Research Archive/Museum of Contemporary Art, Chicago, Bernice and Kenneth Newberger Fund: 250
Museum of Jurassic Technology: 357
Galerie Christian Nagel, Cologne: 132
The Newark Museum/Art Resource, New York: 215
Courtesy G.R. N'Namdi Gallery: 252
Courtesy David Nolan Gallery, New York: 212b
Courtesy the artist and Numark Gallery, Washington, D.C.: 181
© Philip-Lorca diCorcia/Courtesy Pace/MacGill

Gallery, New York: 110
© The artists/Courtesy PaceWildenstein, New York: 89r, 99, 206, 270, 350; Photo: Kerry Ryan McFate: 54–55; Photo: Ellen Labenski: 305t
Maureen Paley, London: 137
© 1986 by Art Spiegelman and Pantheon Books: 374b
Commisioned by Pennsylvania Convention Center Authority: 85t
Courtesy Galerie Emmanuel Perrotin, Paris and Miami: 79, 139
Courtesy Friedrich Petzel Gallery, New York: 45b, 88, 343, 359, 396b
PPOW, New York: 373
Courtesy Fondazione Prada, Milan/Photo: Attilio Maranzano: 394
Courtesy Galeria Joan Prats: 214
Courtesy the artists and the Project, New York: 131t, 150
Courtesy the Project, New York/Collection of Jeanne Greenberg Rohatyn and Nicolas Rohatyn, New York/Photo: Emma Estwick: 299
© The artists/Courtesy Max Protetch Gallery, New York: 77, 78b, 223; Photo: Dennis Cowley: 328b; Photo: Michael Price: 332b
Pruznick/Grey: 399
Courtesy Public Art Fund, New York/Photo: Tom Powel Imaging: 341; Photo: Peter Bellamy: 410
Galeria Ramis Barquet: 279
Courtesy Regen Projects, Los Angeles: 93, 213
© Dusan Reljin 2006: 401
Courtesy the artist and Anthony Reynolds Gallery: 273
© The artists/Courtesy Andrea Rosen Gallery, New York: 60, 111r, 141, 338, 360b
© The Felix Gonzalez-Torres Foundation/ Courtesy of Andrea Rosen Gallery, New York/ Photo: Fred Scruton: 402
Courtesy the artist and Roslyn Oxley9 Gallery, Sydney, Australia: 311b
The Saatchi Gallery, London: 239
Courtesy Tom Sachs Studio: 37r
Sammlung migros Museum für Gegenwartskunst, Zurich/Photo: Andrew Whittuck, London: 179r
The Museum of Modern Art/Licensed by SCALA/Art Resource, New York: 114
© 2006 Bridget Riley/Courtesy Karsten Schubert, London: 80
Courtesy Richard Serra Studio, New York: 385
Courtesy Tony Shafrazi Gallery, New York: 30, 31
Courtesy Jack Shainman Gallery, New York: 311t
Courtesy Sikkema Jenkins & Co.: 37(l), 100, 199, 237t, 272t
Courtesy the artist/The David and Alfred Smart Museum at the University of Chicago/ Purchase, Paul and Miriam Kirkley Fund for Acquisitions: 225t
© The artists/Courtesy Sonnabend Gallery: 44t, 44b, 109, 153, 210, 260b
© Candida Höfer, Cologne/VG Bild-Kunst, Bonn/ Courtesy Sonnabend Gallery: 362
© The artists/Courtesy Sperone Westwater Gallery, New York: 61, 101, 163, 186, 287t
Courtesy Bill Stanton and Janos Marton: 413
Courtesy the artist and the Bernice Steinbaum Gallery: 275
Courtesy Storefront for Art and Architecture, New York: 331t
Courtesy the artist and Stux Gallery, New York: 189
Courtesy the artists and the Frances Young Tang Teaching Museum and Art Gallery, Saratoga Springs, New York/Photo: Kate Ericson and Mel Ziegler: 361
Tate, London/Art Resource, New York: 302
© The artist/Courtesy Timothy Taylor Gallery, London: 356
Courtesy the artist and Through the Flower: 245
© Ellen Page Wilson 1991: 249/Courtesy Tilton Gallery, New York: 243
© Nikki S. Lee/Courtesy Leslie Tonkonow Artworks + Projects, New York: 263
Courtesy Toyota Municipal Museum of Art, Toyota Aichi, Japan: 146r
Courtesy Ubu Gallery, New York: 194
Courtesy Universal Limited Art Editions: 212t
Courtesy the artist and V/Space LAB: 332t
Photo and © Atelier Van Lieshout: 337r
Shoshana Wayne Gallery, Santa Monica, Calif.: 346
Courtesy Barbara Wein Gallery, Berlin: 257
Courtesy Michael Werner Gallery, New York and Cologne: 115, 284, 368r
Courtesy Western Project: 283
Courtesy Whitechapel Gallery Archive, London: 119
© The artists/Courtesy Jay Jopling/White Cube, London: 22t, 59; Photo: Stephen White: 161t; Photo: Diane Bertrand: 202t; Photo: Elfi Tripamer: 303
Courtesy Xu Bing Studio/Photo: Xu Bing: 317t
Courtesy Donald Young Gallery, Chicago: 92
Zabriskie Gallery: 354
Courtesy David Zwirner, New York: 32t, 108, 130b, 146(l), 233
Courtesy David Zwirner, New York and Galerie Eigen + Art, Berlin/Leipzig: 116r
Courtesy the Estate of Jason Rhoades/David Zwirner, New York and Hauser & Wirth, London and Zurich: 49
Courtesy the Estate of Gordon Matta-Clark and David Zwirner, New York: 323
Courtesy David Zwirner, New York and Zeno X Gallery, Antwerp: 103(l)

INDEX

Underlined numbers refer to the illustrations

A

D

E

F